Roger Beard

WINDOWS® ARCHITECTURE I & II
MCSD STUDY GUIDE

WINDOWS® ARCHITECTURE I & II MCSD STUDY GUIDE

Bruce T. Prendergast

IDG BOOKS WORLDWIDE

IDG Books Worldwide, Inc.
An International Data Group Company
Foster City, CA • Chicago, IL • Indianapolis, IN • New York, NY

Windows® Architecture I & II MCSD Study Guide

Published by

IDG Books Worldwide, Inc.

An International Data Group Company

919 E. Hillsdale Blvd., Suite 400

Foster City, CA 94404

www.idgbooks.com (IDG Books Worldwide Web site)

Library of Congress Catalog Card No.: 97-78221

ISBN: 0-7645-3123-9

Printed in the United States of America

10 9 8 7 6 5 4 3 2 1

1P/QS/QW/ZY/FC

Distributed in the United States by IDG Books Worldwide, Inc.

Distributed by Macmillan Canada for Canada; by Transworld Publishers Limited in the United Kingdom; by IDG Norge Books for Norway; by IDG Sweden Books for Sweden; by Woodslane Pty. Ltd. for Australia; by Woodslane New Zealand Ltd. for New Zealand; by Addison Wesley Longman Singapore Pte Ltd. for Singapore, Malaysia, Thailand, Indonesia, and Korea; by Comunicaciones Norma S.A. for Colombia; by Intersoft for South Africa; by International Thomson Publishing for Germany, Austria, and Switzerland; by Toppan Company Ltd. for Japan; by Distribuidora Cuspide for Argentina; by Livraria Cultura for Brazil; by Ediciencia S.A. for Ecuador; by Ediciones ZETA S.C.R. Ltda. for Peru; by WS Computer Publishing Corporation, Inc., for the Philippines; by Unalis Corporation for Taiwan; by Contemporanea de Ediciones for Venezuela; by Computer Book & Magazine Store for Puerto Rico; by Express Computer Distributors for the Caribbean and West Indies. Authorized Sales Agent: Anthony Rudkin Associates for the Middle East and North Africa.

For general information on IDG Books Worldwide's books in the U.S., please call our Consumer Customer Service department at 800-762-2974. For reseller information, including discounts and premium sales, please call our Reseller Customer Service department at 800-434-3422.

For information on where to purchase IDG Books Worldwide's books outside the U.S., please contact our International Sales department at 650-655-3172 or fax 650-655-3297.

For information on foreign language translations, please contact our Foreign & Subsidiary Rights department at 650-655-3021 or fax 650-655-3281.

For sales inquiries and special prices for bulk quantities, please contact our Sales department at 650-655-3200 or write to the address above.

For information on using IDG Books Worldwide's books in the classroom or for ordering examination copies, please contact our Educational Sales department at 800-434-2086.

For press review copies, author interviews, or other publicity information, please contact our Public Relations department at 650-655-3000 or fax 650-655-3299.

For authorization to photocopy items for corporate, personal, or educational use, please contact Copyright Clearance Center, 222 Rosewood Drive, Danvers, MA 01923, or fax 978-750-4470.

is a trademark under exclusive license to IDG Books Worldwide, Inc., from International Data Group, Inc.

ABOUT IDG BOOKS WORLDWIDE

Welcome to the world of IDG Books Worldwide.

IDG Books Worldwide, Inc., is a subsidiary of International Data Group, the world's largest publisher of computer-related information and the leading global provider of information services on information technology. IDG was founded more than 25 years ago and now employs more than 8,500 people worldwide. IDG publishes more than 275 computer publications in over 75 countries (see listing below). More than 60 million people read one or more IDG publications each month.

Launched in 1990, IDG Books Worldwide is today the #1 publisher of best-selling computer books in the United States. We are proud to have received eight awards from the Computer Press Association in recognition of editorial excellence and three from *Computer Currents'* First Annual Readers' Choice Awards. Our best-selling ...For Dummies® series has more than 30 million copies in print with translations in 30 languages. IDG Books Worldwide, through a joint venture with IDG's Hi-Tech Beijing, became the first U.S. publisher to publish a computer book in the People's Republic of China. In record time, IDG Books Worldwide has become the first choice for millions of readers around the world who want to learn how to better manage their businesses.

Our mission is simple: Every one of our books is designed to bring extra value and skill-building instructions to the reader. Our books are written by experts who understand and care about our readers. The knowledge base of our editorial staff comes from years of experience in publishing, education, and journalism — experience we use to produce books for the '90s. In short, we care about books, so we attract the best people. We devote special attention to details such as audience, interior design, use of icons, and illustrations. And because we use an efficient process of authoring, editing, and desktop publishing our books electronically, we can spend more time ensuring superior content and spend less time on the technicalities of making books.

You can count on our commitment to deliver high-quality books at competitive prices on topics you want to read about. At IDG Books Worldwide, we continue in the IDG tradition of delivering quality for more than 25 years. You'll find no better book on a subject than one from IDG Books Worldwide.

John Kilcullen
CEO
IDG Books Worldwide, Inc.

Steven Berkowitz
President and Publisher
IDG Books Worldwide, Inc.

Eighth Annual Computer Press Awards ≥ 1992

Ninth Annual Computer Press Awards ≥ 1993

Tenth Annual Computer Press Awards ≥ 1994

Eleventh Annual Computer Press Awards ≥ 1995

The Value of Microsoft Certification

As a computer professional, your opportunities have never been greater. Yet you know better than anyone that today's complex computing environment has never been more challenging.

Microsoft certification keeps computer professionals on top of evolving information technologies. Training and certification let you maximize the potential of Microsoft Windows desktop operating systems; server technologies, such as the Internet Information Server, Microsoft Windows NT, and Microsoft BackOffice; and Microsoft development tools. In short, Microsoft training and certification provide you with the knowledge and skills necessary to become an expert on Microsoft products and technologies — and to provide the key competitive advantage that every business is seeking.

Microsoft offers you the most comprehensive program for assessing and maintaining your skills with our products. When you become a Microsoft Certified Professional (MCP), you are recognized as an expert and are sought by employers industry-wide. Technical managers recognize the MCP designation as a mark of quality — one that ensures that an employee or consultant has proven experience with Microsoft products and meets the high technical proficiency standards of Microsoft products.

As an MCP, you receive many benefits, such as direct access to technical information from Microsoft; the official MCP logo and other materials to identify your status to colleagues and clients; invitations to Microsoft conferences, technical training sessions and special events; and exclusive publications with news about the MCP program.

Research shows that organizations employing MCPs also receive many benefits:

- A standard method of determining training needs and measuring results — an excellent return on training and certification investments
- Increased customer satisfaction and decreased support costs through improved service, increased productivity, and greater technical self-sufficiency
- A reliable benchmark for hiring, promoting, and career planning
- Recognition and rewards for productive employees by validating their expertise

- Retraining options for existing employees, so they can work effectively with new technologies
- Assurance of quality when outsourcing computer services

Through your study, experience, and achievement of Microsoft certification, you will enjoy these same benefits, too, as you meet the industry's challenges.

Nancy Lewis
General Manager
Microsoft Training and Certification

CREDITS

ACQUISITIONS EDITORS
Anne Hamilton
Tracy Thomsic

DEVELOPMENT EDITOR
Katharine Dvorak

TECHNICAL EDITOR
Adrian Hill

COPY EDITORS
Richard H. Adin
Ami Knox
Carolyn Welch

PROJECT COORDINATOR
Tom Debolski

BOOK DESIGNER
Kurt Krames

GRAPHICS AND PRODUCTION SPECIALISTS
Vincent F. Burns
Renée Dunn
Stephanie Hollier
Linda J. Marousek
Hector Mendoza
Elsie Yim

QUALITY CONTROL SPECIALISTS
Mick Arellano
Mark Schumann

ILLUSTRATOR
Jesse Coleman

PROOFREADERS
Chris Collins
David Wise

INDEXER
Ann Norcross

ABOUT THE AUTHOR

Bruce Prendergast, MCSE and MCSD, has been programming since the 1950s and is an independent consultant in the Los Angeles area. In his spare time Bruce can be found on his mountain bike in the mountains surrounding Los Angeles, as well as absorbed in writing a new novel. Bruce may be contacted via e-mail at Bruce@Prendergast.com.

As always, this book is dedicated to dearest Dianna.

PREFACE

This book is a study guide for the Microsoft Certified Solution Developer (MCSD) core exams:

- Exam No. 70-160: Microsoft Windows Architecture I
- Exam No. 70-161: Microsoft Windows Architecture II

WHY YOU NEED THIS BOOK

The first reason you should buy this book is for the wealth of examples contained within. Even if you're not interested in Microsoft certification, the examples of each technology will kick-start your learning curve. When you're a developer focusing on only one or two technologies, this book can serve as a guide to those technologies with which you are unfamiliar. The second reason you should buy this book is because I have tried to put forth the information that you need to be a successful developer. If I can contribute to making you into a newly minted wizard, then this book is a success. The third reason you should buy this book is because all the Windows Architecture I and II examination answers are in it. No, they're not in a central location where you can practice your short-term memory skills, but the answers are buried in technology discussions and examples. (You must earn the answers!)

I Don't Need to Be Certified; I Am Already an Expert!

That may be true, but as an MCSE/MCSD and a programmer since the 1950s, I may already be an expert programmer, but I still use the certifications as a reminder to stay abreast of the latest technology. We are in the midst of a great technological information explosion. New technology is replaced with still newer technology before you understand the prior technology. I, along with all the rest of you, suffer from *information overloaditis*. It is difficult to stay abreast of the new technologies. The common trap we all fall into is adopting a favorite technology and running with it. We lift our head up from the trenches and the world has passed us by.

I Know Nothing About Microsoft Software (But I Do Use Word and Excel)

I taught the original Windows Open Services Architecture (WOSA) I and II classes at the University of California, Irvine. The students in my WOSA classes were at all levels: entry-level programmers, mainframe programmers who wanted to find out what this GUI stuff is all about, hard-core software experts, and, of course, just users. I know that a great number of my students were (and still are) mainframe programmers. I remember in particular a complete AS/400 programming team enrolling in one of my WOSA classes. They were not interested in certification, but needed to know the correct techniques for using Open Database Connectivity (ODBC).

A student amazed me in one of my WOSA classes at UCI. He was the first class member to successfully pass the WOSA I examination. His profession was job placement, and he wanted to be able to accurately assess job candidates. There were many other students in that class, even some very skilled C++ programmers. So be careful when you start looking for a job with your newly acquired certifications. That recruiter may surprise you.

This brings to mind an experience in my own life. A few years back I was window-shopping for a job. I was at a job fair and approached one table staffed by some executive types. They asked me what I did and I said, "I am a blah-blah and my specialty is SQL." The mercenary farmer only asked me one question: *What is functional dependency?* (See Chapter 41.) This is an incredible question. You take a complete occupation and distill it to four words. Either you know the answer or you do nothing but babble. Please note that you may still babble even though you possess Microsoft SQL Server Administration certification and Microsoft SQL Server Implementation certification. This book fills the gaps not covered by the Microsoft Windows Architecture I and II examinations. Arm yourself with certifications before discussing employment opportunities with recruiters. The recruiter may be a step ahead of you and already be certified.

I Don't Program in C or C++

That's fine. Yes, there is a very little bit of C++ code in the book, but the examples are mostly Visual Basic for Applications (VBA). Microsoft software is evolving to a component architecture, with the components connected by a scripting language such as VBA. This is the ActiveX of today. Approximately one third of the Microsoft

Windows Architecture I certification exam is on component architecture. I can give you a clue right now that the COM interface **IDataObject** must be understood. It is a key interface in COM compound files and is also a key interface for Windows 95 Shell extensions that must be supported for the Window 95 logo.

I believe that you'll find the book meets the middle-of-the-road goals and will not bore or offend C++ developers, while still communicating with Visual Basic developers. The world today is component technology, and this book is targeted at the Visual Basic 5.0 developer. Many C++ interfaces are discussed, but always from a functionality perspective.

The middle-of-the-road perspective also means that this book is not targeted for beginners. Yes, new users of the Microsoft technology will benefit from the examples in this book, but the book is based on and modeled by the Windows Architecture Exam Objectives. The objectives tie together different technologies. Passing the Windows Architecture certifications is a matter of being an active practitioner of Microsoft technologies and then using this book to fill in the missing technologies. I know of a number of instances where individuals with the original WOSA certifications were "blown-away" when they attempted the new Microsoft Windows Architecture examinations. The Windows Architecture certifications will be coveted, and the holder of such certifications is entitled to bragging rights.

Conceptual Difficulties

My teaching of the WOSA class at UCI gave me significant insight into which portions of the Microsoft architecture presented conceptual difficulties to the new student. I believe this book addresses those problem areas.

Will This Book Improve My Skills?

Your understanding of the different technologies discussed in this book will help you select the appropriate technology. Choosing the wrong tool for an application is the most common mistake. Programmers have a weakness: They tend to fall in love with the language they're using and define everything in terms of that language. A C++ programmer will invariably define new applications in terms of C++. The same is certainly true for other tools such as Microsoft Access, which is probably the most often misused tool available.

I also attempt to instill a sense of critical thinking. It is easy to forget that critical thinking is necessary when we're using a Rapid Application Development (RAD) tool such as Microsoft Access or Visual Basic. There is a quote in this book where an individual states, "I can develop an application faster than writing a specification the old way." The point is that RAD tools promote bottom-up design where results are generated quickly before the problem at hand is fully understood.

Do I Need This Book?

Absolutely! You need every possible tool to compete in a very competitive job market. Consider this fact: You are reading this because you want to keep up with technology but you find it very difficult. If you can't keep up, do you think a manager can, or how about a job interviewer? You need a certification to distinguish yourself from everyone else the recruiter is interviewing. He or she probably doesn't understand what you can do, but a certification is certainly never a hindrance to a job search.

Certifications alone are not enough to get a job, however. A job is you, your experiences, your goals, and your aspirations. Certifications in themselves are quite shallow, and are sometimes only an exercise in reciting minutiae, but they do say something else. You care about yourself and are striving to improve, you are goal oriented, and you can follow through on a plan. These are valuable assets for any employer. Certifications are a foundation upon which your employer can build. You have identified yourself as motivated and goal oriented.

I believe that as application functionality moves upward, skill sets move downward. It takes less skill to perform the same task today when compared with any of the older technologies. This opens a window of opportunity for those less skilled to enter the technological labor pool. Certifications will distinguish you as the labor pool broadens.

Some say Microsoft is busy deskilling jobs and automating tasks. It's also called *dumbing down the programmer* by those who cannot accept change. Consider the management of an Oracle database as compared to that of a SQL Server database. Microsoft SQL Server 7.0 will ship sometime after this book is on the shelf. SQL Server is being partitioned into an enterprise, a standard, and a small business version. The small business version of Microsoft SQL Server will not require a Database Administrator (DBA). Other features of Microsoft SQL Server 7.0 include self-tuning and self-healing.

Automating tasks is also evident in Visual Basic 4.0, which now creates ActiveX controls. Creating an OLE control or what is now an ActiveX control was once an eclectic and esoteric task which was the exclusive purview of C++ programmers — that is, until Microsoft Visual Basic 4.0 shipped.

Yes, I know there is a demand for specialty skills, and there always will be. It is estimated that less than only one percent of the current programming population can program a C++ application. I don't consider clicking a wizard and hacking some existing code in the Integrated Development Environment (IDE) as C++ programming. I mean the logical design and application development of an object-oriented application. There is always a demand for talented individuals, and there are far fewer jobs for a rapidly expanding labor pool.

Do I Need Certifications Now?

Yes, you do. I expect the market for individuals with Microsoft certifications to saturate within two or three years. Today, there are about 35,000 individuals with MCSE certifications and about 6,000 individuals with MCSD certifications. The window is still open for additional certified individuals. But in time, the market will saturate, and jobs will only be available to those with certifications and years of experience.

How This Book Is Organized

The book has a natural division of technologies and is divided into five parts. Material is organized in the order of the Microsoft Windows Architecture study guide objectives. Each chapter discusses a distinct architectural topic and starts with an overview of that topic. Each chapter closes with test questions and critical thinking lab exercises to measure your understanding of the issues and to give you practice applying the material you learned from the chapter.

Each chapter also contains examples of the technology at hand. You'll find the examples are as simple as possible to illustrate the issue. This doesn't mean that all examples are simple. When discussing Open Database Connectivity (ODBC), for example, rather than paying lip service to optimizing ODBC, I give you actual working examples of optimized queries. Some of these examples may appear advanced when an issue is illustrated, but the emphasis is on doing it the right way, not just simply doing it.

As the book unfolds you'll find a discussion of many diverse issues, one such topic being database normalization. The original Windows Open Services Architecture I and II certifications are deficient in that you could become a Microsoft Certified Solution Developer without knowing how to normalize a database — a perfect example of an oxymoron. You'll learn how to normalize a database and how to access a database efficiently with different technologies. Most developers are happy to just get the database software working.

Let's briefly review the book organization. As I stated previously, the material is generally in study objective order. Some objectives are covered in a single chapter while other objectives span many chapters, such as component technology and database access technologies.

Part I: Component Technologies

Part I is a very important section of the book. Component architecture is the future and it is now. It is the foundation of all Microsoft technology. Part I is a discussion of the roots of object linking and embedding (OLE), the Component Object Model (COM), and the evolution of OLE to the ActiveX of today. What it is, how to use it, and when to use it are discussed in detail.

Part II: Database Access Technologies
ODBC

This is where the fun starts. In this section I explore the ODBC 3.0 API, which I illustrated using Access 2.0. I did this because Microsoft implemented Unicode in 1995 in their zeal to dominate the Internet. Unicode and the double-byte character set (DBCS) destroyed column-wise and row-wise ODBC binding for SQL results sets using VBA. The ODBC API function **SQLExtendedFetch** with Access 2.0 can bind complete result sets into arrays. By comparison, this makes some of the newer technologies, such as RDO and ODBCDirect, look almost puny. I've coined some of these newer technologies as "refried beans," which I discuss in detail in the ensuing chapters.

I consider ODBC the most important contribution Microsoft has made to the programming community. A new ODBC 3.0 specification exists; however, the

Microsoft implementations are negatively impacted by Unicode implementation. ODBC doesn't implement Unicode; it's the underlying infrastructure that implements Unicode. You'll find Unicode and the companion DBCS discussed in detail in Chapter 42. Using ODBC to access legacy databases should not require Unicode or DBCS. Currently the only circumvention mechanism available to avoid Unicode is the Windows 95 environment or a 16-bit tool such as Access 2.0 in Windows NT. Maybe Microsoft should consider creating an Environment Impact Report before implementing new technologies.

DAO

In this section of Part II, I cover Data Access Objects (DAO) 3.5 extensively with respect to the ODBC API. DAO is the first of several ODBC wrappers that simplify the developer's job. This wrapper simplifies life a little too much, however, and Microsoft Access and the attendant DAO are often misused. The common pitfalls of DAO are discussed in a section called "DAO Tarpits."

Probably the most important feature of this section is acquiring the understanding that Microsoft Access is not a database management system even though it has the appearance of being such. This explains why certain Microsoft developers will not use the word *database* and *Microsoft Access* in the same sentence. Why is this? Sorry, you'll have to read the chapter. I do promise you one thing, however: your Microsoft Access (database) application will eventually crash and *you will not recover it*. It will crash not because of any particular bug, but because certain transaction properties do not exist. I know that Murphy's Law still reigns supreme and your database won't crash until that unique time when you need it the most. If I've piqued your interest, search the book index for the ACID properties.

RDO

Remote Data Objects (RDO) is another ODBC incarnation. It is a thin ODBC wrapper for SQL Server access. This technology first appeared in Visual Basic 4.0 Enterprise edition, and RDO 2.0 shipped with Visual Basic 5.0. ODBCDirect, discussed in the last chapter, is a direct descendent of the RDO technology. You'll find many similarities between RDO and DAO; however, there are also distinct differences. When to use which technology will directly determine the success of your application.

SQL-DMO

So far I've discussed component technologies, ODBC, and three subsequent variations. This section of Part II is a bit different. I use Automation in the form of SQL-DMO (Distributed Management Objects) to manage a registered ODBC data source (DSN). SQL-DMO is a component technology for managing SQL Server from a VBA or C++ environment. Yes, SQL-DMO will return result sets, but its intended purpose is management. I discuss the SQL-DMO from the VBA perspective.

SQL-DMO is an obscure technology, which is surprising when you find how easy it is to use. It also has some very surprising capabilities. Maybe the capabilities of SQL-DMO are not surprising when you find that the Enterprise manager of Microsoft SQL Server is implemented with SQL-DMO.

OLE-DB

This section discusses the OLE-DB technology, which is a marriage of ODBC and component technology. Some OLE-DB technology exists today with Active Data Objects (ADO) and Active Server Pages (ASP). I cover this in detail when building a Web page in a later chapter using Visual InterDev.) It is also the future: Microsoft SQL Server 7.0 will be OLE-DB-based.

Part III: Infrastructure

Operating system awareness

Here we deal with what the operating system can do for us, not what we can do for the operating system. Windows NT is certainly an operating system, but DOS and Windows 3.1 never were, and Windows 95 is hard to describe. Windows 95 looks pretty but it still carries the burden of the INT 21 interrupt and **DoEvents**, the cooperative multitasking tool that must still be used for 16-bit applications.

There are numerous DDE programming examples in this section of Part III. I discuss the Microsoft Windows architecture from two different perspectives: one of the implementers, the other of the user. There are numerous questions on the Microsoft Windows Architecture I examination about operating systems. I discuss all the objectives in detail.

Choosing development tools

In this section I talk about development tools such as Microsoft Visual Basic, Microsoft Visual C++, Microsoft Access, and several other Microsoft development tools. I won't pick any one as a favorite, but I do know this: programmers will "fall in love with the language they are using." You might dislike programming in COBOL very much, but if I gave you a COBOL programming task, within six months you would be extolling the features of the language. I am certain that more than a few of you are language diehards and maybe, just maybe, I can get you to stand back a bit and think of an alternative.

Development methodologies

This chapter discusses the Microsoft Solutions Framework (MSF) methodology and the Microsoft SourceSafe code management system. MSF is contrary to commonly accepted software project development policies and exposes a bottom-up design approach with a learn-as-you-go approach. (The traditional waterfall approach is updated with current technologies and is presented in Chapters 40 and 41.)

Part IV: Internet/Intranet

Part IV is a fun section in which you'll learn how to take the popular Microsoft intranet/Internet tools and do something useful with them. I build a complete Web site starting with FrontPage 98 and embellish the site with Visual InterDev. You will see the technologies we've discussed come to life. I also build an ISAPI DLL for an ISAPI application. You'll also learn to use FrontPage 98, Visual InterDev, Internet Information Server of Microsoft Windows NT 4.0, Microsoft SQL Server Web Assistant, Internet Data Connector (IDC), Microsoft dbWeb, and Office 97 (which is loaded with Internet assistants).

Part V: Applications

Part V is the last section of the book. It starts with a historical perspective for a foundation and continues with an updated version of the waterfall method. (Yes, I know Microsoft's official position is that the waterfall method doesn't work. I say very emphatically that it does, and the failures of the waterfall system are management failures and not failures of the technology.) The section closes out with a discussion of the various application interface issues. These include interface standards, installation, removal, deployment, disabilities, internationalization, and Office 97 and Windows 95 logo requirements.

Chapter 42 is the last and the most important chapter of this book. *Keep the customers happy* is the golden rule of application development. An application bug is quite often a user trying to use an application feature in a manner other than envisioned by the developer. You want the application to be intuitive and at the same time not insult the user's intelligence. This is the reason for standards. There is a penalty for being too clever. Users expect an application to respond in the same manner as all other applications. Simple items such as the order of items in a menu are very important to the user. Is your *Save* or *Delete* command in the proper menu order? Do you ask for verification of data destroying commands? I have some painful memories of a very old Digital Equipment Corporation PDP-11 where I *thought* dir *.* but I *typed* del *.*. Yes, I did recover the data, but only after I did an emergency power-down and worked until the wee hours that night recovering the disk. It takes just a few simple rules to create a successful application.

Resources

The Resources section in the back of the book and on the CD-ROM that accompanies the book contains a wealth of information. You will find exam preparation tips, answers to the chapter Instant Assessment questions, and a review of all the WA I and II exam objectives, as well as a thorough glossary and index.

CD-ROM

The CD-ROM that accompanies this book contains the following materials: an electronic version of the book, excerpts from *Windows NT MCSE Study Guide* (IDG Books Worldwide, 1997) and *MCSE Career Microsoft* (IDG Books Worldwide, 1997), all in fully searchable Portable Document Format; Adobe's Acrobat Reader; ISG Navigator; Internet Explorer 4.0; Transcender exam simulation software; and all of the examples used in the book of all the technologies required for the Microsoft Windows Architecture I and II examinations.

MAPPING WINDOWS ARCHITECTURE I OBJECTIVES

The Windows Architecture I and II examinations are not simple. Object requirements, such as "Compare Data Access Objects (DAO) with other potential components of a solution, such as ODBC or RDO," are general, and do not map to simple answers. Comparative questions require an understanding of each of the identified technologies. This book, rather than serving up "boot-camp style" answers, presents all of the technologies with working examples. Microsoft continues to admonish potential testees to "use the product." Having passed over a dozen Microsoft certifications exams, I can say that a certification test is always easy when the product is used, and it's excruciatingly difficult when you don't use the product.

You will find a Windows Architecture I study guide in Appendix F on the CD-ROM that should prove helpful in studying for the Windows Architecture I certification. Table 1 maps the chapters to the Microsoft Windows Architecture I objectives.

TABLE 1 MAPPING THE WINDOWS ARCHITECTURE I OBJECTIVES

OBJECTIVE TOPIC	TECHNOLOGY	BOOK CHAPTERS
Component Technologies	COM, Automation	1–10
Database Access Technologies	ODBC	11–14
	DAO	15–23
	RDO	24–26
	SQL–DMO	27–28
	OLE–DB	29–32
Operating System Awareness	DDE, NetDDE, Windows Sockets, NetBios, IPX/SPX, DLC, Named Pipes, Memory Mapped Files, Threads, Processes, Registry, TAPI, MAPI, SAPI, LSAPI, SNA API, Crypto API	33
Choosing Development Tools	Visual Basic, Visual J++, Access, C++, FoxPro, Office, BackOffice, Visual Tool Suite	34

continued

TABLE 1 *(continued)*		
OBJECTIVE TOPIC	*TECHNOLOGY*	*BOOK CHAPTERS*
Development Methodologies	Microsoft Solutions Framework, SourceSafe.	35
	Solutions Design Issues	40–41
Internet/Intranet	FrontPage 98, dbWeb, IDC, Visual InterDev, SQL Server Web Assistant, WebBrowser control, Internet Explorer, WinInet control, WebPost control and API, ISAPI, CGI, HTML, HTTP, TCP/IP, Internet download component, code signing	36–39

MAPPING WINDOWS ARCHITECTURE II OBJECTIVES

This is one book for both the Windows Architecture I and II examinations. It is impossible to take a topic such as the Internet and partition it into a Windows Architecture I and a Windows Architecture II perspective. Do what Microsoft admonishes: use the product. Build your own Web site. Use the numerous examples in this book as your starting point. Simply reading my code is not sufficient.

Many of the chapters referenced in Table 2 overlap with Windows Architecture I objectives. Chapters 40, 41, and 42 are unique to the Microsoft Windows Architecture II certification, while the remaining chapters overlap with the Windows Architecture I certification.

You will find a Windows Architecture II study guide in Appendix F on the CD-ROM that should prove helpful in studying for the Windows Architecture II certification. Table 2 maps the chapters to the Microsoft Windows Architecture II objectives.

TABLE 2 MAPPING THE WINDOWS ARCHITECTURE II OBJECTIVES		
OBJECTIVE TOPIC	*TECHNOLOGY*	*BOOK CHAPTERS*
Deployment Issues	Office 97 and Windows 95 logo requirements, Registry, application installation, application removal	42

OBJECTIVE TOPIC	TECHNOLOGY	BOOK CHAPTERS
Solutions Design Issues	Distilling user specifications, business rules, data modeling, application modeling, data normalization	40-41
Internationalization Issues	DBCS, Unicode	42
Choosing Technologies	BackOffice, Office, ODBC, DAO, RDO, ODBCDirect, SQL-DMO, OLE-DB, TAPI, SAPI, MAPI, LSAPI, SNA API, Crypto API	34
Internet and Intranet	FrontPage 98, dbWeb, IDC, Visual InterDev, SQL Server Web Assistant, WebBrowser control, Internet Explorer, WinInet control, WebPost control and API, ISAPI, CGI, HTML, HTTP, TCP/IP, Internet download component, code signing	36-39
User Interface Issues	ToolTips, F1 help, Help menu, .hlp files, accessibility, selecting user interface components, user-interface standards, Win 95 Logo requirements	42

CONVENTIONS USED IN THIS BOOK

The following style conventions are used throughout the book.

Bold — An interface, property, method, or object is set in boldface. An example is the **RecordSet** object of DAO or the **IUnknown** interface of COM.

Italic — Parameters that require values are in italics. You'll find these frequently used in Database Access Technology where we're discussing syntax for creating objects.

CAPITALS — All capital letters are used for directory names, filenames, and acronyms.

Listings — Listings are in a monospaced font.

In addition, several different icons are used throughout this book to draw your attention to matters that deserve a closer look:

concept link

This icon points you to another place in this book (or to another resource) for more coverage on a given topic.

caution Be careful here! This icon points out information that can save you a lot of grief. It's often easier to prevent tragedy than to fix it afterwards.

 exam preparation pointer This icon identifies important advice for those studying to pass the Windows Architecture I and II exams.

 in the real world This icon draws your attention to the author's real-world experiences, which will hopefully help you on the job, if not on the Microsoft Certified Solutions Developer exams.

 note This icon points out an interesting or helpful fact, or some other comment that deserves emphasis.

 tip Here's a little piece of friendly advice, or a shortcut, or a bit of personal experience that might be of use to you.

 web links This icon indicates an online resource that you can access to obtain products, utilities, or other worthwhile information.

Well, that's it. This has been a very broad-brushed view of the material in this book. I promise to do my very best to help you pass the Windows Architecture I and II certification tests. But I intend to give you more than just the material necessary for passing the tests. I am always proud of my students, and I have fond recall of an advanced Microsoft Access class I taught at the University of California, Irvine, last summer: I handed out the final exam three weeks before the quarter ended and didn't collect it until one week after the quarter ended. The exam was to create a Microsoft Access wizard, which they all did. All of my students worked hard and I didn't give a grade less than a B. I hope that you'll be one of my students.

Just in case you do survive the musings of a closet Luddite and actually buy this book and finish it, I award you *in absentia* the Jolt Cola and Cold Pizza Award.

ACKNOWLEDGMENTS

There is always a long list of friends who never fail to help you out. Friends never say no, and my friends didn't say no when I asked for help on the book. I'm lucky that my friends don't know how to say no. In some ways I've taken advantage of each of them. This is a heart-felt thanks to each and every one.

Jim and Mary Panttaja are coauthors of *Microsoft SQL Server Survival Guide*. It was their book and they invited me to help them finish it. Thanks Jim and Mary. You've got me back on the writing path that I abandoned many years ago.

To that special gang at the University of California, Irvine: Jacqueline Badwah, Minh Lam, Rogelio Rodriguez, and Mario Vidalon. Thanks for one of the most fulfilling experiences of my life. I did not realize how much fun teaching could be.

Ah yes, my editors. If you look carefully at the book, you might see faint tinges of pink. It is the blood, sweat, and tears of the IDG Books Worldwide staff working for nearly a year with a cantankerous author. First, there is Anne Hamilton, my acquisitions editor. It took a very long time for our vision of the book to meld. I'm sorry, Anne, for being so stubborn. A very special thanks to Katharine Dvorak, my development editor. She was the buffer between me and my technical editor, Adrian Hill, and my copy editor, Richard H. Adin. I'm certain that both Adrian and Richard asked the question to themselves more than once, "Who is this guy anyway?" Thanks for hanging in there, guys.

Mr. Sreesha Rao and Mr. Dave Seely were my readers for the book. They helped make the book what it is. Their very pointed questions caused many rewrites. They made me realize that I am the master of obfuscation. Thanks, guys.

Mr. Les Gainous is also one of those special people. The book was nearing the end and I needed a technical edit on a few chapters of non-Microsoft material. Les is one of those friends who couldn't say no. He is also one of those unsung wizards in the eclectic world of business rules, data modeling, data normalization, and SQL. Les, thanks for jumping in on such short notice. It is very much appreciated.

Mr. Ron Hudson is another one of those unique friends who can't say no. His help, advice, and consul help make this book unique. Thanks, Ron. Your insight and advice were special and helped make this book unique.

Last, but not least, is Phyllis Murphy. She kept me sane in an insane world. Thanks, Phyllis.

CONTENTS AT A GLANCE

TABLE OF CONTENTS

Component Technologies

The Component Object Model (COM) and Object Linking and Embedding (OLE) have always been arcane subjects. I'll try to demystify the topic in Part I in the following ten chapters:

- **Chapter 1: COM** — Discusses historical issues and sets the background for the Microsoft COM implementation.
- **Chapter 2: Object Interfacing** — Deals with the basics of interface issues.
- **Chapter 3: Interface Issues** — Continues with COM basics and such issues as global naming, type libraries, and the Registry.
- **Chapter 4: Structured Storage** — Continues the layering of COM technology with the introduction of Structured Storage.
- **Chapter 5: Monikers** — Functionality continues to move upward in this chapter with the introduction of monikers.
- **Chapter 6: Uniform Data Transfer** — This is our last stop in Component Technologies before we build our first functional COM application.
- **Chapter 7: Document Linking** — In this chapter we build the first COM application.
- **Chapter 8: Document Embedding** — Presents COM document embedding, which is surprisingly similar to document linking.
- **Chapter 9: Automation** — Presents Automation, a COM technology that does not support linking or embedding.
- **Chapter 10: OLE Controls: Using It All (Well, Almost!)** — This is the pinnacle of COM, where an ActiveX control uses all COM technologies except embedding.

Windows Architecture I

CHAPTER

COM

1

3

About Chapter 1

The *component object model* (COM) is an effort to realize reusable components. Each generation of faster and larger computers fosters seemingly larger and larger programs. Application errors increase with additional program complexity. Thus, Microsoft developed the component object model to attain these very important goals:

- Realize reusability of components

- Manage application complexity

- Eliminate any implementation or distribution issues between the client and its object(s)

- Promote the development of systems that are less fragile and easier to extend

Chapter 1 starts a bit before the beginning of COM and provides thumbnail sketches of prior efforts at code reusability. The history section is abbreviated, but it is important to know that the problem has been wrestled with for 50 years. Microsoft solved the universal-naming problem to make COM a reality. Microsoft didn't define the concept of a *universal unique identifier* (UUID); it borrowed the concept from the Open Systems Foundation (OSF) *distributed computing environment* (DCE) and made it happen. Without Microsoft's efforts, I am sure the standards committee would still be discussing the relative merits of various technologies.

The remainder of this chapter focuses on Microsoft's unique approach to COM to realize code reusability. COM supports encapsulation, inheritance, and polymorphism. COM supports interface inheritance and not implementation inheritance. (It's rather fun to hear the programming purists say, "That's not inheritance!")

IN THE BEGINNING

Component technologies are now while monolithic applications such as a large, compiled FORTRAN program, are relics of the past. Component technologies are not an invention of Microsoft, but rather a natural evolution of computing technology. The early, and certainly primordial, programs were indeed monolithic when compared to a tool with hundreds of components such as Microsoft Word. The compiled legacy applications of the past are best characterized as an immutable binary mass. This changed over time, however, as the concept of shared code evolved to today's component technology.

The evolution started with system libraries where subroutines were copied into the linked application task. These libraries evolved into specialized application libraries, which were still copied into linked space. By the late 1960s, the UNIVAC 1108 with Exec VIII defined an operating system with shared instruction space and private data space. The evolution continued with RSX from Digital Equipment Corporation (DEC), which begat VAX/VMS, which in turn begat Windows NT.

Libraries, shared I-bank instruction sets, and shared *dynamic link libraries* (DLLs) are all part of an effort to reuse code. Microsoft addresses the age-old problem of code reuse with a universal interface in *object linking and embedding* (OLE). A standard interface is known a priori, and the application interrogates the standard interface for additional functionality. The interfaces are reasonably complex to implement; however, Visual Basic 5.0 simplifies the task of creating OLE Controls, which are now called ActiveX controls.

The Microsoft infrastructure development language is C++. Knowledge of C++ is not a prerequisite of this book; COM, however, borrows some notation from C++. If you are not a C++ developer, don't worry. This book is still for you. If you are a C++ developer, you are already familiar with the C++ *scope resolution operator* (::). This book won't teach you programming even though there are many Visual Basic for Applications examples as well as some C++ examples. Please bear with me while a C++ feature that illustrates a notation of COM is presented.

The next paragraph contains a simple C++ example to illustrate (class::method), which is a notation often used in discussions of the COM model. For example, the statement **IUnknown::QueryInterface** is understood to mean "use the **QueryInterface** method of the class **IUnknown**."

The following C++ example illustrates the class Rectangle with the member function Area:

```
Class cRectangle {
int width, height; // private data members
Public:
cRectangle(int ht, int wd); // constructor
  {height = ht; width = wd; }
~cRectangle(); // destructor
int area()// member function (method)
  { return width * height; }
};
```

I embellished the Rectangle class a little bit to illustrate a simple, but reasonably complete, C++ class. I can compute the areas of a rectangle with a class member function reference to **cRectangle::Area**. This distinguishes between another member function reference, **cSphere::Area** of the class Sphere, which is not illustrated. That's all there is to it.

THE ROOTS OF COM

Let's enumerate some useful COM facts. We'll address the evolutionary nature of program communication and show how it evolved into the COM of today.

Program communication is a very old issue.

The Microsoft Architecture deals with a classic problem: program communication. Program communication is fundamental to computing and is an issue that has been with us since the very early days of computing. The difference between the environment today and the environment then is easy to envision.

For example, I once worked for UNIVAC, a large computer mainframe manufacturer. UNIVAC was a leader in computer technology, yet I remember only one notable accomplishment of the company: NASA used a UNIVAC 1108 multiprocessor system for the 1969 Apollo moon shot. If I recall correctly, only thirty-seven or so of the predecessor UNIVAC 1107 systems were sold. I don't know the actual number of UNIVAC 1100s that were sold, but sales were somewhere in the very low thousands. (I do remember the milestone when the 800th unit was shipped.) These numbers appear to be low considering how many desktop computers are sold today.

Still, UNIVAC had difficulty supporting less than one thousand clients using the UNIVAC Exec VIII operating system. Today, Microsoft supports millions of customers. This volume has forced Microsoft to consider standards and code reuse as a matter of corporate survival. It is interesting to note that the initial push for a component architecture with OLE 1.0 came only after Windows 3.1 was a resounding success.

Software libraries enhanced computing and program communication. Libraries were often limited to a specific development language.

Traditional software libraries were specific to one language, but they came in many flavors. Modules that your application required were automatically linked to your executable, giving you your own private copy of the module. System libraries were common with literally hundreds of modules available to FORTRAN and COBOL developers.

What if you had your own copy of a library? That was an entirely different matter. The concept of a system installation of application-oriented libraries came later on the evolutionary computing timeline. The library-install technique began with the very early RSX class systems from Digital Equipment Corporation, which evolved into a fine science in VaxVMS (known today as OpenVMS). This technology is carried forward to Microsoft Windows NT. (Dave Cutler, who today is the chief architect of Windows NT, was an architect of RSX and all its progeny that eventually evolved into OpenVMS.)

The COM interface permits client-server interrogation of services available.

Traditional libraries have unique interfaces. The interfaces were usually well documented and could be used very readily, but only if you read the documentation. Let's contrast that with COM. Client legacy applications interface the services available, but this is only possible with proper documentation. COM is different in that the client object interfaces with a universal and generic interface even when the services available are known. The required interface of all COM-compliant components is the **IUnknown** interface. **QueryInterface** is a method of this interface through which a user interrogates a server that returns available interface information. This is a universal interface, which is only a binary specification. As you learn later, an interface may be implemented in any language, which results in platform independence. I discuss this interrogation mechanism in a detailed discussion of COM in Chapter 2.

A published COM object interface is rigid. Published interfaces cannot be modified, and new services can be added without affecting existing services. New COM services, however, are not published.

As with traditional libraries, the COM interface is rigid. The issue at hand is of maintenance at a later date. A COM interface is never modified and is considered a contract between the client and the interface. New features are implemented as a new interface. Adding a new parameter results in the creation of a new interface, while at the same time inheriting functionality from the prior interface. The existing client is not aware of the new functionality.

Compare that to a traditional library when a new parameter is added to an interface. This cannot be done without significant client expense.

COM gives us a negotiation tool with the **IUnknown::QueryInterface** interface. **IUnknown::QueryInterface** is a rigid COM interface where the client tells the server object, "I want to use this feature. Where is it?" COM publishes a universal interface but not client services, while the legacy model publishes client services and specifications. If you think about this for a minute, you'll realize that this feature significantly reduces code complexity.

The advantage of not publishing services is that new services may be added at a later date (through delegation or aggregation) without informing the client. In other words, new features can be added with zero impact. The client won't use them because it is requesting a service it needs, knows is there, and with which it has a contract. This is very different than strict object-oriented implementations where the smallest change in the base class forces the recompilation of all subclasses. New functionality may be added to a COM component through aggregation and delegation with no effect on the client (well, at least that's the theory) and it does work except when the newly implemented feature has a bug. COM solves what is know as the *fragile base class problem,* which was a major selling point when COM was first introduced.

Implementing **IUnknown** in C++ is illustrated by the following code:

```
interface IUnknown
{
virtual  HRESULT QueryInterface(IID& iid, void ** ppvObj) = 0;
virtual ULONG AddRef() = 0;
virtual UNLOG Release() = 0;
}
```

Implementing **IUnknown** in Visual Basic 5.0 is illustrated by the following code:

```
Implements IUnknown
```

Actually, the **Implements** statement isn't needed for the **IUnknown** interface because it is automatically included with every Visual Basic 5.0 object method.

QueryInterface, **AddRef**, and **Release** are also automatically implemented with any Visual Basic 5.0 component. The implemented class accepts COM **QueryInterface** calls for the specified interface identifier (IID).

Late binding is a feature of COM. Users have additional flexibility and a wider range of choices available.

Traditional libraries are always linked at object-time, as opposed to run-time. The developer — not the user — binds the object. Note that late binding requires COM server-object interrogation with **IUnknown::QueryInterface**. The user is given a choice of services available.

COM gives the user the choice of linking (binding) the objects of choice, while the traditional library model delegates all linking responsibility to the developer.

Program name-space has evolved from private, to departmental, to corporate, to worldwide. The Internet has turned us into a world community; binding to an object now requires a unique name. A UUID names COM objects and their interfaces.

Traditional libraries have name-spaces generic to library usage. These libraries were (and are) used in a heterogeneous environment. The usage is not universal; the client, however, has the responsibility of avoiding name-space collisions.

Within a *Visual Basic for Applications* (VBA) event subroutine, the scope of the variables is limited to the event subroutine. Variable scope has some semblance of a name-space, but it is not an accurate model. The difference is that name-spaces have territorial and jurisdictional constraints. A manufacturing plant has many departments. Rules that exist between the departments within a plant do not apply to relations with other plants of the same corporation. Name-space is not an issue of name collisions within an application, a local area network (LAN), or a wide area network (WAN). The name-space rules, however, were relatively simple. Without a universal naming convention, the rules of the host governed — something akin to "my house, my rules!"

Name-space has evolved from internal names within an application, to departmental name-space, corporate name-space, and, thanks to the Internet, to a universal name-space. This is a far cry from the traditional developer tasked to create a department library. The traditional developer had no global naming problems because one department controlled all application development and the software had no external interfaces. The Internet reinforces the fact that we are one very large community. Naming standards must be global, not departmental.

Microsoft solves the naming problem by borrowing the UUID from the Open Software Foundation's DCE. A UUID identifying an object is known as a *class identifier* (CLSID) and a UUID identifying an interface is known as an *interface identifier* (IID).

COM supports emulation, preserving an investment in older software.

As stated previously, COM is a contract between an interface and a client. This contract is immutable and does not change. Even though new features with new interfaces are added, prior services are still available. It is possible to implement the latest version with no impact on existing applications — if there are no bugs in the latest version.

This is not true with traditional libraries. New libraries inevitably crash applications. There is always a lengthy evaluation period to assess the impact on productions. Rework of the applications can be quite expensive, and the applications may still crash.

It has always been difficult to decide when and if to upgrade an application. If you didn't upgrade to the new library, your application became an orphan without vendor support. The problem compounded if you were more than one library release behind — you were eventually forced to upgrade your application at a considerable expense.

Emulation assumes the characteristics of an object of another type while maintaining its name and original format. The opportunity for emulation exists with older-version client software. Emulation is a retro operation because only older versions, and not newer versions, are emulated. Historically, the client software is modified to conform to the newer server specifications, and this isn't always possible or feasible. COM avoids this problem with the emulation of prior versions or features unique to the older version by using COM library features such as **CoTreatAsClass**. **OleSetAutoConvert** will automatically upgrade an existing component to the newer version level.

Automatic object conversion is the other user option. **OleSetAutoConvert** and **OleDoAutoConvert** are COM library features that support automatic conversion. This option, however, should be used with some caution, as the conversion is not always backward-compatibile.

Reusable components can reduce development costs.

Traditional libraries are reusable; their use, however, is often limited to one language. Subroutine libraries for specific languages were quite common. Developers used assembly language hacks to access library subroutines of other languages. Today, COM is a binary specification and is not limited to any particular language. The only real requirement is that a language supporting COM must have the necessary programming constructs and support the COM library, the interface **IUnknown**, and the methods **QueryInterface**, **Release**, and **AddRef**. Every COM implementation must have a COM library and must support these three methods. Of course, there are other interfaces, but this is the minimal COM implementation.

COM generalizes component interfaces and is a natural step in the evolution of software development. The future of COM is very promising.

Benefits of COM

The benefits of COM are:

- COM supports code reuse between diverse development systems. COM components of an architecture may be used by any language that supports constructs to interface COM server objects. It is a binary specification and is language independent. Yes, an older language might have used a library component of a different language, but that was only with great difficulty and only if the developer knew the proper incantations. It wasn't always possible to share library components.

- The developer is now in control of component installation. If you recall, earlier in the computing evolution timeline the developer had control, but it was a private copy of a library. Library installations eventually evolved to an operating system-level function. It has now moved back to where it should be: developer-controlled installation of components.

- COM objects support distributed applications with the use of a UUID. Applications are no longer limited to a departmental or a locale solution. Enterprise-wide and worldwide applications are now possible. (This is a benefit of the new distributed COM.)

- COM supports a client interrogating a server. Users now have a choice of services. Every COM object is required to support the **IUnknown::QueryInterface**. The client object interrogates this interface of the server with an IID identifying the requested service. A COM client object can build and present a palette of services. The user selects from the available services.

- COM reduces code complexity. While it is true that server complexity increases slightly when developing a COM server (it should reduce, however, with Microsoft Visual Basic 5.0), the overall application complexity decreases. There is only one instance of the server but many instances of server usage by clients. The payoff can be huge. The common code can be developed or purchased and then plugged into the architecture.

- COM supports code reuse with emulation. The COM object can emulate an older server version when an older application version is present. This protects software investments. Contrast this with a legacy application for which existing software must be modified whenever a newer client library is installed.

- Interfaces are rigid in that as new features are added, the original interface remains intact with no loss of functionality. An existing client object is unaware of new server services. This is done through either delegation or aggregation.

- COM objects are integrated with a consistent interface. A COM implementation must support a COM library and all COM objects must support the **IUnknown** interface with the methods **QueryInterface**, **Release**, and **AddRef**. COM does not publish services. It publishes universal and generic interfaces to the server object for client use. The client determines the actual services available with an interrogation process.

- COM objects are extensible. New features added to an existing COM object do not impact existing client code. COM has an immutable law that all existing interfaces cannot change. This is known as a contract between the client and the server.

- The global model of COM supports localization and UNICODE. UNICODE supports foreign languages where the locale identifier is used to designate specific language regions such as France.

- COM is manageable. Type libraries are created from the older *object description language* (ODL) file or the newer *interface description language* (IDL) file. The program `MKTYPLIB.EXE` is used to create a type library with a `.TLB` extension. The information is moved to the Registry at component registration time. The Registry is a central repository of available and active COM components.

COM and the Windows Architecture

That's enough of extolling the virtues of COM for now. Let's discuss COM and the Windows architecture. We begin with an historical perspective and the forces in motion. I want to take you back in time to that period I call the CORBA Wars. I think that I can rightly call the CORBA Wars an internecine war: there were zealots on all sides, and the salvos were epistles grandly stating the virtues of the respective technology. For those of you that recall the period, there were (and still are) different competing technologies, COM, *common object request broker* (CORBA), and IBM's *system object model* (SOM). I won't venture an opinion as to which technology is the best but simply point out that Microsoft supports millions of customers and couldn't wait for negotiated standards from a committee.

 web links **For more information about CORBA, visit its Web site at** `http://www.omg.com`.

These technologies were inspired by the OSF DCE specification mentioned earlier. The DCE specification was an attempt to reduce computational complexity with respect to heterogeneous networking. It identified key issues, but some of the specifications were in error. For example, a DCE *remote procedure call* (RPC) was synchronous. Could that work today? Certainly not; loading an image from the Internet is one example, and there are countless others. Microsoft's solution was to implement COM as an object layer over DCE, as shown in Figure 1-1. Thus, Microsoft implementations are DCE-compliant when possible.

We see some familiar Windows NT features in DCE services. The architecture is not quite the same because threads and RPCs are features of the Windows NT operating system, rather than functions in their own right.

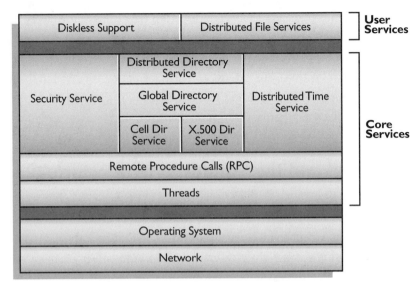

FIGURE 1-1   The DCE over which COM is implemented as an object layer.

This architecture isn't very new, but the issues are. Today Microsoft is working on global directory services. OLE is being used for this implementation, and the technology is rightfully called *OLE directory services* (OLE DS). Specifications exist and some beta code shipped, but Microsoft does not yet have OLE DS implemented. OLE DS uses COM objects to programmatically access directory services on remote systems. This technology is discussed in the database access technology of *OLE database* (OLE DB) later in the book.

Creating enterprise software is not a simple task. Remember that Microsoft was initially a provider of desktop systems and services. Microsoft has developed a very rich infrastructure to support the desktop, and new ventures in that area can be highly leveraged. It has very little software at the enterprise level that can be leveraged. Microsoft must either create new software or purchase the technology.

The rules of the game will change once Microsoft builds enough enterprise software that can be leveraged. Leverage will enable Microsoft to quickly eclipse competitors who currently have technological leads in specific areas.

If you're wondering what *leverage* is about, consider the relatively small amount of time it took for Microsoft to convert *OLE Controls* (OCXs) to ActiveX controls. This wasn't just a renaming of the technology. It is true that ActiveX controls have less capability than the older OCX technology, but ActiveX controls have a distinct advantage on the Internet: quicker response time. ActiveX looks like a winner.

DESIGNED BY COMMITTEE IS NOT ALWAYS AN ATTRACTIVE SOLUTION

I have seen standards that were beneficial. I've also seen languages in which the standards committee lost sight of the original value of the language and added features that tried to mimic other languages. Not all problem solutions are or should be the domain of one language – some problems are better suited to another language. But you couldn't tell the standards committee that. The standards committee language had to do everything. But not everything can be done in one language. I'm certain there are more than a few of you who shudder when you hear the phrase "Designed by Committee."

Before continuing our discussion of COM, let's pause and look at the application interface architecture. COM is only one facet of the Microsoft architecture, but note how the abstraction of these different models appears to be successful.

There are several terms used to describe the application interface architecture; many of these terms, however, may be seen as oversimplifications. The first term is *Windows Operating System Extensions*, which really is correct, but does not effectively convey the complexity of what can be accomplished with this architecture. The second term is *application programming interface* (APIs). This is too low a level and involves the student of Microsoft architecture in needless minutiae because the abstraction level is too low.

You can see from Figure 1-2 why an API is called a Windows Operating System Extension. An API is an application portal to services. Any language may use an API. It is language-independent if the language has the constructs necessary to support an API call.

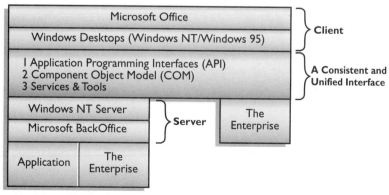

FIGURE 1-2   Microsoft's client–server architecture in a heterogeneous environment.

COM is at the same logical level as an API and appears to serve the same purpose, but it does more than provide an interface. The position of COM in the overall architecture belies the rich functionality available. It is the cornerstone of a new component-based architecture, while at the same time it can be used as a wrapper function for legacy code. I believe that the most important contribution COM can make to the computing community is to provide wrapper functions for legacy code. (I'm certain my perspective is different because much of the adult population appears to have Internet fever.) Desktop access is needed to legacy data, and moving the data to the desktop is unreasonable.

Figure 1-2 should be expanded a little bit because an API is not the only component of the Microsoft Windows architecture. Microsoft defined a *service provider interface* (SPI) at the abstraction level. Not all APIs have a companion SPI, only those involving architectural issues. As an example, internal APIs do not have a companion SPI. The best example of service provider interfaces is the *messaging application program interface* (MAPI). Well-known MAPI service providers include Microsoft's MSMail, IBM's Profs, and Digital Equipment's All-In-One.

Figure 1-3 is a restatement of Windows Operating System Extensions. The consistent and unified interface illustrated in Figure 1-2 is expanded with additional detail. Only two APIs are shown, *Open Database Connectivity* (ODBC) and MAPI, but there are others.

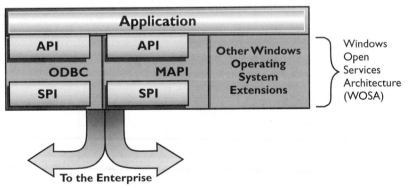

FIGURE 1-3   The API and SPI relationship in Windows architecture.

A generic feature of all Windows Operating System Extensions is the API and SPI interface architecture. Microsoft calls this architecture *open*, as third-party vendors are free to provide services using the SPI. The COM of a client and a server object fits this architecture with the server functioning as a service provider.

I close this discussion of Microsoft architecture with Figure 1-4, a functional API/SPI model. This discussion is not about MAPI; however, the MAPI architecture is the best representation of the relationship between an API and a SPI. MAPI supports **IUnknown** and is a COM-based technology.

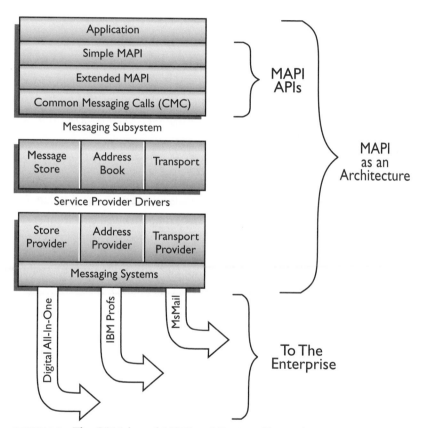

FIGURE 1-4   The COM–based MAPI architecture illustrating the relationship between an API and a SPI.

The process of demystifying OLE/ActiveX and COM has started. These technologies do nothing more than what we have always done as developers, but now we can do it with a little élan. COM allows code reuse, it is extensible, its interfaces are negotiated, older versions can be emulated, and all of its components have a standard interface. Application complexity can be reduced. COM is also a tool for salvaging legacy code.

Microsoft demonstrated wrapping a COBOL CICS transaction within an ActiveX control in spring 1997. This was a major step forward in salvaging legacy software. Rather than rewrite or convert legacy applications, encapsulate them and use remote Automation to control them.

A BASIC COM

COM topics are gradually introduced in the materials that follow. A discussion of the features and functions of basic COM is followed by a discussion of the new COM features, which are named *Distributed COM* (DCOM) and which were introduced in Windows NT 4.0.

What is COM? In the simplest of terms it is a binary interface standard. Any appropriate programming language may be used, but certain guidelines must be followed. We already know that code is reused with Aggregation or Delegation. We also know that there are always two components, a client and a server, that function as service providers. How else can COM be described?

- COM uses the concept of an interface. It is quite unlike a traditional library with service interfaces. The client calls the COM object interface **IUnknown::QueryInterface** to interrogate about rather than to use a service. Object interfaces support the infrastructure and are not client-service specific. Objects are implemented as a DLL for an in-process server within the client address space. Servers implemented on the same machine, but which are not in the client address space, are local servers. A local server and a remote server are implemented as an EXE.

- The COM architecture supports multiple interfaces. Emulation is a feature that supports obsolete object versions. An example is a client expecting version 1.0 support from a version 2.0 server object. Server version 1.0 will be emulated. Polymorphism is the ability to view different objects with the same interface. Emulation is an expression of polymorphism.

- COM objects are used in a multiuser environment. A reference count is maintained for logistical purposes. The object will be released when the reference count is zero.

- COM has a memory management mechanism. Data is passed between the client and server object, and memory is allocated or deallocated as necessary.

- COM objects report error and status information.

- COM supports transparent communication across process boundaries. Communication to remote servers is with a RPC. Clients communicate with local servers via a *light-weight remote procedure call* (LRPC), which is an alias for an *interprocess communication* (IPC) call.

- COM supports a universal naming convention. The requested server is identified dynamically and placed in execution. This may occur across process or machine boundaries.

Those are COM's features, but what does COM look like? COM has grown up a bit in the last few years. Figure 1-4 represents traditional COM, which supported the OLE 2.0 architecture. (The newer features such as Connectable Objects are added later in this section when the current version of COM is discussed.) We layer software, why not layer the complexity issues presented in this book? Starting with COM as it exists today is unreasonably complex. COM is introduced in a gradual fashion starting with the introduction of the older OLE 2.0, which is the foundation for today's technology. OLE 1 was less than useful, but it did identify the problems solved by OLE 2.0 and COM. You should know it's older technology because I am using the older OLE term, which may not be as familiar as the current ActiveX naming convention. You'll also find this same approach in the next section of the book on *Database Access Technologies,* which traces how Open Database Connectivity (ODBC) evolves through each of the access methodologies to arrive at the latest database access technology, which is a merging of COM and OLE with ODBC. As you've already guessed, it is OLE DB. The first ten chapters of this book represent a layering of COM technology, while the rest of the book represents all technologies converging to a common point. Yes, you've guessed right again — the Internet. We'll revisit COM when we build controls for the Internet. But that's not a true sentence. The whole book is about COM. It's a component world today. The Microsoft architecture is component based.

Now back to basics with the traditional COM. Figure 1-5 represents the prior and traditional version of the COM architecture. It supports features and functions of the traditional Windows desktop environment and does not yet support remote objects. You may not be familiar with the terms, but you've used the features every day.

note ✐ **The traditional example of embedding is an Excel spreadsheet in a Word document. In-place activation or visual editing is the use of an older OCX or a newer ActiveX control. Activation of these controls is called *inside-out* as the control is seamlessly integrated with the application and appears to be native to it. My drawing tool for these illustrations is a button on the toolbar that I click to activate the server object.**

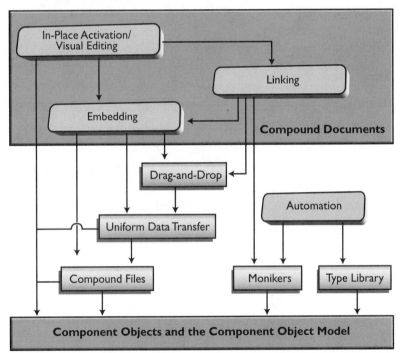

FIGURE 1-5   The traditional version of COM architecture showing COM as a foundation of object services.

Figure 1-5 mixes features and functionality while Figure 1-6 is a simplified version of Figure 1-5 with features and functions separately identified. I believe the concepts are easier to understand if the material is introduced gradually.

You may look at the next few sections as fundamental issues of COM. A discussion of basic COM functions is followed by a discussion of how those features implement the functionality. COM's newer features are introduced after these discussions.

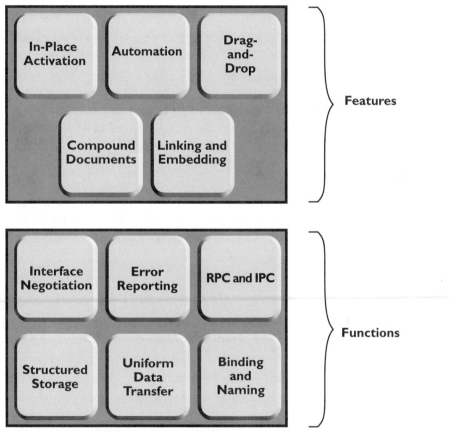

FIGURE 1-6   The features and functions of basic COM are illustrated in a simplified version of Figure 1-5.

Is COM an object model? Yes, it is within the context of COM, but no it isn't within the context of other *object-oriented* (OO) models. Do you compare apples with oranges? Hardly! COM supports the commonly accepted OO features of encapsulation, inheritance, and polymorphism.

Encapsulation

Encapsulation is the isolation of data from direct access by a client. The only client access to the data is with a server method, and direct access to server object data is not possible. The best example is a compound file or a structured file maintained by the server object for the client. There are multiple streams in the compound file representing different objects. A hypothetical example is a Word document with an embedded spreadsheet and an embedded *audio-visual interleave* (AVI) document describing specific features. With the proper permissions, you can read the binary image, but the context and content are unknown.

 concept link

There was a programming example of encapsulation at the beginning of this chapter. By default, a C++ class begins with a private declaration as the default. This means that the declared data members are not directly accessible by the client.

COM is quite interesting in that methods can be encapsulated. Scripting (Automation or OLE Automation) uses the **IDispatch** interface to invoke methods encapsulated within a COM server object. Access to a method of a server object using this interface is with the related DISPID index. This makes a lot of sense when you consider that code space on a remote machine may be different. Windows NT supports the Intel, RISC, MIPS, and PowerPC platforms (at least it used to support MIPS and PowerPC). I am creating this epistle on an Intel toy, but I have Microsoft SQL Server on an Alpha-based machine that supports SQL-DMO (*distributed management objects*), a COM-based OLE technology. I can create VBA scripts on my Intel toy and manage my SQL server over my network. The hardware implementations are diametrically different. Encapsulation can be thought of as asking the server object to perform a task versus the client performing the task. For data, the model is one of an abstraction, but for methods there are physical limitations.

Inheritance

It's apples and oranges time. COM is an interface model and not an implementation model. Implementation inheritance in the classical C++ sense is not supported. In fact, interface inheritance in COM is more robust than implementation inheritance in that it doesn't have the fragile base class problem. This is the problem with strict object-oriented inheritance where changing the parent or root class forces the recompilation of all inherited classes.

Does COM support Inheritance? Yes, it does, with aggregation and delegation. At the infrastructure level, the **IUnknown** interface is required for all COM objects, and all other interfaces in a COM object inherit this interface. At the client level, aggregation or delegation within the object supports methods of older versions. The new server version contains only new methods of which the client may have no knowledge. (For you Internet mavens, doesn't this sound like a cookie factory?) The methods of the older version are aggregated with the new methods for a unified interface. The component has new features but the client doesn't use them because it is unaware of any changes.

How does COM interface inheritance work? Aggregation is the reuse of an object and requires support from the inner object. The aggregated object supports Interface Z and **IUnknown** of the control object in Figure 1-7. The client acquires a pointer to Interface Z through **IUnknown::QueryInterface** of the control object, which makes the services of Interface Z available to the client. It is a bit tricky to aggregate an object because a pointer must be passed to the aggregated object at creation time. This will be a pointer to the controlling object **IUnknown** interface and is done by either **CoCreateInstance** or **IClassFactory::CreateInstance**. When done, **IUnknown** of the control object reports all interfaces through the **QueryInterface** method. This is the reporting of the Interface X and Interface Y along with the inherited Interface Z shown in Figure 1-7. The control object was delegated the responsibility of reporting Interface Z by the aggregated object. Aggregation can be likened to a shell or wrapper where the internal functioning does not change, but a different, and possibly unique, interface is presented to the client.

note **Cookies are code stored on your computer by a Web server to collect and forward information about your computer. They are transparent to the user, but some browsers, such as Microsoft Internet Explorer, offer the option of rejecting cookies.**

Containment is the most common method of reusability. Delegation (also known as containment) is the outer object acting as a client for the inner object. Delegation is not too different from aggregation. The difference is that the control object isolates the delegated object from client access. The significance of this is not readily apparent. Yes, the control object is a wrapper for the delegated object, but think of the practical application of this technology.

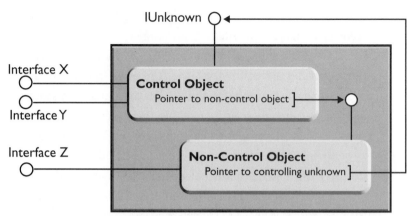

FIGURE 1-7   The internal structure of an aggregate illustrating the client's acquisition of a pointer from the controlling object.

You have built a new COM object and you want to incorporate prior features. You could include the older features by hacking the code by cutting and pasting it, but eventually your new object will suffer from code bloat (fatware).

Another solution is to link the modules of the prior version with modules of the newer version. This solution also suffers from code bloat.

The third alternative is to treat the older version features as components with the new object containing only new features and using the existing or prior features as necessary. This means that newer software versions can be installed without disturbing an existing version. The really profound issue here is that Microsoft has a logical model for reusing code. The original functionality remains intact, and no code hacking is necessary. There are many coding systems, but none of the others has a code-reuse model.

Figure 1-8 illustrates containment. The delegated object is a client of the control object and client access is not possible. The delegated object cannot distinguish control access from a normal client access or access by the control object; in fact, it does not know that direct client access is impossible. Containment is the encapsulation of a delegated object. There is no specific requirement that a delegated object be encapsulated. The delegated object can be any publicly accessible COM component.

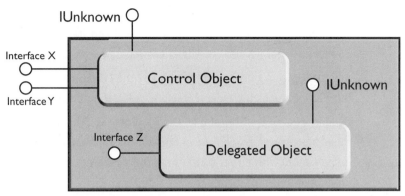

FIGURE 1-8   The delegated object is a client of the control object in delegation (containment) as a code reuse strategy.

Polymorphism

So far we know that COM del supports encapsulation and inheritance. The last question needing an answer is, Does COM support polymorphism? Yes, it does. *Polymorphism* is the ability to view different objects with the same interface. Interface inheritance, where an object can support the new features of the latest version while still supporting an older version, is polymorphic. COM methods such as a **Delete** method that deletes a record from a recordset or that deletes an object from a collection are examples of polymorphism. Aggregation and delegation (containment) are just tools to express polymorphism.

The question remains: Is COM an object-oriented paradigm? I say it is because it exhibits object-oriented properties at the conceptual level. It doesn't matter beyond that because the ultimate goals of component reusability are realized, and that's what counts.

KEY POINT SUMMARY

COM was originally designed as an interprocess or intraprocess communication mechanism; code reusability was a selling benefit. COM has evolved to the point of being a logical model for code reusability.

- COM supports interface inheritance and not implementation inheritance.
- COM is a binary specification. It is language independent.

- A COM object differs from a traditional library that advertises services. All COM objects are required to have a minimal and standard interface. Services are not advertised. The client must query an interface for services.

- All COM objects are required to support the **IUnknown** interface. This interface includes the **QueryInterface**, **AddRef**, and **Delete** methods.

- COM interfaces are immutable. Once used, they cannot be changed. This is called a contract between the client and the server. New features are implemented with either containment or aggregation, and the original functionality is preserved.

- COM supports encapsulation, inheritance, and polymorphism. Aggregation and containment are tools used to express inheritance and polymorphism.

APPLYING WHAT YOU'VE LEARNED

The questions that follow measure your comprehension of this chapter. The issues addressed are the historical perspective, architecture, features, and benefits.

Instant Assessment

1. What is the unique difference between a traditional application library service call and that of a client accessing a COM server object interface?

2. What interface is required of all COM objects?

3. What feature does aggregation or delegation support?

4. What is another name for an application programming interface (API)?

5. What is an SPI and who would use it?

6. Name four benefits of COM.

7. What is emulation?

8. What is a benefit of emulation?

9. What is aggregation?

10. Describe delegation.

11. Describe containment.

12. Describe encapsulation.

13. What are the three commonly accepted criteria for object orientation?

14. Explain the differences between inheritance in C++ and inheritance in COM.

15. What is polymorphism?

16. What is the *fragile base class* problem?

17. How does the COM model avoid the *fragile base class* problem?

 concept link **For answers to the Instant Assessment questions, see Appendix C.**

Lab Exercise

Lab 1.1 *Implementation and interface inheritance*

WA I

Implementation inheritance and interface inheritance are the key differences between COM and traditional *object-oriented programming* (OOP). Consider the problem of two platforms first communicating with COM and then communicating with OOP. COM is implemented on both platforms during the first scenario, and OOP is implemented on both platforms in the second scenario.

- What are the design issues?

- Can you design a system for both scenarios (high level only)?

- What happens when either of the systems fail in either of the scenarios?

- Can you relate the "fragile base class problem" to a computer failing during an OOP scenario?

 Windows Architecture I

CHAPTER

Object Interfacing

2

About Chapter 2

The COM model is all about interface communication. This chapter deals with the concept of an interface and the infrastructure issues of COM.

Two types of interfaces are discussed: the *vtable*, or virtual table, which is a C/C++ pointer table, and **IDispatch**, which is a combination of the pointer table and an interpreted index known as a DISPID. The **IDispatch** interface is the key ingredient of Automation and is introduced here only as an interface.

Chapter 2 also introduces some common interfaces, followed by a map of the generic interfaces of the basic COM model. The chapter closes with the mechanics of instantiating COM servers.

POINTERS AND THE VTABLE

Interface pointers are discussed here in the context of architectural issues and not within the context of software implementation. You already understand the concept of a pointer if you're a C/C++ developer. The **AddressOf** operator in Visual Basic for Applications (VBA), which provides a procedure address used for API callback functions, illustrates the concept of a pointer. Although it is not an interface pointer, it is nonetheless a pointer that illustrates the concept.

The client calls the COM library with a class identifier (CLSID) identifying the object and an interface identifier (IID) identifying the interface. COM loads the server if necessary, and starts it. A pointer is returned to the client if the object was loaded and started successfully. This is not a text on the obscure features of C/C++, even though we do discuss some C/C++ features very briefly. A *pointer* is a virtual address mapping to either a data structure or a method and is a very necessary issue in the COM architecture.

You can probably guess the roots of COM object interfacing — the initial COM models were constructed with C/C++. The natural implementation of an address for data, a structure, or a method in C/C++ is a pointer. C/C++ supports pointers, pointers to pointers, or, as in our case, a pointer to a pointer to a table of pointers. The object provides the implementation of each member function in the interface and creates an array of pointers to those functions called the vtable. This is shared amongst all instances of the object class. To differentiate each instance, the object code allocates according to the object's internal implementation a second structure that contains its private data. The specifications for an OLE interface stipulate that the first 4 bytes in this data structure must be a 32-bit pointer to the vtable. An instance pointer is a pointer to the top of this instance structure; thus a pointer to a pointer to the vtable. It is through this interface pointer that a client accesses the object's implementation of the interface. The use of a pointer table is not new and has been with us since computers were first programmed. It was the common technique used to access operating system functionality before the advent of base-register addressing with memory protection.

An Interface Is a Contract

More than a binary specification, a COM interface is a contract between the client and the interface. COM interfaces are immutable — the function order, function parameters, return values, and operations performed by a COM function never change. What is not specified is the implementation language or how to implement the function. New features are provided with a completely new interface inherited from the prior version. This accounts for interface names such as **IViewData** and **IViewData2**.

The fact that there are no restrictions on how a function is implemented, or what language is used, makes the COM model a binary specification that is platform-independent. The basic COM object interface context we are familiar with is the Visual C++ pointer, but the COM model objects are not limited to any one platform. Windows NT runs on the Digital Equipment Corporation Alpha, a RISC platform with 64-bit addressing, which is quite unlike the Intel CISC platform with 32-bit addressing. The physical implementation of an addressing scheme is interesting, but the important issue is that the logical COM model implementations agree on both platforms.

You should recognize the vtable shown in Figure 2-1. **IUnknown** is the only required pointer and the client must use **IUnknown::QueryInterface** to determine the other pointers. We expand the vtable concept shortly.

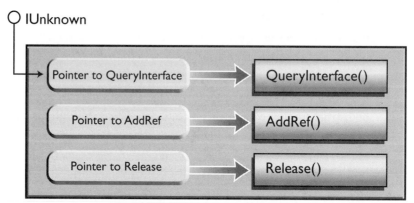

FIGURE 2-1   The IUnknown pointer is the only exposed pointer in this COM object vtable.

Declaring a component object with the related pointers can be done in several ways, and of course they're all done with the C/C++ language. The stout of heart can use nested C structures, C++ nested classes, or C++ multiple inheritances to create the object classes.

BASIC OBJECT INTERFACES

In this section, I discuss briefly the basic functionality of an object. The **IUnknown** interface, which is required for all COM objects, has already been alluded to. Not all object interfaces are discussed, and only the detail necessary to understand the basic issues is provided. For example, the interface **IClassFactory** is discussed, but I make no mention of the **IClassFactory2** interface, which deals with licensing issues. While this interface is important, it is not necessary for an understanding of the overall COM architecture.

IUnknown

All COM interfaces are polymorphic with **IUnknown**. That is, the first three entries of every interface vtable contain pointers to **QueryInterface**, **AddRef**, and **Release**.

The **IUnknown** interface has two responsibilities. The first is locating and returning pointers to an interface based on the client-provided IID. The second responsibility is reference counting. Reference counts control the life of an object. The creator of the object is responsible for establishing the initial value. If the object already exists, then the count is incremented. The **AddRef** method serves both situations. The **IUnknown::Release** decrements the object's reference count. Objects are released when the reference count is zero.

IClassFactory

IClassFactory is one of several steps required for instantiation of a COM object. The **CreateObject** of VBA implies that creating an object is a one-step process. It is a one-step process when only one instance of an object is required. The client calls the COM API function **CoCreateInstance** with the CLSID of the object and IID of the required interface. When successful, a pointer to the requested interface is returned. Figure 2-2 illustrates the **IClassFactory** interface.

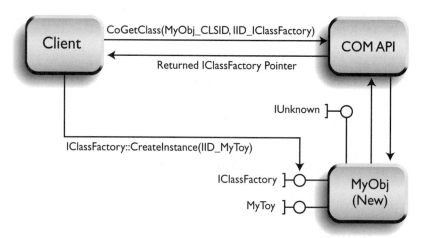

FIGURE 2-2   Using the IClassFactory interface to instantiate an object.

When more than one object is required, the client calls **CoGetClassObject** with the object CLSID and IID_IClassFactory. The client then calls **IClassFactory:: CreateInstance** with the returned **IClassFactory** pointer supplying the IID of the required interface. The **IClassFactory::CreateInstance** method creates an instance of the required object. **CoCreateInstance** is a wrapper for **CoGetClass** and **IClass:Factory::CreateInstance**.The object is later released with **IClassFactory:: Release**. (See "Creating an In-Process Server" and "Creating a Local or Remote Server" later in this chapter.)

IClassFactory is a very necessary component of the COM architecture and a minimal COM implementation requires only two interfaces: **IUnknown** and **IClassFactory**. This has been relaxed with **ActiveX**, which only requires the **IUnknown** interface and the capability to self-register.

IClassFactory::LockServer is the only other method of **IClassFactory**. It keeps the server locked in memory.

IMalloc

The **IMalloc** interface is responsible for memory management. It inherits from **IUnknown** the methods **QueryInterface**, **AddRef**, and **Release**, and implements the methods **Alloc**, **Realloc**, **Free**, **GetSize**, and **DidAlloc**. The methods **Alloc**, **Realloc**, and **Free** are similar to the corresponding C library functions **alloc**, **realloc**, and **free**. The **IMalloc** interface should not be implemented directly, even though it is necessary to any COM implementation. The recommended procedure is to obtain a pointer to the **IMalloc** interface of the task allocator object with the COM library call **CoGetMalloc**. This technique guarantees a thread-safe implementation of **IMalloc**.

The **IMalloc** interface supports allocation, release, size changes, size determinations, garbage collection, and block ownership. **IMalloc** is mentioned in the minimal implementation of a COM as an interface to use. It is not an interface of an object that requires implementation, but rather an interface of the task allocator object.

Marshaling Architecture

Marshaling is the packaging of interface data by a proxy before a remote procedure call (RPC) or local procedure (LPC) sends the data to a local or remote site where a stub unpackages the data. Marshaling is done on an interface-by-interface basis, and not on an object-by-object basis, and is transparent to the application. The primary reason for marshaling is communicating with an object that uses apartment-model threading or with an out-of-process object. (Apartment-model threading only permits one active thread within a COM object while free-threading does not limit the number of threads within a COM object.)

The proxy exists at the client site and is a surrogate for the requested object. It holds a pointer to the requested object and supplies the client with a pointer to itself. A client holding a pointer to a proxy believes that it is the actual object pointer. This is illustrated in Figure 2-3. The stub exists in the server process space. The proxy marshals arguments and unmarshals return values while the stub unmarshals arguments and marshals return values.

COM implements several internal interfaces in managing marshaling. **IRpcProxyBuffer** is implemented at the client site and **IRpcStubBuffer** is implemented at the server site. **IRpcChannelBuffer::SendReceive** does the actual work of sending the marshaled data to the corresponding interface stub. When control is returned to **IRpcChannelBuffer::SendReceive** the contents of the output buffer have been replaced with the returned values.

There are three levels of participation by the client in marshaling. The first level is accepting default marshaling. COM implements default marshaling automatically when the client object has not implemented the **IMarshal** interface. COM will create both the stub and the proxy using **ClassFactory::CreateInstance**.

The second level of participation is with the **IStdMarshalInfo** interface. An object that is using default marshaling can implement this interface and specify the handler to be loaded in the client process. COM starts by requesting the **IStdMarshalInfo** interface. When this interface is not exposed, COM inquires for an **IPersist** interface. If neither exists, a standard handler is used for marshaling.

The last, and obvious, level of participation is the implementation of custom marshaling. Considerations for custom marshaling include:

o Object states are stored in shared memory, and both the client and server process exist on the same machine.

o The objects are immutable, and their state does not change over time.

o Custom marshaling avoids creating a proxy to a proxy.

o Performance enhancements where a custom interface enables a batch and caching capability for a database.

Marshaling support includes the **CoMarshalInterface** wrapper function, which writes proxy initialization data to a stream while **CoUnMarshalInterface** is the COM library function that extracts the data and initializes the proxy. **CoMarshalInterface** will:

1. Query the object for the **IMarshal** interface. Marshaling is transparent to the client. The existence of the **IMarshal** interface on the client object indicates that the object is using custom marshaling. When none is available, **CoMarshalInterface** acquires a pointer to the COM's default **IMarshal** implementation.

2. **IMarshal::GetUnmarshalClass** is called to get the CLSID of the object's proxy.

3. The returned CLSID is written to the stream.

4. The interface pointer is marshaled with **IMarshal::MarshalInterface**.

All other interfaces that may be implemented on an object are exposed in its object proxy through the aggregation of individual interface proxies.

The last issue is the **IStdMarshaling** interface, which must be implemented for any object that supports class emulation. Emulation occurs as a result of selecting *activate-as* in the **Convert** dialog box. The **IStdMarshalInfo** interface determines the correct CLSID for the emulation.

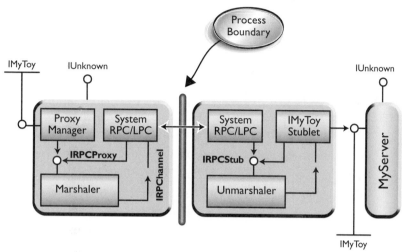

FIGURE 2-3 Marshaling is transparent to the client.

Listing 2-1 is taken from a Windows NT registry. It maps IIDs into proxy/stub CLSIDs. COM looks in the Registry for the proxy and stub under the name **ProxyStubClsid32** for 32-bit systems, and under the name **ProxyStubClsid** for 16-bit systems.

LISTING 2-1 Mapping IIDs on a 16-bit system using ProxyStubClsid in the Registry for default marshaling

```
// maps IIDs into proxy/stub class id
HKEY_CLASSES_ROOT\Interface\{00000000-0000-0000-C000-
  000000000046} = IUnknown
HKEY_CLASSES_ROOT\Interface\{00000000-0000-0000-C000-
  000000000046}\BaseInterface =
HKEY_CLASSES_ROOT\Interface\{00000000-0000-0000-C000-
  000000000046}\NumMethods = 3
HKEY_CLASSES_ROOT\Interface\{00000001-0000-0000-C000-
  000000000046} = IClassFactory
HKEY_CLASSES_ROOT\Interface\{00000001-0000-0000-C000-
  000000000046}\NumMethods = 5
HKEY_CLASSES_ROOT\Interface\{00000001-0000-0000-C000-
  000000000046}\ProxyStubClsid = {0000030E-0000-0000-C000-
  000000000046}
```

This has been an abbreviated tour of the minimal COM object. Let's move on to **IDispatch** and dispinterfaces.

IDISPATCH AND DISPINTERFACES

Our discussion of interfacing COM objects thus far has involved compiled code. What about the scripting supported by tools such as Microsoft Access, Word, Excel, or even the older Visual Basic? These tools are interpreters that use scripts, and the generalized use of address pointers is not possible with these tools. The natural interface for these types of tools is interpretive.

Interpreters need interfaces. Why an interpretive interface? You interface when you want to use one object to control another (Microsoft Access controlling Microsoft Excel is an example). This is OLE Automation, or, simply, Automation, as it is known today. A server exposes its methods and properties, thus enabling client programming.

An object implementing the **IDispatch** interface is by definition an Automation server. An Automation server exposes methods and properties that may be manipulated (programmed) by other objects. The **IDispatch** interface is generic, and an instance of an **IDispatch** interface by an Automation server is called a *dispinterface* and contains these methods:

- *Invoke* — Use a DISPID (index) to call a method or access a property of this dispinterface.
- *GetIDsOfNames* — Convert the text name of a property or a method to DISPID index.
- *GetTypeInfoCount* — Returns 0 if argument is not available, 1 if argument is available.
- *GetTypeInfo* — Retrieves the type information if **GetTypeInfoCount** is successful.

Figure 2-4 is the **IDispatch** vtable interface. The pointer to **IDispatch::Invoke** is an element of the vtable and actual selection of the method or property doesn't occur until the function is entered.

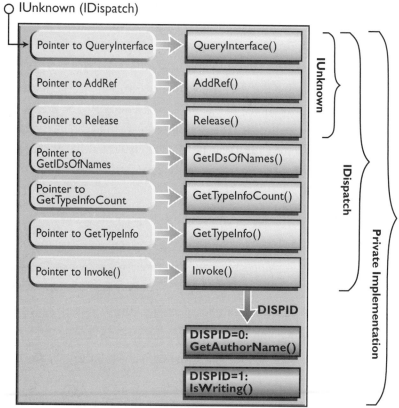

IUnknown (IDispatch)

FIGURE 2-4   The IDispatch vtable interface used by Automation.

The **IDispatch** interface illustrates many of the issues we have discussed:

- The **IDispatch** interface uses the COM model interface inheritance. This is illustrated by the inclusion of the three **IUnknown** methods: **QueryInterface**, **AddRef**, and **Release**.

- The **IDispatch** is certainly polymorphic in that the interface doesn't change when **IDispatch::Invoke** invokes a different method.

- Methods may be added for the pleasure of **IDispatch::Invoke** with no impact on the client. The client isn't aware of the new methods. Compare this to a vtable where any changes require a recompilation of related objects. **IDispatch** methods can be added at run time.

- The **IDispatch** interface gives a choice of either late or early binding.

- Passing data structures through an **IDispatch** interface is awkward and slow. The best that can be done is to wrap the values as properties and use **IDispatch::Invoke** on each property value. A better choice for transferring data is the **IDataObject** interface, which is discussed in Chapter 6.

- The **IDispatch** interface provides encapsulation. Access to values is by method invocation, while a put is by reference.

   Conceptually, the **IDispatch::Invoke** method can be thought of as a switch function, and the DISPID can be thought of as the switch variable. That is an over-simplification of the function, as **IDispatch::Invoke** has additional arguments, including these:

- *DISPID* — An index identifying the property or method.

- *Flags* — The type of call identifying a get, put, or dispatch.

- *Params* — A pointer to a data structure. This array may be new property values, indices for a property get, or variant method arguments.

- *LCID* — The locale identifier identifying the national language.

- *Results* — A pointer to a variant result structure.

- *Exception* — A pointer to a structure named EXCEPINFO for custom error codes.

- *ArgErr* — Invoke will store the index of the first mismatched argument here.

THE DUAL INTERFACE OF IDISPATCH

Automation is a complex process and a significant amount of overhead is involved. What's not readily apparent is the additional cost of converting the parameters that are stored as variants. Implicit type conversion brought about by sloppy client coding techniques contributes still more overhead.

   It's possible to reduce this overhead by creating a dual interface. A dual interface retains all the vtable entries found in the **IDispatch** interface, but it has, in addition, pointers to the methods and properties of the dispinterface. Shouldn't direct access to parameters or methods improve Automation performance? One would think so; however, what's apparent is not always true. Yes, a dual interface helps, but only with an in-process server, which is a server in your address space. A disproportionate amount of Automation overhead is spent in the stub and proxy marshaling code for both the local and remote servers. Figure 2-5 illustrates a dual **IDispatch** interface.

GENERIC INTERFACES

Time to catch our breath again. We know the general communication mechanisms between a client and the server. All COM interfaces use a vtable — a virtual pointer table for interfacing. The only exception is the **IDispatch** interface used by Automation. **IDispatch** uses the **IDispatch::Invoke** method as an interface for scripting clients.

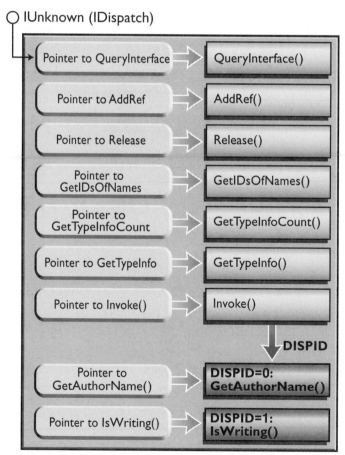

FIGURE 2-5   A dual **IDispatch** interface.

I've barely touched on the generic interfaces available in COM. If I go back to traditional COM and indicate the typical generic COM interfaces, you'll have a better perspective of the interfaces available. I say *typical* because COM is always changing, and I am more interested in the architecture than in the machinations of any particular interface. Figure 2-6 is a roadmap to generic COM interfaces.

note **The topology in Figure 2-6 is not quite correct. Figure 2-6 shows IAdviseSink, IAdviseSink2, and IMessageFilter as *Uniform Data Transfer* (UDT) interfaces. That is not quite true. The scope of these three interfaces extends beyond UDT, and placing them there only illustrates their universal functionality.**

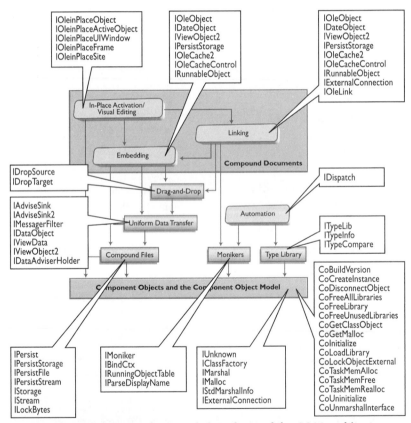

FIGURE 2-6   A roadmap to the generic interfaces of the COM architecture.

COM implements the concept of a library. It is a collection of dynamic link libraries (DLLs) and EXEs whose names and attributes are mapped into the Registry. There is an example of that mapping below, but for now let's look in a little more detail at the COM library.

The pedestrian term for COM library is those system services that start with the letters *Co*. The following list enumerates a few of these system services without an explanation because the name is nearly always indicative of the function. The COM library **Co** functions are:

CoCreateGuid	CoGetClassObject
CoCreateInstance	CoGetCurrentProcess
CoCreateStandardMalloc	CoGetMalloc
CoDisconnectObject	CoGetTreatAsClass
CoDosDateTimeToFileTime	CoInitialize
CoFileTimeNow	CoIsHandlerConnected
CoFileTimeToDosDateTime	CoLockExternal
CoFreeAllLibraries	CoMarshalResult
CoFreeLibraryCoFreeUnusedLibraries	CoMarshalInterface

These are not the only elements of the COM library. There are other support interfaces, many of which are listed in Figure 2-6. Figure 2-7 is my representation of the COM library in which both the client and the object offer services. The COM library is the broker of these services and also offers these services. In this context, a container is also the client.

There's quite a bit more here than meets the eye. Figure 2-6 associates COM interfaces with COM architectural functions and Figure 2-7 shows the COM library used freely by both the client and the object. How are these interfaces managed? Well, if you haven't guessed by now, by the Registry. The Registry (REG) defines a complete topology of the interfaces and their relationships. Let's look at some of the characteristics for the .REG file protocol.

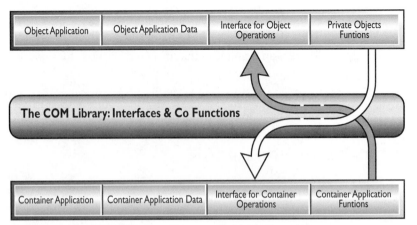

FIGURE 2-7   The COM library acting as a broker of services.

Classes

The Windows NT COM information is located in the Registry hive HKEY_CLASSES_ROOT with information organized in a hierarchical manner. A class entry in the .REG file is formatted similar to the following:

```
HKEY_CLASSES_ROOT\CLSID\{class identifier}\Keyword = Value
```

Typical keywords for a class entry include:

```
LocalServer = <path to 16-bit or 32-bit exe>
LocalServer32 = <path to 32-bit exe >
InprocServer = <path to dll>
InprocServer32 = <path to 32-bit dll>
InprocHandler = <path to dll>
InprocHandler32 = <path to 32-bit dll>
Verb
 verb number = <name, menu flags, verb flags>
 {Examples:
   0 = &Edit, 0, 2
   1 = &Play, 0, 3
   -3 = Hide, 0, 1
   -2 = Open, 0, 1
   -1 = Show, 0, 1}
AuxUserType
```

```
 <form of type>
 {Examples:
   2 = <Short name>    Key 1 is not available!
   3 = <Application Name>}
MiscStatus = <default>
DataFormats = <formats>
 DefaultFile = <format>
 GetSet
   <n> = <format, aspect, medium, flag>
Insertable
ProgID = <ProgID>
TreatAs = <CLSID>
AutoTreatAs = <CLSID>
AutoConvertTo = <CLSID>
Conversion
 Readable
   Main = <format, format, format, . . .>
 Readwritable
   Main = <format, format, format, . . .>
DefaultIcon = <path to exe, index>
Interfaces = <IID, IID, IID, . . .>
VesionIndependentProgID = <Version Independent ProgID>
```

Interfaces

Interfaces entries in the Registry are much simpler than CLSID entries, and the format is essentially the same:

```
HKEY_CLASSES_ROOT\Interface\{interface identifier}\Keyword =
 Value
```

There are only three keywords of interest in a Registry interface entry:

- The first value is always the interface name. It's easily recognized because no assignment operator is associated.

- BaseInterface = < *CLSID of inherited interface*>

- NumMethods = <*The number of methods this interface supports*>

- ProxyStubClsid = <*The CLSID of the component providing marshaling*>

Listing 2-2 shows a snippet from the OLE2.REG file with the interface registration information for **IPersist** and **IPersistFile**. This is a discussion of COM object interface information in the Registry and is not meant to be a discussion of either the **IPersistFile** or **IPersist** interfaces.

LISTING 2-2 COM object interface information found in the Registry

```
HKEY_CLASSES_ROOT\Interface\{0000010B-0000-0000-C000-
   000000000046} = IPersistFile
HKEY_CLASSES_ROOT\Interface\{0000010B-0000-0000-C000-
   000000000046}\BaseInterface = {0000010C-0000-0000-C000-
   000000000046}
HKEY_CLASSES_ROOT\Interface\{0000010B-0000-0000-C000-
   000000000046}\NumMethods = 9
HKEY_CLASSES_ROOT\Interface\{0000010B-0000-0000-C000-
   000000000046}\ProxyStubClsid = {0000030C-0000-0000-C000-
   000000000046}
HKEY_CLASSES_ROOT\Interface\{0000010C-0000-0000-C000-
   000000000046} = IPersist
HKEY_CLASSES_ROOT\Interface\{0000010C-0000-0000-C000-
   000000000046}\NumMethods = 4
HKEY_CLASSES_ROOT\Interface\{0000010C-0000-0000-C000-
   000000000046}\ProxyStubClsid = {0000030C-0000-0000-C000-
   000000000046}
```

The highlights are:

- The CLSID of **IPersistFile** is {0000010B-0000-0000-C000-0000000000046}.

- The base interface for **IPersistfile** is {0000010C-0000-0000-C000-00000000046}. This is COM interface inheritance with the CLSID owned by **IPersist**. The **IPersistFile** interface inherits an interface from **IPersist**; **IPersist**, however, has no interface inheritance.

- **IPersistFile::NumMethods** = 9; there are nine methods available in the **IPersistFile** interface.

- **IPersistFile::ProxyStubClsid** is {0000030C-0000-0000-C000-00000000046}. This CLSID is the **PSGenObject** interface CLSID, which is an in-process server. The server is OLE2PROX.DLL, which does the proxy marshaling.

ProgIDs

I've discussed CLSIDs and interfaces so far. The topic of **ProgIDs** is also important because they are not unique. ProgIDs are a key component in resolving name conflicts.

Every OLE object class that is to appear in an insert object dialog box (hereafter referred to as an *insertable class*), must have a programmatic identifier or **ProgID**.

 note

The ProgID is not guaranteed to be universally unique. It is not more that 39 characters, contains no punctuation, and cannot start with a digit. And the ProgID is the class name for an OLE class.

The two different versions of the ProgID enable the COM library to convert ProgID to CLSID using the construct ROOT\<ProgID>\CLSID. The reverse translation is done using the key ROOT\CLSID\<ProgID>, which is version-dependent. CLSID is a language-independent name in the form <vendor>.<Component>.<Version> such as Word.Document.6.

The structure of a generic Registry ProgID entry structure is illustrated in Listing 2-3. (Not all detail is presented.)

LISTING 2-3 A generic Registry entry illustrating the structure of a ProgID entry

```
CLSID < Main User Type Name> = <ProgID>
CLSID<ProgID> = < Main User Type Name >.version
Insertable    // class is insertable in OLE 2 containers
Protocol
 StdFileEditing
 Server = < full path to the OLE 2 object application >
 Verb
   0 = < verb 0 >
   1 = < verb 1>

   . . .
```

```
VersionIndependentProgID = <VersionIndependentProgID>
CLSID
Shell
 Print
 Open
 Command = < executable application name > %1
```

The registry information presented thus far is from Windows NT, my choice of operating systems. Windows 95 has a Registry; however, the format and the support tools are different than in Windows NT. You can export Registry information in Windows 95 by selecting Export from the Registry menu. These files have the keyword *REGEDIT4* in the preamble, while Windows NT files have the keyword *REGEDIT* in the header.

CREATING AN IN-PROCESS SERVER

Well, we're making progress. We know how COM objects and interfaces are uniquely identified, and we know the architecture of a vtable. How do we use this mechanism? The simplest explanation is to consider the situation in which a client application wishes to start a single instance of a COM server object. The application calls the COM library function **CoCreateInstance** with the *global unique identifier* (GUID) of the desired object and the IID of the desired interface. The COM library delegates the actual task of locating and instantiating an object to the *Service Control Manager* (SCM). SCM searches the Registry and locates the server. The server is started and SCM returns the requested pointer interface to the COM library, which in turn passes the pointer back to the client. (We're not discussing distributed COM (DCOM) yet; we're still dealing with pointers.)

An interesting issue is that COM cannot initialize the new object, but COM does not ask the server to initialize itself. The client does this. The client asks COM for the **IPersistFile** interface by calling **IUnknown::QueryInterface** with the IID of **IPersistFile**. Persistent data exists when this call is successful. The client calls **IPersistFile::Load** to load the persistent data. The object then initializes itself.

The issue of initializing a server introduces the concept of persistent data. This is just another term for *nonvolatile* data.

note ✐ **An IID is either the machine-readable portion of an interface, or 128 bits of chicken tracks. The human-readable interface name of the same interface always starts with a letter *I* and explains names such as IUnknown, IDispatch, and IPersistFile.**

An **IPersist** interface exists when the object exposes any of the **IPersist*** interfaces. There are no specific rules of initialization and an object is free to adopt any technique necessary to initialize. If a file is required for interfacing, the object will expose an **IPersistfile** interface. There is no requirement that a file actually exist. Simply exposing this interface gives the object a chance to initialize itself, even when a file is not used.

The object already knows how to initialize itself. There are no specific rules on initialization and an object may not have a type library. The important fact is that an object must initialize itself. All objects must support a COM library in addition to the **IUnknown** interface. This ensures the object that the required support functionality is available.

Let's expand the detail of creating an in-process server that runs in your address space:

- A client calls the COM library functions **CoGetClassObject** with the CLSID of the desired object and the IID of the desired interface. Because the object is being created, the IID of **IClassFactory** is the other input parameter to **CoGetClassObject**. What is eventually returned to the client is the pointer to **IClassFactory** of the desired object.
- **CoGetClassObject** passes control to the SCM. The job of SCM is to locate the server.
- The functions of SCM include:
  - Looking up the class in the Registry.
  - Looking up the DLL in the Registry.
  - Calling the COM library function **CoLoadLibrary** to load the DLL.
  - Determining the DLL start address with **DLLGetClassObject.**
  - Starting the DLL.
- The DLL creates the class factory.
- The DLL returns the **IClassFactory** pointer to SCM.
- SCM returns the **IClassFactory** pointer to the client.

- The client now uses the returned **IClassFactory** pointer to call **IClassFactory::CreateInstance**. **IClassFactory::CreateInstance** creates the class object and returns a pointer to it. **IClassFactory** also increases the reference by calling **IUnknown::AddRef**.

- The client can later invoke the method **IUnknown::Release** to decrement the reference count. The server will be destroyed when the count goes to zero.

- The object can be used after initialization.

Because **IClassFactory::CreateInstance** creates a pointer to an object, it has the responsibility of incrementing the object reference count by calling **IUnknown::AddRef**. **IUnknown::QueryInterface**, **IOleItemContainer::GetObject**, and **IOleContainer::EnumObjects** are the other interfaces responsible for incrementing the reference count.

This sequence creates an uninitialized instance of an object class. The object can be initialized by one of these methods: **IPersistStorage::InitNew**, **IPersistStorage::Load**, **IPersistStream::Load**, or **IPersistFile::Load**. These methods are discussed in Chapter 4.

The interfaces **IUnknown** and **IClassFactory** are the minimum interfaces an OLE object must support, but an OLE object is not limited to just two interfaces.

CREATING A LOCAL OR REMOTE SERVER

A local or remote server is an executable file, while an in-process server is a DLL. The sequence of events for creating a local server is almost identical to that of a remove server. The only difference is that SCM will provide a pointer to a local object proxy for local servers, or a pointer to a remote object proxy for remote servers. Either way, the process is transparent to the client.

Let's step through the process of creating a local Server:

- A client calls the COM library functions **CoGetClassObject** with the CLSID of the desired object and the IID of the desired interface. The input IID is that of **IClassFactory** because a pointer to **IClassFactory** will be returned to the client.

- **CoGetClassObject** passes control to SCM. The job of SCM is to locate the server.
- SCM does the following:
  - Looks up the class in the Registry.
  - Looks up EXE in the Registry.
  - The server may not be running, in which case the EXE starts with **WinExec**. If the server is already running, then a new process is created with **CreateProcess**.
  - Control is passed to the EXE (**WinMain**).
- EXE does the following:
  - Calls the COM library function **CoInitialize**.
  - Creates the class factory.
  - Calls the COM library **CoRegisterClassObject** with the **IClassFactory** pointer.
  - Control is returned to SCM, which in turn passes control back to the client.
- The client now has the **IClassFactory** pointer and initiates a call to **IClassFactory::CreateInstance** with the CLSID of the object and the IID of the interface.
- The client receives a pointer to the uninitialized object.
- **IUnknown::AddRef** is used by the client to increase the reference count. This ensures that the server will not be destroyed. The client can later invoke the **IUnknown::Release** method to decrement the reference count. The server will be destroyed when the count goes to zero.
- The object can be used after initialization.

This sequence is almost identical to that of an in-process server. The new object can be initialized in the same way with: **IPersistStorage::InitNew**, **IPersistStorage::Load**, **IPersistStream::Load**, or **IPersistFile::Load**. Now you have some insight into the mechanics and overhead costs of OLE servers.

KEY POINT SUMMARY

COM is a binary specification for process communication that is machine independent. COM borrows terminology and constructs from C++, which is the Microsoft host implementation language. Key constructs are the concepts of a vtable, the **IUnknown** and the **IDispatch** interfaces, and the concept of marshaling.

- A vtable is the standard COM interface mechanism in the Microsoft implementation. It is a binary specification and language independent.
- The **IDispatch** interface used by Automation is a combination of a vtable and a dispinterface using **IDispatch::Invoke** with DISPIDs.
- COM objects must initialize themselves.
- **IClassFactory::CreateInstance** creates an instance of a server.
- Object life is managed with the **AddRef** and **Release** methods of **IUnknown**.
- **IUnknown::QueryInterface** is the universal interrogation mechanism of the COM model.
- Transparent marshaling is supported for apartment-model threaded objects and remote objects.

APPLYING WHAT YOU'VE LEARNED

A mastery of the mechanics of COM is required for all levels of developers. Visual Basic 5.0 now supports the creation of ActiveX controls and control creation is no longer limited to C++ developers. The questions that follow test your knowledge of the COM interfacing fundamentals.

Instant Assessment

1. What is a vtable?
2. What interface must all COM objects support?
3. What is the minimum number of interfaces for a COM object? Name the interface.
4. Name the three **IUnknown** methods.

5. Name two unique characteristics of the **IDispatch** interface.

6. What is a dual interface?

7. Under what condition might you use a dual interface?

8. What function is it that the COM library cannot do?

9. What is the role of the Service Control Manager?

10. What is the role of **IUnknown::AddRef** and **IUnknown::Release**?

11. Which component in the COM architecture is responsible for using **IUnknown::AddRef** and **IUnknown::Release**?

12. Identify the COM library component used to start a server.

13. Identify the information that must be supplied to the COM library component identified in Question 12 to successfully start a server.

concept link **For answers to the Instant Assessment questions, see Appendix C.**

Lab Exercise

This laboratory will expand your knowledge of the Registry. It deals with the version-independent ProgID. The basic problem is the latest version of software installed is always the version activated when an icon is double-clicked. The primary goal of this laboratory is to understand the version-independent ProgID mechanism. The secondary goal is to design a Registry protocol that preserves the original version-independent ProgID and which reverts to a version-dependent ProgID. A very crude workaround for this problem is to install a product such as Microsoft Office 97 and then immediately reinstall OfficePro 4.3. Both systems are available; however, double-clicking starts Word 6.*x* and not Word 97.

Lab 2.2 *A shortcoming of the version-independent ProgID*

WA I

Lab 2-2 investigates how to start a COM server. Assume the VBA statements below exist in a Visual Basic context. Statements of this nature are used to print reports from Microsoft Access rather than using the Crystal Reports that comes with Visual Basic.

```
Dim MyObj As Object
Set MyObj = CreateObject("Access.Application")
```

1. Go to your Windows NT Registry and the `HKEY_CLASSES_ROOT` hive.

2. Open the `HKEY_CLASSES_ROOT` hive and select View ⇒ Find.

3. Search for Access.Application.

I found three entries on my system:

- `Access.Application`
- `Access.Application.7`
- `Access.Application.8`

When I expanded these entries I found that *Access.Application* has the same CLSID as *Access.Application.8,* which I expected.

This system has Access 2.0, Access 95, and Access 97 installed. The problem is that when I double-click an icon, Access 97 automatically starts. This is because there is only one class registered for any version of Microsoft Access — .MDB. You can examine the class by searching the `HKEY_CLASSES_ROOT` hive for .MDB.

When I examined that entry I found *Access.Application.8,* which is not what I want. This is the version-independent ProgID discussed earlier. This is a general problem with the design of the Registry, which always uses the last installation version as the version-independent ProgID.

Design a Registry protocol that will provide a floating ProgID. In essence, what is wanted is a version-dependent and not a version-independent ProgID. A version-dependent ProgID will allow the installation of a new version; double-clicking an icon, however, will activate the dependent version and not the most recently installed version.

caution

Do not change the Registry unless you are experienced and understand that a damaged Registry will make the system unbootable. However, do examine the Registry closely until this is understood. I champion a deprecated class whenever a new class is installed. This mechanism would not force unwanted and unneeded application upgrades, and both deprecated and new classes could exist on the same system.

Windows Architecture I

Interface Issues

About Chapter 3

This chapter deals with the fundamental issues of program communication. *Interprogram communication* had to be established before intraprogram communication was possible. The *name-space* domain evolved slowly, primarily because there was no impetus for an international standard, and because name-space was traditionally controlled by the application developer. COM requires a unique object identifier. This started the change towards a global name-space. ActiveX (COM) objects evolved from a machine-oriented and process-oriented technology to the universal name-space of the Internet. Intraprogram communication is now successful on a global basis. This process took nearly 50 years to complete.

The ActiveX control created in this chapter is located in the Visual Basic 5.0 Enterprise Edition **ICheckBook** project in the EXAMPLES/ CHAPTER3 folder on the CD-ROM that accompanies this book.

THE GLOBAL NAME-SPACE PROBLEM

If you're with me so far, you know that my thesis is that the COM model is the natural order of software evolution. The name-space in earlier programming languages was limited. If you wrote a subroutine using an earlier language, your only problem was to ensure that it didn't have the same name as a library subroutine. The result after compiling and linking the subroutine was a binary mass that probably required segmentation to execute properly. The only exposed names were the executable code segment and the FORTRAN Named Common Block names.

 in the real world **I recall a missile reentry program developed in the early 1960s at the Boeing Development Center in Seattle, Washington. The program was written in FORTRAN and used Named Common Blocks. Each common block was named after a brand of beer, a very limited name-space but adequate for the situation. In FORTRAN, Named Common Blocks are a fixed area of memory. Programs were not reentrant, and each new overlay found the information from previous overlays through common blocks. A vexing problem was the reordering of common blocks, which occurred when one or more blocks were no longer in use.**

The developer nearly always created the name-space. I use the word *developer* in the context of both individuals and software development companies. The individuals had complete freedom to create name-spaces of their choice. Only internal standards and policies limited software companies. Users were forced to comply with the vendor-supplied naming conventions.

Here I am only discussing module or subroutine naming. Subroutine parameters were positional with no other context. The source code named parameters internally within the module and the process of compiling and linking masked the names, hence the name *binary mass*.

The Open Systems Foundation (OSF) initially recognized the global naming problem in its distributing computing environment (DCE) specification. Digital Equipment Corporation and Hewlett Packard Corporation worked jointly on a solution to the problem, but the global solution was (and is) the Microsoft implementation of the COM model.

There may be better solutions to the name-space problem than the COM model, but I believe that Microsoft was (and is) in a better position to implement global naming standards than were (are) other companies. Microsoft's size alone dictates a de facto standard.

What I find fascinating is that the software industry approached the 50-year mark before a solution was proposed. I am certain that if we did not have a company the size of Microsoft, we would still be bickering. OSF recognized the problem with its release of the DCE specification in the early 1990s, and Microsoft implemented it with COM.

Solving the Global Name–Space Problem with GUID

Microsoft borrowed the DCE *universal unique identifier* (UUID) concept in solving the name-space problem, and in doing so, renamed it. The designated new name for a UUID is a *global unique identifier* (GUID). The implementation is 128 bits and comes in two versions: one version for object names and the second version for interface names. If you don't understand all the acronyms, here they are:

- Universal unique identifier (UUID) is an OSF DCE concept.
- A globally unique identifier (GUID) is the 128-bit Microsoft implementation of a UUID.
- A COM object class identifier (CLSID) is a GUID.
- A COM object interface identifier (IID) is a GUID.

 note **Please remember that I am discussing older technology. Today, this technology has all been replaced with new and exciting tools. Even though some of this material appears obtuse and a little arcane, it is important to understand the original concepts and the issues involved. It will make life in the trenches a little easier later on.**

The GUID can be guaranteed unique on a global basis. It consists of the current date and time plus a clock sequence to deal with the retrograde motion of clocks, a forcibly incremented counter to deal with high-frequency allocations, and a true globally unique IEEE machine identifier obtained from a network card (the network card is not essential). The *machine identification* is synthesized from machine states when no network card is available. The first GUID example was created on my Intel-based computer.

The following can create a GUID:

- Using the Visual C++ module `UIIDGEN.EXE`: `UUIDGEN.EXE` or `GUIDGEN.EXE` can be used to generate one or more GUIDs at a time. (Figure 3-1 is an example of a GUID created using GUIDGEN.)

```
E:\MSVC40\BIN\uuidgen -n4
6c069860-88a5-11d0-928e-08002b2613ff
6c069861-88a5-11d0-928e-08002b2613ff
6c069862-88a5-11d0-928e-08002b2613ff
6c069863-88a5-11d0-928e-08002b2613ff
```

- Of course if you thrive on Jolt cola and cold pizza, and you are suspicious of software wizards, then you may want to create the GUID yourself and register it with the MFC function **AfxRegisterTypeLib**. The GUID parameter can be declared as:

```
static const GUID myTypeGuid =
{ 0x6c069860, 0x99a5, 0x88a5, 0x11d0, {
0x92, 0x8e, 0x08, 0x00, 0x2b, 0x26, 0x13, 0xff } }
```

The GUID is registered using the constant in the C++ statement:

```
VERIFY(AfxOleRegisterTypeLib(AfxGetInstanceHandle(),
myTypeGuid, "MyCntl.tlb"));
```

- Using `E:\MSVC40\BIN\GUIDGEN`:

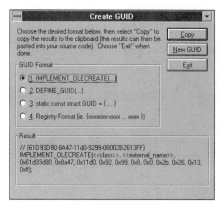

FIGURE 3-1   Creating a GUID with GUIDGEN.

- The COM library function **CoCreateGuid** is used to create a GUID at run time, a unique 128-bit 16-byte integer used for CLSIDs and interface identifiers. **CoCreateGuid** relies on the Win32API function **UuidCreate**. This is done with:

  ```
  HRESULT CoCreateGuid(
  GUID *pguid //Receives a pointer to the GUID on return
  );
  ```

- The Win32 API function **UuidCreate** creates a new UUID with:

  ```
  #include <rpc.h>RPC_STATUS RPC_ENTRY UuidCreate(
  UUID * Uuid
  );
  ```

- Visual Basic 5.0 makes life simpler by creating a GUID automatically.

A GUID in the Registry

What needs a GUID now that I have one? Well, every object class that appears in an **Insert Object** dialog box must have a GUID. Each of these objects is a member of an insertable class. Figure 3-2 shows creating a new object with the **Insert Object** dialog box. Every displayed entry, along with all other companion entries, is a member of an insertable class and requires a GUID. However, not every class object needs a GUID; only those class objects created by COM require one.

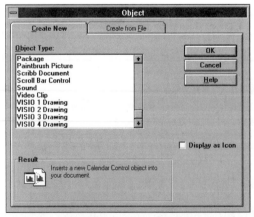

FIGURE 3-2   Creating a new Visio object with the Insert object dialog box.

Let's look at the Registry. I'm using Visio 4.0, which you can see in the dialog box in Figure 3-2. When I go to Administrative Tools ⇒ Registry Editor and open `HKEY_CLASSES_ROOT`, down near the bottom I'll find the Visio 4.0 entries. If I expand the Registry keys, the directory structure shown in Figure 3-3 appears. Notice that Visio 4.0 is an insertable object that requires a CLSID. It's also obvious that version 4.0 is an upgrade from version 3.0.

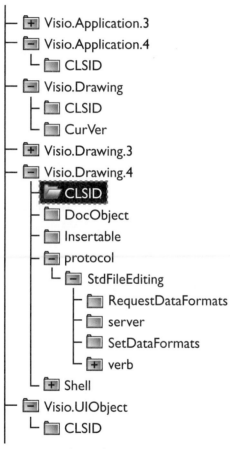

FIGURE 3-3   The registry CLSID.

There are three `Visio.Drawing` entries in Figure 3-3. These entries are ProgIDs. The entry without a version number is the version-independent ProgID. Expanding the CLSID of the version-independent `Visio.Drawing` entry shows that the CLSID is the same as the CLSID of the `Visio.Drawing.4` entry. This is as it should be. The application uses the version-independent Registry entry to find the latest version of the needed object application.

TYPE LIBRARIES

Type libraries contain all of the necessary information to support an object. This information includes descriptions of the object, its methods, and its properties. The information supports accessing, browsing, and getting help on topics.

Creation of type libraries is mentioned almost as a historical note. The integrated development environment (IDE) of the Microsoft tools has automated nearly all aspects of type library management. Microsoft Visual Basic 5.0 (VB) has extended type library management to include COM interfaces specific to type library management. VB keeps everything under the hood and automates the low-level detail. The technology has grown up a bit with numerous new interfaces, methods, and properties.

I'm certain that most of you know how entries appear in the Registry. Objects are registered. It's as simple as that. The COM model is managed with both the Registry and a type library as information sources. The information necessary to instantiate a server object is found in the Registry, while other information comes from type library files created by the MKTYPLIB.EXE or MIDL.EXE compilers.

The MKTYPLIB.EXE compiler is a little long in the tooth, and the *Microsoft Interface Definition Language* (MIDL) compiler is the recommended tool for the 32-bit environment. Both the MIDL.EXE and MKTYPLIB.EXE compilers create a .TLB file.

That's true, but the compilers create much more than just a .TLB file. Figure 3-4 illustrates that compilers can perform more than one task.

The compilers also generate C/C++ header files. The type library infrastructure can be summarized as:

- ○ UUID, Properties, and methods of server objects are stored in a type library. Properties have data types, and methods return values or accept parameters.
- ○ Type library is extended as a .TLB or as a .ODL.
- ○ Object description language (ODL) files are plain-text files.
- ○ MkTypLib creates a type library. Statements are based on the prototype ODL structure of Listing 3-1.

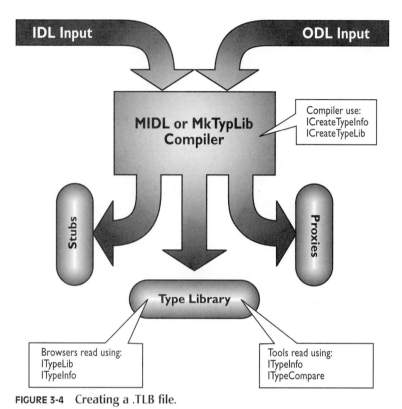

FIGURE 3-4 Creating a .TLB file.

LISTING 3-1 A prototype .ODL file

```
[uuid<GUID>, <helpinfo>, <attributes>]
library <name>
 {
 importlib(<path to another type library>)
 typedef [<attributes>] <basename | struct | enum | union>
 {
 . . .
 } <type>;
 [attributes] module <name>
  {
  <element list>
  };
 [uuid(<GUID>), <helpinfo>, <attributes>]
```

```
interface <name>
 {
 [<attributes>] <return type> [calling convention]
      <function name><arguments>);
 .  .  ..
 }
[uuid(<GUID>), <helpinfo>, <attributes>]
dispinterface <name>
 {
 properties:
      [<attributes>] <type> <name>;

      .  .  .

 methods:
      [<attributes>] <return type> <name> (<arguments>);

      .  .  .

 }
[uuid(<GUID>), <helpinfo>, <attributes>]
dispinterface <name>
 {
 interface <name>;
 }
[uuid(<GUID>), <helpinfo>, <attributes>]
coclass
 {
 [<attributes>] dispinterface < dispinterface name>;
 .  .  .
 [<attributes>] interface < interface name>;
 }
```

A type library is located through the Registry. The CLSID is used to locate the correct entry that identifies the .TLB file. A type library is used by browsers, by OLE Automation checking interfaces at runtime, and by an EXE server for marshaling the dispinterface. Figure 3-5 shows the type library, which contains more than one hundred entries, on the machine I used to type this.

caution I prided myself on being a clever fellow, but I've had a recent change of thought while collecting material for this book. My WinTel toy has about 6GB of hard drive space, and I am always reinstalling an older version of a Microsoft tool for a client. Afterwards, I delete the icons from the desktop and delete the product from the installed directory. Right? Wrong! My HKEY_CLASSES_ROOT hive has stuff from several years back. It is incredible! What I need right now is a tool to purge the HKEY_CLASSES_ROOT hive in the Registry. The lesson here is don't delete, use the uninstall feature of the product.

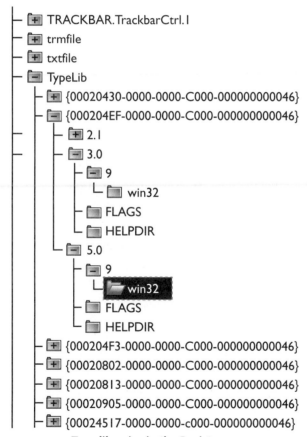

FIGURE 3-5   Type libraries in the Registry.

Building a Type Library

Not all COM objects need a type library. If a type library is necessary, an ODL, or, preferably, an IDL, is created within the Visual C++ environment. The file is input to the MIDL or MKTYPLIB compiler, and the result is a .TLB file. Let's have some fun and build an IDL file. Let's call the object **IAuthor** and the file will be IAUTHOR.IDL.

```
[
 object ,
 uuid(6c069860-88a5-11d0-928e-08002b2613ff),
 pointer_default(unique)
]
interface IAuthor : IUnknown
{
 import "unknwn.idl";
 HRESULT GetAuthorName([out], string, size_is(128)] char *p);
 HRESULT IsWriting([out] BOOL *pBool);
}
```

The IDL file includes my two methods, **GetAuthorName** and **IsWriting**, as well as the inherited methods, **QueryInterface**, **AddRef**, and **Release**. The C++ inheritance is from <drive>:\VC40\INCLUDE\UNKNWN.H and the UNKNWN.IDL file is from the same directory. This interface uses both implementation inheritance and interface inheritance. The implementation inheritance occurs on the Interface line in the IDL file, and the interface inheritance occurs when I import another IDL file to my IDL file on the Import line. This is the equivalent of a cut and paste to the IDL file and gives me my interface inheritance. The COM model doesn't care if the underlying code uses implementation inheritance. All that's really important is that the concept of interface inheritance be adhered to.

Building a Type Library in Visual Basic 5.0

Life is simpler with Visual Basic 5.0. Type libraries are built automatically when the project is built. We'll create a simple ActiveX EXE or DLL with the following dialog. You'll want to create an executable file (EXE) when the ActiveX server does not run in-process. Conversely, an ActiveX DLL will run in-process. Let's name our class **ICheckBook**, which follows the naming conventions for object interfaces.

To create **ICheckBook**, follow these steps:

1. Start Visual Basic 5.0

2. Select **New** and choose either an ActiveX EXE or an ActiveX DLL.

3. From the **View** menu select **Properties Window** and set the class name to **ICheckBook**. The default name should be **Class1**.

4. From the **View** menu, select **Project Explorer**, and double-click **ICheckbook**.

5. Enter the code shown in Listing 3-2 below.

6. From the File menu select **Make Project1.EXE** (or **Make Project1.DLL**)

7. Change the name to **ICheckbook.EXE** (or **ICheckbook.DLL**).

8. Select **OK.**

9. Congratulations! You have just built an ActiveX control. The type library information exists within your new control.

You can browse your new control. From the **View** menu select **Object Browser**.

The control is ready for use. The **Browse** button on the **References** dialog box can be used later to locate your new DLL or EXE file and set a reference to it. Checking your new control in the **References** dialog box will register it.

The VB **Implements** statement can be used with our new class. This is the equivalent of inheritance in C++. There is a restriction with the **Implements** statement not supporting outgoing interfaces (see Chapter 6). This means that any events declared in a class module are ignored.

LISTING 3-2 The ICheckbook property in the Visual Basic ActiveX EXE or DLL

```
Option Explicit
Private dblChkBookBal As Double
Property Get Balance() As Double
 Balance = dblChkBookBal
End Property
Property Let Balance(ByVal dblNewChkBookBal As Double)
 If dblNewChkBookBal < 0 Then
    Err.Raise Number:=vbObjectError + 32112, _
    Description:="Overdraft"
```

```
Else
   dblChkBookBal = dblNewChkBookBal
End If
End Property
```

Registering a Type Library

Server registration can take several forms:

- Registering CLSIDs at object installation through a setup file.
- A self-registering object which is downloaded from the Internet.
- Dynamically registering objects at run time with MFC.
- Selecting **References** ⇒ **Browse** and selecting an ActiveX object from a VBA editor.

Registering a new server is necessary before a client can locate and use your new server. All server CLSIDs must be registered, which is normally done at installation time. The object setup file provides this information. Either system defaults are assumed at object installation, or, at the very minimum, the **CLSID** key and **AppID** key information is required. Important information is the designation of type, which can be in-process, out-of-process local, or out-of-process remote. **RemoteServerName** and **ActivateAtStorage** are also important because they let a client instantiate a server with no built-in server knowledge.

Help in creating a Visual Basic 5.0 setup file is found by selecting the **Help** menu and *Books on Line* from within VB. Enter **Setup** and you'll find displayed all the necessary information topics for using a Setup Wizard to create your new Visual Basic ActiveX control installation files. The setup kit is found in ...\VB\SetupKit. Another choice is using **Regsvr32** when the VB setup wizard isn't wanted.

The second registering technique can be done in C++ at run time. An object may be registered at run time with the MFC function **AfxOleRegisterTypeLib**, which is C++ specific.

```
VERIFY(AfxOleRegisterTypeLib(AfxGetInstanceHandle(),
   myTypeLibGuid, "author.tlb"));
```

Of course, having the server register itself is a very special case. This occurs with Internet downloads where new objects register themselves.

The last example of registering an object is the example server constructed earlier. The **ICheckBook.EXE** file was registered by setting a reference to the executable file dynamic link library while in the **References** dialog box. (A Registry entry was found for **Project1.ICheckBook** along with a CLSID.)

caption

Before you rush to register information in the Registry, remember Windows NT's security issues. I always log on to Windows NT as Administrator, and security is never an issue. I know that is not the way to do it, but my house, my rules. Your system may become inoperable if the Registry is edited incorrectly.

Listing 3-3 is an application registration file from the *Control Developers Kit* (CDK).

LISTING 3-3 The registration file for the Hello application

```
; Registration information for the hello application
;
; IDispatch*     Hello.Application   {D3CE6D43-F1AF-1068-9FBB-
  08002B32372A}
; Type library:  hello.tlb {D3CE6D44-F1AF-1068-9FBB-
  08002B32372A}
; Interface:     IHello   {D3CE6D45-F1AF-1068-9FBB-
  08002B32372A}
;
;;;;;;;;;;;;;;;;;;;;;;;;;;;;;;;;;;;;;;;;;;;
; registration info Hello.Application (defaults to
  Hello.Application.1)
HKEY_CLASSES_ROOT\Hello.Application = OLE Automation Hello
  Application
HKEY_CLASSES_ROOT\Hello.Application\Clsid = {D3CE6D43-F1AF-
  1068-9FBB-08002B32372A}
;;;;;;;;;;;;;;;;;;;;;;;;;;;;;;;;;;;;;;;;;;;
; registration info Hello.Application.1
HKEY_CLASSES_ROOT\Hello.Application.1 = OLE Automation Hello
  1.0 Application
HKEY_CLASSES_ROOT\Hello.Application.1\Clsid = {D3CE6D43-F1AF-
  1068-9FBB-08002B32372A}
```

```
;;;;;;;;;;;;;;;;;;;;;;;;;;;;;;;;
; registration info Hello 1.0
HKEY_CLASSES_ROOT\CLSID\{D3CE6D43-F1AF-1068-9FBB-08002B32372A}
 = IDispatch Hello Example
HKEY_CLASSES_ROOT\CLSID\{D3CE6D43-F1AF-1068-9FBB-
 08002B32372A}\ProgID = Hello.Application.1
HKEY_CLASSES_ROOT\CLSID\{D3CE6D43-F1AF-1068-9FBB-
 08002B32372A}\VersionIndependentProgID =
Hello.Application
HKEY_CLASSES_ROOT\CLSID\{D3CE6D43-F1AF-1068-9FBB-
 08002B32372A}\LocalServer32 = hello.exe
/Automation
;;;;;;;;;;;;;;;;;;;;;;;;;;;;;;;;;
; registration info Hello TypeLib
HKEY_CLASSES_ROOT\TypeLib\{D3CE6D44-F1AF-1068-9FBB-
 08002B32372A}
HKEY_CLASSES_ROOT\TypeLib\{D3CE6D44-F1AF-1068-9FBB-
 08002B32372A}\1.0 = OLE Automation Hello 1.0
Type Library
HKEY_CLASSES_ROOT\TypeLib\{D3CE6D44-F1AF-1068-9FBB-
 08002B32372A}\1.0\HELPDIR =
;Localized language is US english
HKEY_CLASSES_ROOT\TypeLib\{D3CE6D44-F1AF-1068-9FBB-
 08002B32372A}\1.0\409\win32 = hello.tlb
HKEY_CLASSES_ROOT\Interface\{D3CE6D46-F1AF-1068-9FBB-
 08002B32372A} = _DHello
HKEY_CLASSES_ROOT\Interface\{D3CE6D46-F1AF-1068-9FBB-
 08002B32372A}\ProxyStubClsid32 = {00020420-0000-0000-
 C000-000000000046}
HKEY_CLASSES_ROOT\Interface\{D3CE6D46-F1AF-1068-9FBB-
 08002B32372A}\NumMethod = 7
HKEY_CLASSES_ROOT\Interface\{D3CE6D46-F1AF-1068-9FBB-
 08002B32372A}\BaseInterface = {00020400-0000-0000-
 C000-000000000046}
```

We start the analysis of this .REG file by noting the first few comment lines. A different GUID is used to identify the object (this is an OLE Automation example), a type library, and an interface. Reading the file is self-explanatory until we encounter the line with the second CLSID of `00020420-0000-0000-C000-000000000046`. I looked in `OLE2.REG` and found that `OLEAUT32.DLL` owned that CLSID. The name on the line is **ProxyStubClsid**. This means that `OLEAUT32.DLL` will do the marshaling for the server.

```
-- Registration info for OLE Automation private classes
HKEY_CLASSES_ROOT\CLSID\{00020420-0000-0000-C000-000000000046}
 = PSDispatch
HKEY_CLASSES_ROOT\CLSID\{00020420-0000-0000-
 C000-000000000046}\InprocServer = ole2disp.dll
HKEY_CLASSES_ROOT\CLSID\{00020420-0000-0000-
 C000-000000000046}\InprocServer32 = oleaut32.dll
```

The next unexplained issue is the line with the second CLSID of `00020400-0000-0000-C000-000000000046`. This IID was also found in `OLE2.REG`. This is the OLE Automation interface IID that will also use `OLEAUT32.DLL` for marshaling.

```
-- IDispatch
HKEY_CLASSES_ROOT\Interface\{00020400-0000-0000-C000-
 000000000046} = IDispatch
HKEY_CLASSES_ROOT\Interface\{00020400-0000-0000-C000-
 000000000046}\NumMethods = 7
HKEY_CLASSES_ROOT\Interface\{00020400-0000-0000-C000-
 000000000046}\ProxyStubClsid =
  {00020420-0000-0000-C000-000000000046}
HKEY_CLASSES_ROOT\Interface\{00020400-0000-0000-
 C000-000000000046}\ProxyStubClsid32 =
  {00020420-0000-0000-C000-000000000046}
```

The concept of persistent data can be introduced by simply saying that the data is nonvolatile. This topic is discussed in much more detail in Chapter 4, but for now note that the file name of the EXE type library is stored in the Registry. There was a comment line at the top of this .REG file with the type library GUID. That GUID entry contains the EXE server type library file name. Anything stored in that file is by definition persistent and can be used by the EXE server for self-initialization and subsequent late binding. But more on this and other persistent types later.

A benefit of COM is locale sensitivity. UNICODE is a 2-byte character set with which any language can be represented (see Chapter 42). A global name-space without sensitivity to a local language is of little value. UNICODE provides the capability of representing any language, which capability is only a partial solution. The missing element of the global name problem solution is a *localized identifier* (LCID) that can be used with a GUID. Selecting the local language is done with the LCID. If you examine the type library definition line in the prior .REG example, you'll see the localization code for English.

Let's use French, whose locale identifier is 0x40c, as an example. Because I know its LCID, I can construct the header of a hypothetical IDL file with French as the language. The only other task is to convert the property names to French. I will store the generated IDL file as `MYCONTROLFR.IDL` so that I know it is the French version.

```
[
    uuid(xxxxxxxx-xxxx-xxxx-xxxx-xxxxxxxxxxxxxxxx),
    Version(1.0),
    lcid(0x040c)
]
library MyControl
{

    . . .

}
```

We really don't have to worry too much about ODL or IDL files that use our old friend the GUID. IDL files are simpler than the ODL files they replace because they deal only with interfaces. IDL files are constructed manually quite easily. The generation of the numerous other skeleton object files is reasonably automated with Visual C++ wizards, but the creation of an object does not remain a simple process.

The constructs for the MIDL compiler are C/C++ based, and the new MIDL compiler supports all the essential ODL constructs. Complete MIDL compiler documentation can be found in the Microsoft Win 32 software developer's kit (SDK).

Life is now much sweeter with Microsoft Visual Basic 5.0 Enterprise Edition, which does all the under-the-hood type library work for us transparently.

KEY POINT SUMMARY

We learned in Chapter 2 that COM requests an interface with **IUnknown:: QueryInterface**. This isn't possible unless all objects and interfaces are named uniquely. Microsoft is the first software company to successfully solve the global name-space problem and deliver products based on this solution.

o Name-space is the limiting factor of intraprogram communication.

o The concept of a universal unique identifier (UUID) comes from the OSF DCE specification. Microsoft borrowed this concept and named it a globally unique identifier (GUID).

o A COM object class identifier (CLSID) is a GUID.

o A COM object interface identifier (IID) is a GUID.

o All COM objects have a GUID.

o Each COM object interface has an IID.

o Type libraries support objects, and objects cannot be browsed without a type library.

o An object is kept private without a type library.

APPLYING WHAT YOU'VE LEARNED

The questions below will measure your understanding of the global name-space and how it is managed. Some of the issues may appear to be artifacts of the past because modern tools such as Visual Basic 5.0 have automated many of the issues.

Instant Assessment

1. What is the global name-space problem?

2. How is the global name-space problem solved?

3. Explain the differences between a UUID, a GUID, and an IID.

4. Name three methods of creating a UUID.

5. What is the unique requirement of an Insertable Object?

6. When doesn't an object require a GUID?

7. What is the difference between the ODL compiler `MKTYPLIB.EXE` and the IDL compiler MIDL?

8. Name four types of information created by an ODL or IDL compiler.

9. Name two instances where a GUID is necessary.

10. What is persistent data?

concept link **For answers to the Instant Assessment questions, see Appendix C.**

Lab Exercises

This set of laboratories will help you understand that all Microsoft products are component based. This means that each tool supports a type library and the VBA environment.

Lab 3.3 *Surveying your system*

WA I

Lab 3.3 helps you determine the type libraries in your system. Start by doing an inventory of each of your directories and noting the names and locations of all files with the .TLB extension.

1. How many .TLB files only exist in a product path such as `WINWORD`?

2. How many .TLB files exist only in the `SYSTEM` (`SYSTEM32` for Windows NT) directory?

3. List the .TLB files found in other directories that are not in the `SYSTEM` directory.

Lab 3.4 *Visual Basic 5.0 and type libraries*

Lab 3.4 begins with the Visual Basic 5.0 type library, which is accessed differently than other Microsoft products.

WA I

1. Start Visual Basic 5.0.

2. Click **References** from the **Project** menu. The available type libraries are now displayed. When an application doesn't work it is often because the proper type library is not selected. Also notice the **Browse** button. You use this for selecting a type library not found in the combo box on the **References** dialog form.

The next issue is to browse the existing type libraries of a Microsoft Visual Basic project.

1. Select **Object Browser** from the **View** menu. Here you will find the constants, methods, and properties of the type libraries on your system.

2. Browse the type libraries when you're stumped for a method. The method you want to use may be related to a different object.

Lab 3.5 *Word 97 and type libraries*

Each of the following tools supports the VBA environment. By supporting type libraries, each of these tools supports COM objects and illustrates the ubiquity of COM objects in the Microsoft architecture. The VBA code written in either Microsoft Access or VB can be used interchangably with an occasional minor adjustment.

1. Start Word 97.

2. Select **Tools** ⇒ **Macro**.

3. Select **Visual Basic Editor** from the submenu.

4. In Visual Basic Editor, select **Tools** ⇒ **References**. The dialog box shown in Figure 3-6 is displayed.

Browsing a type library in Word 97 is quite similar to browsing a type library in Visual Basic 5.0. While in the editor, select **Object Browser** from the **View** menu.

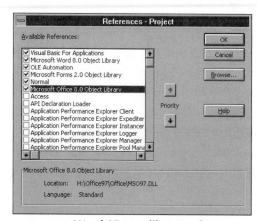

FIGURE 3-6   Word 97 type library references.

Lab 3.6 *Access 97 and type libraries*

WA I

Referencing a type library in Access 97 takes the same amount of work as in Visual Basic 5.0. A control must be placed on a form before a type library can be referenced. To reference the libraries, follow these steps:

1. Start Access 97.

2. Create a new form.

3. Place a control on the form. Clicking a control in the toolbox and painting the control on the form does this.

4. With the control on the form selected, pick an event from the Properties dialog form. This places you in the VBA coding module.

5. Select **Tools** ⇒ **References** to add or change a type library.

6. Select **View** ⇒ **Object Browser** to browse properties, methods, or constants of an Access 97 type library.

Lab 3.7 *Excel 97 and type libraries*

WA I

Type library references in Excel 97 are accessed in the same manner as the Word 97 type library references. To reference the type libraries in Excel 97, follow these steps:

1. Select **Tools** ⇒ **Macro**.

2. Select **Visual Basic Editor** from the submenu.

3. In the editor, select **Tools** ⇒ **References**.

You'll see the now familiar References dialog box displayed. By selecting Object Browser from the View menu, the type libraries may be browsed.

Lab 3.8 *Outlook 97 and type libraries*

WA I

We're still in familiar territory with Outlook 97. The initial step to reference the type libraries is slightly different; however, once in the Visual Basic Editor, the steps are identical to that of Word 97 and Excel 97.

1. Start Outlook 97.

2. Once in Outlook 97, start a new message or double an existing e-mail message. This places you in editing mode.

3. Select **Tools** ⇒ **Macro**.

4. Select **Visual Basic Editor** from the submenu.

5. In the editor, select **Tools** ⇒ **References**.

You'll see the now familiar References dialog box displayed. By selecting Object Browser from the View menu, the type libraries may be browsed.

Lab 3.9 *PowerPoint 97 and type libraries*

This lab almost repeats Lab 3.8. The difference is that in PowerPoint we must have an active slide presentation, while Outlook 97 requires an active message. Either create a new presentation with a blank slide or access an existing presentation. Once this is accomplished, reference the type libraries in PowerPoint 97 with these steps:

1. Start PowerPoint.

2. Select **Tools ⇒ Macro**.

3. Select **Visual Basic Editor** from the submenu.

4. In the editor, select **Tools ⇒ References**.

You'll see the now familiar References dialog box displayed. By selecting Object Browser from the View menu, the type libraries may be browsed.

Lab 3.10 *Microsoft Project 4.1 and type libraries*

This is Project 4.1 circa Windows 95, and it supports type libraries. Project is a task scheduling and planning tool and is not packaged with the standard Microsoft Office products such as Word, Excel, PowerPoint, and Access.

1. Start Microsoft Project.

2. Select **Tools ⇒ Macros**.

3. Select **New** from the dialog box that appears. (Another alternative is to edit an existing project.)

4. Select **OK**.

5. In the editor, select **Tools ⇒ References**.

You'll see the now familiar References dialog box displayed. By selecting Object Browser from the View menu, the type libraries may be browsed.

Windows Architecture I

CHAPTER

Structured Storage

4

About Chapter 4

COM structured storage is a cornerstone of COM implementation. It supports the concept of a file system within a file system. OLE embedding might not exist without this supporting technology. This technology is also indispensable for supporting embedded objects. COM structured storage and its supporting interfaces are the focus of this chapter.

COM STRUCTURED STORAGE

The review of basic COM starts with COM structured storage. Complexity moves upward until we finish with in-place activation of compound documents. Figure 4-1 illustrates the persistent interfaces for COM structured storage.

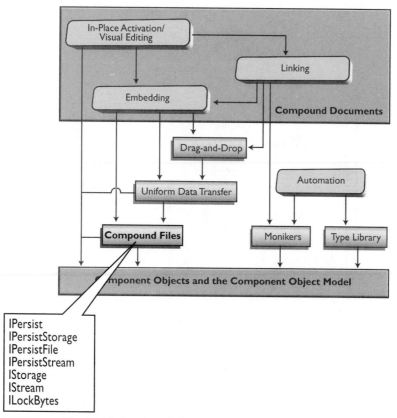

FIGURE 4-1   The COM structured storage stop on our COM technology roadmap.

COM structured storage is the model for compound files in the COM architecture. It is also a technology that enables multiple COM objects to store persistent data within a single file. Compound files are necessary for a component architecture where there is persistent (nonvolatile) data. The data is either used by a component or it is used to initialize a component.

A container uses the COM structured storage model when it asks a server object to initialize itself. Complexity increases when the container has more than one server. The data of each of these servers must be maintained separately. A generalized approach to managing data from multiple sources is suggested, but is not required. The COM structured storage model simplifies data management, but it is not required. Figure 4-2 illustrates the complexity of managing nested data structures.

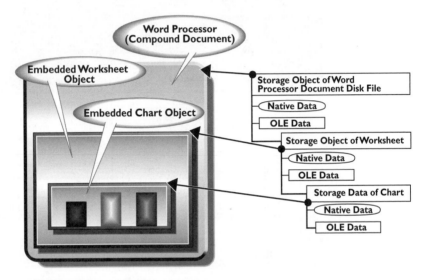

An Example of Compound File Usage

FIGURE 4-2   **The complexity of nested data structures.**

Data comes in two categories. Data can be embedded at the container (client) site or a link may exist to the data source. Commingling data from the container site and the server can create very complex storage issues if the data is stored in flat files.

Managing different types of data is solved with a structured file that is many files in one. Each type of data is assigned to a separate stream within the COM structured storage model. The COM structured storage model isolates the developer from tracking each individual type of data from different sources. Figure 4-2 illustrates the diverse number of streams within a small compound file application.

The complexity of Figure 4-2 is managed with the model of Figure 4-3, which has only four objects. The **LockBytes** object sits between the **RootStorage** object and physical storage or global memory. A **RootStorage** object may have other storage objects (substorages) and files (streams). Other **Storage** objects and **Stream** objects may be subservient to a **Storage** object. *Streams* are the equivalent of files and *storages* are the equivalent of directories, hence the description, "a file system within a file system."

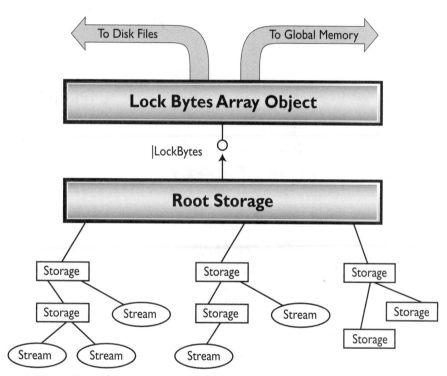

FIGURE 4-3   **Managing storages and streams with the COM structured storage model.**

The **LockBytes** object manages structured storage transparently. It is passive and does not alter data. The **IStorage** and **IStream** interfaces automatically use this functionality for a compound document that can be disk file or global memory based. An **ILockBytes** interface manages a byte array and insulates the developer from the underlying infrastructure issues.

concept link

For a more detailed look at **ILockBytes**, see Chapter 5. This is also where the interaction between the **ILockBytes** interface for synchronous storage and the **IFillLockBytes** wrapper for asynchronous storage is illustrated. (Asynchronous storage is used by a URL moniker for downloading from the Internet.)

Figure 4-4 is a peek at the internal structure of a compound document. You can readily identify some components of a compound file. The elements starting with 5 or 6 are streams and part of an OLE Document. **Book** is the root storage and the **VBA_Project** is a storage object. **CompObj** is the CLSID of the object written with **IStorage::SetClass**.

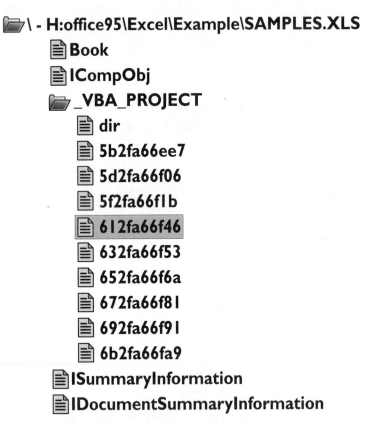

\ - H:office95\Excel\Example\SAMPLES.XLS
    Book
    ICompObj
    _VBA_PROJECT
        dir
        5b2fa66ee7
        5d2fa66f06
        5f2fa66f1b
        612fa66f46
        632fa66f53
        652fa66f6a
        672fa66f81
        692fa66f91
        6b2fa66fa9
    ISummaryInformation
    IDocumentSummaryInformation

FIGURE 4-4   The Win32 document viewer shows the internal structure of a compound file.

Benefits

Structured storage is designed to solve storage problems that do not have a solution in the flat-file models. Compound file benefits include:

- *File system and platform independence* — Compound file systems run on top of existing file systems, making them file-system and platform-independent.

- *Multiple files are encapsulated* — A compound file is externally represented as a single entity. However, within the compound file are many subfiles. This relationship is described as a "file system within a file system."

- *Giving structure to data without structure* — The concept of streams permits the storing of files that are of arbitrary length. While it is true that other file systems do manage *binary large objects* (BLOBS), these other systems have no generalized tools for supporting BLOBS and the management is always ad hoc.

- *Incremental access* — Structures within a compound file may be loaded and saved individually. The complete compound file need not be loaded or saved.

- *Concurrency is supported* — Multiple users or applications can concurrently read or write information within the same compound file.

- *Transactions are supported* — Users of a compound file can read or write in transacted mode. Changes are buffered and are eventually committed or reverted.

- *Low memory save is supported* — A file save mechanism is supported, which requires no additional memory. This allows the user to do a complete save in low memory situations. A traditional save fails because it requires additional overhead memory for the save process.

Storage Objects and IStorage

Storage objects support the concept of a file system within a file system. A storage object is a directory and the streams are individual files. A directory (storage object) can have other storage objects (directories) and files (streams).

StgCreateDocFile creates a root **IStorage** object while an existing compound file is opened with **StgOpenStorage**. The result of either operation is a root

IStorage pointer. At this point **IStorage::OpenStorage** can be invoked to open an existing substorage. The alternative is to invoke **IStorage::CreateStorage** for a new substorage object. Invoking the **Release** method on a storage object releases memory.

A CLSID can be assigned to storages. This enables containers to find and load the object server that created the data.

The **IStorage** interface inherits **QueryInterface**, **AddRef**, and **Release** from the **IUnknown** interface. The **IStorage** interface supports these methods:

IStorage method	CommandLine	Description
Commit	(None)	Ensures that all changes made to the storage are reflected in the parent storage.
CopyTo	Copy	Copies the entire contents of one storage to another. **CopyTo** is a defragmentation tool for compound files. The output streams are contiguous with no lost space between streams.
CreateStorage	Mkdir, Chdir	Creates and opens a new substorage nested within the existing storage object.
CreateStream	(None)	Creates and opens a stream. Transactions are not supported for stream objects.
DestroyElement	Del, Deltree	Deletes a specified storage or stream. If a substorage is deleted, all elements of the substorage are also destroyed.
EnumElements	Dir	Returns a STATSTG enumerator object, which implements **IEnumSTATSTG**.
MoveElementTo	Copy (+Del)	Copies or moves a substorage or a stream from one storage to another.
OpenStorage	Chdir	Opens an existing storage. Opening the same storage object for the same parentstorage object is not permitted.

IStorage method	CommandLine	Description
OpenStream	Copy	Opens an existing stream object. Two instances of the same open stream are not supported. Transactions are not supported for stream objects.
RenameElement	Rename	Renames the specified storage or stream.
Revert	(None)	Discards any transaction-related changes to the storage since the last **IStorage:: Commit**.
SetClass	(None)	Assigns the specified CLSID to this storage object.
SetElementTimes	(None)	The modification, access, and creation times are set if supported by the underlying file system.
SetStateBits	Attrib	Stores up to 32 bits of state information.
Stat	(Varies)	Returns the STATSTG structure for this storage object.

OleLoad is an API function that loads an object nested within a specified storage object. The advantage of using **OleLoad** is that it is a wrapper function and simplifies the object loading process. **OleLoad** call parameters include:

- A pointer to a storage object, an **IStorage** instance.
- The IID of the requested interface that the client will use for communicating with this object.
- A pointer to the object's client site.
- A pointer to the newly loaded object.

OleLoad loads a linked or embedded object into memory. It invokes the **IPersistStorage::Load** method; however, the complete load task is somewhat complex and has six processing steps:

1. **OleLoad** calls **OleDoAutoConvert** to see if an auto conversion is necessary.
2. **OleLoad** gets the object CLSID by invoking **IStorage::Stat** on the object.

3. **OleLoad** calls **CoCreateInstance** to create an instance of a handler. The default handler is used when no handler is available. **OleCreateDefault Handler** creates a default handler.

4. **OleLoad** invokes **IOleObject::SetClientSite** to inform the object of the client site.

5. **IUnknown::QueryInterface** is invoked asking for **IPersistStorage**. If this is successful, **IPersistStorage::Load** is invoked.

6. The client provides the IID of the object interface. **OleLoad** queries the object and returns the requested interface pointer.

OleSave is another helper API function that saves an open storage object in transacted mode. **OleSave** call parameters include:

- A pointer to the object.
- A pointer to the destination storage object.
- TRUE if the destination storage is the same as the load storage; FALSE otherwise.

OleSave is a wrapper function for the standard COM interfaces. The internal **OleSave** steps include:

1. **OleSave** invokes **IPersistStorage::GetClassID** to get the CLSID.
2. The CLSID is written to the storage object with **WriteClassStg**.
3. **IPersistStorage::Save** is invoked to save the object.
4. **IPersistStorage::Commit** is invoked if there are no errors.

Stream Objects and IStream

The stream object is where the data is stored. Streams are analogous to traditional files and can be in compound documents that are disk- or global memory-based. A storage object may have any number of streams; for the sake of simplicity, however, in Figure 4-2 I've only indicated two streams. One is for native data and the other is for presentation data. (Data within COM is managed with Uniform Data Transfer using the FORMATEC and STGMEDIUM structures. Data transfer issues are discussed in Chapter 6.) Figure 4-3 illustrates additional complexity.

Streams do have restrictions. The OLE implementation of the **IStream** interface does not support stream transactions or region locking. The **IStream** methods **LockRegion**, **UnlockRegion**, **Commit**, and **Revert**, have no effect in an OLE compound file implementation.

Streams can be marshaled to another process without using global memory. This increases marshaling performance. The only problem is that both processes share the same storage object pointer. A desirable alternative is to clone the stream object and pass the cloned stream pointer to the other process. Both processes now have access to the same stream object with different pointers.

Memory resources are always an issue with large stream objects. Resource allocation problems occur when the stream size exceeds the system heap size, or the system has a memory size of 50MB or less. Stream buffers are limited to 512 bytes. The solution is to use **SetSize** to preallocate memory in increments of 512 bytes. Use **VirtualAlloc**, which reserves or commits a region of pages in virtual memory, rather than **GlobalAlloc**, which allocates from the heap. The API call **CreateStreamOnHGlobal** creates an **IStream** object on global memory and returns a pointer to that object.

Creating an **IStream** object in a compound file requires a storage object pointer. **StgCreateDocFile** or **StgOpenStorage** returns a root storage object pointer. Either of these operations results in a root **IStorage** pointer. **IStorage::CreateStorage** can be used to create a new substorage, or an existing storage can be opened with **IStorage::OpenStorage**. The resulting substorage pointer is then used with either **CreateStream** or **OpenStream** to create an **IStream** object.

Invoking the **Release** method on a stream is equivalent to closing a file. The stream object is no longer available.

The **IStream** interface inherits **QueryInterface**, **AddRef**, and **Release** from the **IUnknown** interface and implements these methods:

- *Clone* — Creates a new stream object with its own seek pointer referencing the original data.

- *Commit* — Ensures that transacted mode changes are reflected in the parent object. If the stream is open in direct mode, **IStream::Commit** only flushes the buffers to the next storage level object. Transactions are not supported for streams in the OLE compound file implementation.

- *CopyTo* — Copies a specific number of bytes from one stream object to another stream object.

- *LockRegion* — Locks a specific range of bytes in a stream. Not all file system implementations may support this functionality. **IStream::Unlock Region** must be invoked for further access. This method is not supported in an OLE compound file implementation.

- *Read* — Read a specific number of bytes from a stream object starting at the current seek pointer. This task is much more complex than it appears. This occurs when **IStream::Read** is invoked by an asynchronous moniker. Monikers are discussed in Chapter 5. For now, just understand that **IStream::Read** can be either synchronous or asynchronous.

- *Revert* — **IStream::Revert** discards all stream changes since the last **IStream::Commit**. **IStream::Revert** has no effect on streams opened in direct mode and streams using the OLE compound file implementation.

- *Seek* — Positions a pointer in the stream. This method is not available with an asynchronous moniker except to position back in the *data-push* model.

- *SetSize* — Specifies the new size of the stream in bytes.

- *Stat* — Retrieves the STATSTG structure for the stream.

- *UnlockRegion* — Unlocks a previously locked region in a stream. This method is not supported in an OLE compound file implementation.

- *Write* — Writes a specific number of bytes to a stream.

OleLoadFromStream is an API wrapper function for loading an object from a stream. Its call parameters are:

- A pointer to the source stream.
- The IID of the requested interface that the client will use for communication with this object.
- A storage location pointer.

OleLoadFromStream is a fairly simple interface, but it does have one unique requirement. The object CLSID must immediately precede the object's data in the stream or a NULL is returned as the object pointer. **OleLoadFromStream** encapsulates these steps:

- **ReadClassStm** is invoked to read the CLSID from the stream.

- **OleLoadFromStream** will call **CoCreateInstance** to create an instance of a handler. The default handler is used when no handler is available. **OleCreateDefaultHandler** creates a default handler.
- **IPersistStream::Load** is invoked to read the data.
- An **IStream** pointer is returned.

OleSaveToStream is an API wrapper function that saves an object to a stream. Its call parameters are:

- A pointer to the object that is to be saved in a stream. (A CLSID should precede the data. A NULL is written to the stream when a CLSID doesn't exist.)
- A pointer to the target stream.

OleSaveToStream encapsulates the following steps, simplifying the task of saving a stream object:

- **OleSaveToStream** obtains the CLSID by invoking **IPersistStream::GetClassID.**
- The CLSID is written to the stream with **WriteClassStm.**
- **OleSaveToStream** invokes **IPersistStream::Save** with the *dirty* flag set to TRUE.

Storage Features

Access modes, transactioning, element naming, incremental access, and share-ability are features of structured storage. Some features have parallels with comparable technologies and function in the expected manner. Not all features have a parallel, and the concept of sharing in COM is not based on access privileges, but on marshaling with a proxy.

Access modes

The access modes for compound files are comparable to traditional file systems. The user specifies the access mode at file open time with one of the following flags. The flag name is descriptive and includes:

STGM_READ, STGM_WRITE, STGM_READWRITE, STGM_SHARE_DENYNONE, STGM_SHARE_DENYREAD, STGM__SHARE_DENYWRITE, STGM_SHARE_EXCLUSIVE, and STGM_CREATE.

Transactioning

Compound files support the concept of transactions. An **IStorage::Commit** only changes data at the next level. This permits a local undo or revert operation. An example of this is **Undo** in Word, which reverts changes that have not yet been saved to a file.

All changes are lost when an object is released and the transaction has not been committed. The issue is to start at the bottom of the hierarchy and commit all transactions.

Doing a revert at the root level is the equivalent of undoing all lower level transactions in the hierarchy. Exiting from Word without a **Save** is such an example. The user is prompted to verify that this is the desired course of action. Once confirmed, all transactions are reverted.

Element naming

There are element-naming conventions for storages and streams. All element names are stored as Unicode on all platforms. The names are limited to thirty-one characters. The exception is the root storage associated with a disk file, which can have a name as long as the file system allows.

A filename can be any character above 32 (an ASCII space), except the characters <.>, <:>, <\>, </>, and <!>. A leading character with a value less than 32 is reserved for internal COM usage. The leading character is binary with the following rules:

- \000, \001, and \002 specify an OLE-managed element.
- Presentation data is marked as \002OlePres<xxx> when *xxx* is between 000 and 999.
- \001Ole contains object information such as linking status.
- \003 marks an element owned by the code that manages the parent storage.
- \004 is used exclusively by the COM structured storage implementation.
- \005 and \006 are used by COM for OLE Documents.
- \007 to \0x1f are reserved for the operating system.

Incremental access

Incremental access is the reading or editing of a single object within the compound file. Opening a Word document does not require the complete document to be loaded. There is the initial overhead of opening the root storage. This is followed by a sequence of **IStorage::OpenStorage** operations to locate the desired stream and a call to **IStorage::OpenStream** once the stream is located. The remainder of the compound file remains unopened.

A portion of a compound file is now open for editing. Editing a compound file leads to fragmentation of the compound file. A partial solution is to call **IStorage::CopyTo**, which will defragment the compound file but not the internal streams. All streams must be rewritten individually to completely defragment the compound file.

Shareable elements

Compound files are shareable across process boundaries. These are not Win32 shared files in global memory, but the use of custom marshaling to share files. The sharing may extend beyond the platform. A proxy and the object work together with entire state data stored on a shared medium such as disk. This improves performance because other components need not load the objects but instead acquire a copy of the current state information.

LockBytes Object and ILockBytes

The **LockBytes** object provides a layer between the root storage object and the actual storage medium and is not exposed for default compound file implementations. Optionally, the user can allocate a byte array and then create and open a compound file over the byte array and the **LockBytes** object. Opening or creating a compound file with either a default or a custom implementation is enumerated with:

StgCreateDocFile	Opens a new compound file with a default file-based **LockBytes** object. An **IStorage** pointer is returned. The file may be transacted or direct. Options permit the overwriting of existing files.

StgOpenStorage	Opens an existing compound file and functions in the same manner as **StgCreateDocFile**.
StgCreateDocfileOnILockBytes	Creates a custom compound file implementation consisting of several steps:

- Allocates the byte array with **GlobalAlloc**. Do this with care because the space comes from the heap.

- Creates an **ILockBytes** object with **CreateILockBytesOnHGlobal** using the memory handle returned by **GlobalAlloc**. An **ILockBytes** interface pointer is returned.

- Creates the compound file with **StgCreateDocfileOnILockBytes** using the returned **ILockBytes** interface.

- Uses the returned **ILockBytes** pointer to open the file with **StgOpenDocfileOnILockBytes**.

StgOpenDocfileOnILockBytes	Opens a compound file that does not reside on the disk with a provided **ILockBytes** pointer. An **IStorage** pointer is returned.

> **note** The **LockBytes** array object is one of three components that defines storage structures. The other two objects are **Storage** objects and **Stream** objects. Technically there is a **RootObject**; however, it could be considered an instance of a **Storage** object because **Storage** objects can have subservient **Storage** objects.

A call to **StgCreateDocFile** creates an OLE compound-document file containing an **ILockBytes** implementation that associates a byte array with a disk file.

Now the nice part: The **IStream** and **IStorage** interfaces automatically call the **ILockBytes** methods for both types of compound-file storage objects. There is no need to access the **ILockBytes** methods directly.

You may choose to implement your own **ILockBytes** interface. If you do, you should consider custom marshaling by implementing the **IMarshal** interface.

When the OLE implementations of the **IStorage** and **IStream** interfaces are marshaled to another process, the **ILockBytes** interface is also automatically marshaled. Implementing your own **IMarshal** interface prevents this automatic marshaling of the **ILockBytes** interface.

In summary, you do not need to call **ILockBytes** interfaces directly. This is done automatically by the OLE implementation of the **IStorage** and **IStream** interfaces. If you do implement your own version of **ILockBytes**, **StgCreatge-DocfileOnIlockBytes** can be used to create a compound file structure supported by your own **ILockBytes** interface.

The **ILockBytes** interface inherits **QueryInterface**, **AddRef**, and **Release** from the **IUnknown** interface and supports the following methods:

o *ReadAt* — Reads a fixed number of bytes from an offset in the byte array.

o *WriteAt* — Writes a fixed number of bytes to an offset in the byte array.

o *Flush* — Ensures the flushing of internal buffers to the storage device.

o *SetSize* — Changes the size of the byte array. Callers extending a byte array should not rely on STG_E_MEDIUMFULL being returned at the appropriate time because of cache buffering.

o *LockRegion* — Locks a range of bytes on the byte array for write or exclusive access. This function is not available for a global memory implementation.

o *UnlockRegion* — Reverses a previous **LockRegion** call. This function is not available for a global memory implementation.

o *Stat* — Returns a STATSTG structure detailing information about the object, which in turn reflects information about the device.

RootStorage Object and IRootStorage

The **RootStorage** object is optional and not required for implementations that are not file based. Obtaining the **IRootStorage** pointer is done with **IStorage:: QueryInterface**(*IID_IRootStorage*), which uses the **IStorage** pointer that is returned when the compound file was opened or created.

The **IRootStorage** interface inherits **QueryInterface**, **AddRef**, and **Release** from the **IUnknown** interface. **IRootStorage::SwitchToFile** is the only method supported by this interface. This method is designed for use in low memory situations and is used as a full save operation on a compound file only after another operation on the compound file has failed because of low memory. It is possible to implement this interface to function as a **SaveAs** operation; however, Microsoft does not guarantee proper operation in future releases.

When a low memory situation occurs, the **IStorage::CopyTo** method will probably fail because it requires additional memory. The following scenario will function in a zero-free memory environment:

- Obtain the **IRootStorage** interface with **IStorage::Query Interface**(*IID_IRootStorage*).
- Create the new file with **IRootStorage::SwitchToFile**(*pszNewFile*). This uses no extra memory and uses the third handle obtained when the file was opened. (Haven't you ever wondered why it took three handles to open a compound file?)
- The last step is to call **IStorage::Commit**, which commits the data and uses no extra memory.

A root storage object is not required for compound document implementations that are not file based. This explains why there is no **BaseInterface entry** in the Registry entry for the **IStorage** interface shown below.

```
HKEY_CLASSES_ROOT\Interface\{0000000B-0000-0000-C000-
  000000000046} = Istorage

HKEY_CLASSES_ROOT\Interface\{0000000B-0000-0000-C000-
  000000000046}\NumMethods = 18

HKEY_CLASSES_ROOT\Interface\{0000000B-0000-0000-C000-
  000000000046}\ProxyStubClsid = {00000314-0000-0000-C000-
  000000000046}
```

IPersist

IPersist is the base interface for all **IPersist**-type interfaces. It supports the required **IUnknown** methods **QueryInterface**, **AddRef**, and **Release**. **GetClassID** is the only private method of this interface.

IPersistFile

The **IPersistFile** interface is usually implemented by the object application, but it can be implemented by container applications. It is the mechanism for loading or saving documents to or from disk files. The client application is responsible for opening or closing the file. Binding a linked object is the normal use of this interface. This is a link to an embedded object when the application is a container.

The **IPersistFile** interface inherits **QueryInterface**, **AddRef**, and **Release** from the **IUnknown** interface. It also inherits **GetClassID** from the **IPersist** interface. The **IPersistFile** interface also supports these methods:

○ *IsDirty* — A flag is set. The client should call **Save** before releasing the object.

○ *Load* — Loads an object into memory from an absolute path. **IMoniker::BindToObject** invokes this method (see Chapter 5).

○ *Save* — Saves an object to storage. This includes all nested objects. The container must invoke **IPersistFile::SaveCompleted** after this operation is completed.

○ *SaveCompleted* — The container has completed the file save with **IPersist::Save**.

○ *GetCurFile* — Obtains the absolute path of the file associated with the document, or the default filename prompt if no file is available.

○ *LoadFSP* — Loads a document but does not show it to the user.

○ *SaveFSP* — Saves the document. If the file specification parameter (FSP) is null, then the operation is a file save. A non-NULL value for the FSP parameter is **FileSaveAS** or **FileSaveCopyAs**. The container must invoke the function **IPersistFile::SaveCompletedFSP** after the original save is complete.

○ *SaveCompletedFSP* — The container has completed the file save with **IPersist::SaveFSP**.

○ *GetCurFSP* — Returns the file specification name associated with the object or the default file name prompt.

IPersistMemory

An object implements the **IPersistMemory** interface to save itself in memory. The container invokes **IPersistMemory::Load** or **IPersistMemory::Save** to load or unload the object.

The **IPersistMemory** interface inherits **QueryInterface**, **AddRef**, and **Release** from the **IUnknown** interface. It also inherits **GetClassID** from the **IPersist** interface. **IPersistMemory** supports the following methods, which are functionally equivalent to the methods of the **IPersistStream** interface:

- *IsDirty* — A flag is set.
- *Load* — Initializes an object previously stored with **IPersistMemory::Save**.
- *Save* — Saves the current state of an object to a stream object. This call supports a dirty flag.
- *GetMaxSize* — Determines the maximum size for usage with **IPersistMemory::Save**.
- *InitNew* — Initializes the object to a default state.

IPersistMoniker

IPersistMoniker is designed for asynchronous-aware objects. Synchronous objects use the **IMoniker::BindToObject** interface for binding the **IPersistFile**, **IPersistStreamInit**, or **IPersistStorage** interfaces. The difference in techniques is that the **IPersistMoniker** implementation allows control to be given to the object being instantiated rather than binding its persistent data. This technique is used for binding URL monikers in the background after the application has regained control. The **IPersistMoniker** interface cannot be used for synchronous binding.

The **IPersistMoniker** interface does not include an **InitNew** method for initializing an object. The **IPersistStorageInit**, **IPersistMemory**, or **IPersist-Propertybag** method **InitNew** must be used to initialize an object.

The **IPersistMoniker** interface inherits **QueryInterface**, **AddRef**, and **Release** from the **IUnknown** interface. It also inherits **GetClassID** from the **IPersist** interface. The **IPersistMoniker** interface supports these methods:

- *IsDirty* — A flag is set.
- *Load* — Loads an object using a specified moniker.
- *Save* — Saves the object specifying a destination moniker.

o *SaveCompleted*—Notifies the object that the save operation is complete.

o *GetCurMoniker*—Retrieves the moniker for the object's persistent state.

IPersistPropertyBag

The **IPersistPropertyBag** interface is used to save and load individual object properties. Implementers of the **IPersistPropertyBag** interface are free to store the information in any manner the applications desires. It could be name/value pairs as text strings that a Visual Basic program stores. A natural implementation of this interface is a save-as-text operation. The object gives the container the format choice while retaining the decision as to which properties should be saved.

IErrorLog is a companion interface to the **IPropertyBag** interface, which does the actual storage and retrieval of property values, as shown in Figure 4-5. It is used for the logging of errors on a per property basis.

The **IPersistPropertyBag** interface inherits **QueryInterface**, **AddRef**, and **Release** from the **IUnknown** interface. It also inherits **GetClassID** from the **IPersist** interface. The **IPersistPropertyBag** interface supports these methods:

o *InitNew*—Initializes the property bag.

o *Load*—The container uses this method to load the control's properties.

o *Save*—Used by the container to save the object's properties.

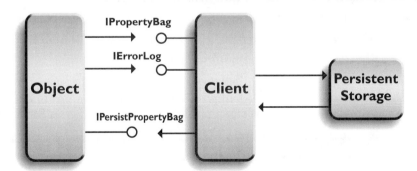

FIGURE 4-5   The IErrorLog is a companion interface to the IPropertyBag interface.

IPersistStorage

Object handlers use the IPersistStorage interface or object applications to support container simple-stream objects such as monikers.

The **IPersistStorage** interface inherits **QueryInterface**, **AddRef**, and **Release** from the **IUnknown** interface. It also inherits **GetClassID** from the **IPersist** interface. The **IPersistStorage** interface supports these methods:

- *IsDirty* — A flag is set.
- *InitNew* — Initializes the storage object.
- *Load* — Loads an object into memory for the container or loads the object in running state for an object handler.
- *Save* — Saves an object to storage, including all nested objects.
- *SaveCompleted* — Terminates the *no scribble storage mode* or the *hands off* mode created by invoking **IPersistStorage::HandsOffStorage**. You can think of this function as releasing a lock.
- *HandsOffStorage* — Sets the state for **IPersistStorage::Save**. Think of it as a interlock until the save function is completed.

IPersistStream

The **IPersistStream** interface is used to support simple stream objects such as monikers. The **IPersistStream** parameters are unique and are only valid during the call in which they are passed. The object does not retain them after the call is completed. An OLE container with embedded or linked objects will use the **IPersistStorage** interface instead of this interface.

The **IPersistSteam** interface inherits **QueryInterface**, **AddRef**, and **Release** from the **IUnknown** interface. It also inherits **GetClassID** from **IPersist** interface. The **IPersistStream** stream supports these methods:

- *IsDirty* — A flag is set.
- *Load* — Initializes an object previously stored with **IPersistStream::Save**.
- *Save* — Saves the current state of an object to a stream object. This call supports a dirty flag.
- *GetMaxSize* — Determines the maximum size for usage with **IPersistStream::Save**.

IPersistStreamInit

The **IPersistStreamInit** interface replaces the **IPersistStream** interface. It is equivalent to the **IPersistStream** interface with the additional method **InitNew**, which initializes an object to a default state.

IOleCache2 (caching) cannot be supported when **IPersistStreamInit** is exposed because **IOleCache2** requires the **IPersistStorage** interface. The alternative is to render the object with **IDataObject::GetData**, which is discussed in Chapter 6.

The **IPersistSteamInit** interface inherits **QueryInterface**, **AddRef**, and **Release** from the **IUnknown** interface. It also inherits **GetClassID** from the **IPersist** interface. The **IPersistStream** stream supports these methods:

o *IsDirty* — A flag is set.

o *Load* — Initializes an object previously stored with **IPersistStream::Save**.

o *Save* — Saves the current state of an object to a stream object. This call supports a dirty flag.

o *GetMaxSize* — Determines the maximum size for usage with **IPersistStream::Save**.

o *InitNew* — Initializes an object to a default state.

KEY POINT SUMMARY

o The COM structured storage model is a file system within a file system. Storages are equivalent to directories and streams are equivalent to files.

o Compound files are the implementation of the COM structured storage model.

o Transactions are not supported for compound files. The Commit method exists; however, compound documents cannot be locked.

o The COM structured storage model supports the concept of persistence.

o Compound files and streams are suited for fragmented data collection or for real-time data collection.

o A compound file system based on the COM structured storage model can be implemented in either global memory or on disk.

APPLYING WHAT YOU'VE LEARNED

Structured storage has roots in COM. It almost has blossomed into an independent technology. Structured storage supports the concept of a compound file, which is loosely termed a "file system within a file system."

Instant Assessment

1. What is the difference between structured storage and compound files?

2. Name the four objects of the COM structured storage model.

3. Which interface uses the **ILockBytes** interface?

4. Are there any restrictions on the **ILockBytes** interface? If there are, what are they?

5. What is the purpose of the one **IRootStorage** method?

6. Name two issues when marshaling a stream object to another process.

7. What are the **IStream** interface limitations?

8. What is the role of **IPersistMoniker**?

9. Compare the role of **IPersistMoniker** and persistent data with **IMoniker::BindToObject** and persistent data.

10. Describe how the **IPersistPropertyBag** interface is used.

11. What are the primary uses of **IPersistStream**, **IPersistStorage**, and **IPersistMemory**?

12. What valuable service does **IStorage::CopyTo** perform besides the utilitarian role of copying a storage object?

 concept link **For answers to the Instant Assessment questions, see Appendix C.**

Lab Exercise

Developers are always faced with advances in technology. The issues raised by technological advances are to first understand the new technology and then to evaluate current applications for possible inclusion of the new technology. There also are ancillary issues such as whether the technology is stable and what its impact is on current production. The technology may be attractive, but the developers often overlook the issue of what the benefits are to the organization.

Lab 4.11 *Converting applications to the structured storage model*

WA I

Evaluate your current systems in terms of the storage structures used. Consider the feasibility and possibility of converting qualifying existing systems to the COM structured storage model. Remember that transactions are supported for compound documents, but not for streams within the compound document.

Possible candidates to consider are applications with numerous small files. These files can be combined within a single compound file. Other candidates are data files that are shared. Microsoft Word, Excel, and Access are tools that currently share data and use compound files. Can your compound file candidate use a standard tool?

What about special features such as a file save in a zero-free memory environment. Your organization may have thousands of desktop systems with limited memory. Can this feature be a benefit?

Factors to consider in your evaluation are direct costs, which should detail all aspects of the implementation cycle. Other factors to consider are the indirect costs of training and the need to run the new system in parallel with the older system during testing. Often overlooked is the need to run two systems in parallel, which can entail the addition of temporary personnel.

Is the technology new? This question isn't directed at Microsoft, but at any software vendor. You can expect a relatively frequent change cycle until the technology stabilizes. This results in unstable systems with lost production.

The most important issue is that of derived benefits. Can you list the benefits? Can these benefits be translated into economic benefits, or, more importantly, will it save the corporation money?

Windows Architecture I

CHAPTER

Monikers

5

About Chapter 5

The next stop on our tour of the COM architecture is binding components with monikers. We're gradually moving upward in functionality. It is hard to tell which portion of the COM technology represents the cornerstone, but binding with monikers wins the prize in my book. A component architecture requires a connection mechanism, which monikers provide.

Monikers are names that can describe the result of a query, a range of cells in a spreadsheet, or a paragraph in a document. They are persistent, intelligent names. Different moniker classes deal with different names, and they encapsulate a type of name and the intelligence to work with that name behind the polymorphic **IMoniker** interface.

A moniker itself is difficult to describe. The physical representation of a moniker is that of a path, while the logical representation is that of an object with intelligence. Needless to say, there's quite a bit under the hood. This chapter is the *why, when,* and *how* of binding components with monikers.

I've also tried to illuminate the operations of binding a URL moniker, as the Internet is almost everywhere.

WHY A MONIKER?

Tags are attached to entities in an object-oriented world. An action has a tag (*name* if you wish, or *method* if you purport to be programmer), and the data upon which the action operates also has a tag. The action may be anything you wish, and many actions do not have data on which to operate. Balancing your checkbook at the end of each month is an action that uses the data of your checkbook stubs and the bank statement.

A characteristic of COM is that instances of an object are not named. Yes, you use the class identifier (CLSID) to request instantiation of an object with **CoCreateInstance**; instantiation of the object, however, is not direct. A pointer to the object is returned and not a name. Technically, it is possible to instantiate an object directly, but this requires that every object requesting instantiation of another object must be aware of all the minutiae required to instantiate the requested object. The moniker solves two problems for the requesting object. It shields the requesting object from the details of instantiation and solves the additional problem of instantiating an object without actually knowing the object name.

Describing a moniker can be put in more pedestrian terms by considering your car as a component object model. Components include such items as the battery, ignition coil, and starter motor, all of which are encapsulated within an assembly, euphemistically called a car. Individual operations are shielded from the vehicle operator. Starting your car means supplying electricity to the starter motor, timing a spark, and supplying gasoline.

These are all packaged behind a moniker called the ignition switch position. The vehicle operator requests an instantiation of the engine running by positioning the ignition switch to the starting position. The battery instantiates the starter motor. Spark is induced as the motor turns, gasoline ignites, and the engine starts. After the engine has started, the starter motor stops because it is no longer needed.

The same is true with a moniker. The moniker disappears after the object is instantiated. Both the ignition switch position and the starter motor are agents to start the engine. Once the gasoline ignites, the engine is started and there is no further need for either agent. A moniker is an agent that connects spreadsheet cells to your Word document. The moniker disappears after the connection is established.

A moniker uses persistent data to instantiate your spreadsheet rows. That data is no longer needed after the connection is established. In the same manner, the intelligence in your car is the connection of the battery, ignition switch, and starter motor to a specific switch position. That switch position is no longer needed after the car starts.

NAMING AND BINDING WITH MONIKERS

Figure 5-1 gives us a fix on our COM roadmap. A moniker is a conceptual connection mechanism to an object. It is often referred to as an *alias*, but this definition is too simple. A *moniker* is a persistent name with intelligence that supports the **IMoniker** interface and which is used to connect COM objects, but is itself a COM object.

 note **Because the IMoniker interface inherits from IStream interface, it understands how to store and retrieve monikers that manage a stream.**

The moniker-binding process starts with the requester establishing a binding context by calling **CreateBindCtx**. This creates a binding context, and the interface **IBindCtx** becomes available. The next step is to declare the binding options with a call to **IBindCtx::SetBindOptions**. The bind context parameter is then passed to **IMoniker::BindToObject** for binding. After completion, the bind context is released by calling **IUnknown::Release**. A simple application can use the function **BindMoniker**, which is a wrapper for **CreateBindCtx** and **IMoniker::BindToObject**. We'll take a closer look at **IMoniker::BindToObject** after we deal with several architectural issues of monikers.

EARLY AND LATE BINDING

This is the *when* of binding. *Early binding* occurs during object compilation (object time), as opposed to binding at run time, which is late binding. Early binding is done by a developer, while *late binding* is done by the user, and may depend upon the context of the application. In general, late binding fosters the Microsoft "docu-centric" approach to work, while early binding is often "application-centric."

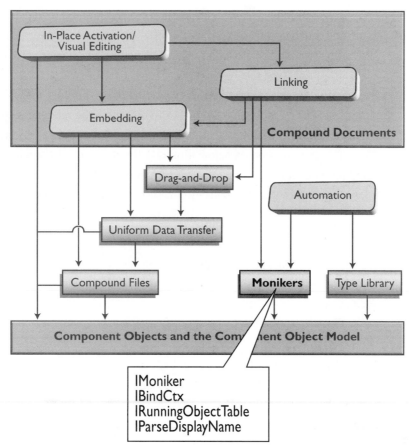

FIGURE 5-1   The Monikers stop on our COM technology roadmap.

Binding types may be categorized as follows:

- A virtual table (vtable) is early binding.
- Dispinterface is late binding.
- A registered type library is required for early binding.
- Dynamic marshaling is required for late binding.

Vtables are addresses, and address pointers do not exist until objects are running. Thus, early binding on a vtable can only occur if the appropriate servers are already running along with the required proxy and stub software (assuming the object does not use the **IDispatch** interface).

Late binding is flexible and easy to use; early binding (compile time) is "type safe" and much faster. The compiler verifies data types during early binding, hence the term "type safe." Late binding depends upon client choices or client-supplied data and is not "type safe."

A dual interface simplifies early binding. Early binding is possible in Visual Basic 5.0 (VB) by adding a reference to an object via the references dialog box and then declaring a variable as a specific object type instead of **As Object**.

The code fragments below illustrate the difference between early and late binding. The binding process doesn't commence in the first example until the **Set** statement is executed. The object in the second example is recognized at load time.

```
Private Sub Late_Binding()
 Dim MyWD As Object
 Set MyWD = CreateObject("word.basic")
 MyWD.Visible = True
 Exit Sub
End Sub
Private Sub Early_Binding()
 Dim MyWD As WordBasic
 Set MyWD = CreateObject("word.basic")
 MyWD.Visible = True
 Exit Sub
End Sub
```

Clients have four techniques for acquiring monikers and all involve late binding, or binding at execution time.

- *Enable Links from Insert Objects* — A moniker is created when an **Insert Dialog** box is used and *Enable Links* is checked on the **Insert Object** dialog box. An example is the *Object* of the Word **Insert** menu.

- *Enable Linking from Clipboard and Drag and Drop Operations* — This is more of a programming issue of enabling links in the FORMATETC structure.

- *Paste Link and PasteSpecial Commands* — These are common entries of an **Edit** menu with Word being a good example. A paste link function is performed.

- *Drag and Drop Linking Feedback* — Another programming issue where the **IDropTarget::Drop** function looks to see if both the Shift and Ctrl keys are pressed. If they are, a paste link action is performed.

MONIKER TYPES

Monikers come in many flavors. There are base types, decomposition types, and synthetic types (which are only used to resolve local syntax issues). Figure 5-2 illustrates a composite moniker. The following list describes the moniker types:

- *File Moniker* — A path in a file system. A file moniker is created with **CreateFileMoniker**. Only a file moniker and an item moniker can be persisted.

- *Item Moniker* — Identifies objects in a container. The object may be smaller than a file, such as a pseudo-object, which is only a portion of an object. Item monikers are created with **CreateItemMoniker**. This moniker may be persisted.

- *Generic Composite Moniker* — Two or more monikers of an arbitrary type that are combined together. This class of monikers is created with **CreateGenericComposite**.

- *Antimonikers* — The inverse of an item, file, or pointer moniker. Antimonikers are used in a relative path construction where the moniker to the left of the antimoniker must be annihilated. An anti-moniker construct has a form similar to \..\. Antimonikers are created with **CreateAntiMoniker**. An antimoniker neutralizes the left context moniker.

- *Pointer Moniker* — A temporary moniker that functions as a pointer to a persistent moniker. The function of a pointer moniker varies depending upon the context. Pointer monikers are created with **CreatePointerMoniker**. In essence, pointer monikers wrap real pointers and are not bindable.

- *Class Moniker* — Represent an object class and bind the class object to the class for which it was created. Class monikers are created with **CreateClassComposite**.

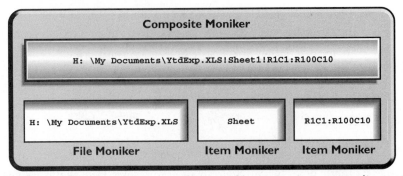

FIGURE 5-2   The file and item monikers combine to create a composite moniker.

 note   **The CLSID identifies monikers. The CLSID** {0000030x-0000-0000-C000-000000000046} **is a CLSID with** *x* **identifying the moniker type. CLSID moniker codess are: 3 for file; 4 for item; 5 for anti; and 6 for pointer monikers.**

UNDER THE HOOD WITH IMONIKER::BINDOBJECT

A nontrivial moniker is represented by constituent monikers. The binding process starts from the right, and the string is decomposed into the different moniker classes. A moniker will always have a left context. A moniker does not exist in isolation and will also have a right context. Normally the right context moniker isn't of immediate interest because it is already bound. This is illustrated in Figure 5-3 where *Item 1* is the current moniker of interest.

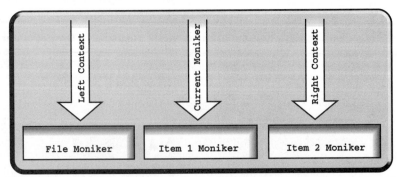

FIGURE 5-3   The right context moniker is already bound to the moniker of current interest (Item 1).

Left context of a moniker is very important. Momentarily we'll find out why it is important, but first we must define two rules:

○ *Rule 1:* During parsing of display names, every container must support **IParseDisplayName**. What better source of name parsing can there be than the container itself parsing the name? It knows what is expected.

○ *Rule 2:* An item moniker requires the moniker in left context to support the **IOleItemContainer** interface. The reason is self-explanatory when you look at the **IOleItemContainer** interface in Figure 5-4, which is unique to the user context. The methods **GetObject**, **GetObjectStorage**, and **IsRunning** are methods that facilitate optimizing the binding process by locating running servers.

The missing keystone is that any **IMoniker** implementation must also implement the **IROTData** interface. This enables registering of an object in the Running Object Table. This puts in place the necessary tools to look at the Running Object Table and to know when the target server is already running. Binding is stopped at the point where the requested object exists in the Running Object Table. This places the importance of the moniker left context in the proper perspective.

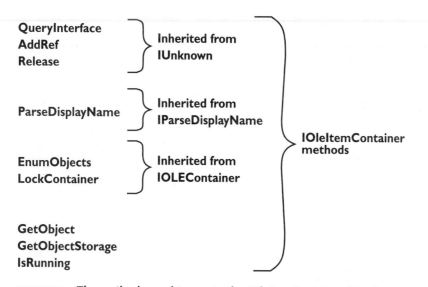

FIGURE 5-4 The methods used to create the IOleItemContainer interface.

We're looking at pure elegance here. Remember that an object with the **IOleItemContainer** interface supports the moniker in left context. This means that as each **IMoniker::BindToObject** binding to the left is initiated, the **IMoniker** interface eventually returns a pointer to communicate either with the object through **IOleItemContainer::GetObject** or with the storage of that object through **IOleItemContainer::GetStorage**. **IOleItemContainer** also parses names for its own objects.

We now have enough information to bind an object. But first, who uses the **IMoniker** interface? The two primary users of binding are a browser that calls the **IMoniker** interface and the **IOleLink** interface that supports embedded monikers of linked objects. Both interfaces share common features.

IOleUILinkContainer is another binding interface; however, it manages the functionality of the Links dialog box and uses the **IOleLink** interface.

I'll keep things simple for now and say that **MyServer** was browsed for **MyToys**. I'll make it still simpler and say that the composite moniker resolves down to just a file moniker. The simple moniker shown in Figure 5-5 assumes that the server is already running.

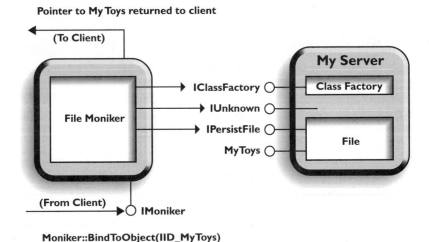

FIGURE 5-5   A simplified illustration of how a simple moniker is bound.

This mechanism is quite similar to the server start sequence discussed earlier. Binding a simple moniker is illustrated in Figure 5-5 and starts with the client calling **IMoniker::BindToObject** with the interface identifier (IID); in this example, it is IID_MyToys. The moniker is resolved to a simple file moniker and calls **GetClassFile** to get the file CLSID. It then calls **IClassFactory::CoCreateInstance** with the CLSID requesting **IPersistFile**. The file name is passed to **IPersistFile::Load**, which loads the file. The moniker then calls **IPersistFile::QueryInterface** *(IID_MyToys)* and the returned pointer is passed back to the client. The very last step, which is not shown, is the client connecting to and using the **MyToys** interface.

This is all well and good, but I haven't used any of the contexts we've developed. So, let's bind a composite moniker, which has a file moniker and an item moniker. Once you see how the mechanism works for a single-item moniker, the additional steps needed for the multiple-item moniker are just recursions.

Just as we did above, the client calls **IMoniker::BindToObject** with the IID. In this example, it is IID_MyToys. The moniker is resolved to a file moniker and an item moniker. The item moniker then calls **LeftContext::BindToObject** *(IID_IOleItemContainer)*. The file moniker knows that it has a filename and calls **GetClassFile** for the file CLSID. The file moniker then calls **IClassFactory:: CoCreateInstance** with the CLSID requesting **IPersistFile**. The file name is passed to **IPersistFile::Load**, which loads the file.

Next, the moniker calls **IUnknown::QueryInterface***(IID_IOleItemContainer)* and returns that pointer to the item moniker. In return, the item moniker calls **IOleItemContainer::GetObject**. There is only one item moniker, and the item moniker has the additional responsibility of calling **IUnknown::QueryInterface** *(IID_MyToys)*. The returned pointer is then passed back to the client. The very last step, which is not shown in Figure 5-6, is the client connecting to and using the **MyToys** interface.

With more than one item moniker, the upward recursion is with each item moniker always calling **LeftContext::BindToObject***(IID_IOleItemContainer)*. The downward recursion is that each item moniker must call **IOleItemContainer::Get-Object** and the last item moniker in the downward recursion has the additional responsibility of calling **IUnknown::QueryInterface**(<IID of requested interface>). Remember that each nested item must support the **IOleItemContainer** interface. The rule is simple: The number of **IOleItemContainer** interfaces must equal the number of item monikers.

This scenario is probably a worst case in which target objects are never running. The concept of the *Running Object Table* (ROT) is introduced in the following section. As you will see, binding is not necessary when an object exists in the ROT; the moniker invokes **IOleItemContainer::GetObject** directly without binding.

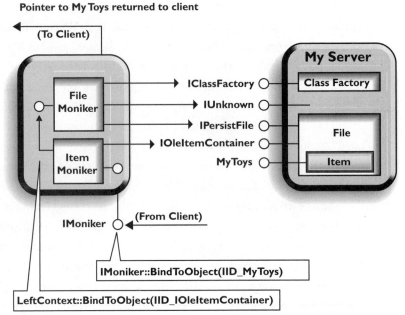

Pointer to My Toys returned to client

FIGURE 5-6   A simplified illustration of how a composite moniker is bound.

SYNCHRONOUS MONIKERS

Synchronous monikers complete the binding process without client interaction. Figure 5-7 is the basic synchronous moniker binding architecture. This is contrasted with the asynchronous moniker binding architecture of Figure 5-9 (shown later) where there is an ongoing dialog between the client and the asynchronous moniker through the **IBindStatusCallback** interface.

IBindCtx

The **IBindCtx** interface is for the management of options, bound objects, and object parameters related to binding. Methods of this interface are not called directly; however, pointers to different methods of this interface are found in many of the **IMoniker** interface calls. These methods are coroutines of the **IMoniker** interface.

The client calls **CreateBindCtx** with a pointer to the moniker for which it intends to request binding. This establishes an environment for the **IMoniker** interface, and the client then calls **IMoniker::BindToObject** with the same pointer.

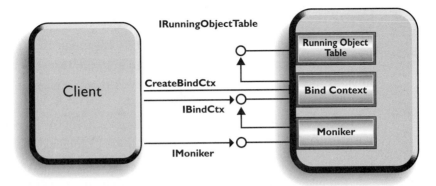

FIGURE 5-7 Synchronous monikers complete the binding process without client interaction.

The **IBindCtx** interface inherits all methods of the **IUnknown** interface, and **IBindCtx** supports the following methods:

- *RegisterObjectBound* — Remembers the passed object as being bound and that it must be released when overall binding is complete.

- *RevokeObjectBound* — The reverse operation of **IBindCtx::RegisterObjectBound**.

- *ReleaseBoundObjects* — Releases all currently bound objects.

- *SetBindOptions* — Remembers the parameters used by **IMoniker** functions.

- *GetBindOptions* — Returns the parameters set with **IBindCtx::SetBindOptions**.

- *GetRunningObjectTable* — Returns access to the Running Object Table. Moniker implementations should use this method rather than the global application programming interface (API) **GetRunningObjectTable**.

- *RegisterObjectParam* — Contextual information is passed to the binding process. String keys are case sensitive. The input consists of a name, under which the object is registered, and the object.

- *GetObjectParam* — Looks up a key in internal tables and returns the associated object.

- *EnumObjectParam* — Enumerates the keys of the internal contextual tables.

IMoniker

IMoniker::BindToObject is the workhorse of moniker binding. **IMoniker** is supported by a host of global API calls in addition to the **IBindCtx** interface. The **IBindCtx** methods are not called directly, but are supported coroutines that manage the moniker infrastructure.

A new moniker class requires the implementation of the **IMoniker** interface and the **IROTData** interface (see the section below, "IRunningObjectTable"). This allows your object to be registered in the Running Object Table.

IMoniker is well equipped for any moniker-binding task encountered. The interface inherits the required **IUnknown** interface. However, it also inherits **GetClassID** from the **IPersist** interface and **IsDirty**, **Load**, **Save**, and **GetMaxSize** from the **IPersistStream** interface. **IMoniker** supports these methods:

- *BindToObject* — Locates and loads the object referenced by a given moniker. The bind process has both a right context and a left context. The left context requires **IOleItemContainer** support, and the right context can involve binding to other objects. There isn't a need for this with the right context object support provided by the **IBindCtx** interface.

- *BindToStorage* — **IMoniker::BindToStorage** communicates with the object storage while **IMoniker::BindToObject** communicates with the object. This interface supports access to **IStorage**, **IStream**, and **ILockBytes**.

- *Reduce* — Compacts the moniker.

- *ComposeWith* — Returns a new moniker composed of the current, the left context, and the right context monikers.

- *Enum* — Enumerates the elements of a composite moniker.

- *IsEqual* — A moniker equality test.

- *Hash* — A moniker hash value. The hash value should rely on internal states and not memory addresses. Hashing is invariant under marshaling, and a marshaled moniker returns the same hash value. Hashed values must be invariant for a global ROT.

- *IsRunning* — The moniker obtains the run status by calling **IBindCtx::GetRunningObjectTable** and interrogating the table.

- *GetTimeOfLastChange* — Provides time and date information for management purposes.

- *Inverse* — Needed for the implementations of **IMoniker::RelativePathTo**. An inverse moniker does not destroy a particular moniker. It destroys all monikers with a similar structure. Not all monikers can have inverse monikers. Objects embedded within other objects cannot have relative paths, and hence cannot have inverse monikers.

- *CommonPrefixWith* — Returns the longest common prefix shared by two monikers.

- *RelativePathTo* — Returns the relative path to a moniker when appended to the end of the current moniker.

- *GetDisplayName* — Returns the current moniker's display name.

- *ParseDisplayName* — Parses a composite moniker's remaining display name. **Moniker::ParseDisplayName** is called by **MkParseDisplayName**. It only parses as much as is appropriate from the tail of the moniker.

- *IsSystemMoniker* — Determines the moniker type.

IParseDisplayName

The **IParseDisplayName** interface is inherited by several other interfaces and only has one method, **ParseDisplayName**. Objects invoking **MkParseDisplayName** or **MkParseDisplayNameEx** use **IParseDisplayName** indirectly.

Compound documents that support links to embedded objects or to pseudo-objects must support the **IOleItemContainer** interface, which is illustrated in Figure 5-4. The **IParseDisplayName** interface is inherited from **IOleItemContainer** and need not be implemented directly.

The alternative is to implement **IParseDisplayName** directly as part of a class object that has access to the interface available by invoking **CoGetClassObject**.

IRunningObjectTable

ROT optimizes binding by maintaining an active running object table. Passive objects are not included in this table; that is, all objects not in the table are by definition passive. **IMoniker::IsRunning** is invoked to see if the object in left context is running. Binding is not necessary if the object is already running and the moniker can call **IOleItemContainer::GetObject** rather than invoking **IMoniker::IBindToObject** on the left context.

Moniker providers use ROT. The moniker provider registers its own objects when it starts running and revokes their registration when they stop running.

The Win32 software developer's kit (SDK) includes a tool for viewing ROT, a sample of which is shown in Figure 5-8.

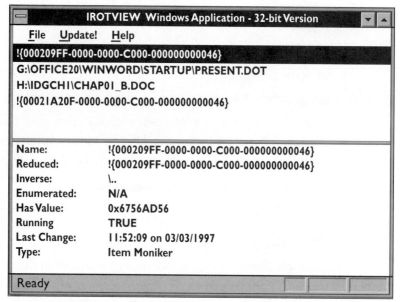

FIGURE 5-8   A Running Object Table viewed using the viewing tool from the Win32 SDK.

Either clients or servers can access ROT by invoking the global API **GetRunningObjectTable**. Moniker implementations must access this table through the bind context that is passed to them and not through the global API. A moniker class accesses ROT by invoking **IBindCtx::GetRunningObjectTable** on the bind context for the current binding operation.

The **IRunningObjectTable** interface inherits all methods of **IUnknown**. **IRunningObjectTable** supports these methods:

- *Register* — Registers the designated object as having entered the running state.

- *Revoke* — Revokes the registered status of an object in ROT. It's assumed that the object is about to stop running. An error occurs if the object is not running.

- *IsRunning* — Tests to determine whether the object in question is running.

- *GetObject* — If the object is running, **GetObject** returns the object as it is actually registered.

- *NoteChangeTime* — Notes any changes in time for use by **IMoniker:: GetTimeOfLastChange**.

- *GetTimeOfLastChange* — Reports the time of the last change. Moniker implementations should use their own implementation of **Moniker:: GetTimeOfLastChange**.

- *EnumRunning* — Enumerates the objects of the type **IEnumMoniker**.

Moniker Support Functions

Moniker support functions are general utilities not supported by an interface. **CreateBindCtx** and **CreateFileMoniker** are good examples of utility supports.

The following are the supporting moniker global API calls:

- *BindMoniker* — A helper function that is a wrapper for CreateBindCtx and **IMoniker::BindToObject**. Calling **Moniker::BindToObject** directly is probably more efficient when there is more than one moniker.

- *CreateAntoMoniker* — An antimoniker that supports the **IMoniker::Inverse** method. An antimoniker removes the last component when appended to the end of a generic moniker.

- *CreateBindCtx* — Allocates and initializes an object linking and embedding (OLE) binding context before **IMoniker::BindToObject** is invoked.

- *CreateFileMoniker* — Creates a file moniker from a pathname.

- *CreateFileMonikerFSP* — Creates a file moniker from a file specification.

- *CreateItemMoniker* — Returns a newly allocated item moniker.

- *CreatePointerMoniker* — A pointer moniker is a wrapper that, when used with different methods of the **IMoniker** interface, returns different values. The function of a pointer moniker varies with each of the **IMoniker** methods. A pointer moniker wraps an existing interface pointer in a moniker that can be passed to those interfaces that require monikers. Pointer monikers allow an object that has no persistent representation to participate in a moniker-binding operation.

  - **BindToObject** — Turns into a **QueryInterface** pointer.

  - **BindToStorage** — Returns a no storage status.

- o **Reduce** — Reduces the moniker to itself.

- o **ComposeWith** — Always does a generic composition.

- o **Enum** — Returns a Null.

- o **IsSystemMoniker** — Returns its own type.

- o **IsEqual** — Tests the other moniker, but only if it is the right type.

- o **Hash** — Returns a constant.

- o **GetTimeOfLastChange** — Returns a not available status.

- o **Inverse** — Returns an antimoniker.

- o **RelativePathTo** — Returns the other moniker.

- o **GetDisplayName** — Returns a NULL.

- o **ParseDisplayName** — Binds to the pointer using **IParseDisplayName**.

- o *CreateGenericComposite* — Returns a newly allocated composite moniker.

- o *GetRunningObjectTable* — Returns a pointer to the Running Object Table. Moniker implementations should not use this API call but should instead use the **IBindCtx::GetRunningObjectTable** method.

- o *MkParseDisplayName* — Parses the input display name to a moniker. This is the inverse of **IMoniker::GetDisplayName**.

- o *MonikerRelativePathTo* — Creates a moniker specifying a relative path.

- o *MonikerCommonPrefixWith* — Returns the longest common path a moniker shares with another moniker.

ASYNCHRONOUS MONIKERS

Asynchronous monikers return control to the client before binding is complete. Figure 5-9 shows the generic asynchronous moniker architecture where the moniker reports binding status back to the client with the **IBindStatusCallback** interface. This is an interim step to URL monikers, which are discussed later in this chapter.

The binding process uses a dialog between the client and the moniker. The client controls the binding process through the **IBinding** interface, while the asynchronous moniker uses the bind context object as a surrogate to return a status report, obtain binding priority, and notify the client of object or data availability.

The client must register the **IBindStatusCallback** interface with the global API **RegisterBindStatusCallback**.

All methods within **IBindStatusCallback** may be called from within **IMoniker::BindToObject** and **IMoniker::BindToStorage**. The client receives a pointer to the **IBind** interface when the moniker calls **IBindStatusCallback:: OnStartBinding**.

The asynchronous moniker supports both a *data-pull* and a *data-push* model. The moniker provides data as it is available in the data-pull model, but is blocked from obtaining additional data until the client has read the current data. The client must read all available data before the moniker can return from **IBindStatusCallBack::OnDataAvailable**. Subsequent calls are made to **IBindStatusCallBack::OnDataAvailable** until the equivalent of a file EOF (end of file) is returned.

The data-push returns an OK status even if the client returns from **IBindStatusCallBack::OnDataAvailable** without reading all the data. The client can elect to skip the data; however, it is possible to use the seek method to position back in the stream and obtain the missing blocks. The backward seek is not available with the data-push model.

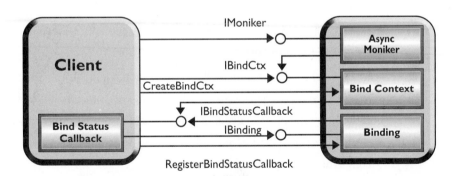

FIGURE 5-9 A generic asynchronous moniker architecture where the moniker reports binding status back to the client.

IAsyncMoniker

The **IAsyncMoniker** is a small, but necessary interface. This interface contains only the **IUnknown** methods, and its existence is simply a signal that an asynchronous moniker exists. Actual binding operations occur within the **IMoniker** interface.

IBindStatusCallback

IBindStatusCallback is the interface used by the methods of **IMoniker::BindToObject** and **IMoniker::BindToObject**. This interface supports callbacks from binding operations that may be in any arbitrary order. Clients can register an **IBindStatusCallback** interface with the global API function **RegisterBindStatusCallback**.

A **BindStatusCallback** object is required for each instance of an asynchronous binding operation. The **IBindStatusCallback** does not identify the type of bind operation associated with a notification.

The **IBindStatusCallback** interface inherits all methods of **IUnknown**. **IBindStatusCallback** implements these methods:

- *GetBindInfo* — This is called by an asynchronous moniker for binding information.

- *GetPriority* — The asynchronous moniker calls this method for the binding priority.

- *OnDataAvailable* — This is called by an asynchronous moniker when data is available. The moniker may be blocked for a data-pull model.

- *OnLowResource* — The client is notified by an asynchronous moniker that resources are low.

- *OnObjectAvailable* — The asynchronous moniker calls this method with a pointer to the new object.

- *OnProgress* — This is used by the asynchronous moniker to report load states.

- *OnStartBinding* — The asynchronous moniker notifies the client which callback methods are registered and available in the **IBind** interface.

- *OnStopBinding* — The client is notified that the binding operation is complete.

- *QueryInterface* — This is used by the asynchronous moniker to query for additional client services.

IBinding

The **IBinding** interface is required for custom asynchronous moniker implementations. It provides client access to the binding process. A pointer to this interface is returned to the client when the moniker calls **IBindStatusCallBack:: OnStartBinding**.

The **IBinding** interface inherits all methods of **IUnknown**. **IBinding** implements these methods:

- *Abort* — The client aborts the bind operation.
- *GetBindResult* — The client queries a protocol-specific binding result.
- *GetPriority* — The client retrieves the bind priority.
- *Resume* — A suspended bind operation is resumed by the client.
- *SetPriority* — The binding priority is established by the client.
- *Suspend* — The binding is suspended by the client.

URL MONIKERS

A URL is associated with an Internet address such as `http://www.microsoft.com`. An *asynchronous URL moniker* adds additional complexity to our moniker architecture, but there really aren't too many changes. Figure 5-9 illustrates asynchronous monikers. Using this architecture, a new data format interface was added on the client side while I replaced the generic **Binding** object with the **Transport Protocol** object, resulting in Figure 5-10. **BindStatusCallback**, **IBindCtx**, and **CreateBindCtx** are still there from the asynchronous monikers of Figure 5-9.

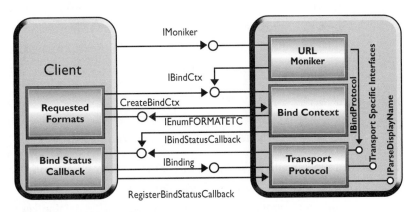

FIGURE 5-10   URL monikers.

How does this all work? It starts with a browser calling **MkParseDisplayName** with a URL. **MkParseDisplayName** returns a pointer to an asynchronous moniker. The browser doesn't know if the returned moniker is asynchronous, so it calls **IsAsyncMoniker**. If the moniker is asynchronous, the browser creates a bind context and registers the **IBindStatusCallback** with the newly acquired bind context. The browser then calls **IMoniker::BindToObject**. The moniker binds to the object and queries the object for the **IPersistMoniker** interface.

CASE 1: The moniker returns a pointer to **IPersistMoniker**.

1. The URL moniker calls **IPersistMoniker::Load** with its own **IMoniker** pointer to the object.

2. The object can choose between a push-data and a pull-data model (blocking versus nonblocking). The object modifies the bind context and registers its own **IBindStatusCallback**. The object then calls **IMoniker::BindToStorage** on the pointer it received through **IPersistMoniker::Load**.

3. The action now moves to the moniker, which creates an asynchronous storage and caches a reference to the wrapper object's **IFillLockBytes** interface. The **IProgressNotify** interface is registered on the root storage, and **IPersistStorage::Load** is called with the asynchronous storage **IStorage** pointer. The moniker calls **IFillLockBytes** as the data arrives using **ILockBytes** on a temporary file.

4. Data is read from storage by the object, and a control is returned to the object when it has sufficient data for self-initialization. The downloader receives a notification on **IProgressNotify** when the object attempts to access data not yet available. The **IProgressNotify::OnProgress** method does not block a data-push model.

CASE 2: **IPersistMoniker** doesn't exist.

The moniker queries for **IPersistStorage**, which indicates a storage object. If a pointer to **IPersistStorage** is returned, these steps occur:

1. The moniker calls **IMoniker::BindToStorage** on itself requesting a blocking **IStorage** interface. Because **IPersistMoniker** doesn't exist, this is a synchronous moniker. Just like the first call to **IPersistMoniker** above, both **IMoniker::BindToStorage** and **IPersistMoniker::Load** bootstrap off the URL moniker.

2. Control returns to the moniker where a reference to the wrapper object's ·
IFillLockBytes interface is cached. The **IProgressNotify** interface is
registered on the root storage, and **IPersistStorage::Load** is called with the
asynchronous blocking storage **IStorage** pointer (see Figure 5-11). The
moniker calls **IFillLockBytes** as the data arrives using **ILockBytes** on a
temporary file.

Eventually the object returns from **IMoniker::BindToObject**, and the
browser has the desired object. The browser queries for **IOleObject** and hosts the
object as a Document Object.

URL Monikers and Asynchronous Downloads

Figure 5-11 illustrates the asynchronous storage model. The unshaded areas of
the figure represent the standard structured storage model of COM. The area of
the figure labeled *DownLoader* induces a wrapper object for asynchronous storage
downloads by URL monikers.

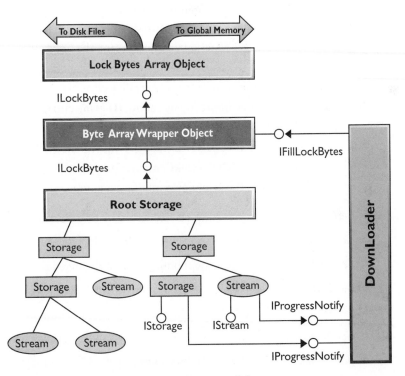

FIGURE 5-11 The asynchronous storage model.

A URL moniker is an evolutionary step for an asynchronous moniker. Figure 5-11 shows a new URL moniker interface, **IProgressNotify**, which is not user callable. Another addition to the URL moniker is the hidden **IBindProtocol** interface of Figure 5-10. These interfaces are not discussed because they are not user callable and there is no immediate need to know their details.

THE OBJECT AND CLIENT MONIKER INTERFACE

These are the interfaces for the desktop. A client uses these interfaces indirectly when cutting, pasting, and linking objects from the desktop. As an example, the **IOleLinkContainer** interface discussed previously is a programmatic interface, while **IOleUILinkContainer** is the client-side equivalent.

IOleLink

Linked objects implement the **IOleLink** interface. The container queries the object for the **IOleLink** interface and assumes the object is not linked when the interface doesn't exist. The **IOleLink** interface must be implemented for linked objects. The container object uses this functionality for locating the link source and the cached presentation data, and to activate the link to the native data.

Not all **IOleLink** functions are called directly. A container invokes **IOleLink::BindToSource** indirectly by calling **IOleObject::DoVerb**.

IOleLink is implemented to support the **Links** dialog box. If the Links dialog box is displayed with **IOleUIEditLinks**, the equivalent **IOleLink** methods are implemented within the **IOleUILinkContainer** interface.

IOleLink inherits the **IUnknown** interface and implements these methods:

- *SetUpdateOptions* — Specifies cached data updating strategy.
- *GetUpdateOptions* — Returns cached data updating strategy.
- *SetSourceMoniker* — Sets the moniker of a newly linked source.
- *GetSourceMoniker* — Returns the moniker identifying the linked source.
- *SetSourceDisplayName* — Sets the display name for a newly linked source.
- *GetSourceDisplayName* — Returns the linked source display name.
- *BindToSource* — Activates the link source by binding the moniker found within the linked source.

- *BindIfRunning* — Activates the link between the source and link source, but only if the link source is already running.

- *GetBoundSource* — Returns the **IUnknown** pointer if the connection is currently active.

- *UnbindSource* — Closes the link between a linked object and a linked source.

- *Update* — Updates the cached data for a linked object (binding to the source may be necessary).

IOleUILinkContainer

The **IOleUILinkContainer** interface must be implemented by container objects using the global API **OleUIEditLinks** function to display a dialog box. This includes the **Links** dialog box, the **Change Source** dialog box, the **Update Links** dialog box, and the **Object Properties** dialog box.

The **Links** dialog box will call back to the container to manipulate container links indirectly. The links of a container and the types of link updating are enumerated with this interface. Updating can be manual or automatic.

This interface inherits all methods of **IUnknown**; no other interfaces are inherited. The implementation of this interface will use **IOleLink** interfaces. The methods of this interface include:

- *GetNextLink* — Enumerates the container links (the container link identifiers are returned in sequence).

- *SetLinkUpdateOptions* — Sets the update option to automatic or manual.

- *GetLinkUpdateOptions* — Returns the link update options.

- *SetLinkSource* — Calls from the **Change Source** dialog box.

- *GetLinkSource* — Calls during dialog box initialization or after returning from the Change Source dialog box.

- *OpenLinkSource* — Calls when the **OpenSource** button is selected from the **Links** dialog box (OLE links will call **IOleObject::DoVerb**).

- *UpdateLink* — Forces links to connect to their source and retrieve current information.

- *CancelLink* — Closes the link when the user selects the Break Link button from the **Links** dialog box.

Marshaling

Late binding requires *dynamic marshaling*, which is a function of the COM library and is supported by the **IStdMarshal** interface. The objects are bound at execution time, which requires the services of a local proxy and a remote stub. (I call marshaling a loose end because it is not on our COM roadmap in Figure 5-1, although it is an essential issue of COM.)

The general concept of marshaling is illustrated in Figure 5-12, where an in-process server handles the *remote procedure call* (RPC) administration. As Figure 5-12 shows, this code is called the proxy. The proxy packages the data (marshals) before sending the data to a remote stub via an RPC channel. Figure 5-12 only shows one RPC channel; however, this is an oversimplification as an RPC channel is usually established with each remote object.

The corresponding code on the server is a stub that *unmarshals* the data before passing it to a server. This process is an example of standard marshaling in that no new objects are created. The dark, vertical bar denotes a process boundary: The target server may exist on the same machine or another machine.

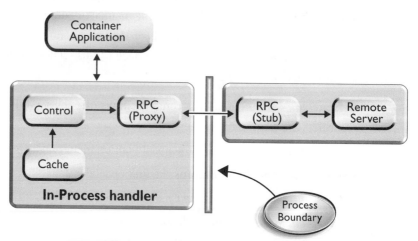

FIGURE 5-12   The RPC (proxy) marshals the data and the stub unmarshals it.

The code in Listing 5-1 is from an OLE 2.0 registration file. It gives us some clues to the nature of such names as **ProxyStubClsid**, **IStdMarshalInfo**, **IRpcChannel**, **IMarshal**, and **IRpcStub**, which are the glue that makes marshaling work. (The **IMarshal** interface is only used for custom marshaling.)

LISTING 5-1 An example of Registry proxy stubs for marshaling from an OLE 2.0
registration file

```
HKEY_CLASSES_ROOT\Interface\{0000000E-0000-0000-C000-
  000000000046} = IBindCtx
HKEY_CLASSES_ROOT\Interface\{0000000E-0000-0000-C000-
  000000000046}\NumMethods = 13
HKEY_CLASSES_ROOT\Interface\{0000000E-0000-0000-C000-
  000000000046}\ProxyStubClsid = {00000312-0000-0000-C000-
  000000000046}

HKEY_CLASSES_ROOT\Interface\{0000000F-0000-0000-C000-
  000000000046} = IMoniker
HKEY_CLASSES_ROOT\Interface\{0000000F-0000-0000-C000-
  000000000046}\BaseInterface = {00000109-0000-0000-C000-
  000000000046}

HKEY_CLASSES_ROOT\Interface\{0000000F-0000-0000-C000-
  000000000046}\NumMethods = 23
HKEY_CLASSES_ROOT\Interface\{0000000F-0000-0000-C000-
  000000000046}\ProxyStubClsid = {0000030C-0000-0000-C000-
  000000000046}
```

Standard marshaling occurs automatically. There may be occasions where custom marshaling is a better choice than standard marshaling. Reasons to consider implementing custom marshaling include:

- Custom marshaling is a consideration when the target server object itself is a proxy for some other object.
- Some objects store their entire state in shared memory. Creating a custom proxy gives immediate access to the storage.
- Some objects have an immutable state after creation — the object cannot change. A custom proxy can create a copy of this immutable state without the overhead of an RPC channel.
- A custom proxy can be used to batch cached data until such time as a commit operation is performed.

Custom marshaling is a bit more complex than standard marshaling. The client starts by calling **IClassfactory::CreateInstance** on the remote server where the stub passes the request to the target object. The returned **IClassFactory** pointer is then passed to **CoGetClassObject** where this process occurs:

1. Within **CoGetClassObject**, COM attempts to acquire the proxy CLSID of the client proxy. The standard marshaling proxy CLSID is used when none is available.

2. COM asks the target object for a marshaling packet. When none is available COM creates a packet supporting standard marshaling.

3. The packet and the proxy CLSID are passed back to the client process.

4. The client creates an instance of the proxy using the CLSID that was just returned. The client then passes the packet to the new proxy.

5. The proxy connects with the target server. An interface pointer is returned to the original **CoGetClassObject** call, and the client can now communicate with the remote server with custom marshaling.

Steps 1 and 2 are wrapped in the COM API function **CoMarshalInterface**, while Steps 4 and 5 are wrapped in the **CoUnmarshalInterface**. Step 3 is specific to COM.

KEY POINT SUMMARY

Monikers and moniker binding are under-the-hood technologies that make COM work. Late binding is always a choice, but late binding cannot work without the help and support of dynamic marshaling.

- Monikers can be synchronous or asynchronous.

- The **IPersistMoniker** interface signals an asynchronous moniker.

- The binding process starts by the client creating a binding context. This is done with the global API call **CreateBindCtx**. The next logical step is the client calling **IMoniker::BindToObject**.

- Active objects are maintained in the Running Object Table. The binding process takes advantage of this and increments the reference count for objects already instantiated. The presence of the Running Object Table realizes binding optimizations.

- The presence of the **IOleLink** interface indicates that an object is linked. It is also the linked object's interface to the linking and binding process with monikers.

APPLYING WHAT YOU'VE LEARNED

Understanding what is under the hood always improves your design skills. Remember the car at the beginning of the chapter? Understanding the interplay between the components is essential when the architecture doesn't work. Is the battery dead? Are the cables in good condition? Is there a spark? All these questions are based on understanding the connection mechanism and relationship of the components to each other. The same strategy applies to COM components.

Instant Assessment: Monikers

1. Which interface must be supported for all item monikers?
2. In binding a composite moniker, which moniker is responsible for determining the pointer for the original IID passed in by the client?
3. When is the first action the client performs related to binding a moniker?
4. What is the second step?
5. Which important interface does **IMoniker** inherit besides **IUnknown**?
6. What is the Running Object Table?
7. What restrictions are there on the global API **GetRunningObjectTable** call?
8. What is the unique characteristic of the **IOleLink** interface?
9. What is the unique characteristic of the **IOleUILinkContainer** interface?
10. Explain the relationship between **MkParseDisplayName**, **IParseDisplayName**, and **IMoniker::GetDisplayName**.

Instant Assessment: Marshaling

1. What is the general meaning of *marshaling* within the COM context?
2. What are the generic names for the COM functions that perform marshaling?

3. What feature of COM requires marshaling?

4. Default marshaling is accomplished with the **IStdMarshal** interface. Provide four reasons for custom marshaling.

 concept link **For answers to the Instant Assessment questions, see Appendix C.**

Lab Exercise

This is an evaluation of your system and the systems you use in your job. The lab assumes that all systems use the Microsoft Windows architecture with a user interface of Microsoft Windows 3.1 or later, including all versions of Windows NT.

Lab 5.12 *Functionality of local systems*

WA I

Enumerate all functionality that is local to a machine and uses OLE. Don't be general and say *Microsoft Excel embedded in a Word document*, but identify the specific application such as *Quarterly Sales Summary for the Southeast Region*. The goal is to identify the impact of the COM moniker technology in daily operations.

Now perform the same task for applications that use linking from a remote source. This includes remote Automation tasks, distributed COM tasks, and intranet/Internet tasks.

Windows Architecture I

Uniform Data Transfer

About Chapter 6

Uniform Data Transfer (UDT) is a key and necessary COM technology, but it is wrong to say UDT was specifically designed for COM. Earlier data transfer technology within the Windows operating system was overly complex with a specific API function for each type of data transfer. Managing API functions, parameters, handles, and buffers resulted in too much complexity with limited functionality. UDT is essential for COM and manages the complexity; however, it is also the garbage collector of prior technologies.

UDT is commonly characterized as the technology that removed the global memory bottleneck. *Dynamic data exchange* (DDE), the predecessor to COM, is a slow and early technology that only uses global memory. This use of global memory did not limit DDE's functionality but did limit its application; consequently large data transfers in DDE are slow. It's also fair to say that OLE 1 suffered the same global memory malady.

UDT addresses both of these issues with two interfaces and two data structures. UDT is a generalized wrapper for device types and data formats. In UDT, formats are expanded beyond the clipboard-only format. UDT represents a single data object with the **IDataObject** interface, which can be used in any transfer protocol such as drag-and-drop, clipboard, or a compound document.

Supporting UDT with data change notifications is the **IAdviseSink** interface. This is a very important interface and is the first step on the path to connectable objects. Even though this is a chapter on UDT, notification mechanisms other than **IAdviseSink** are discussed. These topics are vaguely related to **IAdviseSink**, and their inclusion here is for closure on all notification issues. This chapter completes the thumbnail sketches of basic COM functionality and prepares us for the next two chapters of COM linking and embedding.

IN THE BEGINNING

UDT is our next stop on the COM roadmap (Figure 6-1) as we continue our visit to COM functionality. This section can be summed up in one sentence: Implementing the **IDataObject** interface is synonymous with Uniform Data Transfer. But it was not always this easy. DDE and the early version of OLE were resource hogs, and clipboard data transfers were unduly complex. UDT brought manageability and performance to an emerging and chaotic technology.

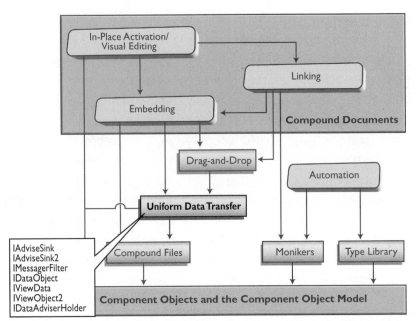

FIGURE 6-1   The Uniform Data Transfer stop on our COM technology roadmap.

UDT is a wrapper that simplifies clipboard data transfer. A data object is created and used with data properties defined within two data structures. Along with the infrastructure issues of managing buffers, handles, and data format specifications, the data consumer deals only with obtaining a pointer to an **IDataObject** interface, rather than using a Windows API function.

The first issue is to understand what existed before OLE 2:

- All transfers were done with API functions.
- Clipboard transfers were limited to a single type (UINT or a CF_* value, which are C/C++ datatypes).
- Structures existed only in memory.
- Transfers were only through global memory.

UDT generalizes data transfers with the **IDataObject** interface. It makes a paradigm shift by introducing the concept of transfer protocols. Rather than moving data to the consumer, the goal of UDT is to supply an **IDataObject** pointer to the consumer. **UDT** separates data from the transfer protocol. The transfer protocols for a compound document, clipboard, or a drag-and-drop operation each function differently. Let's review the four ways of obtaining a pointer to an object.

(These are all general mechanisms, but we'll adapt them to acquiring an **IDataObject** pointer. The process of acquiring the pointer is known as a transfer protocol.)

o *Call an API function that creates an object of only one type.* The pointer returned is to one specific interface type or object type. This technique is illustrated by assuming that you have just installed a new proprietary board in your system. The board manufacturer also supplied a custom dynamic link library (DLL). Your application calls **CoCreateInstance** on the supplied class identifier (CLSID) and creates a specific instance of the proprietary DLL. Your application then uses **IDataObject** member functions to retrieve the data.

There is a variation on this technique used by the clipboard protocol where an **IDataObject** pointer isn't actually created by an API function. An API function places an **IDataObject** pointer on the clipboard and another API function retrieves an **IDataObject** pointer from the clipboard.

o *Call an API function that can create an object based on class type.* Any interface pointer you request is returned. This is the most common object instantiation procedure and is the common technique used for compound documents, a discussion of which starts in Chapter 7. The general procedure is the client calling the COM library functions **CoGetClassObject** with the CLSID of the desired object and requested interface identifier (IID), which in this case is IID_IDataObject. Because the object is being created, the IID of **IClassFactory** is the other input parameter to **CoGetClassObject**. What eventually is returned to the client is the pointer to **IClassFactory** of the desired object. The client calls **IClassFactory:: CreateInstance**, which instantiates the required object.

o *Call a member function of some interface that returns a specific interface pointer on another separate object.* The best example of this is calling **QueryInterface** on an object for an **IDataObject** interface pointer.

o *Implement interface functions on your own objects to which other object users pass their own interface pointers.* This technique is used by drag-and-drop, which is discussed later in this chapter. The process starts with an object registering itself as a drop target in a drag-and-drop operation. **DoDragDrop** is in a loop calling **WindowFromPoint**. When a valid window handle is returned from **WindowFromPoint**, it is checked for an

IDropTarget pointer. If such a pointer exists, a call is marshaled to **IDropTarget::DragEnter** supplying the **IDataObject** pointer from the source object.

Comparing UDT with Prior Technologies

UDT generalizes and expands the prior technologies. Table 6-1 compares **IDataObject** member functions with prior technology.

TABLE 6-1 COMPARING IDATAOBJECT MEMBER FUNCTIONS WITH PRIOR TECHNOLOGY

IDataObject Member Function	Protocol	Equivalent Windows Function or Message
GetData	Clipboard	`GetClipboardData`
	DDE	`WM_DDE_REQUEST, WM_DDE_DATA`
	OLE 1	`OleGetData`
SetData	Clipboard	`SetClipboardData`
	DDE	`WM_DDE_POKE`
	OLE 1	`OleSetData`
QueryGetData	Clipboard	`IsClipboardFormatAvailable`
	DDE	None (`WM_DDE_CONNECT_ADVISE`, not quite the same)
	OLE 1	None
GetCanonicalFormatEtc	Clipboard	None
	DDE	None
	OLE 1	None
EnumFormatEtc	Clipboard	`EnumClipboardFormats` (direction only)
	DDE	None
	OLE 1	None
DAdvise	Clipboard	None
	DDE	`WM_DDE_ADVISE`
	OLE 1	None

IDATAOBJECT MEMBER FUNCTION	PROTOCOL	EQUIVALENT WINDOWS FUNCTION OR MESSAGE
DUnadvise	Clipboard	None
	DDE	WM_DDE_UNADVISE
	OLE 1	None

Mapping IDataObject Functionality to DDE

Table 6-1 doesn't quite give us the complete picture. DDE appears to be mappable to UDT. Table 6-2 leads us to believe that conversion from DDE to UDT is a simple matter. Not so!

TABLE 6-2 COMPARING IDATAOBJECT MEMBER FUNCTIONS WITH DDE MESSAGES

IDATAOBJECT METHOD	DDE MESSAGE
IDataObject::SetData	WM_DDE_POKE
IDataObject::GetData	WM_DDE_RREQUEST
IDataObject::DAdvise	WM_DDE_ADVISE
IDataObject::DUnadvise	WM_DDE_UNADVISE
IDataObject::OnDataChange	WM_DDE_DATA

In spite of the apparent parallel functionality of the **IDataObject** interface and DDE, the mapping is not appropriate because DDE is inherently asynchronous and the **IDataObject** interface is synchronous. There is always an exception to any rule, and **IDataObject::DAdvise** is asynchronous under specific conditions.

That's the first problem. The second problem is the invocation process. An example DDE application starts a conversation with a service such as "Excel" and an example topic of "YearEnd.XLS." OLE 2 starts with a call on **CoCreateInstance** with a CLSID for Excel asking for the **IPersistFile** interface. The file is loaded with **IPersistFile::Load** ("YearEnd.XLS"). A **QueryInterface** call on **IPersistFile** for the **IDataObject** interface follows this.

The third problem area is the clipboard format. **IDataObject** does not support a standard field where a caller can specify a subset of data, whereas a DDE conversation allows a user to request data by specifying an item name and the clipboard format. In summary, converting a DDE application to UDT is not quite as simple as it appears.

Notifications

Notifications of data changes in prior technology were minimal and hand-tooled to specific applications. The developer could sandwich a custom dialog box between **MakeProcInstance** and **FreeProcInstance**. There are the DDE messages WM_DDE_ADVISE and WM_DDE_UNADVISE, but these only apply to DDE. This changes with the introduction of Uniform Data Transfer notifications that occur when data modeled by the **IDataObject** interface changes. The three COM transport protocols—drag-and-drop, clipboard, and compound document—each support the **IAdviseSink** interface for notifications. The **IAdviseSink** interface is a UDT component and is delegated the responsibility of accepting the data changes generated by the data source. The client calls the data source represented by **IDataObject::DAdvise** and supplies the **IAdviseSink** interface pointer used for future notifications. Dismissal of further notifications is accomplished with **IDataObject::DUnadvise**.

The COM model has evolved and the general connection mechanism **IConnectionPointContainer** and **IConnectionPoint** is an outgrowth of the original **IAdviseSink** interface. (Several interfaces are included in this section that deal with COM object communications in general and not just **IDataObject** notifications.)

UNIFORM DATA TRANSFER COMPONENTS

This section discusses the core components of UDT. **IDataAdviseHolder** is included as a component of UDT; its role, however, is that of a helper function to **IDataObject**. It is an optional interface that relieves the **IDataObject** interface of the mundane task of notifying consumers when data changes.

Describing Data with the FORMATETC Structure

UDT deals directly with the earlier performance issues of OLE, which transferred all data through global memory. It didn't take too much data to bring everything to a grinding halt. Data transfer formats are expanded beyond the clipboard-only format. The new FORMATETC (format et cetera) data structure supports both the internal OLE files, disk files, and global memory, whereas the earlier implementations only supported global memory.

 note

The FORMATETC data structure, the STGMEDIUM data structure, the IDataObject interface, and the IAdviseSink interface are the four key components of Uniform Data Transfer.

FORMATETC is the first key element of Uniform Data Transfer structures. It is the data structure with more information than the name implies. Information stored in the FORMATETC structure includes the clipboard data type, a pointer to a target device type, the aspect, which can be the data itself, a thumbnail sketch of the data, an icon, or a preformatted printer image. The general FORMATETC format is:

- A word identifying the format. This is the improved version of the old clipboard format, although the term *clipboard* is used for historical reasons, as the identified structures have nothing to do with the clipboard anymore.

- A pointer to a DVTARGETDEVICE structure which describes the device such as a screen or a printer, for which the data was rendered.

- The aspect (view), which can be native data, an icon, a thumbnail sketch, or preformatted printer output. This represents the detail contained in the rendering.

- An identifier when the data must be split across boundaries. -1 indicates no data split. Otherwise useful only with `DVASPECT_CONTENT` or `DVASPECT_DOCPRINT` to identify the data segment.

- The storage type, which can be global memory, disk file, stream, storage, a bitmap, or a metafile.

Describing Storage with the DVTARGETDEVICE Structure

The DVTARGETDEVICE structure describes the target device with a driver name, a device name, a port name, and the device mode. A pointer to this structure is maintained within the FORMATETC data structure.

The STGMEDIUM structure overlaps a small amount of information found in the FORMATETC data structure. The STGMEDIUM format is:

- The storage type, which can be global memory, disk file, stream, storage, a bitmap, or a metafile. This describes the data location.
- A file handle.
- The filename.
- A pointer to a stream storage object.
- A pointer to a storage object.

IDataObject

The **IDataObject** is implemented for any container or server application that is capable of transferring data. OLE compound document servers must implement **IDataObject** for both embedded and linked objects. The **IDataObject** interface is required for drag and drop operations. It is an optional but recommended interface for clipboard operations.

IDataObject uses the FORMATETC and STGMEDIUM data structures for transfer and rendering data. As shown in Figure 6-2, **IAdviseSink::OnDataChange** is the recipient of **IDataObject** notifications and is the only required method of **IAdviseSink** when used in the context of UDT.

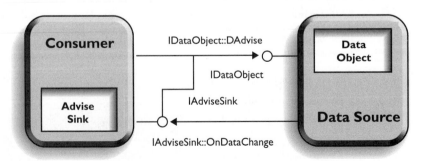

FIGURE 6-2   The IDataObject and IAdviseSink interfaces, which illustrate IAdviseSink receiving notifications from IDataObject.

The **IDataObject** interface inherits all methods of **IUnknown** and implements these methods:

o **GetData**—Transfers data through the STGMEDIUM structure and renders it to the FORMATETC specification. This can be native data, an icon, a thumbnail sketch, or preformatted printer output.

o **GetDataHere**—Transfers data through the STGMEDIUM structure to the client and renders it to the FORMATETC specification. This can be native data, an icon, a thumbnail sketch, or preformatted printer output.

o **QueryGetData**—Asks if the data object is capable of rending data as described in the FORMATETC structure.

o **GetCanonicalFormatEtc**—Creates a logically equivalent FORMATETC structure.

o **SetData**—Sends data to the source as described by the FORMATETC and STGMEDIUM structures.

o **EnumFormatEtc**—Returns a newly created pointer for enumerating the FORMATETC supported by the object.

o **DAdvise**—Connects to **IAdviseSink** and establishes the notification connection.

o **DUnadvise**—Closes the notification link.

o **EnumDAdvise**—Returns a newly created pointer for enumerating the current advisory connections.

IAdviseSink

IAdviseSink occupies a rather unique place in COM. **IAdviseSink** was the first asynchronous COM interface. Until that time, all COM interfaces were synchronous. Almost all the other COM interfaces are still synchronous, except for asynchronous monikers or advisory notifications. (*Asynchronous* means that control is returned immediately to the caller.)

The **IAdviseSink** notification mechanism requires that the client implement **IDataObject::DAdvise** and **IOleObject::Advise**. In-process objects and handlers can optionally implement **IViewObject::SetAdvise**. Performance is an issue when **IAdviseSink::OnDataChange** must be marshaled. An example of this is data contained within an .EXE.

A document change has different contexts. There is the question of knowing when the document is saved, closed, or renamed. There is also the issue of knowing when the document's native data changes and when the document's presentation data changes. Requests for the different types of notifications are listed in Table 6-3.

TABLE 6-3 WHO TO CALL TO REQUEST A DOCUMENT CHANGE NOTIFICATION	
USE THIS METHOD	*TO REGISTER A REQUEST FOR NOTIFICATION WHEN:*
IOleObject::Advise	The document is saved, changed, or closed.
IDataObject::DAdvise	The document's native data changes.
IViewObject::SetAdvise	The document's presentation data changes.

IDataObject::ADdvise is the only UDT advisory request method in Table 6-3. **IOleObject::Advise** is an advisory request mechanism for compound documents, while **IViewObject::SetAdvise** is an advisory request mechanism for rendering objects.

Management of notification registration is simplified with the wrapper interfaces **IDataAdviseHolder** and **IOleAdviseHolder**. These interfaces track advisory connections and send the proper notifications using **IAdviseSink** interface pointers. **IDataAdviseHolder** simplifies life for **IDataObject** while **IOleAdviseHolder** performs the same task for **IOleObject**.

IAdviseSink is an asynchronous interface. This means that synchronous methods cannot be invoked in an **IAdviseSink** method. An example of this restriction is the method **IAdviseSink::OnViewChange** calling the method **IDataObject::GetData**. **IAdviseSink** inherits **IUnknown** and implements the following:

- **OnDataChange** — An advisory is issued when data changes. This is the only required method when the interface is used in a UDT context and the operation is asynchronous.

- **OnViewChange** — An advisory is issued when the object view changes. This method only applies to viewable objects and not data objects.

- **OnRename** — An advisory is issued when the object name changes.

o **OnSave** — An advisory is issued when the object is saved.

o **OnClose** — An advisory is issued when the object is closed.

IDataAdviseHolder

The OLE 2 specification states that any data object may receive multiple calls to **IDataObject::DAdvise**. This means that the data object is responsible for sending notifications to all interested advisory sinks. Delegating this task to the **IDataAdviseHolder** interface solves the logistical problem of managing multiple advisory sinks.

The methods of **IDataAdviseHolder** create and manage advisory connections between a data object and interested advisory sinks. **IDataAdviseHolder** is a custom implementation and is usually unnecessary. The standard OLE implementation can be used.

A custom **IDataAdviseHolder** interface implementation delegates the methods **IDataObject::DAdvise**, **IDataObject::DUnadvise**, and **IDataObject::EnumDAdvise** to the corresponding **IDataAdviseHolder** methods. **CreateDataAdviseHolder** creates a **DataAdviseHolder** object. This is done the first time a **IDataObject::Advise** is received.

Multicasting occurs by **IDataObject** sending its own pointer and flags to **IDataAdviseHolder::SendOnDataChange** when data changes. **IDataAdviseHolder** enumerates the accumulated advisory list and calls **IAdviseSink::OnDataChange** for each member of the list. **IDataAdviseHolder** also calls **IDataObject::GetData** to obtain a rendering if the supplied flags do not include ADVF_NODATA. The acquired rendering is then sent to the sink.

IDataAdviseHolder inherits all methods of **IUnknown** and implements the following:

o **Advise** — Creates a data source and advisory sink connection.

o **Unadvise** — Destroys the connection.

o **EnumAdvise** — Returns a pointer to an enumeration object.

o **SendOnDataChange** — Notifies each waiting and managed advise sink of a data change. The standard advisory service is not the most optimal; better performance occurs with a custom implementation.

OTHER NOTIFICATIONS

The COM notification mechanisms discussed in this section are not limited to notifications from the data object represented by the **IDataObject** interface to the **IAdviseSink** interface. **IAdviseSink** is the recipient of notifications from interfaces other than **IDataObject**.

 concept link

Hopefully, you are not confused. This is indeed a chapter on Uniform Data Transfer, which uses the IAdviseSink::OnDataChange mechanism for data advisories. I elected to collect in the last portion of this chapter other advisory notification mechanisms. All of COM is related and by referencing all notification mechanisms that use the IAdviseSink interface, interfaces such as the IOleObject interface, which is not a data object interface but an embedded object interface, are drawn into the discussion. Be patient. There is a method to my madness, and by the end of the chapter, you'll know the minimum interfaces for an embedded object. This prepares you for the next two chapters, which deal with linked and embedded COM objects.

IAdviseSink2

IAdviseSink2 inherits all methods of **IAdviseSink** and adds the method **OnLinkSrcChange**. An advisory is issued when the link source changes. The link object should invoke **IAdviseSink::OnLinkSrcChange** when the link source is renamed. This is a notification mechanism for compound documents and not the **IDataObject** interface.

IAdviseSinkEx

IAdviseSinkEx inherits all methods of **IAdviseSink** and adds the method **OnViewStatusChange**. An advisory is issued when the view status changes. This is a notification mechanism for compound documents and not the **IDataObject** interface.

IOleAdviseHolder

IOleAdviseHolder does the same service for servers and compound documents that **IDataAdviseHolder** does for data sources and advisory sinks. The **IOleAdvise Holder** is a wrapper for the advisory methods of **IOleObject**.

The **IOleAdviseHolder** implementation is identical to the implementation of **IDataAdviseHolder** in that the data object calls **CreateOleAdviseHolder** the first time **IOleObject::Advise** is invoked. When implementing **IOleObject** on the data object, the **IOleObject::Advise**, **IOleObject::Unadvise**, and **IOle::EnumAdvise** methods are delegated to the **IOleAdviseHolder** interface.

IOleAdvise inherits all methods of **IUnknown** and implements the following:

o **Advise** — Establishes an advisory sink and data object connection.

o **Unadvise** — Destroys the advisory connection.

o **EnumAdvise** — Returns a pointer to an enumeration object.

o **SendOnRename** — Notifies managed advisory sinks of a name change.

o **SendOnSave** — Notifies managed advisory sinks when the data object is saved.

o **SendOnClose** — Notifies managed advisory sinks when an object is closed.

IOleObject

IOleObject defines an embedded object. The **IOleObject** interface is used for managing embedded objects and for embedded objects communicating with the host container. **IOleObject** is to compound documents what **IDataObject** is to data objects. **IOleObject** is also a source of **IAdviseSink** notifications.

With **IOleObject**, things start to come together. In addition to **IDataObject** and **IPersistStorage**, **IOleObject** is an important building block. **IOleObject**, **IPersistStorage**, and **IDataObject** are the three required interfaces for each type of embedded object. They also represent three of the four necessary interfaces that constitute an embeddable but minimal compound document. Before the chapter ends, we'll have introduced all the required interfaces for a minimal compound document.

IOleObject has 21 methods; however, **DoVerb**, **SetHostNames**, and **Close** are the only nontrivial methods. Calls to all other methods are optional. **DoVerb** activates embedded objects, **SetHostNames** communicates container application and document names, and **Close** moves an embedded object from the running state to the loaded state. The **SetExtent**, **InitFromData**, **GetClipBoardData**, **SetColorScheme**, **SetMoniker**, and **GetMoniker** methods are optional and need not be implemented.

IOleObject inherits all methods of **IUnknown** and implements the following:

- **SetClientSite** — Informs the object of its container client site, which sets the **IOleClientSite** pointer.
- **GetClientSite** — Returns the object's client site.
- **SetHostNames** — Supplies an object with the names of its container application and the compound document in which it is embedded.
- **Close** — Changes a running object to the loaded state, optionally saving or discarding changes.
- **SetMoniker** — Notifies an object of its container's moniker, the object's own moniker relative to the container, or the object's full moniker.
- **GetMoniker** — Retrieves an embedded object's moniker.
- **InitFromData** — Initializes a newly created embedded object from selected data. This can be a paste from the clipboard or from data, which resides in the same container.
- **GetClipBoardData** — Transfers a data object from the clipboard.
- **DoVerb** — Invokes an embedded object to perform a selected verb.
- **EnumVerbs** — Enumerates verbs (actions).
- **Update** — Updates the object.
- **IsUpToDate** — Checks the object for being up to date.
- **GetUserClassID** — Returns the object's CLSID. This might change with emulation.
- **GetUserType** — Returns the user-type name.
- **SetExtent** — Sets the object's display area extent.
- **GetExtent** — Retrieves the object's display area extent.
- **Advise** — Establishes an object and advisory sink connection.

- **Unadvise** — Destroys the advisory sink connection.

- **EnumAdvise** — Returns a pointer to an enumeration object.

- **GetMiscStatus** — Returns object status.

- **SetColorScheme** — Sets the color palette the object application should use when editing the specified object.

IViewObject

Object handlers and in-process servers that manage their own presentations implement the **IViewObject** interface. The **IViewObject** is functionally equivalent to **IDataObject**; however, **IViewObject** places a data representation on a device context (hDC), while a data representation is placed on a transfer medium by **IDataObject**.

Device contexts are valid only within a process. This means the **IViewObject** interface cannot be marshaled. This is logical, as a bitmap on the screen is a local rendering dependent upon local attributes and characteristics.

The **IViewObject** interface inherits all methods of **IUnknown** and implements the following:

- **Draw** — Draws the object representation on the device context.

- **GetColorSet** — Returns the local object drawing palette.

- **Freeze** — Locks the drawn representation.

- **Unfreeze** — Unlocks the drawn representation.

- **SetAdvise** — Establishes a connection between the draw object and an advisory sink.

- **GetAdvise** — Returns the latest **SetAdvise** information.

 concept link

The **IViewObject** is a major milestone for us. It is the last object we need to create an embedded object. We'll take a closer look at linked and embedded objects starting in Chapter 7.

 note

The **IPersistStorage**, **IDataObject**, **IOleObject**, and **IViewObject** interfaces collectively represent a minimal and embeddable compound document object.

IViewObject2

The **IViewObject2** object extends the **IViewObject** object with one additional method. **GetExtent** returns the size of the view object from cache. **IViewObject2** inherits all methods of **IUnknown** and **IViewObject**.

IViewObjectEx

The **IViewObjectEx** interface inherits all methods on **IUnknown**, **IViewObject**, and **IViewObject2**. **IViewObjectEx** provides support for flicker-free drawings, hit testing on nonrectangular objects, and control sizing. The additional methods implemented are:

- **GetRect** — Returns a rectangle describing the requested drawing aspect.
- **GetViewStatus** — Identifies supported drawing aspects and returns opacity information.
- **QueryHitPoint** — Asks if a point is within a given object aspect.
- **QueryHitRect** — Asks if a point in a rectangle is within the object drawing aspect.
- **GetNaturalExtent** — Returns container-sizing hints for the object to use as the user resizes the object.

IMessageFilter

That about covers object communication with advisory sinks. However, advisory sink messages are always asynchronous. Nearly all messaging in COM is synchronous; that is, the client loops until the message is complete. COM supports three messaging classes:

- *Synchronous* — The client loops until the response is received. This is the common COM communication mechanism.
- *Asynchronous* — Messages may be delivered at any time. COM supports five asynchronous methods:
  - **IAdviseSink::OnDataChange**
  - **IAdviseSink::OnViewChange**
  - **IAdviseSink::OnRename**

- o **IAdviseSink::OnSave**

- o **IAdviseSink::OnClose**

- o *Input-Synchronized*— These are methods of compound documents that must complete to save user input before control is returned to the requester. (We discuss these interfaces in Chapters 7 and 8 when we discuss linking and embedding of compound documents.) These are the COM input-synchronized methods:

  - o **IOleWindow::GetWindow**

  - o **IOleInPlaceActiveObject::OnFrameWindowActivate**

  - o **IOleInPlaceActiveObject::OnDocWindowActivate**

  - o **IOleInPlaceActiveObject::ResizeBorder**

  - o **IOleInPlaceWindow::GetBorder**

  - o **IOleInPlaceUIWindow::RequestBorderSpace**

  - o **IOleInPlaceUIWindow::SetBorderSpace**

  - o **IOleInPlaceFrame::SetMenu**

  - o **IOleInPlaceFrame::SetStatusText**

  - o **IOleInPlaceObject::SetObjectRects**

Message filtering with **IMessageFilter** is used to resolve synchronous message deadlocks and is not directly related to advisory sinks. **IMessageFilter** is a recommended but optional interface. The interface provides OLE servers and applications with the ability to selectively handle incoming and outgoing OLE messages while waiting for responses from synchronous calls. Messages can be rejected or deferred and attempted at a later time. **IMessageFilter** presents a dialog box to resolve deadlocks, giving the user an opportunity of dealing with the deadlock. An example of a blocking task is Excel computing formulas in the background at the behest of a Word document and ignoring incoming messages.

Another example of a deadlock is a client with a message loop inside **IRpcChannelBuffer::SendReceive**. The remote server is not responding and the application is deadlocked. COM notifies a message filter when a timeout condition or another blocking condition occurs. This allows the user to timeout as well as handle any other incoming calls that occur. As you can see, **IMessageFilter** does more than just filter messages. It is a concurrency manager.

The **IMessageFilter** object is created with the COM library function **CoCreateMessageFilter**. Once registered, COM will call the message filter rather than the default messaging implementation.

IMessageFilter inherits all interfaces from **IUnknown** and implements:

- **HandleIncomingCall** — A single entry point for all incoming calls.

- **RetryRejectedCall** — A dialog box is presented to the user with retry, cancel, or task switch options.

- **MessagePending** — A Windows message arrived while OLE is waiting to respond to a remote call.

CONNECTABLE OBJECTS

Connectable objects are a generalization of the advisory sink dialog. In fact, advisory sink messages are just a subset of the message functionality supported. When an object supports one or more outgoing interfaces it is said to be connectable. A source can have as many outgoing interfaces as it likes, where each interface is composed of a distinct set of member functions and each function represents a single event, notification, or request. Connectable objects are a feature of the COM model and are not limited to OLE controls even though connectable objects are often associated with OLE controls. The mechanics of a connectable object are illustrated in Figure 6-3.

The **IAdviseSink–IDataObject** advisory architecture is limited in that a client can only pass an **IAdviseSink** interface pointer to **IDataObject**. Compare this with the **IConnectionPoint** interface, which can be passed the pointer of any interface. An **IConnectionPointContainer** may support more than one **IConnectionPoint** interface and more than one **IConnectionPoint** interface may use the same **IConnectionPointContainer** interface. Any sink can be connected to any number of data objects. Figure 6-4 shows more than one sink connected to an object, while Figure 6-5 shows a sink connected to more than one object.

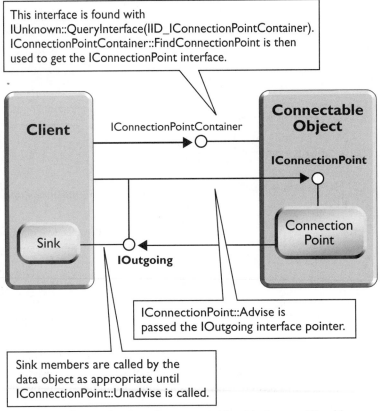

This interface is found with
IUnknown::QueryInterface(IID_IConnectionPointContainer).
IConnectionPointContainer::FindConnectionPoint is then
used to get the IConnectionPoint interface.

IConnectionPoint::Advise is
passed the IOutgoing interface pointer.

Sink members are called by the
data object as appropriate until
IConnectionPoint::Unadvise is called.

FIGURE 6-3 The mechanics of a connectable object are outlined here.

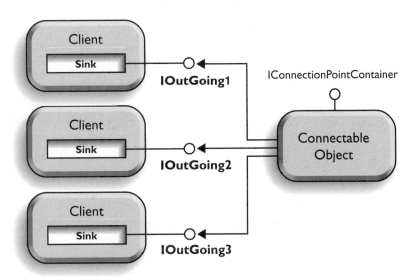

FIGURE 6-4 A IConnectionPointContainer can support more than one
IConnectionPoint interface (a many-to-one connection).

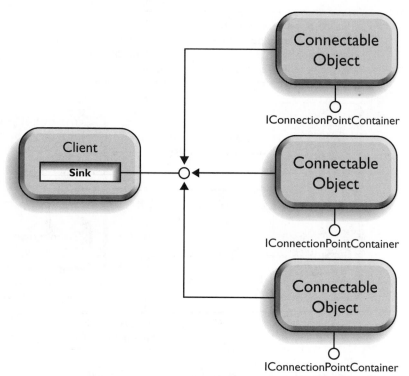

FIGURE 6-5   More than one IConnectionPoint interface may use the same IConnectionPointContainer interface (a one-to-many connection).

IConnectionPointContainer

A connectable object has the **IConnectionPointContainer** interface implemented. It generalizes the object communication process and provides more than just advisory messages for sinks. A connectable object supports:

- The capability to connect and disconnect sinks to the objects for the outgoing IIDs. (This is the basic support offered the **IAdviseSink** interface by the **IDataObject**.) Connections are established with **IConnectionPoint:: Advise** and the connection is broken with **IConnectionPoint::Unadvise**.

- Event sets from outgoing interfaces.

- The capability to enumerate the IIDs of outgoing interfaces.

- The capability to enumerate the existing connections to a particular interface.

IConnectionPointContainer supports all the methods of **IUnknown**. **Find ConnectionPoint** and **EnumConnectionPoints** are the two additional methods supported by **IConnectionPointContainer**.

Connecting to a connectable object starts by invoking **IUnknown:: QueryInterface** with **IID_IConnectionPointContainer**. A pointer is returned to the **IConnectionPointContainer** if the object is connectable. The client then has two choices: either ask the **FindConnectionPoint** method for a particular connection or ask **EnumConnectionPoints** to return an enumeration object.

IConnectionPoint

The **IConnectionPoint** object is the client side of connectable objects. **IConnectionPoint** supports all methods of **IUnknown** and these methods:

- **GetConnectionInterface** — Returns the IID of the outgoing managed interface.

- **GetConnectionPointContainer** — Returns a pointer to the connectable object, which is the parent's **IConnectionPointContainer** interface.

- **Advise** — Creates a connection between the connectable object and a client's sink. (The sink implements the outgoing interface for the connectable object.)

- **Unadvise** — Destroys a sink connection previously created with **IConnectionPoint::Advise**.

- **EnumConnections** — Returns an enumeration object of the current connections for this connection point.

DRAG AND DROP: A TRANSFER PROTOCOL

Drag and drop is a standard feature of the Microsoft Windows environment. It is a transfer protocol that requires the **IDataObject** interface. Figure 6-6 shows the relationship of drag and drop to the linking and embedding features of compound documents.

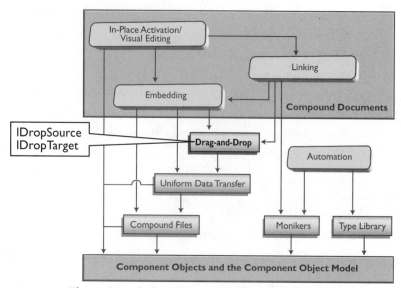

FIGURE 6-6   The various drag and drop interfaces are illustrated here.

Drag and drop eliminates traditional application borders. Using *interwindow dragging,* objects can be copied or moved from one application window to another application window.

Drag and drop is an extension of the clipboard. Quite often very little must be changed in the code to implement drag and drop. Rather than selecting an object, copying it to the clipboard, and then pasting it, drag and drop permits everything to be done in one operation.

Objects may be dragged from one container to another container using *inter-object dragging.* Objects may also be dropped over icons such as printers or mailboxes that will process them.

Drag and drop is implemented with the two interfaces **IDropSource** and **IDropTarget**. Each interface has assigned responsibilities that enable smooth drag and drop operations. **DoDragDrop** is an API function that implements a loop used for tracking mouse and keyboard movement.

IDropSource

This is the first of two interfaces necessary to implement drag and drop. Any object containing data that can be dropped onto another interface implements **IDropSource**. **IDropSource** is responsible for the following:

o Providing the drop target with the **IDataObject** and **IDropSource** interfaces.

o Generating pointer and source feedback.

o Determining when the drag has been canceled or a drop has occurred.

o Performing any action on the original data caused by the drop operation, such as deleting the data or creating a link to it.

IDropSource inherits all methods of **IUnknown** and implements the following methods:

o **QueryContinueDrag** — Returns the keyboard state and determines whether the escape key has been pressed.

o **GiveFeedback** — Provides feedback from the source application during drag and drop operations (as illustrated later in Figure 6-8).

The architecture of drag and drop is shown in Figure 6-7 with both the **IDataObject** and **IDropSource** interfaces implemented at the source.

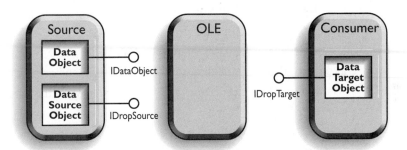

FIGURE 6-7   The drag and drop architecture.

IDropTarget

The **IDropTarget** interface is implemented for all applications that can accept data. Any drag and drop application target must first be registered by calling **RegisterDragDrop** and passing the **IDropTarget** interface as an argument.

IDropTarget has the following responsibilities:

o Registering and revoking each drop target window.

o Determining the drag source effect at any given time.

o Drag scrolling.

o Target feedback.

o Integrating data when a drop occurs or if the drag is canceled.

IDropTarget supports all methods of **IUnknown** in addition to these methods:

o **DragEnter** — Determines the effect on the target window and whether the window can accept the data.

o **DragOver** — Provides feedback on the state of the drag operation to the user and to **DoDragDrop**.

o **DragLeave** — Causes the drop target to remove its feedback.

o **Drop** — Drops the data on the target application.

API functions that support drag and drop are:

o **RegisterDragDrop** — This API function must be called for each window able to accept dropped objects.

o **RevokeDragDrop** — This API function revokes the previous registration of an application window for drag and drop operations.

o **DoDragDrop** — This API function is used to initiate a drag-and-drop operation in a loop calling **WindowFromPoint** with the current mouse coordinates. Called by the drag source when a drag-and-drop operation starts. **DoDragDrop** calls **IDropTarget::DragEnter** when the mouse pointer passes over a window that is a registered drop target. The window is found by calling **WindowFromPoint** with the current mouse coordinates. When a valid window handle is returned from **WindowFromPoint**, it is checked for an **IDropTarget** pointer. If such a pointer exists, a call is marshaled to **IDropTarget::DragEnter** supplying the **IDataObject** pointer from the source object.

DoDragDrop calls **IDropSource::QueryContinueDrag** during each loop iteration to determine whether the operation should continue. Consistent operation is assured with **IDropTarget::DragOver** and **IDropSource:: GiveFeedback** paired giving the user the most up-to-date feedback information. Figure 6-8 identifies the relationships of a drag and drop operation.

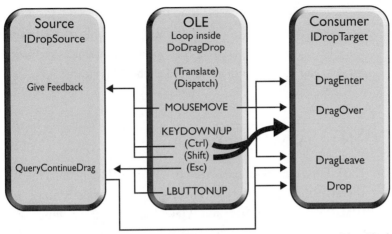

FIGURE 6-8   The relationships of a drag and drop operation are identified in this illustration.

CLIPBOARD: A TRANSFER PROTOCOL

IDataObject supports the drag and drop, clipboard, and compound document transfer protocols. As with other transfer protocols, the clipboard transfer does not transfer actual data, but instead transfers an **IDataObject** pointer.

Setting up the FORMATETC data structure and the STGMEDIUM data structure can represent significant work. Using Uniform Data Transfer with the clipboard is optional. However, UDT must be used with for compound documents.

There must be an anticipation of clipboard operations within the application. The object is started with **OleInitialize** rather than **CoInitialize**. This gives OLE a clipboard-handling window. Correspondingly, **OleUninitialize** is called rather than **CoUninitialize** when destroying the object. This ensures proper cleanup of OLE's clipboard window.

Managing clipboard operations is relatively simple once the FORMATETC and the STGMEDIUM data structures are initialized. Clipboard operations are supported by these three UDT operations:

- *OleSetClipboard*—Places an **IDataObject** pointer on the clipboard.
- *OleGetClipboard*—Retrieves an **IDataObject** pointer from the clipboard. The consumer must call **Release** when it is finished with the pointer.
- *OleFlushClipboard*—Flushes the clipboard.

Separating the protocols from the data creates an issue for clipboard operations. Recipients of clipboard data must be capable of delayed rendering when using UDT. The data source manages delayed rendering by capturing a snapshot of the data and holding onto it until the clipboard is cleared.

KEY POINT SUMMARY

This completes a thumbnail sketch of basic COM functionality. We discussed the **IPersistStorage** interface in Chapter 4. The **IPersistStorage** interface and the **IDataObject**, **IOleObject**, and **IViewObject** interfaces, which were discussed in this chapter, constitute a minimal and embeddable compound document object. This sets the stage for Chapters 7 and 8, which discuss compound document linking and embedding. Of course, there are many frills missing, but the object is still a compound document. The functionality discussed so far includes:

- Structured storage with compound files
- Uniform Data Transfer
- Naming and binding with monikers
- Marshaling
- Drag and drop, clipboard, and compound document transfer protocols

The **IDispatch** interface of Automation (formally OLE AAutomation) was discussed briefly along with type libraries in a previous chapter. We pause now for a review before moving on to the next chapters, in which we look at compound documents that support linking, embedding, and in-place activation or visual editing.

- UDT is a wrapper and a generalization of what used to be clipboard-only data transfers. Formats and device types are now generalized.
- The basic UDT technology consists of the **IDataObject** and **IAdviseSink** interfaces and the STGMEDIUM and FORMATETC data structures.
- An object must implement the **IDataObject** interface to support UDT.
- Drag and drop requires the **IDataObject** interface.
- The **IDataObject–IAdviseSink** connection is the first COM asynchronous object link.
- Connectable objects communicate asynchronously and are a generalization of the **IDataObject–IAdviseSink** technology.

APPLYING WHAT YOU'VE LEARNED

Objects are the now and the future of developers. A COM developer cannot be successful unless the functionality of each object is understood. In this chapter, we looked at Uniform Data Transfer through the **IDataObject** interface. We also traced the evolution of notifications with COM. The questions and the lab will measure your understanding of UDT and notification issues.

There are several questions on the Microsoft Windows Architecture I examination pertaining to Uniform Data Transfer. The questions below address the issues raised by those questions.

Instant Assessment: Uniform Data Transfer

1. When is an application using Uniform Data Transfer?

2. Discuss the benefits of Uniform Data Transfer.

3. Identify the data structures associated with Uniform Data Transfer and describe the contents of each structure.

4. Describe the programming restriction that arises when implementing your own version of the **IAdviseSink** interface.

5. What interfaces are required to implement an advisory connection?

6. Explain the role of the interfaces **IDataAdviseHolder** and **IOleAdviseHolder**.

7. What interfaces define an embedded object?

8. You are building a container application. What are the three nontrivial methods of the **IOleObject** interface that must be implemented?

9. What method activates an embedded object?

10. Explain the difference between **IViewData** and **IDataObject**.

11. What is a limitation of the **IViewObject** interface?

12. What is the relationship between the **IAdviseSink** and **IConnectionPoint** interfaces?

13. What defines a connectable object?

Instant Assessment: Drag and Drop

1. What does drag and drop eliminate?

2. Drag and drop is an extension of what Microsoft operating system feature?

3. Name the two interfaces responsible for drag and drop operations and indicate when they should be implemented.

4. What is a requirement of the drag and drop target object?

5. What is the function of **DoDragDrop**?

concept link **For answers to the Instant Assessment questions, see Appendix C.**

Lab Exercise

Memory was a bottleneck for DDE and OLE 1.0. Both DDE and OLR 1.0 were originally implemented in an era when the memory of personal computers was limited to 16MB and 4-8MB was the norm. That has changed, and the larger memory models of current systems mask the inefficiencies of older technologies such as dynamic data exchange. For example, my personal development system is 131MB and global memory is not an issue. DDE applications still exist, and new DDE applications are still sold. It is difficult to benchmark DDE with the expanded memory models; Lab 6.12, however, should convince you of the cost effectiveness of using COM on the desktop.

Lab 6.13 *Going cold-turkey with no drag and drop*

MCSD

WA I

For one day, use your personal system normally — well, almost normally. Do not use any drag-and-drop operations, but copy everything to the clipboard. From the clipboard, copy the data to the target destination. You might function for a short period without drag and drop, but you will quickly appreciate the benefits of COM.

Windows Architecture I

CHAPTER

Document Linking

7

About Chapter 7

The last few chapters built the necessary infrastructure that is the nuts and bolts under the COM hood. We've discussed a lot of the gritty details, such as **IDispatch** and **IUnknown**, and the higher level functionality, such as the **IDataObject** interface of Chapter 6. This is the first COM chapter where interfaces start to assume the semblance of an application. The COM model comes to life in this chapter with the linking of documents. The concepts of a document and of a container object are introduced. Linked documents must have a parent container object. The prior chapters have been somewhat abstract and this chapter is a bit more practical. We take all the interfaces and assemble them into an application. (If you want to peek ahead, Figure 7-10 is where a linked OLE Document based on COM comes together.)

The **IOleLink** interface was introduced in Chapter 5 as the bridge between a document and binding. It is repeated here, as this is its proper location in the architecture. The mere presence of the **IOleLink** interface means the document is linked. Without this interface it is not linked. Linking requires the **IOleItemContainer** interface introduced in Chapter 5.

The data of a linked document is maintained at the source, while embedded data is maintained in the compound object. Embedded data comes in two flavors: native data, which is a copy of the original data, and presentation data that is a cached view of the native data. We take a closer look at embedded data in Chapter 8.

BEFORE YOU'RE CONFUSED

This chapter starts to put everything together with linked compound documents as the main topic. The problem is with the word *embedded*. I consider any compound document as being *embedded within a container*. Embedding a document in a container is independent of the type of data the document supports, which may be either embedded data or linked data. *Embedded data* or *linked data* classifies the type of compound document; as the chapter unfolds you'll find that there is very little difference between either class of compound document. Chapter 8 discusses compound documents with embedded data in more detail.

The word *document* is used in the context of modeled data. A spreadsheet represents data, yet when modeled with COM interfaces, it becomes an OLE Document: more precisely, a COM compound document. *Linked data* is represented by a *linked document,* and *embedded data* is referred to as an *embedded document,* which is not precisely correct. It is an embedded document independent of having embedded data. An embedded object with links to data is loosely referred to as a *linked object*. This definition isn't precise, but it suffices because we now understand the problem — the definition of embedded.

COMPOUND DOCUMENTS

OLE Documents represent an interaction model. A compound document refers to the embedding of one document within another document, or linking a document to an external document.

> **note** The use of the term *document* in this context does not just refer to word processing documents; it also includes spreadsheets, charts, drawings, and forms, as well as video or sound clips.

> **concept link** To understand the concept of compound documents requires defining two new concepts: a container and a server. Container and server functionality varies slightly for linked and embedded documents. The differences are discussed later for documents with linked data and documents with embedded data.

OLE Documents support the compound document transfer protocol discussed in Chapter 6. It is the means of integrating data from any arbitrary compound document (a persistent file; see Chapter 4). The container is the host and manages compound document integration.

The unit of exchange for the OLE-document protocol is the compound document content object, or simply the content object. The content object is unstructured and has no intrinsic identifier. Assigning a class identifier (CLSID) to the content object provides the necessary unique identification. The CLSID also marks the compound document type and identifies the server code that knows how to manipulate that data at the container's request. Container objects encapsulate their internal data formats and code behind a set of interfaces that define the prototype. These interfaces provide for persistence, structured data exchange, viewing, caching, and activation of the user interface in which the user can manipulate that data.

Data objects that retain their native full-featured editing and operating capabilities in their own container when moved or copied are called embedded objects. These objects are edited within the container using in-place or visual editing. This is different than a linked document, which is edited in a separate window.

OLE DOCUMENT DEFINITION, FEATURES, AND BENEFITS

WA I

Compound documents form half the keystone of component technology. The other half of the keystone is the OLE controls (now called ActiveX), which are discussed in Chapter 10. The features and benefits of linked and embedded documents and common characteristics are listed below. There is a very subtle distinction between an OLE component and an OLE document. Both use the Uniform Data Transfer (UDT) compound document transfer protocol; an OLE document, however, must support linking or embedding.

Common Characteristics of Compound Documents

The following are the common characteristics of compound documents:

o An OLE component object communicates with the compound document transfer protocol defined by Uniform Data Transfer.

- Business solutions can be built with prefabricated components.

- Rather than an Independent Software Vendor (ISV) building a complete application, a customized component can be used to add functionality to an existing application.

- An OLE Document object communicates with compound document transfer protocol defined by Uniform Data Transfer and supports at least one of the basic linking or embedding interfaces.

- OLE Documents may be used for word processing text, tabular data from a spreadsheet, a sound recording, or pictures created in another application.

- OLE Documents can seamlessly incorporate data from numerous sources including bitmaps, objects, and data of different formats.

- The sharing of general purpose interface mechanisms gives greater commonality between applications.

- Microsoft coined the word "document-centric." This means that applications are less "application-centric." Users can focus on the data needed to create the documents rather than the applications responsible for the data.

- OLE Documents allow applications to interoperate, and end users need not be concerned with managing and switching between various object applications.

Characteristics of Linked Documents

The following are the common characteristics of linked documents:

- Object linking means that an image of the object is cached in the container document along with the moniker that refers to the location of the object's actual data. The persistent state (actual data) exists elsewhere, and the moniker is stored in the document as a data link.

- Objects can be linked to or embedded in another object (or even part of an object) in the same OLE document. Changing a linked object changes the original and can affect the image that other users have of this object.

- Linked data may be read-only, meaning that it will only be displayed or played back.

- Data may be stored as a link to the original data with only a presentation copy available in the OLE Document.

- Documents can share data so that one copy of an object can serve many users.

- Linked objects are edited in a separate window. The target server is started, and a new window opens for editing. Double-click an Excel-linked object, and Excel will start with the object presented.

Characteristics of Embedded Documents

The following are the common characteristics of embedded documents:

- The entire object is embedded within the container. Restated, the object's persistent state is kept within the document itself.

- A copy of the data is stored in the OLE Document when the object is embedded. The data is not updated by the system, and the user is responsible for updating the data. Updating locally embedded data does not affect the source data.

- Embedded objects are edited in-place, which is editing within the container. This is discussed in Chapter 8.

Figure 7-1 is illustrative of constructing an application with embedded objects. The application represents a collection of embedded objects, however most of the data is not embedded. The features of Figure 7-1 roughly parallel what I am current using, Microsoft Word. The active document I am editing will be linked, however other data such as a spelling dictionary will be embedded within the spell checker.

DISPLAYING A DOCUMENT

When displaying an OLE-embedded or OLE-linked object in its presentation or content form (as opposed to displaying the object as an icon), a cached metafile description is generally used. The object can be indistinguishable from native objects.

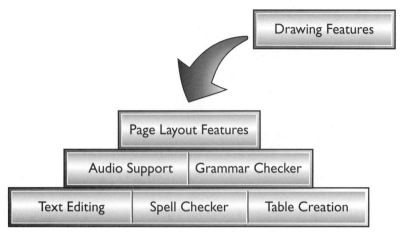

FIGURE 7-1   An application is built with components.

The **Show Objects** command is used to visually identify OLE-embedded or OLE-linked objects. Dashes should appear around the linked object, and a thin line one pixel wide should appear around any embedded objects. If the link object is not current, then the dashed lines use the inactive text color. Lines are around the highest level only.

In the original Windows Open System Architecture (WOSA) examinations, Microsoft made an issue of title bar conventions when displaying an OLE Document. There are differences between Windows 3.1 and Windows 95 when displaying an object. The rules for title bar content when displaying an active OLE Document are listed below. The point is to have all Documents respond visually in the same manner. A clever application will not be used when its presentation or usage style differs from the norm. Unique applications increase training costs, and the goal is to reduce the total cost of ownership, not increase it. I say that with tongue-in-cheek because Windows 95 represents a major paradigm shift for Windows 3.1 users who were only recently weaned from MS-DOS. Internet Explorer 4.0 and Windows 98 will cause another paradigm shift. I don't know the figure, but retraining costs incurred by Corporate America for Microsoft software is probably in the billions.

Microsoft preaches standards with WOSA, but those standards apply only to Microsoft programmers. There are published guidelines for user interfaces, but because Microsoft has a monopoly on the desktop it doesn't have to practice what it preaches, especially when marketing is more important than customer desires.

This is a tautology because an entity with a monopoly never considers the needs of the market. It's a sliding scale. The new entrepreneurial company always puts market needs first while a monopoly always places its own self-interests first. The bottom line is that you and I are given rules of the road for presenting objects in a uniform manner; Microsoft, however, is free to change the desktop style whenever it wishes, especially when it perceives a market threat. I've talked to many users who are very comfortable with Microsoft Windows 3.1. For whatever reason, they dislike Windows 95. They can't understand the need to change.

That's enough soapbox for now. Let's get back to the rules of the road for displaying embedded objects. A default label generally accompanies an embedded or linked object document stored as the icon. The icon's default label is one of the following for an OLE-embedded object:

- Name of the object (example: file name without the extension)
- The object's registered short-type name
- The object's registered full-type name
- "Document" if an object has no name, no short name type, and no registered name type

 The icon label is the file name for an embedded object with linked data.

LINKING COMPOUND DOCUMENTS

This is our first stop on our tour of compound documents. Figure 7-2 illustrates linking an Excel spreadsheet to a Word document. A linked OLE Document is always small. The native data is maintained at the source and the OLE Document only maintains presentation data. All attached users see the changes immediately when a linked document is edited. Links can be nested and combined with embedded objects.

A linked OLE object cannot be edited unless the source is active. Double-clicking the object activates the source. If original data is edited at the source, all other users who share the data have the reflected changes. Linked objects open in their own window for editing. A link may play in-place, but not be edited in-place.

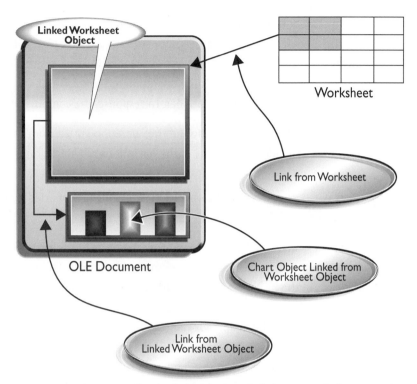

FIGURE 7-2   This example of a linked compound document links an Excel spreadsheet to a Word document.

 tip   **Updating from a link source is automatic by default. Manual updating can be accomplished by setting the linked object's Update property to *Manual*. When the user creates an OLE link, it is by default an automatic link.**

An OLE-linked object includes a cached copy of the source's type at the time of the last update. When the type of a link's source changes, all links derived from that source object contain the old type and operations until either an update occurs or the link source is activated. In addition to the type (class), an OLE-linked object has two other properties: the name of the source and the updating basis.

What happens when the application is moved? Nothing happens if the path is still relative or the source wasn't moved, because the link is adaptable. Source location information is maintained in the Registry. This must be updated when the source is moved. An alternative is to use the linking-to application of the Links dialog box to reestablish the link.

An OLE-linked object includes a cached copy of its source's type at the time of the last update. When executing an operation on a link object, the link object compares the cached type with the current type of the link source. If they are the same, the linked object forwards the operation to the source. If they are different, the linked object informs the container. In response, the container can either:

o Execute the new type's operation, if the operation issued from the old link is syntactically identical to one of the operations registered for the source's new type; or

o Display a message box, if the operation is no longer supported by the link source's type.

A link is maintained with three properties: Type (or class), the name of the source data, and its updating basis (automatic or manual). These properties are on a link page in the linked object's property sheet supplied by the container. A container application can supply a **Links** command that displays a dialog box for altering the properties. The dialog box has the commands: **Cancel, Update Now, Open Source, Change Source, Break Link,** and **Help**.

So by now you're probably wondering how this is managed. Like all other features in this chapter, linked OLE objects are managed with the interfaces, as shown in Figure 7-3. Figure 7-3 identifies our current position in the COM roadmap. As you can see from the roadmap, we're are about to build our first COM application with a linked document.

You should recognize some of the interfaces from earlier discussions. Let's discuss the new interfaces before delving into document linking.

CONTAINERS

Linking requires two components, a server and a container. Each has unique interfaces. We start with the simplest one—the container that is a host for compound documents provided by the server. This example presents a general case and not a container capable of supporting all the embedding or in-place activation features. We discuss this container type in Chapter 8.

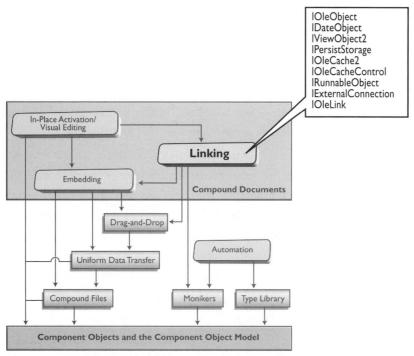

FIGURE 7-3 Interfaces for Linking Compound Documents.

Let's look at some container characteristics:

- A container can contain multiple nested, linked, or embedded OLE objects. Objects can be linked to or embedded in another object (or even as part of an object) in the same OLE Document. Changing a linked object will change the original and can affect the image that others have of this object. Only one object at a time may be active within a container.

- The container determines the selection behavior and appearance of embedded or linked objects. When a user selects an object, the object is displayed with an appropriate selection appearance for that type.

- Objects are blended with the features of the container. An object may display some adornments such as row or column headers; however, it may inherit from the container toolbars, menus, or supplemental palette windows. The operations available for an OLE-linked object are those supplied by its container and those supplied by the source. Toolbar negotiation is a good example.

- A container has adaptable links, which are maintained with monikers. COM maintains both an absolute moniker and a relative moniker as an aid in maintaining links when a file is moved. Windows NT tracks moved files, which is also an aid in maintaining links. An object may be linked to a complete or partial object (pseudo-object), with relative links. It is possible to move the destination, or both the source and destination may be moved together. The link is maintained as long as it is relative.

- OLE containers "export" properties to an object. This is done when the properties of the object do not match those of the container. The object inherits these properties and transforms its appearance to be more consistent with the object's container. To a user, the objects appear "smart" because they know how to transform themselves to match their container. This process saves the user time because the user does not need to adjust the object's properties before or after embedding it in the target container.

- When selecting access to an object, interaction with the object content is not provided. Select commands are made available to interact with the object as a whole. Only after activating the object is user access permitted to object content. The object is activated with **IOleObject::DoVerb**(*Verb*). **DoVerb** operations for a linked object are discussed in "Building an Application" later in this chapter. The scenario for in-place activation of an object with embedded data is discussed in Chapter 8.

- The container can only retrieve those commands from the Registry that have been registered by the object's type.

- Outside-in or inside-out activation is permitted; the container, however, uses an activation style that is appropriate to the native style of activation. Even though an object has registered as inside-out activation, the container may not permit this.

- Outside-in activation requires an explicit user action. This is the typical case for containers that often embed large objects and treat them as whole units.

- Inside-out activation interaction with an object is direct. Inside-out objects are indistinguishable from native data. Inside-out activation requires close cooperation between the container and the object.

IOleContainer and IOleItemContainer

A container is a relatively simple stand-alone application that serves as a host for either linked or embedded data. The container requires an instance of the **IOleClientSite** and **IAdviseSink** interfaces for each contained object. When the content objects are linked, the **IOleItemContainer** interface is also supported for monikers. Both **IOleContainer** and **IOleItemContainer** were included in the discussion of monikers in Chapter 5. They are mentioned here because this is their proper place in the COM architecture.

A generic container is illustrated in Figure 7-4. The **IOleItemContainer** interfaces are not needed if the Documents are not linked. **IOleItemContainer** is required to resolve an item moniker.

Figure 7-4 illustrates container concepts and not server concepts. Hence, moniker resolution is not illustrated; for file moniker resolution, the **IPersistFile** interface would be paired at the outer content object level with **IOleItem Container**. The same is true of **IPersistStorage**. The **IPersistStorage** interface is normally exposed on the inner content object for item moniker resolution. The **IOleItemContainer** interface is not supported on the inner-most content object. Figure 7-7, later in the chapter, represents a reasonably complete application with link sourcing; however, it is a server and without any container interface.

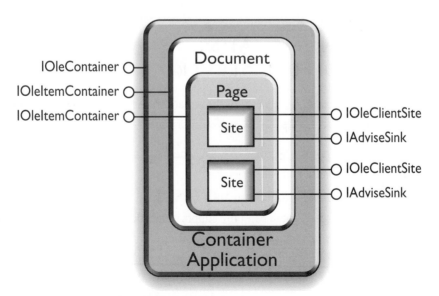

FIGURE 7-4 A generic container structure.

IOleClientSite

We now have a new interface, **IOleClientSite**, which is the linked object's view of the local context. Think of this as an object that is wearing rose-colored glasses as it surveys its surrounding context. The interface supports all methods of **IUknown** and implements the following:

- **GetContainer** — Returns a pointer to the embedding container's **IOleContainer** interface.

- **OnShowWindow** — Notifies a container when an object's window becomes visible or invisible.

- **GetMoniker** — Returns the container's moniker, the object's moniker relative to the container, or the object's full moniker.

- **RequestNewObjectLayout** — Called when a compound document asks for more or less room.

- **SaveObject** — Requests that the object attached to this client be saved.

- **ShowObject** — Asks the container to display the object.

The container uses **IOleObject::SetClientSite** to pass the content object the **IOleClientSite** interface pointer.

OBJECT HANDLER, MINI, LOCAL, AND FULL SERVERS

The container is only part of the equation. Let's look at the different types of server options before discussing server interfaces:

- *Full Server* — Similar to Excel, these are freestanding and support both linked and embedded objects.

- *Miniserver* — Similar to MS-Graph, which is shipped with Microsoft Word and Access, these can only support embedded objects and can only run in the context of a container application. A miniserver does not save its data to disk files and, consequently, cannot support linking. The data is usually saved to a container's compound file. Both full- and miniservers are implemented as an EXE and are called local servers.

- *In-Process Server* — Similar to a miniserver but implemented as a dynamic link library (DLL) rather than as an EXE. No local procedure call (LPC) is required because it exists in the same address space as the application.

- *In-Process Object Handler* — Exists simply to display an object without the overhead of having to load a local server. It has minimal functionality.

Distinguishing between the different types of servers or handlers is important. For example, a data cache object must write directly to the container's window. The container owns the presentation window. This means that object rendering must be implemented as either an in-process server or as an in-process handler. It cannot be implemented as part of a local server such as Excel. COM provides default handlers. Later in this chapter, Figure 7-10 illustrates both a default object handler and a default cache handler.

Let's start with the minimal compound document we discovered in Chapter 6, which are the **IPersistStorage**, **IDataObject**, **IOleObject**, and **IViewObject** interfaces. It is a simple example that sources a whole object and not a partial (pseudo) object. I've added the **IOleCache2** interface (added below) and the **IViewObject2** interface for a realistic compound document model. Let's look at the role of each interface.

- **IOleObject** does all the work. **IOleObject::DoVerb** starts the object, and **IOleObject::Close** stops the object.

- **IDataObject** (Chapter 6) manages the data extent and is used by containers when requesting a copy of specific data. It is also the interface through which the default handler (see Figure 7-10 later) asks for presentation data such as a bitmap or a metafile.

- The **IPersistStorage** (Chapter 4) interface manages the native data. It ensures that the document is presented incrementally.

- **IOleCache2** manages the presentation data that is available to the container of the object even when the server application is not running or is unavailable. This interface is discussed below. **IOleCache** is the base class, and **IOleCache2** is the desired implementation.

- **IViewObject2** (Chapter 6) manages object renderings onto a device context. **IViewObject2** is normally used by the default handler (see Figure 7-10 later).

- **IClassFactory** (Chapter 2) is responsible for object instantiation.

IOleObject

You should be familiar with most of the interfaces mentioned above. The **IPersist***
interfaces control persistence, while the **IDataObject** interface controls Uniform
Data Transfer. The new interface is **IOleObject**, which is the primary interface
through which a linked or embedded object provides functionality to the container.
It's not really new; we discussed this interface in Chapter 6. The **IOleObject** interface defines the content object. The object application must implement **IOleObject**,
IDataObject, and **IPersistStorage** for each type of embedded object it supports.

IOleObject supports all methods of **IUnknown** and implements:

○ **SetClientSite** — Informs a newly created or loaded embedded object of its
client site in the container.

○ **GetClientSite** — Queries an object for the pointer to its current client site
in the container.

○ **SetHostNames** — Specifies window title information to display when an
object is open for editing.

○ **Close** — Transitions an embedded object back to the loaded state.

○ **SetMoniker** — Notifies the object of either its own moniker or its
container's moniker.

○ **GetMoniker** — Returns a connectable moniker to the object.

○ **InitFromData** — Initializes an object with the supplied data.

○ **GetClipBoardData** — Returns an exact copy of clipboard data.

○ **DoVerb** — Requests that an object perform one of its verbs.

○ **EnumVerbs** — Enumerates available verbs for an object in verb number order.

○ **Update** — Ensures object data or view caches are current.

○ **IsUpToDate** — Recursively checks to see if an object is up-to-date.

○ **GetUserClassID** — Returns the CLSID corresponding to
IOleObject::GetUserType.

○ **GetUserType** — Determines the human-readable identification.

○ **SetExtent** — Sets the logical rectangular limits.

○ **GetExtent** — **IOleObject::GetExtent** returns the current extent, while
IViewObject2::GetExtent allocates an extent from cache.

○ **Advise** — Sets an advisory connection for the notification of close, save,
rename, and link source changes to the object.

- **Unadvise** — Deletes an advisory connection.

- **EnumAdvise** — Enumerates the advisory connection for an object.

- **GetMiscStatus** — Returns miscellaneous status information.

- **SetColorScheme** — Specifies the color palette to use when editing the object.

concept link

Figures 7-5, 7-6, and 7-7 each represent different complexity levels of a compound document. The figures also represent the assembling of the technologies of the prior chapters. **IClassFactory** was discussed in Chapter 2, the **IPersist*** interfaces were discussed in Chapter 4, and **IDataObject** was discussed in Chapter 6. **IOleObject** was introduced in Chapter 6 only because it sources notifications to **IAdviseSink**. Its proper place is in this chapter. Binding with a moniker cannot be discussed meaningfully without the **IOleItem Container** interface so it was discussed in Chapter 5; however, its proper place is in this chapter.

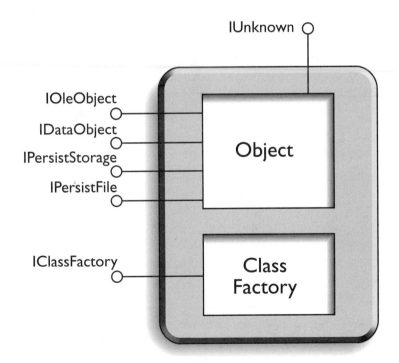

Link Source Server

FIGURE 7-5 A compound document embedded in a local server.

Figure 7-5 is too simple and only represents a compound document. Figure 7-6 represents an application with a portion of a linked object known as a pseudo-object. **IPersistFile** and **IOleItemContainer** are exposed on the document, while **IPersistStorage** is exposed on the embedded object. This is the expected architecture for moniker binding.

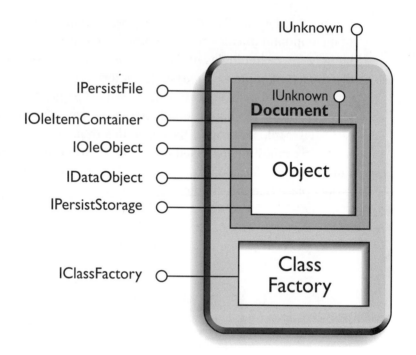

Link Source Server

FIGURE 7-6   An application with a portion of a linked object known as a pseudo-object.

We can actually do something useful with the server illustrated in Figure 7-6. Let's not stop here as we peel back layers of complexity. We'll go one level deeper to illustrate the necessary connections.

Figure 7-7 provides us with a clue as to the purpose of **IOleItemContainer**. You may think of **IOleItemContainer** as the rental office for local sites. The container provides both services and resources to the client objects, and Figure 7-7 shows the interfaces used for each interior object. **IOleItemContainer** is an extension of **IOleContainer**. Containers that use item monikers must implement

IOleItemContainer. This interface is discussed extensively in Chapter 5; thus, this material should only be a review. Refer to Chapter 5 for **IOleItemContainer**'s participation in the moniker binding process.

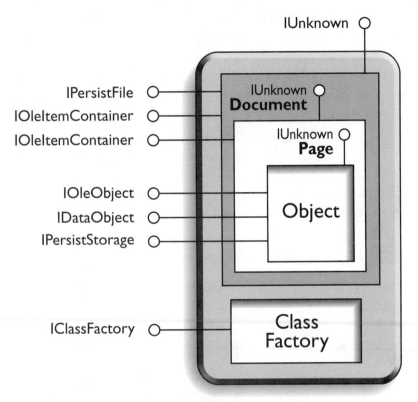

Link Source Server

FIGURE 7-7   A link source for an embedded object.

IOleItemContainer inherits all methods of **IUnknown**. It aggregates the method **IParseDisplayName** and inherits the methods of **IOleContainer**. **IOleItem Container** supports these methods:

o **GetObject** — Returns an item moniker as part of the binding process.

o **GetObjectSource** — Returns a storage pointer for the named object.

o **IsRunning** — Returns the object's running status.

BUILDING AN APPLICATION

So far we've assembled a container with embedded content objects and the supporting interfaces. We also presented different levels of server complexity. The application is not complete and is not "runnable" without additional help from either an in-process server or an in-process handler. A handler that looks like an in-process server is the final element of the object linking equation. The basic data flow of an in-process handler is shown in Figure 7-8. This is a default handler with generic interfaces; implementing a custom handler, however, is always an option for the developer. Figure 7-9 expands Figure 7-8 to show the complete in-process handler supporting data flow for a linked object. The container owns the presentation window. Rendering is done by the in-process handler, which must run in the address space of the container. Marshaling is used to communicate with the object application.

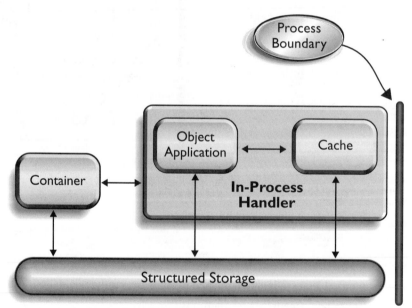

FIGURE 7-8   The basic data flow of an in-process handler.

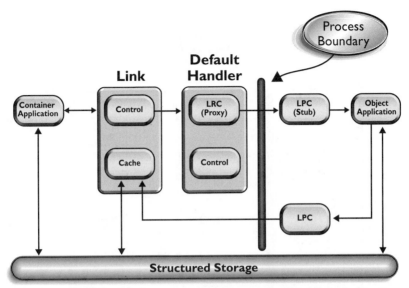

FIGURE 7-9   The complete in-process handler supporting a linked object's data flow.

We know the functionality of the default handler. Let's consider the COM interfaces necessary for the default handler to connect the container site and server object and build our application. We start with the rule that a DLL object application must implement **IExternalConnection**, **IRunnableObject**, and the **IOleObject** interfaces. It generally implements at least **IDataObject** and **IPersistStorage**. **IPersistStorage::Save** and **IOleObject::Update** both must call **IOleCache2::UpdateCache** to update the cache nodes.

Even though some of the common interfaces are not shown, everything is put together in Figure 7-10, which represents the complete application. The in-process handlers have been merged with the content object, a container, and a cache handler. The linked object architecture of Figure 7-10 shouldn't be intimidating; we've discussed most of the interfaces previously. Note that the default object handler is aggregated with the default cache handler.

Interfaces such as **IOleItemContainer** are not exposed in Figure 7-10. Detail is missing from both the Default Object Handler and the Object Server. Even without all the detail, Figure 7-10 does illustrate the general interface interactions.

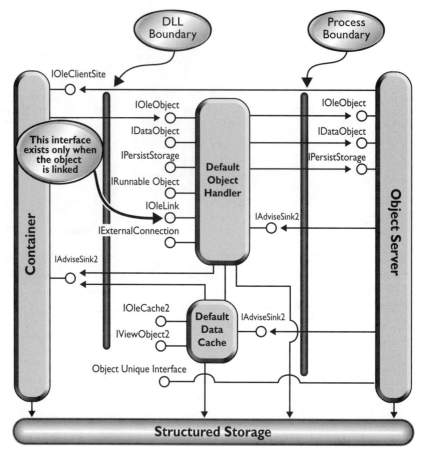

FIGURE 7-10   A complete application with interfaces for a linked object.

Let's review the function of each interface and then fill in the missing pieces for those interfaces we have yet to discuss. (Not all interfaces are illustrated.)

- **IOleClientSite** — Provides the object's view of the context and is implemented by a container site. (Do not confuse this with a container document, which is managed with the **IOleItemContainer** interface.)

- **IAdvise2** — Receives asynchronous notifications. Equivalent to **IAdviseSink** with the added function **LinkSrcChanged**.

- **IOleObject** — The primary interface through which a linked or embedded object supplies functionality to the container. **IOleObject** represents a content object.

- **IDataObject** — Implements Uniform Data Transfer.

- **IPersistStorage** — Manages the **IStorage** interface.

- **IRunnableObject** — Manages transition to and from the running state.

- **IOleLink** — Signals that the item is linked.

- **IOleCache2** — An extension of **IOleCache** that enables an object to control what data is cached. It is very important because it saves a cached picture of the last image the user saw.

- **IViewObject2** — Renders the object using cache data.

- **IExternalConnection** — Required for silent updates of linked data. A link used by external objects to manage the lock count. Guarantees that data will not be lost on a broken connection.

Figure 7-10 is due some explanation beyond the enumeration of interfaces. We've built the application piecemeal, but its complexity is still formidable. Let's start first with the dual exposed **IOleObject** interfaces on both the Default Object Handler and the Object Server. The simple explanation is that both are content objects, but that doesn't suffice. Consider the scenario of a user opening a Word document. This makes Word the container in Figure 7-10. During the compound document loading process, structured storage items (streams) are encountered for Excel. Word loads a default in-process handler over the default cache object, which forces a delegation of the cache object. Word then passes the Excel data storage pointer to the **IPersistStorage** interface on the newly constructed in-process default handler. **IViewObject2** is used by Word to display the cached Excel data. Word finishes initialization and everything is displayed; however, Excel hasn't started. There is no reason to start Excel until the user asks for activation.

At some later time, the user selects *Open* from the pop-up menu displayed on a mouse right-click. Word passes the verb to **IOleObject::DoVerb** to open the spreadsheet. (The OLE specifications state that the *Open* verb will open a presentation in a new window, which it eventually does.)

IOleObject::DoVerb is invoked on the in-process handler and not the local server, which in this case is Excel. This puts in motion a server instantiation mechanism with moniker binding (see Chapter 2 and Chapter 5), roughly described by these steps:

- OLE (from **DoVerb** on the default in-process handler implementation) calls **IMoniker::BindToObject***(IID_IOleObject)*. This starts the retrieval process for the moniker stored within the in-process default handler object. (We've skipped some detail here such as **IBindCtx**. See Chapter 5 for additional detail.)

o **GetClassFile** is called. It calls **StgOpenStorage** and **ReadClassStg** and tries to retrieve the CLSID. (Recall that the CLSID immediately precedes the stream data and was placed there by **OleSaveToStream**. See Chapter 4.)

o When no CLSID is found, **GetClassFile** searches the Registry for the ProgID representing that file extension. The ProgID is then used to locate a CLSID stored in the Registry. If this fails, **BindToObject** fails.

o Assuming that nothing has failed, **BindToObject** calls **CoCreateInstance** for Excel with the supplied CLSID.

o The file moniker calls **IClassFactory::CreateInstance**. **IUnknown::QueryInterface** is called on the returned pointer asking for the **IPersistFile** interface.

o The file moniker next loads the file with a call to **IPersistFile::Load**.

o The **IPersistFile** interface is released by the file moniker by first calling **IPersistFile::QueryInterface**(*IID_IOleObject*), which retrieves the **IOleObject** pointer on the Excel object. This is followed by a call to **IPersistFile::Release**. This chicanery works since the OLE 2 design specification states that **IOleObject**, **IDataObject**, and **IPersistStorage** must be on the same interface as the source server's **IPersistFile** interface.

o The file moniker's last act is to return the just acquired Excel **IOleObject** pointer to the in-process default handler implementation of **IOleObject::DoVerb**.

o The **IOleObject::DoVerb** in-process handler implementation uses the returned **IOleObject** pointer and delegates the original *Open* verb to the local Excel server that is now running.

o Excel data changes are communicated back to the cache, and the in-process handler interfaces with the two **IAdviseSink2** interfaces.

I said Figure 7-10 represented a linked object. Yes, it does. But it is also an embedded object. Remove the **IOleLink** interface and it becomes an embedded object. So, technically speaking, a linked object is an extension of an embedded object. We've established our introduction to Chapter 8. A linked object and an embedded object share common features. Each maintains a cache, each uses container functionality, and each requires its own storage object.

A container cannot tell the difference between a linked and an embedded object. The presence of the **IOleLink** interface signals a linked object. COM supplies default **IOleLink** implementation; the developer, however, always has the choice of providing a custom installation. **IOleLink** supplies the tools for managing the serialized moniker found in the object's storage, and the moniker supplies the external data location.

Supporting Cast Members in Our Application

There are four new interfaces that haven't been mentioned yet: **IExternal Connection**, **IRunnableObject**, **IOleLink**, and **IOleCache2**. I'll throw in **IOleCache** because **IOleCache2** inherits from it. I'll also throw in **IOleCacheControl** to complete the picture. We're familiar with many of the supporting characters in our application. Here are some cast members from Figure 7-10 we've not discussed before and an update on some with which we have a passing acquaintance.

IExternalConnection

The **IExternalConnection** interface is not required for linking, but a developer is probably foolish for not implementing this interface. **IExternalConnection** is one of the three required interfaces for a DLL implementation. The other two required interfaces are **IRunnableObject** and **IOleObject**.

The **IExternalConnection** interface is a tool used for managing silent updates of linked data. The interface is a mechanism to track external locks on an embedded object, which ensures an orderly shutdown of the object. This prevents possible data loss during shutdown that occurs with unsaved changes when a connection is broken.

This interface supports all methods of **IUnknown** and implements these methods:

- **AddConnection**—Signals the creation of a strong external connection. A strong connection is created with locks or a moniker binding.

- **ReleaseConnection**—Signals the release of an external connection.

This interface should be implemented with all embeddable compound-document objects that support links to themselves. (Rows in a spreadsheet are an example.) An in-place container uses the **OleLockRunning** API function to manage the lock states of an object. The stub manager has the responsibility of calling **IExternalConnection** whenever the connection status changes.

IRunnableObject

Object handlers and DLL object applications can determine when to transition into the running state and when to become a contained state. Silent (automatic) updates are supported. The default object handler supports **IOleContainer:: LockContainer**, as must any other DLL object implementation. **IRunnableObject** inherits all methods of **IUnknown** and implements:

- **GetRunningClass** — Returns CLSID of the running object.
- **Run** — Places an object in run state.
- **IsRunning** — Determines whether an object is running.
- **LockRunning** — Locks a running object into run state or unlocks a running object. (The object is closed on the last unlock.)
- **SetContainedObject** — Indicates the object is embedded in an OLE container.

IOleLink

The **IOleLink** interface supplies the necessary functionality to manage the object's moniker and update the linked object. An object is considered embedded in the absence of this interface. **IOleLink** inherits all methods of **IUnknown** and implements these methods:

- **SetUpdateOptions** — Sets the linked object's update options.
- **GetUpdateOptions** — Retrieves an object's update options.
- **SetSourceMoniker** — Stores the source moniker inside the object.
- **GetSourceMoniker** — Retrieves the source moniker from the object.
- **SetSourceDisplayName** — Parses a linked object's display name and stores that name within the object.

- **GetSourceDisplayName** — Retrieves the display name from the object.
- **BindToSource** — Binds the moniker contained within the linked object.
- **BindIfRunning** — Binds to the source if it is running with **IOleLink:: BindToSource**.
- **GetBoundSource** — Retrieves the object connected to the link source.
- **UnbindSource** — Unbinds an object from a linked source.
- **Update** — Updates a linked object with the latest link source data.

IOleCache

This interface supports caching and wasn't used directly in Figure 7-10; however, **IOleCache** inherits all methods of **IUnknown** and supports these methods:

- **Cache** — Specifies the data format and other data to be cached within an embedded object.
- **Uncache** — Deletes a cache connection.
- **EnumCache** — Enumerates present cache connections.
- **InitCache** — Fills cache with either clipboard or drag-and-drop data.
- **SetData** — Fills cache from the indicated storage medium.

IOleCache2

IOleCache2 is an extension of **IOleCache**, which enables cache updating by a client object. **IOleCache2** inherits all methods of **IOleCache** and **IUnknown**, and, in addition, supports these methods:

- **UpdateCache** — Updates cache using supplied parameters.
- **DiscardCache** — Flushes memory caches. (**IDataObject::GetData** will revert to disk files.)

IOleCacheControl

This is the last tidbit on linking minutiae. **IOleCacheControl** is a specialized interface that a container does not need. It is used exclusively by object handlers and DLL object applications as the cache connection to the **IDataObject** implementation. This interface supports all methods of **IUnknown** and these methods:

- **OnRun** — Notifies the cache that the compound document has entered run state. (This creates a data advisory sink between the running object and cache.)

- **OnStop** — Notifies the cache that it should terminate any existing connections previously established by **IOleCacheControlOnRun**.

KEY POINT SUMMARY

Compound documents are an interaction model and come in two styles — embedded or linked. A linked document is almost a trivial extension of an embedded document. Except for the **IOleLink** interface, a container cannot distinguish between an embedded and a linked document. The major difference is that linked documents have a link to the data source embedded in the content object (serialized moniker), while an embedded object has a copy of the data.

- An OLE Document is an object that supports either basic linking or embedding.

- Linked documents can be text, tabular data, a sound recording, a video recording, or pictures created by an application. This is not an inclusive list, only illustrative.

- All copies of a linked document reflect changes made by other users. This differs from embedded documents, which have a copy of the data. Editing of embedded documents does not affect other users.

- Linked documents may play in-place but cannot be edited in-place. They will open in their own windows for editing.

- Linked documents always use the least resources. Native data remains at the source.

- A container can support multiple levels of linking.

- Linked objects blend with the properties of the container. The container exports ambient properties to the object. These are display properties, and not properties of the linked source.

APPLYING WHAT YOU'VE LEARNED

Here are a few review questions before we move on to embedding documents in the next chapter.

Instant Assessment

1. What is an OLE Documents representation?

2. What is the definition of an OLE component?

3. What is the definition of an OLE Document?

4. Explain compound document embedding.

5. Explain compound document linking.

6. What is the compelling reason to use linked OLE Documents instead of embedded documents?

7. What is an adaptable link?

8. An object is selected. When can object editing start?

9. What is outside-in activation?

10. What is inside-out activation?

11. Name an example of a full server.

12. When is a miniserver used?

13. What is an in-process server?

14. What is an in-process object handler?

15. The presence of what interface indicates a linked object?

16. What are the three nontrivial interfaces required for an object handler implementation?

 concept link   **For answers to the Instant Assessment questions, see Appendix C.**

Lab Exercise

Lab 7.14 measures the cost of linking versus embedding. Any object may be used, but one classic example is embedding a spreadsheet into a Word document. For this lab, let's assume you are using a Word document for the container.

There are two ways to measure the resources involved. The first is save the document on a periodic basis and monitor the size. You can also use the About button on the Word toolbar and monitor global memory.

Lab 7.14 *Linking objects conserves resources*

WA I

1. Create a Word document and save it. Note the file size. You should save two copies of this blank document. We'll use the second copy later for measuring the cost of embedding documents.

2. Create an Excel spread sheet with data. An easier choice is to locate a .BMP file and link it to the Word document. But don't stop there. Link in three more copies. This gives a total of four linked images. If your container is Word, go to the **Insert** menu and select **Object**. A dialog box is presented. Always **Create from File**. The object will be linked or embedded depending upon your position in this scenario.

3. Save the Word document and look at the file size. Subtract the original size and divide the extra space by four and you have a rough approximation of the cost of linking.

4. Repeat the above sequence, but this time embed the object. Be sure you start with a new blank Word document.

5. Compare the results.

Windows Architecture I

CHAPTER

Document Embedding

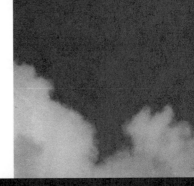

8

About Chapter 8

We now know that document linking is just an extension of document embedding. This chapter and the previous chapter are collectively a discussion of OLE Documents, with this chapter focusing on the mechanics of in-place activation of an embedded document, which is a feature of OLE Documents.

Our old friend **IOleLink** is not found in this architecture. All of the interfaces supporting an embedded document are the same as those supporting a linked document. The differences are the interfaces that are necessary to support in-place activation and the absence of the **IOleLink** interface. Even though this chapter is titled "Document Embedding," the topic is in-place activation of embedded documents and the supporting interfaces. We closed Chapter 7 after building an application and taking a close look at activating a linked object. We do the same in this chapter. As you've probably guessed, some new characters are added to our supporting cast. Because the topic is embedded document activation, it seems natural that most of the new characters are container-related OLE Document features. The new container interfaces include **IOleInPlaceSite**, **IOleInPlaceFrame**, and **IOleInplaceUIWindow**; **IOleInplaceObject** and **IOleInplaceActive Object** are the new server interfaces. (You can see how this all fits together by peeking ahead at Figure 8-8, which is our application from Chapter 7 that is now capable of in-place activation.)

Before We Begin

This chapter is about only one issue: the in-place activation of a single Excel spreadsheet. There are a few general issues about embedded objects at the start of the chapter; however, use the illustrations as your guides to the chapter:

- *Figure 8-1* — The multiple levels of an Excel spreadsheet are identified.

- *Figure 8-2* — An embedded object with exposed sizing handles is activated.

- *Figure 8-3* — The structured storage for the Excel spreadsheet is represented. Note that the class identifier (CLSID) is stored in the data object, not in the container data stream (Word in our example) as it is with linked documents.

- *Figure 8-4* — Data flow for an embedded object. This is also the data flow for Figures 8-1, 8-2, 8-4, and 8-8, which is the completed application.

- *Figure 8-5* — Our roadmap to the COM architecture, which identifies the interfaces required for in-place activation.

- *Figure 8-6* — An in-place capable container with the interfaces necessary for in-place activation exposed. This container is the same container as in Figures 8-4 and 8-8. Its presence is implied in Figures 8-1 and 8-2.

- *Figure 8-7* — An in-place capable server with the necessary in-place activation interfaces. This server is the same server as in Figures 8-4 and 8-8. Its presence is implied in Figures 8-1 and 8-2.

- *Figure 8-8* — The server of Figure 8-7 is merged with the container of Figure 8-6 along with our new interfaces and an in-process default handler to form our application. Figures 8-1, 8-2, 8-3, 8-4, and 8-8 are all different representations of the same embedded spreadsheet application.

Figure 8-8 is a bit complex. I will ease you into the more arcane issues of COM with a bit less frustration. This is one of the more difficult chapters in this book. If you comprehend this chapter, then Chapter 10, which is OLE Controls or ActiveX components, will be a piece of cake because it is an extension of this material. Good eating!

COMPOUND DOCUMENT EMBEDDING AND IN-PLACE ACTIVATION

OLE linking uses the least memory resources because the data is kept at the source. Each embedded object is a copy of the original data. Consequently, embedded objects require significantly more resources than OLE linked objects that only store a link to the source.

Editing will affect all shared users of linked documents, but editing of embedded documents will not affect other users. For this reason, in-place activation of linked documents is possible, but is not recommended. Data is stored locally in the container with an embedded document. OLE embedded documents retain their native, full-featured editing and operating capabilities in the container, and are edited in-place within the container and not in a separate window. Edits made to the data become a part of the document immediately and automatically, just like edits to native data. The user's last view of the data is cached and is known as presentation data. Both the presentation data and native date are changed with in-place editing. The presentation data does not change until the user edits the data with another in-place activation.

OLE embedded objects participate in the undo stack of the window in which they are activated. Changes can be abandoned if the topmost container includes an explicit command that prompts the user to save or discard changes to the container's file.

The user places a copy of the data in the container. The container can be another object or an OLE Document. Documents may be embedded within documents, as illustrated in Figure 8-1. Any of the traditional document embedding mechanisms can be used, an example being the Word **Insert** menu and the *Object* entry. When the **Link to Data** checkbox is not checked, the data is embedded in the container, which in this case is Word. The only difference between a linked document and an embedded document is the **IOleLink** interface. Object handlers play the same role for embedded documents that is played for linked documents.

 note **Recognize in Figure 8-1 that the worksheet is the chart container, while the OLE Document is said to be the spreadsheet's container.**

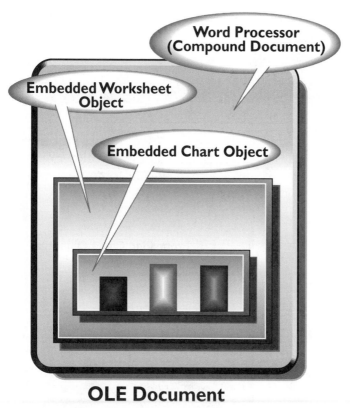

OLE Document

FIGURE 8-1   The multiple levels of an embedded Excel spreadsheet are identified.

The user can open OLE embedded objects in the active window. The object will have a 45-degree angle "hatched" pattern when the object is opened in its own window. This pattern is only displayed when the active object's menus appear in the topmost container's menu bar. Figure 8-1 is opened in its own window by double-clicking the object. This is a VISIO object, and the double-clicking results are shown in Figure 8-2.

OLE embedded documents support both outside-in and inside-out activation. Outside-in activation is the normal double-click sequence where the user "drills-down" on an object. A double-click from the mouse is required for each nested layer of the object. An object may be marked as OLEMISC_ACTIVATEWHEN-VISIBLE. This is still outside-in activation even though the top layer is activated automatically when visible. An object marked as OLEMISC_INSIDEOUT only requires one mouse click. When the mouse is clicked over a nested embedding, all layers are activated. This is inside-out activation where the object appears as native container data.

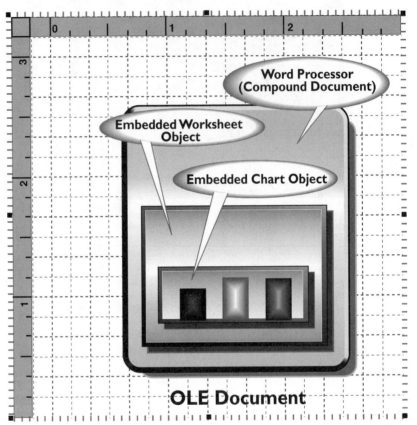

FIGURE 8-2 An embedded and activated object with exposed sizing handles.

Let's interrupt our chain of thought for a moment and look at what the compound file might be for this object. I have often referred to compound files as a multiheaded hydra, in that there can be numerous streams open simultaneously. Figure 8-3 shows the native data, the presentation data (the last user view), and the CLSID stored within a data object. Moniker binding is not required with an embedded object because the CLSID is known directly.

Figure 8-4 is the data flow for an embedded object, and it is also the data flow for Figures 8-1, 8-2, and 8-3. Note that the object application, the container application, and the default object handler all have access to structured storage.

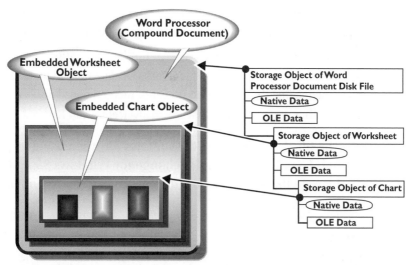

FIGURE 8-3   Compound storage structure for an embedded document.

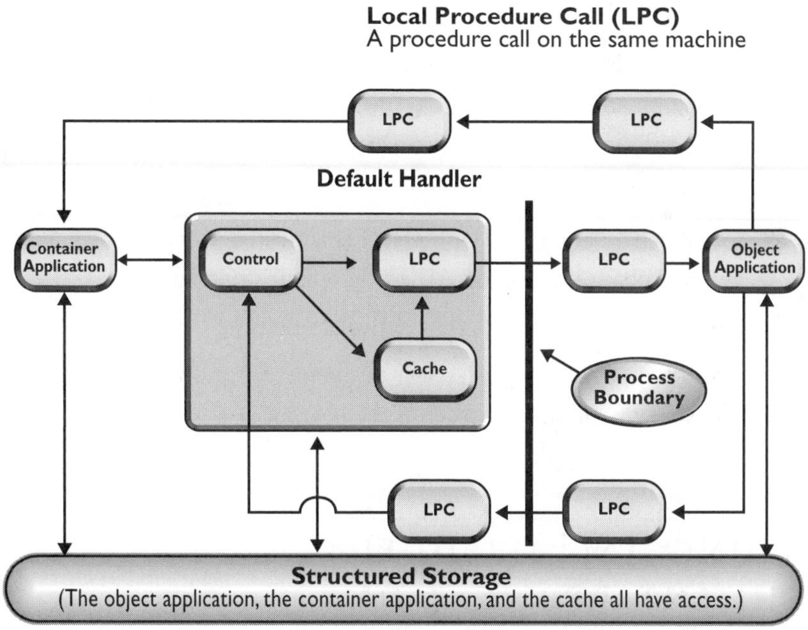

Local Procedure Call (LPC)
A procedure call on the same machine

FIGURE 8-4   The data flow of an embedded object.

We're now back on track with in-place activation. *Visual editing* is sometimes referred to as *in-place activation*, where a user double-clicks the object to

edit the object in-place. This is different than editing a linked object that opens in its own window. Visual editing is a document-centric approach that insulates the user from the underlying mechanisms. In-place activation is commonly associated with embedded documents; it is possible, however, to do in-place activation on linked documents. The procedure is not recommended because of the surprise that the other users will get when you inadvertently edit a linked document.

 note **The title bar changes with Windows 3.1 when using in-place editing. The title bar does not change for Windows 95 and later systems, as the title bar always displays the top-level container's name.**

In-place activation merges menus, places a hatch pattern around the object's border, and changes the menu bar to reflect the new controls. The degree of change to the container's interface is determined solely by the container. This determination is made independent of the embedded object's capability. It is common to merge toolbars and menu bars, but this is not a requirement.

The following is a list of the characteristics of visual editing:

- ALT+ENTER is now the recommended shortcut key for the Properties command.
- OLE embedded objects can be supported by a pop-up menu using the SHIFT+F10 key.
- When an embedded OLE object is activated, it may display "adornments" and change menu bars. The title remains unchanged.
- Only a single level may be active at one time.
- If the object's menus appear in the menu bar, then a hatched pattern is shown around the border of the object.

BUILDING AN EMBEDDED DOCUMENT APPLICATION

We already know that the **IOleLink** interface distinguishes a linked object from an embedded object, so let's move on to the finer details of in-place activation. The absence of key interfaces signals when an embedded document cannot be in-place activated. Figure 8-5 identifies the new interfaces needed to give our embedded document in-place activation or visual editing.

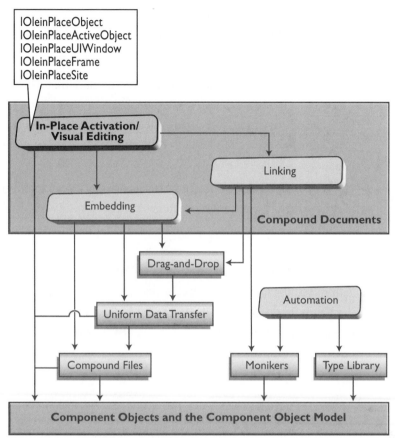

FIGURE 8-5 Our roadmap to the COM architecture, which identifies the interfaces required for in-place activation.

TITLE BAR RULES ARE NOT CLEAR

An argument to **IOleInPlaceUIWindow:: SetActiveObject** (an interface discussed later in this chapter) has a pointer to a string that contains a name which describes the object. The following is a quote from the Win32 PlatForm SDK documentation on **IOleInPlaceUI Window::SetActiveObject**.

Note to Implementers:

The Microsoft Windows User Interface Design Guide *recommends that an in-place container ignore the* pszObjName *parameter passed in this method. The guide says, "The title bar is not affected by in-place activation. It always displays the top-level container's name."*

Let's see how these interfaces are used for in-place activation.

The container in Figure 8-6 has three new supporting interfaces for embedded document activation (visual editing):

- **IOleInPlaceFrame** — A new container-level interface that defines the concept of a frame and controls the container's top-level frame window. Only one of these interfaces is permitted per container. The interface manages merging the top-level user interface such as menu items and toolbars.

- **IOleInPlaceUIWindow** — This interface is used by object applications to negotiate border space on the document or frame window. It establishes a communication channel between the object and each frame and document window.

- **IOleInPlaceSite** — The duo is now a trio. The site representation object within the container is increased by one new member and now consists of the **IOleInPlaceSite**, **IOleClientSite**, and **IAdviseSink**. **IOleInPlaceSite** marks a site as in-place capable. Each embeddable site will expose these three interfaces.

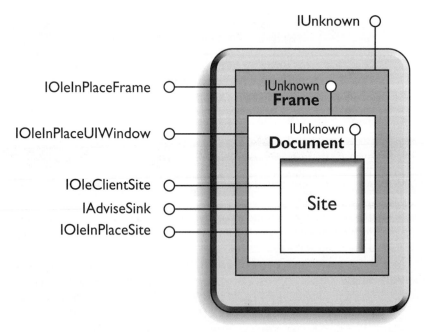

FIGURE 8-6   An in-place capable container with the interfaces necessary for in-place activation exposed.

The server illustrated in Figure 8-7 supports two new interfaces for in-place activation. One manages activation and deactivation while the other is quite elusive, existing only during activation.

- The interface **IOleInPlaceObject** marks objects as in-place capable. This interface can always be found with **QueryInterface** on any other interface of the object.

- The active object presents the **IOleInPlaceActiveObject,** which isn't found by the other interfaces. Consequently, **IOleInPlaceActiveObject** supplies its own **QueryInterface** definition. You can think of **IOleInPlaceActiveObject** as only a temporary interface. The **IOleInPlaceActiveObject** pointer is supplied by the object to the document with a call to **IOleInPlaceUIWindow:: SetActiveObject** and then to the container with a call to **IOleInPlaceFrame:: SetActiveObject**.

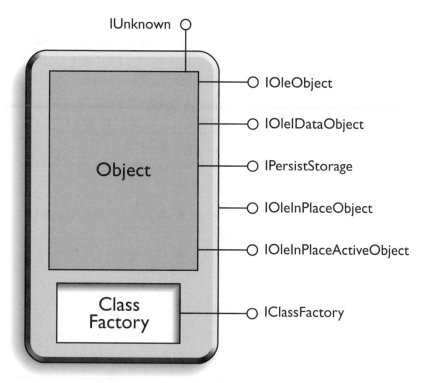

FIGURE 8-7   **An in-place capable server with the necessary in-place activation interfaces.**

Figure 8-8 is built from three major pieces. The container of Figure 8-6 represents the container of Figure 8-8. The object server of Figure 8-8 was derived from Figure 8-7. The default handler is the same one we encountered in Chapter 7. Figure 8-8 is greatly simplified and detail is omitted. However, it should be very obvious that there is significant overhead with in-place activation. Why? Because all the server interfaces must be marshaled to the container. Figure 8-4 is the equivalent of Figure 8-8. It represents the data flow for Figure 8-8. The local procedure calls (LPC) of Figure 8-4 are synonymous with a marshaling proxy and stub. The notation is just simplified. Remember that the server exists in a different address space than the container and in-process default handler. Now you should have an idea of why COM is so complex and servers don't always start immediately.

What are the missing links? In-place activation starts with **IOleObject:: DoVerb**. The object then calls the container with **IOleClientSite::QueryInterface** looking for **IOleInPlaceSite**. The container returns a pointer to **IOleInPlaceSite** if it exists. The object opens as a regular embedded object when this interface doesn't exist. The in-place activation site exists, but can it be used? The next call is to the site itself asking for in-place activation support. This is done with the pointer just returned, and the object calls **IOleInPlaceSite::CanInPlaceActivate** asking permission to in-place activate. (COM is quite polite. Later we learn where it warns the container of its intentions.) We now have the missing interface rules for both linked and embedded objects:

- An object is linked when the **IOleLink** interface is supported.

- An object server must expose the **IOleInPlaceObject** interface and the container must expose the **IOleInPlaceSite** interface to enable in-place activation. That doesn't always guarantee in-place activation, as you will discover in the next section.

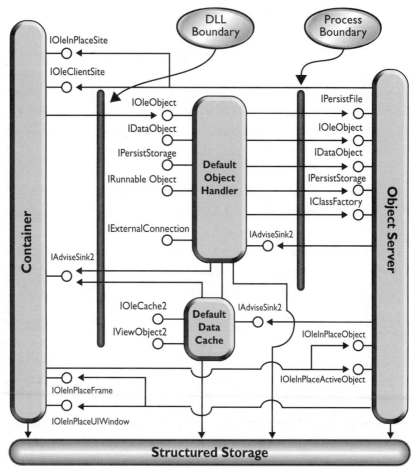

FIGURE 8-8 This embedded document is capable of in-place activation.

ACTIVATING AN EMBEDDED DOCUMENT

These are the necessary steps to activate an embedded document. The invocation mechanism is different than the linked document activation discussed in Chapter 7. That mechanism uses a moniker encountered in the Word stream to instantiate the Excel server. Binding is not necessary with server instantiation of an embedded document because the server CLSID, server data, and cache presentation are all stored together in the embedded data object as shown in Figure 8-2. Let's assume this is an Excel activation from Word, similar to the activation example of Chapter 7.

Things start very easily for embedded documents during the loading process. As before, Word encounters the cache data object during the load process and loads a default in-process handler over the default cache object. This forces a delegation of the cache object. Word then passes the Excel cache data storage pointer to the **IPersistStorage** interface on the newly constructed in-process default handler. **IViewObject2** is used by Word to display the cached Excel data. Word finishes initialization and everything is displayed; Excel, however, hasn't started. There is no reason to start Excel until the user asks for activation.

At some later time the user double-clicks an embedded document and Word passes the *Edit* verb to the in-process default handler implementation of **IOleObject::DoVerb**. (The OLE specifications state that the *Edit* verb will open a presentation in a window of the host container.)

IOleObject::DoVerb is invoked on the in-process handler and not the local server, which in this case is Excel. This puts in motion a standard server instantiation mechanism (Chapter 2), roughly described by these steps:

1. OLE (from **DoVerb** on the default in-process handler implementation) calls **CoGetClassObject** with the Excel CLSID obtained from the embedded storage object and requests the **IClassFactory** interface. The **IOleLink** interface is missing and **DoVerb** knows this is an embedded document object.

2. **DoVerb** calls **IClassFactory::CreateInstance**. The returned object pointer is used to call **IUnknown::QueryInterface** and locates the **IPersistStorage** interface.

3. The object is initialized with a call to **IPersistStorage::Load**.

4. The **IPersistStorage** interface is released by the in-process default handler implementation of **DoVerb** by first calling **IPersistStorage::QueryInterface** (*IID_IOleObject*), which retrieves the **IOleObject** pointer on the Excel object. The **IPersistStorage::Release** follows this. This chicanery works because the OLE 2 design specification states that **IOleObject**, **IDataObject**, **IPersistStorage**, and **IPersistFile** must all be on the same interface.

5. The in-process default handler implementation of **IOleObject::DoVerb** uses the returned **IOleObject** pointer and now delegates the original *Edit* verb to the local Excel server, which is now running. Up to this point, everything is classical COM object instantiation.

6. The object, Excel in our case, knows it has work to do because it was passed an *Edit* verb. An **IOleClientSite** pointer was passed to Excel along with the *Edit* verb and Excel calls **IOleClientSite::QueryInterface** asking for the **IOleInPlaceSite** interface. The container supports embedding when this interface exists. If it doesn't exist, the object will be opened in a separate window.

7. The container site exists, but can it be used? The server now calls **IOleInPlaceSite::CanInPlaceActive**. A negative reply will always be received if the container is displayed in an aspect other than DVASPECT_CONTENT. As in the last step, the alternative is always a separate window.

8. In-place activation needs the document and frame context. The interfaces **IOleInPlaceFrame** and **IOleInPlaceUIWindow** are each in different interfaces (see Figure 8-6), and are not available through **IOleInPlaceSite:: QueryInterface**. An alternate mechanism is to call **IOleInPlaceSite:: GetWindowContext** that returns the **IOleInPlaceFrame** and **IOleInPlaceUIWindow** interfaces.

9. The server declares its intention of in-place activation by calling **IOleInPlaceSite::OnInPlaceActivate**. This tells the container to allocate the necessary structures. The object's editing window is moved to the container, merging container and server menus and creating toolbars.

10. The document is now in the in-place active state. Nothing further is done when the requested state is OLEIVERB_INPLACEACTIVE.

11. When we want to proceed further to full activation, the container is warned of our intentions by calling **IOleInPlaceSite::OnUIActivate**. The **IOleInPlaceActiveObject** pointer is supplied by the object to the document with a call to **IOleInPlaceUIWindow::SetActiveObject** and then to the container with a call to **IOleInPlaceFrame::SetActiveObject**.

12. Several housekeeping steps remain and we'll skip those steps. Menus must be merged, toolbars displayed, and accelerator keys managed. The interfaces are now established and the embedded object looks quite like a custom control. Housekeeping is done and the object is activated.

13. Excel data changes are communicated back to the cache and the in-process handler interfaces with the two **IAdviseSink2** interfaces.

We're nearly through with our discussion of compound documents, so let's quickly move through the supporting interfaces we've just illustrated for in-place activation.

SUPPORTING CAST MEMBERS IN OUR APPLICATION

It's not a "cast of thousands," so how about a cast of the "valuable few"? These are the definitions of the new interfaces introduced in this chapter to support in-place activation of embedded documents.

IOleWindow

This interface is the fountainhead of all **IOleInPlace*** interfaces; yet it hides in the background. This interface isn't shown in Figure 8-5, but all **IOleInPlace*** interfaces inherit all methods of this interface. Interfaces that inherit from **IOle Window** include these: **IOleInPlaceObject**, **IOleInPlaceActiveObject**, **IOleInPlace UIWindow**, **IOleInPlaceFrame**, **IOleInPlaceSite**, **IOleInPlaceSiteEx**, **IOleInPlace SiteWindowless**, and **IOleInPlaceObjectWindowless**. This interface inherits all methods of **IUnknown** and implements these methods:

- **GetWindow** — Returns the window handle of the window participating in the in-place activation. This can be a frame, document, parent, or in-place object window.

- **ContextSensitiveHelp** — Determines when help mode should be entered during in-place activation.

IOleInPlaceObject

The immediate container manages the activation and deactivation of an in-place object through the **IOleInPlaceObject** interface. This interface also determines how much of the in-place object should be visible.

IOleInPlaceObject inherits all methods of **IOleWindow** and **IUnknown**. **IOleInPlaceObject** implements these methods:

o **InPlaceDeactivate** — Deactivates an in-place object and discards the object's undo state.

o **UIDeactivate** — Deactivates and removes the user interface supporting in-place activation.

o **SetObjectRects** — Determines how much of the in-place object is visible.

o **ReactivateAndUndo** — Reactivates an object.

IOleInPlaceActiveObject

This interface is the communication channel between the document window containing the in-place object and the outermost window frame. The communications include message translation, window state (active or deactivated), and the document state (active or deactivated). The interface also notifies the object when to resize its borders and manages modeless dialog boxes.

This interface is not available through any **QueryInterface**. It is supplied by the object to the document with a call to **IOleInPlaceUIWindow::SetActiveObject** and then to the container with a call to **IOleInPlaceFrame::SetActiveObject**. These methods must be called in this order. The container uses this pointer in processing **IOleInPlaceFrame::SetMenu**.

This interface inherits all methods of **IOleWindow** and **IUnknown**. **IOleInPlaceActiveObject** implements these methods:

o **TranslateAccelerator** — Translates messages from the active object's message queue.

o **OnFrameWindowActivate** — Notifies the active object when the container's top-level frame is activated or deactivated.

o **OnDocWindowsActivate** — Notifies the active in-place object when the container's document window is activated or deactivated.

o **ResizeBorder** — Notifies the object when to resize its border space with supplied parameters.

o **EnableModeless** — Enables or disables a modeless dialog box.

IOleInPlaceUIWindow

This is a container interface, which is used to negotiate border space on the document or frame window. This interface inherits all methods of **IOleWindow** and **IUnknown**. **IOleInPlaceUIWindow** implements these methods:

- **GetBorder** — Returns a RECT (see Win32 application programming procedure [API] documentation) structure for active use of toolbars and similar controls.

- **RequestBorderSpace** — Requests border space around the active in-place object's frame window.

- **SetBorderSpace** — Allocates border space requested in the **IOleInPlaceUIWindow::GetBorder** call.

- **SetActiveObject** — Establishes a direct channel between the active in-place object and the frame and document windows.

IOleInPlaceFrame

Container applications use this interface to control the display and placement of the composite menu, keystroke accelerator translation, context-sensitive help mode, and modeless dialog boxes. This interface inherits all methods of **IOleWindow**, **IOleUIWindow**, and **IUnknown**. **IOleInPlaceFrame** implements these methods:

- **InsertMenus** — Called by the object application to allow the container to insert its menu groups in the composite menu.

- **SetMenu** — The composite menu is installed into the window frame containing the object being activated.

- **RemoveMenus** — A request from the object application to the container application. The container is asked to remove its menu elements from the composite menu.

- **SetStatusText** — Text is set and displayed in the container's frame window status line.

- **EnableModeless** — A frame's modeless dialog box is enabled or disabled.

- **TranslateAccelerator** — Accelerator keystrokes that are targeted for the container's frame are translated.

IOleInPlaceSite

This interface is implemented by container applications and is used to interact with the object's in-place client site. This interface inherits all methods of **IOleWindow** and **IUnknown**. **IOleInPlaceSite** implements these methods:

- **CanInPlaceActivate** — Determines if the object can be activated in-place.
- **OnInPlaceActivate** — Notifies the container when one of its objects is being activated in-place.
- **OnUIActivate** — Notifies the container that in-place activation is about to occur and the container's menu will be replaced with the in-place composite menu.
- **GetWindowContext** — The in-place object retrieves the window interfaces that form the window object hierarchy. Also returns the position in the parent window.
- **Scroll** — The in-place object requests to the container to scroll the in-place object by the supplied pixel count.
- **OnUIDeactivate** — Notifies the container that it should reinstall its user interface and take focus.
- **OnInPlaceDeactivate** — Sends a notification to the container that the object is no longer active.
- **DiscardUndoState** — The active object sends a request for the container to discard its Undo State.
- **DeractivateAndUndo** — The active object sends this to the container when a user invokes Undo immediately after activating an object.
- **OnPosRectChange** — The in-place object calls this when the active object's extents have changed.

COMPOUND DOCUMENT OPTIMIZATIONS

The following interfaces are not part of the original OLE implementation using COM; they came about as a result of ActiveX Controls 96 and the need to improve the functionality of OLE/ActiveX controls on the Internet. They are included in this chapter strictly for closure because they all inherit from **IOleWindow**.

IOleInPlaceSiteEx

This is an add-on interface to **IOleInPlaceSite.** It avoids unnecessary screen flashing when an object is activated or deactivated. This interface inherits all methods of **IOleWindow, IOleInPlaceSite**, and **IUnknown. IOleInPlaceSiteEx** implements these methods:

- **InInPlaceActivateEx** — The embedded object calls this interface at activation to determine if it needs redrawing.

- **OnInPlaceDeactivateEx** — The container is notified whether the object needs to be redrawn at deactivation.

- **RequestUIActivate** — The container is notified that the object is about to enter the UI-active state.

IOleInPlaceSiteWindowless

IOleInPlaceSiteWindowless works with **IOleInPlaceObjectWindowless** to implement an environment where an in-place object can be activated without requiring a window or the associated window resources.

Small controls do not need a window. The **IOleInPlaceSiteWindowless** interface addresses these matters:

- It is an extra burden on a control to have a window that isn't needed or wanted.

- The **IOleInPlaceSiteWindowless** interface supports nonrectangular controls, a feature not previously available.

- Requiring a window prevents the control from being transparent.

Windowless objects are an extension of normal compound documents. The windowed and windowless objects both use the same definitions for OLE states. The only difference is that windowless objects do not consume window resources. The container provides the services to the object, which are normally associated with a window.

A windowless object in a client server application should query its site for the **IOleInPlaceSiteWindowless** interface. The object calls the container with **IOleInPlaceSiteWindowless::CanWindowlessActivate** when the interface exists.

The object should behave like a standard compound document and create a window environment when the **IOleInPlaceSiteWindowless** interface does not exist.

Windowless objects must be in-place active to receive mouse or keyboard messages. Windowless objects obtain services from the container for capturing the mouse, setting focus, obtaining a device context, or deciding to paint.

The **IOleInPlaceSiteWindowless** interface is derived from the interface **IOleInPlaceSiteEx** and inherits all methods of **IOleWindow**, **IOleInPlaceSite**, **IOleInPlaceSiteEx**, and **IUnknown**. **IOleInPlaceSiteWindowless** implements these methods:

- **AdjustRectangle** — Adjusts a rectangle when it is partially or entirely covered by opaque objects.

- **CanWindowlessActivate** — Informs an object when its container can support a windowless in-place activation.

- **GetCapture** — Determines whether mouse capture is available to the active in-place windowless object.

- **GetDC** — Returns a handle to the device context (see Win32 API documentation).

- **GetFocus** — Determines whether an active in-place windowless object has keyboard focus.

- **InvalidateRect** — Enables an object to invalidate a specified rectangle of its in-place image on the screen.

- **InvalidateRgn** — Enables an object to invalidate a specified rectangle of its in-place image on the screen.

- **OnDefWindowMessage** — Invokes default-message handling for the object.

- **ReleaseDC** — Releases the device context obtained with **IOleInPlaceSiteWindowless::GetDC**.

- **ScrollRect** — Scrolls through an area with the in-place object's image on the screen.

- **SetCapture** — Enables the capturing of all mouse messages for an in-place windowless object.

- **SetFocus** — Sets the keyboard focus to an in-place windowless object.

IOleInPlaceObjectWindowless

IOleInPlaceObjectWindowless is the other half of the windowless object equation. This interface enables a windowless object to process window messages and participate in drag and drop operations.

Small controls do not need windows. The container is expected to implement the **IOleInPlaceSiteWindowless** interface. The object must act as a normal compound document when the **IOleInPlaceSiteWindowless** interface does not exist.

IOleInPlaceObjectWindowless is derived from **IUnknown**, **IOleWindow**, and **IOleInPlaceObject**. **IOleInPlaceObjectWindowless** implements these methods:

- **OnWindowMessage** — Dispatches a message from the container to a windowless object.

- **GetDropTarget** — Supplies the **IDropTarget** interface for a windowless object.

KEY POINT SUMMARY

In-place activation of embedded objects is quite powerful and eases the user's burden. This comes at a significant cost:

- In-place activation of embedded documents promotes management problems where there may be multiple copies of the data, each of which is different.

- Applications supporting embedded documents are complex to develop. It's fair to say that any application that supports OLE Documents is complex to develop and this includes both linked and embedded documents. The easiest-to-use applications are always the most difficult to implement.

- Embedded documents are resource intensive. A private copy of the native data is stored in the container object.

- Editing an embedded document changes both the presentation and native data immediately.

- Editing an embedded document does not affect other users.

- Embedded documents are edited in their own window.

- An embedded document merges menus and toolbars.

APPLYING WHAT YOU'VE LEARNED

Embedding an object is almost a cliché when Excel is embedded in Word. Many other Microsoft tools, however, support embedded objects. The questions that follow will test your understanding of the embedded document architecture, while the laboratories will show you that a container is not always a container. That is, the containers respond differently to an embedding of the same object. Your goal as a developer is to always have your tools respond in the same manner. Unconventional software is very error-prone even though the implementation is very clever. Function should always come before form and form should not be unique.

Instant Assessment

1. What is another name for in-place activation?

2. Explain the difference between an embedded document and a linked document.

3. What interface does the object request of the container when in-place activation starts?

4. Assume that the interface **IOleInPlaceSite** exists. What is the next logical step for in-process activation?

5. You have implemented an embedded application. The user complains that the screen flashes too much. Which interface is faulty (or which did you forget to implement)?

6. Explain a windowless object implementation.

7. What type of object is a candidate for a windowless object implementation?

8. Which container interface must exist before an object can do a windowless activation?

9. When will a windowless control be activated as a normal object?

10. When will the edited data of an embedded object be saved?

 concept link **For answers to the Instant Assessment questions, see Appendix C.**

Lab Exercises

These labs are designed to acquaint the new Microsoft user with embedding objects. There are two methods for doing this. For these exercises, we'll use the mouse and embed our object using menus. The other method is to drag and drop, which is found in an earlier section.

I've created a small object with VISIO, which you can use for testing object embedding. The file BLOB.BMP is located on the CD-ROM in the <unit>\EXAMPLES\CHAPTER8 folder that accompanies this book.

Lab 8.15 *Visual Basic 5.0 and object embedding*

WA I

1. Start Visual Basic 5.0.

2. Select **Toolbox** from the **View** menu if no toolbox is present.

3. Click an **Image** control and paint it on the form.

4. Click a **Picture** control and paint it on the form.

5. Click an **OLE** control and paint it on the form. The **OLE** control responds with a dialog box.

6. Select **Create Form File** and browse the path of BLOB.BMP.

7. Set the **Picture** property of both the **Image** control and the **Picture** control to the path for BLOB.BMP.

8. Run the form.

9. Double-click all controls.

In-place activation occurs for only the **OLE** control. Neither the **Image** control nor the **Picture** control, which is an extended version of the **Image** control, will activate.

Lab 8.16 *Word 97 and object embedding*

WA I

Inserting an object in Word 97 is easy. It is possible to center an object by moving the cursor in slightly from the left margin. If this is done, then the space bar can be used to move the image right or the delete key can move the image left.

1. Open Word 97.

2. Insert the image by selecting **Object** from the **Insert** menu of Word 97.

3. Select **Create From File** and **Browse**.

4. Locate `BLOB.BMP` file and click **OK**. It may take several seconds before the image appears.

5. Click an area of the document away from the embedded image.

6. Now go back and double-click the image. The image should open up in Paintbrush.

Lab 8.17 *Access 97 and object embedding*

WA I

Access 97 reacts quite differently to embedding an object. Access 97 is an automation controller and has the capability of managing embedded objects.

1. Open Access 97.

2. Create a blank form.

3. Select **Object** from the **Insert** menu.

4. Browse your system until you find `BLOB.BMP` or any other .BMP file.

5. Click **OK**.

After a few seconds, the object will appear on the form. Look at it very carefully. Access 97 has packaged the object within an OLE container. It is in an unbound object frame, which you can inspect using the property window of Access 97.

Access 97 and Visual Basic are each different in subtle ways. Both can support embedded objects; Access 97, however, has an **Insert** menu while Visual Basic 5.0 does not.

1. Select an **Image** control and paint it on the form.

2. Answer the dialog box by selecting **Create from File** and browse for `BLOB.BMP`. Do the same with the **Unbound Object Frame**.

You should have three copies of `BLOB.BMP` on the form. Two copies are in an **Unbound Object Frame** and one copy is in an **Image** control.

3. Set the **Enabled** property of the **Unbound Object Frames** to *Yes* and set the **Locked** property of those it controls to *No*. Note that the **Image** control does not have an **Enabled** or **Locked** property.

4. Start Access 97. The **Unbound Object Frames** will activate in place while the **Image** control cannot be activated.

In-place activation also works for **Bound Object** Frame.

Lab 8.18 *Excel 97 and object embedding*

WA I

Objects may be embedded in Microsoft Excel 97.

1. Start Excel.

2. Select a cell in the center of the screen.

3. Select **Object** from the **Insert** menu.

4. Select **Create From File** and browse for BLOB.BMP.

5. After the image is displayed, click on another cell and then double-click the image. Paintbrush will start.

6. Return to Excel.

Note that you can drag the image. The image was not embedded in the cell, but was placed on top of the worksheet.

Lab 8.19 *Outlook 97 and object embedding*

WA I

Objects may also be embedded in Microsoft Outlook 97. Start Outlook 97.

1. Double-click an existing e-mail message or create a new message.

2. Tap the space bar to move the cursor in slightly and then select **Object** from the **Insert** menu.

3. Select **Create From File** and browse for BLOB.BMP.

4. After the image is displayed, double-click it. Paintbrush will open.

Lab 8.20 *PowerPoint 97 and object embedding*

WA I

Microsoft PowerPoint 97 can have embedded objects. In-place activation, however, cannot be done when in **Slide Show** mode. An object may be embedded on an individual slide or it may be embedded in the master slide, which makes it visible on all other slides.

1. Start PowerPoint 97.

2. Create a new presentation or open an existing presentation.

3. For an object that should be visible on all slides, such as a logo, select **Master ⇒ Slide Master** from the **View** menu.

4. Embed the object by selecting **Object** from the **Insert** menu.

5. Select **Create From File** and browse for BLOB.BMP.

6. After the image is displayed, double-click it. Paintbrush will open.

Lab 8.21 *Microsoft Project 4.1 and object embedding*

WA I

An object may be embedded in Microsoft Project 4.1. Like Excel 97, Project 4.1 opens with default working document and an object can be embedded directly.

1. Start Project 4.1.

2. Embed the object by selecting **Object** from the **Insert** menu.

3. Select **Create From File** and browse for BLOB.BMP.

4. After the image is displayed, double-click it. Paintbrush will open.

Windows Architecture I

Automation

About Chapter 9

This chapter is about a different technology based on COM. *Automation* or what used to be known as *OLE Automation* is the exposing of properties and methods for manipulation by a client application. This technology is separate from OLE technology, which is also based on COM. The confusion comes about because both OLE Documents (linking and embedding) and Automation may be used by an object, but each are separate technologies based on COM. Unfortunately, the term OLE has been loosely applied to any technology based on COM, which is not correct. OLE Automation does not support linking and embedding of documents. It only supports the exposing of properties and methods for manipulation by a client application, which is now known as Automation.

Automation is the **IDispatch** interface discussed in Chapter 2. We briefly discuss some Automation issues in this chapter, and then step into examples of Automation.

AUTOMATION: A DIFFERENT COM TECHNOLOGY

Welcome to Automation. It's been a long trip getting here, but the difficulty was worth it. The previous pages are just fluff if you're a C/C++ programmer. The material presented thus far, however, may be a little bit eclectic to the Microsoft technology newcomer.

This section is where we start to tie everything together. You'll shortly discover that COM interfaces are everywhere, and the **IUnknown** interface is ubiquitous in the Microsoft architecture. Figure 9-1 represents an OLE Automation object that uses the classic COM **IUnknown** interface, first introduced in Chapter 2. Automation uses COM, but it is not OLE linking or embedding. (Embedding and linking are not features of Automation.) *OLE Automation* is the capability of an application object (application server) to define a set of properties and commands and make them accessible to other applications to enable programming. The public exposure of these properties and commands allows one application to contain code that manipulates another application.

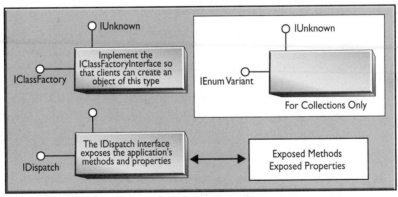

FIGURE 9-1   An OLE Automation (Automation) Object.

An Automation object contains the **IUnknown** interface, which has become a ubiquitous component of the Microsoft architecture. I said earlier in this book that component technology is now. There is no better way to demonstrate that than by Figure 9-2, which illustrates that all methods of Microsoft Visual Basic 5.0 are members of the **IUnknown1** interface. Obviously, this interface inherits from the **IUnknown** interface.

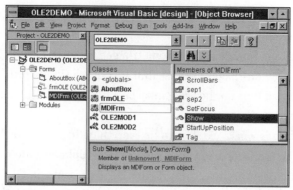

FIGURE 9-2   IUnknown is a ubiquitous feature of Microsoft architecture.

Automation uses COM and the supporting infrastructure. You should recognize the interfaces from Figure 9-1. The key difference is that Automation does not support the linking or embedding that are features of OLE compound documents. The key infrastructure issues of Automation include:

- A storage mechanism that can support transactions and incremental loading and storing which promotes efficient use of memory. This is the structured storage of COM, which is available to all COM participants. There is no requirement to use structured storage with Automation files because the files are generally not compound files.

- The ability to associate a logical name with an object is required for unique object identification. This requirement exists for both OLE Documents and Automation objects. The global unique identifier (GUID) and interface identifier (IID) are used in both technologies.

- A mechanism for interprocess communications that combines data in a package before sending it. The mechanism can service all applications regardless of whether they support OLE Documents. (This is an example of marshaling, which was discussed in Chapter 5.)

- The application that creates an object need not support OLE; however, the accepting application must support OLE.

- Both OLE Documents and Automation use the Registry to locate servers. Server and parameter attributes are stored in type libraries.

OLE Automation refers to the ability of an application to define a set of properties and commands and make them accessible to other applications to enable programmability. Two components participate in Automation: a client and an Automation object or server.

- An *OLE Automation controller* or client is an application that can manipulate exposed components belonging to another application.
- The application that exposes the components is called the *OLE Automation server.*

The role of an Automation controller is to use the inherent features of the application to manipulate the exposed methods and properties of an OLE Automation server. *Being a good OLE client is a requirement for being an OLE Automation application controller.* An OLE client is a program that can store and display OLE objects, which may be either linked or embedded.

Programmability is a key issue in being a good OLE Automation controller, as this is the primary tool used to manipulate the OLE Automation server. This is different than an OLE server, which is a program that can edit and create OLE objects for other programs to display and store. OLE servers provide objects (either linked or embedded) that OLE clients can display.

Choosing an application controller is a function of the type of data. The first question to ask is, "What type of data will the integrated solution present or be allowed access to?" Microsoft Access supports OLE Automation and has visual editing. Access is the tool of choice for storing and manipulating data. It can be tightly integrated with Microsoft Excel, which is a good OLE Automation server. Microsoft Excel, however, is a better choice when your data is worksheet-related.

note **Microsoft Visual Basic is not designed for any particular type of data, but it is an excellent container for OLE objects. Visual Basic also supports OLE Automation and has visual editing support.**

I suspect there is some confusion about now because nearly all Microsoft products support Visual Basic for Applications (VBA). The supporting of VBA does not make a tool an Automation controller. In the weakest sense, it is performing Remote Automation using VBA.

Another way to look at Automation is to note that only Microsoft Access and Microsoft Visual Basic support the embedding of OLE objects in controls. This provides the container through which methods and properties are exposed.

I repeat the statement *being a good OLE client is a requirement for being an OLE Automation application controller* in Table 9-1. The rules are not hard and fast, as VBA is ubiquitous in Microsoft Office 97, but in the strictest sense, Table 9-1 represents practical and reasonable choices. Yes, I suppose Excel could be an Automation controller in some circumstances, but there are limitations, such as the lack of drag-and-drop control.

TABLE 9-1 FACTORS IN CHOOSING AN AUTOMATION CONTROLLER					
	GOOD OLE CLIENT	*GOOD OLE AUTOMATION CLIENT*	*OLE AUTOMATION SERVER*	*VISUAL EDITING*	*CONTROLLER*
Word	X		X	X	
Project	X		X	X	
Access	X	X		X	X
Excel	X	X	X	X	
Visual Basic	X	X		X	X
Visio			X	X	

Table 9-1 shows that Visual Basic and Access are not OLE servers because they cannot be controlled.

 note **Visual Basic is probably the best choice for the centralized control model because it is not designed to handle any particular type of data.**

Figure 9-3 illustrates a very simple application consisting of numerous components. This is obviously a standalone application and a reasonably realistic architecture is tiered. I'm sure most of you have dealt with a two-tier architecture where the client is linked to the server.

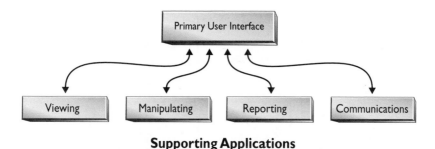

Supporting Applications

FIGURE 9-3 A centralized control model composed of several applications.

AUTOMATION AS A PORTAL
TO NEWER TECHNOLOGY

Automation will remain with us but it is just the first of many steps to newer and more advanced technologies. The first logical step after Automation is *Remote Automation*. Technology has advanced beyond Remote Automation and Microsoft delivered distributed COM (DCOM) with Windows NT 4.0. Still another technology step is the Distributed Transaction Coordinator (DTC) of Microsoft SQL Server 6.5. That is evolving into the Microsoft Transaction Server (MTS).

Figure 9-4 represents a component application, whose architecture is one of assembling building-block components. The unique feature of Figure 9-4 is that all the components are in a near proximity, which means the same address space.

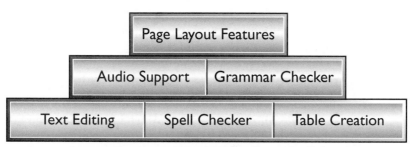

FIGURE 9-4 A conventional component application with all the components sharing the same address space.

Take Figure 9-4 and provide both lateral and longitudinal separation. Rename the functions and you have the tiered architecture of Figure 9-5.

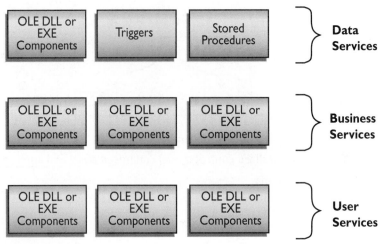

FIGURE 9-5   A generic three-tier business application.

There is no upper limit to the number of tiers in an architecture. It is always a matter of the problem at hand. The smallest nontrivial tiered architecture has three tiers. These tiers can be reasonably divided into user services, business services, and data services. Figure 9-5 illustrates such an architecture. The objects in this architecture communicate with DCOM, but that is not a requirement. User services and business services may exist on the same host. Remote business rules are not a requirement for a tiered architecture, and Figure 9-5 is a logical model and not a physical model. The transparency is in the stub and proxy mechanism that supports marshaling (see Chapter 5). Substituting a stub and a proxy on the client system changes a *local procedure call* (LPC) to a *remote procedure call* (RPC). Microsoft promised that the implementation of DCOM would be transparent and it was.

note   **The layers in an architecture can increase very quickly. A departmental roll-up application can have three tiers. That may feed into a regional roll-up application, which in turn may feed into a corporate roll-up.**

Figure 9-5 will have business rules as the second tier. Both the second and third tier will be shared applications; hence, the need for an object-oriented architecture.

Figure 9-5 is quite fascinating. It is history in the making. Automation is the first step in separating business rules from the coding process. Business rules are still embedded in code today, but the separation of processing functions has started an evolutionary process. The earlier COBOL programs were very primitive. They had both data definitions and business rules embedded in the code. That has changed, and today data definitions have evolved into the modern relational database where data definitions are no longer embedded in the code but are embedded within the data. This is a true separation of function and data. This same type of paradigm shift must also occur for business rules, which shift is currently in the very early and formative stages of doing. A tiered architecture isolates functionality; the business rules, however, are still embedded in code. To put this in perspective, this is the current frontier of computing technology. I fully expect to see business rule engines on the market within the next five years. These engines will bring business rules to a par with data definitions, which are managed by database engines.

Let's step back in time and look at an old COBOL program. COBOL has a File Definition section known as a FD. The shortcoming of this is that file specifications are embedded in the program. It took the programming community 30 years to evolve out of the primordial ooze of computing to the point where data definitions are not defined within the data. This is the power of the relational database. It separated data from the process.

Guess what! We're still primitive. Business rules can evolve only *after* data evolves, and business rules haven't evolved yet. When a developer writes a trigger, that's a business rule. It's embedded in code (the process). The evolution of business rules starts with a change to a multitier architecture that is fueled by Automation. Creating a tiered architecture moves the business rules from the process to an intermediate level; however, the business rules are still embedded in code.

Business rules today are managed reactively. They should be managed proactively with an officer of the corporation adjusting rules dynamically to changing business conditions. This can't happen until business rules are separated from the code (process).

You can liken the business rule issue of today to that of the COBOL FD. File definitions are buried in the COBOL FD, and a programmer must modify the program to change the data definition. The same issue is true of business rules today. A programmer must modify a trigger or stored procedure to effect a business rule change. Like the data definition buried in the program, a business rule is buried in still another program, in this case a trigger, a stored procedure, or a component of a tiered architecture.

AUTOMATION EXAMPLES

This is not a section on integrated applications, but rather a sampling of Automation examples from various Microsoft products. With these examples I've tried to illustrate that everything today is component technology. Tools such as Microsoft Access and Microsoft Visual Basic are not monolithic products; rather they are the integration of numerous Automation components.

All examples have been tested. The configuration and resources may be different than your configuration, and not all examples may run. Most of the examples deal with Microsoft Office 97, Microsoft Access 97, Microsoft Visual Basic 5.0 Enterprise Edition, and Microsoft SQL Server 6.5. You must adjust server names and paths. Some examples will not run unless you have access to a SQL Server database.

The Internet work in this book uses Windows NT 4.0 Server service release 3. The Windows NT Server system uses Visual Studio 97 Enterprise Edition, which includes Visual InterDev for our Internet work (Chapters 36–39). All other examples within this book, including this chapter, were developed using Windows NT 3.51 workstation service release 5. Office 97 service release 1 is installed on that system. Office 95 was reinstalled after Office 97 was installed, making Office 95 the default for creating Automation objects. Microsoft Visual Basic 5.0 Enterprise Edition service release 1 is also installed on the system. Some examples do not work as originally envisioned, and the comments in both the code and chapter text indicate the deviations. Microsoft publishes millions of lines of code, and I must report that I have encountered code that appears to have never been tested. This isn't unreasonable when the code volume is considered.

When the examples do not function, it may be because your system or tool service release level does not agree with the service level with which the examples were developed. All tools were current with the appropriate service release when the examples were initially developed. Some examples failed during my review because of service release updates. These have been corrected. Except for Office 97, the most common problem was related to proper type library selection. Type libraries do overlap, and I have no rules other than to tell you to browse the type library you have selected and ascertain that it has the object, properties, and methods that you need. You will find with Office 97 and Visual Basic 5.0 that a great deal of your debugging is done by browsing type libraries and not with snapshot tracing.

A secondary issue is that some examples only work with Office 95. They do not work with Office 97. There were severe problems with Word 97's Object Word. There were no problems with WordBasic for either Word 95 or Word 6.0. Code for Object Word is not interchangable with code for WordBasic.

Another issue is the order of tool installation. I installed OfficePro 4.3 in a directory named OFFICE93, Office 95 is installed in a directory named OFFICE95, and Office 97 is installed in the OFFICE97 directory. The order of installation is important, and this relates to the default ProgID in the Registry. When installing Office 97 last, double-clicking a .DOC file will start Word 97. Note that Word 95 and Word 6 are still available though an icon. As stated previously, Office 95 was installed last on the development system.

concept link
You'll find an Automation example using Microsoft Internet Explorer in Chapter 38.

All examples for the book are in the EXAMPLES folder of the CD-ROM that accompanies this book. For example, the Automation examples for this chapter are found in the folder <unit>\EXAMPLES\CHAPTER9. In this folder, you will find AUTO.VBP, which is a Visual Basic 5.0 (VB) project for all the VB examples in this chapter. You will also find AUTO.MDB, which is an Access 97 database that contains Automation examples. The MDB database is a copy of the examples in the AUTO.VBP project. I did this because it begs the question a little too much to show an Access example from Access. Although the Option Explicit statement is not visibly displayed in any of the code fragments, it exists in the module declaration section for all examples. The examples in this book are all complete code fragments that will execute; well, they executed at least twice for me: once when I developed them, and once during my review of this book.

The code in Listing 9-1 registers the drive where you have placed the EXAM-PLES folder. You may leave the CD-ROM mounted at all times, and when prompted, enter the CD-ROM unit. The alternative is to drag the folder to any other unit on your system. Listing 9-1 expects the EXAMPLES directory to be in the root of the designated drive. When requested, the routine will place the unit in the Registry. You will be prompted for the unit until it is registered; however, there is no requirement that the unit containing the EXAMPLES folder be registered. It is important to understand how Listing 9-1 functions. You'll find questions on this topic in the Windows Architecture II examination on this topic.

LISTING 9-1 **Registering the unit for the EXAMPLES folder**

```
Function GetUnit() As String
' (C) 1998 Bruce T. Prendergast
' DBA Prendergast Consulting
' DBA PCS
' IDG Books Worldwide ISBN 0-7645-3123-9
'
' Listing 9-1 Registering the EXAMPLES unit
'
' Places the EXAMPLES folder unit in the registry
' under with the key:
' HKEY_CURRENT_USER
'    \SOFTWARE
'      \VB and VBA Program Settings
'        \WindowsArchitecture
'          \Examples
'            \Unit
'
    Dim Saved_Unit As String   ' Unit in Registry
    Dim Input_Unit As String   ' User supplied unit
    Dim Msg As String          ' Canned message
    Dim LoopCount As Integer   ' Loop Limiter
    Dim Unit_Path As String    ' Resulting unit path
    Dim Answer As String       ' User answer
    Msg = "Windows Architecture Location not " & _
        "Registered" & vbCrLf & "What is the unit " & _
        " where the EXAMPLES directory is stored?"
'
' get the registered unit from the registry
'
    GetSetting "WindowsArchitecture", "Examples", "Unit",_
        Saved_Unit
    If Len(Saved_Unit) = 0 Then
      Unit_Path = ""
      LoopCount = 3
      On Error GoTo GarbageIn
ResumeInput:
```

```
        While Unit_Path = "" And LoopCount > 0
          Input_Unit = InputBox(Msg, _
          "Examples are not Registered")
          Saved_Unit = UCase$(Input_Unit)
          LoopCount = LoopCount - 1
          Unit_Path = CurDir(Saved_Unit & ":\Examples")
        Wend
        If Unit_Path = "" Then
          MsgBox "Invalid Unit designation. " & _
          "Program Terminating"
          End
        End If
        Answer = ""
        While Answer <> "Y" And Answer <> "N"
          Answer = InputBox( _
          "Do you wish to register the EXAMPLES " & _
          "directory (Y/N)", "Examples Not Registered")
          Answer = UCase$(Answer)
        Wend
        If Answer = "Y" Then
          SaveSetting "WindowsArchitecture", _
          "Examples", "Unit", Saved_Unit
          MsgBox "Examples registered with key: " & _
          "WindowsArchitecture\Examples\Unit"
        End If
      End If
    GetUnit = Saved_Unit
    Exit Function
GarbageIn:
    Resume ResumeInput
End Function
```

DAO from Visual Basic

We start with *Data Access Objects* (DAO), a component of Microsoft Access, which has been with us for a very long time. DAO is commonly used from Visual Basic and offers these advantages:

- Visual Basic can use DAO to query either an Access or a SQL Server database.

- DAO is a component of Microsoft Access and has a smaller memory footprint than Microsoft Access.

- Microsoft Access requires a run-time license while DAO does not.

Accessing DAO is illustrated with:

```
Set MyWS = DBEngine.Workspaces(0)
```

This statement is the common shorthand notation, and the **DAO** declaration is assumed because it is the parent object of **DBEngine**. The formal statement is shown below, where a user-defined variable is instantiated with an instance of an Access **Workspace** object. This is the form we'll use in this example because we explicitly want **DAO** and want to avoid loading Access.

```
Set MyWS = DAO.DBEngine.Workspaces(0)
```

note **There are numerous other database access technologies discussed in this book. Although we're discussing Automation here, there are other implementations of database access that are *lean and mean*. Remote Data Objects (RDO) (Chapters 24 through 26) are a component of Microsoft Visual Basic Enterprise Edition. The corresponding implementation of RDO within Microsoft Access is ODBCDirect (derived from Open Database Connectivity, which is discussed in Chapter 18), where DBEngine and an ODBCDirect Workspace object is used. Our example here uses an Access Workspace object by default. The ODBCDirect implementation is a still smaller footprint than this example, but it is limited to ODBC databases only and cannot query an Access database.**

The DAO example below is from Visual Basic 5.0. You'll note from the comments in the code fragment that I had a few problems with DAO 3.5, so the example uses the Microsoft DAO 3.0 Object Library. This example has a colorful history, so I'll step though the various events:

- The goal of the example is to show how DAO from Visual Basic is used. The ProgID **Access.Application** causes all of Access to be loaded while the ProgID **DAO.DBEngine** only loads DAO, which is all we need. **DAO.DBEngine** doesn't work with the DAO 3.5 Object Library, but it does work with the DAO 3.0 Object Library. That's good enough and time moves on.

- Some time after the example was created, and before my review of the material, service release 1 for Visual Basic 5.0 Enterprise Edition was installed. The host operating system is Windows NT WS 3.51 service release 5.

- During my review, the example failed to work for either the DAO 3.0 Object Library or the DAO 3.5 Object Library.

- Office 95 was reinstalled and the example worked again, but only for the DAO 3.0 Object Library.

The reference is created in the code module by selecting **Tools** ⇒ **References** ⇒ **Microsoft DAO 3.0 Object Library**.

It must create a workspace and a database before creating a pass-through query to a SQL Server. This example will not work unless Microsoft SQL Server is installed. You can find this example on the CD-ROM that accompanies this book in the AUTO.VBP project of the EXAMPLES\CHAPTER9 folder. Listing 9-3 is the Access 97 version of Listing 9-2. Listing 9-2 has a smaller memory footprint because only DAO is loaded, while Listing 9-3 accesses DAO from within Access and all of Microsoft Access is loaded.

LISTING 9-2 Using DAO from Visual Basic

```
Private Sub DAO_fromVisualBasic_Click()
' (C) 1998 Bruce T. Prendergast
' DBA Prendergast Consulting
' DBA PCS
' IDG Books Worldwide ISBN 0-7645-3123-9
'
' Listing 9-2 DAO from Visual Basic
'
  Dim MyDAO As DBEngine
  Dim MyWS As Workspace
  Dim MyDB As Database
  Dim MyFld As Field
  Dim MyQry As QueryDef, MyRS As Recordset
'
' the stament below gets a type mismatch
' with DAO 3.5. It works fine with DAO 3.0
```

```
'
  Set MyDAO = CreateObject("DAO.DBEngine")
'
' get a workspace
'
  Set MyWS = CreateWorkspace("", "admin", "")
  If Dir("MyDB.mdb") <> "" Then Kill "MyDB.mdb"
'
' create a new database
'
  Set MyDB = MyWS.CreateDatabase("MyDB.mdb", _
  dbLangGeneral, dbEncrypt)
'
' The zero-length string creates a temporary query
'
  Set MyQry = MyDB.CreateQueryDef("")
  Dim SourceConnectStr As String
  SourceConnectStr = "ODBC;DATABASE=Pubs;UID=sa;" & _
    "PWD=;DSN=Thor;"
'
' This is a pass-through query so the connect
' string is set first, which stops Jet from
' parsing the SQL placed in the SQL property
' of the QueryDef.
'
  MyQry.Connect = SourceConnectStr
  MyQry.ReturnsRecords = True
  MyQry.SQL = "sp_who" ' an SQL Server stored procedure
'
' Now create the snapshot and print the returned data
'
  Set MyRS = MyQry.OpenRecordset()
'
' enumerate fields
'
  Debug.Print "Fields: Name, Type, Value"
```

```
   For Each MyFld In MyRS.Fields
      Debug.Print " "; MyFld.Name; " "; MyFld.Type; _
      " "; MyFld.Value
   Next MyFld
   MsgBox "SQL Pass-Through query completed successfully"
   Exit Sub
End Sub
```

DAO from Microsoft Access

There were enough problems with the Visual Basic 5.0 version using DAO to merit
redoing it again in Microsoft Access 97. Listing 9-3 is located in the Microsoft
Access 97 AUTO.MDB database in the EXAMPLES\CHAPTER9 folder on the
CD-ROM, or the unit where you have relocated the EXAMPLES folder.

LISTING 9-3 Using DAO from Microsoft Access

```
Private Sub DAO_from_Access_Click()
' (C) 1998 Bruce T. Prendergast
' DBA Prendergast Consulting
' DBA PCS
' IDG Books Worldwide ISBN 0-7645-3123-9
'
' Listing 9-2 Access 97 DAO
'
   Dim MyWS As Workspace, MyDB As Database
   Dim MyFld As Field
   Dim MyQry As QueryDef, MyRS As Recordset
   Set MyWS = DBEngine.Workspaces(0)
   Set MyDB = MyWS.Databases(0)
'
' The zero-length string creates a temporary query
'
   Set MyQry = MyDB.CreateQueryDef("")
   Dim SourceConnectStr As String
   SourceConnectStr = "ODBC;DATABASE=Pubs;" & _
      "UID=sa;PWD=;DSN=Thor;"
```

```
'
' This is a pass-through query so the connect
' string is set first, which stops Jet from
' parsing the SQL placed in the SQL property
' of the QueryDef.
'

  MyQry.Connect = SourceConnectStr
  MyQry.ReturnsRecords = True
  MyQry.SQL = "sp_who" ' SQL Server stored procedure
'
' Now create the snapshot and print the returned data
'
  Set MyRS = MyQry.OpenRecordset()
'
' enumerate fields
'
  Debug.Print "Fields: Name, Type, Value"
  For Each MyFld In MyRS.Fields
    Debug.Print " "; MyFld.Name; " "; MyFld.Type; _
    " "; MyFld.Value
  Next MyFld
  MsgBox "SQL Pass-Through query completed successfully"
  Exit Sub
End Sub
```

Microsoft Access from Microsoft Visual Basic

Microsoft Visual Basic does not have a native report writer. Crystal Reports ships with Visual Basic, but it is a third-party product. Listing 9-4 creates an instance of Access 95 to print a report. The object variable is defined within the event routine and goes out of scope when the event ends. A practical application should declare the variable at the form level, which preserves it over events. As stated previously, this application will have a very large memory footprint. Note that a specific version of Microsoft Access is instantiated.

The reference for this application is created in the code module by selecting: **Tools ⇒ References ⇒ Microsoft DAO 3.0 Object Library**. This is a Visual Basic 5.0 example located in the AUTO.VBP project folder on the CD-ROM.

This is not a recommended solution for a distributed application because Microsoft Access requires a run-time license for each client unless the Access Developers Toolkit (ADT) is used. Crystal Reports should be your choice for a distributed application.

LISTING 9-4 Creating Access reports from Visual Basic

```
Private Sub Access_Automation_Click()
' (C) 1998 Bruce T. Prendergast
' DBA Prendergast Consulting
' DBA PCS
' IDG Books Worldwide ISBN 0-7645-3123-9
'

' Listing 9-4 Automation From Visual Basic
'
  Dim MyObj As Access.Application
  Set MyObj = CreateObject("Access.Application.7")
  With MyObj
    .OpenCurrentDatabase _
    "H:\Office95\Access\Samples\Northwind.mdb"
    .Visible = True
    .DoCmd.OpenReport "Products by Category", acPreview
  End With
  Set MyObj = Nothing
End Sub
```

Microsoft Excel from Visual Basic

This is an example of calling Microsoft Excel 97 from Microsoft Access 97. Listing 9-5 is the VBA fragment that creates the Excel example, and Listing 9-6 is a very simple interaction mechanism for rotating the spreadsheet. A reference must be created to the Excel type library before compiling the VBA script. The reference is created in the code module by selecting **Tools** ⇒ **References** ⇒ **Microsoft Excel 8.0 Object Library**.

This example is located in the Microsoft Access 97 AUTO.MDB database in the EXAMPLES\CHAPTER9 folder on the CD-ROM, or the unit where you have relocated the EXAMPLES folder.

LISTING 9-5 Controlling Excel 97 from Access 97

```
Private Sub Excel_from_Access_Click()
' (C) 1998 Bruce T. Prendergast
' DBA Prendergast Consulting
' DBA PCS
' IDG Books Worldwide ISBN 0-7645-3123-9
'
' Listing 9-5 Controlling Excel from Access
'
' These are form level variables to preserve them
'
'Dim MyXL As Object
'Dim MyChrt As Object
'Dim xl3DColumn As Integer
'
' This is late binding
'
  Dim i As Integer
  xl3DColumn = -4100 'xl constant for 3D Column chart
  Set MyXL = CreateObject("Excel.Application")
  With MyXL
    .Visible = True
    .Workbooks.Add
    .Range("a1").Value = 4
    .Range("a2").Value = 1
    .Range("a3").Value = 3
    .Range("a4").Value = 2
    .Range("a1:a4").Select
  End With
  Set MyChrt = MyXL.Charts.Add()
  MyChrt.Type = xl3DColumn
  For i = 30 To 180 Step 10
    MyChrt.Rotation = i
  Next
End Sub
```

A command button exists on the form that rotates the Excel spreadsheet. The code in Listing 9-6 rotates the spreadsheet with small incremental steps.

LISTING 9-6 **Interacting with Excel by rotating the spreadsheet**

```
Private Sub Rotate_Excel_Click()
' (C) 1998 Bruce T. Prendergast
' DBA Prendergast Consulting
' DBA PCS
' IDG Books Worldwide ISBN 0-7645-3123-9
'
  If MyChrt Is Nothing Then Exit Sub
  IRotate = (IRotate + 15) Mod 180
  MyChrt.Rotation = IRotate
'
' This code assumes that Excel is the
' next sibling window
'
  SendKeys "%{TAB}"
  DoEvents
End Sub
```

These are the form level variables used in Listings 9-5 and 9-6:

```
Option Compare Database
Option Explicit
Dim MyXL As Object
Dim MyChrt As Object
Dim xl3DColumn As Integer
Dim IRotate As Integer
```

As you can see from the main code, the spreadsheet constants are wired into the VBA code. The application works by starting the Access 97 MDB `AUTO.MDB`. There is only one form in this MDB. Click the command button **Excel 95 from Access 97**. The application starts Excel with Automation. The chart is then rotated 180 degrees with Automation. Reduce the screen size by clicking the **Min** button of Excel and drag the Excel window down until you can see the **Rotate Excel Chart** command button on the Access 97 form. Click that button and it will rotate in

15-degree increments. Turn to the labs at the end of this chapter for more examples of adding features to this application.

OLE Messaging

This is an example of e-mail using OLE Messaging. The implementation uses late binding to send a message to Microsoft Outlook 97. Microsoft Outlook 97 is the default e-mail provider on a Windows NT workstation. (Microsoft Exchange server is an alternate e-mail provider choice.) The example requires references to the OLE/Messaging Object Library, which are created in the code module by selecting **Tools ⇒ References ⇒ OLE/Messaging 1.0 Object Library**.

The message in Listing 9-7 was sent to an e-mail recipient with the name Dudley Doright. I am reasonably sure that Dudley Doright is not a valid mailbox on your system. Create a new mailbox with the name Dudley Doright or modify the example code in Listing 9-7 to reflect an existing e-mail recipient on your system. This example is located in the Microsoft Access 97 AUTO.MDB database in the EXAMPLES\CHAPTER9 folder on the CD-ROM, or the unit where you have relocated the EXAMPLES folder.

LISTING 9-7 Sending e-mail with OLE messaging

```
Sub Create_Message()
' (C) 1998 Bruce T. Prendergast
' DBA Prendergast Consulting
' DBA PCS
' IDG Books Worldwide ISBN 0-7645-3123-9
'
'   Listing 9-7 OLE Messaging
'

  Dim objSession As Object, objMessage As Object, _
  objRecip As Object
  Set objSession = CreateObject("MAPI.SESSION")
  objSession.Logon
  Set objMessage = objSession.Outbox.Message.Add
  objMessage.Subject = "I've caught Snidley Whiplash"
  Set objRecip = objMessage.Recipients.Add
  objRecip.Name = "Dudley DoRight"
```

```
    objRecip.Type = mapiTo
    ' mapiTo is an OLE messaging-defined constant = 1
    objMessage.Update
    objMessage.Send showDialog:=True
    objSession.Logoff
End Sub
```

Microsoft Office Binder

This example is slightly more complicated. Microsoft Access 97 directs Word 97 to build a Binder 97 binder. This takes two object library references and both are selected while in the code module. The first library is selected with **Tools ⇒ References ⇒ Microsoft Word 8.0 Object Library**. The second library is selected with **Tools ⇒ References ⇒ Microsoft Binder 8.0 Object Library**. This example is located in the Microsoft Access 97 AUTO.MDB database in the EXAMPLES\CHAPTER9 folder on the CD-ROM, or the unit where you have relocated the EXAMPLES folder.

    This example will not work as constituted because the files referenced are local to the development system. Use the example as a prototype skeleton to place your files within the bindery. The application is unique with respect to other examples in this chapter. The example in Listing 9-8 uses Automation on two different objects. This example must use Word 97 (Word 8.0) and not Word 6 or Word 95 (Word 7.0).

LISTING 9-8   The Access 97 VBA code that creates Figure 9-6

```
Private Sub Access97_Word97_Binder97_Click()
' (C) 1998 Bruce T. Prendergast
' DBA Prendergast Consulting
' DBA PCS
' IDG Books Worldwide ISBN 0-7645-3123-9
'
' Listing 9-8 create a binder
' Use Word 97 and Binder 97 from Access 97
'
    Dim MyBnd As OfficeBinder.Binder
    Dim MyWrd As Word.Application
    Dim MyDoc As Document
```

```
        Dim MyFont As Font
        Set MyBnd = CreateObject("Office.Binder")
        MyBnd.Visible = True
        Set MyWrd = CreateObject("Word.Application.8")
        Documents.Add
        Set MyFont = New Font
        MyFont.Bold = True
        MyFont.Italic = True
        MyFont.Size = 22
        MyFont.Name = "Arial"
        ActiveDocument.Paragraphs(1).Range.Font = MyFont
        With ActiveDocument.Content
          .InsertBefore "Component Technology"
        End With
        ActiveDocument.SaveAs filename:="E:\IDGExamp\BindSum.DOC"
        MyWrd.Quit
        Set MyWrd = Nothing
        MyBnd.Sections.Add filename:="E:\IDGMASTR\ch01.doc"
        MyBnd.Sections.Add filename:="E:\IDGMASTR\ch02.doc"
        MyBnd.Sections.Add filename:="E:\IDGMASTR\ch03.doc"
        MyBnd.Sections.Add filename:="E:\IDGMASTR\ch04.doc"
        MyBnd.Sections.Add filename:="E:\IDGMASTR\ch05.doc"
        MyBnd.Sections.Add filename:="E:\IDGMASTR\ch06.doc"
        MyBnd.Sections.Add filename:="E:\IDGMASTR\ch07.doc"
        MyBnd.Sections.Add filename:="E:\IDGMASTR\ch08.doc"
        MyBnd.Sections.Add filename:="E:\IDGMASTR\ch09.doc"
        MyBnd.Sections(1).Name = _
          "IDG Chapter 1-10 ComponentTechnology"
        MyBnd.SaveAs filename:="E:\IDGExamp\MyIDGbinder.obd", _
        saveOption:=bindDisplayDialog
        Exit Sub
    End Sub
```

Figure 9-6 illustrates the results of the Microsoft Binder 97 example in Listing 9-8.

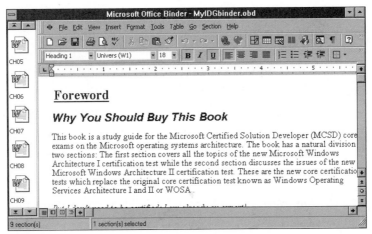

FIGURE 9-6   Listing 9-8 creates this binder.

Microsoft PowerPoint

PowerPoint raises some interesting issues. You may be accustomed to using PowerPoint for slide show presentations. You clicked the mouse when you wanted and everything progressed nicely. But what if your slide presentation is in a kiosk? Automation is the natural choice.

Figure 9-7 illustrates that PowerPoint 97 supports component technology. The page is nothing special. I picked *Corporate Home Page* while in the setup

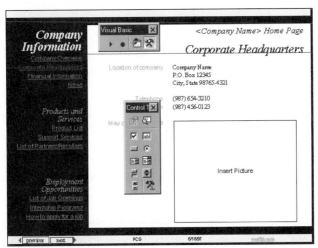

FIGURE 9-7   A Web page created in PowerPoint 97 showing that PowerPoint supports component technology.

wizard. I dropped the VBA toolboxes on the form to illustrate the issue that PowerPoint is far from being a static presentation medium.

You can also embed ActiveX controls on a PowerPoint page. This is another alternative to using either Microsoft Front Page or Microsoft Visual InterDev to create Web pages, which we discuss later in the book.

This is a standard PowerPoint presentation. A text box and a command button are embedded on the master slide. Anything on the master slide is always visible to all slides of the presentation. The purpose of the example is to illustrate that interaction with a PowerPoint slide is possible.

 concept link

The lab exercise in Chapter 37 builds a PowerPoint Internet kiosk presentation.

This example is located in the Microsoft PowerPoint 97 AUTO.PPT presentation in the EXAMPLES\CHAPTER9 folder on the CD-ROM, or the unit where you have relocated the EXAMPLES folder.

The code below is in the click event of the command button. Start the presentation in PowerPoint 97. Clicking the command button will toggle the text box.

```
Private Sub CommandButton1_Click()
Static Icount
Icount = (Icount + 1) Mod 2
If Icount = 0 Then
TextBox1 = ""
Else
TextBox1 = "Ouch, you clicked me!"
End If
End Sub
```

Microsoft Project

This is a small example that sets up a schedule for turning in chapters of a book to your publisher. (Don't believe it — it is much too simplistic when all of the edit cycles are considered!) A fictitious chapter-writing schedule is created with Listing 9-9, and Figure 9-8 shows the bogus results of the example. The example is located in the Microsoft Access 97 AUTO.MDB database in the EXAMPLES\CHAPTER9 folder on the CD-ROM, or the unit where you have relocated the EXAMPLES folder.

LISTING 9-9 A fictitious chapter-writing schedule

```
Private Sub MSProject4p1_Click()
' (C) 1998 Bruce T. Prendergast
' DBA Prendergast Consulting
' DBA PCS
' IDG Books Worldwide ISBN 0-7645-3123-9
'
' Listing 9-9 Project 4.1 and a fictitious schedule
'
  Dim MyProj As Object, MyDoc As Object
  Dim MyTask As Object
  Dim MySuccessor As Object
  Dim i As Integer
  Set MyProj = CreateObject("MSProject.Application")
  MyProj.Visible = True
  MyProj.FileNew SummaryInfo:=False
  Set MyDoc = MyProj.ActiveProject
'
' create the tasks
'
  For i = 1 To 9
    MyDoc.Tasks.Add Name:="Chapter " & i
  Next i
  For i = 1 To 9
    If i = 1 Then Set MyTask = _
      MyDoc.Tasks("Chapter " & i)
    MyTask.ActualDuration = 1440
    If i < 9 Then
      Set MySuccessor = _
        MyDoc.Tasks("Chapter " & i + 1)
      MyTask.LinkSuccessors MySuccessor
    Set MyTask = MySuccessor
    Set MySuccessor = Nothing
    End If
  Next i
  Set MyTask = Nothing
```

```
    MyProj.FileSave
    MyProj.Quit
End Sub
```

Microsoft Word

Some book editors do not want graphics embedded within a chapter sent to them in Microsoft Word. As an author, I need the graphics to maintain a perspective. The example in Listing 9-10 keeps us both happy. I insert the graphics I need to maintain my perspective, and then use this example to strip the graphics from my chapter before I e-mail it. Listing 9-10 is the VBA code that strips the graphics from my Word document.

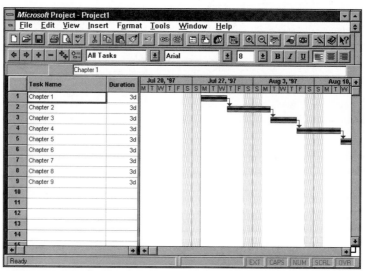

FIGURE 9-8   The result in Microsoft Project of creating the schedule with Listing 9-9.

The source document for this example is from Word 6.0, which requires the use of the Microsoft WordBasic 95 Type Library. (This library cannot be used with Word 97.) This code fragment uses WordBasic to strip embedded graphics from a .DOC file. The output file is then given the prefix of "NG" before being e-mailed to my editor. This example is located in the Microsoft Access 97 `AUTO.MDB` database in the `EXAMPLES\CHAPTER9` folder on the CD-ROM, or the unit where you have relocated the `EXAMPLES` folder.

LISTING 9-10 I keep my editor happy by stripping inserted objects from my manuscript

```
Private Sub FileStrip_Click()
'(C) 1998 Bruce T. Prendergast
' DBA Prendergast Consulting
' DBA PCS
' IDG Books Worldwide ISBN 0-7645-3123-9
'
' The routine strips graphics from a Word
' document. Editors don't like to work on
' documents with embedded graphics.
'
' New files have the prefix "NG", which indicates
' "No Graphics"
'
' Uses: Microsoft WordBasic 95 Type Library
'
' The input document type is Word 6.0
'
  Dim iGraphPos As Long
  Dim objWord As Object
  Dim iPos As Integer
  Dim iNewSlash As Integer
  Dim strFile As String
  Dim strPath As String
  Dim strFullPath As String
  Dim strResp As Variant
'
  While UCase(strResp) <> "Y" And _
      UCase(strResp) <> "N"
    strResp = InputBox( _
          "Do You wish to continue (Y/N)?", _
    "Strip Graphics")
    If strResp = "" Then Exit Sub
    If UCase$(strResp) = "N" Then Exit Sub
  Wend
'************************************************
```

```
'** step 1 - get full path   **
'**********************************************
  strFullPath = ""
  strFullPath = _
      InputBox(".DOC File Name with full path")
  If strFullPath = "" Then Exit Sub
'
'**********************************************
'** step 2 - build path **
'**********************************************
'
  DoCmd.Hourglass True
  iPos = 1
  While InStr(iPos, strFullPath, "\", _
      vbBinaryCompare) > 0
    iNewSlash = InStr(iPos, strFullPath, _
          "\", vbBinaryCompare)
    iPos = iPos + iNewSlash
  Wend
  strPath = Mid$(strFullPath, 1, iNewSlash - 1)
  strFile = Mid$(strFullPath, iNewSlash + 1)
'
'**********************************************
'** step 3 - strip the graphics **
'**********************************************
'
  Set objWord = CreateObject("Word.basic")
  With objWord
    .FileOpen Name:=strPath & "\" & strFile
    .StartOfDocument
    iGraphPos = .GetSelStartPos()
    .EditGoTo "g"
    While iGraphPos <> .GetSelStartPos()
      iGraphPos = .GetSelStartPos()
      .EditClear
      .EditGoTo "g"
```

```
      Wend
      .FileSaveAs strPath & "\NG" & strFile
      .FileClose 1
      Set objWord = Nothing
    End With
    DoCmd.Hourglass False
    Exit Sub
End Sub
```

Microsoft SQL Server

Chapter 27 covers SQL-DMO (Distributed Management Objects) at length, so this
is a short-and-sweet example. After all, I am just showing that Automation is ubiquitous in the Microsoft architecture. We'll get quite a bit fancier later on, so be
patient. Listing 9-11 enumerates the databases supported by a SQL Server known
as *Thor*.

This example is located in the Microsoft Visual Basic 5.0 AUTO.VBP project
in the EXAMPLES\CHAPTER9 folder on the CD-ROM that accompanies this book,
or the unit where you have relocated the EXAMPLES folder.

LISTING 9-11 Using SQL-DMO to report SQL Server supported databases

```
Private Sub SQLDMO_VB50_Click()
'(C) 1998 Bruce T. Prendergast
' DBA Prendergast Consulting
' DBA PCS
' IDG Books Worldwide ISBN 0-7645-3123-9
'
' Listing 9-11 SQL Server (SQL OLE Automation)
' from Visual Basic 5.0
'
  Dim MySQL As Object
  Dim MyDB As Object
  Dim MyStr As String
  Dim SourceConnect As String
  On Error GoTo SQLDMOError
  Set MySQL = CreateObject("SQLOLE.SQLServer")
```

```
        MySQL.Connect "Thor", "sa", ""
        Debug.Print "Databases on Thor"
        For Each MyDB In MySQL.Databases
          Debug.Print "Database: " & MyDB.Name
        Next
        MySQL.Disconnect
        Exit Sub
SQLDMOExit:
        Exit Sub
SQLDMOError:
        MsgBox Err.Description
        Resume SQLDMOExit
End Sub
```

KEY POINT SUMMARY

Understanding Automation in the Microsoft architecture is necessary to become a successful developer. Rather than writing a custom application, the successful and smart developer uses Automation on the available components and delivers a timely solution. The solution is probably more robust than a custom application because it includes proven and existing components that are already in use. That is not to say there won't be bugs, but they should certainly be fewer.

- Automation is the new name for OLE Automation.

- Automation uses COM, but the technology does not support linking or embedding. An OLE Document supports either linking or embedding.

- Automation is the exposing of methods and properties for manipulation by a client object.

- OLE and Automation may be combined within an object. There is no restriction on an object only supporting one technology.

- The **IDispatch** interface signals an Automation server.

- Automation is a ubiquitous feature of the Microsoft component technology.

APPLYING WHAT YOU'VE LEARNED

The following questions will test your understanding of Automation. The laboratories illustrate Automation with either Visual Basic 5.0 or Access 97 controlling the editing of Word 97, Word 95, or Word 6 .DOC files.

Instant Assessment

1. What is the definition of Automation?

2. What distinguishes Automation from an OLE Document?

3. Explain what a dual interface is.

4. Explain the statement, *being a good OLE client is a requirement for being an OLE Automation application controller.*

5. Explain why Microsoft Visual Basic cannot be an OLE Automation server.

6. Name the three nontrivial tiers of an architecture. Which are candidates for Automation?

7. In what way are business rules primitive?

 concept link   **For answers to the Instant Assessment questions, see Appendix C.**

Lab Exercises

This is where we use Automation to supply intelligence to our objects. The project we pursue in the next series of labs is Automation using a VBA code fragment to edit a Word 6, Word 95, or Word 97 document.

WordBasic is used for editing the Word 6 or Word 95 document, and Object Word is used for the Word 97 document. The required libraries are shown below. Don't mix and match libraries. It does work but there are always complications.

o Word 6.0 Microsoft WordBasic Object Library

o Word 95 Microsoft WordBasic 95 Object Library

o Word 97 Microsoft Word 8.0 Object Library

There are two versions of the VBA for this example. The first uses the WordBasic model, which is 900+ references with no object model. The second example uses the new object model of Word 97. Remember that you can't mix and match Word 97 with either Word 6 or Word 95. Feel free to use the editor of your choice.

The first task is to create the following text in the editor of your choice. I prefer Word 95 for this demonstration. You might save the file under various names such as TEST1.DOC, TEST2.DOC, and TEST3.DOC. This will keep you from having to restore the original files after every Automation example.

This is the text to use in the example, and it is also the file AUTO.DOC in the EXAMPLES\CHAPTER9 folder on your CD-ROM:

Dear Reader,

Thank you for buying this book.

$Author$

The Automation example consists of a small VBA fragment, which modifies the text of the .DOC file. I hope you can see the import of this. VBA may be used to create custom letters that can be tuned to the unique attributes of the target recipient.

The VBA code for Word 6 or Word 95 is shown below. If you have problems, this example can be found in the AUTO.MDB Access 97 database in the EXAMPLES\ CHAPTER9 folder on the CD-ROM or the unit where you have relocated the EXAMPLES folder.

```
Private Sub VBA_Test_Click() ' This line need not be entered
'
'Automation example
'
Dim objWord As Object
DoCmd.Hourglass True
Set objWord = CreateObject("Word.Basic")
With objWord
.FileOpen Name:="E:\IDGEXAMP\AUTO.DOC"
.StartOfDocument
.EditReplace Find:="$Author$", _
Replace:="Bruce T. Prendergast", _
WholeWord:=1, ReplaceOne:=1
.FilePrint ' this may be replaced with a .FileClose 1
End With
Set objWord = Nothing
DoCmd.Hourglass False
```

```
Exit Sub
End Sub' This Line need not be entered.
```

The VBA code for Word 97 using the new object model is:

```
Private Sub Command1_Click() ' This line need not be entered
'
' Word 97 example for search replace
'
Dim MyRange As Object
Dim objWord As Object
Dim MyDoc As Document
Set objWord = CreateObject("Word.application")
objWord.Documents.Add "E:\IDGEXAMP\AUTO.DOC"
Set MyRange = ActiveDocument.Content
With MyRange.Find
.ClearFormatting
.Text = "$Author$"
With .Replacement
.ClearFormatting
.Text = "Bruce T. Prendergast"
End With
.Execute Replace:=wdReplaceAll, _
Format:=True, MatchCase:=True, MatchWholeWord:=True
End With
ActiveDocument.SaveAs "E:\idgch1ex\test1.doc"
ActiveDocument.Close
Set MyRange = Nothing
Set objWord = Nothing
Exit Sub
End Sub   ' This line need not be entered
```

Lab 9.22 *Visual Basic 5.0 and Automation with WordBasic*

Our first victim is Visual Basic 5.0.

MCSD
WA I

1. Open Visual Basic 5.0 and place a command button on a form. If the toolbox isn't present then select **Toolbox** from the **View** menu.
2. Select a command button in the toolbox and paint it on the form.

3. Double-click the command button that displays the VBA editing environment.

4. Enter the code illustrated above for Word 6 or Word 95. You'll have to adjust the location of the .DOC file. The original AUTO.DOC file is in your EXAMPLES\CHAPTER9 folder.

Before running the application, select **Project ⇒ References** and verify that either the Microsoft WordBasic Object Library for Word 6 or the Microsoft WordBasic 95 Object Library is selected.

5. After the text is entered in the command button, click **Event** and select **Start With Full Compile** from the **Run** menu. **Option Explicit** was not used because this is a very small application. Every nontrivial form and every module should have the **Option Explicit** statement which catches spelling errors.

6. Go to either Word 6 or Word 95 and verify your results.

```
Private Sub Command1_Click()
DoCmd.Hourglass True
Dim objWord As Object
Set objWord = CreateObject("Word.Basic")
With objWord
.FileOpen Name:="E:\IDGEXAMP\AUTO.DOC"
.StartOfDocument
.EditReplace Find:="$Author$", _
Replace:="Bruce T. Prendergast", _
WholeWord:=1, ReplaceOne:=1
.FileClose 1
End With
Set objWord = Nothing
DoCmd.Hourglass False
Exit Sub
End Sub
```

Lab 9.23 *Visual Basic 5.0 and Automation with Object Word 97*

WA I

1. Open Visual Basic 5.0 and place a command button on the form. If the toolbox isn't present then select **Toolbox** from the **View** menu.

2. Select a command button in the toolbox and paint it on the form.

3. Double-click the command button that displays the VBA editing environment.

4. Enter the code illustrated for Word 97 above. (It is not necessary to enter the first and last lines of the sample VBA text.)

Before running the application, select **Project ⇒ References** and verify that the Microsoft Word 8.0 Object Library is selected. This is a different library than the one we used for the WordBasic model.

5. After the text is entered in the command button click **Event**, select **Start With Full Compile** from the **Run** menu. **Option Explicit** was not used because this is a very small application. Every form and every module should have the **Option Explicit** statement which catches spelling errors.

6. Go to Word 97 and verify your results.

Lab 9.24 *Access 97 and Automation with WordBasic or Object Word*

WA I

Repeat the same exercise as in Lab 9.23 for Access 97 (remember to use the right library), then follow these steps:

1. Start Access 97 and create a blank form. (Ascertain that the Toolbox Wizard is *Off* on the toolbox.)

2. Select a command button and paint it on the form.

3. Select **Event ⇒ Code Builder** from the properties window.

4. Enter the appropriate WordBasic or Object Word VBA code and test it.

5. While in the VBA editor, verify the proper libraries by selecting **References** from the **Tools** menu.

6. Run the code and test it.

Windows Architecture I

OLE Controls: Using It All (Well, Almost!)

About Chapter 10

This chapter is the culmination of component technology. We started in Chapter 1 with intertask/intratask communications issues. Subsequent chapters added new technology, while building on the technology of previous chapters. Chapter 7 saw us use the COM infrastructure for linking OLE Documents. Remember that an OLE Document is a COM object that supports linking or embedding. Additional pieces came together in Chapter 8 with embedded documents and in-place activation. A somewhat disjointed technology named Automation appeared in Chapter 9. Automation technology is based on COM but does not support linking or embedding.

This chapter is about OLE Controls. They represent all the technologies we've discussed so far, including Automation, except for linking. (Controls do not support linking.) This chapter adds the two missing OLE Control features: properties and events.

OLE CONTROLS

OLE Controls are the next logical extension of COM. Microsoft introduced the first *OLE Custom Control (OCX)* in 1994 when the Windows architecture was undergoing an upgrade to the 32-bit model. Microsoft Visual Basic 3.0 was quite successful with the *Visual Basic custom control (VBX)*; however, it was only 16 bits and conversion to 32 bits was not simple. An additional requirement for the Windows architecture upgrade was that any replacement for a VBX must not be limited to only Visual Basic. These factors spawned the OLE Control, which is 32 bits, not specific to any Microsoft tool, and Unicode-compliant.

To this point, COM supported OLE Documents with linking and embedding and OLE Automation or Automation. A COM component did not yet support its own interface. Automation was a one-way dialog. An application controller manipulates exposed methods of a server. This is adequate for simple problems. What was needed is functionality that exposes both incoming and outgoing interfaces. The roots of this functionality begin with **IAdviseSink**, which is a one-way dialog. A successor to this interface is connectable objects that use the **IConnectionPoint** interface. This interface goes beyond a two-way dialog by supporting event sets, the enumeration of interface identifiers (IIDs) (available functionality), the ability to connect and disconnect advisory sinks, and the ability to enumerate connections to a particular outgoing interface. (By the way, this interface is the workhorse of Microsoft Visual InterDev, which is the new Internet development tool.)

The COM model used for OLE Documents and OLE Automation did not have a model for properties. Properties were exposed by an Automation virtual table (vtable), but there was no logical model. OLE Controls needed a standard for specifying their own interface. They also needed a generalized way of handling properties. To this point, properties were accessed with a **DISPID**, which is implementation-specific. Figure 10-1 is a dual **IDispatch** interface with the property **IsWriting**. **IDispatch::Invoke** recognizes the entry as a property when a flag is set. The **IDispatch::Invoke** method supports these flags:

- **DISPATCH_METHOD** — The referenced element is a method. Both this flag and the **DISPATCH_PROPERTYGET** flag may be set when a property has the same name.

- **DISPATCH_PROPERTYGET** — The referenced element is retrieved as a property or data member.

- **DISPATCH_PROPERTYPUT** — The referenced element is changed as a property or data member.

- **DISPATCH_PROPERTYPUTREF** — Changes to the referenced element are by reference rather than value assignment. Only valid when the property accepts a reference to an object.

The other missing element is events. An event is a notification of a state change in a property. Common events in the Visual tools are **On_Click**, **On_LostFocus**, and **On_Change**. The solution here is definitional. Methods exist and objects have both incoming and outgoing interfaces. An event is an invoked method that creates an outgoing message to a waiting advisory sink.

Rename a few things, use everything we've developed so far, and add a model for property pages and you have an OLE Control. OLE Controls are considered the pinnacle of COM technology. OLE Controls don't quite use all the technology we've developed — they support embedding but not linking.

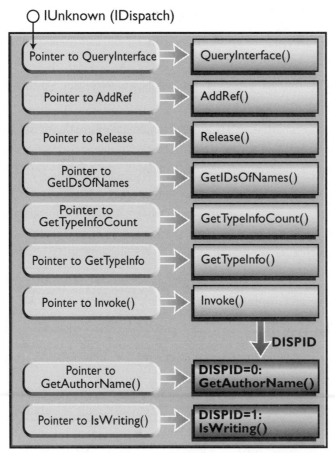

○ IUnknown (IDispatch)

Pointer to QueryInterface	QueryInterface()
Pointer to AddRef	AddRef()
Pointer to Release	Release()
Pointer to GetIDsOfNames	GetIDsOfNames()
Pointer to GetTypeInfoCount	GetTypeInfoCount()
Pointer to GetTypeInfo	GetTypeInfo()
Pointer to Invoke()	Invoke()

↓DISPID

Pointer to GetAuthorName()	DISPID=0: GetAuthorName()
Pointer to IsWriting()	DISPID=1: IsWriting()

FIGURE 10-1   A dual IDispatch interface with a property.

OLE Features

The original OLE Control specification permitted a control to maintain its own interface, send events to a control container, let a container set properties, and negotiate interfaces. An OLE Control adds several new interfaces to COM, which makes it a superset of the COM interfaces discussed thus far. An OLE Control can be used as an Automation object or as a data source for compound document control.

OLE Controls can be created by Microsoft C++ or Microsoft Visual Basic starting with version 4.0. Microsoft Access, Microsoft Visual Basic, and Microsoft Internet Explorer are the popular COM containers for OLE Controls. The nominal OLE Control implementation is as an in-process server.

Features of the OLE Control using the COM model include:

- Events that are fired by the control. This is the control accessing a method of the control container.

- OLE Controls that are 32-bit Unicode-based. (Note that Unicode is expensive in terms of memory.)

- Ambient Properties. These are environmental properties of the container and the control adapts to these properties to interface seamlessly. An example is the default background color.

- Extended Properties. The control may support extended properties such as position, size, layout, or automatic headers and footers for displayed pages. There is no limit on these properties and they are specific to the implementation.

- An OCX supports object embedding and Automation, but not linking.

OLE Benefits

The benefits of OLE Controls (OCX) include the following:

- OLE Controls are not limited to only Visual Basic as are VBXs.

- OLE Controls are easier to develop than a VBX. This is certainly demonstrated in Visual Basic 5.0.

- An OCX uses the COM model. This means that emulation or conversion is supported. A control can emulate an earlier version, or an older version can be upgraded.

- An OLE Control promotes reusable software, in that it is a component and may be "plugged-in." The component can be an off-the-shelf or custom-developed.

OLE Controls are transparent to the user. An OLE Control starts with inside-out activation, while an OLE Document always starts with outside-in activation. Inside-out activation means the control is integrated seamlessly with the container and is activated by only one click of the mouse button versus the double-click required for in-place activation.

OLE Controls Interface Architecture

This is a book on Microsoft architecture and as such, it is not my intent to make you conversant with every COM interface. You should recognize most of the interfaces illustrated in Figure 10-2, but here we'll only look at the interfaces for properties. This is new technology for a control — everything else is refried beans.

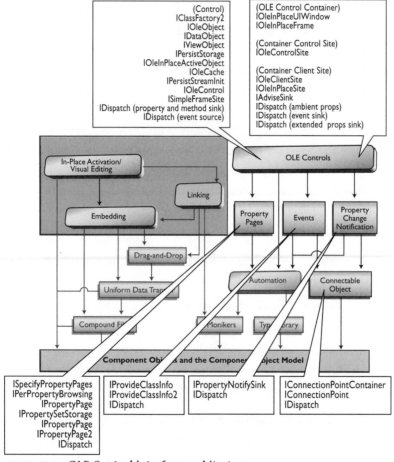

FIGURE 10-2   OLE Control interface architecture.

Figure 10-2 is the road map for this chapter. As you can see, OLE Controls use nearly all of COM. There are a few new ones that we'll discuss shortly. The interfaces indicated by the captions at the top of Figure 10-2 represent the cumulative technology discussed through and including Chapter 8.

At the bottom of Figure 10-2 are the **IConnectionPointContainer** and **IConnectionPoint** interfaces that were both discussed previously in this chapter. Connectable objects are used extensively with OLE Controls. Properties and events are the remaining OLE Control technologies not discussed thus far. We start now with properties.

OLE Control Properties

Properties are a feature new to OLE Controls. A control may not have properties, however, the majority of the new interfaces shown in Figure 10-2 concern properties. Properties existed in the COM model before OLE Controls, but the design was not formalized. The COM model updated for OLE Controls provides a complete protocol for managing properties and property pages of an OLE Control. Figure 10-3 is a closer look at the details of property page communication. (You might want to review the **IPersistPropertyBag** interface covered in Chapter 4.)

There is a missing link in Figure 10-3. The missing interface is the persistent storage implementation and the developer of an OLE Control has several persistent storage options. The following list outlines the persistent storage choices for the developer, which are also the persistent storage choices indicated in Figure 10-3:

o Implement the **IPropertyStorage** interface for a single property to a file implementation.

o Implement the **IPropertySetStorage** interface for a group of properties to a file implementation.

o Create or use a compound file implementation with **StgCreateDocFile** or **StgOpenStorage** (see Chapter 4). **IStorage::QueryInterface** is interrogated for **IPropertySetStorage** once this is accomplished.

exam preparation pointer

Questions on the Windows Architecture I test concern creating or using a compound file implementation with StgCreateDocFile or StgOpenStorage. Review very carefully the IPersistStream and IPersistStorage interfaces.

o Implement the **IPropertyBag** interface (see Chapter 4). The container implements this interface which the object interfaces.

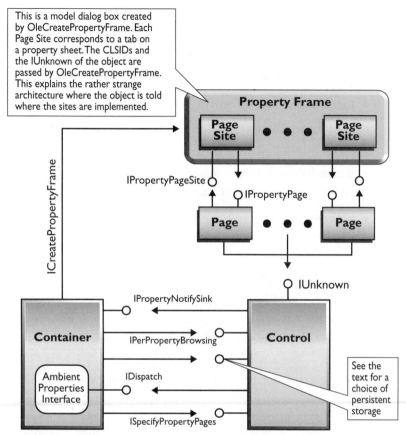

This is a model dialog box created by OleCreatePropertyFrame. Each Page Site corresponds to a tab on a property sheet. The CLSIDs and the IUnknown of the object are passed by OleCreatePropertyFrame. This explains the rather strange architecture where the object is told where the sites are implemented.

Property Frame

Page Site ● ● ● Page Site

ICreatePropertyFrame

IPropertyPageSite ○

○ IPropertyPage

Page ● ● ● Page

○ IUnknown

IPropertyNotifySink

Container

IPerPropertyBrowsing

Control

Ambient Properties Interface

IDispatch

ISpecifyPropertyPages

See the text for a choice of persistent storage

FIGURE 10-3   Control property pages with a displayed property page.

ISpecifyPropertyPages

ISpecifyPropertyPages is the elementary property interface. Its existence signals that the control supports properties. This interface implements all methods of **IUnknown** and implements the method **GetPages**. This method returns all CLSIDs that this object wants displayed.

An object signals its ability to interact with one or more property pages by implementing this interface. **ISpecifyPropertyPages::GetPages** returns a counted array of CLSIDs to the client that collectively describes the property pages that the object wants displayed. This interface and the **IPropertyPage**, **IPropertyPageSite**, and **ISpecifyPropertyPages** interfaces collectively manage property pages as shown in Figure 10-3. All of the functionality described here, enables properties to be worked within a page on an object-by-object basis along with property frames.

IPerPropertyBrowsing

Property pages of an object can be accessed with the **IPerPropertyBrowsing** interface. This interface is required for all objects that a client can browse. This interface supports all methods of **IUnknown** and implements the following:

- **GetDisplayString** — Returns a text description of the specified property.
- **MapPropertyToPage** — Returns the CLSID of the property page for property manipulation.
- **GetPredefinedStrings** — Returns a pointer array that can be used by **IPerPropertyBrowsing::GetPredefinedValue**.
- **GetPredefinedValue** — Returns a value based on a pointer returned by **IPerPropertyBrowsing::GetPredefinedString**.

IPropertyNotifySink

The **IPropertyNotifySink** interface is implemented on the control container and accepts property change notifications from the OLE Control. The object is required to call **IPropertyNotifySink** for only those properties marked with the **Bindable** or **RequestEdit** attributes in the object's type information. When properties are so marked, the control will call **IPropertyNotifySink::OnChanged** whenever a change occurs or will call **IPropertyNotifySink::OnRequestEdit** whenever an edit request occurs. The exception to these rules is object initialization and object loading time. This interface inherits all methods of **IUnknown** and these are the only two methods of **IPropertyNotifySink**.

IPropertyPage

The in-process object implements this interface to the actual property page. A different property page object is required for each unique property page within a property sheet. It is through this interface that the property frame supplies the necessary commands and information to each property page in the sheet. The sequence of events for Figure 10-3 starts with **OleCreatePropertyFrame** creating a modal dialog, and then attempting to instantiate and initialize the property page using the supplied CLSIDs. (**IOleCreatePropertyFrameIndirect** performs the same type of function and is not illustrated.) A properly managed dialog box (modal) should only display controls for those properties defined within the property sheet. The page should have the Windows style **WS_CHILD**; it should not have a style related to a frame, caption, system menus, or controls.

IPropertyPage implements all methods of **IUnknown** and implements the following:

- **SetPageSite** — Initializes a property page and provides the page with a pointer to the **IPropertyPageSite** interface. The interface is used for property frame communication.

- **Activate** — Creates the dialog box window for the property page.

- **Deactivate** — Destroys the window created with Activate.

- **GetPageInfo** — Returns a PROPPAGEINFO structure with property information.

- **SetObjects** — Provides an array of the **IUnknown** pointers of the objects affected by the property sheet in which this property page must be displayed.

- **Show** — Makes the property dialog box visible or invisible.

- **Move** — Resizes and repositions the property page dialog box with the frame.

- **IsPageDirty** — Indicates whether the page has changed since the last activation.

- **Apply** — Applies current property page values to underlying objects specified through **SetObjects**.

- **Help** — Invokes help in response to a user request.

- **TranslateAccelerator** — Provides a pointer to a MSG structure for keystroke translation.

IPropertyPage2

IPropertyPage2 is an extension of **IPropertyPage** that tells the page which property to highlight or to receive focus when the page is activated. The interface implements all methods of **IUnknown**, **IPropertyPage**, and the method **EditProperty**, which identifies the property to receive focus when the page is activated.

IPropertyPageSite

IPropertyPageSite is the last of the property page interfaces. It is the interface that provides the main features for a property site object. A property page site is created for each property page within the property frame. The property page site stores some state global data and this interface provides access to that data for all property pages. The interface receives notifications when changes occur from the page through **IPropertyPageSite::OnStatusChange**. The frame in turn initiates a call to **IPropertyPage::IsPageDirty** when a change occurs. The return value is then used to either enable or disable the frame's apply button. Initially, the button is disabled.

IPropertyPageSite supports all methods of **IUnknown** and implements:

- **OnStatusChange** — Called when the user has changed property values on the property page.

- **GetLocaleID** — Returns the locale identifier. The property pages are then adjusted to the country-specific setting.

- **GetPageContainer** — The IUnknown pointer for the object representing the entire property frame dialog box is returned. This object contains all the property pages.

- **TranslateAccelerator** — Passes a keystroke to the property frame.

DISTRIBUTED COM

Microsoft delivered Distributed COM (DCOM) with Windows NT 4.0. Recall the proxy and stub used for marshaling and the **IMarshal** interface. These interfaces were on the same machine and used *Local Procedure Calls* (LPC), which communicate between different processes on the same machine. Figure 1-15 from Chapter 1 is updated below in Figure 10-4 with DCOM protocols. This change is transparent to the client and the only difference will be the response time of an RPC as compared to an LPC.

DCOM is just one step of a long road down which Microsoft would like to lead us. The first step was Remote Automation. DCOM is the second step. Parallel to the second step is the Distributed Transaction Coordinator of Microsoft SQL Server. The third step is the Microsoft Transaction Server 1.0, and shortly after you see this book at your local bookstore, Microsoft will start shipping Transaction Server Version 2.0.

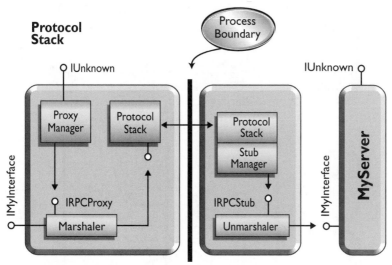

FIGURE 10-4   Marshaling is transparent to the client.

DCOM Benefits

Distributed COM was first shipped with Windows NT 4.0 and promises to revolutionize distributed applications. Before DCOM, scaling an application was always increasing the database server size. DCOM changes the architecture where scaling an application is distributing additional components and not necessarily increasing the size of the database server.

DCOM is scalable

Objects are added as requirements change. Monolithic applications are not scaleable except to the extent of purchasing a significantly larger, and certainly a much more expensive, computer. The first step in distributing an application is to decompose it into generic scaleable components. Figure 10-5 represents a monolithic application; Figure 10-6 illustrates the decomposition and distribution of the application.

Scaling an application can result in a bottleneck. I've anticipated that with the architecture of Figure 10-6 where there are two database servers. I assume these are Microsoft SQL Servers that can be synchronized with replication, or that a roll-up function can be used periodically. This basic strategy is valid for corporate roll-up from regional offices.

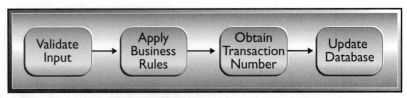

FIGURE 10-5   A monolithic application.

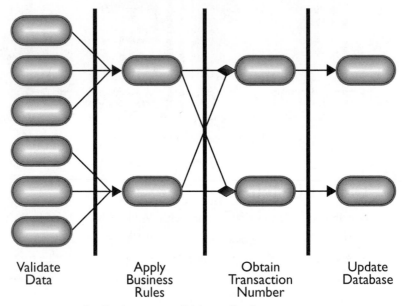

Validate   Apply   Obtain   Update
Data   Business   Transaction   Database
                  Rules   Number

FIGURE 10-6   Distributing a monolithic application.

Placing COM components in an architecture is not enough. The generic functions of Figure 10-6 make sense; however, the success of using DCOM for Remote Automation depends upon the function. An opportunity to use a DCOM component is the remote generation of a report. The client can control report generation without passing the data down the wire to the client. The key question to ask before distributing a component is: "Will distributing this component cause a bottleneck or increase processing costs?"

Interaction rates, dispersion, and component size are issues to consider when creating a distributed architecture. A high interaction rate dictates a local component that is best implemented as an in-process server.

Component size may reduce the flexibility of deployment. The component may not be large when compared with a monolithic application, but ease and speed of deployment are essential. Remember that components are not anchored to a particular system — the deployment costs should be considered. The last issue is that smaller components increase network traffic. Validation of data and business rules could be combined in Figure 10-6; however, the choice is specific to the problem at hand.

DCOM is language neutral

The components in Figure 10-6 are also not restricted to any particular tool. DCOM components developed on Digital Equipment Corporation's OpenVMS in either BLISS or C/C++ can be used by components that are WinTel-based. DCOM is based on the COM model, which is a binary specification and thus, language-independent.

Local components on a WinTel system are developed with the preferred tool of choice. Initial DCOM objects are first implemented in Visual Basic for a proof of concept. Formal implementation is done at a later date in either C++ or Java to take advantage of DCOM's free-threading/multithreading and thread pooling.

DCOM is efficiently managed

The DCOM architecture requires a periodic keep-alive message from the client. Client keep-alive messages are pooled to preserve bandwidth and they are also piggybacked on other messages. As do all COM objects, DCOM objects have a reference count. The component will be released in three *ping* cycles when the client doesn't respond. Garbage collection is automatic.

A BINARY MASS DOES NOT CONTAIN COMPONENTS

I recently received a brochure from Digital Equipment Corporation extolling the virtues of a new FORTRAN 90 compiler. This compiler generates code for Windows 95, Windows NT, UNIX, or OpenVMS. I thought about it for a few moments and realized that legacy software has something of value that we've all overlooked. Microsoft has been so busy making systems easy to use for individuals who shouldn't have a system, that they have overlooked some very important factors. A vice president of Microsoft was recently promising to make software *as reliable as mainframe software*. I say Microsoft can't make it happen. The concept of a binary mass, which is immutable over time, is what makes legacy software reliable. Both FORTRAN and COBOL create immutable binary masses, which is compiled and linked code without components (see Chapter 33).

DCOM Components and Reuse

Microsoft promotes the reuse of COM components. True, the COM client has a contract with an interface, but the factors are complex. I don't accept Microsoft's position on the reusability of software. Their own delivery of new releases of Microsoft Office is a case in point. Microsoft demonstrates new products and new versions, but always with new data.

I was at an SQL summit several weeks ago. The Microsoft representative did some rather dazzling tricks, but it was all with new data he created. Microsoft is legendary in not supporting older versions. Software may be able to be salvaged at the internal component level, but Microsoft doesn't let us salvage anything. Yes, software may be salvaged at a very low level, but, the bottom line is cost to the consumer. I can't translate the supposedly reusability with attendant reduced costs of COM to the bottom line of a balance sheet. I see the forced conversions and the lack of support for prior versions as actually costing the client.

As a result, we are forced into conversion efforts we don't necessarily want. My preferred system of choice is Windows NT 3.51 Workstation with service pack (sp) 5. I consider it reliable. I became very suspicious of Windows NT 4.0 when I learned that the printer and display GDI drivers were moved into the kernel. This now makes Windows NT 4.x vulnerable to third-party drivers. My suspicions were confirmed with sp2 for Windows NT, which created chaos. Unfortunately, the cure was worse than the problem. Microsoft corrected sp2 problems with sp3 in time for us to create an Internet Web site in Chapter 37.

To restate the paragraph, yes there is reuse of DCOM components. However, the benefit of reusing DCOM components is offset with infrastructure and conversion costs at a level different than the DCOM component. The real picture should be examined from the perspective of the total cost of ownership, and not the cost saved by reusing individual components.

In my opinion, component software has significantly increased software costs. Building a component architecture increases two abstract software-engineering terms. The first is program volume and your application volume now consists of all numerable components in the architecture. Increased program volume is related to software errors, or what is euphemistically called *bugs*. The component application has potential failure rates that can be orders of magnitude greater that a compiled and linked binary mass.

Program complexity also increases in a component technology. A more pedestrian view is that a chain is no stronger than the weakest link. It is intuitively apparent to me, and hopefully to you, my reader, that as program complexity increases, so does the failure rate.

ActiveX

Microsoft renames technologies on a regular basis. Microsoft first attached the name OLE to almost all technologies that used the earlier COM model. (MAPI is one notable exception.) Microsoft then concluded that it must have a new name for COM technology used with an Internet or Intranet. Hence, the name *ActiveX*.

ActiveX is nothing new. It is all the COM technology discussed thus far in this book. Yes, it contains additional technology that I haven't discussed, and other technology that evolved after the rite of passage. The technology was evolving independent of the name change. I reason that we would still have the same technology today, even without a name change. Microsoft, however, compartmentalize COM technology a bit better with ActiveX. Linking and embedding, or what was known as OLE Documents, is now known as OLE technology. So an OLE Control is really an ActiveX control. Most of you should be familiar with the aliasing of an API function. Microsoft marketing is just aliasing a technology.

ActiveX Performance Enhancements

The Internet has helped us all, even indirectly when we don't use it. Before the Internet, component technology was OLE with OLE Automation, OLE Controls, and OLE Compound Documents. Each of these technologies suffered from the same affliction: code bloat. The advent of the Internet forced Microsoft to rethink COM, which resulted in a reduced footprint and performance enhancements. However, Microsoft may be going too far. Now I think they are afflicted with *hammeritis*, which is to give someone a hammer and everything becomes a nail. If Microsoft has it their way, everything will be a COM object. On second thought, maybe they're afflicted by *COMitis*.

Okay, I'm off my soapbox for now. Let's take a look at what I consider the neat stuff: all the enhancements to COM that came about as a result of trying to use an OLE Control on the Web. Those issues discussed previously will just be mentioned. The performance enhancements discussed here are outlined in the Microsoft document, *ActiveX Controls 96*. This white paper is found in the OC96 directory of the Microsoft ActiveX Development Kit published by the Microsoft Developer Network (MSDN).

Many of the interfaces briefly mentioned below were discussed previously within the context of a COM Document. They are mentioned briefly here, as they are also used in an OLE Control. You'll find references to earlier material for each of the previously introduced interfaces.

IPointerInactive

The Internet forced some rather nice performance improvements, and this is one of them. The **IPointerInactive** interface is new and permits drag-and-drop operations for inactive objects. Minimizing the active object count results in an obvious performance boost. The interface is implemented by giving intelligence to the activation process. OLE 2.0 has only two states: active and inactive, and that isn't enough for drag-and-drop operations over inactive objects.

The **IPointerInactive** interface removes the need for controls to be activated when visible. It is now the responsibility of the container to forward all mouse movements to controls which must conform to the OCX96/ActiveX Controls 96 specification. This reduced the considerable overhead of activating all of the visible controls when loading forms. Inactive controls still need some way of interacting with the user. For example, a control might want to act as the drop target, or respond to the mouse, but being inactive prevents them from doing this, as they have no window. **IPointInactive** provides this capability.

This interface uses the COM library definition:

```
#define OLEMISC_IGNOREACTIVATEWHENVISIBLE . . .
```

The importance of this definition is that an object with this flag set, assuming, of course, that the container understands the flag and uses **IPointInactive**, should ignore the flag OLEMISC_ACTIVEWHENVISIBLE and not do in-place activation when the object becomes visible. The object itself determines when in-place activation should occur.

IPointInactive inherits all methods of **IUnknown** and implements the following:

- **GetActivationPolicy** — Returns the present activation policy for the object. Occurs when the mouse is over the object. The object may or may not request activation.
- **OnInactiveSetCursor** — Called by the container for the inactive object under the mouse pointer. This occurs with the receipt of a WM_SETCURSOR message.
- **OnInactiveMouseMove** — Indicates to an inactive object that the mouse pointer is over the object.

IViewObject::Draw

The **IViewObject** interface was presented in Chapter 6, as the companion to **IDataObject**. **IViewObject** renders the data presentation while **IDataObject** manages the data. These comments here are specific to only one method of the **IViewObject** interface. This is not to imply that **Draw** is the only method of **IViewObject**, but that the *ActiveX Controls 96* specification optimizes the **Draw** method. The net result of the enhancement is to reduce the unnecessary selecting and deselecting of the font, brush, and pen when rendering an object. OLE 2 has the restriction that all GDI objects selected into the hDC passed to **IViewObject::Draw** be deselected before returning. The problem is solved with the **DVASPECTINFO** structure passed as a parameter to **IViewObject::Draw**.

IViewObjectEx and IOleInPlaceSiteEx

The **IViewObjectEx** and **IOleInPlaceSiteEx** interfaces were discussed previously. **IViewObjectEx** was discussed in Chapter 6, while **IOIleInPlaceSiteEx** is discussed in Chapter 8. The changes promote a flicker-free environment. Changes were also made to **IViewObjectEx** to support non-rectangular objects.

IOleInPlaceSiteWindowless and IOleInPlaceObjectWindowless

These interfaces were discussed in Chapter 8. Both of these interfaces are derived from **IOleInPlaceSiteEx**. They enable an object to be windowless and use the services of the container. The net result is small, irregular objects that can be transparent and irregular. It also enables an object to draw itself when active.

IQuickActivate

This is a new interface for minimizing the overhead of loading a control into a container. The net result is the combining of the load-time and initialization-time handshaking into one call. Reducing the handshaking process down to the one call is accomplished with the **QACONTAINER** structure with default parameters based on other controls.

Before the **IQuickActivate** interface, the process of activating a control was a serialized process involving calls to **QueryInterface** and the container's **IDispatch** interface. Activating a control can be reduced to one call when the control supports the **IQuickActivate** interface. A container that supports quick activation queries a control for the **IQuickActivate** interface. When this interface exists, the container fills up a QACONTAINER structure with pointers to the key interfaces needed by the control and calls **IQuickActivate::QuickActivate**.

IQuickActivate inherits all methods of **IUnknown** and implements:

- **QuickActivate** — The QACONTAINER structure is passed to the method. In return, the control supplies required parameters in QACONTROL.
- **SetControlExtent** — Called by the container to set the control extent.
- **GetControlExtent** — Called by the container to get the control extent.

IOleUndoManager

The **IOleUndoManager** interface is not necessarily a performance issue, however Microsoft enhanced the COM model to implement multilevel undo and redo. These actions also incorporate undo actions performed on contained controls. These changes incorporate three new interfaces and an undo manager is required because of the complexity.

Undo information is saved on a stack. Not everything can be restored when the stack is not large enough. The only objects contributing to the undo stack are the active objects with a user interface. Windowless objects and inactive objects do not participate in the undo process.

IOleUndoManager inherits all methods of **IUnknown** and implements:

- **Open** — This is equivalent to **IOleParentUndoUnit::Open**. The undo manager is opened.

- **Close** — This is equivalent to **IOleParentUndoUnit::Close**. The undo manager is closed.

- **Add** — This is equivalent to **IOleParentUndoUnit::Add**. The undo manager places the unit on the undo stack and discards the entire redo stack when it is the base state. The undo manager places new items in the undo stack when in the undo mode and new units on the redo stack when in redo mode.

- **GetOpenParentState** — Returns false on no open parent, otherwise it delegates the open unit's GetParentMethod.

- **DiscardFrom** — Discards the specified undo item and all other undo items below in the undo stack. The undo manager must first search the undo stack for the item with **IOleParentUndoUnit::FindUnit**.

- **UndoTo** — The undo manager is instructed to perform undo actions down to and including a specified undo unit.

- **RedoTo** — The undo manager is instructed to perform redo actions down to and including a specified redo unit.

- **EnumUndoable** — Enumerates the top-level units in the undo stack.

- **EnumRedoable** — Enumerates the top-level units in the redo stack.

- **GetLastUndoDescription** — Fetches the description from the top of the undo stack.

- **GetLastRedoDescription** — Fetches the description from the top of the redo stack.

- **Enable** — Used by the container to enable or disable the undo manager. Useful for objects that does not support multilevel undo operations.

IOleUndoUnit

The undo unit is responsible for undo or redo operations. When there is no undo manager, the **IOleUndoUnit** performs the undo or redo directly, and nothing is placed on either stack. The converse is true when the undo manager exists, and the undo or redo unit is placed on the appropriate stack.

IOleUndoUnit inherits all methods of **IUnknown** and implements:

- **Do** — The undo unit has the responsibility of placing itself on the property stack. This occurs by calling **IOleUndoManager::Open** or **IOleUndoManager::Add**. The state of the undo unit determines the stack that will be used. Parent units should place themselves on the appropriate undo or redo stack before calling this method for their children.

- **GetDescription** — Fetches the description of the undo unit. The caller must release this string and all units are required to provide a user-readable description.

- **GetUnitType** — Determines whether special handling is required. The CLSID and the type ID must uniquely identify the unit.

- **OnNextAdd** — A parent notifies the last undo unit that a new undo unit has been added.

IOleParentUndoUnit

The **IOleParentUndoUnit** interface is supported by units that are capable of containing other units. It inherits all methods of **IUnknown** and **IOleUndoUnit** and implements:

- **Open** — Creates a new parent undo unit. The stack is left open and new units are passed to the stack until it is closed.

- **Close** — The most recent undo unit is closed. An optional parameter is provided for closing the stack.

- **Add** — The undo manager or the parent undo unit must accept any undo unit passed. Blocking is the only exception to this rule.

- **GetParentState** — Returns state information on the inner most open parent undo unit.

- **FindUnit** — Normally called by the undo manager to locate an undo unit. The parent looks in its own list first. When the unit isn't found, a delegation is done to each child that is a parent. A child is designated as a parent if the interface **IOleParentUndoUnit** is found with **QueryInterface**.

My general observations are that Microsoft has added a little too much complexity here. If I change the foreground color and some other attributes of a control, I would expect to reset them myself. Common implementations of software typically provide a reset to installation defaults. This is probably not possible when the control you'll use 15 minutes from now hasn't been downloaded from the Web yet. I am sure they'll provide a good rationale for this feature; however, it adds to the overall application complexity and I'm not convinced it is needed.

ICategorizeProperties

ICategorizeProperties is one of the nicer features on the improvements Microsoft made for controls. This is a control interface that returns the categories of properties supported by the control. Containers can now determine which properties are not supported. I've listed the standard categories below; however, because this is a specification, I'm sure the list is augmented.

```
#define PROPCAT_Nil -1
#define PROPCAT_Misc -2
#define PROPCAT_Font -3
#define PROPCAT_Position -4
#define PROPCAT_Appearance -5
#define PROPCAT_Behavior -6
#define PROPCAT_Data -7
#define PROPCAT_List -8
#define PROPCAT_Text -9
#define PROPCAT_Scale -10
#define PROPCAT_DDE -11
```

ICategorizeProperties inherits all methods of **IUnknown** and implements:

- **MapPropertyToCategory** — Returns the category ID for the passed DISPID.
- **GetCategoryName** — Returns the text name of the requested category.

CoGetClassObjectFromURL

Component technology is quickly drawing to a close. This COM library function, while not a performance enhancement, is the workhorse of Internet downloads. The Internet Download Component architecture is illustrated in Figure 10-7.

FIGURE 10-7   Internet download component architecture.

 **concept link**   **URL Moniker** in Figure 10-7 is the URL implementation of **IMoniker**, which was discussed previously in Chapter 5.

CoGetClassObjectFromURL does everything necessary to download and install a new component. Microsoft Internet Explorer uses this code when it encounters a CODEBASE attribute inside an OBJECT tag. **CoGetClassObjectFromURL** uses the **IBindStatusCallBack** interface for communication with the client. **CoGetClassObjectFromURL** returns an **IClassFactory** object for a CLSID. When no CLSID is given, it interprets the Internet MIME type stored in *szContentType,* an argument to **CoGetClassObjectFromURL**.

An existing object is instantiated by **CoGetClassObjectFromURL**. New objects are downloaded from *szCodeURL,* an argument to **CoGetClassObjectFromURL** or from an Object Store on the Internet Search Path.

 concept link   The **CoGetClassObjectFromURL** is presented here in the context of COM. This material is presented again in the context of the Internet in Chapter 39.

CoGetClassObjectFromURL performs the following functions:

- Downloads the appropriate files which may be .CAB, .INF, or .EXE using URL Monikers.
- Calls **WinVerifyTrust()** to verify that all downloaded components are safe to install.
- Ascertains the self-registration of all COM components.
- Adds Registry entries to track downloaded code.
- Calls **CoGetClassObject** for the desired CLSID.

ICodeInstall

All clients of **CoGetClassObjectFromURL** must declare this interface. It provides a window for displaying the user verification of downloaded code. **IBindStatusCallback::QueryInterface** requests the **ICodeInstall** interface during the binding setup.

    ICodeInstall inherits all methods of **IUnknown** and implements:

- **GetWindow** — The Component Download function uses this method for user verification of downloaded code.

- **OnCodeInstallProblem** — This method solicits the client response to a download error.

COMPONENT TECHNOLOGY IN REVIEW

In theory, COM is a dream come true for developers. In reality, the promises are held at bay by uneven implementation problems, created by the increase in application volume and interface complexity.

Poor Reliability

It is true that the COM model reduces interface complexity with a standard interface; however, this reduction in complexity is offset by an increase in the number of interfaces. Microsoft appears to have overlooked some very important software engineering factors. COM increases two programming metrics: application volume and application complexity. Bugs increase as either of these metrics increases, and the increase is not linear! I see a definite deterioration in service levels between Microsoft OfficePro 4.3, Microsoft Office 95, and Microsoft Office 97. The vanilla stuff works great with Microsoft Office 97, but try and do some real work and you are major toast. Microsoft delivered a service pack for Office 97 in late 1997. Word 97 is now usable, but some problems still remain with Object Word. The deterioration in service level for Office 97 still exists.

Forced Upgrades

I got a good dose of this recently when I was running quite well with Microsoft SQL Server 6.0 and Microsoft Access 2.0. (You'll find out shortly that the ODBC

API function **SQLExtendedFetch** when used in a *before Unicode* environment makes ODBCDirect and RDO both look rather anemic.) Recently, I downloaded some goodies from the Microsoft Web site (www.microsoft.com). I tried to use SQL Server 6.0 and Access 2.0 subsequent to this, and to my dismay, the system started regurgitating error messages that my stored procedures were out of date and that I must upgrade to Microsoft SQL Server 6.5. I have Microsoft SQL Server 6.5, but it is installed on another boot and I was trying to preserve this outstanding combination of Access 2.0 and SQL Server 6.0. So much for reusability! The problem is that downloads will install new DLLs. It's Microsoft's policy that a service release is not just to fix bugs, but is a vehicle to implement new features. As long as this is a policy, there can be no software stability. The unfortunate client who needs the service pack to correct a problem will, in all inevitability, host new problems in the *green* code representing the new features.

The COM Contract Doesn't Benefit the Enterprise

Yes, version control works, but it is version control that is forcing an upgrade and not the version control with reusability put out by the Microsoft marketing spin-makers. Microsoft dictates the version you should use, and you have no choice but to upgrade! When the client doesn't upgrade, the software is *orphaned*. An example of orphaned software is that no Windows 3.1 user can use 32-bit tools. That does not help the bottom line of an enterprise. The small gains made with the reusability of software at the interface level does not even begin to offset the expense of implementing the next Microsoft release of a product. Microsoft's theme of software reusability with the COM model is quite hollow where users get no reusability at all at the application level. The reusability of COM is useful to Microsoft developers only, and not the consumers.

Immutability of Applications

There's much more to a system than writing methods behind an interface. It is an issue of strategic planning with software upgrades controlled by the enterprise and not the software vendor. It is deciding when and how to upgrade; not the Microsoft-forced upgrades. A component application, at least in theory, could use a new DLL every day. Of course, it's absurd that such an environment should exist anywhere except at Microsoft, where systems are referenced by build numbers. Your application task changes when a new DLL is installed from a service pack. The component application does not possess the immutability of legacy software where a legacy application changes only when recompiled and relinked by the developer. You install a service pack to repair a problem with your modems and your accounting applications develop a problem.

I believe the maelstrom of software change must slow down and software must become reliable. My thesis is very simple: Production applications and the operating system itself should be a binary mass, at least to the point that it is immutable over time. I discussed this point earlier in the book with a deprecated class. Preserve existing production applications by either deprecating their class or providing each new version release of a product has a new class. That's the way COM works. Each new interface, even if it inherits from another interface, gets a new CLSID. New products versions should have new classes. Why can't Microsoft product releases function in the same manner as COM?

The second issue is that a user should have a choice in protecting an existing technology from *versionitis* and declare it as immutable. I've done that, but my personal system is 131MB with 8GB and many boots where I hide technology from other boots. It shouldn't be this way. I can't continue to keep all prior versions on-line forever. We'll be measuring blips in the sales of disk drives with each new release of a Microsoft product.

Making the operating system immutable to change may not be possible because the basic Microsoft Windows architecture is numerable DLLs, many of which are dependent on other DLLs. I believe the DLL concept is flawed because the concept of a DLL sponsors volatility. I have 20/20 hindsight like everyone else, and it is easy to take issue with concepts. That is an apology, because I am sure a great deal of work was spent on the DLL concept; however the DLL concept is still lacking. Along with the volatility is the fact that DLL use is not controlled. DLLs are used by both the system and applications, and updates to system DLLs are an implied update to an application. At this late date there is really not much that can be done. Commonality of code may have gone too far. A DLL library for the exclusive use of the operating system is the first step in controlling DLL use and insulates the application from operating system upgrades. We don't have that, and volatility is too high. The concept of a DLL library is good to a point. However, the level at which Microsoft creates new software has made the concept of a DLL library very questionable. There are simply too many changes with no stability and everything is co-dependent. It is a maelstrom of change.

In spite of the apparent sales volume, I have no long-term expectations for the Windows architecture. It is too volatile. Mainframes are known to be reliable. The relief may be mainframe servers for thin Java clients. UNIX still remains a viable alternative. If the UNIX camp loses too many sales, they'll retrench and provide a prettier interface, as that is one of the few features which Microsoft offers. Yes, Microsoft has lots of clever software, but none of it is useful unless it is stable, and it is not. I give Microsoft an *A*+ for user interface design and an *C*- for system engineering.

This brings us to the end of component technology. The Open Database Connectivity (ODBC) journey is next. ODBC is the root technology for database access, and we'll explore all the current variations of this outstanding technology. It is the start of the longest journey in the book. Persevere.

KEY POINT SUMMARY

COM technology is not mature. We can't do without it, so we'll have to learn to live with it. Maybe my small voice and the voice of you, my reader, can convince Microsoft that reliability is more important than features. The key points below address the theme of this chapter, that OLE Controls are the pinnacle of COM.

- An ActiveX is an alias for an OLE Control. Microsoft marketing decreed that, henceforth, OLE Controls shall be know as ActiveX controls.

- OLE Controls are the pinnacle of COM technology. They incorporate all prior COM technology except linking. This includes Automation.

- OLE Controls added support for properties and property pages to the COM model.

- Events are a new feature of OLE Controls.

- OLE Controls are 32-bit and support Unicode.

- OLE Controls use inside-out activation because they integrate seamlessly with the container object. This is compared to outside-in activation of an OLE embedded document.

APPLYING WHAT YOU'VE LEARNED

This chapter builds on previously presented COM technology. Key features missing with COM was a formal model for properties. The extensions to COM include new objects that model properties.

The missing ingredient for an OLE Control is the concept of an event. This is definitional because COM already supports methods. Rename specific methods and you have events. Use events with the connectable objects (see Chapter 5), and the picture of an OLE Control is complete. The questions below will test your general understanding of these issues.

Instant Assessment

1. Name a new feature of OLE Controls.

2. OLE Controls are considered the pinnacle of COM technology in that they use nearly all COM features. What key COM feature is missing with OLE Controls?

3. What new feature did OLE Controls bring to the COM model?

4. How are events implemented within OLE Controls?

5. What activation method is used for OLE Controls?

6. Explain how DCOM benefits a credit card application.

7. What is the purpose of the **IPointerInactive** interface?

 concept link   **For answers to the Instant Assessment questions, see Appendix C.**

Lab Exercises

I'm sure you've heard of Java. It is an interpretive tool that "plays in the sandbox." In other words, it cannot write to a client disk. The concept makes Java a desirable tool for Internet access, while ActiveX is a desirable tool for intranet use.

Lab 10.25 *Do you agree with ActiveX for an intranet and Java for the Internet?*

WA I

Evaluate your current LAN and WAN applications as to which technology to use: Java or ActiveX. Your considerations should take into account the nature of the application as well as the operating environment. Windows NT is certainly more secure than Windows 95. Use, as general guidelines, Java for the Internet and ActiveX for an intranet. (We'll revisit these issues when we discuss the Internet in Chapters 36-39.)

○ Start by identifying the required minimal client functionality. Does the client need ActiveX controls? Why isn't HTML satisfactory? Present the minimal reliable functionality. Answer the objections. The resulting system should be a usable compromise. It may not have any ActiveX controls.

○ Is security an issue? ActiveX may have code signing; however, the inherent unreliability of COM obviates the value of code signing.

○ Consider the browsers the clients will use. ActiveX should only be used on an Intranet or with Microsoft Internet Explorer. Yes, there are other browsers out there which are supposed to support ActiveX, but can you be sure they got it right?

○ Impose standards on developers. Force a justification for each ActiveX control. Remember that Microsoft ActiveX controls do not have a standard such as American National Standards Institute (ANSI). Microsoft is free to deprecate any function, feature, or component (see Chapter 39).

Lab 10.26 *Doing it better the second time*

WA I

We now know that a significant amount of logic can be embedded into a control. Microsoft technology, through the use of controls, supports what are known as *Microsoft Active Documents*. This is because the concept of a container object is ubiquitous in the Microsoft architecture. It is possible, for example, to drag a Word document onto Microsoft Internet Explorer. The menu bars merge and the document is now displayed in Internet Explorer.

Lab 10.26 focuses on Microsoft Active Documents and consists of two parts:

○ Make a survey of your Visual Basic standalone applications. If an application creates a document, consider converting the application to a control that supports the concept of Active Documents. The concept is much more intuitive. Rather than providing a filename to a standalone application, drag-and-drop is used to drop a file object onto the newly created control.

○ Make note of common functionality when surveying your Visual Basic applications. Justify creating a control that encapsulates the common functionality.

Database Access Technologies

II

The chapters are presented in order of technological evolution. This part is composed of five sections:

- **Chapters 11-14: Open Database Connectivity (ODBC)** — Access 2.0 is used to present the ODBC API.

- **Chapters 15-23: Data Access Objects (DAO)** — Both Jet and ODBCDirect are presented. ODBCDirect is a descendant of Remote Data Objects (RDO).

- **Chapters 24-26: Remote Data Objects (RDO)** — A database access technology limited to Microsoft Visual Basic Enterprise Edition.

- **Chapters 27-28: SQL Distributed Management Objects (SQL-DMO)** — Automation is used for remote management of Microsoft SQL Server.

- **Chapters 29-32: OLE-DB** — COM is used for the underpinnings of the new pretender to the throne of database connectivity, OLE-DB.

Windows Architecture I

CHAPTER

ODBC

11

About Chapter 11

The chapter begins with a description and a brief history of *Open Database Connectivity* (ODBC). This is followed by a discussion of the ODBC architecture and the different roles played by the ODBC application, the ODBC data source, the ODBC driver manager, the ODBC network software, and the ODBC driver. The chapter closes with a discussion of ODBC benefits.

ODBC: A Database Connectivity Standard

This chapter is quite interesting because it describes the evolution of database connectivity technology and the evolution of Microsoft, the company. ODBC is a base technology, and subsequent database access technologies are wrappers to this technology.

ODBC came about in an era when the primary focus of Microsoft was connectivity between the desktop and the enterprise. The focus has now changed to the Internet. Spin-off technologies for the enterprise, such as corporate intranets, are useful to the enterprise, but corporate needs that do not fit the Internet model are likely to be ignored by Microsoft, as Microsoft's focus remains the Internet and other issues are ancillary to it.

Microsoft's obsession with the Internet influences its software. For example, the focus on the Internet has given Microsoft an "e-mail"-type mentality where result sets from servers are now encapsulated within objects. Encapsulation of data is acceptable when using the Internet; however, using this technology with an AS/400 DB2 database may not be acceptable.

There is a question of where we are and where we're going. ODBC is the first heterogeneous database access technology. It is not the last one. The core ODBC technology evolves through various other database access technologies, and eventually evolves into OLE-DB, which is also a heterogeneous database access technology. ODBC is an open technology while OLE-database (see Chapters 29–32), the new pretender to the throne of database connectivity, is not. ODBC is a charter member of the Windows Open Services Architecture (WOSA), while OLE-DB is the latest member of the new Windows architecture. ODBC 3.0 is certainly an open technology with X/Open and ISO compliance, but OLE-DB is not an open technology; it is a proprietary Microsoft architecture with no published standards.

Structured Query language (SQL) and ODBC are standards for *relational database management system* (RDBMS) connectivity. A feature of ODBC is a common ODBC SQL language.

ODBC is a specification for a database *application programming interface* (API). This specification is independent of any one particular *database management system* (DBMS). The natural consequence of this is that ODBC is a tool for heterogeneous connection of different databases.

The ODBC specification is language-independent, even though the Microsoft ODBC implementation is a C/C++ version. Chapter 14 has examples based on

Visual Basic for Applications (VBA), which improves the readability of the examples. Dependency on the implementation language does present issues, however.

The first issue is that the SQL data type SQL_VARCHAR does not map into a C/C++ data type. The compromise is to declare a variable length string in VBA, preinitialize the string to binary zero, and then declare the data type as SQL_C_CHAR. This is a relatively minor compromise if the maximum string lengths are known. But the fact remains that SQL data types should all map to the underlying data types of the implementation language for ODBC even if it is language-independent.

The second issue is using the ODBC API from VBA. Microsoft says you can do it and publishes examples. The issue is the binding of columns to be used with **SQLExtendedFetch** where the columns are character arrays. The C/C++ implementation is to increment the array address. It is a bit more difficult with VBA, but it can be done. This probably explains why ODBC articles always provide unbound column examples using **SQLGetData**. (See the **SQLExtendedFetch** example in Chapter 14.)

Unicode is the third issue. The *double-byte character set* (DBCS) of Unicode is two bytes. Microsoft publishes techniques for Unicode mapping, but the real problem is that Unicode is not an integrated data type. It is an ad hoc add-on technology that is looking for a problem to solve. It is not needed for communication with legacy databases, which is why ODBC was implemented. Microsoft's zeal in providing Internet technology ignores the fact that bread-and-butter computer systems of corporate America are still COBOL-based. Unicode is a hindrance in communicating with legacy databases.

concept link   **See "Translating the Character Sets" in Chapter 3 for more information about Unicode.**

note   **This chapter reflects the recently released ODBC 3.0 specification. ODBC 3.0 currently meets all X/Open and ISO/IEC Call-Level Interface (CLI) specifications using SQL as its database access language. Prior releases of ODBC were based on preliminary specifications and did not fully implement all features. ODBC 3.0 specifications are a superset of the X/Open CAE Specification, Data Management: SQL Call-Level Interface (CLI) and ISO/IEC 9075-3: 1995 (E) Call-Level Interface (SQL/CLI). ODBC 3.0 fully implements this specification, and prior versions were based on the preliminary version of this specification but didn't fully implement it.**

An ODBC driver written to the X/Open and ISO CLI specifications will work with any ODBC 3.0 application. All ODBC 3.0 drivers are required to support the Core Interface conformance level specification (see "ODBC Driver API Conformance Levels" in Chapter 12). This means that an ODBC driver will support all features used by a standards-compliant application.

Microsoft ODBC contains features beyond the call-level specifications of ISO/IEC and X/Open CLI standards. The following is an *inclusive* list and includes accumulated features from prior versions. Connection pooling and bulk operations are two of the new and important features of ODBC 3.0.

Microsoft ODBC has these features:

- Multirow fetches by a single function call
- Binding to an array of parameters
- Bookmark support, including fetching by bookmark, variable-length bookmarks, and bulk update and delete by bookmark operations on discontiguous rows
- Row-wise binding
- Binding offsets
- Support for batches of SQL statements, either in a stored procedure or as a sequence of SQL statements executed through **SQLExecute** or **SQLExecDirect**
- Positioned updates and delete operations, and batched updates and delete operations by function call (**SQLSetPos**)
- Exact or approximate cursor row counts
- Catalog functions that extract information from the information schema without the need for supporting information schema views
- Escape sequences for outer joins, scalar functions, date-time literals, interval literals, and stored procedures
- Code-page translation libraries
- Reporting of a driver's ANSI-conformance level and SQL support
- On-demand automatic population of implementation parameter descriptor
- Enhanced diagnostics with row and parameter status arrays
- Date-time, interval, numeric/decimal, and 64-bit integer application buffer types

- Asynchronous execution

- Stored procedure support, including escape sequences, output parameter binding mechanisms, and catalog functions

- Connection enhancements including support for connection attributes and attribute browsing

ODBC History

Dr. E. F. Codd created *Structured Query Language* (SQL) at IBM in the 1970s. SQL became an American National Standards Institute (ANSI) standard in 1986 and is the standard used in relational database implementations today. Microsoft conforms to current standards and supports SQL-92 in SQL Server 6.5, while other desktop products, such as Microsoft Access support specialized dialects of SQL including fragments of SQL-92, SQL-89, and proprietary Microsoft SQL implementations. Microsoft Access does not have a standardized SQL implementation. Embedded SQL, a nonstandard form of SQL that can be compiled into a C++ program, is available in the MSDN library.

SQL implementation typically occurred in three forms:

- **Embedded**, where the SQL statements are compiled directly into the program

- **SQL modules**, where an application program invokes system resident modules

- **Call-level interface (CLI)**, which consists of functions to pass SQL statements to the DBMS and receive results from the DBMS

As the definition of an enterprise changed, there was a need to go beyond departmental or even corporate level computing. Of the three types of SQL interfacing, the CLI interface is the only possible choice for a heterogeneous DBMS interface. Both embedded SQL and SQL modules are dependent upon local operating system implementation features. Hence, ODBC, a heterogeneous relational database interface specification, was born.

ODBC is a call-level interface, but it is also much more. To understand why, some knowledge of the computing industry before ODBC is necessary. Before Microsoft arrived, the computing community consisted of mainframes, which were being encroached upon by minicomputers. Minicomputers were introduced around 1969. These were large, single-board systems that had no immediate impact on mainframes. Databases started with mainframes and were traditionally supplied by the mainframe manufacturer; hence there was no urgency to provide common interfaces or conversion tools. It would be heresy for a hardware manufacturer to provide a common interface, or conversion tools. Why would a manufacturer want to make it easy to convert to another manufacturer's hardware?

There were a number of third-party databases, but these were mostly in the IBM market. Burroughs, National Cash Register (NCR), Univac, and Control Data (CDC) all had their own unique database management systems. They were not necessarily relational in the true sense because Dr. Codd's relational theory was new and still being developed. Databases evolved over time, but it was not quite as bad as the Tower of Babel. There was one common unifying thread — Structured Query Language (SQL). Nothing was shared and even SQL was fractured into varying dialects. Standards eventually evolved for SQL, but that didn't stop vendors from adding proprietary extensions. The stage was now set for Microsoft with ODBC and a common SQL. ODBC unified heterogeneous databases with a single architecture, a common interface, and a common SQL for all applications.

ODBC solves the problem of heterogeneous database access by standardizing an interface. ODBC does all of the following:

o Defines a call-level interface that meets internationally recognized standards.

o Defines a common SQL grammar. (Application programs write to the ODBC SQL grammar and the driver translates the SQL to the SQL of the target data source. SQL statements that are not recognized are passed directly to the data source. The Microsoft SQL Server USE <database name> is an example.)

o Manages multiple databases simultaneously. (This permits the heterogeneous interconnection of different databases; ODBC, however, is not a heterogeneous database join engine, nor is it a distributed transaction processor. Applications that use ODBC are responsible for any cross-database functionality.)

o Exposes numerous database features; however, the driver is not required to expose all features to the application. (A database driver need not support all database features.)

ODBC Architecture

ODBC architecture consists of five components: the application, the driver manager, the ODBC driver, the network software, and the data source. We start with a discussion of the problems solved by the ODBC architecture. The relationship of WOSA to ODBC is next, and the section closes with a sketch of each ODBC architecture component.

The Database Access Problem

ODBC is the Windows architecture solution for connecting to different databases in a heterogeneous environment. ODBC is not always the optimal solution for communicating with a single database; it is, however, the optimal solution for communicating with more than one database in a heterogeneous environment.

The native API of the data source is always the optimal database connectivity solution when communicating with a single database, which is certainly not a heterogeneous environment. It exposes the application program to data source version changes. An example of this is that the Microsoft SQL Server DB-LIB, the native SQL Server API, only communicates with Microsoft SQL Server. Changes to DB-LIB or the DB-LIB interface can impact the application program. The application is not isolated from underlying system changes. This doesn't happen with ODBC, which insulates the application from data and source version changes. ODBC provides the additional benefit of heterogeneous database communication.

ODBC is just one component of the *Microsoft Windows Architecture* (WA). The WA solution provides a single API to interface various enterprise computing networks. A single interface hides the complexities of communicating in a heterogeneous environment from the developer and from the user. The high-cost labor-intensive task of communication in a heterogeneous environment is reduced to only one interface. A single WA interface enables seamless integration of applications with multiple services across multiple computing environments. Costs are significantly reduced because developers only need to learn one API for all implementations. This makes it possible to build long-term stable enterprise solutions.

Service Provider Interface Model

The Microsoft Windows Architecture model of a *service provider interface* (SPI) and an API insulates the application from implementation details. Figure 11-1 illustrates how ODBC conforms to this model with both an application interface and an enterprise interface.

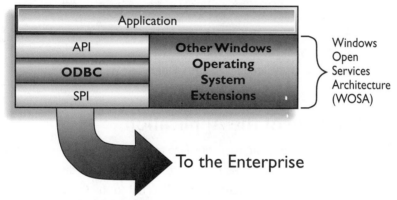

FIGURE 11-1   Windows Operating Systems Architecture.

Figure 11-2 illustrates additional detail of the ODBC model and helps explain how the ODBC model works.

The ODBC API provides a common interface for all applications. Figure 11-2 illustrates more than one application interfacing the same DBMS and the possibility of an application communicating with more than one DBMS. The vendor-provided ODBC drivers have the role of service providers in this model. Each component of Figure 11-2 has a unique role to play. The identifiable components are the application, the data source, the driver manager, the driver, and the network software, each of which are discussed in the sections that follow.

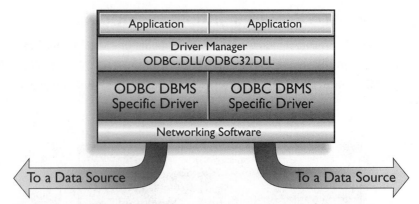

FIGURE 11-2   **ODBC in the Windows Operating System Architecture.**

The Role of the Application

The *application* is the user interface to the system. It uses the ODBC API to submit SQL statements and retrieve results, and does not directly interface the ODBC driver. All application requests are directed to the ODBC driver manager, which interfaces with the driver. This insulates the application from data source and network implementation issues. The role of the application is best understood by enumerating the data retrieval tasks. The application:

- Creates a data structure before connecting to a data source with user supplied connection information.
- Optionally declares the start of a transaction. Transactions are only necessary for updates, and are optional but recommended.
- Creates one or more SQL statements and supplies any needed parameters.
- Assigns a cursor name to a possible result set, or optionally allows the ODBC driver to assign a cursor name. Not all statements will create a result set.
- Submits the query for immediate execution or as a prepared statement.
- Assigns and initializes column storage and retrieves the result set if necessary.
- Retrieves and manages any error information returned from the ODBC driver.
- Completes each transaction by either rolling it back or committing it.

- Terminates the connection when processing is complete, and releases all allocated structures.

The Role of the ODBC Data Source

A *data source* is a collection of objects. These objects are the platform where the DBMS resides, the DBMS that resides on that platform, and the data the user wants to access. This aggregation of objects is technically not classified as a data source until the data source is registered. Microsoft SQL Server is a relational database, but it is not an ODBC data source until it is registered.

Registering a data source can be done from Control Panel or, as illustrated below in Figure 11-3, from the ODBC panel of the ODBC software developer's kit (SDK). The ODBC SDK is a component of the Microsoft SQL Server Programmers Toolkit and is found in the Microsoft SQL Server workstation version.

 No, I didn't make a mistake. Figure 11-3 is indeed the ODBC 2.5 interface. This SDK still supports 16-bit drivers while the ODBC 3.0 SDK is without the 16-bit ODBC Administrator icons. Both SDKs are installed.

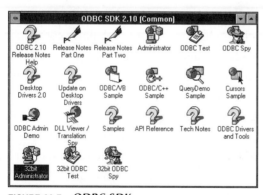

FIGURE 11-3   ODBC SDK.

Registering your data source is just a matter of double-clicking the 16-bit or 32-bit icons. If you do that, you'll see a display similar to Figure 11-4, which was created by double-clicking the 32-bit ODBC Administrator icon.

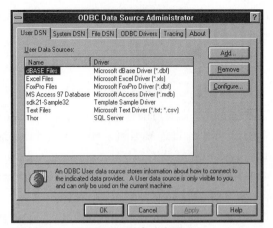

FIGURE 11-4   ODBC 3.0 Administrator.

The Role of the ODBC Driver Manager

The *ODBC driver manager* is the gateway to the data source. The driver manager:

o Forwards application calls to the ODBC driver.

o Satisfies some information and initialization requests without invoking the ODBC driver.

o Is responsible for loading and starting the ODBC driver. (Earlier ODBC drivers were not cached, which resulted in prohibitive connection time. This is the primary reason that earlier applications that used ODBC maintained the connection to the data source. Recent ODBC driver managers cache the ODBC driver, eliminating the need to maintain the connection. The ODBC 3.0 Driver Manager advances the technology with connection pooling. Connections are drawn from the pool when the application calls **SQLConnect** or **SQLDriverConnect**, and are returned to the pool when the application calls **SQLDisconnect**.)

o Optionally logs application calls.

o Manages error and state checking.

The Role of the ODBC Driver

The *ODBC driver* has the responsibility of converting the ODBC SQL to the SQL of the proprietary database. If the ODBC doesn't recognize the SQL command (such as the Microsoft SQL Server USE command), the ODBC driver forwards the SQL statement directly to the data source in what is called pass-through mode.

A developer who writes an ODBC driver to access file data is required to supply a database engine that supports at least the minimal SQL functionality. This is not true with OLE-DB, our goal for the future. An OLE-DB *provider* is a wrapper around file data and *provider* is not required to support a SQL engine. This explains why the OLE-DB memory footprint is quite small for file access; there's no SQL engine.

The ODBC driver also has the responsibility of creating and maintaining a connection with the data source. A SQL query is forwarded to the data source, and a result set is returned to the application task. The driver:

- Connects to and disconnects from the data source requested by the application.

- Submits application requests to the data source. The application requests may be modified by the driver before submission to the data source.

- Translates to or from other formats when requested by the application. This is limited to escape sequences or to a conversion function on a specific column, such as converting from SQL_SMALLINT to SQL_CHAR.

- Returns result sets to the client application.

- Captures and formats errors for client analysis.

- Creates and manages cursors if necessary. This operation is transparent to the application.

- Initiates a required data source transaction when necessary. This action is invisible to the application.

The Role of Network Software

The *network software*, as defined in the ODBC architecture and illustrated in Figure 11-2, is only a logical definition. It is not ODBC software, but is all the software that comprises the supporting infrastructure. This consists of transport protocols and operating system support at both the ODBC client application site and at the data source site. Another view is that network software in the ODBC context is all the software between the client ODBC driver and the target data source, which is usually SQL Server.

ODBC Benefits

The byproduct of standards is nearly always reduced costs. Code reuse occurs, application complexity is reduced, and client satisfaction increases. These are only local benefits, however. There are other benefits as well, such as the creating of new software markets and the solution to problems that were heretofore too expensive to solve.

ODBC should be thought of in a global context where companies merge on almost a daily basis. ODBC is an ideal solution for the corporation with a newly acquired division with an incompatible DBMS. Connecting the disparate databases with ODBC is relatively inexpensive compared to converting the database. Data warehouses are an example of where economics dictates a connectivity solution rather than a conversion solution.

ODBC exposes database capabilities, making heterogeneous database connections possible. ODBC does not supplant database capabilities. An ODBC connection to a simple database will not transform it into a full-featured relational database engine. Nor are ODBC driver writers expected to implement functionality not already found in the underlying database.

ODBC should also be recognized as a major advancement in DBMS technology. Before ODBC, all connectivity solutions were proprietary. Microsoft has turned database connectivity into a commodity we can all afford. Microsoft has given us a positive example of their leadership capability with ODBC.

These are ODBC's benefits:

- ODBC is vendor-neutral. ODBC drivers from different vendors can be used interchangeably by an application when the drivers support the application's required conformance levels.

- ODBC is open. Microsoft has obtained a broad consensus from many vendors. In addition to the SQL Access Group (SAG), ODBC is the connectivity tool of choice for many Web tools.

- ODBC is powerful. It supports both on-line transaction processing (OLTP) and decision support systems (DSS). Many features are available including transactions, scrollable cursors, system table transparency, array fetch and update, catalog functions, a flexible connection model, and stored procedures.

- ODBC permits DBMS access from more than one location. More than one server may be accessed from the same application.

- ODBC allows users access to access more than one DBMS from within a single application. Varied data sources are available, and third-party drivers for ODBC 3.0 are now shipping. The Intersolve ODBC 3.0 driver supports: ALLBASE; dBase; INFORMIX; SQL/400; Btrieve; Digital Alpha Workstations; INGRESS; SQL/DS; Centura SQLBase; Digital AlphaServer ES; Microsoft SQL Server; Sybase SQL Server 4; Clipper; Microsoft .XLS files; NetWare SQL; Sybase System 10; DB2; Foxbase; Oracle; Teradata; DB2/2; FoxPro; Paradox; Text files; DB2/6000; IMAGE/SQL; PROGRESS; and XDB.

- ODBC simplifies application development. The developer creates a single application and only changes the ODBC drivers to communicate with another DBMS.

- ODBC is a portable API. The same interface and access technology may be used on different platforms. ODBC conforms to the Windows Open Services Architecture.

- ODBC insulates applications from changes to the underlying network and DBMS. Any modifications made to the supporting network infrastructure or the target DBMS will not affect current ODBC applications.

- ODBC promotes the use of SQL. ODBC 3.0 is X/Open ISO compliant.

- ODBC helps corporations protect their DBMS investments and the acquired DBMS developer skills. At the same time, "downsizing" or "rightsizing" can still be used to contain costs.

KEY POINT SUMMARY

ODBC presents a uniform interface with a standardized SQL for heterogeneous interconnection of different databases. ODBC is not a heterogeneous database join engine, nor is it a distributed transaction processor. Applications that use ODBC are responsible for any cross-database functionality.

- ODBC is a standard.

- ODBC defines a common SQL. Applications are written to the ODBC SQL standard, and not the SQL of specific databases. This approach allows an application to be moved to another database by changing ODBC drivers.

- ODBC is language-independent.

- ODBC is vendor-neutral.

- ODBC is portable.

- ODBC insulates an application from the flux of the underlying network infrastructure and DBMS.

- ODBC uses a CLI.

- ODBC is a connectivity mechanism for registered ODBC data sources.

- There are only four components in the ODBC architecture: the application, the driver manager, the driver, and the data source.

- The application only interfaces the driver manager.

- ODBC drivers expose database functionality. They do not enhance it.

- An ODBC data source must provide a minimal SQL engine. This means the developers writing ODBC file drivers must supply a SQL engine with minimum functionality.

APPLYING WHAT YOU'VE LEARNED

An understanding of the ODBC architecture is necessary for a successful ODBC application. The questions below measure your understanding of the ODBC architecture and are an aid in preparing for the Microsoft Windows Core examinations.

The ODBC lab prepares you for developing an ODBC application. Unfortunately, many developers build ODBC applications without the services of the ODBC software developer's kit (SDK).

Instant Assessment

1. Name the major components of the ODBC architecture.

2. Name five benefits of the ODBC architecture.

3. What role does the ODBC driver play in the Microsoft Windows Architecture?

4. Explain the role of each component in the ODBC architecture.

 concept link   **For answers to the Instant Assessment questions, see Appendix C.**

Lab Exercise

Lab 11.27 *Preparing for an ODBC application*

WA I

Lab 11.27 assumes that your desktop system supports ODBC. You'll need a registered data source later in this section for the labs and examples.

1. Go to Control Panel and select the ODBC icon.

2. Investigate the registered data sources for your system.

3. You should have a copy of the ODBC SDK installed. ODBC Test from the ODBC SDK is recommended for debugging ODBC applications. Acquire and install the ODBC SDK. It is available through the Microsoft Developer Network (MSDN). You will find it on CD-ROM 1 of the MSDN 1997 subscription. The SDK is also available from Microsoft Press as ISBN 1-57231-516-4.

Windows Architecture I

ODBC Drivers

About Chapter 12

Chapter 12 outlines the mechanics of how *Open Database Connectivity* (ODBC) is used as a standard. The chapter starts with the definition of both the *application program interfaces* (API) and SQL conformance levels, which define the standard, and closes with a discussion of ODBC driver architecture.

Drivers are written to conformance levels, and it is up to the vendor as to which level a driver is written. Next in the chapter is an ODBC API quick reference associating the API function with the conformance level. The reference contains a description of each API function. Comparing application requirements against the quick reference will quickly determine the API conformance level that is necessary for a driver.

ODBC DRIVER API CONFORMANCE LEVELS

The vendor-neutral environment of ODBC is created by defining three levels of APIs and three levels of SQL grammar conformance. A unique benefit of this approach is that the application can communicate with diverse databases, each having varying dialects of SQL. A single application program is written using ODBC SQL. Different drivers translate the SQL for different databases. Changing the database driver is the only necessary change to communicate with a different data source. Communicating to diverse databases without application reprogramming is a significant ODBC benefit.

The SQL driver is responsible for converting the ODBC SQL to the SQL of the proprietary database. If the ODBC driver doesn't recognize the SQL command, (such as the SQL Server USE statement), the ODBC driver forwards the SQL directly to the data source in what is called pass-through mode.

caution

This database independence is possible only with compliance to the API and SQL grammar conformance levels. Driver writers are encouraged to support the Level 1 API (at a minimum); however, not all ODBC drivers support the same level of interoperability. This problem can be eased with still another layer of software, a leveling library (see Figure 12-1).

You may wonder, "Why must I use ODBC SQL in my application? If I provide Transact-SQL (Microsoft SQL Server T-SQL), it will be passed through directly to SQL Server without translation." The answer is that if you're using data source SQL statements, the application is not functioning in a heterogeneous environment and ODBC is the wrong choice. The optimal interface is always the native API of the data source. A heterogeneous interface will always have more overhead than the native API. A skilled manager of a client-server project will not allow unnecessary dependencies to be built into the application, and a native language is a dependency.

ODBC is a standard, but that is where it ends. Developers see ODBC as a means to an end and use the DBMS-specific (syntactically) SQL. They'll write an application using Transact-SQL of Microsoft SQL Server. The developer knows that Transact-SQL-specific statements will be passed directly to SQL Server when the ODBC driver doesn't recognize it. This is precisely what ODBC is not. ODBC is a standard for heterogeneous interconnection of databases. If you are writing an application in Transact-SQL using ODBC, then this is a major programming error. The developer should always use the native API when writing an application to a vendor-specific application. Developers use ODBC because it is relatively easy and convenient to use. They probably don't even know that a native API exists.

A different perspective is that desktop software is often an adjunct to an enterprise. The Information Systems (IS) manager is responsible for what is euphemistically called legacy systems and for desktop systems. The IS manager may be conversant with desktop software issues at other than a superficial level, but it may not be the level necessary for strategic planning.

Some rules of the road for considering an ODBC implementation are:

- When only one database must be accessed, the best performance is always from the native API. Don't use ODBC just because it is convenient. Whatever the usage is today, it will be double next year, and double the year after. Starting with less than the best is not a good strategy in software development.

- As a developer, you are probably not aware of all strategic planning issues within your enterprise. Arbitrarily using vendor-specific SQL constructs limits the application portability and may hinder strategic deployment.

- Use only American National Standards Institute (ANSI)-standard SQL constructs. Avoid using vendor-specific SQL implementations. Vendor-specific SQL implementations will lock you into the current vendor. Vendor-specific features also have a *creep* factor. You're seduced, and the feature is gradually enhanced. Your conversion costs escalate to the point where conversion to another DBMS system becomes prohibitive. In other words, you're hooked!

- Always write to ODBC SQL specifications. This maintains software portability.

Microsoft always ships a level of ODBC that is compatible with the current release of Microsoft SQL Server. This is all well and good. However, Microsoft still doesn't understand the Enterprise. The SQL-92 upgrade wasn't a singular update. Pieces of SQL-92 shipped with different upgrades to SQL Server. The syntax of some SQL statements changed between SQL Server releases 6.0 and 6.5 and application performance was negatively impacted. This places the Enterprise at risk.

The solution to this problem of whipsawing is quite simple: always code application SQL to the ODBC standard, and never implement a version of Microsoft SQL Server that is incomplete at the standards implementation level.

This may be a difficult rule to enforce because the application only uses ODBC and Microsoft SQL Server. Your application developers will want to write statements directly in Transact-SQL. They do not understand the problem of dependency. These problems can be avoided with proper application program management.

We're all stubborn and don't seem able to learn from history. Software manufacturers from the legacy era shipped a COBOL compiler with full current compliance to industry standards. There were no partial shipments. If COBOL-66 shipped, it included all ANSI specifications. Another compiler wasn't shipped until the standards changed. Microsoft fails to recognize that an incremental upgrade to the enterprise is no different than a complete upgrade. A new release is quite often ready to ship before the Enterprise has completely evaluated the last incremental release.

What is important about SQL Server, for example, is that all development energy should focus on compliance with industry standards, and neither time nor money should be spent on items such as the SQL Server 6.5 Web Wizard until a robust and standards-compliant version is shipped. The Web Wizard is fine, but it should be an optional add-on only after standards implementations are complete. Microsoft software does not have a reputation for being robust, and additional and unsolicited software features simply increase the probability of a software failure. What makes a thin client appealing is that it involves less software and is, by definition, more reliable.

Different levels of conformance are found at the tool level. Microsoft Visual Basic supports the Level 1 API and the Core SQL Grammar, while Microsoft Access supports the Level 1 API and the Minimum SQL Grammar.

 note

ODBC specifications are currently changing. ODBC 2.5 represents the 32-bit release and ODBC 3.0 is the X/Open standards-compliant release.

 exam preparation pointer

The API and SQL Grammar conformance levels should be memorized if you're studying for the core Microsoft Windows Open Systems Architecture (WOSA) examinations. They are not covered in the new Microsoft Windows Architecture (WA) examinations.

The conformance levels are valuable from the perspective of knowing which driver is appropriate and when additional functionality must be added by the application. The bottom line is that the application program must provide missing functionality, and this can significantly increase development costs.

Core API

The following list outlines the minimal functionality an ODBC driver must support to qualify for CORE API support designation. (Functionality, however, is not limited to this list.)

- Allocate and free environment, connection, and statement handles.
- Connect to data sources. Use multiple statements on a connection.
- Prepare and execute SQL statements. Execute SQL statements immediately.
- Assign storage for parameters in a SQL statement and result columns.
- Retrieve data from a result set. Retrieve information about a result set.
- Commit or roll back transactions.
- Retrieve error information.

Level 1 API

This list outlines the minimal functionality an ODBC driver must support to qualify for Level 1 support designation. (Functionality, however, is not limited to this list.)

- Core API functionality.
- Connect to data sources with driver-specific dialog boxes.
- Set and inquire values of statement and connection options.
- Send part or all of a parameter value (useful for long data).
- Retrieve part or all of a result column value (useful for long data).
- Retrieve catalog information (columns, special columns, statistics, and tables).
- Retrieve information about driver and data source capabilities, such as supported data types, scalar functions, and ODBC functions.

Level 2 API

The following list outlines the minimal functionality an ODBC driver must support to qualify for Level 2 API support designation. (Functionality, however, is not limited to this list.)

- Core and Level 1 functionality.
- Browse connection information and list available data sources.
- Send arrays of parameter values. Retrieve arrays of result column values.
- Retrieve the number of parameters and describe individual parameters.
- Use a scrollable cursor.
- Retrieve the native form of an SQL statement.
- Retrieve catalog information (privileges, keys, and procedures).
- Call a translation DLL.

ODBC DRIVER SQL GRAMMAR CONFORMANCE LEVELS

The ODBC SQL conformance levels correspond roughly to the SQL Access Group SQL CAE specification (1992).

Minimum SQL Grammar

This list outlines the minimal functionality an ODBC driver must support to qualify for minimum SQL grammar support designation. (Functionality, however, is not limited to this list.)

- Data Definition Language (DDL): `CREATE TABLE` and `DROP TABLE`.
- Data Manipulation Language (DML): simple `SELECT`, `INSERT`, `UPDATE SEARCHED`, and `DELETE SEARCHED`.
- Expressions: Simple (such as A > B + C).
- Data types: `CHAR`, `VARCHAR`, or `LONG VARCHAR`.

Core SQL Grammar

The following list outlines the minimal functionality an ODBC driver must support to qualify for Core SQL grammar support designation. (Functionality, however, is not limited to this list.)

- Minimum SQL grammar and data types.

- ALTER TABLE, CREATE INDEX, DROP INDEX, CREATE VIEW, DROP VIEW, GRANT, and REVOKE.
- Full SELECT.
- Expressions: subquery, set functions such as SUM and MIN.
- Data types: DECIMAL, NUMERIC, SMALLINT, INTEGER, REAL, FLOAT, DOUBLE PRECISION.

Extended SQL Grammar

The following list outlines the minimal functionality an ODBC driver must support to qualify for extended SQL grammar support designation. (Functionality, however, is not limited to this list.)

- Minimum and Core SQL grammar and data types.
- Outer joins, positioned UPDATE, positioned DELETE, SELECT FOR UPDATE, and unions.
- Expressions: scalar functions such as SUBSTRING and ABS, date, time, and time stamp literals.
- Data types: BIT, TINYINT, BIGINT, BINARY, VARBINARY, LONG VARBINARY, DATE, TIME, TIMESTAMP.
- Batch SQL statements.
- Procedure calls.

ODBC API QUICK REFERENCE

The following tables (Tables 12-1 – 12-10) list the client-side ODBC API functions by category with the standards compliance level, conformance level, function name, description, and ODBC version when introduced. Deprecated functions are noted. Use this quick reference when designing your ODBC application and identify the basic functionality needed. Correlate this with ODBC functionality and identify the conformance level necessary for your application.

exam
preparation
pointer Unfortunately, I cannot tell you which ODBC functions are referenced on the Windows Architecture I examination. The only clue I can give you is to be sure that you understand data retrieval, transactions, and obtaining connection, statement, or data source information.

TABLE 12-1 MANAGING THE DATA SOURCE CONNECTION

COMPLIANCE	CONFORMANCE	ODBC FUNCTION	DESCRIPTION
Deprecated ODBC 1.0	Core	**SQLAllocConnect**	Allocate memory for a connection handle. An environment handle is required. See **SQLAllocHandle**.
ISO 92 ODBC 3.0	Core	**SQLAllocHandle**	Allocate an environment, connection, statement, or descriptor handle.
ODBC ODBC 1.0	Level 2	**SQLBrowseConnect**	Iterative enumeration of data source attributes and attribute values.
ISO 92 ODBC 1.0	Core	**SQLConnect**	Connect to a registered data source.
ISO 92 ODBC 1.0	Core	**SQLDisconnect**	Close a connection associated with a connection handle.
ODBC ODBC 1.0	Level 1	**SQLDriverConnect**	An alternative to **SQLConnect** with extended connection parameters.
Deprecated ODBC 1.0	Core	**SQLFreeConnect**	Release a connection handle and free the associated memory. See **SQLFreeHandle**.
ISO 92 ODBC 3.0	Core	**SQLFreeHandle**	Free an environment, connection, statement, or description handle.

TABLE 12-2 MANAGING THE ENVIRONMENT

COMPLIANCE	CONFORMANCE	ODBC FUNCTION	DESCRIPTION
Deprecated ODBC 1.0	Core	**SQLAllocEnv**	Allocate memory for an environment handle. See **SQLAllocHandle**.
Deprecated ODBC 1.0	Core	**SQLFreeEnv**	Release the environment handle and free the associated memory. See **SQLFreeHandle**.
ISO 92 ODBC 3.0	Core	**SQLGetEnvAttr**	Returns the setting of an environment attribute.
ISO 92 ODBC 3.0	Core	**SQLSetEnvAttr**	Sets an environment attribute.

TABLE 12-3 OBTAINING INFORMATION ABOUT A DRIVER AND DATA SOURCE

COMPLIANCE	CONFORMANCE	ODBC FUNCTION	DESCRIPTION
ISO 92 ODBC 1.0	Level 2	**SQLDataSources**	Lists data source names.
ODBC ODBC 2.0	Level 2	**SQLDrivers**	List drivers. A function of the driver manager.
ISO 92 ODBC 1.0	Level 1	**SQLGetFunctions**	Returns supported ODBC function information. May be driver or driver manager implemented.
ISO 92 ODBC 1.0	Level 1	**SQLGetInfo**	Returns general driver and data source information specific to a connection handle.
ISO 92 ODBC 1.0	Level 1	**SQLGetTypeInfo**	Returns data source information about the data types that are supported.

TABLE 12-4 SETTING AND RETRIEVING DRIVER OPTIONS

COMPLIANCE	CONFORMANCE	ODBC FUNCTION	DESCRIPTION
ODBC ODBC 3.0	Level 1	**SQLBulkOperations**	Performs bulk inserts or updates.
ISO 92 ODBC 3.0	Core	**SQLGetConnectAttr**	Returns the current setting of a connection attribute.
Deprecated ODBC 1.0	Level 1	**SQLGetConnectOption**	Gets the value of a connection option.
ISO 92 ODBC 3.0	Level 1	**SQLGetStmtAttr**	Returns the value of a statement attribute.
Deprecated ODBC 1.0	Level 1	**SQLGetStmtOption**	Returns the current value of a statement option. See **SQLGetStmtAttr**.
ISO 92 ODBC 3.0	Level 1	**SQLSetConnectAttr**	Returns the setting of a connect attribute.
Deprecated ODBC 1.0	Level 1	**SQLSetConnectOption**	Sets the setting of a connect option. See **SQLGetConnectAttr**.
ISO 92 ODBC 3.0	Level 1	**SQLSetStmtAttr**	Sets the value of a statement attribute.
Deprecated ODBC 1.0	Level 1	**SQLSetStmtOption**	Sets the value of statement option. See **SQLSetStmtAttr**.

TABLE 12-5 PREPARING SQL STATEMENTS

COMPLIANCE	CONFORMANCE	ODBC FUNCTION	DESCRIPTION
Deprecated ODBC 1.0	Core	**SQLAllocStmt**	Allocates memory for a statement handle. See **SQLAllocHandle**.
ISO 92 ODBC 1.0	Core	**SQLPrepare**	Prepares a SQL statement for execution. Use this statement whenever statement execution is repeated.

continued

TABLE 12-5 *(continued)*

COMPLIANCE	CONFORMANCE	ODBC FUNCTION	DESCRIPTION
ODBC ODBC 2.0	Level 1	**SQLBindParameter**	Binds a buffer to a parameter marker in a SQL statement.
ISO 92 ODBC 3.0	Core	**SQLCloseCursor**	Close a cursor opened on a statement.
Deprecated ODBC 1.0	Level 2	**SQLParamOptions**	Permits bulk updates. An application can specify multiple values for a set of parameters assigned by **SQLBindParameter**. See **SQLSetStmtAttr**.
ISO 92 ODBC 1.0	Core	**SQLGetCursorName**	Returns the cursor name associated with a statement handle.
ISO 92 ODBC 1.0	Core	**SQLSetCursorName**	Associates a cursor name with a statement handle.
Deprecated ODBC 1.0	Core	**SQLSetParam**	Binds data to a parameter. See **SQLBindParameter**.
Deprecated ODBC 1.0	Level 2	**SQLSetScrollOptions**	Sets result set scrolling options. See **SQLSetStmtAttr**.

TABLE 12-6 SUBMITTING REQUESTS

COMPLIANCE	CONFORMANCE	ODBC FUNCTION	DESCRIPTION
ISO 92 ODBC 1.0	Core	**SQLExecDirect**	The fastest way to submit a SQL statement for a one-time execution. The statement may be preparable, but need not be prepared.
ISO 92 ODBC 1.0	Core	**SQLExecute**	Executes a prepared statement.
ODBC ODBC 1.0	Level 2	**SQLNativeSQL**	Returns the driver-translated SQL string.
ODBC ODBC 1.0	Level 2	**SQLDescribeParam**	Returns the description of a parameter marker associated with a prepared SQL statement.

COMPLIANCE	CONFORMANCE	ODBC FUNCTION	DESCRIPTION
ISO 92 ODBC 1.0	Level 2	**SQLNumParams**	Returns the parameter count of a SQL statement.
ISO 92 ODBC 1.0	Level 1	**SQLParamData**	Used with **SQLPutData** to supply parameter data at execution time.
ISO 92 ODBC 1.0	Level 1	**SQLPutData**	Sends characters or binary data to the driver at execution time.

TABLE 12-7 RETRIEVING RESULTS AND INFORMATION ABOUT RESULTS

COMPLIANCE	CONFORMANCE	ODBC FUNCTION	DESCRIPTION
ISO 92 ODBC 1.0	Core	**SQLBindCol**	Assigns the storage and data type for a result set column.
ISO 92 ODBC 3.0	Core	**SQLColAttribute**	A generalized version of **SQLDescribeCol**.
Deprecated ODBC 1.0	Core	**SQLColAttributes**	A generalized version of **SQLDescribeCol**.
ISO 92 ODBC 1.0	Core	**SQLDescribeCol**	Returns the result descriptor, which contains the column name, type, precision, scale, and nullability. This function cannot be used for bookmarks.
Deprecated ODBC 1.0	Core	**SQLError**	Returns error or status information. See **SQLGetDiagRec**.
Deprecated ODBC 1.0	Level 2	**SQLExtendedFetch**	An extended version of **SQLFetch**. An array is returned for each bound column. See **SQLFetchScroll**.
ISO 92 ODBC 1.0	Core	**SQLFetch**	Retrieves a row from a result set. Only the driver returns data for columns bound to storage locations with **SQLBindCol**.
ISO 92 ODBC 3.0	Core	**SQLFetchScroll**	Retrieves the specified row set from a result set. Retrieval is absolute or relative.

continued

TABLE 12-7 *(continued)*

COMPLIANCE	CONFORMANCE	ODBC FUNCTION	DESCRIPTION
ISO 92 ODBC 1.0	Level 1	**SQLGetData**	Retrieves data for a single unbound column.
ODBC ODBC 1.0	Level 2	**SQLMoreResults**	Determines if additional results are available for a statement handle.
ISO 92 ODBC 1.0	Core	**SQLNumResultCols**	Returns the number of columns in a result set.
ISO 92 ODBC 1.0	Core	**SQLRowCount**	Returns the row count of a SQL UPDATE, INSERT, or DELETE statement.
ODBC ODBC 1.0	Level 2	**SQLSetPos**	Sets the cursor position in a row set.

TABLE 12-8 OBTAINING DATA SOURCE SYSTEM TABLE INFORMATION (CATALOG FUNCTIONS)

COMPLIANCE	CONFORMANCE	ODBC FUNCTION	DESCRIPTION
ODBC ODBC 1.0	Level 2	**SQLColumnPrivileges**	Returns as a result set the column names and privileges for a table associated with a statement handle.
X/Open ODBC 1.0	Level 1	**SQLColumns**	Returns as a result set the table column names associated with a statement handle.
ODBC ODBC 1.0	Level 2	**SQLForeignKeys**	Returns as a result set the list of foreign keys in a table and a list of foreign keys in other tables that refer to the primary key in the referenced table.
ODBC ODBC 1.0	Level 2	**SQLPrimaryKeys**	Returns as a result set the primary key column names.
ODBC ODBC 1.0	Level 2	**SQLProcedureColumns**	Returns as a result set the list of input and output parameters and column names that make up a result set for a specific procedure.

COMPLIANCE	CONFORMANCE	ODBC FUNCTION	DESCRIPTION
ODBC ODBC 1.0	Level 2	**SQLProcedures**	Returns as a result set a list of procedure names at the data source.
X/Open ODBC 1.0	Level 1	**SQLSpecialColumns**	Returns as a result set the optimal set of columns that uniquely identify a row and the columns that are automatically updated when any value in a row is changed.
ISO 92 ODBC 1.0	Level 1	**SQLStatistics**	Returns the statistics and indexes for a table.
ODBC ODBC 1.0	Level 2	**SQLTablePrivileges**	Returns a list of tables and the associated privileges for each table. The information is returned as a result set.
X/Open ODBC 1.0	Level 1	**SQLTables**	Returns a list of data source tables.

TABLE 12-9 MANAGING DESCRIPTORS

COMPLIANCE	CONFORMANCE	ODBC FUNCTION	DESCRIPTION
ISO 92 ODBC 3.0	Core	**SQLCopyDesc**	Copies descriptor information from one handle to another.
ISO 92 ODBC 3.0	Core	**SQLGetDescField**	Returns the current setting of a single field within a descriptor record.
ISO 92 ODBC 3.0	Core	**SQLGetDescRec**	Returns multiple fields from a descriptor record.
ISO 92 ODBC 3.0	Core	**SQLGetDiagField**	Returns the current value of a field in a diagnostic record.
ISO 92 ODBC 3.0	Core	**SQLGetDiagRec**	Returns multiple fields from a diagnostic record.
ISO 92 ODBC 3.0	Core	**SQLSetDescField**	Sets the value of a single field in a descriptor record.
ISO 92 ODBC 3.0	Core	**SQLSetDescRec**	Sets multiple fields in a descriptor record.

TABLE 12-10 TERMINATING A STATEMENT			
COMPLIANCE	*CONFORMANCE*	*ODBC FUNCTION*	*DESCRIPTION*
ISO 92 ODBC 1.0	Core	**SQLCancel**	Cancels the processing associated with a statement handle.
ISO 92 ODBC 3.0	Core	**SQLEndTran**	Requests a commit or rollback for all active operations on all operations associated with a connection.
ISO 92 ODBC 1.0	Core	**SQLFreeStmt**	Stops processing, closes all cursors, pending results are discarded, and all resources are released (an option) for a specific statement handle.
Deprecated ODBC 1.0	Core	**SQLTransact**	Requests a commit or a rollback on all active statement handles associated with a connection. See **SQLEndTran**.

ODBC DRIVER LEVELING

Not all ODBC drivers are created equally. ODBC drivers conform to vendor-specified conformance levels; consequently all drivers may not be equal. The problem occurs in a heterogeneous environment where an application must communicate with two different databases, and the conformance level between the drivers does not agree. The problem and the solution are illustrated in Figure 12-1.

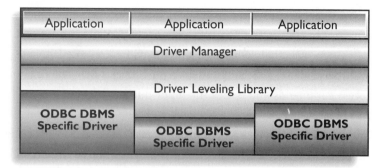

FIGURE 12-1   A driver-leveling library.

in the
real world

A library developed by Q+E, (recently merged with Intersolve),
provides a uniform ODBC interface that gives the same level of
functionality to the application interface, even though each driver
might support a different level of conformance. Q+E (Intersolve)
developed and marketed a driver-leveling library. Explorer is the
current Intersolve name for this product. Intersolve may be found
at http://www.intersolve.com.

A second use of a leveling library is when user requirements exceed driver
capability. The general problem is that the application program must provide
missing driver functionality. An ODBC leveling library can reduce the application-
programming task.

ODBC DRIVER ARCHITECTURE

The simplest classification scheme for driver architecture is to note where the
SQL statements are processed. The single-tier driver will process the SQL statements while the multitier driver passes the SQL statements to the data source.

Single-Tier Drivers

Single-tier drivers are commonly used for flat-file access. A single-tier driver
processes SQL statements locally. In the case of a flat file, the driver writer provides
a minimal SQL implementation. A driver that accesses an xBase file is an example
of a single-tier driver implementation. Single-tier drivers have a file-based engine

rather than a DBMS-based engine. Microsoft Access is an example of a single-tier driver in that the SQL statements are processed locally and not sent to a DBMS.

Any driver that sends SQL statements to a remote DBMS is classified as a multitiered driver. The single-tier driver converts SQL statements locally to file access commands and issues the input-output (I/O) commands to retrieve the data. A single-tier driver is associated with non-SQL-based databases. The definitions are not clear-cut, and Microsoft Access can be used with either a file-based single-tier driver or with a DBMS-based multitiered driver. When used with Microsoft Access, the single-tiered file driver accesses the .MDB file of Access directly. Figure 12-2 illustrates both a single-tier local file-based data source and a single-tier remote file-based data source.

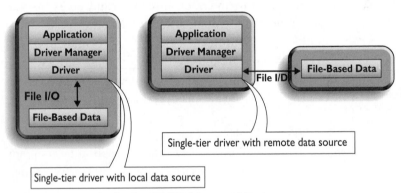

FIGURE 12-2   Two single-tier ODBC driver architectures.

Two-Tier Drivers

There are two variations of a two-tier driver. The first variation is with SQL statements passed to a data source. The data source can be local as we observed in single-tier drivers, but this is not the norm. Figure 12-3 illustrates the first variation of a two-tier driver: the driver does not process the SQL statement, but, passes the statement to a SQL engine at the data source.

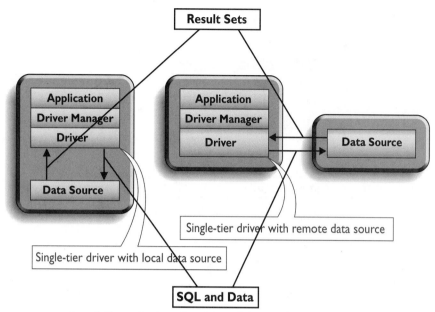

FIGURE 12-3   A variation of a two-tier ODBC driver architecture.

The second variation of a two-tier driver is used by proprietary databases that are not SQL based. A two-tier driver may pass SQL statements that are partially parsed or it may pass basic file I/O operations to the data source. In either case, the data source uses an ODBC Gateway to the proprietary database.

Another interesting feature is that the non-SQL data source can have a SQL engine that resides on either the data source or at the client site. Each version has an ODBC Gateway at the data source; the SQL engine, however, can reside on either the client or at the data source. The ODBC Gateway software can support SQL-based and non-SQL-based data sources. Figure 12-4 illustrates a two-tier driver with a remote SQL engine. The variation with a client-based SQL engine is not illustrated.

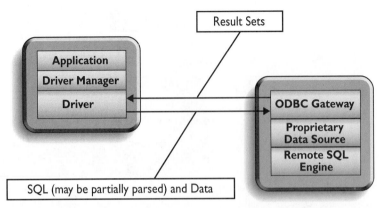

FIGURE 12-4   A two-tier ODBC driver with a remote SQL Engine.

Three-Tier Drivers

Only one aspect distinguishes a three-tier driver from a two-tier driver. The two-tier driver has gateway software residing at the data source, while the three-tier driver has gateway software residing on an intermediary system. Other than the location of the gateway software, the configuration variations between a two- and a three-tier driver are the same. Figure 12-5 illustrates a three-tier driver.

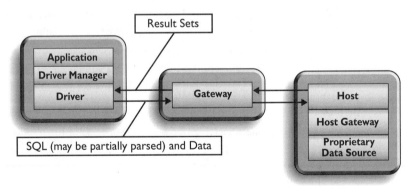

FIGURE 12-5   A three-tier ODBC driver architecture as a gateway.

Key Point Summary

API and SQL Grammar conformance levels define the ODBC driver. This makes software interchangeable and any driver can be used that meets a standard. The conformance levels normalize database access. Conformance levels make ODBC drivers vendor-neutral. Each driver's required functionality should work identically; however, this does not prevent a vendor from adding extra functionality.

- ODBC drivers have an API and a SQL conformance level.
- The ODBC vendor chooses the level of conformance for its driver product.
- Missing functionality must be added by the application. As an example, an application requiring a scrollable cursor needs an ODBC driver with a Level 2 API conformance level.
- A single-tier ODBC driver is used for file systems.
- A three-tier ODBC architecture is commonly used as a bridge.
- An ODBC driver must support a local or a remote SQL engine. The remote SQL engine may be a SQL server, but the ODBC driver developer is required to supply a minimal SQL engine for a file access. Providing a minimal SQL engine is not a burden to the new OLE-DB. An OLE-DB driver (*provider*) does not require a minimal SQL engine for mailbox access. Compare that with an ODBC mailbox driver, which does require a minimal SQL engine.

Applying What You've Learned

A keen understanding of API and SQL Grammar conformance levels is required for a successful ODBC application. The developer analyzes the client requirements and selects an ODBC driver that meets these minimum requirements. When an ODBC driver does not meet the requirements, the developer then either provides the additional functionality in the application or removes the requirement from the specification. The following questions test your understanding of conformance levels with respect to application requirements.

Instant Assessment

1. Explain the purpose of conformance levels.

2. Discuss ODBC driver functionality versus client application requirements.

3. The application design requires a time stamp for transactions. Which conformance level is required?

4. The client wishes to do a browse connect. Which conformance level is required?

5. The client wants optimal performance with prepared SQL statements. Which API conformance level is required?

6. Which ODBC API conformance level supports a scrollable cursor?

7. Explain what a single-tier driver is.

8. What is the difference between a single-tier and a two-tier ODBC driver?

9. What is the basic difference between a two-tier and a three-tier ODBC driver?

10. What is a driver-leveling library?

 concept link   **For answers to the Instant Assessment questions, see Appendix C.**

Lab Exercise

Lab 12.28 *Looking under the hood of an ODBC driver*

 MCSD
WA I

Acquire the ODBC software developer's kit (SDK). Sources for this include the Microsoft Web site at htp://www.microsoft.com or the Microsoft FTP site at ftp://ftp.microsoft.com. The ODBC 3.0 SDK (with documentation) is also available from Microsoft Press. It is preferable that you obtain the SDK appropriate for the level of ODBC your site uses.

 caution   **Do not use the ODBC 3.0 SDK with Windows 3.1 and 16-bit applications. ODBC 3.0 is 32 bits.**

Our goal to use ODBC Test to survey your ODBC environment. If you do not have the ODBC 3.0 SDK, you'll start by using **SQLAllocEnv**. After you have an environment, use **SQLAllocConnect**. Now use **SQLGetConnectOption** and browse the connection options. Continue until you are comfortable using ODBC Test.

The exercise assumes you are using ODBC SDK 3.0.

1. Select the ODBC SDK icon and double-click **ODBC Test**.

2. Click the **Connection** menu and select *Full Connect*. This assumes that SQL Server is already started. If it isn't, go to the SQL Server Service Manager and start SQL Server.

3. Let's look at ODBC functions supported by this driver. Start by again clicking the **Connection** menu and select *SQLGetFunctions*. You will be presented with a result set that enumerates all supported functions. The value SQL_TRUE indicates the function is supported.

4. We could look at each attribute individually, but instead let's look at the complete connection functionality. The quantity of information provided will surprise you; it scrolls for several seconds. Start by again clicking the **Connection** menu and select *Get Info All*.

5. We'll move over to statements. From the **Statement** menu, select *Show Cursor Settings*. A dialog box is presented with the default cursor settings. Although we won't show further functionality, the value of the ODBC SDK cannot be overstated.

Windows Architecture I

ODBC Applications

About Chapter 13

I n the last two chapters, we *discussed* Open database Connectivity (ODBC); this chapter is where we *do* it. Chapter 13 is about programming an ODBC application, which may appear complex when compared to using *Data Access Objects* (DAO) of Microsoft Access or *Remote Data Objects* (RDO) of Visual Basic. It isn't, however. Programming an ODBC application is a matter of understanding the issues and using an organized approach. ODBC will always have higher performance. Both DAO and RDO represent ODBC wrappers and will have an apparent ease of use until an unsolvable issue is encountered. (Both RDO and DAO use objects, and objects have performance issues related to thread models. See Chapter 33.)

All the key programming issues are discussed in this chapter, beginning with the ODBC application guidelines, followed by a series of ODBC functionality topics, including cursors, transactions, concurrency, transaction isolation levels, and the ACID properties. The ACID properties are characteristics of a database transaction: atomicity, consistency, integrity, and durability. These are defined later in the chapter, but for now a database is not a true database unless it exhibits these properties for transactions.

The ODBC programming protocol is discussed next. ODBC statements must be in the correct order or an ODBC state transition error occurs. Included with the programming protocol are a few notes on debugging with ODBC Test.

The chapter closes with a section called "ODBC Tarpits." Programming ODBC is the programming of two languages. The first language is C++ or a VBA scripting tool, either of which host SQL statements. Poorly written SQL statements account for many ODBC performance problems.

ODBC APPLICATION GUIDELINES BEFORE PROGRAMMING

ODBC applications are special. As you learned in Chapter 12, there are API and SQL conformance levels. There are two choices when your client application requirements cannot be satisfied with the ODBC drivers available. You can:

- Reduce the application functionality and inform the client, or
- Provide the required functionality in the application.

A good example of this is backward-scrolling cursors. Although backward-scrolling cursors are not recommended, the application must provide the missing functionality.

Another example is **SQLBrowseConnect**. You have a hard choice to make if your driver does not support Level 2 API conformance and your client wishes to do a browse connect.

ODBC application development can be a very easy or a very difficult task. To properly address all of the development issues, follow these guidelines:

- Completely understand the client's requirements. There is no substitute for thinking or hard work. Don't be tempted to start programming with the modern *rapid access development* (RAD) tools until all aspects of the requirements are understood. The power of the new modern programming tools is such that it tempts us to do a bottom-up design, which is always a sure path to a disaster. It is excruciatingly hard to resist programming until each detail is completely understood.

- Survey the ODBC drivers available and compare driver functionality with your requirements. If the application requirements are clear, then this is the time for hard choices. Decide whether the application will supply any missing functionality. Select your third-party driver.

- Ensure you have a programming specification and have selected an ODBC driver. This step is critical. You must test your newly acquired driver before you start programming. This is a precautionary measure to verify that your driver supports your required functionality. The ODBC driver can be tested as illustrated in Figure 13-1 with ODBC Test from the ODBC SDK.

- Test the ODBC drivers against your specifications. One of the greatest mistakes in ODBC programming is to consider the application as monolithic. Now is the time to consider the ODBC architecture with a division of labor. This can be the writing of stored procedures for SQL Server, or it can be a slightly more elegant solution with a tiered architecture.

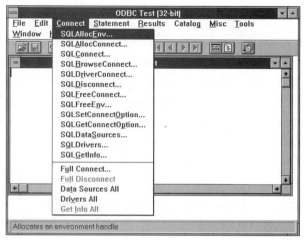

FIGURE 13-1   32-bit ODBC Test.

- Acquire an intimate understanding of the driver and the data source. Use this knowledge to compare supported data source functionality with client requirements. An intimate knowledge of the data source is necessary to write a good ODBC application. The developer determines missing data source functionality by calling **SQLGetInfo**, or by using ODBC Test. Questions can be answered as to transaction support, cursor behavior on commit or rollback, the support of multiple active statements per connections, scalar functions supported, and the data types supported. A successful ODBC programmer must have an intimate understanding of the data source's characteristics.

PROGRAMMING YOUR ODBC APPLICATION

Programming an ODBC application involves managing the handles that represent data structures and the calling of ODBC API functions.

Handles

The ODBC environment requires four different classes of handles. Their allocation sequence is ordered and an error occurs if handles are not allocated in the proper order.

An ODBC application starts with these three steps:

1. The first step is to allocate an environment handle to determine the data access context. This is an opportunity to collect and cache driver information before the application commences any data operations. The most important issue of the environment is the registering of the ODBC version. This is done with **SQLSetEnvAttr** and setting the `SQL_ATTR_APP_ODBC_VER` attribute. This establishes the deprecation level for ODBC 3.0, which automatically maps older API functions to the new ODBC 3.0 functions.

2. The second step is to allocate a connection handle, or at least to go through the motions of doing such. The application issues a connection allocation request to the driver manager. The driver manager recognizes the request but doesn't perform the task immediately. The driver manager allocates the connection handle only after the application has selected a data source driver. An environment handle may have one or more connection handles.

caution

Connections have been a traditional problem with ODBC. Earlier versions of ODBC did not cache the driver, hence the additional time necessary to load the driver. There is also the issue of limited connections to SQL Server. ODBC 3.0 pools connections, and this factor alone is a strong impetus to upgrade existing ODBC applications.

3. The third step is to allocate and use a statement handle. Not all ODBC API calls require a statement handle. It is associated with a SQL statement, and common usage is the binding of parameters along with both direct and prepared statement executions. Overlooked by many ODBC programmers is the fact that a statement handle may be reused. The statement context may dictate otherwise, but the release of just the column or parameter buffers is certainly more efficient than the complete deallocation of all statement handle resources.

Error reporting in ODBC is slightly more complex than in the average application. There are the typical error messages for such items as invalid argument types, invalid data, and the like, but there is also something additional. ODBC reports state transition errors when a handle is not in the proper state. The three handles — environment, connection, and statement — each have three states: unallocated, allocated, and connected. State transition errors occur when the programming protocol is not adhered to and ODBC API functions are referenced in the wrong order. A discussion of the programming protocol is just ahead, so let's finish this discussion of handles by introducing the new handles of ODBC 3.0.

There are two divisions of labor — the application and the driver — and two classes of data — rows and parameters. The new handles are identified when the word *driver* is replaced with the word *implementation*, and all combinations of labor and metadata are enumerated.

The new descriptor types for ODBC 3.0 are listed next along with a description of the information maintained by each descriptor.

- **Application Parameter Descriptor (APD)** — Application buffers bound to parameters in a SQL statement. Information includes addresses, lengths, and C data types.

- **Implementation (Driver) Parameter Descriptor (IPD)** — Parameter information as to SQL data types, lengths, and nullability.

- **Application Row Descriptor (ARD)** — Application buffers bound to columns in a result set. Information includes addresses, lengths, and C data types.

- **Implementation (Driver) Row Descriptor (IRD)** — Column information as to SQL data types, lengths, and nullability.

Microsoft helps us out with these new descriptors. They are allocated automatically when a statement is allocated.

Transactions

Transactions are required in SQL 92, which ODBC 3.0 supports. The default transaction state for ODBC is *autocommit*. This means that a statement is committed automatically when it completes.

The ODBC 3.0 API function **SQLEndTran** supports a commit or rollback option. This statement is only used in manual-commit mode.

ODBC transactions are not explicitly initiated. An implicit default transaction begins when the application initiates database operations.

The cursor behavior of a transaction, which is either committed or rolled back, is data source-dependent and is dictated by one of these actions occurring:

- The commit or rollback closes the cursor and deletes all query plans for prepared statements.

- The commit or rollback closes the cursor and preserves the query plan for prepared statements.

- The commit or rollback closes the cursor and deletes all query plans for prepared statements.

Determining the cursor behavior is an important step in application initialization. The cursor behavior for a COMMIT and a ROLLBACK operation should be determined with **SQLGetInfo** after connecting to the data source. The attributes to interrogate are SQL_CURSOR_COMMIT_BEHAVIOR and SQL_CURSOR_ROLLBACK_BEHAVIOR. Possible return values include:

- SQL_CB_DELETE — Close cursor and delete prepared statement along with query plan.

- SQL_CB_CLOSE — Close cursor. (Prepared statements and query plans are preserved.)

- SQL_CB_PRESERVE — Cursor and query plan are preserved. (**SQLCloseCursor** is used to close the cursor.)

SQLExecute, **SQLExecDirect**, **SQLBulkOperations**, **SQLSetPos**, or **SQLCloseCursor** automatically commit a transaction when in autocommit mode.

Transaction Isolation Levels

Transaction isolation is the degree of interaction between multiple concurrent transactions. There is, however, a simple rule that describes the issue. Maximum consistency (highest transaction isolation level) is also the lowest concurrency level. Conversely, the highest concurrency level yields the lowest consistency level. Maximum performance (I'll call it apparent performance) yields the lowest consistency level. There is no clear answer other than to use the lowest possible transaction isolation level consistent with the ODBC application design.

There are four transaction isolation levels. These levels are defined by the occurrence (or lack of) of the following phenomena:

- **Dirty Read**, which is the reading of transaction data of another application before the data is rolled back. The data read is considered dirty if there is a possibility that the transaction can be rolled back. The data may or may not exist within the database even though it was read by an application.

- **Nonrepeatable Read**, which occurs when the application reads a row and gets a different result each time. Another application updated the row before the second read occurred.

- **Phantom Read**, which is a row that matches a search criteria but isn't seen by the application. A second application has added a new row that meets the search criteria after the initial rows were read.

The different transaction isolation levels can now be enumerated. For example, assume there are two independent applications. Application A has an open transaction with *repeatable read* as the transaction isolation level. It is possible for application B to experience a *phantom read* while the transaction for application A remains open. Table 13-1 relates read phenomena to the different transaction isolation levels.

TABLE 13-1 READ PHENOMENA AND TRANSACTION ISOLATION LEVELS			
TRANSACTION ISOLATION LEVEL	*DIRTY READS*	*NONREPEATABLE READS*	*PHANTOM READS*
Read uncommitted	X	X	X
Read committed		X	X
Repeatable read			X
Serializable			

To better understand Table 13-1, a definition of each transaction isolation level term is needed:

- **Read uncommitted** — No transaction isolation occurs. Transactions running at this level are typically read-only.

- **Read committed** — The transaction is forced to wait until write-locked applications release data locks.

- **Repeatable read** — The transaction waits until write-locks on rows are released by other applications. The transaction holds a read-lock on all rows it returns to the application and write-locks on all rows it changes, deletes, or inserts.

- **Serializable** — The application holds read-locks on all rows affected by a read. A write-lock is placed on all rows affected by a change, delete, or insertion.

Concurrency

Increasing the level of transaction isolation reduces the level of *concurrency*. ODBC offers these four methods of concurrency control by a cursor:

o **Read-only** — The data is read-only, and the cursor cannot update or delete data.

o **Locking** — The cursor establishes the lowest locking level consistent with application design. Very low concurrency levels occur when the locking design choice is repeatable read or serialize.

o **Optimistic concurrency using row versions** and **optimistic concurrency using values** — Row versioning is a feature of an Oracle database, while values such as time stamps are a feature of Sybase and Microsoft SQL Server. Optimistic concurrency adopts the strategy of not locking the row until the update occurs. The current time stamp is compared with the prior time stamp to see if the data has changed. Conversely, pessimistic locking locks the row immediately. A developer uses this approach when collisions are commonplace and expected.

ACID, Consistency, and Measuring Database Transactions

An important feature of any database is transactions. The ACID properties declare the requirements necessary for consistent transactions:

o **Atomicity** — Either all or none of the transactions changes are present when the transaction completes.

o **Consistency** — The transaction respects all business rules and referential integrity. Inconsistent updates can be done, but will violate system integrity.

o **Isolation** — Transactions are isolated. SQL Server uses the SET statement:

```
SET TRANSACTION ISOLATION LEVEL
READ COMMITTED | READ UNCOMMITTED |
REPEATABLE READ | SERIALIZABLE
```

The SQL Server transaction isolation levels are maintained for all Recordsets of the transaction. On the other hand, Microsoft Access does not have a unified approach. Various RecordSet options can be used, such as **dbSeeChanges**, however, the options must be set for every RecordSet, which is an error-prone mechanism. Microsoft Access does have the **IsolateODBCTrans** for the **Workspace** object, but that just isolates one transaction from another and does not manage transaction isolation levels.

o **Durability**—Once the commit occurs, the transactions must be present even if the system fails. SQL Server supports this property with write-ahead into a log; Microsoft Access, however, does not. SQL Server will recover all closed transactions during recovery and will purge all open transactions. Microsoft Access does not have a log, and a system failure can mean loss of the database and the possible logical loss of the related disk. Microsoft Access is commonly used as a server, which is a serious architectural error. A solution is to back up the Access database before posting transactions. Another solution is to replicate the Access database on other sites. Either of these solutions for the **Durability** property issue is ad hoc and is not integrated into the Microsoft Access architecture. They each require operator intervention, whereas the log file and recovery mechanism of SQL Server is ingrained in the SQL Server architecture. Failure to support the **Durability** property is a good reason to not use Microsoft Access as a Server.

Block Cursors

I am sure that everyone is familiar with the screen cursor. It helps the user manage the screen. An ODBC cursor has the same role. There are different cursor models, and each model manages a returned result set in a different manner. *Block cursors* (also known as *fat cursors*) are the default for an application using ODBC 3.0. A block cursor is a returned rowset that cannot be scrolled; that is, the user cannot scroll back and forth between rows. An ODBC 3.0 application uses block cursors by setting the rowset size, binds the rowset buffers with **SQLColBind**, and calls either **SQLFetch** or **SQLFetchScroll**.

Cursor management in ODBC 3.0 is enhanced with the addition of cursor offsets. Column bindings are changed without an additional reference to **SQLColBind**. (This feature is not available for ODBC 2.0.)

Block cursors return multiple rows. Support for block cursors is an inherent feature of ODBC 3.0. **SQLFetch** always returns a multiple row result set in ODBC 3.0, while an ODBC 2.0 application returns only a single row forward cursor. The situation changes slightly when an ODBC 3.0 application calls **SQLFetch** using an ODBC 2.0 driver. The ODBC will only return one row unless the driver supports **SQLExtendedFetch**.

Block cursors are efficient. **SQLGetData** operates on a single column of a single row, and is not efficient. It is not designed for fetching data from multiple rows. Its intended use is the retrieval of long data, data that occurs in segments and cannot be retrieved in a single **SQLGetData** call. Long data can be either character or binary data.

Scrollable Cursors

Scrollable cursors are another cursor model. The user, through the client application, can scroll the returned rows of a result set. The scrollable cursor models are related to transaction isolation levels discussed above. The transaction isolation level determines the change detection threshold for scrollable cursors. Scrollable cursors come in these four flavors:

- **Static** — No data changes are detected by the client application. This is equivalent to the snapshot type recordset of the Microsoft Jet engine.

- **Dynamic** — These cursors detect all changes, but are difficult to implement; and, of course, difficult software is always error prone. The change detection threshold is managed by setting the `SQL_ATTR_TXN_ISOLATION` connection attribute.

- **Keyset-driven** — A keyset-driven cursor is almost a hybrid of static and dynamic cursors. The change detection threshold is managed by setting the `SQL_ATTR_TXN_ISOLATION` connection attribute. This cursor can detect deleted rows but not the addition of new rows.

  The complete keyset for the result set is saved when the cursor is opened. Rows deleted by another application are detectable; newly added rows, however, are not detectable. Looking at `SQL_STATIC_SENSITIVITY` with **SQLGetInfo** will determine if keyset-driven cursors can detect their own deletes.

- **Mixed**—A combination of a keyset-driven and a dynamic cursor. Rowset size should be less than the keyset size for a mixed cursor. A mixed cursor is equivalent to a dynamic cursor when the keyset size is set to 1. It is equivalent to a keyset-driven cursor when the keyset size is equal to the result set size.

The cursor will always detect deletions when scrolling within the keyset established when the cursor opened. The cursor assumes dynamic cursor behavior when the client application scrolls beyond the keyset size initially established and is unable to determine deleted rows. A rowset refresh will establish a new keyset and will return the cursor behavior to that of a keyset-driven cursor so long as the client application does not scroll beyond the established keyset limits.

Cursor Library Support

ODBC supports a block scrollable cursor for any driver that is Level 1 API compliant. The supported cursors are static and forward only. The cursor library also supports positioned update and delete statements for result sets created by SELECT statements.

Programming Protocol

The ODBC API is a series of single API functions that must be called in a prescribed order. An ODBC application follows an organized flow, or protocol, with ODBC API calls performing specific functions. Figure 13-2 illustrates the overall control flow of connecting to a data source and processing SQL statements.

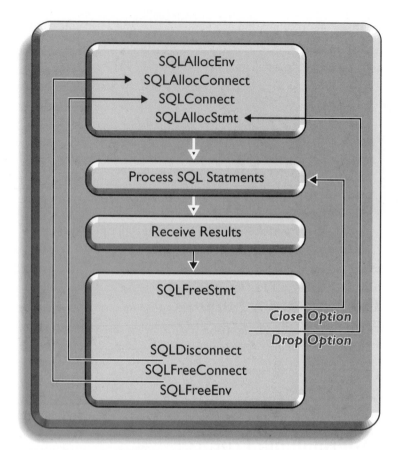

FIGURE 13-2   Basic ODBC programming protocol.

SQL processing detail is expanded in Figure 13-3; however, not all of the API functionality is shown. The example illustrated in Figure 13-3 is not an optimal solution, but it serves the purpose of illustrating additional API call sequence detail. You'll note that **SQLDescribeCol** is used. This is an arbitrary choice, and **SQLColAttributes** is a generalized alternative to using **SQLDescribeCol**. Optimal performance is obtained by calling **SQLColAttributes**, **SQLDescribeCol**, and **SQLNumResultCols** after a statement execution. These functions may execute slower for data sources that emulate statement preparation, or may not be supported by the target data source.

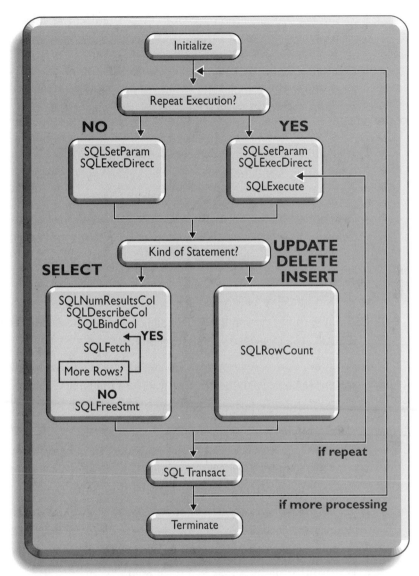

FIGURE 13-3 Advanced ODBC programming protocol.

Figures 13-2 and 13-3 represent logical flow of an ODBC application. Figure 13-2 represents ODBC functions used in resource allocation and controlling flow of an ODBC application. Figure 13-3 represents the ODBC functions used for building a query and processing query results. The programming steps using ODBC 3.0 functions are outlined below. As an example, the function **SQLAllocHandle**(STMT) is used rather than the deprecated ODBC 2.0 **SQLAllocStmt**. (See Chapter 12 for a list of deprecated functions.) These steps are procedural in nature:

1. Connecting to the data source consists of allocating an environment and a connection handle. The API functions called in this step are **SQLAllocHandle**(ENV), **SQLSetEnvAttr**, **SQLAllocHandle**(DBC), **SQLConnect**, and **SQLSetConnectAttr**.

2. This is a reminder to call **SQLSetEnvAttr** and set SQL_ATTR_ODBC_VER before using **SQLConnect**. It is the only opportunity to institute a behavioral change with ODBC 3.0 behavior changing to ODBC 2.*x*.

3. The cursor behavior for a COMMIT and a ROLLBACK operation is determined with **SQLGetInfo** after connecting to the data source. The attributes to interrogate are SQL_CURSOR_COMMIT_BEHAVIOR and SQL_CURSOR_ROLLBACK_BEHAVIOR. (See "Transactions," earlier in this chapter, for further detail.)

4. The application then initializes. Possible functions are **SQLGetInfo**, **SQLAllocHandle**(STM), and **SQLSetStmtAttr**.

5. Execution starts with any of the catalog functions such as **SQLColumns**, **SQLProcedures**, **SQLStatistics**, or it may be the binding of parameters with **SQLBindParameter** followed by **SQLExecDirect**. **SQLPrepare** and **SQLExecute** are other options.

6. Result sets are now returned. **SQLNumResultCols** counts the number of result set columns. Using **SQLDescribeCol** is optional if the column data types are already known. The application loops on **SQLDescribeCol** followed by **SQLBindCol** for each bound column in the result set. **SQLFetch** retrieves the data directly into the bound variables. Use **SQLGetData** when the columns are unbound or for long data. **SQLSetPos** moves the cursor.

7. The ODBC application uses **SQLRowCount** to verify that the expected number of rows is correct for the update or delete.

8. **SQLEndTran** follows an update of delete operation in the ODBC programming protocol. It is used to commit or rollback a transaction, but only when transaction processing is in manual mode. **SQLEndTran** is not applicable to query or catalog operations.

9. Finally, the connection is closed using the API functions **SQLFreeHandle** (STMT), **SQLDisconnect**, **SQLFreeHandle**(DBC), and **SQLFreeHandle**(ENV).

Debugging an ODBC Application

No discussion of programming is complete without a mention of debugging tools. ODBC has a trace mechanism for debugging an ODBC application. The trace output that follows is generated from the first example in the Examples section below. It was created by selecting Options ⇒ ODBC Trace from the ODBC 2.0/2.5 Administrator. ODBC Test is an invaluable tool in debugging an ODBC application. Listing 13-1 is the trace output from ODBC Test of the ODBC 2.1 SDK for the Access 2.0 query using ODBC 2.0/2.5:

```
USE Pubs
SELECT au_fname, au_lname FROM authors;
```

LISTING 13-1 Trace output from an OBDC Test for an Access 2.0 query using ODBC 2.0/2.5

```
SQLAllocEnv(phenv1DEF0000);
SQLAllocConnect(henv1DEF0000, phdbc32D70000);
SQLConnect(hdbc32D70000, "Thor", 4, "sa", 2, "", 0);
SQLAllocStmt(hdbc32D70000, phstmt32A70000);
SQLExecDirect(hstmt32A70000, "USE Pubs", 127);
SQLExecDirect(hstmt32A70000, "SELECT au_fname, au_lname FROM
  authors;", 128);
SQLFetch(hstmt32A70000);
SQLNumResultCols(hstmt32A70000, pccol);
SQLGetData(hstmt32A70000, 1, 1, rgbValue, 33, pcbValue);
SQLGetData(hstmt32A70000, 2, 1, rgbValue, 33, pcbValue);
SQLFreeStmt(hstmt32A70000, 1);
SQLDisconnect(hdbc32D70000);
SQLFreeConnect(hdbc32D70000);
SQLFreeEnv(henv1DEF0000);
```

The same query was run in Listing 13-2 with the ODBC 3.0 SDK using Access 95. Note the richness of content. The trace was started with the ODBC 3.0 dialog shown in Figure 13-4.

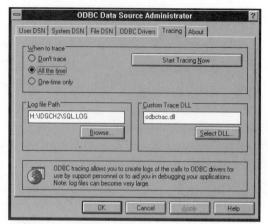

FIGURE 13-4   ODBC 3.0 Administrator dialog box.

Listing 13-2 is the trace output from ODBC Test of the ODBC 3.0 SDK for the ODBC 3.0 query:

```
USE Pubs
SELECT au_fname, au_lname FROM authors;
```

Note the differences in output. The ODBC Test from the ODBC 3.0 SDK provides finer detail of the operations associated with an ODBC query. All of the output for the simple query of the PUBS database is shown in Listing 13-2. Use ODBC Test of the ODBC 3.0 SDK with caution. You may fill your disk with trace output!

LISTING 13-2 Tracing a query that uses ODBC 3.0

```
MSACCESS 7b:76    ENTER SQLAllocConnect
    HENV   0x092a18e0
    HDBC * 0x001761d0
MSACCESS 7b:76    EXIT SQLAllocConnect with return code 0
(SQL_SUCCESS)
    HENV   0x092a18e0
    HDBC * 0x001761d0 ( 0x092a2d28)
MSACCESS 7b:76    ENTER SQLConnect
    HDBC   0x092a2d28
    UCHAR *    0x0018555c [ 4] "Thor"
    SWORD 4
```

```
        UCHAR *     0x001854dc [ 2] "sa"
        SWORD 2
        UCHAR *     0x001c53a4
        SWORD 0
MSACCESS 7b:76    ENTER SQLConnectW
        HDBC   0x092a2d28
        WCHAR *     0x092a0cc0 [ 8] "Thor"
        SWORD 8
        WCHAR *     0x092a2de8 [ 4] "sa"
        SWORD 4
        WCHAR *     0x092a2df8
        SWORD 0
MSACCESS 7b:76 EXIT SQLConnectW with return code 1
  (SQL_SUCCESS_WITH_INFO)
```

(Additional output omitted for brevity)

ODBC TARPITS

In the discussion that follows, I assume you have some SQL knowledge, because a requirement for successful ODBC programming is a working knowledge of SQL.

Performance is always an issue when data is shipped over the wire. This section is an enumeration of ODBC performance issues where some of the issues are common sense. A mechanical facility with ODBC API functions is not necessarily a guarantee of successful ODBC application. The successful ODBC programmer understands the characteristics and idiosyncrasies of the target data source, has a keen understanding of the problem at hand, and has the ability to recognize when programming tasks should be delegated.

A Division of Labor

You should always conduct a careful assessment of the architecture before you begin ODBC coding. Even though all tasks may be performed at the client site, there are certainly some intermediate steps that should be performed at the server. Stored procedures at the server always improve the performance of a client server application. A well-crafted ODBC application solution is not always a monolithic application program. It is architecture with the sharing of responsibilities.

A Procedural Solution

The greatest risk is in believing a good ODBC solution exists when in fact one doesn't. As stated previously, writing ODBC calls is a very straightforward process. The problem is that ODBC is only the messenger and the real issue is the use of ODBC, not the ODBC code itself. The specific problem is writing procedural code in a loop.

Procedural code that processes individual rows is not efficient. SQL deals with sets. If the client requires a browse capability, an optional solution is to download result sets to the client and browse the data locally. Replace code loops with SQL statements. **SQLGetData** in a loop is an example of a procedural solution. The proper solution is either column-wise binding or row-wise binding and using **SQLExtendedFetch** to retrieve a complete rowset result set rather than a single-row result set.

Bookmarks

Bookmarks are off by default. Turn unneeded bookmarks off in ODBC 2.0 with **SQLSetStmtOption** and in ODBC 3.0 with **SQLSetStmtAttr**.

Buffers

Always allocate a large enough *buffer*. A diagnostic record is created every time a record is truncated. This can be a major performance issue. An error message is created for each truncated row. Always allocate enough buffer space and avoid truncation.

Comparing Columns

The goal of any SQL query is to retrieve data. The goal of the developer is to construct a query that is search-limited. A search-limited query always compares a column value to a constant and will not scan the complete table. The constant allows the SQL engine to use index tables and limit the query. A query that is not search-limited, by definition performs a complete table scan. This is a major performance issue when the table has millions of rows. Comparing different columns in the same table is never search-limited, and is always a table scan. The query breaks the search-limited rule of not comparing a column with a constant. The problem is easily understood when you understand that each row must be read *before* it can be considered for inclusion in the result set.

Data Source Catalog

The ODBC application is probably not the only client of Microsoft SQL Server. The SQL server system control tables must be queried for catalog information. This operation is expensive, involves complex queries on the server with many joins, and may impact other users. The data comes from dynamic catalog functions such as **SQLTables**, **SQLColumns**, and **SQLPrimaryKeys**. A wise choice is to cache the information when the application starts. The same caching rule also applies to the static catalog functions such as **SQLGetTypeInfo**.

Expressions in a SQL Query

The expression `sales * 12 > 48000` is not search-limited because the column must be retrieved and the calculation performed before the comparison is made. Combining constants results in the expression `sales > 4000`, which is search-limited.

Limiting a Result Set

Common sense says don't pull any more data down the wire than is absolutely necessary. This applies to both unneeded rows and columns. This issue is also one of addressing scalability. Large result sets can be inappropriate for a list box. Data limiting doesn't apply only to query requests. It also applies to information functions such as **SQLTables**, which can return thousands of rows.

List Boxes

Care must be exercised when designing the application form. A query is required for each list box and this can make the form startup time prohibitive. Limit the number of list boxes on the application form.

Managing a BLOB

A BLOB is a large binary object that can be either binary or character data. The data isn't returned in a result set for a BLOB when the bound control for the BLOB is hidden. A BLOB should only be loaded when requested by the user.

Mixed Mode Expressions

Search limiting cannot be done with *Nulls*. A column that allows Nulls is changed from the CHAR type to the VARCHAR type by Microsoft SQL Server at column-definition time. Consequently, any query looking at that column results in a mixed mode expression (CHAR compared with VARCHAR) and the resulting query is not search-limited. A mixed mode expression is a form of expression calculation, which by definition is not search-limited.

An integer column with nulls and an integer column without nulls are not considered different data types. A column that the developer declares as CHAR and allows Nulls is changed by SQL Server to VARCHAR. SQL Server does not change the data type of an integer column when nulls are allowed. This means that an expression that involves columns of integer data that allow nulls is not considered a mixed mode expression.

Output Data Binding

Data from an unbound column can be obtained directly by calling **SQLGetData**. The preferable alternative is to use **SQLBindCol,** which binds a program variable to the column. The same choices exist here that exist for preparing a SQL statement. **SQLGetData** is an acceptable approach for a single value of data retrieved once. **SQLBindCol** is only done once for each output column of the query.

These are nice words, but it is somewhat idealistic to say that all columns should be bound. The Microsoft implementation of ODBC is C/C++ based. This means that column binding must be a mapping from a SQL data type to a C data type. C does not have an equivalent data type for the SQL data type VARCHAR, which means you cannot bind a VARCHAR column. The compromise is to create a variable length string and initialize it to a zero value and then declare it as a SQL_C_CHAR data type.

The other binding issue is Unicode, which has no C data type mapping. Characters are no longer 8-bit, but are now 16 bits. Characters and bytes are no longer synonymous. Any Microsoft-based application that uses Visual Basic for Applications is at risk when using character input/output (I/O).

Byte arrays are a means to avoid the problems of binding Unicode characters (see Chapter 42). The code fragment below illustrates the general technique. A byte array is not subject to Unicode machinations.

```
Private Type First_Array
 First_Name(20) as Byte
 cbFirst_Name as Long
End Type
 . . .
Dim User as First_Array
RetCode = SQLBindCol(hstmt, SQL_C_CHAR, User. First_Name(0),
 20, User.cbFirst_Name)
```

Preparing a SQL Statement

SQL statements can be executed directly with the **SQLExecDirect** statement, or the query can be prepared (compiled) with **SQLPrepare** and executed with **SQLExecute**. A query plan is created when a SQL statement is prepared. The **SQLExecute** statement lets the same statement be reused without compiling a new query plan. **SQLExecDirect** can be used for single-statement execution; however, the use of **SQLPrepare** and **SQLExecute** is preferred when statement execution is repeated.

Primary Keys

Always bind the primary key column. This keeps rows in a result set unique when using a cursor.

Recombining Strings

Data that is returned to the application as null-terminated strings must have the termination character stripped before the strings are recombined. The application program using string operators or functions normally performs this task.

Record Length

Buffer length is different than record length. The record length reflects the original record size even if truncation has occurred. Don't blindly use the record length. Compare the record length against the buffer length before using it. The problem is that although no data is lost because the query can be reissued, each truncated record does result in an error message. This can dramatically affect network bandwidth.

Search Limited

Microsoft SQL Server uses a cost-based optimizer for query optimization. Within this context there are only two types of queries: those that are search-limited and those that are not. A query which is not search-limited will always do a table scan, which is usually the least desirable scenario. This is not always true because a table scan may be more efficient when the query selectivity is low.

A search-limited query uses an inclusion operator to compare a column in a table with a constant. The general syntax for such an expression is:

```
<column> <inclusion operator> <constant> [ AND ... ]
```

Some examples are:

```
fname = 'Bruce'
lname= 'Prendergast'
title='wannabe author'
fname = 'Bruce' AND lname = 'Prendergast'
salary < 10000
```

`<`, `>`, `=`, `BETWEEN`, and `LIKE` are the inclusion operators. All columns of a joined expression must be in the same table. `BETWEEN` is really not an inclusion operator for a search argument. It is converted in the optimizer parsing phase to two search arguments using the operators `>` and `<` joined by the `AND`.

`LIKE` is a qualified inclusion operator in that `LIKE <character string>%` is search-limited while `LIKE %<character string>` is not search-limited.

Nonsearch arguments are those operators that force more than one scan of the target table. The operators `NOT`, `NOT IN ()`, `!=`, and `<>` are not search-limited arguments. To find members that are not in a result set, the SQL engine must first find those elements that are members of the original set. The `NOT IN` members are those members not contained in the original set. This process requires two table scans.

It is possible to convert some nonsearch argument operators. The expression `<column> <> 0` can be converted to `<column> > 0` if the number is positive.

Expressions with the `OR` operator are not search-limited because the `OR` operator is the union of two distinct queries. By definition the operator `<>` is not search-limited. Converting the to an expression of the form `column > 0 OR column < 0` is still not search-limited because the expression uses the `OR` operator.

SQLExtendedFetch

There are always two ways to perform a task—a wrong way and a right way. **SQLFetch** returns a single row while **SQLExtendedFetch** returns multiple rows. **SQLFetch** is certainly the wrong choice as a data retrieval mechanism for backward scrolling. (I am assuming the application is doing backward scrolling because your ODBC driver doesn't support it.) Your code includes a loop of **SQLFetch** followed by a **SQLFreeStmt**. The appropriate implementation is **SQLExtendedFetch**, which returns a row set simplifying the local cursor implementation.

 note **This issue applies to ODBC 2.0 only because SQLFetch in ODBC 3.0 supports block cursors.**

KEY POINT SUMMARY

Several key issues were discussed in this chapter. The first was that the order in which the ODBC functions are used must be understood for a successful ODBC application. Recall that ODBC uses a call-level interface (CLI) and does not use object models.

The second major issue was to understand that a client-server application using ODBC forms an interaction model. Without other users, there are no problems. The ODBC interaction model is controlled by the transaction isolation levels set by other applications with open transactions. Of course this is not an issue when there is no common table or row. Let's imagine a fun scenario:

The Vice President of Finance is scrolling the yearly profit and loss statement. Another task is posting year-end information, and there is a detail line item where XYZ Corporation made a $1,000,000 purchase. This gives the company a small profit for the year. The Vice President captures this information because the transaction is open and the transaction isolation level is set to **read uncommitted** (dirty read).

The transaction is rolled back because the XYZ Corporation $1,000,000 entry is an error. The transaction is rerun with corrected input and the company now has a small loss for the year. The Vice President of Finance still has the report showing the small company profit. He showed it to the CEO and . . . .

Microsoft Access is not a DBMS because it does not support the **durability** property of a transaction. Microsoft Access does not support transaction isolation levels, another reason for never using Access as a server.

The other key issue for the developer is to understand which ACID properties of a transaction are supported by the target DBMS. Without proper ACID property support, the developer must provide a scenario for contingencies.

- ODBC function statements must be issued in the proper order. A state transition error occurs when statements are issued in the wrong order.
- Three handles control ODBC: the environment handle, the connection handle, and the statement handle.
- Each handle has three states: unallocated, allocated, and connected.
- Block cursors are the default in ODBC 3.0.
- ODBC 3.0 is enhanced with cursor offsets. This means that every row need not be bound. This feature is not available in ODBC 2.0.
- ODBC3.0 supports SQL 92. Autocommit transactions are the default.
- ODBC 3.0 has four new descriptors that are allocated automatically by ODBC 3.0. They are the Application Parameter descriptor (APD), Implementation (Driver) Parameter Descriptor (IPD), Application Row Descriptor (ARD), and Implementation (Driver) Row Descriptor (IRD).
- ODBC supports a cursor library for those drivers that are Level 1 compliant.
- A transaction rolls back all open transactions for the particular environment.

APPLYING WHAT YOU'VE LEARNED

The questions below are quite comprehensive. If you know the answers and understand the issues, then you are well on your way to becoming a competent and proficient ODBC developer.

Instant Assessment

1. Explain the concept of a search-limited expression. Give several examples of search limited expressions.

2. What is the fastest processing technique for a single SQL statement? What is the fastest processing technique for repeated statements?

3. Explain why a SQL query with the NOT IN operator is not search-limited.

4. What is the problem with calculations in a query expression?

5. What is unique about a SQL expression containing an OR clause?

6. What advantage does preparing a SQL statement offer?

7. What is a state transition error?

8. What is a fat cursor?

9. What is the unique characteristic of a static cursor?

10. Explain the operating principles of a dynamic cursor.

11. What are the limitations of a keyset-driven cursor?

12. Name a limitation of the Microsoft implementation of ODBC in C/C++.

13. What important function must be performed after an environment handle is allocated?

14. Describe the differences between the ODBC 2.*x* **SQLFetch** and the ODBC 3.0 **SQLFetch**.

15. Name a new and very useful connection attribute that enhances performance.

16. Describe long data and how to process it.

17. **SQLGetData** has a unique property. What is it?

18. What new binding feature is not supported in ODBC 2.0? Is it a performance issue?

19. What is a catalog function?

20. Name the catalog functions.

21. When is **SQLDescribeCols** used?

22. When is the ODBC API function **SQLEndTran** used?

23. What happens to a SQL statement that the ODBC driver cannot translate?

24. What is the scope of a transaction?

25. Describe using the API function **SQLExecute**.

26. What is the default transaction mode for ODBC?

27. What determines cursor behavior for commit or rollback operations?

28. When is a cursor closed automatically?

29. Describe a performance issue with manual commit transactions.

30. Compare optimistic concurrency with pessimistic concurrency.

31. Describe ODBC cursor library support.

concept link   **For answers to the Instant Assessment questions, see Appendix C.**

Windows Architecture I

ODBC Examples

About Chapter 14

Chapter 14 is a collection of ODBC examples. The examples are ordered by increasing complexity. Not all ODBC API functions are illustrated, but the examples are representative of all the general categories. The examples include connecting, disconnecting, catalog functions, statement options, connection options, transactions, input parameters, output parameters, queries, rowset size, keyset size, statement concurrency, and positioned updates.

All ODBC examples are located on the CD-ROM that accompanies this book. The examples use ODBC 2.0 and Microsoft Access 2.0. The Access ODBC.MDB is located in the EXAMPLES\CHAPTER14 folder of your CD-ROM. ODBC 2.0/2.5 and Access 2.0 are used for the examples because the software is upward-compatible but not downward-compatible. The choice of Access 2.0 is based on several factors:

- I assume that many readers of this book are not conversant with Visual C++. This makes Microsoft Access or Microsoft Visual Basic the middle-of-the-road tools using the ODBC API.

- Access 2.0 is 16-bit and does not use Unicode.

- Many of my associates are still programming Access 2.0 applications. It appears that Microsoft Access 2.0 is still widely used.

- Microsoft Access 2.0 is upward-compatible with other Microsoft Access releases. Converting ODBC 2.0 to ODBC 3.0 requires some work because of all the API calls that changed from ODBC.DLL to ODBC32.DLL. Older ODBC functionality is supported though deprecated in ODBC 3.0. This means that deprecated functions are likely to disappear from the next ODBC release.

ODBC WITHOUT UNICODE

The main form of the ODBC.MBD is shown in Figure 14-1. The captions on the command buttons of Figure 14-1 identify the demonstrated functionality. The click event of each command button contains the related code fragment.

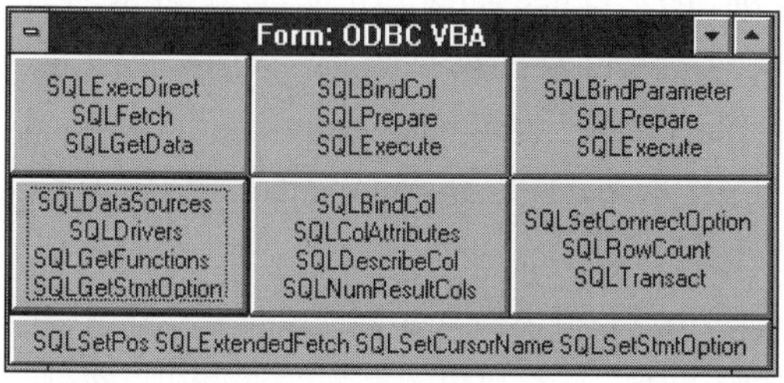

FIGURE 14-1   Access 2.0 ODBC.MDB on the CD-ROM.

The ODBC example presented in this chapter demonstrates sophisticated issues using column-wise binding with a **SQLExtendedFetch**. Listing 14-1 is the code behind the bottom command button in Figure 14-1. Although not illustrated in this chapter, the code examples for the other command buttons are found in the Access 2.0 MDB in the EXAMPLES\CHAPTER14 folder on the CD-ROM that accompanies this book. A second cursor is used for a positioned update that may be rolled back if the transaction fails. My only choices in demonstrating these examples are C++ or Microsoft Access 2.0. I elected to use Microsoft Access 2.0 because of the readability of the code. I can't use the ODBC API with either Access 95 or Access 97 because of the column binding issues of Unicode. That doesn't mean that Access 95 and Access 97 do not use ODBC. Indeed they do; however, it is encapsulated within *Data Access Objects* (DAO). It should be obvious that Microsoft Access 2.0 is still a viable product, especially when dealing with foreign databases. It does not have the burden of a Unicode character set.

The ODBC example in this chapter uses ODBC 2.0/2.5 and Microsoft Access 2.0, which is 16-bit. The natural choice for Access 2.0 is ODBC 2.0/2.5 with 16-bit drivers. Many ODBC 2.0 functions are deprecated in ODBC 2.0. As an example, **SQLAllocEnv**, **SQLAllocConnect**, and **SQLAllocStmt** are deprecated functions in ODBC 3.0. They are replaced with the new ODBC 3.0 function **SQLAllocHandle**, which expects a parameter identifying the allocation type.

The example uses the ODBC SDK naming convention with respect to ODBC parameters. The naming conventions are described in both the ODBC 2.0 SDK and the ODBC 3.0 SDK. As an example of a naming convention, *szSqlStr* is a null-terminated string where the SQL statement is stored. *SqlStr* represents the contextual functionality. The string size is represented by the parameter *cbSqlStr*, which is the count in bytes of a string with a contextual functionality of *SqlStr*. Another example is *pcbColDef,* which is defined as a pointer to a byte count for the *ColDef* parameter. The usage will be clear from the code context. Variables that are not ODBC parameters have meaningful names and are understood in the context in which they are used. *au_fname* is a column name in the *Pubs* database, *authors* table of Microsoft SQL Server.

The example in Listing 14-1 (ODBC7_Click) is one instance of how an ODBC application should be done. The primary functionality of this example is **SQLExtendedfetch**, and not **SQLGetData**, which is only useful as a teaching aid. Yes, there is a lot of work, but after you've done it a few times, it is simply a matter of cutting and pasting along with using the tool kit you've developed. Use these techniques with C++ and you'll blow the doors off any other database access technology. Remember that the other database access technologies are only ODBC wrappers and a wrapper always adds overhead. Other technologies incur overhead by binding into variants, which is not true with ODBC and C++. A column binds into a native C++ type when the application is implemented in C++. As you may have guessed, Microsoft has threading model problems.

You have threading model control in C++. There are currently four threading models. Don't be impressed with the easy-to-use database access technologies. Everything of value has a price, and anything of real value does not have a cheap price. This ODBC API example took several days to construct and there were some problems. The development time for this example can be reduced significantly by using DAO of Microsoft Access or RDO of Visual Basic. It is a zero-sum gain: either reduce the development cycle by using DAO or RDO and incur additional operational overhead and application limitations, or lengthen the development cycle with the ODBC API and reduce operational overhead and reduce application limitations. The bottom line: ODBC for the enterprise and DAO or RDO for the desktop. (See Chapters 15–23 on DAO and Chapters 24–26 on RDO.)

A keyset and a rowset size is set using **SQLSetStmtOption**. No binding options are set because column-wise binding is the default. The cursor type is set to keyset-driven and a cursor is created.

Now comes the interesting part. This is a **SQLExtendedFetch** that will return multiple rows. If the result set is small, this is the equivalent of binding the complete result set. It the result set is large, then this example is the equivalent of binding a complete rowset. Note that both RDO and DAO support the **GetRows** method that provides good query performance. However, the ancillary issues of threading model problems, variants, incurred overhead, and the very nature of COM, which is objects using marshaling to communicate with other objects, reduces the attractiveness of using such a technology in the enterprise. (Does all that COM minutiae start to make sense now?) The use of DAO or RDO on the desktop cannot be faulted. The **GetRows** method optimizes data retrieval for DAO and RDO; the method, however, does not support a positioned update.

I was unable to bind a VBA array; I did, however, successfully bind a zero-initialized string. A C++ array binds with no difficulty, and many of the implementation difficulties I encountered with VBA do not exist for applications coded in C++.

The string size is the rowset size times the column width. The rather ugly expressions later in the code are just the starting character position calculations for the VBA **MID$** function. This behavior makes sense when you consider that ODBC expects a C-type data structure and increments that structure address by the column width.

I did encounter a problem when binding arrays. ODBC 2.0 sets all column widths to the width of the last column bound. This is ODBC 2.0 and there isn't any hope for a patch. Because this is character data, I set all column widths to the same value of 20 characters. Note that this is not Unicode software.

The position update requires a second cursor. The SQL syntax for a positioned update SELECT statement includes the phrase FOR UPDATE OF, which is different syntax than a conventional SELECT statement. The positioned update statement has the phrase WHERE CURRENT OF, which references the cursor positioned by the other statement. This synchronizes the statement handles because both statement handles are using the same cursor. **SQLTransact** is included to roll back the positioned update when an error occurs.

To create an **ODBC7_Click** program, follow these steps (also refer to Listing 14-1):

1. Call the function **Create_Connection** to establish all handles.

2. Use **SQLSetConnectOption** to set transaction to AUTOCOMMIT.

   The connection parameter is identified by *fOption,* which is set to

SQL_AUTOMMIT. The SQL_AUTOCOMMIT_ON value to set this connection option is in parameter *vParam*.

3. Set statement concurrency using **SQLSetStmtOption** and setting the parameter *fOption* to SQL_CONCUR_ROWVER.

4. Set cursor type using **SQLSetStmtOption** and setting the parameter *vParam* to SQL_CURSOR_KEYSET_DRIVEN.

5. Set keyset size using **SQLSetStmtOption** and setting the parameter *vParam* to a local constant, in this case 20.

6. Set rowset size using **SQLSetStmtOption** and setting the parameter *vParam* to a local constant, in this case 20.

7. Create a cursor using **SQLSetCursorName** and name it *C1*.

8. Use **SQLExecDirect** for connecting to the *Pubs* database of Microsoft SQL Server. A prepared statement isn't used because there are no parameters and this statement is not repeated.

9. Use **SQLFreeStmt** with the parameter value SQL_UNBIND to clean up the statement.

10. Construct a query asking for the columns *au_fname* and *au_lname* against the *authors* table of the *Pubs* database.

11. Use **SQLPrepare** to prepare the query identified by the statement handle *hstmt* of the statement *szSqlStr* with length *cbSqlStr*.

12. Use **SQLExecute** to execute a prepared statement the *hstmt* handle.

13. Use **SQLNumResultCols** to verify the number of result columns for the statement handle *hstmt*.

14. Use a loop to call **SQLDescribeCol** to save the column types in an array.

15. Bind each output column using **SQLBindCol** and the parameter values in the array *fCType()*.

16. Set *fFetchType* to SQL_FETCH_NEXT and use **SQLExtendedFetch** to bind a complete keyset into the bound arrays. SQL_FETCH_NEXT is used because this is a keyset-driven cursor.

17. Scroll through the data using the *iact* variable. The calculated variable *fidx* is the found or starting index of the data. The data length is held in the array *cblname()*.

18. When a user elects to change a value, set *fOption* to `SQL_POSITION` and *flock* to `SQL_LOCK_NO_CHANGE`. Position the cursor using the original statement handle *hstmt*.

19. Clean up the position update handle *hstmtU* by using **SQLFreeStmt** with the option `SQL_UNBIND`.

20. Construct a SQL positioned update statement that uses the phrase `WHERE CURRENT OF <cursor name>`. In this case, the name is *C1*.

21. Prepare the positioned statement *hstmtU* using **SQLPrepare**.

22. Bind the new input value. This is the value the client changed. Use **SQLBindParameter** on statement handle *hstmtU*.

23. Execute the position update using **SQLExecute** on statement handle *hstmtU*.

24. Examine the row count of the statement handle *hstmtU* with the **SQLRowCount** function. If the value is not one row, the transaction is forced to fail.

25. If the update fails, set the transaction parameter *fType* to the value `SQL_ROLLBACK` and use **SQLTransact** to rollback the transaction. **SQLTransact** uses the environment handle *henv* and the connection handle *hdbc*. It does not use a statement handle.

26. Otherwise, use *fType* to set the value of `SQL_COMMIT` and use **SQLTransact** to commit the transaction.

27. Loop back on the keyset index. There is no rowset logic. The implementation of this is left as an exercise to the reader.

28. Use the function **Release_Connection** to release all handles and the connection.

LISTING 14-1 SQLSetPos, SQLExtendedFetch, SQLSetCursorName, and SQLSetStmtOption

```
Sub ODBC7_Click ()
'(C) 1998 Bruce T. Prendergast
' DBA Prendergast Consulting
' DBA PCS
' IDG BooksWorldwide ISBN 0-7645-3123-9
'
' Listing 14-1 SQLSetPos, SQLExtendedfetch,
' SQLSetCursorName, and SQLSetStmtOption.
' Demonstrate a positioned update
'
```

```
            Const ROWS = 20
    '
    '   SQLError parameters
    '
        Dim ErrCode As Integer
        Dim ErrorMsg As String * MAX_STRING_LENGTH
        Dim cbErrorMsg As Integer
        Dim NativeError As Long
        Dim SqlState As String * MAX_STRING_LENGTH
    '
    '   SQLSetPos
    '
        'Dim hstmt as Long        ' duplicated
        'Dim irow as Integer      ' duplicated
        'Dim fOption as integer   ' duplicated
        Dim fLock As Integer      ' SQL_LOCK_NO_CHANGE,
                                  ' SQL_LOCK_UNLOCK,
                                  ' or SQL_LOCK_EXCLUSIVE
    '
    '   SQLTransact
    '
        'Dim henv as Long         ' duplicated
        'Dim hdbc as Long         ' duplicated
        Dim fType As Integer      ' SQL_COMMIT or SQL_ROLLBACK
    '
    '   SQLNumResultCols
    '
        Dim cCol As Integer
    '
    '   SQLDescribeCol
    '
        Dim szColName As String * 64
        Dim cbColNameMax As Integer    ' maximum returned name
        Dim pcbColName As Integer      ' Return name size
        Dim pfSQLType As Integer       ' attribute we're looking
                                         for
```

```
        Static pcbColDef(ROWS) As Long    ' output data column
                                            precision
        Dim pibscale As Integer            ' Output scale
        Dim pfNullable As Integer          ' SQL_NO_NULLS,

                            '        SQL_NULLABLE,

          ' or SQL_NULLABLE_UNKNOWN
'
'       SQLNumParams
'
        'Dim hstmt as Long          ' duplicated
        Dim pcPar As Integer        ' returned parameter count
'
'       SQLSetConnectOption
'
        'Dim hdbc as Long           ' duplicated
        Dim fOption As Integer      ' Set to SQL_AUTOCOMMIT
        Dim vParam As Long          ' Set to SQL_AUTOCOMMIT_OFF
'
'       SQLRowCount
'
        'Dim hstmt as Long                  ' duplicated
        Dim pcRow As Long                   ' returned row count
'
'       Initialize VARCHAR strings
'
        Static lname(ROWS) As String        ' storage for last name
        Static fname(ROWS) As String        ' storage for first name
        Static cbfname(ROWS) As Long        ' SQLBindCol
        Static cblname(ROWS) As Long        ' SQLBindCol
        Dim tfname As String                ' debug
        Dim tlname As String                ' debug
        Dim tsizemax As Long                ' debug
'
'       SQLExecDirect parameters
```

```
        '

            Dim RetCode As Integer
            Dim szSqlStr As String * 128     ' SQL query storage
            Dim cbSqlStr As Long             ' byte count for query
        '

        '   SQLBindParameter
        '

            'Dim hstmt As Long               ' Duplicated
            Dim icol As Integer              ' binding column
            Dim ipar As Integer              '
            Dim fParamType As Integer        '
            Static fCType(2) As Integer      '
            Dim fSQLType As Integer          '
            Dim cbColDef As Long             '
            Dim ibScale As Integer           '
            Dim rgbValue As String * 64      '
            Dim cbValueMax As Long           '
            Dim pcbValue As Long             '
        '

        '   SQLSetCurorName
        '

            'Dim hstmt as Integer            ' duplicated
            Dim szCursor As String * 64      ' cursor name
            Dim cbCursor As Integer          ' size of cursor
        '

        '   SQLExtendedFetch
        '

            'Dim hstmt as Integer        ' duplicated
            Dim fFetchType As Integer    ' FETCH_NEXT
            Dim iRow As Long             ' row to fetch
            'Dim pcRow As Long        ' duplicated (See SQLRowCount)
            Static rgfRowStatus(ROWS) As Integer ' row status values
            Dim iAct As Integer      ' SQLExtendedFetch loop variable
        '

        '   use common code
        '
```

```
    If Not Create_Connection() Then
        Exit Sub
    End If
'
'   set connect options
'
    fOption = SQL_AUTOCOMMIT
    vParam = SQL_AUTOCOMMIT_ON
    RetCode = BTPSQLSetConnectOption(hdbc, fOption, vParam)
    If RetCode <> SQL_SUCCESS Then
        MsgBox "SQLSetConnectOption failed"
        GoTo SetPos_error
    End If
'
'   set statement options. I'll be using SQLExtendedFetch
'   and column-wise binding is the default so I won't set
'   the binding type.
'
    fOption = SQL_CONCURRENCY
        vParam = SQL_CONCUR_ROWVER
    RetCode = BTPSQLSetStmtOption(hstmt, fOption, vParam)
    If RetCode <> SQL_SUCCESS Then
        MsgBox "SQLSetStmtOption on concurrency failed"
        GoTo SetPos_error
    End If
    fOption = SQL_CURSOR_TYPE
        vParam = SQL_CURSOR_KEYSET_DRIVEN
    RetCode = BTPSQLSetStmtOption(hstmt, fOption, vParam)
    If RetCode <> SQL_SUCCESS Then
        MsgBox "SQLSetStmtOption on cursor type failed"
        GoTo SetPos_error
    End If
    fOption = SQL_ROWSET_SIZE
        vParam = ROWS
    RetCode = BTPSQLSetStmtOption(hstmt, fOption, vParam)
    If RetCode <> SQL_SUCCESS Then
```

```
            MsgBox "SQLSetStmtOption on rowset size failed"
            GoTo SetPos_error
        End If
        szCursor = "C1" & Chr$(0)
        cbCursor = SQL_NTS
        RetCode = BTPSQLSetCursorName(hstmt, ByVal szCursor,
        cbCursor)
        If RetCode <> SQL_SUCCESS Then
            MsgBox "SQLSetCursorName on cursor creation failed"
            GoTo SetPos_error
        End If
        '
        '   connect to the Pubs database on SQL Server
        '
        szSqlStr = "USE Pubs" & Chr$(0)        ' on SQL Server
        cbSqlStr = Len(szSqlStr) - 1
        RetCode = BTPSQLExecDirect(hstmt, szSqlStr, cbSqlStr)
        If (RetCode <> SQL_SUCCESS) And (RetCode <>
                            SQL_SUCCESS_WITH_INFO) Then
            MsgBox "Could not connect to Pubs database "
            GoTo SetPos_error
        End If
        '
        '   clean up the statement
        '
        RetCode = BTPSQLFreeStmt(hstmt, SQL_UNBIND)
        '
        '   The first and last name query
        '
        szSqlStr = "SELECT au_fname, au_lname FROM authors"
            szSqlStr = szSqlStr & " FOR UPDATE OF au_fname,
            au_lname"
        cbSqlStr = Len(szSqlStr)
        RetCode = BTPSQLPrepare(hstmt, szSqlStr, cbSqlStr)
        If RetCode <> SQL_SUCCESS Then
            MsgBox "SQLPrepare failed"
```

```
        GoTo SetPos_error
    End If
'
'   Execute a prepared statement. I'll get a warning message
'   that concurrency has changed, which I'll ignore
'
    RetCode = BTPSQLExecute(hstmt)
     If (RetCode <> SQL_SUCCESS) And (RetCode <>
                    SQL_SUCCESS_WITH_INFO) Then
        MsgBox "SQLExecute failed"
        GoTo SetPos_error
    End If
'
'   Get output column count
'
    RetCode = BTPSQLNumResultCols(hstmt, cCol)
    If RetCode <> SQL_SUCCESS Then
        MsgBox "SQLNumResultCols error"
        GoTo SetPos_error
    End If
'
'   find the column sizes
'
    cbColNameMax = 63
    For icol = 1 To cCol
        RetCode = BTPSQLDescribeCol(hstmt, icol,
                    szColName, cbColNameMax, pcbColName,
                    pfSQLType, pcbColDef(icol - 1),
                    pibscale, pfNullable)
'
'   construct the bind arguments. Set C data type to SQL data
'   type
'
        If pfSQLType = SQL_VARCHAR Then
            fCType(icol - 1) = SQL_C_CHAR
```

```
                Else
                    fCType(icol - 1) = pfSQLType
                End If
            Next icol
        '

        '   initialize the output area
        '

            For iRow = 0 To ROWS - 1
                fname(iRow) = String$(pcbColDef(0), 0)
                lname(iRow) = String$(pcbColDef(1), 0)
            Next iRow
        '

        '   Bind the first and last names
        '

            RetCode = BTPSQLBindCol(hstmt, 1, fCType(0), ByVal
                        fname(0),
                        pcbColDef(0), cbfname(0))


            If RetCode <> SQL_SUCCESS Then
                MsgBox "SQLBindCol error on first parameter"
                GoTo SetPos_error
            End If
            RetCode = BTPSQLBindCol(hstmt, 2, fCType(1), ByVal
                        lname(0),
                        pcbColDef(1), cblname(0))
            If RetCode <> SQL_SUCCESS Then
                MsgBox "SQLBindCol error on second parameter"
                GoTo SetPos_error
            End If
        '

        '   get a rowset
        '

            fFetchType = SQL_FETCH_NEXT
            iRow = 1
            RetCode = BTPSQLExtendedFetch(hstmt, fFetchType,
                    iRow, pcRow, rgfRowStatus(0))
```

```
    If RetCode <> SQL_SUCCESS Then
        MsgBox "SQLExtendedFetch error"
        GoTo SetPos_error
    End If
'
'
'   at this point I have a rowset in cursor C1. It is simple
'   and is only one row. It could have been more. It is
'   keyset-driven and I can loop on rows, or the values could
'   have been placed in a combo box. So, let's do something
'   important and change a first name.
'
    For iAct = 0 To pcRow - 1
'
'   is the row deleted
'
        If rgfRowStatus(iAct) <> SQL_ROW_DELETED Then
'
'   does the user want to change it
'
            rgbValue = InputBox("Change First Name, C/R for
No",
                                    "Change First Name",
"No")
            If rgbValue <> "No" Then
'
' change it
'
                fOption = SQL_POSITION
                fLock = SQL_LOCK_NO_CHANGE
                RetCode = BTPSQLSetPos(hstmt, iAct, fOption,
                                    fLock)
                If RetCode <> SQL_SUCCESS Then
                    MsgBox "SQLSetPos error"
                    GoTo SetPos_error
                End If
'
```

```
'    clean up the statement from prior usage
'
              RetCode = BTPSQLFreeStmt(hstmt, SQL_UNBIND)
'
'    update
'
              szSqlStr = "UPDATE authors SET au_fname = ? "
                  szSqlstr = szSqlStr & "WHERE CURRENT OF
                  C1;"
              cbSqlStr = Len(szSqlStr)
              RetCode = BTPSQLPrepare(hstmt, szSqlStr,
              cbSqlStr)
              If RetCode <> SQL_SUCCESS Then
                  MsgBox "SQLPrepare failed"
                  GoTo SetPos_error
              End If
'
'    bind the parameter
'
              ipar = 1                    ' the first one
              fParamType = SQL_PARAM_INPUT  '
              fSQLType = SQL_VARCHAR        ' SQL data type
              ibScale = 0      ' not used for char
              cbValueMax = 32  ' buffer size maximum for
                                    text
              pcbValue = Len(rgbValue) ' Input length
              RetCode = BTPSQLBindParameter(hstmt, ipar,
                  fParamType, fCType(iRow), fSQLType,
                  pcbColDef(iRow), ibScale, rgbValue,
                  cbValueMax, pcbValue)
              If RetCode <> SQL_SUCCESS Then
                  MsgBox "SQLBindParameter failed"
                  GoTo SetPos_error
              End If
'
'    Execute a prepared statement
```

```
'
                    RetCode = BTPSQLExecute(hstmt)
                    If RetCode <> SQL_SUCCESS Then
                        MsgBox "SQLExecute failed on Pubs
                        database"
                        GoTo SetPos_error
                    End If
                    RetCode = BTPSQLRowCount(hstmt, pcRow)
                    If pcRow <> 1 Then
'

'   unable to update row, roll it back

'
                        fType = SQL_ROLLBACK
                        RetCode = BTPSQLTransact(henv, hdbc,
                        fType)
                        MsgBox "Transaction rolled back.  Row
                        count was:
                                                        " &
Str$(pcRow)
                    Else
                        fType = SQL_COMMIT
                        RetCode = BTPSQLTransact(henv, hdbc,
                        SQL_COMMIT)
                        MsgBox "Transaction committed"
                    End If
                End If
            End If
        Next iAct
        RetCode = Release_connection()
        Exit Sub
SetPos_error:
    MsgBox "RetCode is: " & Str$(RetCode)
    ErrCode = BTPSQLError(henv, hdbc, hstmt, SqlState,
  NativeError, ErrorMsg, MAX_STRING_LENGTH, cbErrorMsg)
    MsgBox "Error message: " & Mid$(ErrorMsg, 1, cbErrorMsg)
    MsgBox "SQL State: " & SqlState
```

```
        MsgBox "Native error code: " & Str$(NativeError)
        RetCode = Release_connection()
        Exit Sub
    End Sub
```

KEY POINT SUMMARY

- ◦ ODBC is easily misused because it has a CLI. A mechanical facility with ODBC functions does not guarantee a successful ODBC solution; you have a procedural solution when rows are pulled down the wire from the data source within a loop. The ideal update mechanism remains a SQL statement. A SQL statement processes many rows, whereas a procedural loop invariably processes only one row at a time.

- ◦ There is ODBC life beyond **SQLGetData** and **SQLPutData**. ODBC authors invariably use these functions in ODBC examples. The problem is that the examples are often not extended beyond these simple functions and the reader is left with the impression that ODBC is simple and easy to use. **SQLGetData** and **SQLPutData** should only be used as teaching tools. This chapter uses **SQLGetData** only as the first step to our ultimate goal: **SQLExtendedFetch**.

- ◦ Surprisingly, the ODBC API can be used from Access. This is a confusing point to many developers because Microsoft Access hosts its own version of ODBC known as the Desktop Driver Set.

APPLYING WHAT YOU'VE LEARNED

The Lab Exercises are divided into two categories. The first category is converting all but one of the examples to the ODBC 3.0 API. The second category is embellishing the examples with additional functionality. You must have access to SQL Server to complete the laboratories.

Lab Exercises

Lab 14.29 *Converting to ODBC 3.0*

This Lab Exercise converts some of the examples from Access 2.0 and ODBC 2.0/2.5 to ODBC 3.0 and Access 97. Unicode isn't a factor in these examples. Listing 14-1 and listings 14-2, 14-3, and 14-10 on the CD-ROM must be converted. Remember that there are deprecated ODBC 2.0 functions in these examples. You shouldn't start this exercise unless you have the ODBC 3.0 SDK that is available from Microsoft Press. Your starting point is to change the library references of all ODBC API declarations from ODBC.DLL to ODBC32.DLL.

Lab 14.30 *Finishing the ODBC conversions*

The goal of this lab is to convert to ODBC 3.0 the examples represented by Listings 14-4, 14-5, 14-6, and 14-7 on the CD-ROM. You did the majority of the conversion work in Lab 14.29 and this exercise should be relatively easy.

Lab 14.31 *Creating a useful ODBC example of your own*

Unlike Access and DAO, which can bind data to a control, ODBC binds data to program variables. It is the developer's responsibility to present the data to the user. This is relatively easy using the **AddItem** method of both Microsoft Access and Visual Basic.

This is a "tough love" lab exercise. The task is easily accomplished in other database access technologies such as DAO, but we're going to use ODBC to construct a database browse application. You have the option of extending this application to a general query-by-form application, but here we'll only browse.

1. The application starts with only one combo box. This combo box (or list box) presents a list of the databases available to the user. Clear all other information when a user selects a database.

2. Present the database name in a conspicuous manner and populate a list or combo box with table names from the database.

3. Follow the same general procedure as above, and present the table name in a conspicuous manner. Present a new combo box with a list of column names.

4. When the user selects a column, present the values in a list box.

5. Provide two text boxes for upper and lower values and an option button for the type of logical test.

Lab 14.32 *Back to Access 2.0 and ODBC 2.0/2.5*

WA I

The **SQLExtendedFetch** example of Listing 14-9 has limited user interface capability. All data is displayed with a message and a dialog box. Although the database access technique is satisfactory, the user interface is far less than desirable. Provide a user-friendly interface where the information is displayed in a list box or a combo box and the user selects the row information that is to be updated. You should be able to capitalize on the skills you acquired in the last laboratory, except that Access 2.0 does not have an **AddItem** method. For this example, you'll want to use a **CallBack** function to fill the list box or combo box.

Listing 14-9 only updates a single column of a single row. The smart way to implement this laboratory is to pool all updates to a single row in one command. You can add that logic if you wish; however, we're dealing with user interactions in real time and this should not affect network bandwidth. This is a judgment call. Always pool updates for widely used applications; single-user applications, such as this example, can update only one column at a time.

Windows Architecture I
Windows Architecture II

CHAPTER

Data Access Objects

15

About Chapter 15

Chapter 15 is an introduction to *Data Access Objects* (DAO). Microsoft Jet Engine and the DAO are feature rich; however, this richness comes with a price. Jet and DAO are not scalable, and even put the enterprise at risk when used as servers. (You'll find out why in this chapter.) Jet and DAO are offspring of the ad hoc period in computing where users attempted to define their own data management systems. Legacy systems existed, but they were not responsive to user needs. Hence a generation of ad hoc systems evolved that were clever and very fast. These systems are PC-based and include Clipper, dBase, Paradox, and FoxPro, to which Microsoft Access owes a debt of gratitude. For the most part these systems are flat-file and use *Open Database Connectivity* (ODBC) single-tier drivers. None of these systems exhibit the ACID properties of a transaction, a key topic of this chapter and the reason that neither Jet nor DAO should be used as a server. Jet and DAO have other limitations, which are also discussed in this chapter. Finally, the chapter closes with a graded introduction to the DAO architecture.

DAO: A Wrapper for ODBC

The Desktop Driver Set is the name given to the ODBC components embedded within DAO and the Microsoft Jet Engine. The Jet Engine first saw life with Microsoft Access, and is now a component accessible by any Microsoft Office product using Visual Basic for Applications (VBA). The products supporting VBA include Access, Visual Basic, Excel, Word, and Visual C++. There are others, but suffice it to say, VBA is now ubiquitous in Microsoft products. Microsoft Visual Basic and Microsoft Access are the principal vehicles for DAO. There are two flavors of ODBC discussed in this chapter. The first flavor of ODBC is the ODBC Desktop Driver Set used by Jet, and the second flavor is the new ODBCDirect, which doesn't require the Jet Engine. The prior chapters on ODBC were difficult, but I did represent ODBC in other than the C/C++ language.

Try to think of Remote Data Objects as the new Ferrari on the block. Then continue with the automobile analogy and liken ODBC to an MG TC or TD, but preferably an MG TC. You are in control of all aspects of your environment when driving an MG or when programming ODBC. This is quite unlike DAO, where functionality is encapsulated into objects. (Of course, Detroit knows how to package automobiles, and they manufactured a car for many years that was known as the "plastic pachyderm.")

There is no finesse in a car with an automatic transmission, but it does make it easier to drive. These cars only did one thing very well and that was to go very fast in a straight line. DAO is somewhat the same in that it is very easy to use but lacks finesse. Jet and DAO are the slowest database access technologies. Jet is feature rich and DAO uses the ODBC Desktop Driver Set, which involves significant handshaking. DAO is slower than ODBCDirect, which takes the minimalist approach with fewer features, which means less overhead. Of course the "plastic pachyderm" is also a slower car, limited by poor suspension and the laws of physics, so Detroit gave it a very large engine. They reasoned that a car going very fast in a straight line would give you the illusion of speed. (I leave it to the reader to guess the identity of the "plastic pachyderm.") We can do the same with DAO and install it in a Pentium 200 if it appears to be slow. The "plastic pachyderm" of database access technologies is Jet and DAO.

The second flavor of ODBC is ODBCDirect, which are DAO objects without the Microsoft Jet Engine. ODBCDirect is a new feature of DAO 3.5 and Visual Basic 5.0. ODBCDirect is like a model kit: you build it yourself and it has the barest of essentials. Like the minimal kit car, ODBCDirect is also a member of the minimal-ist genre supporting only the essentials. This means that ODBCDirect does not support bound controls. ODBCDirect does not possess a SQL engine, and *Data Definition Language* (DDL) operations, updateable joins, or heterogeneous joins cannot be performed directly. ODBCDirect is an ODBC data source access tech-nology, and DDL SQL statements can still be passed to the ODBC data source.

The details of DAO begin in Chapter 16. This chapter addresses general DAO issues and introduces the DAO architecture. Chapter 13 contained a section on the ODBC tarpits; this chapter also has a DAO tarpits section. The issues are not the same, but it is very easy to make basic mistakes because of the very high func-tionality of DAO.

WHAT IS DAO?

The DAO objects support the concept of a workspace enabling access to Microsoft Jet Databases, Microsoft Jet-connected ODBC databases, and installable *indexed sequential access method* (ISAM) databases. DAO is a set of hierarchical objects organized in a rigid order. The objects are not object-oriented in the program-ming sense, but hierarchical in the classical sense. Object collections are defined, and both properties and methods of collections or objects are accessible to an application program using VBA.

DAO objects encapsulate both properties and methods. This is quite unlike the *call-level interface* (CLI) of ODBC. The DAO is a wrapper for ODBC functions, along with other methods and properties. The use of ODBC functions is implicit, not explicit, in that ODBC functions are not directly called when executing a DAO method.

Even though the DAO objects must be instantiated in a particular order, there is an inherent flexibility in the capabilities of the different objects. A record-set may be opened from a SQL statement, a database object using a query, another recordset, or a database object using a table.

A Feature-Rich (Maybe Too Rich) and Very Useful Tool

Microsoft Access, along with the Microsoft Jet Engine and DAO, offer a rich and varied set of tools for application development. It is a simple task to click a few buttons, use a wizard, and create bound forms that are instantly usable. Unfortunately, that ease of use leads to a reputation of a badly abused, and often misused, product. The rightful place for a tool such as Microsoft Access and the DAO is the desktop.

I consider Microsoft Access seductive in that what appears to be a very simple task often turns out to be quite complex. Internally, Microsoft Access has a large number of "tricks" to enhance performance, and Access 97 looks to be the best of the breed. That still does not make the product an enterprise server. Even though Microsoft has added numerous performance "tricks" to Jet and DAO, performance will always suffer because of poor application design.

Microsoft DAO and the Jet engine are paired with a very good report writer. It's nice to have a great query engine, but an application needs more than just a query engine. Visual Basic, for example, does not have a report writer. Programmers in Visual Basic must either rely on the Jet Engine and the report writer of Microsoft Access or resort to Crystal Reports. Programmers in Visual Basic can access all features of the DAO with the **DBEngine** property of the **Application** object. It isn't necessary to use Crystal Reports when programming in Visual Basic.

The Microsoft Access Jet Engine has a sophisticated query optimizer, along with numerous other features that are beneficial to the desktop user. However, Microsoft Access and DAO cannot compete with Microsoft SQL server on issues such as lock management, memory management, concurrency, multiple users, and transaction isolation.

I am in no way critical of Microsoft Access with Jet and DAO. I consider it an outstanding product and the most useful computing tool available today with the exception of Microsoft Word. Microsoft Access remains a client-side tool and not an enterprise server. To use architectural terms, the product, while absolutely outstanding in terms of capability, is not scalable.

THE SCALABILITY OF FEATURE-RICH TOOLS IS OFTEN OVERLOOKED

The scenario starts easily enough. A need is identified and Microsoft Access is evaluated as the correct tool for the task. But is it really adequate? Typically, the evaluation is done in terms of immediate needs and with no thought being given to long-terms needs. The application is developed, and within a year there are 200 users, each frustrated in not being able to complete his or her task.

I was asked to look at a Microsoft Access application by a client. An "A" student at a local college created the application. The application has 200 users, and there are many performance problems. Microsoft Access is the wrong tool for the task the client wanted performed. The client, however, couldn't afford the correct solution – a top-down design starting with organizational needs and long-term goals based on using Microsoft SQL Server – because the analysis to determine long-term needs could cost an order of magnitude more than the actual programming. Had the client performed a problem analysis initially, it would have been obvious why Microsoft Access is the wrong tool. The bottom line is that users are implementing applications directly without first performing a problem analysis. An analysis should identify inappropriate tool selection before the implementation is started.

In Chapter 40 there is a quotation that states: "an application can be generated faster than a specification can be written the old way." When no specification is written, this in turn implies that little or no problem analysis is done. Missing is an understanding of the real problem with the RAD tool delivering a partial solution to an apparent and possibly wrong problem.

In other words, bottom-up design where development is done before the problem is understood. Immediate results present an aura of an application even though it is incomplete and quite possibly wrong. The ease with which an application can be generated and the immediacy of results with a RAD tool masks the fact that there is no formal specification, which is the real application cost. A RAD tool saves costs not by reducing coding time, but by abrogating the analysis phase. It is easy to lose sight of the actual cost of program development with rapid application development (RAD) tools. In the legacy world (read that as mainframe), the coding process represented 10 to 15 percent of the total life-cycle costs. The remainder of the time was invested in different analysis and design phases. It's easier to program today, and deployment costs are typically measured in development time, so where has the analysis time gone? Is it a feature of RAD tools that no system analysis is done? It certainly appears that way.

Creating a specification in the legacy world promotes critical thinking. Creating an application with a RAD tool does not promote critical thinking. A *real* solution is created using a tool and a formal specification, while an *apparent* solution is created by a RAD tool without a formal specification. If you're lucky, once in a while an *apparent* solution is a *real* solution. This explains why information costs are increasing and productivity has been declining at a steady rate since 1987 (see Chapter 40).

Why can't the analysis phase of a COBOL project be dropped and declared as a RAD tool? Isn't that what is happening? Remember that the physical coding phase of a legacy application only represents 10 to 15 percent of the total life-cycle costs. Dropping the analysis phase means maintenance costs will be high, the project will never fulfill the requirements, and another project will be started within two years to replace this one. Doesn't this sound familiar?

The Reputation Isn't Deserved

Jet ODBC with DAO has a reputation for being slow. That's not quite true. It does do a fair amount of handshaking, but it is still ODBC. It can also be stated that ODBC has performance problems. **SQLNumResultCols** returns the number of columns of a result set, but there is no need to call **SQLNumResultCols** if the application already knows the returned column count a priori. This is the performance issue with Jet ODBC. It must issue generic ODBC calls to process a result set. It calls **SQLNumResultCols** to get the column count and then calls **SQLDescribeCol** for each column in the result set. Jet is not slow. Yes, you can write tighter code that is not generic, but there is always the problem of portability. After 39 years of programming, my philosophy is to always write code at the highest possible functional level.

The VBA programmer has several choices. Use the Jet engine with the embedded desktop driver set and DAO, or use either the ODBC API or ODBCDirect and bypass Jet as illustrated in Figure 15-1. Granted, bypassing Jet is possible, but I always look to the next generation of hardware to solve performance issues. Microsoft designed Access and Jet as client-side tools for Microsoft SQL Server. Jet only has a performance problem when an architectural design error exists.

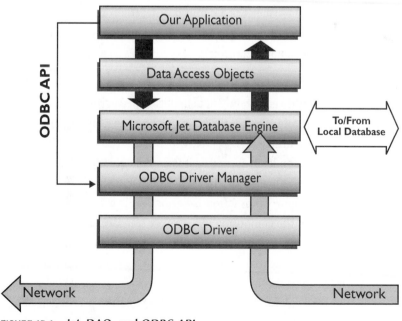

FIGURE 15-1 Jet, DAO, and ODBC API.

Jet Is Not a Server, but Jet and ODBCDirect Communicate with Servers

The Microsoft Jet Database Engine is not a server even though there are many existing applications called servers that are reported to function successfully. Although Microsoft Access was built to appear to be a server, several key features are missing. The first missing feature is support for the **durability** property of a transaction; the second missing feature is a meaningful implementation of transaction isolation levels. Both of these issues were discussed in Chapter 11 with respect to ODBC.

An important feature of any database is transactions. Microsoft Access supports transactions; however, a useful database transaction should exhibit these **ACID** properties:

- **Atomicity** — Either all or none of the transactions changes are present when the transaction completes.

- **Consistency** — The transaction respects all business rules and referential integrity. Inconsistent updates can be done, but violate system integrity.

- **Isolation** — Transactions are isolated. The isolation is realized by using locks, separate workspaces, and the **IsolateODBCTrans** property.

- **Durability** — Once the commit occurs, the transactions must be present even if the system fails. SQL Server supports this property and Microsoft Access does not. Microsoft Access survives as a server only when transactions are small.

Durability is certainly not supported in Microsoft Access. If you create a long transaction and lose power during the transaction posting, then chaos ensues. This is quite unlike SQL Server, which has a transaction log and guarantees that the data is completely posted or it is completely rolled back.

Another issue is that, as discussed previously in Chapter 11, Microsoft Access does not support transaction isolation levels even though these levels are standards within the computing industry for transaction management.

Yes, DAO has ad hoc options such as **dbSeeChanges**, but these options are subject to the vagaries of the developer and are error prone. The fact is, DAO supports "dirty reads," and unless the developer is aware of such an issue, consistency of the Jet database is compromised. The **Isolation** property (I of ACID) of transactions is not violated but is very difficult to manage because every **OpenRecordset** method must use **dbSeeChanges** and have the proper error recovery logic. As you can well see, this is not an easily managed task, and the task both complicates and prolongs the coding cycle. It is much easier with SQL Server to SET TRANSAC-TION ISOLATION LEVEL REPEATABLE READ.

Even using **dbSeeChanges** presents a problem. What if the other user rolls back the transaction? The only safe mechanism for posting transactions to an Access database is with exclusive use of the database. This doesn't solve the ACID problem, but at least the problem of "dirty reads" is put to rest.

One of the ACID properties is violated, and one is very difficult to manage. Is that enough to convince you that Access is really a client-side tool and not a server-side tool? Microsoft Access was not designed as a server, although it is used as one all too often. Let me say it again: Microsoft Access is a desktop database; it is not an enterprise server. The good news is that ODBCDirect is a tool for connecting to ODBC data sources that support transactions properly.

DAO TARPITS

DAO Tarpits is an enumeration of what not to do with DAO, or, in some cases, how to improve the performance of DAO. Issues mostly involve queries, which can be local or remote, because queries are the primary consumer of system resources.

 If you're just learning DAO and Jet or ODBCDirect, feel free to skip this section. This section requires a working knowledge of Jet, DAO, and SQL, which is the internal query language of the Jet Engine. Mark this section and come back to it after you develop your first application.

The following enumeration of issues is by no means exhaustive because there are many programming issues that do not fall within the scope of DAO. The enumerated issues are common traps for Access developers. Access appears very easy to use, and I am sure that many Access users (and developers) do not understand SQL. Many of the issues discussed here are related to incorrect SQL usage.

1. Heterogeneous joins between different data sources is possible; however, Jet will read rows from both data sources and attempt to do the SQL JOIN locally. This is a major no-no because tables are pulled down the wire and joined locally.

2. Columns in a SQL JOIN should be indexed. Indexes are created automatically when a relationship is established.

3. Avoid expressions in a SQL expression. This automatically forces a table scan. The reason is that each row must be accessed and the expression calculated before applying the selection criteria. This always forces a table scan.

4. The GROUP BY should be placed in the same table as the aggregate. This is really not a DAO issue, but one of SQL, because the issue also applies to SQL Server.

   - For example, this issue occurs when joining tables. If you're grouping by **Part Number**, then make sure that **Part Number** and the aggregate column come from the same table.

   - The example below illustrates GROUP BY from the same table as an aggregate. It also illustrates doing a GROUP BY and an aggregate before a JOIN. Be sure both sides of the join are indexed.

   - To illustrate this issue, let's start with:

     ```
     SELECT tblInv.[Part Name], Count(tblLots.[Lot ID])
       AS [On Hand] FROM tblInv
          INNER JOIN tblLots ON tblInv.[Inv ID] = tblLots.[Inv
       ID]
     GROUP BY tblInv.[Part Name],tblLots.[Inv ID]
     ```

   - The solution to building a query from the same table as the aggregate is to break the original query down into two distinct queries. The first query uses the aggregate COUNT on **tblLots** and the GROUP BY. We'll call this **CountQuery**.

     ```
     SELECT DISTINCTROW tblLots.[Inv ID],
     COUNT(tlbLots.[Lot ID]) AS [On Hand]
     FROM tblLots GROUP BY tblLots[Inv ID]
     ```

   - The last query is combining the GROUP BY query with a JOIN on **tblInv**.

     ```
     SELECT DISTINCTROW tblInv.[Part Name],CountQuery.[On
       Hand]
     FROM CountQuery
     INNER JOIN tblInv ON CountQuery.[Inv ID] = tblInv.[Inv
       ID]
     ```

5. You may have heard of mixed mode expressions where integer data and floating point data are mixed in one expression. It doesn't work quite that way with SQL server. *Render onto SQL Server only those functions of SQL Server.* Paraphrasing this, domain aggregate functions of Jet such as **DMax**, **DMin**, and **DLookup** are not recognized by SQL Server. Jet will compute the values locally and send the information as parameters.

   The SQL Server and Access date functions are not compatible. When a JOIN occurs on a field with an Access date function, Jet pulls the remote table *down the wire* and makes the row selection locally.

6. You've seen many references to procedural code loops. SQL is set-theoretic based, and procedural loops are always slower.

7. There are examples in the following DAO chapters of cloning SQL server tables locally. An obvious alternative to this is SQL Server replication. This issue falls into the category of denormalization; consider, however, maintaining infrequently updated tables on the client side.

8. I've mentioned table scans before. They are exactly what the name implies, a complete scan of the table. Table scans can be avoided by placing an index on the appropriate field. I know this sounds trivial, but it's easy to forget.

9. If you are using procedural loops rather than SQL, do not use a **Find** unless the field is indexed.

10. Rushmore is a cost-base optimizer. Compact the Access database whenever data changes significantly. Compacting recovers fragmented space and updates table statistics for use by the query optimizer. Starting with DAO 3.0, tables are reorganized in primary key order during compacting, which is the equivalent of a clustered index. The clustered index may be kept indefinitely as long as the table isn't updated.

11. Use **CacheStart**, **CacheSize**, and **FillCache** for Jet ODBC sources. There is an example later in the subsequent DAO chapters. ODBCDirect has it's own cache. Consider using **GetRows** to improve performance of unbound forms. A specified number of rows is placed directly into a **Variant** array for easy access by VBA.

12. During table attachment, Jet selects the first unique index (if any) as the primary index. The ODBC API function **SQLStatistics** returns clustered, hashed, and other indexes in that order. Selection of an index is

alphabetical with the order. Rename an index to force Jet to select a different index.

13. When an index doesn't exist on an attached table, a pseudoindex can be created locally.

```
CREATE UNIQUE INDEX myIndex
ON attachedTable(Col1, Col2, ...)
```

14. Always use **DB_APPENDONLY** (DAO 2.0) or **dbAppendOnly** for DAO 3.0/3.5. This prevents the query from being populated with bookmarks from all rows in the table.

15. Although the choice is arbitrary, use a dynaset-type **Recordset** object for result sets of more than 500 rows. Use a snapshot-type **Recordset** object for result sets that are less than that.

16. Always wrap transactions around all database edits. It improves buffering and tables are restored when an error occurs. DAO transactions have shortcomings so the smaller the transaction size, the better because DAO doesn't have a recovery log, which violates the **D** of the database ACID properties discussed above.

17. Use object variables that reduce resolution time. Starting with the statement:

```
MyValue = Forms!{Inventory]![On Hand]
```

This can be reduced to:

```
Dim MyFrm as Form
Set MyFrm = Forms![Inventory]
MyQuantity = MyFrm![On Hand]
```

or better yet:

```
MyQuantity = Me![On Hand]
```

The technique can be enhanced even further with repeated use of an object within loops:

```
With Me
 MyQuantity = ![On Hand]

 . . .

End With
```

18. Never make floating-point (**single** or **double**) numbers primary keys. They may work satisfactorily in Access, but conversion to another platform is not precise and records appear as *#Deleted*. The records aren't deleted; the floating-point keys did not convert precisely on SQL Server.

19. SQL Server only accepts SQL statements that can be processed in a single SQL statement. SQL Server will not process a statement with a DISTINCT clause containing local expressions.

20. SQL Server does not support multiple outer joins. Jet will only send a single outer join to SQL Server.

21. Jet can attach a SQL Server view. It will be treated as an attached table with no indexes. A pseudoindex can be created locally with:

```
CREATE UNIQUE INDEX myIndex
ON attachedView(Col1, Col2, ...)
```

22. Remote tables should have a TIMESTAMP field. ODBC looks at each field to determine whether the row has changed when the table does not have a TIMESTAMP column. With a TIMESTAMP column, ODBC only looks at the TIMESTAMP field to determine whether the row has changed. A TIMESTAMP field can be added with:

```
ALTER TABLE RemoteTable ADD versionCol TIMESTAMP
```

23. This is an admonition of experience. Always code to an American National Standards Institute (ANSI) standard and avoid clever vendor tricks. It insures portability. The resources saved are quite often illusory, and even though the technique looks clever, it remains *green* code that you are beta testing for your favorite vendor.

It's natural to code directly to the target server. The problem is you may never know when the same application is expected to access another server in a heterogeneous environment. Always code to an ANSI standard. The heterogeneous interconnect standard is ODBC SQL. Microsoft SQL Server is currently SQL 92. Microsoft, however, has not demonstrated its ability to include all changes to a standard within a single release. Microsoft is in the software sales business, and it is in Microsoft's best interest to sell as much software as possible, even if it means selling incremental releases of SQL Server with only partial upgrades to a standard.

I haven't determined how many different dialects of SQL exist in the Jet Engine, but coding to ODBC SQL permits ready access to other databases such as Oracle, Ingress, and Sybase. It also prevents the whipsawing that occurs when Microsoft dribbles out incremental upgrades.

An example of not coding to a standard is joins over aggregation. This is ad hoc design that is a byproduct of using RAD without sufficient preliminary design.

DAO TODAY

DAO is an Automation component available to the enterprise. DAO is available in all popular Microsoft tools including Access, Excel, PowerPoint, Project, and Visual Basic. Previously, DAO was only available in Microsoft Access and Visual Basic. (You might want to review the Automation examples in Chapter 9.)

An Automation Component

The DAO of yesteryear is a shadow of today's DAO. *Data Access Objects* were a component of only Microsoft Access. That changed with the use of Visual Basic for Applications as the universal scripting language for Microsoft Office and BackOffice. The introduction of the **DBEngine** property of the **Application** object makes all collections and objects of DAO available to all components supporting the **Application** object. VBA is available in Microsoft Access, Excel, PowerPoint, Project, and Visual Basic.

The component nature of the current Microsoft toolset is evidenced by VBA's extension of the **Dim** statement by the optional phrase **WithEvents**. The syntax for this statement is:

```
Dim [WithEvents] varname[([subscripts])] [As [New] type], . . .
```

The **WithEvents** keyword specifies that *varname* is an object variable that responds to events triggered by an ActiveX object. This syntax is probably heresy to dyed-in-the-wool Basic programmers. **Dim** statements have traditionally been declarations for allocating storage, and **WithEvents** is certainly not a storage declaration attribute. Depending on vendor-specific language enhancements is the norm today.

FREEDOM OF EXPRESSION LEADS TO NONPORTABILITY

In that former world (legacy to those who think the computer industry started with the Commodore), the directions from management were to maintain maximum application portability by not using any vendor-dependent language constructs.

Applications are now feature-rich with the latest vendor-dependent features, and no standards exist. This vendor-dependency started after users took control of their own destiny by doing their own applications. Users with bootleg systems were not answerable to any authority. Lack of discipline, inadequate technical skills, and the use of tools that promoted the generation of spaghetti code undid 30 years of discipline. The issue continues with bootleg intranet systems. Microsoft wants everyone to love ActiveX controls. If you do, then you must have a Microsoft Windows system.

Black is white and up is down because we are all now dependent upon proprietary software from a single vendor and there are no standards except those that the vendor sets. Microsoft is so large that if the product sells, it is by definition a standard.

The **Application** object has the new property **DBEngine**. This exposes the DAO methods and properties to any Automation client that has access to the **Application** object. DAO is now available to any Automation client that supports the required interfaces.

Any tool such as Visual Basic, Access, or Excel, which supports a **Modules** collection and a **Module** object, has a *Tools* toolbar with an entry of *References*. This is the **References** collection of the **Application** object and is the gateway to Automation type libraries (.TLB). The **Reference** object obtains references set to another application's or project's type library. A type library is one or more files that describe objects along with their exposed methods and properties.

An Enterprise Tool

DAO 3.5, which shipped with Office 97, is now a very rich enterprise connection tool to ODBC databases. The **Connections** collection and the **Connection** object are new in DAO 3.5 and support connections to an ODBC database without using the Microsoft Jet Engine. This minimizes the application footprint significantly.

Along with the new **Connections** collection, two new recordset types are now available, which brings to five the different recordset techniques that can be used to access or update data. (You'll find an example of these five access types in the **OpenRecordset** section later in this chapter.)

- **Table** — Unique to the DAO **Workspace** object. **Table** is one of the original recordset definitions of Microsoft Access and the earlier version of Jet and DAO.

- **Snapshot** — Another original Access DAO recordset definition. The data is captured at a point in time, and updates or deletions are not visible to the client. This recordset type is equivalent to an ODBC **Static** cursor.

- **Dynaset** — A keyset recordset that may have either pessimistic or optimistic locking. **Dynaset** is the last of the three original recordset definitions. Deleted rows can be detected, but newly added rows will be undetected. This recordset type is equivalent to the ODBC keyset cursor.

- **Forward-Only** — This is a new recordset. It uses a minimal amount of resources. The ODBC default cursor is forward-only with a snapshot type record. This recordset, however, is equivalent to a snapshot without a cursor.

- **Dynamic** — This is a new recordset type. It is reserved for access to ODBC-registered data sources. It is used by ODBCDirect, which is the name given to using the **Connections** collection and the **Connection** object without the Jet Engine. One very nice feature of ODBCDirect is the ability to define asynchronous operations.

Another valuable enterprise feature is the enhanced support for batches in DAO 3.5 — that is, the **BatchCollisionCount** and **BatchCollisions** properties of the **Recordset** object. These and other new features of DAO 3.5, along with the replication features of SQL Server, are all that is necessary to build a distributed database where SQL Server replicates to local or regional databases. Microsoft Access along with Jet and ODBCDirect send batch transactions back to SQL Server.

DAO Architecture

The DAO and VBA are the vital ingredients of Microsoft Access. DAO provides the resources, and VBA is the mechanism used to manipulate the resources. Within the objects are the methods and properties that are used to manipulate data.

I'm a little loose with my terms in that Access Basic is the scripting language for Access 2.0 and not VBA. VBA didn't join us until Access 95. I'll use VBA as a generic reference.

Figure 15-2 is a closer look at the DAO Architecture. (Figure 15-3 is offered only for closure of Microsoft Access objects, which are not discussed in this book.) This is the current DAO architecture for Access 97 Version 8.0 using Jet 3.5. The only architectural difference between Microsoft Access 2.0 using DAO 2.0 and Access using DAO 3.0/3.5 is the addition of the new **Error** object in DAO 3.0 and the new **Connection** object in DAO 3.5. There are, however, many programming differences.

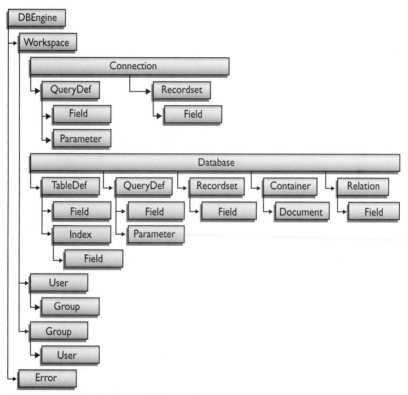

FIGURE 15-2   DAO 3.5 object hierarchy.

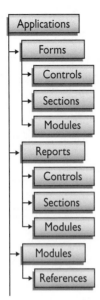

FIGURE 15-3   Microsoft Access object hierarchy.

DAO Architecture Detail

Following is a breakout of the methods and properties of all DAO objects. Methods or properties designated with the ⟨(D)⟩ character are applicable to ODBCDirect only. Properties or methods applicable only to Microsoft Jet are indicated with ⟨(J)⟩.

The **Properties** collection is a member of every DAO object except the **Error** object and the **Connection** object. The **Properties** collection is defined in the **Users** object of the **Workspace** collection.

 note Microsoft publishes the methods **BeginTrans**, **Commit Trans**, and **Rollback** as methods of the **DBEngine** object and of the **Workspace** object. I believe this to be an error because using these methods at **DBEngine** level will either commit or rollback all transactions of all **Workspace** objects, either of which is incorrect. Previous versions of the DAO have these methods defined at the **Workspace** object level, which is correct.

```
DBEngine
  Methods: CompactDatabase(J), CreateDatabase(J),
           CreateWorkspace, Idle(J), OpenConnection(D),
```

```
              OpenDatabase, RegisterDatabase, RepairDatabase(J),
              SetOption(J)
Properties: DefaultPassword, DefaultType, DefaultUser,
              IniPath(J), LoginTimeout, SystemDB(J), Version
Errors Collection
   Methods: Refresh
   Property: Count
   Error Object:
       Properties: Description, HelpContext, HelpFile, Number,
                   Source
Workspaces Collection
   Methods: Append, Refresh
   Property: Count
   Workspace Object
       Methods: BeginTrans, Close, CommitTrans,
                CreateDatabase, CreateGroup, CreateUser,
                OpenConnection(D), OpenDataBase, Rollback
       Properties: Connection(D), DefaultCursorDriver(D),
                   IsolateODBCTrans, Name, Type(D), Username
       Users Collection
          Methods: Append, Delete, Refresh
          Property: Count
          Properties Collection
             Method: Append, Delete, Refresh
             Property: Count
             Property Object
                Properties: Inherited(false in (D)), Name,
                            Type, Value
                Properties Collection (all DAO objects except
                 Connection and Error)
    User Object
       Methods: CreateGroup, NewPassWord
       Properties: Name, PassWord, PID
       Groups Collection
          Methods: Append, Delete, Refresh
          Property: Count
```

```
            Group Object
                Method: CreateUser
                Properties: Name, PID
        Users Collection (See Users collection of Workspace
         object)
        Connections Collection
            Method: Refresh
            Property: Count
            QueryDefs Collection (See QueryDefs collection of
             Database object)
            RecordSets Collection (See Recordsets collection of
             Database object)
        Connection Object
    Methods: Close, Cancel, CreateQueryDef, Execute,
     OpenRecordSet
        Properties: Connect, Database, Name, QueryTimeout,
                    RecordsAffected, StillExecuting, Updatable
        Databases Collection
            Method: Refresh
            Property: Count
        Database Object
    Methods: Close, CreateProperty, CreateQueryDef,
             CreateRelation, CreateTableDef, Execute,
             MakeReplica, NewPassword, OpenRecordSet,
             PopulatePartial, Synchronize
        Properties: CollatingOrder, Connect, Connection(D),
                    DesignMasterID, Name, QueryTimeout,
                    RecordsAffected, Replicable(user_defined),
                    ReplicaID, Updatable, V1xNullBehavior,
                    Version
        Relations Collection
    Methods: Append, Delete, Refresh
                Property: Count
                Relation Object
                Method: CreateField
                    Properties Collection (See Users collection
```

```
                  of Workspace object)
             Properites: Attributes, ForeignTable, Name,
                     PartialReplica, Table
             Fields Collection (See Relation object of
              Databases collection)
             Methods: Append, Delete, Refresh
             Property: Count
             Field Object
         Methods: AppendChunk, CreateProperty, GetChunk
         Properties: AllowZeroLength, Attributes,
                     CollatingOrder, DataUpdatable,
                     DefaultValue, FieldSize, ForeignName,
                     Name, OrdinalPosition, OriginalValue,
                     Required, Size, SourceField,
                     SourceTable, Type, ValidationOnSet,
                     ValidationRule, ValidationText,
                     Value, VisibleValue(D)
      Containers Collection
          Method: Refresh
          Property: Count
          Container Object
          Properties: AllPermissions, Inherit, Name, Owner,
                     Permissions, UserName
          Properties Collection (See Users collection of
           Workspace object)
          Documents Collection
          Method: Refresh
          Property: Count
          Document Object
         Properties: AllPermissions, Container, DateCreated
                     KeepLocal(User_defined), LastUpdated,
                     Name, Owner, Permissions,
                     Replicable(user_defined), UserName
    Recordsets Collection
          Method: Refresh
          Property: Count
```

```
                    Recordset Object
                    Fields Collection (See Relation object of
                     Databases collection)
                    Properties Collection (See Users collection of
                     Workspace object)
    {Table}         Methods: AddNew(J), CancelUpdate(J), Clone(J),
                             Close(J), Delete(J), Edit(J),
                             GetRows(J), Move(J), MoveFirst(J),
                             MoveLast(J), MoveNext(J),
                             MovePrevious(J), OpenRecordset(J),
                             Seek(J), Update(J)
                    Properties: BOF(J), Bookmark(J), Bookmarkable(J),
                             DateCreated(J), EditMode(J), EOF(J),
                             Index(J), LastModified(J),
                             LastUpdated(J), LockEdits(J),
                             Name(J), Nomatch(J),
                             PercentPosition(J), RecordCount(J),
                             Restartable(J, always false),
                             Transactions(J), Type(J),
                             Updatable(J), ValidationRule(J),
                             ValidationText)(J)
    {Dynaset}       Methods: AddNew, Cancel(D), CancelUpdate,
                             Clone(J), Close, CopyQueryDef(J),
                             Delete, Edit, FillCache(J),
                             FindFirst(J), FindLast(J), FindNext(J),
                             FindPrevious(J), GetRows, Move,
                             MoveFirst, MoveLast, MoveNext,
                             MovePrevious, NextRecordset(D),
                             OpenRecordset(J), Requery, Update
                    Properties: AbsolutePosition,
                             BatchCollisionCount(D),
                             BatchCollisions(D), BatchSize(D),
                             BOF, Bookmark, Bookmarkable,
                             CacheSize, CacheStart(J),
                             Connection(D), EditMode, EOF,
                             Filter(J), LastModified, LockEdits,
```

Name, Nomatch(J), PercentPosition,
RecordCount, RecordStatus(D),
Restartable, Sort(J),
StillExecution(D), Transactions(J),
Type, Updatable, UpdateOptions(D),
ValidationRule(J), ValidationText(J)

{Snapshot}   Methods: AddNew(D), Cancel(D), CancelUpdate(D),
Clone(J), Close, CopyQueryDef(J),
Delete(D), Edit(D), FindFirst(J),
FindLast(J), FindNext(J),
FindPrevious(J), GetRows, Move,
MoveFirst, MoveLast, MoveNext,
MovePrevious, NextRecordset(D),
OpenRecordset(J), Requery, Update(D)
Properties: AbsolutePosition,
BatchCollisionCount(D),
BatchCollisions(D), BatchSize(D), BOF,
Bookmark, Bookmarkable, CacheSize(D),
Connection(D), EditMode, EOF, Filter(J),
LastModified(D), LockEdits, Name,
Nomatch(J), PercentPosition,
RecordCount, RecordStatus(D),
Restartable, Sort(J), StillExecution(D),
Transactions(J, always false), Type,
Updatable(always false in Jet),
UpdateOptions(D), ValidationRule(J),
ValidationText(J)

{Forward only}   Methods: AddNew(D), Cancel(D),
CancelUpdate(D), Close,
CopyQueryDef(J), Delete(D), Edit(D),
FindFirst(J), FindLast(J),
FindNext(J), FindPrevious(J),
GetRows(Forward only w/o bookmark),
MoveNext, NextRecordset(D), Requery,
Update(D)
Properties: BatchCollisionCount(D),

```
                               BatchCollisions(D), BatchSize(D),
                               BOF, Connection(D), EditMode, EOF,
                               Filter(J), Name, RecordCount,
                               RecordStatus(D), Restartable,
                               StillExecution(D), Transactions(J,
                               always false), Type, Updatable(always
                               false in Jet), Type,
                               UpdateOptions(D), ValidationRule(J),
                               ValidationText(J)
   {Dynamic}    Methods: AddNew(D), Cancel(D), CancelUpdate(D),
                               Close(D), Delete(D), Edit(D),
                               GetRows(D), Move(D), MoveFirst(D),
                               MoveLast(D), MoveNext(D),
                               MovePrevious(D), NextRecordset(D),
                               Requery(D), Update(D)
                Properties: AbsolutePosition(D),
                               BatchCollisionCount(D),
                               BatchCollisions(D), BatchSize(D),
                               BOF(D), Bookmark(D), Bookmarkable(D),
                               CacheSize(D), Connection(D),
                               EditMode(D), EOF(D), LastModified(D),
                               LockEdits(D), Name(D),
                               PercentPosition(D), RecordCount(D),
                               RecordStatus(D), Restartable(D),
                               StillExecution(D), Type(D),
                               Updatable(D), UpdateOptions(D)
         QueryDefs Collection
         Methods: Append, Delete, Refresh
                 Property: Count
                 QueryDef Object
                 Fields Collection (See Relation object of
                   Databases collection)
                 Parameters Collection
                 Method: Refresh
                 Property: Count
                 Parameter Object
```

```
                Properties: Name, Value, Type
        Methods: Close, CreateProperty(J), Execute, OpenRecordset
                Properties: Cache(D), Connect, DateCreated(J),
                            KeepLocal(J, user_defined),
                            LastUpdated(J), LogMessages(J),
                            MaxRecords, Name, ODBCTimeout,
                            Prepare(D), RecordsAffected,
                            Replicable,(J),ReturnsRecords(J),
                            SQL, StillExecuting(D), Type,
                            Updatable
TableDefs Collection
Methods: Append, Delete, Refresh
                Property: Count
                TableDef Object
                Methods: CreateField, CreateIndex,
                        CreateProperty, OpenRecordset,
                        RefreshLink
                Properties: Attributes, ConflictTable Connect,
                            DateCreated,
                            KeepLocal(user_defined),
                            LastUpdated, Name, RecordCount,
                            Replicable(user_defined),
                            ReplicaFilter, SourceTablename,
                            Updatable, ValidationRule,
                            ValidationText
            Fields Collection (See Relation object of
            Databases collection)
            Indexes Collection
            Methods: Append, Delete, Refresh
            Property: Count
            Index Object
        Fields Collection (See Relation object of
        Database collection)
        Methods: CreateField, CreateProperty
        Properties: Clustered, DistinctCount, Foreign,
                    IgnoreNulls, Name, Primary, Required,
                    Unique
```

A NEW SOFTWARE METHODOLOGY

Supposedly knowledgeable pundits in the software industry say that an application's development costs using a RAD tool such as Visual Basic or Microsoft Access is one-tenth the cost of doing the same project in COBOL. They point out, however, that the long-term maintenance costs for a RAD application can be as much as 20 times the COBOL maintenance costs. I propose a new software methodology. Just develop new applications and never maintain existing applications. New tools nearly always have more features that supposedly improve productivity. When maintenance time arrives, don't do it. Take the latest tool available on the market and build a new application. This was tongue in cheek when I wrote it, but I am starting to believe it. Microsoft has millions of customers. Fix a bug for me, and a bug is created for thousands of other users. Exclusive of mechanical errors, most bugs are a result of usage style where the feature is used in a manner not envisioned by the developer.)

KEY POINT SUMMARY

Microsoft Access is a very rich and powerful desktop tool. It is very easy to misuse Microsoft Access, and abrogating the analysis phase to determine Access's appropriateness is a recipe for disaster. Microsoft Access is not a server in the formal sense; however, I am sure that Microsoft Access servers will continue to be deployed. Microsoft Access is a component of the Microsoft Office suite and not a member of the Microsoft BackOffice suite. If Microsoft intended Access to be an enterprise tool, I believe Microsoft would have placed it in the Microsoft BackOffice suite. Its rightful place is as a local tool on the desktop and not as an enterprise server.

- VBA is now ubiquitous in Microsoft Products.
- Type libraries are also ubiquitous, which means that DAO is also ubiquitous through type library support.
- DAO is feature-rich and is easily misused.
- Jet and DAO are not servers, even though an application can be developed that appears to function as a server.
- Jet and DAO permit "dirty reads," are not scalable, and do not support the ACID properties.

- ODBCDirect is a direct descendant of the RDO of Visual Basic Enterprise Edition. It is a very thin ODBC wrapper, whereas Jet and DAO form a very rich ODBC wrapper.

- DAO is a host for ODBCDirect.

APPLYING WHAT YOU'VE LEARNED

These questions specifically address the issue of inappropriate tool selection. You'll find that understanding these issues is valuable in preparing for the Windows Architecture examinations.

Instant Assessment

1. Name the four key words that represent the ACID properties of a database and provide a brief phrase describing each property.

2. How do Jet and DAO fail to satisfy the fourth of the ACID properties?

3. The DAO hierarchy is very rich. What is the rigid restriction that must be imposed on DAO objects?

4. You are developing a complex form with many controls to be used in a decision support system (DSS) environment. (A DSS is a read-only database.) In your case, it is Microsoft SQL Server. Your choices include the ODBC API, DAO, RDO, and ODBCDirect. Which database access technology is appropriate for your application?

5. You are tasked with designing a corporate roll-up function. Transactions are gathered from branch offices and posted on a batch basis to a centralized Microsoft SQL Server database. Which database access technology is appropriate?

6. Management wishes to create reports in Microsoft Access from an AS/400 system. Which database access technology is correct?

 concept link **For answers to the Instant Assessment questions, see Appendix C.**

MCSD Windows Architecture I

Working with DAO

16

About Chapter 16

Normally garbage collection comes last, when everything is cleaned up. You can think of this chapter as Jet Data Access Objects (DAO) garbage collection, in that it deals with miscellaneous DAO issues. We discuss the common methods of all collections and the default collections of objects. The chapter closes with a discussion of the **Containers** collection. This chapter is a prelude to our discussion of DAO objects, which starts with the next chapter.

The examples in this chapter may be found in the Access 97 `CHAPTER16.MDB` database located in the `EXAMPLES\CHAPTER16` folder of the CD-ROM located at the back of this book.

Working with Collections

All collections have a **Count** property and some collections have the **Append**, **Delete**, and **Refresh** methods. The following sections discuss the features of collections. This is followed by a discussion of the methods of DAO objects.

Some collections function differently. For example, when a new **Querydef** object is created, it is automatically appended to the **QueryDefs** collection. Removing a **QueryDef** object from the **QueryDefs** collection may be done with **Delete** method or **Close** method. Objects from the **Databases** collection are not removed with the **Close** method; however, objects in the **Recordsets**, **QueryDefs**, or **Workspaces** collections are removed when closed. Jet ignores the **Close** method on the default **Workspace** object.

Close

I begin by mixing apples with oranges. This section's theme is the methods common to collections. I break that rule slightly and open with the **Close** method of numerous DAO objects. (With the discussion here, it won't be repeated for each subsequent object discussion.)

Syntax:

> *Object*.**Close**

Where:

> *Object:* One of: **Connection** object, **Database** object, **QueryDef** object, **Recordset** object, or **Workspace** object

The default **Workspace** object cannot be closed. Closing an object terminates all dependent open objects. Closing a **Workspace** object releases all pending edits and data is lost. Objects should be closed starting with the reverse hierarchical order of the **Recordset** object.

An object always remains open unless explicitly closed or the module terminates, in which case the local variables go out of scope. Global objects remain open until explicitly closed.

note *Going out of scope* **is a formal term given to leaving an environment such as a subroutine. Local variables are defined within the subroutine and exiting the subroutine forces an inplicit release of local variables.**

An error occurs when you use **Close** if the **Database**, **QueryDef**, **Recordset,** or **Workspace** object is already closed. You avoid this problem by setting the object type variable to **Nothing** when the object is closed and later test it before attempting the **Close**. Resources are released when an object is set to the value **Nothing**.

The code below is a true exercise in futility but it does demonstrate how to use the **Close** method. It is futile because the **Dim** statement declares a local variable that goes out of scope when the subroutine or function is exited. The other reason why it is a futile exercise is that the default workspace cannot be closed.

```
Dim MyWs as Workspace
Set MyWs = DBEngine.Workspaces(0)
. . .
MyWS.Close
```

Count

Syntax:

> *Object*.**Count**

Where:

> *Object:* One of: **Errors**, **Connections**, **Containers**, **Databases**, **Fields**, **Groups**, **Indexes**, **Parameters**, **Properties**, **QueryDefs**, **Recordsets**, **Relations**, **TableDefs**, **Users**, or **Workspaces**

Count is the only property of all collections while **Refresh** is the only common method. It is illustrated for the **Errors** collection of the **DBEngine** object with:

```
For MyErr = 0 to DBEngine.Errors.Count - 1
. . .
Next MyErr
```

The count is implied using the **With** statement of VBA. This code fragment also illustrates enumerating the **Errors** collection.

```
For each MyErr in DBEngine.Errors
. . .
Next MyErr
```

Append

Syntax:

> *Object*.**Append**

Where:

> *Object:* (See Table 16-1) One of: **Fields**, **Groups**, **Indexes**, **Properties**, **QueryDefs**, **Relations**, **TableDefs**, **Users**, or **Workspaces**

New items are added to a collection with the **Append** method. There appears to be some confusion as to when an object is appended. The **Append** method is listed as a method of the **QueryDefs** collection even though a **QueryDef** object is automatically appended to the **QueryDefs** collection. The rules listed in Table 16-1 should clarify this issue.

TABLE 16-1 RULES FOR APPENDING OBJECTS TO A DAO COLLECTION

OBJECT	*COLLECTION*	*WHEN YOU CAN APPEND*
Workspace	Database	Never; use the OpenDatabase method
Database	Containers	Never
Database	Recordsets	Never; use the OpenRecordset method
Connection	Workspaces	Never; use the OpenConnection method
Container	Documents	Never
Index	Fields	When the Index object is a new, unappended object
QueryDef	Fields	Never
QueryDef	Parameters	Never
Recordset	Fields	Never
Relation	Fields	Never
TableDef	Fields	When the Updatable property of the TableDef is True
TableDef	Indexes	When the Updatable property of the TableDef is True
Database, Field, QueryDef, TableDef	Properties	When the Database, Field, Index, QueryDef, TableDef or TableDef is persistent

Table 16-1 represents restrictions. There is no restriction on using the **Append** method with either the **Users** or **Groups** collection.

Adding a new field to a **TableDef** is illustrated in Listing 16-1. The example creates a table and appends two new fields. It closes by appending the newly created table to the **TableDefs** collection.

LISTING 16-1 Appending **TableDef** and **Field** objects to a collection

```
Private Sub Append_Fields_Click()
'(C) 1998 Bruce T. Prendergast
' DBA Prendergast Consulting
' DBA PCS
' IDG Books Worldwide ISBN 0-7645-3123-9
'

' Listing 16-1 Appending fields to a collection.
'

Dim MyDB As Database
Dim MyWS As Workspace
Dim MyTblDf As TableDef
Dim MyFld As Field
Set MyWS = DBEngine.Workspaces(0)
Set MyDB = MyWS.Databases(0)
'

' the statement below can optionally
' replace the previous two statements
'

'Set MyDB = DBEngine(0)(0)
'

' just in case the table already exists
'

On Error Resume Next
'

' use the delete method of a collection
'

MyDB.TableDefs.Delete "tblAccounts"
Set MyTblDf = MyDB.CreateTableDef("tblAccounts")
'
```

```
' create a field
'
Set MyFld = MyTblDf.CreateField("Account Name", dbText)
'
' declare the size before it is appended to the table
'
MyFld.Size = 30
MyTblDf.Fields.Append MyFld
Set MyFld = MyTblDf.CreateField("Amount Due", dbCurrency)
MyTblDf.Fields.Append MyFld
Set MyFld = MyTblDf.CreateField("Last Payment Date", dbDate)
MyTblDf.Fields.Append MyFld
'
' append the table now that the fields are appended
'
MyDB.TableDefs.Append MyTblDf
'
' refresh the collection now that a table is appended
'
MyDB.TableDefs.Refresh
MsgBox "Table and fields created successfully"
Exit Sub
End Sub
```

Delete

The **Delete** method and the **Close** method for objects are related. Not all collections have a **Delete** method — the **Connections** collection is one example of a collection without the **Delete** method. Closing some objects removes them from the collection to which they are appended. The **Delete** method must be used for objects appended to collections other than the **Databases**, **Recordsets**, or **Workspaces** collections.

Syntax:

Object.**Delete**

Where:

> *Object:* An object of type **Collection**. One of: **Fields**, **Indexes**, **Groups**, **Properties**, **QueryDefs**, **Relations**, or **Users**.

Refresh

Refresh is the last method of a collection. This method adjusts ordinal numbers of collection members and makes all ordinal numbers monotonic. Additionally, **Refresh** may change the order of objects within a collection. Applications in a multiuser environment should be refreshed before they are used when the collection is subject to change. The **Refresh** method should be used immediately before referencing the collection.

Syntax:

> *Object.***Refresh**

Where:

> *Object:* An object of type **Collection**. One of: **Errors**, **Connections**, **Containers**, **Databases**, **Documents**, **Fields**, **Groups**, **Indexes**, **Parameters**, **Properties**, **QueryDefs**, **Recordsets**, **Relations**, **TableDefs**, **Users**, or **Workspaces**

WORKING WITH DEFAULT COLLECTIONS

Default collection provides a shortcut mechanism for addressing lower level methods and properties. Figure 16-1 illustrates abstract default collections, but a pragmatic example is always easier to understand. The **RecordSet** collection has the **Fields** collection as the default collection. Assume for the moment that the **Fields** collection contains two fields named *lname* and *fname* with respective ordinals of 0 and 1. Assume also that the collection belongs to the **Recordset** object *MyRS*. The default collection is illustrated below, where all four lines are equivalent and the first two lines use the default collection; that is, the **Fields** collection is not referenced. You'll note that the default property of a **Field** collection is the **Value** property.

```
MyRS!lname ="Bruce"
```

```
MyRS("lname") = "Bruce"
MyRS.Fields("lname").Value = "Bruce"
MyRS.Fields(0).Value = "Bruce"
```

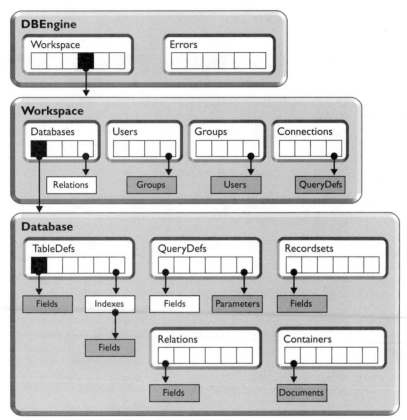

FIGURE 16-1   DAO and default collections.

The DAO default collections are listed in Table 16.2. Using default collections improves performance. The statement:

```
MyRS("lname") = "Bruce"
```

executes faster than the statement:

```
MyRS.Fields("lname").Value = "Bruce"
```

Both of the statements are functionally equal and the second statement takes longer to execute. DAO only searches for a name in the **Fields** collection of the first statement, whereas DAO must search a **Fields** collection and then search the **Properties** collection in the second example. The rule of thumb is to count the "dots." The statement with the higher "dot" count will always take longer to execute. Using the default collections means fewer characters to type, and improves performance. Table 16-2 lists the DAO default connections.

TABLE 16-2 DEFAULT COLLECTIONS FOR DAO OBJECTS

OBJECT	DEFAULT COLLECTION
Connection	Querydefs
Container	Documents
Database	Recordsets (ODBCDirect default) TableDefs(Jet Default)
DBEngine	Workspaces (no DBEngine object is available)
Form	Controls
Group	Users
Index	Fields
QueryDef	Parameters
Recordset	Fields
Relation	Fields
Report	Controls
TableDefs	Fields
User	Groups
Workspace	All open Databases

DAO and Microsoft Jet also have default objects that are implied and not referenced. These three statements are functionally identical:

```
Forms!MyForm
Access.Forms!MyForm
Access.Application.Forms!Myform
```

Neither the **Access** nor the **Access.Application** components of the **Forms** expressions are explicitly stated. The presence of the objects is implied.

Table 16-3 identifies all collections and objects of DAO. Restrictions limiting objects only to a Jet workspace are indicated.

 note Every DAO object has a **Properties** collection.

TABLE 16-3 DISTINGUISHING BETWEEN JET AND ODBCDIRECT OBJECTS		
COLLECTION	*OBJECT*	*DESCRIPTION*
Connections	Connection	Connection information. ODBCDirect workspace only.
Containers	Container	Predefined object storage. Jet workspaces only.
Databases	Database	An open database.
Documents	Document	Predefined object storage information. Jet workspaces only.
Errors	Error	Object-related errors.
Fields	Field	A column that is a component of a table, query, index, relation, or a recordset.
Groups	Group	A group of users. Jet workspace only.
Indexes	Index	Uniqueness or predefined table ordering. Jet workspace only.
Parameters	Parameter	Parameter definition for a parameter query.
Properties	Property	A user-defined or a built-in property.
QueryDefs	QueryDef	A saved query definition.
Recordsets	Recordset	Records of a base table or a query.
Relations	Relation	Relationships between fields in tables and queries. Jet workspace only.
TableDefs	TableDef	A save table definition. Jet workspaces only.
Users	User	A session. Jet workspace only.
Workspaces	Workspace	A session of the Jet database engine. DAO 3.5 supports an ODBCDirect workspace.

WORKING WITH CONTAINERS

The **Containers** collection of a **Database** object consists of all the saved objects that define a database. The Microsoft Jet database engine predefines some of the containers, and others are defined by Microsoft Access. **SysRel** is a special system container that defines the layout of the **Relationships** window. This container is not modified in VBA. Figure 16-2 illustrates the **Containers** collection in the DAO hierarchy. The general DAO hierarchy is shown in Figure 16-2. The very dark areas of Figure 16-2 represent default collections and the shaded area at the bottom is the **Containers** collection of a **Database** object.

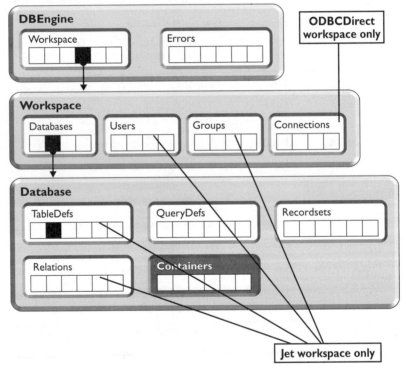

FIGURE 16-2   The **Containers** collection in the DAO hierarchy.

Table 16-4 identifies the contents of each container collection. The definitions here are somewhat complex, and if you don't understand them immediately, don't worry. Figure 16-2 shows that the **Containers** collection is contained by the **Database** object. That's easy enough, however it is a **Containers** collection of

Container objects and each **Container** object contains a **Documents** collection of **Document** objects.

TABLE 16-4 THE CONTAINERS COLLECTION RELATIONSHIPS

COLLECTION/OBJECT	IS CONTAINED BY	CONTAINS
Containers collection (of containers)	Database object	Containers object
Containers object	Containers collection	Documents collection

DAO provides several types of **Containers** objects, but every database contains at least the three shown in Table 16-5. The **Databases**, **Tables**, and **Relationships** containers are defined by Jet while the **Forms**, **Scripts**, **Reports**, and **Modules** containers are defined by Access.

TABLE 16-5 CONTAINERS DEFINED BY JET

COLLECTION/OBJECT	IS CONTAINED BY	CONTAINS
Databases	Workspaces	Saved databases
Tables	Databases	Saved tables and queries
Relationships	Databases	Saved relationships

TABLE 16-6 CONTAINER CONTENTS

CONTAINER NAME	IS DEFINED BY	CONTAINS
Databases	Jet Database Engine	Databases
Tables	Jet Database Engine	TableDefs and QueryDefs
Relationships	Jet Database Engine	Relationships
Forms	Microsoft Access	Forms
Reports	Microsoft Access	Reports
Scripts	Microsoft Access	Macros
Modules	Microsoft Access	Modules

Note that the **Connections** collection is not listed in Table 16-6. The containers listed in this table are features of Jet and Microsoft Access, hence ODBCDirect objects do not have containers. The Microsoft ODBCDirect documentation states that an ODBCDirect **QueryDef** object is temporary, but Microsoft never states the reason why. So now you know. All ODBCDirect objects must be temporary because a container is a feature of Jet and Microsoft Access and not DAO. The hierarchy for relating containers and documents is shown in Figure 16-3.

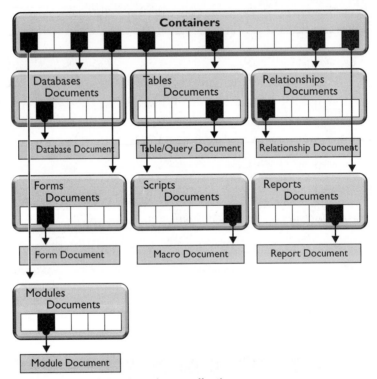

FIGURE 16-3   DAO 3.5 Containers collection.

Containers are used for system management. A container object has six properties: **AllPermissions**, **Inherit**, **Name**, **Owner**, **Permissions**, and **UserName**. Care should be used when modifying these properties. For example, the **Permissions** field might contain a number like 1048575 that isn't documented.

Each **Container** object in a **Containers** collection has a **Documents** collection. This is the default collection for a **Container** object. The **Container** objects are Microsoft Access database objects and not DAO objects.

The **Document** object contains the **AllPermissions, Container, DateCreated, KeepLocal** (user-defined), **LastUpdated, Name, Owner, Permissions, Replicable** (user-defined), and **UserName** properties.

Addressing a document within a container is relatively simple. Just use the collection name. After the container is addressed, the individual objects can be enumerated. Listing 16-2 enumerates the documents of a **Forms** collection.

LISTING 16-2 Enumerating the documents of a **Forms** collection

```
Private Sub Append_Fields_Click()
'(C) 1998 Bruce T. Prendergast
'    DBA Prendergast Consulting
'    DBA PCS
'    IDG Books Worldwode ISBN 0-7645-3123-9
'
'    Listing 16-1 Appending fields to a collection.
'
    Dim MyDB As Database
    Dim MyWS As Workspace
    Dim MyTblDf As TableDef
    Dim MyFld As Field
    Set MyWS = DBEngine.Workspaces(0)
    Set MyDB = MyWS.Databases(0)
    '
    '    The statement below can optionally
    '    replace the previous two statements
    '
    'Set MyDB = DBEngine(0)(0)
    '
    '    just in case the table already exists
    '
    On Error Resume Next
    '
    '    use the delete method of a collection
    '
    MyDB.TableDefs.Delete "tblAccounts"
    Set MyTblDf = MyDB.CreateTableDef("tblAccounts")
```

```
'
'    create a field
'
Set MyFld = MyTblDf.CreateField(_
        "Account Name", dbText)
'
'declare the size before appending
'
MyFld.Size = 30
MyTblDf.Fields.Append MyFld
Set MyFld = MyTblDf.CreateField(_
        "Amount Due", dbCurrency)
MyTblDf.Fields.Append MyFld
Set MyFld = MyTblDf.CreateField(_
        "Last Payment Date", dbDate)
MyTblDf.Fields.Append MyFld
'
'    append the table now that the fields are appended
'
MyDB.TableDefs.Append MyTblDf
'
'    refresh the collection after the table appending
'
MyDB.TableDefs.Refresh
MsgBox "Table and fields created successfully"
Exit Sub
End Sub
```

KEY POINT SUMMARY

This chapter identified the collections and objects of Jet and ODBCDirect. The chapter also presented the **Containers** collection and the **Documents** collection, both of which are used for managing DAO objects.

Using the proper notation is important and affects performance. The DAO default collections provide a shorthand notation for object, method, or property access. Default collections enhance performance by minimizing the "dot" count. Other important facts learned in this chapter are:

- The default **Workspace** object cannot be closed, although other **Workspace** objects may be closed.

- The **Delete** method is not available to the **Databases**, **Recordsets**, or **Workspaces** collections.

- **Count** is a method of all collections.

- The **Containers** collection is a feature of Jet and Microsoft Access, hence there are no **Container** objects for ODBCDirect objects. All ODBCDirect objects are temporary.

- The default collection of an object provides a shorthand notation for accessing the object.

APPLYING WHAT YOU'VE LEARNED

The questions below assess your understanding of the DAO hierarchy. The questions focus on issues related to collections. Your understanding of these issues is necessary for a successful DAO implementation.

Instant Assessment

1. Name the first object in the DAO hierarchy.

2. Name a property of all collections.

3. Which DAO object does not have a default collection?

4. Give an example of a default collection.

5. Name an object that is automatically appended to a collection.

6. Discuss the **Refresh** method of a collection.

7. When does DAO ignore the **Close** method?

8. Name two methods to remove a **QueryDef** from the **QueryDefs** collection.

9. Name a collection where objects cannot be removed with the **Delete** method.

10. Name four objects that share the same collection.

11. What is the purpose of containers?

12. What is a unique characteristic of **Container** objects?

 For answers to the Instant Assessment questions, see Appendix C.

Lab Exercises

Lab 16.33 *Using default collections*

Given a **Recordset** object named **MyRS** and a **Field** object named **Client**. Write four different versions of an expression that will yield the contents of the **Client** field.

Lab 16.34 *Using proper object syntax*

Given an Access form named **form1** with a text box named **text1**. Write the complete syntax for yielding the contents of the text box into a program variable.

Lab 16.35 *Comparing DAO with ODBC*

The goal of this laboratory is to compare ODBC and DAO. ODBC uses a call-level interface (CLI) so it is difficult to compare DAO and ODBC. This means that comparing details is not meaningful, but comparing major functionality is meaningful. One significant feature of DAO is the **Containers** collection, which is useful for managing DAO objects represented as **Document** objects. This feature does not exist in ODBC. Start your analysis by listing only the compelling features of each technology, and not the detailed features. Remember that ODBC represents a standard, while DAO is dependent upon the proclivities of the vendor.

Can you justify using ODBC in lieu of DAO because of the adherence to standards? Can you identify the guidelines for selecting technology within your organization. Which database technology is best for your organization?

Windows Architecture I
Windows Architecture II

CHAPTER

Working with the DBEngine Object

17

About Chapter 17

Beginning with this chapter, we look at the objects in the default hierarchical order: **DBEngine**, **Workspaces**, **Connections**, **Databases**, **TableDefs**, **QueryDefs**, and ending with the **Recordsets** collection. We pick up related collections such as the **Fields** and **Relationships** collections along the way.

As the objects are discussed, an example is given for each method of the object. Output from the examples is presented, and the reader is encouraged to try the examples and replicate the results. All examples are found in the DAO.MDB on the CD-ROM that accompanies this book. The example MDBs are written for Access 97, which is not the lowest common Microsoft Access denominator. Microsoft Access 2.0 and Access 95 are mentioned when appropriate. *Data Access Objects* (DAO) properties are listed by name for each object but are not discussed in detail. Some of the properties must be used for the examples.

The examples in this chapter may be found in the Access 97 CHAPTER17.MDB database located in the EXAMPLES\CHAPTER17 folder of the CD-ROM located at the back of this book.

THE DBENGINE OBJECT

The **DBEngine**(see Figure 17-1) is the first object used in the DAO hierarchy to obtain access to other objects. It is not a member of a collection, and **DBEngine** objects cannot be created.

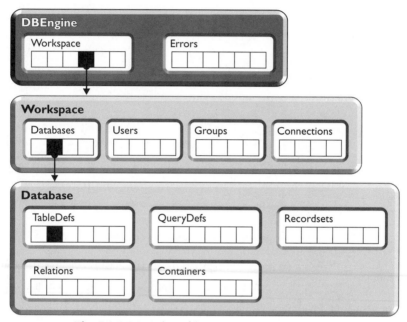

FIGURE 17-1   The DAO DBEngine object.

DBEngine Object Definition

Methods: **BeginTrans**, **CommitTrans**, **CompactDatabase**(J), **CreateDatabase**(J), **CreateWorkspace**, **Idle**(J), **OpenConnection**(D), **OpenDatabase**, **RegisterDatabase**, **RepairDatabase**(J), **Rollback**, and **SetOption**(J)

Properties: **DefaultPassword**, **DefaultType**, **DefaultUser**, **IniPath**(J), **LoginTimeout**, **SystemDB**(J), and **Version**

Collections: **Errors**

Legend: D = ODBCDirect, J = Jet

Workspaces is the default collection in **DBEngine** as illustrated in Figure 17-1. The **DBEngine** object should not be confused with the **DBEngine** property of the **Application** object which gives Automation clients access to the DAO, a topic discussed in Chapter 9.

The following code illustrates the use of the **DBEngine** object from Microsoft Access:

```
Set MyWS = DBEngine.Workspaces(0)
Set MyDB = MyWS.Databases(0)
'
' the statement below can optionally
' replace the previous two statements
'
Set MyDB = DBEngine(0)(0)
```

The **DBEngine** is available to any tool supporting a **Reference** library and Visual Basic for Applications (VBA). The following statement is from a working example of Chapter 9:

```
Set MyDAO = CreateObject("DAO.DBEngine")
```

There's a bit more to this than meets the eye. A review of the DAO example in Chapter 9 of the Component Technology section shows that a **Workspace** object must be created when using DAO through Automation. This is because Microsoft Access has a default **Workspace** object, whereas DAO does not.

 The Microsoft implementation of the **DBEngine** object appears to be in error. The methods **BeginTrans**, **CommitTrans**, **RollBack**, and **OpenConnection** are listed as methods of the **DBEngine** object but are actually methods of both the **Workspace** object and the **DBEngine** object. Prior to DAO 3.5, **BeginTrans**, **CommitTrans**, and **RollBack** were methods of only the **Workspace** object. Using **BeginTrans**, **CommitTrans**, and **RollBack** at the **DBEngine** object level affects all transactions of all workspaces, which is neither logical nor desirable. The documentation for the **BeginTrans**, **CommitTrans**, and **RollBack** methods makes no mention of the **DBEngine** object; however, when the **DBEngine** object is browsed, the **BeginTrans**, **CommitTrans**, and **RollBack** methods are visible. I do not consider the **BeginTrans**, **CommitTrans**, and **RollBack** methods of the **DBEngine** to be legitimate.

Our discussion starts here with the first legitimate method of the **DBEngine** object.

CompactDatabase

The **CompactDatabase** method of **DBEngine** can be used from Access Basic. The Jet Engine uses a query optimizer that Microsoft calls *Rushmore* technology. The query optimization is cost-based and must have accurate input-output (I/O) statistics on all tables to optimize queries correctly. Updating table statistics for use by the optimizer is done only when the database is compacted. The database should be compacted after every bulk operation. The table statistics reflect only the results of the last table compaction and not the current contents.

Consider compacting the database when transactions are rolled back. False statistics exist in the tables, and the compaction will restore table statistics.

Tables are rewritten to primary key order during compaction. This effectively creates a clustered index, a feature first available with DAO 3.0.

The database should be compacted after activities such as posting transactions from a transaction table using right-outer joins. This assumes, of course, that the postings were done in exclusive mode. The issue is to compact the database whenever a significant amount of new information is added that can change query selectivity. An example is an order entry environment where batches are submitted. Query selectivity may be affected adversely when batches do not contain a random mix of data. For example, submitting all new orders of customers whose last names start with the character range A-J is not random.

Syntax:

DBEngine.**CompactDatabase** *OldDBName, NewDBName, Locale, Options*

Where:

OldDBName: The database must be closed with no other users connected. The name may be a *uniform naming convention* (UNC) name such as "\\MyServer\MyShare\MyDir\MyDB.MDB".

NewDBName: Full path name of the new database

Locale: Optional; a **Variant** specifying a collating order for the new database

Jet 2.0 intrinsic constants

DB_LANG_GENERAL	English, German, French, Portuguese, Italian, and Modern Spanish
DB_LANG_ARABIC	Arabic
DB_LANG_CZECH	Czech
DB_LANG_CYRILLIC	Russian
DB_LANG_DUTCH	Dutch
DB_LANG_GREEK	Greek
DB_LANG_HEBREW	Hebrew
DB_LANG_HUNGARIAN	Hungarian
DB_LANG_ICELANDIC	Icelandic
DB_LANG_NORWDAN	Norwegian and Danish
DB_LANG_POLISH	Polish
DB_LANG_SWEDEN	Swedish and Finnish
DB_LANG_SPANISH	Traditional Spanish
DB_LANG_TURKISH	Turkish

Options

DB_ENCRYPT	Encrypt while compacting
DB_DECRYPT	Decrypt while compacting
DB_VERSION10	Create an Access 1.0 version database
DB_VERSION11	Create an Access 1.1 version database
DB_VERSION20	Create an Access 2.0 version database
DB_VERSION30	Create an Access 2.0 version database

Jet 3.0/3.5 Intrinsic Constants

dbLangGeneral	English, German, French, Portuguese, Italian, and Modern Spanish
dbLangArabic	Arabic
dbLangChineseSimplified	Simplified Chinese
dbLangChineseTraditional	Traditional Chinese
dbLangCyrillic	Russian
dbLangCzech	Czech
dbLangDutch	Dutch

dbLangGreek	Greek
dbLangHebrew	Hebrew
dbLangHungarian	Hungarian
dbLangIcelandic	Icelandic
dbLangJapanese	Japanese
dbLangKorean	Korean
dbLangNordic	Norwegian and Danish (Jet 1.0 only)
dbLangNorwdan	Norwegian and Danish
dbLangPolish	Polish
dbLangSlovenian	Slovenian
dbLangSwedfin	Swedish and Finnish
dbLangThai	Thai
dbLangTurkish	Turkish
Options	
dbEncrypt	Encrypt while compacting
dbDecrypt	Decrypt while compacting
dbVersion10	Create an Access 1.0 version database
dbVersion11	Create an Access 1.1 version database
dbVersion25	Create an Access 2.5 version database
dbVersion30	Create an Access 3.0 version database (version 3.5 compatible)

CreateWorkspace

Creating a workspace is the equivalent of creating a new session. It is a method of **DBEngine**, and the new workspace is deleted when closed. The default workspace cannot be closed.

Syntax:

DBEngine.**CreateWorkSpace** (*Name, User, Password, Type*)

Where:

Name: The name of the new workspace.

User: An existing user name.

Password: The password for the existing account.

Type: The constants **dbUseJet** or **dbUseODBC.**

Creating a new workspace is illustrated in Listing 17-1. An alternate workspace is an option to consider when posting transactions using the **CommitTrans** or **Rollback** methods of a workspace, which will roll back or commit all transactions. An additional workspace can be created for temporary work, preserving the current work. The additonal workspace can be either a Jet workspace or an ODBCDirect workspace.

LISTING 17-1 Creating a workspace

```
Private Sub Create_Workspace_Click()
'(C) 1998 Bruce T. Prendergast
'   DBA Prendergast Consulting
'   DBA PCS
'   IDG BGooks Worldwide ISBN 0-7645-3123-9
'
'   Listing 17-1 Create a workspace
'
    Dim MyWS As Workspace, MyNewWS As Workspace, _
        MyUserName As Variant
    Dim I As Integer
    MyUserName = DBEngine.Workspaces(0).UserName
    Debug.Print
    Debug.Print "Enumeration of DBEngine"
    Debug.Print
    '
    ' Enumerate all workspaces.
    '
    Debug.Print "Workspaces: Name, UserName"
    For Each MyWS In DBEngine.Workspaces
        Debug.Print "<1>"; MyWS.Name;
        Debug.Print ", "; MyWS.UserName
    Next MyWS
    Debug.Print
```

```
'
' Enumerate a property
'
Debug.Print "DBEngine.Version: "; _
    DBEngine.Version
Debug.Print
'
' create a new WS and do it again.
'
Set MyNewWS = DBEngine.CreateWorkspace( _
    "NewWS", MyUserName, "", dbUseJet)
DBEngine.Workspaces.Append MyNewWS
For Each MyWS In DBEngine.Workspaces
    Debug.Print "<2>"; MyWS.Name;
    Debug.Print ", "; MyWS.UserName
Next MyWS
Debug.Print
MsgBox "Creating a workspace was successful"
Exit Sub
End Sub
```

The enumeration of the new workspace is shown in Listing 17-2. I did an append to the **Workspaces** collection only to show you that another workspace was created. It was not necessary to do this, and the new workspace can be used immediately.

LISTING 17-2 The results of Listing 17-1

```
Enumeration of DBEngine
Workspaces: Name, UserName
<1>#Default Workspace#, admin
DBEngine.Version: 3.5

<2>#Default Workspace#, admin
<2>NewWS, admin
```

Idle

This is a Jet method and isn't necessary in a single-user environment unless there are multiple instances of an application. When in doubt use the **Idle** method. The method may actually improve Access performance in a multiuser environment.

The **Idle** method gives the Jet Engine an opportunity to finish or perform background tasks. A lock may be released from the user prospective, but the actual release is not complete until all associated tasks are complete. Continual and repeated use of the **Idle** method may indicate either slow and inadequate hardware, poor application design, or too many users.

DoEvents should be used when DAO is being used from a 16-bit cooperative multitasking environment and is not required for Windows NT. Using this method with Window 3.1, Windows for WorkGroups, and Windows 95 is illustrated in the code below. (The technique is only applicable to DAO 2.0/2.5/3.0.)

```
DBEngine.Idle DB_FREELOCKS
DoEvents
```

Control to the application is not returned until all read locks are released when the intrinsic constant **DB_FREELOCKS** is used. In DAO 3.0, the intrinsic constant is renamed to **dbFreeLocks**.

DAO 3.5 uses the property **dbFlushCache** with the **Idle** method, as shown below.

```
DBEngine.Idle dbFlushCache
```

RegisterDatabase

You may use Jet to attach tables in other Access databases. Open Database Connectivity (ODBC) data sources such as Microsoft SQL Server must be registered before being accessed by Jet. Microsoft recommends registering databases using the Windows Control Panel ODBC setup icon. However, if you do elect to use the **Register Database** method, then you are encouraged by Microsoft to use the *silent* option, which is no dialog box. Listing 17-3 registers a database. If the data source is already registered, then it is updated. No changes are made when the data source is registered and the attempted registration fails for any reason.

note ⫤ **If the registration is done in a Windows NT or a Windows 95 environment, the Registry is updated rather than the** ODBC.INI **file.**

LISTING 17-3 Registering a database as a data source and opening a registered database

```
Private Sub Register_Data_Source_Click()
'(C) 1998 Bruce T. Prendergast
'   DBA Prendergast Consulting
'   DBA PCS
'   IDG BGooks Worldwide ISBN 0-7645-3123-9
'
'   Listing 17-3 Registering a data source
'
    Dim MyWS As Workspace, MyDB As Database
    Dim MyErr As Error
    Dim Attr As String
    '
    ' Build keywords string.
    '
    Attr = "Description=SQL Server on server Thor" _
        & Chr$(13)
    Attr = Attr & "OemToAnsi=No" & Chr$(13)
    Attr = Attr & "Network=DBNMPNTW" & Chr$(13)
    Attr = Attr & "Address=\\Thor\PIPE\SQL\QUERY" _
        & Chr$(13)
    Attr = Attr & "Database=Pubs"
    '
    ' Update the Registry (ODBC.INI in WFW and Win 3.1)
    '
    DBEngine.RegisterDatabase "Thor", "SQL Server", _
        True, Attr
    '
    ' The code below is shown as inline however the
    ' code above is a one-time event. This is the
    ' acid test! Is it there?
    '
    Set MyWS = DBEngine.Workspaces(0)
```

```
On Error GoTo No_Database
Set MyDB = MyWS.OpenDatabase( _
    "Thor", False, False, "ODBC;")
MsgBox "Data source registration was successful"
Exit Sub
No_Database:
For Each MyErr In DBEngine.Errors
    MsgBox MyErr.Description
Next MyErr
End Sub
```

I was prompted for a password because I didn't declare one when connecting to SQL Server. I didn't get any errors, and I logged onto the SQL Server using a separate process after executing the above code. The following output from **isql/w** of SQL Server indicates that a connection was made to the *Pubs* database:

SPID	STATUS	LOGINAME	HOSTNAME	BLK	DBNAME	CMD
1	sleeping	sa		0	master	MIRROR HANDLER
2	sleeping	sa		0	master	LAZY WRITER
3	sleeping	sa		0	master	CHECKPOINT SLEEP
4	runnable	sa		0	master	RA MANAGER
10	sleeping	sa	THOR	0	master	AWAITING COMMAND
11	sleeping	sa	THOR	0	master	AWAITING COMMAND
12	sleeping	sa	THOR	0	pubs	AWAITING COMMAND
13	runnable	sa	THOR	0	master	SELECT

(1 row(s) affected)

The appropriate network drivers are installed at initial product installation. The driver installed is based upon the operating system in use. Microsoft Access 2.0, Access 95, and Access 97 all assume an operating environment. Access 2.0 assumes a Windows 3.1 environment, Access 95 assumes a Windows 95 environment, and Access 97 assumes a Windows 95 environment or a Windows NT 4.0 environment. These products also function very well on Windows NT 3.51. The general problem is the documentation assumes a specific driver for an assumed environment. If I want to register a database on Windows NT, then I can't use the DBNMP3 driver stated in the documentation. I must use DBNMPNTW as listed in Table 17-1.

TABLE 17-1 NETWORK PROTOCOL DRIVERS FOR WINDOWS 3.1, WINDOWS 95, WINDOWS NT, AND MS-DOS			
NET-LIBRARY	*WINDOWS NT, WINDOWS 95*	*WINDOWS 3.1, WFW 3.11*	*MS-DOS*
Named Pipes	DBNMPNTW.DLL	DBNMP3.DLL	DBNMPIPE.EXE
NWLink IPX/SPX	DBMSSPXN.DLL	DBMSSPX3.DLL	DBMSSPX.EXE
Bayan Vines	DBMSVINN.DLL	DBMSVIN3.DLL	DBMSVINE.EXE
TCP/IP	DBMSSOCN.DLL	DBMSSOC3.DLL	Not Available
Multi-Protocol	DBMSRPCN.DLL	DBMSRPC3.DLL	Not Available

The last issue is the pipe name. The default pipe for SQL Server is:

```
\\Thor\PIPE\SQL\QUERY
```

Your server is probably not named **Thor** and may not use the default pipe. Contact your SQL Server administrator if you have trouble connecting. All servers can't use the same pipe, and if more than one server is installed, the pipe name is probably different.

RepairDatabase

If you have Version 2.0, then you should upgrade to Jet 2.5, which is the service pack ACCSVC.EXE found in the monthly subscription to Microsoft TechNet. It will locate errors in the database that version 2.0 cannot. If you find yourself with errors such as *1709 Undocumented Jet Engine error,* then consider upgrading. When you upgrade, you will have the equivalent of the Jet 2.5 16-bit version found in Microsoft Visual Basic 4.0.

Of course, all versions of Microsoft Access have birthing problems. You'll want to install the Access 95 service pack, which corrects a memory leak. This replaces the Windows component VBA232.DLL in the Windows NT SYSTEM 32 directory.

caution A few words of caution on repairing a database are appropriate here. The Access 2.0 recovery strategy is to first repair the database and then compact it. This strategy actually caused problems in Access 95. The current database compaction strategy, exclusive of Microsoft Access 2.0, is to compact the database first and only repair the database if necessary.

Repair of a database is illustrated with:

DBEngine.**RepairDatabase** "C:\MYDB.MDB"

SetOption

This method temporarily overrides the Microsoft Windows Registry settings and is applicable to only Jet workspaces.

Syntax:

DBEngine.**SetOption** *Parameter, NewValue*

Where:

Parameter: A **Long** which is one of: **dbPageTimeout**, **dbSharedAsyncDelay**, **dbExclusiveAsyncDelay**, **dbLockRetry**, **dbUserCommitSync**, **dbImplicitCommitSync**, **dbMaxBufferSize**, **dbMaxLocksPerFile**, **dbLockDelay**, **dbRecycleLVs**, **dbFlushTransactionTimeout**

NewValue: A **Variant** value which will set the new *Parameter* value. The constants below correspond with Registry keys in the path. The Registry key for the constant **dbPageTimeout** is shown below:

```
Jet\3.5\Engines\Jet\3.5\PageTimeout
```

Values for some of the parameters are:

○ **dbPageTimeout** — The expiration time in milliseconds of cache data which is not read-locked. The default is 5000. DWORD in Window 95 or Windows NT 4.0; REG_DWORD in Windows NT 3.51.

○ **dbSharedAsyncDelay** — The time in milliseconds to defer the asynchronous flush of a shared database. The default is zero. DWORD in Window 95 or Windows NT 4.0; REG_DWORD in Windows NT 3.51.

o **dbExclusiveAsyncDelay** — The time in milliseconds to defer the asynchronous flush of an exclusive database. The default is 2000. `DWORD` in Window 95 or Windows NT 4.0; `REG_DWORD` in Windows NT 3.51.

o **dbLockRetry** — Retry count for a locked page. The default is 20. `DWORD` in Window 95 or Windows NT 4.0; `REG_DWORD` in Windows NT 3.51.

o **dbUserCommitSync** — **Yes** instructs the system to wait for a commit; **No** indicates no wait. The default is **Yes**. String for Windows 95 or Windows NT 4.0, `REG-SZ` for Windows NT 3.51.

o **dbImplicitCommitSync** — **No** instructs the system to proceed without waiting for the commit to finish; **Yes** instructs the system to wait for the commit to finish. The default is **No**. String for Windows 95 or Windows NT 4.0; `REG-SZ` for Windows NT 3.51.

o **dbMaxBufferSize** — The size of the internal cache in kilobytes (K). Computed as (TotalRam in MB - 12) / 4) + 512K. Default for 32MB is 5632K. `DWORD` in Window 95 or Windows NT 4.0; `REG_DWORD` in Windows NT 3.51.

Figure 17-2 illustrates the default Jet 3.5 initialization constants.

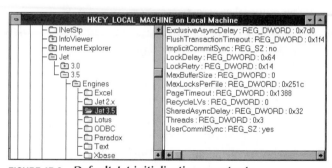

FIGURE 17-2   Default Jet initialization constants.

THE ERRORS COLLECTION

Error handling is enhanced starting with DAO 3.0. The **Err** function and **Error** statement of DAO 2.0 are replaced with the DAO 3.0 **Errors** collection of the **DBEngine**. The **Errors** collection handles only errors created by DAO operations and is detailed below. Do not confuse the **Error** object, which is for DAO errors, with the **Err** object, which is for run-time errors.

***Errors** Collection Definition*

> Methods: **Refresh**

> Property: **Count**

***Error** Object*

> Methods: **Clear**, **Raise**

> Properties: **Description**, **HelpContext**, **HelpFile**, **LastDLLError**, **Number**(Default), **Source**

The older technique using the **Err** function and the **Error** statement still works and is supported for backward compatibility. Existing programs will continue to function, but expanded error information is now available. The new technique doesn't work for DDE errors.

The **Error** object contains both an error number and a description. The description can also be found using the **AccessError** method of the **Application** object:

```
Application.AccessError(lngErrorCode)
```

The **Errors** collection will return all ODBC errors. The first **Error** object returns the lowest level error, with each subsequent level returning a higher level of error.

Applications are not always simple. *Error unwinding* is not discussed in this book, but it is the process of capturing an error and then creating another artificial error to pass error processing back to another level in a layered application. VBA error handlers cannot handle their own errors, but go back to the call tree until a handler is found. The developer can take advantage of this feature by capturing the original error and then forcing another error in the error handler. This starts the unwind process. The **Errors** collection makes this easy by preserving the original error information. An unwind process may be started using the **Raise** method with a user defined error code:

```
Err.Raise lngUserErrorCode
```

The **Errors** collection has the user-defined error at **DBEngine.Errors(0)**, and the original errors are preserved in **DBEngine.Errors(1) — DBEngine.Errors (DBEngine.Errors.Count-1)**. You'll note that the **Errors** collection is not refreshed when using the **Raise** method. This is because the **Err** object is for Access run-time errors, and the **Errors** collection and **Error** objects are for DAO errors. If **Err.Number** does not match **DBEngine.Errors(0)**, then the error is a run-time error or a user-defined error.

LISTING 17-4 **Enumerating the Errors collection**

```
Private Sub Error_Enumeration_Click()
'(C) 1998 Bruce T. Prendergast
'    DBA Prendergast Consulting
'    DBA PCS
'    IDG BGooks Worldwide ISBN 0-7645-3123-9
'
'    Listing 17-4 Enumerating the Errors collection
'
    Dim MyDB As Database
    Dim MyWS As Workspace
    Dim MyQdf As QueryDef
    Dim MyErr As Error
    Set MyWS = DBEngine.Workspaces(0)
    Set MyDB = MyWS.Databases(0)
    On Error GoTo DAO_Error
    Set MyQdf = MyDB.OpenRecordset( _
        "I donot Exist")
    Stop
DAO_Error:
    MsgBox "Error Count : " & _
        DBEngine.Errors.Count
    For Each MyErr In DBEngine.Errors
        MsgBox "DAO Error Description: " & _
```

```
                    MyErr.Description
               MsgBox "DAO Error Source: " & MyErr.Source
               MsgBox "DAO Error Number: " & MyErr.Number
          Next MyErr
          MsgBox "Error enumeration complete"
          Exit Sub
     End Sub
```

KEY POINT SUMMARY

We're gradually moving through the DAO objects. The **DBEngine** object is the primary topic of this chapter. It is the first object in the DAO hierarchy, and it plays a key role in Access database performance. The **CompactDatabase** method of the **DBEngine** object improves Access performance. Indexes are placed in clustered primary key order. The **DBEngine** object is a parent to both a jet **Workspace** object and an ODBCDirect **Workspace** object. Both types of workspace objects may exist simultaneously.

- DAO is ubiquitous in the Microsoft Architecture and may be used by any tool supporting VBA and a Reference library.
- DAO does not have a default Workspace object, whereas Microsoft Access does.
- The **Errors** collection is an element of DAO. Only DAO errors are reported in the **Errors** collection.
- A DAO **Workspace** object supports either Jet or ODBCDirect. A Jet and an ODBCDirect workspace can both exist simultaneously.

APPLYING WHAT YOU'VE LEARNED

The following questions will assess your understanding of the **DBEngine** object. The questions are designed to measure your comprehension of the **DBEngine** object.

Instant Assessment

1. What is another name for a workspace?

2. Name two benefits of compacting a DAO 2.0/3.0/3.5 database.

3. Name a DAO 3.0/3.5 benefit of database compaction.

4. When should a database be compacted?

5. Name the two types of **Workspaces** and describe the differences.

6. Name the DAO entity that contains the methods **BeginTrans**, **CommmitTrans**, and **Rollback**.

7. What are the **RepairDatabase** issues?

8. When can a **Workspace** object be closed?

9. What unique feature of VBA can be used to unwind errors?

 concept link   **For answers to the Instant Assessment questions, see Appendix C.**

Lab Exercise

Lab 17.36 *Using DAO in the enterprise*

 MCSD — WA I

Chapter 3 includes laboratories that access type libraries using the References entry of the appropriate **Tools** menu. The objective of this laboratory is to use Automation to instantiate the DAO from different Microsoft tools. We know that Visual Basic, Excel, Word, PowerPoint, and OutLook each support VBA. This laboratory will step the process of creating a pass-through query to Microsoft SQL Server from within Microsoft Excel using DAO. It is left as an exercise for the reader to create a corresponding query in either PowerPoint or OutLook.

 concept link   **The code in Listing 17-5 is located in the Access 97** `CHAPTER17.MDB` **database in the** `EXAMPLES\CHAPTER17` **folder on the CD-ROM that accompanies this book.**

LISTING 17-5 DAO from Excel

```
Private Sub DAO_from_Excel_Click()
'(C) 1998 Bruce T. Prendergast
' DBA Prendergast Consulting
' DBA PCS
' IDG Books Worldwide ISBN 0-7645-3123-9
```

```
'
' Listing 17-5 Using DAO in Excel 97
'
MsgBox "This code is not intended to be used from Access"
Exit Sub
'
'****************************************************
'cut all lines below this for pasting into Excel 97
'****************************************************
'
Dim MyDAO As DBEngine
Dim MyWS As Workspace
Dim MyDB As Database
Dim MyFld As Field

Dim MyQry As QueryDef, MyRS As Recordset
'
' the stament below gets a type mismatch
' with DAO 3.5 but works fine with DAO 3.0
'
Set MyDAO = CreateObject("DAO.DBEngine")
'
' get a workspace
'
Set MyWS = CreateWorkspace("", "admin", "")
If Dir("MyDB.mdb") <> "" Then Kill "MyDB.mdb"


'
' create a new database
'
Set MyDB = MyWS.CreateDatabase("MyDB.mdb", _
dbLangGeneral, dbEncrypt)
'
' the zero-length string creates a temporary query
```

```
'
Set MyQry = MyDB.CreateQueryDef("")
Dim SourceConnectStr As String
SourceConnectStr = "ODBC;DATABASE=Pubs;UID=sa;" & _
"PWD=;DSN=Thor;"
'
' this is a pass-through query so the connect
' string is set first tostop Jet from
' parsing the SQL placed in the SQL property
' of the QueryDef.
'
MyQry.Connect = SourceConnectStr
MyQry.ReturnsRecords = True
MyQry.SQL = "sp_who" ' an SQL Server stored procedure
'
' now create the snapshot and print the returned data
'
Set MyRS = MyQry.OpenRecordset()
'
' enumerate fields
'
Debug.Print "Fields: Name, Type, Value"
For Each MyFld In MyRS.Fields
Debug.Print " "; MyFld.Name; " "; MyFld.Type; " "; MyFld.Value
Next MyFld
MsgBox "SQL pass-through query completed successfully"
Exit Sub
'
'*************************************************
'cut all lines above this for pasting into Excel 97
'*************************************************
'
End Sub
```

To create a pass-through query in Excel 97 using DAO (the SQL Server **sp_who** stored procedure of SQL Server 6.5 is called from Excel 97 using DAO), follow these steps:

1. Start Access 97.

2. Open the CHAPTER17.MDB in the EXAMPLES\CHAPTER17 folder of the CD-ROM located in this book.

3. Cut the indicated text from the **DAO_From_Excel** click event located on the Chapter17 form.

4. Start Excel 97

5. From the Excel **Tools** menu, select Macro.

6. Select Visual Basic Editor.

7. From the Visual Basic Editor **Tools** menu, select References.

8. Select and check Microsoft DAO 3.0 Object Library. (Note: This is supposed to work with DAO 3.5. Unfortunately, this example only works with DAO 3.0 on my test system. You should try DAO 3.5 first.)

9. From the Visual Basic Editor **Tools** menu, select Macros.

10. Enter your macro name.

11. Click create.

12. Paste in the cut text by selecting Edit ⇒ Paste.

13. Run the macro. Assuming that you have access to SQL Server, you should expect the message: "SQL pass-through query completed successfully".

Congratulations! You just called a Microsoft SQL Server stored procedure from Excel 97 using DAO.

Windows Architecture I

CHAPTER

Working with the Workspace Object

18

About Chapter 18

A **Workspace** object is the equivalent of a session and is where the rubber hits the road. It is a major intersection at which the choice is to follow the superhighway to Microsoft Access and nirvana, or to make that right turn and go cross-country with ODBCDirect.

Chapter 18 reveals your personality. You are either a conspicuous consumptionist and use Microsoft Access, or you are a minimalist and use ODBCDirect. This choice is between using an ODBCDirect **Workspace** object created with the intrinsic constant **dbUseODBC** or **dbUseJet** for Microsoft Access. We can't create the **Workspace** object here; that was done previously with the **DBEngine** object.

The examples in this chapter may be found in the Access 97 CHAPTER18.MDB database located in the EXAMPLES\CHAPTER18 folder of the CD-ROM located at the back of this book.

THE WORKSPACES COLLECTION

The **Workspaces** collection is next in the DAO hierarchy. Unlike **DBEngine**, **Workspace** objects can be created and the **Workspaces** collection is the default collection of the **DBEngine** object. Figure 18-1 is our next stop on the DAO roadmap.

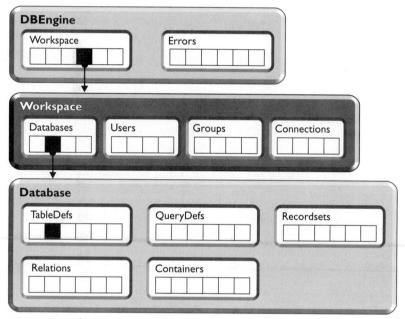

FIGURE 18-1   The Workspace object.

Count is the only property of the **Workspaces** collection that has only the **Append** and **Refresh** methods.

Workspaces Collection Definition

    Methods: **Append, Refresh**

    Property: **Count**

Workspace Object

    Collections: **Databases**(default), **Groups, Users**

    Methods: **BeginTrans, Close, CommitTrans, CreateDatabase, CreateGroup, CreateUser, OpenConnection**(D), **OpenDatabase, Rollback**

Properties: **Connection**(D), **DefaultCursorDriver**(D), **IsolateODBCTrans**, **Name**, **Type**(D), **UserName**

Legend: D = ODBCDirect

The is the start of a natural dichotomy in the DAO. A workspace may be either a Jet workspace or an ODBCDirect workspace.

BEGINTRANS, COMMITTRANS, AND ROLLBACK

Transactions improve system performance by buffering data until it is committed. They also provide a mechanism for rolling back an update when it is in error. Transactions are available to either a Jet **Workspace** object or to an ODBCDirect **Workspace** object.

Syntax:

Object.[**BeginTrans** | **CommitTrans** | **Rollback**]

Where:

Object: An object of type **Workspace**

An application may create multiple workspaces. The same data source may have overlapping transactions from different workspaces. The **IsolateODBCTrans** property insures that the transactions from different workspaces do not interact. Transactions are global to a workspace, and transactions to more than one database can be rolled back with a single **Rollback** method.

PATIENCE IS A VIRTUE WITH TRANSACTIONS

Impatient users create grief for themselves. The system may be two hours into a batch transaction and the impatient user aborts the process. What is often forgotten is that the rollback will take just as long as the original transaction. The impatient user aborts the rollback and loses the database. Wait until the rollback is complete, and remember that patience is a virtue.

There are some simple rules for creating useful transactions:

o Never update the same row twice. This does not mean that more than one value can be changed, but don't change a value and then change the same value later in the transaction. This is an issue of repeatability when the transaction is rolled back.

o Don't do inconsistent updates. An inconsistent delete is the removing of the parent entity orphaning child entities in a one–many relation. An inconsistent update includes an inconsistent delete. The value of the parent is replaced with a new value, which orphans child entities.

o Always update all tables in the same order. Other transactions may be running and locks can be held by the other transactions. Adopting an updating protocol for the order of table updating minimizes deadlocks.

o Make the transaction as short as possible. Transactions are not meant to be long, drawn out affairs. The ideal transaction is very short and very simple. Nesting of transactions is possible, but avoid them if at all possible. SQL Server supports nested transactions; however, the Microsoft Jet database engine does not support nested transactions to ODBC data sources such as SQL Server. Significant rework is required to upsize a nested Access transaction to Microsoft SQL Server.

o Transactions should exhibit the **ACID** properties:

  o **Atomicity:** Either all or none of the transaction's changes are present when the transaction completes.

  o **Consistency:** The transaction respects all business rules and referential integrity. Inconsistent updates can be done, but violate system integrity.

  o **Isolation:** Transactions are isolated. The isolation is realized by using locks, separate workspaces, and the **IsolateODBCTrans** property.

  o **Durability:** Once the commit occurs, the transactions must be present even if the system fails. SQL Server supports this property and Microsoft Access does not.

Some databases may not support transactions. The **Transaction** property of the **Recordset** object can be tested before attempting transactions.

Nesting transactions are supported but not recommended because SQL Server does not support nested transactions. In Access, the innermost transactions are rolled back first. ODBCDirect workspaces do not support nested transactions.

note 🖊 **Transactions are automatically rolled back if you close your work-space without saving or rolling back pending transactions.**

Listing 18-1 is an example of rolling back a transaction. It is not a recommended procedure because there is user interaction during an open transaction. This is an example of how *not* to create a transaction. Locks remain open on SQL Server while the system is waiting for a user response.

The example is of a local table, which is satisfactory when no other users are affected. This technique gives less than satisfactory performance when this application is upgraded to SQL Server.

LISTING 18-1 User interaction during a transaction – a poor design

```
Private Sub Change_Title_Click()
'(C) 1998 Bruce T. Prendergast
' DBA Prendergast Consulting
' DBA PCS
' IDG Books Worldwode ISBN 0-7645-3123-9
'
' Listing 18-1 Undesired transaction user interaction
'
    Const MB_ICONQUESTION = 32
    Const YES = 6
    Const YES_NO = 4
    Dim CRLF As String, EmployeeName As String
    Dim Message As String, Prompt As String
    Dim MyWorkspace As Workspace, MyDatabase As Database, _
        MyTable As Recordset
    CRLF = Chr$(13) & Chr$(10)
    Prompt = "Change title to Account Executive?"
    Set MyWorkspace = DBEngine.Workspaces(0)
    Set MyDatabase = MyWorkspace.Databases(0)
    Set MyTable = MyDatabase.OpenRecordset("Employees", _
        DB_OPEN_TABLE)
    MyWorkspace.BeginTrans        ' Start of transaction.
    Do Until MyTable.EOF
        If MyTable![Title] = "Sales Representative" Then
```

```
        EmployeeName = MyTable![Last Name] & ", " & _
            MyTable![First Name]
        Message = "Employee: " & _
                        EmployeeName & CRLF & CRLF
        If MsgBox(Message & Prompt, MB_ICONQUESTION & _
            YES_NO, "Change Job Title") = YES Then
            MyTable.Edit     ' Enable editing.
            MyTable![Title] = "Account Executive"
            ' Change job title.
            MyTable.Update  ' Save changes.
        End If
    End If
    MyTable.MoveNext          ' Move to next record.
Loop
If MsgBox("Save all changes?", MB_ICONQUESTION + YES_NO, _
    "Save Changes") = YES Then
    MyWorkspace.CommitTrans ' Commit changes.
Else
    MyWorkspace.Rollback     ' Undo changes.
End If
MyTable.Close                ' Close table.
End Sub
```

A Poorly Constructed Transaction

The **On error GoTo** statement is always used to capture transaction errors. This technique is used in the example shown in Listing 18-2, but it suffers from being too simplistic. The error is captured and reported with the transaction rolled back. It is certainly better than Listing 18-1; however, no error unwind processing is done. The error processing is adequate if the error occurs in a single layer application. A very complex application requires the unwinding of errors with progressive error information passed back to higher levels of the application.

Listing 18-2 illustrates the use of **On error GoTo** to establish the transaction failure address. If for any reason an error occurs, the transaction is rolled back and the database remains unchanged.

LISTING 18-2 Capturing an error in a poorly constructed transaction

```
Private Sub Poor_Transaction_Click()
'(C) 1998 Bruce T. Prendergast
' DBA Prendergast Consulting
' DBA PCS
' IDG Books Worldwide ISBN 0-7645-3123-9
'
' Listing 18-2 A procedural solution
'
' This example illustrates a transaction rollback,
' however it is a very poor example since all the
' work is done as a procedure. SQL is always the
' desired solution
'
    Dim MyRs As Recordset
    Dim MyDB As Database
    Dim MyWS As Workspace
    Dim Criteria As String
    Dim User_Input As Integer
    '
    '   an artificial user input
    '
    User_Input = 5
    Set MyWS = DBEngine.Workspaces(0)
    Set MyDB = MyWS.Databases(0)
    Set MyRs = MyDB.OpenRecordset("tblInventory", _
        dbOpenDynaset)
    Criteria = "[On Hand] > " & User_Input
    MyRs.FindFirst Criteria

    On Error GoTo Transaction_Failure
    If MyRs.NoMatch Then
        MsgBox "No records to update"
        Exit Sub
    Else
        MyWS.BeginTrans
```

```
        MyRs.Edit
    End If
    '
    '   update the data
    '
    With MyRs
        ![cost] = ![cost] + ![cost] / 10
    End With
    MyRs.Update
    MyWS.CommitTrans
    MsgBox "Poor transaction was successful"

exit_after_error:
    MyRs.Close
    MyDB.Close
    Exit Sub
Transaction_Failure:
    MsgBox Error$
    MyWS.Rollback
    MsgBox "Update failed, and rolled back"
    Resume exit_after_error
End Sub
```

A Properly Constructed Transaction

Listing 18-3 is a properly constructed transaction, but it is deficient in terms of coding style: it uses hard-coded values for parameters, which is not a good practice. Additionally, it suffers slightly because the **RecordsAffected** property of a Jet database returns a zero for a non-**Null** result set.

 concept link **See the Parameters collection discussion in Chapter 22 on using parameters with a QueryDef object.**

Listing 18-3 uses the **AffectedRecords** property of a **Database** or **QueryDef** object. It returns the number of records affected by the most recently invoked **Execute** method. The value of this property is that it can be checked from within the transaction, and when the number of records affected by the action query (deletes, updates, or inserts) is different than expected the transaction can be rolled back.

LISTING 18-3 **A properly constructed transaction**

```
Private Sub Proper_Transaction_Click()
'(C) 1998 Bruce T. Prendergast
' DBA Prendergast Consulting
' DBA PCS
' IDG Books Worldwide ISBN 0-7645-3123-9
'
' Listing 18-3 A proper solution
'
'    This example illustrates a transaction rollback,
'    and is a good example since the update is done
'    in SQL and not in a procedure.
'
    Dim MyQdf As QueryDef
    Dim MyDB As Database
    Dim MyWS As Workspace

    Set MyWS = DBEngine.Workspaces(0)
    Set MyDB = MyWS.Databases(0)
    '
    '    An SQL statement rather than a procedural update
    '
    Set MyQdf = MyDB.CreateQueryDef("")
    MyQdf.SQL = "UPDATE tblInventory SET [Cost] = " _
            & "[Cost]+[Cost]/10 WHERE [On Hand] > " & 5
    Debug.Print MyQdf.SQL
    '
    '    update the data
    '
    On Error GoTo Transaction_Failure
    '
    '    dbfailOnError will create an
    '    error for locked records
    '
    MyWS.BeginTrans
    MyQdf.Execute dbFailOnError
```

```
    If MyQdf.RecordsAffected <> 987654321 Then
        MsgBox "Transaction Failure: " & _
                "inappropriate row count" & _
        vbCrLf & "Transaction rolled back"
        MyWS.Rollback
        Exit Sub
    End If
    MyWS.CommitTrans
    MsgBox "Proper transaction was successful"
exit_after_error:
    Exit Sub
Transaction_Failure:
    MsgBox Error$
    MyWS.Rollback
    MsgBox "Update failed, and rolled back"
    Resume exit_after_error
End Sub
```

CreateDatabase

This **Workspace** object method creates a new database object.

Syntax:

    Set *Database* = *Workspace*.**CreateDatabase**(*DatabaseName, Locale* [, *Options*])

Where:

    DataBase: An object of type **Database**.

    Workspace: An object of type **Workspace**.

    DatabaseName: A string expression for the new database name. It represents a full path such as C:\MYDATA.MDB or a uniform naming convention (UNC) expression of the form: \\MyServer\MyShare\MyDir\MyDB.MDB. Access will supply the .MDB extension if necessary.

    Locale: DAO 2.0 Intrinsic constants as follows:

DB_LANG_GENERAL	English, German, French, Portuguese, Italian, and Modern Spanish
DB_LANG_ARABIC	Arabic
DB_LANG_CZECH	Czech

DB_LANG_CYRILLIC	Russian
DB_LANG_DUTCH	Dutch
DB_LANG_GREEK	Greek
DB_LANG_HEBREW	Hebrew
DB_LANG_HUNGARIAN	Hungarian
DB_LANG_ICELANDIC	Icelandic
DB_LANG_NORWDAN	Norwegian and Danish
DB_LANG_POLISH	Polish
DB_LANG_SWEDEN	Swedish and Finnish
DB_LANG_SPANISH	Traditional Spanish
DB_LANG_TURKISH	Turkish

Options: Intrinsic values for DAO 2.0:

DB_ENCRYPT	Encrypt while compacting
DB_DECRYPT	Decrypt while compacting
DB_VERSION10	Create an Access 1.0 version database
DB_VERSION11	Create an Access 1.1 version database
DB_VERSION20	Create an Access 2.0 version database

Locale: DAO 3.0/3.5 intrinsic constants as follows:

dbLangGeneral	English, German, French, Portuguese, Italian, and Modern Spanish
dbLangArabic	Arabic
dbLangChineseSimplified	Simplified Chinese
dbLangChineseTraditional	Traditional Chinese
dbLangCyrillic	Russian
dbLangCzech	Czech
dbLangDutch	Dutch
dbLangGreek	Greek
dbLangHebrew	Hebrew
dbLangHungarian	Hungarian
dbLangIcelandic	Icelandic

dbLangJapanese	Japanese
dbLangKorean	Korean
dbLangNordic	Norwegian and Danish (Jet 1.0 only)
dbLangNorwdan	Norwegian and Danish
dbLangPolish	Polish
dbLangSlovenian	Slovenian
dbLangSpanish	Traditional Spanish
dbLangSwedfin	Swedish and Finnish
dbLangThai	Thai
dbLangTurkish	Turkish

Options: Intrinsic values for DAO 3.0/3.5:

dbEncrypt	Encrypt while compacting
dbDecrypt	Decrypt while compacting
dbVersion10	Create an Access 1.0 ver database
dbVersion11	Create an Access 1.1 ver database
dbVersion25	Create an Access 2.5 ver database
dbVersion30	Create an Access 3.0 ver database (version 3.5 compatible)

Creating a new database is illustrated in Listing 18-4.

LISTING 18-4 Creating a new database

```
Private Sub Create_Database_Click()
'(C) 1998 Bruce T. Prendergast
' DBA Prendergast Consulting
' DBA PCS
' IDG Books Worldwide ISBN 0-7645-3123-9
'
' Listing 18-4 Creating a database
'

    Dim MyWS As Workspace
    Dim MyDB As Database
    Dim CurDB As Database
```

```
        Set MyWS = DBEngine.Workspaces(0)
        '
        '    just in case the .mdb already exists
        '
        On Error Resume Next
        Kill "MyNewDB.mdb"
        Set CurDB = MyWS.Databases(0)
        Set MyDB = MyWS.CreateDatabase _
            ("MyNewDB.mdb", dbLangGeneral, dbVersion30)
        MyDB.QueryTimeout = CurDB.QueryTimeout
        MyDB.Close
        CurDB.Close
        MsgBox "Creating a database was successful"
        Exit Sub
End Sub
```

CreateGroup and CreateUser

CreateGroup and **CreateUser** are methods of **Workspace** objects. **CreateGroup** is also a method of a **User** object and **CreateUser** is a method of a **Group** object.

Syntax:

> **Set** *Variable* = *Object*.**CreateGroup**([*Name* [, *PID*]])

Where:

> *Variable:* A variable of type **Group**.

> *Object:* The variable name of the **Workspace** object used to create the new **Group** object.

> *Name:* A string expression uniquely identifying the user.

> *PID:* A string expression of -four to twenty characters.

Syntax:

> **Set** *Variable* = *Object*.**CreateUser**([*Name* [, *PID* [, *Password*]]])

Where:

> *Variable:* A variable of type **User**.

> *Object:* The variable name of the **Workspace** object used to create the new **User** object.

Name: A string expression uniquely identifying the user.

PID: A string expression of -four to twenty characters.

Password: Up to fourteen characters with any ASCII character except a null. Passwords are cleared with a zero length string.

Creating a group, a user, and a user in a group

Listing 18-5 illustrates the creation of a unique user, a group, and a user within a group, and Listing 18-6 illustrates the results.

LISTING 18-5 Creating a user, a group, and a user in a group

```
Private Sub Create_User_Click()
'(C) 1998 Bruce T. Prendergast
' DBA Prendergast Consulting
' DBA PCS
' IDG Books Worldwide ISBN 0-7645-3123-9
'
' Listing 18-5 Creating a user, a group, and a user in a group
'
    Dim NewGrp As Group, SQLGrpPID As Variant
    Dim MyWS As Workspace
    Dim MyUsr As User
    Dim MyGrp As Group
    Dim I As Integer

    SQLGrpPID = "The21IDG"
    Set MyWS = DBEngine.Workspaces(0)
    '
    '   this is debug stuff
    '
    On Error Resume Next
    MyWS.Groups.Delete "SQL Users"
    MyWS.Users.Delete "Bruce"

    Set NewGrp = MyWS.CreateGroup(_
            "SQL Users", SQLGrpPID)
    MyWS.Groups.Append NewGrp
```

```
MyWS.Groups.Refresh
'
' Enumerate all group accounts.
'
Debug.Print "Groups: Name (Groups)"
For Each MyGrp In MyWS.Groups
    Debug.Print "  "; MyGrp.Name
Next MyGrp
Debug.Print
'
' Group created, now create the user
'
Dim NewUser As User
Dim UserPIN As String
UserPIN = "sksid16"
Set NewUser = MyWS.CreateUser("Bruce", UserPIN)
MyWS.Users.Append NewUser
MyWS.Users.Refresh
'
' Now Enumerate all user accounts.
'
Debug.Print "Users: Name (Users)"
For Each MyUsr In MyWS.Users
    Debug.Print "  "; MyUsr.Name
Next MyUsr
'
' add user to new group
'
Set NewGrp = NewUser.CreateGroup("SQL Users")
NewUser.Groups.Append NewGrp
NewUser.Groups.Refresh
Debug.Print "Number of SQL Users is: " _
        & MyWS.Groups![SQL Users].Users.Count
Debug.Print "Users: Name  [SQL Users]"
For Each MyUsr In MyWS.Groups![SQL Users].Users
    Debug.Print "  "; MyUsr.Name
Next MyUsr
```

```
        Debug.Print
        MyWS.Groups.Delete "SQL Users"
        MyWS.Users.Delete "Bruce"
        MsgBox "Creating users and groups was successful"
        Exit Sub
    End Sub
```

LISTING 18-6 The results from Listing 18-5

```
Groups: Name (Groups)
Admins
Users
SQL Users
Users: Name (Users)
admin
Creator
Engine
Bruce
Number of SQL Users is: 1
Users: Name [SQL Users]
Bruce
```

OpenConnection

This **Workspace** object method opens a connection to an ODBC database. The method is available only from an ODBCDirect workspace and returns a **Connection** object. The object is similar to a **Database** object of Jet; the **Connection** object, however, does not use the Jet engine.

Syntax:

> Set *Connection* = *Workspace*.**OpenConnection**(*DBName, Options, Read-Only, Source*)

Where:

> *Connection:* A variable of type **Connection**.

> *Workspace:* An optional variable of type ODBCDirect **Workspace**.

> *DBName:* This field has several considerations:

- o This field may be a UNC name of the form:
  `\\MYSERVER\MYSHARE\MYDIR\MYDB.MDB`

- o A zero-length string in which case a dialog box is presented when the *Source* is ODBC.

- o Use **Databases**(0) if the reference is the current database.

Options: One of: **dbDriverNoPrompt, dbDriverPrompt, dbComplete, dbCompleteRequired**, or **dbRunAsync**.

- o **dbDriverNoPrompt**: The connection string provided in *DBName* and *Source* is used.

- o **dbDriverPrompt**: The ODBC data sources dialog box is presented.

- o **dbDriverComplete**: The *Source* argument has all the necessary connect information.

- o **dbCompleteRequired**: The behavior is **dbDriverComplete** with all prompts disabled.

- o **dbRunAsync**: The connection is made asynchronously.

Read-Only: A Boolean **True** when the database is opened for read-only access.

Source: An ODBC connection string.

Opening an ODBCDirect connection

Listing 18-7 illustrates establishing a connection to SQL Server with DAO ODBCDirect.

LISTING 18-7 Connecting to SQL Server

```
Private Sub Open_Connection_Click()
'(C) 1998 Bruce T. Prendergast
' DBA Prendergast Consulting
' DBA PCS
' IDG Books Worldwide ISBN 0-7645-3123-9
'
' Listing 18-7 Opening an ODBCDirect Connection
'
    Dim MyODWS As Workspace, MyDB As Database
    Dim MyCon As Connection
```

```
Dim MyErr As Error
Dim c As Connection
On Error GoTo Unable_To_Connect
'
'    create an ODBCDirect workspace
'
Set MyODWS = CreateWorkspace(_
        "MyODBCWS", "admin", "", dbUseODBC)


'
'    connect
'
Set MyCon = MyODWS.OpenConnection(_
        "MyConnection", dbDriverNoPrompt, True, _
    "ODBC;DATABASE=Pubs;UID=sa;PWD=;DSN=Thor;")
'
'    verify that the connection exists
'
For Each c In MyODWS.Connections
    Debug.Print "Connection: " & c.Name
Next c
MsgBox "ODBCDirect connection was successful"
Exit Sub
Unable_To_Connect:
    For Each MyErr In DBEngine.Errors
        MsgBox MyErr.Description
    Next MyErr
End Sub
```

OpenDatabase

This **Workspace** object method opens a specified database in a session and returns a reference to an object of type **Database**. The open database is automatically appended to the **Databases** collection. The **Database** object is removed from the **Databases** collection when the database is closed.

Syntax:

Set *Database* = *Workspace.***OpenDatabase***(DBName, Options, Read-Only, Source)*

Where:

Database: A variable of type **Database**.

Workspace: A variable of type **Workspace**.

DBName: This field has several considerations:

- This field may be a UNC name of the form: \\MYSERVER\MYSHARE\ MYDIR\MYDB.MDB

- A zero-length string in which case a dialog box is presented when the *Source* is ODBC.

- Use **Databases**(0) if the reference is the current database.

Options: A Boolean **True** when the database is opened for exclusive use or **False** for Jet databases. One of: **dbDriverNoPrompt**, **dbDriverPrompt**, **dbComplete**, or **dbCompleteRequired** for ODBCDirect workspaces.

Read-Only: A Boolean **True** when the database is opened for read-only access.

Source: A string expression described in Table 18-1.

TABLE 18-1 JET DBNAME STRINGS AND SOURCE STRINGS FOR DATABASE TYPES

DATABASE	DBNAME	SOURCE
Microsoft Access	"drive:\path\filename"	None
dBase III	"drive:\path"	"dbase III;"
dBase IV	"drive:\path"	"dBase IV;"
Paradox 3.x	"drive:\path"	"Paradox 3.x;"
Betrieve	"drive:\path\file.DDF"	"Btrieve;"
FoxPro 2.0	"drive:\path"	"FoxPro 2.0;"
FoxPro 2.5	"drive:\path"	"FoxPro 2.5;"
ODBC	zero-length string	"DATABASE = DefaultDatabase; UID = user; PWD = PassWord; DSN = DataSourceName;"

The following is an example Jet or ODBCDirect connection string to an ODBC data:

```
"ODBC;DATABASE=Pubs;UID=sa;PWD=;DSN=Thor;")
```

The connection string of Remote Data Objects (RDO) varies slightly.

KEY POINT SUMMARY

DAO supports the traditional Jet workspaces and the new ODBCDirect workspaces. The ODBCDirect workspace can only access ODBC data sources and doesn't require the Jet Engine.

- A **Workspace** object is either an ODBCDirect or a Jet workspace. It can't be both simultaneously; however, a workspace of each type may exist simultaneously.
- The **Workspaces** collection is the default collection of the DBEngine object.
- Transactions are a feature of a **Workspace** object.
- All open transactions of all database or connection objects are rolled back with the Rollback method.
- Jet or ODBCDirect transactions both violate the **ACID** properties of a database.

APPLYING WHAT YOU'VE LEARNED

These questions measure your understanding of managing transactions with either the Jet **Workspace** object or the ODBCDirect **Workspace** object.

Instant Assessment

1. What is a characteristic of **Workspace** transactions?
2. The Microsoft DAO 3.5 documentation illustrates the transaction methods **BeginTrans**, **CommitTrans**, and **Rollback** as methods of the **DBEngine**. Explain why this is wrong?
3. What happens to a transaction when a **Workspace** object is closed?

4. What is the difference between SQL Server and DAO transactions?

5. What constitutes a poorly constructed transaction?

6. What happens when an object is set to **Nothing**?

7. What is the default collection of a **Workspace** object?

8. What is an inconsistent update?

9. Name the **ACID** properties.

10. Which **ACID** property does Jet and DAO not support?

11. Explain the actions of the **Close** method in the following fragment:

```
Dim MyWS as Workspace
Set MyWS = DBEngine.Workspaces(0)

. . .

MyWS.Close
```

12. What is the meaning of DSN when opening, registering, or connecting to a database?

13. Explain why Listing 18-7 uses the **DBEngine** when it is enumerating the **Errors** collection of DAO.

14. Listing 18-5 uses the **Refresh** method of a **Workspace** object to refresh the **Groups** and the **Users** collections. Other than exposing new members of these collections, what other action occurs?

 concept link   **For answers to the Instant Assessment questions, see Appendix C.**

Lab Exercise

Lab 18.37 *When less is better: Use ODBCDirect rather than Jet*

WA I
WA II

The objective here is an evaluation of existing Access applications. Identify your current Microsoft Access applications that use ODBC data sources. Is the ODBC data source their only database access? Candidates for conversion to ODBCDirect are those Access applications that only access ODBC data sources. Can the applications be converted to ODBCDirect? The first benefit of converting to ODBCDirect is a reduced application memory footprint. The second benefit is improved performance when compared to accessing the ODBC data source with the ODBC Desktop Driver Set of Jet.

Windows Architecture I

Working with the Connection Object

About Chapter 19

Chapter 19 is about the **Connection** object, which is the first object in the ODBCDirect object in the Data Access Objects (DAO) hierarchy. The **Connection** object is used with Open Database Connectivity (ODBC) data sources. It is a desktop link to a remote server in the enterprise. It is not designed to supplant Jet and DAO on the desktop, but rather to function as a link in a component-connected enterprise.

The examples in this chapter may be found in the Access 97 CHAPTER19.MDB database located in the EXAMPLES\CHAPTER19 folder of the CD-ROM located at the back of this book.

THE CONNECTIONS COLLECTION

This is our third stop in the DAO hierarchy. **Connections** are new with DAO 3.5. The name given to the technology is ODBCDirect.

- The Microsoft Jet Database Engine is not loaded, which reduces the application footprint. It also means that you do not have to buy a Microsoft Access license for each client. The footprint issue is not valid with a virtual memory system.

- ODBCDirect is designed for access to ODBC data sources only, and the **OpenConnection** method is tuned for remote database connectivity.

- Server-side features such as server-side cursors are now available.

- Asynchronous queries are supported.

- ODBCDirect supports batch updating.

Limitations exist for ODBCDirect. These features are supported by Jet but are not available in ODBCDirect:

- Updatable joins

- Heterogeneous joins

- Data Definition Language (DDL) operations

- ODBCDirect objects are not persistent and cannot be stored in a database

- Bound forms

The **Connection** object in ODBCDirect is the equivalent of the **Database** object in Jet. The ODBCDirect **Connection** object is the parent of a **QueryDefs** and a **Recordsets** collection, both of which are child objects of the Jet **Database** object. The Microsoft Jet Database Engine provides a very rich functionality. It has always supported asynchronous queries, and control was given back to the application before the **Recordset** object was fully populated. Jet makes data available before the query completes.

An ODBCDirect **QueryDef** object is also asynchronous; however, data is not available until the query completes. The Jet engine is superior to ODBCDirect in many ways, so look at ODBCDirect as the minimum functionality necessary to complete a task. ODBCDirect is a very thin ODBC wrapper.

An ODBCDirect **Connection** object requires an ODBCDirect **Workspace** object. Figure 19-1 tells us that the **Connection** object is our next stop in the DAO roadmap. So that you're not confused, the **DBEngine** reference in Figure 19-1 is the **DBEngine** object of DAO and not the Jet database engine. ODBCDirect does not load the Jet database engine.

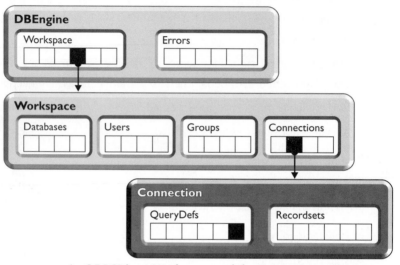

FIGURE 19-1   An ODBCDirect Workspace and the Connection collection.

Connections *Collection Definition*

Method: **Refresh**

Property: **Count**

Connection Object

Collections: **QueryDefs**(default), **Recordsets**

Methods: **Cancel, Close, CreateQueryDef, Execute, OpenRecordset**

Properties: **Connect, Database, Name, QueryTimeout, RecordsAffected, StillExecuting, Transactions, Updatable**

The **Connection** object of DAO 3.5 appears as an additional layer between the application and the data source. The **Database** property of a connection returns a **Database** object while the **Connection** property of a **Database** object returns a **Connection** object.

Actually, the **Connection** object is not an additional layer. The **Connection** object was added as an ad hoc implementation and the resulting mechanism is that a **Database** object is automatically created whenever a **Connection** object is created. Conversely, the **Database** object is automatically deleted whenever the **Connection** object is deleted. The Microsoft documentation states that an OBDCDirect **Connection** supports the **QueryDefs** collection and the **Recordsets** collection. The **Connection** object is nothing but a surrogate for the **Database** object, which is the actual collection manager.

The **Connection** object is simple meat and potatoes. It is a no-frills database connectivity technology. The enumeration of the **Connection** object properties illustrates a minimal yet effective database interface:

- **Connect** — Read-only in an existing **Connection** object.
- **Database** — The automatic **Database** object created when the connection object was created.
- **Name** — Connection name, read-only.
- **QueryTimeout** — This is self-explanatory.
- **RecordsAffected** — Number of records affected by an action query using the **Execute** method. It will not return a meaningful row count for an SQL DROP TABLE action query.
- **StillExecuting** — Used with an asynchronous **QueryDef** object, with a **MoveLast** on a **Recordset** object, opening a **Recordset** object, the **Execute** method of a **Connection** object, or the **OpenConnection** method.
- **Transactions** — Determines if the **Connection** object supports transactions.
- **Updatable** — Determines if the **Connection** object is updatable. **Recordset** objects may have individual read-only fields.

Cancel

This method cancels the execution of a pending asynchronous method for ODBCDirect workspaces. Listing 19-1 is an example of this method. The **Cancel** method should be wrapped up in a transaction because using the **Cancel** method outside a transaction can leave the data in an unknown state.

Syntax:

> *object.***Cancel**

Where:

object: Cancel the **Execute** of an **OpenConnection** method when *object* is a **Connection** or cancel the execution of a **Querydef** object. Cancel the **MoveLast** or **OpenRecordset** when *object* is a **Recordset.** The asynchronous connection example of Listing 19-1 uses the **Cancel** method to terminate a connection request after a timed interval.

LISTING 19-1   An asynchronous connection with a Close and a Cancel

```
Private Sub Asynchronous_Connection_Open_Click()
'(C) 1998 Bruce T. Prendergast
'    DBA Prendergast Consulting
'    DBA PCS
'    IDG Books Worldwide ISBN 0-7645-3123-9
'
'    Listing 19-1 Establishing an Asynchronous
'    Connection with a timer.
'
     Dim MyODWS As Workspace, MyDB As Database
     Dim MyCon As Connection
     Dim MyErr As Error
     Dim WaitTime As Single
     On Error GoTo Async_Connect_Error
     '
     '    create an ODBCDirect workspace
     '
     Set MyODWS = CreateWorkspace("MyODBCWS", _
          "admin", "", dbUseODBC)
     '
     '    connect
     '
     Set MyCon = MyODWS.OpenConnection("MyConnection", _
          dbDriverNoPrompt + dbRunAsync, True, _
          "ODBC;DATABASE=Pubs;UID=sa;PWD=;DSN=Thor;")
```

```
'
'    if no connection is made in 10 seconds then
'    assume that SQL server is not available
'
'
'    note to the reader. The loop is just for
'    illustrative purposes only. Actual code
'    should implement a form timer event.

WaitTime = Timer
While (Timer - WaitTime) < 5
Wend
Do While MyCon.StillExecuting
    If MsgBox("No connection yet—keep waiting?", _
            vbYesNo) = vbNo Then
        MyCon.Cancel
        MsgBox "Connection cancelled!"
        MyODWS.Close
        Exit Sub
    Else
        WaitTime = Timer
        While (Timer - WaitTime) < 5
        Wend
    End If
Loop
MyCon.Close
Set MyCon = Nothing
MyODWS.Close
MsgBox "Asynchronous connection was successful"
Exit Sub
Async_Connect_Error:
    For Each MyErr In DBEngine.Errors
        MsgBox MyErr.Description
    Next MyErr
End Sub
```

CreateQueryDef

This method of the **Connection** object creates a **QueryDef** object. ODBCDirect **QueryDef** objects are temporary. We learned previously that the ODBCDirect **Workspace** object does not support containers, a requirement for object persistence.

Syntax:

Set *QueryDef* = *Connection*.**CreateQueryDef**([*Name*] [, *SQLText*])

Where:

QueryDef: An object of type **QueryDef**.

Connection: A object of type **Connection**.

Name: An optional unique string expression of type **Variant** identifying the **QueryDef**. All ODBCDirect **Querydef** objects are temporary.

SQLText: An optional valid SQL statement that defines the **QueryDef**. The string is of type Variant. A SQL statement may be placed in the *SQL* property of the **Querydef** object when this field is omitted.

We're currently discussing the **Connection** object. You will learn in subsequent discussions of the **QueryDef** object that Jet and ODBCDirect treat a **QueryDef** object differently. A Jet **QueryDef** object is prepared when it is stored, whereas an ODBCDirect **QueryDef** must have the **Prepare** property set before the SQL text is saved in the **SQL** property of the **QueryDef** object. This and other features of an asynchronous ODBCDirect **QueryDef** are illustrated in Listing 19-2.

concept link

You'll find additional details about an asynchronous ODBCDirect QueryDef in Chapter 22, which discusses QueryDef objects.

LISTING 19-2 A prepared and asynchronous ODBCDirect QueryDef

```
Private Sub ODBCDirect_QueryDef_Click()
'(C) 1998 Bruce T. Prendergast
'    DBA Prendergast Consulting
'    DBA PCS
'    IDG Books Worldwide ISBN 0-7645-3123-9
'
'    Listing 19-2 A prepared and Asynchronous
'    ODBCDirect QueryDef
'
```

```
Dim MyODWS As Workspace, MyDB As Database
Dim MyCon As Connection
Dim MyErr As Error
Dim MyQdf As QueryDef
Dim WaitTime As Single
Dim MyFld As Field
Dim MyRS As Recordset
On Error GoTo Unable_To_Connect
'
'    create an ODBCDirect workspace
'
Set MyODWS = CreateWorkspace( _
    "MyODBCWS", "admin", "", dbUseODBC)
'
'    connect
'
Set MyCon = MyODWS.OpenConnection( _
    "MyConnection", dbDriverNoPrompt, True, _
    "ODBC;DATABASE=Pubs;UID=sa;PWD=;DSN=Thor;")
Set MyQdf = MyCon.CreateQueryDef("")
'
'    The prepare property must be set
'    before the SQL property is set
'    The statement below is useless since
'    the default is dbQPrepare, but illustrating
'    the relationship is necessary. dbQUnprepare
'    should be used when the SQL statement has
'    character parameters with leading wild-card
'    characters
'
MyQdf.Prepare = dbQPrepare
MyQdf.SQL = "SELECT au_fname FROM authors " & _
    "WHERE au_lname ='Green'"
'
'    run the query asynchronously
'
```

```
MyQdf.Execute dbRunAsync
WaitTime = Timer
While (Timer - WaitTime) < 5
Wend
Do While MyQdf.StillExecuting
    If MsgBox("No query yet—keep waiting?", _
            vbYesNo) = vbNo Then
        MyQdf.Cancel
        Exit Sub
    Else
        WaitTime = Timer
        While (Timer - WaitTime) < 5
        Wend
    End If
Loop
'
'   create a recordset
'
Set MyRS = MyQdf.OpenRecordset()
'
'   show the field from the recordset
'   and enumerate the fields collection
'
MsgBox "First name is: " & MyRS![au_fname]
For Each MyFld In MyRS.Fields
    MsgBox "Value is: " & MyFld.Value
Next MyFld
MsgBox "ODBCDirect Querydef was successful"
Exit Sub
Unable_To_Connect:
For Each MyErr In DBEngine.Errors
    MsgBox MyErr.Description
Next MyErr
End Sub
```

Execute

The **Execute** method of a **Connection** or **Database** object runs an SQL statement or an action query.

Syntax:

> *Object.***Execute**(*Source* [, *Options*])
>
> *Querydef.***Execute** ([*Options*])
>
>> See the **Execute** method of the **Database** for a detailed discussion.

OpenRecordset

OpenRecordset is the **Connection** or **Database** object method for opening a **Recordset**. The syntax for opening a recordset of a **QueryDef**, **Recordset**, or a **TableDef** object is:

> **Set** *Recordset = Object.***OpenRecordset**([*Type* [, *Options* [, *Lockedits*]]])
> The syntax for opening a recordset using a **Connection** or a **Database** object is:
> **Set** *Variable = Object.***OpenRecordset**(*Source* [, *Type* [, *Options* [, *Lockedits*]]])
> See the **OpenRecordset** method of the **Database** object for a detailed discussion of this method.

KEY POINT SUMMARY

ODBCDirect is a member of the minimalist genre of database access technologies. ODBCDirect can only access ODBC data sources. ODBCDirect objects are not persistent in that they cannot be saved in a database. The global ODBCdirect object exists for the life of the application, and local ODBCDirect objects exist for the life of the function. This means that queries must be compiled for each instance of a subroutine or function. Once within the function or subroutine, the query need only be compiled once.

- ODBCDirect is a minimal ODBC wrapper without a database. It does not support the Jet Database Engine. DAO is a host for ODBCDirect.

- The ODBCDirect Connection object piggybacks on the DAO Database object. This is done by the automatic creation of a **Database** object whenever a **Connection** object is created. The **Connection** object delegates (do you remember delegation from the Component Object Model?) the ODBCDirect **QueryDefs** and **Recordset** collections to the **Database** object.

- A database can be opened with a traditional call to the **OpenDatabase** method, or a database can be opened with the **OpenConnection** method. The **OpenConnection** method is tuned for remote database connectivity.

- ODBCDirect does not support:
  - User-defined properties
  - Bound forms
  - Updatable joins
  - The **FindFirst**, **FindNext**, or **FindPrevious** methods
  - Crosstab queries (the SQL TRANSFORM statement can be used)
  - Heterogeneous data access

APPLYING WHAT YOU'VE LEARNED

The questions below measure your comprehension of the key points in this chapter. ODBCDirect is specifically designed for access to ODBC data sources. Your understanding of ODBCDirect functionality is the key to selecting the appropriate database access tool.

Instant Assessment

1. Name four distinct features of an ODBCDirect connection.

2. Name four distinct limitations of an ODBCDirect connection.

3. What is a unique feature of creating an ODBCDirect connection?

4. Name the two collections of the **Connection** object.

5. What **Connection** object property is useful for checking the validity of a transaction?

6. What is the default collection of a **Connection** object?

7. Explain the relationship between a **Connection** object and a **Database** object.

 concept link   **For answers to the Instant Assessment questions, see Appendix C.**

Lab Exercises

The first lab exercise asks you to convert an existing application to ODBCDirect. The second lab exercise illustrates using ODBCDirect from PowerPoint to query SQL Server from a PowerPoint slide.

Lab 19.38 *ODBCDirect is not always appropriate*

WA I

Assuming that you have existing Microsoft Access applications in your shop, on paper list the features of the Access applications. Factors to consider are bound or unbound forms, DDL operations, heterogeneous joins, and updatable joins. Can you justify ODBCDirect on a performance basis? For the sake of discussion, assume that your performance increases 25 percent when you convert to ODBCDirect.

Take an existing Microsoft Access application using Jet and convert it to ODBCDirect of DAO. If you don't have one, then you can quickly create one by attaching tables from the *Pubs* database in SQL Server. Use the Forms Wizard to create your forms. Once you have the application operational, convert the forms to use ODBCDirect of DAO. Note the programming effort. You may not finish the project because you'll quickly find that it is labor intensive. You've just learned an important lesson. It's called a zero-sum gain: when it's easy to use, there's a lot going on under the hood. When there's not much going on under the hood, the developer must work proportionally harder. A stripped-down hotrod is not always a good choice. This laboratory does not require ODBCDirect; however, if you are a minimalist, and always try to use the least resources, then ODBCDirect is for you. Factors to consider in the conversion:

o Does the Access application use bound forms? ODBCDirect doesn't support bound forms.

o Are persistent objects required? ODBCDirect doesn't support persistent objects that take the form of saved **QueryDef** objects. This also means that queries must always be compiled before the first use in a function or subroutine.

o Are DDL operations used? ODBCDirect does not support DDL operations.

o Are there user-defined properties? ODBCDirect does not support user-defined properties.

Lab 19.39 *Animating PowerPoint 97 with ODBCDirect*

WA I

This lab requires SQL Server 6.5, Access 97, and PowerPoint 97. We're building a PowerPoint presentation with intelligence that will be used in a kiosk. We'll only look at a portion of that application. We'll use DAO and ODBCDirect to animate a PowerPoint slide.

1. Open Access 97.

2. Cut the indicated text of Listing 19-3 from the CHAPTER19.MDB located in the EXAMPLES\CHAPTER19 folder on the CD-ROM that accompanies this book (the code listing is also reprinted in Listing 19-3).

3. Open PowerPoint 97.

4. Create a PowerPoint presentation.

5. Select a slide.

6. While in *Slide View,* from the View menu, select *Toolbars ⇒ Visual Basic.*

7. Click Toolbox.

8. Draw a command button on the slide.

9. Paste in the cut text to the command button Click event.

10. From the Tools Menu, select *References.*

11. Select *Microsoft DAO 3.5 Object Library.*

12. Return to *Slide View* by selecting *return from Visual Basic* in the File menu.

13. Start the slide show.

14. Click the command button.

15. A message box should display: "Current author count: 23."

Congratulations! You have just animated a PowerPoint slide.

LISTING 19-3 Using ODBCDirect from PowerPoint

```
Private Sub DAO_From_PowerPoint_Click()
'(C) 1998 Bruce T. Prendergast
' DBA Prendergast Consulting
' DBA PCS
' IDG Books Worldwide ISBN 0-7645-3123-9
'

' Listing 19-3 ODBCDirect and DAO from PowerPoint
'

MsgBox "This example is intended for PowerPoint"
Exit Sub
```

```
'*****************************************
' cut below for pasting into PowerPoint
'*****************************************

Dim MyODWS As Workspace, MyDB As Database
Dim MyCon As Connection
Dim MyErr As Error
Dim MyQdf As QueryDef
Dim WaitTime As Single
Dim MyFld As Field
Dim MyRS As Recordset
On Error GoTo Unable_To_Connect
Set MyODWS = CreateWorkspace("MyODBCWS", "admin", "",
 dbUseODBC)
'
' connect
'
Set MyCon = MyODWS.OpenConnection("MyConnection",
 dbDriverNoPrompt, True, _
"ODBC;DATABASE=Pubs;UID=sa;PWD=;DSN=Thor;")

Set MyQdf = MyCon.CreateQueryDef("")
MyQdf.SQL = "SELECT count (*) FROM authors"
MyQdf.Execute
Set MyRS = MyQdf.OpenRecordset()
MsgBox "Current author count: " & MyRS(0)
Exit Sub
Unable_To_Connect:
For Each MyErr In DBEngine.Errors
MsgBox MyErr.Description
Next MyErr

'*****************************************
' cut above for pasting into PowerPoint
'*****************************************
End Sub
```

Windows Architecture I

CHAPTER

Working with the Database Object

20

About Chapter 20

We're taking the high road with this chapter. In this chapter, the **Workspace** object is your session, and the **Database** object is your workbench from where you launch your endeavors. The Jet **Database** object has the **TableDefs**, **Querydefs**, **Recordsets**, **Relations**, and **Containers** collections.

There are many examples in this chapter, quite a few of which are the way *not* to do something. There are also several examples of creating objects. For example, Listing 20-5 uses only DAO to build two tables, add fields and indexes, and finishes by adding a relationship to the two tables.

All examples in this chapter are located in the CHAPTER20.MDB located in the EXAMPLES\CHAPTER20 folder on the CD-ROM that accompanies this book.

THE DATABASES COLLECTION

Figure 20-1 tells us that the **Databases** collection is the next stop in the DAO hierarchy. The first stop was **DBEngine** followed by **Workspaces** and **Connections.** A **Database** object represents an open database. A **Database** collection represents all those objects in the database within a session. **TableDefs** are the default collection with a Jet **Database** object.

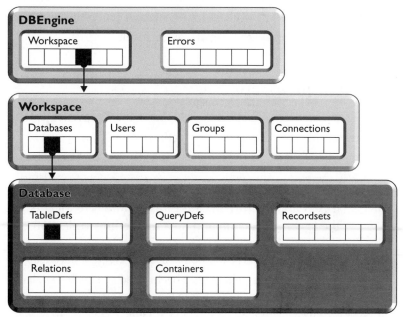

FIGURE 20-1   TableDefs are the default collection with a Jet Database object.

Databases Collection Definition

> **Property**: Count
>
> **Database** Object
>
> Methods: **Close, CreateProperty**(J), **CreateQueryDef, CreateRelation**(J), **CreateTableDef**(J), **Execute, MakeReplica**(J), **NewPassword**(J), **OpenRecordset, PopulatePartial, Synchronize**(J)
>
> Properties: **CollatingOrder**(J), **Connect, Connection**(D), **DesignMasterID**(J), **Name, QueryTimeout, RecordsAffected, Replicable**(J), **ReplicaID**(J), **Updatable, V1zNullBehavior, Version**

Collections: **Containers**(J), **Properties**, **Querydefs**(J), **Recordsets**(D default), **Relations**(J), **Tabledefs**(J default)

Legend: D = ODBCDirect, J = Jet

The **Connection** object of DAO 3.5 appears as an additional layer between the application and the data source. The **Database** property of a **Connection** object returns a **Database** object while the **Connection** property of a **Database** object returns a **Connection** object.

Figure 20-1 illustrates the **TableDefs** collection as the default collection for a **Database**. This is only true for Jet. The default collection for a **Database** object in a ODBCDirect **Workspace** is the **Recordsets** collection.

CreateProperty

This is the first collection that supports the **Properties** collection. With the **CreateProperty** collection, user-defined properties may be appended to the **Properties** collection.

 note I did not show the **Properties** collection in the Data Access Objects (DAO) architecture because it is common to all collections except the **Errors** collection and the **Connections** collection.

The **CreateProperty** method is used to create a new user-defined **Property** object in a **Properties** collection. This method applies to **Database** objects, **Index** objects, **QueryDef** objects, and **TableDef** objects. It also applies to **Field** objects in **Fields** collections of **QueryDef** and **TableDef** objects. Before we discuss user-defined properties, let's define the **Property** object and the **Properties** collection with Figure 20-2.

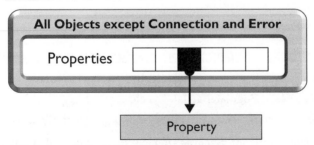

FIGURE 20-2   Default Properties collection.

Properties *Collection Definition*

Methods: **Append, Delete, Refresh**

Property: Count

Property Object

Properties: **Inherited, Name, Type, Value**

The properties for **Form, Report,** and **Control** objects differ from DAO properties. Property objects:

o Do not have an **Inherited** property.

o Have a **Category** property that cannot be set.

o Can't be enumerated.

o User-defined properties can be accessed with the syntax:

```
Object.Properties!Name
```

o Built-in properties are accessed with the syntax:

```
Object.Name
```

o You can reference built-in or user-defined properties with the syntax:

```
Object.Properties("Name")
```

Syntax (DAO 2.0):

Set *variable* = *Object*.**CreateProperty**([*Name* [, *Type* [, *Value*]]])

Syntax (DAO 3.0/3.5):

Set *variable* = *Object*.**CreateProperty**([*Name* [, *Type* [, *Value* [, *fDDL*]]]])

Where:

Variable: A variable of type **Property.**

Object: A variable name of the **Database, Field, Index, QueryDef** or **TableDef** object you are using.

Name: A string expression which uniquely identifies the new property name.

Type: One of the following intrinsic constants (Type settings for a **Field, Parameter,** or **Property** object):

MICROSOFT ACCESS 2.0 INTRINSIC DATA TYPES

DB-BOOLEAN	**Yes/No**
DB_DATE	**Date/Time**

continued

MICROSOFT ACCESS 2.0 INTRINSIC DATA TYPES (continued)

DB_TEXT	**Text**
DB_MEMO	**Memo**

MICROSOFT ACCESS 2.0 ACCESS BASIC INTRINSIC DATA TYPES

DB_INTEGER	**Integer**
DB_LONG	**Long**
DB_CURRENCY	**Currency**
DB_SINGLE	**Single**
DB_DOUBLE	**Double**

MICROSOFT ACCESS 2.0 JET ENGINE INTRINSIC DATA TYPES

DB_BYTE	**Byte**
DB_LONGBINARY	**Long Binary**

MICROSOFT ACCESS 2.0 INTRINSIC TYPE SETTINGS FOR A QUERYDEF OBJECT

DB_QSELECT	**Select**
DB_QACTION	**Action**
DB_QCROSSTAB	**Crosstab**
DB_QDELETE	**Delete**
DB_QUPDATE	**Update**
DB_QAPPEND	**Append**
DB_QMAKETABLE	**Make-Table**
DB_QDDL	**Data-Definition**
DB_QSQLPASSTHROUGH	**Pass-Through**
DB_QSETOPERATION	**Union**
DB_QSPTBULK	Used with **DB_QSQLPASSTHROUGH** to specify an update query

MICROSOFT ACCESS 2.0 INTRINSIC TYPE SETTINGS FOR A TABLEDEF OBJECT

DB_OPEN_TABLE	**Table**
DB_OPEN_DYNASET	**Dynaset**
DB_OPEN_SNAPSHOT	**Snapshot**

DAO 3.0 DATA TYPES FOR FIELD, PARAMETER, OR PROPERTY OBJECTS

dbBoolean	**Yes/No**
dbByte	**Byte**
dbCurrency	**Currency**
dbDate	**Date/Time**
dbDouble	**Double**
dbGuid	**GUID**
dbInteger	**Integer**
dbLong	**Long**
dbLongBinary	**Long Binary** (OLE Object)
dbMemo	**Memo**
dbSingle	**Single**
dbText	**Text**

DAO 3.0 QUERYDEF OBJECT INTRINSIC DATA TYPES

dbQAction	**Action**
dbQAppend	**Append**
dbQCrosstab	**Crosstab**
dbQDDL	**Data-Definition**
dbQDelete	**Delete**
dbQMakeTable	**Make-Table**
dbQSelect	**Select**
dbQSetOperation	**Union**
dbQSPTBulk	Used with **dbQSQLPassThrough** to specify an update query
dbQSQLPassThrough	**Pass-Through**
dbQUpdate	**Update**

DAO 3.0 RECORDSET OBJECT INTRINSIC DATA TYPES

dbOpenDynaset	**Dynaset**
dbOpenSnapshot	**Snapshot**
dbOpenTable	**Table**

DAO 3.5 data types for Field, Parameter, or Property objects

dbBigInt	**Big Integer**
dbBigBinary	**Binary**
dbBoolean	**Yes/No**
dbByte	**Byte**
dbChar	**Char**
dbCurrency	**Currency**
dbDate	**Date/Time**
dbDecimal	**Decimal**
dbDouble	**Double**
dbFloat	**Float**
dbGuid	**GUID**
dbInteger	**Integer**
dbLong	**Long**
dbLongBinary	**Long Binary** (OLE object)
dbMemo	**Memo**
dbNumeric	**Numeric**
dbSingle	**Single**
dbText	**Text**
dbTime	**Time**
dbTimeStamp	**Time Stamp**
dbVarBinary	**VarBinary**

DAO 3.5 QueryDef object intrinsic data types

dbQAction	**Action**
dbQAppend	**Append**
dbCompound	**Compound**
dbQCrosstab	**Crosstab**
dbQDDL	**Data-Definition**
dbQDelete	**Delete**
dbQMakeTable	**Make-table**
dbQProcedure	**Procedure** (ODBCDirect)

dbQSelect	**Select**
dbQSetOperation	**Union**
dbQSPTBulk	Used with **dbQSQLPassThrough** to specify an update query
dbQSQLPassThrough	**Pass-Through**
dbQUpdate	**Update**

DAO 3.5 RECORDSET OBJECT INTRINSIC DATA TYPES

dbOpenDynamic	ODBCDirect workspaces only
dbOpenDynaset	**Dynaset**
dbOpenForward	**Forward Only**
dbOpenSnapshot	**Snapshot**
dbOpenTable	**Table**

Value — A **Variant** containing the initial value of the property.

FDDL — The user cannot delete or change this property without the **dbSecWriteDef** permission when this property is **True**. The default value is **False**.

The type and class of property added to a database is a choice of the designer. In the following example, a **Property** *Encrypted* is appended to the **Database** object and the object is enumerated. It is left to the imagination of the reader what else can be done with this feature. Database repair dates, database compacting dates, data posting dates are just a few of the possibilities. Listing 20-1 creates a user-defined property.

LISTING 20-1 Creating a user-defined property

```
Private Sub User_Defined_Click()
'(C) 1998 Bruce T. Prendergast
'    DBA Prendergast Consulting
'    DBA PCS
'    IDG Books Worldwide ISBN 0-7645-3123-9
'
'    Listing 20-1 Creating a user-defined property
'
```

```
Dim MyDB As Database
Dim MyPro As Property
Dim MyWS As Workspace
Set MyWS = DBEngine.Workspaces(0)
Set MyDB = MyWS.Databases(0)
'
' Next two lines are debugging
'
On Error Resume Next
MyDB.Properties.Delete ("Encrypted")
'
' Create new Property object.
'
Set MyPro = MyDB.CreateProperty("Encrypted")
'
' Set other properties of MyProperty.
'
MyPro.Type = DB_BOOLEAN
MyPro.Value = True
MyDB.Properties.Append MyPro
'
' Enumerate all properties of current database.
'
Debug.Print "Properties of Database "; MyDB.Name
For Each MyPro In MyDB.Properties
    Debug.Print
    If Not MyPro.Name = "Connection" Then
        Debug.Print "Type: "; MyPro.Type & _
            " Value: "; MyPro.Value & _
            " Inherited: "; MyPro.Inherited & _
            " Name:" & MyPro.Name
    End If
Next MyPro
MsgBox "Creating a UDF property was successful"
Exit Sub
End Sub
```

Listing 20-1 generated the output in Listing 20-2. The value of the *Inherited* property of the new user-defined **Property** is false because it did not inherit anything, but did the enumeration at the hierarchical level where the new **Property** was added. Another example of using the **Name**, **Type**, and **Value** properties is shown during the discussion of a **QueryDef** object.

LISTING 20-2 The results of Listing 20-1

```
Properties of Database H:\Access 97 MDBs\IDG\DAO.mdb
Type: 12 Value: H:\Access 97 MDBs\IDG\DAO.mdb Inherited: False
  Name:Name


Type: 12   Value:          Inherited: False   Name:Connect
Type: 1    Value: True     Inherited: False   Name:Transactions
Type: 1    Value: True     Inherited: False   Name:Updatable
Type: 3    Value: 1033     Inherited: False   Name:CollatingOrder
Type: 3    Value: 60       Inherited: False   Name:QueryTimeout
Type: 12   Value: 3.0      Inherited: False   Name:Version
Type: 4    Value: 0        Inherited: False   Name:RecordsAffected
Type: 15   Value:          Inherited: False   Name:ReplicaID
Type: 15   Value:          Inherited: False   Name:DesignMasterID
Type: 10   Value: 07.53    Inherited: False   Name:AccessVersion
Type: 4    Value: 3512     Inherited: False   Name:Build
Type: 1    Value: True     Inherited: False   Name:Encrypted
```

 note The **Connection** property was not included in the enumeration of Listing 20-2 because the MDB is Jet.

If you look carefully at the output of Listing 20-2, the **Inherited** property is false for each built-in property. It has a Boolean value and may be tested for inheritance. If the value is **True** for a **Recordset**, then the value was inherited from the parent **TableDef**. The same is true for a **QueryDef**. If a user-defined property is created for a **Querydef**, then the **Inherited** property is **True** in any underlying **Recordset**.

CreateQueryDef

This method of the **Database** object creates a **QueryDef** object. The **Connection** object, which was the topic of Chapter 19, also creates **QueryDef** objects. This chapter discusses the properties and methods of the **Database** object.

Syntax:

Set *QueryDef* = *Database*.**CreateQueryDef**([*Name*] [, *SQLText*])

Where:

QueryDef: A variable of the type **QueryDef** which represents the object we wish to create.

Database: A variable of type **Database**.

Name: A unique string expression identifying the **QueryDef**. Set this value to a zero-length string to create a temporary **QueryDef**. If you provide anything for a name other than a zero-length string, the **QueryDef** is automatically appended to the **QueryDef** collection.

SQLText: A valid SQL statement that defines the **QueryDef**. This value can be set with the SQL property after the **QueryDef** is appended to the collection. If you place SQL text here, then Jet assumes that it is Access-compatible SQL. Foreign-dialect SQL is placed in the SQL property field after the **Connect** property is set.

A **Querydef** object created without a name is a temporary **Querydef**. A query plan is created each time the **Querydef** is executed. When a name is given to a **QueryDef** object, it becomes a stored **QueryDef** object and can be considered a compiled SQL statement. An execution plan for a stored **QueryDef** object is remembered from the first execution.

The compilation of a Jet **QueryDef** object is implicit, whereas the ODBCDirect compilation is explicit with the **Prepare** property. This is because the **QueryDef** object of an ODBCDirect **Connection** object is temporary.

Creating a Jet QueryDef and the use of the SQL property

When SQL is defined for a Jet database, it cannot use foreign syntax. Listing 20-3 does not set the **Connect** property, therefore, the SQL parameter of the QueryDef will be parsed by Jet. A pass-through query must set the **Connect** property first, causing Jet to bypass parsing of the SQL property.

LISTING 20-3 Using the Jet QueryDef SQL property

```
Private Sub Jet_QueryDef_Click()
'(C) 1998 Bruce T. Prendergast
'    DBA Prendergast Consulting
'    DBA PCS
'    IDG Books Worldwide ISBN 0-7645-3123-9
'
'    Listing 20-3 The Jet QueryDef SQL property
'
     Dim MyDB As Database
     Dim MyQry As QueryDef
     Dim MyRS As Recordset
     Dim MyWS As Workspace
     Dim MyFld As Field
     Set MyWS = DBEngine.Workspaces(0)
     Set MyDB = MyWS.Databases(0)
     '
     '    just in case we're still practicing
     '
     On Error Resume Next
     MyDB.QueryDefs.Delete "Inventory"
     Set MyQry = MyDB.CreateQueryDef("Inventory")
     MyQry.SQL = "SELECT [Product Name] FROM " & _
         "tblInventory WHERE [On Hand] < 5;"
     Set MyRS = MyQry.OpenRecordset("Inventory", _
         dbOpenSnapshot)
     For Each MyFld In MyRS.Fields
         Debug.Print MyRS![Product Name]
     Next MyFld
     MsgBox "Jet SQL QueryDef was successful"
     Exit Sub
End Sub
```

Accessing SQL Server stored procedures (pass through query)

Listing 20-4 only addresses the SQL Server stored procedure *sp_who*; however, it can be used as a model for accessing SQL Server. Just substitute the name of your

SQL Server stored procedure for *sp_who* in the **QueryDef** SQL property field. The **QueryDef** name was set to a zero-length string thereby creating a temporary query not appended to a collection. The **Connect** property was set before the SQL property and Jet doesn't attempt to parse the SQL property.

LISTING 20-4 A pass-through query to SQL Server

```
Private Sub SQL_Pass_Through_Click()
'(C) 1998 Bruce T. Prendergast
'    DBA Prendergast Consulting
'    DBA PCS
'    IDG Books Worldwide  ISBN 0-7645-3123-9
'
'    Listing 20-4 SQL Pass-through to SQL Server
'
    Dim MyWS As Workspace, MyDB As Database
    Dim MyFld As Field
    Dim MyQry As QueryDef, MyRS As Recordset
    Set MyWS = DBEngine.Workspaces(0)
    Set MyDB = MyWS.Databases(0)
    '
    '    The zero-length string creates a temporary query
    '
    Set MyQry = MyDB.CreateQueryDef("")
    Dim SourceConnectStr As String
    SourceConnectStr = "ODBC;DATABASE=Pubs;UID=sa;" & _
        "PWD=;DSN=Thor;"
    '
    '    This is a pass-through query so the connect
    '    string is set first which stops Jet from
    '    parsing the SQL placed in the SQL property
    '    of the QueryDef.
    '
    MyQry.Connect = SourceConnectStr
    MyQry.ReturnsRecords = True
    MyQry.SQL = "sp_who"   ' SQL Server Stored procedure
    '
```

```
'    Create the snapshot and print the data
'
Set MyRS = MyQry.OpenRecordset()
'
' enumerate fields
'
Debug.Print "Fields:  Name,  Type,  Value"
For Each MyFld In MyRS.Fields
    Debug.Print " "; MyFld.Name; _
       " "; MyFld.Type; " "; MyFld.Value
Next MyFld
MsgBox "SQL Pass-Through query was successful"
Exit Sub
End Sub
```

Listing 20-4 generated:

```
spid         3     1
status       10    sleeping
loginame     10    sa
hostname     10
blk          10    0
dbname       10    master
cmd          10    MIRROR HANDLER
```

CreateRelation

The **CreateRelation** method of the **Database** object is used to create relations. This method is specific to Jet databases.

Syntax:

Set *Variable* = *Database*.**CreateRelation**([*Name* [, *Table* [, *ForeignTable* [,*Attributes*]]]])

Where:

Variable: A variable of type **Relation**.

Database: A variable of type of type **Database**.

Name: A string expression that uniquely identifies the new **Relation** object.

Table: A string expression that identifies the primary table. In the relation, it is the referenced table.

ForeignTable: A string expression that uniquely identifies the foreign table. The table must exist or an error occurs.

Attributes: A **Long** variable with the following intrinsic values:

JET 2.0 INTRINSIC CONSTANTS

DB_RELATIONUNIQUE	Relationship is one-to-one
DB_RELATIONDONTENFORCE	Not enforced, no referential integrity
DB_RELATIONINHERITED	Relations exist in a noncurrent database that contains the two attached tables
DB_RELATIONLEFT	The relation is a left join
DB_RELATIONRIGHT	The relation is a right join
DB_RELATIONUPDATECASCADE	Updates cascade
DB_RELATIONDELETECASCADE	Deletions cascade

JET 3.0/3.5 INTRINSIC CONSTANTS

dbRelationUnique	Relationship is one-to-one
dbRelationDontEnforce	Not enforced, no referential integrity
dbRelationInherited	Relations exist in a noncurrent database that contains the two attached tables
dbRelationUpdateCascade	Updates cascade
dbRelationDeleteCascade	Deletions cascade

Attributes within a relation are read-only once the **QueryDef** object is appended to a collection. Attributes may be combined by addition.

dbRelationUpdateCascade + dbRelationDeleteCascade

A **Relation** contains a **Fields** collection that must be used in building the **QueryDef** object.

Creating tables, fields, indexes, and a relationship

Listing 20-5 is a very comprehensive example that creates tables, adds fields to those tables, indexes the tables, and then creates a relationship between the tables. It doesn't take too much more logic to convert Listing 20-5 into a minimal database wizard.

LISTING 20-5 Creating tables, fields, indexes, and a relationship

```
Private Sub Creating_Relations_Click()
'(C) 1998 Bruce T. Prendergast
'   DBA Prendergast Consulting
'   DBA PCS
'   IDG Books Worldwide ISBN 0-7645-3123-9
'
'   Listing 20-5 Creating relations
'
'   Create an Order and an OrderDetail table
'   with fields and a relation
'

    Dim MyRltn As Relation
    Dim MyDB As Database
    Dim MyFld As Field
    Dim MyWS As Workspace
    Dim MyTdf As TableDef
    Dim MyIdx As Index

    Set MyWS = DBEngine.Workspaces(0)
    Set MyDB = MyWS.Databases(0)
    '
    '   clear everything out
    '
    On Error Resume Next
    MyDB.Relations.Delete "Orders and Detail"
    MyDB.TableDefs.Delete "Orders"
    MyDB.TableDefs.Delete "Detail"
    '
    '   Here we go, Primary key first!
    '
    Set MyTdf = MyDB.CreateTableDef( _
        "tblOrders")
    Set MyFld = MyTdf.CreateField( _
        "OrderID", dbLong)
    MyFld.Attributes = dbAutoIncrField
    MyTdf.Fields.Append MyFld
```

```
'
'   name the index
'
Set MyIdx = MyTdf.CreateIndex( _
    "Orders Primary Key")
'
'   and the index field
'
MyIdx.Fields.Append MyIdx.CreateField( _
    "OrderID")
MyIdx.Primary = True
MyTdf.Indexes.Append MyIdx
'
'   Two fields for the Orders table
'
Set MyFld = MyTdf.CreateField( _
    "Order Date", dbDate)
MyTdf.Fields.Append MyFld
'
Set MyFld = MyTdf.CreateField( _
    "Customer Number", dbLong)
MyTdf.Fields.Append MyFld
'
'   append to the TableDefs collection
'
MyDB.TableDefs.Append MyTdf
'
'   Let's build the foreign table
'
Set MyTdf = MyDB.CreateTableDef( _
    "tblDetail")
Set MyFld = MyTdf.CreateField( _
    "DetailID", dbLong)
MyFld.Attributes = dbAutoIncrField
MyTdf.Fields.Append MyFld
'
'   name the index
```

```
'
Set MyIdx = MyTdf.CreateIndex( _
    "Detail Primary Key")
'
'   and the index field
'
MyIdx.Fields.Append MyIdx.CreateField( _
    "DetailID")
MyIdx.Primary = True
MyTdf.Indexes.Append MyIdx
'
'   Two fields for the Detail table
'
Set MyFld = MyTdf.CreateField( _
    "Part Number", dbLong)
MyTdf.Fields.Append MyFld
Set MyFld = MyTdf.CreateField( _
    "Quantity", dbLong)
MyTdf.Fields.Append MyFld
Set MyFld = MyTdf.CreateField( _
    "OrderID", dbLong)
MyTdf.Fields.Append MyFld
'
'   append to the TableDefs collection
'
MyDB.TableDefs.Append MyTdf
'
'   create a relation
'
Set MyRltn = MyDB.CreateRelation( _
    "Orders and Detail", _
    "tblOrders", "tblDetail")
'
MyRltn.Attributes = dbRelationUpdateCascade _
    And dbRelationDeleteCascade
'
'   PK is the field of the relation
```

```
      '
      Set MyFld = MyRltn.CreateField("OrderID")
      '
      '   PK is set as ForeignName of Detail Table
      '
      MyFld.ForeignName = "OrderID"
      MyRltn.Fields.Append MyFld
      '
      ' Save Relation definition
      '
      MyDB.Relations.Append MyRltn
      MyDB.TableDefs.Refresh
      MyDB.Relations.Refresh
      MsgBox "Creating a relation was successful"
      Exit Sub
End Sub
```

Figure 20-3 illustrates the results of running Listing 20-5 and selecting:

```
Tools | Relationships
```

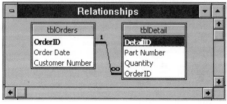

FIGURE 20-3   The results of Listing 20-5.

CreateTableDef

The Jet **CreateTableDef** method of a **Database** object serves several purposes. It can be used to create virtual tables when connecting to a remote source, such as SQL Server or dBase, or it can be used for creating local tables.

Syntax:

Set *Variable* = *Database*.**CreateTableDef**([*Name* [, *Attributes* [, *Source* [,*Connect*]]]])

Where:

> *Variable*: A variable of type **TableDef**.
>
> *Database*: A variable of type **Database**.
>
> *Name:* A string expression that uniquely identifies the **TableDef** object.
>
> *Attributes:* A **Long** variable using the intrinsic values:

JET 2.0 INTRINSIC CONSTANTS FOR TABLEDEF ATTRIBUTES

DB_ATTACHEXCLUSIVE	A Jet database is attached in exclusive mode
DB_ATTACHSAVEPWD	Remember the user ID and password with the connection information for Jet databases
DB_SYSTEMOBJECT	The table is a system table
DB_HIDDENOBJECT	A hidden table for temporary use
DB_ATTACHEDTABLE	Non–ODBC attached table such as Microsoft Access or Paradox
DB_ATTACHEDODBC	Attached table is on Microsoft SQL Server, Sybase, or Oracle

JET 3.0/3.5 INTRINSIC CONSTANTS FOR TABLEDEF ATTRIBUTES

dbAttachExclusive	A Jet database is attached in exclusive mode
dbAttachSavedPWD	Remember the user ID and password with the connection information for Jet databases
dbSystemObject	The table is a system table
dbHiddenObject	A hidden table for temporary use
dbAttachedObject	Non–ODBC attached table such as Microsoft Access or Paradox
dbAttachedODBC	Attached table is on Microsoft SQL Server, Sybase, or Oracle

> *Connect:* A connect string for a pass-through query or an attached table.

Creating a **TableDef** object was illustrated in Listing 20-5.

Connecting to an ODBC source (SQL Server) with a TableDef object

A **TableDef** object is an efficient mechanism for Jet to connect to an ODBC source such as SQL Server. Listing 20-6 illustrates this procedure. It is interesting that the Form Wizard can be used on the attached table with almost-immediate access to SQL Server data. Of course the data is read-only, but this is quite acceptable for a decision support system (DSS) where data is not updated.

LISTING 20-6 Jet attaching a SQL Server table

```
Private Sub TableDef_Connection_Click()
'(C) 1998 Bruce T. Prendergast
'    DBA Prendergast Consulting
'    DBA PCS
'    IDG Books Worldwide ISBN 0-7645-3123-9
'
'    Listing 20-6 attachning a SQL Server table
'
     Dim MyWS As Workspace
     Dim MyDB As Database
     Dim MyTblDf As TableDef

     Set MyWS = DBEngine.Workspaces(0)
     Set MyDB = MyWS.Databases(0)


     '
     '    debugging
     '
     On Error Resume Next
     MyDB.TableDefs.Delete "PubsAuthors"

     Set MyTblDf = MyDB.CreateTableDef( _
          "Pubs authors")
     Dim SourceConnectStr As String
     SourceConnectStr = "ODBC;DATABASE=Pubs;" & _
          "UID=sa;PWD=;DSN=Thor;"
     '
```

```
'    Declare ODBC SQL Server data source          .
     '
    MyTblDf.Attributes = dbAttachedODBC
     '
    '   connect
     '
    MyTblDf.Connect = SourceConnectStr
    MyTblDf.SourceTableName = "authors"
    MyDB.TableDefs.Append MyTblDf
    MsgBox "TableDef attach was successful"
End Sub
```

Figure 20-4 shows the newly created *Pubs authors* table created in Listing 20-6.

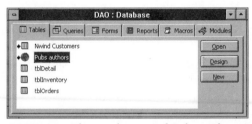

FIGURE 20-4   The newly created Pubs authors table (see Listing 20-6).

Using the Access 97 Form Wizard is not restricted to Jet tables. The Form Wizard can also be used on attached tables, which is a relatively effortless process.

Connecting to a non-ODBC external table with TableDef

Connecting to a non-ODBC source is not that much different than connecting to an ODBC SQL data source. The NorthWind (a sample database shipped Microsoft Access) application Customers table is attached to a local Access database with the following code fragment shown in Listing 20-7. The results of the attachment are shown in Figure 20-4.

LISTING 20-7 Jet attaching a non-ODBC database

```
Private Sub Connect_Non_ODBC_Click()
'(C) 1998 Bruce T. Prendergast
```

```
'    DBA Prendergast Consulting
'    DBA PCS
'    IDG Books Worldwide ISBN 0-7645-3123-9
'
'    Listing 20-7  Jet attaching a non-ODBC database
'
     Dim MyWS As Workspace, MyDB As Database
     Dim MyTblDf As TableDef

     Set MyWS = DBEngine.Workspaces(0)
     Set MyDB = MyWS.Databases(0)
     On Error Resume Next
     MyDB.TableDefs.Delete "Nwind Customers"
     Set MyTblDf = MyDB.CreateTableDef( _
         "Nwind Customers")
     MyTblDf.Connect = _
         ";DATABASE=H:\Office95\Access\" & _
         "Samples\NorthWind.MDB"
     MyTblDf.SourceTableName = "Customers"
     MyDB.TableDefs.Append MyTblDf
     MsgBox "Non-ODBC attach was successful"
     Exit Sub
End Sub
```

Execute

There are two forms of the **Execute** method. The first executes an action query.

Syntax

> *QueryDef.***Execute** *Options*

See the **Execute** method of the **QueryDef** object for a discussion of this form. The **Execute** method of a **Database** or **Connection** object runs an SQL statement.

Syntax:

> *Object.***Execute**(*Source* [, *Options*])

Where

> *Object:* The **Database** or **Connection** object name.

Source: The SQL statement or action query to be executed.

Options: One or more of the intrinsic constants described below.

MICROSOFT ACCESS JET 2.0

DB_DENYWRITE	Deny write permission to other users
DB_INCONSISTENT	The default, which is set when updates may change both the one-side and the many-side of a relation
DB_CONSISTENT	Only the many-side of a relation will be updated
DB_SQLPASSTHROUGH	SQL pass-through
DB_FAILONERROR	Roll back updates if an error occurs

MICROSOFT ACCESS JET 3.0/3.5

dbDenyWrite	Deny write permission to other users
dbInconsistent	The default, which is set when updates may change both the one-side and the many-side of a relation
dbConsistent	Only the many-side of a relation will be updated
dbSQLPassThrough	SQL pass-through
dbFailOnError	Roll back updates if an error occurs
dbSeeChanges	Generate a run-time error if another user is changing your data
dbRunAsync	New for DAO 3.5 (ODBCDirect only) – Execute **QueryDef** or **Connection** objects asynchronously
dbExecDirect	New for DAO 3.5 (ODBCDirect only) – Do not call the **SQLPrepare** ODBC application programming interface (API) functions before executing a **QueryDef** or **Connection** object

The **Execute** method executes a SQL statement on either a specified **Connection** or **Database** object. The method is only valid for action queries. An error occurs when this method is used on other types of queries, except executing a SQL pass-though in an ODBCDirect **Workspace** will *not return an error* even if a **Recordset** object isn't returned. This method is best used when it is nested in a transaction. The benefits are an implicit caching of the data during the transaction with the secondary benefit of locks being released in an orderly fashion.

tip

The option **dbFailOnError** should be used on every update or delete query. This insures that an error is returned when rows are locked.

The **Execute** method may be paired with the **StillExecuting** property and the **dbRunAsync** constant to manage asynchronous queries of an ODBCDirect **Workspace**.

Listing 20-8 illustrates most of these issues. Note that there are two SQL statements that will be rolled back on an error. It's not a desirable technique in a transaction, but if both statements are related, the operation may be satisfactory. The issue is repeatability, which was discussed in Chapter 11.

LISTING 20-8 Using the Execute method and dbFailOnError

```
Private Sub Database_Execute_Click()
'(C) 1998 Bruce T. Prendergast
'    DBA Prendergast Consulting
'    DBA PCS
'    IDG Books Worldwide ISBN 0-7645-3123-9
'
'    Listing 20-8 The Execute method with dbFailOnError
'
    Dim MyDB As Database
    Dim MyWS As Workspace
    Dim MyErr As Error
    Set MyWS = DBEngine.Workspaces(0)
    Set MyDB = MyWS.Databases(0)
    On Error GoTo Database_Execute_Error
    MyWS.BeginTrans
    MyDB.Execute "DELETE FROM tblCustomers;", _
        dbFailOnError
    MyDB.Execute "UPDATE tblInventory SET " & _
        "[cost] = [cost] + [cost]/10;", dbFailOnError
    MyWS.CommitTrans
    MsgBox "Database Execute was successful"
Recovery_Exit:
    MyDB.Close
```

```
        Exit Sub
Database_Execute_Error:
    For Each MyErr In DBEngine.Errors
        MsgBox MyErr.Description
    Next MyErr
    MyWS.Rollback
    MsgBox "Transaction failed and rolled back"
    Resume Recovery_Exit
End Sub
```

OpenRecordset

This is the **Connection** or **Database** object method for opening a **Recordset**. Opening a base table in the database is the fastest way to retrieve data; the data, however, cannot be filtered with Access Basic.

The syntax to open a recordset of a **QueryDef**, **Recordset,** or a **TableDef** object is:

Set *Recordset = Object.***OpenRecordset**([*Type* [, *Options* [, *Lockedits*]]])

There are several different techniques for creating a **Recordset** object. See the **OpenRecordset** method of a **TableDef** object for further details on this technique.

The syntax to open a recordset using a **Connection** or a **Database** object is:

Set *Variable = Object.***OpenRecordset**(*Source* [, *Type* [, *Options* [, *Lockedits*]]])

Where:

Object: A variable of either type **Connection** or type **Database**.

Variable: A variable of type **Recordset**.

Source: This field may be a SQL statement, a query name, or a table name.

Type: An intrinsic integer that identifies the data type of the new **Recordset** object.

DAO 2.0 INTRINSIC TYPE SETTINGS

DB_OPEN_TABLE	Table
DB_OPEN_DYNASET	Dynaset
DB_OPEN_SNAPSHOT	Snapshot

DAO 3.0/3.5 INTRINSIC TYPE SETTINGS

dbOpenTable	Table
dbOpenDynaset	Dynaset
dbOpenSnapshot	Snapshot
dbOpenDynamic	New for DAO 3.5, it is similar to an ODBC dynamic cursor – ODBCDirect workspaces only
dbForwardOnly	New for DAO 3.5 – forward-only type Recordset object

Options: **Recordset** options as defined by the following intrinsic constants:

DAO 2.0 OPTIONS

DB_DENYWRITE	Other users cannot change/add records
DB_DENYREAD	Other users cannot view records
DB_READONLY	Your access is read-only; other users can modify records
DB_APPENDONLY	Records may be appended
DB_INCONSISTENT	Updates may be made to both the one-side and the many-side
DB_CONSISTENT	Updates may be made to the one-side or to the many-side only when the one-side exists
DB_FORWARDONLY	The **Recordset** is a forward-scrolling snapshot

DAO 3.0 OPTIONS

dbAppendOnly	Records may be appended
dbDenyWrite	Other users cannot change/add records
dbDenyRead	Other users cannot view records
dbReadOnly	Your access is read-only; other users can modify records
dbInconsistent	Updates may be made to both the one-side and the many-side
dbConsistent	Updates may be made to the one-side or to the many-side only when the one-side exists
dbForwardOnly	The **Recordset** is a forward-scrolling snapshot
dbSQLPassThrough	The *Source* query is passed to an ODBC backend server
dbSeeChanges	Generates a run-time error when another user is changing your data

DAO 3.5 OPTIONS

dbAppendOnly	Records may be appended
dbDenyWrite	Other users cannot change/add records
dbDenyRead	Other users cannot view records
dbExecDirect	ODBCDirect workspace only; bypasses the use of **SQLPrepare**
dbForwardOnly	Creates snapshot-type recordset (Jet only)
dbReadOnly	Your access is read-only; other users can modify records
dbRunAsync	ODBCDirect databases only

DAO 3.5 OPTIONS

dbInconsistent	Updates may be made to both the one-side and the many-side
dbConsistent	Updates may be made to the one-side or to the many-side only when the one-side exists
dbSQLPassThrough	The Source query is passed to an ODBC backend server
dbSeeChanges	Generates a run-time error when another user is changing your data

Lockedits: **Recordset** options as defined by the following intrinsic constants (This field is applicable to DAO 3.5 only):

dbReadOnly	Deletions and updates are not permitted
DbPessimistic	Lock the record when editing starts (this assumes numerous collisions)
dbOptimistic	Lock the record only when the update occurs
dbOptimisticValue	Use optimistic concurrency based on row values (ODBCDirect workspaces only)
dbOptimisticBatch	Enables batch optimistic updating (ODBCDirect workspaces only)

There are restrictions on the use of the option **dbOpenTable**. It cannot be used with a **Querydef** object, a dynaset or snapshot-type **Recordset**, or a **TableDef** object that represents a linked table. Restated, the table cannot be a virtual table.

Executing the MoveLast method or the MoveFirst method or setting the PercentPopulation property to 100 populates the Recordset object.

It is possible in DAO to read data that is being changed. The *Options* constant **dbSeeChanges** can be set in a multiuser environment. This is done because a read is permitted (dirty read; see Chapter 11 on transaction isolation levels) and the data just read may not exist. DAO does not have a clean technique for handling consistency of a recordset. SQL Server uses a transaction isolation level metaphor to handle dirty reads.

Opening a Recordset from a Database object using a SQL statement

Listing 20-9 is an example of creating a **Recordset** object from a SQL statement on a local table in a current database.

LISTING 20-9 Opening a **Recordset** from a Database object with a SQL Statement

```
Private Sub RecordSet_From_SQL_Click()
'(C) 1998 Bruce T. Prendergast
'    DBA Prendergast Consulting
'    DBA PCS
'    IDG Books Worldwide ISBN 0-7645-3123-9
'
'    Listing 20-9 Recordset from a SQL statement
'
    Dim intI As Integer
    Dim MyDB As Database
    Dim MyWS As Workspace
    Dim MyRS As Recordset
    Set MyWS = DBEngine.Workspaces(0)
    Set MyDB = MyWS.Databases(0)
    Set MyRS = MyDB.OpenRecordset( _
        "SELECT [Product Name] FROM " & _
        "tblInventory WHERE [On Hand] < 10;")
    With MyRS
        If Not MyRS.NoMatch Then
            While Not .EOF
                MsgBox "Name is: " & _
                    ![Product Name]
```

```
                .MoveNext
              Wend
          End If
      End With
      MsgBox "Recordset from SQL was successful"
      Exit Sub
  End Sub
```

Opening a Recordset from a Database object using a query

Just so you're not confused, the **Recordset** we are opening here is only for the **Database** object. Other alternatives are to open a **Recordset** from a **QueryDef**, **Recordset**, or **TableDef** object.

We continue our example using the same table we used earlier. The **QueryDef** is automatically appended to the **QueryDef** collection for later use. This is obviously one-time code and you need not create a new **QueryDef** each time. You get an error when creating a **QueryDef** and the name already exists in the **QueryDef** collection. Listing 20-9 created a **Recordset** object from a SQL statement. Listing 20-10 creates a **Recordset** object from a **QueryDef** object.

LISTING 20-10 Creating a Recordset with QueryDef from a Database objectf

```
Private Sub RecordSet_From_QueryDef_Click()
'(C) 1998 Bruce T. Prendergast
'    DBA Prendergast Consulting
'    DBA PCS
'    IDG Books Worldwide ISBN 0-7645-3123-9
'
'    Listing 20-10 Recordset from a QueryDef
'
    Dim MyDB As Database
    Dim MyWS As Workspace
    Dim MyRS As Recordset
    Dim MyQdf As QueryDef
    Set MyWS = DBEngine.Workspaces(0)
    Set MyDB = MyWS.Databases(0)
    '
```

```
'    clear debug stuff
'
On Error Resume Next
MyDB.QueryDefs.Delete "Inventory Query"
Set MyQdf = MyDB.CreateQueryDef( _
    "Inventory Query")
MyQdf.SQL = "SELECT [Product Name] " & _
    "FROM tblInventory WHERE [On Hand] < 10;"
Set MyRS = MyDB.OpenRecordset( _
    "Inventory Query")
With MyRS
    If Not MyRS.NoMatch Then
        While Not .EOF
            MsgBox "Name is: " _
                & ![Product Name]
            .MoveNext
        Wend
    End If
End With
MsgBox "Recordset from QueryDef was successful"
Exit Sub
End Sub
```

Opening a Recordset from a Database object using a table

The same table is reused for this example, but this time the table is opened directly. Before we create the **Recordset**, let's mention some restrictions for this technique:

1. The table must not be an attached table. Test the **Connect** property setting. If the **Connect** property hasn't been set then you can use **dbOpenDynaset**.

2. *Source* must not be a SQL statement.

3. *Object* must not be a **QueryDef** or a **Recordset.**

ODBC performance is improved by using the **dbForwardOnly** option for your cursors. Listing 20-11 creates a **Recordset** object from a **Tabledef** object and is the last example of creating **Recordset** objects.

LISTING 20-11 **Creating a Recordset with TableDef from a Database object f**

```
Private Sub Recordset_From_Table_Click()
'(C) 1998 Bruce T. Prendergast
'   DBA Prendergast Consulting
'   DBA PCS
'   IDG Books Worldwide ISBN 0-7645-3123-9
'
'   Listing 20-11 Recordset from a Tabledef
'
    Dim MyDB As Database
    Dim MyWS As Workspace
    Dim MyRS As Recordset
    Set MyWS = DBEngine.Workspaces(0)
    Set MyDB = MyWS.Databases(0)
    Set MyRS = MyDB.OpenRecordset( _
        "tblInventory", dbOpenDynaset)
    '
    '   This example illustrates an issue only.
    '   The procedural loop below is a very
    '   poor solution. SQL statements
    '   should be used whenever possible.
    '
    With MyRS
        If Not MyRS.NoMatch Then
            While Not .EOF
                If ![On Hand] < 10 Then
                    MsgBox "Name is: " & _
                        ![Product Name]
                End If
                .MoveNext
            Wend
        End If
    End With
    MsgBox "Recordset from a table was successful"
    Exit Sub
End Sub
```

The three examples illustrate different techniques to create a **Recordset** from a **Database** object. Creating a **Recordset** from a table always gives the fastest access to the data when the table is local. The slowest access is by creating a **Recordset** on a remote table.

THE USERS COLLECTION

The **Users** collection contains all stored **User** objects of a **Workspace** or **Group** object (Microsoft Jet workspaces only). This DAO object provides user-level security for Access with **User** objects. Access permissions are set for a database, tables, queries, forms, reports, macros, and groups using **Document** objects to enforce the security.

You may append a new **User** object to the **Users** collection of a group. This gives a user account the access permissions for that **Group** object. You may also append a **Group** object to the **Groups** collection of a **User** object. The **Refresh** method must be used because of the interlocking relationship between the **Users** and the **Groups** collections.

The **Name**, **PID,** and **Password** properties of a new **User** object may be set. Only the **Name** property of an existing **User** object may be examined.

Syntax:

Users Collection Definition

>   Property: **Count**

>   Methods: **Append, Delete, Refresh**

User Object

>   Collections: **Groups**

>   Methods: **CreateGroup, NewPassword**

>   Properties: **Name, Password, PID**

CreateGroup

The **CreateGroup** method is used to append a group to a **Groups** collection of a **User** object or a **Workspace** object. The **CreateGroup** method of the **User** object is identical to the **CreateGroup** method of a **Workspace** where a new group is appended to the **Groups** collection of a **Workspace** object. The only difference between the two methods is that the object type must be set in the **CreateGroup** method of the User object.

The **User** object acquires all the permissions of an appended **Group** object. Management of the system is simplified by giving permissions to groups only and not to users. The required **Group** object is appended to the **User** object that needs the permissions.

Creating a **Group** object or a **User** object is a method of the **Workspace** object. See the **Workspace** object for an example of creating a user, a group, and a user in a group.

NewPassword

The **NewPassword** method enables a user to change his or her password. Only a member of the **Admins** group can change other passwords. Passwords are case sensitive.

Syntax:

*UserObject.***NewPassword** *OldPassword, NewPassword*

Where:

UserObject: A **User** object from the **Users** collection of a **Database** object.

OldPassword: The original password enclosed in quotes.

NewPassword: The new password enclosed in quotes. A zero-length string ("") can be used to clear a password.

Changing a password is illustrated by:

```
DBEngine.Workspaces(0).Users("Skywalker").NewPassword
 "r2d2","3cpo"
```

THE GROUPS COLLECTION

The **Groups** collection is a collection of **Workspace** or **User** objects. A **Group** object represents a set of users who have common access permissions. This is the preferred approach to managing users. Things can quickly get out of hand when permissions must be managed for all users individually.

These methods, objects, and properties define the Groups collection:

Groups Collection Definition

 Property: **Count**

 Methods: **Append**, **Delete**, **Refresh**

Group Object

 Collections: **Users** (Default)

 Methods: **CreateUser**

 Properties: **Name**, **PID**

Creating a **Group** object or a **User** object is a method of the **Workspace** object. See the **Workspace** object for an example of creating a user, a group and a user in a group.

CreateUser

This method creates a **User** object in a **Users** collection of a **Group** object that will have all the permissions of the **Group** object.

Syntax:

 Set *Variable* = *Object*.**CreateUser**(*[Name* [, *PID* [, *Password*]]])

Where:

 Variable: A variable of type **User**.

 Object: The variable name of the **Group** object used to create the new **User** object.

 Name: A string expression uniquely identifying the user.

 PID: A string expression of -four to twenty characters.

 Password: Up to fourteen characters with any ASCII character except a null. Passwords are cleared with a zero-length string.

See the **Workspace** object for an example of creating a user, a group, and a user in a group.

KEY POINT SUMMARY

The topic of this chapter is the **Database** object. The goal of this chapter is to compare the **Database** object functionality to the **Connection** object of ODBCDirect. Both the ODBCDirect **Connection** object and the Jet **Database** object support the creation of a **QueryDef** object. Both the ODBCDirect and the Jet **QueryDef** objects may be prepared. Only the Jet **QueryDef** objects have persistence.

- ODBCDirect does not support DDL statements. DDL statements can only be used from a **Database** object created from a Jet **Workspace** object.
- Neither the **Error** object nor the **Connection** object has a **Properties** collection.
- User-defined properties are available in DAO.
- A **QueryDef** object is compiled when it is stored, which is implicit. An ODBCDirect **QueryDef** object cannot be stored, but it does have the **Prepare** property.
- A Jet **QueryDef** object with a zero-length name is a temporary **QueryDef** object.
- The **Connect** property of a pass-through query must be set before the SQL properties are set. Jet will attempt to parse the string as Access SQL in lieu of a **Connect** property value.

APPLYING WHAT YOU'VE LEARNED

The following questions will measure your understanding of the material and this chapter. Determining the appropriateness of a database access technology is done though an understanding of the particular database access technology's functionality. An example is the asynchronous connection discussed in Chapter 19. That feature is quite valuable from a client interface perspective. Users get annoyed easily when they are unable to interact. Remember that an ODBCDirect query must be prepared every time it is created.

Instant Assessment

1. What collection is a member of every DAO object except the **Connection** object and the **Error** object?

2. Explain the difference between the **Execute** method of a **Database** or **Connection** object and the **Execute** method of a **QueryDef** object.

3. What is the default collection for the **Connection** object?

4. Of what use is the **Cancel** method?

5. What is unique about a **QueryDef** object of a **Connection** object?

6. Explain the difference between the **OpenRecordset** method of a **Connection** or **Database** object and the **OpenRecordset** method of a **QueryDef** object, **Recordset** object, or **TableDef** object.

7. Explain the difference in addressing a user-defined property and a built-in property.

8. What is the purpose of the option **dbFailOnError** when used with the **Execute** method?

9. What is the issue of the **Connect** property of a Jet **Querydef** object?

10. Discuss user-defined properties and the **Inherited** property.

11. Discuss SQL statements and the **QueryDef** object.

12. How is a Jet **QueryDef** object appended to the **QueryDefs** collection?

13. How is a temporary Jet **QueryDef** object created?

14. How is the property **ReturnsRecords** used?

15. How can a relation be changed in VBA code?

16. What does it mean to *Prepare* a SQL statement?

17. When is an ODBCDirect **QueryDef** object compiled?

18. When is a Jet **QueryDef** object compiled?

 concept link **For answers to the Instant Assessment questions, see Appendix C.**

Lab Exercise

Lab 20.40 *Comparing ODBCDirect and Jet query performance*

WA I
WA II

This laboratory compares the performance of ODBCDirect and Jet queries that are either prepared or unprepared. The results of your testing will validate compiling (preparing) queries.

This laboratory assumes existing data on a remote SQL server. The objective is very simple: Measure the difference in performance between a prepared and an unprepared query. The table should be of reasonable size so that SQL Server must make an intelligent search. SQL Server will always do a table scan on small tables, because it is faster to read the table directly than to use an index.

Queries from this and other chapters can be used for your project. Your server must be a registered ODBC source. You'll note that the server I used for the examples in the book is named *Thor*. You'll want to change that name.

The queries should be repeated and their average response time measured. You can use a **Timer** control for this. Identify a table of reasonable size for the query.

You might consider doing the testing in off-hours because other network traffic will distort your results.

	Average Response Time
Jet Prepared Query	_____
Jet Unprepared Query	_____
ODBCDirect Query	_____
ODBCDirectQuery (Prepared)	_____

 Windows Architecture I

CHAPTER

Working with the TableDef Object

21

About Chapter 21

This chapter expands our definitions slightly. Recall that a **Workspace** object is a session, and a **Database** object is the workbench. The **TableDef** object is where the data is stored. We can call the storage location shelves, drawers, or bins. But this is only part of the picture. These are physical storage locations similar to Jet's support of local databases. Data Access Objects (DAO) also supports logical or virtual tables when the data is not local. The local representation is a map showing where the table is located.

This chapter also includes the **Fields** collection, which is the default collection of the **TableDef** object. Recall that ODBCDirect does not support Data Definition Language (DDL) statements. This means that ODBCDirect does not have a **TableDefs** collection.

Finally, the chapter closes with the **Relations** collection. This is a collection of **Database** objects; the tables, however, have relations.

The examples in this chapter are located in the Access 97 CHAPTER21.MDB located in the EXAMPLES\CHAPTER21 folder of the CD-ROM that accompanies this book.

THE TABLEDEFS COLLECTION

The next stop in the DAO default hierarchy is the **TableDefs** collection, as illustrated in Figure 21-1. The **TableDefs** collection has the **Fields** collection as the default collection.

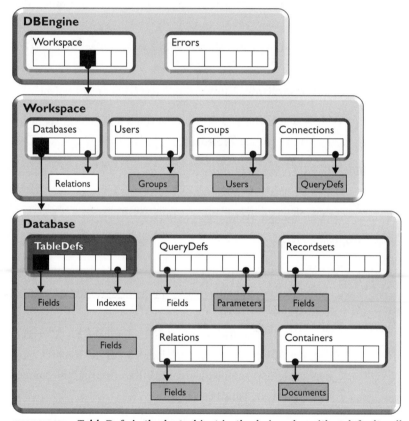

FIGURE 21-1   TableDefs is the last object in the heirarchy with a default collection.

The parent of the **TableDefs** collection is the **Database** object. **TableDef** objects are not available to **Connection** objects of an ODBCDirect **Workspace** object. A **TableDef** object can accomplish the following:

- Maintain attached tables by reading and writing the **Connect** and **SourceTableName** properties, and using the **Refresh** method.

- Maintain validation conditions by reading or writing the **ValidationRule** and **ValidationText**.

Recordset object option types that are available for the **Tabledef** object **OpenRecordset** method include:

- **dbOpenTable**: A table-type **Recordset** object (Jet)

- **dbOpenDynamic**: A dynamic-type **Recordset** object, like an Open Database Connectivity (ODBC) dynamic cursor. (ODBCDirect)

- **dbOpenDynaset**: A dynaset-type **Recordset** object, like an ODBC keyset cursor

- **dbOpenSnapshot**: A snapshot-type **Recordset** object, like an ODBC static cursor

- **dbOpenForwardOnly**: A forward-only-type **Recordset** object

Tabledefs use the standard collections addressing technique and can be accessed with the syntax: **Tabledefs**(*"Name"*)

Tabledefs *Collection Definition*

Collections: **Fields**(default), **Indexes**

Methods: **Append**, **Delete**, **Refresh**

Property: **Count**

Tabledef *Object*

Methods: **CreateField, CreateIndex, CreateProperty, OpenRecordSet, Refreshlink**

Properties: **Attributes, ConflictTable, Connect, DataCreated, KeepLocal**(user_defined)**, LastUpdated, Name, RecordCount, Replicable**(user_defined)**, ReplicaFilter, SourceTableName, Updatable, ValidationRule, ValidationText**

The discussion for the **TableDefs** collection and the **Tabledef** object continues the policy of only discussing the methods of objects within a collection.

 concept link

See Chapter 16 for a discussion of the Append, Delete, and Refresh methods.

CreateField

A **Field** object may be created for an **Index**, **Relation**, or a **TableDef** object.

Syntax:

Set *Variable = Object*.**CreateField**([*Name* [, *Type* [, *Size*]]])

Where:

Name: An optional **Variant** of type **String** that uniquely names the new **Field** object

Variable: A variable of type **Field**

Object: A variable of type **TableDef** (A **Field** object can also be created for an **Index** object and a **Relation** object.)

Type: An integer intrinsic constant of the following (type settings for a **Field**, **Parameter**, or **Property** object):

JET 2.0/2.5 INTRINSIC DATA TYPES VALUES

DB_DATE	Date/Time
DB_TEXT	Text
DB_MEMO	Memo
DB-BOOLEAN	Yes/No
DB_INTEGER	Integer
DB_LONG	Long
DB_CURRENCY	Currency
DB_SINGLE	Single
DB_DOUBLE	Double
DB_BYTE	Byte
DB_LONGBINARY	Long Binary

JET 3.0 INTRINSIC DATA TYPES VALUES

dbDate	Date/Time
dbText	Text
dbMemo	Memo
dbBoolean	Yes/No
dbInteger	Integer
dbLong	Long
dbCurrency	Currency

continued

Jet 3.0 intrinsic data types values (continued)

dbSingle	Single
dbDouble	Double
dbByte	Byte
dbLongBinary	Long Binary (OLE Object)

Jet 3.5 intrinsic data type values

dbBigInt	Big Integer
dbBigBinary	Binary
dbBoolean	Yes/No
dbByte	Byte
dbChar	Char
dbCurrency	Currency
dbDate	Date/Time
dbDecimal	Decimal
dbDouble	Double
dbFloat	Float
dbGuid	GUID
dbInteger	Integer
dbLong	Long
dbLongBinary	Long Binary (OLE Object)
dbMemo	Memo
dbNumeric	Numeric
dbSingle	Single
dbText	Text
dbTime	Time
dbTimeStamp	Time Stamp
dbVarBinary	VarBinary

Size: The maximum size in bytes for a **dbText** or **DB_TEXT** field

Construction of a **Field** object for a **TableDef** object is not complete until the **Attributes** property of the **Field** object is set. The **Attributes** property of a **Field** object can be set with the following intrinsic constants. The values are of type **Long**, and summing the constants can set multiple values.

JET 2.0/2.5 INTRINSIC VALUES FOR FIELD ATTRIBUTES

CONSTANT	DESCRIPTION
DB_FIXEDFIELD	Fixed length field. This is the default for numeric fields.
DB_VARIABLEFIELD	A variable length field. Used only for text fields.
DB_AUTOINCRFIELD	Auto incrementation of a **Long** type for new records. Value is read-only.
DB_UPDATABLEFIELD	Field can be changed.
DB_DESCENDING	Applies only to **Field** objects in an **Index** collection. The default sorting order is ascending.

JET 3.0/3.5 INTRINSIC FIELD ATTRIBUTE VALUES

CONSTANT	DESCRIPTION
dbFixedField	Fixed length field. This is the default for numeric fields.
dbVariableField	A variable length field. Used only for text fields.
dbAutoincrField	Auto incrementation of a **Long** type for new records. Value is read-only.
dbUpdatableField	Field can be changed.
dbDescending	Applies only to **Field** objects in an **Index** collection. The default sorting order is ascending.
dbSystemField	New for DAO 3.5. Jet only. Replica information is stored here. Not deletable.
dbHyperLinkField	New for DAO 3.5. Contains hyperlink information for memo fields only.

concept link See Chapter 20 for an example of using **Fields**, **Relations**, **Indexes**, and **Tabledefs**.

CreateIndex

This is our next stop in the **TableDefs** methods enumeration. An index is a necessary ingredient for efficient data retrieval.

Syntax:

Set *Variable* = *Tabledef*.**CreateIndex**([*Name*])

Where:

Variable: A variable of type **Index**

TableDef: A variable of type **TableDef**

Name: A string variable that uniquely identifies the new **Index** object

CreateProperty

The **CreateProperty** method is used to create a new user-defined **Property** object in a **Properties** collection. This method applies to **Database** objects, **Index** objects, **QueryDef** objects, and **TableDef** objects. It also applies to **Field** objects in **Fields** collections of **QueryDef** and **TableDef** objects. Refer to the **CreateProperty** method of the **Database** object for a description of using this method.

OpenRecordset

The **OpenRecordset** method of the **Database** or **Connection** object creates a **Recordset** object from a source name identifying a query, a table, or a SQL statement. The source name is known a priori with the **OpenRecordset** method of a **TableDef** object, and a source name parameter need not be specified. All parameters of the **OpenRecordSet** method of the **TableDef** object are optional. Creating a **Recordset** object from a **TableDef** object is the optimal access data technique; the data, however, cannot be filtered with **Filter** property of Access Basic.

Syntax:

Set *Recordset* = *Object*.**OpenRecordset**([*Type* [, *Options* [, *Lockedits*]]])

Where:

Variable: A variable of type **Recordset**

Object: The name of a **QueryDef**, **Recordset**, or **TableDef**. When *Object* is of type **Recordset**:

- It cannot be a forward-scrolling snapshot or an ODBCDirect **Recordset** object

- *Variable* type and *Object* type must agree when *Object* is a dynaset- or snapshot-type **Recordset**. *Type* must be a dynaset-type **Recordset** object when *Object* is a table-type **Recordset** object.

Type: An intrinsic integer that identifies the data type of the new **Recordset** object

DAO 2.0 TYPE SETTINGS FOR A RECORDSET OBJECT

DB_OPEN_TABLE	Table
DB_OPEN_DYNASET	Dynaset
DB_OPEN_SNAPSHOT	Snapshot

DAO 3.0 TYPE SETTINGS FOR A RECORDSET OBJECT

dbOpenTable	Table
dbOpenDynaset	Dynaset
dbOpenSnapshot	Snapshot

DAO 3.0/3.5 INTRINSIC TYPE SETTINGS

dbOpenTable	Table
dbOpenDynaset	Dynaset
dbOpenSnapshot	Snapshot
dbOpenDynamic	New for DAO 3.5, this is similar to an ODBC dynamic cursor and is for ODBCDirect workspaces only.
dbForwardOnly	New for DAO 3.5, this is a forward-only type Recordset object and a snapshot-type Recordset without a cursor.

Options: **Recordset** options as defined by the following intrinsic contstants:

ACCESS 2.0 OPTIONS SETTINGS FOR A RECORDSET OBJECT

DB_DENYWRITE	Other users cannot change or add records.
DB_DENYREAD	Other users cannot view records.

continued

DB_READONLY	The access is read-only. Other users can modify records.
DB_APPENDONLY	Records may be appended.
DB_INCONSISTENT	Updates may be made to the one-side and the many-side.
DB_CONSISTENT	Updates may be made to the one-side or to the many-side only when the one-side exists.
DB_FORWARDONLY	The **Recordset** is a forward-scrolling snapshot.

DAO 3.0/3.5 OPTIONS SETTINGS FOR A RECORDSET OBJECT

dbDenyWrite	Other users cannot change or add records.
dbDenyRead	Other users cannot view records.
dbReadOnly	Your access is read-only. Other users can modify records.
dbAppendOnly	Records may be appended.
dbInconsistent	Updates may be made to the one-side and the many-side.
dbConsistent	Updates may be made to the one-side or to the many-side only when the one-side exists.
dbForwardOnly	The **Recordset** is a forward-scrolling snapshot.
dbSQLPassThrough	The *Source* query is passed to an ODBC backend server.
dbSeeChanges	Generates a run-time error when another user is changing your data.

Lockedits: **Recordset** options as defined by the following intrinsic constants (this field is applicable to DAO 3.5 only):

dbReadOnly	Deletions and updates are not permitted.
dbPessimistic	Locks the record when editing starts. This assumes numerous collisions.
dbOptimistic	Locks the record only when the update occurs.
dbOptimisticValue	Uses optimistic concurrency based on row values (ODBCDirect workspaces only).
dbOptimisticBatch	Enables batch optimistic updating (ODBCDirect workspaces only).

Opening a Recordset using a QueryDef object

The examples in this chapter start by illustrating the creation of a **Recordset** object from a **QueryDef** object. The **QueryDef** is automatically appended to the **QueryDef** collection for later use. This is one-time code and you need not create a new **QueryDef** each time. An error occurs if you create a **QueryDef** and the name already exists in the **QueryDefs** collection. Creating a **Recordset** object from a **QueryDef** object is illustrated in Listing 21-1.

LISTING 21-1 Opening a Recordset object from a QueryDef object

```
Private Sub RecordSet_From_QueryDef_Click()
'(C) 1998 Bruce T. Prendergast
'    DBA Prendergast Consulting
'    DBA PCS
'    IDG Books Worldwide ISBN 0-7645-3123-9
'
'    Listing 21-1 RecordSet Object from a QueryDef
'
    Dim MyDB As Database
    Dim MyWS As Workspace
    Dim MyRS As Recordset
    Dim MyQdf As QueryDef
    Set MyWS = DBEngine.Workspaces(0)
    Set MyDB = MyWS.Databases(0)
    '
    '    clear debug stuff
    '
    On Error Resume Next
    MyDB.QueryDefs.Delete "Inventory Query"
    Set MyQdf = MyDB.CreateQueryDef( _
    "Inventory Query")
    MyQdf.SQL = "SELECT [Product Name] FROM " & _
        "tblInventory WHERE [On Hand] < 10;"
    Set MyRS = MyDB.OpenRecordset( _
        "Inventory Query")
    With MyRS
        If Not MyRS.NoMatch Then
```

```
                        While Not .EOF
                            MsgBox "Name is: " _
                                & ![Product Name]
                            .MoveNext
                        Wend
                End If
            End With
            MsgBox "Recordset from QueryDef was successful"
            Exit Sub
    End Sub
```

Opening a Recordset using a TableDef object

The **tblInventory** table of CHAPTER21.MDB (found on the CD-ROM that accompanies this book) is reused for this example, illustrated in Listing 21-2, but this time it is opened directly. The **OpenRecordset** method cannot be used on attached tables. If it is necessary to verify that the table is not attached, use the **Connect** property. Use the **dbForwardOnly** option to improve cursor performance.

LISTING 21-2 Creating a Recordset object from a TableDef object

```
Private Sub Recordset_From_TableDef_Click()
'(C) 1998 Bruce T. Prendergast
'    DBA Prendergast Consulting
'    DBA PCS
'    IDG Books Worldwide ISBN 0-7645-3123-9
'
'    Listing 21-2 Recordset Object from a TableDef
'
    Dim MyDB As Database
    Dim MyWS As Workspace
    Dim MyRS As Recordset
    Dim MyTdf As TableDef
    Set MyWS = DBEngine.Workspaces(0)
    Set MyDB = MyWS.Databases(0)
    Set MyTdf = MyDB.TableDefs("tblInventory")
    Set MyRS = MyTdf.OpenRecordset( _
        dbOpenDynaset, dbReadOnly + dbForwardOnly)
```

```
'
'    This example illustrates a poor programming
'    practice. The procedural loop below is a very
'    technique and SQL statements should be used
'    whenever possible.
'

With MyRS
    If Not MyRS.NoMatch Then
        While Not .EOF
            If ![On Hand] < 10 Then
                MsgBox "Name is: " _
                    & ![Product Name]
            End If
            .MoveNext
        Wend
    End If
End With
MsgBox "Recordset from TableDef was successful"
Exit Sub
End Sub
```

Opening a Recordset using a Recordset object

You need to use your imagination here. This next example, illustrated in Listing 21-3, builds on our prior example, but considers the initial **Recordset** object our base without a filter. An additional **Recordset** object is created from this base. The practical application here is a base **Recordset** and different filtered subsets. The user selects filters from a combo box. The application may permit the user to scroll different filtered recordsets in different list boxes.

LISTING 21-3 Creating a Recordset object from a Recordset object

```
Private Sub Recordset_From_Recordset_Click()
'(C) 1998 Bruce T. Prendergast
'    DBA Prendergast Consulting
'    DBA PCS
'    IDG Books Worldwide ISBN 0-7645-3123-9
'
```

```
'    Listing 21-3 Creating a RecordSet from a RecordSet
'

Dim MyDB As Database
Dim MyWS As Workspace
Dim MyRS As Recordset
Dim MyRSa As Recordset
Set MyWS = DBEngine.Workspaces(0)
Set MyDB = MyWS.Databases(0)
'
'    first recordset is a dynaset, keys only
'
Set MyRS = MyDB.OpenRecordset( _
"tblInventory", dbOpenDynaset)
MyRS.Filter = "[On Hand] < " & 10
'
'    filtered recordset is a snapshot
'
Set MyRSa = MyRS.OpenRecordset( _
    dbOpenSnapshot, dbForwardOnly + dbReadOnly)
With MyRSa
    If Not MyRS.NoMatch Then
        While Not .EOF
            MsgBox "Name is: " _
                & ![Product Name]
            .MoveNext
        Wend
    End If
End With
MsgBox "Recordset from a Recordset was successful"
Exit Sub
End Sub
```

RefreshLink

The **RefreshLink** method is used for attached tables. If the **Connect** property of the table is set, then the **RefreshLink** method is used to reestablish the connection. It is also used when you change the Connect property of a **TableDef**. Listing

21-4 is an example of such a function. Listing 21-4 consists of two routines. The main routine calls the **ReconnectTable** function, which is a refresh link to SQL Server. Note that the **TableDef** object must be removed from the **TableDefs** collection when the table name is changed.

As this connection string to a table on a Web HTML page shows, connection strings are no longer just issues of connecting to Access or SQL Server tables:

```
"HTML Import;DATABASE=http://www.myserver.com/samples/
 page1.html"
```

LISTING 21-4 Using the RefreshLink method to refresh a connection

```
Private Sub Refresh_Link_Click()
'(C) 1998 Bruce T. Prendergast
'    DBA Prendergast Consulting
'    DBA PCS
'    IDG Books Worldwide ISBN 0-7645-3123-9
'
'    Listing 21-4 Refreshing a SQL Server Link
'
    Dim MyWS As Workspace
    Dim MyDB As Database
    Dim MyTblDf As TableDef
    Dim MyErr As Error
    Dim SourceConnectStr As String
    On Error GoTo Refresh_Error
    Set MyWS = DBEngine.Workspaces(0)
    Set MyDB = MyWS.Databases(0)
    SourceConnectStr = _
        "ODBC;DATABASE=Pubs;UID=sa;PWD=;DSN=Thor;"
    If Not ReconnectTable(SourceConnectStr, _
        "Pubs Authors", "authors") Then
        Set MyTblDf = MyDB.CreateTableDef( _
            "Pubs authors")
        '
        '    Declare ODBC SQL Server data source
        '
        MyTblDf.Attributes = dbAttachedODBC
```

```
            '
            '   connect
            '
            MyTblDf.Connect = SourceConnectStr
            MyTblDf.SourceTableName = "authors"
            MyDB.TableDefs.Append MyTblDf
            Set MyTblDf = Nothing
            MsgBox _
                "TableDef creation was successful"
            Exit Sub
        End If
        MsgBox "TableDef refresh was successful"
Normal_Exit:
        Exit Sub
Refresh_Error:
        For Each MyErr In DBEngine.Errors
            MsgBox MyErr.Description
        Next MyErr
        Resume Normal_Exit
End Sub
Function ReconnectTable(tdfPath As String, _
    tdfName As String, tblName As String) As Integer
'(C) 1998 Bruce T. Prendergast
'    DBA Prendergast Consulting
'    DBA PCS
'    IDG Books WorldWide ISBN 0-7645-3123-9
'
'    Listing 21-4 Function for Refreshing a link
'
    Dim MyWS As Workspace
    Dim MyDB As Database
    Dim MyTblDf As TableDef
    Set MyWS = DBEngine.Workspaces(0)
    Set MyDB = MyWS.Databases(0)
    For Each MyTblDf In MyDB.TableDefs
        '
```

```
'    Is this the one?
'

     If MyTblDf.Name = tdfName Then
'

'    Yes, try to reattach
'

         MyTblDf.Connect = tdfPath
         MsgBox "connect string is set"
         On Error Resume Next
         MyTblDf.RefreshLink
         If Err <> 0 Then
             ReconnectTable = False
             Exit Function
         End If
         ReconnectTable = True
         Exit Function
     End If
Next MyTblDf
ReconnectTable = False
Exit Function
End Function
```

THE FIELDS COLLECTION

This is the last stop in our trip through the default collections. There are other collections that we discuss later, but the **Fields** is the first discussed collection that does not have a default collection.

Fields Collection Definition

    Methods: **Append, Refresh, Delete**

    Property: **Count**

Field Object of *Index* Object

    Methods: **CreateProperty**(J)

    Properties: **Attributes, DataUpdatable, Name, Required, Type, Value**

    Legend: ODBCDirect = D, Jet = J

Field *Object of* ***QueryDef*** *Object*

Methods: **CreateProperty**(J)

Properties: **AllowZeroLength**(J), **Attributes**, **CollatingOrder**(J), **DataUpdatable**, **DefaultValue**(J), **Name**, **OrdinalPosition**, **Required**, **Size**, **SourceField**, **SourceTable**, **Type**, **ValidationRule**(J), **ValidationText**(J)

Legend: ODBCDirect = D, Jet = J

Field *Object of* ***Recordset*** *Object*

Methods: **AppendChunk**, **GetChunk**

Properties: **AllowZeroLength**(J), **Attributes**, **CollatingOrder**(J), **DataUpdatable**, **DefaultValue**(J), **FieldSize**, **Name**, **OrdinalPosition**, **OriginalValue**(D), **Required**, **Size**, **SourceField**, **SourceTable**, **Type**, **ValidateOnSet**(J), **ValidationRule**(J), **ValidationText**(J), **Value**, **VisibleValue**(D)

Legend: ODBCDirect = D, Jet = J

Field *Object of* ***Relation*** *Object*

Method: **CreateProperty**(J)

Properties: **DataUpdatable**, **ForeignName**, **Name**

Legend: ODBCDirect = D, Jet = J

Field *Object of* ***TableDef*** *Object*

Methods: **CreateProperty**(J)

Properties: **AllowZeroLength**(J), **Attributes**, **DataUpdatable**, **DefaultValue**(J), **Name**, **OrdinalPosition**(J), **Required**, **Size**, **SourceField**, **SourceTable**, **Type**, **ValidationRule**(J), **ValidationText**(J)

Legend: ODBCDirect = D, Jet = J

No methods are discussed for the **Fields** collection.

THE INDEXES COLLECTION

The **Indexes** collection is the most overlooked collection in Microsoft Access. An index can be the key to a successful Microsoft Access or DAO application. Developers simply forget to use an index. The **TableDef** is the only object with an **Indexes** collection in Microsoft Access.

Indexes *Collection Definition*

Methods: **Append, Refresh, Delete**

Property: **Count**

Index *Object*

Collections: **Fields**(default)

Methods: **CreateField, CreateProperty**

Properties: **Clustered, DistinctCount, Foreign, IgnoreNulls, Name, Primary, Required, Unique**

When an index doesn't exist on an attached table, a pseudo index can be created locally. The index is maintained locally and the source data is not changed. Views on SQL Server are a good example. A local index on large SQL Server views will dramatically improve performance. A pseudo index is created with the following Access SQL statement. You should place a similar SQL string in the **SQL** property of a **QueryDef** object before using the **Execute** method.

```
CREATE UNIQUE INDEX myIndex
 ON attachedTable(Col1, Col2, ...)
```

Jet will create a local version of the primary key index automatically for attached SQL Server tables.

DAO does not have a clustered index, and the **Clustered** property is only **True** if the attached SQL Server table has a clustered index. A database is compacted in logical key order rather than physical order in DAO 3.0/3.5, giving the effect of a clustered primary key. The effect quickly fades when new rows are appended to the table.

The **Required** property of a **Field** object can be set requiring non-**Null** values.

An index can be updated only if the **Updatable** property of the **TableDef** is **True**.

Relationships that enforce referential integrity will have an index created by Jet automatically with the **Foreign** property set to **True**.

Management of **Nulls** can be accomplished with the **Required** and **IgnoreNulls** properties.

REQUIRED VALUE	IGNORENULLS VALUE	NULL IN INDEX FIELD
False	**True**	**Null** values are allowed; no index created.
False	**False**	**Null** values are allowed; an index entry is added.
True	**True** or **False**	**Null** values are not allowed; no index is created.

CreateField

A **Field** object may be created for an **Index**, **Relation**, or a **TableDef** object. (See the **CreateField** method of the **TableDef** object for details.)

CreateProperty

The **CreateProperty** method is used to create a new user-defined **Property** object in a **Properties** collection. This method applies to **Database** objects, **Index** objects, **QueryDef** objects, and **TableDef** objects. It also applies to **Field** objects in **Fields** collections of **QueryDef** and **TableDef** objects. Refer to the **CreateProperty** method of the **Database** object for a description of using this method.

THE RELATIONS COLLECTION

The **Relations** collection is a collection of a **Database** object. The object has a single method and determines the relationship between tables in a database.

Relations Collection Definition

    Collections: **Field**(default)

    Methods: **Append**, **Delete**, **Refresh**

    Property: **Count**

    Relation Object

        Methods: **CreateField**

        Properties: **Attributes**, **ForeignTable**, **Name**, **Table**

CreateField

The **Relation** object has only one method, which is **CreateField**. (See the **CreateField** method of the **TableDef** object for details. See **Workspace** object for an example of creating tables, fields, indexes, and a relation.)

KEY POINT SUMMARY

This chapter focused on the **TableDef** object. Examples of creating a **Recordset** object from **Tabledef**, **QueryDef**, or other **Recordset** objects were presented. Accessing a table directly is the optimal data retrieval technique.

- The **Tabledefs** collection is a feature of Jet.
- Remote tables can be attached; **Recordset** objects, however, cannot be created from attached **TableDef** objects. The **OpenRecordset** method of the **Database** or **QueryDef** object must be used to create a **Recordset** object of an attached table.
- Performance of remote tables is improved with local indexes, known as pseudoindexes.
- **Recordset** objects can be created from **TableDef** objects, **QueryDef** objects, or other **Recordset** objects.
- **Recordset** objects created with the **OpenRecordset** method of the **TableDef** object cannot be filtered using the **Filter** property.

APPLYING WHAT YOU'VE LEARNED

The following questions will test your understanding of different data retrieval techniques. This knowledge is essential to understanding the appropriateness of the different database access technologies.

Instant Assessment

1. What is fastest access method for retrieving data?

2. What are the limitations of this method?

3. What is the slowest possible access technique to a table?

4. What are the limitations to opening a table-type **Recordset** object from a **Database** object?

5. What is the default collection for a **TableDef** object?

6. **Recordset** objects may be opened from **QueryDef**, **Recordset**, or **TableDef** objects. What is the restriction on creating a **Recordset** object from another **Recordset** object?

7. List the five **Recordset** types with a brief description of each.

8. What is the only DAO object with an **Indexes** collection?

9. Compare **TableDef** operations in ODBCDirect with **TableDef** operations in Jet.

 concept link   **For answers to the Instant Assessment questions, see Appendix C.**

Lab Exercise

WA I

Lab 21.41 *Improve remote table performance with pseudoindexes*

Lab 21.41 explores improving attached table performance with pseudoindexes. Attach a table, preferably on Microsoft SQL Server. Ascertain that the table is large enough to make an index effective. The SQL Server optimizer calculates the cost of accessing data. Table scans are always the most efficient access techniques for small tables.

1. Pick a column in the attached table and construct a query that looks for a specific value. Ascertain that SQL Server does not have an index on that column. This query should not be a pass-through query. Issue the query and measure the performance. Call this *Query_1*.

2. Construct a local index or pseudoindex on that table. Issue the query and again measure the performance. It should have improved dramatically. Call this *Query_2*.

3. Break the table attachment. Create a pass-through query to SQL Server. SQL server should not have the column of interest indexed. Issue the query and measure the performance. Call this *Query_3*.

4. Repeat *Query_3*, but with an index on the SQL Server column of interest. Call this *Query_4*.

MCSD Windows Architecture I

CHAPTER

Working with the QueryDef Object

22

About Chapter 22

Chapter 22 brings us closer to the data. The **Workspace** object is the session, the **Database** object is the workbench, and a **Querydef** object is a plan for locating and retrieving the data. In keeping with the vernacular, I'll call it a scheme. This chapter is about planning and scheming. The result of this planning and scheming will be a **QueryDef** object that can be used to retrieve the data. The scheme can be simple and direct or it can be prepared, that is, compiled. Pay close attention to the subtle differences between a Jet **QueryDef** object and an ODBCDirect **QueryDef** object.

The examples in this chapter are located in the Access 97 CHAPTER22.MDB located in the EXAMPLES\CHAPTER22 folder of the CD-ROM that accompanies this book.

THE QUERYDEFS COLLECTION

Our current stop in the DAO hierarchy is the **QueryDefs** collection, illustrated in Figure 22-1. The **QueryDefs** collection is a collection of an ODBCDirect **Connection** object or a Jet **Database** object.

ODBCDirect objects are not persistent; that is, they're not saved to disk. An ODBCDirect **QueryDef** object is released when the ODBCDirect **Workspace** object is closed or the **QueryDef** object goes out of scope. (*Going out of scope* means that all local variables and objects are released when the subroutine exits.) Supplying a zero-length string for the **QueryDef** object name creates jet temporary queries. A Jet **QueryDef** object is automatically appended to the **QueryDefs** collection, but only when an object name is supplied.

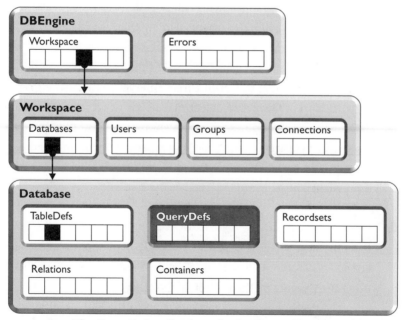

FIGURE 22-1   The QueryDefs collection of a database object.

QueryDefs Collection Definition

   Methods: **Append, Refresh, Delete**

   Property: **Count**

   QueryDef Object

Collections: **Fields**, **Parameters**(default)

Methods: **Cancel**(D), **Close**, **CreateProperty**(J), **Execute**, **OpenRecordset**

Properties: **CacheSize**(D), **Connect**, **DataCreated**(J), **KeepLocal**(J), **LastUpdated**(J), **LogMessages**(J), **MaxRecords**, **Name**, **ODBCTimeout**, **Prepare**(D), **RecordsAffected**, **Replicable**(J), **ReturnsRecords**(J), **SQL**, **StillExecuting**(D), **Type**, **Updatable**

Legend: ODBCDirect = D, J = Jet

You can create a **QueryDef** object from the query-by-example (QBE) window of Microsoft Access or by using the **CreateQueryDef** method of a **Database** or a **Connection** object. A **QueryDef** object only has two collections: **Fields** and **Parameters**, which is the default collection.

A new Jet **QueryDef** object is appended automatically to the **QueryDefs** collection. A **QueryDef** object with name set as a zero-length string is a temporary **QueryDef** object and is not appended to the **QueryDefs** collection. An ODBCDirect **QueryDef** object is always temporary and is never saved.

An appended Jet **QueryDef** object's query plan is compiled automatically. This is different than the ODBCDirect **QueryDef** object. The **Prepare** property of an ODBCDirect **QueryDef** object may be set to either **dbQPrepare** (default) or **dbQUnprepare**. The values are equivalent to the ODBC API functions **SQLPrepare** and **SQLExecDirect.** Using **dbQUnprepare** is recommended for ODBCDirect queries with parameters that are character strings. An SQL statement with the expression:

```
LIKE '%<character string>'
```

has unknown selectivity and a new query plan should be compiled with each query. This is accomplished by setting the **Prepare** property to **dbQUnprepare** and using the **Execute** method option **dbExecDirect**.

The **Prepare** property must be set before the **SQL** property is set. This is only a minor performance issue because **dbPrepare** is the default for the **Prepare** property and overriding **dbPrepare** with **dbExecDirect** creates another query plan compilation, which results in two consecutive query plan compilations.

It's all well and good to discuss the merits of preparing or not preparing a query when using SQL Server but the bottom line is that the SQL Server statement UPDATE STATISTICS must be used to update table statistics. The client can change the data, but unless the SQL Server statistics are current, preparing a query is an exercise in futility.

Well, not quite futile. Even though the table statistics on the server are inaccurate, a prepared **QueryDef** object with parameters is still useful. It is not only the question of a query plan, but also that of binding parameters.

The **QueryDefs** collection functions in the same manner as the **Connections**, **Databases**, **Recordsets**, and **Workspaces** collections in that a new object is automatically appended to the collection. There is no need to use the **Append** method.

 See Chapter 16 for further details on the **Append** method.

Execute

There are two **Execute** methods of DAO. The first method is used for a **Connection** or a **Database.**

Syntax:

*Object.***Execute**(*Source* [,*Options*)

 See the **Execute** method in Chapter 20 for further details of using this method with a **Connection** object or a **Database** object.

 The **Execute** method is the same for a **QueryDef**, **Connection**, or **Database** object in all cases. Only the option field changes depending on the object type. The issue is the context of where the **Execute** method is used.

The **Execute** method of a **QueryDef** object runs an action query. An action query performs an update, deletion, or an addition.

Syntax:

*QueryDef.***Execute**([*Options*])

Where:

QueryDef: The **QueryDef** object name.

Options: One or more of these intrinsic constants:

*Microsoft Access Jet 2.0*

DB_DENYWRITE	Denies write permission to other users.
DB_INCONSISTENT	The default. Set when updates may change both the one-side and the many-side of a relation.

continued

DB_CONSISTENT	Updates may be made to the one-side or to the many-side only when the one-side exists.
DB_SQLPASSTHROUGH	SQL pass-through.
DB_FAILONERROR	Rolls back updates if an error occurs.

MICROSOFT ACCESS JET *3.0/3.5*

dbDenyWrite	Denies write permission to other users.
dbInconsistent	The default. Set when updates may change both the one-side and the many-side of a relation.
dbConsistent	Updates may be made to the one-side or to the many-side only when the one-side exists.
dbSQLPassThrough	SQL pass-through.
dbFailOnError	Rolls back updates if an error occurs.
dbSeeChanges	Generates a run-time error if another user is changing your data.
DbRunAsync	New for DAO 3.5 (ODBCDirect only) Execute **QueryDef** or **Connection** objects asynchronously.
dbExecDirect	New for DAO 3.5 (ODBCDirect only). Do not call the **SQLPrepare** ODBC API functions before executing a **QueryDef** or **Connection** object.

A query with hard-coded parameters: a poor practice

Listing 22-1 is an action query embedded within a transaction. The **Parameters** collection of a query should be used for query parameters. The example is a simple query without a parameter. It is a poor example of a query because the criteria is "hard-coded" into the VBA code, but we'll improve on that later.

LISTING 22-1 An action query embedded in a transaction

```
Private Sub Proper_Transaction_Click()
'(C) 1998 Bruce T. Prendergast
'    DBA Prendergast Consulting
'    DBA PCS
'    IDG Books Worldwide ISBN 0-7645-3123-9
'
'    Listing 22-1 An example of a Proper Transaction
```

```
'
'   This example illustrates a transaction rollback,
'   and is a good transaction example since the update
'   is done in SQL and not in a procedural loop.
'

    Dim MyQdf As QueryDef
    Dim MyDB As Database
    Dim MyWS As Workspace

    Set MyWS = DBEngine.Workspaces(0)
    Set MyDB = MyWS.Databases(0)
    '
    '   An SQL statement rather than a procedural update
    '
    Set MyQdf = MyDB.CreateQueryDef("")
    MyQdf.SQL = "UPDATE tblInventory SET [Cost] = " & _
        "[Cost]+[Cost]/10 WHERE [On Hand] < " & 5
    '
    '   update the data
    '
On Error GoTo Transaction_Failure
    '
    '   dbfailOnError will create an
    '   error for locked records
    '
MyWS.BeginTrans
MyQdf.Execute dbFailOnError
    '
    '   only one record is expected to be updated
    '
If MyQdf.RecordsAffected <> 1 Then
    MsgBox "Transaction count inappropriate." _
        & vbCrLf & " Transaction rolled back."
    MyWS.Rollback
    Exit Sub
End If
MyWS.CommitTrans
```

```
        MsgBox "Proper transaction was successful"
exit_after_error:
    Exit Sub
Transaction_Failure:
    MsgBox Error$
    MyWS.Rollback
    MsgBox "Update failed, and rolled back"
    Resume exit_after_error
End Sub
```

OpenRecordset

Opening a **Recordset** object from a **QueryDef** object has the same form and syntax as opening a **Recordset** object from a **TableDef** object.

concept link

See Chapter 21 for further details of working with the TableDef object.

Just opening a recordset is not very interesting, so I included some interesting examples in this section. The first example is quite simple; however, the complexity of subsequent examples escalates. In order of appearance they are:

1. A query with a parameter prompted from the user.

2. A query with each query parameter bound to a control on the form. I think you'll enjoy this one. It really simplifies those query-by-form problems.

3. Cloning an attached SQL Server table to a local table.

4. Cloning a SQL Server query to a local table.

5. Returning multiple result sets to different tables from SQL Server.

The query in Listing 22-1 is enhanced in Listing 22-2 with the use of the **Parameters** collection. Our first enhancement is to use a parameter set in VBA. The example shows a parameter receiving a prompted user value.

LISTING 22-2 A query with a parameter

```
Private Sub Parameterized_Query_Click()
'(C) 1998 Bruce T. Prendergast
'    DBA Prendergast Consulting
```

```
'   DBA PCS
'   IDG Books Worldwide ISBN 0-7645-3123-9
'
'   Listing 22-2 An example of a Parameterized Query
'
    Dim MyDB As Database
    Dim MyWS As Workspace
    Dim MyRS As Recordset
    Dim MyQdf As QueryDef
    Set MyWS = DBEngine.Workspaces(0)
    Set MyDB = MyWS.Databases(0)
    '
    '   clear debug stuff
    '
    On Error Resume Next
    MyDB.QueryDefs.Delete "Inventory Query"
    Set MyQdf = MyDB.CreateQueryDef( _
    "Inventory Query")
    MyQdf.SQL = "SELECT [Product Name] FROM " & _
        "tblInventory WHERE [On Hand] < [Limit];"
    MyQdf.Parameters("Limit") = _
        InputBox("Minimum Stocking Level", _
        "Items below this Threshold", 1)
    Set MyRS = MyQdf.OpenRecordset()

    With MyRS
        If Not MyRS.NoMatch Then
            While Not .EOF
                MsgBox "Name is: " & _
                    ![Product Name]
                .MoveNext
            Wend
        End If
    End With
    MsgBox "Parameterized QueryDef was successful"
    Exit Sub
End Sub
```

The statement:

```
MyQdf.Parameters("Limit") = InputBox("Minimum Stock Levels",
 "Threshold", 1)
```

does not create a **Parameter** object. Creation of a **Parameter** object is done automatically when the SQL source text is stored in the SQL **Property** field in the previous statement. Access recognizes that *Limit* is not a field of the table *tblInventory* and assumes that it is a parameter. The results of the **InputBox** function are saved in the **Value** property which is the default property for the **Parameter.**

Binding QueryDef parameters to controls

We can further enhance the example in Listing 22-2 by binding parameters to controls on a form. This is done using the **Eval** function of VBA and is illustrated in Listing 22-3. To do this, the control names on the form must be the same as the names in the **Parameters** collection of the query. A slight modification of the previous code fragment illustrates this.

I call this a binding parameter; however, it is not binding in the sense that the **RecordSource** property of a form and the **ControlSource** are set. All controls are unbound with the **ControlSource** property set to **Null** and the binding only occurs in the sense that the parameter name matches the control name.

LISTING 22-3 Binding parameters from a form

```
Private Sub Parameter_Binding_Click()
'(C) 1998 Bruce T. Prendergast
'    DBA Prendergast Consulting
'    DBA PCS
'    IDG Books Worldwide ISBN 0-7645-3123-9
'
'    Listing 22-3 Parameter Binding from a Form
'

    Dim MyDB As Database
    Dim MyWS As Workspace
    Dim MyRS As Recordset
    Dim MyQdf As QueryDef
    Dim MyPrm As Parameter
```

```
    Dim MyFrm As Form


    Set MyWS = DBEngine.Workspaces(0)
    Set MyDB = MyWS.Databases(0)
    '
    '   clear debug stuff
    '
    On Error Resume Next
    MyDB.QueryDefs.Delete "Inventory Query"

    Set MyQdf = MyDB.CreateQueryDef("Inventory Query")
    MyQdf.SQL = "SELECT [Product Name] FROM " & _
        "tblInventory WHERE [On Hand] < [Threshold];"
'********************
'   start scaffolding
'********************
    Me!Threshold = 5
'******************
'   end scaffolding
'******************
    '
    '   bind the query to the form
    '
    Set MyFrm = Screen.ActiveForm
    For Each MyPrm In MyQdf.Parameters
        MyPrm.Value = Eval("Forms![" & _
            MyFrm.Name & "]!" & MyPrm.Name)
    Next MyPrm
    Set MyRS = MyQdf.OpenRecordset()
    With MyRS
        If Not MyRS.NoMatch Then
            While Not .EOF
                MsgBox "Name is: " & _
                    ![Product Name]
                .MoveNext
            Wend
        End If
```

```
      End With
      MsgBox "Bound QueryDef was successful"
      Exit Sub
End Sub
```

What is nice about the above example is that all controls on the form that have the same name as the respective **QueryDef** parameter are automatically bound to the form. Because I am using the **Parameters** collection of a **Querydef** object, all other controls are ignored. The expression:

```
MyPrm.Value = Eval("Forms![" & MyFrm.Name & "]!" & MyPrm.Name)
```

retrieves data from a control on the form that has the same name as the query parameter.

Cloning a SQL Server table locally

Browsing data has always been a problem in a multiuser environment. The typical approach it to issue a query and then browse the recordset. If this is a multiuser environment, then lock conflicts will abound. Bound forms will have the greatest problem because there is no lock control. Unbound forms will function better with error recovery on a lock failure and with the use of optimistic locking.

The problems are magnified with SQL Server read, intent, and update locks. The solution is to use a make-table action query and do a SELECT INTO a table. The table can then be browsed off-line from the server with no lock conflicts, which is equivalent to a snapshot. New records that are added or changed locally will not be reflected on SQL Server. SQL Server can be updated with regular batch postings. The ideal use of this approach is in a decision support system (DSS) where data is not updated on a regular basis, and updates, when they occur, need not be reflected immediately. The local tables can be refreshed on a regular basis.

There is one small downside to this approach. You may create a very large table that may not be manageable on the client side. Another local data management technique is the **GetRows** method that is discussed later in this chapter.

A code fragment to create a table is shown in Listing 22-4. The incoming data comes through an attached table and a make-table is used on the attached SQL Server table to create the local copy. Be very careful if you do this because SQL Server tables can be very large. Your best option is a query that only brings over a portion of the SQL Server table.

Cloning a SQL Server table locally using an attached table

```
Private Sub SQL_Server_To_Local_Click()
'(C) 1998 Bruce T. Prendergast
'   DBA Prendergast Consulting
'   DBA PCS
'   IDG Books Worldwide ISBN 0-7645-3123-9
'
'   Listing 22-4 Cloning a SQL Server Table
'   to a Local Table
'
    Dim MyDB As Database
    Dim MyWS As Workspace
    Dim MyTdf As TableDef
    Set MyWS = DBEngine.Workspaces(0)
    Set MyDB = MyWS.Databases(0)
    '
    '   debugging
    '
    On Error Resume Next
    MyDB.TableDefs.Delete "Pubs Authors"
    MyDB.TableDefs.Delete "Pubs Authors Local"
    DoCmd.Hourglass True
    Set MyTdf = MyDB.CreateTableDef("Pubs Authors")
    Dim SourceConnectStr As String
    SourceConnectStr = "ODBC;DATABASE=Pubs;" & _
        "UID=sa;PWD=;DSN=Thor;"
    '
    '   Declare ODBC SQL Server data source
    '
    MyTdf.Attributes = dbAttachedODBC
    '
    '   connect
    '
    MyTdf.Connect = SourceConnectStr
    MyTdf.SourceTableName = "authors"
    MyDB.TableDefs.Append MyTdf
```

```
MyDB.TableDefs.Refresh
'

'   clone the table

'
MyDB.Execute "SELECT [Pubs Authors].* " & _
    "INTO [Pubs Authors Local] " & _
    "FROM [Pubs Authors];"
DoCmd.Hourglass False
MsgBox "Cloning SQL Server table was successful"
Exit Sub
End Sub
```

Creating a local table for browsing query results

Listing 22-5 is a refinement of the previous example. Only selected columns are cloned. A WHERE clause will reduce the returned result set further.

The browse problem in the preceding example was solved with only a make-table query from a table. This example solves the same problem; however, the make-table query has another query as a source.

Cloning tables from SQL Server is relatively easy. Problems can arise, however, with name collisions from shared **QueryDefs**. These examples only illustrate the basic principle and the reader should take proper precautions to prevent name collisions.

LISTING 22-5 Cloning a SQL Server query into a local table

```
Private Sub SQL_Server_Query_Clone_Click()
'(C) 1998 Bruce T. Prendergast
'   DBA Prendergast Consulting
'   DBA PCS
'   IDG Books Worldwide ISBN 0-7645-3123-9
'

'   Listing 22-5 Cloning an SQL Server
'   Result Set to a Local Table
'

Dim MyDB As Database
Dim MyWS As Workspace
Dim MyTdf As TableDef
```

```
    Dim MyBQdf As QueryDef
    Dim MyQdf As QueryDef
    Dim ConnectStr As String
    Set MyWS = DBEngine.Workspaces(0)
    Set MyDB = MyWS.Databases(0)
    '
    '    debugging
    '

    On Error Resume Next
    MyDB.TableDefs.Delete "Pubs Authors Local"
    MyDB.QueryDefs.Delete "MyBaseQD"
    Set MyBQdf = MyDB.CreateQueryDef( _
        "MyBaseQD", "Select au_id, au_fname, " & _
        "au_lname FROM authors")
    MyBQdf.ReturnsRecords = True
    ConnectStr = "ODBC;DATABASE=Pubs;UID=sa;" & _
        "PWD=;DSN=Thor;"
    MyBQdf.Connect = ConnectStr
    Set MyQdf = MyDB.CreateQueryDef("")
    MyQdf.SQL = "SELECT MyBaseQD.* INTO " & _
        "[Pubs Authors Local] FROM MyBaseQD;"
    '
    '    clone the table
    '

    MyQdf.Execute
    DoCmd.Hourglass False
    MsgBox "Cloning SQL Server query was successful"
    Exit Sub
End Sub
```

Returning multiple resultsets in a query from SQL Server

Life with a server can be very complicated. Microsoft SQL Server has update locks, shared locks, page locks, and table locks. We'll complicate life for SQL Server a bit more by defining a pass-through query which returns multiple resultsets. A SELECT INTO SQL statement moves an incoming query into the local tables. A pass-through query is established by setting the **Connect** property before setting the **SQL** property.

The pass-through query in Listing 22-6 is composed of two SQL statements. The results of the first query are placed in the table *CloneTable* and the results of the second query are placed in the table *CloneTable1*. If there were a third query it would be found in the table *CloneTable2*.

As previously stated, you must take precautions against name collisions. This technique only works if the previous clone tables are deleted.

The query is not simple. Ignoring housekeeping issues, the query is constructed by establishing a base query that consists of multiple SQL statements, each of which is separated by a semicolon. An example of this technique is the **SQL** property of the *MyQdf* **QueryDef** object in Listing 22-6 that consists of two SQL statements. The **Execute** method of the **Database** object with the accompanying SELECT INTO SQL statement creates the tables. The data source for creating the local tables is not the remote tables of SQL Server, but the incoming data defined by the base query definition.

LISTING 22-6 Cloning multiple SQL Server queries to a local table

```
Private Sub Cloning_Multiple_SQL_Server_Tables_Click()
'(C) 1998 Bruce T. Prendergast
'    DBA Prendergast Consulting
'    DBA PCS
'    IDG Books Worldwide ISBN 0-7645-3123-9
'
'    Listing 22-6 Cloning Multiple SQL Server Tables
'
    Dim MyDB As Database
    Dim MyWS As Workspace
    Dim MyQdf As QueryDef
    Dim MyTdf As TableDef
    Dim SourceConnectStr As String
    Set MyWS = DBEngine.Workspaces(0)
    Set MyDB = MyWS.Databases(0)
    DoCmd.Hourglass True
    '
    '   build my table attachments to SQL Server
    '
    On Error Resume Next
```

```
MyDB.TableDefs.Delete "Pubs Authors"
MyDB.TableDefs.Delete "Pubs Titles"
'
'   trash the clone tables
'
MyDB.TableDefs.Delete "CloneTable"
MyDB.TableDefs.Delete "CloneTable1"

Set MyTdf = MyDB.CreateTableDef("Pubs Authors")
'
'   Declare ODBC SQL Server data source
'
MyTdf.Attributes = dbAttachedODBC
'
'     connect
'
SourceConnectStr = "ODBC;DATABASE=Pubs;UID=sa;" & _
        "PWD=;DSN=Thor;"
MyTdf.Connect = SourceConnectStr
MyTdf.SourceTableName = "authors"
MyDB.TableDefs.Append MyTdf
MsgBox "Pubs database authors table is attached"
'
'   now attach the titles table
'
Set MyTdf = MyDB.CreateTableDef("Pubs Titles")
'
'   Declare ODBC SQL Server data source
'
MyTdf.Attributes = dbAttachedODBC
'
'   connect
'
MyTdf.Connect = SourceConnectStr
MyTdf.SourceTableName = "titles"
MyDB.TableDefs.Append MyTdf
```

```
          MsgBox "Pubs titles table is attached"
          '
          '    create the base SQL Server query.
          '
          MyDB.QueryDefs.Delete "MyBaseQD"
          Set MyQdf = MyDB.CreateQueryDef("MyBaseQD")
          MyQdf.Connect = SourceConnectStr
          MyQdf.SQL = "SELECT au_id,au_lname,au_fname " & _
              "FROM authors;" & _
              "SELECT title_id,title FROM titles;"
          MyQdf.ReturnsRecords = True
          MyDB.Execute "Select * into CloneTable from MyBaseQD;"
          '
          '    at this point the results of the query
          '    are in two local tables and may be scrolled
          '    locally with no SQL Server interaction.
          '
          MyDB.TableDefs.Refresh
          MsgBox "Multiple SQL Server query cloning was successful"
          DoCmd.Hourglass False
          Exit Sub
      End Sub
```

KEY POINT SUMMARY

You can consider the **QueryDef** object the workhorse of database access technology. Data Definition Language (DDL) statements are usually a one-time affair that occurs when the database is created. After that, the query is the vehicle for all other work. A query either returns data or is an action query that performs updates, deletions, or additions. Writing efficient queries is the Holy Grail of all database developers. Poor query performance may negate outstanding engineering in other areas.

There were several examples presented in this chapter of cloning remote tables locally. This technique is acceptable for DSS where the database is read-only.

The technique is not acceptable for online transaction processing (OLTP) systems that are being updated on a regular basis. The key points of this chapter are:

- Both the **Connection** object and the **Database** object can create a **QueryDef** object.

- DAO and Microsoft Access use a Jet **QueryDef** object.

- An ODBCDirect **QueryDef** object is used in accessing an ODBC data source.

- ODBCDirect **QueryDef** objects are not prepared automatically, unlike the appended Jet **QueryDef** object.

- ODBCDirect **QueryDef** objects are temporary; they have no persistence.

- A Jet **QueryDef** object is automatically appended to the QueryDefs collection, but only when an object name is supplied.

- A pass-through query is done in Jet by setting the **Connect** property before setting the **SQL** property.

APPLYING WHAT YOU'VE LEARNED

A successful query requires an understanding of the index structure, the size of the table, and the characteristics of the data. Small tables can be indexed, but the index won't be used because the optimizer considers using the index for small tables as inefficient. Indexes are a necessity for large tables. A query that is run repeatedly should be prepared. These and other issues are the crux of a successful database application. A successful database solution requires an understanding of the technology. The questions below address your understanding of this technology. There is a direct correlation between timely query results and client satisfaction. The user has expectations and doesn't expect a query from a million-row table with joins to perform instantly.

Instant Assessment

1. How is an ODBCDirect **QueryDef** deleted?

2. What are **dbQPrepare** and **dbQUnprepare** and how are they used?

3. Why would you not want a statement prepared?

4. What is the relationship between the **QueryDef** object properties **Prepare** and **SQL**?

5. What is the default collection for the **Fields** object?

6. What is the only object with an **Indexes** collection?

7. Explain the **Clustered** property of the **Index** object.

8. When is an index automatically created by the Jet Engine?

9. When is a **Parameter** object created?

10. What is at risk when cloning tables in a multiuser environment?

11. What constitutes a good query?

 concept link   **For answers to the Instant Assessment questions, see Appendix C.**

Lab Exercise

Lab 22.42 *Monitoring locks on SQL Server with an open query*

Lab 22.42 requires SQL Server. The issue is to send an unprepared parameter query to SQL Server and examine the lock status on SQL Server when a query is awaiting parameters.

MCSD

WA I

1. Prepare a parameter query for SQL Server. Identify the table of interest on SQL Server.

2. Go to SQL Server and verify that no other users have access to the table.

3. Go to **iSQL/W** and execute the stored procedure *sp_lock*. This procedure displays the outstanding locks.

4. Go back to your workstation and issue the query but don't provide the parameter.

5. While the parameter is pending, go back to **iSQL/W** and reissue the stored procedure *sp_lock*. You should find a lock outstanding.

6. Finish the query by providing the parameter. Verify that SQL Server locks are now normal.

Consider repeating this lab exercise for an action query. The point of both laboratories is that an unprepared query that requires a parameter will lock tables until the parameter value is supplied. Depending on SQL Server status of the resulting SET TRANSACTION ISOLATION LEVEL statement, another user might be able to read a locked table. No transactions, however, can proceed with outstanding locks.

Windows Architecture I

Working with the Recordset Object

About Chapter 23

We're at the end of the road in our discussion of Data Access Objects (DAO). After working through Chapters 15 to 22, we now have a session, a workbench, and a devious plan. Here we reap the fruits of our efforts.

Chapter 23 is the last chapter on DAO, and in this chapter we look at all aspects of the **Recordset** object. The **Recordset** object is either our data or a set of keys that locates and retrieves our data for us. You might want to scrutinize the examples in this chapter fairly closely. Maintaining open cursors can be expensive except, of course, when it is a snapshot-type cursor with read-only data instead of a dynaset with keys. Several examples show cloning a resultset to local tables for browsing. This reduces the load on the network and on SQL Server. (I don't champion the use of server-side cursors, as the less work that SQL Server does, the better it is.)

The examples in this chapter are located in the Access 97 CHAPTER23.MDB located in the EXAMPLES\CHAPTER23 folder of the CD-ROM that accompanies this book.

THE RECORDSETS COLLECTION

Nothing can be more frustrating than an application that fails to perform properly. The first step in developing a useful Access application is a clear understanding of the different modes of data access and which to use. We begin with the properties and methods of the **Recordsets** collection and the listing of a **Recordset** object. A list of method restrictions and a list of property restrictions follow this. These restrictions apply to ODBC snapshot-type **Recordset** objects created with the **DB_FORWARDONLY** restriction (**dbForwardOnly** in DAO 3.0/3.5). Working examples follow the restrictions.

Figure 23-1 is the DAO roadmap for this chapter. It indicates that this is our last stop in the DAO hierarchy. The **Recordsets** collection is a collection of the Jet **Database** object.

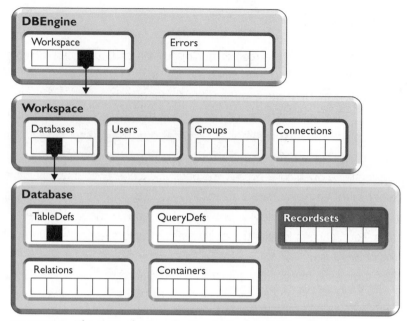

FIGURE 23-1   The Recordsets collection is the last DAO collection.

Recordsets Collection Definition

   Methods: **Refresh**

   Property: **Count**

Recordset Object

   Collections: **Fields**

   Methods: **AddNew**, **Cancel**(D), **Clone**(J), **Close**, **CopyQueryDef**(J), **Delete**, **Edit**, **FillCache**(J), **FindFirst**(J), **FindLast**(J), **FindNext**(J), **FindPrevious**(J), **Move**, **MoveFirst**, **MoveLast**, **MoveNext**, **MovePrevious**, **NextRecordset**(D), **OpenRecordset**(J), **Requery**, **Seek**(J), **Update**

   Properties: **AbsolutePosition**, **BatchCollisionCount**(D), **BatchCollisions**(D), **BatchSize**(D), **BOF**, **Bookmark**, **Bookmarkable**, **CacheSize**, **CacheStart**(J), **Connection**(D), **DataCreated**(J), **EditMode**, **EOF**, **Filter**(J), **Index**(J), **LastModified**, **LastUpdated**(J), **LockEdits**, **Name**, **NoMatch**(J), **PercentPosition**, **RecordCount**, **RecordStatus**(D), **Restartable**, **Sort**(J), **StillExecuting**(D), **Transactions**(J), **Type**, **Updatable**, **UpdateOptions**(D), **ValidationRule**(J), **ValidationText**(J)

   Legend: ODBCDirect = D, Jet =J

Table 23-1 lists the methods of DAO 2.5/3.0 and DAO 1.*x*. Snapshot-type **Recordset** objects created with **DB_FORWARDONLY** (**dbForwardOnly** in DAO 3.0) do not support the methods marked with an asterisk (*). Empty cells indicate that the method is not supported.

TABLE 23-1 DAO 2.5/3.0 AND DAO 1.*x* METHODS

METHOD	DAO 2.5/3.0 RECORDSET DYNASET	SNAPSHOT	TABLE	DAO 1.x RECORDSET DYNASET	SNAPSHOT	TABLE
AddNew	Yes		Yes	Yes		Yes
CancelUpdate	Yes		Yes			
Clone	Yes	Yes*	Yes	Yes	Yes*	Yes
Close	Yes	Yes	Yes	Yes	Yes	Yes
CopyQuerydef	Yes	Yes				
Delete	Yes		Yes	Yes		Yes
Edit	Yes		Yes	Yes		Yes
FillCache	Yes					
FindFirst	Yes	Yes*		Yes	Yes*	
FindLast	Yes	Yes*		Yes	Yes*	
FindNext	Yes	Yes*		Yes	Yes*	
FindPrevious	Yes	Yes*		Yes	Yes*	
GetRows	Yes	Yes	Yes			
Move	Yes	Yes	Yes			
MoveFirst	Yes	Yes*	Yes	Yes	Yes*	Yes
MoveLast	Yes	Yes*	Yes	Yes	Yes*	Yes
MoveNext	Yes	Yes	Yes	Yes	Yes	Yes
MovePrevious	Yes	Yes*	Yes	Yes	Yes*	Yes
OpenRecordset	Yes	Yes*	Yes			
Requery	Yes	Yes				
Seek			Yes			Yes
Update	Yes		Yes	Yes		Yes

Table 23-2 lists the methods of DAO 3.5 **Recordset** object methods. Blank cells indicate that the method is not supported.

TABLE 23-2 DAO 3.5 RECORDSET METHODS

METHOD	TABLE	DYNASET	SNAPSHOT	FORWARD-ONLY	DYNAMIC
AddNew	Jet	Both	ODBC*	ODBC	ODBC
Cancel		ODBC	ODBC	ODBC	ODBC
CancelUpdate	Jet	Both	ODBC*	ODBC	ODBC
Clone	Jet	Jet	Jet		
Close	Jet	Both	Both	Both	ODBC
CopyQuerydef		Jet	Jet	Jet	
Delete	Jet	Both	ODBC*	ODBC	ODBC
Edit	Jet	Both	ODBC*	ODBC	ODBC
FillCache		Jet			
FindFirst		Jet	Jet		
FindLast		Jet	Jet		
FindNext		Jet	Jet		
FindPrevious		Jet	Jet		
GetRows	Jet	Both	Both	Both	ODBC
Move	Jet	Both	Both	No Bookmark	ODBC
MoveFirst	Jet	Both	Both		ODBC
MoveLast	Jet	Both	Both		ODBC
MoveNext	Jet	Both	Both	Both	ODBC
MovePrevious	Jet	Both	Both		ODBC
NextRecordset		ODBC	ODBC	ODBC	ODBC
OpenRecordset	Jet	Jet	Jet		
Requery		Both	Both	Both	ODBC
Seek	Jet				
Update	Jet	Both	ODBC*	ODBC	ODBC

TABLE 23-2 LEGEND

<*>	Driver dependent
<ODBC>	ODBCDirect workspaces
<Jet>	Jet and DAO 3.5
<Both>	Jet and DAO 3.5 or ODBCDirect workspaces

Table 23-3 lists the properties of DAO 2.5/3.0 and DAO 1.x. Snapshot-type **Recordset** objects created with **DB_FORWARDONLY (dbForwardOnly** in DAO 3.0) do not support the properties marked with an asterisk (*). Blank cells indicate that the property is not supported.

TABLE 23-3 DAO 2.5/3.0 AND DAO 1.x PROPERTIES

	DAO 2.5/3.0 RECORDSET			*DAO 1.x RECORDSET*		
PROPERTY	*DYNASET*	*SNAPSHOT*	*TABLE*	*DYNASET*	*SNAPSHOT*	*TABLE*
AbsolutePosition	R/W	R/W*				
BOF	R	R	R	R	R	R
Bookmark	R/W	R/W*	R/W	R/W	R/W	R/W
Bookmarkable	R	R*	R	R	R	R
CacheSize	R/W					
CacheStart	R/W					
DateCreated			R			R
EditMode	R	R	R			
EOF	R	R	R	R	R	R
Filter	R/W	R/W		R/W	R/W	
Index			R/W			R/W
LastModified	R		R	R		R
LastUpdated			R			R
LockEdits	R/W		R/W	R/W		R/W
Name	R	R	R	R	R	R

continued

TABLE 23-3 *(continued)*

DAO 2.5/3.0 RECORDSET			*DAO 1.x RECORDSET*		
PROPERTY	DYNASET	SNAPSHOT	TABLE	DYNASET	SNAPSHOT	TABLE
NoMatch	R	R	R	R	R	R
PercentPosition	R/W	R/W*	R/W			
RecordCount	R	R	R	R	R	R
Restartable	R	R	False			
Sort	R/W	R/W		R/W	R/W	
Transactions	R	False	R	R	False	R
Type	R	R	R	R	R	R
Updatable	R	False	R	R	False	R
ValidateOnSet	R/W	R	R/W			
ValidationRule	R	R	R			
ValidationText	R	R	R			

Table 23-4 lists the properties of DAO 3.5 **Recordset** object properties. Blank cells indicate that the property is not supported.

TABLE 23-4 DAO 3.5 RECORDSET PROPERTIES

PROPERTY	TABLE	DYNASET	SNAPSHOT	FORWARD-ONLY	DYNAMIC
AbsolutePosition		R/W	R/W		R/W ODBC
BatchCollision Count		R ODBC	R ODBC	R ODBC	R ODBC
BatchCollisions		R ODBC	R ODBC	R ODBC	R ODBC
BatchSize		R/W ODBC	R/W ODBC	R/W ODBC	R/W ODBC
BOF	R Jet	R Both	R Both	R Both	R ODBC
Bookmark	R/W Jet	R/W Both	R/W Both		R/W ODBC
Bookmarkable	R Jet	R Both	R Both		R ODBC

PROPERTY	TABLE	DYNASET	SNAPSHOT	FORWARD-ONLY	DYNAMIC
CacheSize		R/W Jet R ODBC	R ODBC		R ODBC
CacheStart		R/W Jet			
Connection		R/W ODBC	R/W ODBC	R/W ODBC	R/W ODBC
DateCreated	R Jet				
EditMode	R Jet	R Both	R Both	R Both	R ODBC
EOF	R Jet	R Both	R Both	R Both	R ODBC
Filter		R/W Jet	R/W Jet	R/W Jet	
Index	R/W Jet				
LastModified	R Jet	R Both	R ODBC*		R ODBC
LastUpdated	R Jet				
LockEdits	R/W Jet	R/W Jet R ODBC	R/W Jet R ODBC		R ODBC
R ODBC		R ODBC			
Name	R Jet	R Both	R Both	R Both	R Both
NoMatch	R Jet	R Jet	R Jet		
PercentPosition	R/W Jet	R/W Both	R/W Both		R/W ODBC
RecordCount	R Jet	R Both	R Both	R Both	R ODBC
RecordStatus		R ODBC	R ODBC	R ODBC	R ODBC
Restartable	R Jet A/F	R Both	R Both	R Both	R ODBC
Sort		R/W Jet	R/W Jet		
StillExecution		R/W ODBC	R/W ODBC	R/W ODBC	R/W ODBC
Transactions	R Jet	R Jet	R Jet A/F	R Jet A/F	
Type	R Jet	R Both	R Both	R Both	R ODBC
Updatable	R Jet	R Both	R ODBC* R Jet A/F	R ODBC* R Jet A/F	R ODBC
UpdateOptions		R/W ODBC	R/W ODBC	R/W ODBC	R/W ODBC
ValidateRule	R Jet	R Jet	R Jet	R Jet	

continued

TABLE 23-4 *(continued)*					
PROPERTY	TABLE	DYNASET	SNAPSHOT	FORWARD-ONLY	DYNAMIC
ValidationText	R Jet	R Jet	R Jet	R Jet	
ValidationText	R Jet	R Jet	R Jet	R Jet	

TABLE 23-4 LEGEND

<*>	Driver dependent
<R>	Read-only
<R/W>	Read/write
<A/F>	Always false
<ODBC>	ODBCDirect workspaces
<Jet>	Jet and DAO 3.5
<Both>	Jet and DAO 3.5 or ODBCDirect workspaces

AddNew, Edit, and Update

Syntax:

> *Object*.{**AddNew** | **Edit** | **Update** }

Where:

> *Object:* A table-type or a dynaset-type **Recordset** object

These methods are used to add new records or to edit existing records in a **Recordset** object. After using **AddNew** or **Edit**, the **Update** method must be used to save the changes. The changes are lost if the procedure terminates, the object is closed, or the **Database** object is closed before the **Update** method is applied. Moving to another record before using the **Update** method also loses the changes.

If the **Recordset** is not positioned to the last record, then the **AddNew** method adds those records that are positioned beyond the current record. When the new record does not exist in the current **Recordset** object, a **MoveLast** method is performed followed by an **AddNew** method that appends the new record to the **Recordset** object. A **FindFirst** method is executed first when it is not known that the record exists. When the record doesn't exist, the cursor is correctly positioned beyond the last record after the **FindFirst** operation. This is the correct position for appending a new record, and the **AddNew** method is executed. The **Edit** method is executed when a record is located as a result of a **FindFirst** operation. This technique is illustrated in Listing 23-1 where a **FindFirst** is executed followed by a test of the **NoMatch** property that results in either the **Edit** or **AddNew** methods being executed.

New records are always inserted at the end of a **Recordset** or **Dynaset** object. This is done independent of sort or collating order. Records with an index are returned in index order.

Newly inserted records will appear in the proper order for a **TableDef** object that has an index. This does not mean that the base table is clustered, but that the index is updated on an insert. If a new data page must be added when using the **AddNew** method, the locking is pessimistic.

Using AddNew, Edit, and Update on an unbound form with unbound controls

Listing 23-1 illustrates the **AddNew**, **Edit**, and **Update** methods. The code fragment represents prototype code for an unbound form save record click-event. The section marked as *scaffolding* simulates user-entered data.

LISTING 23-1 Using AddNew, Edit, and Update on an unbound form

```
Private Sub AddNew_Edit_Update_Click()
'(C) 1998 Bruce T. Prendergast
'    DBA Prendergast Consulting
'    DBA PCS
'    IDG Books Worldwide ISBN 0-7645-3123-9
'
'    Listing 23-1 AddNew, Edit, & Update
'    on an unbound form
'
    Dim MyRS As Recordset
    Dim MyDB As Database
    Dim MyWS As Workspace
    Dim Criteria As String
    Dim User_Input As String
    Dim MyErr As Error
    '
```

```
'    Note: This is prototype code only.
'    Use it for a RECORD SAVE command
'    button Click event for an unbound
'    form
'
'    The text boxes on the screen will be
'    jammed with data simulating a user
'    entering data and clicking a save button
'********************
'    begin scaffolding
'********************
With Me
    ![Last Name] = "Whiplash"
    ![First Name] = "Snidley"
    ![Credit Limit] = 5
    ![Credit Used] = 0
    ![Credit Type] = "Deadbeat"
End With
'******************
'    end scaffolding
'******************
If IsNull(Me![Last Name]) Then
    Me![Last Name].SetFocus
    Exit Sub
End If
User_Input = Me![Last Name] & ""
If Len(Trim$(User_Input)) = 0 Then
    Me![Last Name].SetFocus
    Exit Sub
End If
'
'    Do the DAO thing
'
Set MyWS = DBEngine.Workspaces(0)
Set MyDB = MyWS.Databases(0)
Set MyRS = MyDB.OpenRecordset( _
```

```
        "tblEmployees", dbOpenDynaset)
    Criteria = "[Last Name] = " & _
        Chr$(34) & User_Input & Chr$(34)
    MyRS.FindFirst Criteria
    On Error GoTo Transaction_Failure
    MyWS.BeginTrans
    If MyRS.NoMatch Then
        MyRS.AddNew
    Else
        MyRS.Edit
    End If
    '
    '   move the data
    '
    With MyRS
        ![Last Name] = Me![Last Name]
        ![First Name] = Me![First Name]
        ![Credit Limit] = Me![Credit Limit]
        ![Credit Used] = Me![Credit Used]
        ![Credit Type] = Me![Credit Type]
        .Update
        MyWS.CommitTrans
    End With
    With Me
        ![Last Name] = Null
        ![First Name] = Null
        ![Credit Limit] = Null
        ![Credit Used] = Null
        ![Credit Type] = Null
    End With
    MsgBox "Addnew, Edit, and Update was successful."
exit_after_error:
    MyRS.Close
    MyDB.Close
    Set MyRS = Nothing
    Set MyDB = Nothing
```

```
        Me![Last Name].SetFocus
        Exit Sub
Transaction_Failure:
        For Each MyErr In DBEngine.Errors
            MsgBox MyErr.Description
        Next MyErr
        MyWS.Rollback
        MsgBox "Update failed, and rolled back"
        Resume exit_after_error
End Sub
```

Using FindFirst, NoMatch, Bookmark, and RecordsetClone to synchronize a bound form

Find methods cannot be used on bound forms. The fragment in Listing 23-2 demonstrates a technique that uses the **FindFirst** method on a cloned **Recordset** object. The example locates a record using a value from a text box. The section of code in Listing 23-2 marked as *scaffolding* simulates user input to the text box. This example uses a click-event text box. Another practical implementation of this code is the **AfterUpdate** event of a combo box that is query driven. Listing 23-2 synchronizes the cloned **Recordset** object with the form **Recordset** object using the **Bookmark** property of a form.

LISTING 23-2 Synchronizing a bound form with RecordSetClone

```
Private Sub Synchronize_with_RecordSetClone_Click()
'(C) 1998 Bruce T. Prendergast
'    DBA Prendergast Consulting
'    DBA PCS
'    IDG Books Worldwide ISBN 0-7645-3123-9
'
'    Listing 23-2 Synchronizing a bound form
'    with RecordSetClone
'
    Dim MyCS As Recordset
    Dim Criteria As String
    Dim User_Input As String
'
```

```
'*******************
'   begin scaffolding
'*******************
    Me!Synchronize.SetFocus
    Me!Synchronize = "Widget"
'*****************
'   End Scaffolding
'*****************
    User_Input = Screen.ActiveControl & ""
    If Len(Trim$(User_Input)) = 0 Then
        Exit Sub
    End If
    Criteria = "[Product Name]=" & Chr$(34) & _
            Trim$(User_Input) & Chr$(34)
    Set MyCS = Me.RecordSetClone
    '
    '   locate the criteria in the cloned recordset
    '
    MyCS.FindFirst Criteria
    If Not MyCS.NoMatch Then
        '
        '   Synchronize the bound form with the bookmark
        '
        Me.Bookmark = MyCS.Bookmark
        MsgBox "Synchronization is complete"
    End If
    Exit Sub
End Sub
```

CancelUpdate

Syntax:

   *Object.***CancelUpdate**

Where:

   Object: A table-type or a dynaset-type **Recordset** object

This method is new with DAO 3.0 and applies only to table-type or dynaset-type **Recordset** objects of DAO 3.0. There are five recordset types: table, dynaset, snapshot, forward-only, and dynamic. Only the table-type, dynaset-type, and dynamic-type (new with DAO 3.5) are updatable; hence the **CancelUpdate** method only applies to these **Recordset** types. The method cancels all changes made with either an **Edit** method or an **AddNew** method if the **Update** was not done. This is equivalent to an *object*.**Move** 0 in DAO 2.0. This method is more efficient than moving to another record and back, which will also cancel the changes.

Clone

Syntax:

Set *CloneRecordset* = *OriginalRecordSet*.**Clone**

Where:

CloneRecordset: An object of type **Recordset**

OriginalRecordset: An object of type **Recordset**

The **Clone** method is used to create multiple or duplicate **Recordset** objects. Opening a cloned **Recordset** object is much faster and more efficient than opening a new **Recordset** object. This method cannot be used on forward-scrolling snapshots. This technique is useful for an application that requires multiple current records.

Cloned records lack a current record. A current record can be established with any of the **Move** methods or you may use the **Bookmark** property to establish one.

Creating a cloned **Recordset** from a **QueryDef** object does not rerun the query. Closing the underlying **Recordset** does not close the cloned **Recordset**, nor does closing the cloned **Recordset** close the underlying **Recordset**.

If the **Bookmark** property of a **Recordset** is used in an Access Basic module, then the **Option Compare Binary** statement must be placed in the **Declarations** section of the module.

The **Index** property of a table-type **Recordset** object is not copied with the **Clone** method. It must be set manually.

The **Clone** method of a **Recordset** object is different than the **RecordsetClone** property of a form that was illustrated in Listing 23-2.

CopyQueryDef

CopyQueryDef is a new feature of DAO 3.0. The **CopyQueryDef** method for a **QueryDef** object works very much like the **Clone** method for a **Recordset** object. This method is used to create a duplicate **QueryDef** object only after a **Recordset** has been created with the **OpenRecordset** method. If a **Querydef** did not create the **Recordset**, then an error message is given.

Syntax:

Set *Object* = *Recordset*.**CopyQueryDef**

Where:

Object: An object of type **QueryDef**

Recordset: An object of type **Recordset** created by an object of type **QueryDef**

Delete

The **Delete** method normally removes an object from a collection. The **Delete** method for the **Recordset** object removes the current record. The **Recordset** object is removed from the **Recordsets** collection when it is closed.

Syntax:

Recordset.**Delete**

Where:

Recordset: A table-type or a dynaset-type **Recordset** object

There are always two ways to solve a problem, the wrong way and the right way. The wrong way to do a delete is illustrated by the VBA fragment in Listing 23-3. It deletes a row using the **Delete** method of the **Recordset** object. SQL statements are always faster than DAO operations. SQL statements smooth the migration path to SQL Server when the application is upgraded; applications written with only DAO **Recordset** object methods, however, are not upsizable to SQL Server and must be recoded.

 concept link

The VBA fragment in Listing 23-3 wraps a transaction around the Delete method, which reverses the delete process when an error occurs. Listing 23-4 uses SQL for the delete operation.

Poor technique: deleting rows with DAO methods

Listing 23-3 illustrates the VBA **Delete** method. The example only deletes one row of a table, and the use of VBA in a procedural loop is acceptable. Procedural loops are not an acceptable coding practice for manipulating rows in a relational database because a procedural loop on a set of data induces unneeded and unwanted overhead. SQL statements are always the preferred technique. Listing 23-4 illustrates the use of a SQL statement to delete rows.

LISTING 23-3 Poor technique: deleting rows with DAO methods

```
Private Sub Deleting_With_DAO_Click()
'(C) 1998 Bruce T. Prendergast
'    DBA Prendergast Consulting
'    DBA PCS
'    IDG Books Worldwide ISBN 0-7645-3123-9
'
'    Listing 23-3 Deleting with DAO
'
     Dim MyRS As Recordset
     Dim MyDB As Database
     Dim MyWS As Workspace
     Dim Criteria As String
     Dim MyErr As Error
     Dim User_Input As String

     Set MyWS = DBEngine.Workspaces(0)
     Set MyDB = MyWS.Databases(0)
     Set MyRS = MyDB.OpenRecordset( _
         "tblInventory", dbOpenDynaset)
     User_Input = InputBox( _
                 "Inventory Item to Delete", _
         "Delete from Inventory")
     If Len(Trim$(User_Input & "")) = 0 Then
         MsgBox "Nothing to delete, exiting"
         Exit Sub
     End If
     Criteria = "[Product Name] = " & _
```

```
            Chr$(34) & User_Input & Chr$(34)
     MyRS.FindFirst Criteria
     If MyRS.NoMatch Then
          Exit Sub
     End If
     On Error GoTo DAO_Delete_Failure

     If MyRS.NoMatch Then
          Exit Sub
     End If
     MyWS.BeginTrans
     '
     '   It's there so delete it
     '
     MyRS.Delete
     MyWS.CommitTrans
     MsgBox "Delete method was successful"
DAO_Delete_Failure_Exit:
     MyRS.Close
     MyDB.Close
     Set MyRS = Nothing
     Set MyDB = Nothing
     Exit Sub
DAO_Delete_Failure:
     For Each MyErr In DBEngine.Errors
          MsgBox MyErr.Description
     Next MyErr
     MyWS.Rollback
     MsgBox "Delete failed and rolled back"
     Resume DAO_Delete_Failure_Exit
     Exit Sub
End Sub
```

Proper technique: deleting rows with SQL

The data within a relational database is organized as sets of data. SQL statements
are designed to process sets of data. A procedural loop on a set of data induces

unneeded and unwanted overhead. The proper technique for manipulating data sets is with a SQL statement. Listing 23-4 illustrates deleting rows with a SQL statement.

LISTING 23-4 **Proper technique: deleting rows with SQL**

```
Private Sub Deleting_With_SQL_Click()
'(C) 1998 Bruce T. Prendergast
'    DBA Prendergast Consulting
'    DBA PCS
'    IDG Books Worldwide ISBN 0-7645-3123-9
'
'    Listing 23-4 Deleting the proper Way, with SQL
'

    Dim MyDB As Database
    Dim MyWS As Workspace
    Dim MyErr As Error
    Dim MySQL As String
    Dim User_Input As String

    Set MyWS = DBEngine.Workspaces(0)
    Set MyDB = MyWS.Databases(0)
    User_Input = InputBox( _
        "Inventory Item to Delete", _
        "Delete from Inventory")
    If Len(Trim$(User_Input & "")) = 0 Then
        MsgBox "Nothing to delete, exiting"
        Exit Sub
    End If
    MySQL = "DELETE * from tblInventory WHERE " & _
        "[Product Name] = " & Chr$(34) & _
        User_Input & Chr$(34) & ";"
    On Error GoTo SQL_Delete_Failure
    MyWS.BeginTrans
    MyDB.Execute MySQL, dbFailOnError
    MyWS.CommitTrans
```

```
    MsgBox "SQL delete was successful"
SQL_Delete_Failure_exit:
    MyDB.Close
    Set MyDB = Nothing
    Exit Sub
SQL_Delete_Failure:
    For Each MyErr In DBEngine.Errors
        MsgBox MyErr.Description
    Next MyErr
    MyWS.Rollback
    MsgBox "Delete failed and rolled back"
    Resume SQL_Delete_Failure_exit
    Exit Sub
End Sub
```

FillCache

The **FillCache** method is used to buffer records from a Jet-connected ODBC source. Records will not be cached when the data source isn't Jet-connected ODBC. The method can only be used on dynaset-type **Recordset** objects. ODBCDirect has its own caching mechanism. The Jet Database Engine will always check the cache first before retrieving data from the data source.

Updated records are not reflected in the cache. **FillCache** only fetches records not already cached. To refresh the cache, follow these steps:

1. Set the **CacheSize** property to zero.

2. Set **CacheSize** to the original value.

3. Use **FillCache** to refresh the cache.

Syntax:

*Recordset.***FillCache** [*Rows* [,*Start*]]

Where:

Recordset: A **Recordset** representing a **QueryDef** or a **TableDef** that contains data from an ODBC data source

Rows: An integer representing the number of rows to fill in the cache

Start: A string representing a bookmark. The cache is filled starting at the point indicated by the bookmark

Scrolling through the *authors* table in the *pubs* database of SQL Server is illustrated in Listing 23-5. The example in Listing 23-5 uses Jet caching. Performance is the modern equivalent of the technologists quest for the Holy Grail. The developer is continually searching for performance enhancements.

Improve Jet performance with caching

Listing 23-5 illustrates using the **FillCache** method. The ideal implementation is a **CacheEmpty** event, which doesn't exist. The only choice for the application is to count rows and refresh the cache at the desired threshold. The logic of Listing 23-5 is that it waits until the cache is empty before replenishing the cache. Ideally, the best time to refresh the cache is when the cache is at 50 percent or less and not when the cache is empty.

LISTING 23-5 Improve Jet performance by caching

```
Private Sub Caching_With_Jet_Click()
'(C) 1998 Bruce T. Prendergast
'    DBA Prendergast Consulting
'    DBA PCS
'    IDG Books Worldwide ISBN 0-7645-3123-9
'
'    Listing 23-5 Improving Jet performance
'    with caching
'
     Dim MyDB As Database
     Dim MyWS As Workspace
     Dim MyTdf As TableDef
     Dim MyTblFld As Field
     Dim MyRS As Recordset
     Dim CacheIndex As Integer
     Dim SourceConnectStr As String

     Set MyWS = DBEngine.Workspaces(0)
     Set MyDB = MyWS.Databases(0)
     '
     '    clean house
     '
```

```
On Error Resume Next
MyDB.TableDefs.Delete "Pubs Authors"
'
'    build my table attachment to SQL Server
'
Set MyTdf = MyDB.CreateTableDef("Pubs Authors")


'
'   Declare ODBC SQL Server data source
'
MyTdf.Attributes = dbAttachedODBC
'
'    connect
'
SourceConnectStr = "ODBC;DATABASE=Pubs;" & _
    "UID=sa;PWD=;DSN=Thor;"
MyTdf.Connect = SourceConnectStr
MyTdf.SourceTableName = "authors"
MyDB.TableDefs.Append MyTdf
'
'    number of authors records in cache
'
Const AuthorsCache% = 25
Set MyRS = MyTdf.OpenRecordset(dbOpenDynaset)
'
'   set cache size
'
MyRS.CacheSize = AuthorsCache
'
'    Loop through the records
'
CacheIndex = 0
MyRS.FillCache
If MyRS.RecordCount = 0 Then
    MsgBox "No records, exiting"
    Exit Sub
```

```
            End If
            Do Until MyRS.EOF
                CacheIndex = CacheIndex + 1
                If CacheIndex Mod AuthorsCache = 0 Then
                    MyRS.CacheStart = MyRS.Bookmark
                    MyRS.FillCache
                End If
                Debug.Print MyRS![au_id], _
                    MyRS![au_fname], MyRS![au_lname]
                MyRS.MoveNext
            Loop
            MyRS.Close
            MsgBox "Jet cache example was successful"
            Exit Sub
        End Sub
```

FindFirst, FindLast, FindNext, and FindPrevious

These methods will locate a record based on a search criteria. The search criteria is constructed as a WHERE clause string without the keyword WHERE. The record satisfying the search criteria becomes the current record.

Syntax:

Recordset.{**FindFirst** | **FindLast** | **FindNext** | **FindPrevious**} *Criteria*

Where:

Recordset: A **Recordset** object representing type dynaset or snapshot

Criteria: A string expression which is a SQL WHERE expression without the keyword WHERE

tip **Always check the NoMatch property after using a Find method.**

You should never use a **Find** operation on a remote attached table. Every **Find** operation uses SQL for locating the record. Using **Find** adds the overhead of the Rushmore query optimizer. Additionally, it returns only one record at a time from a remote data source. You can improve the situation by using the **FillCache** method; your best choice, however, is always to have a SQL statement do a bulk operation. Any **Find** operation can and should be replaced with a SQL statement.

The **Seek** method is another alternative. Microsoft documentation states that you cannot use the **Seek** method on an attached table, but you can open the table directly. See Listing 23-11 for an example of the **Seek** method.

concept link   **See Listings 23-1, 23-2, and 23-3 for examples of the FindFirst method.**

GetRows

GetRows is a new method of DAO 3.0 and is supported by both Jet and ODBCDirect. With the **GetRows** method you can specify how many rows to return. It is an extension of the **SQLExtendedFetch** ODBC application programming interface (API) function. The data returned by the **GetRows** method is moved into an unbound array.

Syntax:

*VariantArray = Recordset.***GetRows**(*NumberOfRows*)

Where:

VariantArray: A variable name of type **Variant**

Recordset: A Dynaset-type, Snapshot-type, or a Table-type **Recordset** object

NumberOfRows: The number of rows to return

The created array has two dimensions. The first subscript in the array is the relative field number starting with zero. The second subscript in the array is the relative row number within the array. The expression *VariantArray(1, 2)* addresses the second field of the third row.

The requested number of rows may not be returned because the **Recordset** object encountered an end-of-file condition. You can determine the returned row count with an expression that is similiar to:

```
ReturnRowCount = Ubound(VariantArray, 2) + 1
```

Improving Jet or ODBCDirect performance with GetRows

To illustrate the **GetRows** method, we use the *authors* table from the *pubs* database on SQL Server. Listing 23-6 illustrates the **GetRows** method.

LISTING 23-6 Improving Jet or ODBCDirect performance with GetRows

```
Private Sub SQL_Server_GetRows_Click()
'(C) 1998 Bruce T. Prendergast
'   DBA Prendergast Consulting
'   DBA PCS
'   IDG Books Worldwide ISBN 0-7645-3123-9
'
'   Listing 23-6 Improving ODBCDirect with GetRows
'
    Dim MyWS As Workspace
    Dim MyDB As Database
    Dim MyFld As Field
    Dim RetRows As Variant
    Dim RetCount As Integer
    Dim i As Integer
    Dim MyQry As QueryDef, MyRS As Recordset

    Set MyWS = DBEngine.Workspaces(0)
    Set MyDB = MyWS.Databases(0)
    '
    '   A zero-length string creates a temporary query
    '
    Set MyQry = MyDB.CreateQueryDef("")
    Dim SourceConnectStr As String
    SourceConnectStr = "ODBC;DATABASE=Pubs;UID=sa;" & _
        "PWD=;DSN=Thor;"
    '
    '   This is a pass-through query so the
    '   connect string is set first that
    '   stops Jet from parsing the SQL placed
    '   in the SQL property of the QueryDef.
    '
    MyQry.Connect = SourceConnectStr
    MyQry.ReturnsRecords = True
    MyQry.SQL = "SELECT au_id, au_fname, " & _
        "au_lname FROM authors;"
```

```
'
'   Create the snapshot and print the data
'
Set MyRS = MyQry.OpenRecordset()
'
'   Loop through the records. I am not using the
'   resultset row count but am depending on the
'   actual returned rows from a keyset
'
Do Until MyRS.EOF
    RetRows = MyRS.GetRows(10)
    RetCount = UBound(RetRows, 2) + 1
    For i = 0 To RetCount - 1
        Debug.Print RetRows(0, i);
        Debug.Print RetRows(1, i);
        Debug.Print RetRows(2, i)
    Next i
Loop
MsgBox "SQL GetRows query was successful"
Exit Sub
End Sub
```

Improve performance with SQL Count, avoiding the Recordset property RecordCount

The **GetRows** method requires a known record count, and the **RecordCount** property returns the count of records accessed. A count on a recordset is determined by executing the **Movelast** method on the recordset, an action that reads each row and impacts performance. The proper technique is to use the SQL aggregate **Count**. Listing 23-7 illustrates counting rows with the SQL aggregate function.

The SQL aggregate **COUNT** is quite efficient. When an index exists on a table, the SQL Server optimizer will read the index file for the row count. One or two disk accesses is much more efficient than reading the complete table. The Rushmore optimizer of the Jet Database Engine also accesses the index when an index exists. Of course, there is an obvious problem when there are no indexes. When there are multiple indexes available, SQL Server picks the best one, that is, the index that consumes the least resources.

A linked **TableDef** object will always have a record count of -1.

An interesting feature of Listing 23-7 is the use of the **Fields** collection and the default properties to return the value.

The expression:

*Recordset.***Fields**(*Ordinal*)

returns the value when the name of a field isn't known but the ordinal position in the **Fields** collection is known.

LISTING 23-7 Improving performance with SQL Count

```
Private Sub SQL_Count_Click()
'(C) 1998 Bruce T. Prendergast
'   DBA Prendergast Consulting
'   DBA PCS
'   IDG Books Worldwide ISBN 0-7645-3123-9
'
'   Listing 23-7 Improving performance with SQL
'
    Dim MyWS As Workspace, MyDB As Database
    Dim MyFld As Field
    Dim MyQry As QueryDef, MyRS As Recordset
    Set MyWS = DBEngine.Workspaces(0)
    Set MyDB = MyWS.Databases(0)
    '
    '   A zero-length string creates a temporary query
    '
    Set MyQry = MyDB.CreateQueryDef("")
    Dim SourceConnectStr As String
    SourceConnectStr = "ODBC;DATABASE=Pubs;UID=sa;" & _
        "PWD=;DSN=Thor;"
    '
    '   This is a pass-through query so the connect
    '   string is set first that stops Jet from
    '   parsing the SQL placed in the SQL property
    '   of the QueryDef.
    '
```

```
    MyQry.Connect = SourceConnectStr
    MyQry.ReturnsRecords = True
    MyQry.SQL = "Select COUNT(*) FROM authors ;"
    '
    '   Create the snapshot and print the returned data
    '
    Set MyRS = MyQry.OpenRecordset()
    '
    '   I can use the Fields collection and the
    '   default Value property to return the value
    '
    MsgBox "Record count is: " & MyRS.Fields(0)
    MsgBox "SQL aggregate Count was successful"
    Exit Sub
End Sub
```

Move

The **Move** method moves the current position of a record in a **Recordset** object. Trappable errors occur when attempting to move to an invalid bookmark or record position.

Syntax:

Recordset.**Move** *Rows* [, *Start*]

Where:

Recordset: A **Recordset** object name

Rows: A signed **Long** integer that represents the number of rows to move. This must be a positive value for forward-scrolling snapshots. The number of rows to move is relative to the current record position unless the *Start* parameter is specified.

Start: The name of a bookmark represented as a **String**.

Use of the move command is illustrated in Listing 23-8 with an event procedure that saves the contents of controls on an unbound form. After the record is saved, the **LastModified** property is used in the **Move** method to set the **CurrentRecord** property of the **Recordset**. This enables the application to scroll to the next row following the row just saved.

Recreating the CurrentRecord property with the Move method

Listing 23-8 also illustrates the move method with a special case. After the current row is updated, no current record exists. A current record is created by moving to a bookmark after an update or by using either of the two special uses of the **Move** method:

- MOVE 0 — This use of the **Move** method restores the previous version of the row or record, which reverts the last changes.

- MOVE 0, .LastModified — This use of the **Move** method makes the most recently modified record the current record. This should be done when changing records while browsing. Listing 23-8 is an example of this technique.

LISTING 23-8 Recreating the CurrentRecord property with the Move method

```
Private Sub Save_and_Scroll_Click()
'(C) 1998 Bruce T. Prendergast
'    DBA Prendergast Consulting
'    DBA PCS
'    IDG Books Worldwide ISBN 0-7645-3123-9
'
'    Listing 23-8 Recreating the CurrentRecord property
'
    Dim MyRS As Recordset
    Dim MyDB As Database
    Dim MyWS As Workspace
    Dim Criteria As String
    Dim User_Input As String
    Dim MyErr As Error
'*******************
'    begin scaffolding
'*******************
    Me![Last Name] = "Whiplash"
    Me![First Name] = "Snidley"
    Me![Credit Limit] = 5
    Me![Credit Used] = 0
    Me![Credit Type] = "Deadbeat"
```

```
'*******************
'   end scaffolding
'*******************
If IsNull(Me![Last Name]) Then
    Me![Last Name].SetFocus
    Exit Sub
End If
User_Input = Me![Last Name] & ""
If Len(Trim$(User_Input)) = 0 Then
    Me![Last Name].SetFocus
    Exit Sub
End If
'
'   Do the DAO thing
'
Set MyWS = DBEngine.Workspaces(0)
Set MyDB = MyWS.Databases(0)
Set MyRS = MyDB.OpenRecordset( _
    "tblEmployees", DB_OPEN_DYNASET)
User_Input = Trim$(Me![Last Name])
Criteria = "[Last Name] = " & Chr$(34) & _
    User_Input & Chr$(34)
MyRS.FindFirst Criteria

On Error GoTo Save_and_Scroll_Failure
MyWS.BeginTrans
If MyRS.NoMatch Then
    MyRS.AddNew
Else
    MyRS.Edit
End If
'
'   move the data
'
With MyRS
    ![Last Name] = Me![Last Name]
```

```
            ![First Name] = Me![First Name]
            ![Credit Limit] = Me![Credit Limit]
            ![Credit Used] = Me![Credit Used]

            ![Credit Type] = Me![Credit Type]
            .Update
        End With
        MyWS.CommitTrans
        '
        '  move to the new record since it may
        '   be the last record
        '
        MyRS.Move 0, MyRS.LastModified
        '
        '   Try to get the next one
        '
        MyRS.Move 1
        If MyRS.EOF Then
            With Me
                ![Last Name] = Null
                ![First Name] = Null
                ![Credit Limit] = Null
                ![Credit Used] = Null
                ![Credit Type] = Null
            End With
        Else
            With MyRS
                Me![Last Name] = ![Last Name]
                Me![First Name] = ![First Name]
                Me![Credit Limit] = ![Credit Limit]
                Me![Credit Used] = ![Credit Used]
                Me![Credit Type] = ![Credit Type]
            End With
        End If
        Me![Last Name].SetFocus
        MsgBox "Save and Scroll example was successful"
    Save_and_Scroll_Failure_exit:
```

```
    MyRS.Close
    MyDB.Close
    Set MyRS = Nothing
    Set MyDB = Nothing
    Me![Last Name].SetFocus
    Exit Sub
Save_and_Scroll_Failure:
    For Each MyErr In DBEngine.Errors
        MsgBox MyErr.Description
    Next MyErr
    MyWS.Rollback
    MsgBox "Update failed, and rolled back"
    Resume Save_and_Scroll_Failure_exit:
End Sub
```

MoveFirst, MoveLast, MoveNext, and MovePrevious

These methods have the greatest potential for misuse in DAO. The methods permit record positioning without a condition. Index usage with the **Seek** method on a table or bulk operations with a SQL statement are preferred alternatives to the use of these methods.

Syntax:

Recordset.{**MoveFirst** | **MoveLast** | **MoveNext** | **MovePrevious**}

Where:

Recordset : A dynaset-type **Recordset** object, snapshot-type **Recordset** object, or table-type **Recordset** object

MoveFirst, **MoveLast**, and **MovePrevious** cannot be used on forward-scrolling snapshots.

Poor technique: updating records with MoveNext, Update

Listing 23-9 illustrates the use of the **MoveFirst** and **MoveNext** methods and should not be used as a model for an application. It is a recreation of Listing 3-21, which used SQL for the update. As stated previously, always use SQL whenever possible. It's always faster, and upgrades to SQL Server are less painful.

LISTING 23-9 Poor technique: updating Records with MoveNext, Update

```
Private Sub Updating_With_DAO_Click()
'(C) 1998 Bruce T. Prendergast
'    DBA Prendergast Consulting
'    DBA PCS
'    IDG Books Worldwide ISBN 0-7645-3123-9
'
'    Listing 23-9 Updating records with
'    MoveFirst, Update. This is a procedural
'    solution and is considered poor technique.
'
    Dim MyRS As Recordset
    Dim MyWS As Workspace
    Dim MyDB As Database
    Dim MyTdf As TableDef
    Set MyWS = DBEngine.Workspaces(0)
    Set MyDB = MyWS.Databases(0)
    Set MyTdf = MyDB.TableDefs("tblInventory")
    Set MyRS = MyTdf.OpenRecordset(dbOpenDynaset)
    '
    '    This example fails programming standards
    '    by not encapsulation an update in a
    '    transaction and using a procedural loop
    '    when an SQL statement would accomplish
    '    the same task.
    '
    With MyRS
        .MoveFirst
        Do Until .EOF
            If ![Cost] > 100 Then
                .Edit
                ![Cost] = ![Cost] * 0.9
                .Update
            End If
            .MoveNext
        Loop
```

```
        .Close
    End With
    MsgBox "Poor technique using MoveFirst, " & _
        "Update completed successfully"
    Exit Sub
End Sub
```

OpenRecordset

A complete discussion of opening a **Recordset** object from a **QueryDef** object, a **Recordset** object, or a **TableDef** object may be found in the **OpenRecordset** method of the **Tabledef** object in Chapter 21.

Requery

This method updates the data in a **Recordset** object if the **Restartable** property of the **Recordset** object is true. If the optional **QueryDef** parameter is specified, then the **Restartable** property is ignored.

Syntax:

> *RecordSet.***Requery** [*NewQueryDef*]

Where:

> *Recordset:* A dynaset-type or a snapshot-type **Recordset** object

> *NewQueryDef:* This parameter was a new feature of Access 95 and may be the name of the original **QueryDef** object or it may be a new **QueryDef** object. If it is the original **QueryDef** object name, then the data is recreated with the **OpenRecordset** method of a **QueryDef** object. If necessary, parameters of the **QueryDef** object can be changed before running **Requery**.

Requery on Restartable Recordsets

Listing 23-10 illustrates using the **Requery** method. The code fragment is an **After_Update** event for a combo box. The contents of the combo box are used to access a record and display it on an unbound form. Both the **Recordset** object and the **Database** object are declared as **Static** variables so that they do not pass out of scope. The **Recordset** object and the **Database** object are defined when the **Recordset** object has a value of **Nothing.**

Listing 23-10 combines a static **Database** object and a static **Recordset** object with the **Recordset** object **Requery** method and the **Restartable** property. The purpose of this code fragment is to maintain the static objects and requery whenever necessary. Thus far, all the **Recordset** object methods presented always instantiate the object. This is not a common technique, but it does represent another alternative when dealing with unbound forms.

LISTING 23-10 Requery on Restartable Recordsets

```
Private Sub Restartable_Recordsets_Click()
'(C) 1998 Bruce T. Prendergast
'    DBA Prendergast Consulting
'    DBA PCS
'    IDG Books Worldwide ISBN 0-7645-3123-9
'
'    Listing 23-10 Requery a restartable
'    recordset. This example must be run more
'    than once. The first pass creates the
'    recordset object in a static variable.
'    The object is requeried on each subsequent
'    pass.
'
     Static MyDB As Database
     Static MyRS As Recordset
     Dim Criteria As String
     Dim User_Input As String
'********************
'    begin scaffolding
'********************
     Me![Last Name] = "Whiplash"
     Me![First Name] = "Snidley"
     Me![Credit Limit] = 5
     Me![Credit Used] = 0
     Me![Credit Type] = "Deadbeat"
'******************
'    end scaffolding
'******************
```

```
        If IsNull(Me![Last Name]) Then
            Exit Sub
        End If
        If MyRS Is Nothing Then
            Set MyDB = DBEngine.Workspaces(0).Databases(0)
            Set MyRS = MyDB.OpenRecordset( _
                "tblEmployees", dbOpenDynaset)
        Else
            If MyRS.Restartable Then
                MyRS.Requery
            End If
        End If
        User_Input = Trim$(Me![Last Name])
        Criteria = "[Last Name] = " & Chr$(34) & _
            User_Input & Chr$(34)
        MyRS.FindFirst Criteria
        If MyRS.NoMatch Then
            With Me
                ![First Name] = Null
                ![Credit Limit] = Null
                ![Credit Used] = Null
                ![Credit Type] = Null
            End With
        Else
        '
        '   move the data
        '
            With MyRS
                Me![First Name] = ![First Name]
                Me![Credit Limit] = ![Credit Limit]
                Me![Credit Used] = ![Credit Used]
                Me![Credit Type] = ![Credit Type]
            End With
        End If
        MsgBox "Restartable example was successful"
        Exit Sub
    End Sub
```

Seek

Microsoft Access's **Seek** method is the quickest way to access a record. It requires an index and is not burdened with the overhead of query optimization, which looks for the least-cost path. Optimizing isn't necessary because a table is opened directly.

Syntax:

> *Table.***Seek** *Comparison, Key1, Key2, . . .*

Where:

> *Table:* The name of an existing table-type **Recordset** object
>
> *Comparison:* A relation sting expression such as: "<", "<=", "=", "> =", or ">".
>
> *Key1, Key2:* The **Seek** method requires an existing index and these values correspond to fields in the index for the **Recordset** object.

The **Seek** method is a carryover from the halcyon days of the xBase systems and may not be a good choice. Direct access is always fast, but xBase systems are not relational even though they may present a relational interface. (Do you recall a single-tier ODBC driver from Chapter 12?)

Searches using string comparison values "=", "> =", or ">" start the search at the beginning of the recordset. Searches using comparison strings "<" or "<=" start the search at the end of the recordset and traverse backwards.

Always check the success of the **Seek** operation using the **NoMatch** property of the **Recordset** object.

> note ◀ **Field types must agree. If the comparison value is numeric, then the corresponding *Key* field must be numeric.**

The **Seek** method cannot be used on attached tables. Attached tables must be opened as dynaset-type **Recordset** objects, and the **Seek** method only applies to table-type **Recordset** objects. The **Seek** method may be used in an indexed sequential access method (ISAM) database when opened with the **OpenDatabase** method. **Find** and **Seek** are not available to a **Recordset** object in an ODBCDirect **Workspace**.

Using Seek on a table

Listing 23-11 illustrates the use of the **Seek** method on a table.

LISTING 23-11 **Using Seek on a table**

```
Private Sub Table_Seek_Click()
'(C) 1998 Bruce T. Prendergast
'    DBA Prendergast Consulting
'    DBA PCS
'    IDG Books Worldwide ISBN 0-7645-3123-9
'
'    Listing 23-11 a Table seek, the fastest
'    table access method
'
     Dim MyRS As Recordset
     Dim MyWS As Workspace
     Dim MyDB As Database
     Dim PartDescription As String
     Dim NewCost As Currency
     Set MyWS = DBEngine.Workspaces(0)
     Set MyDB = MyWS.Databases(0)
     Set MyRS = MyDB.OpenRecordset("tblInventory")
     '
     '    set the key to use
     '
     MyRS.Index = "Product Name"
     PartDescription = ""
     While (Len(PartDescription) = 0)
         PartDescription = InputBox( _
             "Enter Part Description")
         If Len(PartDescription) = 0 Then
             MsgBox "No part number specified"
             Exit Sub
         End If
         NewCost = 0
         While (NewCost = 0)
             NewCost = InputBox("Enter New Cost")
             If NewCost = 0 Then
                 Exit Sub
             End If
         Wend
```

```
                  With MyRS
                       .Seek "=", PartDescription
                       If .NoMatch Then
                            MsgBox "Part Number not found"
                       Else
                            .Edit
                            ![Cost] = NewCost
                            .Update
                       End If
                  End With
             Wend
             MyRS.Close
             MsgBox "Seek demonstration was successful"
             Exit Sub
        End Sub
```

KEY POINT SUMMARY

Jet supports direct record access by use of the different methods discussed in this chapter. This is a carryover from the days of flat file systems such as Paradox and dBase. Tables have relationships in a relational database, and direct access of tables is possible but is not recommended. SQL statements are recommended.

Microsoft continues to improve Jet performance. Jet supports caching, and both Jet and ODBCDirect support the **GetRows** method.

- DAO and Jet have a caching scheme that enhances the performance of **Recordset** objects.
- Both Jet and ODBCDirect support the **GetRows** method, which enhances performance.
- Cloning a Jet **Recordset** object is preferable to creating a new Jet **Recordset** object.
- The **FillCache** method is used to buffer records from an ODBC source. The method can only be used on dynaset-type **Recordset** objects.

This is the last DAO chapter. If you're still with me, persevere. Remote Data Objects (RDO) is next.

APPLYING WHAT YOU'VE LEARNED

These questions measure your understanding of how to use the **Recordset** object methods. Most of these questions are performance related. Your comprehension of this material will aid your understanding of the advantages and disadvantages of DAO database access technology. An intimate knowledge of DAO, ODBCDirect, RDO, ODBC, and OLE-DB is required to select the appropriate database access technology.

Instant Assessment

1. What happens when an **AddNew** and a **Move** operation are performed?

2. Why must a **MoveLast** or a **FindFirst** method be used before executing the **AddNew** method?

3. Where are newly inserted rows placed in a table?

4. When should the **CancelUpdate** method be used on a **Recordset** object?

5. Explain the **RecordCount** property.

6. A cloned record can be created with the **Clone** method of the **Recordset** object. Name two features of a cloned **Recordset** object.

7. What recordset type cannot be cloned?

8. When can the **FillCache** method of a **Recordset** object be used?

9. What is the syntax for retrieving values from a **Recordset** object when the field names are not known?

10. Name two requirements of the **Recordset** object **Seek** method.

11. Identify a restriction of the **Seek** method?

concept link **For answers to the Instant Assessment questions, see Appendix C.**

Lab Exercise

Lab 23.43 *Testing GetRows of Jet versus GetRows of ODBCDirect*

The object of Lab 23.43 is to compare the Jet and ODBCDirect **GetRows** methods. You should be able to cut and paste Listing 23-6 from the Access 97 CHAPTER23.MDB located in the EXAMPLES\CHAPTER23 folder of the CD-ROM that accompanies this book. Like many other labs, this lab also needs a remote SQL Server.

Create a Jet pass-through query. Be sure to set the **Connect** property before placing the SQL text in the **SQL** property. A Jet **QueryDef** object is compiled automatically. Setting the **Name** property of the Jet **QueryDef** object to a zero-length string makes it a temporary query. It also means that it is not a prepared query. Test the query and measure the response.

Use the same SQL text to create an ODBCDirect query. Because an ODBC-Direct **QueryDef** object is not compiled automatically, an ODBCDirect query can be compared to a Jet query. The required ODBCDirect coding is different and you must modify the code slightly. Remember that this query requires an ODBCDirect **Workspace** object and an ODBCDirect **Connection** object. Test the query and measure the response.

The network should be idle and you should repeat these tests. A fresh boot of the client and server flushes all caches. Both SQL Server and Windows NT maintain caches, and a fresh system boot is the only mechanism for ensuring that all caches are flushed.

Windows Architecture I

CHAPTER

RDO

24

About Chapter 24

This chapter is about Remote Data Objects (RDO). RDO first saw the light of day with Visual Basic 4.0 Enterprise Edition. Version 2.0 of RDO was delivered with Visual Basic 5.0 Enterprise Edition. Microsoft Access developers have their own version with ODBCDirect of Data Access Objects (DAO) 3.5.

ODBCDirect of the last chapter is the DAO equivalent of RDO. Microsoft Access developers clamoring for a lean and mean version of DAO will believe that ODBCDirect was developed just for them. I don't believe that to be true, and to understand why, we must look at the grand plan of component technology that Microsoft espouses.

The examples in this chapter may be found in the `CHAPTER24.VBP` Visual Basic 5.0 Enterprise Edition project located in the `EXAMPLES\CHAPTER24` folder of the CD-ROM located at the back of this book.

The examples in Chapters 24 to 26 use RDO 2.0 of Visual Basic Enterprise 5.0. The RDO 2.0 library is also used; however, the examples follow the RDO 1.0 syntax rules. This makes the examples usable in either RDO 1.0 or RDO 2.0.

RDO AS A TRANSITION TECHNOLOGY

What is the position of RDO in this ever-changing flux of database access technology software? RDO was the first OCX data control. The concept of an OCX data control was further polished with RDO version 2.0. ODBCDirect is a feature of DAO 3.5 and not a control in its own right, although it maintains the characteristics of RDO. There are advantages to both RDO and ODBCDirect. Neither has an SQL engine and ODBCDirect does not need the Jet engine. Microsoft Access developers will believe that ODBCDirect was developed just for them, as will Microsoft Visual Basic developers believe that RDO was developed just for them. This is not true on either count. It is all part of a grand plan by Microsoft to migrate everything — and I do mean everything — to component technology.

Is this the end of the road? Certainly not. Microsoft has already disavowed each of these technologies. Microsoft's publicly stated goal is to replace DAO and RDO with OLE-DB, a technology that is discussed later in this chapter. The import of this is that there is no foreseeable stability in database access software. So, in addition to the bug rate of Microsoft software, adopting these technologies is a dead-end path, unless, of course, you're an Internet maven. The only hope for a corporation in this maelstrom of change is to adopt the ODBC standard and avoid other database access technologies until Microsoft realizes its goal and stabilizes the software. But don't look for this to happen soon. Additionally, as of this date, OLE-DB is a bit sluggish.

I find quite interesting the material put forth by Microsoft's spin-doctors. Of course, the material is dated, but not too badly because RDO and ODBCDirect are both recent technologies. The literature for these technologies gives many promises of performance and extols their many virtues, but ignores the fact that all the features already exist in ODBC.

THE RDO DESIGN GOALS

By now you understand that RDO is a very thin ODBC wrapper. A natural question is: "If the wrapper is so thin, why have one at all?" I enumerate the design goals of RDO below and you can make your own decisions. For my part, I prefer what I call traditional ODBC because it has a standard and is not subject to the biannual mutations put forth by Microsoft.

Recall that ODBC is a Call Line Interface (CLI). It is not an object-oriented technology. I believe that RDO is only proof of the concept to move database access technologies to a component-based technology. RDO represents only one of many steps of *Where Do You Want to Go Today?* (the home page of Microsoft's Web site). The only feature missing from ODBC is object-oriented program management.

I COUNTED THE VOTES

The Visual Basic 4.0/5.0 keyword **Item** is defined as:

- A property in Visual Basic 5.0 documentation-on-line

- A method in Visual Basic 4.0 documentation-on-line

- A method in Visual Basic 4.0 Language Reference, Microsoft book number 58514

- A method in Visual basic 5.0 Language Reference ISBN 1-57231-507-5

There are other problems and the keyword **Item** is not an isolated issue. This chapter and subsequent RDO chapters use the RDO definitions found in Visual Basic 4.0.

High Performance ODBC Data Source Access

Microsoft has the ODBC application programming interface (API) along with the Visual Basic SQL (VBSQL) API, which is now a little long in tooth. Microsoft's goal was to leverage existing technology and enhance access to registered ODBC data sources. I don't see a leveraging occurring when the wrapper is so thin that the ODBC handles are visible, and ODBC can be used directly. Reverting to the ODBC API from RDO is possible, which is the back door that I mentioned. I tend to think of leveraging as doing something that couldn't be done otherwise.

Microsoft stacked the deck when they touted RDO as having superior performance to DAO. It's similar to comparing apples and oranges. RDO has built-in caching, while DAO does not. Any published performance differences are meaningless. Benchmark each technology's comparable features, and the performances may differ slightly.

The ODBC API can be accessed directly from DAO. An Access application can use the ODBC API directly, which is faster than a technology such as RDO, which is an ODBC wrapper. The ODBC API has minimal overhead because it can be used without objects and is a call-level interface. The extra RDO layer only adds overhead, which is illustrated in Figure 24-1. Figure 24-1 compares the basic architecture of RDO and DAO.

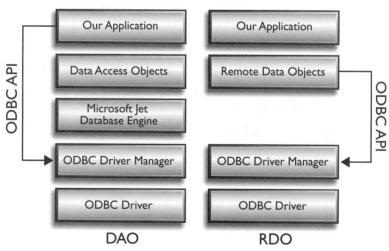

FIGURE 24-1 DAO, RDO, and the ODBC API.

Manage Return Codes

Capturing return codes from Microsoft SQL Server-stored procedures is difficult, that is, if you're not using the ODBC API. The one significant change in this area is the definition of the **rdoParameter** object. Each RDO prepared SQL statement has an **rdoParameters** collection. It could be argued that this is an improvement over ODBC, but the ODBC developer achieves the same result with a user-defined data type.

Manage Multiple Result Sets

Managing multiple result sets can be an issue. Microsoft C++ supports thread management and multiple resultsets are not an issue with C++. It is an issue with Microsoft Visual Basic. Version 4.0 is an interpreted language while version 5.0 is compiled; neither supports thread management. Lack of thread management in Visual Basic requires some enhancement to support multiple result sets. To be fair, Visual Basic 5.0 can do thread management only after some chicanery with a callback function. The point is, thread management is not designed into Visual basic 5.0.

This problem is one of application design. Each combo or list box on the desktop requires a separate query. Good programming practices limit the number of combo or list boxes on the desktop. **SQLMoreResults** is an ODBC API function, so the technology here is not new.

Microsoft should pay as much attention to the client-server paradigm as they have to the Internet. I'm certain you've noticed the **URL BindMoniker** process that gives control to the browser long before the browser page is complete. This technology doesn't exist for the client-server environment. Yes, a query is asynchronous, but access to the data is not possible until the query completes. I note that Microsoft Access has always had the feature of background population of data with the user able to access the currently loaded data.

Limit the Returned Rows

This is a nonissue because ODBC enables the developer to specify both the row set size and the returned result set size.

WHEN YOU DON'T READ THE ERROR MESSAGES

Not too long ago, I bid on converting a Novell xBase system to Microsoft SQL Server. It was for a local steel company and my bid included two servers that would mirror each other. For whatever reason, I didn't win the bid.

About six months later I got a telephone call. A programmer had come to work the previous night and shut down the SQL Server. The next morning the company could not restore its SQL Server from backup. The company had never tested its backups and I concluded that either the tape drive was defective or the database was corrupted and the generated backups were bad. As it turned out, the database was corrupted and the company had been making defective backups for months. The problem was that no one had ever looked at the log file for errors. My idea of a good backup is a pager that notifies the DBA of a failure.

The company was down for most of a month and had to hire a specialty company to recover its data. I estimate the company lost many times the cost of the mirrored system I had bid. Quoting myself from *Microsoft SQL Server Survival Guide*, "Enterprise problems require enterprise solutions."

Preset the Fatal Error Threshold

I can't ever imagine doing this. It is the responsibility of the application to filter the error messages. Setting a property and forgetting it is inviting disaster. I firmly believe that all error messages should be logged and reported. E-mail the error to the database administrator (DBA). If that doesn't work, e-mail it to the DBA's supervisor. Do whatever you must to draw attention to errors.

My point is not to suppress any messages, and not to provide any mechanism to suppress error messages. Take proactive action when an error occurs.

Use Server-side Cursors

The general consensus is thumbs down on server-side cursors. The DBA is always striving to improve server performance, and the last thing the DBA needs are client cursors wandering around on the server.

Execute Queries Asynchronously

Asynchronicity can be managed with threads in the application in lieu of adding complexity to the query mechanism.

Expose ODBC Handles

Why expose ODBC handles? Use ODBC directly. Of course, you can't always do this.

Reduce Memory Footprint

This is not a good design parameter. From my perspective, hardware became cheaper than labor in about 1975. It continues to get cheaper. Moore's law continues to be true, and computer power increases by fifty percent (I'm just being conservative, it's actually much more than fifty percent) or more every eighteen months. Windows NT is a virtual memory operating system. The footprint is meaningless because executable code is mapped into a virtual address space and memory is demand-paged as necessary. This is a nonissue.

The design goals that I've listed are from the Microsoft RDO documentation. My comments appear negative, but are not. The appearance is a result of my bias. My bias is what I call *meat and potatoes* computing. This paradigm is the everyday, realistic computing an enterprise does to stay in business. It certainly involves Microsoft software, but more importantly, it involves legacy software. Microsoft seems to have forgotten its roots. It is pushing hard for a component-everything world at the expense of all else. Considering the capabilities of RDO as compared to ODBC, I will choose ODBC over RDO because ODBC is a standard that can be depended on.

RDO: Slightly Better than DAO, But...

Let's start by quickly reviewing transaction isolation levels and the atomicity, consistency, integrity, and durability (ACID) properties of RDO. These issues were discussed in the section on ODBC, so you can skip the following review material if you recall the issues.

Transaction Isolation Levels

Transaction isolation is the degree of interaction between multiple concurrent transactions. There is, however, a simple rule that describes the issue: maximum consistency (highest transaction isolation level) is also the lowest concurrency level. Conversely, the highest concurrency level yields the lowest consistency level. Maximum performance (I call it apparent performance) yields the lowest consistency level. There is no clear answer other than to use the lowest possible transaction isolation level consistent with the ODBC application design.

There are four transaction isolation levels described in Table 24-1. The occurrence (or lack of) of the following phenomena defines these levels:

o **Dirty Read** is the reading of transaction data of another application before the data is rolled back. The data read is considered dirty if there is a possibility that the transaction can be rolled back. The data may or may not exist within the database even though it was read by an application.

o **Nonrepeatable Read** occurs when the application reads a row and gets a different result each time. Another application updated the row before the second read occurred.

o **Phantom Read** is a row that matches a search criterion but isn't seen by the application. A second application has added a new row that meets the search criterion after the initial rows were read.

note ▌ A **HoldLock** is not a lock, but an optimizer hint for the Microsoft SQL Server `SELECT` statement that maintains shared locks until a transaction is committed, rolled back, or the SQL statement completes. Maintaining a lock is the equivalent of the **Serializable** transaction isolation level.

TABLE 24-1 READ PHENOMENA AND TRANSACTION ISOLATION LEVELS

TRANSACTION ISOLATION LEVEL	DIRTY READS	NONREPEATABLE READS	PHANTOM READS
Read Uncommitted	X	X	X
Read Committed		X	X
Repeatable Read			X
Serializable			

Table 24-1 is understood when each term is defined:

- **Read Uncommitted:** No transaction isolation occurs. Transactions running at this level are typically read-only.

- **Read Committed:** The transaction is forced to wait until write-locked applications release data locks. This prevents the transaction from reading dirty data. The transaction holds a read lock if it only reads the row or a write lock if it updates or deletes the row. The transaction releases the read lock when it moves off the current row. Write locks are released when the transaction is rolled back or committed.

- **Repeatable Read:** The transaction waits until write-locks on rows are released by other applications. The transaction holds read-locks on all rows it returns to the application and write-locks on all rows it changes, deletes, or inserts.

- **Serializable:** The application holds read-locks on all rows affected by a read. A write-lock is placed on all rows affected by a change, delete, on insertion.

Concurrency

Increasing the level of transaction isolation reduces the level of concurrency. ODBC offers three distinct methods of concurrency control by a cursor and two categories of optimistic concurrency:

- **Read-Only:** The data is read-only and the cursor cannot update or delete data.

- **Locking:** The cursor establishes the lowest locking level consistent with application design. Very low concurrency levels occur when the locking design choice is Repeatable Read or Serialize.

- **Optimistic concurrency using row versions and optimistic concurrency using values:** Row versioning is a feature of an Oracle database, while values such as timestamps are a feature of Sybase and Microsoft SQL Server. Optimistic concurrency adopts the strategy of not locking the row until the update occurs. The current timestamp is compared with the prior timestamp to see if the data has changed. Conversely, pessimistic locking locks the row immediately. A developer uses this approach when collisions are commonplace and expected.

IF YOU CAN'T TRUST THE DOCUMENTATION, WHAT CAN YOU TRUST?

Table 24-1 reflects the ODBC 3.0 definition of transaction isolation levels with the **Repeatable Read** and **Serializable** isolation levels not equivalent. Microsoft SQL Server 6.5 documentation erroneously states that the **Repeatable Read** isolation level and the **Serializable** isolation level are equivalent. **Phantom Reads** cannot logically occur for a single SQL statement using the **Repeatable Read** isolation level. A single SQL statement in a transaction makes the **Repeatable Read** isolation level equivalent to the **Serializable** isolation level. **Phantom Reads** can occur when there is more than one SQL statement in the transaction at the **Repeatable Read** isolation level and the **HoldLock** optimizer hint is not used. The **Serializable** isolation level and the **Repeatable Read** isolation level are not equivalent when the transaction contains more than one SQL statement. The following is a quotation from *Microsoft SQL Server 6.5*, Books-On-Line:

"REPEATABLE READ or SERIALIZABLE: Indicates that "dirty reads," nonrepeatable reads, and phantom values cannot occur. REPEATABLE READ and SERIALIZABLE are interchangeable."

Database ACID Properties

An important feature of any database is transactions. The **ACID** properties declare the requirements necessary for consistent transactions:

- **Atomicity:** Either all or none of the transaction's changes are present when the transaction completes.

- **Consistency:** The transaction respects all business rules and referential integrity. Inconsistent updates can be done, but violate system integrity.

- **Isolation:** Transactions are isolated. SQL Server uses the SET statement:

```
SET TRANSACTION ISOLATION LEVEL
READ COMMITTED | READ UNCOMMITTED |
REPEATABLE READ | SERIALIZABLE
```

The SQL Server transaction isolation levels are maintained for the all-row sets of the transaction. On the other hand, Microsoft Access does not have a unified approach. Various recordset options can be used such as **dbSeeChanges**; however, the options must be set for every recordset, which is an error-prone mechanism. Microsoft Access does have the **IsolateODBCTrans** for the **Workspace** object, but that just isolates transactions from each other and does not manage transaction isolation levels.

The situation is different with RDO. A trappable error occurs with optimistic concurrency. The user then has the responsibility of refreshing the current row with **Move** 0 and then reapplying the **Edit** or **AddNew** methods. In DAO, the trappable error doesn't occur unless **dbSeeChanges** is used.

o **Durability:** Once the commit occurs, the transactions must be present even if the system fails. SQL Server supports this property with a log. Recoverability is guaranteed with SQL Server but not with Microsoft Access.

It should be obvious that RDO doesn't violate the rules on ACID properties because it doesn't have a database. It does, however, have concurrency problems. Concurrency must be set for every result set. Like Microsoft Access, the default concurrency for RDO is a "dirty read." I recommend against using either RDO transactions or Microsoft Access transactions on a database that has transaction isolation levels such as Microsoft SQL Server. The failure to use SET TRANSAC-TION ISOLATION LEVEL * can result in dirty or phantom reads as illustrated in Table 24-1.

RDO permits reading from locked pages even with pessimistic locking in effect for the **LockEdits** property of the **rdoResultset** object. RDO does not have the **dbSeeChanges** property of Microsoft Access and the possession of this property will not help matters. Simply changing DAO object names to RDO object names is not the conversion issue. The **LockEdits** property of a DAO **OpenRecordset** object is shown first.

DAO LockEdits Intrinsic Constants

dbPessimistic	Pessimistic concurrency is always the lowest level locking possible to ensure consistency. This is always at the expense of concurrency.
dbReadOnly	No updates allowed.
dbOptimistic	Record ID-based. Compares new and old record ID to see if changes have been made since the record was last accessed.
dbOptimisticValue	Value based. Each field is compared for changes, which is a very inefficient mechanism.
dbOptimisticBatch	Enables batch optimistic values.

The **LockType** property of an RDO **rdoOpenResultset** method is shown next.

RDO LockType Intrinsic Constants

rdConcurLock Pessimistic concurrency is always the lowest level locking possible to ensure consistency. This is always at the expense of concurrency.

rdConcurReadOnly No updates allowed.

rdConcurRowver Record ID-based. Compares new and old record ID to see if changes have been made since the record was last accessed.

rdConcurValues Value-based. Each field is compared for changes, which is a very inefficient mechanism.

ODBCDirect and RDO manage concurrency similarly. The only difference is that ODBCDirect has support for batch activities. Why, then, did Microsoft insist on changing intrinsic constants if they serve the same purpose? Microsoft apparently did not have you or me in mind when it was done. It is not clear why ODBCDirect and RDO do not have the same naming conventions. The technologies of ODBCDirect and RDO are very closely related. Microsoft appears to ignore conversion costs to newer or different technologies. An undue burden is placed on the developer by the renaming of intrinsic constants between releases and the fact that intrinsic constant naming rules apply only to the individual technologies.

Performance

I discussed this in our discussion of Microsoft Access and I'll repeat the argument here: Hardware is too fast today to believe that there are performance problems. Performance problems are solved with distributing the application.

There is another much more effective technique of managing performance. It's a matter of controlling user expectations. Managing expectations will do wonders for any enterprise. Of course, you can manage expectations about everything. Do I mind if my computer doesn't respond immediately? No, certainly not, because the expense is direct and very personal. That issue is often forgotten.

Looking at a specific driver's performance is not the issue. Flaws in architectural design will cost far more than the false economy of discussing the relative performance of one driver versus another driver. When you strip software down to its minimum essentials, you create dependencies that are neither scalable nor portable. Your stripped down driver may run faster, but it is a very hollow victory when the savings you realize are nothing compared to the cost of losing scalability and portability.

A relational database was one of the first stepping stones from the primordial ooze of computing. The relational database separated the definition of the data from the process. Traditional legacy programs have the definition of the data embedded within the program. When you reduce a database access tool to its barest essentials, you force the programmer to involuntarily place dependencies in the code (process), and that is what we are striving to avoid.

Consider the work that Microsoft Access must do for a query. (This discussion is in terms of ODBC so and you might want to review some of its functions.) When Microsoft Access doesn't know how many columns are in the incoming query, it calls **SQLNumResultCols** for the number of columns of a result set. Of course, if this information is buried in the code and known a priori, there is no reason to call this function.

The next task is to call **SQLDescribeCol** for each column in the result set. Our stripped down version of database access technology doesn't need to do this either because everything is assumed or known a priori about the columns. The next step in the process is to use a loop, on the columns based on the **SQLNumResultCols** count. Within that loop, the functions **SQLDescribeCol** and **SQLBindCol** are called successively for each column. This need not be done for every query, just the first one. This environment has the definition of the data defined within the data. Data definitions can be changed without impacting the process.

What happens when the definitions change in our stripped down hotrod? Tilt! The program stops running because the definitions of the data were not contained within the data. This doesn't usually happen with managed software in an enterprise, but when we're dealing with rapid application development (RAD) tools such as Visual Basic and PowerBuilder, the tail wags the dog. What do I mean by that? I mean that developers are setting the rules because technology is moving too fast for management to understand the issues.

If you learn anything from me, it is to understand that Microsoft is in the tool business. Tools are always a bottom-up design issue. Microsoft makes it incredibly easy to commit the sins of programming we've tried to avoid for years.

RAD tools promote programming before you really know what the problem is. The second issue is that of Microsoft's promoting technologies that are supposed to give higher performance but don't. This is a false economy; the supposed savings are not realistic because memory and CPU capability are always very cheap compared to labor costs. The hidden cost is the loss of scalability or portability coupled with Microsoft's disregard of the conversion costs.

A properly designed ODBC API application is the correct choice for enterprise applications. Yes, RDO and DAO can be used for desktop applications, but enterprise problems need enterprise solutions.

RDO AND DAO

RDO has the look and feel of DAO. It is simpler to program than DAO because there are fewer objects. There are some minor changes you must make because a DAO **Workspace** object is the equivalent of an **rdoEnvironment** object. There is a lot of parallelism, but there is not a one-to-one mapping of RDO objects to DAO objects. Table 24-2 enumerates the basic differences between RDO and DAO.

TABLE 24-2 MAPPING DAO TO RDO

DAO ITEM	*EQUIVALENT RDO ITEM*
DBEngine	rdoEngine
User	n/a
Workspace	rdoEnvironment
Database	n/a
Connection*	rdoConnection
TableDef	rdoTable
Index	n/a
Recordset	rdoResultset
Table	n/a
Dynaset	Keyset
Snapshot	Static

continued

TABLE 24-2 *(continued)*	
DAO ITEM	*EQUIVALENT RDO ITEM*
Dynamic*	Dynamic
Forward-Only*	Forward-Only
Field	rdoColumn
QueryDef	rdoPreparedStatement
Parameter	rdoParameter
* = new with ODBCDirect	

Binding in DAO is with the **data** control and the equivalent binding in RDO is with the *Remote Data Control* (RDC). Many of the RDO methods have the same name as the corresponding DAO method. Converting to RDO from DAO is not difficult.

Both RDO and DAO recordset (rowset if you're speaking RDOese) types are discussed below. They are nearly the same except RDO doesn't support a table-type cursor.

o **Table**: One of the original recordset definitions of Microsoft Access and the earlier version of Jet and DAO. RDO does not support this cursor type.

o **Snapshot**: Another original Access DAO recordset definition. The data is captured at a point in time and updates or deletions are not visible to the client. This recordset type is equivalent to an ODBC Static cursor. This is the RDO static-type rowset.

o **Dynaset**: A keyset recordset that may have either pessimistic or optimistic locking. The last of the original three recordset definitions. Deleted rows can be detected but newly added rows go undetected. This rowset type is a **Keyset** cursor in the ODBC API, the DAO ODBCDirect, and in RDO.

o **Forward-only**: This is a new recordset that uses a minimum of resources. If you recall from the last chapter, the ODBC default cursor is forward-only with a snapshot-type record. This recordset is equivalent to a **Snapshot** without a cursor. A forward-only cursor is available in the DAO ODBCDirect or in RDO. Only one row is visible.

- **Dynamic:** This is a new recordset type and it is reserved for access to ODBC-registered data sources. The dynamic-type cursor is limited to ODBCDirect in DAO and RDO. It is not available to Jet. A **Dynamic** cursor is equivalent to a **Dynaset** or **Keyset** cursor except that new rows are added to the keyset. A simpler way of saying this is that the keyset membership is not fixed. Bookmarks are not available with a **Dynamic** cursor.

Neither ODBCDirect of DAO nor RDO require a query processor. Microsoft touts this as reducing the footprint, which is a specious argument in a virtual memory system. With respect to ODBCDirect, the DAO reincarnation of RDO, it is an issue of automation objects not requiring a Microsoft Access license.

Microsoft Access has always had asynchronous queries. Data was available from queries while population of the result set occurred in the background. Microsoft states that ODBCDirect and RDO both support asynchronous queries. That is true: the application can continue execution and the **StillExecuting** property of RDO can be interrogated. The data, however, is not available until the query terminates. The problem with this implementation is that the **rdoResultset** object is not valid until the query completes. Microsoft may have created a problem for itself with this design approach. *I believe that it is a very basic design error to encapsulate result sets.* Encapsulation of process components is a very well understood technology, but the encapsulation of result sets is contrary to processing data; on the other hand, it is what you might expect if the orientation is from an e-mail perspective. Be patient and wait. Microsoft is afflicted with *COMitis,* which is to make everything a component. It may yet recover.

RDO AND ODBC

I consider ODBC a core technology. It is a standard, and the technology is not burdened with esoteric programming constructs. I don't mean to say that object-oriented programming isn't useful or valid, but there is a time and a place for everything. The very rich ODBC API function library supports every conceivable database access need.

RDO is an ODBC wrapper. The touted features of RDO are really ODBC API features. RDO exposes the ODBC environment handle **hEnv**, the connection handle

hDbc, and the statement handle **hStmt**. This exposes all facets of ODBC to the developer. Objects do not enhance ODBC. Objects simply make it easy for someone not skilled in using the ODBC API to access a relational database. Remember that Microsoft is intent on de-skilling and automating tasks. This makes its products usable by a larger community, which, in turn, increases its sales. RDO is another version of refried beans. RDO is nothing more than ODBC in a control.

WHAT IS RDO?

RDO is an independent database access technology designed for and used by Microsoft Visual Basic Enterprise Edition. RDO is designed specifically for the client-server environment and 32-bit systems. It is not a good technology choice for a Microsoft Access database.

RDO cannot be redistributed except as a technology within an OLE Automation server. RDO is only available in Microsoft Visual Basic Enterprise Edition. RDO may be used in a VBA environment of another tool only when Microsoft Visual Basic Enterprise Edition is installed on the same machine.

RDO objects support the concept of a **rdoEnvironment** object enabling access to remote-registered ODBC databases. This environment is similar to the **Workspace** object of Microsoft Access.

RDO is relational database oriented. To impress us that this is a relational database connectivity tool, Microsoft has changed its vernacular to agree with the terminology used in relational databases. Records are now called rows and fields are now called columns.

RDO is a very thin ODBC wrapper designed specifically for client-server environments. It is quite similar to ODBCDirect in that it does not support Data Definition Language (DDL) operations, updatable joins, or heterogeneous joins. Neither RDO nor ODBCDirect support bound forms, although a data control is available for each. Both DAO and RDO have a remote data control for binding purposes. These controls are not the same as the RDO control in Visual Basic Enterprise Edition named **MSRDC20.OCX** or Access 97's RDC named **MSRDC32.OCX**.

RDO is implemented as a series of objects. These objects have a strict hierarchical relationship, and the objects must all be instantiated in a specific order. Of course the order is also logical because a result set must have a query, a query must have a connection, a connection must have an environment, and an environment must have an engine. The objects are not object-oriented in the programming sense, but hierarchical in the classical sense. Object collections are defined, and both properties and methods of collections or objects are accessible to a Visual Basic Enterprise Edition application program.

RDO uses the ODBC API implicitly with RDO objects calling the ODBC driver manager. This is quite unlike the call-level interface of ODBC. RDO is an ODBC API wrapper for ODBC functions along with other methods and properties. The use of ODBC functions is implicit — not explicit — in that ODBC functions are not directly called when executing a RDO method.

RDO lacks some of Microsoft Access's flexibility in creating a result set. RDO can create a result set from a table, a SQL string, or from an **rdoPreparedStatement**. A result set cannot be created from another result set or from another query, both of which are features of Microsoft Access.

RDO ARCHITECTURE

The RDO architecture presented here is that of RDO version 1.0. The RDO examples in this section were tested with Visual Basic Enterprise Edition 5.0 and the Microsoft Remote Data Object Library 2.0. RDO 1.0 syntax is used in the examples so that they may run with either RDO 1.0 or RDO 2.0. The **rdoPreparedStatement** object in this library was replaced with the **rdoQuery** object. The essential enhancement to this object is persistence at design time for setting parameters. This is an advanced feature not necessary to an architectural understanding of RDO. The examples as constituted will work with either Visual Basic Enterprise Edition 4.0 or 5.0. To recap, this chapter uses 1.0 architecture with a 2.0 library. This makes the examples usable with either enterprise version of Visual Basic.

Figure 24-2 is a close look at the DAO architecture; Figure 24-3 is the RDO architecture. You can see that the RDO architecture is much simpler. You can see the parallels between the ODBCDirect of DAO in Figure 24-2 and the RDO architecture in Figure 24-3.

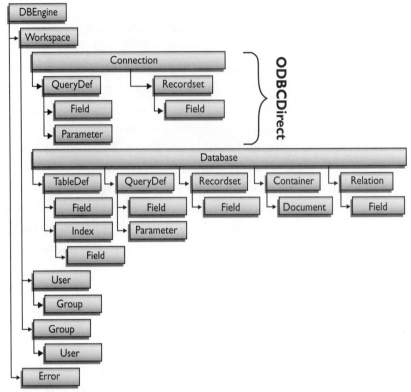

FIGURE 24-2   DAO 3.5 object hierarchy.

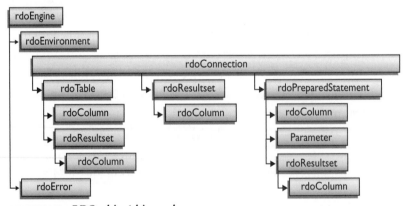

FIGURE 24-3   RDO object hierarchy.

RDO Architecture Detail

The following is a breakout of the methods and properties of all RDO objects. All objects are listed in their hierarchical order.

```
rdoEngine
 Methods: rdoCreateEnvironment, rdoRegisterDataSource
 Properties: rdoDefaultCursorDriver, rdoDefaultErrorThreshold,
 rdoDefaultLoginTimeout, rdoDefaultPassword, rdoDefaultUser,
 rdoVersion
 rdoErrors Collection
     Methods: Clear, Item
     Property: Count
     Error Object
         Properties: Description, HelpContext, HelpFile, Number,
         Source, SQLRetCode, SQLState
 rdoEnvironments Collection
     Methods: Item
     Property: Count
     Environment Object
         Methods: BeginTrans, Close, CommitTrans,
         OpenConnection, RollbackTrans
         Properties: CursorDriver, hEnv, LoginTimeout, Name,
         Password, UserName
         rdoConnections Collection
     Methods: Item
     Property: Count
             rdoConnection Object
                 Methods: BeginTrans, Cancel, Close, CommitTrans,
                 CreatePreparedStatement, Execute, OpenResultSet,
                 RollbackTrans
                 Properties: AsyncCheckInterval, Connect, hDbc,
                 Name, QueryTimeout, RowsAffected, StillExecting,
                 Transactions, Updatable, Version
```

```
rdoPreparedStatements Collection
    Methods: Item
    Properties: Count
    rdoPreparedStatement Object
        Methods: Cancel, Close, Execute,
        OpenResultset
        Properties: BindThreshold, Connect,
        ErrorThreshold, hStmt, KeysetSize,
        LockType, LogMessages, MaxRows, Name,
        QueryTimeout, RowsAffected, RowsetSize,
        SQL, StillExecution, Type, Updatable
        rdoColumns Collection
            Methods: Item
            Properties: Count
            rdoColumn Object
                Methods: AppendChunk, ColumnSize,
                GetChunk
                Properties: AllowZeroLength,
                Attributes, ChunkRequired, Name,
                OrdinalPosition, Required, Size,
                SourceColumn, SourceTable, Type,
                Updatable, Value
        rdoParameters Collection
            Methods: Item
            Properties: Count
            rdoParameter Object
                Properties: Direction, Name, Type,
                Value
    rdoResultSets Collection
        Methods: Item
        Properties: Count
        rdoResultset Object
            Methods: AddNew, Cancel,
            CancelUpdate, Close, Delete, Edit,
            GetRows, MoreResults, Move,
```

```
                    MoveFirst, MoveLast, MoveNext,
                    MovePrevious, Requery, Update
                    Properties: AbsolutePosition, BOF,
                    Bookmark, Bookmarkable, EOF, hStmt,
                    LastModified, LockEdits, Name,
                    PercentPosition, Restartable,
                    RowCount, StillExecuting,
                    Transactions, Type, Updatable
                    rdoColumns Collection (see
                    rdoPreparedStatement Object)
             rdoTables Collection
                Methods: Refresh, Item
                Properties: Count
                rdoTable Object
                    Methods: OpenResultset, Refresh
                    Properties: Name, RowCount, Type,
                    Updatable
                    rdoColumns Collection (see
                    rdoPreparedStatement Object)
```

WORKING WITH DEFAULT COLLECTIONS

In Figure 24-4, it is apparent that the **rdoEngine** is the only object without a collection even though it has a default collection. Another way of saying this is that no new **rdoEngine** objects can be created. There is only one RDO engine.

Result sets may be created from a connection directly. This means the SQL statement is neither prepared nor compiled. Tables and prepared statements also create result sets. Neither Figure 24-3 nor Figure 24-4 agrees with the Microsoft documentation. I have added the objects in the shaded area of Figure 24-4 to represent the fact that an **rdoResultset** may be created from both an **rdoTable** and an **rdoResultset**. This is a hierarchical relationship and not an object-oriented relationship even though objects have collections. Table 24-3 enumerates the RDO default collections.

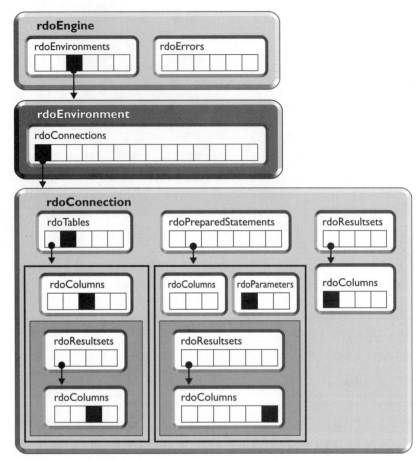

FIGURE 24-4   RDO default collections.

TABLE 24-3 DEFAULT COLLECTIONS OF RDO OBJECTS

OBJECT	DEFAULT COLLECTION
rdoResultset	rdoColumns
rdoConnection	rdoTables
rdoPreparedStatement	rdoParameters
rdoTable	rdoColumns

Default collection provides a shortcut mechanism for addressing lower level methods and properties. The **rdoResultset** collection has the **rdoColumns** collection, which is the default collection. Assume for the moment that the **Fields** collection contains two fields named *au_fname* and *au_lname* with ordinals of zero and one, respectively. Assume also that the collection belongs to the **rdoResultset** object **MyRS**. The following default collection illustrates where all four lines are equivalent and the first two lines use the default collection; that is, the **rdoColumns** collection is not referenced. Note that the default property of an **rdoColumn** object is the **Value** property.

```
Debug.Print MyRS!au_fname
Debug.Print MyRS("au_fname")
Debug.Print MyRS.rdoColumns("au_fname").Value
Debug.Print MyRS.rdoColumns(0).Value
```

WORKING WITH COLLECTIONS

All collections have a **Count** property and an **Item** property. Other than the **Clear** method of the **rdoErrors** collection, there are no other methods or properties of collections. There are, however, many properties and methods of objects within these collections, many of which have parallels in DAO.

Unlike DAO objects, RDO objects cannot be saved. All objects are automatically appended to their respective collection. When appropriate, a **Close** operation deletes an object from a collection.

Count

Count is the only property of all collections. The **Count** property of the **rdoErrors** collection is illustrated in the code fragment below.

A collection can be enumerated without knowing the collection count. Listing 24-1 illustrates the **For Each** construct of the **rdoErrors** collection.

LISTING 24-1 Enumerating the errors collection of RDO

```
Private Sub Enumerating_Click()
'(C) 1998 Bruce T. Prendergast
' DBA Prendergast Consulting
' DBA PCS
' IDG Books Worldwide ISBN 0-7645-3123-9
```

```
'
' Listing 24-1 Enumerating ODBC errors in RDO
'
    Dim RdoEnv As rdoEnvironment
    Dim RdoCon As rdoConnection
    Dim RdoPre As rdoPreparedStatement
    Dim MyRS As rdoResultset

    Dim MyErr As rdoError
    Dim c As rdoConnection
    Dim ConnectMode As Integer
    Dim WaitTime As Integer
    On Error GoTo Unable_To_Connect
        '
    '    create an RDO environment
    '
    ConnectMode = True
    Set RdoEnv = rdoEngine.rdoEnvironments(0)
    '
    '    connect with RDO connect string
    '
    Set RdoCon = RdoEnv.OpenConnection("", _
                rdDriverNoPrompt, False, _

        "DATABASE=Pubs;UID=sa;PWD=;DSN=Thor;")
    '
    ' a successful connection. Reset the connect
        '     mode so that all errors are printed.
    '
    ConnectMode = False
    '
    ' prepare a statement
    '
    Set RdoPre = RdoCon.CreatePreparedStatement("MyPS", _
      "SELECT au_lname, au_fname " & _
      "FROM authors " & _
      "WHERE au_lname LIKE 'G%' ")
```

```
'
' start an asynchronous query
'
Set MyRS = RdoPre.OpenResultset(rdOpenForwardOnly, _
    rdConcurReadOnly, rdAsyncEnable)
MsgBox "Breakpoint 1"
WaitTime = Timer
While (Timer - WaitTime) < 5
Wend
Do While RdoPre.StillExecuting
    If MsgBox("No query yet—keep waiting?", _
            vbYesNo) = vbNo Then
        RdoPre.Cancel
        Exit Sub
    Else
        WaitTime = Timer
        While (Timer - WaitTime) < 5
        Wend
    End If
Loop
While Not MyRS.EOF
    Debug.Print MyRS(0), MyRS(1)
    MyRS.MoveNext
Wend
MsgBox "RDO prepared statement was successful"
Exit Sub
Unable_To_Connect:
    For Each MyErr In rdoEngine.rdoErrors
        '
        ' this is a connection and I expect warning
        ' messages. Ignore just the With_Info messages
        ' such as "connecting to pubs", etc.,
        '
        If ((MyErr.SQLRetcode <> rdSQLSuccessWithInfo) Or _
          (ConnectMode <> 0)) Then
            MsgBox MyErr.Description & " State:" & _
            MyErr.SQLState & " SQLRetCode:" & _
```

```
                    MyErr.SQLRetcode & " NativeErrorCode:" & _
                    MyErr.Number
            End If
        Next MyErr
        Resume Next
End Sub
```

Item

Item is the only method of all collections. The method returns a specific member of a collection. It is the default method of all collections and is the ordinal one based. The following two lines are equivalent:

```
Debug.Print rdoCon(1)
Debug.Print rdoCon.Item(1)
```

Clear

Clear is only a method of the **rdoErrors** collection. It clears all objects from the **rdoErrors** collection.

Key Point Summary

RDO is a feature of Microsoft Visual Basic Enterprise. RDO can only be used when Microsoft Visual Basic Enterprise is installed on the same system, which limits the usability of the technology. Granted, the software occupies a smaller footprint than Access; a better choice for the developer is ODBCDirect of DAO 3.5, which needs neither an Access license nor Visual Basic Enterprise. RDO may only be redistributed when embedded in an Automation server. Your understanding of this technology may be moot because Microsoft has already announced that both DAO and RDO will be replaced by the new OLE-DB database access technology (see Chapters 29 to 32). These issues were discussed in this chapter:

- RDO is a very thin ODBC wrapper.

- The ODBCDirect technology is a direct descendant of RDO; however, Microsoft changed the nomenclature when creating ODBCDirect.

- RDO is a component of Visual Basic Enterprise Edition.

- RDO is designed as a client-server tool to access ODBC data sources.

- RDO is a 32-bit-only tool.

- RDO cannot be redistributed except as an embedded technology in an Automation server.

- RDO does not support bound forms, DDL statements, updatable joins, or heterogeneous joins. However, a RDC control is available.

APPLYING WHAT YOU'VE LEARNED

An understanding of each of the database access technologies is one of the keys for selecting the proper database access technology. These questions assess your understanding of the RDO issues discussed in this chapter. The laboratory measures the performance of a DAO, RDO, and an ODBCDirect query. An understanding of the performance issues will enhance your ability to select the appropriate database access technology.

Instant Assessment

1. Name the first object in the RDO hierarchy.

2. Name a property of all collections.

3. Which RDO object does not have a default collection?

4. Give an example of a default collection.

5. Name an object that is automatically appended to a collection.

6. When does RDO ignore the **Close** method?

7. Name a collection where objects cannot be removed with the **Close** method.

8. Name three objects that share the same collection.

9. Name two DAO and Jet features not available in RDO.

 concept link   **For answers to the Instant Assessment questions, see Appendix C.**

Lab Exercise

Lab 24.44 *Comparing Jet, ODBCDirect, and RDO query performance*

WA I

The goal of Lab 24.44 is to measure the performance of RDO versus ODBCDirect and DAO. A remote SQL Server should be available.

Choose a table with a reasonable amount of data. A minimal amount of data is not always an effective measure of performance.

Construct these three queries. The first query is a DAO pass-through query. Don't be afraid to use some tricks. Remember that we are comparing DAO performance against RDO. The first trick is to use the **GetRows** method. This will stop Jet from pinging the server on every new row. The other trick is to use caching. Remember that RDO is already cached and the performance comparisons between Jet and RDO are blatantly dishonest.

The second query is an ODBCDirect query that returns the same information. The third query is RDO. Use the same SQL text for the RDO query.

You'll find that Jet is slower than RDO, but not by the margins publicized.

 Windows Architecture I

CHAPTER

Working with RDO Objects

25

About Chapter 25

This is dirty fingernails time again. Chapter 25 discusses Remote Data Objects (RDO) in the default hierarchical order: **rdoEngine**, **rdoError**, **rdoEnvironment**, **rdoConnection**, and **rdoTable**. **rdoPreparedStatement, rdoResultset, rdoColumn,** and **rdoParameter** are reserved for the next chapter.

An example is given for the common method of an object in the discussion of the object. The reader is encouraged to try the examples and replicate the results. RDO properties are listed by name for each object but are not discussed in detail. However, some of the properties must be used to make the examples work.

This chapter uses RDO 2.0 of Visual Basic Enterprise 5.0. The Remote Data Objects 2.0 library is used, but the examples follow the RDO 1.0 syntax rules. This makes the examples usable in either RDO 1.0 or RDO 2.0.

Just in case you've thumbed directly to this chapter, Microsoft has significant errors in RDO 2.0 of Visual basic 5.0. The Visual Basic 4.0/5.0 keyword **Item** is defined as:

- A property in Visual Basic (VB) 5.0 documentation-on-line
- A method in Visual Basic 4.0 documentation-on-line
- A method in Visual Basic 4.0 Language Reference (Microsoft book 58514)
- A method in Visual Basic 5.0 Language Reference (ISBN 1-57231-507-5)

There are other problems such as using the Visual Basic 5.0 object browser and "seeing" the **Add** method of the **rdoEnvironments** collection. Try to use the method and you will quickly realize that the documentation borders on pure fiction. A new **rdoEnvironment** object is automatically appended to the **rdoEnvironments** collection, and an **Add** method isn't needed. Additionally, the **Add** method doesn't work even though it is documented in VB 5.0 and can be browsed.

The examples in this chapter may be found in the CHAPTER25.VBP Visual Basic 5.0 Enterprise Edition project located in the EXAMPLES\ CHAPTER25 folder of the CD-ROM located at the back of this book.

This chapter and subsequent RDO chapters use the RDO 1.0 definitions as defined in Visual Basic 4.0. Exceptional new RDO 2.0 features such as events of the RDO 2.0 **rdoConnection** object are discussed, but the context of the chapter remains RDO 1.0.

THE RDOENGINE OBJECT

The **rdoEngine** is the first object used in the RDO hierarchy to obtain access to other objects. It is not a member of a collection, and **rdoEngine** objects cannot be created; the **rdoEngine**, however, can be initialized. The **rdoEngine** and the **rdoEnvironments** collection of Figure 25-1 are our first stop in the RDO architecture.

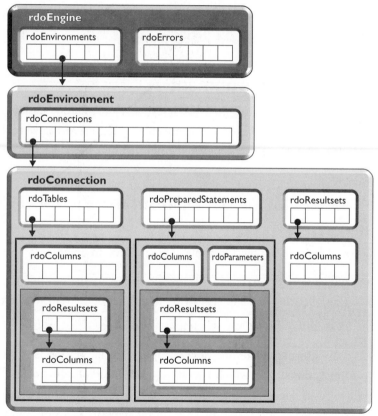

FIGURE 25-1   The rdoEngine.

rdoEngine Object Definition

Methods: **rdoCreateEnvironment, rdoRegisterDataSource**

Properties: **rdoDefaultCursorDriver, rdoDefaultErrorThreshold, rdoDefaultLoginTimeout,**

rdoDefaultPassword, rdoDefaultUser, rdoVersion, rdoLocaleID

Collections: **rdoEnvironments, rdoErrors**

A **rdoEngine** represents a remote Open Database Connectivity (ODBC) data source. This object is the first object in the hierarchy and is a predefined object.

Before creating this object you must set a reference to the **Microsoft Remote Data Object 1.0** library for Visual Basic Enterprise Edition 4.0 or to **Microsoft Remote Data Object 2.0** library for Visual Basic Enterprise Edition 5.0.

The ODBC data source must be registered before accessing it with the **rdoEngine**.

rdoCreateEnvironment

This method creates the equivalent of a session. More than one session can be created, and each session can have many connections. The newly created **rdoEnvironment** object is automatically appended to the **rdoEnvironments** collection.

Syntax:

Set *rdoEnviron* = **rdoEngine.rdoCreateEnvironment**(*Name, User, Password*)

Where:

rdoEnviron: An object variable of type **rdoEnvironment**

Name: A **String** variable representing the user name

User: A **String** variable identifying the owner of the **rdoEnvironment** object

Password: A **String** variable representing the user password

An alternative method of creating the initial session is to use the default **rdoEnvironments**(0), which is created when the **rdoEngine** object is initialized. When this is done the *Name* parameter is initialized from **rdoDefaultUser** and the *Password* parameter is initialized from **rdoDefaultPassword**. An example of this technique is shown in Listing 25-1.

A **rdoEnvironment** object is removed from the **rdoEnvironments** collection when it is closed. The **rdoEnvironment**(0), which is the default session object, cannot be closed.

Only the **UserName** and **Timeout** properties can be modified after a **rdoEnvironment** object is created.

 note

Transactions are global to an environment. When a CommitTrans operation is performed, all of the open transactions of all connections of the rdoEnvironment object are committed.

`LISTING 25-1` Starting the rdoEngine

```
Private Sub Starting_rdoEngine_Click()
'(C) 1998 Bruce T. Prendergast
' DBA Prendergast Consulting
' DBA PCS
' IDG Books Worldwide ISBN 0-7645-3123-9
'
' Listing 25-1 starting the rdoEngine
'
    Dim RdoEnv As rdoEnvironment
    Dim RdoCon As rdoConnection
    Dim MyErr As rdoError
    Dim c As rdoConnection
    Dim ConnectMode As Integer
    On Error GoTo Unable_To_Connect
    '
    '   create an RDO environment
    '
    ConnectMode = True
    Set RdoEnv = rdoEngine.rdoEnvironments(0)
    '
    '   connect with RDO connect string
    '
    Set RdoCon = RdoEnv.OpenConnection( _
        "", rdDriverNoPrompt, True, _
        "DATABASE=Pubs;UID=sa;PWD=;DSN=Thor;")
```

```
        '
        ' a successful connection. Reset the connect
        ' mode so that all errors are printed.
        '
        ConnectMode = False
        '
        '   verify that the connection exists
        '
        For Each c In rdoEngine.rdoErrors
            Debug.Print "Connection: " & c.Name
        Next c
        '
        ' this is an experiment
        '
        rdoEngine.rdoEnvironments(0).Close
        MsgBox "RDO connection completed successfully"
        Exit Sub
Unable_To_Connect:
        For Each MyErr In rdoEngine.rdoErrors
            '
            ' this is a connection and I expect warning
            ' messages. Ignore just the With_Info messages
            ' such as "connecting to pubs", etc.,
            '
            If ((MyErr.SQLRetcode <> rdSQLSuccessWithInfo) Or _
              (ConnectMode <> 0)) Then

              MsgBox MyErr.Description & " State:" & _
                MyErr.SQLState & " SQLRetCode:" & _
                MyErr.SQLRetcode & " NativeErrorCode:" & _
                MyErr.Number
            End If
        Next MyErr
        Resume Next
End Sub
```

rdoRegisterDataSource

RDO only communicates with registered ODBC data sources. The **rdoRegister DataSource** method registers a new data source or updates existing registered data sources.

Syntax:

> *rdoEngine*.**rdoRegisterDataSource** *DSName, Driver, Silent, Attributes*

Where:

DSName: The name of the data source. Typically, the Windows NT Server name, although this isn't a requirement.

Driver: A string variable identifying the ODBC driver name. This is not a dynamic link library (DLL) name but the registered ODBC name, which is typically *SQL Server*. The *Driver* name must be registered before the data source can be registered.

Silent: No dialog box is shown when this value is **True**. An error occurs for missing information. Set the parameter to **False** and note the parameters in the dialog box. Once they are recorded correctly, permanently set this parameter to **True**.

Attributes: These are the parameter values of the dialog box entered in carriage return-delimited string format.

 concept link **Listing 25-2 illustrates registering an ODBC data source.**

THE RDOERRORS COLLECTION

The **rdoErrors** collection is the accumulation of errors that occur during execution. It is an accumulation because an error at a lower level quite often precipitates other errors.

rdoErrors Collection Definition

Methods: **Clear**, **Item**

Properties: **Count**

rdoError object

Methods: none

Properties: **Description, HelpContext, HelpFile, Number, Source, SQLRetCode, SQLState**

The **rdoEngine** supports the **Errors** collection. The **rdoDefaultErrorThreshold** property of the **rdoEngine** contains the default value for the **ErrorThreshold** property of the **RemoteData** object and the **rdoPreparedStatement** object. The **rdoDefaultErrorThreshold** property does not limit errors unrelated to either the **RemoteData** object or the **rdoPreparedStatement** object. For the reasons that have been discussed, errors should not be inhibited.

The secondary issue is that error logging significantly impacts performance, even though the errors are of a warning nature. Identify all errors and take corrective measures to prevent their occurrence. It is not always the unreported fatal error that is a problem, but the numerous *With_Info* messages which subtract from the overall performance of a system.

This is not a course on programming; simply exposing the error and crashing the application is not sufficient. Visual Basic for Applications (VBA) has the feature that an error handler cannot handle an error that occurs within the error handler. This can be used to our advantage. When an error occurs, do the necessary bookkeeping and then execute the **RAISE** statement. The parameter values for this command will have been filled in, and the next error handler in the stack will process the error message. This is called *unwinding the stack*.

The primary cause of an error is the first object in the stack or **rdoErrors**(0). The errors in the stack always represent only one error. The multitude of error objects is each of the different software layers reporting their disenchantment with the miscreant service.

The **rdoError** object has no methods while the **rdoErrors** collection has only the **Clear** method, which clears the collection. You'll find that all the RDO program examples have simple error reporting. Listing 25-2 illustrates using the **rdoRegisterDataSource** and the enumeration of the **rdoErrors** collection.

LISTING 25-2 Registering an ODBC data source and enumerating the Errors collection

```
Private Sub Register_DataSource_Click()
'(C) 1998 Bruce T. Prendergast
' DBA Prendergast Consulting
```

```
' DBA PCS
' IDG Books Worldwide ISBN 0-7645-3123-9
'
' Listing 25-2 Registering a data source and
' enumerating the errors collection.
'

    Dim RdoEnv As rdoEnvironment
    Dim RdoCon As rdoConnection

    Dim MyErr As rdoError
    Dim c As rdoConnection
    Dim ConnectMode As Integer
    On Error GoTo Unable_To_Connect

    Dim Attr As String
    '
    ' Build keywords string.
    '
    Attr = "Description=SQL Server on server Thor" & _
      Chr$(13)
    Attr = Attr & "OemToAnsi=No" & Chr$(13)
    Attr = Attr & "Server=Thor" & Chr$(13)
    Attr = Attr & "Network=DBNMPNTW" & Chr$(13)
    Attr = Attr & "Address=\\Thor\PIPE\SQL\QUERY" & _
      Chr$(13)
    Attr = Attr & "Database=Pubs"

    '
    '   create an RDO environment
    '
    Set RdoEnv = rdoEngine.rdoEnvironments(0)
    '
    ' Update the Registry
    '
    rdoEngine.rdoRegisterDataSource "Thor", _
      "SQL Server", True, Attr
    '
```

```
' The code below is shown as inline however
' the code above is a one-time event.
'
ConnectMode = True
'
'    connect with RDO connect string
'
 Set RdoCon = RdoEnv.OpenConnection( _
     "", rdDriverNoPrompt, True, _
     "DATABASE=Pubs;UID=sa;PWD=;DSN=Thor;")
'
' a successful connection. Reset the connect
' mode so that all errors are printed.
'
ConnectMode = False
'
'    verify that the connection exists
'
For Each c In rdoEngine.rdoErrors
    Debug.Print "Connection: " & c.Name
Next c

MsgBox "Data source registration was successful"
Exit Sub
Unable_To_Connect:
    For Each MyErr In rdoEngine.rdoErrors
       '
       ' this is a connection and I expect warning
       ' messages. Ignore just the With_Info messages
       ' such as "connecting to pubs", etc.,
       '
       If ((MyErr.SQLRetcode <> rdSQLSuccessWithInfo) Or _
         (ConnectMode <> 0)) Then
           MsgBox MyErr.Description & " State:" & _
           MyErr.SQLState & " SQLRetCode:" & _
           MyErr.SQLRetcode & " NativeErrorCode:" & _
           MyErr.Number
```

```
        End If
      Next MyErr
      Resume Next
      Exit Sub
End Sub
```

THE RDOENVIRONMENTS COLLECTION

The **rdoEnvironment** object of Figure 25-2 is our next step in the RDO hierarchy.

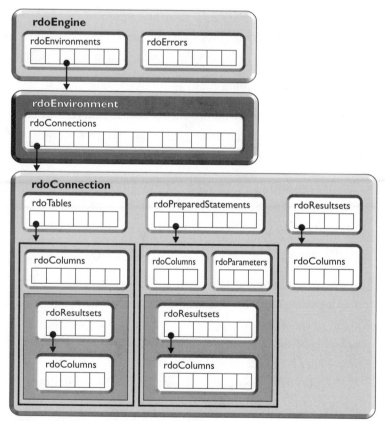

FIGURE 25-2   The rdoEnvironment object.

A session is an environment. It is a host for connections. It contains open databases, transactions are global to an environment, and it operates within a security context. New environments are automatically appended to the **rdoEnvironments** collections, and **rdoEnvironment** objects are removed from the collection when the object is closed. The default environment cannot be closed and has the name *Default_Environment*, which is the object **rdo Environments**(0). The **rdoCreateEnvironment** method is not used to create the default **rdoEnvironments**(0). **rdoEnvironments**(0) is created automatically at the first reference.

rdoEnvironments *Collection Definition*

> Methods: **Item**
>
> Properties: **Count**
>
> ***rdoEnvironment*** *object*
>
>> Methods: **BeginTrans, Close, CommitTrans, OpenConnection, RollbackTrans**
>>
>> Properties: **CursorDriver, hEnv, LoginTimeout, Name, Password, UserName**
>>
>> Collections: **rdoConnections**

Be aware that the ODBC driver may choose a server-side cursor, which may not be desired. The rules governing cursor selection are set with the **CursorDriver** property, which has these optional values:

rdUseIfNeeded (0) — The ODBC driver will choose the appropriate style of cursors. Server-side cursors are used if they are available.

RdUseODBC (1) — RDO uses the ODBC cursor library.

RdUseServer (2) — RDO uses server-side cursors.

There is nothing innately wrong with these parameters, but the placement of this property in the **rdoEnvironment** object rather than in the **rdoResultset** object is highly questionable. We may see a few design changes here, but then maybe not after you read the next chapter. Mix and match are possible, and changing this property does not affect existing connections.

The **rdoEnvironment** object exposes the ODBC environment handle **hEnv** to all objects of the environment. This makes all ODBC application programming interface (API) environment functions available to the RDO environment.

BeginTrans, CommitTrans, and RollbackTrans

These methods are used to mange transactions from the RDO environment. Nested transactions are only supported if your data source supports them.

Syntax:

> *Object*.**BeginTrans** | **CommitTrans** | **RollbackTrans**

Where:

> *Object:* Either a **rdoEnvironment** object or a **rdoConnection** object

A transaction example is shown in Listing 25-3. An update is made to the *Authors* table of the *Pubs* database on Microsoft SQL Server. The transaction is immediately rolled back, the target column is interrogated for the current value, and the appropriate message is issued.

 note **The transaction example illustrated in Listing 25-3 was tested with both a rdoConnection object and a rdoEnvironment object. I encourage you to always use a rdoEnvironment object so you'll not forget that transactions are global to the environment.**

The example in Listing 25-3 has three distinct error-handling routines. The first captures any errors during a connection. The second routine performs a **RollbackTrans** on an error and reports all messages. The last error-handling routine is actuated after the rollback is complete.

LISTING 25-3 A RDO transaction

```
Private Sub Transaction_Click()
'(C) 1998 Bruce T. Prendergast
' DBA Prendergast Consulting
' DBA PCS
' IDG Books Worldwide ISBN 0-7645-3123-9
'
' Listing 25-3 an RDO transaction
'

    Dim RdoEnv As rdoEnvironment
    Dim RdoCon As rdoConnection
    Dim RdoPre As rdoPreparedStatement
```

```
Dim MyRS As rdoResultset

Dim MyErr As rdoError
Dim c As rdoConnection
Dim ConnectMode As Integer
On Error GoTo Unable_To_Connect
'
'    create an RDO environment
'
ConnectMode = True
Set RdoEnv = rdoEngine.rdoEnvironments(0)


'
'    connect with RDO connect string
'
Set RdoCon = RdoEnv.OpenConnection( _
    "", rdDriverNoPrompt, False, _
    "DATABASE=Pubs;UID=sa;PWD=;DSN=Thor;")
'
' a successful connection. Reset the connect
' mode so that all errors are printed.
'
ConnectMode = False
'
' prepare a statement
'
Set RdoPre = RdoCon.CreatePreparedStatement( _
    "MyPS", "UPDATE authors " & _
    "SET au_fname='John' " & _
    "WHERE au_id = '172-32-1176'")
'
' Do the action query
'
On Error GoTo Transaction_Error
RdoEnv.BeginTrans
```

```
    RdoPre.Execute
    RdoEnv.RollbackTrans
    On Error GoTo Normal_Error
    '
    ' now lets see that we didn't change anything
    '
    RdoPre.Close
    Set RdoPre = RdoCon.CreatePreparedStatement( _
      "MyPS", "SELECT au_fname " & _
      "FROM authors " & _
      "WHERE au_id = '172-32-1176'")
    Set MyRS = RdoPre.OpenResultset( _
      rdOpenForwardOnly, rdConcurReadOnly)
    If MyRS(0) <> "Johnson" Then
      MsgBox "Rollback failed"
      Exit Sub
    Else
      MsgBox "RDO Transaction was successful"
    End If
    Exit Sub
Unable_To_Connect:
    For Each MyErr In rdoEngine.rdoErrors
        '
        ' this is a connection and I expect warning
        ' messages. Ignore just the With_Info messages
        ' such as "connecting to pubs", etc.,
        '
        If ((MyErr.SQLRetcode <> rdSQLSuccessWithInfo) _
          Or (ConnectMode <> 0)) Then
          MsgBox MyErr.Description & " State:" & _
            MyErr.SQLState & " SQLRetCode:" & _
            MyErr.SQLRetcode & " NativeErrorCode:" & _
            MyErr.Number
        End If
    Next MyErr
```

```
        Resume Next
Transaction_Error:
    RdoEnv.RollbackTrans
    MsgBox "Transaction failed and rolled back"
Normal_Error:
  For Each MyErr In rdoEngine.rdoErrors
    MsgBox MyErr.Description & " State:" & _
      MyErr.SQLState & " SQLRetCode:" & _
      MyErr.SQLRetcode & " NativeErrorCode:" & _
      MyErr.Number
    Next MyErr
    Resume Error_Exit
Error_Exit:
    Exit Sub
End Sub
```

Close

The **Close** method may be used for any **rdoEnvironment** object other than the default environment object. Open transactions in an environment are rolled back on a close. Action queries that are not wrapped in a transaction may be terminated with unpredictable results.

Syntax:

   Object.**Close**

Where:

   Object: An object of type **rdoEnvironment, rdoConnection, rdoPreparedStatement, rdoResultset**

   RDO objects are closed when the object variable goes out of scope or the **Close** method is explicitly applied to the object. Objects are closed automatically when they go out of scope. RDO objects are not persistent and closing a RDO object removes it from the respective collection.

OpenConnection

The **rdoConnection** object is used for managing data source connections. Browsing typically takes two connections. One is used for updating and the other is used for queries.

As stated previously, the RDO syntax we're discussing is RDO 1.0 of Visual Basic 4.0 and not RDO 2.0 of Visual Basic 5.0. RDO 2.0 supports the *Options* parameter of the **OpenConnection** method, which permits opening a connection asynchronously. Listing 19-1 of Chapter 19 is an example comparable to the RDO 2.0 **OpenConnection** method, which is not discussed here.

Syntax:

> **Set** *rdoCon = rdoEnv*.**OpenConnection**(*DSName, Prompt, ReadOnly, Connect*)

Where:

rdoCon: A variable of type **rdoConnection**

RdoEnv: A Variable of type **rdoEnvironment**

DSName: A **String** containing the data source name. The name must be a registered ODBC data source. If no name is provided, the user is prompted unless *Prompt* is set to **rdDriverNoPrompt**. In this situation, an error occurs.

Prompt: One of: **rdDriverNoPrompt**, **rdDriverPrompt**, **rdDriverComplete**, or **rdDriverCompleteRequired**

ReadOnly: The database is open read-only when this field is **True**.

Connect: A **String** representing the connection parameters to the database. It should be the same as the data access objects (DAO) connect string except the clause *"ODBC;"* is not used.

All RDO examples contain code for opening a connection, and additional examples are unwarranted. The primary issue with a connection is that it remain open until closed.

THE RDOCONNECTIONS COLLECTION

Figure 25-3 tells us that our next stop in the RDO hierarchy is the **rdoConnection** object.

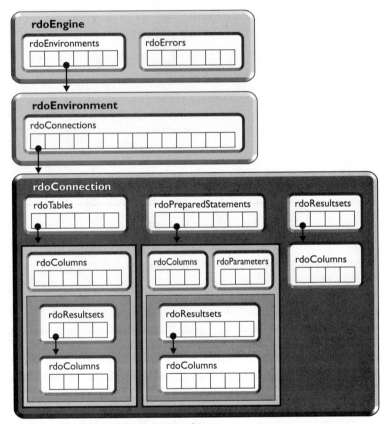

FIGURE 25-3:   The rdoConnection object.

The **rdoConnection** object is a requirement for manipulating a database. Queries may be issued directly from a connection, but they are not prepared.

rdoConnections Collection Definition

Methods: **Clear, Item**

Properties: **Count**

rdoConnection object

Methods: **BeginTrans, Cancel, Close, CommitTrans, CreatePreparedStatement, Execute, OpenResult, SetRollbackTrans**

Properties: **AsyncCheckInterval, Connect, hDbc, Name, QueryTimeout, RowsAffected, StillExecuting, Transactions, Updatable, Version**

Numerous tasks can be performed from a connection, including:

- An action query may be run or a SQL statement passed to a database.

- A result set may be opened with **rdoOpenResultset**.

- A prepared SQL statement can be created with **rdoCreatePreparedStatement**.

- The **rdoConnection** object supports transactions. The number of rows can be tested. For example, a transaction can be rolled back with **RollbackTrans** if the number of rows is incorrect. The **RowsAffected** property applies to both the **rdoConnection** object and the **rdoPreparedStatement** object.

- A **rdoConnection** object exposes the ODBC connection handle **hDbc**, the **rdoConnection** object.

- We're discussing RDO 1.0 of Visual Basic 4.0, but there is an interesting new feature of the RDO 2.0 **rdoConnection** object. RDO 2.0 introduces the concept of managing the **rdoConnection** object with events. Table 25-1 enumerates the new **rdoConnection** object events of RDO 2.0.

TABLE 25-1 RDOCONNECTION EVENTS OF RDO 2.0

EVENT	WHEN FIRED
BeforeConnect	Before ODBC is called to establish the connection
Connect	After a connection is established
Disconnect	After a connection is closed
QueryComplete	After a query of this connection completes
QueryTimeout	After the QueryTimeout period is exhausted

BeginTrans, CommitTrans, and RollbackTrans

Microsoft's documentation for the **rdoConnection** object appears to be in error. The methods **BeginTrans**, **CommitTrans**, and **RollBackTrans** are listed as methods of the **rdoConnection** object but are actually methods of the **rdoEnvironment** object. Transactions span all connections of a **rdoEnvironment** object. It is illogical to have transactions at the connection level in the RDO hierarchy. Please see the **rdoEnvironment** object for comments on using these methods.

Cancel

The **Cancel** method cancels pending results or instructs the remote data source to stop work on the query.

Syntax:

> *Object.***Cancel**

Where:

> *Object:* An object variable of type **rdoConnection**, **rdoPreparedStatement**, or **rdoResultset**

The **Cancel** method may be used on an asynchronous result set. All remaining rows of the current result set are flushed. These result sets are created with the **rdAsyncEnable** parameter from either the **Execute** or **OpenResultset** method.

The **MoreResults** method of the **rdoResultset** object flushes the current result set. The next pending result is current, if there is one. Listing 25-4 illustrates an asynchronous query and the **Cancel** method.

LISTING 25-4 An asynchronous query using StillExecuting and Cancel

```
Private Sub Asynchronous_Click()
'(C) 1998 Bruce T. Prendergast
' DBA Prendergast Consulting
' DBA PCS
' IDG Books Worldwide ISBN 0-7645-3123-9
'

' Listing 25-3 A prepared and asynchronous RDO query
'

    Dim RdoEnv As rdoEnvironment
```

```
Dim RdoCon As rdoConnection
Dim RdoPre As rdoPreparedStatement
Dim MyRS As rdoResultset
Dim WaitTime As Long

Dim MyErr As rdoError
Dim c As rdoConnection
Dim ConnectMode As Integer
On Error GoTo Unable_To_Connect
'
'    create an RDO environment
'
ConnectMode = True
Set RdoEnv = rdoEngine.rdoEnvironments(0)
'
'    connect with RDO connect string
'
 Set RdoCon = RdoEnv.OpenConnection( _
   "", rdDriverNoPrompt, False, _
   "DATABASE=Pubs;UID=sa;PWD=;DSN=Thor;")
'
' a successful connection. Reset the connect
' mode so that all errors are printed.
'
ConnectMode = False
'
' prepare a statement
'
Set RdoPre = RdoCon.CreatePreparedStatement( _
   "MyPS", "SELECT au_lname, au_fname " & _
   "FROM authors " & "WHERE au_lname LIKE 'G%' ")
'
' start an asynchronous query
'
Set MyRS = RdoPre.OpenResultset(rdOpenForwardOnly, _
   rdConcurReadOnly, rdAsyncEnable)
```

```
                WaitTime = Timer
                While (Timer - WaitTime) < 5
                Wend
                Do While RdoPre.StillExecuting
                    If MsgBox("No query yet—keep waiting?", _
                            vbYesNo) = vbNo Then
                        RdoPre.Cancel
                        Exit Sub
                    Else
                        WaitTime = Timer
                        While (Timer - WaitTime) < 5
                        Wend
                    End If
                Loop
                While Not MyRS.EOF
                   Debug.Print MyRS(0), MyRS(1)
                   MyRS.MoveNext
                Wend
                MsgBox "Prepared statement was successful"
                Exit Sub
        Unable_To_Connect:
                For Each MyErr In rdoEngine.rdoErrors
                   '
                   ' this is a connection and I expect warning
                   ' messages. Ignore just the With_Info messages
                   ' such as "connecting to pubs", etc.,
                   '
                   If ((MyErr.SQLRetcode <> rdSQLSuccessWithInfo) Or _
                     (ConnectMode <> 0)) Then
                     MsgBox MyErr.Description & " State:" & _
                     MyErr.SQLState & " SQLRetCode:" & _
                     MyErr.SQLRetcode & " NativeErrorCode:" & _
                     MyErr.Number
                   End If
                Next MyErr
                Resume Next
        End Sub
```

Close

A closed object is automatically removed from a collection. Objects that cannot be closed include **rdoEngine**, **rdoError**, **rdoParameter**, **rdoColumn**, **rdoTable**, and **rdoEnvironments**(0).

Objects that can be closed include **rdoEnvironment**, **rdoConnection**, **rdoPreparedStatement**, **rdoResultset**, and **rdoConnection**.

Syntax:

Object.**Close**

Where:

Object: An object variable of type **rdoConnection**, **rdoPreparedStatement**, **rdoResultset**, or **rdoEnvironment**

A connection is not released unless it is specifically closed. This applies to either global variables or form variables. A connection made with local variables in scope is automatically released when the subroutine terminates.

CreatePreparedStatement

A prepared SQL statement is a reusable statement, and it may contain parameters. Any statement that is used repeatedly should be prepared.

You may not be able to prepare a SQL statement when there is an unpopulated resultset pending on the data source that only supports single operations.

Syntax:

Set *rdoPre* = *rdoCon*.**CreatePreparedStatement**(*Name, SQLString*)

Where:

rdoPre: A variable of type **rdoPreparedStatement**

RdoCon: A variable of type **rdoConnection**

Name: A required field even though it may be a zero-length string. An error occurs if *Name* exists in the **rdoPreparedStatements** collection. This also includes a zero-length string.

SQLString: A **String** variable containing a valid SQL statement

concept link **See Listing 25-4 for an example of a prepared asynchronous query.**

Execute

This is a method of both the **rdoConnection** object and the **rdoPreparedStatement** object. The method executes an action query or a query that does not return rows.

Syntax:

rdoCon.**Execute** *Source* [,*Options*]

rdoPre.**Execute** [*Options*]

Where:

rdoCon: A variable of type **rdoConnection**

rdoPre: A variable of type **rdoPreparedStatement**

Source: A **String** variable containing a valid SQL statement or the name of an existing **rdoPreparedStatement** object

Options: The optional intrinsic constant **rdAsyncEnable** declares an asynchronous query.

concept link

See Listing 25-4 for an example of using the Execute method with an asynchronous query.

OpenResultset

This method creates a new **rdoResultset** object. A **rdoResultset** object can be created from the **rdoConnection** object by supplying a **rdoTable** name, a valid SQL statement, or the name of an existing **rdoPreparedStatement**. A **rdoResultset** object can be also be created from a **rdoTable** object or a **rdoPreparedStatement** object.

Syntax:

Set *rdoRes* = *rdoCon*.**OpenResultset**(*Source* [, *Type* [, *LockType* [, *Options*]]])

Set *rdoRes* = *Object*.**OpenResultset**(*Type* [, *LockType* [, *Options*]])

Where:

rdoRes: A variable of type **rdoResultset**

Object: Either a **rdoTable** object or a **rdoPreparedStatement** object. The **rdoTable** object must be refreshed before creating a resultset.

Source: A **rdoTable** name, a **rdoPreparedStatement** name, or a valid SQL statement that may return rows

Type: One of these intrinsic constants: **rdOpenForwardOnly**, **rdOpenStatic**, **rdOpenKeyset**, or **rdOpenDynamic**

LockType: One of these intrinsic constants: **rdConcurLock** (pessimistic), **rdConcurReadOnly** (default), **rdConcorRowver** (optimistic on row ID), or **rdConcurValues** (optimistic on row values)

Options: The optional intrinsic constant **rdAsyncEnable** declares an asynchronous query.

Listing 25-4 illustrates opening an asynchronous resultset from a **rdoPreparesStatement** object.

THE RDOTABLES COLLECTION

The **rdoTables** collection represents the database definitions. The tables in the database can be enumerated, the columns in a table can be enumerated, and the column attributes can be listed. No schema definitions such as foreign keys are available.

rdoTables Collection Definition

> Methods: **Item**
>
> Properties: **Count**
>
> *rdoTable Object*
>
>> Methods: **OpenResultset**, **Refresh**
>>
>> Properties: **Name**, **RowCount**, **Type**, **Updatable**
>>
>> Collections: **rdoColumns**

OpenResultset

See the **rdoConnection** object for a discussion of this method. A result set from a **rdoTable** object is not recommended. It is the equivalent of a SQL SELECT *, and all rows of all tables will be in the result set. The best choice is where table names are enumerated in a list box as outlined in Listing 25-5. Clicking a table name, clicking a column name, and displaying the properties in a tabular control such as a grid accomplish drill-down.

Refresh

The **Refresh** method must be used to populate the **rdoTables** collection before use. Listing 25-5 is an example of this method. Frequent use of this method is not recommended if your SQL Server has numerous users.

Syntax:

> *rdoCon*.**rdoTables.Refresh**

Where:

> *rdoCon:* An object of type **rdoConnection**

LISTING 25-5 Enumerating the rdoTable object

```
Private Sub rdoTables_Click()
'(C) 1998 Bruce T. Prendergast
' DBA Prendergast Consulting
' DBA PCS
' IDG Books Worldwide ISBN 0-7645-3123-9
'
' Listing 25-5 enumerating the rdoTables collection.
'
    Dim RdoEnv As rdoEnvironment
    Dim RdoCon As rdoConnection
    Dim RdoPre As rdoPreparedStatement
    Dim rdoTbl As rdoTable
    Dim rdoCol As rdoColumn
    Dim MyRS As rdoResultset
    Dim i As Integer
    Dim MyErr As rdoError
    Dim c As rdoConnection
    Dim ConnectMode As Integer
    On Error GoTo Unable_To_Connect
    '
    '   create an RDO environment
    '
    ConnectMode = True
    Set RdoEnv = rdoEngine.rdoEnvironments(0)
    '
```

```
'    connect with RDO connect string
'
Set RdoCon = RdoEnv.OpenConnection( _
   "", rdDriverNoPrompt, False, _
   "DATABASE=Pubs;UID=sa;PWD=;DSN=Thor;")
'
' a successful connection. Reset the connect
' mode so that all errors are printed.
'
ConnectMode = False
RdoCon.rdoTables.Refresh
'
' enumerate all tables in this database
'
For Each rdoTbl In RdoCon.rdoTables
   Debug.Print "Table name is :" & rdoTbl.Name
Next rdoTbl

MsgBox "rdoTables enumeration is complete"
'
' assume that the loop above placed the table
' names in a combo or list box. Pick a table
' and enumerate the columns. I am assuming that
' the name was picked from a list box in the
' fragment below.
'
' enumerate all columns of a selected table
'
Set rdoTbl = RdoCon.rdoTables("authors")
For Each rdoCol In rdoTbl.rdoColumns
   Debug.Print "Column name is: " & rdoCol.Name
Next rdoCol
MsgBox "Column names of " & rdoTbl.Name & _
   " enumerated successfully"
'
' carrying your imaginagion a little further,
```

```
' you have just clicked a column name in a list
' box. This enumerates those properties.
'
'
' we'll leave it at the "authors" table and
' assume for the moment that the "au_fname"
' column was clicked
'
Set rdoCol = rdoTbl.rdoColumns("au_fname")
  '
  ' these are the rdoColumn properties.
  ' They are not in a collection and are
  ' enumerated directly
  '
  Debug.Print "AllowZeroLength: " & _
    rdoCol.AllowZeroLength
  Debug.Print "Attributes: " & _
    rdoCol.Attributes
  Debug.Print "ChunkRequired: " & _
    rdoCol.ChunkRequired
  Debug.Print "Name: " & rdoCol.Name
  Debug.Print "OrdinalPosition: " & _
    rdoCol.OrdinalPosition
  Debug.Print "Required: " & rdoCol.Required
  Debug.Print "Size: " & rdoCol.Size
  Debug.Print "SourceColumn: " & _
    rdoCol.SourceColumn
  Debug.Print "SourceTable: " & _
  rdoCol.SourceTable
  Debug.Print "Type: " & rdoCol.Type
  Debug.Print "Updatable: " & rdoCol.Updatable
  '
  ' the next line can't be enumerated since
  ' this is a rdoTables collection and not
  ' a result set.
  '
```

```
    'debug.print "Value: " & rdoCol.Value

    MsgBox "Column Enumeration was successful"
    Exit Sub
Unable_To_Connect:
    For Each MyErr In rdoEngine.rdoErrors
        '
        ' this is a connection and I expect warning
        ' messages. Ignore just the With_Info messages
        ' such as "connecting to pubs", etc.,
        '
        If ((MyErr.SQLRetcode <> rdSQLSuccessWithInfo) Or _
          (ConnectMode <> 0)) Then
          Debug.Print MyErr.Description & " State:" & _
            MyErr.SQLState & " SQLRetCode:" & _
            MyErr.SQLRetcode & " NativeErrorCode:" & _
            MyErr.Number
        End If
    Next MyErr
    Resume Next
End Sub
```

KEY POINT SUMMARY

This chapter presented a thumbnail sketch of the **rdoEngine**, **rdoEnviroments** collection, **rdoErrors** collection, **rdoEnvironments** collection, **rdoConnection** collection, and the **rdoTables** collection. These are objects at the top of the RDO hierarchy and do not represent all RDO objects. We discuss the remaining RDO objects in Chapter 26.

RDO and ODBCDirect of DAO 3.5 are closely related. We discussed RDO 1.0 in this chapter for the reasons stated at the beginning of the chapter. RDO 1.0 predates ODBCDirect and the differences between ODBCDirect and RDO 1.0 are evolutionary. The evolution continues with events added to the **rdoConnection** object of RDO 2.0. How far the evolution will proceed is unknown because Microsoft has stated that both RDO and DAO are to be replaced with OLE-DB.

- ODBCDirect of DAO and RDO have a lot of similarities at both the functional and the execution levels.

- Subtle differences exist in specific areas. The **dbSeeChanges** intrinsic constant of DAO is not needed because trappable concurrency errors occur automatically in RDO.

- Data Definition Language (DDL) statements are not available in RDO. The application must use the remote server's DDL statements.

APPLYING WHAT YOU'VE LEARNED

These questions measure your understanding of the major RDO objects. The lab exercise for this chapter is the construction of a table browser using the code from Listing 25-5 as the starting point.

Instant Assessment

1. What is the default collection of the **rdoEngine** object?

2. Explain the difference in optimistic concurrency in RDO as compared to DAO.

3. You have two **rdoConnection** objects, each with a result set. The **rdoEnvironment** object is not the default environment. What happens when it is closed?

4. You are attempting to register a data source using RDO. It fails and you can find nothing wrong with your VBA code. What is the likely problem?

5. What is a unique characteristic of the **rdoEnvironments**(0) object?

6. You have an error. There are many error messages and it is quite confusing because every layer of the system has its own interpretation of the problem. Where is the primary RDO error message located?

7. What must be done before accessing the **rdoTables** collection?

8. What is the scope of a transaction?

9. Why is RDO not a good choice for heterogeneous connection of the enterprise?

10. You have developed this killer application that uses RDO. What must be done to license the software?

 concept link **For answers to the Instant Assessment questions, see Appendix C.**

Lab Exercise

Lab 25.45 *Converting Listing 25-5 to a table browsing tool*

WA I

This is a programming project. The **rdoTables** example in Listing 25-5 exposed the tables, columns, and column attributes of a table. You'll find most of the necessary code to retrieve tables, column names, and column properties in Listing 25-5. The **Debug.Print** will be replaced with the **AddItem** method of a combo or list box for the different logical steps. Operation of the application is as follows:

- The user is connected to a data source. You can make this automatic to a local data source or prompt the user to select from a list of data source names.

- Once connected to the data source, the application displays the available table names in a list or combo box.

- The user selects a table name and the column names for that table, and the table properties are displayed.

- The last step is for the user to select a column and have the application display the column's properties.

Windows Architecture I
Windows Architecture II

Working with the rdoPreparedStatement Object

26

About Chapter 26

Chapter 25 discussed Remote Data Objects (RDO) infrastructure issues. Chapter 26 is where the work is done with the discussion of the **rdoPreparedStatements**, **rdoResultsets**, **rdoColumns**, and **rdoParameters** collections.

Several methods are shared between collections. (I won't repeat my discussion of methods in this chapter, but I will refer you to the appropriate collection.) There are no surprises here. Many methods of RDO retain the name of the equivalent DAO method. There are a few new methods and properties such as the statement handle property **hStmt**. RDO is a Spartan technology that supplies the basic functionality for most ODBC data source access requirements. The developer can optionally use the **hStmt** handle to access additional features of the ODBC API directly. The ODBC API is an alternate source for required functionality that is missing in RDO.

The examples in this chapter may be found in the CHAPTER26.VBP Visual Basic 5.0 Enterprise Edition project located in the EXAMPLES\CHAPTER26 folder of the CD-ROM located at the back of this book.

The RDO chapters use RDO 2.0 of Visual Basic Enterprise 5.0. The Remote Data Objects 2.0 library is used; however, the examples follow the RDO 1.0 syntax rules. This makes the examples usable in either RDO 1.0 or RDO 2.0.

THE RDOPREPAREDSTATEMENTS COLLECTION

The **rdoPreparedStatements** collection is a collection of **rdoConnection** objects that manage a query. **rdoPreparedStatement** is also the object that exposes **hStmt**, the statement handle of ODBC. This object is the workhorse of RDO and all query management is done by it. The **rdoPreparedStatements** collection in the RDO architecture is shown in Figure 26-1.

With DAO Microsoft always admonished developers to "Be sure and prepare your query." There was even a question or so on the old Windows Operating Systems Architecture test about query preparation. With RDO there is no choice. Use this collection and all queries are prepared.

Features of the **rdoPreparedStatement** object are outlined as follows:

o Binary large objects (BLOBS) can be managed. The **BindThreshold** sets the column size in bytes. Data larger than this threshold must use the **AppendChunk** and **GetChunk** methods of the **rdoColumn** object.

- The data source connection is read-only from this object.

- The error threshold can be set. I don't recommend this, but the **ErrorThreshold** property of the **rdoPreparedStatement** may be set to a specific severity level. Consult your Microsoft SQL Server documentation.

- This object exposes the ODBC statement handle **hStmt**.

- Set the keyset size with the method **KeysetSize**. A zero value results in a keyset driver cursor. A value other than zero results in a mixed cursor where keys in the keyset are keyset driven and keys not in the keyset are dynamic driven.

- Concurrency is managed by setting the **LockType** property to one of these intrinsic constants: **rdConcurReadOnly**, **rdConcurLock**, **rdConcurRowVer**, or **rdConcurValues**.

- ODBC logging is set with the **LogMessages** method, which sets the log file path.

- The **MaxRows** property defines the maximum number of rows in a resultset.

- The query time out period can be set with the **QueryTimeout** property.

- The number of returned rows is found in the **RowsAffected** property. This property can be tested against an expected value and if the value is wrong, the transaction can be aborted.

- The maximum returned rowset size is managed with the **RowsetSize** property.

- The SQL source statement is set or stored in the **SQL** property.

- The status of an executing asynchronous query can be interrogated with the **StillExecuting** property.

- The **Type** property is one of these intrinsic constants: **rdOpenForwardOnly**, **rdOpenkeyset**, **rdOpenDynamic**, **rdOpenStatic**.

- The updatability of the remote data source is found in the **Updatable** property.

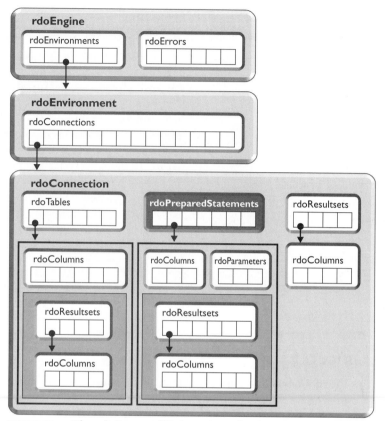

FIGURE 26-1   The rdoPreparedStatements collection in the RDO architecture.

rdoPreparedStatement *Collection Definition*

     Methods: **Item**

     Properties: **Count**

rdoPreparedStatement *Object*

        Methods: **Cancel, Close, Execute, OpenResultset**

        Properties: **BindThreshold, Connect, ErrorThreshold, hStmt, KeysetSize, LockType, LogMessages, MaxRows, Name, QueryTimeout, RowsAffected, RowsetSize, SQL, StillExecuting, Type, Updatable**

        Collections: **rdoColumns, rdoParameters**

WE COUNTED THE VOTES BEFORE – THIS IS THE LAST TIME

Microsoft has significant errors in RDO 2.0 of Visual basic 5.0. The Visual Basic 4.0/5.0 keyword **Item** is defined as follows:

- As a property in Visual Basic (VB) 5.0 documentation-on-line
- As a method in Visual Basic 4.0 documentation-on-line
- As a method in Visual Basic 4.0 Language Reference, Microsoft book 58514
- As a method in Visual Basic 5.0 Language Reference ISBN 1-57231-507-5

There are other problems such as being able to use the Visual Basic 5.0 Object Browser and "see" the **Add** method of the **rdoEnvironments** collection. This is a bogus method. Try to use the method and you will quickly realize that the documentation borders on pure fiction. A new **rdoEnvironment** object is automatically appended to the **rdoEnviroments** collection and an **Add** method isn't needed, and doesn't work even though it is documented only in VB 5.0 and can be browsed.

This chapter will use the RDO 1.0 definitions as defined in Visual Basic 4.0. Exceptional new RDO 2.0 features are discussed such as events of the RDO 2.0 **rdoConnection** object, however the context of the chapter remains RDO 1.0.

Cancel

See the **rdoConnection** object (Chapter 25) for a discussion of this method.

Close

See the **rdoConnection** object (Chapter 25) for a discussion of this method.

Execute

See the **rdoConnection** object (Chapter 25) for a discussion of this method.

OpenResultset

See the **rdoConnection** object (Chapter 25) for a discussion of this method. I'm not going to repeat the **OpenResultset** discussion, but Listing 26-1 provides an interesting example. I've stripped off some of the RDO veneer and used the ODBC API. The example uses the **hStmt** of the **rdoResultset** object and not the **hStmt** of the **rdoPreparedStatement** object. This example uses ODBC 3.0, which is the ODBC32.DLL.

The **SQLError** and the **SQLNumResultCols** API functions are both declared in the declaration section of the form as **Private**. A few constants are hardcoded because I didn't want to bring in whole libraries for just two API references.

I have included all the necessary debug code in case the example doesn't work on your system. The ODBC API error code follows ODBC conventions and not RDO code conventions. No error event occurs; the return code must be tested for a legitimate value. Listing 26-1 goes under the thin ODBC wrapper of RDO and calls ODBC API functions directly.

LISTING 26-1 An rdoResultset Object and the ODBC API

```
Private Sub ODBC_API_Click()
'(C) 1998 Bruce T. Prendergast
' DBA Prendergast Consulting
' DBA PCS
' IDG Books Worldwide ISBN 0-7645-3123-9
'
' Listing 26-1 A prepared query and the ODBC API
'
    Dim RdoEnv As rdoEnvironment
    Dim RdoCon As rdoConnection
    Dim RdoPre As rdoPreparedStatement
    Dim MyRS As rdoResultset
    Dim RetCode As Integer
    Dim ipCol As Integer              ' row count
    '
    '
    '   SQLError parameters
    '
    Const MAX_STRING_LENGTH = 128
    Dim ErrCode As Integer
    Dim ErrorMsg As String * MAX_STRING_LENGTH
    Dim cbErrorMsg As Integer
    Dim NativeError As Long
    Dim SqlState As String * MAX_STRING_LENGTH
    Const SQL_Success = 0
    '/* SQLError defines */
```

```
Const SQL_NULL_HENV = 0
Const SQL_NULL_HDBC = 0
Const SQL_NULL_HSTMT = 0
Dim MyErr As rdoError
Dim c As rdoConnection
Dim ConnectMode As Integer
On Error GoTo Unable_To_Connect
'
'   create an RDO environment
'
ConnectMode = True
Set RdoEnv = rdoEngine.rdoEnvironments(0)
'
'   connect with RDO connect string
'
Set RdoCon = RdoEnv.OpenConnection( _
  "", rdDriverNoPrompt, False, _
  "DATABASE=Pubs;UID=sa;PWD=;DSN=Thor;")
'
' a successful connection. Reset the connect
' mode so that all errors are printed.
'
ConnectMode = False
'
' prepare a statement
'
Set RdoPre = RdoCon.CreatePreparedStatement( _
  "MyPS", "SELECT au_lname, au_fname " & _
  "FROM authors " & _
  "WHERE au_lname LIKE 'G%' ")

Set MyRS = RdoPre.OpenResultset( _
  rdOpenForwardOnly, rdConcurReadOnly)
'
' get the result set row count
'
```

```
      RetCode = BTPSQLNumResultCols(MyRS.hstmt, ipCol)
   '

 ' this error code analysis follows ODBC conventions
 ' and not RDO conventions
   '

   If RetCode <> SQL_Success Then
       MsgBox "ODBC API call failed with code:" & _
         Str$(RetCode)
       ErrCode = BTPSQLError(RdoEnv.henv, _
         RdoCon.hdbc, RdoPre.hstmt, SqlState, _
          NativeError, ErrorMsg, _
          MAX_STRING_LENGTH, cbErrorMsg)
       MsgBox "RetCode is: " & Str$(RetCode)
       MsgBox "Error message: " & Mid$(ErrorMsg, _
         1, cbErrorMsg)
       MsgBox "SQL State: " & SqlState
       MsgBox "Native error code: " & _
       Str$(NativeError)
       Exit Sub
    End If
    If ipCol <> 2 Then
      MsgBox "ipcol is: " & Str$(ipCol)
      MsgBox "SQLNumResultCols returned wrong value"
      Exit Sub
    End If
    While Not MyRS.EOF
      Debug.Print MyRS(0), MyRS(1)
      MyRS.MoveNext
    Wend
    MsgBox "ODBC API with RDO Prepared statement " & _
      "was successful"
    Exit Sub
Unable_To_Connect:
    For Each MyErr In rdoEngine.rdoErrors
       '

       ' this is a connection and I expect warning
```

```
        ' messages. Ignore just the With_Info messages
        ' such as "connecting to pubs", etc.,
        '
        If ((MyErr.SQLRetcode <> rdSQLSuccessWithInfo) _
          Or (ConnectMode <> 0)) Then
          MsgBox MyErr.Description & " State:" & _
            MyErr.SqlState & " SQLRetCode:" & _
            MyErr.SQLRetcode & " NativeErrorCode:" & _
            MyErr.Number
        End If
      Next MyErr
      Resume Next
    End Sub
```

THE RDORESULTSETS COLLECTION

A **rdoResultset** is an object that represents the rows returned from a query. A result set is created by (see **rdoConnection::OpenResultset** in Chapter 25 for the precise syntax):

- Opening a **rdoResultset** object from an **rdoConnection** using the name of an existing **rdoTable** object, the name of a **rdoPreparedStatement** object, or a SQL statement.
- Opening a **rdoResultset** object from an existing **rdoTable** object or an existing **rdoPreparedStatement** object.

The **rdoResultset** object has most of the properties of the DAO **Recordset** object. The only property that I've noticed missing is the **RecordsetClone** property, which is useful in synchronizing a bound form. However, this property isn't needed because RDO supports data-aware controls and not bound forms.

rdoResultset Collection Definition

Methods: **Item**

Properties: **Count**

rdoResultset Object

Methods: **AddNew, Cancel, CancelUpdate, Close, Delete, Edit, GetRows, MoreResults, Move, MoveFirst, MoveLast, MoveNext, MovePrevious, Requery, Update**

Properties: **AbsolutePosition, BOF, Bookmark, Bookmarkable, EOF, hStmt, LastModified, LockEdits, Name, PercentPosition, Restartable, RowCount, StillExecuting, Transactions, Type, Updatable**

 note Both the **rdoResultset** object and the **rdoPreparedStatement** object expose the ODBC statement handle **hStmt**.

AddNew

AddNew adds a new row to a rowset. The newly added row may or may not be visible to other applications. This is a function of the cursor type.

The row that was current before the new row was added remains the current row. Setting the **Bookmark** property to the **LastModified** property can set the new row current.

A pending **AddNew** operation can be canceled with the **CancelUpdate** method but only before the row is updated with the **Update** method. Figure 26-2 illustrates the general sequence of operations.

Syntax:

*rdoRes.***AddNew**

Where:

rdoRes: An object of type **rdoResultset**

The record (row) editing facilities of RDO appear to be identical to those of DAO. The **CancelUpdate** method method is supported in both DAO and RDO and has the advantage of canceling an update without manipulation the cursor. The editing and updating techniques of RDO are illustrated in Listing 26-2. Listing 26-2 also illustrates the **CancelUpdate** method and the rolling back of a transaction. The successful transaction rollback is verified.

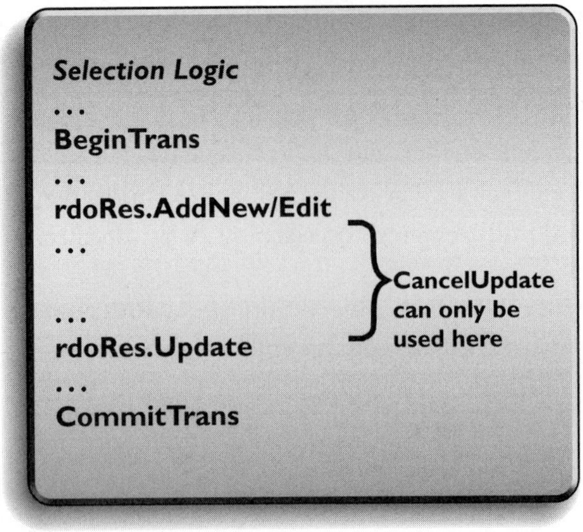

```
Selection Logic
...
BeginTrans
...
rdoRes.AddNew/Edit
...

...                    }  CancelUpdate
rdoRes.Update             can only be
...                       used here
CommitTrans
```

FIGURE 26-2   Using AddNew, Edit, CancelUpdate, and Update.

LISTING 26-2 Canceling an update with CancelUpdate and rolling back a transaction with RollbackTrans

```
Private Sub Updating_Rowsets_Click()
'(C)1998 Bruce T. Prendergast
' DBA Prendergast Consulting
' DBA PCS
' IDG Books Worldwide ISBN 0-7645-3123-9
'
' Listing 26-2 Canceling an update and rolling
' back a transaction
'
    Dim RdoEnv As rdoEnvironment
    Dim RdoCon As rdoConnection
    Dim RdoPre As rdoPreparedStatement
    Dim MyRS As rdoResultset

    Dim MyErr As rdoError
    Dim c As rdoConnection
    Dim ConnectMode As Integer
    On Error GoTo Unable_To_Connect
    '
```

```
'   create an RDO environment
'
ConnectMode = True
Set RdoEnv = rdoEngine.rdoEnvironments(0)
'
'   connect with RDO connect string
'
Set RdoCon = RdoEnv.OpenConnection( _
  "", rdDriverNoPrompt, False, _
  "DATABASE=Pubs;UID=sa;PWD=;DSN=Thor;")
'
' a successful connection. Reset the connect
' mode so that all errors are printed.
'
ConnectMode = False
'
' prepare a statement
'
Set RdoPre = RdoCon.CreatePreparedStatement( _
  "MyPS", "SELECT au_fname, au_lname, au_id " & _
  "FROM authors " & _
  "WHERE au_id = '172-32-1176'")
Set MyRS = RdoPre.OpenResultset(rdOpenDynamic, _
  rdConcurLock)
'
' Do the action query
'
On Error GoTo Transaction_Error
RdoEnv.BeginTrans
With MyRS
  .MoveFirst
  Do While Not .EOF
    If !au_id <> "172-32-1176" Then
      .MoveNext
    Else
'
      ' found it, edit it, and change our mind
```

```
                    '
                    .Edit
                    !au_fname = "John"
                    .CancelUpdate
                    Exit Do
                End If
            Loop
        End With
        '
        ' a null transaction rollback, but it should work
        '
        RdoEnv.RollbackTrans
        MyRS.Close
        On Error GoTo Normal_Error
        '
        ' now lets see that we didn't change anything
        '
        RdoPre.Close
        Set RdoPre = RdoCon.CreatePreparedStatement( _
            "MyPS", "SELECT au_fname " & _
            "FROM authors " & _
            "WHERE au_id = '172-32-1176'")
        Set MyRS = RdoPre.OpenResultset(rdOpenDynamic, _
            rdConcurLock)
        If MyRS(0) <> "Johnson" Then
            MsgBox "CancelUpdate failed"
            Exit Sub
        Else
            MsgBox "RDO CancelUpdate was successful"
        End If
        Exit Sub
Unable_To_Connect:
    For Each MyErr In rdoEngine.rdoErrors
        '
        ' this is a connection and I expect
        ' warning messages. Ignore just the
```

```
        ' With_Info messages such as
        ' "connecting to pubs", etc.,
        '
        If ((MyErr.SQLRetcode <> rdSQLSuccessWithInfo) _
          Or (ConnectMode <> 0)) Then
          MsgBox MyErr.Description & " State:" & _
            MyErr.SqlState & " SQLRetCode:" & _
            MyErr.SQLRetcode & " NativeErrorCode:" & _
            MyErr.Number
        End If
      Next MyErr
      Resume Next
Transaction_Error:
    RdoEnv.RollbackTrans
    MsgBox "Transaction failed and rolled back"
Normal_Error:
  For Each MyErr In rdoEngine.rdoErrors
    MsgBox MyErr.Description & " State:" & _
      MyErr.SqlState & " SQLRetCode:" & _
      MyErr.SQLRetcode & " NativeErrorCode:" & _
      MyErr.Number
    Next MyErr
    Resume Error_exit
Error_exit:
    Exit Sub
End Sub
```

Cancel

See the **rdoConnection** object (Chapter 25) for discussion of this method.

CancelUpdate

CancelUpdate flushes the copy buffer. This is the only change that is made before using the **Edit** or **AddNew** methods. It has the same effect as moving to another row. All changes are lost. Listing 26-3 illustrates the **CancelUpdate** method.

Syntax:

   *rdoRes.***CancelUpdate**

Where:

   rdoRes: A variable of type **rdoResultset**

Close

See the **rdoConnection** object (Chapter 25) for discussion of this method.

Delete

This method deletes the current row of an updatable rowset. A current row must exist when using this method or an error will occur.

The cursor must be positioned to another row after the deletion even though the deleted row is no longer accessible. The **CancelUpdate** method is not applicable to a deletion. A deleted row can only be restored with the **RollbackTrans** method on a **rdoEnvironment** object.

A delete may fail for numerous reasons. Factors to consider on a delete failure include:

o There is no current row.

o The **rdoConnection** object or the **rdoResultset** object is read-only.

o Columns in the row are not updatable.

o The row doesn't exist, it has already been deleted.

o The row or data page is locked by another user.

o The user permissions do not allow a delete operation.

Syntax:

   *rdoRes.***Delete**

Where:

   rdoRes: A variable of type **rdoResultset**

Edit

This method updates a row in a rowset. Changes are placed in the copy buffer until removed with the **CancelUpdate** method, the cursor is moved to another row, or the **Update** method is used to update the row.

The **LockEdits** field manages concurrency. Concurrency is the ability of other users to access the system while an update is in process. This requires an understanding of pessimistic and optimistic locking:

- *Pessimistic Locking* — The ODBC data source determines when row or page locking is used. Row or table locking occurs when the editing starts. This point is identified by the execution of the **Edit** method. The lock is released after the **Update** method completes.

- *Optimistic Locking* — The row or page is not locked until an attempt is made to update the row with the **Update** method. This is called optimistic locking because the developer believes that there will be few lock collisions. This is an intuitive judgment call on the part of the developer and performance from optimistic locking may be less than when using pessimistic locking. The **Update** method manages the concurrency and reads the current version of the newly locked row. An error is returned when either the row values or the row ID (see Table 26-1) don't match the row in the rowset at the start of the edit as marked by the **Edit** method.

The **LockEdits** property is set **true** for pessimistic locking which can be either row or page locking An error occurs when the row or page is lock and pessimistic concurrency is in use. The **LockEdits** field is set false for optimistic concurrency. With optimistic concurrency the new row is compared with the previous version and an error occurs if another user has changed the row. The **LockEdits** property is set when the resultset is opened and is an integer that specifies the type of concurrency control. A default concurrency of **rdConcurReadOnly** is assumed. Table 26-1 enumerates the values available to the *LockType* parameter of the **OpenResultset** method.

The **Edit** method fails when:

- A current row doesn't exist.
- The **rdoConnection** or **rdoResultset** object is read-only.
- Columns in the row are not updatable.

- o The **EditMode** property indicates an edit is already in process.
- o Another user locks the row or data page.

TABLE 26-1 LOCKTYPE PARAMETER VALUES OF THE OPENRESULTSET METHOD

INTRINSIC CONSTANT	DESCRIPTION
rdConcurLock	Pessimistic Concurrency
rdConcurReadOnly	Read-Only (Default)
rdConcurRowwerOptimistic	Optimistic concurrency based on row ID
rdConcurValuesOptimistic	Optimistic concurrency based on row values

Syntax:

> *rdoRes.***Edit**

Where:

> *rdoRes:* A variable of type **rdoResultset**

concept link   **See Listing 26-2 for an example that uses this method.**

GetRows

This method retrieves one or more rows into a **Variant** variable and should be considered when performance is an issue with a remote server. This method further partitions the concept of a resultset with multiple keysets. A logical approach is to have a keyset size, which is an integral number of **GetRows** block sizes. A suggested value is 100 for a keyset size and 20 for the **GetRows** method row count.

This technique overcomes the problem of trying to use the ODBC API function **SQLExtendedFetch** with Unicode. If you recall, there is a DAO example of using the **GetRows** method in Chapter 23. The Microsoft Access 2.0 version of this is an example in Chapter 14 that uses the ODBC API function **SQLExtendedFetch**. (The ODBC example in Chaper 14 does not use Unicode.)

GetRows will not retrieve data for any column where the **ChunkRequired** property is true.

Syntax:

varArray = *rdoRes*.**GetRows**(*Rows*)

Where:

varArray: A variable of type **Variant**.

rdoRes: An object of type **rdoResultset**.

Rows: A number of type **Long**.

Listing 26-3 uses the RDO **GetRows** method to return values into a variant array that is indexed by row and column. The number of rows returned is unpredictable and the code in Listing 26-3 calculates the returned row count with the **Ubound** function of VBA.

LISTING 26-3 Improving RDO performance with GetRows

```
Private Sub GetRows_Click()
'(C) 1998 Bruce T. Prendergast
' DBA Prendergast Consulting
' DBA PCS
' IDG Books Worldwide ISBN 0-7645-3123-9
'
' Listing 26-3 Using GetRows in RDO
'
    Dim RdoEnv As rdoEnvironment
    Dim RdoCon As rdoConnection
    Dim RdoPre As rdoPreparedStatement
    Dim MyRS As rdoResultset

    Dim RetRows As Variant    ' returned row array
    Dim RetCount As Long      ' returned row count
    Dim i As Integer          ' scratch integer

    Dim MyErr As rdoError
    Dim c As rdoConnection
    Dim ConnectMode As Integer
    On Error GoTo Unable_To_Connect
    '
```

```
'   create an RDO environment
'
ConnectMode = True
Set RdoEnv = rdoEngine.rdoEnvironments(0)
'
'   connect with RDO connect string
'
Set RdoCon = RdoEnv.OpenConnection( _
  "", rdDriverNoPrompt, False, _
  "DATABASE=Pubs;UID=sa;PWD=;DSN=Thor;")
'
' a successful connection. Reset the connect
' mode so that all errors are printed.
'
ConnectMode = False
'
' Open a resultset directly
'
Set MyRS = RdoCon.OpenResultset( _
  "SELECT au_lname, au_fname, au_id " & _
  "FROM authors ", _
  rdOpenForwardOnly, rdConcurReadOnly)
'
' get the rows 10 at a time
'
Do Until MyRS.EOF
  RetRows = MyRS.GetRows(10)
  '
  ' Loop through the records. I am not
  ' using the resultset row count but
  ' am depending on the actual returned
  ' rows from a keyset
  '
  RetCount = UBound(RetRows, 2) + 1
  For i = 0 To RetCount - 1
    Debug.Print RetRows(0, i);
    Debug.Print RetRows(1, i);
```

```
            Debug.Print RetRows(2, i)
        Next i
    Loop
    MsgBox "RDO GetRows example was successful"
    Exit Sub
Unable_To_Connect:
    For Each MyErr In rdoEngine.rdoErrors
        '
        ' this is a connection and I expect warning
        ' messages. Ignore just the With_Info messages
        ' such as "connecting to pubs", etc.,
        '
        If ((MyErr.SQLRetcode <> rdSQLSuccessWithInfo) _
            Or (ConnectMode <> 0)) Then
            MsgBox MyErr.Description & " State:" & _
            MyErr.SqlState & " SQLRetCode:" & _
            MyErr.SQLRetcode & " NativeErrorCode:" & _
            MyErr.Number
        End If
    Next MyErr
    Resume Next
End Sub
```

MoreResults

The current result set is cleared and a value of **True** is returned when additional result sets are pending. The **BOF** and **EOF** properties are both set to **True** when there are no further result sets.

Cancel flushes the current result set; however, it will also flush all pending result sets.

Syntax:

varBool = rdoRes.**MoreResults**

Where:

varBool: A variable of type **Boolean**

rdoRes: An object of type **rdoResultset**

The **MoreResults** implementation is incomplete. It is useful, however, when loading a Visual Basic form that has many combo or list boxes that must be populated. The limitation of this implementation is that action queries can be included, but the **RowsAffected** property is not exposed, thus making an action query useless in this environment. The **RowsAffected** property may not appear to be useful when updating a single table; however, a relational database is complex with referential dependencies. The **RowsAffected** property is needed for any action query involving any relational database.

Let's drop the mentality of a Visual Basic developer and assume the mindset of a database administrator or database analyst. A common task is the posting of transactions to a database. When the transaction fails, it must be debugged. A hypothetical example is using the **MoreResults** method after a query followed by an action query. Both queries have the same WHERE clause. The **RowsAffected** property is interrogated after the action query and when the row count is in error, the transaction is rolled back. A result set is still available for debugging, even though the transaction was terminated with the **RollbackTrans** method. Of course, this isn't possible since **RowsAffected** is not exposed, and **MoreResults** doesn't support action queries. At this point, the **MoreResults** implementation is sadly incomplete and is not very useful. RDO is a technology for only ODBC data sources and not flat file systems. It's relatively easy to write singular read-only queries, and the **MoreResults** method has marginal benefit as implemented. Listing 26-4 illustrates using the **MoreResults** method.

Listing 26-4 is a query combined with an action query. Either save this example or remember the technique.

LISTING 26-4   Processing multiple queries with MoreResults

```
Private Sub MoreResults_Click()
'(C) 1998 Bruce T. Prendergast
' DBA Prendergast Consulting
' DBA PCS
' IDG Books Worldwide ISBN 0-7645-3123-9
'
' Listing 26-4 Using the MoreResults method
'

    Dim RdoEnv As rdoEnvironment
    Dim RdoCon As rdoConnection
    Dim RdoPre As rdoPreparedStatement
```

```
Dim MyRS As rdoResultset

Dim MyErr As rdoError
Dim c As rdoConnection
Dim ConnectMode As Integer
Dim MySQL As String
On Error GoTo Unable_To_Connect
'
'   create an RDO environment
'
ConnectMode = True
Set RdoEnv = rdoEngine.rdoEnvironments(0)
'
' I must use ODBC for multiple queries
'
RdoEnv.CursorDriver = rdUseOdbc
'
'   connect with RDO connect string
'
Set RdoCon = RdoEnv.OpenConnection( _
  "", rdDriverNoPrompt, False, _
  "DATABASE=Pubs;UID=sa;PWD=;DSN=Thor;")
'
' a successful connection. Reset the connect
' mode so that all errors are printed.
'
ConnectMode = False
On Error GoTo Normal_Error
'
' Build two statements
'
Set MyRS = RdoCon.OpenResultset( _
  " SELECT au_lname, au_fname, au_id " & _
  " FROM authors " & _
  " WHERE au_id = '172-32-1176'" & _
  " SELECT title_id, title FROM titles", _
  rdOpenForwardOnly, rdConcurReadOnly)
```

```
        Debug.Print MyRS!au_fname; " "; MyRS!au_lname; _
          " "; MyRS!au_id
        Do While MyRS.MoreResults
          Do Until MyRS.EOF
            Debug.Print MyRS!title_id; " "; MyRS!Title
            MyRS.MoveNext
          Loop
        Loop
        MsgBox "RDO Multiple Query was successful"
        Exit Sub
Unable_To_Connect:
        For Each MyErr In rdoEngine.rdoErrors
          '
          ' this is a connection and I expect warning
          ' messages. Ignore just the With_Info messages
          ' such as "connecting to pubs", etc.,
          '
          If ((MyErr.SQLRetcode <> rdSQLSuccessWithInfo) _
            Or (ConnectMode <> 0)) Then
            MsgBox MyErr.Description & " State:" & _
              MyErr.SqlState & " SQLRetCode:" & _
              MyErr.SQLRetcode & " NativeErrorCode:" & _
              MyErr.Number
          End If
        Next MyErr
        Resume Next
Normal_Error:
      For Each MyErr In rdoEngine.rdoErrors
        MsgBox MyErr.Description & " State:" & _
          MyErr.SqlState & " SQLRetCode:" & _
          MyErr.SQLRetcode & " NativeErrorCode:" & _
          MyErr.Number
      Next MyErr
      Resume Error_exit
Error_exit:
      Exit Sub
End Sub
```

Move, MoveFirst, MoveLast, MoveNext, and MovePrevious

Each of these methods is standard for moving around within a result set. Movement is relative to the current position of to a bookmark. Movement is always relative to the current row unless a bookmark is specified.

An error occurs when using the **Move** method and there are no rows.

The **BOF** and **EOF** properties are set when positioning before the first row or after the last row, respectively.

Syntax:

rdoRes.**Move** *Rows* [, *Start*]

rdoRes.{**MoveFirst | MoveLast | MoveNext | MovePrevious**}

Where:

rdoRes: An object of type **rdoResultset**

Rows: A signed **Long** that specifies the number of rows to position

Start: A variable of type **Variant** identifying a bookmark

Most examples use one of these methods.

Requery

The data in a **rdoResultset** is updated with this method. Previous bookmarks are lost after performing a **Requery**. A new result set is created when **rdoParameter** objects have changed. Objects with their **Restartable** property set to **False** cannot use this method.

Syntax:

rdoRes.**Requery**

Where:

rdoRes: An object of type **rdoResultset**

An example usage of the **Requery** method is a click event of a combo box where parameters are updated from text boxes.

```
myRes.Parameters(0) = txtf_name
myRes.Paremamters(1) = txtl_name
MyRes.Requery
```

Update

This is the last of the **rdoResultset** object methods. The row set is updated from the data placed in the copy buffer by either **Edit** or **AddNew**. **CancelUpdate** can be used until the **Update** method is applied. After that, only the **RollbackTrans** method can reverse the changes.

Syntax:

> *rdoRes*.**Update**

Where:

> *rdoRes:* An object of type **rdoResultset**

THE RDOCOLUMNS COLLECTION

rdoColumns is the default collection of the **rdoPreparedStatement, rdoResultset**, and **rdoTable** objects. **rdoColumn** objects need not be closed. They are automatically closed when the **rdoPreparedStatement** or **rdoResultset** object is closed.

The **rdoColumns** keyword is typically not used when referencing a column value. The default property of an **rdoColumn** object is the **Value** property and all four lines below are equivalent.

```
Debug.Print MyRS!au_fname
Debug.Print MyRS("au_fname")
Debug.Print MyRS.rdoColumns("au_fname").Value
Debug.Print MyRS.rdoColumns(0).Value
```

rdoColumns Collection Definition

> Methods: **refreshItem**
>
> Properties: **Count, Item**
>
> > **rdoColumn** Object
> >
> > > Methods: **AppendChunk, ColumnSize, GetChunk**
> > >
> > > Properties: **AllowZeroLength, Attributes, ChunkRequired, Name, OrdinalPosition, Required, Size, SourceColumn, SourceTable, Type, Updatable, Value**

rdoColumn objects are infrequently used. Quite possibly, the only time you'll ever use the **rdoColumns** object is in the management of BLOBS.

The size of a BLOB is determined by the **ColumnSize** property. The code snippet below illustrates the essentials of managing a BLOB. The **AppendChunk** method is used for storing blocks of data and is not used in the example below which retrieves data.

The chunk size is arbitrary and is set to 512 bytes in the sample code.

```
lColSiz = rdoRes!rdoCol.ColumnSize
if iColSiz = -1 then
 varTmp = rdoRes!rdoCol.GetChunk(512)
 varBlob=Nothing
 while len(varTmp) >0
   varBlob = varBlob & varTmp
   varTmp = rdoRes!rdoCol.GetChunk(512)
 Wend
Else
 If iColSiz > 0 then
   varBlob = rdoRes!rdoCol.GetChunk(iColSiz)
 End If
End If
```

The **BindThreshold** property of the **rdoPreparedStatement** object determines the maximum size of a bindable column. Data that exceeds this threshold must be managed with the **GetChunk** and **AppendChunk** methods. The default value for the **BindThreshold** property is 1024 bytes.

AppendChunk and GetChunk

The **AppendChunk** method writes successive blocks of BLOB data to storage. No size argument is required. The target column must have a data type of either **rdTypeLongVARBINARY** or **rdTypeLongVARCHAR**.

The **AppendChunk** method must be used when the **ChunkRequired** property is **True**. An error occurs when using **AppendChunk** and there is no current row.

Syntax:

*rdoRes.rdoCol.***AppendChunk** *Source*

*varBlob = rdoRes.rdoCol.***GetChunk***(Bytes)*

Where:

rdoRes: An object of type **rdoResultset**

rdoCol: An object of type **rdoColumn**

Source: A string expression containing the data

VarBlob: A variable of type **Variant**

Bytes: The size of the requested chunk

ColumnSize

This method returns the size in bytes of either a **rdTypeLongVARBINARY** or **rdTypeLongVARCHAR** variable.

Syntax:

*varSize = rdoRes.rdoCol.***ColumnSize**

Where:

varSiz: A variable of type **Variant** or **Long**

rdoRes: An object of type **rdoResultset**

rdoCol: An object of type **rdoColumn**

THE RDOPARAMETERS COLLECTION

The **rdoParameters** collection is a collection of the **rdoPreparedStatement** object. The **rdoParameter** object encapsulates both input and output parameters of a query. Input parameters are commonly used as query selection criteria and output parameters are the returned results of stored procedures on the remote data source. The returned value is not considered a result set.

Creating a parameter query uses the ODBC syntax of embedding the <?> character in the query text. The position of the <?> determines the relative argument number in the parameters collection. In the SQL string:

```
MySQL = "{ ? = call sp_password (?, ?) }"
```

the first parameter is an output parameter and the last two are input parameters.

Parameters have a **Direction** property that must be set before using the query. This is illustrated below where the **Direction** properties and the default **Value** properties are set.

```
Dim rdoPre as rdoPreparedStatement
Set MyPW = rdoPre.CreatePreparedStatement("MyPW",MYSQL)
With MyPW
 .rdoParameters(0).Direction = rdParamReturnValue
 .rdoParameters(1).Direction = rdParamInput
 .rdoParameters(2).Direction = rdParamInput
 .rdoParameters(1) = "Yoda"
 .rdoParameters(2) = "Jedi"
End With
```

rdoParameters *Collection Definition*

    Methods: **Item**

    Properties: **Count**

    rdoParameter *Object*

        Properties: **Direction**, **Name**, **Type**, **Value**

KEY POINT SUMMARY

This is the last RDO chapter. We've learned that RDO has the look and feel of DAO while maintaining the image of a lean and mean database access technology. Required application functionality not available in RDO is immediately available in the ODBC API. Listing 26-1 illustrated mixing RDO and ODBC API functionality.

- Query preparation is automatic with the **rdoPreparedStatement** object. The feature is an option in ODBCDirect. Preparation is automatic in DAO when a **QueryDef** object is saved.

- ODBC API function calls can be intermixed with RDO object statements.

- The processing functionality of RDO is almost identical to that of DAO and ODBCDirect. There are subtle name differences.

APPLYING WHAT YOU'VE LEARNED

The questions below will assess your understanding of the material in this chapter. The questions are not simple and are the type of questions to expect on any Microsoft certification examination. The examinations are relatively easy when the product is used and excruciatingly difficult when the product is not used. You have been presented with many programming examples. Success on the examinations is both understanding and using the technology.

The first lab exercise addresses the issue of converting an application between different database access technologies. The second lab exercise measures the comparative performance of the **GetRows** method in Jet, ODBCDirect or RDO. This is the last database access technology until we marry COM with ODBC and get OLE-DB in Chapters 29–32. As a refresher, the last laboratory of the chapter is an enumeration of the unique characteristics of each of the database access technologies we've discussed so far. This includes ODBC, Jet, ODBCDirect, and RDO.

Instant Assessment

1. The **rdoPreparedStatement** object has a parallel in the DAO **QueryDef** object. What feature is an option with a DAO **QueryDef** object but is built-in with the **rdoPreparedStatement** object?

2. A **Delete** method has failed on a row in a result set. Give six reasons for this problem.

3. An **Edit** method has failed on a row of a result set. Give five reasons for this problem.

 concept link   **For answers to the Instant Assessment questions, see Appendix C.**

Lab Exercises

These laboratories compare the relative performance of the **GetRows** method in Jet, ODBCDirect, and RDO. The results will be useful in your selection of the appropriate database access technology.

Lab 26.46 *Converting RDO application to Jet or ODBCDirect*

Because many of you may not have Microsoft Visual Basic Enterprise Edition, the lab is to select an example from the RDO section of this book and convert it to Jet and DAO or to ODBCDirect of DAO. The simplest choice is ODBCDirect. Don't try to convert the **OpenResultset** example (Listing 26-1) because it uses the ODBC API. A Jet **QueryDef** object does not have the **hStmt** property. RDO examples from this chapter that are candidates for converting to DAO include:

- *Listing 26-2* — The example features the **Edit**, **AddNew**, **CancelUpdate**, and **Update** methods. Each of these methods is represented by a comparable DAO method.

- *Listing 26-3* — This is an example of the RDO **GetRows** method. Both Jet and ODBCDirect support a **GetRows** method.

Lab 26.47 *Comparing Jet, ODBCDirect, and RDO GetRows performance*

After completing Lab 26.47 you will have three versions of the **GetRows** method. Measure and compare the **GetRows** method performance in Jet, ODBCDirect, and RDO. Queries are prepared automatically in RDO. Queries are not prepared automatically in ODBCDirect. You must prepare an ODBCDirect query to attain the same RDO performance. Compare the performance before and after preparing the ODBCDirect queries.

Lab 26.48 *Identifying the unique characteristics of ODBC, Jet, ODBCDirect, and RDO*

The Windows Architecture core examinations will test your understanding of when to select the appropriate database access technology. The database access technologies to consider are ODBC, Jet (Access), ODBCDirect, and RDO. Make a list identifying the unique characteristics of each technology. As the first hint, both RDO and ODBCDirect only communicate with ODBC data sources. Another hint is that Jet is designed for the desktop and not for connecting to enterprise ODBC data sources, while ODBC is designed for connection to enterprise ODBC data sources. That doesn't mean that Jet cannot communicate with a remote database, but that it wasn't designed for it. Unfortunately, developers have favorite implementation languages and will not always pick the appropriate language.

Windows Architecture I
Windows Architecture II

CHAPTER

SQL-DMO

27

About Chapter 27

Chapter 27 describes Microsoft SQL Server Distributed Management Objects (SQL-DMO). It compares the architectural differences between objects of Remote Data Objects (RDO) and Data Access Objects (DAO) and SQL-DMO objects. SQL-DMO objects have unique features that are not found in either RDO or DAO objects. The chapter closes with a discussion of two views of the SQL-DMO architecture. The first view is an enumeration by object of the properties and methods of all SQL-DMO objects, and the detail illustrates the object dependencies of SQL-DMO.

The examples in this chapter may be found in the CHAPTER27.VBP Visual Basic 5.0 Enterprise Edition project located in the EXAMPLES\ CHAPTER27 folder of the CD-ROM located at the back of this book.

WHAT IS SQL–DMO?

SQL-DMO is an automation tool for the management of Microsoft SQL Server. SQL-DMO is a set of 32-bit COM objects from which automation tools can be built for either Windows NT or Windows 95. SQL-DMO objects encapsulate the native SQL Server DB-LIB API. The SQL-DMO implementation is complete, and the SQL Server Enterprise Manager is written using SQL-DMO. SQL-DMO objects can be invoked from any tool that supports the OLE 2.0 COM standard. SQL-DMO administrative scripts for SQL Server can be created in the Microsoft Visual C++ development system or in any tool supporting VBA. Practical use of SQL-DMO is from Visual Basic or Visual C++.

SQL-DMO is an attractive alternative for reducing enterprise infrastructure costs. A single database administrator can manage multiple SQL Server sites. SQL-DMO gives the SQL Server administrator the ability to tailor management tools to an individual management style. It is also a mechanism for delivering selected portions of SQL Server to a client without the necessity of licensing the SQL Server Enterprise manager.

As defined from the SQL Server perspective, SQL-DMO is an element of a comprehensive framework called *SQL Distributed Management Framework* (SQL-DMF), which is an integrated framework of objects, services, and components used to manage Microsoft SQL Server. From the developer perspective, SQL-DMO is an Automation tool for remotely managing SQL Server.

The topmost object is the **Application** object, which cannot be directly connected. The initial connection is to the **SQLServer** object. The **Application** object is the parent object, and all other objects are available through this object. The **Application** object isn't referenced directly, and there can only be one instance of the **Application** object. (The **Application** object supports only the **Quit** method.)

SQL-DMO has several object-packaging techniques that simplify manageability. The first technique partitions a collection into lists. The Microsoft SQL-DMO documentation provides numerous lists. Listing 27-1 enumerates the startup procedures of a remote SQL Server using the **ListStartupProcedures** list.

 caution

Some caution must be used when interpreting the SQL-DMO vocabulary. What is referred to as a QueryResults object is in more precise terms the QueryResults collection of QueryResult objects. The individual QueryResult object is identified by the CurrentResultSet property of the QueryResults object. Chapters 27 and 28, the SQL-DMO

chapters, will use the published Microsoft definition of a SQL-DMO object.

The second technique is to place a group of properties in a collection and assign a collection name. Because the properties are members of a collection, the VBA **With ... End With** construct for enumerating class members can be used. This encapsulation of properties simplifies management and development tasks.

A **QueryResults** object is another example of encapsulation. The results of a SQL Server query are encapsulated within an object. Within the object encapsulation are the properties and methods of the object and properties of the resultset contained within the object.

Encapsulation has been carried to a higher level in SQL-DMO with a SQL Server query encapsulated within a method. RDO, JET, and ODBCDirect of DAO 3.5 do not encapsulate queries within a method. Any Enum*Lists* method of SQL-DMO is a SQL Server query that returns a **QueryResults** object. An example of such a method is the **EnumDirectories** list of the **SQLServer** object.

Using SQL-DMO

This section covers the basics of starting and using SQL-DMO objects. These are the preliminary issues. The section starts with the basic infrastructure and closes with SQL-DMO error processing.

Initialization

SQL-DMO requires a 32-bit environment and can be used from either a tool that supports Microsoft Visual Basic for Applications (VBA) or from Microsoft C++. The requirements for using SQL-DMO are outlined below.

Visual Basic 4.0 requires the `SQLOLE32.TLB` type library, while Visual Basic 5.0 requires a reference to the **Microsoft SQLOLE Object Library** (which is the `SQLOLE65.TLB`). The C++ file requirements are found in the Microsoft Documentation.

Starting SQL-DMO

A SQL-DMO application must first create a SQLServer object before connecting to a server. The initial SQL-DMO object is created with statement of the form:

```
Public objSQLServer as NEW SQLOLE .SQLServer
. . .
objSQLServer. connect "aserver", "alogin", "apassword"
```

A second syntax for instantiating SQL-DMO is with:

```
Dim objSQLServer as SQLOLE.SQLServer
Set objSQLServer = CreateObject("SQLOLE.SQLServer")
```

There is a third choice for instantiating SQL-DMO. It falls into the category of late-binding. It is done when no reference is possible to the SQLOLE library.

```
Dim objServer as Object
Set objServer = CreateObject("SQLOLE.Server")
```

Referencing SQL-DMO Objects

The objects of SQL-DMO are used in the same manner as objects from either RDO or DAO. Collection elements are referenced by ordinals or with quoted names. If the database *Pubs* has an ordinal of 1, then both **Set** statements below are equivalent. Ordinals are 1-based.

```
Dim objDatabase as SQLOLE.Database
Set objDatabase=objSQLServer.Databases("Pubs")
Set objDatabase = objSQLServer.Database(1)
```

Managing Objects

SQL-DMO has the standard object manipulation methods. **Add** appends an object to a collection while the **Remove** method removes an object from a collection. The **Refresh** method also fulfills its traditional role.

The **For...With** constructs are used for collection enumeration. SQL-DMO has partitioned collections into lists. For example, the **StoredProcedures** collection of the **SQLServer** object is partitioned to a **ListStartupProcedures** list. Accessing only those startup procedures might use a dialog similar to Listing 27-1.

LISTING 27-1 Using a list name in lieu of a collection name

```
Private Sub ListStartupProcedures_Click()
'(C) 1998 Bruce T. Prendergast
' DBA Prendergast Consulting
' DBA PCS
'
' Listing 27-1 Using ListStatupProcedures of SQL-DMO
'
  Dim objSQLDMO As New SQLOLE.SQLServer
  objSQLDMO.Connect "thor", "sa", ""
  Dim objListStrtProc As SQLOLE.StoredProcedure
  For Each objListStrtProc In _
  objSQLDMO.ListStartupProcedures
    With objListStrtProc
      MsgBox .Name
    End With
  Next objListStrtProc
  Set objSQLDMO = Nothing
  Exit Sub
End Sub
```

Listing 27-1 is a model of simplicity for connecting a SQL-DMO object to Microsoft SQL Server. Neither a DAO **Workspace** object nor a RDO **connection** object is required.

The other issue is the list name. The list name in the example above is **ListStartupProcedures,** which replaces the name of the parent **StoredProcedures** collection.

Error Processing

There are two distinct error processing mechanisms. The first error retrieval mechanism occurs with early vtable-binding. Visual Basic implementations supporting early Virtual table (vtable)-binding use the Visual Basic **Err** object to return application error information. **Error.Description** retrieves the standard error description while the expression **Err.Number-vbObjectError** calculates the

SQL-DMO error number. The name of the SQL-DMO component in error is found in **Err.Source**.

The second error processing mechanism is with a DISPID and late binding, which does not support the **Err** object, but supports the **Err** and **Error** function. Usage is illustrated by:

```
If Err <> 0
Debug.Print "Error from SQL-DMO " & Err & ": " & Error(Err)
```

COMPARING SQL-DMO, JET, RDO, AND ODBCDIRECT

Table 27-1 tells us that all SQL-DMO, Jet, RDO, and ODBCDirect implement COM objects. Only SQL-DMO does not have an engine, and it is a technology based only on COM. A SQL-DMO connect is simpler to establish than Jet, RDO, or ODBCDirect. SQL-DMO requires only the **SQLServer** object, and no engine is necessary to make a connection to SQL Server. Listing 27-1 illustrates the simplicity of establishing a SQL-DMO connection. The simplicity of SQL-DMO is a precursor of what is to come with OLE-DB (see Chapters 33-36). SQL-DMO is a technology for managing SQL Server remotely; however, like RDO, SQL-DMO is a proof of concept for new technology. That is not to say that SQL-DMO is or will be deprecated but that the techniques proven in SQL-DMO will be used in OLE-DB. SQL-DMO simplifies the object model. This is an interim step to OLE-DB where the object model is simplified further and objects may be instantiated without observing the rigid object hierarchy of Jet, ODBDirect, or RDO. Table 27-1 enumerates the infrastructure of connecting to SQL Server from the RDO, ODBCDirect, Jet, and SQL-DMO.

SQL-DMO and the UserData Property

Unique to SQL-DMO objects is the **UserData** property. This property has the **Long** attribute and can be used by the client application for setting flags. The property is not used by SQL-DMO, and its expected use is for automated management procedures in the SQL-DMO application.

TABLE 27-1 INFRASTRUCTURE OF CONNECTING TO JET, ODBCDIRECT, RDO, AND SQL-DMO

TECHNOLOGY	OBJECT	METHOD
Jet	DBEngine	Predefined
	Workspace object	Instantiated
	Database object	Instantiated
	QueryDef object	Instantiated and parameterized
ODBCDirect	DBEngine	Predefined
	Workspace object	Instantiated
	Connection object	Instantiated and parameterized
RDO	RDOEngine	Predefined
	Environment object	Instantiated
	Connection object	Instantiated and parameterized
SQL-DMO	SQLServer object	Predefined
	Connection object	Instantiated and parameterized

Default Collections

Like RDO and DAO, SQL-DMO has default collections. Default collections are a shorthand mechanism for accessing objects. Table 27-2 lists SQL-DMO's default collections.

TABLE 27-2 SQL-DMO DEFAULT COLLECTIONS

PARENT OBJECT	DEFAULT COLLECTION
Configuration	ConfigValues
Executive	Tasks
SQLServer	Databases
Database	Tables
Table	Columns

An example of using a default collection is *ParentObject!Name*. Using this syntax the *Pubs* database is accessed with the SQL-DMO statement **objSQLServer!***Pubs*. This is the equivalent of **objSQLServer.Databases***("Pubs")*.

SQL-DMO Collections, Methods, Objects, and Properties

Listing 27-2 is the objects, methods, and properties of SQL-DMO. The objects in the listing are arranged in object hierarchical order with the **Application** object first. All properties are read-write except those properties identified with the suffix <R>, which are read-only. Those properties identified with the suffix <BC> can be written *before the connection* is established. <BA> is used with the **Text** property of the **Default** object to indicate a write *before adding* the new default property.

Guide to SQL-DMO Collections, Methods, Objects, and Properties

LISTING 27-2 Objects, properties, and methods of the SQL-DMO architecture

```
Application
   Properties: Application(R), DBLibraryVersionString(R),
   FullName(R), Name(R), Parent(R), TypeOf(R), UserData,
   VersionMajor(R), VersionMinor(R)
   Methods: Quit
   Backup Object
Properties: Application(R), DiskDevices, DumpDevices,
DumpExpirationDate, DumpInitDeviceBefore, DumpRetainDays,
FloppyDevices, LoadFileNumber, LoadTableBatchPages, Parent(R),
SkipTapeHeader, TapeDevices, TypeOf(R), UnloadTapeAfter,
UserData
       Collections: Properties(R)
         Property Object
           Properties: Application(R), Get(R), Name(R),
           Parent(R), Set(R), Type(R), TypeOf(R), UserData, Value
```

```
                Collections: Properties (see above)
          HistoryFilter Object
             Properties: Application(R), CategoryName, CompletionTypes,
          EndDate, EventID, EventTypes, MessageID, MinimumRetries,
          MinimumRunDuration, MinimumTimesSkipped, OldestFirst,
          Parent(R), Severity, Source, StartDate, TaskID, TaskName,
          TypeOf(R), UserData
                Collections: Properties
                   Property Object (see Backup Object)
          Names Object (a collection of strings and not an objects
          collection)
                Properties: Application(R), Parent(R), TypeOf(R), UserData
                Methods: FindName, Insert, Replace
                Methods (string only) : Add, Remove, Refresh
          Permission Object
                Properties: Application(R), Granted(R), Grantee(R),
                ObjectID(R), ObjectName(R), ObjectOwner(R), ObjectType(R),
                ObjectTypeName(R), Parent(R), PrivilegeType(R),
                PrivilegeTypeName(R), TypeOf(R), UserData
                Lists: ListPrivilegeColumns
                Collections: Properties (see Backup Object)
          Collections: SQLServers(R), Properties
                Property Object (see Backup Object)
                SQLServer Object
                   Properties: Application(R), ApplicationName(BC),
                   AutoReConnect, CommandTerminator, Configuration(R),
                   ConnectionID(R), DistributionDatabase(R),
                   DistributionServer(R), DistributionWorkingDirectory,
                   Executive(R), HostName(BC), IntegratedSecurity(R),
                   Language, Login(BC), LoginSecure(BC), LoginTimeout(BC),
                   MaxNumericPrecision(R), Name(BC), NetPacketSize(BC),
                   NextDeviceNumber(R), Parent(R), Password(BC),
                   ProcessID(R), QueryTimeout, Registry(R), SaLogin(R),
                   Status(R), TrueLogin(R), TrueName(R), TypeOf(R),
                   UserData, UserProfile(R), VersionMajor(R),
                   VersionMinor(R), VersionString(R)
                   Methods: BeginTransaction, Close,
```

```
CommandShellImmediate(CommandShell),
CommandShellWithResults, CommitTransaction, Connect,
Continue, Disconnect, ExecuteImmediate,
ExecuteWithResults, KillDatabase, KillProcess, Pause,
ProcessInputBuffer, ProcessOutputBuffer, PurgeHistory,
ReadBackupHeader,ReadErrorLog, ReConnect,
RemoveSubscriberSubscriptions, RollbackTransaction,
SaveTransaction, Start, StatusInfoRefetchInterval,
ShutDown, UnloadODSDLL, VerifyConnection
Lists: EnumAvailableMedia, EnumDirectories,
EnumErrorLogs, EnumHistory, EnumLocks, EnumProcesses,
EnumPublicationDatabases, EnumServerAttributes,
EnumSubscriberSubscriptions, EnumSubscriptionDatabases,
EnumVersionInfo, ListStartupProcedures
Configuration Object
   Properties: Application(R), Parent(R),
   ShowAdvancecOptions, TypeOf(R), UserData
   Methods: ReconfigureCurrentValues,
   ReconfigureWithOverride
   Collections: ConfigValues(R), Parameters(R),
   Properties(R)
     ConfigValue Object
       Properties : Application(R), CurrentValue,
       Description(R), DynamicReconfigure(R), ID(R),
       MaximumValue(R), MinimumValue(R), Name(R),
       Parent(R), RunningValue(R), TypeOf(R), UserData
       Collections: Properties (see backup Object)
  Executive Object
   Properties: AlertSystem(R), Application(R), AutoStart,
   LimitHistoryRows, LimitHistoryRowsMax, Parent(R),
   RestartSQLServer, RestartSQLServerInterval, Status(R),
   TypeOf(R), UserData
   Methods: BeginAlter, CancelAlter, DoAlter,
   ReassignLoginTasks, Refresh, RemoveLoginTasks, Start,
   Stop
   Lists: EnumQueuedTasks, EnumSubSystems,
ListSubSystemTasks
```

```
Collections: Properties(R), Tasks(R)
  Property Object (See Backup Object)
  Task Object
    Properties: ActiveEndDate, ActiveStartDate,
    Application(R), Command, Database, DateCreated(R),
    DateModified(R), Description,
    EMailCompletionLevel, EmailOperator, Enabled,
    FrequencyInterval, FrequencyRecurrenceFactor,
    FrequencyRelativeInterval, FrequencySubDay,
    FrequencySubDayInterval, FrequencyType, ID(R),
    LastRunCompletionLevel(R), LastRunDate(R),
    LastRunDuration(R), LastRunRetries(R),
    LogHistoryCompletionLevel, Name, NextRunDate(R),
    Owner(R), Parent(R), RetryAttempts, RetryDelay,
    RunPriority, SubSystem, TagAdditionalInfo,
    TagObjectID, TagObjectType, TargetSQLServer,
    TypeOf(R), User, UserData
    Methods: BeginAlter, CancelAlter, DoAlter, Invoke,
    PurgeHistory, Reassign, Refresh, Remove
    Lists: EnumHistory
    Collections: Properties (see Backup Object)
  AlertSystem Object
    Properties: Application(R), FailSafeOperator,
    ForwardingServer, ForwardingSeverity,
    NofificationMethod, PagerCCTemplate,
    PagerSendSubjectOnly, PagerSubjectTemplate,
    PagerToTemplate, Parent(R), TypeOf(R), UserData
    Methods: BeginAlter, CancelAlter, DoAlter, Refresh
    Collections : Properties (see Backup Object)
Registry Object
  Properties: Application(R), AutostartLicensing,
  AutostartMail, AutostartServer, CaseSensitive(R),
  CharacterSet(R), ErrorLogPath, MailAccountName,
  MailPassword, MasterDBpath, NTEventLogging(R),
  NumberOfProcessors(R), Parent(R), PerfMonMode,
  PhysicalMemory(R), RegisteredOrganization(R),
  RegisteredOwner(R), SortOrder(R), SQLRootPath,
```

TapeLoadWaitTime, TypeOf(R), Userdata

Collections: Properties (see Backup Object)

IntegratedSecurity Object

Properties: Application(R), AuditLevel, DefaultDomain, DefaultLogin, ImpersonateClient, MapDollarSign, MapPoundSign, MapUnderscore, Parent(R), SecurityMode, SetHostName TypeOf(R), UserData

Methods: GrantNTLogin, Refresh, RevokeNTLogin

Lists: EnumAccountInfo, EnumNTDomainGroups

Collections: Properties (see Backup Object)

Collections: Alerts(R), Databases(R), Devices(R), Languages(R), Logins(R), Operators(R), Properties(R), RemoteServers(R)

Alert Object

Properties: Application(R), CountResetDate, DatabaseName, DelayBetweenResponses, Enabled, EventCategory(R), EventDescriptionKeyword, EventID(R), EventSource(R), HasEMailNotification(R), HasPagerNotification(R), ID(R), IncludeEventDescription, LastOccuranceDate, LastResponsedate, MessageID, Name, NotificationMessage, OccuranceCount, Parent(R), Severity, TaskName, TypeOf(R), UserData

Methods: AddNotification, BeginAlter, CancelAlter, DoAlter, Refresh, Remove, RemoveNotification, UpdateNotification

Lists: EnumNotifications

Collections: Properties (see Backup Object)

Database Object

Properties: Application(R), CreateDate(R), CreateForLoad(BA), DataSpaceUsage(R), DBOLogin(R), DBOption(R), IndexSpaceUsage(R), ID(R), MinimumSize(R), Name, Owner(R), Parent(R), Size(R), SpaceAvailable(R), SpaceAvailableInMB(R), Status(R), SystemObject(R), TransactionLog(R), TypeOf(R), UserData, UserName, UserProfile(R), Version(R)

Methods: CheckAllocations, CheckCatalog, CheckPoint,

```
                         CheckTables, CheckTextAllocsFast,
                         CheckTextAllocsFull, Dump, ExecuteImmediate,
                         ExecuteWithResults, ExtendOnDevices,
                         GenerateBackupSQL, GetDataTypeByName,
                         GetMemoryUsage, GetObjectByName, Grant,
                         IsValidKeyDataType, Load, ManualSyncCompleted,
                         ManualSyncPending, RecalcSpaceUsage, Remove, Revoke,
                         SetOwner, Shrink, SpaceAllocatedOnDevice
                         Lists: EnumCandidateKeys, EnumDependencies,
                         EnumLocks, ListDatabasePermissions, ListDevices,
                         ListObjectPermissions, ListObjects
                    DBObject Object
                       Properties: CreateDate(R), ID(R), Name, Owner(R),
                       Parent(R), SystemObject(R), Type(R), TypeName(R),
                       TypeOf(R), UserData
                       Methods: Remove, Script
                       Lists: EnumDependencies, ListPermissions,
                       ListUserPermissions
                       Collections: Properties (see Backup Object)
                    DBOption Object
                       Properties: ColumnsNullByDefault, DBOUseOnly,
                       EnablePublishing, EnableSubscribing,
                       NoCheckpointOnRecovery, Offline, Parent(R),
                       ReadOnly, SelectIntoBulkCopy, SingleUser,
                       TruncateLogOnCheckpoint, TypeOf(R), UserData
                       Methods: Refresh
                       Collections: Properties (see Backup Object)
                    TransactionLog Object
                       Properties: Application(R), CreateDate(R),
                       IsLogOnSeparateDevice(R), LastDump(R), Parent(R),
                       Size(R), SpaceAvailable(R), SpaceAvailableinMB(R),
                       TypeOf(R), UserData
                       Methods: DedicateLogDevices, Dump,
                       GenerateBackupSQL, Load, SpaceAllocatedOndevice,
                       Truncate, UndedicateLogDevices
                       Lists: ListDevices
                       Collections: Properties (see Backup Object)
```

```
SystemDatatype Object
  Properties: AllowIdentity(R), AllowNulls(R),
  Application(R), IsNumeric(R), MaximumLength(R),
  Name(R), Parent(R), TypeOf(R), UserData
  Collections: Properties (see Backup Object)
Collections: Defaults(R), Groups(R), Properties(R),
Publications(R), Rules(R), StoredProcedures(R),
SystemDatatypes(R), Tables(R),
UserdefinedDatatypes(R), Users(R), Views(R)
  Default Object
    Properties: Application(R), CreateDate(R),
    ID(R), Name, Owner(R), Parent(R), Text(BA),
    TypeOf(R), UserData
    Methods: BindToColumn, BindToDataType, Remove,
    Script, UnbindFromColumn, UnbindFromDatatype
    Lists: ListBoundColumns, ListBoundDataTypes
    Collections: Properties (see Backup Object)
  Group Object
    Properties: Application(R), ID(R), Name(BA),
    Parent(R), SystemObject(R), TypeOf(R), UserData
    Methods: Remove, Script
    Lists: ListDatabasePermissions,
    ListObjectPermissions, ListUsers
    Collections: Properties (see Backup Object)
  Property Object (see Backup Object)
  Publication Object
    Properties: Application(R), Description,
    Enabled, ID(R), InitialSyncMethod,
    InitialSyncTask(R), Name, Parent(R),
    ReplicationFrequency, Restricted, TypeOf(R),
    UserData
    Methods: BeginAlter, CancelAlter, DoAlter,
    Remove
    Lists: EnumFullSubscribers
    Collections: Articles, Properties(R)
      Article Object
        Properties: Application(R),
```

```
                    CreationScriptPath, DeleteCommand,
                    Description, DestinationTableName,
                    FilterClause, ID(R), InitialSyncObjectName,
                    InsertCommand, Name, Parent(R),
                    PreCreationMethod, ReplicateAllColumns(R),
                    ReplicationFilterProcName, ReplicationType,
                    TableName(BA), TypeOf(R), UpdateCommand,
                    UserData
                    Methods: AddReplicatedColumns, BeginAlter,
                    CancelAlter, DoAlter, Remove,
                    RemoveReplictedColumns,
                    ScriptDestinationTable
                    Lists: ListReplicatedColumns,
                    Collections: Properties(R), Subscriptions(R)
                      Property Object (see Backup Object)
                      Subscription Object
                         Properties: Application(R),
                         DestinationDatabase, InitialSyncType,
                         Parent(R), ServerName, Status,
                         TypeOf(R), UserData
                         Methods: BeginAlter, CancelAlter,
                         DoAlter, Remove
                         Collections: Properties (see Backup
                         Object)
                 Property Object (see Backup Object)
              Rule Object
                 Properties: Application(R), CreateDate(R),
                 ID(R), Name, Owner(R), Parent(R), Text(BA),
                 TypeOf(R), UserData
                 Methods: BindToColumn, BindToDataType, Remove,
                 Script, UnbindFromColumn, UnbindfromDatatype
                 Lists: ListBoundColumns, ListBoundDataTypes
                 Collections: Properties (see Backup Object)
              StoredProcedure Object
                 Properties: Application(R), CreateDate(R),
                 ID(R), Name, Owner(R), Parent(R), Startup(BA),
                 SystemObject(R), Text(BA), Type(R), TypeOf(R),
```

UserData
Methods: Grant, Remove, Revoke, Script
Lists: EnumDependencies, EnumParameters,
ListPermissions, ListUserPermissions
Collections: Properties (see Backup Object)
SystemDatatype Object
Properties: AllowIdentity(R), AllowNulls(R),
Application(R), IsNumeric(R), MaximumLength(R),
Name(R), Parent(R), TypeOf(R), Userdata
Collections: Properties (see Backup Object)
Table Object
Properties: Application(R), Attributes(R),
ClusteredIndex(R), CreateDate(R),
DataSpaceUsed(R), ID(R), IndexSpaceUsed(R),
Name, Owner(R), Parent(R), PrimaryKey(R),
Rows(R), SystemObject, TypeOf(R), UserData
Methods: BeginAlter, CancelAlter, CheckTable,
CheckTextAllocfast, CheckTextAllocsFull,
DoAlter, DoAlterWithNoCheck, Grant,
InsertColumn, RecalcSpaceUsage,
RecompileReferences, Refresh, Remove, Revoke,
Script, TruncateData, UpdateStatistics
Lists: EnumDependencies, EnumStatisticsUpdates,
EnumReferencedKeys, EnumReferencedTables,
EnumReferencingKeys, EnumReferencingTables,
ListArticles, ListPermissions,
ListUserPermissions
Collections: Checks(R), Columns(R), Indexes(R),
Keys(R), Properties(R), Triggers(R)
  Check Object
    Properties: Application(R),
    ExcludeReplication, Name, Parent(R),
    Text(BA), TypeOf(R), UserData
    Methods: Remove, Script
    Collections: Properties (see Backup Object)
  Column Object
    Properties: AllowNulls(BA), Application(R),

```
                              DataType(BA), Default, DRIDefault(R), ID(R),
                              Identity(BA), IdentityIncrement(BA),
                              IdentitySeed(BA), InPrimaryKey(BA),
                              Length(BA), Name, NumericPrecision(BA),
                              NumericScale(BA), Parent(R),
                              PhysicalDataType(R), Rule, TypeOf(R),
                              UserData
                              Methods: Remove
                              Lists: ListKeys
                              Collections: Properties (see Backup Object)
                    Index Object
                              Properties: Application(R), FillFactor(BA),
                              ID(R), Name, Parent(R), SpaceUsed(R),
                              Type(BA), TypeOf(R), UserData
                              Methods: GenerateCreationSQL,
                              IndexedColumns, Rebuild, RecalcSpaceUsage,
                              Remove, Script, UpdateStatistics
                              Lists: EnumStatistics, ListIndexedColumns
                              Collections: Properties (see Backup Object)
                    Key Object
                              Properties: Application(R), Clustered(BA),
                              FillFactor(BA), Name, Parent(R),
                              ReferencedKey(R), ReferencedTable, Type,
                              TypeOf(R), UserData
                              Methods: Remove, Script
                              Collections: KeyColumns(R), Properties(R),
                              ReferencedColumns(R)
                                KeyColumn Object (names, not an object
                                collection)
                                Property Object (see Backup Object)
                                ReferencedColumn Object (names, not an
                                object collection)
                    Property Object (see Backup Object)
                    Trigger Object
                              Properties: Application(R), CreateDate(R),
                              ID(R), Name, Owner(R), Parent(R),
```

         SystemObject(R), Text(BA), Type(BA),
         TypeOf(R), UserData
         Methods: Remove, Script,
         Lists: Enumdependencies
         Collections: Properties (see Backup Object)
    UserDefinedDatatype Object
      Properties: AllowIdentity(R), AllowNulls(BA),
      Application(R), BaseType(BA), Default, ID(R),
      Length(BA), Name, NumericPrecision(BA),
      NumericScale(BA), Owner(R), Parent(R), Rule,
      TypeOf(R), UserData
      Methods: Remove, Script
      Lists: ListBoundColumns, UserDefinedDatatype
      Collections: Properties (see Backup Object)
    User Object
Properties: Application(R), Group, ID(R), Login(BA)
Name(BA), Parent(R), SystemObject(R), TypeOf(R),
UserData
         Methods: AddAlias, Remove, RemoveAlias, Script
         Lists: List Aliases, ListDatabasePermissions,
         ListObjectPermissions, ListOwnedDevices
         Collections: Properties (see Backup Object)
Device Object
   Properties: Application(R), Default,
   DeviceNumber(R), FirstPage(R), LastPage(R),
   MirrorName(R), MirrorState(R), Name, Parent(R),
   PhysicalLocation(BA), Size(BA), SkipTapeLabel,
   SpaceAvailable(R), Status, SystemObject(R), Type,
   TypeOf(R), UserData
   Methods: Mirror, ReadBackupHeader, ReMirror, Remove,
   SwitchToMirrorDevice, SwitchToMirrorTemp,
   UnMirrorDevice, UnMirrorTemp
   Lists: ListDatabases
   Collections: Properties (see Backup Object)
Language Object
   Properties: Alias, Application(R), DateFormat(BA),

```
        Days(BA), FirstDayOfWeek(BA), ID(R), Months(BA),
        Name(BA), Parent(R), ShortMonths(BA), TypeOf(R),
        Upgrade(R), UserData
        Methods: Day, Month, Remove, ShortMonth
        Collections: Properties (see Backup Object)
Login Object
        Properties: Application(R), Database, Language,
        ID(R), Name(BA), Parent(R), SystemObject(R),
        TypeOf(R), UserData
        Methods: AliasName, Remove, Script, SetPassword,
        UserName
        Lists: ListTasks
        Collections: Properties (see Backup Object)
Operator Object
        Properties: Application(R), EMailAddress, Enabled,
        ID(R), LastEMailDate(R), LastPageDate(R), Name,
        PagerDays, PagerAddress, Parent(R),
        SaturdayPagerEndTime, SaturdayPagerStartTime,
        SundayPagerEndTime, SundayPagerStartTime,
        WeekdayPagerEndTime, WeekdayPagerStartTime,
        TypeOf(R), UserData
        Methods: AddNotification, BeginAlter, CancelAlter,
        DoAlter, Refresh, Remove, RemoveNotification,
        UpdateNotification
        Lists: EnumNotifications
        Collections: Properties (see Backup Object)
Property Object (see Backup Object)
RemoteServer Object
        Properties: Application(R), ID(R), Name(BA),
        NetName, Options(R), Parent(R), SubscriberInfo(R),
        TopologyX(R), TopologyY(R), TypeOf(R), UserData
        Methods: BeginAlter, DoAlter, CancelAlter,
        ExecuteImmediate, ExecuteWithResults, Refresh,
        Remove, SetOptions, SetTopologyXY(Reserved),
        Subscribe, UnSubscribe
        Lists: EnumArticles, EnumPublicationDatabases,
```

```
EnumPublications, EnumPublicationsSyncTask,
EnumSubscriptionDatabases, EnumSubscriptions,
EnumTasks
Collections: Properties(R), RemoteLogins(R)
   Property Object (see Backup Object)
   RemoteLogin Object
      Properties: Application(R), LocalName(BA),
      Parent(R), RemoteName(BA), Trusted, TypeOf(R),
      UserData
      Methods: Remove
      Collections: Properties (see Backup Object)
```

SQL-DMO PROPERTY OBJECT

Every SQL-DMO object has a **Properties** collection except the **Property** object. (I hope that is clear.) Recall that objects are elements of collections. A **Property** object with a collection would be a self definition, and that is not correct. A **Property** object is related to every object property. The **Property** object is not available to C++. (If my attempts to clarify this topic have led to further obfuscation, please move on because there is nothing on either Windows Architecture examination relating to the **Properties** collections of SQL-DMO.)

Property Object Properties

Application	The **Application** object
Get	**True** if the property can be read
Name	Property Name
Parent	Parent object
Set	**True** if the value can be changed
Type	Visual Basic property type
TypeOf	SQLOLE_OBJECT_TYPE value
UserData	Application data, long

SQL-DMO Architecture

Figure 27-1 shows the SQL-DMO architecture. The **Application** object is the top object in the hierarchy. It cannot be referenced except as a property of another object. It is the parent of all other application objects, and there can only be one **Application** object. The **Application** object cannot be instantiated.

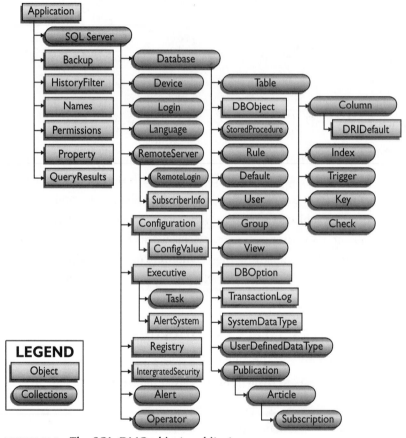

FIGURE 27-1   The SQL-DMO object architecture.

Figure 27-1 illustrates the concept of encapsulated properties within an object. The **Application** object has several of these objects.

KEY POINT SUMMARY

SQL-DMO is an Automation tool (Chapter 9) that encapsulates the native SQL Server DB-LIB API. SQL-DMO is a tool for the remote management of SQL Server. The SQL-DMO implementation is complete, and the SQL Server Enterprise Manager is implemented using SQL-DMO.

Microsoft appears to be focusing most of their energy on Internet technologies. Because of this we've enjoyed an unusually long period (two years) of relative stability with SQL Server 6.5 and SQL-DMO. My hope is that this stability of the technology will continue after the release of Microsoft SQL Server 7.0, which is scheduled to be released this year. Highlights of this chapter are:

- While SQL-DMO can query SQL Server, SQL-DMO is a SQL Server management tool and not a SQL Server query tool.

- SQL-DMO does not require an engine and is a COM technology.

- SQL-DMO has a unique object packaging within the Microsoft toolset. Properties are encapsulated as subservient objects (collections), and collections are partitioned as lists.

- SQL-DMO, while unique, inherits many standard object constructs from RDO and DAO.

- While SQL-DMO has many properties and methods, it is a relatively simple object model. It has more objects than RDO or DAO, but it is easier to use.

APPLYING WHAT YOU'VE LEARNED

These questions will measure your understanding of the position that SQL-DMO occupies in the Microsoft architecture. The questions will also measure your understanding of the conceptual differences between SQL-DMO and the previously discussed RDO and DAO implementations.

Instant Assessment

1. SQL-DMO has collections that are similar to both RDO and DAO. What is the relationship of a list to a collection?

2. How has SQL-DMO improved property management?

3. What characteristic does SQL-DMO share with RDO?

4. What is the top object in the SQL-DMO object hierarchy? How is it accessed?

5. All SQL-DMO objects have a very unique property. What is the name of that property and what is it used for?

6. Compare the use of SQL-DMO to connect to Microsoft SQL versus the use of DAO to connect to Microsoft SQL Server.

7. What is a Microsoft C++ limitation with respect to SQL-DMO properties?

 concept link   **For answers to the Instant Assessment questions, see Appendix C.**

Windows Architecture I
Windows Architecture II

CHAPTER

Working with Application Scope Objects

28

About Chapter 28

Chapter 28 is the first of five chapters that takes a close look at Microsoft SQL Server Distributed Management Objects (SQL-DMO). The **Application** object is the focus of this chapter.

An **Application** object is temporary and cannot be persisted. The **Quit** method of the **Application** object closes all connections to SQL Server and releases all existing SQL-DMO objects. SQL-DMO objects cannot be persisted. A good example is the **QueryResults** object. Another example is the **Backup** object, which is a collection of properties that are passed to a method or another object for a dump process.

The examples in this chapter may be found in the Visual Basic 5.0 Enterprise Edition project CHAPTER28.VBP located in the EXAMPLES\ CHAPTER28 folder of the CD-ROM located at the back of this book. This project is the SQL-DMO tool we'll use in all further SQL-DMO examples.

Understanding the **QueryResults** object of **Application** object is necessary for both the Windows Architecture I and II examinations.

THE SQL–DMO APPLICATION

Figure 28-1 is the SQL-DMO application we explore. The operation is fairly simple. Provide a server, user identification, and a password. Click the **Login** button and the **Application** menu is enabled. From the **Application** menu there are several choices, which include *Application*, *Backup*, *Permissions*, and *Query Results*. These are the examples for this chapter. The **Application** object appears when *Application* is clicked.

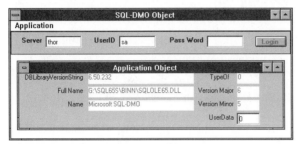

FIGURE 28-1   The Application object.

THE APPLICATION OBJECT

The **Application** object is the parent of all SQL-DMO objects. There can only be one instance of an **Application** object.

   Quit is the only method of the **Application** object. No other SQL-DMO objects can be referenced after using the **Quit** method.

Application Object Properties

Application	The **Application** object; a self reference
DBLibraryVersionString	The DB-Library version string
FullName	The filename and full path of the SQL-DMO component object layer
Name	The SQL-DMO component object layer name
Parent	The **Application** object; a self reference

TypeOf	SQLOLE_OBJECT_TYPE value
UserData	Temporary application storage that is not used by SQL-DMO

Quit is the only method of the Application object. Listing 28-1 requires the statement:

```
Public objSQLDMO as New SQLOLE.SQLServer
```

This statement is defined in the declaration section of the CHAPTER28.BAS Module within the CHAPTER28.VBP Visual Basic 5.0 Enterprise Edition project.

Listing 28-1 instantiates the **objSQLDMO** object. The properties of the resulting **Application** object are enumerated in Listing 28-1. This is the same **Application** object displayed in Figure 28-1.

LISTING 28-1 Creating the SQL-DMO Application object form of Figure 28-1

```
Private Sub Form_Load()
'(c) 1998 Bruce T. Prendergast
' DBA Prendegast Consulting
' DBA PCS
' IDG Books Worldwide ISBN 0-7645-3123-9
'
' Listing 28-1Initializing the Application object form
' of Figure 28-2
'

  Dim Response As Integer
  Response = CenterForm(Me)
  Dim objApplication As SQLOLE.Application

  Set objApplication = objSQLDMO.Application
  With objApplication
    txtDBLibraryVersionString = .DBLibraryVersionString
    txtFullName = .FullName
    txtName = .Name
    txtTypeOf = .TypeOf
    txtVersionMajor = VersionMajor
    txtVersionMinor = .VersionMinor
    txtUserData = .UserData
```

```
        End With
        Exit Sub
End Sub
```

WORKING WITH THE BACKUP OBJECT

A **Backup** object is rather unique. It is not an object with storage persistence; it is a packaging of parameters that are then passed to either a **Dump**, **Load**, **GenerateBackupSQL** method of a **TransactionLog** object, or to a **Database** object, or to the **SQLServer.ReadBackupHeader** method. The **Backup** object has no methods.

Backup Object Properties

Application	The **Application** object
DiskDevices	Delimited list of disk devices (Uses the SQL-DMO **MultiString** format for the full path, hard disk device, and optional volume name)
DumpDevices	Delimited list of dump devices (Uses the SQL-DMO **MultiString** format for the full path, hard disk device, and optional volume name)
DumpExpirationDate	Dump cannot be overwritten before this date
DumpInitDeviceBefore	A flag that determines if the device should be initialized before the dump starts
DumpRetainDays	The period in days to retain the dump
FloppyDevices	A **MultiString** list of floppy disk devices and volume specifiers
LoadFileNumber	The file to load from a tape or disk device
LoadTableBatchPages	The number of data pages to load between transaction commits
Parent	The **Application** object
SkipTapeHeader	A flag to skip American National Standards Institute (ANSI) tape headers when dumping to or loading from a tape device

TapeDevices	A **MultiString** list of tape devices that includes the full path, file name, and an optional volume
TypeOf	`SQLOLE_OBJECT_TYPE` value
UnloadTapeAfter	A flag for automatically rewinding and unloading the tape after the operation is complete
UserData	Temporary application storage that is not used by SQL-DMO

Let's take a look under the hood of the **Backup** object. Remember that it only plays a very small role in the grand scheme of Microsoft SQL Server database backup. Figure 28-2 is the result of selecting **Application** ⇒ **Backup** from our SQL-DMO application.

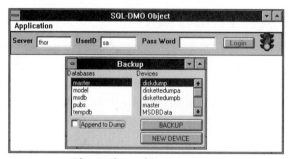

FIGURE 28-2   The Backup object.

The form should be self-explanatory. A **Database** object and a **Device** object are selected and a check box determines if the dump is to be appended. The code from the BACKUP command button is shown in Listing 28-2.

LISTING 28-2   Creating a database backup with SQL-DMO

```
Private Sub cmdBackup_Click()
'(c) 1998 Bruce T. Prendergast
' DBA Prendergast Consulting
' DBA PCS
' IDG Books Worldwide ISBN 0-7645-3123-9
'
' Listing 28-2 Using the SQL-DMO Backup object
' of Figure 28-3
```

```
Dim objBackup As New SQLOLE.Backup
Dim intResp As Integer
Dim msg As String
'
' is there a backup device
'
If IsNull(lboDevices) Then Exit Sub
'
' has one been selected?
'
If lboDevices.ListIndex = -1 Then
  MsgBox "Disk device is not selected"
  Exit Sub
End If
'
' has a database been selected?
'
If IsNull(lboDatabases) Then Exit Sub
If lboDatabases.ListIndex = -1 Then
  MsgBox "No database selected"
  Exit Sub
End If
msg = "This will backup the database " & _
  lboDatabases & " to " & lboDevices & _
  ". Continue?"
intResp = MsgBox(msg, vbOKCancel + _
  vbCritical + vbDefaultButton2, _
  "Warning: Database Backup")
If intResp <> vbOK Then Exit Sub
'
' create a backup object
'
objBackup.DumpDevices = lboDevices.Text
'
' check for appending dump
If chkAppend.Value = True Then
```

```
        objBackup.DumpInitDeviceBefore = 0
    Else
        objBackup.DumpInitDeviceBefore = 1
    End If
    '
    ' Let's do it
    '
    MousePointer = 11
    On Error GoTo Backup_error
    objSQLDMO.Databases( _
        CStr(lboDatabases)).Dump objBackup
Normal_exit:
    MousePointer = 0
    Exit Sub
Backup_error:
    MsgBox "Error: " & Err.Number & " " & _
        Err.Description + " from " & Err.Source
    Resume Normal_exit
End Sub
```

There are two other very important features of the **Backup** form. The space used and allocated is displayed by double-clicking either the **Databases** or **Devices** list box. The control used to display the space used and allocated is the GRAPH32.OCX control. It is the **Pinnacle-BPS Graph Control** found by selecting **Project ⇒ Components ⇒ Pinnacle-BPS Graph Control of Visual Basic 5.0**. Figure 28-3 shows the database space allocation.

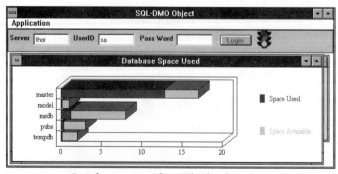

FIGURE 28-3   Database usage from the backup form.

The code to create the graph of Figure 28-3 uses the **Database** object, which hasn't been discussed. The code, shown in Listing 28-3, is easy to understand so we shouldn't be too far ahead of ourselves.

LISTING 28-3 Creating the graph of Figure 28-3

```
Private Sub Form_Load()
'(C) 1998 Bruce T. Prendergast
' DBA Prendergast Consulting
' DBA PCS
' IDG Books Worldwide ISBN 0-7645-3123-9
'
' Listing 28-3 Creating Figure 28-4 from the
' Databases collection
'
 Dim i As Integer
  Dim Result As Boolean
  Dim objDatabase As SQLOLE.Database
  Dim sngSize As Single
  Result = CenterForm(Me)
  Graph1.NumPoints = objSQLDMO.Databases.Count
  Graph1.NumSets = 2
  Graph1.ThisSet = 1
  i = 0
  For Each objDatabase In objSQLDMO.Databases
    i = i + 1
    Graph1.ThisPoint = i
    Graph1.LabelText = objDatabase.Name
    sngSize = CSng(objDatabase.SpaceAvailableInMB)
    Graph1.ThisSet = 1
    Graph1.GraphData = CSng(objDatabase.Size) - sngSize
    Graph1.ThisSet = 2
    Graph1.GraphData = sngSize
  Next objDatabase
  Exit Sub
End Sub
```

The last feature of Figure 28-3 is creating a new **Device** object, which is illustrated in Figure 28-4 and Listing 28-4. This is also getting ahead of ourselves, but a bit of preannouncing reduces the burden of the subsequent chapters.

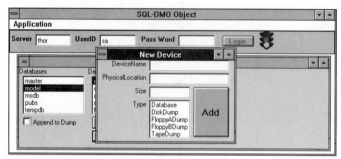

FIGURE 28-4   The new device form.

LISTING 28-4   Creating a new device with SQL-DMO

```
Private Sub cmdAdd_Click()
'(C)1998 Bruce T. Prendergast
' DBA Prendergast Consulting
' DBA PCS
' IDG Books Worldwide ISBN 0-7645-3123-9
'
' Listing 28-4 Creating a new device in Figure 28-5
'
  Dim objDevice As New SQLOLE.Device
  Dim strNoNo As String
  Dim strName As String
  Dim i As Integer
  '
  ' a valid device name
  '
  strName = Trim$(txtName & "")
  If Len(strName) = 0 Then
    MsgBox "Please specify a device name"
    Exit Sub
  End If
```

```
strNoNo = "./[];=\:|," & Chr$(34)
For i = 1 To Len(strNoNo)
  If InStr(1, strName, Mid$(strNoNo, i, 1)) Then
    MsgBox "Invalid device name"
    Exit Sub
  End If
Next i
'
' a valid physical location
'
On Error GoTo File_Error
If (GetAttr(txtPhysicalLocation) And vbDirectory) = 0 Then
  MsgBox "Physical Location must be a valid directory"
  Exit Sub
End If
On Error GoTo Normal_error
'
' limit is 1-100 megabytes for size
'
If Val(txtSize) < 1 Or Val(txtSize) > 100 Then
  MsgBox "Device limit is 1-100 megabytes"
  Exit Sub
End If
'
' must select a device type
'
If lboType.ListIndex = -1 Then
  MsgBox "Please select a device type".
  Exit Sub
End If
'
' build device
'
With objDevice
  .Name = strName
  .PhysicalLocation = txtPhysicalLocation & _
```

```
      "\" & strName
    .Size = Val(txtSize)
    .Type = lboType.ItemData(lboType.ListIndex)
  End With
  objSQLDMO.Devices.Add objDevice
  objSQLDMO.Devices.Refresh
Normal_exit:
  Exit Sub
File_Error:
  MsgBox "Invalid physical location"
  Resume Normal_exit
Normal_error:
  MsgBox "Error: " & Err.Number & " " & _
    Err.Description + " from " & Err.Source
  Resume Normal_exit
End Sub
```

That's enough of the **Backup** object! Let's move on to the next **Application** scope object.

Working with the HistoryFilter Object

The **HistoryFilter** object is the repackaging of properties for use by another object. The **HistoryFilter** object is used by the **EnumHistory** or **PurgeHistory** methods of the **SQLServer** or **Task** object. Using this method from a **SQLServer** object is illustrated with:

```
objSQLServer.PurgeHistory HistoryFilter := objHistoryFilter
```

HistoryFilter Object Properties

Application	The **Application** object
CategoryName	Included event category name
CompletionTypes	SQLOLE_COMPLETION_TYPE value
EndDate	Include all tasks before this end date

EventID	Included event ID
EventTypes	`SQLOLE_EVENT_TYPE` value
MessageID	Included message ID
MinimumRetries	Minimum retry count
MinimumRunDuration	Date, minimum run time
MinimumTimesSkipped	Minimum number of times a task was skipped
OldestFirst	If **True**, then task list is sorted in ascending time of task occurrence
Parent	The **Application** object
Severity	Included **Severity** level
Source	Included event source
StartDate	Include all tasks after this date and time
TaskID	Task ID (You must be the task owner or the system administrator when passing this to **SQLServer.PurgeHistory**)
TaskName	Task name (You must be the task owner or the system administrator when passing this to **SQLServer.PurgeHistory**)
TypeOf	`SQLOLE_OBJECT_TYPE` value
UserData	Temporary task storage

WORKING WITH THE PERMISSIONS OBJECT

A **Permissions** object is another of those strange objects without a permanent habitat. SQL-DMO defines a series of lists, some of which are permission lists. These lists are read-only and are not objects with storage persistence.

Permissions Object Properties

Application	The **Application** object
Granted	If **True**, then the privilege is granted

Grantee	The database user or group for whom this privilege applies
ObjectID	The object ID
ObjectName	Name
ObjectOwner	Database user owning the object
ObjectType	`SQLOLE_OBJECT_TYPE` value
ObjectTypeName	The object type name to which this privilege applies
Parent	The **Application** object
PrivilegeType	`SQLOLE_PRIVILEGE_TYPE` value
PrivilegeTypeName	Identifier
TypeOf	`SQLOLE_OBJECT_TYPE` value
UserData	Temporary storage (long)

Methods

ListPrivilegeColumns	*ColumnList = Permission.**ListPrivilegeColumns***

This method returns a list of **Column** objects included in a SELECT or UPDATE privileges for a table or view. Creating a **ColumnList** object is a two-step process. The first step is to create a **Permission** object list, which is illustrated below.

```
Dim objPermissionList As Object
Dim objPermission As SQLOLE.Permission
Dim objSQLDMO As New SQLOLE.SQLServer
Dim objDatabase As SQLOLE.Database
'
' connect to SQL server
'
objSQLDMO.Connect "thor", "sa", ""
Set objDatabase = objSQLDMO.Databases("Pubs")
'
' build a permissions list
'
Set objPermissionList =
  objDatabase.Tables("authors").ListPermissions
```

A **PermissionList** object now exists and privilege columns can be found by enumerating the **PermissionList** object.

```
Dim PrivList As Object
For Each objPermission In objPermissionList
Set PrivList = objPermission.ListPrivilegeColumns
'
' evaluate list
'
Next objPermission
End Sub
```

Selecting **Application** ⇒ **Permissions** in our SQL-DMO application captured Figure 28-5. The *Pubs* database was selected followed by selecting the only view.

The grid control `GRID32.OCX` is found with **Project** ⇒ **Components** ⇒ **Microsoft Grid Control**. Listing 28-5 is the supporting code for the form. The mouse is used to adjust grid column widths.

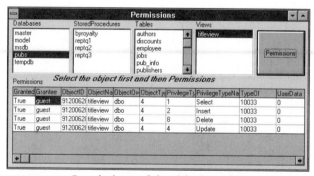

FIGURE 28-5 Permissions of the **titleview** object in the Pubs database.

LISTING 28-5 Creating the permissions of Figure 28-5

```
Private Sub DisplayPermissions()
'(C) 1998 Bruce T. Prendergast
' DBA Prendergast
' DBA PCS
' IDG Books Worldwide ISBN 0-7645-3123-9
'
' Listing 28-5 A common subroutine used to display
```

```
' permissions. The subroutine is called from the
' click event of the Stored procedures, Tables, or
' Views list boxes of Figure 28-6.
'

  Dim i As Integer
  Dim objPermissionList As Object
  Dim objPermission As SQLOLE.Permission
  Dim objDatabase As SQLOLE.Database
  '
  ' got to have a database
  '
  If lboDatabases.ListIndex = -1 Then
    MsgBox "Please select a database"
    Exit Sub
  End If
  On Error GoTo Permission_error
  '
  ' get the permissions
  '
  Set objDatabase = objSQLDMO.Databases( _
    CStr(lboDatabases))
  Select Case PermissionIndex
    Case 1
      Set objPermissionList = _
        objDatabase.ListObjectPermissions()
    Case 2
      Set objPermissionList = _
        objDatabase.StoredProcedures( _
        CStr(lboStoredProcedures)).ListPermissions
    Case 3
      Set objPermissionList = _
        objDatabase.Tables(CStr(lboTables)).ListPermissions
    Case 4
      Set objPermissionList = _
        objDatabase.Views(CStr(lboViews)).ListPermissions
  End Select
```

```
MousePointer = 11
Grid1.Cols = 10
Grid1.FixedCols = 0
Grid1.Rows = objPermissionList.Count + 1
Grid1.Row = 0
Grid1.Col = 0: Grid1.ColWidth(0) = 600: _
  Grid1.Text = "Granted"
Grid1.Col = 1: Grid1.ColWidth(1) = 700: _
  Grid1.Text = "Grantee"
Grid1.Col = 2: Grid1.ColWidth(2) = 700: _
  Grid1.Text = "ObjectID"
Grid1.Col = 3: Grid1.ColWidth(3) = 700: _
  Grid1.Text = "ObjectName"
Grid1.Col = 4: Grid1.ColWidth(4) = 700: _
  Grid1.Text = "ObjectOwner"
Grid1.Col = 5: Grid1.ColWidth(5) = 700: _
  Grid1.Text = "ObjectType"
Grid1.Col = 6: Grid1.ColWidth(6) = 800: _
  Grid1.Text = "PrivilegeType"
Grid1.Col = 7: Grid1.ColWidth(7) = 1200: _
  Grid1.Text = "PrivilegeTypeName"
Grid1.Col = 8: Grid1.ColWidth(8) = 1000: _
  Grid1.Text = "TypeOf"
Grid1.Col = 9: Grid1.ColWidth(9) = 800: _
  Grid1.Text = "UserData"
i = 0
If Grid1.Rows > 0 Then
  For Each objPermission In objPermissionList
    With objPermission
      i = i + 1
      Grid1.Row = i
      If objPermission.Granted = -1 Then
        Grid1.Col = 0:  Grid1.Text = "True"
      Else
        Grid1.Col = 0: Grid1.Text = "False"
      End If
```

```
                    Grid1.Col = 1: Grid1.Text = .Grantee
                    Grid1.Col = 2: Grid1.Text = .ObjectID
                    Grid1.Col = 3: Grid1.Text = .ObjectName
                    Grid1.Col = 4: Grid1.Text = .ObjectOwner
                    Grid1.Col = 5: Grid1.Text = .ObjectType
                    Grid1.Col = 6: Grid1.Text = .PrivilegeType
                    Grid1.Col = 7: Grid1.Text = .PrivilegeTypeName
                    Grid1.Col = 8: Grid1.Text = .TypeOf
                    Grid1.Col = 9: Grid1.Text = .UserData
                End With
            Next objPermission
        End If
    Normal_exit:
        MousePointer = 0
        Exit Sub
    Permission_error:
        MsgBox "Error " & Err.Number & ": " & _
            Err.Description, vbCritical
        Resume Normal_exit
    End Sub
```

WORKING WITH THE QUERYRESULTS OBJECT

A **QueryResults** object is created with the **ExecuteWithResults** method of the **SQLServer**, **Database**, and **RemoteServer** objects. It is also created by any of the **Enum*Items*** methods. The results are a snapshot that is stored in memory and that cannot be changed. The object supports methods useful for extracting data from a **QueryResults** objects.

QueryResults Object Properties

Application	The **Application** object
Columns	Column count of the current result set
CurrentResultSet	A **Long** identifying the current result set; 1-based

Parent	The **Application** object
ResultSets	Result set count
Rows	Row count of current result set
TypeOf	`SQLOLE_OBJECT_TYPE` value
UserData	Temporary application storage **Long**, which is not used by SQL-DMO

Methods

ColumnMaxlength	*lngMaxLength = QueryResults.***ColumnMaxLength** ([**Column:=**] *lngColumn*)
ColumnName	*strName = QueryResults.***ColumnName**([**Column:=**] *lngColumn*)
ColumnType	*tDatatype = QueryResults.***ColumnType**([**Column:=**] *lngColumn*)
GetColumnBool	*bolColumnData = QueryResults.***GetColumnBool**([**Row : =**] *lngRow* , [**Column:=**] *lngColumn*)
GetColumnDouble	*dblColumnData = QueryResults.***GetColumnDouble**([**Row : =**] *lngRow* , [**Column:=**] *lngColumn*)
GetColumnFloat	*fltColumnData = QueryResults.***GetColumnFloat**([**Row : =**] *lngRow* , [**Column:=**] *lngColumn*)
GetColumnLong	*lngColumnData = QueryResults.***GetColumnLong**([**Row : =**] *lngRow* , [**Column:=**] *lngColumn*)
GetColumnString	*strColumnData = QueryResults.***GetColumnString**([**Row : =**] *lngRow* , [**Column:=**] *lngColumn*)
GetRangeString	*strOutput = QueryResults.***GetRangeString**([[**Top :=**] *lngTop,*] [[**Left :=**] *lngLeft,*] [[**Bottom :=**] *lngBottom,*] [[**Right :=**] *lngRight,*] [[**RowDelim:=**] *strRowDelimiter,*] [[**ColDelim:=**] *strColDelimiter,*] [[**ColWidths:=**] *mstrColWidths,*])
Refresh	*QueryResults.***Refresh**

That's all for methods of the **QueryResults** object. Time for some action. Figure 28-6 is the result of using the SQL-DMO application and selecting

Application ⇒ Query Results. The form output is the result of selecting the *Pubs* database and entering the displayed query.

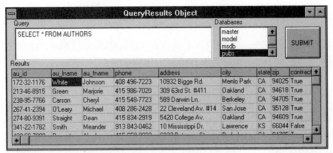

FIGURE 28-6   Using ExecuteWithResults to create a QueryResults object.

Listing 28-6 is the code for creating the **QueryResults** object and is found under the **SUBMIT** command button of Figure 28-6. The code places the results encapsulated within the **QueryResults** object into the Microsoft Grid Control (GRID32.OCA).

LISTING 28-6 Creating a QueryResults object

```
Private Sub cmdSubmit_Click()
'(C)1998 Bruce T. Prendergast
' DBA Prendergast Consulting
' DBA PCS
' IDG Books Wordlwide ISBN 0-7645-3123-9
'
' Listing 28-6 Displaying the SQL-DMO QueryResults
' object in the Microsoft Grid control (GRID32.OCA)
'
  Dim i As Integer
  Dim j As Integer
  Static objQRS As SQLOLE.QueryResults

  If IsNull(txtQuery) Then Exit Sub
  If lboDatabases.ListIndex = -1 Then
    MsgBox "Please select a database"
    Exit Sub
```

```vb
    End If

    On Error GoTo query_error
    MousePointer = 11
    Set objQRS = objSQLDMO.Databases( _
      CStr(lboDatabases)).ExecuteWithResults(txtQuery)
    If objQRS.Rows > 0 Then
      Grid1.Cols = objQRS.Columns
      Grid1.FixedCols = 0
      Grid1.Rows = objQRS.Rows + 1
      Grid1.Row = 0
      For i = 0 To Grid1.Cols - 1
        Grid1.Col = i
        Grid1.Text = objQRS.ColumnName(Column:=i + 1)
        Grid1.ColWidth(i) = objQRS.ColumnMaxLength( _
          Column:=i + 1) * 100
      Next i
      For j = 0 To objQRS.Rows - 1
        Grid1.Row = j + 1
        For i = 0 To objQRS.Columns - 1
          Grid1.Col = i
          Grid1.Text = objQRS.GetColumnString( _
            Row:=j + 1, Column:=i + 1)
        Next i
      Next j
    End If
Normal_exit:
  MousePointer = 0
  Exit Sub
query_error:
  MsgBox "Error " & Err.Number & ": " & _
    Err.Description, vbCritical
  Resume Normal_exit
End Sub


Private Sub Form_Load()
```

```
'(c) 1998 Bruce T. Prendergast
' DBA PCS
' DBA Prendergast Consulting
'
Dim Result As Integer
Dim objDatabase As SQLOLE.Database

Result = CenterForm(Me)
lboDatabases.Clear
For Each objDatabase In objSQLDMO.Databases
   lboDatabases.AddItem objDatabase.Name
Next objDatabase
Exit Sub
End Sub
```

SQL-DMO is an elegant object model. Encapsulating all attributes of the result set in the **QueryResults** object eliminates application dependencies. The first loop of Listing 28-6 uses **ColumnName** method to extract the column names. Multiplying the **ColumnMaxLength** by 100 gives an approximate column width in pixels. This isn't too important because the mouse can be used to resize the grid control columns.

The second loop extracts the column values. The indexes take a little fussing because the result set is 1-based and the **Grid** control is 0-based.

A stored procedure works quite well in our SQL-DMO application. Listing 28-6 is quite flexible. Nearly all the logic of the **QueryResults** object application is listed in Listing 28-6. Figure 28-6 is the first example using this form and Figure 28-7 is the second example. The code is surprising in general, considering the small number of lines necessary to realize the output. Column names were not changed. The user does have the option of changing column sizes with the mouse.

In spite of the apparent generality and flexibility of SQL-DMO queries, Microsoft does not recommend using SQL-DMO as a general SQL Server query tool. I suspect that the reason the SQL-DMO would not be an effective query tool is because COM is apartment-model threaded (see Chapter 33). This means that an SQL-DMO application is not scaleable, while a C++ application is scaleable. A C++ application can control the threading model with the Win32 API. This is something that Visual Basic cannot do. Yes, you can set threading flags in Visual Basic, or the clever developer does some chicanery with the callback function.

Neither of these techniques will yield a robust and scaleable application. Clever tricks are to be avoided at all costs for enterprise endeavors. Flags give some apparent relief, but a flag is too general to be helpful. It is set when the application is compiled and is immutable during execution. Until threading control is designed into the Visual Basic implementation and thread control is no longer an immutable flag set at compilation time or the results of clever chicanery, Microsoft Visual Basic does not have thread control. Multiple threads may run with very special circumstances in Visual Basic, but there is no thread control in Visual Basic such as that exhibited by C++ and the Win 32 API. This is a very important issue and there is a question in one of the Windows Architecture examinations which asks if SQL-DMO supports queries. You must answer that within the context of the question. Yes, it does; however, the application is not scaleable.

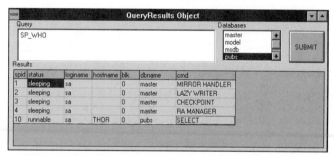

FIGURE 28-7   Creating a QueryResults object with a stored procedure.

KEY POINT SUMMARY

SQL-DMO is surprisingly easy to use. Since SQL-DMO uses Automation, it is not scaleable with the OLE 2.0 standard, which is apartment model-threaded. This is quite acceptable for a DBA-managing SQL Server. It is not acceptable for an enterprise multi-user application. The chapter focused on the **Application** object and highlights of this chapter include:

- Surprisingly, SQL-DMO can be used for effective queries. A question on the Microsoft Windows Architecture I certification test asks if SQL-DMO supports queries.

- The **Application** object is the parent of all objects in the SQL-DMO architecture.

- The **Application** object cannot be instantiated. The **SQLOLE.SQLServer** object is the object that is instantiated.

- No other SQL-DMO objects need be instantiated, although it is advisable to do so for the simplicity of object addressing. Overhead in object addressing is measured in the "dot" count. This is a general issue of addressing COM object in Jet, ODBCDirect, RDO, or SQL-DMO. Minimize the "dot" count by instantiating the object of interest and the application performance improves.

APPLYING WHAT YOU'VE LEARNED

Here are a few quick questions that assess your understanding of the SQL-DMO **Application** object.

Instant Assessment

1. What is a unique characteristic of **Application** scope objects?

2. Identify where a **Backup** object is used in the SQL-DMO architecture.

3. What methods does the **Backup** object support?

 concept link **For answers to the Instant Assessment questions, see Appendix C.**

Lab Exercise

Lab 28.49 *Comparing SQL-DMO, ODBCDirect, and RDO query performance*

WA I
WA II

Lab 28.49 is a comparative analysis of a SQL Server query from SQL-DMO, DAO, and RDO. I don't include ODBC in this list of technologies because it is a call-level interface (CLI) and not an object-oriented technology. (This lab requires SQL Server since the common characteristic of SQL-DMO, ODBCDirect, and RDO is that each is a technology for accessing an ODBC data source.)

Select a table with a reasonable amount of data where measuring performance is meaningful. Construct three different versions of the same query. In the first version of the test application, use SQL-DMO, in the second version, use ODBCDirect, and in the third version, use RDO. Make everything comparable as to result set size and row count within each query. SQL-DMO only supports snap-shot-type result sets. This means that the ODBCDirect and RDO should be for-ward-only-type result sets.

 tip **The SQL Server Pubs database is not large enough for meaningful testing. You may have to construct new test tables or or build a row populating application.**

Build timing into the application and use it to measure the performance of each technology. Restart your system after each test to ensure that the cache is clear. You should be surprised by the results of your testing.

OLE-DB

29

About Chapter 29

Chapter 29 is about OLE-DB and understanding how the architecture works. It is not at the communication level of component object model (COM) interfaces, but at a somewhat higher functional level. This higher level requires an understanding of the two basic concepts: that of *consumer* and *provider* (which may be either a *service provider* or a data *provider*). The OLE-DB components, which are enumerators, data source objects, sessions, commands, and rowsets, are subservient to these roles.

The version of OLE-DB used in this book is OLE-DB 1.1. The International Software Group (ISG) markets OLE-DB software tools. An evaluation copy of the ISG Navigator can be found in the `ISGSOFT` folder of the CD-ROM that accompanies this book. ISG Navigator is OLE-DB 1.5 compliant and provides data access to more data sources on more platforms with better performance and lower cost than any other data access software. The ISG Navigator arrived too late to be included in any examples in this book, but you'll find examples of using this tool in the March 1998 edition of the *Visual Basic Programmers Journal.*

OLE-DB in the Windows Architecture

Let's look again at the current Microsoft database access architecture before the imposition of OLE-DB. Figure 29-1 is from Chapter 24. We'll take a traditional view of database access architecture and impose the new OLE-DB architecture of *consumers* and *providers*.

The Internet/intranet phenomena have changed the definition of a task. Figure 29-2 illustrates the OLE-DB architecture from a familiar perspective. The primary consumer is now either a traditional application or an Internet/intranet browser. The application of Figure 29-2 can call ODBC through any of the traditional mechanisms such as Jet Desktop Driver Set, ODBCDirect, RDO, or the traditional ODBC API. The other access path for ODBC data is through OLE-DB. ODBC and ODBC drivers remain intact; however, layered above ODBC is an OLE-DB provider that exposes an OLE-DB interface. The application is somewhat more complex in that it may now be an Internet/intranet browser.

There is some detail missing in Figure 29-2. The *provider* definitions are correct, but the ADO/OLE-DB connections are simplified. Additional OLE-DB interface detail is illustrated in Figure 29-3. Figure 29-2 represents a meshing of the architecture of Figure 29-1 with the architecture of Figure 29-3.

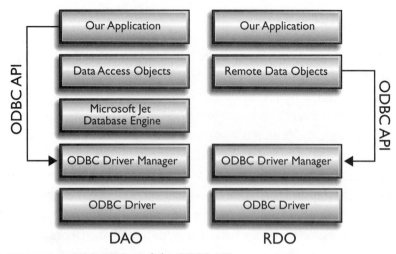

FIGURE 29-1   DAO, RDO, and the ODBC API.

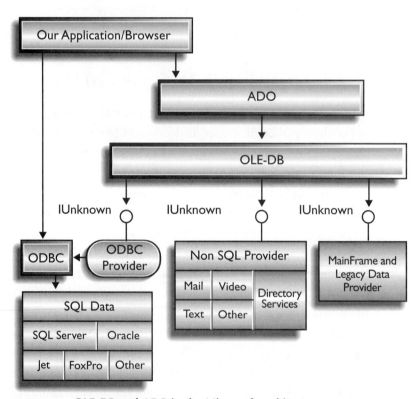

FIGURE 29-2   OLE-DB and ADO in the Microsoft architecture.

Figure 29-2 illustrates an ambitious undertaking for Microsoft. OLE-DB provides key solutions to many of the current industry problems regarding accessing legacy data:

○ OLE-DB provides a universal data interface.

○ Providers are wrappers of non-Structured Query Language (SQL) data.

○ An OLE-DB provider need not provide a SQL engine, which is a requirement with ODBC drivers.

○ ADO is an OLE-DB wrapper.

○ OLE-DB is the vehicle for the long-awaited Microsoft Directory Services. This single issue has hindered the acceptance of Windows NT in the enterprise, although it can be argued that Windows NT is a success in spite of this shortcoming.

○ Converting millions of lines of COBOL applications is not realistic, and OLE-DB provides the technology for creating inexpensive wrappers for legacy applications. This may be the most important feature of OLE-DB.

In Figure 29-3, all the objects, except the application, are COM based. The application may be COM based, but this is not a requirement.

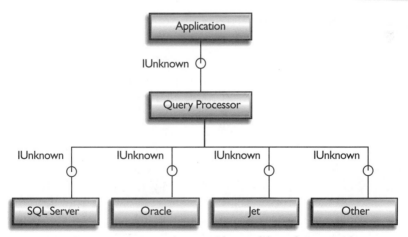

FIGURE 29-3 A consumer, a service provider, and four data providers.

CONSUMERS AND PROVIDERS

With OLE-DB, Microsoft has added new names to database access vocabulary. An application is now called a *consumer* in the context of OLE-DB; however, a consumer in the OLE-DB sense is not limited to an application. Any component that consumes an OLE-DB interface is a consumer.

Another new word in the OLE-DB vocabulary is that of *provider*. Any component that exposes an OLE-DB interface is a provider. The query processor of Figure 29-3 is a provider to the application, which is a consumer. The query processor of Figure 29-3 is also a consumer of the interfaces exposed by the underlying database components. Each of the database components is a provider because each exposes an OLE-DB interface.

The third term is *service provider*. That's the function of the query processor in Figure 29-3. It consumes interfaces from database providers, performs a service with or on the data, and is, in turn, a provider to another consumer. A service provider does not own the data, while a *data provider* owns the data. A service provider can be both a consumer and a provider as illustrated by the query processor of Figure 29-3.

OLE-DB OBJECTS

The OLE-DB architecture has only seven objects. Figure 29-4 illustrates the OLE-DB object hierarchy. (The object hierarchy differs slightly from that of ADO, which is discussed in Chapter 31.) The sections that follow discuss the basic functionality of each of these seven objects.

WORKING WITH THE ENUMERATOR OBJECT

Enumerators are used for locating data sources. A specific enumerator directly searches for directories or Registry entries, whereas a generic enumerator searches for data sources or other enumerators. The optional and mandatory interfaces of the **TEnumerator** CoType are found in Table 30-1 of Chapter 30.

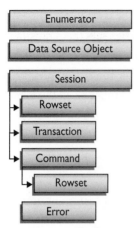

FIGURE 29-4   The OLE-DB object hierarchy.

Calling **CoCreateInstance** with the class identifier (CLSID) of the enumerator creates an enumerator. The consumer requests the **ISourcesRowset** interface because the other significant interfaces are optional.

ISourcesRowset::GetSourcesRowset returns data sources and enumerators, and **IParseDisplayName::ParseDisplayName** is used on a returned display name. The returned result from this method is a moniker that the consumer binds to instantiate the object.

The **IDBInitialize** interface only exists if the enumerator requires initialization. The **IDBProperties** interface must be exposed whenever the **IDBInitialize** interface is exposed.

Initializing an Enumerator

When the enumerator is in an uninitialized state, only the following can be done without eliciting an error:

- Call **QueryInterface** for **IUnknown, IDBInitialize, IDBProperties**, or **ISupportErrorInfo**.

- Call the **IUnknown** methods **AddRef** or **Release** on any interface obtained by **QueryInterface**.

- Initialize elements of the **Initialization** property group by calling methods of **IDBProperties**.

- Call methods of either **IDBInitialize** or **ISupportErrorInfo**.

IDBProperties::GetPropertyInfo tells the consumer which properties must be initialized, and **IDBProperties::SetProperties** sets the requisite property value. **IDBInitialize::Initialize** is called after all properties are set.

All operations are logical. The consumer must disconnect from a database before connecting to another database or a file must be closed before switching to another file.

The **Enumerator** object is uninitialized with **IDBInitialize::Uninitialize**. An **Enumerator** object must be uninitialized before it can be reinitialized.

Enumerators in the Registry

Enumerators are found in the Registry in two locations. The first location is the HKEY_CLASSES_ROOT, which must have these enumerator subkeys and values:

EnumeratorProgID = FriendlyDisplayName

*EnumeratorProgI***CLSID** *= EnumeratorCLSID*

The second location is the HKEY_CLASSES_ROOT\CLSID subkey, which must have these values and subkeys:

EnumeratorCLSID = FriendlyDisplayName

*EnumeratorCLSID***ProgID** *= EnumeratorProgID*

*EnumeratorCLSID***VersionIndependentProgID** *= VersionIndependentProgID*

*EnumeratorCLSID***InprocServer32** *= EnumeratorDLLFileName*

*EnumeratorCLSID***InprocServer32\Threading Model = Apartment | Free | Both**

*EnumeratorCLSID***OLE DB Enumerator =** *Description*

THREADING MODELS

The enumerator Registry entry, *EnumeratorCLSID***InprocServer32\Threading Model,** specifies the threading model. *Apartment-model* threading is the use of one primary or controlling thread per COM object. Other threads are queued and handled sequentially by the object's parent thread. The issues here are of re-entrance and code reuse. This is contrasted by *free-threading* where there may be many threads active simultaneously within an object. Single-threaded providers only work reliably with single-threaded consumers. A single-threaded consumer can work with any type of object.

Free-Thread Provider Responsibilities

Microsoft does not have a unified thread architecture. The good citizenship rules for a provider with free-threading are:

- Implement the necessary guard mechanisms to make all threads "thread-safe."
- Guarantee an operation with no deadlocks or lock starvation.
- Shield consumers or other threads from the effects of **IRowsetUpdate::Update** or **IRowsetResynch::ResynchRows**. This is done by making all update operations atomic.

 note An atomic update is the smallest possible unit of work and is typically represented by the amount involved with a single SQL statement. An example of a non-atomic transaction is a transaction with two SQL statements. With an atomic update, the transaction isolation levels **Repeatable Read** and **Serializable** are equivalent.

- Make immediate mode operations such as **IRowsetChange::SetData**, **IRowsetChange::Change::DeleteRows** atomic.
- Guarantee a minimum level of marshaling support by aggregating an **IMarshal** object obtained from **CoCreateFreeThreadedMarshaler**.

Apartment-Model Provider Responsibilities

The good citizenship rules for a provider with apartment-model threading are:

- Provider assumes the OLE-DB object will always receive calls on the same thread.
- The apartment-model must use a proxy-stub mechanism to accept calls from other apartments.
- The provider guarantees that all rowsets created by the rowset are also apartment-model and belong to the same thread as their ancestor rowset.

- Apartment-model OLE-DB object does not share its state with other objects on different threads. The only exception is an ancestor/descendant relationship such as **IColumnsRowset::GetColumnsRowset**.

- The provider furnishes marshaling support in terms of stubs and proxies. This is because OLE automatically creates a host-provider thread in the client when the new object is created.

Free-Thread Consumer Responsibilities

The good citizenship rules for a consumer with free-threading are:

- Call **CoInitializeEx** on each thread with a null pointer as the first parameter and `COINIT_MULTITHREADED` as the second parameter to initialize the object as free-threaded.

- Transfer pointers directly when the other thread is free-threaded and the pointers correspond to free-threaded objects.

- To transfer a free-threaded object to an apartment, it is necessary to marshal the pointer at the source and unmarshal it at the destination.

Apartment-Model Consumer Responsibilities

The good citizenship rules for a consumer with apartment-model threading:

- Implement a message queue.

- Call **CoInitialize** or **OLEInitialize** on the thread.

- Marshal to other apartments using **CoMarshalInterface** and **CoUnmarshalInterface**.

- Interact with a free-threaded server if the free-threaded server aggregates with a generic **CoCreateFreeThreadedMarshaler** and if the apartment-model is well behaved.

Thread-Safe Implementation

Independent of the threading model, the OLE-DB developer is responsible for creating a thread-safe application. Serializing shared data does this. It is the provider's responsibility to ensure thread-safety with objects that are returned from interface method calls directly. It's the client's responsibility to ensure thread-safe callback objects.

A service provider implements a thread-safe object by serializing access to shared data within the object, insuring that one thread does not inadvertently replace the work of another thread. A service provider can implement serialized access to data in three ways:

- **Serialize each method of a provider object** — Provide every object with its own critical section, which calls the Win32 API function **EnterCriticalSection** at the beginning of every method and the function **LeaveCriticalSection** at the end. This option has two drawbacks: a high overhead and the possibility of deadlock. Deadlock can occur if, for example, the thread-safe object calls an OLE-DB support object or an object returned indirectly through one of the copy methods.

- **Serialize the provider** — Use a single critical section for all objects, calling **EnterCriticalSection** when the provider is loaded and **LeaveCriticalSection** when the provider is unloaded. This option provides the most simplicity, but suffers in performance when used with multithreaded clients.

- **Serialize data structures** — Create a small number of critical sections to be associated with crucial shared-data structures. The data are isolated from the object and placed, for example, in memory or in a parent object. Access to the data is handled through an internal interface. This option offers the best balance between performance and simplicity.

Threads and Transactions

All consumers accessing a shared object such as a rowset through different threads are assumed to be within the same transaction.

General Guidelines for Error Objects

- Free-thread objects should produce free-thread error objects.
- Apartment-thread model OLE-DB objects should produce apartment-thread model error objects that are associated to the same thread.

Unresolved Threading Issue

The threading model of **IPersist*** objects is indeterminate. This issue will not be addressed until a later version of OLE-DB.

Threads and Notifications

Rowset objects are free-thread, and **IConnectionPointContainer** can handle apartment-thread model or free-thread listeners. A listener is a consumer that has requested that a provider send it notifications of various events (see Chapter 6, **IAdviseSink** and **IConnectpointContainer**). The rowset creator must use **CoMarshalInterface** because the rowsets are free-thread. When **IConnection PointContainer** receives an interface from **IRowsetNotify**, **CoMarshalInterface** must be used to move the interface to another thread. The receiving interface must extract the pointer with **CoUnmarshalInterface**. A **Rowset** object has the obligation of keeping track of the threads of each listener.

WORKING WITH THE DATA SOURCE OBJECT

A **Data Source** is the initial object instantiated by a provider. The consumer doesn't call **CoCreateInstance** directly. This task is done at the behest of the consumer during the binding process. For example, **IMoniker::BindToObject** will eventually call **GetClassFile**, **CoCreateInstance**, and **IPersistFile::Load**(*pszFile*) for a file moniker. The optional and mandatory interfaces of the **TDataSource** CoType are found in Table 30-1 of Chapter 30.

The presence of the interfaces **IDBInitialize** and **IDBProperties** indicates that a data source can be accessed without the use of an **Enumerator** object. A consumer dedicated to a particular data source can use an enumerator to bypass this.

Initializing a Data Source Object

Data Source objects are always created in an uninitialized state, and only the following can be done without eliciting an error:

o Call **QueryInterface** for **IUnknown**, **IDBDataSourceAdmin**, **IDBInitialize**, **IDBProperties**, **IPersist**, **IPersistFile**, or **ISupportErrorInfo**.

- Call the **IUnknown** methods **AddRef** or **Release** on any interface obtained by **QueryInterface**.

- Initialize elements of the Initialization property group by calling methods of **IDBProperties**.

- Call methods in **IDBDataSourceAdmin**, **IDBInitialize**, **IPersist**, **IPersistFile**, or **ISupportErrorInfo**.

    IDBProperties::GetPropertyInfo tells the consumer which properties must be initialized, and **IDBProperties::SetProperties** sets the requisite property value. **IDBInitialize::Initialize** is called after all properties are set. **IDBDataSource Admin::CreateDataSource** is available for creating and initializing a new **Data Source** object.

    All operations are logical. The consumer must disconnect from a database before connecting to another database or a file must be closed before switching to another file.

    The **Data Source** object is uninitialized with **IDBInitialize::Uninitialize**. A **Data Source** object must be uninitialized before it can be reinitialized.

Persisting a Data Source Object

A **Data Source** object can be persisted; however, none of the child objects such as sessions, commands, or rowsets, can be persisted. Security is managed by the DBPROP_AUTH_PERSIST_AUTHINFO property, and encryption is managed by the DBPROP_AUTH_PERSIST_ENCRYPTED property. A provider may make these properties read-only to prevent the saving of sensitive information.

    IPersistFile::Save saves the **Data Source** object in either an initialized or an uninitialized state. **IPersist::Load** retrieves the object and may return DB_E_ALREADYINITIALIZED. When this value is not returned, the consumer initializes the newly loaded **Data Source** object by calling **IDBInitialize::Initialize**.

    When a provider persists a **Data Source** object, it only persists enough information to return the object to the original persisted state. A provider is not required to save consumer set properties of other groups.

    When **IPersistFile** is not supported, the consumer can retrieve all properties with **IDBProperties::GetProperties** and call **IPersist::GetClassID** for the CLSID. The consumer saves these values for later re-creation of the data source.

WORKING WITH THE SESSION OBJECT

The primary purpose for a **Session** object is to define a transaction. The optional and mandatory interfaces of the **TSession** CoType are found in Table 30-1 of Chapter 30.

A **Session** object is created with **IDBCreateSession::CreateSession** on the **Data Source** object. Each **Data Source** supports multiple sessions.

The **Session** object is the first object where meaningful work can be accomplished. The consumer can create a simple rowset with **IOpenRowset::Open Rowset,** which all providers must support. The alternative is to create a **Command** object on the session with **IDBCreateCommand::CreateCommand**, fill in the appropriate properties, and call **ICommand::Execute** to create a rowset. Not all providers support commands.

Tables are created and indexes modified with **ITableDefinition** and **IIndexDefinition**; however, providers are not required to support these interfaces. **ITableDefinition** may be the only definition mechanism available for simple arrays of data.

WORKING WITH THE COMMAND OBJECT

A **Command** object is subservient to a **Session** object as illustrated in Figure 29-4. A **Command** object is created on the **Session** object with the method **IDBCreate Command::CreateCommand**. A **Command** object permits the execution of a text statement against a data source, which is typically a SQL statement. The optional and mandatory interfaces of the **TCommand** CoType are found in Table 30-1 of Chapter 30.

Commands are used for data definition and data manipulation. A degenerate case of data manipulation is the creation of a rowset from the SQL SELECT statement.

Providers are not required to support commands that are generally used to support a relational database management system. A simple text data source will generally not have commands.

Calling **QueryInterface** on a **Session** object creates a **Command** object. The consumer calls **IDBCreateCommand::CreateCommand** when an interface is returned. Commands are not supported when no interface is returned.

Command text is set with **ICommandText::SetCommandText**. The text is provider-specific and, consequently, the consumer must pass the text's global unique identifier (GUID). For most situations this will be the `DBGUID_DBSQL` property, which signifies American National Standards Institute (ANSI) SQL.

The level of ANSI SQL support is determined by the `DBPROP_SQLSUPPORT` property. Supported values include `DBPROPVAL_SQL_NONE`, `DBPROPVAL_SQL_ODBC_MINIMUM`, `DBPROPVAL_SQL_ODBC_CORE`, and `DBPROPVAL_SQL_ODBC_EXTENDED`. These levels correspond to the levels of SQL conformance defined in the ODBC version 2.5 specification and are cumulative. Setting a level automatically sets all bits at lower levels. **ICommand::Execute** will execute the statement and instantiates a **Rowset** object. A pointer to a **Rowset** object is returned to the consumer.

Preparing a Command

Command properties may be set with **ICommandProperties::SetProperties**. All providers are required to support **IColumnsInfo::GetColumnInfo**, whereas **IColumnsRowset::GetColumnsRowset** is an optional provider interface. Command text must be set to use either of these methods and the command must be prepared, but only if the provider supports it.

Commands that are to be executed more than once should be prepared. Preparation (compilation) is done with **ICommand::Prepare**. Providers are not required to support preparation.

Parameters are supported with the <?> as a marker. It uses the same construction as ODBC parameters. Providers indicate the support for parameters by implementing the interface **ICommandWithParameters**. Parameters are set with **ICommandWithParameters::SetParameterInfo**.

Parameters are created by first creating an **Accessor** object that describes the parameters. The handle to the **Accessor** object and the data buffer containing the parameters are passed to **ICommand::Execute**.

Command States

Preparing a command introduces the concept of states. A command may be in one of the following states:

Initial   No command text.

Unprepared   Command text is set, statement is not prepared.

Prepared   Command has been compiled.

Executed   Command has been executed.

The first list below outlines the error codes, and the second list outlines the methods and the resulting error codes returned from the various command states. The error codes and the error-state table have a direct parallel with the SQLState values of ODBC. Error codes include: OK S_OK, NC DB_E_NOCOMMAND, NP DB_E_NOTPREPARED, OO DB_E_OPENOBJECT.

Error States

Method	Initial	Unprepared	Prepared	Executed
IColumnsInfo				
GetColumnInfo	NC	OK[1] | NP[2]	OK	OK
MapColumnIDs	NC	OK[1] | NP[2]	OK	OK
IColumnsRowset				
GetAvailableColumns	NC	OK[1] | NP[2]	OK	OK
GetColumnsRowset	NC	OK[1] | NP[2]	OK	OK
Icommand				
Cancel	OK	OK	OK	OK
Execute	NC	OK	OK	OK
GetDBSession	OK	OK	OK	OK
ICommandPrepare				
Prepare	NC	OK	OK	OK[3] | OO[4]
Unprepare	OK	OK	OK	OK[3] | OO[4]
ICommandProperties				
GetProperties	OK	OK	OK	OK

Method	Initial	Unprepared	Prepared	Executed
ICommandText				
GetCommandText	NC	OK	OK	OK
SetCommandText	OK	OK	OK	OK[3] | OO[4]
ICommandWithParameters				
GetParameterInfo	OK[5] | NC[6]	OK[5] | NP[2,6]	OK	OK
MapParameterNames	OK[5] | NC[6]	OK[5] | NP[2,6]	OK	OK
SetParameterInfo	OK	OK	OK	OK[3] | OO[4]

[1]**ICommandPrepared** *is not supported.*
[2]**ICommandPrepare** *is supported.*
[3]**Execute** *did not create a rowset.*
[4]**Execute** *created a rowset.*
[5]**SetParameterInfo** *has been called.*
[6]**SetParameterInfo** *has not been called.*

Multiple Result Sets

Multiple result sets require the mandatory interface **IMultipleResults**. Multiple result sets are returned when the text comprises multiple separate text statements or when more than one set of parameters is passed to a command.

The consumer creates multiple result sets by requesting the **IMultiple Results** interface when calling **ICommand::Execute**. A **Multiple Results** object is returned by this method.

The **Multiple Results** object is used to retrieve results; providers, however, are not required to support **Multiple Results** objects or the **IMultipleResults** interface.

IMultipleResults::GetResults returns result sets in the order of creation. The DBPROP_MULTIPLERESULTS property determines when it is necessary to release the current **Rowset** object before another **Multiple Results** object is returned.

WORKING WITH THE ROWSET OBJECT

The **Rowset** object is the workhorse of OLE-DB. The object exposes relational data or data from simple tables in terms of **Rowset** objects. The first object is the **TRowset** CoType and the second object is the **TTRansactionOptions** CoType. The optional and mandatory interfaces of both CoTypes are found in Table 30-1 of Chapter 30.

Each interface has an assigned responsibility. **IRowset** contains methods for fetching rows; **IAccessor** describes column bindings; **IColumnsInfo** provides column information; **IRowsetInfo** describes the rowset; and **IConvertType** provides datatype conversion information. A consumer uses **IRowset** for sequentially traversing rows, which may include backward traversing.

Opening a Rowset

A rowset will always be created even when there are no rows. New rows may be inserted in the rowset, and column metadata may be interrogated.

The first source for rowsets of OLE-DB is equivalent to ODBC catalog functions with the **IColumnsRowset::GetColumnsRowset**, **IDBSchemaRowset:: GetRowset**, and **ISources::GetSourcesRowset**. These are read-only rowsets for column, schema, and data source metadata.

All providers must support the second source for OLE-DB rowsets. This is **IOpenRowset::OpenRowset** on a session object. **IOpenRowset** is a mandatory interface of the **Session** object and is not an interface of the **Rowset** object. This is a simple table interface, and the rowsets are the equivalent of a wild card select on a table that has the form SELECT * FROM *table*.

The third source of a rowset is from the sequence **IDBCreate::Create Command** on a **Session** object, initializing **Command** object properties and text, and calling **ICommand::Execute** on a **Command** object.

All rowsets must support **IRowset, IAccessor, IColumnInfo, IRowsetInfo**, and **IConvertType**. **IRowsetLocate** may be exposed even though the consumer does not request it. **IRowsetUpdate** cannot be exposed unless specifically requested by the consumer because the presence of this interface changes the behavior of the **IRowsetChange** interface. This is because the interface identifier (IID) of **ICommand::Execute** is usually an IID of one of the interfaces listed for the **TRowset** CoType.

Fetching and Releasing Rows

Rows are fetched by various methods. **IRowset::GetNextRows, IRowsetLocate:: GetRowsAt, IRowsetLocate::GetRowsByBookmarks,** and **IRowsetScroll::Get**

RowsAtRatio will all fetch multiple row handles with a single call. There is no concept of a single current row although **IRowset::GetNextRows** will obtain the next sequential row.

Any pattern of rows can be held if the **IRowsetLocate** interface is supported. The consumer may be required by the provider to release current rows before again calling **GetNextRows** when the provider does not support **IRowsetLocate**. This is because a rowset that does not implement the **IRowsetLocate** interface is a sequential rowset.

Row handles are reference counted. **IRowset::Release** releases a rowset and the row handle. **IRowset::Release** must be called for each fetch of a row, and once for each call to **IRowset::AddRefRows** for the associated row.

Row handles are not released with implicit row deletion. This includes operations such as **IRowsetChange::DeleteRows**, **IRowsetUpdate::Update** on a row with a pending deletion, or **IRowsetUpdate::Undo** on a row with a pending insert. The consumer must still call **IRowset::ReleaseRows** to release the row.

The next fetch position is maintained by **GetNextRows**. **IRowsetIndex::Seek** changes the next position, and **IRowset::RestartPosition** resets the rowset to the rowset's position at the time of its creation.

A rowset that is supported with a reversible fetch direction, where **GetNext Rows** is called in one direction and **GetNextRows** is called with no skip in the other direction, will have the last row read as the next row to read when the read direction is reversed.

Rowsets support negative position counts from a bookmark or from a current position. This is calculated by computing the current absolute position and applying the negative offset. For example, -1 is the previous row.

Row Uniqueness

Exposing the interface **IRowsetIdentity** provides unique rows to the consumer even though duplicate rows may exist within the rowset. Setting the DBPROP_LITERALIDENTITY property to VARIANT_TRUE assures that each row is unique. When DBPROP_LITERALIDENTITY is set to VARIANT_FALSE, the consumer can call **IRowset::IsSameRow** to determine the uniqueness of a row. Testing for uniqueness is necessary when a rowset handle is passed to a consumer from one of the **IRowsetNotify** methods because the consumer may already own the handle. Microsoft promises chaos when providers do not support the **IRowsetIdentity** interface.

Deferred Columns

Data may be deferred. The DBCOLUMNFLAGS_MAYDEFER property returned by **IColumnsInfo::GetColumnsInfo** is set when a column is deferred. When this flag is set a provider is not required to retrieve data from the data source until **IRowSet::GetData** is called. Discrepancies may occur for deferred row accesses when the consumer is not using a **Repeatable Read** isolation level or better. The consumer can be warned of a row version problem by looking at the DBCOLUMN-FLAGS_ISROWVER property. A consumer requests a deferred column by setting the DBPROP_DEFERRED property. OLE objects are always deferred. Deferring a column is the act of creating a transaction log entry with before and after versions of the data. After all log entries are made, the data is applied. The immediate update is the opposite and changes the column directly.

Column data may also be cached. A newly read row is cached when the DBCOLUMNFLAGS_CACHEDEFERRED property is set. The value is changed by **IRowsetChange::SetData** or **IRowset::ResynchRows**. The cache is not released until the row handle is released.

Calls to **GetData** may return different values when the flag DBCOLUMN-FLAGS_CACHEDEFERRED is not set. A call to **ResynchRows** is necessary to reflect underlying column changes.

Changing Data

Data is changed by consumers with the **SetData**, **DeleteRows**, and **InsertRow** methods in **IRowsetChange**. A rowset is in *immediate update* mode when the **IRowsetUpdate** interface is not exposed. Changes are transmitted to the data source immediately when any of the prior methods of **IRowsetChange** are invoked. Pending changes are transmitted to the source with a call to **IRowsetUpdate::Update**. Both changes made by **IRowsetUpdate::Update** and any of the methods of **IRowsetChange** become visible to other transactions running at the **Read Uncommitted** isolation level. Rowsets created within the context of a transaction can be aborted or committed by calling **ITransaction::Commit** or **ITransaction::Abort**. A read-only rowset is created by not requesting the **IRowsetChange** or the **IRowsetUpdate** interfaces.

Immediate Versus Delayed Update Mode

The provider deferred update model has several advantages when working with rowsets from a remote data source, including these advantages:

- Multiple changes to the same row may leave a row in an indeterminate state. This occurs with multicolumn key changes. Buffering the row until the changes are complete avoids this problem.

- The response time is not necessarily improved, but network traffic is reduced by buffering rowset changes.

- Buffering the changes locally provides an opportunity for a local undo function.

Row States

The method **IRowsetUpdate::GetRowStatus** returns a row status. **IRowsetUpdate:: GetPendingRows** places all rows within the rowset in a pending state. Table 29-1 enumerates the DBPENDINGSTATUS properties and row states.

TABLE 29-1 DBPENDINGSTATUS ROW STATES	
DBPENDINGSTATUS Intrinsic Value	*Row State*
DBPENDINGSTATUS_NEW	Pending insert
DBPENDINGSTATUS_CHANGED	Pending update
DBPENDINGSTATUS_DELETED	Pending delete
DBPENDINGSTATUS_UNCHANGED	No changes pending
DBPENDINGSTATUS_INVALIDROW	Row is deleted

WORKING WITH THE TRANSACTION OBJECT

A transaction consists of two objects, which are described in Table 30-1 of Chapter 30.

All work done within the scope of a new **Session** object is committed immediately after each method call. Once a **Session** object enters a transaction, all work done within the scope of the **Session** object also falls within the scope of the transaction.

The interface **ITransactionLocal** inherits from **ITransaction**. When the provider supports transactions, local transactions are also available. **ITransaction Local::StartTransaction** starts a local transaction.

Transaction Retention

The flag *fRetaining* can be set for either **ITransaction::Commit** or **ITransaction:: Abort**. When *fRetaining* is **False**, new units of work may or may not be within the scope of a transaction independent of the prior action. Conversely, when *fRetaining* is **True**, any additional work may or may not be done within the scope of a transaction. This is confusing. Table 29-2 makes the relationship between *fRetaining* and DBPROP_COMMITPRESERVE or DBPROP_ABORTPRESERVE clear.

TABLE 29-2 THE RELATIONSHIP BETWEEN *fRetaining* AND RESULTING TRANSACTION MODES

DBPROP_ABORTPRESERVE OR DBPROP_COMMITPRESERVE	fRetaining	ROWSET STATE AFTER COMMIT	RESULTING TRANSACTION MODE OF SESSION
FALSE	FALSE	zombie	implicit/autocommit
FALSE	TRUE	zombie	explicit/manual
TRUE	FALSE	preserved	implicit/autocommit
TRUE	TRUE	preserved	explicit/manual

Rowset Preservation

Microsoft introduced the concept of a *zombie* state. A rowset is in a *zombie* state when the only method available is **Release** for the release of row handles and rows. Every other interface will return the error code E_UNEXPECTED.

The first situation to consider is the DBPROP_COMMITPRESERVE property set to VARIANT_TRUE after returning from **ITransaction::Commit**. In this situation the rowset is not a *zombie* and remains accessible even though it has been committed. The rowset assumes the *zombie* state when DBPROP_COMMITPRESERVE is set to VARIANT_FALSE after returning from **ITransaction::Commit**.

A parallel situation exists for `DBPROP_ABORTPRESERVE` being set to `VARI-ANT_FALSE` when returning from **ITransaction::Abort**. The rowset is a *zombie* and is not accessible. The rowset is accessible after the **ITransaction::Abort** when `DBPROP_ABORTPRESERVE` is set to `VARIANT_TRUE`.

Nested Transactions

Transactions may be nested. Changes within the inner transaction are not seen by the parent transaction until the inner transaction is committed.

A nested transaction is started with **ITransationLocal::StartTransaction**, which returns the transaction level **pulTransactionLevel* = 1 for the root transaction. Transactions may be aborted or committed with **ITransactionLocal::Abort** or **ITransactionLocalCommit**. The *fRetaining* flag also exists for local transactions, and the status of this flag determines when remaining work within the object still is within the scope of a local transaction.

Transaction Objects

The consumer calls **ITransactionObject::GetTransactionObject** to obtain the current transaction object. This enables the consumer to abort a transaction at other than the lowest level. Calling **ITransactionLocal::Commit** or **ITransactionLocal::Abort** is the equivalent of calling **ITransaction::Commit** or **ITransaction::Abort** on a **Transaction** object.

Calling **Commit** or **Abort** with *fRetaining* set to **False** terminates the transaction and turns the **Transaction** object into a *zombie*.

Event Notification

The **Transaction** object may support event notification. **ITransactionOutcome Events** is a notification sink. The consumer calls **IUnknown::QueryInterface** for the **IConnectionPointContainer** interface on the **Session** object. The consumer then acquires the **IConnectionPoint** interface for **IID_TransactionOutComeEvent** and passes its **ITransactionOutcomeEvents** interface to the returned connection point. The **Session** object now notifies each registered **ITransactionOutcome Events** interface of the outcome of a transaction.

Coordinated Transactions

A provider that supports coordinated transactions exposes the **ITransactionJoin** interface. The **Commit** and **Abort** methods follow the *zombie* rules discussed earlier for the *fRetaining* flag.

It is an error to call **ITransaction::JoinTransaction** when the session is already participating in either a local or a coordinated transaction.

ITransactionLocal::StartTransaction may be used within a coordinated transaction. The transaction is nested and follows all rules discussed earlier for nested transactions.

WORKING WITH THE ERROR OBJECT

This is the last of the OLE-DB thumbnail sketches. Errors with OLE-DB objects are supported by the **TErrorObject** CoType. The optional and mandatory interfaces of the **TErrorObject** CoType are found in Table 30-1 of Chapter 30.

Every method returns an error code. The return codes are of type HRESULT with the codes divided into success and warning codes, and error codes. Codes beginning with S_ or B_S_ are either success or warning codes. Returned codes that are neither S_OK nor S_FALSE are usually error codes. DB_S_ENDOFROWSET is a code returned from **IRowset::GetNextRows**, which indicates a success even though no rows are returned.

Error codes that begin with E_ or DB_E_ are failures with no useful work being performed. Errors that return the code DB_E_ERRORSOCCURRED have allocated memory to return additional information. The consumer must release this additional memory. **IMalloc::Free** is used to free the provider allocated memory for OLE-DB interfaces such as **IRowsetUpDate::Update** that return an array of status values.

All functions will return S_OK or E_FAIL. Some functions that allocate memory will return E_OUTOFMEMORY as a reminder to the consumer to request less rows.

Some methods will return the code DB_S_ERRORSOCCURRED when one or more errors occur. Some providers return this code when there are no errors and one or more warning messages.

Methods that operate on more than one item return `DB_S_ERRORSOC-CURRED` when at least one item is processed successfully. The error code `DB_E_ERRORSOCCURRED` is returned when no items are processed successfully.

Automation Components Returning an Error

Unlike other technologies that return a status code, OLE-DB returns an error object. There are two types of errors: OLE-DB errors and automation errors. Following are the steps taken by the automation component when an error is detected:

- The automation component with an error calls **CreateErrorInfo**, which returns a pointer to a generic error object that you can use with **QueryInterface** on **ICreateErrorInfo** to set its contents. You can then pass the resulting object to **SetErrorInfo**. The generic error object implements both **ICreateErrorInfo** and **IErrorInfo**.

- **ICreateErrorInfo** is now called with the error description and GUID of the offending component.

- The component calls **QueryInterface** to retrieve the **IErrorInfo** interface pointer. This pointer identifies the **Error** object to all Automation components.

- **SetErrorInfo** in the automation dynamic link library (DLL) is called, and is passed the **IErrorInfo** interface pointer. **SetErrorInfo** replaces its own **Error** object with the new **Error** object and increments the new **Error** object reference count.

- The component calls **Release** to decrement its reference count, which effectively transfers ownership of the **Error** object from the component causing the error to the automation DLL.

An Automation Consumer Retrieving an Error Object

The user (consumer) must now retrieve an automation error. The automation DLL maintains one error object per thread. The returned error information is contained in a generic error object, and the steps below are necessary to retrieve the error information from the generic error object.

- The automation consumer calls **QueryInterface** on the component that returned the error code, which retrieves an **ISupportErrorInfo** interface pointer for the component. **ISupportErrorInfo** must be exposed by all components that create error objects.

- The automation consumer calls **InterfaceSupportErrorInfo** with the IID of the interface which returned the error code. S_OK is returned if error objects are supported and S_FALSE when error objects are not supported.

- The automation consumer calls the **GetErrorInfo** in the automation DLL. An **IErrorInfo** interface is returned with the reference count decremented. This effectively transfers ownership of the **Error** object to the consumer.

- The automation consumer calls methods of **IErrorInfo** to retrieve error information.

- The final step is to call **Release** on the **Error** object, which releases it.

OLE–DB Error Records

An automation **Error** object has the interface **IErrorInfo** and only supports one error message. It also has the limitation that no vendor-specific information can be returned.

An OLE-DB **Error** object exposes the interfaces **IErrorInfo** and **IError Records** while supporting multiple error records with vendor-specific information. The error records are defined with the C++ structure:

```
typedef  struct tagERRORINFO {
 HRESULT hrError; // error code returned
 DWORD   dwMinor; // provider specific error code
 CLSID   clsid;   // CLSID of object returning the error
 IID     iid;     // IID of interface generating the error
                  // may be different than IID of calling
                       method
 DISPID  dispid;  // method that returned the error
 }  ERRORINFO
```

A Provider Returning an OLE-DB Error Object

OLE-DB errors are not a single value, but are an array of error codes. Automation only supports a single error and not an array of errors. The steps below create an OLE-DB error object with an **IErrorInfo** and an **IErrorRecords** interface that effectively represents an array of error codes.

- The provider calls **GetErrorInfo** in the automation DLL. Ownership of the current **Error** object is returned. An **Error** object only exists if a lower-level object has already created it. The provider only has temporary ownership of an **Error** object and loses that ownership when returning the **Error** object to the automation DLL.

- An OLE-DB **Error** object is created if none exists. The provider calls **CoCreateInstance** with the CLSID_EXTENDEDERRORINFO class ID or **IClassFactory::CreateInstance** on a class factory **Error** object created earlier for this class.

- **IErrorRecords::AddErrorRecord** is called to add one or more error records.

- The provider calls **QueryInterface** to retrieve an **IErrorInfo** pointer on the **Error** object.

- The provider calls the automation DLL method **SetErrorInfo** and passes the **IErrorInfo** interface pointer.

- The last provider task is to call **Release**, which effectively passes ownership of the **Error** object to the automation DLL.

When a Consumer Retrieves an OLE-DB Error Object

These are the steps necessary for a consumer to retrieve OLE-DB errors:

- The consumer calls **QueryInterface** on the component returning the error to retrieve the **ISupportErrorInfo** interface.

- The consumer next calls **InterfaceSupportsErrorInfo**. S_OK signifies the interface supports error objects, and S_FALSE indicates no error object support.

○ The consumer next calls the **GetErrorInfo** of the automation DLL, which returns an **IErrorInfo** interface pointer. This function also decrements the reference count, releasing the **Error** object to the consumer.

○ The consumer next calls **QueryInterface** for an **IErrorRecords** interface.

○ The consumer now calls methods in **IErrorRecords**. **IErrorRecords:: GetErrorInfo** which returns an **IErrorInfo**-specific record. Note that **IErrorInfo** pointer on this interface returns pointers to records, whereas the **IErrorInfo** reference above transfers a pointer to an error object.

○ Lastly, the consumer calls **Release** on the **Error** object.

KEY POINT SUMMARY

OLE-DB is the new database access technology from Microsoft. The entry level for database programmers is raised with the additional burden of understanding COM interfaces. This includes the additional complexity of managing threads, error objects, and notification sinks, which is beyond the traditional issue of understanding transactions, queries, stored procedures, SQL, and data definition language constructs. The major OLE-DB issues include:

○ OLE-DB is COM based.

○ OLE-DB is a universal database access technology.

○ OLE-DB is incomplete and is still in development.

○ The security and remote data access aspects of ADO are incomplete.

APPLYING WHAT YOU'VE LEARNED

OLE-DB is a new database access technology. A successful OLE-DB developer must understand COM and OLE-DB. These questions, while related to database aspects of OLE-DB, require an intimate knowledge of COM and how interfaces function (see Chapters 1–10).

Instant Assessment

1. Name all the different methods that may be used to create a rowset. Briefly describe the different characteristics of these rowsets.

2. What interfaces must all rowsets support?

3. Discuss the three roles objects play in the OLE-DB environment.

4. Explain the difference between an automation error and an OLE-DB error.

5. What is a characteristic of the error code DB_S_ERRORSOCCURRED?

6. What is apartment-model threading? How do apartment-model threads communicate? What is the major problem with apartment-model threads?

7. When is the cache for a rowset released?

8. What is a *zombie* rowset?

 concept link **For answers to the Instant Assessment questions, see Appendix C.**

Lab Exercises

The first lab exercise is a cost/benefit analysis of converting an existing application to OLE-DB. The second laboratory assumes there is an existing RDO or DAO application that does not use transaction isolation levels. The goal of the lab is to convert the application to OLE-DB and use transaction isolation levels.

Lab 29.50 *Evaluate the costs and benefits of converting a DAO or RDO application to OLE-DB*

 This lab exercise is a cost/benefit analysis of converting an existing RDO or DAO application to OLE-DB. Assess the cost of converting one of your DAO or RDO applications to OLE-DB. Costs include code conversion, beta testing, parallel testing, and lost time due to system failures.

Lab 29.51 *Use transaction isolation levels in OLE-DB*

 Consider redesigning one of your applications to fully use OLE-DB transaction isolation levels. OLE-DB and Microsoft SQL Server support these transaction properties; RDO local transactions and Jet transactions, however, do not support them. The first question to ask is whether transaction isolation levels will benefit your enterprise.

Working with OLE-DB Interfaces

30

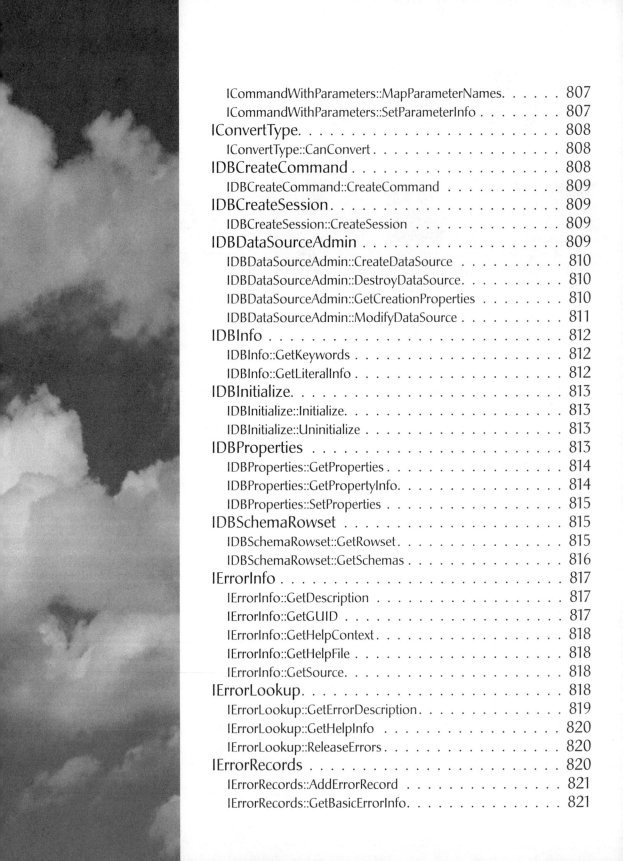

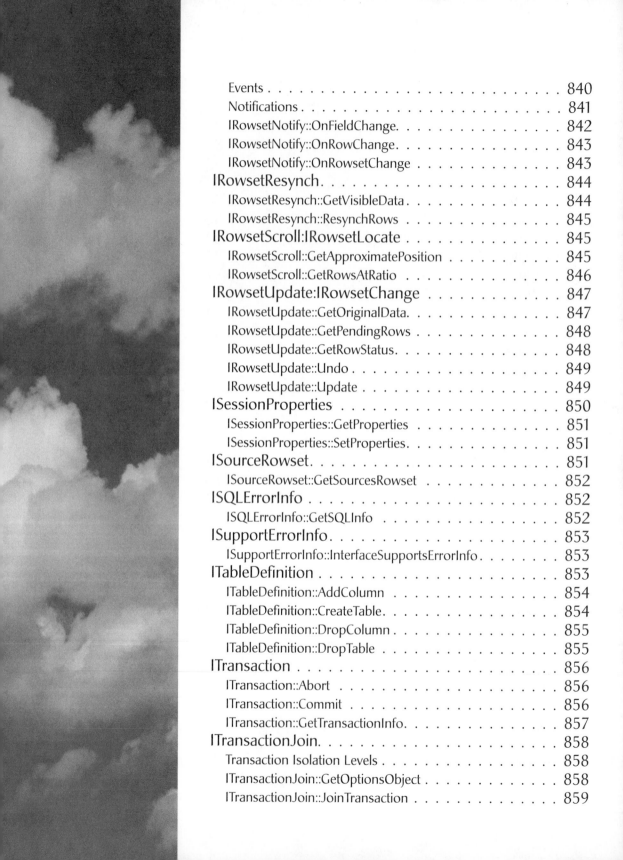

About Chapter 30

In Chapter 30, we look in detail at all the component object model (COM) interfaces. Chapter 29 gave us an overview, whereas this chapter presents the dirty details of COM interfacing. All OLE-DB interfaces are discussed — at least the ones that are currently published.

This chapter makes use of your newly acquired knowledge of COM objects . The COM **IConnectionPointContainer** interface (see Chapter 6) is the workhorse of connectable objects, and you'll see good examples of this with rowset notifications and the **IRowsetNotify** interface.

OLE-DB is quite complex. Taken singularly, any individual topic is manageable. However, when all aspects of OLE-DB are considered, the resulting system is one of formidable complexity. The net result is a system that is very complex to build, debug, and manage. Complexity factors include a lack of COM skills, error handling, COM event notifications with **IRowsetNotify**, and thread management. The Open Database Connectivity (ODBC) developer may have few of these skills and development of a new system could be quite protracted. Traditional ODBC-developer skill sets include Structured Query Language (SQL), stored procedures, data definition language (DDL) statements, triggers, and Visual Basic or C/C++.

The most difficult issue of all is the apartment-model threading discussed in Chapter 29. Apartment-model threads effectively force serialization at an object level, but when viewed from a system design perspective the serialization may not be necessary. Apartment-model serialization is an issue of implementation technique and not of system design. Apartment-model threading is a definite limiting factor in OLE-DB performance in a multiuser environment.

BEFORE WE BEGIN

OLE-DB is a series of COM interfaces. An object such as a **Session** object or a **Command** object consists of both mandatory and optional interfaces. Table 30-1 enumerates the optional and mandatory interfaces of OLE-DB. This table can be used as a reference for the remainder of the chapter.

TABLE 30-1 OLE-DB MANDATORY AND OPTIONAL INTERFACES

CoType Name	*Object Name*	*Mandatory Interfaces*	*Optional Interfaces*
TEnumerator	Enumerator	IParseDisplayName, ISourcesRowset	ODBInitialize, IDBProperties, ISupportErrorInfo
TDataSource	Data Source	IDBCreateSession, IDBInitialize, IDBProperties, IPersist	IDBDataSourceAdmin, IDBInfo, IPersistFile, ISupportErrorInfo
TSession	Session	IGetDataSource, IOpenRowset, ISessionProperties	IDBCreateCommand, IDBSchemaRowset, IIndexDefinition, ISupportErrorInfo, ITableDefinition, ITransactionJoin, ITransactionLocal, ITransactionObject
TCommand	Command	IAccessor, IColumnsInfo, ICommand, ICommandProperties, ICommandText, IConvertType	IColumnsRowset, ICommandPrepare, ICommandWith Parameters, ISupportErrorInfo
TMultipleResults	Multiple Results	IMultipleResults	
TRowset	Rowset	IAccessor, IColumnsInfo, IConvertType, IRowset, IRowsetInfo	IColumnsRowset, IConnectionPoint Container, IRowsetChange, IRowsetIdentity, IRowsetLocate, IRowsetResynch, IRowsetScroll, IRowsetUpdate, ISupportErrorInfo

continued

TABLE 30-1 *(continued)*			
CoTYPE NAME	*OBJECT NAME*	*MANDATORY INTERFACES*	*OPTIONAL INTERFACES*
TIndex	Index	IAccessor, IColumnsInfo, IConvertType, IRowset, IRowsetIndex, IRowsetInfo	IRowsetChange, ISupportErrorInfo
TTransaction	Transaction	IConnectionPoint Container, ITransaction	ISupportErrorInfo
TTransaction Options	Transaction Options	ITransactionOptions	ISupportErrorInfo
TErrorObject	Error	IErrorInfo, IErrorRecords	
TCustomError Object	Custom Errors		ISQLErrorInfo

IACCESSOR

The enumeration of OLE-DB objects starts with **IAccessor**. This is the first OLE-DB object; objects are enumerated in alphabetical order. All rowsets and commands must implement the **IAccessor** interface, which supplies binding information through the DBBINDING structure for rowset data, parameter data, or both. As Table 30-1 indicates, the **IAccessor** interface is a mandatory interface for **Command** objects, **Rowset** objects, and **Index** objects.

Accessor objects are associated with a **Rowset** object. In the interest of efficiency, **Accessor** objects can be created on the **Command** object and inherited by newly created **Rowset** objects. The consumer has the responsibility of verifying that **Accessor** objects created on a **Command** object are still valid after the command is changed. An **Accessor** object on a **Command** is released when the **Command** reference count or the **Accessor** reference count reaches zero. A child **Accessor** is not affected when the parent **Accessor** object is released on a zero reference count.

Rowset objects inherit **Accessor** objects from the parent **Command** object. **Accessor** object handles, flags, and bindings are identical for the **Accessor** object of a rowset that was inherited from a **Command** object.

Accessors may lose the parent and parent accessors may lose their children. An inherited **Acccessor** object is released when the reference count reaches zero. The parent accessor is not released.

The **IAccessor** object uses the DBBINDING structure, outlined as follows.

```
typedef struct tagDBBINDING {
  ULONG       iOrdinal;    // column or parameter ordinal
  ULONG       obValue;     // value byte offset in consumer
                           //   buffer
  ULONG       obLength;    // data alignment based on hardware
  ULONG       obstatus;    // length byte offset in consumer
                           //   buffer
  ITypeInfo * pTypeInfo;   // Reserver, should be Null
  DBOBJECT *  pObject;     // Pointer to DBOBJECT structure
                           //
                           // typedef struct tagDBOBJECT {
                           // DWORD dwFlags;
                           // IID iid;
                           // } DBOBJECT;
                           //
  DBINDEXT *  pBindExt;    // Pointer to DBBINDEXT structure
                           //
                           // typedef struct tagDBBINDEXT {
                           // BYTE * pExtension;
                           // ULONG ulExtension;
                           // } DBBINDEXT;
                           //
  DBPART      dwPart;      // One of: DBPART_VALUE, _LENGTH,
                           // or _STATUS.
  DBMEMOWNER  dwMemOwner;  // Either
                           // DBMEMOWNER_CLIENTOWNED
                           // or DBMEMOWNER_PROVIDEROWNED.
  DBPARAMIO   eParamIO;    // One of: DBPARAMIO_NOTPARAM,
                           // _INPUT, or _OUTPUT
```

```
ULONG        cbMaxLen;    // Max size in bytes
DWORD        dwFlags;     // Reserved
DBTYPE       wType;       // Data type
BYTE         bPrecision;  // Digits of precision, numeric
                             types
BYTE         bScale;      // Fraction digits for numeric
                             types
} DBBINDING;
```

IAccessor::AddRefAccessor

The **IAccessor::AddRefAccessor** method increases the reference count of an existing **Accessor** object.

The following adds a reference count to an existing **Accessor** object:

```
HRESULT    AddRefAccessor (
HACCESSOR hAccessor,
ULONG *    pcRefCount);
```

hAccessr   Accessor handle.

PcRefCount   Pointer to returned reference count.

IAccessor::CreateAccessor

The **CreateAccessor** method creates an **Accessor** object from a DBBINDING structure.

The following creates an **Accessor** object from a set of bindings using a DBBINDING structure:

```
HRESULT     CreateAccessor (
DBACCESSORFLAGS     dwAccessorflags,
ULONG               cBindings,
const DBBINDING     rgBindings[],
ULONG               cbRowSize,
HACCESSOR *         phAccessor,
DBBINDSTATUS        rgStatus[]);
```

dwAccessorFlags	One of: DBACCESSOR_PASSBYREF, DBACCESSOR_PARAMETERDATA, Or DBACCESSOR_OPTIMIZED.
Cbindings	Input accessor binding count.
rgBindings []	Input array of DBBINDING structures.
CbRowSize	Input byte count allocated to an array of parameters.
PhAccessor	Pointer to a returned accessor handle; **Null** on an error.
rgBindingStatus []	An array of returned DBBINDSTATUS values. One of: DBBINDSTATUS_OK, _UNSUPPORTEDCONVERSION, _BADBINDINFO, _BADSTORAGEFLAGS, or _NOINTERFACE.

IAccessor::GetBindings

The **GetBindings** method returns the bindings of an **Accessor** object.

```
HRESULT     GetBindings (
  HACCESSOR           hAccessor,
  DBACCESSORFLAGS * pdwAccessorflags,
  ULONG *             pcBindings,
  DBBINDING **        prgBindings);
```

hAccessor	Accessor handle.
pdwAccessorflags	Pointer to a returned bitmask or status. DBACCESSOR_INVALID on an error.
pcBindings	Pointer to returned binding count.
prgBindings	Pointer to a returned array pointer of DBBINDING structures. *prgBindings* is a **Null** pointer when *pcbindings* is zero or an error occurs. The consumer must release this buffer with **IMalloc::Free**.

IAccessor::ReleaseAccessor

The **ReleaseAccessor** method decrements the reference count of an **Accessor** object. The **Accessor** object and all dependent resources are released when the reference count reaches zero.

```
HRESULT    ReleaseAccesor (
 HACCESSOR   hAccessor,
 ULONG *     pcRefCount);
```

hAccessor   Accessor handle.

pcRefCount   Pointer to returned reference count. None returned if **Null**.

IColumnsInfo

IColumnsInfo is one of two interfaces that expose column metadata. **IColumns Rowset** provides complete data while **IColumnsInfo** is a simpler interface for the common data. **IColumnsInfo** is a required interface for all commands and rowsets.

Commands that expose **ICommandPrepare** can only access **IColumnsInfo** when the command is prepared or the rowset is instantiated. DB_E_NOTPREPARED is the expected response from calling a method of **IColumnInfo** before the command is prepared.

These interfaces and methods use the DBCOLUMNINFO structure outlined below:

```
typedef  struct   tagDBCOLUMNINFO {
 LPOLESTR        pwszName;
 ITypeInfo *     pTypeInfo;
 ULONG           iOrdinal;
 DBCOLUMNFLAGS   dwFlags;
 ULONG           ulColumnSize;
 DBTYPE          wType;
 BYTE            bPrecision;
 BYTE            bScale;
 DBID            columnid;
 }  DBCOLUMNINFO
```

IColumnsInfo::GetColumnInfo

The **GetColumnInfo** method returns column metadata in a DBCOLUMNINFO array.

```
HRESULT    ReleaseAccesor (
  ULONG *            pcColumns,
  DBCOLUMNINFO **    prgInfo,
  OLECHAR **         ppStringsBuffer);
```

pcColumns	Pointer to returned column count.
prgInfo	Pointer to a returned array pointer of DBCOLUMNINFO structures. The consumer must release this buffer with **IMalloc::Free**.
ppStringsBuffer	Pointer to where a returned pointer of string value names is returned. **Null** pointer returned on an error or no string names. The consumer must release this buffer with **IMalloc::Free**.

IColumnsInfo::MapColumnIDs

The **MapColumnIDs** method returns an array of ordinals based on an array of column IDs.

```
HRESULT    MapColumnIDs (
  ULONG         cColumnIDs,
  const DBID    rgColumnIDs[],
  ULONG         rgColumns[]);
```

cColumnIDs	The number of column IDs to map.
rgColumnIDs[]	The array of column IDs to map.
rgColumns[]	Array of mapped column ordinals.

IColumnsRowset

This interface returns complete column metadata in a rowset. Advanced providers expose this interface, which is optional for commands and rowsets.

IColumnsRowset uses both the DBPROPSET structure and the DBPROP structures.

```
typedef struct tagDBPROPSET {
  DBPROP *        rgProperties;     //DBPROP structures array
  ULONG           cProperties;      //Property count to get
  GUID            guidPropertySet;  //Property group GUID
}DBPROPSET;

typedef struct tagDBPROP {
  DBPROPID        dwPropertyID;
  DBPROPOPTIONS   dwOptions;
  DBPROPSTATUS    dwStatus;
  DBID            colid;
  VARIANT         vValue;
}DBPROP;
```

IColumnsRowset::GetAvailableColumns

The **GetAvailableColumns** method returns a list of optional metadata columns that can be supplied in a metadata rowset.

```
HRESUL    GetAvailableColumns (
  ULONG *      pcOptColumns,
  DBID **      prgOptColumn);
```

pcOptColumns   Pointer to returned element count.

prgOptColumns   Pointer to a returned array pointer of optional metadata columns this provider can supply. **IMalloc::Free** must be used by the consumer when this array is no longer needed. **Null** pointer returned on an error or **pcOptColumns* is zero.

IColumnsRowset::GetColumnsRowset

IColumnsRowset::GetColumnsRowset returns a read-only metadata rowset for each column in the current rowset. This interface uses the DBPROPSET structure to pass an array of DBPROP structures:

```
HRESULT    GetColumnsRowset (
  IUnknown *    pUnkOuter,
  ULONG         cOptColumns,
```

```
const DBID    rgOptColumns[],
REFIID        riid,
ULONG         cPropertySets,
DBPROPSET     rgPropertySets[],
IUnknown **   ppColRowset);
```

pUnkOuter   Pointer to the controlling **IUnknown** interface when the rowset is being created as part of an aggregate; otherwise a **Null** pointer.

cOptColumns   Element count of *rgOptColumns*.

rgOptColumns[]   Specifies the columns for which metadata is requested.

riid   Interface identifier (IID) of the requested rowset interface.

cPropertySets   Count of DBPROPSET structures in *rgPropertySets*.

rgPropertySets[]   Array pointer of DBPROPSET properties and values to be set. Ignored when *cPropertySets* is zero.

ppColRowset   Pointer to where a pointer is returned for a metadata rowset. It is a **Null** pointer on an error. The rowset is empty when called by a command that does not return rows.

ICOMMAND

The **ICommand** interface is required for all **Command** objects. A single command may be executed more than once and the parameters may vary.

The DBPARAMS structure is used by this interface:

```
struct   DBPARAMS {
 void *      pData;
 ULONG       cParamSets;
 HACCESSOR   hAccessor;
};
```

ICommand::Cancel

The current command is cancelled with the **Cancel** method.

```
HRESULT  Cancel();
```

ICommand::Execute

This method executes the command constructed by the **ICommandText** interface using the supplied DBPARAMS structure.

```
HRESULT    Execute (
  IUnknown *     pUnkOuter,
   REFIID        riid,
  DBPARAMS *     pParams,
  LONG *         pcRowsAffected,
  IUnknown **    ppRowset);
```

pUnkOuter	Pointer to the controlling **IUnknown** interface when the rowset is being created as part of an aggregate; Otherwise a **Null** pointer.
riid	Requested IID of the rowset returned in **ppRowset*.
pParams	Pointer to a DBPARAMS structure.
pcRowsAffected	Pointer to a returned row count for an update, delete, or insert operation. Either a <-1> or the total number of rows affected when *riid* is IID_IMULTIPLERESULTS. Undefined when not an update, delete, or an insert. No count is returned for a **Null** pointer.
ppRowset	Pointer to where a pointer is returned for a rowset. It is a **Null** pointer on an error. The rowset is empty when called by a command that does not return rows.

ICommand::GetDBSession

The **GetDBSession** method returns the **Session** object interface pointer of the session that created the command.

```
HRESULT    GetDBSession (
  REFIID        riid,
  IUnknown **    ppSession);
```

riid	The interface on which to return the pointer.
ppSession	A pointer to memory in which to return the session pointer. **ppSession* is **Null** on a failure.

ICOMMANDPREPARE

ICommandPrepare compiles a SQL statement. When a provider supports command preparation **IColumnsInfo::GetColumnInfo**, **IColumnsInfo::MapColumnIDs**, **IColumnsRowset::GetAvailableColumns**, and **IColumnsRowset::GetColumns Rowset**, all must have the command prepared before being called.

ICommandPrepare::Prepare

Compile a command (optimize).

```
HRESULT    Prepare (
   ULONG        cExpectedRuns);
```

cExpectedRuns   Expected execution count for the optimizer.

ICommandPrepare::Unprepare

Discard the current command execution plan.

```
HRESULT  UnPrepare ();
```

ICOMMANDPROPERTIES

This is a mandatory interface for all **Command** objects.

This interface specifies to the **Command** object the required properties from the **Rowset** property group that must be supported by rowsets returned by **ICommand::Execute** method.

The consumer uses the DBPROPIDSET structure to pass an array of DBPROPID values.

```
typedef struct   tagDBPROPIDSET {
  DBPROPID *  rgPropertyIDs;
  ULONG       cPropertyIDs;
  GUID        guidPropertySet;
} DBPROPIDSET;
```

ICommandProperties::GetProperties

The **GetProperties** method returns the list of properties in the **Rowset** property group for the current rowset.

```
HRESULT     GetProperties (
  const ULONG          cPropertyIDSets,
  const DBPROPIDSET    rgPropertyIDSets[],
  ULONG *              pcPropertySets,
  DBPROPSET **         prgPropertySets);
```

cPropertyIDSets	rgPropertyIDSets count.
rgPropertyIDSets[]	An array of DBPROPIDSET structures.
pcPropertySets	Pointer to the number of DBPROPSET structures returned in prgPropertySets.
prgPropertySets	A pointer to returned array pointer of DBPROPSET structures. Each structure contains at least one property supported by the provider.

The provider allocates this memory which the consumer releases with **IMalloc::Free**.

When *cPropertyIDSets* is not zero, one structure is returned for each property specified in *rgPropertyIDSets[]*.

When *cPropertyIDSets* is zero, one structure is returned for each property set that contains at least one property belonging to the **Rowset** property group.

ICommandProperties::SetProperties

This method sets properties in a **Rowset** property group.

```
HRESULT     SetProperties (
  ULONG          cPropertySets,
  DBPROPSET      rgPropertySets[]);
```

cPropertySets	rgPropertySets count.
rgPropertySets[]	An array of DBPROPSET structures containing properties and values.

ICommandText:ICommand

ICommandText inherits from **ICommand** and is a mandatory on all commands. A **Command** object can have only one text command; the current text command replaces the previous text command.

ICommandText::GetCommandText

This method returns the last text command set by **ICommandText:: SetCommandText**.

```
HRESULT    GetCommandText (
  GUID *        pguidDialect,
  LPOLESTR *    ppwszCommand);
```

pguidDialect   A pointer to a GUID that describes the syntax and rules for parsing the command text.

ppwszCommand   A pointer to where the command text pointer will be returned. A **Null** pointer is returned on an error. The consumer releases the command text buffer with **IMalloc::Free**.

ICommandText::SetCommandText

Replaces the command text with the current text. Meaningful error checking does not occur until **ICommandPrepare::Prepare** or **ICommand::Execute**.

```
HRESULT    GetCommandText (
  REFGUID    rguidDialect,
  LPOLESTR   pwszCommand);
```

rguidDialect   A GUID that specifies the syntax and rules for parsing the command text.

pwszCommand   A memory pointer to the command text. Methods such as **ICommand::Execute** and **ICommand::Prepare** return DB_E_NOCOMMAND until new command text is set.

ICOMMANDWITHPARAMETERS

All providers that support parameters must support this interface. Any provider that returns `DBPROPVAL_SQL_ANSI92_INTERMEDIATE` or `DBPROPVAL_SQL_ANSI92_FULL` can support parameters.

This is an optional interface that encapsulates parameters. A new query plan (preparation) is not required when the parameters are scalars.

This interface uses the DBPARAMINFO structure.

```
typedef struct   tagDBPARAMINFO {
  DBPARAMFLAGS    dwFlags;        // one of:
                                       DBPARAMFLAGS_ISINPUT,
                                  //_ISOUTPUT, _ISSIGNED,
                                     ISNULLABLE, or
                                  //_ISLONG
  ULONG           iOrdinal;       //1-based ordinal
  LPOLESTR        pwszName;       //Parameter name
  ITypeInfo *     pTypeInfo;      //ITypeInfo describes the type
  ULONG           ulParamSize;    //Maximum length or all bits
  DBTYPE          wType;          //Indicator of type
  BYTE            bPrecision;     //Maximum digits for numeric
                                       type
  BYTE            bScale;         //Maximum fractional digits
}  DBPARAMINFO;
```

ICommandWithParameters::GetParameterInfo

ICommandWithParameters::GetParameterInfo returns a list of command parameters, their names, and their values. The list is returned as information stored in the DBPARAMINFO structure.

```
HRESULT    GetParameterInfo (
  ULONG *         pcParams,
  DBPARAMINFO **  prgParamInfo,
  OLECHAR **      ppNamesBuffer);
```

pcParams   A pointer to memory where the parameter count is returned.

prgParamInfo   A pointer to a returned array pointer of DBPARAMINFO parameter information structures. The consumer releases this buffer with **IMalloc::Free**.

ppNamesBuffer   A pointer to memory when a pointer to the parameter names are returned. The consumer releases this buffer with **IMalloc::Free**.

ICommandWithParameters:: MapParameterNames

ICommandWithParameters::MapParameterNames returns an array of ordinals when given an array of parameter names.

```
HRESULT    MapParameterNames (
  ULONG             cParamNames,
  const OLECHAR *   rgParamNames[],
  LONG              rgParamOrdinals[]);
```

cParamNames   Parameter names input count.

rgParamNames[]   An input array of parameter names used to determine the ordinals.

rgParamOrdinals[]   Returned array of name ordinals

ICommandWithParameters::SetParameterInfo

This interface specifies the data type of each parameter using a DBPARAMBIND-INFO structure.

```
typedef struct tagDBPARAMBINDINFO {
  LPOLESTR       pwszDataSourceType;//Data type name pointer
  LPOLESTR       pwszName;          //Parameter name
  ULONG          ulParamSize;       //Maximum length or all
                                    bits
  DBPARAMFLAGS   dwFlags;           //See DBPARAMINFO
                                    structure
  BYTE           bPrecision;        //Maximum digits, numeric
                                    type
```

```
    BYTE              bScale;                //Maximum fractional
                                                          digits
} DBPARAMBINDINFO;
HRESULT    SetParameterInfo (
  ULONG              cParams,
  const ULONG        rgParamOrdinals[],
  const DBPARAMBINDINFO     rgParamBindInfo[]);
```

cParams	Input parameter count.
rgParamOrdinals[]	Input array or parameter ordinals.
rgParamBindInfo[]	Input array of DBPARAMBINDINFO structures.

IConvertType

IConvertType is a mandatory interface for commands, rowsets, and index rowsets. The interface has only one method that provides type conversion availability on a command or rowset.

IConvertType::CanConvert

```
HRESULT    CanConvert (
  DBTYPE            wFromType,
  DBTYPE            wToType,
  DBCONVERTFLAGS    dwConvertFlags);
```

wFromType	Source conversion type.
wToType	Target conversion type.
dwConvertFlags	Flag which determines if the conversion is on a rowset or command; either DBCONVERTFLAGS_COLUMN or DBCONVERTFLAGS_PARAMETER.

IDBCreateCommand

The **IDBCreateCommand** is the interface used to create a **Command** object on a session.

IDBCreateCommand::CreateCommand

```
HRESULT    CreateCommand (
  IUnknown *        pUnkOuter,
  REFIID            riid,
  IUnknown **       ppCommand);
```

pUnkOuter	Pointer to the controlling **IUnknown** interface when the command is being created as part of an aggregate; otherwise a **Null** pointer.
riid	Requested IID of the rowset returned in **ppCommand*.
ppCommand	Pointer where the newly created **Command** object pointer will be returned.

IDBCREATESESSION

The **DBCreateSession** interface creates a **Session** object on a **Data Source** object.

IDBCreateSession::CreateSession

```
HRESULT    CreateSession (
  IUnknown *        pUnkOuter,
  REFIID            riid,
  Iunknown **       ppDBSession);
```

pUnkOuter	Pointer to the controlling **IUnknown** interface when the session is being created as part of an aggregate; otherwise a **Null** pointer.
riid	Requested IID of the rowset returned in **ppSession*.
ppDBSession	Pointer to memory where the newly created **Session** object pointer will be returned.

IDBDATASOURCEADMIN

IDBDataSourceAdmin is an optional interface for managing **Data Source** objects. Objects may be destroyed, created, or modified.

IDBDataSourceAdmin::CreateDataSource

This interface creates a **Data Source** object and, optionally, a **Session** object.

```
HRESULT    CreateDataSource (
 ULONG           cPropertySets,
 DBPROPSET       rgPropertySets[],
 IUnknown *      pUnkOuter,
 REFIID          riid,
 IUnknown **     ppSession);
```

cPropertySets	DBPROPSET structure count in *rgPropertySets*[].
rgPropertySets[]	An array of DBPROPSET structures. See **IColumnsRowset::GetColumnsRowset**. This argument is ignored when *cPropertySets* is zero.
pUnkOuter	Pointer to the controlling **IUnknown** interface when the session is being created as part of an aggregate; Otherwise a **Null** pointer.
riid	Requested IID of the rowset returned in **ppSession*.
ppSession	Pointer to memory where the newly created **Session** object pointer will be returned.

IDBDataSourceAdmin::DestroyDataSource

This method destroys the current data source and leaves the **Data Source** object in an uninitialized state.

```
HRESULT  DestroyDataSource ();
```

IDBDataSourceAdmin::GetCreationProperties

This method returns only those data-source creation properties supported by the provider. The property information is returned in a DBPROPINFOSET structure, which describes an array of DBPROPINFOSET structures.

```
typedef struct    tagDBPROPIDSET {
 DBPROPID *       rgPropertyIDs;
 ULONG            cPropertyIDs;
```

```
   GUID              guidPropertySet;
} DBPROPIDSET;

typedef  DWORD  DBPROPID;
HRESULT   GetCreationProperties (
 ULONG             cPropertyIDSets,
 const DBPROPIDSET  rgPropertyIDSets[],
 ULONG *           pcPropertyInfoSets,
 DBPROPINFOSET **   prgPropertyInfoSets,
 OLECHAR **        ppDescBuffer);
```

cPropertyIDSets	The number of DBPROPIDSET structures in *rgPropertyIDSets*.
rgPropertyIDSets[]	An array of DBPROPIDSET structures.
pcPropertyInfoSets	A pointer to memory where the *prgPropertyInfoSets* count is returned.
prgPropertyInfoSets	A pointer to where an array pointer of DBPROPINFOSET structures are returned. The consumer releases this buffer with **IMalloc::Free**.
ppDescBuffer	A pointer to memory where a pointer for **pwszDescription* strings of the DBPROPINFO structure are returned. The consumer releases this buffer with **IMalloc::Free**.

IDBDataSourceAdmin::ModifyDataSource

This method modifies the current data source.

```
HRESULT   CreateDataSource (
 ULONG        cPropertySets,
 DBPROPSET    rgPropertySets[]);
```

cPropertySets	DBPROPSET structure count in *rgPropertySets*[].
rgPropertySets[]	An array of DBPROPSET structures containing properties and values to be set. See **IColumnsRowset::GetColumnsRowset**. This argument is ignored when *cPropertySets* is zero.

IDBINFO

IDBInfo is an optional provider interface. It returns literals and keywords supported by the provider.

IDBInfo::GetKeywords

```
HRESULT    GetKeyWords (
  LPOLESTR *    ppwszKeywords);
```

ppwszKeywords   A pointer to memory in which to return the pointer to a string of comma-delimited keywords.

IDBInfo::GetLiteralInfo

This method returns information on literals used in text commands, the **ITableDefinition** interface, and the **IIndexDefinition** interface. Literal information is returned in a DBLITERALINFO structure.

```
typedef struct    tagDBLITERALINFO {
  LPOLESTR      pwszLiteralValue;
  LPOLESTR      pwszInvalidChars;
  LPOLESTR      pwszInvalidStartingChars;
  DBLITERAL     lt;
  BOOL          fSupported;
  ULONG         cchMaxLen;
} DBLITERALINFO;
HRESULT    GetLiteralInfo (
  ULONG              cLiterals,
  const DBLITERAL    rgLiterals[],
  ULONG *            pcLiteralInfo,
  DBLITERALINFO **   prgLiteralInfo;
  OLECHAR **         ppCharBuffer);
```

cLiterals   The literal count being inquired about. All literal information returned when zero.

rgLiterals[]	An array of literals about which to return information. The corresponding entry of *prgLiteralInfo* returns **FALSE** in the *fSupported* argument for an invalid entry.
pcLiteralInfo	Pointer to the returned literal count. Set to zero if an error other than DB_E_ERRORSOCCURRED is returned.
prgLiteralInfo	A pointer to returned pointer of a DBLITERALINFO structures array pointer. **IMalloc::Free** is used by the consumer to release this buffer.
ppCharBuffer	A pointer to memory where a pointer for all string values of type *pwszLiteralValue, pwszInvalidChars,* and *pwszInvalid StartingChars* are stored. **IMalloc::Free** is used by the consumer to release this buffer.

IDBINITIALIZE

IDBInitialize is an optional interface for **Enumerator** objects and a mandatory interface for **Data Source** objects. The methods of this interface initialize or uninitialize **Enumerator** or **Data Source** objects.

IDBInitialize::Initialize

Initialize an **Enumerator** or a **Data Source** object.

```
HRESULT  Initialize ();
```

IDBInitialize::Uninitialize

Uninitialize an **Enumerator** or a **Data Source** object.

```
HRESULT  Uninitialize ();
```

IDBPROPERTIES

The methods of the **IDBProperites** interface set or get the properties of an **Enumerator** or a **Data Source** object.

IDBProperties::GetProperties

This method returns properties in the Data Source object, Data Source Information group, Data Source Initialization group, or the Enumerator Initialization property group.

```
HRESULT     GetProperties (
 ULONG                cPropertyIDSets,
 const DBPROPIDSET    rgPropertyIDSets[],
 ULONG *              pcPropertySets,
 DBPROPSET **         prgPropertySets);
```

cPropertyIDSets   The number of DBPROPIDSET structures in *rgPropertyIDSets*.

rgPropertyIDSets[]   An array of DBPROPIDSET structures.

pcPropertySets   A pointer to memory for the returned *prgPropertySets* count.

prgPropertySets   A pointer to a returned array pointer of DBPROPSET structures. Each structure contains at least one property supported by the provider.

The provider allocates this memory that the consumer releases with **IMalloc::Free**.

When *cPropertyIDSets* is not zero, the DBPROPSET structures are returned in the same order as the DBPROPIDSET structures specified in *rgPropertyIDSets*[].

IDBProperties::GetPropertyInfo

This method returns information about all properties supported by the provider.

```
HRESULT     GetCreationProperties (
 ULONG                cPropertyIDSets,
 const DBPROPIDSET    rgPropertyIDSets[],
 ULONG *              pcPropertyInfoSets,
 DBPROPINFOSET **     prgPropertyInfoSets,
 OLECHAR **           ppDescBuffer);
```

cPropertyIDSets   The number of DBPROPIDSET structures in *rgPropertyIDSets*.

rgPropertyIDSets[]	An array of DBPROPIDSET structures.
pcPropertyInfoSets	A pointer to where the *prgPropertyInfoSets* count is returned.
prgPropertyInfoSets	A pointer to where a pointer to an array of DBPROPINFOSET structures is returned.
ppDescBuffer	A pointer to where a pointer for **pwszDescription* strings of the DBPROPINFO structure is returned. **IMalloc::Free** must be used by the consumer to release this buffer.

When *cPropertyIDSets* is not zero, the DBPROPINFOSET structures are returned in the same order as the DBPROPIDSET structures specified in *rgPropertyIDSets*[].

IDBProperties::SetProperties

This method will set properties in the **Data Source**, **Data Source Initialization** group, or an **Enumerator Initialization** property group.

```
HRESULT    SetProperties (
  ULONG          cPropertySets,
  DBPROPSET      rgPropertySets[]);
```

cPropertyIDSets	The number of DBPROPSET structures in *rgPropertySets*.
rgPropertySets[]	An array of DBPROPSET structures containing properties and values to set.

IDBSCHEMAROWSET

The **IDBSchemeRowset** is an optional interface on **Session** objects that returns advanced schema information.

IDBSchemaRowset::GetRowset

This method returns a rowset schema.

```
HRESULT    GetRowset (
  IUnknown *      pUnkOuter,
```

```
REFGUID        rguidSchema,
ULONG          cRestrictions,
const VARIANT  rgRestrictions[],
REFIID         riid,
ULONG          cPropertySets,
DBPROPSET      rgPropertySets[],
IUnknown **    ppRowset);
```

pUnkOuter	Pointer to the controlling **IUnknown** interface when the rowset is created as part of an aggregate. It is a **Null** when **IDBSchemaRowset** is not being aggregated.
rguidSchema	GUID identifying the schema rowset.
cRestrictions	Restriction value count.
rgRestrictions[]	An array of restriction values applied in the order of restriction columns.
riid	IID of the requested rowset interface.
cPropertySets	Count of DBPROPSET structures in *rgPropertySets*.
rgPropertySets	An array of DBPROPSET structures containing properties.
ppRowset	A memory location where the pointer to the rowset is returned. This rowset is read-only. An empty rowset is returned in the absence of schema information.

IDBSchemaRowset::GetSchemas

This method will return a list of schema rowsets accessible by **IDBSchema:: GetRowset**.

```
HRESULT    GetSchemas (
  ULONG *            pcSchemas,
  GUID **            prgSchemas,
  ULONG **           prgRestrictionSupport);
```

pcSchemas	Pointer to where a returned schema count is stored. Always a minimum of three because all providers must support TABLES, COLUMNS, and PROVIDER_TYPES.

prgSchemas	A pointer to where a returned pointer to an array of GUIDs is returned.
prgRestrictionSupport	A pointer to where a pointer to an array of ULONGS is returned, one pointer for each supported schema rowset. An entry is collectively named `DBSCHEMA_ASSERTIONS` with:

bit 0: CONSTRAINT_CATALOG,

bit 1: CONSTRAINT_SCHEMA, and

bit 2: CONSTRAINT_NAME.

IERRORINFO

Recall from Chapter 29 that **IErrorInfo** is defined by automation and is not adequate to support the many levels of errors within OLE-DB. This interface returns an error message, the name of the component, and the GUID of the interface in which the error occurred. The name and topic of the Help file is also returned.

IErrorInfo::GetDescription

```
HRESULT     GetDescription (
  BSTR *        pbstrDescription);
```

pbstrDescription   Pointer to a memory location where a string pointer is returned.

IErrorInfo::GetGUID

This method returns the GUID of the interface that defined the error.

```
HRESULT     GetGUID (
  GUID *       pguid);
```

pguid   Pointer to a memory location in which to return the GUID of the interface that defined the error.

IErrorInfo::GetHelpContext

This method returns the error Help context ID.

```
HRESULT    GetHelpContext (
 DWORD *      pdwHelpContext);
```

pdwHelpContext   Pointer to a memory location in which to return the Help
context ID.

IErrorInfo::GetHelpFile

This method returns the fully qualified path of the Help file that describes the
error.

```
HRESULT    GetHelpFile (
 BSTR *       pbstrHelpFile);
```

pbstrHelpFile   Pointer to a memory location in which to return a string that is
a fully qualified path to the Help file.

IErrorInfo::GetSource

This method returns the name of the component causing the error.

```
HRESULT    GetSource (
 BSTR *       pbstrSource);
```

pbstrSource   Pointer to a memory location where the component name is
returned.

IErrorLookup

The **IErrorLookup** interface is mandatory for all OLE-DB providers that support
Error objects. The methods of this interface return an error message, source, Help
file path, and context ID based on a return code.

   IErrorLookup is called by code within the OLE-DB software developer's kit
(SDK). Consumers should not call it.

   Error information is returned in an ERRINFO structure.

```
typedef struct  tagERRORINFO {
 HRESULT         hrError;    // Error code returned by method
 DWORD           dwMinor;    // Provider-specific error code
 CLSID           clsid;      // Object CLSID that returned the
                                error
 IID             iid;        // IID of interface generating the
                                error
 DISPID          dispid;     // If defined, this identifies the
                                method
}ERRORINFO;
```

IErrorLookup::GetErrorDescription

An internal method that returns the error message and the source name.

 There is no supplied documentation in the OLE-DB 1.1 SDK with respect to the DISPARAMS structure, which is a vendor-specific structure.

```
HRESULT    GetErrorDescription (
 HRESULT        hrError,
 DWORD          dwLookupID,
 DISPARAMS *    pdispparams,
 LCID           lcid,
 BSTR *         pbstrSource,
 BSTR *         pbstrDescription);
```

hrError   Error code returned by method.

dwLookupID   Provider-specific error code.

pdispparams   Pointer to error parameters; **Null** pointer if none.

lcid   Locale ID.

pbstrSource   A pointer in which to return the pointer for the component name. **SysFreeString** must be used to release this pointer.

pbstrDescription   A pointer in which to return the pointer for the error description. **SysFreeString** must be used to release this pointer.

IErrorLookup::GetHelpInfo

An internal method that returns the Help file path and the topic context ID.

```
HRESULT    GetHelpInfo (
  HRESULT        hrError,
  DWORD          dwLookupID,
  LCID           lcid,
  BSTR *         pbstrHelpFile,
  DWORD *        pdwHelpContext);
```

hrError   Error code returned by method.

dwLookupID   Provider-specific error code.

lcid   Locale ID.

pbstrHelpFile   A memory pointer in which to return the pointer for the
                   Help file fully qualified path. It is a **Null** when no file exists.
                   The consumer must free this string with **SysFreeString**.

pdwHelpContext   A memory pointer in which to return the Help context ID.

IErrorLookup::ReleaseErrors

An internal method to release all dynamic error information. Recall that an OLE-DB error may have many error records.

```
HRESULT    ReleaseErrors (
  const DWORD      dwDynamicErrorID);
```

dwDynamicErrorID   Dynamic error ID.

IERRORRECORDS

Consumers use the **IErrorRecords** interface to retrieve OLE-DB error records and providers use it to add new error records. Consumers call **QueryInterface** to obtain a pointer to this interface after retrieving an **Error** object with **GetErrorInfo** in the automation dynamic link library (DLL).

If the **Error** object exists, providers will use the same retrieval mechanism. If an **Error** doesn't exist, a provider uses a class factory or **CoCreateInstance** to create the **Error** object while requesting that a pointer to this interface be returned.

concept link

For more information about working with the Error object, see Chapter 29.

IErrorRecords::AddErrorRecord

A provider uses the **AddErrorRecord** method to add error records.

```
HRESULT     AddErrorRecord (
 ERRORINFO *      pErrorInfo,
 DWORD            dwLookupID,
 DISPPARAMS *     pdispparams,
 IUnknown *       punkCustomError,
 DWORD            dwDynamicErrorID);
```

pErrorInfo	A pointer to an ERRORINFO structure.
dwLookupID	A vendor-specific error code. It may also be the code `IDENTIFIER_SDK_ERROR`, which says ignore the vendor lookup service and use the OLE-DB SDK lookup service.
pdispparams	Pointer to a DISPPARAMS structure of error parameters. It is provider-specific and not documented in the OLE-DB 1.1 SDK.
punkCustomError	Interface pointer to a custom error object; it is **Null** if none.
dwDynamicErrorID	Zero when the lookup service uses error information that is hard-coded in the lookup service.

IErrorRecords::GetBasicErrorInfo

This method returns the return code and a provider-specific error number.

```
HRESULT    GetBasicErrorInfo (
 ULONG     ulRecordNum,
 ERRORINFO * pErrorInfo);
```

ulRecordNum	A zero-based error record number.
pErrorInfo	A pointer to an ERRORINFO structure associated with *ulRecordNum*.

IErrorRecords::GetCustomErrorObject

This method returns a pointer to an interface on the **Custom Error** object.

```
HRESULT      GetCustomErrorObject (
  ULONG          ulRecordNum,
  REFIID         riid,
  IUnknown **    ppObject);
```

ulRecordNum   A zero-based error record number.

riid   IID of interface to return.

ppObject   A pointer to memory in which to return a pointer to the **Custom Error** object.

IErrorRecords::GetErrorInfo

This method returns an interface on the specified record.

```
HRESULT      GetErrorInfo (
  ULONG          ulRecordNum,
  LCID           lcid,
  IErrorInfo **  ppErrorInfo);
```

ulRecordNum   A zero-based error record number.

lcid   Locale ID.

ppErrorInfo   A pointer to memory in which to return the **IErrorInfo** object pointer.

IErrorRecords::GetErrorParameters

This method returns error parameters associated with an error record. The DISP-PARAMS structure is provider-specific and not included in the OLE-DB 1.1 SDK documentation.

```
HRESULT      GetErrorParameters (
  ULONG          ulRecordNum,
  DISPPARAMS *   pdispparams);
```

ulRecordNum   A zero-based error record number.

pdispparams   Pointer to a provider-specific DISPPARAMS structure. The consumer allocates this buffer.

IErrorRecords::GetRecordCount

This method returns the record of an OLE-DB **Error** object.

```
HRESULT    GetRecordCount(
 ULONG *      pcRecords);
```

pcRecords   A pointer to memory where the **Error** object record count is returned.

IGetDataSource

The **IGetDataSource** interface is mandatory for a **Session** object. It has one method, which returns the interface pointer to the **Data Source** object.

IGetDataSource::GetDataSource

```
HRESULT    GetDataSource (
 REFIID       riid,
 IUnknown **   ppDataSource);
```

riid   IID on which to return the pointer.

ppDataSource   Pointer to memory where the returned **Data Source** object pointer is returned. It is a **Null** on an error.

IIndexDefinition

IIndexDefinition is an optional interface, but it is a mandatory interface for all providers that support creation and dropping of indexes.

This interface uses the DBINDEXCOLUMNDESC structure.

```
typedef struct {
  DBID *           pColumnID;       // base table ID column
  DBINDEXCOLORDER eIndexColOrder;  //DBINDEXCOLORDER_ASC or
                                    //DBINDEXCOLORDER_DESC
} DBINDEXCOLUMNDESC
```

IIndexDefinition::CreateIndex

A new index is created with this method.

```
HRESULT    CreateIndex (
  DBID *               pTableID,
  DBID *               pIndexID,
  ULONG                cIndexColumnDescs,
  const DBINDEXCOLUMNDESC    rgIndexColumnDescs[],
  ULONG                cPropertySets,
  DBPROPSET            rgPropertySets[],
  DBID **              ppIndexID);
```

pTableID	Table DBID pointer.
pIndexID	ID pointer of the new index that will be created.
cIndexColumnDescs	DBINDEXCOLUMNDESC structure count.
rgIndexColumnDescs[]	An array of DBINDEXCOLUMNDESC structures.
cPropertySets	DBPROPSET structure count.
rgPropertySets[]	An array of DBPROPSET structures.
ppIndexID	A pointer to memory where the pointer to the DBID of the newly created index is returned.

IIndexDefinition::DropIndex

This method will drop an index on a base table.

```
HRESULT    DROPIndex (
  DBID *     pTableID,
  DBID *     pIndexID);
```

pTableID   Pointer to DBID of the base table.

pIndexID   Pointer to DBID of the index which will be dropped. The index must belong to the table specified in *pTableID*. A **Null** value will drop all indexes.

IMULTIPLERESULTS

IMultipleResults is a mandatory interface on all **Multiple Results** objects. The Providers that support multiple-result sets set the DBPROP_MULTIPLERESULTS property of the **Data Source** Information group.

A multiple-results set is created when a consumer calls **ICommand::Execute** with an *riid* of IID_IMultipleResults.

IMultipleResults::GetResult

This method returns the next results set from a series of result sets.

```
HRESULT     GetResult (
 IUnknown *     pUnkOuter,
 LONG           lReserved,
 REFIID         riid,
 LONG *         pcRowsAffected,
 IUnknown **    ppRowSet);
```

pUnkOuter   Pointer to the controlling **IUnknown** interface when the results set is being created as part of an aggregate; otherwise a **Null** pointer.

lReserved   Must be zero.

riid   The requested interface to return in *ppRowSet*.

pcRowsAffected Pointer to where the count of deleted, inserted, or modified rows will be returned.

ppRowSet   A pointer to memory where the next **Rowset** object pointer will be returned. *ppRowSet* is ignored when *riid* is IID_NULL.

IOPENROWSET

IOpenRowset is a required interface for a **Session** object. It has one method that generates a rowset of all rows in a single base table or index.

IOpenRowset::OpenRowset

```
HRESULT    OpenRowset (
  IUnknown *     pUnkOuter,
  DBID *         pTableID,
  DBID *         pIndexID,
  REFIID         riid,
  ULONG          cPropertySets,
  DBPROPSET      rgPropertySets[],
  IUnknown **    ppRowSet);
```

pUnkOuter	Pointer to the controlling **IUnknown** interface when the rowset is being created as part of an aggregate; otherwise a **Null** pointer.
pTableID	Table DBID. *pTableID* must uniquely identify the table when *pIndexID* is **Null**.
pIndexID	Index DBID. *pIndexID* must uniquely identify the index when *pTableID* is **Null**.
riid	The requested interface to return in *ppRowSet*. This must be an interface the rowset *ppRowSet* supports even when no rowset is created.
cPropertySets	Input DBPROPSET structure count.
rgPropertySets[]	An array of DBPROPSET structures with properties and values to set.
ppRowSet	A pointer to memory where the **Rowset** object pointer will be returned.

IROWSET

An **IRowset** is the base rowset interface and requires both the **IAccessor** and **IRowsetInfo** interfaces. Acquiring a rowset is not a single step, but instead is a series of smaller steps:

1. The **IRowsetInfo::GetProperties** interface is used to return the rowset's capabilities.

2. The rowset characteristics or the metadata is determined. (The consumer examines the metadata and determines the columns required.)

3. The column (ordinal) order is determined by either the **IColumnsInfo** interface, which returns common metadata, or with **IColumnsRowset**, which returns more extensive metadata. Columns may be mapped with **IColumnsInfo::MapColumnIDs**. (The ordinals acquired are necessary for binding, which is done with **IAccessor::CreateAccessor**.)

4. A rowset is acquired with methods such as **GetNextRows** or **IRowsetLocate::GetRowsAt**. The consumer inserts new data by calling **IRowsetChange::InsertRow** while changing data occurs by calling **IRowsetChange::SetData**.

5. The consumer accesses the data in the rows by passing to **GetData** a row handle, an accessor handle, and a pointer to a consumer-allocated row buffer. (There can be more than one copy of data from a row, with each copy having been by a different accessor. There is no recommended technique for consumer row buffer allocation, and the consumer can use any appropriate allocation mechanism. Large objects may be truncated and the consumer should check rowset status for DBSTATUS_S_TRUNCATED.)

6. The consumer allocates space for bound columns that have a type indicator of DBTYPE_BYTES or DBTYPE_BYREF. The consumer can request the binary large object (BLOB) columns be delivered as **ILockBytes**, **IStorage**, **ISequentialStream**, or **IStream** objects. This approach takes advantage of COM-structured storage that already supports streams. It is possible to build an OLE-DB provider on top of the OLE object storage system.

7. **ReleaseRows** releases all the rows, **IAccessor::ReleaseAccessor** releases all accessors, and **IUnknown::Release** is called by all interfaces exposed by the rowset to release the rowset.

IRowset::AddRefRows

This method increases the reference count of an existing row handle.

```
HRESULT     AddRefRows (
  ULONG        cRows,
  const HROW   rghRows[],
  ULONG        rgRefCounts[],
  DBROWSTATUS rgRowStatus[]);
```

cRows   Row handle count.

rghRows[]   An array of row handles.

rgRefCounts[] Returned array or reference counts.

rgRowStatus[] Returned array of status values. Set to `DBROWSTATUS_S_OK` or `DB_S_ERRORSOCCURRED` when an error occurs incrementing a reference count.

IRowset::GetData

This method retrieves data from a rowset's copy.

```
HRESULT     GetData (
  HROW         hRow,
  HACCESSOR    hAccessor,
  void *       pData);
```

hRow   Row handle.

hAccessor Accessor handle. This may be **Null** if *cBinding* was zero in **IAccessor::CreateAccessor**. No data is returned when *hAccessor* is **Null**.

pData   A pointer to data storage. The allocation of this buffer is a consumer responsibility.

IRowset::GetNextRows

The consumer uses this method to fetch rows sequentially.

```
HRESULT     GetNextRows (
  HCHAPTER        hReserved,
```

```
LONG        lRowsOffset,
LONG        cRows,
ULONG *     pcRowsObtained,
HROW **     prghRows );
```

hReserved	Reserved.
lRowsOffset	Signed count of rows to skip before fetching new rows. The sign of cRows determines the direction. When this value is zero and cRows is negative, the last row read is the next row to read.
cRows	Number of rows to fetch. cRows may be negative for fetching backwards when the property DBPROP_CANFETCHBACKWARDS is VARIANT_TRUE.
pcRows	Obtained A pointer to memory when the fetched row count is saved. All rows may not be fetched when the consumer does not have proper permissions.
prghRows	A pointer to memory where space is allocated for row handles. When *prghRows is **Null** on input the provider allocates memory for the handles and returns a pointer to the handle buffer address. The consumer is responsible for releasing provider-allocated buffer space with **IMalloc::Free**.

IRowset::ReleaseRows

```
HRESULT       ReleaseRows (
ULONG           cRows,
const HROW      rghRows[],
DBROWOPTIONS    rgRowOptions[],
ULONG           rgRefCounts[],
DBROWSTATUS     rgRowStatus[]);
```

cRows	Row handle count. No action is take when *cRows* is zero.
rghRows[]	An array of row handles.
rgRowOptions	An array of *cRows* elements that is reserved for future use, and which should be a **Null** pointer, is described by:
	`typedef DWORD DBROWOPTIONS`
rgRefCounts[]	An array of reference counts.

rgRowStatus[]   Set to `DBROWSTATUS_S_OK` or `DB_S_ERRORSOCCURRED` when an error occurs decrementing a reference count.

IRowset::RestartPosition

The consumer uses this method to set the fetch position back to the original position.

```
HRESULT    RestartPosition (
ULONG      hReserved);
```

hReserved   Reserved for future use.

IRowsetChange

The **IRowChange** interface is used for deleting, inserting, or changing existing rows. This interface requires the **IAccessor** and **IRowset** interfaces.

The existence of the **IRowsetChange** interface does not mean that deleting, inserting, and changing existing rows is available, but that at least one of these capabilities is supported. The `DBPROP_UPDATABILITY` property reports on which of these capabilities is supported by the interface. The `DBPROP_UPDATABILITY` property is found with **IRowsetInfo::GetProperties** and a `DBPROP_ROWSET` structure is returned with the rowset properties.

When the interface **IRowsetUpdate** is exposed on a rowset, updates are deferred until the user calls **IRowsetUpdate::Update**. This is known as a *deferred* update. Deferring a column (see Chapter 29) is the act of creating a transaction log entry with before and after versions of the data. After all log entries are made the data is applied. This mechanism also supports a consumer undoing the changes. The immediate update is the opposite of a deferred update and changes the column directly. A deferred or immediate update is independent of the locking type, which may be optimistic or pessimistic.

Changes are accomplished immediately when **IRowsetChange** is called and the **IRowsetUpdate** interface is not exposed on a rowset which is an *immediate* mode update.

Rowset updates quite often fail. These failures are usually security issues or an attempted breach of schema or constraint integrity. The properties

DBPROP_COLUMNRESTRICT or DBPROP_ROWRESTRICT are set to VARIANT_TRUE, which determines which access rights are restricted on either a column or a row basis. These properties should be checked before attempting an update.

IRowsetChange::DeleteRows

The consumer uses this method to delete rows in a rowset.

```
HRESULT     InsertRow (
 HCHAPTER    hReserved,
 ULONG       cRows,
 const HROW  rghRows[],
 DBROWSTATUS rgRowStatus[]);
```

hReserved	Reserved for future use.
cRows	Row handle count. No action is take when *cRows* is zero.
rghRows[]	An array of row handles. The response to deleting a row with a duplicate handle is provider-specific. An error status is possible.
rgRowStatus[]	Set to DBROWSTATUS_S_OK or DB_S_ERRORSOCCURRED when an error occurs decrementing a reference count.

IRowsetChange::InsertRow

The consumer uses this method to create and insert a new row in the rowset.

```
HRESULT     InsertRow (
 HCHAPTER    hReserved,
 HACCESSOR   hAccessor,
 void *      pData,
 HROW *      phRow);
```

hReserved	Reserved for future use.
hAccessor	Accessor handle. This may be **Null**, which creates a default value row.
pData	Pointer to user-provided data with offsets corresponding to bindings.
phRow	Pointer to where the new row handle is returned.

IRowsetChange::SetData

The consumer uses this method to change the value of columns in a rowset.

```
HRESULT     SetData (
  HCHAPTER    hRow,
  HACCESSOR   hAccessor,
  void *      pData);
```

hRow   Row handle.

hAccessor   Accessor handle. This may be **Null** if *cBinding* was zero in
              IAccessor::CreateAccessor. No data is set when *hAccessor* is **Null**.

pData   Pointer to user-provided data with offsets to corresponding
              bindings.

IROWSETIDENTITY:IROWSET

IRowsetIdentity inherits all properties and methods of **IRowset**. Handles that represent the same underlying row always exhibit the same data and state.

The provider may support row identity even when a consumer has not requested the **IRowsetIdentity** interface. The interface is not disabled when not used.

IRowsetIdentity::IsSameRow

The consumer has a need to compare returned row handles with known row handles upon notification when using the **IRowsetNotify** mechanism. The property DBPROP_LITERALIDENTITY is VARIANT_TRUE when row handles can be compared on a binary basis.

```
HRESULT     IsSameRow (
  HROW        hThisRow,
  HROW        hThatRow);
```

hThisRow   Active row handle.

hThatRow   Active row handle.

IRowsetIndex

The **IRowsetIndex** interface exposes indexes of a rowset. It is the primary rowset interface for indexes. A rowset may have more than one index.

An index is opened when the rowset is opened. This is accomplished by passing the index DBID to **IOpenRowset::OpenRowset** when opening the rowset. A pointer to an index rowset is returned.

IRowsetChange manages index deletions and insertions. Deleting the old value and inserting a new value changes an index. An update capability does not exist for indexes.

IRowsetIndex::GetIndexInfo

This method returns index rowset capabilities.

```
HRESULT     GetIndexInfo (
  ULONG *              pcKeyColumns,
  DBINDEXCOLUMNDESC **  prgIndexColumnDesc,
  ULONG *              pcIndexProperties,
  DBPROPSET **         prgIndexProperties);
```

pcKeyColumns	Key column count pointer.
prgIndexColumnDesc	An array of DBINDEXCOLUMNDESC structures (see the **IIndexDefinition** interface).
pcIndexProperties	Pointer to the count of DBPROPSET structures in *prgIndexProperties*.
prgIndexProperties	Pointer to where a pointer to an array of DBPROPSET structures is returned. The provider allocates the buffer and the consumer releases it with **IMalloc::Free**. It is **Null** when the **pcIndexProperties* is zero.

IRowsetIndex::Seek

This method directly positions to a key value based on a range set by the **IRowsetIndex::SetRange** method.

```
HRESULT    Seek (
 HACCESSOR    hAccessor,
 ULONG        cKeyValues,
 void *       pData,
 DBSEEK       dwSeekOptions);
```

hAccessor	Accessor handle. Key values must be bound in the proper order. DB_E_BADBINDINFO or DBSTATUS_E_BADACCESSOR will occur when keys are not bound in the proper order.
cKeyValues	Binding count for *hAccessor*.
pData	A pointer to data values on which to seek. Data is placed at offsets corresponding to offsets in the accessor.
dwSeekOptions	One of: DBSEEK_FIRSTEQ; _LASTEQ; _GE; _GT; _LE; or _LT.

IRowsetIndex::SetRange

This methods limits the visible row entries of **IRowset::GetNextRows** or **IRowset::Seek**.

```
HRESULT    SetRange (
 HACCESSOR    hAccessor,
 ULONG        cStartKeyValues,
 void *       pStartData,
 ULONG        cEndKeyValues,
 void *       pEndData,
 DBRANGE      dwRangeOptions);
```

hAccessor	Accessor handle. Key values must be bound in the proper order. DB_E_BADBINDINFO or DBSTATUS_E_BADACCESSOR will occur when keys are not bound in the proper order.
cStartKeyValues	Starting key binding count for *hAccessor*.
pStartData	A pointer to data values on which to seek. Data is placed at offsets corresponding to offsets in the accessor.
cEndKeyValues	End key binding count for *hAccessor*.
pEndData	A pointer to data values on which to seek. Data is placed at offsets corresponding to offsets in the accessor.

dwSeekOptions	One or more of: `DBRANGE_INCLUSIVESTART`; `_EXCLUSIVESTART`; `_INCLUSIVEEND`; `_EXCLUDENULLS`; `_PREFIX`; or `_MATCH`. **pEndData* is a **Null** pointer when DBRANGE_PREFIX is used.

I ROWSET INFO

The **IRowsetInfo** interface returns rowset metadata and must be implemented by all **Rowset** objects. The interface has three methods. These methods get properties, get a referenced rowset, or get the creator interface pointer, which can be either a **Session** object or a **Command** object.

IRowsetInfo::GetProperties

```
HRESULT    GetProperties (
  const ULONG      cPropertyIDSets,
  const DBPROPSET  rgPropertyIDSets[],
  ULONG *          pcPropertySets,
  DBPROPSET **     prgPropertySets);
```

cPropertyIDSets	Count of DBPROPIDSET structures in *rgPropertyIDSets*.
rgPropertyIDSets[]	An array of DBPROPIDSET structures.
pcPropertySets	Pointer to counter of DBPROPSET structures returned in *prgPropertySets*.
prgPropertySets	A pointer to a returned array pointer of DBPROPSET structures. Each structure contains at least one property supported by the provider.

The provider allocates the memory that the consumer releases with **IMalloc::Free**.

When *cPropertyIDSets* is not zero, the DBPROPSET structures are returned in the same order as the DBPROPIDSET structures specified in *rgPropertyIDSets*[].

IRowsetInfo::GetReferencedRowset

This method returns a rowset pointer for a referenced bookmark.

```
HRESULT    GetReferencedRowset (
 ULONG            iOrdinal,
 REFIID           riid,
 IUnknown **      ppReferencedRowset);
```

iOrdinal	Bookmark column for the related rowset. Column zero is present in a rowset as a bookmark if, and only if, the rowset property DBPROP_BOOKMARKS is VARIANT_TRUE. Reading column zero provides the *self bookmark*.
riid	IID of interface pointer requested to return in *ppReferencedRowset*.
ppReferencedRowset	Pointer to the requested rowset interface pointer.

IRowsetInfo::GetSpecification

This method returns an interface pointer to the creator object, which may be a **Session** object or a **Command** object.

```
HRESULT    GetSpecification (
 REFIID        riid,
 IUnknown **   ppSpecification);
```

riid	IID of interface where the pointer is returned.
ppSpecification	A memory pointer to where the interface pointer is returned. It is a **Null** on an error.

IROWSETLOCATE:ROWSET

The methods of the **IRowsetLocate:Rowset** interface enable a consumer to access rows in an arbitrary manner. Rowsets without this interface are considered *sequential*. **IRowsetLocate** inherits from **IRowset** and is the base object of **IRowsetScroll**.

IRowsetLocate::Compare

```
HRESULT    GetReferencedRowset (
 HCHAPTER      hReserved,
```

```
ULONG           cbBookmark1,
const BYTE *    pBookmark1,
ULONG           cbBookmark2,
const BYTE *    pBookmark2,
DBCOMPARE       pComparison);
```

hReserved	Reserved for future use.
cbBookmark1	Byte count of first bookmark.
pBookmark1	Pointer to first bookmark. The first bookmark may be `DBBMK_FIRST` or `DBBMK_LAST`, which are the first and last rows of the rowset.
cbBookmark2	Byte count of second bookmark.
pBookmark2	Pointer to second bookmark. The second bookmark may be `DBBMK_FIRST` or `DBBMK_LAST`, which are the first and last rows of the rowset.
pComparison	A pointer to memory which is returned. It is one of: `DBCOMPARE_LT; _EQ; _GT; _NE;` or `_NOTCOMPARABLE`.

IRowsetLocate::GetRowsAt

This method uses an offset from a bookmark to fetch rows.

```
HRESULT     GetRowsAt (
  HWATCHREGION    hReserved1,
  HCHAPTER        hReserved2,
  ULONG           cbBookmark,
  const BYTE *    pBookmark,
  LONG            lRowsOffset,
  LONG            cRows,
  ULONG *         pcRowsObtained,
  HROW **         prghRows);
```

hReserved1	Reserved for future use.
hReserved2	Reserved for future use.
cbBookmark	Bookmark byte count.

pBookmark	Pointer to bookmark. This bookmark may be `DBBMK_FIRST` or `DBBMK_LAST`, which are the first and last rows of the rowset.
lRowsOffset	Signed row count from bookmark to target row.
cRows	Maximum number of rows to fetch. No rows are fetched when *cRows* is zero. Negative numbers indicate a backward fetch, which only occurs when the property `DBPROP_CANSCROLLBACKWARDS` is `VARIANT_TRUE`.
pcRowsObtained	Pointer to the obtained row count.
prghRows	A pointer to where a pointer to an array of row handles is returned. The provider allocates this when *prghRows* is **Null**. The consumer must use **IMalloc::Free** to release this array.

IRowsetLocate::GetRowsByBookmark

This method fetches rows that match a list of bookmarks.

```
HRESULT     GetRowByBookmark (
HCHAPTER        hReserved,
ULONG           cRows,
const ULONG     rgcbBookmarks[],
const BYTE *    rgpBookmarks[],
HROW            rghRows[],
DBROWSTATUS     rgRowStatus[]);
```

hReserved	Reserved for future use.
cRows	Row count to fetch. No rows are fetched when *cRows* is zero.
rgcbBookmarks[]	The count in bytes for each bookmark.
rgpBookmarks[]	An array of pointers to bookmarks for each row. `DBBMK_FIRST` and `DBBMK_LAST` are invalid bookmarks. Duplicates are returned and the reference count is incremented appropriately.
rghRows []	An array of *cRows* in which to return row handles.
rgRowStatus[]	Set to `DBROWSTATUS_S_OK` or `DB_S_ERRORSOCCURRED` when an error occurs incrementing a reference count.

IRowsetLocate::Hash

The method calculates hash values for the specified bookmarks.

```
HRESULT     HASH (
  HCHAPTER          hReserved,
  ULONG             cBookmarks,
  const ULONG       rgcbBookmarks[],
  const BYTE *      rgpBookmarks[],
  DWORD             rgHashedValues[],
  DBROWSTATUS       rgBookmarkStatus[]);
```

hReserved	Reserved for future use.
cBookmarks	Bookmarks to hash. No bookmarks are hashed when *cBookmarks* is zero.
rgcbBookmarks[]	The count in bytes for each bookmark.
rgpBookmarks[]	An array of pointers to bookmarks for each row. DBBMK_FIRST and DBBMK_LAST are invalid bookmarks. Duplicate hashes are returned for duplicate bookmarks.
rgHashedValues[]	An array of *cBookmarks* hash values.
rgBookmarkStatus[]	Set to DBROWSTATUS_S_OK or DB_S_ERRORSOCCURRED when an error occurs while hashing a bookmark.

IROWSETNOTIFY

The **IRowsetNotify** interface is a callback mechanism for synchronizing objects on a consumer's rowset. It will not synchronize shared tables, external programs, or other users. This mechanism is not to be used for transaction notification. Each transaction may consist of many rows and this mechanism is inappropriate for high volume notifications. **ITransactionOutcomeEvents** should be used for transaction notifications.

IConnectionPointContainer is an optional interface for a **Rowset** object. The client calls **IConnectionPointContainer::FindConnectionPoint** asking for support of IID_IRowSetNotify. **FindConnectionPoint** responds with an interface address when this IID is supported. The consumer's **IRowsetNotify** address is then supplied by the consumer to the interface returned from **FindConnectionPoint**.

The connection is established. This mechanism is identical to that of **IAdviseSink**, which was discussed in Chapter 6.

Events

Events consist of phases. The consumer is given a chance to abort an event at each phase point. When this happens, other listeners are notified of the phase failure.

EVENT VALUE	DESCRIPTION
DBEVENTPHASE_OKTODO	Informs a listener of a pending event. The listener _ must respond with S_OK for the event to proceed or with S_FALSE to cancel. When a listener cancels an event, all other listeners that have already been called are called back with DBEVENT_FAILEDTODO.
DBEVENTPHASE_ABOUTTODO	Informs a listener that _OKTODO was _ approved by all other listeners. When a listener cancels an event, all other listeners that have already been called are called back with DBEVENT_FAILEDTODO.
DBEVENTPHASE_SYNCHAFTER	Informs a listener that the event has occurred. The listener synchronizes with the rowset and verifies that there is no reason to cancel the event. When a listener cancels this event, all other listeners that have already been called are called back with DBEVENT_FAILEDTODO.
DBEVENTPHASE_FAILEDTODO	Informs a listener that the event failed. The _ listener reverses all changes and synchronizes with the current rowset state.
DBEVENTPHASE_DIDEVENT	Informs a listener that the event completed and that all listeners are synchronized and agree to commit the event's changes. A listener must comply with this event.

The final phase of an event is always `DBEVENTPHASE_FAILEDTODO` or `DBEVENTPHASE_DIDEVENT` and all providers must support these two phases. The provider-supported phases are determined by calling **IDBProperties::GetProperties** and examining the `DBPROP_NOTIFICATIONS` property.

Notifications can be economical. Changes are grouped for single-phase events such as `DBREASON_ROW_ACTIVATE` or `DBREASON_ROW_RELEASE`. When a method changes multiple rows and a single-phase event is generated, the provider makes a single call to **IRowset::OnRowChange** and passes an array containing the row handles of all affected rows.

The number of calls to **OnRowChange** is managed by `DBPROP_NOTIFICA-TIONGRANULARITY` for multiphase events such as `DBPROP_ROW_UNDOCHANGE` or `DBPROP_ROW_UPDATE`.

Notifications

Only the methods that generate a notification are listed below. For example, **IRowset::GetData** does not generate a notification and therefore is not listed.

METHOD	DBREASON Generated	PHASES
IUnknown::Release	_ROWSET_RELEASE	DIDEVENT
IRowset::GetNextRows	_ROW_ACTIVATE[1]	DIDEVENT
	_ROWSET_FETCHPOSITIONCHANGE	All Phases
IRowset::ReleaseRows	_ROW_RELEASE	DIDEVENT
IRowset::RestartPosition	_ROWSET_FETCHPOSITIONCHANGE	All Phases
	_ROWSET_CHANGED[2]	All Phases
IRowsetChange::DeleteRows	_ROW_DELETE	All Phases
IRowsetChange::InsertRow	_ROW_INSERT	All Phases
IRowsetChange::SetData	_ROW_FIRSTCHANGE[3]	All Phases
	_COLUMN_SET	All Phases
	_COLUMN_RECALCULATED	DIDEVENT
IRowset::Seek	_ROWSET_FETCHPOSITIONCHANGE	All Phases
IRowsetLocate::GetRowsAt	_ROW_ACTIVATE	DIDEVENT
IRowsetLocate:: GetRowsByBookmark	_ROW_ACTIVATE	DIDEVENT

METHOD	DBREASON Generated	PHASES
IRowsetResynch::ResynchRows	_ROW_RESYNCH	All Phases
IRollScroll::GetApproximatePosition	_ROW_ACTIVATE	DIDEVENT
IRowsetUpdate::Undo	_ROW_UNDOCHANGE	All Phases
IRowsetUpdate::Update	_ROW_UPDATE	All Phases

[1]*Only one DBREASON is listed even though other DBREASONs may be appropriate.*
[2]**IRowsetChange::SetData** *generates this reason only when column metadata changes.*
[3]DBREASON_ROW_FIRSTCHANGED *is only generated the first time for a row.*

IRowsetNotify::OnFieldChange

This method notifies a consumer when a field changes.

```
HRESULT     OnFieldChange (
  IRowset *      pRowset,
  HROW           hRow,
  ULONG          cColumns,
  ULONG          rgColumns[],
  DBREASON       eReason,
  DBEVENTPHASE   ePhase,
  BOOL           fCantDeny);
```

pRowset   A rowset pointer. This pointer identifies one of potentially many rowsets.

hRow   Row handle of a changed column. The consumer must call **IRowset::AddRefRows** to guarantee that this row is valid after the method returns.

cColumns   Column count in *rgColumns*[].

rgColumns[]   An array of columns in the row was changed.

eReason   Reason for change. The method returns S_OK or DB_S_UNWANTEDREASON when the reason is not recognized.

ePhase   Event phase.

fCantDeny   When **True**, the consumer cannot return S_FALSE and veto the event.

IRowsetNotify::OnRowChange

This method notifies a consumer when a row changes.

```
HRESULT      OnRowChange (
 IRowset *      pRowset,
 HROW           cRows,
 const HROW     rghRows[],
 DBREASON       eReason,
 DBEVENTPHASE   ePhase,
 BOOL           fCantDeny );
```

pRowset	A rowset pointer. This pointer identifies one of potentially many rowsets.
cRows	Row handle count in *rghRows*[].
rghRows[]	An array of row handles for rows that are changing.
eReason	Reason for change. The method returns S_OK or DB_S_UNWANTEDREASON when the reason is not recognized.
ePhase	Event phase.
fCantDeny	When **True**, the consumer cannot return S_FALSE and veto the event.

IRowsetNotify::OnRowsetChange

This method notifies a consumer when a rowset changes.

```
HRESULT      OnRowsetChange (
 IRowset *      pRowset,
 DBREASON       eReason,
 DBEVENTPHASE   ePhase,
 BOOL           fCantDeny );
```

pRowset	A rowset pointer. This pointer identifies one of potentially many rowsets.
eReason	Reason for change. The method returns S_OK or DB_S_UNWANTEDREASON when the reason is not recognized.
ePhase	Event phase.

fCantDeny   When **True**, the consumer cannot return S_FALSE and veto the event.

IROWSETRESYNCH

The **IRowsetResynch** method retrieves rows that are currently visible to the transaction. **IRowsetSynch** is used to implement optimistic concurrency and for fixing a row in a disconnected environment, which is the environment that exists after a collison that occurrs during an optimistic update. The **Rowset** object must also expose **IRowsetIdentity** when **IRowsetSynch** is exposed.

IRowsetSynch is not useful at isolation levels of REPEATABLE READ or higher. Data at this level, which has already been read, does not change. When a consumer requests **IRowsetSynch**, it is exposed even though the interface is not useful at isolation levels of REPEATABLE READ or higher.

The rowset must have a mechanism of obtaining data from the data source. When the property DBPROP_OTHERUPDATEDELETE is VARIANT_FALSE for static cursor such as a snapshot or forward-only cursor, the consumer must have an alternate mechanism for obtaining the data. The **IRowsetSynch** interface is limited to dynamic or keyset-driven cursors without an alternate rowset source.

IRowsetResynch::GetVisibleData

This method gets the data visible to a transaction for the specified row.

```
HRESULT    GetVisibleData (
HROW       hRow,
HACCESSOR  hAccessor,
void *     pData);
```

hRow   Row handle.

hAccessor   Accessor handle. No data is retrieved for a **Null** handle.

pData   Pointer to consumer-allocated buffer.

IRowsetResynch::ResynchRows

This method obtains data from the data source and refreshes rows that are visible to the transaction.

```
HRESULT     ResynchRows (
  ULONG             cRows,
  const HROW        rghRows[],
  ULONG *           pcRowsResynched,
  HROW **           prghRowsResynched,
  DBROWSTATUS**     prgRowStatus);
```

cRows	Resynchronization row count.
rghRows[]	An array of row handles to be synchronized.
pcRowsResynched	A pointer to when an array of row handles is returned on which synchronization was attempted. This is all the rows in the rowset when *cRows* is zero. **ResynchRows** increments the reference count.
prgRowStatus	A pointer memory for an array of status values. Set to DBROWSTATUS_S_OK or DB_S_ERRORSOCCURRED when an error occurs. No row status is returned when *prgRowStatus* is **Null**.

IRowsetScroll:IRowsetLocate

The **IRowsetScroll:IRowsetLocate** interface inherits **IRowsetLocate** and enables consumers to fetch rows at approximate positions in the rowset. This interface is useful when precision positions are not required within a rowset.

IRowsetScroll::GetApproximatePosition

This method obtains the approximate position of a row corresponding to a bookmark.

```
HRESULT     GetApproximatePositionRows (
  HCHAPTER        hReserved,
  ULONG           cbBookmark,
```

```
const BYTE *    pBookmark,
ULONG *         pulPosition,
ULONG *         pcRows);
```

hReserved   Reserved for future use.

cbBookmark   Bookmark length in bytes. When *cbBookmark* is zero, *pBookmark* is ignored, **pcRows* is set to the row count, and no position is returned in **pulPosition*.

pBookmark   Pointer to a bookmark that can be DBBMK_FIRST or DBBMK_LAST, which represent the first and last rows of the rowset. The consumer is not required to have permission to read the row.

pulPosition   A pointer to memory where the rowset position is returned. This value is one-based. No position is returned when *pulPosition* is **Null**. **pulPosition* is set to zero when **pcRows* is zero. **pulPosition* is not changed on an error.

pcRows   A pointer to memory where the total row count is returned. **pcRows* is not changed on an error. **pcRows* is zero for no rows.

IRowsetScroll::GetRowsAtRatio

This method fetches rows from a fractional position in a rowset.

```
HRESULT     GetRowsAtRatio (
 HWATCHREGION   hReserved1,
 HCHAPTER       hReserved2,
 ULONG          ulNumerator,
 ULONG          ulDenominator,
 LONG           cRows,
 ULONG *        pcRowsObtained,
 HROW **        prghRows);
```

hReserved1   Reserved for future use.

hReserved2   Reserved for future use.

ulNumerator   Numerator for calculation of fractional position.

ulDenominator   Denominator for calculation of fractional position.

cRows	Row count to fetch.
pcRowsObtained	Pointer when the actual number of rows fetched is returned. **GetRowsAtRatio** only fetches those rows for which the consumer has permissions.
prghRows	A pointer to memory where the pointer to an array or row handles is stored. When *prghRows* is **Null**, the provider allocates the buffer that the consumer must release with **IMalloc::Free**.

IRowsetUpdate:IRowsetChange

IRowsetUpdate is an optional interface that inherits from **IRowsetChange** and is a buffering mechanism for changes to the database. A consumer undo capability is supported.

This interface caches each row of a rowset changed with **IRowsetChange:: SetData**. **IRowsetUpdate** should not be exposed on a rowset when the consumer does not request it.

IRowsetUpdate::Update implements the concept of *deferred update mode*. Rowset changes made when the **IRowsetUpdate** interface is not exposed are immediate.

IRowsetUpdate::GetOriginalData

This method fetches the most recent changes to the data source. Pending changes are not fetched.

```
HRESULT     GetOriginalData (
  HROW        hRow,
  HACCESSOR   hAccessor,
  void *      pData);
```

hRow	Row handle.
hAccessor	Accessor handle. This may be **Null** if *cBinding* was zero in **IAccessor::CreateAccessor**. No data is returned when *hAccessor* in **Null**.
pData	A pointer to a consumer-allocated buffer.

IRowsetUpdate::GetPendingRows

This method returns rows with pending changes.

```
HRESULT    GetPendingRows (
  HCHAPTER             hReserved,
  DBPENDINGSTATUS      dwRowStatus,
  ULONG *              pcPendingRows,
  HROW **              prgPendingRows,
  DBPENDINGSTATUS **   prgPendingStatus);
```

hReserved	Reserved for future use.
dwRowStatus	The type of status requested. One or more of: DBPENDINGSTATUS_NEW, DBPENDINGSTATUS_CHANGED, or DBPENDINGSTATUS_DELETED.
pcPendingRows	Pointer to returned row count of rows with pending changes.
prgPendingRows	A pointer to where a pointer of row handles is returned. Allocated by the provider when *prghPendingRows* is **Null** and the consumer must use **IMalloc::Free** on this array.
prgPendingStatus	A pointer to where a pointer to an array of DBPENDINGSTATUS values is returned. These values correspond with row handles in **prgPendingRows*. The buffer must also be released with **IMalloc::Free**.

IRowsetUpdate::GetRowStatus

This method returns the row status of selected rows.

```
HRESULT    GetRowStatus (
  HCHAPTER          hReserved,
  ULONG             cRows,
  const HROW        rghRows[],
  DBPENDINGSTATUS   rgPendingStatus[]);
```

hReserved	Reserved for future use.
cRows	Input row count. No status is returned when *cRows* is zero.
rghRows[]	Array of row handles.

rgPendingStatus[]   An array of row states. One of: `DBPENDINGSTATUS_NEW`, `DBPENDINGSTATUS_CHANGED`, `DBPENDINGSTATUS_UNCHANGED`, or `DBPENDINGSTATUS_DELETED`.

IRowsetUpdate::Undo

This method will undo any changes since the last fetch or when **Update** was called.

```
HRESULT     Undo (
 HCHAPTER          hReserved,
 ULONG             cRows,
 const HROW        rghRows[],
 ULONG *           pcRows,
 HROWS **          prgRows,
 DBROWSTATUS **    prgRowStatus);
```

hReserved   Reserved for future use.

cRows   Undo row count. All pending changes are undone. When *cRows* is zero, all pending changes to all rows in the rowset are undone.

rghRows[]   Array of row handles to undo. No errors are returned.

pcRows   Returns attempted undo row count.

prgRows   A pointer to where a pointer of row handles on which an undo was attempted is returned. Allocated by the provider when *prghRows* is **Null**. The consumer must use **IMalloc::Free** on this array.

prgRowStatus   A pointer memory to where a pointer for an array of status values is returned. Set to `DBROWSTATUS_S_OK` or `DB_S_ERRORSOCCURRED` when an error occurs. No row status is returned when *prgRowStatus* is **Null**.

IRowsetUpdate::Update

This method transmits any changes to the data source since either the last fetch or when **Update** was last called.

```
HRESULT      Update (
 HCHAPTER          hReserved,
 ULONG             cRows,
 const HROW        rghRows[],
 ULONG *           pcRows,
 HROWS **          prgRows,
 DBROWSTATUS **    prgRowStatus);
```

hReserved   Reserved for future use.

cRows   Update row count. All pending changes are undone. When *cRows* is zero, all pending changes to all rows in the rowset are undone.

rghRows[]   Array of row handles to update. **prgRowStatus* contains the resulting error status. See *prgRows* below when *rghRows*[] is **Null**.

pcRows   Returned attempted update row count.

prgRows   A pointer to where a pointer of row handles on which an update was attempted is returned. Allocated by the provider when *prgRows* is **Null** and the consumer must use **IMalloc::Free** on this array.

When *rghRows* is **Null** the returned *prgRows* array will be all rows with a pending status and **Update** will increment the reference count for rows located in *rghRows*[]. This may bring into existence rows that have a pending change and a zero reference count.

prgRowStatus A pointer to memory to where an array of status values is returned. Set to DBROWSTATUS_S_OK or DB_S_ERRORSOCCURRED when an error occurs. No row status is returned when *prgRowStatus* is **Null**. **Update** does not add a reference count to the rows returned in **prgRows*. *prgRowStatus* is allocated by the provider and the consumer must use **IMalloc::Free** on this array.

ISessionProperties

ISessionProperties is a mandatory interface for **Session** objects. This interface returns property information a **Session** object supports and the current setting of those properties.

ISessionProperties::GetProperties

```
HRESULT     GetProperties (
 ULONG              PropertyIDSets,
 const DBPROPIDSET rgPropertyIDSets[],
 ULONG *           pcPropertySets,
 DBPROPSET **      prgPropertySets);
```

cPropertyIDSets	DBPROPIDSET structure count for *rgPropertyIDSets*[].
rgPropertyIDSets[]	An array of DBPROPIDSET structures.
pcPropertySets	Pointer to returned DBPROPSET structure count.
prgPropertySets	A pointer to memory where a pointer is returned for an array of DBPROPSET structures. When *cPropertyIDSets* is zero, each structure returned has at least one property belonging to the **Session** property group. When *cPropertyIDSets* is not zero each structure returned corresponds with a property set specified in *rgPropertyIDSets*.

prgPropertySets is allocated by the provider and the consumer must use **IMalloc::Free** on this array.

ISessionProperties::SetProperties

This method sets properties in the **Session** property group.

```
HRESULT     SetProperties (
 ULONG       cPropertySets,
 DBPROPSET   rgPropertySets[]);
```

cPropertySets	DBPROPSET structure count for *rgPropertySets*[].
rgPropertySets[]	An array of DBPROPSET structures containing properties and values to set.

ISOURCEROWSET

The **ISourceRowset** interface returns a rowset or data sources and enumerators visible from the current enumerator.

ISourceRowset::GetSourcesRowset

```
HRESULT     GetSourcesRowset (
  IUnknown *      pUnkOuter,
  REFIID          riid,
  ULONG           cPropertySets,
  DBPROPSET       rgPropertySets[],
  IUnknown **     ppSourcesRowset);
```

pUnkOuter	Pointer to the controlling **IUnknown** interface when the rowset is being created as part of an aggregate; otherwise a **Null** pointer.
riid	IID of the interface of where to return the requested rowset interface.
cPropertySets	Count of DBPROPSET structures in *rgPropertySets*.
ppSourcesRowset	Pointer to the returned pointer of the metadata rowset. A **Null** pointer on an error.

ISQLErrorInfo

The **ISQLErrorInfo** interface returns SQLSTATE and native error codes.

ISQLErrorInfo::GetSQLInfo

```
HRESULT     GetSQLInfo (
  BSTR *      pbstrSQLState,
  LONG *      plNativeError);
```

pbstrSQLState	Pointer to a five character string where an American National Standards Institute (ANSI) SQL state code is returned. The consumer must release this memory with **SysFreeString**.
plNativeError	A pointer to a native error code. This value is not necessarily the same as *dwMinor* of **IErrorRecords::GetErrorInfo**.

ISUPPORTERRORINFO

The same mechanism is used for retrieving automation and OLE-DB error objects. The presence of this interface indicates support for OLE-DB error reporting.

ISupportErrorInfo::InterfaceSupportsErrorInfo

```
HRESULT     InterfaceSupportsErrorInfo (
 REFIID       riid);
```

riid   IID of requested interface. S_OK is returned indicating that automation and OLE-DB error objects can be returned. S_FALSE is returned when the interface cannot return either automation or OLE-DB error objects.

Retrieving an OLE-DB Error Object:

- The consumer calls **QueryInterface** to retrieve a pointer to **ISupportErrorInfo**.

- The consumer calls **ISupportErrorInfo::InterfaceSupportsInfo** and passes the IID of the OLE-DB object which created the error.

- When S_OK is returned, the consumer calls **GetErrorInfo**. The result of this call is an **IErrorInfo** interface pointer on the OLE-DB object. Any error object should be discarded by the consumer when S_FALSE is returned by **ISupportErrorInfo::InterfaceSupportsInfo**.

ITABLEDEFINITION

The **ITableDefinition** interface exposes methods to create, drop, and alter tables on the data source using the DBCOLUMNDESC structure:

```
typedef struct   tagDBCOLUMNDESC {
  LPOLESTR        pwszTypeName;     //Equivalent to TYPE_NAME in
                                    //PROVIDER_TYPES schema
                                         rowset.
  ITypeInfo *     pTypeInfo;        //NULL pointer or abstract
                                         data type
  DBPROPSET *     rgPropertySets;   //Array of DBPROPSET
                                         structures
```

```
  CLSID *          pclsid;           //CLSID of OLE column object.
                                     //IID_NULL when more than one
                                     //class can reside in column.
  ULONG            cPropertySets;    // DBPROPSET structure Count
  ULONG            ulColumnSize;     //maximum lenght for this
                                        column
  DBID             dbcid;            //ColumnID
  DBTYPE           wType;            //Data type. Corresponds to
                                     //DATA_NAME column in
                                     //PROVIDER_TYPES schema
                                        rowset.
  BYTE             bPrecision;       //Digits of precision, numeric
                                        type
  BYTE             bScale;           //Fraction digits, numeric
                                        type
}DBCOLUMNDESC;
```

ITableDefinition::AddColumn

```
HRESULT     AddColumn (
  DBID *          pTableID,
  BCOLUMNDESC * pColumnDesc,
    DBID **       ppColumnID);
```

pTableID   Table DBID.

pColumnDesc   Pointer to a DBCOLUMNDESC structure.

ppColumnID   Pointer to where a pointer to a new column DBID is returned.

ITableDefinition::CreateTable

This method creates a new table. One very nice feature is the creation of an empty rowset for the insertion of new rows.

```
HRESULT     CreateTable (
  IUnknown *      pUnkOuter,
  DBID *          pTableID,
  ULONG           cColumnDesc,
```

```
DBCOLUMNDESC   rgColumnDescs[],
REFIID         riid,
ULONG          cPropertySets,
DBPROPSET      rgPropertySets[],
DBID **        ppTableID,
IUnknown **    ppRowset);
```

pUnkOuter	Pointer to the controlling **IUnknown** interface when the optional rowset *ppRowset* is being created as part of an aggregate; otherwise a **Null** pointer.
pTableID	Pointer to the ID of the table to create.
cColumnDescs	Element count of *rgColumnDescs*.
rgColumnDescs[]	An array of DBCOLUMNDESC structures.
riid	IID of the requested rowset interface. Ignored when *ppRowset* is **Null**.
cPropertySets	Count of DBPROPSET structures in *rgPropertySets*.
rgPropertySets	An array of DBPROPSET structures.
ppTableID	Pointer to the returned pointer for the table ID.
ppRowset	Pointer to a returned pointer for a newly created empty rowset. Not created when *ppRowset* is **Null**.

ITableDefinition::DropColumn

This method drops a column from a base table.

```
HRESULT     DropColumn (
DBID *      pTableID,
DBID *      pColumnID);
```

pTableID	Pointer to table ID.
pColumnID	Pointer to columnID.

ITableDefinition::DropTable

This method drops a base table in the data source.

```
HRESULT     DropColumn (
   DBID *      pTableID);
```

pTableID   Pointer to table ID.

ITRANSACTION

The **ITransaction** interface supports a transaction commit, a transaction abort, or a transaction obtains status. Not all the code is yet implemented in this interface. There are placeholders for future code involving the Microsoft Distributed Transaction server.

ITransaction::Abort

The **Abort** method aborts the current transaction.

```
HRESULT     Abort (
   BOID *      pboidReason,
   BOOL        fRetaining,
   BOOL        fAsynch);
```

pboidReason   Optional pointer to the reason for aborting the transaction. Pointer may be **Null**. (I can find no documentation on this parameter.)

fRetaining   The flag *fRetaining* can be set for either **ITransaction::Commit** or **ITransaction::Abort**. When *fRetaining* is **False** new units of work are not within the scope of a transaction independent of the prior action. Conversely, when *fRetaining* is **True** any additional work is done within the scope of a transaction.

fAsynch   When **True** an asynchronous abort is performed and the consumer must use **ITransactionOutcomeEvents** to learn the transaction status.

ITransaction::Commit

The **Commit** method commits the current transaction.

```
HRESULT      Commit (
COMMIT          fRetaining,
DWORD           grfTC,
DWORD           grfRM);
```

fRetaining   The flag *fRetaining* can be set for either **ITransaction::Commit** or **ITransaction::Abort**. When *fRetaining* is **False** new units of work are not within the scope of a transaction independent of the prior action. Conversely, when *fRetaining* is **True** any additional work is done within the scope of a transaction.

grfTC   One of:

- XACTTC_ASYNC —An asynchronous commit is performed.

- XACTTC_PHASEONE —When specified, the call to **Commit** returns after phase one of a two-phase commit.

- XACTTC_PHASETWO —When specified, the call to **Commit** returns after phase two of a two-phase commit.

- XACTTC_SYNC —Synonym for XACTTC_PHASETWO.

grfRM   Must be zero. Implementation appears to be incomplete in this area.

ITransaction::GetTransactionInfo

The **GetTransactionInfo** method uses the XACTTRANSINFO structure to acquire transaction information.

```
typedef struct tagXACTTRANSINFO {
    XACTUOW         uow;     // transaction associated wotk
    ISOLEVEL        isoLevel;                // isolation level
    ULONG           isoFlags;                // zero
    DWORD           grfTCSupported;          // XACTTC flags
    DWORD           grfRMSupported;          // zero
    DWORD           grfTCSupportedRetaining; // zero
    DWORD           grfRMSupportedRetaining; // zero
}XACTTRANSINFO;


HRESULT     GetTransactionInfo (
    XACTTRANSINFO *     pInfo);
```

pInfo   Pointer to a caller allocated XACTTRANSINFO structure.

ITransactionJoin

Providers supporting distributed transactions expose the ITransactionJoin interface. It is poorly documented and some structures, such as the options structure returned by **GetOptionsObject,** are not defined. OLE-DB does not yet support distributed transactions.

Transaction Isolation Levels

ISOLATIONLEVEL_UNSPECIFIED	Applicable only to **ITransactionJoin:: JoinTransaction**; invalid for **ITransactionLocal** or for setting an isolation level while in autocommit mode
ISOLATIONLEVEL_CHAOS	Cannot overwrite the dirty data of other transactions at higher isolation levels
ISOLATIONLEVEL_READUNCOMMITTED	
ISOLATIONLEVEL_BROWSE	Synonym for _READUNCOMMITTED
ISOLATIONLEVEL_READCOMMITTED	
ISOLATIONLEVEL_CURSORSTABILITY	Synonym for _READCOMMITTED
ISOLATIONLEVEL_REPEATABLEREAD	
ISOLATIONLEVEL_SERIALIZABLE	
ISOLATIONLEVEL_ISOLATED	Synonym for _SERIALIZABLE

ITransactionJoin::GetOptionsObject

```
HRESULT    GetOptionsObject (
  ITransactionOptions **        ppOptions);
```

ppOptions   Pointer to where a pointer is returned for an undocumented transaction option object.

ITransactionJoin::JoinTransaction

```
HRESULT    JoinTransaction (
  IUnknown *      pUnkOuter,
  ISOLEVEL       isoLevel,
  ULONG     isoFlags,
  ITransactionOptions ** ppOtherOptions);
```

pUnkOuter	Pointer to the controlling **IUnknown** interface of the transaction coordinator. **QueryInterface** can be called for for the transaction coordinator for **ITransaction**.
isoLevel	Isolation level.
isoFlags	Must be zero.
ppOtherOptions	An optional pointer that may be Null. This is an undocumented transaction option object.

ITRANSACTIONLOCAL:ITRANSACTION

ITransactionLocal inherits from **ITransaction** and is the **Session** object interface for transactions.

ITransactionLocal::GetOptionsObject

```
HRESULT    GetOptionsObject (
  ITransactionOptions **      ppOptions);
```

ppOptions	Pointer to where a pointer is returned for an undocumented transaction option object.

ITransactionLocal::StartTransaction

```
HRESULT    StartTransaction (
  ISOLEVEL       isoLevel,
  ULONG       isoFlags,
  ITransactionOptions *      pOtherOptions,
  ULONG *        pulTransactionLevel );
```

isoLevel	Isolation level.
isoFlags	Must be zero.
pOtherOptions	An optional pointer that may be Null. This is an undocumented transaction option object.
pulTransactionLevel	A pointer to memory where the new transaction level is returned.

ITRANSACTIONOBJECT

The method of the **ITransactionObject** interface returns a transaction object.

ITransactionObject::GetTransactionObject

The consumer calls **ITransactionObject::GetTransactionObject** to obtain the current transaction object. This enables the consumer to abort a transaction at other than the lowest level. Calling **ITransactionLocal::Commit** or **ITransactionLocal::Abort** is the equivalent of calling **ITransaction::Commit** or **ITransaction::Abort** on a **Transaction** object.

```
HRESULT     GetTransactionObject (
  ULONG             ulTransactionLevel,
  Itransaction **   ppTransactionObject);
```

ulTransactionLevel	The supplied transaction level.
ppTransactionObject	A pointer to memory where the transaction object pointer is returned.

ITRANSACTIONOPTIONS

The **ITransactionOptions** interface gets and sets options of a transaction using the XACTOPT structure.

```
typedef struct tagXAXTOPT   {
  ULONG           ulTimeout;  //timeout, milliseconds, 0=infinite
  unsigned char szDescription[MAX_TRAN_DESC];
}XACTOPT
```

ITransactionsOptions::GetOptions

```
HRESULT     GetOptions (
  XACTOPT *      pOptions);
```

pOptions   Pointer to an XACTOPT structure.

ITransactionOptions::SetOptions

```
HRESULT     SetOptions (
  XACTOPT  *      pOptions);
```

pOptions   Pointer to an XACTOPT structure.

KEY POINT SUMMARY

OLE-DB is new and all the promised features are not quite there yet. Microsoft states that OLE-DB is the future. In this chapter, we melded database access technologies with COM. To be fair, Data Access Objects (DAO) and Remote Data Objects (RDO) have always used COM; the consumer has no mechanism to change the underlying plumbing of the architecture. Chapter 32 shows that Active Data Objects (ADO), the layer above OLE-DB, has many features in common with both RDO and DAO. OLE-DB represents a paradigm shift in database access technology. Some of the significant issues of this chapter are:

- OLE-DB is complex. A different interface is required for nearly every task.

- The presence of an interface indicates feature support. Each interface has an assigned responsibility. **IRowset** contains methods for fetching rows; **IAccessor** describes column bindings; **IColumnsInfo** provides column information; **IRowsetInfo** describes the rowset; and **IConvertType** provides datatype conversion information. A consumer uses **IRowset** for sequentially traversing rows, which may include backward traversing.

- The absence of interfaces is also indicative of features. A read-only rowset is created by not requesting the **IRowsetChange** or the **IRowsetUpdate** interfaces.

- The OLE-DB implementation is incomplete.

- OLE-DB supports transaction isolation levels.

o OLE-DB introduces events for synchronizing objects attached to a **Rowset** object with the **IRowsetNotify** interface.

APPLYING WHAT YOU'VE LEARNED

These questions measure your understanding of the OLE-DB concepts. None of these questions are on the Windows Architecture core examinations.

Instant Assessment

1. What is the role of an **Accessor** object?

2. Name the interfaces that supply column metadata.

3. Name the methods that must be prepared before being called.

4. What is a unique characteristic of the **IErrorLookup** interface?

5. What is a unique characteristic of the **IRowsetUpdate** interface?

6. What are the intrinsic constants DBBMK_FIRST and DBBMK_LAST?

7. Describe the mechanism for establishing a notification connection.

8. What is the relationship between the **ITransaction** and the **ITransactionLocal** interfaces?

 concept link **For answers to the Instant Assessment questions, see Appendix C.**

Lab Exercise

Lab 30.52 *Evaluating your use of OLE-DB*

WA I

OLE-DB represents a universal database access technology. It's a given that we already have database technologies. ODBC, DAO, RDO, and ODBCDirect function satisfactorily within their original design constraints. Excluding the Internet or intranet where ADO, the OLE-DB wrapper, is used extensively, can you attach a value to a SQL query that can both access a mailbox and an ODBC database in the same SQL statement?

Evaluate your current use of current database access technologies. Do you need universal database access in any of your current applications?

OLE-DB's hope for the future is wrappers (providers) for legacy data. If your organization has legacy data, can you justify using this new technology? Remember that ODBC is a standard and OLE-DB is very proprietary.

Windows Architecture I
Windows Architecture II

CHAPTER

Active Data Objects

31

About Chapter 31

OLE-DB and the Active Data Objects (ADO) wrapper are the two new kids on the block. This chapter provides a thumbnail sketch of the ADO architecture along with a comparative look at Data Access Objects (DAO) and Remote Data Objects (RDO). OLE-DB and ADO are still incomplete, with all features not yet in place. One of the ADO features missing is row versioning control. ADO does support optimistic locking; however, the control is not there.

ADO: THE BEST OF BREED

ADO and OLE-DB promise to be the best of breed for database access. Microsoft finally acknowledged that transaction isolation levels are needed on the client and on the server. Unfortunately, supporting the atomicity, consistency, integrity, and durability (ACID) properties appears to be a vendor-specific issue, and the actual implementations may be uneven. Microsoft spin-doctors repeatedly state that OLE-DB/ADO will support the ACID properties, but there is no evidence of ACID property support. The **Field** object does support an **OriginalValue** property, but this doesn't go very far when compared to the functionality of the Microsoft SQL Server log.

Transaction ACID Properties

Let's start by quickly reviewing the ACID properties of a transaction. These issues were discussed previously in the chapters that covered RDO and ODBC, and are updated here for OLE-DB and ADO, the OLE-DB wrapper.

An important feature of any database is transactions. The **ACID** properties declare the following requirements necessary for consistent transactions:

- **Atomicity** — Either all or none of the transactions changes are present when the transaction completes.

- **Consistency** — The transaction will respect all business rules and referential integrity. Inconsistent updates can be done, but will violate system integrity.

- **Isolation** — The SQL Server transaction isolation levels are maintained for all row sets of the transaction. Transactions are isolated. SQL Server uses the SET statement:

```
SET TRANSACTION ISOLATION LEVEL
READ COMMITTED | READ UNCOMMITTED |
REPEATABLE READ | SERIALIZABLE
```

- **Durability** — Once the commit occurs, the transactions must be present even if the system fails. SQL Server supports this property with a log. Recoverability is guaranteed with SQL Server but not with Microsoft Access.

The issue of ACID properties and OLE-DB/ADO is provider specific. The consumer has the responsibility of determining provider support for OLE-DB and ADO, the OLE-DB wrapper.

Transaction Isolation Levels

Both OLE-DB and ADO support transaction isolation levels. *Transaction isolation* is the degree of interaction between multiple concurrent transactions. There is, however, a simple rule that describes the issue. *Maximum consistency* (highest transaction isolation level) is also the lowest concurrency level. Conversely, the highest concurrency level will yield the lowest consistency level. *Maximum performance* (I'll call it apparent performance), will yield the lowest consistency level. There is no clear answer other than to use the lowest possible transaction isolation level consistent with the application design. An important issue here is that an OLE-DB provider may not support the requested isolation level, but may support transaction at the next highest level. The OLE-DB developer will want to interrogate the DBPROPSET_DBSOURCEINFO structure for the DBPROP_SUPPORTEDTXNISOLEVELS property that defines the supported transaction levels. The ADO developer will want to examine the **IsolationLevel** property of the **Connection** object.

There are four transaction isolation levels. These levels are defined by the occurrence (or lack) of the following phenomena:

- **Dirty Read** is the reading of transaction data of another application before the data is rolled back. The data read is considered dirty if there is a possibility that the transaction can be rolled back. The data may or may not exist within the database even though it was read by an application.

- **Nonrepeatable Read** occurs when the application reads a row and gets a different result each time. Another application updated the row before the second read occurred.

- **Phantom Read** is a row that matches a search criterion but isn't seen by the application. A second application has added a new row that meets the search criterion after the initial rows were read.

Table 31-1 enumerates the different transaction isolation levels.

TABLE 31-1 TRANSACTION ISOLATION LEVELS			
TRANSACTION ISOLATION LEVEL	*DIRTY READS*	*NONREPEATABLE READS*	*PHANTOMS*
Read Uncommitted	X	X	X
Read Committed		X	X
Repeatable Read			X
Serializable			

Table 31-1 is understood when each term is defined:

- **Read Uncommitted** — No transaction isolation occurs. Transactions running at this level are typically read-only.

- **Read Committed** — The transaction is forced to wait until write-locked applications release data locks.

- **Repeatable Read** — The transaction waits until write-locks on rows are released by other applications. The transaction holds a read-lock on all rows it returns to the application and write-locks on all rows it changes, deletes, or inserts.

- **Serializable** — The application holds read-locks on all rows affected by a read. A write-lock is placed on all rows affected by a change.

ADO Transaction Isolation Levels

We've seen the optimistic approach in both DAO and RDO. OLE-DB optimistic locking is dramatically different and doesn't support row versioning. However, OLE-DB and ADO are both take-charge approaches where the consumer controls the fate of a transaction rather than trusting to the whims of the computer gods.

ADO transaction isolation levels are specified in the **IsolationLevel** property of the **Connection** object and are parallel to those of OLE-DB:

adXactUnspecified   The provider is using a different and unknown isolation level.

adXactChaos   Inhibit a transaction overwriting pending changes of a transaction with a higher isolation level.

adXactBrowse	Other transactions may view uncommitted transactions.
adXactReadUncommitted	Same as **adXactBrowse**.
adXactCursorStability	Transaction data cannot be viewed by other transactions until committed (default).
adXactReadCommitted	Same as **adXactCursorStability**.
adXactRepeatableRead	Changes cannot be seen from other transactions; a requery will bring an update rowset.
adXactIsolated	Transactions are isolated.
adXactSerialize	Same as **adXactIsolated**.

OLE-DB Transaction Isolation Levels

The OLE-DB transaction isolation level is a parameter of the method **ITransactionLocal::StartTransaction**:

`ISOLATIONLEVEL_UNSPECIFIED`	Applicable only to **ITransactionJoin::JoinTransaction**. Invalid for **ITransactionLocal** or for setting isolation level while in autocommit mode.
`ISOLATIONLEVEL_CHAOS`	Cannot overwrite the dirty data of other transactions at higher isolation levels.
`ISOLATIONLEVEL_READUNCOMMITTED`	
`ISOLATIONLEVEL_BROWSE`	Synonym for `_READUNCOMMITTED`
`ISOLATIONLEVEL_READCOMMITTED`	
`ISOLATIONLEVEL_CURSORSTABILITY`	Synonym for `_READCOMMITTED`
`ISOLATIONLEVEL_REPEATABLEREAD`	
`ISOLATIONLEVEL_SERIALIZABLE`	
`ISOLATIONLEVEL_ISOLATED`	Synonym for `_SERIALIZABLE`

Managing Concurrency

RDO, Jet, and ADO each manage optimistic concurrency differently. Jet, for example, sets the property **dbSeeChanges** for each recordset. This is an error-prone mechanism. Microsoft Access does have the **IsolateODBCTrans** for the **Workspace** object, but that just isolates transactions from each other and does not manage transaction isolation levels.

The situation is different with RDO and ADO where a trappable error occurs with optimistic concurrency. The user then has the responsibility of refreshing the current row with **Move** 0 and then reapplying the **Edit** or **AddNew** methods. In DAO the trappable error doesn't occur unless **dbSeeChanges** is used.

RDO permits reading from locked pages even with pessimistic locking in effect for the **LockEdits** property of the **rdoResultset** object. RDO does not have the **dbSeeChanges** property of Microsoft Access, and the possession of this property will still not help matters. Unlike DAO and RDO, dirty reads can be controlled in ADO and OLE-DB. Maximum consistency is always at the expense of concurrency; however, it is possible in ADO to eliminate dirty reads since ADO and OLE-DB both support transaction isolation levels. To be fair, any database access technology that uses Microsoft SQL Server transactions will have transaction isolation level support. It's only the local transactions of RDO and DAO that do not support transaction isolation levels.

OLE-DB has two notification mechanisms. The first is **IRowsetNotify**, which established connection sinks for rowset changes and synchronization. This interface is mentioned here because an event occurs with each row and the **IRowsetNotify** interface is not appropriate for a transaction.

The second notification mechanism uses the **ITransactionOutcomeEvents** as a notification sink. The consumer calls **QueryInterface** for the interface **IConnectionPointContainer** on the session. The returned **IConnectionPoint** interface for IID_TransactionOutcomeEvent is passed to the consumer **ITransactionOutcomeEvents** interface.

I do not know how row versioning is done in ADO. ADO row versioning control is hidden from the user, and there is a possibility that row versioning is maintained with a GUID. The point I wish to make is that Microsoft does not have a unified approach to row versioning. Row versioning in Microsoft products take these forms:

o **TimeStamp**—An error is reported when the time stamp is changed.

- **Value Based** — The row is scanned and an error is reported when a value is changed. This is often done in lieu of a time stamp.
- **RowID** — A unique row identifier. The problem here is that we do not know the row ID type used in ADO. I suspect with ADO that it is a GUID since the technology is a manifestation of COM objects. The problem arises with other databases such as Informix, Sybase, Ingress, or Oracle that may be using a different row versioning mechanism. ADO is still too new and there are too many unknowns.

When Converting Between ADO, DAO, and RDO

The intrinsic constants relating to optimistic and pessimistic locking for ADO, DAO, and RDO are listed below. The constants illustrate some of the differences between the database access technologies. The fact that there are many common methods such as **Move** or **MoveNext** does not mean that all functionality is comparable. The comparison is started with intrinsic constants for the **LockEdits** property of a DAO **Recordset** object.

DAO LockEdits Intrinsic Constants

dbPessimistic	Pessimistic concurrency is always the lowest level locking possible to ensure consistency. This is always at the expense of concurrency.
DbReadOnly	No updates allowed.
DbOptimistic	Record ID based. Compares new and old record ID to see if changes have been made since the record was last accessed.
DbOptimisticValue	Value based. Each field is compared for changes. A very inefficient mechanism.
DbOptimisticBatch	Enables batch optimistic values

These are the intrinsic constants of the **LockType** property of an RDO **rdoOpenResultset** method.

RDO LockType Intrinsic Constants

rdConcurLock	Pessimistic concurrency is always the lowest level locking possible to ensure consistency. This is always at the expense of concurrency.

RdConcurReadOnly No updates allowed.

rdConcurRowver   Record ID based. Compares new and old record ID to see if changes have been made since the record was last accessed.

rdConcurValues   Value based. Each field is compared for changes. A very inefficient mechanism.

Lock type is established with the *LockType* parameter of the **Open** method of either an OLE-DB **Connection** object or an OLE-DB **Recordset** object.

OLE-DB LockType Intrinsic Constants

adLockReadOnly   No updates allowed, read-only.

AdLockPessimistic   Pessimistic concurrency.

AdLockOptimistic   Row is locked when the update is attempted.

AdLockBatchOptimistic Optimistic batch updates

Performance

ADO is the newest database access technology from Microsoft. It is an OLE-DB wrapper that is simple and smaller than the DAO or RDO predecessors. A selling pitch for this new technology is its reduced footprint and speed. This is a specious argument because a virtual memory management system is a standard feature of modern operating and desktop systems.

The application footprint is not a factor in a virtual memory system. All dynamic link libraries (DLLs) are shared, and only one copy of the DLL is loaded irrespective of the number of users. Of course, if you're using Windows 95 you may have a memory problem. After all, what else can be done with a DOS derivative? The bottom line is that memory is cheap and footprint size should never be an issue.

The issue of speed is also highly questionable. Published tests of ADO in computer magazines indicate that ADO is indeed much faster than either DAO or RDO. However, these tests were done without significant thread loading. A common testing technique is to compare a single-threaded DAO or RDO application with an OLE-DB application. Microsoft must love these articles because there can't be a better sales pitch than this when an independent third-party touts the product. And, of course, Microsoft cannot be faulted when product performance fails to materialize. The performance issue here is the nonreentrancy of Microsoft code and the use of apartment-model threads. Apartment-model threading within an object imposes an unwanted and unneeded serialization. This serialization is one of implementation technique and not system design. OLE-DB performance will be an issue in a multiuser environment until Microsoft converts all of its code to the free-threading model.

No one can predict performance. Assembling and testing a system resembles medieval alchemy. The actual performance is not known until the system is tested under realistic load conditions. However, I believe there will be significant performance issues with OLE-DB and the ADO wrapper, the magnitude of which is unknown. Deploying a distributed architecture is a very recent experience. DCOM was shipped with Windows NT 4.0 and is a relatively new technology. I find it interesting that Microsoft is committing everything to OLE-DB and a component architecture when the DCOM technology has not yet proven that it is scaleable. (I know of a major seven-tier distributed component system based on the Microsoft architecture that failed.)

Within the discipline of mathematics there is the concept of a zero-sum game. What is a loss to one player is a gain to another player. The stock market has been likened to a zero-sum game. One or more losers offset each winner in the stock market. I believe OLE-DB is also a zero-sum game. ADO, which is the user interface to OLE-DB, is very easy to use, and this ease of use comes at the expense of the complexity of the underlying OLE-DB. The concept is easily understood if all the tasks necessary to support a database are considered. Both DAO and RDO have a reasonable division of labor with Microsoft SQL Server and the supporting ODBC infrastructure. The division of labor between ADO and OLE-DB is not equitable.

A properly designed ODBC application programming interface (API) application is the correct choice for enterprise applications. Yes, RDO, DAO, and OLE-DB can be used for desktop applications, but enterprise problems need enterprise solutions. Maybe when Microsoft can demonstrate adequate OLE-DB performance and its implementation of software is executed with the precision necessary for a corporation, not that of a *Doom II* player, can OLE-DB be considered as a viable database access technology.

If you're a Webbie, you know that Microsoft Visual Interdev uses ADO by default when creating active server pages. ODBC is a not a viable choice for this scenario.

RDO, DAO, and ADO

DAO, RDO, and ADO all have the same look and feel. ADO is far simpler for development because it has a smaller number of objects and a correspondingly smaller number of methods and properties. The intrinsic constants have yet to be standardized so you'll find yourself making transliterations of the intrinsic constants depending upon your choice of using either DAO, RDO, or ADO.

Method names are common. There are some minor transliterations you must make because a DAO **Workspace** object is the equivalent of a **rdoEnvironment** object. An OLE-DB **Command** object is not the equivalent of a DAO **Workspace** object or a **rdoEnvironment** object, but it is close enough. There is parallelism, but there is not a one-to-one mapping of RDO objects, DAO objects, or OLE-DB objects. Table 31-2 enumerates the basic differences between RDO, DAO, and OLE-DB.

TABLE 31-2 EQUIVALENT DAO, RSO, AND OLE-DB OBJECTS

DAO OBJECT	*EQUIVALENT RDO OBJECT*	*EQUIVALENT OLE-DB OBJECT*
DBEngine	rdoEngine	adodb
User	n/a	n/a
Workspace	rdoEnvironment	Command
Database	n/a	n/a
Connection	rdoConnection	Connection
TableDef	rdoTable	n/a
Index	n/a	n/a
Recordset	rdoResultset	Recordset
Table	n/a	n/a
Dynaset	Keyset	Keyset
Snapshot	Static	Static
Dynamic	Dynamic	Dynamic
Forward-Only	Forward-Only	ForwardOnly
Field	rdoColumn	Field
QueryDef	rdoPreparedStatement	
Parameter	rdoParameter	Parameter

MICROSOFT IS STILL UNDECIDED

Microsoft went to great lengths to convince the software community that RDO is a *proper* database access technology. Within RDO, references to fields and recordsets are replaced by references to columns and rows. It gives the appearance of trying to convince the relational database community that Microsoft does indeed understand the genre. The naming nomenclature is still muddled because OLE-DB uses rows and columns while ADO, the OLE-DB wrapper, uses fields and records.

Binding in DAO is with the **data** control and the equivalent binding in RDO is with the **Remote Data Control** (RDC). Many of the RDO methods have the same name as the corresponding DAO methods. Converting to RDO from DAO is not difficult. Neither is converting an application from DAO or RDO to ADO difficult.

 note **Binding with ADO is with what used to be the Advanced Data Control (ADC). This was renamed recently to Remote Data Service (RDS). Converting to ADO is a trivial exercise when the required functionality exists. Row versioning by record ID will probably be included in a later release.**

RDO rowset, DAO recordset, and ADO recordsets are discussed below. They are nearly the same except RDO and ADO do not support a table-type cursor. These are the record types supported by the current Microsoft database access technology:

- **Table** — One of the original recordset definitions of Microsoft Access and the earlier version of Jet and DAO. RDO and ADO do not support this cursor type.

- **Snapshot** — Another original Access DAO recordset definition. The data is captured at a point in time, and updates or deletions are not visible to the client. This recordset type is equivalent to an ODBC, RDO, or ADO **Static** cursor or static-type rowset.

- **Dynaset** — A keyset type recordset that may have either pessimistic or optimistic locking. The last of the original three recordset definitions. Deleted rows can be detected, but newly added rows go undetected. This rowset type is a **Keyset** cursor in the ODBC API, in the DAO ODBCDirect, in ADO, and in RDO.

○ **Forward-Only** — This is a new recordset that uses the minimum amount of resources. As discussed in Chapter 30, the ODBC default cursor is forward-only with a snapshot-type record. This recordset is equivalent to a **Snapshot** without a cursor. A forward-only cursor is available in DAO ODBCDirect, ADO, or RDO. Only one row is visible.

○ **Dynamic** — This is a new recordset type. It is reserved for access to ODBC-registered data sources. The dynamic-type cursor is limited to ODBCDirect in DAO, ADO, and RDO. It is not available to Jet. A **Dynamic** cursor is equivalent to a Jet **Dynaset** or **Keyset** cursor of ADO or RDO, except that new rows are added to the keyset. A simpler way of saying this is that the keyset membership is not fixed. Bookmarks are not available with a dynamic cursor.

Figure 31-1 illustrates the basic architecture of DAO, RDO, and ADO.

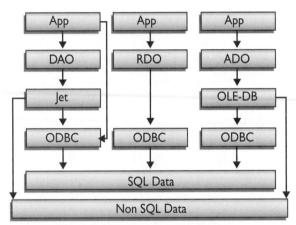

FIGURE 31-1   DAO, RDO, and the ODBC API.

The shortest path to a Structured Query Language (SQL) data source is still the ODBC API. Only one application in Figure 31-1 is illustrated using the ODBC API. In general, the mix and match of ODBC functionality is not possible. The ODBC API is separate from the ODBC desktop driver set of Microsoft Access. It is possible to access the ODBC API from RDO because the ODBC handles are exposed.

Yes, you can use the ODBC API in an application that uses ADO; however, the two technologies do not communicate except through an OLE-DB provider. ADO is an object-oriented technology whereas ODBC is a call-level interface (CLI).

ADO has a reduced footprint, which is meaningless in a multi-user environment. The value of the small ADO footprint is with Web-based applications. The attractiveness of the ODBC API is the **SQLExtendedFetch**, which binds all columns of a result set. ADO is clever; however, the encapsulation of a result set gives it an e-mail flavor. The complexity of OLE-DB far exceeds that of ODBC. ODBC developers wishing to create an OLE-DB application must now learn the COM technology. What is fun about Figure 31-1 is that the shortest path to ODBC data is still the ODBC API.

Neither ODBCDirect of DAO nor RDO require a query processor. ADO, which uses OLE-DB, doesn't technically require a query processor; however, it does require a provider. Provider resources will vary depending upon the data source.

DAO, RDO, ADO, AND ODBC

ODBC remains a core technology. It is a standard, and the technology is not burdened with esoteric programming constructs. DAO is a fat ODBC wrapper whereas RDO is a very thin ODBC wrapper. I don't mean to say that object-oriented programming isn't useful or valid, but there is a time and a place for everything. The very rich ODBC API function library supports every conceivable database access needed for the enterprise. Of course, if you need animated e-mail, then ADO is a necessary component of the Internet/intranet equation.

DAO and RDO are both ODBC wrappers. It is not correct to refer to ADO as an ODBC wrapper. ADO uses ODBC today through a provider interface, but it is reasonable to expect that ADO, and its parent OLE-DB, will eventually function without ODBC. ODBC is a standard over which Microsoft has little control and is ubiquitous in the enterprise today. OLE-DB is proprietary. Microsoft is busy porting component object model (COM) implementations to different platforms. By the time the implementations are successfully ported, OLE-DB, and its offspring ADO, will be firmly entrenched in the enterprise. Other database access implementations may be developed, but no market will exist. Sane people do not tinker with software that works.

The ODBC API can be used without objects because it is a call-level interface. Adding objects to an application increases the application volume and application complexity, which in turn increases the potential for application errors. Objects do not enhance ODBC. They simply make it easy to use for someone not skilled in using the ODBC API to access a relational database. This makes its products usable by a larger community, which increases its sales. ADO is another step in this direction.

WHAT IS ADO?

ADO is the glue of an Internet/intranet architecture, but Microsoft is trying to use it for everything else. It is COM-based and is the necessary flesh to the bones of distributed COM (DCOM), which first appeared in Windows NT 4.0. ADO has its rightful place in the single-user environment, but it is far from a proven product in a multiuser environment.

ADO is not relational database oriented; it is the promised universal database interface where a query can be constructed to pull data from relational databases, nonrelational databases, and nondatabase sources such as e-mail boxes. Whether that future will be realized is speculative. Microsoft has demonstrated the technology, but implementation is not yet complete.

ADO is like RDO in that it does not support data definition language (DDL) operations. The supporting OLE-DB does support DDL operations.

ADO shares a kinship with DAO in supporting heterogeneous joins. Microsoft introduced relational database technology to the mass of users who do not understand database design or normalization. When your Internet link slows to a crawl, contemplate all those new ADO users who are doing heterogeneous database joins over the Internet or your intranet.

Bound forms are not supported by ADO, RDO, or ODBCDirect; however, a data control is available for each. Both DAO and RDO have a RDC for binding purposes. These controls are not the same with the RDC control in Visual Basic Enterprise Edition named **MSRDC20.OCX** and the RDC of Access 97 named **MSRDC32.OCX**.

Binding is available in ADO with the ADC. The newest version of this ADO/OLE-DB component was renamed RDS, and it is backward compatible with ADC. Current features of RDS include data binding in an active hypertext markup language (HTML) environment.

 web links **This technology is still in development, but a beta version is available from the ADC Web site at**: http://www.microsoft.com/adc.

ADO is based upon objects that are roughly parallel to the underlying OLE-DB COM model objects. A hierarchical relationship exists between the ADO objects, but it is not strict. The user can open a recordset directly, ignoring the need to create a **Connection** object first. ADO automatically creates a default connection object.

RDO objects use the ODBC API implicitly with RDO objects calling the ODBC driver manager. This is quite unlike the call-level interface of ODBC. RDO is an ODBC API wrapper for ODBC functions along with other methods and properties. The use of ODBC functions is implicit, not explicit, in that ODBC functions are not directly called when executing a RDO method.

RDO lacks some of Microsoft Access's flexibility in creating a result set. RDO can create a result set from a table, a SQL string, or a **rdoPreparedStatement**. A result set cannot be created from another result set or from another query, both of which are features of Microsoft Access. A different type of flexibility is available with ADO, which can specify the **Source** argument of an **Open** method as a **Command** object variable, a SQL statement, a stored procedure, or a table name.

ADO does not use the ODBC API and depends on an ODBC provider for accessing ODBC data sources. This situation is best described by saying that ADO is not an ODBC wrapper, but that ADO uses an ODBC wrapper that is equivalent to a *Provider* exposing an ODBC wrapper.

ADO Architecture

The ADO architecture is that of OLE-DB software developer's kit (SDK) version 1.1. Version 1.5 is expected to ship in the near future, so many changes in the SDK can be expected.

Figures 31-2, 31-3, and 31-4 are a look at the respective architectures of DAO, RDO, and ADO. The RDO architecture is simple compared to DAO, and ADO simplifies database access even further.

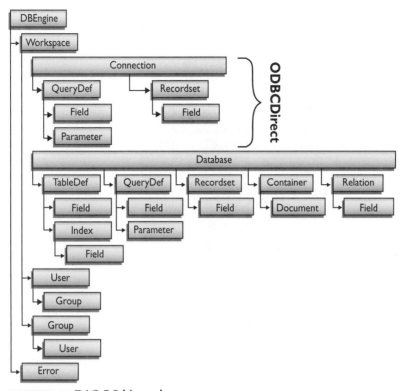

FIGURE 31-2 DAO 3.5 hierarchy.

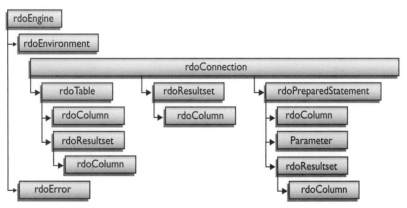

FIUGRE 31-3 RDO hierarchy.

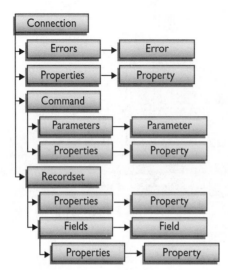

FIGURE 31-4   ADO hierarchy.

ADO ARCHITECTURE DETAIL

The following is a breakout of the methods and properties of all ADO objects. All objects are listed in their hierarchical order.

```
Connection Object
  Methods: BeginTrans, Close, CommitTrans, Execute, Open,
  RollbackTrans
  Properties: Attributes, CommandTimeout, ConnectionString,
              ConnectionTimeout, DefaultDatabase,
              IsolationLevel, Mode, Provider, Version
  Errors Collection
    Method: Clear
    Properties: Count, Item
Error Object
    Methods: Description, HelpContext, HelpFile, NativeError,
              Number, Source, SQLState
  Properties Collection
    Method: Refresh
    Properties: Count, Item
    Property Object
```

```
     Properties: Attributes, Name, Type, Value
Command Object
 Methods: CreateParameter, Execute
 Property: ActiveConnection, CommandText, CommandTiemout,
           CommandType
 Properties Collection
  Method: Refresh
  Properties: Count Item
  Property Object
   Properties: Attributes, Name, Type, Value
 Parameters Collection
  Methods: Append, Delete, Refresh
  Properties: Count, Item
  Parameter Object
   Property: Attributes, Direction, Name, NumericScale,
             Precision, Size, Type, Value
Recordset Object
 Methods: AddNew, CancelBatch, CancelUpdate, Clone, Close,
          Delete, GetRows, Move, MoveFirst, MoveLast,
          MoveNext, MovePrevious, NextRecordset, Open,
          Requery, Resync, Supports, Update, UpdateBatch
 Property: AbsolutePage, AbsolutePosition, ActiveConnection,
           BOF, Bookmark, CacheSize, CursorType, EditMode,
           EOF, Filter, LockType, MaxRecords, PageCount,
           PageSize, RecordCount, Source
 Properties Collection
  Method: Refresh
  Properties: Count, Item
  Property Object
   Properties: Attributes, Name, Type, Value
 Fields Collection
  Methods: Append, Delete, Refresh
  Properties: Count, Item
  Properties Collection
   Method: Refresh
   Properties: Count, Item
```

```
Property Object
  Properties: Attributes, Name, Type, Value
Field Object
  Methods: AppendChunk, GetChunk
  Properties: ActualSize, Attributes, DefinedSize, Name,
              NumericScale, OriginalValue, Precision, Type
```

WORKING WITH DEFAULT COLLECTIONS

ADO has only four collections: **Errors**, **Fields**, **Properties**, and **Parameters**. Objects of these collections may be addressed in the same manner as illustrated below for the **Field** object. Each of the constructs in each group is equivalent.

Field Object

recordset.Fields.Item(0)

recordset.Fields.Item("name")

recordset.Fields(0)

recordset.Fields("name")

recordset(0)

recordset("name")

recordset!["name"]

Parameter Object

command.Parameters.Item(0)

command.Parameters.Item("name")

command.Parameters(0)

command.Parameters("name")

command(0)

command("name")

command!["name"]

Property Object

object.Properties.Item(0)

object.Properties.Item("name")

object. Properties(0)

object. Properties("name")

object(0)

object("name")

object!["name"]

Error Object

connection.Errors.Item(0)

connection.Item(0)

Default collections provide a shortcut mechanism for addressing lower-level methods and properties. The **Value** property is the default property for the **Field**, **Parameter**, and **Property** objects.

Working with Collections

All collections have a **Count** property and the **Item** method. The **For...Each** construct can be used to enumerate ADO collections in the same manner as the RDO and DAO collections. Unlike DAO objects, RDO and ADO objects cannot be saved. Only **Parameter** objects can be appended to the **Parameters** collection.

Append

This method is only available in the ADO parameters collection.

Clear

Clear is only a method of the **Errors** collection, which clears all objects from the **Errors** collection.

Count

Count is the only common property of all collections.

Delete

This is a method of the **Parameters** collection and the **Recordset** object. It deletes a member of a collection or the current record respectively.

Refresh

This is a method of the **Fields**, **Parameters**, and **Properties** collection. It is not available to the **Errors** collection.

Item

Item is a default method of all collections. The method returns a specific member of a collection. It is the default method of all collections and is zero-based. This is a bit confusing because the RDO **Item** method is one-based. This can be a minor source of confusion when converting an RDO application to ADO.

note I call **Item** a method because it returns something from a collection. A property is a specific value while a method may return different values. The Microsoft ADO documentation calls **Item** a property.

ADO PROPERTIES

This chapter closes with an enumeration of all ADO properties.

AbsolutePage	**Recordset** object. Used in conjunction with the **PageSize** property, which defaults to 10. The consumer sets **PageSize** to the number of records per page. **AbsolutePage** is the absolute page number of the desired record. Useful for Web applications or providers that do not support indexing.
AbsolutePosition	**Recordset** object. Move to a specific record based on a one-based ordinal. It is not to be used in lieu of a record number because deletes affect absolute position. Cache for the current recordset is reloaded starting with the specified record.
ActiveConnection	**Command** object. Read/write. Setting to **Nothing** disassociates the current **Command** object for reuse with provider-supplied **Parameter** objects cleared and associated data source resources released. Consumer **Parameter** objects are not cleared. Closing a **Connection** object sets **ActiveConnection** to **Nothing**.
	Recordset object. Read-only when **Source** property is a valid **Command** object. Can be set to a valid **Connection** object or a valid connection string. Provider may return a valid **Connection** object.
	ActiveConnection inherits from the *ActiveConnection* parameter of the **Open** method.
	ActiveConnection inherits **Command** object **ActiveConnection** when **Source** property is set.
ActualSize	**Field** object. **ActualSize** may be less than **DefinedSize**. Read-only.

Attributes

Connection object. The values are a power of 2 and represent bit postions. The aggregate properties supported is the sum of the different numbers.

adXactCommitRetaining <1341072 >: CommitTrans starts a new transaction.

adXactAbortretaining <262144>: RollbackTrans starts a new transaction.

Parameter object.

adParamSigned <16>: Accepts signed values, default.

adParamNullable <64>: Accepts **Null** values.

adParamLong <128>: Accepts **Long** binary data.

Field object.

adFldMayDefer <2>: Retrieve only when requested.

adfFldUpdatable <4>: Writable.

adFldUnknownUpdatable <8>: Provider cannot determine if consumer can write field.

adFldFixed <16>: Contains fixed-length data.

adFldIsNullable <32>: Accepts **Null** values.

adFldMayBeNull <64>: Null values may be read.

adFldLong <128>: Long binary and **AppendChunk** and **GetChunk** may be used.

adFldRowID <256>: Field contains some kind of record ID. Type of record ID is not specified.

adFldRowVersion <512>: A date or timestamp field.

adFldCacheDeferred <4096>: Provider caches field.

Property object.

adPropNotSupported <0>: Property is not provider supported.

adPropRequired <1>: Value required before data source initialization.

adPropOptional <2>: Value is optional before data source initialization.

adPropRead <512>: Consumer readable.

adPropWrite <1024>: Consumer writable.

BOF

Recordset object. **True** when before the first record. **EOF** and **BOF** are **True** when there are no records. No current record when either **EOF** or **BOF** are **True**. **EOF** and **BOF** remain **False** after deleting the last record and do not change until an attempt is made to reposition the current record.

Bookmark

Recordset object. Returns or sets the bookmark position that identifies the current record position. Bookmarks of the **Clone** method are identical to original bookmarks.

CacheSize

Recordset object. Default is 1 for forward-only cursors, 10 for other cursors. **Resync** method refreshes cache. Zero is not a valid value.

CommandText

Command object. Sets or returns the text version of a query in a **Command** object. Provider specific. May contain a SQL statement, table name, or a stored procedure call. Zero-length string is the default. The query is prepared when calling either the **Execute** or **Open** methods and the **Prepared** property is **True**.

CommandTimeout

Connection or **Command** object. Elapsed time until ADO declares an error. A zero value is an indeterminate wait.

CommandType

Command object. Type of **CommandText** property data.

adCmdtext <1>: Textual.

adCmdTable <2>: Table name.

adCmdStoredProc <4>: Stored procedure call.

adCmdUnknown <8>: Unknown, default.

ConnectionString

Connection object. Five parameters to the connection string: *Provider, Data Source, User, Password,* and *File Name*. String is a series of *arguments = value* statements separated by a semicolon. The connection string cannot have both a *Provider* and a *File Name*.

ConnectionTimeout

Connection object. Elapsed time until ADO declares an error. A zero value is an indeterminate wait. Read-only when connection is open.

Count	**Errors, Fields, Parameters,** and **Properties** collections. Object count within collection.
CursorType	**Recordset** object. Set to one of:
	adOpenForwardOnly <0>: Equivalent to a static cursor with forward-only scrolling.
	adOpenKeyset <1>: Cannot see row additions or row deletions by other users. Changes to rows by other users are visible. Supports **adBookmark, adHoldRecords, adMovePrevious,** and **asResync.** See **Supports** method.
	adOpenDynamic <2>: Additions, changes, and deletions by other users are visible. Supports **adMovePrevious.** See **Supports** method.
	adOpenStatic <3>: Additions, changes, and deletions by other users are not visible. Supports **adBookmark, adHoldRecords, adMovePrevious,** and **adResync.** See the **Supports** method.
DefaultDatabase	**Connection** object. Resolves to the name of a provider database.
DefinedSize	**Field** object. Consumer-defined size, which may be greater than **ActualSize.**
Description	**Error** object. Error description.
EditMode	**Recordset** object. Returns one of:
	adEditNone <0>: Not in edit mode.
	adEditInProgress <1>: Current record is modified and not saved.
	adEditAdd <2>: Addnew has been invoked but the record hasn't been saved yet.
EOF	**Recordset** object. **True** when after the last record. **EOF** and **BOF** are **True** when there are no records. No current record when either **EOF** or **BOF** are **True. EOF** and **BOF** remain **False** after deleting the last record and do not change until an attempt is made to reposition the current record.

Filter	**Recordset** object. Filtered **Recordset** becomes the current cursor. May affect **AbsolutePosition**, **Absolutepage**, **RecordCount**, and **PageCount**. Uses a criteria string with SQL syntax. The criteria string is the equivalent of a SQL WHERE clause without the keyword WHERE. Only <*> and <%> are allowed as wild card characters and they must be the last character in the string. Must not be **Null**.
	Sets and returns a **Variant** value, which may be an array of bookmarks, a criteria string concatenated with AND, or one of the following:
	adFilterNone <0>: Removes the current filter.
	adFilterPendingRecords <1>: View only changed records not yet sent to server. Applicable to batch update mode only.
	adFilterAffectedRecords <2>: View records of **Delete**, **Resync**, **UpdateBatch**, or **CancelBatch** methods.
	adFilterFetchedrecords <3>: View records currently in cache.
HelpContext	**Error** object. Returns a context ID as a **Long** to a topic in a Microsoft Windows Help file.
HelpFile	**Error** object. Returns a fully qualified string to a Microsoft Windows Help file.
IsolationLevel	**Connection** object.
	adXactUnspecified <-1>: Indeterminate isolation level.
	adXactChaos <16>: Cannot overwrite changes from highly isolated transactions.
	adXactBrowse <256>: Uncommitted transaction may be read.
	adXactReadUncommitted <256>: Equivalent to **adXactBrowse**.
	adXactCursorStability <4096>: Default. Transactions are viewable after committing.
	adXactReadCommitted <4096>: Equivalent to **adXactCursorStability**.
	adXactRepeatableRead <65536>: Cannot see other transaction changes; a requery fetches new records.

adXactIsolated <1048576>: Transactions are isolated.

adXactSerializable <1048576>: Equivalent to **adXactIsolated**.

Item   **Errors**, **Fields**, **Parameters**, and **Properties** collections. Returns a specific member of a collection by name or ordinal number.

LockType   **Recordset** object. **adLockBatchOptimistic** should be either a keyset or static cursor. Uses **Supports** method to determine functionality. Provider may substitute lock types. Read/write when closed, read-only when open.

adLockReadOnly <1>: Read-only.

adLockPessimistic <2>: Records locked when editing starts.

adLockOptimistic <3>: Records locked when **Update** method is called.

adLockBatchOptimistic <4>: Required for batch update mode.

MaxRecords   **Recordset** object. **Long**. Limits the number of records returned by provider. Zero requests all records.

Mode   **Connection** object. Indicates the rules for modifying data of a **Connection**.

adModeUnknown <0>: Indeterminate permissions.

adModeRead <1>: Read-only.

adModeWrite <2>: Write-only.

adModeReadWrite <3>: Read/write permission.

adModeShareDenyRead <4>: Deny shared reads.

adModeShareDenyWrite <8>: Deny shared writes.

adModeShareExclusive <12>: Deny other reads/writes.

adModeShareDenyNone <16>: Exclude all others.

Name   **Field**, **Parameter**, or **Property** object. Property name. An ordinal or the property name can be used to retrieve an object.

NativeError   **Error** object. Database-specific error code.

Number   **Error** object. A **Long** that uniquely identifies an error.

NumericScale   **Parameter** or **Field** object. Number of digits to the right of the decimal point.

OriginalValue	**Field** object. The value before any changes or the value before the last **Update** or **BatchUpdate** call. The same value that is returned by a **CancelUpdate** or **CancelBatch** method call.
PageCount	**Recordset** object. Number of pages in the **Recordset** object. See **PageSize** and **AbsolutePage**.
PageSize	**Recordset** object. Determines number of records for a logical page. Useful for Web applications when indexing is not available.
Prepared	**Command** object. Provider compiles and saves a compiled copy of the query before the **Command** object's first execution.
Precision	**Parameter** or **Field** object. Maximum number of digits used to represent a value.
Provider	**Connection** object. Name of the provider for the connection. When there is no provider, the default is MSDASQL (Microsoft ODBC Provider for OLE DB).
RecordCount	**Recordset** object. The number of records in a **Recordset** object. When the recordset does not support approximate position of bookmarks, determining the number of records can be a resource drain.
	The **RecordCount** method may be very inefficient when **adApproxPosition** is not supported. Use the **Supports** method to verify provider support of the **adApproxPosition** before calling the **RecordCount** method of a **Recordset** object.
Size	**Parameter** object. The maximum size in bytes read or written from the **Value** property of a **Parameter** object.
Source	**Recordset** object. Specifies the **Recordset** source by setting the **Source** property to a **Command** object variable, a SQL statement, a stored procedure, or a table name.
	The **ActiveConnection** property of a **Recordset** object inherits the **ActiveConnection** property of a **Command** object when the **Source** property is set to a **Command** object variable.
	Error object. The name of the object or application that created the error.
SQLState	**Error** object. Returns a five-character ANSI SQL standard error code.

Status	**Recordset** object. The status of a **Recordset** object as a result of calling **Delete**, **Resync**, **UpdateBatch**, or **CancelBatch**.

adRecOK <0>: Record successfully updated.

adrecNew <1>: New record.

adRecModified <2>: Modified record.

adRecDeleted <4>: Deleted record.

adRecUnmodified <8>: Record is unmodified.

None of the following status codes save the record.

adRecInvalid <16>: Invalid bookmark.

adrecMultipleChanges <64>: Affects multiple records.

adRecPendingChanges <128>: Refers to a pending insert.

adRecCanceled <256>: Cancels operation.

adRecCantRelease <1024>: Existing record locks.

adRecConcurrencyViolation <2048>: Optimistic concurrency is in use.

adrecIntegrityViolation <4096>: Integrity constraint violation.

adRecMaxChangesExceeded <8192>: Too many pending changes.

adRecObjectOpen <16384>: Conflict with an open storage object.

adRecOutOfMemory <32768>: Computer is out of memory.

adRecPermissionDenied <65536>: Insufficient permissions.

adRecSchemaViolation <131072>: Violates structure of the underlying database.

adRecDBDeleted <262144>: Already deleted.

Type	**Field**, **Parameter**, or **Property** object. Parameter is read/write.

adBigInt <20>: 8-Byte unsigned integer.

adBinary <128>: Binary.

adBoolean <11>: Boolean.

adBSTR <8>: Null terminator Unicode.

adChar <129>: String.

adCurrency <6>: 8-Byte signed integer scaled 10,000.

adDate <7>: Date.

adDBDate <133>: *yyyymmdd*.

adDBTime <134>: *hhmmss*.

adDBTimeStamp <135>: *yyyymmddhhmmss* plus a fraction in the billionths.

adDecimal <14>: Exact numeric with fixed precision and scale.

adDouble <5>: Double precision floating point.

adEmpty <0>: No value specified.

adError <10>: 32-Bit error code.

adGUID <72>: GUID.

adDispatch <9>: IDispatch pointer on a COM interface.

adInteger <3>: 4-Byte signed integer.

adIUnknown <13>: IUnknown pointer on a COM interface.

adLongVarBinary <205>: Long binary; Parameter object only.

adLongVarChar <201>: Long string.

adLongVarWChar <203>: Long Null-terminated string; Parameter object only.

adNumeric <131>: An exact numeric value with fixed precision and scale.

adSingle <4>: Single-precision floating point.

adSmallInt <2>: 2-Byte signed integer.

adTinyInt <16>: 1-Byte signed integer.

adUnsignedBigInt <21>: 8-Byte signed integer.

adUnsignedInt <19>: 4-Byte unsigned integer.

adUnsignedSmallInt <18>: 2-Byte unsigned integer.

adUnsignedTinyInt <17>: 1-Byte unsigned integer.

aduserDefined <132>: User-defined variable.

adVarBinary <204>: Binary; Parameter object only.

adVarChar <200>: String; Parameter object only.

adVariant <12>: Automation variant.

	adVarWChar <202>: Null-terminated Unicode character · string; Parameter object only.
	adWchar <130>: Null-terminated Unicode character string.
UnderlyingValue	Field object. The value currently visible to the transaction and which may be the result of an update. The value used by the **Resync** method to replace the Value property.
Value	**Field, Parameter**, or **Property** object. Returns the value of the property.
Version	Properties collection. Provider version is returned as a dynamic property.

KEY POINT SUMMARY

Microsoft has stated that ADO will replace DAO and RDO. ADO has the look and feel of both DAO and RDO. Maybe with only one database access technology, we can retreat from this Tower of Babel that Microsoft has been building. ADO is easy to use, and the current common use of ADO is with Web pages. ADO has not yet proved to be scaleable even though Microsoft states that it is their database access technology of the future. These are some of the major issues of this chapter:

o   ADO is intended to be the universal database access technology.

o   The rigid object implementation hierarchy of RDO and DAO is relaxed in ADO with ADO's automatic creation of default objects as necessary. A **Connection** object isn't needed to open a **Recordset** object. One is created by the system automatically.

o   Row versioning properties are missing from ADO.

o   There are only four collections in ADO: **Errors, Fields, Parameters**, and **Properties**.

o   ADO supports transaction isolation levels, which means dirty reads can be managed.

- The durability component of the **ACID** properties is not yet visible even though Microsoft states that ADO supports the **ACID** properties. The architecture of OLE-DB/ADO indicates that **ACID** properties support is a provider-specific issue. There is nothing yet available that can be likened to the functionality of the Microsoft SQL Server log.
- ADO does not support DDL statements, whereas OLE-DB supports DDL.

APPLYING WHAT YOU'VE LEARNED

These questions will assess your understanding of ADO. You should be able to answer these questions directly since parallel functionality exists in RDO and DAO.

Instant Assessment

1. It was stated that a memory footprint is not an issue in a virtual memory system such as Windows NT. Why?

2. What is the default property for the **Field**, **Parameter**, and **Property** objects?

3. Name the collections that support the **Append** method.

4. Name the collections or objects that support the **Delete** method.

5. Name the collections or objects that support the **Clear** method.

concept link **For answers to the Instant Assessment questions, see Appendix C.**

Lab Exercise

Lab 31.53 *Converting from DAO or RDO to ADO*

WA I

The task for Lab 31.53 is the conversion of an existing DAO or RDO application to ADO. There is a second choice. Either convert an existing DAO or RDO application to ADO or convert an ADO example from Chapter 32 to either DAO or RDO. There are numerous ADO examples in Chapter 32 that can be used for this purpose. Completion of either of these conversion tasks is a useful mechanism for exposing conversion issues.

Windows Architecture I
Windows Architecture II

CHAPTER

Working with Active Data Objects

32

About Chapter 32

Chapter 32 provides thumbnail sketches of all Active Data Object (ADO) methods and contains numerous examples. The examples use Microsoft Visual Basic 5.0 Enterprise Edition and were tested with the Microsoft OLE DB ActiveX Data Object 1.0 Library of Visual Basic Enterprise Edition 5.0.

The examples in this chapter are located in the Visual Basic 5.0 Enterprise Edition Chapter32.VBP project located in the EXAMPLES\CHAPTER32 folder of the CD-ROM that accompanies this book.

ADO METHODS

With previous database access technologies, the developer knows apriori the support offered by database access technologies such as Data Access Objects (DAO) and Remote Data Objects (RDO). Interrogating the data source was and still is a good programming practice with ODBC. Developing an ADO application requires the ODBC developer mindset since the consumer must interrogate the provider as to the level of support available. This is quite unlike ODBC, which has Application Programming Interface (API) and structured query language (SQL) conformance levels and performance is guaranteed. The consumer interrogated ODBC and knew by conformance level the functionality available. With ADO and OLE-DB, the inquiry is done at the individual feature level. One reason for this is ADO and OLE-DB are proprietary to Microsoft and no standards exist. This means that the level of support from each provider may be uneven. The main reason is that OLE-DB and the companion ADO are universal access technologies. It is not realistic to have conformance levels when comparing an Oracle database to an e-mail box. The ADO developer should use the **Supports** method when applicable to identify provider resources levels. Yes, a provider may support an attribute or resource, but the level of support will not be even. As an example, a provider may support updates, but this support may not extend to a multi-table join.

ADO Error Handling

ADO, like DAO, has two sources of errors. The first source is ADO errors and the second source is from the supporting Visual Basic. ADO errors are found in the

Errors collection of a **Connection** object. This sounds simple, but it isn't. The first example in the following section does not have a **Connection** object. The **Recordset** object is opened directly. Constructs such as:

```
MyCon.Errors(0).Description
```

are meaningless without a **Connection** object. A reasonable construct uses the **ActiveConnection** property to access the implicit **Connection** object created by ADO when a **Recordset** object is opened without a connection. Listing 32-1 uses the **ActiveConnection** property.

AddNew

AddNew is a method of the **Recordset** object that adds one or more new records to an existing recordset. The consumer should verify that the data source supports the **AddNew** method before attempting to add a new record. The recordset must be refreshed with the **Requery** method when bookmarks are not supported.

Syntax:

> *Recordset*.**AddNew** *Fields, Values*

Where:

> *Recordset:* An object of type **Recordset**.
>
> *Fields:* A **Variant** representing a single name or a **Variant** array of names.
>
> *Values:* A **Variant** representing a single value or a **Variant** array of values.

When the **AddNew** method uses the optional *Fields* and *Values* parameters, the **Recordset** object is updated immediately and the **Update** method need not be used.

LISTING 32-1 Using AddNew to insert a new record

```
Private Sub AddNew_Click()
'(C)1998 Bruce T. Prendergast
' DBA Prendergast Consulting
' DBA PCS
' IDG Books Worldwide ISBN 0-7645-3123-9
'

' Listing 32-1 Using the ADO AddNew method
'
```

```
Dim fldValues(3)
Dim fldNames(3)
Dim MyErr As Error
Dim MyRS As Recordset
'
' declare and create object
'
On Error GoTo ADO_Error
Set MyRS = CreateObject("ADODB.Recordset")
'
' open it
'
MyRS.Open "Select * From Authors", _
   "DATABASE=pubs;UID=sa;PWD=;DSN=THOR", _
   adOpenDynamic, adLockOptimistic
If Not MyRS.Supports(adAddNew) Then
   MsgBox "Cannot add new records"
   Set MyRS = Nothing
   Exit Sub
End If
'
' build a new record
'
fldNames(0) = "au_id": fldNames(1) = _
   "au_fname": fldNames(2) = "au_lname": _
   fldNames(3) = "Contract"
   fldValues(0) = "123-45-6789": _
   fldValues(1) = "Sally": _
   fldValues(2) = "Silly": fldValues(3) = 0
'
' add the record (THIS IS IMMEDIATE)
'
MyRS.AddNew fldNames, fldValues
'
' must be a requery if bookmarks are not supported
'
If Not MyRS.Supports(adBookmark) Then
```

```
      MyRS.Requery
    End If
    '
    ' Delete test data.
    '
    MyRS.Delete
    MsgBox "ADO AddNew method completed successfully"
normal_exit:
    Set MyRS = Nothing
    Exit Sub
ADO_Error:
    If MyRS.ActiveConnection.Errors.Count = 0 Then
      MsgBox "Error is: " & Err.Number
      MsgBox Err.Description
    Else
        '
        ' note how the ActiveConnection links the recordset
        ' back to the Errors collection of the connection
        '
      For Each MyErr In MyRS.ActiveConnection.Errors
        MsgBox "Error: " & MyErr.Number & " " & _
          MyErr.Description
      Next MyErr
    End If
    Resume normal_exit
    Exit Sub
End Sub
```

Append

Append is a method of the **Parameters** collection of a **Command** object. Objects representing query parameters are appended to the **Parameters** collection. The **Type** must be set before the object is appended and the **Size** property must be greater than zero for variable length data. A **Parameter** object is created with the **CreateParameter**, which has the optional arguments *Name, Type, Direction, Size,* and *Value.* The example in Listing 32-2 specifies only the *Type* and *Direction.*

Syntax:

> *Collection.***Append** *Parameter*

Where:

> *Collection:* The **Parameters** collection.

> *Parameter:* An object of type **Parameter**.

LISTING 32-2 Appending a parameter to the Parameters collection

```
Private Sub Append_Click()
'(C)1998 Bruce T. Prendergast
' DBA Prendergast Consulting
' DBA PCS
' IDG Books Worldwide ISBN 0-7645-3122-9
'
' Listing 32-2 Using the ADO Append method
'
  Dim MyCon As Connection
  Dim MyCmd As Command
  Dim MyPar As Parameter
  Dim MyRS As Recordset
  Dim MyErr As Error
  '
  ' declare and create a connection
  '
  On Error GoTo ADO_Error
  Set MyCon = New ADODB.Connection
  MyCon.ConnectionString = _
    "DATABASE=pubs;UID=sa;PWD=;DSN=THOR"
  '
  ' switch to no error handling
  '
  On Error Resume Next
  MyCon.Open
  Set MyCmd = New ADODB.Command
  '
  ' link command to connection
  '
```

```
MyCmd.ActiveConnection = MyCon
'
' build a command
'
MyCmd.CommandText = _
  "SELECT au_fname, au_lname " & _
  "FROM authors where au_id= ?"
'
' build the parameter
'
Set MyPar = MyCmd.CreateParameter( _
  , adChar, adParamInput)
MyPar.Size = 11
MyPar.Value = "172-32-1176" ' ssn of White Johnson
MyCmd.Parameters.Append MyPar
Set MyPar = Nothing
'
' get the data
'
Set MyRS = MyCmd.Execute
'
MsgBox MyRS(0) & " " & MyRS(1)
MsgBox MyRS.Status
If MyRS(0) <> "Johnson" Or MyRS(1) <> "White" Then
  MsgBox "failed to find record"
  Set MyRS = Nothing
  Set MyCmd = Nothing
  Set MyCon = Nothing
  Exit Sub
End If
MsgBox "ADO Append method was successful"
normal_exit:
  Set MyRS = Nothing
  Set MyCmd = Nothing
  Set MyCon = Nothing
  Exit Sub
ADO_Error:
```

```
   If MyCon.Errors.Count = 0 Then
     MsgBox "Error is: " & Err.Number
     MsgBox Err.Description
   Else
   For Each MyErr In MyCon.Errors
       MsgBox "Error: " & MyErr.Number & " " & _
         MyErr.Description
     Next MyErr
   End If
   Resume normal_exit
   Exit Sub
End Sub
```

AppendChunk, GetChunk

The **AppendChunk** method appends large amounts of text or binary data to a **Field** or **Parameter object** (see Listing 32-3). The **adFldLong** bit must be set in the **Attributes** property of the **Field** object before the **AppendChunk** method may be used.

GetChunk also requires the **adFldLong** bit set in the **Attributes** property of the **Field** object.

The same condition exists for the **Parameter** object, but the names are different. The **adParamLong** bit of the **Attributes** property of a **Parameter** object has the same bit position as the **adFldLong** bit of the **Field** object **Attributes** property. This bit must be set before **AppendChunk** may be used on a **Parameter** object.

The first instance of **AppendChunk** replaces the original data while subsequent usage functions as an append operation.

Syntax:

   {*Field* | *Parameter*}.**AppendChunk** *Data*

   Set *Variable* = *Field*.**GetChunk**(*ByteCount*)

Where:

   Field: An object of type **Field.**

   Parameter: An object of type **Parameter.**

   Data: A **Variant** containing the source data.

   Variable: A **String** or a **Variant** of type **String.**

   ByteCount: The number of bytes to retrieve.

LISTING 32-3 Using AppendChunk on a Parameter object

```
Private Sub AppendChunk_Click()
'(C)1998 Bruce T. Prendergast
' DBA Prendergast Consulting
' DBA PCS
' IDG Books Worldwide ISBN 0-7645-3123-9
'
' Listing 32-3 Using ADO AppendChunk
'
    Dim MyCon As Connection
    Dim MyCmd As Command
    Dim MyPar As Parameter
    Dim MyRS As Recordset
    Dim MyErr As Error
    '
    ' declare and create a connection
    '
    On Error GoTo ADO_Error
    Set MyCon = New ADODB.Connection
    MyCon.ConnectionString = _
        "DATABASE=pubs;UID=sa;PWD=;DSN=THOR"
    MyCon.Open

    Set MyCmd = New ADODB.Command
    '
    ' link command to connection
    '
    MyCmd.ActiveConnection = MyCon
    '
    ' build a command
    '
    MyCmd.CommandText = _
        "SELECT au_id, au_fname, au_lname FROM authors"
    '
    ' build a character glob, or is it blob?
    '
```

```
Set MyPar = MyCmd.CreateParameter( _
  , adChar, adParamInput)
MyPar.Name = "ParamTest"
MyPar.Size = 4096
'
' make sure AppendChunk will work. adParamLong
' has the same bit number as adFldLong of the
' Field object
'
MyPar.Attributes = adParamLong
MyPar.Value = ""
MyCmd.Parameters.Append MyPar
Set MyPar = Nothing
'
' get the data
'
Set MyRS = MyCmd.Execute
'
' build a pile of first and last names
'
While Not MyRS.EOF
  MyCmd.Parameters("ParamTest").AppendChunk _
    MyRS(0) & "|" & MyRS(1) & "|"
  MyRS.MoveNext
Wend
MsgBox "AppendChunk method was successful"
normal_exit:
  Set MyRS = Nothing
  Set MyCmd = Nothing
  Set MyCon = Nothing
  Exit Sub
ADO_Error:
  If MyCon.Errors.Count = 0 Then
    MsgBox "Error is: " & Err.Number
    MsgBox Err.Description
  Else
  For Each MyErr In MyCon.Errors
```

```
        MsgBox "Error: " & MyErr.Number & " " & _
            MyErr.Description
      Next MyErr
    End If
    Resume normal_exit
    Exit Sub
End Sub
```

BeginTrans, CommitTrans, RollbackTrans

The **BeginTrans**, **CommitTrans**, and **RollbackTrans** methods manage transactions for a **Connection** object. **BeginTrans** returns a number indicating the current level when nesting transactions. <1> is the top-level transaction. A new transaction is started when the current transaction is committed with **CommitTrans** and the **Attributes** property of the **Connection** object is set to **adXactCommitRetaining**. A new transaction is started when the current transaction is rolled back with **RollbackTrans** and the **Attributes** property of the **Connection** object is set to **adXactAbortRetaining**.

Listing 32-4 sets the **IsolationLevel** property of a **Connection** object to **adXactSerializable**. The transaction retention level in Listing 32-4 is set to **adXactAbortRetaining** and verified.

Syntax:

> [*Level* =]*Connection*.**BeginTrans**

> *Connection*.{**CommitTrans** | **RollbackTrans** }

Where:

> *Level:* Optional **Long** returned transaction level.

> *Connection:* An object of type **Connection**.

LISTING 32-4 Using BeginTrans, CommitTrans, and RollbackTrans

```
Private Sub BeginTrans_Click()
'(C)1998 Bruce T. Prendergast
' DBA Prendergast Consulting
' DBA PCS
' IDG Books Worldwide ISBN 0-7645-3123-9
'
```

```
' Listing 32-4 Using ADO Transactions
'

  Dim MyCon As Connection
  Dim MyCmd As Command
  Dim MyErr As Error
  Dim AffectedByMe As Integer
  Dim TransactionOpen As Boolean
  '
  ' declare and create a connection
  '
  On Error GoTo ADO_Error
  Set MyCon = New ADODB.Connection
  MyCon.ConnectionString = _
    "DATABASE=pubs;UID=sa;PWD=;DSN=THOR"
  MyCon.Open
  '
  ' set transaction isolation level
  '
  MyCon.IsolationLevel = adXactSerializable
  '
  ' start a new transaction on a rollback
  '
  MyCon.Attributes = adXactAbortRetaining

  Set MyCmd = New ADODB.Command
  '
  ' link command to connection
  '
  MyCmd.ActiveConnection = MyCon
  '
  ' build a command
  '
  MyCmd.CommandText = _
    "INSERT jobs (job_desc, min_lvl, max_lvl)" & _
      "VALUES('Hacker',10,10)"
  TransactionOpen = True
  MyCon.BeginTrans
```

```
'
' Delete the record and check AffectedRecords property
'
  MyCmd.Execute AffectedByMe
If AffectedByMe <> 1 Then
    MsgBox "Incorrect Add count: " & AffectedByMe
End If
'
' Roll it back
'
MyCon.RollbackTrans
'
' lets look at the the transaction retaining status
'
If (MyCon.Attributes And adXactAbortRetaining) = 0 Then
    MsgBox "Transaction retention status error"
End If
'
' we're still in a transaction
' reset the retention status and abort it
'
MyCon.Attributes = 0
MyCon.RollbackTrans
MsgBox "ADO Transaction was succesful"
normal_exit:
    Set MyCmd = Nothing
    Set MyCon = Nothing
    Exit Sub
ADO_Error:
    If TransactionOpen Then MyCon.RollbackTrans
    If MyCon.Errors.Count = 0 Then
        MsgBox "Error is: " & Err.Number
        MsgBox Err.Description
    Else
        For Each MyErr In MyCon.Errors
            MsgBox "Error: " & MyErr.Number & " " & _
                MyErr.Description
```

```
    Next MyErr
  End If
  Resume normal_exit
  Exit Sub
End Sub
```

CancelUpdate

CancelUpdate is a method of the **Recordset** object. It cancels changes made to the current record before the **Update** method is called. The prior current record becomes the current record when **CancelUpdate** is called after an **AddNew** call and if **Update** has not yet been called. Changes to a record after an **Update** can only be reversed with the **RollbackTrans** method of a **Connection** object.

Syntax:

> *Recordset*.**CancelUpdate**

Where:

> *Recordset:* An object of type **Recordset**.

Clear

Clear is the only method of the **Errors** collection. ADO automatically clears the collection before logging new errors. The **Filter** property or **Delete**, **Resync**, **UpdateBatch**, or **CancelBatch** may log warning messages that do not inhibit application execution.

Syntax:

> *Collection*.**Clear**

Where:

> *Collection:* The **Errors** collection.

Clone

The **Clone** method is a mechanism for creating duplicate **Recordset** objects without requerying the data source. Closing the original **Recordset** object does not close the cloned **Recordset** object and, conversely, closing the cloned **Recordset** object does not close the original **Recordset** object. Changes made to the parent **Recordset** object are available in all cloned copies, independent of cursor type.

 note

ADO is unlike Microsoft Access which allows any form-bound recordset to be cloned. The application must ascertain that an ADO Recordset object supports bookmarks or the Recordset object cannot be cloned, as illustrated in Listing 32-5.

Syntax:

> **Set** *Duplicate* = *Original*.**Clone**

Where:

> *Duplicate:* An object of type **Recordset**.
>
> *Original:* An object of type **Recordset**.

LISTING 32-5 Parent records visible in cloned recordset

```
Private Sub Clone_Click()
'(C)1998 Bruce T. Prendergast
' DBA Prendergast Consulting
' DBA PCS
' IDG Books Worldwide ISBN 0-7645-3123-9
'
' Listing 32-5 Using ADO Supports and Clone methods
'
  Dim fldValues(3)
  Dim fldNames(3)
  Dim MyErr As Error
  Dim MyRS As Recordset
  Dim MyCS As Recordset
  Dim FoundSally As Boolean
  '
  ' declare and create object
  '
On Error GoTo ADO_Error
Set MyRS = CreateObject("ADODB.Recordset")
  '
  ' open it
  '
```

```
MyRS.Open "Select * From Authors", _
  "DATABASE=pubs;UID=sa;PWD=;DSN=THOR", _
  adOpenKeyset, adLockOptimistic
'
' bookmarks must be supported for cloning
'
If Not MyRS.Supports(adBookmark) Then
  MsgBox "Cloning not supported on this recordset"
  Set MyRS = Nothing
  Exit Sub
End If
'
' build the clone recordset
'
Set MyCS = MyRS.Clone
'
' build a new record
'
fldNames(0) = "au_id"
fldNames(1) = "au_fname"
fldNames(2) = "au_lname"
fldNames(3) = "Contract"
fldValues(0) = "123-45-6789"
fldValues(1) = "Sally"
fldValues(2) = "Silly"
fldValues(3) = 0
'
' add the record (THIS IS IMMEDIATE)
'
MyRS.AddNew fldNames, fldValues
'
' Sally Silly should now be visible on the
' cloned recordset
'
MyCS.MoveFirst
FoundSally = False
Do While Not MyCS.EOF
```

```
                    If MyCS(1) = "Silly" And MyCS(2) = "Sally" Then
                       FoundSally = True
                       Exit Do
                    End If
                    MyCS.MoveNext
                 Loop
                 If Not FoundSally Then
                    MsgBox "Error in cloned recordset"
                    Set MyRS = Nothing
                    Set MyCS = Nothing
                    Exit Sub
                 End If
                 MsgBox "ADO Clone method completed successfully"
              normal_exit:
                 Set MyRS = Nothing
                 Set MyCS = Nothing
                 Exit Sub
              ADO_Error:
                 If MyRS.ActiveConnection.Errors.Count = 0 Then
                    MsgBox "Error is: " & Err.Number
                    MsgBox Err.Description
                 Else
                    For Each MyErr In MyRS.ActiveConnection.Errors
                       MsgBox "Error: " & MyErr.Number & " " & _
                          MyErr.Description
                    Next MyErr
                 End If
                 Resume normal_exit
                 Exit Sub
              End Sub
```

Close

The **Close** method closes a **Connection** object or a **Recordset** object and all dependent objects.

The actions that occur when a **Connection** object is closed are:

- The **Command** object persists, but the **ActiveConnection** property is set to **Nothing**.

- The command object is reusable at a later time.

- The **Command** object's **Parameters** collection is cleared.

- Any pending changes to an open **Recordset** object are rolled back. Closing a **Connection** object with an outstanding transaction will generate an error.

- Transaction objects are rolled back automatically when the **Connection** object falls out of scope.

    The actions that occur when a **Recordset** object is closed are:

- Associated data and exclusive access are released.

- An error is generated when an edit is in progress.

- All changes since the last **UpdateBatch** are lost when closing a **Recordset** object during batch updating.

- Closing a **Recordset** object does not close a cloned **Recordset** object.

- The **Recordset** object remains available for later reuse.

Syntax:

　　Object.**Close**

Where:

　　Object: An object of type **Connection** or type **Recordset**.

CreateParameter

The **CreateParameter** method creates a new **Parameter** object.

Syntax:

　　Set *Parameter* = *Command*.**CreateParameter**(*Name, Type, Direction, Size, Value*)

Where:

　　Parameter: An object of type **Parameter**.

　　Command: An object of type **Command**.

　　Name: A **String** representing the **Parameter** object name.

　　Type: Optional, a **Long** that specifies the **Parameter** object's data type.

One of:

adBigInt <20>: 8-Byte unsigned integer.

adBinary <128>: Binary.

adBoolean <11>: Boolean.

adBSTR <8>: **Null-**terminator Unicode.

adChar <129>: String.

adCurrency <6>: 8-Byte signed integer scaled 10,000.

adDate <7>: Date.

adDBDate <133>: *yyyymmdd*.

adDBTime <134>: *hhmmss*.

adDBTimeStamp <135>: *yyyymmddhhmmss* plus a fraction in the billionths.

adDecimal <14>: Exact numeric with fixed precision and scale.

adDouble <5>: Double-precision floating point.

adEmpty <0>: No value specified.

adError <10>: 32-Bit error code.

adGUID <72>: Global unique identifier (GUID).

adDispatch <9>: **IDispatch** pointer on a COM interface.

adInteger <3>: 4-Byte signed integer.

adIUnknown <13>: **IUnknown** pointer on a COM interface.

adLongVarBinary <205>: Long binary; **Parameter** object only.

adLongVarChar <201>: Long string.

adLongVarWChar <203>: Long **Null**-terminated string; **Parameter** object only.

adNumeric <131>: An exact numeric value with fixed precision and scale.

adSingle <4>: Single-precision floating point.

adSmallInt <2>: 2-Byte signed integer.

adTinyInt <16>: 1-Byte signed integer.

adUnsignedBigInt <21>: 8-Byte signed integer.

adUnsignedInt <19>: 4-Byte unsigned integer.

adUnsignedSmallInt <18>: 2-Byte unsigned integer.

adUnsignedTinyInt <17>: 1-Byte unsigned integer.

aduserDefined <132>: User-defined variable.

adVarBinary <204>: Binary; **Parameter** object only.

adVarChar <200>: String; **Parameter** object only.

adVariant <12>: Automation **Variant**.

adVarWChar <202>: **Null**-terminated Unicode character string; **Parameter** object only.

adWchar <130>: **Null**-terminated Unicode character string.

Size: Optional; a **Long**; the maximum length in bytes or characters.

Value: Optional; a **Variant** specifying the **Parameter** object's value.

 concept link   See Listing 32-2 for an example of the **CreateParameter** method.

Delete

The **Delete** method deletes the current record of a **Recordset** object or a **Parameter** object from the **Parameters** collection.

The current record is deleted immediately when in immediate mode. If it is marked for deletion from the cache, the actual deletion doesn't occur until **UpdateBatch** is called. Batch updating only exists when the **LockType** property is set to **adLockBatchOptimistic**.

Syntax:

Recordset.**Delete** *AffectRecords*

Collection.**Delete** *Index*

Where:

Recordset: An object of type **Recordset**.

AffectRecords: One of:

adAffectCurrent <1>: Delete current record only.

adAffectGroup <2>: Delete the records satisfying the **Filter** property.

Collection: An object of type **Collection**.

Index: A **String** identifying the **Parameter** object.

note   A trappable error only occurs when no records can be deleted. No trappable error occurs when at least one of the intended records can be deleted.

The **Delete** method may not be supported on the **Recordset** object. The consumer has the obligation of calling the **Supports** method to verify record deletion support. Listing 32-6 is an example of most of the issues involving deleting a record.

The example starts by creating a complete recordset of the original table. A **Recordset** object is created with arguments supplied to both the **Source** and **ActiveConnection** parameters. A **Connection** object is needed for a later transaction. The following steps then occur:

o The original recordset is filtered.

o A transaction is opened and the record is deleted.

o The Errors collection is interrogated for an error because a delete failure is not usually fatal to application execution.

o The deleted recordset is filtered and verified.

o The transaction is rolled back because this is only a demonstration.

LISTING 32-6 Deleting a record and verifying the delete with a filter

```
Private Sub Delete_Click()
'(C)1998 Bruce T. Prendergast
' DBA Prendergast Consulting
' DBA PCS
' IDG Books Worldwide ISBN 0-7645-3123-9
'

' Listing 32-6 Filtering deleted rows in ADO
'

  Dim MyCon As Connection
  Dim MyCmd As Command
  Dim MyPar As Parameter
  Dim MyRS As Recordset
  Dim MyRSCount As Integer
  Dim MyErr As Error
  Dim TransactionStarted As Boolean
  '

  ' declare and create a connection
  '

  On Error GoTo Filter_Error
  Set MyCon = New ADODB.Connection
```

```
MyCon.ConnectionString = _
  "DATABASE=pubs;UID=sa;PWD=;DSN=THOR"
'
' switch to no error handling
'
On Error Resume Next
MyCon.Open
Set MyCmd = New ADODB.Command
'
' link command to connection
'
MyCmd.ActiveConnection = MyCon
'
' this is cleanup from prior efforts
'
MyCmd.CommandText = _
  "Delete FROM jobs WHERE job_desc ='Hacker'"
MyCmd.Execute
'
' now for a fresh start
'
On Error GoTo Filter_Error
MyCmd.CommandText = _
  "INSERT jobs (job_desc, min_lvl, max_lvl)" & _
  "VALUES('Hacker',10,10)"
MyCmd.Execute
'
' get the data
'
Set MyRS = New ADODB.Recordset
MyRS.Open "select * from jobs", _
  MyCon, adOpenKeyset, adLockOptimistic, adCmdText
If Not MyRS.Supports(adDelete) Then
  MsgBox "Cannot delete records"
  Set MyRS = Nothing
  Set MyCon = Nothing
  Set MyCmd = Nothing
```

```
      Exit Sub
   End If
   '
   ' set the filter, a string filter here
   '
   On Error Resume Next
   '
   ' should be one record
   '
   MyRS.Filter = "job_desc LIKE 'Hack*'"
   '
   ' Lets look at the filtered set
   '
   MyRS.MoveFirst
   MyRSCount = MyRS.RecordCount
   If (MyRS(1) <> "Hacker") Or (MyRSCount <> 1) Then
     MsgBox "Filter original failure"
     Set MyRS = Nothing
     Set MyCon = Nothing
     Set MyCmd = Nothing
     Exit Sub
   End If
   MyCon.BeginTrans
   TransactionStarted = True
   '
   ' delete only filtered records
   '
   MyRS.Delete adAffectGroup
   If MyCon.Errors.Count > 0 Then
     MsgBox MyCon.Errors(0).Description
   Else
       '
       ' filter the deleted records, a filter constant here
       '
     MyRS.Filter = adFilterAffectedRecords
     MyRS.MoveFirst
```

```
    MyRSCount = MyRS.RecordCount
    If MyRSCount <> 0 Then
      MsgBox "Filter delete failure"
    End If
  End If
  MyCon.RollbackTrans
  MsgBox "Filtering deleted rows was successful"
Normal_exit:
  Set MyRS = Nothing
  Set MyCon = Nothing
  Set MyCmd = Nothing
  Exit Sub
Filter_Error:
  If TransactionStarted Then MyCon.RollbackTrans
  If MyCon.Errors.Count = 0 Then
    MsgBox "Error is: " & Err.Number
    MsgBox Err.Description
  Else
    For Each MyErr In MyCon.Errors
      MsgBox "Error: " & MyErr.Number & " " & _
        MyErr.Description
    Next MyErr
  End If
  Resume Normal_exit
End Sub
```

Execute

Execute is a method of the **Command** or **Connection** object. A new **Recordset** object is always returned and the **Recordset** will be closed and can be ignored for action queries which add, delete, or change records. The **RecordsAffected** count is returned only for action queries even though the documentation implies that a query returns a record count.

Input query parameters are optional and can be used to selectively override **Parameter** objects in the **Parameters** collection. Output parameters are not supported.

Defaults for a **Recordset** object created with the **Execute** method are **adOpenForwardOnly** for cursor type and **adLockReadOnly** for lock type.

The **AffectedRecords** property is different than the **RecordCount** property. **AffectedRecords** gives the record count of affected records as a result of an action query. The **RecordCount** property returns the total number of records in a **Recordset** object. If the **Recordset** object supports approximate positioning with the **adApproxPosition** attribute or bookmarks, the returned value will be the exact number of records in the **Recordset** object. This count is independent of **Recordset** object population. If the **Recordset** object does not support approximate positioning, this property may be a significant drain on resources because all records will have to be retrieved and counted to return an accurate **RecordCount** value.

adApproxPosition is an intrinsic value of the **CursorType** property of the **Recordset** object. The ADO **CursorType** documentation has no reference to this intrinsic value even though the value may be browsed in the Visual Basic 5.0 Object Browser.

Syntax:

Set *Recordset* = *Command*.**Execute**(*RecordsAffected, Parameters, Options*)

Command.**Execute** *RecordsAffected, Parameters, Options*

Set *Recordset* = *Connection*.**Execute**(*CommandText, RecordsAffected, Options*)

Connection.**Execute** *CommandText, RecordsAffected, Options*

Where:

Recordset: Object of type **Recordset**.

Command: Object of type **Command**.

Connection: Object of type **Connection**.

RecordsAffected: Optional; **Long**; the number of added, deleted, or changed records.

Parameters: A **Variant** array of input parameters passed to a SQL statement.

Options: One of: **adCmdText<1>, adCmdTable<2>, adCmdStoredProc<4>,** or **adCmdUnknown<8>.**

CommandText: **String**. One of: Table name, SQL statement, or stored procedure name.

Please see Listing 32-4 for an example of the **Execute** method.

GetRows

The **GetRows** method retrieves a block of rows into an array. An optional parameter can be used to identify specific fields.

Syntax:

> **Set** *Array* = *Recordset*.**GetRows**(*Rows, Start, Fields*)

Where:

> *Array:* Returned **Variant** data array. The first subscript identifies the field while the second subscript identifies the row. The array size is automatically calculated by **GetRows**.

> *Recordset*: An object of type **Recordset**.

> *Rows*: Optional. **Long** row count. Default is **adGetRowsRest** (-1).

> *Start*: Optional. A **String** or **Variant** bookmark for the starting record.

> *Fields:* Optional. **Variant** represents an array of one or more field names or ordinal numbers that identify the fields of interest.

Move, MoveFirst, MoveLast, MoveNext, MovePrevious

The **Move** method provides logical navigation between records of a recordset. Operation is as expected with moving beyond the last record or before the first record creating the end-of-file (EOF) and beginning-of-file (BOF) conditions, respectively. Attempting to move beyond either the EOF or BOF creates an error.

The **CacheSize** property and the **Move** method can be used to support backward and forward scrolling for forward-only recordsets. The provider replenishes the cache when a **Move** method is executed that is beyond the scope of the current cache.

Syntax:

> *Recordset*.{**MoveFirst** | **MoveLast** | **MoveNext** | **MovePrevious** }

> *Recordset*.**Move** *NumberOfRecords, Start*

Where:

> *Recordset:* An object of type **Recordset**.

> *NumberOfRecords:* **Long** record count.

> *Start:* A **String** or a **Variant** that evaluates a bookmark.

NextRecordset

NextRecordset clears the current **Recordset** object and returns the next **Recordset** object. Multiple **Recordset** objects are created by concatenating at least two SQL statements separated by semicolons (see Listing 32-7). As an example:

```
SELECT * FROM authors;SELECT * FROM titles
```

returns two **Recordset** objects. Multiple recordsets are only available in the **CommandText** property of a **Command** object.

LISTING 32-7 Processing multiple Recordset objects

```
Private Sub NextRecordset_Click()
'(C)1998 Bruce T. Prendergast
' DBA Prendergast Consulting
' DBA PCS
' IDG Books Worldwide ISBN 0-7645-3123-9
'
' Listing 32-7 Using the ADO NextRecordset method
'
  Dim MyCon As Connection
  Dim MyCmd As Command
  Dim MyPar As Parameter
  Dim MyRS As Recordset
  Dim MyErr As Error
  Dim RecordsAffected As Long
  '
  ' declare and create a connection
  '
  On Error GoTo ADO_Error
  Set MyCon = New ADODB.Connection
  MyCon.ConnectionString = _
    "DATABASE=pubs;UID=sa;PWD=;DSN=THOR"
  '
  ' switch to no error handling
  '
  On Error Resume Next
  MyCon.Open
```

```
   Set MyCmd = New ADODB.Command
   '
   ' link command to connection
   '
   MyCmd.ActiveConnection = MyCon
   '
   ' get the data
   '
   MyCmd.CommandText = _
     "Select * FROM authors;SELECT * FROM titles"
   Set MyRS = MyCmd.Execute(RecordsAffected, , adCmdText)
   '
   ' the first recordset
   '
   MsgBox MyRS(0) & " " & MyRS(1) & " " & MyRS(2)
   '
   ' the second recordset
   '
   Set MyRS = MyRS.NextRecordSet
   MsgBox MyRS(0) & " " & MyRS(1) & " " & MyRS(2)
   MsgBox "NextRecordset completed successfully"
   MyRS.Delete
Normal_exit:
   Set MyRS = Nothing
   Set MyCmd = Nothing
   Set MyCon = Nothing
   Exit Sub
ADO_Error:
   If MyRS.ActiveConnection.Errors.Count = 0 Then
     MsgBox "Error is: " & Err.Number
     MsgBox Err.Description
   Else
     For Each MyErr In MyRS.ActiveConnection.Errors
       MsgBox "Error: " & MyErr.Number & " " & _
         MyErr.Description
     Next MyErr
```

```
        End If
        Resume Normal_exit
        Exit Sub
End Sub
```

Open

The **Open** method either opens a connections to a data source using a **Connection** object or opens a cursor using a **Recordset** object.

Syntax:

*Connection.***Open** *ConnectionString, UserID, Password*

*Recordset.***Open** *Source, ActiveConnection, CursorType, LockType, Options*

Where:

Connection: An object of type **Connection**.

Recordset: An object of type **Recordset**.

ConnectionString: The five parameters to the connection string are: *Provider, Data Source, User, Password,* and *File Name.* String is a series of *argument = value* statements separated by a semicolon. The connection string cannot have both a *Provider* and a *File Name*.

UserID: Optional user name; **String**.

Password: Optional password; **String**.

Source: Optional. The *Source* is a SQL statement, table name, stored procedure call, or a **Variant** that evaluates whether a **Command** object is valid.

ActiveConnection: Optional. *ActiveConnection* is a **Variant** that evaluates a **Connection** object or a **String** with connection definitions.

CursorType: Optional. One of: **adOpenForwardOnly <0>** (which is the default), **adOpenKeyset <1>**, **adOpenDynamic <2>**, or **adOpenStatic <3>**.

LockType: Optional. One of: **adLockReadOnly <1>**, **adLockPessimistic <2>**, **adLockOptimistic <3>**, or **adLockBatchOptimistic <4>**.

Options: Optional. One of: **adCmdText <1>**, **adCmdTable <2>**, **adCmdStoredProc <4>**, or **adCmdUnknown <8>**.

See Listing 32-1 for an example of opening a cursor on a **Recordset** object and Listing 32-3 for an example of opening a connection using a **Connection** object.

Refresh

The **Refresh** method refreshes a **Fields**, **Parameters**, or **Properties** collection.

Fields collection

No visible changes occur to the **Fields** collection when using the **Refresh** method. When bookmarks are supported changes to the underlying database structure are retrieved with the **Requery** method or the **MoveFirst** method.

Parameters collection

Using the **Refresh** method on the **Parameters** collection of a **Command** object retrieves either provider-side parameter information for stored procedures or a parameterized query specified in the **Command** object. The collection is empty when the provider does not support stored procedure calls or parameterized queries. Accessing a **Parameter** object automatically refreshes the **Parameters** collection.

The following conditions should exist before using the **Refresh** method on a **Command** object's **Parameters** collection:

- A valid **Command** object and a valid **Connection** object must exist.
- The **ActiveConnection** property of the **Command** object must be set to a valid **Connection** object.
- The **CommandText** property of the **Command** object must be set to a valid command.
- Unless the consumer initially sets the **Size** property to a nominal value, ADO allocates the maximum possible space for variable-length objects in the **Parameters** collection.

Properties collection

The provider populates the **Properties** collection with exposed dynamic properties. This functionality is beyond ADO built-in property support.

Syntax:

> *Object*.**Refresh**

Where:

> *Object:* One of: **Fields**, **Parameters**, or **Properties** collections.

Requery

The **Requery** method refreshes the current cursor. This is because cursor properties such as **CursorType**, **LockType**, and **MaxRecords** are read-only when the cursor is open. The method is equivalent to calling **Close** immediately followed by a call to **Open**.

Syntax:

Recordset.**Requery**

Where:

Recordset: An object of type **Recordset**.

Resync

The **Resync** method resynchronizes records in the current **Recordset** object. This method lets a consumer see underlying changes made by other consumers when the **Recordset** object is either a static or forward-only cursor. Deleted records return an error and the consumer must check the **Errors** collection for deleted records on a **Resync**. **Resync** cancels any pending batch updates.

Syntax:

Recordset.**Resync** *AffectRecords*

Where:

Recordset: An object of type **Recordset** object.

AffectRecords: One of:

adAffectCurrent <1>: Refreshes current record.

adAffectGroup <2>: Refreshes records satisfying the **Filter** property.

adAffectAll <3>: Refreshes all records in the **Recordset** object independent of the **Filter** property setting.

Supports

The **Supports** method determines functionality of a **Recordset** object.

There is a minor error in the documentation of this method. The **Set** statement is only used for objects and a variable of type **Boolean** is not an object.

Syntax:

> **Set** *Boolean = Recordset*.**Supports***(CursorOptions)* (Published syntax)
>
> *Boolean = Recordset*.**Supports***(CursorOptions)* (Correct syntax)

Where:

> *Boolean:* A variable of type **Boolean**.
>
> *Recordset:* An object of type **Recordset**.
>
> *CursorOptions:* One of:
>
> **adAddNew <16778240>**: **AddNew** method is permitted.
>
> **adApproxPosition <16384>**: **AbsolutePosition** and **AbsolutePage** are permitted. A record count is the physical reading of each record without this support.
>
> **adBookmark <8192>**: Bookmarks are supported.
>
> **adDelete <16779264>**: Record deletion is permitted.
>
> **adHoldRecords <256>**: Record retrieval and manipulation are permitted without committing pending changes.
>
> **adMovePrevious <512>**: **Move** and **MovePrevious** are permitted.
>
> **adResync <131072>**: Cursor may be updated with visible data from underlying database.
>
> **adUpdate <16809984>**: **Update** method is permitted.
>
> **adUpdateBatch <65536>**: Batch updating is permitted.
>
> See Listing 32-1 for an example of this method.

Update

The **Update** method updates the underlying database with accumulated changes to a record. Using the **Update** method isn't necessary with a single record because ADO automatically calls **Update** when positioning to a new record. This is the *immediate mode* supported by the underlying OLE-DB.

The **Update** method provides optional updating capabilities for multiple fields. Because ADO does not support an **Edit** mode it is quite unlike prior database access technologies such as Microsoft Access. Consequently, pessimistic locking starts when the **Recordset** object is created and not when editing starts. This may be a bit confusing and more than one database may operate in an almost exclusive mode until developers fully understand the different update strategy. Changes made before the **Update** method is called may be canceled with the **CancelUpdate** method.

Syntax:

Recordset.**Update** *Fields, Values*

Where:

Recordset: An object of type **Recordset**.

Fields: Optional. *Fields* is a **Variant** variable or array of one or more field names or field ordinal numbers.

Values: Optional. *Values* is a **Variant** variable or array of one or more field values that correspond to the ordinals or names of the *Fields* argument.

UpdateBatch

The **UpdateBatch** method infers that the **Recordset** object is operating in the *deferred mode* supported by the underlying OLE-DB. Batch mode is established when the **Recordset** object is created by setting the **LockType** property of the **Recordset** object to **adLockBatchOptimistic.**

Batch operations can only be used with a static or keyset cursor. Batch updating is the preferred update mechanism for records with multiple key fields because batch updating eliminates the inconsistent states that occur during partial updates.

The provider caches multiple changes in batch update mode and only writes the accumulated changes to the underlying data source only when the client calls the **UpdateBatch** method. The process starts with the client calling the **AddNew** method without arguments. This sets the **EditMode** property to **adEditAdd**. ADO will now cache any column changes locally. When the client calls the **Update** method a new row is added to the rowset (recordset) and the **EditMode** property is reset to **adEditNone**. The changes are still not posted to the underlying database. The client eventually posts the changes to the underlying database with the **UpdateBatch** method.

The **UpdateBatch** method may generate errors and the consumer must check the **Errors** collection for error messages. A run-time error only occurs when none of the records can be updated. The errors in the **Recordset** object can be located by setting the **Filter** property to **adFilterAffectedRecords**. The **Status** property of each record in the resulting **Recordset** is then examined to determine the record status. A good choice is to wrap the update within a transaction and have the complete update roll back when conflicts cannot be resolved.

Syntax:

> *Recordset*.**UpdateBatch** *AffectRecords*

Where:

> *Recordset:* An object of type **Recordset**.
>
> *AffectRecords:* Optional. One of:
>
> **adAffectCurrent <1>**: Writes current record changes only.
>
> **adAffectGroup <2>**: Writes changes satisfying the **Filter** property.
>
> **adAffectAll <3>**: This is the default. It writes all pending changes.

WHERE TO FIND ADO

That finishes the thumbnail sketch of the ADO methods. The next several paragraphs highlight those niches in your system where you can put into practice some of the ADO techniques acquired in this chapter. Use the dialogs that follow to help you locate the ADO object library that is required before any of the tools can use ADO.

Access 97

Start Access 97. The **References** menu is found in the Visual Basic editor. Create a new database and place a control on a blank form. Use the **Properties** page and activate the Visual Basic Editor through an event of the control. Once in the editor, select: **Tools** ⇒ **References** ⇒ **Microsoft OLE DB ActiveX Data Objects 1.0**. You can now repeat in Microsoft Access 97 any of the ADO examples found in this chapter.

Excel 97

Using ADO in Excel is identical to using ADO in Microsoft Word 97. Start Excel 97. Select: **Tools** ⇒ **Macro** ⇒ **Visual Basic Editor**. After the editor has started select: **Tools** ⇒ **References** ⇒ **Microsoft OLE DB ActiveX Data Objects 1.0**. You can now repeat in Microsoft Excel 97 any of the ADO examples found in this chapter.

OutLook 97

Start Microsoft Outlook 97. Either edit an existing e-mail message or start the creation process for a new e-mail message. Once in the e-mail editor, which in this case defaults to Word 97, select: **Tools** ⇒ **Macro** ⇒ **Visual Basic Editor**. After the editor has started select: **Tools** ⇒ **References** ⇒ **Microsoft OLE DB ActiveX Data Objects 1.0**. You can now repeat in Outlook 97 any of the ADO examples found in this chapter.

PowerPoint 97

Using ADO in Microsoft PowerPoint is identical to using ADO in Microsoft Word 97 or Microsoft Excel. Start Excel 97. Create a blank presentation or open an existing presentation and select: **Tools** ⇒ **Macro** ⇒ **Visual Basic Editor**. After the editor has started select: **Tools** ⇒ **References** ⇒ **Microsoft OLE DB ActiveX Data Objects 1.0**. You can now repeat in Microsoft PowerPoint 97 any of the ADO examples found in this chapter.

Visual Basic 5.0

This system has Visual Basic 5.0 Enterprise edition installed, which was used for all the examples in this chapter. From a Visual Basic project select: **Project** ⇒ **References** ⇒ **Microsoft OLE DB ActiveX Data Objects 1.0**. You can now repeat in Microsoft Visual Basic any of the ADO examples found in this chapter.

Visual InterDev

Although Microsoft Visual InterDev uses ADO, any discussion of ADO and the Internet/intranet is deferred until Chapter 36.

Word 97

Start Microsoft Word 97. Select: **Tools** ⇒ **Macro** ⇒ **Visual Basic Editor**. After the editor has started select: **Tools** ⇒ **References** ⇒ **Microsoft OLE DB ActiveX Data Objects 1.0**. You can now repeat in Word 97 any of the ADO examples found in this chapter.

KEY POINT SUMMARY

ADO has many of the familiar methods and properties of both DAO and RDO, but there are significant differences. The ADO developer must be vigilant and must always test for support of a resource with the **Supports** method before attempting to use that resource. This is a commonplace mindset for ODBC programmers who use ODBC catalog functions, but it is a new skill that the DAO or RDO developer must acquire.

ADO does not support an edit method. Changes to a record are immediate after moving off the record unless in batch mode.

The **Errors** collection is a collection of the **Connection** object. When an error occurs, the **ActiveConnection** property of a **Recordset** object provides the link to the appropriate **Connection** object.

Row versioning is implicit in optimistic locking. Row versioning by record ID, which was introduced in RDO, is not available in ADO.

Transaction isolation levels are supported giving the developer the ability to accurately manage consistency. Microsoft spin doctors continue to state that the atomicity, consistency, integrity, and durability (ACID) properties are supported, but there is no evidence of it. In particular, the log of Microsoft SQL server represents the durability component which is not visible in either ADO or OLE-DB.

APPLYING WHAT YOU'VE LEARNED

These questions assess your understanding of ADO objects, properties, methods. There are subtle differences between ADO and the predecessor RDO and DAO technologies.

Instant Assessment

1. Name the four ADO collections.

2. What is the issue when the **Recordset** object attribute **adApproxPosition** is not supported?

3. Identify the basic difference between editing a record in DAO and editing a record in ADO.

4. What is batch mode?

5. How is batch mode initiated?

6. What common characteristic does the DAO **Errors** collection share with the ADO **Errors** collection?

7. Explain how to use the **Supports** method.

8. What is the common issue for the **Delete**, **Resync**, **UpdateBatch**, and **CancelBatch** methods?

 concept link   **For answers to the Instant Assessment questions, see Appendix E.**

Lab Exercise

Lab 32.54 *Converting RDO or DAO to ADO*

MCSD
WA I
WA II

Select an existing RDO or DAO application and supercharge it by converting it to ADO. If you don't have an application to convert, see Chapters 24-26 for RDO examples to convert or see Chapters 15-23 for DAO examples to convert to ADO.

Infrastructure

Part III is composed of the following three chapters:

- **Chapter 33: Operating System Awareness** — The Microsoft family of operating systems is examined. Other topics include the Windows architecture, protocols, interprocess communication, and internal issues such as threads, processes, and memory management.

- **Chapter 34: Choosing Development Tools** — The tool selected for an application is often the wrong tool because it is a favorite tool.

- **Chapter 35: Development Methodologies** — Microsoft Visual SourceSafe and Microsoft Solutions Framework are the only topics of this chapter.

Windows Architecture I

CHAPTER

Operating System Awareness

33

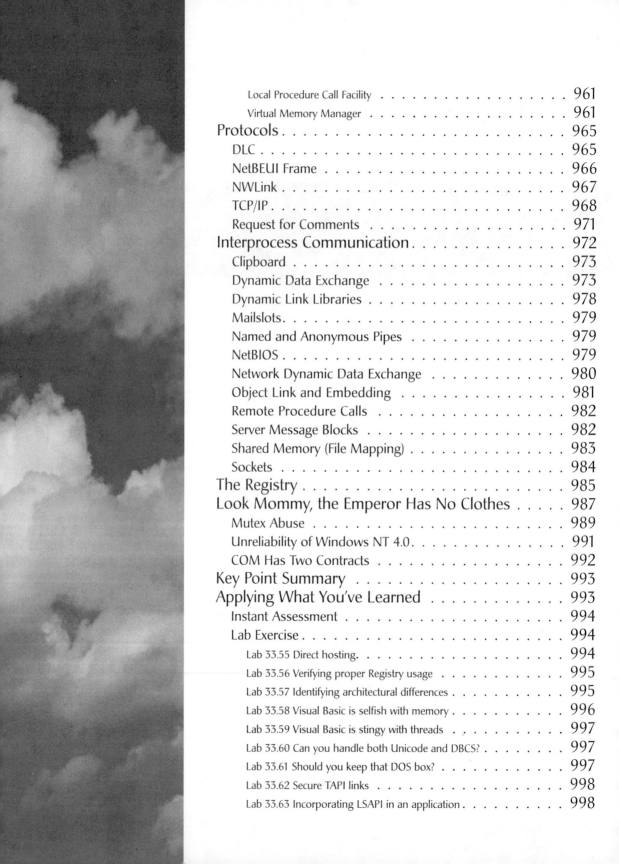

About Chapter 33

C hapter 33 starts with a quick look at the differences between the current alternatives in the Microsoft architecture: Windows NT and Windows 95. The Windows architecture is then examined from the top to provide an overall perspective. A thumbnail sketch of the components representing architectural issues follows. This architecture will soon be dated because of the forthcoming Windows 98.

All of the Windows Architecture I examination operating system awareness objectives are discussed in this chapter.

THE MICROSOFT WINDOWS FAMILY

In this section I discuss the Microsoft Windows Family to help you understand the distinct differences between Windows NT and Windows 95.

The first factor to consider is price. The retail price of Windows 95 is less than that of Windows NT Workstation. (Windows NT Server is not comparable in price with Windows 95 because it is an enterprise tool, and all licenses may cost thousands of dollars.) The next factors to consider are the architectural issues.

Hardware Platforms

- *Windows 95* — The hardware requirements for Windows 95 are less than that of Windows NT. Windows 95 is targeted for 386/486 class systems. 8MB is the minimum memory; however, 16MB is recommended from experience. The amount of memory is a function of user tasks, thus a minimum of 32MB is recommended for power users.

- *Windows NT* — The minimum recommended system is a Pentium class or higher system. Windows NT will run on 16MB of RAM, which is the minimum recommended; however, serious users will require 64MB or more. Windows NT server systems that support SQL Server typically start at 128MB and extend to 500MB or more.

Software Compatibility

- *Windows 95* — Supports nearly all MS-DOS and Windows 3.1 or Windows 3.11 applications. Windows 95 will support older DOS device drivers.

- *Windows NT* — Supports no applications that access the hardware directly. Direct hardware access in Windows NT is considered a breach of security. Windows 3.1 16-bit applications and DOS applications run in a single virtual DOS machine (VDM). This means that a corrupt DOS or Windows 3.1 application destroys other applications. Windows NT 4.0 provides the option of running 16-bit applications in a private VDM.

Hardware Compatibility

- *Windows 95* — Offers support for more than 4,000 devices. A device detection code and dynamic configuration scheme is used to manage devices.

- *Windows NT* — Supports approximately 3,000 devices. There is some device detection for devices on a hardware compatibility list (HCL). Device support is generally static. The rule of thumb with Windows NT is not to buy a device unless it appears on the HCL.

The PC hardware environment is limited by the number of interrupt request lines (IRQs). Devices cannot share an IRQ in Windows NT. An example might be a serial printer port and a modem line. Sharing an IRQ was possible on older systems; both devices just couldn't be used at the same time.

New with Windows NT 4.0 Workstation is the 10-connection limitation. This was not a limitation with Windows NT 3.51 workstation. The issue here is that Microsoft doesn't want Windows NT workstation used on the Internet as a Web page host.

Reliability

- *Windows 95* — Reliability has improved significantly when compared to Windows 3.1 and 3.11. This is not because Microsoft software has fewer bugs (it actually has more), but because in Windows 3.1/3.11 the GDI (graphical display interface), User, and Kernel stacks (internal memory stacks) are each 64K. In Windows 3.1/3.11, memory crashes were often caused by an empty stack. The "out of memory" message was reported when the stacks were depleted even though the system had 16MB or more of RAM.

o   *Windows NT* — Windows NT is very reliable. The operating system utilizes hardware memory protection and an errant task cannot destroy the operating system. Windows NT 3.1/3.5/3.51 are reliable, with Windows NT 3.51 the most reliable. Each of these systems supports a client-server relationship for the printer and GDI drivers.

Security

o   *Windows 95* — Windows 95 really doesn't have any security. It does have share-based security based on a local area network (LAN), but this is quite outmoded today where the push is to an Internet/intranet environment. The security model of the desktop environment should be rethought in light of the paradigm shift, which is now occurring to a browser-based environment. Windows 95 does have support for server-based logon validation, but as stated previously, this is an outmoded security model.

o   *Windows NT* — Everything is secure within Windows NT. The security issues are often the system manger not understanding how to secure the system. This complete security is possible because everything within Windows NT is considered an object, and each object has an access control list (ACL) that controls access to the object. Windows NT provides industrial strength security.

Performance

o   *Windows 95* — Performance is improved with the multitasking model of Windows 95, however multitasking is limited to 32-bit applications. The performance increases that come with a 32-bit addressing model and application multitasking is offset significantly by the introduction of Unicode, which is a 16-bit character set. Unicode is necessary for communicating on an international basis; however, very few of us do that. Windows 95 does not support Unicode directly; however, 32-bit applications support Unicode (See Chapter 42 for additional Unicode details). The Internet is certainly international, but that is not an excuse for making everything Unicode-based. The very least to expect is that Unicode should be a configuration option for the operating system. Unicode is an undue burden when communicating with legacy applications.

note **Windows 95 supports the Win32 application programming interface (API). An application developed for Windows 95 generally can run unchanged on Windows NT. Windows 95 ignores Win32 API function calls that are Windows NT specific. This includes API calls relating to security.**

o *Windows NT*—Windows NT is self-tuning and uses preemptive multi-tasking for all applications, not just the 32-bit applications. Windows NT is also Unicode. Microsoft warned us that Unicode was coming, but it was insidious and was there all the time. The effect of Unicode didn't appear until 32-bit applications were deployed. The client is unaware of Unicode with 16-bit applications such as Microsoft Office Pro 4.3, which includes Access 2.0. Other related 16-bit applications include Open Database Connectivity (ODBC) circa 2.0/2.5 and SQL Server with 16-bit applications (16-bit ODBC drivers sans Unicode). These applications provide good performance. (Don't discard SQL Server 6.0 and Access 2.0. They are still quite useful when used with the ODBC API.)

Windows NT provides values and benefits that are not realized with Windows 95. The most important feature of Windows NT is the complete security model, which has a Department of Defense (DOD) rating of C2. The other issue is to understand the different architecture models will change the reliability and performance. My system is Windows NT 3.51 workstation service pack (sp) 5. I will have nothing less. It is a multiboot system that allows me to boot in DOS, Windows 3.1 (my Compuserve character-based e-mail reader), Windows 95, Windows NT 3.51 Server, Window NT 4.0 workstation (my Internet port), and Window NT 4.0 Server, where I play with new Microsoft software.

My Windows NT 3.51 system appears to be slower than my Windows NT 4.0 system, and indeed it is, but it is only the display speed that is an issue. The GDI and printer drivers were moved into the Kernel in Windows 4.0. Formatting print files is not an issue because it is buffered and is a background task. When I say Windows NT 3.51 appears to be slower, it is only the appearance on the screen;

internal computational processes are no slower or faster on either version of Windows NT. My immediate recommendation is to purchase a copy of Windows NT 3.51 while they are still available in the distribution channels. Although it is true that NT 3.51 does not support the Internet Information Server, there are many enterprise tasks that require the reliability of NT 3.51.

WINDOWS ARCHITECTURE

We've discussed the benefits of the different operating systems. Here we take a larger view of the architecture. Microsoft calls this the *Microsoft Windows Open System Architecture* (WOSA), but I prefer to call it the *Windows Operating System Architecture*. This is because of the service provider interface (SPI), and the application provider interface or API (yes, I know it is supposed to be the *Application Programming Interface*). We discussed Windows NT workstation and Windows 95 in the previous section. Figure 33-1 illustrates the relationship of the desktop operating system to the API interface.

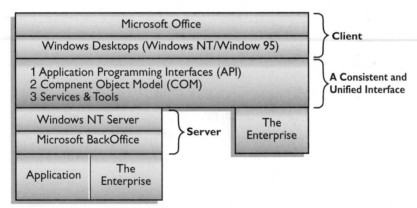

FIGURE 33-1 Windows NT and Windows 95 in the Microsoft architecture.

Let's further define the concept of a service provider interface and an application programming interface. Both of these interface models are shown in Figure 33-2. Both form the basis for the complete Microsoft architecture.

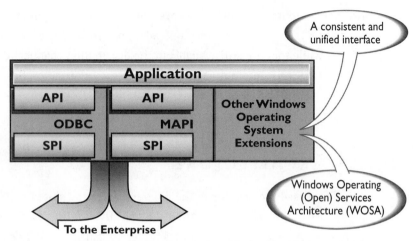

FIGURE 33-2   The API and the SPI relationship in the Windows architecture.

Let's pause briefly and consider Figure 33-2. Microsoft considers WOSA to be an "open" architecture because it is open on both sides. The *Messaging API* (MAPI) has service providers such as fax and telephony, and the interfaces sandwich the technology. This explains the furor a few years back when Microsoft announced MAPI. Lotus thought it could provide value-added content and expand the scope of Lotus Notes, its flagship product. Lotus was quite dismayed to realize that Microsoft provided all the value-added content and that third party vendors were limited to either writing an application or providing device drivers. Lawsuits were threatened, but this all ended when IBM purchased Lotus. My comment is this: The architecture is uniform and consistent, but certainly not open; hence Windows Operating System Architecture. Figure 33-3 takes a closer look at MAPI.

That's WOSA. Microsoft has many APIs in the WOSA architecture. Let's look at the major WOSA APIs.

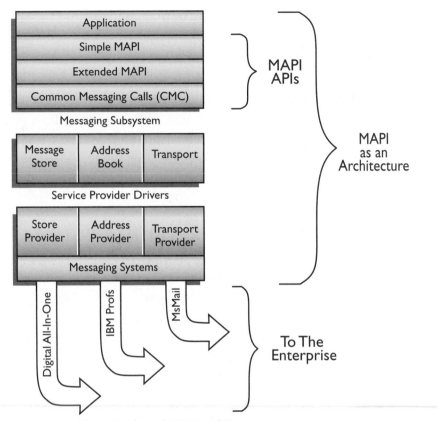

FIGURE 33-3 The COM-based MAPI architecture.

System Network Architecture (the APPC API, CPI-C API, and LUA API)

System Network Architecture (SNA) is an IBM network and communications architecture. Microsoft supports SNA with a fully WOSA-compliant SNA server. Associated with the SNA server are three programming interfaces supported by WOSA:

- The first SNA API is APPC, which supports program-to-program communications in a distributed processing environment. Communication may be within a system or within a network. Transaction programs cooperate together to perform remote database queries, copy a remote file, or receive electronic mail. The APPC API allows programs to communicate using IBM's logical unit (LU) type 6.2 protocol.

- The second SNA API supported by WOSA is CPI-C, which also uses the LU 6.2 protocol to communicate with programs on a peer-to-peer basis. The difference between APPC and CPI-C is that CPI-C communicates with programs within the IBM Systems Application Architecture (SAA).

- The final SNA protocol supported in the WOSA environment is the Logical Unit Application (LUA) programming interface, which allows workstations to communicate with host applications using the LU 0, 1, 2, or 3 protocols. LUA/Request Unit Interface or LUA/Session Level Interface APIs that need direct access to LU types 0, 1, 2, and 3 data streams are supported.

Open Database Connectivity API

Microsoft has a right to be proud of ODBC (see Chapters 11–14). It is ubiquitous within the computer community and nearly every communication protocol has either an ODBC wrapper or an ODBC interface.

ODBC is a standard within the computer industry, and Microsoft has shipped ODBC 3.0, which is ISO 92 compliant. Some ODBC functions are X/Open compliant because ODBC 3.0 is a superset of X/Open version 1.0.

 tip **The value of ODBC is for heterogeneous interconnection of computer systems. The native API will always be faster when a heterogeneous database connection is not desired.**

Messaging API

MAPI is not a single API but architecture consisting of three different APIs. The relationship of these APIs is illustrated in Figure 33-3. Each API has a unique role in the MAPI architecture.

- *Simple MAPI* — An API that consists of the 12 most common API calls. The API is designed to make it easy to add messaging to existing applications. Simple MAPI applications can be a form-routing application or a calendar and scheduling program. The API can be used from either the Visual Basic for Applications (VBA) or the C/C++ environment.

- *Common messaging calls (CMC)* — An API designed to be independent of the actual messaging service. It uses a set of ten high-level functions for mail-enabled applications. CMC was developed in concert with the X.400

API Association (XAPIA). CMC is the choice for heterogeneous messaging and is the preferred API when multiple platforms must be supported, multiple messaging services must be supported, or detailed knowledge of the underlying message service is not required. CMC applications are considered *mail-enabled*.

o *Extended MAPI* — Has advanced features such as folders and attachments. Extended MAPI has a rather unique definition of an address book. The address book consists of one or more lists of message recipients, and each list is a container. You can liken it to the **Containers** collection of Access (not DAO). Recipients can be a single user or a distribution list.

Extended MAPI supports unified logons, which means that your original logon is remembered and users are not required to enter name and password for each new application.

Extended MAPI consists of two physical components, which are further divided into four logical components. The first physical component is the MAPI *run-time* dynamic link library (DLL) which acts as a broker between clients and service providers. The DLL is integrated into the Windows operating system as part of the messaging subsystem.

The MAPI run-time DLL contains a set of COM objects that support MAPI functionality. These objects support MAPI initialization, starting a MAPI session, managing memory, administering profiles, and displaying a standardized user interface.

The second physical component is the spooler system, which is an integral part of the Windows operating system. The logical extended MAPI components are:

o *Transport provider* — Uses the SPI portion of the WOSA API-SPI model. Transport providers may be for plain old telephone service (POTS), fax, or cellular phones. A transport provider runs in the context of the spooler.

o *Message store* — A Microsoft-provided component of extended MAPI. Messages are stored automatically when a service provider is temporarily unavailable. Folders exist within the message store and are hierarchical. These features do not exist in CMC or simple MAPI. A message store provider runs within the client context.

o *Message spooling* — A feature provided by the Microsoft operating system. The message is spooled to the service provider in the same manner output is spooled to a printer. Message spooling runs within the context of the operating system.

- *Address book* — May be provided by third-parties. The address book provider runs within the client context.

License Service API

License service API (LSAPI) does not conform to the WOSA model of an API and a SPI; however, it is an API that provides a unified and consistent interface to license management. The purpose of LSAPI is to provide an interface to separate the application code from license policy. The application and the LSAPI-compliant application are both provided by the third-party vendor. The LSAPI-compliant model consists of:

- An LSAPI-enabled application. A very key point is that LSAPI does not enforce licensing policy. It is only a consistent interface between an application and a licensing policy application.
- The standard LSAPI function layer (which is the `LSAPI32.DLL`).
- An LSAPI-compliant license product. This product includes a database for storing access tokens or license data. It establishes the licensing policy for the LSAPI-enabled application and manages all licensing resources such as rights to run, releasing those rights when they are no longer needed. A benefit of the LSAPI API is that one LSAPI-compliant product may be used for many LSAPI-enabled applications.

Sockets

There are sockets and there are sockets. Microsoft Sockets 1.1 was Transmission Control Protocol/Internet Protocol (TCP/IP)-based and used the sockets paradigm of the Berkeley Software Distribution (BSD) UNIX. Windows Sockets 2 has Sockets 1.1 as a subset and is now a multiprotocol interface, as illustrated in Figure 33-4. The Windows Sockets 2 interfaces conform to the WOSA model with both a service provider and an application provider interface. Windows Sockets 2 is protocol independent. You might have already used this new paradigm with SQL Server Multiprotocol.

The difference between Windows Sockets 1.1 and Sockets 2 is in the sockets interface. The protocol stack vendor supplies the DLL that implements the interface to the protocol stack in Sockets 1.1. Microsoft supplies the interface to the protocol stack in Sockets 2. This makes the protocol stack a consistent and unified interface. Protocol stack vendors no longer supply proprietary interfaces to their protocol stacks.

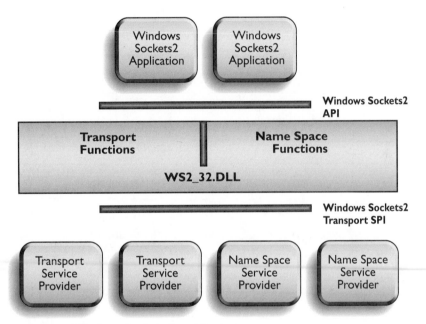

FIGURE 33-4 **Windows Sockets 2 architecture.**

Windows Sockets 2 includes new functionality beyond TCP/IP. It also includes the Microsoft Winsock 1.1 specification, which supports only the TCP/IP protocol. Figure 33-5 shows the relationship of Sockets 1.1 and Sockets 2.

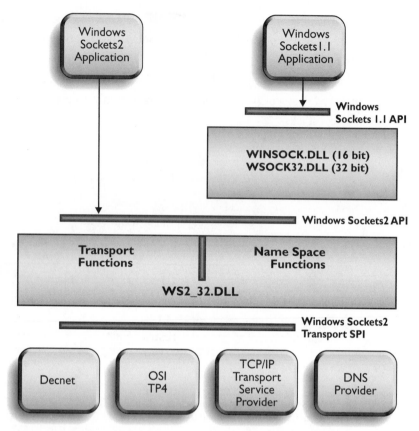

FIGURE 33-5   Sockets 2 maintains compatibility with Sockets 1.1.

Cryptographic API

The CryptoAPI ships with Microsoft NT 4.0, Microsoft Internet 3.0 and beyond, and OEM service release 2 of Windows 95. The CryptoAPI provides services that enable application developers to add cryptography to their Win32 applications. The CryptoAPI uses the WOSA initiative with the concept of a service provider. Individual modules are known as cryptographic service providers (CSPs). The base provider is the Microsoft RSA Base Provider and is bundled with the operating system.

The CryptoAPI is related to the code signing of Chapter 39. Both represent security tools available to the Win32 developer. Table 33-1 is a list of the CryptoAPI functions.

TABLE 33-1 CRYPTO API FUNCTIONS	
FUNCTION CATEGORY	*FUNCTIONS*
Context	CryptAcquireContext, CryptReleaseContext, CryptSetProvParam, CryptGetProvParam, CryptSetProvider
Key Encryption	CryptGenKey, CryptDeriveKey
Data Encryption	CryptEncrypt, CryptDecrypt
Key Exchange	CryptDestroyKey, CryptSetKeyParam, CryptGetKeyParam, CryptExportKey, CryptImportKey, CryptGenRandom, CryptGetUserKey
Hashing and Signature	CryptSetHashParam, CryptGetHashParam, CryptCreateHash, CryptHashData, CryptHashSessionKey, CryptGetHashValue, CryptDestroyHash, CryptSignHash, CryptVerifySignature

web links

A product incorporating the CryptoAPI cannot be exported directly. For information on export restrictions, visit the Business Software Alliance's home page, http://www.bsa.org.

Telephony Application Programming Interface

Telephony application programming interface (TAPI) is the Microsoft WOSA API for telephone communication. It supports the WOSA model with both a service provider interface and an application programming interface.

TAPI 2.0 ships as a component of Windows NT Server 4.0 and Windows NT Workstation 4.0 operating systems. TAPI 2.0 uses the WOSA model and abstracts the hardware layer, which provides both developers and users with network and device independence. TAPI is the only Microsoft platform that enables applications to access PSTN, ISDN, PBX, and IP networks. TAPI features include:

- Automated phone dialing
- Caller identification
- Conferencing and collaboration
- Data access (news feeds, stock quotes, and general information services)
- Data transmission (faxes, electronic mail); a MAPI service provider

- Direct telephone network connections
- Remote computer control
- Voice mail

Speech API

Microsoft has delivered the Speech API (SAPI) Software Developer's Kit 1.0. SAPI offers tangible benefits other than those illustrated by science fiction movies. The basic SAPI functionality includes:

- *Reading dynamic text* — This is a SAPI action that I'm sure you are familiar with. Reporting computerized bank balances or the time are two examples of this benefit.
- *Proofreading* — This is also characterized as a SAPI benefit.
- *User event notification* — SAPI facilitates the reporting of informational event messages. Event notification messages exist now but they get lost behind other windows or screen savers when ignored. Modal dialog boxes can stop the system until the requisite response is given. Voice informational messages can report the status of background tasks such as Internet uploads or large print tasks.

SAPI humanizes the computer. The user's computer interface is friendly, and communication is not limited to message and dialog boxes. SAPI also facilitates a hands-free computing environment. This makes the computer accessible on an assembly line when coupled with portable heads-up displays. SAPI will streamline computer access and simplify tasks (but, unfortunately, computers are still not as powerful as those of "Star Trek" fame).

Consoles

The Win32 API supports a character-based I/O interface for character-mode applications. The console interface is processor-independent. A console consists of an input buffer and one or more screen buffers. Buffers are queued and each buffer contains information about an event. Events include key-press, key-release, and mouse events. A screen buffer is a two-dimensional array of character and color data.

There are two different levels of console access. High-level is the equivalent of standard input to retrieve data stored in a character buffer. The second level of access is low-level with the application receiving detailed information about keyboard and mouse events. Table 33-2 lists the Win32 API functions supporting character-mode consoles.

TABLE 33-2 WIN32 API FUNCTIONS SUPPORTING CONSOLES

FUNCTION	DESCRIPTION
GetConsoleScreenBufferInfo	Retrieves the window size, screen buffer size, and color attributes.
SetConsoleWindowInfo	Changes the size of the console window.
SetConsoleScreenBufferSize	Changes the size of the screen buffer.
SetConsoleTextAttribute	Sets the color attributes.
SetConsoleTitle	Sets the console window title.
GetConsoleTitle	Retrieves the console window title.

THE MESSAGING MODEL: AN INTERNAL ARCHITECTURAL ISSUE

Microsoft Windows NT architecture is decidedly different than traditional operating systems. It is the first distributed operating system. By distributed I mean that operating system tasks are delegated to more than one box. This architecture is possible because of messaging. Everything in the Windows architecture is message-based. It is a message-switching environment. This means it can be distributed because messages can be sent over a network. Hence, features such as the *Windows Internet Naming Service* (WINS) can function on a separate platform. Another example is the *Dynamic Host Configuration Protocol* (DHCP) server, which leases TCP/IP addresses. This, too, can be an independent server.

The concept of a primary domain controller (PDC) with backup domain controllers (BDC) is another example of workload distribution. The PDC and DBC do logon verification.

Workload distribution extends to the application area where SQL Server supports replication to other SQL Server replication sites. System management of

SQL Server is not always easy, and some sites have discontinued the practice. However, SQL Server is still a distributed product. Microsoft recommends that it be installed on a dedicated box. A large enterprise will have many SQL Server boxes, with each box supporting a different endeavor. There could be a SQL Server box outside the firewall supporting an active server page of an *Internet Information Server* (IIS). Within the firewall is the original SQL Server, which replicates to the SQL outside the firewall. Of course, there are other production SQL Servers.

The concept of a server is nearly always synonymous with an application that can be distributed. The IIS is not such an animal. It appears to be an extension of Windows NT 4.x Server.

 note **The Windows programming model is event driven and graphical object oriented. Events are new and they're not new.**

We've discussed the vtable of COM in earlier chapters. We illustrated the original definitions of an object linking and embedding (OLE) control where an event is created by calling a method. A popular VBA trick is to call an event routine such as `On_Click` that directly simulates an event. One area where that we haven't explored is the message map of the *Microsoft Foundation Class* (MFC), one of which is shown below for a keypress and a mouse button. It processes events in much the same manner as VBA.

```
BEGIN_MESSAGE_MAP(CMainWin, CFrameWind)
 ON_WM_CHAR()
 ON_WM_LBUTTON()
END_MESSAGE_MAP()
```

MANAGING THE WINDOWS ARCHITECTURE

So far we have discussed the Microsoft Windows family and looked at the architecture from the top down using the WOSA perspective. In this section, we look at the nuts and bolts of the Windows operating system's internals. We build on these internals in later sections to acquire still higher functionality such as interprocess communication. The architecture continues to flow upward until we have distributed COM (DCOM). DCOM is a portion of the WOSA initiative; we've come full circle.

MICROSOFT DIDN'T INVENT EVENT PROGRAMMING, THEY POPULARIZED IT

We've had hardware events since the early 1960s. I recall a FORTRAN-buffered input-output (I/O) package that used the concept of *end-action*. The package was named *NTRAN* and all buffer maintenance occurred during end-action. The end-action was performed in FORTRAN. It wasn't an esoteric concept written in machine language and buried within the bowels of the operating system. An I/O completion status was checked, buffers were added or removed from the chain, and control was returned to the inter- rupted task. The operating system cooperated with I/O scheduling techniques, which are incorporated in the disk hardware today. The performance was phenomenal. Access times on FH-432 flying head drums were in the 4 millisecond region; with gather-reads and scatter-writes, the average access time were typically a millisecond or less (it was quite often around a half-millisecond). I chuckle to myself when some young technophile thinks he has a hot SCSI 10-millisecond disk.

The context of the following sections is Windows NT-based. Windows NT and Windows 95 both support the Win32 API. They each have a virtual memory manager and they each have a Registry. The only caveat is that the Windows NT Registry and the Windows 95 Registry are not compatible; however, Microsoft promised to remedy that with Windows 98.

Processes

A *process* is a program loaded into memory. It is all the resources necessary for that program and includes code, data, files, pipes, and synchronization objects. A process has a private virtual address space. This address space is shared with all threads (discussed in the next section) of the process. A process is an instance of a program that is loaded into memory and prepared for execution.

A process is also an object within the Windows NT context. It has a process ID, a base priority, and an exit code. This is comparable to a file object, which has a byte offset, a sharing code, and an open mode. A process does not execute code; it is simply the address space where the data and code reside.

Multitasking can be accomplished with additional processes. The Win32 API **CreateProcess** function creates a new process and its primary thread. The new process executes the specified executable file. This is quite expensive in terms of resources. Communication between processes entails additional overhead because global variables within the process cannot be addressed directly. All threads within a process occupy the same address space and can address the process's global variables directly. Synchronization objects must be used to avoid "deadlock" or "race" conditions when multitasking. This applies to both threads within the same process and separate processes.

> note 📝 **Windows 95 supports the concept of a process but only for 32-bit applications.**

Threads

A *thread* is a unit of execution in a process. Contained within a thread are all the necessary parameters to control execution. This includes an entry point, an area for register saves used during context switching, and control parameters such as base page limits.

As stated above, threads execute; processes do not. A thread is a Windows NT concept; 16-bit Windows uses the concept of a module and tasks but has only one thread. Threads are supported in Windows along with thread multitasking. However, Windows 95 only supports a unit processor and all multithreaded applications will run as though single-threaded on the same processor.

The first thread is always called the primary thread. Any thread of any process can use `CreateThread` and `CreateProcess` to create additional threads or processes.

Object ownership is mixed within a process. All Graphical Display Interface (GDI) objects (pens, brushes, and bitmaps) are owned by the process. Most user objects(windows, menus, and accelerator tables) are owned by the thread. Only three user objects (icons, cursors, and windows classes) are owned by the process. All other user objects are owned by the thread.

Windows NT attempts to present an image of a lively system. Every thread in the owning process is given a priority boost at the completion of input or output. The priority drops back one level as each time slice is completed without additional I/O. The priority continues to drop until the thread returns to the base priority. A thread's dynamic priority is never less than the base priority. The scheduler boosts the priority of the priority class associated with the foreground window until it is greater than or equal to the priority class of the background process.

Scheduling

Thread *scheduling* is done on the basis of process classes. A process class (priority class) has five members. Normal scheduling has four useful priority classes: high, normal foreground, normal background, and low or idle classes.

Figure 33-6 should reduce the confusion as to the priority scheduling of a new thread. A common misconception is that scheduling is done on thread priority. This is not true. The thread plays no part in the initial scheduling selection. Threads are first selected on the basis of priority class. Only after the priority class is selected is the relative priority level within the priority class given consideration. The thread's *normal* priority within the *high, normal foreground, normal background,* and *idle* is the base priority.

Within a priority class there are 5 possible levels (lowest, below normal, normal, above normal, and highest). This gives a maximum of 5 priority levels (-2 to +2) per priority class. The base (normal) priority is always relative zero within a priority class. For example, the High priority class has an absolute base priority of 13, but for selection purposes, the available priority scheduling levels are -2, -1, 0, +1, and +2. All threads are started with normal priority level, (0) relative to the base priority. The thread priority is a combination of the priority level and the base priority. The priority levels for the different priority classes are listed below and are illustrated in Figure 33-6.

- *Real time priority* — level 24
- *High priority* — level 13
- *Normal foreground priority* — level 9
- *Normal background priority* — level 7
- *Low priority* — level 4

Kernel

The *Kernel* schedules threads and manages objects. It does not implement policy because that is the responsibility of the executive. The Kernel does make policy decisions as to when a process should be removed from memory.

Real Time	High	Normal Foreground	Normal Background	Idle
31 Time Critical				
30				
29				
28				
27				
26 Highest				
25 Above Normal				
24 Normal				
23 Below Normal				
22 Lowest				
21				
20				
19				
18				
17				
16 Idle				
15	TimeCritical/Highest	TimeCritical	TimeCritical	TimeCritical
14	Above Normal			
13	Normal			
12	Below Normal			
11	Lowest	Highest		
10		Above Normal		
09		Normal	Highest	
08		Below Normal	Above Normal	
07		Lowest	Normal	
06			Below Normal	Highest
05			Lowest	Above Normal
04				Normal
03				Below Normal
02				Lowest
01	Idle	Idle	Idle	Idle

FIGURE 33-6   Windows NT priorities and scheduling classes.

The Kernel supports *symmetric multiprocessing* (SMP). Any thread can run on any processor in a SMP environment. Multiple threads of the same process may execute simultaneously. This is advantageous because servers may use multiple threads to process requests from more than one client. Convenient mechanisms exist for threads to share objects, including shared memory and a message passing facility.

The objects managed by the Kernel can be divided into two classes. The first class is **Dispatcher** objects, which include events, mutants, mutexes, semaphores, critical sections, threads, and timers. (Mutants were supported in Windows NT 3.1 but have disappeared from the documentation. I included them as a fun name.) Each of these is described as follows:

o *Event* — used to synchronize an action with the occurrence of an event.

o *Mutant* — a user mode extension of the mutex (see below); provides exclusive access to a resource; replaced by a critical section and no longer documented.

o *Mutex* — originally restricted to Kernel use only; provides exclusive access to a resource. There appears to be some confusion within the Microsoft architecture because mutex, which is supposed to be a Kernel-level synchronization object, is now used in the user environment.

o *Semaphore* — think of a semaphore as a flag person where a new road is being constructed. The flag person limits the number of cars in one direction while a semaphore limits the number of accesses or uses of a resource.

o *Critical section* — functions like a mutex in the user environment and is limited to a single thread within the process. It is not accessible from other processes. It is the replacement for a mutant.

o *Threads* — dispatched by the Kernel and controlled by a **Process** object. Hardware protection starts when the thread is initially dispatched. The number of threads within is not limited and Windows NT schedules threads on a central processing unit (CPU)-independent basis when the hardware system supports more than one CPU. This is symmetric multiprocessing compared to asymmetric multiprocessing where one CPU may be dedicated to the operating system and another CPU to user tasks.

o *Timer* — used to record the passage of time.

The kernel supports as **Control** objects an asynchronous procedure call, an interrupt, a process, and a profile:

o *Asynchronous procedure call* — breaks into the execution of a specified thread and causes a procedure to be called. This is a Kernel-mode activity where an asynchronous procedure call (APC) interrupts a user-mode thread's execution.

o *Interrupt* — connects an interrupt source to an interrupt service routine using the interrupt dispatch table. Interrupts are unique to a processor.

o *Process* — the virtual address space and control information for controlling the execution of threads. A process object contains a list of ready process threads, total accumulated thread execution time, a base priority, and a thread affinity.

o   *Profile* — an object used for performance-profiling, which may be either a system or a user.

Executive

Everything within Windows NT is an object. The Object manager, Process Manager, I/O Manager, and Virtual Memory Manager manage objects. All subsystems manage objects. The object-oriented nature of the Windows NT is illustrated by noting that the Windows NT Executive does not distinguish between a file handle and an object handle.

Object Manager

The Object Manager manages the global namespace for Windows NT. It tracks the creation and use of an object by any process. Common objects tracked include:

Directory objects	Object-type objects
Symbolic Link objects	Semaphore and Event objects
Process and Thread objects	Section and Segment objects
Port objects	Device objects
File Systems objects	File objects

Process Manager

We've discussed process quite a bit. You've probably already guessed that the Process Manager manages the creation and deletion of process objects. It also tracks **Process** objects and **Thread** objects. The Process Manager imposes any policy, hierarchy, or grouping rules for processes.

The Process Manager works with the Security Manager, which assigns each process a *security access token*. The tokens are used by the Process Manager to impose interprocess protection.

I/O Manager

The I/O manager manages all Windows NT input and output. Contained within the I/O manager are file system managers, network drivers, device drivers, and a cache manager. The I/O manager supports both synchronous and asynchronous I/O. I/O completion routines use the asynchronous procedure call (callbacks) discussed earlier.

The *Cache Manager* manages cache for the complete system. The Cache Manager uses many features of the *Virtual Memory Manager* (VMM) for file-caching. It also offers special services such as *lazy write* and *lazy read,* which significantly improve file-system performance. Associated with the *lazy write* is a *lazy commit,* which marks the data as committed and later writes the data to disk when time is available. Of course, there is a time and a place for everything. SQL Server cannot write the log file immediately and cannot support the database transaction ACID properties with either a *lazy write* or a *lazy commit.*

Local Procedure Call Facility

We're already familiar with the proxy/stub mechanism used for marshaling within COM. This is an integral feature of Windows NT. The mechanism was transparently upgraded in Windows NT 4.0 to support DCOM. Figure 33-7 illustrates remote procedure calls (RPC) that use the COM convention of calling the client stub a *proxy* and the remote stub a *stub.*

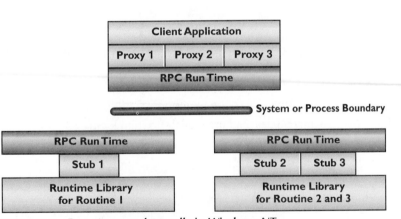

FIGURE 33-7 Remote procedure calls in Windows NT.

Virtual Memory Manager

The evolution of the memory model within the Windows architecture has been very painful. It is based on the memory model set by IBM with the first PC, circa 1981. The segmented memory model of Figure 33-8 represents DOS and Windows 3.1 memory architecture. The early PC system voraciously consumed available memory, and Figure 33-8 represents every possible trick. There was a design error in the early Intel chips and the A20 line gave access to an additional 64K page called the High Memory Area. What was a design error quickly became a feature.

note 🖋 **This memory model was based on 64K memory pages. Swapping applications to or from extended or expanded memory was always messy.**

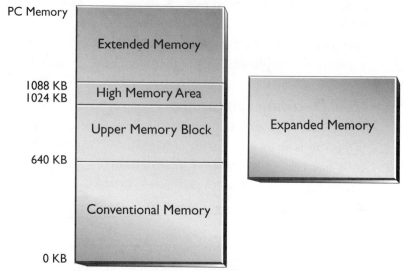

FIGURE 33-8   The early segmented memory model of DOS and Windows 3.1.

The complexity of the memory is significantly reduced with the Windows NT/Windows 95 flat memory model shown in Figure 33-9.

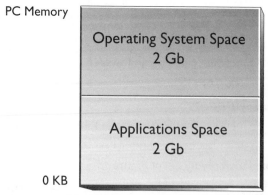

FIGURE 33-9   The flat memory model of Windows NT and Windows 95.

Developing applications in the 32-bit flat memory model is simpler. No more **GlobalLock** or **LocalLock**. **VirtualLock** doesn't move the memory page to a low page address like the Win 3.1 API function **GlobalPageLock**.

Windows 95 virtual memory management does not use extended memory, expanded memory, or A20 memory. `VMM32.VXD` and `KRNL386` are the new Windows 95 memory management modules, which replace and extend the Windows 3.1's `WIN386.EXE` and `KRNL386`. Windows NT was initially designed as a virtual memory management system. It is reasonable to assume that the virtual memory model of Windows 95 is based on Windows NT technology.

Virtual memory refers to the fact that the operating system can allocate more memory than the computer has available. A virtual memory page is 512 bytes and can have the states *Free, Reserved, Committed,* and *Not Present.*

The VMM is flexible with the functions **VirtualAlloc**, **VirtualFree**, **VirtualLock**, **VirtualProtect** and **VirtualQuery**. **VirtualAlloc** can allocate memory, which is committed later when needed. Windows 95's exception handling can automate this with page faults which occur when the referenced page is not in memory.

The selector level protection of Windows 3.1 is replaced with read-only code pages in Windows 95. Windows 95 and Windows NT all memory protection is done through paging.

GDI, User, and Kernel stacks were limited to 64K in Windows 3.1. The stacks are no longer limited to the 16-bit model. The "out of memory" message is now an ancient artifact of the Windows 3.1 segmented memory model.

There are two choices of stack management in Windows 95 and Windows NT. The first choice is the **VirtualXxxx** functions, which have 4K granularity. The second choice is the **HeapAlloc**, **HeapFree**, **HeapRealloc**, **HeapSize**, **HeapCreate**, and **HeapDestroy** functions. These functions have a granularity of 4 bytes with very low overhead when compared to the **VirtualXxxx** functions that have 4K granularity.

Virtual memory management is a model where memory pages are mapped a linear address space. A task earns pages in a working set (the set of pages currently in use) by referencing a nonexistent page, a page fault. (Earning pages is a concept of the Virtual Memory Manager [VMM] where a page fault adds a newly referenced page to the working set.) VMM loads the requested page into memory and maps it to a physical address that need not agree with the virtual address. Even though tasks enjoy a flat virtual address space, the physical representation need not be flat (linear) as illustrated in Figure 33-10.

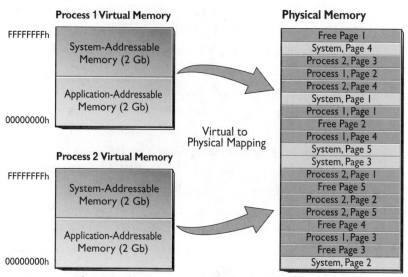

FIGURE 33-10   The virtual memory model is flat but the physical model is not.

Physical memory pages are demand paged. Committed pages are those pages that constitute the working set. When page faults occur, pages are retrieved from the page pool in memory or from the page file on disk. Older pages must be flushed to the page file on disk if the desired page is not in memory, hence the name demand paging, as shown in Figure 33-11.

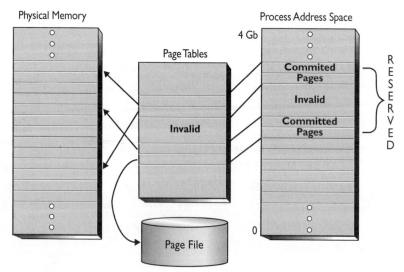

FIGURE 33-11   Demand paging with virtual memory management.

The committed pages of a task are called the working set. The code pages are read-only and constitute no loss to application functionality when pages are removed. The task must re-earn those pages with additional page faults. This is precisely what happens in Windows NT during a low memory situation. VMM will prune pages from active applications and use those pages to support a file copy. The only problem with this is that VMM doesn't give those pages back to the task and the task must re-earn them with page faults. This explains why task execution slows with a file copy. The rule of thumb is to ignore Microsoft's minimum memory requirements and buy as much memory as you can afford. Ignore the 16MB minimum with 32MB recommended. Think in terms of 64MB or, better yet, 128MB. This is a lesson I learned many years ago with VAX/VMS (OpenVMS). Virtual memory systems are like users with disk quotas: Each will use everything given regardless of the initial size.

PROTOCOLS

The Windows architecture includes the TCP/IP, NWLink, NetBEUI, and DLC transport protocols. These protocols support various interprocess communication mechanisms, which are discussed in the next section. Windows operating systems use these protocols for heterogeneous communication with systems such as the OpenVMS (DECNet), MAC, Novell, Unix, and OS/2 clients. The basic functionality of each of these protocols is sketched below:

- *DLC* — Data Link Control Protocol
- *NetBEUI* — NetBIOS Extended User Interface Protocol
- *NWLink* — Novell IPX/SPX Compatible Protocol
- *TCP/IP* — Transmission Control Protocol/Internet Protocol

DLC

Data Link Control is an IBM protocol for communicating with printers and has become a de facto standard for printers. The protocol enables a printer to be connected directly to a network without a supporting operating system. Windows NT DLC works with either token ring or Ethernet MAC drivers and can transmit and receive Digital/Intel/Xerox (DIX) format frames when bound to an Ethernet MAC.

NetBEUI Frame

NetBIOS is an IBM protocol and the first PC protocol. It is also the native Microsoft Windows operating system protocol. The original protocol has evolved with different variations. The following definitions should clarify the naming issues:

- *NetBEUI* — NetBIOS Extended User Interface, a transport layer protocol base, which originally included the NetBIOS interface.
- *NetBIOS* — A programming interface, although included with the original NetBEUI, the interface is now used by higher-level programs such as print and file services for protocols other then NetBEUI.
- *NBF* — NetBEUI Frame, which is enhanced NetBEUI.
- *NBT* — NetBIOS on TCP/IP (see TCP/IP).
- *NWNBLink* — The NetBIOS implementation within NWLink (see NWLink below).

NetBEUI Frame (NBF) is the native Windows NT protocol, and as such enables interprocess communication with NetBIOS, Named Pipes, Mailslot, NetDDE, RPC over NetBIOS, and RPC over Named Pipes using NBF. NBF does not support sockets or RPC over Sockets programming.

NetBEUI is not a routable protocol and a practical NBF network is 100 or less nodes. The stated Microsoft guideline for usage as a departmental network is 20 to 200 nodes. For very large networks, use TCP/IP. For small networks NBF is the fastest transport protocol supported in the Microsoft architecture.

NetBEUI and NBF provide for both *connectionless* and *connection-oriented* traffic. *Connectionless* traffic may be *reliable* and *unreliable*. *Unreliable connectionless* messaging is used for NetBEUI or NBF. No guarantee of delivery is made, and the sender is not notified that the message has been sent. If the sender *is* notified that the message has been sent and not when it has been delivered, then it is called *reliable connectionless*. If the sender isn't notified when the message is sent, then it is *unreliable connectionless*. In either case, delivery is not guaranteed. This mechanism is similar to the User Datagram Protocol (UDP) of TCP/IP. *Connection-oriented* messages will always have an acknowledgment and delivery is guaranteed.

NWLink

NWLink is the Microsoft implementation of both the IPX (internetwork packet exchange) network layer and SPX (sequenced packet exchange) transport protocols. NWNBLink is the NetBIOS implementation within NWLink.

The Windows NT implementation supports direct hosting, which completely bypasses the NetBIOS interface, allowing direct access to the IPX binding. This significantly improves network performance; however, it can only be initiated by a Windows NT. Since the Windows NT Redirector does not support direct hosting, a Windows NT computer cannot initiate a direct hosting session. Supplied with Windows NT on a CD-ROM is a protected mode redirector, `VREDIR386`, for use with Windows for Workgroups direct hosting. IPX enables direct hosting by supporting Socket IDs for use by applications. Novell has a NetBIOS implementation within the IPX protocol. The Microsoft implementation of this protocol (NBIPX) can be bypassed when both a Socket ID and the IPX protocol is available. These sockets are implemented at the Windows NT Server Service level, enabling a bypassing of the Windows NT Redirector. This is equivalent to bypassing the *Transport Layer* in the Open System Interconnect (OSI) model and connecting directly to the *Session layer*.

NWLink can be used with many different frame types on a network. Supported are Ethernet, Token Ring, FDDI, and ArcNet topologies. Use caution, however. On Ethernet networks, the standard framing format for Netware 2.2 and Netware 3.1 is 802.3. Starting with Netware 4.0 the default frame format is 802.2. On Windows NT, both frame types of NWlink can be bound to the same network interface card.

Even though Windows NT can bind NWLink to more than one network interface card, Windows NT is not capable of acting as an IPX router. How is that for an outdated statement? Steelhead is the code name for a set of new routing and internetworking capabilities for use with Windows NT Server version 4.0. Steelhead enables software routing over IP and IPX networks without the need for hardware routers.

TCP/IP

Microsoft provides a complete implementation of the *Transmission Control Protocol/Internet Protocol* (TCP/IP). Windows NT enhances the TCP/IP implementation with the *Dynamic Host Configuration Protocol* (DHCP) and *Windows Internet Naming Service* (WINS).

DHCP dramatically simplifies TCP/IP configuration management issues and relieves the user of configuration responsibilities. TCP/IP ports are leased by DHCP and address configuration is automatic.

WINS, a Microsoft-specific implementation, is implemented very efficiently. Within WINS, Microsoft has given TCP/IP a higher level of functionality with the implementing of NetBIOS naming conventions. Users specify resources using uniform naming conventions (UNC), and WINS automatically resolves the IP address for Address Resolution Protocol (ARP) to use in resolving the media access control (MAC) address.

The TCP/IP utility library is very rich. One of the more popular protocols in that library is the File Transfer Protocol (FTP) which is ACSII-based. FTP is a session-oriented protocol used extensively on the Internet for downloading files. The Microsoft Windows TCP/IP implementation functions with these environments:

- Internet
- Windows for Workgroups
- Windows NT (including RAS)
- LAN Manager for UNIX Host
- LAN Manager
- Pathworks for OpenVMS (DECNet)
- IBM Mainframes
- TCP/IP Hosts
- NFS Hosts

The OSI model consists of seven layers. TCP/IP remaps those seven layers to a four-layer conceptual model, as shown in Figure 33-12.

Figure 33-12 shows us that TCP/IP consists of five protocols: TCP, UDP, ICMP, IP, and ARP. TCP/IP has wide interoperability in a wide area network (WAN), but does not have a reputation for being fast. This is due in part to the large size of the protocol stack, which contains five complete protocols.

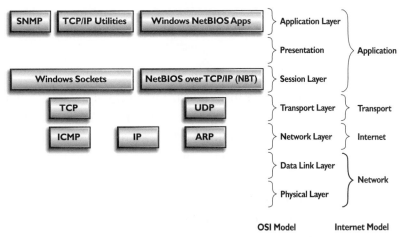

FIGURE 33-12 Mapping Internet protocols to the OSI model.

Transport Control Protocol

TCP is a connection-oriented protocol with data transmitted in segments. Data is transmitted as a stream; that is, without defined boundaries. A session must be established before a connection-oriented protocol can be used. Sessions communicate between port numbers, with some ports reserved for dedicated use.

TCP is a reliable protocol, and unlike a broadcast or a datagram, a reliable protocol requires an acknowledgment (ACK). Reliability is obtained by identifying each segment. If an ACK is not returned, the sender retransmits the data. If the data is received damaged, it is discarded because the sender will automatically retransmit. Segments are reassembled correctly at the destination.

User Datagram Protocol

UDP is a connectionless protocol and does not require a session. Unlike TCP, messages in UDP are not sent as a data stream. The reliability is the responsibility of the application and no acknowledges are required. The arrival of datagrams and the correct sequencing of packets are not guaranteed. It is not a broadcast message because the destination port and IP address of the recipient are required. It's like mail. I send you a letter and expect you'll get it, but there is no guarantee that you will. *Unreliable connectionless* messaging is when the sender is not notified that the datagram has been sent. *Reliable conectionless* messaging is when the sender is notified that the datagram has been sent. In both cases, the user is not notified of the receiver's receipt of message. UDP ports are distinct and separate from TCP ports even though some of them use the same port number.

Internet Control Message Protocol

All TCP/IP implementations have the Internet Control Message Protocol (ICMP), which provides all error and message reporting. To ensure delivery, ICMP messages are contained within IP datagrams. Common ICMP messages are echo request, echo reply, redirect, source quench, and destination unreachable.

Internet Protocol

IP is a connectionless protocol responsible for routing and addressing packets between hosts. This means that a session need not be established before exchanging data. An acknowledgment is not required and is the responsibility of the upper layer TCP. With a connectionless protocol, packets might be lost, delivered out of sequence, or duplicated.

Address Resolution Protocol

ARP obtains hardware addresses using a broadcast. The hardware addresses are mapped to corresponding IP addresses and saved in cache.

Simple Network Management Protocol

SNMP is used for the reporting of management and status information. Although originally developed as a tool for use in monitoring bridges and routers, Microsoft has expanded SNMP to include reporting for:

- Windows NT systems
- LAN Manager Servers
- Gateways or Routers
- Mainframes or Minicomputers
- Terminal Servers
- Wiring Hubs

SNMP is implemented as an agent in Windows NT. SNMP agents perform **get**, **get-next**, and **set** operations requested by the SNMP management system. **Trap** is the only operation initiated by SNMP agent software. The **trap** operation alerts SNMP management systems to such things as disk failures, password violations, and quota failures. The exact information returned can be determined by examining the Management Information Base (MIB) returned by the SNMP agent. SNMP is actively used in the Microsoft Systems Management Server (SMS).

Request for Comments

This is some fun material that is both TCP/IP-related and Internet-related. Changes to the Internet and the TCP/IP protocol are started by posting a Request for Comment (RFC). An RFC is a public document, and over the years many RFCs have been posted. For example, RFC 1945 defines the HyperText Transport Protocol (HTTP) 1.0. Anyone can submit an RFC and the rules for submission are found in RFC 1543. To locate any RFC, use your favorite Internet search engine.

RFCs are not limited to technical material. This poem is found in RFC 968. (This is public information and distribution is unlimited.)

Twas the Night Before Start-up
Vint Cerf, 1985 (RFC 968)

Twas the night before start-up and all through the net,
  not a packet was moving; no bit nor octet.
The engineers rattled their cards in despair,
  hoping a bad chip would blow with a flare.
The salesmen were nestled all snug in their beds,
  while visions of data nets danced in their heads.
And I with my datascope tracings and dumps
  prepared for some pretty bad bruises and lumps.
When out in the hall there arose such a clatter,
  I sprang from my desk to see what was the matter.
There stood at the threshold with PC in tow,
  an ARPANET hacker, all ready to go.
I could see from the creases that covered his brow,
  he'd conquer the crisis confronting him now.
More rapid than eagles, he checked each alarm
  and scrutinized each for its potential harm.
On LAPB, on OSI, X.25!
  TCP, SNA, V.35!

His eyes were afire with the strength of his gaze;
>   no bug could hide long; not for hours or days.
A wink of his eye and a twitch of his head,
>   soon gave me to know that I little to dread.
He spoke not a word, but went straight to his work,
>   Fixing a net that had gone plumb berserk;
And laying a finger on one suspect line,
>   he entered a patch and the net came up fine!
The packets flowed neatly and protocols matched;
>   the hosts interfaced and the shift-registers latched.
He tested the system, from Gateway to PAD;
>   Not one bit was dropped; no checksum was bad.
At last he was finished and wearily sighed
>   and turned to explain why the system had died.
I twisted my fingers and counted to ten;
>   an off-by-one index had done it again...

INTERPROCESS COMMUNICATION

Next is a brief discussion of the interprocess communication mechanism available in the Windows architecture. Interprocess communication calls (IPCs) exist as layers above protocols or other system functions. IPCs discussed in this section include dynamic data exchange (DDE), network dynamic data exchange (NetDDE), named pipes, memory-mapped files, and NetBIOS.

The issue for this section is data sharing, which is commonly done with IPC. There are many different techniques, and to select the correct technology, basic questions must be answered. Issues to consider include:

- Does the application need to be networkable?

- Must the application be interoperable?

- Is the application tightly coupled or loosely coupled? (A loosely coupled application communicates in a general way. A tightly coupled application communicates with a very strictly defined interaction mechanism.) The clipboard is an example of a loosely coupled communication medium.

- Is performance an issue? DDE is an older technology with marginal performance.

- Does the user or the application choose the other application?
- Is the application character mode-based or Windows-based?

Clipboard

The Clipboard is a very loosely coupled exchange medium in that an application need not agree on the format of the data being transferred via the Clipboard. Communication with the Clipboard uses global memory and is always within the process.

Dynamic Data Exchange

DDE is one of the original Windows IPC mechanisms. It is a protocol-based messaging scheme. It has a problem in that messaging occurs with global memory. Hence it is not useful with large files. The DDE's shortcomings were a motivating factor in the design of structured storage and Uniform Data Transfer in COM. Today DDE is still available with the Win32 API, which makes it available to both Windows 95 and Windows NT. (It is also still available with Windows 3.1 and Access 2.0 or Visual Basic 3.0 or earlier; however, using DDE with these tools is not recommended because of the performance issue.) The current solution is COM. OLE provides the necessary functionality. DDE functions on a client-server basis. A dialog is called a conversation. The following are some DDE definitions:

- *Cold link* — A one-time transfer similar to a clipboard transfer.
- *Warm link* — Server notifies client when data changes. Client must request data.
- *Hot link* — Server sends data updates to the client when changed.

DDE is supported in C++ and VBA environments. VBA DDE commands include:

DDEInitiate initiates a connection with a named application and a topic. The first parameter is the *application name,* which is typically MSAccess, Excel, or WinWord. A special *topic* is **System**, which initiates a conversation on other topics and data formats supported. A channel number is returned as a function value. **DDEInitiate** is illustrated by:

```
intChan = DDEInitiate("Excel", "System")
```

DDRequest requests data using a returned channel number and an *item*. A request with a *topic* value of **Topics** returns a list of topics available. The data is returned as function values. **DDERequest** is illustrated by:

```
ExcelTopics = DDERequest(intChan, "Topics")
```

A DDE conversation involves a topic and an item. Microsoft Access supports as topics the following:

- The *system* topic supports these items:
  - *SysItems* — A list of items supported by Microsoft Access.
  - *Formats* — A list of supported clipboard formats available to Access.
  - *Status* — Either **Busy** or **Ready**.
  - *Topics* — A list of open databases.
- A database name (database topic) and items TableList, QueryList, FormList, ReportList, MacroList, and ModuleList.
- A table name (tablename topic). The item format for the tablename topic is: databasename; TABLE tablename.
- A query name (queryname topic). The item format for the queryname topic is: databasename; QUERY queryname.
- A Microsoft Access SQL string (sqlstring topic). This is the only DDE topic that supports a **DDEPoke** command. The item format for the SQL is: databasename; SQL sqlstring. A valid SQL string is limited to 255 characters. The SQL statement must be broken into fragments, as illustrated below, when the string length exceeds 255 characters. The $<;>$ is the terminator and the last character entered.

```
Chan = DDEInitiate("MSAccess","Northwind;SQL")
DDEPOKE Chan, "SQLText", "SELECT *"
DDEPOKE Chan, "SQLText", "FROM Orders"
DDEPOKE Chan, "SQLText",";"
strResp = DDERequest(Chan, "NextRow")
```

The example above used the keyword **NextRow** as the item for the SQL topic. Here is the complete list of items for the SQL topic:

- *All* — All the data in the table including column names.
- *Data* — All data rows with no column names.

- *FieldNames* — A single row list of column names.

- *FieldNames;T* — The column names are in the first row and supported data types are listed in the second row. Most standard Access data types are supported. Notably missing is a GUID.

- *NextRow* — Retrieves the next row of a table or query.

- *PrevRow* — Retrieves the previous row of a table or query.

- *FirstRow* — First row of the table or query.

- *LastRow* — Last row of the table or query.

- *FieldCount* — Retrieves the column count in the table or query.

- *SQLText* — Where the SQL statement is constructed. See example above.

- *SQLText;n* — The size of tab-delimited SQL results.

Normally the application server returns data upon request. **DDEPoke** places a new value in an *item* location of a *topic*. A good example is changing the value in a spreadsheet. An example of **DDEPoke** is:

```
DDEPoke intChan, "R1C4","78.93"
```

DDEExecute can send command strings to the application server. The parameters are the channel number and the command string. **DDEExecute** is illustrated by:

```
DDEExecute intChan "[OPEN(""1996_TAXES.XLS"")]"
```

A DDE conversation is terminated with **DDETerminate**. The only parameter is the channel number. Terminating a DDE conversation is illustrated by:

```
DDETerminate intChan
```

Listing 33-1 is a DDE example using a SQL statement on an Access database. Note that there are error messages within the code. DDE runs most of the time with DAO 3.0. I gave up trying to make DDE work with DAO 3.5.

LISTING 33-1 Using SQL and DDE on an Access database

```
Private Sub cmdOutput_Click()
'(C)1998 Bruce T. Prendergast
' DBA Prendergast
' DBA PCS
```

```
' IDG Books Worldwide ISBN 0-7645-3123-9
'
' Listing 33-1 SQL and DDE on an Access database
'
  Dim Results
  Dim StartTime As Long
  Dim ChannelsIgnored As Integer
  Dim strItem As String
  Dim strOutput As String
  Dim Channel_1              'DDE Channels
  Dim Channel_2              '
  Dim MyAccess As Object     '
Restart_DDE:
  Set MyAccess = CreateObject("Access.Application")
  DoEvents
    '
  ' channel 1 is used to open the database. It can't
  ' be used for data retrieval since the topic is
  ' SYSTEM. Channel 2 is used for data retrieval.
  '
  Channel_1 = DDEInitiate("MSAccess", "System")
  DoEvents
  Results = "Busy"
  StartTime = Timer
  While Results <> "Ready"
    If Timer - StartTime > 100 Then
      MsgBox "Unable to start MSAccess"
      Set MyAccess = Nothing
      DDETerminate Channel_1
      Exit Sub
    End If
    Results = DDERequest(Channel_1, "Status")
  Wend
  On Error Resume Next
  DDEExecute Channel_1, _
    "[OpenDatabase E:\IDGExamp\DDESRVR.MDB]"
```

```
  If Err = 285 Then
    DoEvents
    '
    ' I've got to say this is a bug. We
    ' dropped into this code with a READY
    ' status. It always works the second time
    '
    ChannelsIgnored = ChannelsIgnored + 1
    MsgBox "Restart count is: " & _
      Str$(ChannelsIgnored)
    If ChannelsIgnored < 4 Then
      Set MyAccess = Nothing
      GoTo Restart_DDE
    End If
    MsgBox "Apparent DDE error"
    GoTo Normal_Exit
  End If
  On Error GoTo 0
  strItem = "E:\IDGExamp\DDESRVR.MDB;" & _
    "SQL Select * FROM Inventory;"
  Channel_2 = DDEInitiate("MSAccess", strItem)
  txtOutput = DDERequest(Channel_2, "Data")
Normal_Exit:
  Set MyAccess = Nothing
  Exit Sub
Error_Trap:
  MsgBox Error$
  Resume Normal_Exit
```

concept link

Figure 33-13 illustrates all the DDE examples except the DDEPOke function to a database. All of the examples in Figure 33-13 use DAO 3.0. Listing 33-1 created the data in the lower-right corner of Figure 33-13. You'll find a Visual Basic 5.0 Enterprise Edition project entitled DDECLIENT.VBP and an Access 97 MDB entitled DDESERVER .MDB in the EXAMPLES\CHAPTER33 folder of the CD-ROM that accompanies this book.

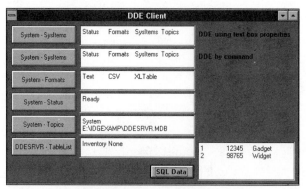

FIGURE 33-13   **DDE examples on the CD-ROM.**

In summary, DDE is not useful with DAO 3.5. It functions most of the time with DAO 3.0 and a second restart appears to be sufficient. DDE is not efficient for large data structures, and one can only guess that support for an older technology is waning.

Dynamic Link Libraries

DLLs in Windows 3.1 can share data directly. File sharing is the recommended technique for data sharing with a DLL in the Win32 API.

A DLL has its own data segment within 16-bit Windows. This housed static and global variables but was limited to 64K. In the Win32 API, both code and data are mapped into the process space and the data space is no longer limited. Each Win32 application maintains a private copy of the DLL data. The data sharing techniques of older style DLLs are no longer viable.

There is only one physical copy of DLL code in Win32 and it is mapped into the user portion of the process address space of many different applications. A DLL mapped in such a manner has an associated usage count that is incremented on a per process basis and decremented when the process exits.

In the Win 3.1 API, a DLL is loaded as a component of the application. This is different in the Win32 API where a DLL is mapped into process space. It may be mapped at a different address in each process that uses the DLL. Each process can use **GetProcAddress** to locate the DLL.

Mailslots

Mailslots offer a one-way interprocess communication capability. Any process can create a mailslot and become a mail server. Other processes (properly called mail-slot clients) gain access to the mailslot by name. Messages can also be sent to the mail server. Messages broadcast within a domain are limited to 400 characters; individual messages are limited to the size specified by the mailslot creator.

Named and Anonymous Pipes

Named pipes can operate between unrelated processes and across a network. The programming operations are simple with reads and writes. Opening a pipe is not difficult. Child processes can inherit attributes of a pipe. Microsoft SQL Server uses named pipes as the primary communication link.

An *anonymous* pipe operates much like a named pipe, but it cannot be used over a network. The common use for an anonymous pipe is for a parent process communication with a child process. The parent process creates the anonymous pipe and the child process inherits the pipe handles. Pipes are typically used by the parent process for redirecting I/O to a child process. An anonymous pipe cannot be used between unrelated processes.

NetBIOS

NetBIOS is useful for porting existing IBM NetBIOS applications to the Windows environment. It is the standard in the personal computing environment and is supported in the three Microsoft transport protocols NBT, NBF, and NWLink. NetBIOS is the oldest of the Microsoft protocols, and as such, there are several variations:

- *NetBEUI* — NetBIOS Extended User Interface, a transport layer protocol base, which includes the original IBM NetBIOS interface.

- *NetBIOS* — A programming interface. Although included with the original NetBEUI, the interface is now used by higher-level programs such as print and file services for protocols other then NetBEUI.

- *NBF* — NetBEUI Frame (enhanced NetBEUI).

o *NBT* — NetBIOS on TCP/IP (see TCP/IP).

o *NWNBLink* — the NetBIOS implementation within NWLink (see NWLink).

Figure 33-14 illustrates NetBIOS in the Windows Architecture.

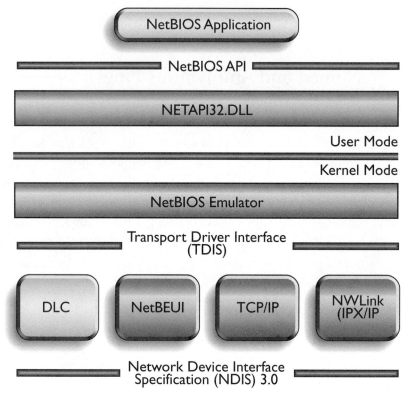

FIGURE 33-14   NetBIOS in the Windows Architecture.

Network Dynamic Data Exchange

Network Dynamic Data Exchange (NetDDE) is an extension of DDE over a NetBIOS-compatible network. The NetDDE server monitors DDE requests looking for an application name that has the form \\<ServerName>\NDDE$. NetDDE is transparent to the DDE application. Only the application name is changed. Figure 33-15 illustrates NetDDE in the Windows architecture.

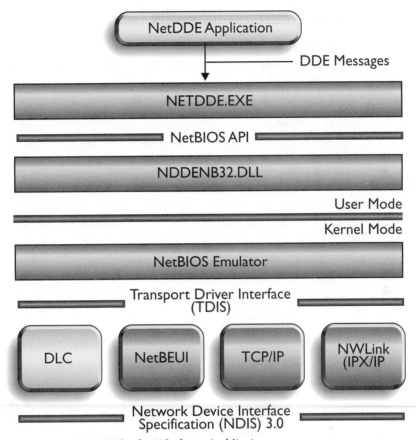

FIGURE 33-15   NetDDE in the Windows Architecture.

Object Link and Embedding

The general topic in the first ten chapters of this book is COM, which includes *Object Linking and Embedding* (OLE). OLE is a technology that manages compound documents. Any file than contains OLE objects is called a *container*. Containers are typically compound documents that consist of linked or embedded objects.

Remote Procedure Calls

Remote procedure call (RPC) work between processes on the same computer or with processes on remote computers. An RPC can be characterized as a "DLL over a network."

Windows Win32 RPC is compliant with the Open Software Foundation's (OSF) Distributed Computing Environment (DCE) initiative. This means that an RPC-enabled application can communicate with foreign systems that are also RPC compliant. RPC automatically supports data conversion between different hardware architectures. The byte ordering differences between the Intel and the RISC architectures are transparent to the RPC application. RPC clients are *tightly coupled*. RPC can be used with Named Pipes, NetBIOS, and Windows Sockets.

Server Message Blocks

The *Server Message Block Protocol* (SMB) was developed jointly by Microsoft, Intel, and IBM. It is the native file-sharing protocol in the Windows 95 and Windows NT operating systems. It is also available on other platforms such as UNIX and VMS. SMB is a layer above the transport protocol, which has four message types:

- *Session control messages* — commands that start and end a redirector connection to a shared resource on a server.

- *File messages* — used by the redirector to gain access to server files.

- *Printer messages* — used to send data to a print queue and obtain print queue status.

- *Message messages* — used for exchanging messages with another workstation.

The *common Internet file system* (CIFS) is an enhanced version of the SMB protocol. CIFS runs over TCP/IP and uses the Internet's global *Domain Naming Service* (DNS) for scalability. Microsoft has submitted the CIFS 1.0 protocol specification to the Internet Engineering Task Force (IETF) as an Internet draft document and is working with interested parties for CIFS to be published as an Informational Request for Comments (RFC). CIFS (SMB) has been an Open Group (formerly X/Open) standard for PC and UNIX interoperability since 1992 (X/Open CAE Specification C209). The SMB protocol provides interoperability between systems such as those listed below. There are many other systems that support SMB and CIFS, but this list suffices to illustrate common interoperability:

o MS OS/2 LAN Manager

o Microsoft Windows for Workgroups

o Microsoft Windows 95

o Microsoft Windows NT

o MS-DOS Lan Manager

o Digital Equipment Corporation Pathworks

o Microsoft LAN manager for UNIX

o 3COM 3+Open

o MS-Net

Shared Memory (File Mapping)

Shared memory is implemented as file mapping in the Win32 API (see Figure 33-16). A process creates a named file on a block of shared memory. Other processes use the same name and either call **CreateFileMapping** or **OpenFile Mapping** to obtain a handle to the file-mapping object. Caution is required because event objects, semaphore objects, mutex objects, and file mapping objects all occupy the same name space. An error occurs when an object of a different class owns the requested name.

The acquired file-mapping handle is passed to **MapViewOfFile**, which maps a file view into the process address space. A view is called coherent when all views are derived from the same *file-mapping object*.

Virtual addresses may vary between processes, and **MapViewOfFileEx** maps the file view to specific addresses.

A mapped file is a block of memory, not a file. Reading or writing is done with **ReadProcessMemory** and **WriteProcessMemory**. Mapped files cannot be accessed from other computers.

Storage pages associated with a mapped file view are sharable and not global. The storage pages are not available to other processes unless the file is mapped. When file mapping is used and sharing isn't desired, the file should be opened for exclusive use and the file handle should be kept open until reading or editing is complete.

tip   A synchronization object such as a semaphore should be used when multiple processes have write access to the shared memory.

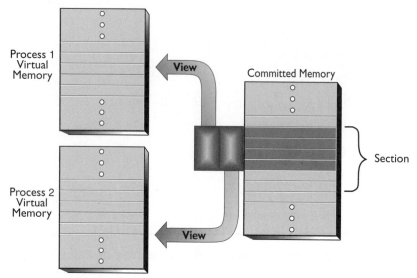

FIGURE 33-16   Shared memory files in the Win32 API.

Sockets

We've been here before (see "Sockets" in the Windows Architecture section earlier in this chapter), but in the context of the WOSA API-SPI model. So you won't be confused, the WOSA Sockets 2.0 version is represented by the WS2_32.DLL, which is the service provider interface, while WINSOCK32.DLL is the application provider interface (API).

Let's take another look at sockets from the API level. Sockets supports RPC and is supported by the TCP/IP and IPX/IP transport protocols. The basis for Windows Sockets is the University of California, Berkeley version. Figure 33-17 illustrates Sockets in the Windows architecture.

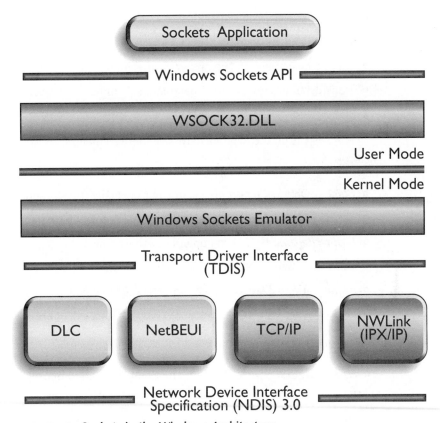

FIGURE 33-17   Sockets in the Windows Architecture.

THE REGISTRY

The Registry was covered extensively in Chapters 1 to 10 on component technology. The following information is a topical review of the essentials.

The Windows Registry is Unicode based and is the repository for all hardware and software configuration parameters. It replaces the older WIN.INI and CONFIG.SYS files of the 16-bit Windows 3.1 system. The benefits of a centralized repository for configuration information include:

- Reduces the likelihood of syntactical errors.
- Uses Control Panel to standardize the user interface.
- Configuration data is secure.
- Provides atomic edits.

- Registry is recoverable after system crashes.
- Tracking and enumerating hardware.
- User-, application-, and computer-related information is separate.
- Track dynamic configuration parameters. Enumerate, track and configure applications, device drivers and operating system parameters.

A key within the Registry may have these elements:

- *Name* — String used to gain access to the key
- *Class* — Optional object class name not normally used by applications
- *Security descriptor* — Optional and normal security inheritances apply
- *Last write time* — Time stamp of last value change
- *Value(s)* — Zero or more pieces of information
- *Name* — Up to 32767 Unicode characters (65534 bytes); Nulls are allowed
- *Type* — Types with values below 0X7FFFFFFF are system reserved

Data entry points in the Windows NT Register include:

- *HKEY_CLASSES_ROOT* — OLE and Shell application information; an alias for `HKEY_LOCAL_MACHINE\SOFTWARE\CLASSES`
- *HKEY_CURRENT_USER* — Defines preferences of the current user
- *HKEY_LOCAL_MACHINE* — Defines system/hardware configuration
- *HKEY_USERS* — Defines the user's current and default configurations; user profiles appear as subtrees; `HKEY_CURRENT_USER` is an alias to the current user

By definition, values in `HKEY_CURRENT_USER` override similar values in `HKEY_LOCAL_MACHINE`.

The Registry API interface is with **RegSaveKey** and **RegLoadKey**. The user can read and write the equivalent of a Windows 3.1 .INI file with the Win32 API functions **GetPrivateProfileString** and **WritePrivateProfileString**. The key is:

```
HKEY_LOCAL_MACHINE\Software\Microsoft\Windows NT\
  CurrentVersion\IniFileMapping
```

`HKEY_LOCAL_MACHINE` has five subkeys: Hardware, Security, SAM, Software, and System. Only the Software and System subkeys are writable by a user.

LOOK MOMMY, THE EMPEROR HAS NO CLOTHES

Penelope and her mother, Gervia, have come to town for the parade. This is Penelope's first parade and she is having a marvelous time. Penelope is about four years old, with an infectious smile and curly brown hair. If you say hello to Penelope, she'll hide behind her mother's skirt. After a few moments she'll peek out at you. Peeking from behind her mother's skirt, Penelope is momentarily distracted as the parade comes into view. Penelope is amazed and inadvertently blurts, "Mommy, the Emperor has no clothes."

The title of this section should tell you that the material here is not on either of the Windows Architecture core examinations. This is not an essay on scatology. What is expressed in this section are my opinions, based on nearly forty years of experience. As I see it, serious flaws exist in the Windows Architecture and Microsoft exacerbates these issues by trying to be all things to all users.

ESTABLISHING MY CREDENTIALS

I suppose a human trait is that we all have 20/20 hindsight. I'm afflicted too; however, critical and objective thinking is always a part of any significant endeavor.

I am approaching 61 years of age and what I say in these few paragraphs is not an ego trip. My value systems have evolved with time, and I'm sure your value systems have also. If nothing else, I may be a bit too confident. I do believe that I have written over a million lines of code in my programming career, and if I haven't, it feels that way.

The window in my career applicable to operating systems is from about 1964 to 1972. This might sound like old technology to you, but it's not. By the late 1960s we had four-ring multiprocessor systems (Windows NT is only two rings, zero and three). The Apollo moon shot used a Univac 1108 Multiprocessor system. We also had features such as reentrant FOR-TRAN where code banks were shared. Compare that to the Windows architecture that didn't get shared code in a DLL until the Win32 API. The operating system used preemptive multitasking and exclusive locks, which were not needed for a unit processor environment.

I am somewhat amused by popular computer book authors who state that their career started with the TRS-80 or the Commodore, and then proceed to call Microsoft technology new. It is not. We had free-threading applications in the early 1970s. Microsoft is currently struggling with this same issue and is using a multiprocessor synchronization object, the mutex, to solve it. That is a brief sketch of the technology of the period. It didn't all exist in the early 1960s, but it certainly existed by 1972, which is when I exited the operating system arena for other software endeavors.

continued

continued

I may be off a year or so in my time frames since this was a long time ago. Until 1964 I was performing operating system maintenance on computers such as a GE 225, Philco 2000, IBM 7094/7044 Hasp system, and a Univac 1107 for Boeing Aerospace Division in Seattle, Washington. In 1964, I was given the project of establishing remote communications between the Boeing Developmental Center and several remote sites. There were other people involved such as the Univac hardware engineers and the Univac 1004 programmer (a remote printer/card reader). I wrote a cross-assembler and linker that ran on the Univac 1107 and used these tools to write my own real-time operating system for a Univac 418, which supported 10 Telpak-A lines (40.8 KB full-duplex). That might not sound like much today, but that was hot stuff 30 years ago. The Univac 418 operating system cross-booted from the Univac 1107. The system was converted to the Univac 1108 in 1965.

Many intervening events occurred, and I was later doing contract work in Huntsville, Alabama, designing wire routing programs for missiles. Univac found me in Huntsville. I was offered double my Boeing salary if I would go to East Hartford, Connecticut, and implement a Boeing-type Univac 1108-418 system for United Aircraft. I did, and when the project was finished, I was on special assignment for a Univac regional vice president. I spent some time on the ill-fated United Airlines project in Chicago, where I wrote some device drivers for Exec VIII, the new Univac operating system. I did find some quirky timing bugs in the 1108 instruction set. My stint in Chicago wasn't long, and I currently admire anyone who lives in Chicago during the winter. Exec VIII was new; there were lots of bugs; and there were no days off. Burnout came quickly. I recall a period of about six months where I would drive to Boston once a week, collect a stack of Exec VIII panic dumps,

and then return to my home in Connecticut where I would work into the wee hours of the morning analyzing octal memory dumps.

My coworkers from Boeing were all at a new startup company in Texas named University Computing Company (UCC). They talked me into coming to Texas, which wasn't difficult because of my unrelenting workload at Univac. However, UCC didn't know what to do with me. I was essentially a staff consultant. I spent most of a year writing my own version of a multiprogrammed operating system for the Univac 1108. Things were going very well for me until one of the owners of the company (and also Richard Nixon's campaign chairman for Texas) sent me a personal letter asking for a $5,000 contribution to Nixon's 1968 campaign fund (I still have the letter somewhere). I didn't contribute the $5,000 and figured my career with UCC was going nowhere. That was the fall of 1968.

By the spring of 1969, I was encamped in Southern California as a computer scientist for Computer Sciences Corporation. The job started very strangely. I was given a small office with somewhere between six and eight feet of system specifications. No one talked to me other than a polite hello. I spent two or three weeks trying to figure out what they were doing. It was a new Univac operating system named CSTS (Computer Sciences Time Sharing).

After about three weeks, I became friendly enough with the programmers in the bullpen to start casual conversations. When I found out what they were doing, I made suggestions. The immediate feedback was: "Yes, Mr. Prendergast." The guys and gals in the bullpen were members of the technical staff (MTS A, MTS B, and MTS C). I was the computer scientist (the company at that time had about 5,000 programmers and only 200 computer scientists, which I found out belatedly was an honor). I had the title, but my self-image was that of the consummate hacker, and I had been expecting to be assigned a programming task. It turns out that my task was to build the complete operating system. I was the computer scientist of the integration group.

At Computer Sciences Corporation there were three groups: engineering, integration, and quality assurance. The rules were simple: engineering built to published specifications, and it was within my authority to refuse any software from engineering. The integration staff built scaffolding for temporary functional support and rolled it out when the line item was delivered. The quality assurance gang took a perverse delight in breaking anything delivered by integration.

Those were the fun days. It was truly Jolt Cola and cold pizza time. Do you recall the panic dumps I used to take home to Connecticut and pore over trying to glean the smallest clue as to why the Exec VIII crashed? I vowed that would never happen again. The host development system for CSTS system was Univac Exec II. It was rolled out and CSTS was booted. I wrote a complete panic analysis routine that identified all the structures and threads, dumped all the stacks, listed the anomalies and suggested the probable cause for failure. The programmers who thought I was invading their turf did not take this very kindly. Eventually they grew to like it. CSTS was completed in the spring of 1972 on schedule and went on to become the standard Department of Defense operating system for more than ten years. It might have lasted longer; however, the very expensive Univac computers were supplanted by minicomputers during the 1980s. Today those minicomputers are being replaced by desktop personal computer systems. I am sorry to say that the apparent engineering standards of today do not approach those we had 25 years ago. When the CSTS project wound down in 1972, many of the staff departing for Digital Equipment Corporation and a new exciting system called RSX. I was humored many years later to see some RSX internals and note that the structure names and notations were strikingly similar to those of CSTS. And now that I've posted my Armchair Quarterback License, let's get on with it.

Mutex Abuse

A locking mechanism must exist for resources that can be accessed from more than one CPU (a symmetric multiprocessor). An interlocking mechanism isn't required for a uniprocessor. The problem is that the mutex is the recommended solution to many software design problems, which are not multiprocessor related.

An interlocking mechanism isn't needed in a uniprocessor environment; it is a question of an architectural design error. The solution to the problem is quite simple: Assign a resource to a priority level appropriate for the resource. A thread executes a **Raise** (it could be an implicit **Drop**) to the priority level of the resource. If no other thread is on the queue to the resource, the requesting thread owns the resource implicitly, because it is the first on the queue and is executing. The thread executes a **Drop** (possibly an implicit **Raise)** when the resource is released, which returns it to the original thread level, causing normal thread scheduling to occur. The resource is protected, no explicit interlocking occurs, and requesters are queued on a first in-first out (FIFO) basis. The resource is still protected.

The following is a Microsoft quote from the Microsoft Developer Network on the use of mutexes:

As already mentioned in the preceding section, NT mutex objects have built-in features that provide system (kernel-mode only) threads mutually exclusive, deadlock-free access to shared resources in SMP machines. Every NT mutex object has two basic built-in features that provide this protection for resources shared between or among system threads:

Ownership

The NT Kernel assigns ownership of a given mutex to a single thread at a time, which has the following effects:

- *Raises the owning thread's runtime priority to the lowest real-time priority if that thread's priority is not already in the real-time range*

- *Prevents the owning thread's process from leaving the balance set: that is, from being paged out to secondary storage*

- *Prevents the delivery of normal kernel-mode asynchronous procedure calls (APCs): that is, from being preempted by an APC unless the Kernel issues an APC_LEVEL software interrupt to run a special kernel APC, such as the I/O Manager's IRP completion routine that returns results to the original requestor of an I/O operation*

What's the problem? None from the documentation; but real practice is not the same. Apparently the apartment-model threading issue of COM objects is to be solved with a mutex within the COM object. Refer to Figure 33-6, the Windows NT priorities and scheduling classes. Note that the classes *High*, *Normal Foreground*, *Normal background*, and *Idle* all have a common real-time range. The following quote is offered from *Inside COM* (Microsoft Press, 1997), which was written by a Visual C++ development team member:

Free threads are created and managed with the usual Win32 threading functions, such as CreateThread, ResumeThread, WaitForMultipleObjects, WaitForSingleObject, CreateMutex, and CreateEvent. Using the standard threading objects, such as mutexes, critical sections, and semaphores, you protect access to your component's internal data, making the component thread safe.

Enough said about the mutex. It is obvious that the Windows architecture is being corrupted when a Kernel-level SMP synchronization object is used to solve a user-level programming issue. Windows NT 4.0 supports free-threading; however, apartment-model threads are the default. It appears a component-based architecture reverts to one basic priority: real-time.

Alas poor mutex, I knew him well (my apology to Shakespeare).

Unreliability of Windows NT 4.0

Reliability is not quite the same with Windows NT 4.0. GDI, and printer drivers have been moved into the Kernel. Yes, there is a performance enhancement, but it is only an apparent enhancement. I say it is an *apparent* improvement because it improves response time to the user who is using the system on an interactive basis. The same benefits could have been realized by upgrading the hardware.

Moore's Law is a rule of thumb that computer performance will double every 12 to 18 months. Moore's Law is still with us today; and I doubled the apparent performance of my own personal system by uprading my video card.

The problem that exists now is that a faulty GDI or printer driver will crash an entire operating system. Microsoft states that duplication of software functionality and the difficulty of software component management are the primary reasons for this architectural change. The change was made to make life easier for Microsoft programmers without considering what effect a reduction in reliability of the product has within corporate America. Microsoft has reverted Windows NT to the level of older Novell systems, where a Netware Loadable Module (NLM) was sent to Novell to be certified before being loaded into a Novell network. Any failure in an NLM run in Kernel mode on ring zero corrupts the complete operating system.

The following statement is from a Microsoft white paper:

Dave Leinweber, Mark Ryland, Microsoft Corporation April 1996

However, this design was leading to a large amount of duplication of system functions that, ultimately, would have negatively affected both system size and performance.

System size? A non-issue. I can buy 64MB of memory for $200 and a 3.5GB hard disk for $179. Performance? No, Moore's Law still prevails. These are words you probably would expect to come from me since I come from an era where memory prices could approach hundreds of thousands of dollars. These are very lame excuses for providing a significantly lower level of reliability to Windows NT 4.0, which is now dependent upon third-party device drivers.

These words are difficult to swallow in light of the fact that Microsoft sells *Source Safe* as a tool for managing software. The sad fact is that duplicity of functionality is precisely what you do want. Legacy systems had this with a system library and a user library. It was a feature that added to the immutability of both the operating system and the application. One of the largest design gaffes of the Windows architecture is that both the application and the operating system share the same library. Two libraries provide an implicit firewall.

COM Has Two Contracts

Windows NT 4.0 is less reliable than prior versions. Microsoft introduced DCOM with NT 4.0. Microsoft's complete future is predicated by components. The future does not look bright, even though the software is very clever. Consider that a component application has an increased volume and interface complexity. Increasing either of these automatically increases the probability of a software anomaly (or bug). But there is something worse than implicitly increasing the volume and complexity of an application. It deals with the very roots of COM and the concepts of aggregation and delegation.

The COM model will *never* be reliable because the client is always exposed to new code even though the new features are not used directly. Compare this to a legacy library. The closest a production application comes to new library features is that they may coexist on the same disk. Legacy applications such as FORTRAN and COBOL have a feature that is often overlooked. This is the immutability of the application. The application is a binary mass. (I have clients who have legacy programs that haven't been compiled in years.) COM has an immutable interface and that's all. Microsoft touts this interface as a contract with the client. Indeed, it is a contract, but you don't know who owns the contract today, and you can be sure the contract will be sold tomorrow (which is done though the coding mechanism of aggregation or delegation). The selling of the interface contract appears to be itself a Machiavellian contract with Mephistopheles, because the interface contract is promised to be resold forever. The poor unsuspecting COM client does not know whether the new contract owner is malevolent or benevolent, hence the continuing unreliability of COM.

If you think issues are muddled now, they will get worse. As I type this, COM+ is in the wings. I know nothing about it except for a news release that stated that it uses object inheritance. What happened to aggregation and delegation? The

Microsoft implementation architecture certainly appears to be confused. Stay tuned to the Microsoft channel for your next adventure in code-soup. This is CodeMan signing off for now, wishing bits and bytes to y'all!

KEY POINT SUMMARY

This chapter is a broad-brush view of the Windows architecture. We've looked at platforms, operating systems, protocols, and interprocess communication. In each area, the Microsoft architecture offers alternatives. Microsoft is trying to maintain a consistent unified interface with the WOSA initiative. Some efforts are not as successful as others, but the effort is there.

- The Windows architecture represents the first distributed operating system.
- All the popular transport protocols are represented in the Windows architecture. Microsoft has enhanced some of the protocols such as the direct hosting feature of NWNBLink. Not to be overlooked are important tools such as DHCP.
- Numerous IPC mechanisms exist. It is only a question of pick-and-choose. An RPC can be used for heterogeneous interconnection or memory files for process to process communication.
- Managing a Windows system is standardized with a Registry. All hardware and software configuration parameters are maintained there. This is also the repository of COM registrations.

APPLYING WHAT YOU'VE LEARNED

These questions will measure your understanding of the material in this chapter. The most important issue is to select the right technology for the task. This includes the proper selection of a platform, an operating system, the appropriate protocol, and an interprocess communication mechanism.

Instant Assessment

1. Name three major issues to consider when deciding between Windows NT workstation and Windows 95.

2. Explain the difference between a DLL in Windows 3.1 and a Win32 DLL (either Windows 95 or Windows NT).

3. Explain how the virtual memory manager (VMM) allocates task memory.

4. What is committed memory and how is it acquired?

5. What is the primary limitation with DDE?

6. What is the difference between a process and a thread?

7. What is a new limitation of Windows NT workstation 4.0?

8. Which protocol stack is necessary for your application to use FTP?

9. Describe thread scheduling in Windows NT.

concept link **For answers to the Instant Assessment questions, see Appendix C.**

Lab Exercises

Lab 33.61 takes a look at some of the issues of protocol performance. It illustrates the differences in architecture between the IPX/SPX protocols and the NetBIOS protocol, which affects performance.

Lab 33.55 *Direct hosting*

WA I

Microsoft states that a client-initiated direct hosting session between Windows NT computers yields a twenty percent increase in performance. This overhead reduction occurs when the NetBIOS layer at the server is bypassed and the client connects directly to the redirector. This laboratory requires a Windows NT server and two Windows 95 clients. The Windows NT server protocol stack must be configured for both the NWLink NetBIOS protocol and the NWLink IPX/SPX protocol. To install these protocols, refer to your Windows NT Server installation procedures.

The client may be a Windows 95 or Windows for Workgroups system (Windows NT Server and Windows NT workstation cannot direct host). The client computer is configured for only the NWLink IPX/SPX protocol. Direct hosting occurs automatically between Windows 95 clients where NetBIOS over IPX is not necessary. To test direct hosting:

1. Unselect *I Want To Enable NetBIOS Over IPX/SPX* in the NetBIOS tab of the IPX/SPX protocol properties dialog box for the two Win95 client systems. Transfer large files between these two Windows 95 systems and measure their performance. These systems will always be in direct hosting mode.

2. Transfer these same files between a Windows 95 system and a Windows NT Server that has the NWLink NetBIOS protocol and not the NWLink IPX/SPX protocol on the protocol stack. The server should be dedicated for this test and will be much slower than the Windows 95-to-Windows 95 test.

3. Add the NWLink IPX/SPX protocol to the server protocol stack and repeat the test. The performance should approach that of the Windows 95-to-Windows 95 test.

Lab 33.56 *Verifying proper Registry usage*

WA I

This lab exercise verifies proper Registry usage. What we'll do is verify that the programs on the Desktop (a supporting icon) are registered within the Registry. An installed application should appear under the key:

```
HKEY_CURRENT_USER\Software\<Company>\Application\<version>\
   <settings>
```

The exercise starts by identifying those companies with products on the Desktop. The company name should appear in the Registry. For example, this system has the following registry key:

```
HKEY_CURRENT_USER\Software\Microsoft\Access\7.0\<settings>
```

This Registry entry states that Access 95 is installed. When you do not find a Registry entry for the product in question that has an icon on the Desktop, the application was installed incorrectly. Search your Registry for the installed applications.

Lab 33.57 *Identifying architectural differences*

WA I

We know that Windows 95 supports the Double Byte Character Set (DBCS) and the Single Byte Character Set (SBCS). SBCS is a fancy name for the ANSI character set we've had for approximately 30 years. Windows NT supports Unicode; Windows 95 does not. All 32-bit tools, such as Access and Visual Basic, also support Unicode. This means that a 32-bit tool such as Visual Basic converts characters to ANSI when passing them to a DLL and converts the characters back to Unicode when returning them.

The lab exercise requires an older tool, Microsoft Access 2.0. The purpose is to measure the overhead of Unicode and the impact on performance. The exercise consists of the following steps:

1. Write an algorithm that creates a very large text file using Access Basic of Access 2.0. You can use a random number generator to create the characters. Write these characters to a file.

2. Within either Visual Basic 4/0/5.0 or Access 95/97, use the same algorithm to create another file. Make sure the file has the same number of records. Compare file sizes when complete. Are they equal. Why or why not?

Lab 33.58 *Visual Basic is selfish with memory*

WA I

This lab exercise demonstrates memory management. What we'll do is we'll watch as the working set of a Visual Basic project expands with page faults as a project is loaded. However, when we select **Remove Project** from the Visual Basic File menu, the working set does not return to the original size. It might on your system when you have other processes in operation. Use these steps for repeating this exercise on your system:

1. Start Visual Basic 5.0. (Don't load a project yet.)

2. Size Visual Basic so that at least a third of the screen is free.

3. Start Windows NT performance monitor.

4. Size the Performance Monitor and Visual Basic so both screens are visible.

5. While in Windows NT Performance Monitor set:

   o For *Object,* select **Process** and **Working Set**

   o For *Instance,* select **VB5**

   o Select **ADD**

6. You should see a straight line as Windows NT Performance Monitor starts. With both Visual Basic 5.0 and Windows NT Performance monitor visible, load a project in Visual Basic. The working set grows as the project is loaded.

7. After the working set is loaded, select **Remove Project** from the **File** menu. The working set does not shrink, but it may shrink on a very active system.

Lab 33.59 *Visual Basic is stingy with threads*

This lab exercise looks at thread scheduling. Like the previous lab, this exercise uses Windows NT Performance Monitor. It also uses Microsoft SQL Server. The application is found on the CD-ROM that accompanies this book and is the Visual Basic 5.0 CHAPTER25.VBP project located in the EXAMPLES\CHAPTER25 folder. To repeat this lab exercise on your system, do the following:

1. Start SQL Server.
2. Start Visual Basic 5.0.
3. Load and start the CHAPTER25.VBP project. Size the Visual Basic window for enough room for Windows NT Performance Monitor.
4. Start Windows NT Performance Monitor and set:
   o For *Object* select **Process** and **Thread Count**
   o For *Instance* select **VB5**
   o Select **ADD**
5. Start the Visual Basic project
6. With both the Windows NT Performance Monitor and the CHAPTER25.VBP project visible, select different command buttons from the application window. You will see the thread count increase and then decrease as the application starts and finishes execution.

Lab 33.60 *Can you handle both Unicode and DBCS?*

DBCS or ANSI is the Windows 95 character set. DBCS is used in the Far East, whereas Windows NT uses Unicode. The problem is your management cannot decide in which country to market the new software system. You realize that your software must support both Unicode and the DBCS. Can you do it? Write string manipulation code that will handle either DBCS or Unicode. You'll find all the information you need in the Visual Basic online documentation. Just don't read this lab exercise and move on. There are examination questions on this topic!

Lab 33.61 *Should you keep that DOS box?*

The Win32 API supports a character based I/O interface for character-mode applications. This lab exercise is a hypothetical evaluation of converting character-mode applications to a Win32 environment while maintaining a character-mode interface. Isn't hardware cheaper than software development time? Take an existing DOS application and justify converting the application to the 32-bit environment while maintaining the character-mode interface. It reminds me of an IBM 1401 that was emulated on an IBM 360, that was emulated on an IBM 370, and the list goes on. Isn't it a matter of accepting the paradigm shift? Why not keep a box dedicated to DOS applications?

Lab 33.62 *Secure TAPI links*

WA I
WA II

Consider the requirements for an application that provides secure telephone links. The application will use both TAPI and CryptoAPI. Is such an application practical? It certainly isn't with Plain Old Telephone Service (POTS), which is analog. TAPI does support the Internet protocol. You'll want to also use the Speech API (SAPI). This application will give you secure conversations over the Internet.

Lab 33.63 *Incorporating LSAPI in an application*

WA I
WA II

The goal of this lab exercise is to build a component that may be incorporated in applications, which makes them LSAPI-enabled. The concept of a component reduces the problem of including specific code in an application. As a hint, see the Microsoft Developer Network (MSDN) article entitled *How to Incorporate the LSAPI in an Application*.

Windows Architecture I

Choosing Development Tools

About Chapter 34

C hapter 34 is about choosing the right product and the right tool for the task. Developers have a propensity to define an application solution in terms of the tool with which they have the most familiarity. An Access developer inevitably suggests an Access solution, and a Microsoft Foundation Class (MFC) developer will propose an MFC solution.

This chapter is about three Microsoft product suites: Microsoft BackOffice, Microsoft Office, and Microsoft Visual Studio. The first of these suites is an aggregation of products purchased individually, while the remaining two suites are collections of products purchased collectively.

MICROSOFT BACKOFFICE

Welcome to the Microsoft BackOffice. As the name implies, these products are tools for the enterprise. BackOffice products support high connectivity (that is, many clients). BackOffice products represent gateways to enterprise resources from Microsoft Office clients.

Windows NT Server

Microsoft Windows NT Server is a powerful enterprise network server operating system with multiple platform support. It features integrated utilities and protocols for heterogeneous connections to other enterprise resources. Features of Windows NT Server include:

o *Multiple-platform support* — Currently supported on the Digital Equipment Corporation Alpha and the Intel 80386, 80486, and Pentium class platforms. (The MIPS, R4000, and R4400 platforms are no longer supported.) NT Server can be a uniprocessor or a symmetric multiprocessor supporting up to eight central processing units (CPUs). Redundant array of independent disks (RAID) 1 and RAID 5 are supported along with clustering. Clustering provides node failover and is a recent addition to the Microsoft Windows NT architecture. Clustering complements RAID 5, which provides disk drive redundancy with "hot-swappable drives," which are rebuilt automatically.

- *An enterprise server* — Windows NT Server is the host for other applications such as Exchange Server, SQL Server, Systems Management Server, SNA Server, Proxy Server, Transaction Server, Merchant Server, Internet Information Server, and Index Server.

- *Enterprise management* — Windows NT Server administration tools let the system administrator manage the entire network from a computer running Windows 3.1, Windows 95, Windows for Workgroups 3.1*x*, Windows NT Workstation, and Windows NT Server. Management features include domain control capability, trust capabilities, centralized user profiles, and directory replication. Systems Management Server (SMS) is a tool for managing a network of hardware and software from a single location.

- *Enterprise connectivity* — The protocols TCP/IP, NWLink IPX/SPX, NetBEUI, AFP, and DLC support enterprise connectivity. Higher level connectivity is provided with remote procedure calls (RPC) conforming to industry standards. Remote access is available using X.25, ISDN, or plain old telephone service (POTS). Services for the Macintosh provide connectivity with Apple systems. Migration tools are available for Microsoft LAN Manager and NetWare. The Open Database Connectivity (ODBC) protocol is used for connection to heterogeneous databases.

Figure 34-1 illustrates Windows NT Server 4.0 hosting Microsoft BackOffice enterprise tools. The BackOffice family products are discussed in the sections that follow. Note that all products are Internet/intranet related except SQL Server, SNA Server, and Systems Management Server.

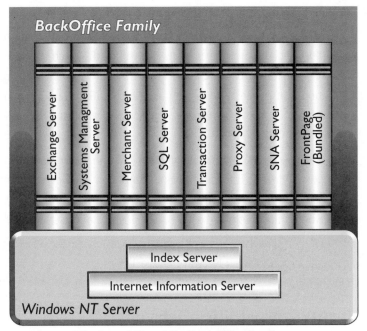

FIGURE 34-1   Windows NT and the BackOffice family.

Exchange Server

Microsoft Exchange Server replaces Microsoft Mail with a product designed specifically for the Internet/intranet. It is not a rewrite of prior technology; it's a new product. Exchange Server is accessible using the Microsoft Exchange client, the Microsoft Outlook 97 desktop information manager, a Web browser, or an Internet newsreader. Exchange Server supports the messaging and collaboration standards X.400, X.500, and messaging application programming interface (MAPI). Exchange Server also supports nearly all of the standard Internet protocols including SMTP, POP3, NNTP, LDAP, HTTP, HTML, and SSL. Supported protocols include:

- *SMTP* — Simple Mail Transport Protocol
- *HTTP* — Hypertext Transport Protocol
- *HTML* — Hypertext Markup Language
- *TCP/IP* — Transmission Control Protocol/Internet Protocol
- *POP3* — Post Office Protocol version 3 as specified in Request for Comment (RFC) 1725

- *NNTP*— Network News Transport Protocol

- *LDAP*— Lightweight Directory Access Protocol over TCP/IP connections. LDAP supports directory operations such as read, search, add, and remove. LDAP is a derivative of the CCITT X.500 Directory Access Protocol (DAP). LDAP does not support the session or presentation layers of the open systems interconnect (OSI) model resulting in reduced overhead. DAP supports the OSI model.

- *SSL*— Secure Sockets Layer, which encrypts Internet connection messages. Microsoft Internet Information Server, NetScape Commerce Server, NetScape Enterprise Server, and O'Reilly WebSite support SSL. Secure hyperlinks begin with `https://` instead of the standard `http://`.

- *IPX/SPX*— Internetwork packet exchange/sequenced packet exchange protocols used in Novell NetWare networks

Internet Information Server

Microsoft's *Internet Information Server* (IIS) is a built-in Web server within Windows NT Server 4.0 and is the key component in the Microsoft Internet architecture. It is not supported on Windows NT Server versions prior to NT server 4.0. It is not a separate product and is integral to Windows NT Server. IIS installs and runs as a native Windows NT service. This tight integration with Windows NT Server provides several advantages:

- Integrated with Windows NT Server 4.0 directory and security services
- Support for open development solutions
- Access to BackOffice components
- Integration with existing databases

IIS supports the *Internet Server API* (ISAPI). IIS supports database programmability with the *Internet database connector* (IDC) and active server pages created from Microsoft Visual InterDev. Active HTML is the newest technology to be supported by IIS. IIS still supports both NCSA and CERN-style image map files, which facilitates porting from UNIX systems.

IIS supports active server pages, Visual Basic Script, and JScript, and is compatible with any scripting engine supporting Perl, REXX, or Python.

Index Server

Index Server is a free, downloadable component of Windows NT Server 4.0. It is also defined as a component of Microsoft BackOffice Server. Index Server supports HTML, text, and all Microsoft Office documents in their native format. Index Server automatically builds an index of your Web server that is easily searched from any Web browser.

Index Server automatically indexes the full text and properties of files on your server, whether it is an intranet, an Internet, or simply a file-and-print server. Index Server allows you to search all of your Web documents, including Microsoft Word and Microsoft Excel. Built-in database connectivity enables easy access to your data from any browser.

Index Server uses content filters, which are associated with individual document formats, to extract the textual information contained within a native document format. Content filters comply with the component object model (COM) **IFilter** interface specifications published by Microsoft. Software authors expose their contents to Index Server by writing a content filter.

Index Server supports browsing by network administrators, Webmasters, and end users. Searching is facilitated by full-text indexing, query by properties, wildcard with expression matching, customizable forms, and logical combinations of each. Index Server goes to the document level and beyond, whereas other Web Servers only search at the HTML page level. Index Server accomplishes the indexing as a background process and requires no user input. Minimum demands are made of system resources.

FrontPage

FrontPage is unique in that it is an end user Web authoring tool for quickly creating Web pages that is also defined as a component of Microsoft BackOffice Server. It is bundled with BackOffice Server.

We discuss FrontPage in more detail in Chapter 36, where we look at the issues of building a Web page with FrontPage.

Proxy Server

A *Proxy Server* is not a Web server. It is a buffer between the local network and the Internet. Requests are forwarded from a client machine inside a firewall to a remote server outside the firewall. A network administrator controls both inbound and outbound connections. Controlling the port number and Internet protocol (IP) domain is the common method of limiting access. Limiting services to clients is another administrator option. Firewall traffic is logged and alarms are activated upon attempted breaches.

The economic advantages include caching at the Proxy Server, which reduces demands made on the local Internet service provider (ISP). The Proxy Server also reduces the number of Internet connection points.

Features of Proxy Server include:

- Compliance with the CERN-proxy standard
- Support for WinSock Proxy
- Support for Secure Sockets Layer
- Support for Internet relay chat (IRC) as defined in Request for Comments (RFC) 1459
- Support for Transmission Control Protocol/Internet Protocol (TCP/IP) and IPX/SPX transport protocol
- Tight integration with the Windows NT Server networking, security, and administrative interface
- SMTP
- LDAP
- RealAudio (streaming audio)
- RealVideo (streaming video)

Transaction Server

The Microsoft Windows architecture fostered the client-server architecture that started in the early 1990s. Unfortunately, the client-server architecture, although promising huge rewards, has not delivered. Yes, there are client-server success stories, but on closer look many of these applications were never good candidates for a mainframe implementation. *Computerworld* magazine regularly reports client-server project failure rates in excess of 70 percent. The causes of failure are categorized as the project was too costly; the project failed to deliver the required functionality; and the end result was operationally too slow. Microsoft Transaction

Server (MTS) attempts to address these issues with a scalable architecture and reduced complexity.

The client-server system failures are of the two-tier variety: a client and a server. This architecture is not scalable because each client requires a server connection. Moving to a larger server does not always solve the problem because this increases the contention for resources within the server. Required connection resources to SQL Server are an example. Each client requires 37KB. The server becomes massive in terms of physical resources, and the system is deemed a failure because of the exorbitant costs.

Transaction Server addresses this issue with a tiered architecture. The architecture is divided into three layers: the first layer is the presentation services to the client; the second layer is the business rules; and the third layer is the data object. This architecture is scalable because individual clients no longer have direct connections to the database. Scaling up this architecture involves a larger database, but it also involves the deploying of additional middle-tier business objects which are essentially commodity level. Scaling costs are reduced significantly.

MTS also addresses the issue of excessive development costs. MTS does this by providing all the necessary plumbing (resource management such as threads, buffers, and synchronization objects) of an application server. The developer creates a standalone component and installs the component in MTS. The plumbing is added automatically. An example is the transparency of transaction support to the developer because MTS integrates with Microsoft Distributed Transaction Coordinator, which was first delivered with SQL Server 6.5.

note **MTS supports any tool that produces an ActiveX dynamic link library (DLL). This includes Visual C++, Visual Basic, and Visual J++. MTS is heterogeneous in the enterprise and supports HTTP from a browser and distributed COM (DCOM) over a network.**

Merchant Server

Merchant Server is a Web server specifically designed for Internet commerce. Clients connect to the Web side, browse for production information, select items for purchase, and purchase them. Merchant Server is compatible with any standard browser, and purchases are permitted only if their browser supports secure transactions.

Merchant Server requires Windows NT Server 3.51 or later, and SQL Server 6.5 or later can be used for database management. Other relational databases such as Oracle may be used if they support Open Database Connectivity (ODBC) 2.5 or higher. A feature of Merchant Server is its capability to create Web pages on-the-fly. This lets the merchandiser target customer segments, spotlight featured products, and provide up-to-the-minute pricing.

SQL Server

Microsoft SQL Server is a relational database management system (RDBMS) that conforms to SQL92 specifications. It supports all Windows operating system protocols such as TCP/IP, SPX/IPX, and NetBIOS Extended User Interface Protocol (NetBEUI). It is a robust RDBMS with a transaction log to ensure data recovery.

SQL Server supports replication to other databases. Replication can be scheduled or done manually. It need not be a complete table. SQL Server Enterprise Manager (SEM) allows graphical management of multiple SQL Servers. Enterprise management of SQL Server sites can also be done using automation and SQL-DMO. SQL Server supports the transaction properties of atomicity, consistency, integrity, and durability (ACID). SQL Server also supports transaction isolation levels. SQL Server is always the choice for mission-critical applications. Microsoft Access does not support ACID properties of a transaction and is too often used for mission-critical applications.

SQL Server functions in either a two-tier or a three-tier architecture as an enterprise database or as a backing database for a Web page. It supports applications with local stored procedures.

Systems Management Server

SMS is an inventory and control system for both hardware and software in the enterprise. From a single location network administrators can inventory resources, deploy software, troubleshoot problems, reconfigure systems, provide help-desk services, provide one-on-one training, and run diagnostics. SMS supports unattended upgrades from a central location. SMS requires SQL server as a repository for inventory information.

SMS is deployed over a network with the TCP/IP Simple Network Management Protocol (SNMP). Events in a Windows NT event log may be forwarded to other systems such as HP OpenView or IBM NetView via a SNMP trap.

SMS supports Windows 3.1, Windows 95, Windows for Workgroups 3.11, Windows NT Workstation 3.5 or later, MS-DOS 5.0 and later, IBM OS/2 2.*x* and OS/2 Warp, and Macintosh System 7.

System Network Architecture Server

SNA Server is the Microsoft architecture's gateway to the IBM world of DB2 relational databases on an IBM mainframe or AS/400. C2 security is extended to SNA data. SNA Server runs on any Windows NT Server version 3.5 or later.

SNA Server is easily managed with a NetView console. Windows NT alerts are supplied as events in the NetView console, and users can issue any Windows NT command from the NetView console. Networking options include Novell Netware, Banyan Vines, IBM LAN Server, and TCP/IP-based networks.

MICROSOFT OFFICE

Microsoft Office is a collection of desktop tools represented by Access, Binder, Excel, Outlook, PowerPoint, and Word. Each of these products is discussed briefly in the following sections. Microsoft Project is discussed in this section even though it is not considered to be a member of Microsoft Office.

An object model represents all of these tools, which leads to a second definition of Microsoft Office as a collection of objects that represents all the aforementioned tools. For example, the **Application** object is the top object in the hierarchy of each of these tools. All tools support Visual Basic for Applications (VBA). Tight application integration is a reality, with VBA common to all tools and with each tool represented by an object model.

Access

Microsoft Access 97 is a 32-bit, multithreaded, Internet-enabled, relational database management system for personal or desktop use. Access is rich with tools and wizards, and the Access Jet 3.5 Engine hosts the Rushmore query optimizer. Access also features Structured Query Language (SQL) with SQL89, SQL92, and Microsoft enhancements. Jet 3.5 also ships with Excel, Visual Basic, and Visual C++.

Access Basic has been replaced with VBA, which is a superset of Access Basic. All tools in the Microsoft Office framework now support VBA. Code written for Excel may be used without change in Visual Basic or Access. The Jet Database Engine provides referential integrity, inner and outer joins, and an object interface, known as data access objects (DAO). DAO is accessible to any tool that supports VBA.

Access can now be used as both an automation server and an automation controller. Before Access 95, Access was limited to the singular role of automation controller. This means that DAO and all of Microsoft Access are now accessible to programmers from outside the Microsoft Access development environment. Any application supporting VBA can now be an automation controller using DAO. Access reports can now be created and printed from tools such as Excel or Visual Basic.

Database replication is supported beginning with Access 95. Complete databases can be replicated to departments. Such an environment provides redundancy and distributes the workload. Jet database replication is not available to either Visual C++ or Excel. An additional restriction is that briefcase replication is only available to Access.

Microsoft Access is a very rich and powerful application development tool. Its greatest shortcoming is that applications are too easy to develop, hence the issue of developing an application before the issue is understood. This isn't a handicap when Access is used as a prototyping tool.

Access is not the product of choice for mission-critical applications. Access supports transactions, but it does not support transaction isolation levels or the ACID properties discussed previously.

Binder

Microsoft Binder is an organization tool. It is a component of Office 97 and is used to group documents. Word documents and Excel spreadsheets are examples of two documents that can be bound together. Either the Word document or the Excel spreadsheet is editable from Binder. This paradigm enhances Microsoft's docu-centric approach of dealing with the issues and not the supporting infrastructure.

 note **Binder does not support VBA although Binder objects can be built with VBA. Binder is Internet enabled.**

Excel

Microsoft Excel is a spreadsheet tool that uses an object-oriented model and supports VBA. Like Access, Excel is both an automation controller and an automation server. Excel can use DAO objects, and Excel objects can be manipulated by Access. Excel does not solve specific problems, but is a tool used in numerous industries for general problem-solving. Excel is supported on the Windows, Windows NT, and Macintosh platforms. Excel 97 is Internet enabled.

Outlook

Outlook 97 is a personal information manager that supports VBA and that is Internet enabled. It supports these features:

o *InBox* — An inbox for e-mail. Messages can be received at home, on the road, and at work. Outlook is a client of Microsoft Exchange Server.

o *Calendar* — Personal time scheduling with the tools Data Navigator and TaskPad.

o *Contacts* — A business and personal contact address book.

o *ToDo* — Both a business and a personal tasks to-do lists. Tasks can be prioritized and assigned.

o *Journaling* — History tracking of any activity on a timeline basis.

o *Notes* — The electronic equivalent of sticky notes.

o *Editor* — An installation selection offers the choice of Microsoft Word as the e-mail editor.

PowerPoint

Microsoft PowerPoint is a slide presentation tool. PowerPoint 97 supports VBA and is Internet enabled. ActiveX can be embedded directly on a slide. PowerPoint 97 supports an object model. PowerPoint objects may be created and properties set from any tool supporting VBA.

Project

Microsoft Project is a task-scheduling tool. Tasks are entered with a start date and duration. Tasks can be designated as recurring. Data is entered into a Gantt chart but can be displayed in Pert chart format. Milestones can be set and changed, and tasks can be deleted. Project 4.1 supports VBA. Project 98 has not yet shipped but is expected to be Internet enabled.

Word

Word shouldn't need too much of an introduction. It is the oldest member of Microsoft Office. Word 97 supports an object model and VBA; prior versions supported WordBasic. Word 97 is Internet enabled and can be integrated with other products that support the document paradigm. For example, all preliminary illustrations for this book were created with VISIO, a third-party drawing tool, and embedded in the preliminary version of the manuscript.

MICROSOFT VISUAL STUDIO

Microsoft Visual Studio 97 is an aggregation of the Microsoft Visual tools set. Visual Studio includes Visual Basic 5.0, Visual C++ 5.0, Visual J++ 1.1, Visual InterDev, and Visual FoxPro. The Enterprise Edition adds Visual SourceSafe 5.0, SQL Server 6.5 Developer Edition, and Transaction Server Developer Edition.

SQL Server

(See Microsoft BackOffice.)

Transaction Server

(See Microsoft BackOffice.)

Visual Basic

Visual Basic is the workhorse of the Microsoft tools set. It does not support the object-oriented paradigm of either FoxPro or Visual C++. It has roots in the original Basic of Kemeny and Kurtz of the mid-1960s. The first Microsoft product was a Basic compiler so it is natural that Visual Basic is its scripting flagship.

The latest version of Visual Basic supports callback functions, a feature previously limited to Visual C++, the output is complied, and it creates ActiveX components.

Visual Basic is the de facto scripting tool for the Windows architecture. ActiveX components inserted into Microsoft Transaction Server automatically become multiuser objects. Another Microsoft tool, Microsoft Visual Modeler, automatically creates the necessary Visual Basic components of a three-tiered architecture. The developer describes the entities and their properties, and the code is generated automatically.

Visual C++

Visual C++ is the second oldest language in the Microsoft language inventory. The predecessors to Visual C++ are a long line of C compilers. There are assembly languages, but Visual C++ is as close as you can get to gun metal in the current architecture. Visual C++ is a very rich language and is the underlying machinery for all of the Microsoft architecture. Visual C++ is the language of choice for concurrency control and threading issues. Some applications may function well with Visual Basic; however, Visual C++ is the language of choice for mission critical applications. Prove the concept with Visual Basic and implement an enterprise solution with Visual C++. Only Visual C++ and Visual FoxPro support object-oriented programming. Visual C++ supports Visual SourceSafe.

Visual FoxPro

Microsoft Visual FoxPro maintains a link with the older dBASE file systems and at the same time occupies a niche at the high end of the professional developers market. Visual FoxPro is only one of two Microsoft products supporting object-oriented programming — Visual C++ being the other.

Visual FoxPro is completely integrated into the Microsoft architecture and supports Visual SourceSafe and other Microsoft Office tools for integrated solutions. A developer extends Visual FoxPro by creating ActiveX automation servers. Solutions are not limited to Microsoft Office and can be Internet based.

Visual InterDev

Visual InterDev is the newest Microsoft tool. It automates the process of creating a Web page. Visual InterDev creates active server pages, simplifying the task of creating database-driven Web applications. The tool has numerous database wizards and programmable data access components. The tool is powerful enough to give credence to the concept of a "17-year-old Web master." The tool creates hundreds, possibly thousands, of lines of code automatically. Visual InterDev can be integrated with Visual SourceSafe.

Visual InterDev works in concert with the Microsoft Front Page 97 Web authoring tool. Database access is added to a Web page created by Front Page 97. The limitation is that once Visual InterDev incorporates a control design time (DTC) into the Web page, Front Page 97 can no longer edit it. Front Page 98 addresses this issue.

Visual J++

Visual J++ is the Microsoft implementation of the Sun JAVA language. It is loosely classified as a C++ derivative. J++ does not, however, have the ambiguous language constructs of C++.

An application can be constructed in pure Java and can run on any platform that supports a Java virtual machine. Visual J++ is one of three Microsoft tools available for building ActiveX components. (The other two tools are Visual Basic and C++.) Java is the glue of choice for multiple-platform deployment.

Visual SourceSafe

Visual SourceSafe is a document management tool from Microsoft. It is a project-oriented version control tool that performs the role of librarian, historian, security guard, and custodian of computer files. Files may be checked out with up to 64 characters describing the reason for the check out. Check-in comments are limited to 32K.

SourceSafe maintains the master copy. By default, files are checked out to single users. The default may be changed, permitting more than one user at the same time. Read-only privileges are maintained where necessary for security.

Visual SourceSafe supports any type of file, text or binary, created in Access, Visual FoxPro, Visual Test, Visual Basic, or Visual C++.

SourceSafe supports modular or object-oriented structures. Files can be organized into an unlimited hierarchy to support new versions, maintenance of existing versions, or new projects. Files may be shared between projects.

CHOOSING A DEVELOPMENT TOOL

This is a quick review of topics relating to the Microsoft tools set. This is a useful guide for the Windows Architecture I examination.

- *Access* — A desktop database management system well suited to non-mission-critical applications. Database ACID properties and transaction isolation levels are not supported. The richness of the Access tool set makes it an ideal prototyping tool. Access supports VBA, but the output is not compiled.

- *ActiveX* — Visual J++, Visual C++, and Visual Basic can create an ActiveX control. Access, Excel, and Visual FoxPro cannot create an ActiveX control.

- *Binder* — A component of Microsoft Office that organizes documents. Documents can be edited from Binder. Binder does not support VBA or the Internet, but the tools creating the documents support VBA and the Internet.

- *CallBack* — Visual Basic 5.0 now supports the concept of a callback function with the **AddressOf** method. Previously this functionality was limited to Visual C++.

- *dBASE* — Only Visual FoxPro supports dBASE file systems functionality. Access may import data from a dBASE file, but it does not support the dBASE programming functionality.

- *Excel* — A spreadsheet tool that is a component of Microsoft Office. Excel is Internet enabled but does not support ActiveX control creation. It does support Jet database replication and VBA, but VBA is not compiled.

- *FrontPage* — A user tool for creating Web pages. The created Web page can be enhanced with database access using Visual InterDev.

- *Index Server* — A free downloadable server that indexes documents on the Web server. Indexing goes below the traditional HTML indexing to text within a document.

- *Internet Information Server* — The Microsoft Server that supports the concept of a Web page. IIS is an integral component of Windows NT 4.0 Server.

- *Merchant Server* — A Web server designed especially for the Internet store. A special feature is the capability to target promotional items easily. Users shop with a shopping cart and make purchases. A secure link is required.

- *Object-oriented* — Only Visual FoxPro and Visual C++ support object-oriented polymorphism and inheritance for an application.

- *Office* — There are two definitions of Office. The first is the collection of Microsoft tools represented by Access, Binder, Excel, Outlook, PowerPoint, and Word. Project is a user tool, but it must be purchased separately. All tools of Microsoft Office have an object model. Most support VBA, Binder being the notable excepting. The second definition of Microsoft Office is defined as the composite collection of all objects defined within the tools mentioned above. The **Application** object is at the top of the hierarchy in each of these tools.

- *Outlook* — E-mail, address books, correspondence, and customer appointments. Microsoft Outlook is a client of Exchange Server.

- *PowerPoint* — A slide presentation tool that supports VBA and ActiveX controls, and is Internet aware.

- *Proxy Server* — A firewall between the enterprise and the Internet. Reduces costs by caching Web pages and reducing the number of connections.

- *Replication* — Windows NT supports directory replication; SQL Server supports database replication. Excel, Visual Basic, Visual C++, and Access support Jet database replication. Visual FoxPro and Visual J++ do not support Jet database replication.

- *SNA Server* — As in Systems Network Architecture, an IBM paradigm. SNA Server is a bridge from the Microsoft architecture in the WOSA tradition to the legacy systems of IBM.

- *SQL Server* — Microsoft's version of a relational database management system. Conforms to the current SQL92 standard. Robust, with transaction isolation levels and a transaction log for recovery. Replication to other databases is supported. Management is with SQL-DMO and automation, or from SQL SEM.

- *Systems Management Server* — Unattended installation of applications in an enterprise, inventory of hardware and software, remote diagnostics, help desk support, and one-on-one training.

- *Transaction Server* — A server that dramatically reduces the cost of implementing a tiered architecture. Transaction Server provides all the plumbing necessary to convert single-user objects to multiuser objects. A promise of a tiered architecture is scalability. A tiered architecture doesn't require a database connection for every user.

- *Visual Basic* — The original Microsoft developer tool and the flagship in the new multitiered client-server architecture. Visual Basic 5.0 features callback functions, compiled output, and ActiveX controls creation.

- *Visual C++* — The second oldest Microsoft tool. A very rich developer tool supporting an object-oriented paradigm with polymorphism and inheritance. The tool of choice for enterprise applications. ActiveX controls can be created.

- *Visual FoxPro* — A very rich developer's tool that supports an object-oriented paradigm with polymorphism and inheritance. FoxPro is the tool of choice for dBASE applications. FoxPro does not support VBA or Access replication and cannot create ActiveX controls.

- *Visual J++* — Microsoft supports two flavors of Visual J++ (JAVA). The first is pure Java for platform independence. The second version is ActiveX dependent, which reduces functionality in a multiplatform environment.

- *Visual SourceSafe* — A project-oriented version control system integrated with the tools of Microsoft Office. Both modular and object-oriented hierarchies are supported. Modules are checked in or out with a reason for each. Files may be shared with other projects. Automatic merging on check-in when a file is shared. Merge conflicts must be managed manually. Check-out comments are limited to 64 bytes, while check-in comments are limited to 32K.

Replication Crosses Many Boundaries

Replication comes in four flavors within the Microsoft architecture. The first flavor of replication is with Windows NT. Replication in this context supports a domain with the replication of user profiles and logon scripts from the Windows NT Primary Domain Controller (PDC) to Backup Domain Controllers (BDC).

The second flavor of replication is with SQL Server. The paradigm is that of a publisher with a distribution server, publications, and subscriptions. Complete databases may be published or only portions of a table. A good example of SQL server replication is the support of a Decision Support System (DSS), which is a database with read-only data. The queries of a DSS are optimized for efficiency with many indexes because there are no updates. The primary database is an On-Line Transaction Processing (OLTP) system with a high transaction rate. Changes from the OLTP system are replicated on a periodic or scheduled basis to the DSS system.

Another flavor of replication is Microsoft Access. Replication in Microsoft Access is quite valuable to the enterprise. A popular use of Access replication is with notebook computers of sales personnel, and the eventual synchronization with the parent database. Distributing the processing is the other valuable Access replication role. Small to medium databases can be replicated to remote sites and the database synchronized with the master on a scheduled basis. Access replication also solves the problem of Access not supporting the ACID properties of a transaction.

The last flavor of replication is with Microsoft Exchange replicating public newsgroup folders included in news feeds. When new items are posted to a replica of a newsgroup public folder, the change is replicated to the server running the Internet News Service.

KEY POINT SUMMARY

Microsoft has a very rich tool suite. An overlap of functionality exists between tools, and a common problem is the selection of the wrong tool for an application. An example of a poor tool choice is using Access for financial transactions or for any mission-critical application.

- The first key point is to understand the benefits and liabilities of each tool.
- The second key point is to understand the requirements of the application.

APPLYING WHAT YOU'VE LEARNED

The questions below will help prepare you for the Choosing Development Tools section of the Windows Architecture I examination.

Instant Assessment

We've discussed nearly all the Microsoft tools. A few minor ones, which are end-user oriented and of not much interest to the developer, were skipped. These questions will aid you in making the correct tool choice.

1. Which BackOffice product automates the installation of enterprise software?
2. SMS requires the cooperation of another Microsoft BackOffice product. What is the name of that product?
3. You are unable to complete a purchase from a store on the Internet. You believe the Web site is supported by Microsoft Merchant Server. What is the likely problem?
4. How do you establish a secure link on the Web?
5. You are building a tiered client-server application. What is the suggested development tool to use with Microsoft Transaction Server?
6. What is the development tool of choice for building controls in a multiple-platform environment?
7. You wish to use Jet database replication. Which Microsoft Office tools support Jet replication?
8. Which BackOffice Server provides connectivity to an AS/400 DB2 relational database?
9. Which Microsoft tools support callback functions?
10. There are two definitions of Microsoft Office. The second definition is the composite collection of all objects defined in the Microsoft Office tool collection. What is the most common object?
11. Visual FoxPro is a very powerful development tool. What are the two distinguishing characteristics of Visual FoxPro?

 concept link   **For answers to the Instant Assessment questions, see Appendix C.**

Lab Exercise

Lab 34.64 *Comparing Access and Visual Basic performance*

WA I

Lab 34.64 demonstrates the advantages of Visual Basic compared to Microsoft Access. The lab uses a simple algorithm to compute prime numbers. A prime number is any number that is only divisible by itself and unity (one).

Microsoft Access is easy to use; in fact, too easy. Visual Basic is not that much more difficult, but it does compile executable programs, which are much faster than the interpretive programs of Access. You'll want the Visual Basic program to be compiled. You can test your code in the integrated development environment (IDE) of Visual Basic, but before doing your timing tests, create a compiled executable.

You'll find a Visual Basic 5.0 project PRIME_SIEVE.VBP and an Access 97 PRIME_SIEVE.MDB database in the EXAMPLES\CHAPTER34 folder of the CD-ROM that accompanies this book. The code for both is identical except for setting the hourglass. Run both of these applications. Be sure you run the executable version of PRIME_SIEVE.VBP. Visual Basic 5.0 is significantly faster. This benchmark should convince you to switch from Access to Visual Basic. I certainly hope so. The code for the Access version is shown in Listing 34-1.

LISTING 34-1 **Access version of prime number sieve**

```
Private Sub Prime_Number_Sieve_Click()
Dim n(Range) As Double ' for RANGE see Declarations
Dim p(Range) As Double ' found primes
Dim start As Double
Dim i As Long ' temporary loop counter
Dim k As Long
Dim StartTime As Double
Dim FinishTime As Double
Dim ElapsedTime As Double
Dim count As Long ' accumulated prime count
DoCmd.Hourglass True
StartTime = Time

For i = 2 To Range
n(i) = 0
```

```
Next i

count = 0
start = Sqr(Range) ' don't need to do upper half

For k = 2 To Range
If n(k) >= 0 Then
count = count + 1
p(count) = k
If k <= start Then
For i = k To Range Step k
n(i) = -1
Next i
End If
End If
Next k
FinishTime = Time
ElapsedTime = FinishTime - StartTime
MsgBox "Elapsed prime number sieve time: " & ElapsedTime
DoCmd.Hourglass False
' For i = 1 To count
' Debug.Print p(i); " ";
' Next i
Debug.Print
Exit Sub
End Sub
```

Adjust the following statement in the declarations section of the form in both the Access version and the Visual Basic version before executing the foregoing code.

```
Private Const Range As Long = 500000
```

The value <500000> is the range of numbers to search for prime numbers. You'll have to adjust the number of primes based on the speed and size of your system. All we did is construct a computational loop to measure the difference between Access, which is interpretive, and Visual Basic 5.0, which is compiled.

Note that I commented out a small print loop at the bottom of the code. The code is there for debugging. If it is enabled, it will skew your timing results with disk I/O.

Lab 34.65 *Combining components for a solution*

WA I

Lab 34.65 is an exercise in combining components in a solution. We'll use a component from BackOffice, Office, and the Visual Tool Suite. The components are Excel, Visual Basic, and SQL Server. The application need not do anything useful other than demonstrate component connectivity.

The laboratory is divided into two steps. The first step is to create a spreadsheet in Excel and populate the spreadsheet with data from SQL Server. The second step is to control Excel from Visual Basic with Automation. This lab exercise can be kick-started by taking advantage of the Excel DAO macro in Listing 17-5 of Chapter 17.

Lab 34.66 *Replication and database durability*

WA I
WA II

We know Microsoft Access does not maintain a write-ahead log such as that maintained by SQL Server. The write-ahead log of SQL Server enables SQL Server to roll back incomplete transactions during system recovery. Design and implement an Access application that replicates an Access database to other users. The frequency of replication depends on the application requirements. There should not be too many users, probably less than ten.

Lab 34.67 *MAPI and OLE Messaging*

WA I
WA II

OLE Messaging is a Messaging API (MAPI) wrapper. The goal of this laboratory is to add OLE Messaging to an existing application. Listing 9-7 of Chapter 9 is an example of using OLE Messaging that will help you get started. Select a production program and use OLE Messaging to signal major application failures.

Windows Architecture I

CHAPTER

Development Methodologies

35

About Chapter 35

C hapter 35 discusses two topics: Microsoft Visual SourceSafe (VSS) and Microsoft Solutions Framework (MSF). VSS is a file-versioning control system that is useful to the iterative development process of MSF.

This chapter contains the material necessary to know to pass the Development Methodologies section of the Windows Architecture I core examination.

MICROSOFT SOLUTIONS FRAMEWORK

I begin with a series of quotes from Chapter 1 of the Microsoft Solutions Framework as published in Microsoft Software Development Kit (MSDK) 2.0:

A key motivation behind Microsoft Solutions Framework stems from a philosophy captured in a five-part action plan:

- *Self-assessment*

- *Skills acquisition*

- *Process evaluation*

- *Architectural planning*

- *Learning by doing*

The ability to provide solutions for new problems and new users who are frequently inexperienced in both computer systems and business databases.

The process is iterative: the planning process and the building process are both candidates for continuous improvement.

Teams gain more experience and skills through iterative refinements of the application.

Microsoft does not have a methodology. It is the combination of a successful discipline for software development, plus experienced people adept at applying it, that contributes to Microsoft's success in software product development.

Build project plans bottom-up rather than top-down, with each project team role taking responsibility for it's own delivery commitments.

The Microsoft Solutions Framework (MSF) advocates planning and building concurrently.

The quoted material gives you some understanding of what MSF is. Before we proceed, let's define the difference between *top-down* and *bottom-up*. Top-down is the traditional perspective. The ultimate goals are defined and then decomposed. The decomposition continues downward through many levels until each objective is of a size deemed capable of being implemented. The decomposition then becomes a plan of implementation. The lowest level represents all the required tasks. Figure 35-1 illustrates the top-down approach where an objective is decomposed to the lowest level.

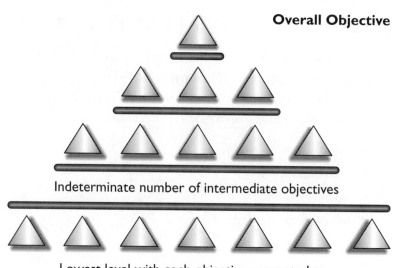

Overall Objective

Indeterminate number of intermediate objectives

Lowest level with each objective converted to
a task which may not all be programming tasks

FIGURE 35-1   Top-down design or the waterfall method.

A feature of the waterfall method is that programming doesn't start until the problem at hand is understood. Another feature of the waterfall method is that a task doesn't start until the previous milestone is complete. This is not quite the same with a bottom-up approach, which permits programming to start before the problem is understood. MSF enables programmers to start before the functional specifications are approved and before the problem is understood. (We return to this discussion after we understand a bit more about MSF.)

Team Model

Many of the strategies put forth by MSF are classic within the computer industry. MSF espouses an orderly approach to implementing a computer application. The logical steps are conceptual design, logical design, and physical design. The logical and physical steps are unique because they involve the concept of a tiered architecture with client, business, and data services. MSF uses a team model, and each team member has a specific role in each of the design phases. We start by defining the roles of team members:

- *Product Management* — User advocate with strong business analytical skills.

- *Program Management*—Traditional management skills with day-to-day coordination.

- *Development*—Builds a system to functional specification.

- *User Education*—Publishes end-user documentation and other related instructional materials.

- *Test and Quality Assurance (QA)*—Verifies compliance with all team deliverables.

- *Logistics*—Installs, migrates, and ensures a smooth rollout.

Teams are not always large and more than one role may be assigned to more than one individual. Combining roles can be both risky and synergistic as shown in Figure 35-2.

	Product Management	Program Management	Development	Test/QA	User Education	Logistics
Product Management		No			Yes	Yes
Program Management	No		No		Yes	Yes
Development		No		No		
Test/QA			No			
User Education	Yes	Yes				
Logistics	Yes	Yes				

FIGURE 35-2 **Risk and synergy in team roles.**

Figure 35-2 illustrates that combining the roles of developer and quality assurance are risky. Although that is true, what is also true is that combining development and product management roles is also risky because the developer has a high familiarity with the physical model. This familiarity may bias consideration of issues other than the physical model.

PROCESS MODEL

Microsoft Solutions Framework uses a milestone-based process model. The reasoning given for this model is that the waterfall process client-server model is task-focused and not process-focused. However, any model must have tasks to measure completion schedules. Not identifying tasks exposes project management to large scale surprises. Basic negative issues with the process model that MSF espouses include:

- *Programming while learning*—The skill sets are not in place and developers use the project to learn.

- *No distinct time frame*—Development of software is an iterative process. The developer keeps working until it is right. The problem here is likely to be an inadequate conceptual design.

- *Scope creep*—The project slowly expands because there are no specified deliverables.

- *Indefinite scope*—The project starts before the scope is completely defined, thus the budgetary requirements are not known until after the project is started.

Microsoft seems to justify the use of an iterative process model on the iterative nature of user interface design. When iterations occur with user interface design, it is likely a failure in the conceptual model, which is predicated on business problems and usage scenarios. The usage scenarios are simply incomplete.

 concept link

Chapters 40 and 41 present a more traditional approach to application development. The traditional Waterfall methodology is updated to reflect our current level of technology.

Milestones

The MSF process model includes milestones. *Milestones* are linked to roles in the team model. The first milestone is Vision/Scope, which is owned by product management. Microsoft states the process model has clear ownership and accountability. Yes, it does have accountability but only for roles of the Team Model and no specific accountability is charged other than the indicated four milestones of Figure 35-3. However, the program manager is not restricted from including other milestones to avoid surprises. This is difficult because development is iterative and actually starts before the Version/Scope document is approved.

Risk-driven scheduling is another feature of the milestone-based process model. Development of the at-risk components is started early in the project. This is very commendable, but one can't help wondering if the component is at risk because of a skill-set deficiency or inadequate usage scenarios.

Another characteristic of the milestone-based process model is versioned releases. The obvious question to ask is: "Why versioned releases?" Microsoft needs versioned releases because it is in the software business. Something this release, something more the next release, and maybe a little bit more the next release, and so on. Users don't need versioned releases. The product, if all team roles are fulfilled, meets specifications. But then again, if the project is being used as a learning tool, you may need a versioned release because you didn't know what you were doing when you started.

in the real world

I recently purchased a FORTRAN 90 compiler from Digital Equipment Corporation and installed it in Microsoft Visual Studio 97 Enterprise Edition. It generates code for UNIX, OpenVMS, Windows NT, and Windows 95. It is not a versioned release. It meets the FORTRAN 90 specifications. It is a complete product with no planned versioned product and that is the way it should be.

Figure 35-3 illustrates Microsoft's vision of accountability with MSF. Note that *Code complete* and *Product release* have two owners. Note also that all roles are participating to some degree for the complete life of the project. Development will gear up, but it is certainly busy long before the Vision/Scope document is approved.

in the real world

My view of a Vision/Scope document is something that was done on someone else's nickel and it is the reason for starting the project. I can hear it now: "Yeah, we just got a new project to help manufacturing cut costs. What do you guys want to build?" The obvious problem is the project starts without a scope.

exam preparation pointer

It will be to your advantage to remember the milestones of Figure 35-3 for the Windows Architecture I core examination.

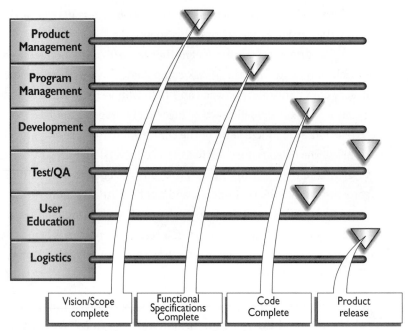

FIGURE 35-3   Ownership of process model milestones.

Conceptual Design

Let's assume that your program manager is experienced and prepared the Vision/Scope document before the project started. Approval of this document makes it a baseline and any modifications must be through change control. The Conceptual Design document is the next deliverable. It specifies the business problem and usage scenarios. This document is the most important document of the project. Failure to properly address user needs and business needs inevitably results in significant rework during the development cycle.

Let's digress a moment and look back at the legacy world. There were three unique skill sets. The lowest was the coder who worked under direct supervision of a programmer. The coder was eventually promoted to programmer, but only after learning requisite skills, such as how to formulate a problem and how to debug an application.

Programmers were a step up the ladder. They did programming, but some of their duties included analysis. Not too much, and at a low level. The next step up the ladder was the analyst. The analyst did not program. The analyst's job involved conceptual level planning and requirements analysis. The analyst also possessed interview skills and could construct usage scenarios.

What is the point of this discussion? It's quite simple: The legacy world has a hierarchy of skill sets. Each skill set is acquired through time and experience. Today there is only one skill set, the developer (not a coder, programmer, or analyst). Certification can raise a coder to the level of programmer, but it cannot raise a coder to the level of analyst.

Logical design is sandwiched between physical design and conceptual design. The team role of development is key in both the logical and physical design steps. The problem is that the boundary between logical design and conceptual design is blurred. The MSF Team Role of Development is allowed to participate in conceptual design. This is a serious mistake because developers do not have the requisite interview or usage-scenario skills. This helps explain the iterative nature of software design when using the Microsoft paradigm. Let's look at MSF team roles during conceptual design:

- *Product Management* — Responsible for obtaining user interviews. Continues user advocate role. Unfortunately, Figure 35-3 indicates the role can be combined with the *Development* role.

- *Program Management* — Owner of the Conceptual Design document. Validates enterprise architecture. Manages overall design. Assures smooth transition from conceptual design to logical design.

- *Development* — Examines completeness and consistency in the statement of business policy. Considers risks.

- *User Education* — Usability issues and training requirements. May be a surrogate user. Implements usage scenarios as a surrogate user.

- *Test and Quality Assurance (QA)* — Testability issues are examined from the perspective of user advocate. Verifies compliance with requirements.

- *Logistics* — Examines the overall infrastructure and rollout issues.

Logical Design

As expected, the next step is the logical design. The result of the logical design process is a functional design document. Focus now changes to the Development role in the MSF Team Model:

- *Product Management* — Verifies that the logical model reflects the user's view of the system. Also verifies linkage between the conceptual and logical models. It is a problem when this role is combined with the Development role.

- *Program Management* — Continues overall project management. Looks for concurrence among project teams. Assures smooth transition from conceptual design to logical design.

- *Development* — Derives the logical and physical models. Verifies adequate detail is available.

- *User Education* — Verifies usability issues and training of logical design. Reviews user interfaces and data views.

- *Test and Quality Assurance (QA)* — Continues examining testability issues from the perspective of user advocate. Verifies compliance with requirements.

- *Logistics* — Examines the overall infrastructure and rollout issues.

My closing comment on MSF is this: don't use it. I know there are many compelling white papers that paint marvelous MSF success stories, but all the success stories I've read always used Microsoft Consulting Services (MCS). The white papers could more honestly be used as public relations material for MCS and not MSF. The faults of MSF are numerous. I am sorry, but I cannot accept iterative development while learning. I've had some discussion with members of the Microsoft staff about MSF and have gotten very disparaging remarks on the waterfall method. Users of the waterfall method should take the responsibility for system failures; it is not the fault of the process itself. A common problem with the waterfall method is the failure to partition the overall objectives into manageable goals. The bottom line is that MSF fits with the need for instant gratification. Our profession shares in this need by programming an application before the problem is understood.

VISUAL SOURCESAFE

Microsoft Visual SourceSafe is a project-oriented source code control system. It works in concert with the Microsoft espoused philosophy of incremental software releases. It runs on Windows 95, Windows NT, MS-DOS, Windows 3.1, and Macintosh platforms.

Only one copy of the source code is maintained. Users check out a copy noting the reason. Correspondingly, the edited copy is checked back in with reasons noted. The default is checkout to a single user, but a file may be checked out to more than one user. **Allow Multiple Checkouts** can be set on the **General Options Tab** of the **Tools** menu. This enables multiple copies of a file to be checked out. Changes are automatically merged when the file is checked back in. When there are multiple checkouts of the same file, a file cannot be checked in if conflicts arise during the merge process. The user must resolve the differences using the differences command to identify the reason for the conflict.

Visual SourceSafe is not limited to the local system with file sharing occurring across projects, platforms, and networks. The type of file is not a limitation; the file type may be text or binary such as user instructions, program source files, binary files, or anything that requires source control. Any size project and any number of users can be supported. Reversion to an earlier version is an integral feature of Visual SourceSafe. Visual SourceSafe simultaneously performs the roles of project librarian, historian, security guard, and custodian.

Visual SourceSafe as a Librarian

SourceSafe has many advantages, the most important of which is keeping files secure. The librarian role of SourceSafe can be described as:

- Prevents accidental file deletion.
- Organizes files in any structure necessary to support the project, which may be hierarchical or object-oriented. Subprojects are also supported.
- Checks files in and out with reasons for each.
- Enables users on different projects, platforms, or on a network to share files. (Only one master copy is maintained. Development of cross-platform applications is supported.)
- Enables stored files to be any type of binary or text file. This includes compound files from Microsoft Word, and source or binary files from Microsoft tools.
- Enables more than one user to checkout a file. (The default is single-user checkout.) Changes are merged automatically at check-in, but check-in is not permitted when merge errors exist.
- Tracks modules with a where-used feature that aids reusability.

Visual SourceSafe as a Historian

A current copy of project files is not enough. The history of each module is important. Excessive changes signal the need to redesign modules. SourceSafe as a historion will:

- Track versions with older versions always available.
- Track date and time of changes to all files.
- Print module activity by project or file as a report or save it to a file.
- Maintain a journal file with a record of all user commands.
- Display differences for resolving merge issues.

Visual SourceSafe as a Security Guard

Visual SourceSafe includes an administrator for managing projects. The administrator is responsible for maintaining a list of users for each project. Each user has a password and the administrator may change the password at any time, locking out the user. Users by default have read/write privileges but an administrator can limit a user to read-only privileges.

Visual SourceSafe as a Custodian

SourceSafe provides features and services for working with other products. These include:

- A command line interface for batch files and integrating with other products.
- A PVCS (third party tool)-to-Visual SourceSafe conversion utility.
- A Microsoft Delta-to-SourceSafe conversion utility.
- Integration with Microsoft tools such as Visual Basic 4.0 and 5.0. (SourceSafe was initially shipped with Visual Basic 4.0 Enterprise Edition and is available through the **AddIn** menu.)

KEY POINT SUMMARY

An iterative approach to software development is not acceptable to corporate America, however Microsoft has no choice. Microsoft doesn't have the clients that we have. Without real customers and good usage scenarios, Microsoft makes a lot of good guesses and has evolved an iterative approach that is successful because of the high skill level of the individuals involved (MCS).

Another issue of the iterative approach is that individual component design failures are masked. This masking covers a multitude of sins such as inadequate skill sets, poor usage scenarios, incomplete problem comprehension, and a bottom-up attitude of the developer implementing his or her image of what the system should be and not implementing the user's image.

- Microsoft Solutions Framework is a process-oriented framework for creating multitiered client-server applications.

- Each team role owns or shares a project milestone. MSF does not support individual ownership.

- Visual SourceSafe is a file-independent versioning control system for source control.

APPLYING WHAT YOU'VE LEARNED

The questions below deal with core issues of both Microsoft Solution Framework and Visual SourceSafe. In the proper context, the questions address all issues of the Development Methodologies section of the Windows Architecture I examination.

Instant Assessment

1. Microsoft Solutions Framework supports the tiered architecture paradigm. Name the services offered by each of the tiers.

2. Name the major milestones of the MSF Process model.

3. Microsoft makes a significant issue of ownership within MSF. Describe ownership within MSF.

4. You are starting a new Web site with multiple developers and you know that all the Visual Basic and C++ developers use SourceSafe. Can you use SourceSafe to protect your Web pages?

5. Describe the procedure to use with SourceSafe to keep a module under version control.

6. A new project is starting that can reuse modules in the current project. How does SourceSafe support different projects with common modules?

concept link    **For answers to the Instant Assessment questions, see Appendix C.**

Lab Exercises

The following lab exercises test your project management skills with Microsoft Solutions Framework as well as your skills as a project leader.

Lab 35.68 *Microsoft Solutions Framework and budgets*

If you haven't guessed, the Process Model of Microsoft Solutions Framework (MSF) appears to be designed for companies like Microsoft with essentially unlimited budgets. The Process Model lets the developer iterate until the software is right. Learning while doing is emphasized. This is the very last thing you want with a limited budget.

You are a new project manager and want to make a good impression. Your management has decided that Microsoft Solutions Framework will be the methodology. You've been given a budget, and there is some slack, but not much. Try and put together a project plan for a project that has an estimated fifteen percent of the components categorized as high risk items and five percent of the components categorized as very high risk items. There are no simple solutions. When it's your project, you'll find that MSF engenders too many risks for prudent project management; however, MSF gives the developers a deeper sense of project participation. Following are some of the considerations:

○ Cheat and address the difficult issues before the project starts. Remember that you are on someone else's nickel with this approach. The more you can get done off budget, the better off you are. Once the project officially starts, you're on your own budget.

- Place a higher emphasis on the earlier design sections. This is difficult to do because the staffing for a MSF project does not include the concept of analysts. MSF team members are all developers.

- Cheat a little bit and go back for additional budget; use the additional funds for staff analyst(s), but don't give them titles as analysts.

- Cheat again, but this time keep two sets of books. One set of books is the MSF approach and the second set of books is the Waterfall method (see Chapters 40 and 41). Keep out of the alligator pits with the Waterfall method books, which are your personal tools and are not public. Use the MSF books to make the developers feel warm and fuzzy.

- That's enough! Remember that anything ethical or legal is acceptable within the norms of good taste and style. Be as creative as possible. You don't want surprises on delivery day. Here's another one of Bruce's rules: "The schedules given by developers are vocalizations of aspirations and have no basis in fact." With that rule in mind, you must develop your own yardstick for measuring project progress. I consider anything without hard dates and schedules a disaster waiting to happen.

Lab 35.69 *Jump-starting internationalization*

WA I

You're a new project leader and you want to make a good impression. Your current task is to design a SourceSafe directory structure for your project. Design this directory structure with the knowledge that the project will be sold internationally and must be internationalized (see Chapter 42). This means keeping the localizations files separate from core files.

Lab 35.70 *Securing the application*

WA II

An application will be sold that requires encryption. You also plan to export the application, and you don't expect to be able to obtain an export license because of the technology used within your encryption algorithms (see Chapter 33). Design a SourceSafe directory structure for your project that will accommodate a domestic and an export version. Use an existing production application for this analysis. There are business choices which must be made. Is the export version a complete product? How much of the application is encrypted?

Internet/Intranet

Part IV is composed of the following four chapters:

- **Chapter 36: Internet and Intranet Architecture—** Historical issues and protocols including Gopher, FTP, HTTP, HTML, Sockets, UDP, TCP, ICMP, IP, ARP, SLIP, and PPP. Common Gateway Interface (GCI), Internet Server API (ISAPI), Internet Data Connector (IDC), FrontPage 98, and Visual Interdev are introduced.

- **Chapter 37: Anatomy of a Web Site—** A Web site is built using the Internet Data Connector (IDC) and Active Server Pages (ASP).

- **Chapter 38: Internet Tools for the Trenches—** CGI and ISAPI architecture. An ISAPI DLL and an ISAPI application is constructed.

- **Chapter 39: Internet Applications with Elan—** Client-side and server-side scripting are discussed here, which includes all objects of the Internet Information Server (IIS) scripting model.

Windows Architecture I
Windows Architecture II

CHAPTER

Internet and Intranet Architecture

36

About Chapter 36

Welcome to the Internet/intranet. Chapter 36 is devoted to the Internet/intranet issues of the Windows Archictecture I core examination. I start with a brief description of Internet architecture followed by a discussion of Internet protocols. All protocols are illustrated along with their dependencies. I then discuss using the Internet from the perspective of publishing. Web browsing is not discussed except for a few comments and an example of a browsing tool. Different modes of Web publishing are discussed using different Internet technologies and tools such as the *Common Gateway Interface* (CGI), Internet Server Application Programming Interface (ISAPI), dbWeb, Internet Data Connector (IDC), FrontPage 98, and Active Server Pages (ASP) of the Microsoft Internet Information Server (IIS).

The Web site created in this chapter is located in the EXAMPLES\ CHAPTER37\MYWEB folder of the CD-ROM that accompanies this book. The Web is placed in the CHAPTER37 folder because most of the Web site work is accomplished there. The results of creating an Access 97 Active Server Page (ASP) are located in the EXAMPLES\CHAPTER36 folder of the CD-ROM that accompanies this book.

THE INTERNET

The Internet began life as a research project sponsored by the Defense Advanced Research Projects Agency (DARPA) in the 1960s. The Internet has evolved into millions of computers connected in a global network.

The interconnection of computers is made possible by the *World Wide Web* (WWW or "Web"), which was invented as a communication tool by Tim Berners-Lee at the European Laboratory for Particle Physics (CERN) in 1989. The Web functions with clients accessing Web servers. It is not too different from the file server of yesteryear, but the technology is at a much higher level. Today there are six popular Web servers. Two of these are freeware/shareware, and the other four are commercial Web servers. The commercial Web servers are from Netscape, Microsoft, Apache, and O'Reilly. One freeware/shareware Web server is the CERN version, and the second is from the National Center for Supercomputing Applications (NCSA).

 web links

The NCSA Web server is commonly known as Mosaic and is downloadable from the NCSA File transfer protocol (FTP) site `ftp://ncsa.uiuc.edu`.

Web browsers are the clients that communicate with Web servers using the common Hypertext Transport Protocol (HTTP). The information they communicate is written in the hypertext markup language (HTML). HTML is based on the standard generalized markup language (SGML). HTTP uses a universal resource locator (URL) to uniquely identify sites. Associated with each site is an Internet protocol (IP) address such as 120.110.050.001, which is in the dotted decimal notation. The IP address has three address classes that are determined by subnet mask size. The IP address is 32 bits that are broken down into 8-bit octets. Table 36-1 defines the submask bits for each address class.

TABLE 36-1 INTERNET PROTOCOL ADDRESS CLASSES

ADDRESS CLASS		BITS USED FOR SUBNET MASK		DOTTED DECIMAL	
Class A	11111111	00000000	00000000	00000000	255.0.0.0
Class B	11111111	11111111	00000000	00000000	255.255.0.0
Class C	11111111	11111111	11111111	00000000	255.255.255.0

A practical example is to consider an address. We'll use the IP address 131.107.16.200. This is a Class B address and is defined as follows:

o *Network ID*—131.107.y.z

o *Host ID*—w.x.16.200

o *Subnet Mask*—255.255.0.0

This is a very simplistic view of an IP address, and there are advanced issues such as a custom subnet mask (subnetting) that are beyond the scope of this book.

A URL is defined as *Protocol://ServerAddress/Path* where the server address is also known as the *domain*. Common Internet protocols include HTTP, FTP, and Gopher, all of which are defined in the following sections. There are other protocols such as Network News Transfer Protocol, which has a URL of *nntp://newsgroup-name* or the News Protocol, which has a URL of *news:newsgroupname*. Another Internet protocol is the MailTo protocol with a URL of *mailto:username@domain*. HTTP is layered on top of the Transmission Control Protocol/Internet Protocol (TCP/IP) suite discussed previously in Chapter 34 and is illustrated in Figure 36-1.

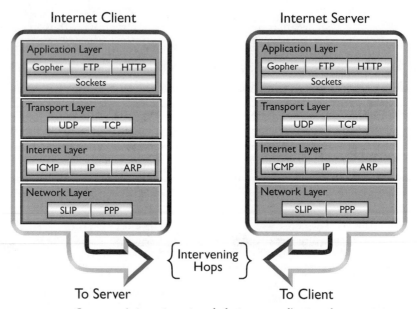

FIGURE 36-1   Common Internet protocols between a client and server.

Note that Figure 36-1 defines *Intervening Hops*. The Internet is a global network of inter-connected computers, and the only direct connection is to your local Internet service provider. An Internet connection starts with the local server looking up the requested site name and matching that name with an IP address. The lookup process is with a Domain Name Service (DNS). Once the IP address is established, the local server connects logically to the requested site. The connection is not quite direct but goes through an intervening and indeterminate number of hops until the TCP/IP information packet reaches the ultimate destination. There is minimal interaction with the encountered servers as the TCP/IP packets make the hops between servers, and for all practical purposes, the connection is direct. This is one of the reasons a TCP/IP data packet pack has a *time-to-die* mechanism. Too many hops and the packet dies automatically. This is quite unlike the captain in the Wagner opera *The Flying Dutchman* who was doomed to sail forever until rescued.

An intranet is defined as an Internet network that is completely contained within a commercial enterprise. Such a network permits a direct connection server connection. An Extranet is an intranet to which selected outside (outside the enterprise) vendors have access.

Application Layer Protocols

Only the popular application layer protocols are illustrated in Figure 36-1. Listed below are the current application layer protocols of the TCP/IP suite. Protocols such as the Domain Host Configuration Protocol (DHCP) are not within the public domain and are Microsoft-specific implementations.

- *Archie* — A catalog of 1,000+ anonymous FTP servers identifying the location of FTP-retrievable files.

- *DHCP* — Microsoft Domain Host Control Protocol. Autoconfiguration with leased IP addresses.

- *DNS* — Domain Naming Service. Maps computer names to IP addresses. Microsoft has a proprietary implementation of this protocol.

- *Finger* — Returns information on a specific Internet site.

- *FTP* — File Transfer Protocol. Used for copying files between Internet sites.

- *Gopher* — Distributed document retrieval and navigation. Resources are cumulatively known as "gopherspace."

- *HTTP*— Hypertext Transfer Protocol. The most common Internet protocol.
- *IRC*— Internet relay chat. A text-based real-time conversation system.
- *MUD*— Multiuser dungeon and dragons game.
- *NFS*— Transparent Internet client file access.
- *NNTP*— Network News Transport Protocol. Electronic news groups.
- *PEM*— Privacy Enhanced Mail. Encrypted mail protocol using either RSA or DES.
- *POP2 or POP3*— Post Office Protocol version 2 or 3. Stores and forwards electronic mail.
- *SMTP*— Simple Mail Transport Protocol. Used between two Internet message transfer agents.
- *SNMP*— Simple Network Management Protocol. Remote administration of TCP/IP machines.
- *Telnet*— Telecommunications Network Protocol. Log in to remote host.
- *USENET*— Uses NNTP to manage a collection of newsgroups and message boards, which is a hierarchical bulletin board system.
- *VERONICA*— Very Easy Rodent-Oriented Netwide Index. Gopherspace search of computerized archives.
- *WAIS*— Wide Area Information Server. Z39.50 content indexing and information retrieval standard.
- *Whois*— Returns Internet user information registered with InterNic.
- *WWW (W3)*— World Wide Web. Protocol for distributed hypertext document searching, navigation, and retrieval.

Except for DHCP, these protocols all have UNIX roots. The protocols of common interest in the Microsoft environment are DHCP, DNS, FTP, NNTP, SMTP, SNMP, and WWW. WWW is commonly known as HTTP. A universal example of the HTTP protocol is the popular address `http://www.microsoft.com`. Another well-known Internet address is `ftp://ftp.microsoft.com`.

exam
preparation
pointer

For the Windows Architecture I core examination you need to understand when to use HTML, FTP, GOPHER, and NNTP.

Transport, Internet, and Network Layer Protocols

The TCP/IP protocols User Datagram Protocol (UDP), TCP, Internet Control Message Protocol (ICMP), IP, and Address REsolution Protocol (ARP) are transport layer and Internet layer protocols (discussed in Chapter 33). Serial Line Internet Protocol (SLIP) and Point-to-Point Protocol (PPP) are categorized as connection protocols, which are the client means of connecting to a remote host.

- *Point-to-Point Protocol* — The standard in Internet connectivity. A dial-up client running PPP can connect to a network running internetwork packet exchange (IPX), TCP/IP, or the NetBIOS Extended User Interface Protocol (NetBEUI) protocols.

- *Serial Line Interface Protocol* — An older Internet protocol that Microsoft clients such as Windows 95 use only on a dial-out basis.

concept link

That about covers our venture into Internet protocols. See Chapter 33 for additional TCP/IP protocol information. The Microsoft 70-59 TCP/IP exam deals with the minutiae of the TCP/IP protocol suite, which is beyond the scope of this book.

HYPERTEXT TRANSFER PROTOCOL

HTTP is the layer between TCP/IP and the *Hypertext Markup Language* (HTML). Win32 Internet API functions (see Chapter 38) work with HTTP 1.0 servers. (The HTTP 1.1 specification is currently in review.) The HTTP clients are the popular browsers, or you can build your own browser using the WebBrowser control and Win32 Internet API functions. HTTP 1.0 is defined in the WWW Request For Comment (RFC) 1945 and is downloadable from `http://www.w3.org/protocols/rfc1945/rfc1945`.

HTTP is a stateless protocol. That means a connection must be established for every message. The message sequence is terminated with a disconnect. The server maintains state information by storing *cookies* at the client. A cookie is a small token of information that is stored by the Web server at the client site. Cookies are a means by which, under HTTP protocol, a server or a script can maintain state information on the client workstation. These cookies reflect the current client profile.

Request headers are sent to the HTTP server as part of a request message. These headers can be modified by the client to exercise a finer control of the HTTP server. The request header fields of WWW RFC 1945 include: **Authorization**, **From**, **If-Modified-Since**, **Referer**, and **User-Agent**.

Response header fields include **Location**, **Server**, and **WWW-Authenticate**. The response from the HTTP server consists of a *Single-Response* or a *Full-Response*, each of which is defined below.

```
Response = Single-Response | Full-Response
Single-Response = [ Entity - Body]
Full-Response = Status-line *( General-Header
                    | Response-Header
                    | Entity-Header )
                  CRLF
                  [ Entity-Body ]
```

Status messages include the following:

```
200 OK                      400 Bad Request
201 Created                 401 Unauthorized
202 Accepted                403 Forbidden
204 No Content              404 Not Found
301 Moved Permanently       500 Internal Server Error
302 Moved Temporarily       501 Not Implemented
304 Not Modified            502 Bad Gateway
                            503 Service Unavailable
```

The general message categories are:

- *1xx* — Informational. Not used and reserved for future use.
- *2xx* — Success. The action was successfully received, understood, and accepted.
- *3xx* — Redirection. Further action is required.
- *4xx* — Client error; probably bad syntax.
- *5xx* — Server error.

Entity header fields include **Allow**, **Content-Encoding**, **Content-Length**, **Content-Type**, **Expires**, and **Last-Modified**.

Microsoft architecture manages HTTP with four Win32 Internet API functions: **HttpAddRequestHeaders**, **HttpOpenRequest**, **HttpQueryInfo**, and **HttpSendRequest**. These functions manage the three different HTTP request methods shown below, and which are described in Chapter 38:

```
<form Method="GET" action="/myweb/GetP?name=bruce">
<form Method="HEAD" action="/myweb/HeadP?name=bruce">
<form Method="POST" action="/myweb/PostP">
```

- *GET* — This method is not the default server input for technology such as Active Server Pages Microsoft Internet Information Server. It is used primarily with Internet Server API (ISAPI) extensions. The GET method retrieves name value pairs appended to the request URL after a (?).

  The produced data is returned and not the source text of the process. The GET method returns an HTTP header followed by an HTTP entity-body.

- *HEAD* — This method is identical to the GET method. The only difference is that an HTTP entity-body is not returned. The headers are identical to the GET method with the same arguments.

- *POST* — Both an HTTP header and an HTTP entity-body are returned by the server. The source text of the process may be returned. Only the POST method can create a new resource, or more precisely, a HTTP header followed by a HTTP entity-body. This is an HTML page, and you'll see an example of this with the ISAPI DLL created in Chapter 39.

  The server is requested to accept the entity enclosed in the request as a new subordinate to the entity identified within the POST method request parameters, hence a new page on the stack for the browser.

Hypertext Markup Language

We now know that the Internet supports more than just Web pages. The previous section presented a rich list of application layer protocols. Our focus here is not on protocols for communication, but the content described by HTML for Web page communication.

A FAVORITE QUESTION AT A MICROSOFT PRESENTATION

It seems that at every Microsoft *show-and-tell* editor. Of course, the audience isn't given an involving HTML, the presenter asks the audi- opportunity to answer, but the answer is ence the name of the most popular Web page *Notepad.*

An HTML document is a plain-text file that contains *elements* recognized by HTML browsers. The HTML document can display text, multimedia objects, and hyperlinks. A *hyperlink* is formatted text pointing to another HTML document.

Elements are the basic building blocks of an HTML document. An HTML document consists of a start tag, an included character string, and an end tag. The start tag is preceded by < and ends with >. The end tag starts with /< and ends with >. An example of displaying a sentence in bold with HTML is illustrated by:

```
<B> This sentence is displayed in bold.</B>
```

Elements may be embedded within other elements, and the next example has the last word of the sentence rendered in both bold and italics:

```
<B> The last word is rendered in both bold and
 <I>italics</I>.</B>
```

An example of a complete, but very simple HTML document is:

```
<!DOCTYPE HTML PUBLIC "-//IETF//DTD HTML//EN">
<HTML>
<HEAD>
<TITLE>Simple Example HTML Document</TITLE>
</HEAD>
<BODY>
<P>A very simple HTML example document.
</BODY>
</HTML>
```

Every HTML 3.2-compliant document is supposed to begin with the !DOC-TYPE element. !DOCTYPE specifies to the browser which version of HTML is being used. The next element in this basic document is HTML, which informs the browser that the content of the file is written in HTML. The matching end tag (</HTML>) is the last tag in the file.

An HTML document follows conventional layout procedures. The HEAD tags delineate the document heading, and the TITLE tags appear with the heading. A browser displays the text of the TITLE element in its title bar. Common elements, such as a menu bar or an image that is repeated for other documents, may appear in the header section.

The BODY element follows the header section and indicates the start of the main content of the document. The BODY element encloses the body text, images, and multimedia objects. The P element inserts a new paragraph within a BODY element with a carriage return and line feed. The end tag </P>, which is typically omitted, indicates the following text is the start of a new paragraph.

HTML can link between other documents or to reference points within the existing document. A hyperlink is a "hot spot" with anchor tags that set the HREF attribute to a new destination address. The hyperlink uses an A element of anchor to associate text or a graphic to another document or to another location within the current document. An example from what is probably the World's most popular Web site is:

```
<P>Click <A HREF="//www.microsoft.com/">here</A> to visit the
  Microsoft Web site.
```

The Web site address is enclosed in double quotation marks. The double quotation marks are optional unless the attribute value contains spaces. The intrinsic constant &QUOT may be used when you want to enclose a value that contains double quotation marks.

The second example of a hyperlink is an anchor point within the existing document. The anchor point must first be defined as shown here:

```
<A NAME="usingie40"></A><H2>Using Internet Explorer 4.0</H2>
```

In the context above, you can think of the anchor point as a program label. The line below illustrates a hyperlink back to the HTML document anchor point (program label equivalent).

```
<P>For more information, see <A HREF="#usingie40">Using
  Internet Explorer 4.0</A>
```

Control is transferred to the anchor point *usingie40* when the hyperlink *Using Internet Explorer 4.0* is clicked.

This is not a book on HTML so we won't delve too much further into HTML fundamentals. There are numerous examples of HTML later in the chapter to illustrate the use of different elements. Table 36-2 enumerates HTML tags.

TABLE 36-2 HTML QUICK REFERENCE

TAG	DESCRIPTION
!	Comments. The browser will not display text between tags.
!DOCTYPE	HTML version used in the current document.
A	Stands for anchor. HREF= attribute creates hyperlinks. NAME= attribute creates a named reference.
ADDRESS	A mailing address.
APPLET	Embeds a Java applet. See OBJECT.
AREA	The shape of a "hot spot" in a client-side image map.
B	Makes text bold. See STRONG.
BASE	A document's URL.
BASEFONT	The base font value.
BGSOUND	Include background sounds that play during initial load.
BIG	Increase the font size.
BLOCKQUOTE	A quotation in text.
BODY	Delineate the beginning and the end of the document body. See HEAD.
BR	Insert a line break.
CAPTION	A caption for a table. Valid only within the TABLE element.
CENTER	Used for text and image centering.
CITE	A citation. Used to present a book, paper, or other published source material.
CODE	A code fragment.
COL	Set column properties.
COLGROUP	Set the properties of one or more columns as a group.
COMMENT	A comment, which is not displayed by a browser.
DD	Definition data. Used to format the text for a definition. See DL, DT.
DFN	A definition. Formats a defined term.
DIR	A directory list.

TAG	DESCRIPTION
DIV	A document division. Related elements are grouped together within a document.
DL	A definition list. Used for a list of defined terms. See DT, DD.
DT	A definition term. Used to format the defined term. See DL, DD.
EM	Emphasizes text, usually by rendering the text in italics.
EMBED	Indicates an embedded object. See OBJECT.
FONT	The font style, size, and color.
FORM	Identifies a form for user data entry. See INPUT for a list of form elements.
FRAME	Specifies an independent window or frame within a page. See FRAMESET.
FRAMESET	Specifies frame layout within a page. See FRAME.
Hn	Text is rendered in a heading style, which is normally a larger font than the body text. *n* is a value from 1 to 6.
HEAD	The HTML document heading.
HR	Draws a horizontal rule. Used for section separation.
HTML	Declares the file as an HTML document.
I	Text is rendered in italics.
IMG	Inserts a graphic file.
INPUT	Denotes a form control such as a check box or radio button. See FORM.
ISINDEX	An index is present.
KBD	Indicates text keyboard text. Fixed-width and bold type.
LI	An item in a list. Adds special character or number depending on use. See UL.
LINK	The relationship between documents. Appears only in the HEAD element.
LISTING	Rendered in a fixed-width text type.
MAP	A collection of hot spots for a client-side image map.
MARQUEE	Text is displayed in a scrolling marquee.
MENU	A list of items.
META	Data about data. Provides information about the document and not the document proper. Useful for client query and search engine indexing.

continued

TABLE 36-2 *(continued)*

TAG	DESCRIPTION
NOBR	Turns off line breaking.
NOFRAMES	Limits the viewable content only to browsers that do not support frames.
OBJECT	Equivalent to embedding. Inserts an OLE Control.
OL	An ordered list. Each item has a number or letter reference. See UL, LI.
OPTION	A choice in a list box.
P	A new paragraph. Inserts a paragraph break.
PARAM	Sets object properties.
PLAINTEXT	Equivalent to a monospaced font. Text is a fixed-width type without processing elements.
PRE	Displays raw text exactly as typed with all line breaks and spacing.
S	Text is in a strikethrough type.
SAMP	Sample text. See CODE.
SCRIPT	Include a script.
SELECT	A list box or dropdown list.
SMALL	Reduces the font size.
SPAN	Applies style information to the enclosed text.
STRIKE	Strikethrough text type. See S.
STRONG	Equivalent to bold. See B.
SUB	Text is a subscript.
SUP	Text is a superscript.
TABLE	Table creation. See TH, TR, and TD for row and column definitions.
TBODY	The table body.
TD	Used for creating a cell in a table.
TFOOT	The table footer.
TH	Used to create a row or column heading in a table.
THEAD	The table header.
TEXTAREA	A box for user text input.
TITLE	A document title. Found in the browser title bar.
TR	Creates a table row.

TAG	DESCRIPTION
TT	Teletype designation. Text is displayed as a fixed-width type.
U	Underline text.
UL	Lines are formatted as bulleted text list. See LI.
VAR	Place holder text for a variable. Displays text in a small, fixed-width font.
WBR	Inserts a soft line break in a block of NOBR text.

WHEN IT STARTED: THE FIRST WAVE

The Internet phenomenon is still relatively new. It wasn't too many years ago when the Internet phenomenon started. The first Microsoft effort at a Web page was to port the CGI protocol to Windows NT. CGI isn't scaleable within the Windows NT architecture, and this was followed by ISAPI.

Common Gateway Interface

CGI is a program that executes for each required Web page action. A CGI program enables interactive communication with the Web page, and the program can be written in any language. (This may be the last and only opportunity for FORTRAN to participate in Web technology.) CGI is a standard for all Web servers and is a protocol used by a standalone executable for communicating with an Internet or intranet server. Consequently, the response time can be very poor, and the applications are not scalable. CGI is a UNIX-based application and does not port well to the Windows NT environment. Each CGI application is run in a separate process, and the overhead is horrific.

web links

CGI applications are typically written in the Practical Extraction and Reporting Language (PERL). This is freeware and is available from http://www.activeware.com. **Another source is** ftp://ftp.microsoft.com/bussys/winnt/winnt-public/reskit/nt351/perl.exe.

CGI depends upon the multipurpose Internet mail extension (MIME) protocol. The extensions supported by MIME include:

- *Text* — Plain text or rich text formats (RTF).
- *Multipart* — Mixed, alternative, or parallel messaging structures.
- *Message* — RFC 822 (encapsulated) with external body.
- *Image* — JPEG (JPG) or GIF (still image data).
- *Audio* — Either audio or voice data.
- *Video* — MPEG (MPG).
- *Application* — Binary data (ODA, Postscript, or octet-stream).
- *X-Private* — Private messages exchanged with bilateral agreements.

Figure 36-2 is an example of a CGI application.

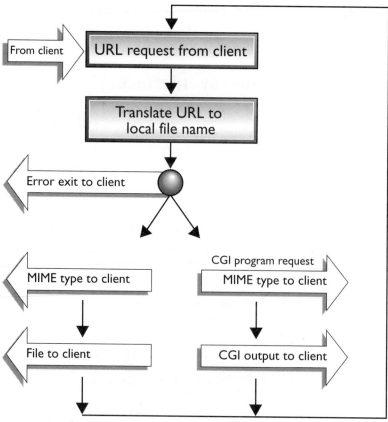

FIGURE 36-2 The structure of a CGI application.

Internet Server API

In some respects, ISAPI and CGI are functionally equivalent. They both deliver the same level of functionality, but a different implementation technique realizes a significantly higher level of performance with ISAPI. The ISAPI Internet functionality is encapsulated within a dynamic link library (DLL), which runs in the same process space as the Internet Information Server, and reduces overhead significantly. The application is now scalable. The overall architecture remains about the same as CGI with the only difference being the call to an in-process DLL; CGI creates a new process. Another CGI limitation is that there is no history. There are a series of CGI environment variables, but these are not enough for a generalized application.

THE SECOND WAVE

We're still dealing with a bit of history here. Microsoft didn't believe the Internet would actually happen. It did and Microsoft nearly missed out. My own image of Microsoft joining the Internet phenomena is a cartoon character chasing a train down the railroad tracks who is able to grasp the caboose railing at the last moment. That is how close I think Microsoft came to missing out on the Internet. Of course, that analogy is probably true of most of the computer industry. Now we know that an elephant can really run. Unfortunately the Microsoft single-mindedness goal of Internet domination is at the expense of other worthy enterprise endeavors. The topics discussed in this section are the Internet Database Connector (IDC) and dbWeb, both of which are not current technologies. These technologies are apparently being replaced, with OLE-DB/ADO used along with design-time controls in an Active Server Page. There is nothing wrong with that, but when does Microsoft deprecate Active Server Pages? Corporations need stability and that is not forthcoming from Microsoft.

Internet Database Connector

IDC is a component of Microsoft Internet Information Server. It is a tool that accepts input from a browser and executes Structured Query Language (SQL) statements against an Open Database Connectivity (ODBC) data source. Resulting output is returned to the client as an HTML document. This is not an interactive

Internet technology and is falling out of favor with Microsoft. Figure 36-3 illustrates the IDC architecture.

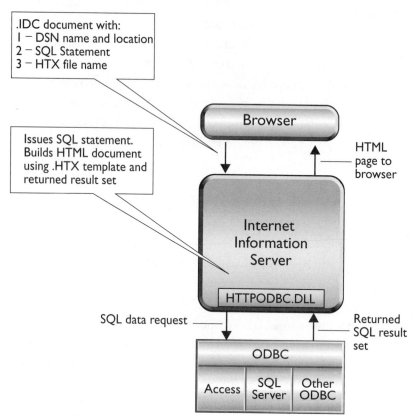

.IDC document with:
1 – DSN name and location
2 – SQL Statement
3 – HTX file name

Issues SQL statement.
Builds HTML document
using .HTX template and
returned result set

Browser

HTML
page to
browser

Internet
Information
Server

HTTPODBC.DLL

SQL data request

Returned
SQL result
set

ODBC

Access | SQL Server | Other ODBC

FIGURE 36-3   The IDC architecture.

An application is not limited to any one particular technology. The HTTPODBC.DLL of IDC can be combined with ISAPI to create very complex applications. ISAPI also has the concept of a filter to customize an application with features such as authentication or logging. The combination of all these technologies is shown in Figure 36-4, where a filter is placed between the browser and access to the Internet Information Server.

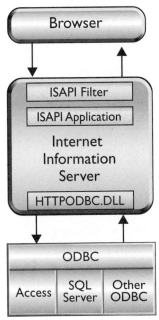

FIGURE 36-4   Combining ISAPI and IDC.

Both `.IDC` and `.HTX` (hypertext markup language extension) files can be created in Notepad, but tools such as FrontPage 98 and Microsoft Access have automated this process. The IDC and HTX files are templates, and are illustrated below in Listings 36-1 and 36-2.

LISTING 36-1   A vacuous IDC file

```
Datasource:
Username:
Password:
DefaultParameters:
RequiredParameters:
Expires:
Template:
SQLStatement:
```

The only note of caution on the IDC template file is that the **Datasource** parameter must always be a "System DSN" (data source name).

LISTING 36-2 An example of an HTX file

```
<html>
<head>
</head>
<%BeginDetail%>
<%Item%>, <%Description%><br>
<%EndDetail%>
</html>
```

The *Item* and *Description* parameters are column names of the SQL statement in the .IDC file.

Let's create a small example of an IDC file from Access 97 (see Figure 36-5 and Listing 36-3). We'll start with the small Access database we used for the dynamic data exchange (DDE) examples in Chapter 33. Open DDESRVR.MDB in Access 97 and use the following scenario to create an IDC/HTX file:

- Select Tables and open the **Inventory** table in design mode.
- Select **SaveAs HTML**.
- Select **Next**.
- Select *Inventory*.
- Select **Next**.
- Select **Browse**.
- Select DEFAULT.HTM.
- Select **Select**.
- Select **Dynamic HTX/IDC**.
- Select **Finish**.

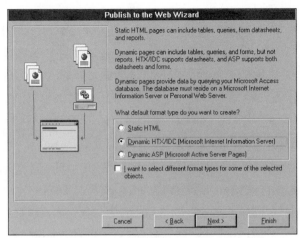

FIGURE 36-5 Access 97 and publishing to the Web with HTX/IDC.

LISTING 36-3 The HTX create in Figure 36-5

```
<HTML>
<TITLE>Inventory</TITLE>
<BODY BGCOLOR="#FFFFFF">
<TABLE BORDER=1 BGCOLOR=#ffffff CELLSPACING=0><FONT
 FACE="Arial"
 COLOR=#000000><CAPTION><B>Inventory</B></CAPTION>
<THEAD>
    <TR>
        <TH BGCOLOR=#c0c0c0 BORDERCOLOR=#000000 ><FONT SIZE=2
                                    FACE="Arial"
COLOR=#000000>ItemID</FONT></TH>
        <TH BGCOLOR=#c0c0c0 BORDERCOLOR=#000000 ><FONT SIZE=2
                                    FACE="Arial"
COLOR=#000000>PartNumber</FONT></TH>
        <TH BGCOLOR=#c0c0c0 BORDERCOLOR=#000000 ><FONT SIZE=2
                                    FACE="Arial"
COLOR=#000000>Description</FONT></TH>
    </TR>
</THEAD>
<TBODY>
    <%BeginDetail%>
```

```
        <TR VALIGN=TOP>
            <TD BORDERCOLOR=#c0c0c0  ALIGN=RIGHT><FONT
SIZE=2
                FACE="Arial"
COLOR=#000000><%ItemID%><BR></FONT>
            </TD>
            <TD BORDERCOLOR=#c0c0c0  ALIGN=RIGHT><FONT
SIZE=2
                FACE="Arial"
COLOR=#000000><%PartNumber%><BR></FONT>
            </TD>
            <TD BORDERCOLOR=#c0c0c0 ><FONT SIZE=2
 FACE="Arial"
COLOR=#000000><%Description%><BR></FONT>
            </TD>
        </TR>
    <%EndDetail%>
</TBODY>
<TFOOT></TFOOT>
</TABLE>
</BODY>
<BR><BR>
<IMG SRC = "msaccess.jpg">
</HTML>
```

Note the *BeginDetail* and *EndDetail* elements of the .HTX file in Listing 36-3. This is the section where the data is displayed. You'll want to remember these for the Windows Architecture I core examination. Other than the HTX extensions, the file appears as a normal HTML document.

SQL Server Web Assistant

You might have noticed in Figure 36-5 that one of the options is static HTML. This is a form of HTML that cannot be interacted with by either the client or the Web server. This is referred to as *push* technology, where a static page is published on a periodic basic. Microsoft SQL Server 6.5 publishes static HTML with the SQL Server Web Assistant, an example of which is shown in Figure 36-6. No examples are provided for this easy-to-use tool. The SQL Web Assistant can also publish a page on a data change. An easy example is the posting of product price changes.

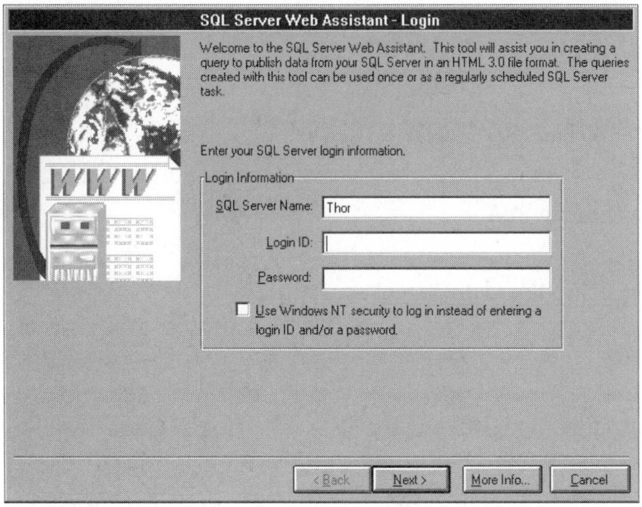

FIGURE 36-6 SQL Server 6.5 Web Assistant.

HTML from Office 97

Microsoft published a series of *Internet Assistants*. These tools served the purpose of converting Office 95 documents to HTML format. This capability is now embedded in Office 97, and all Office 97 applications can save their data as HTML documents. The general mechanism is the **SaveAs** command from the **File** menu.

Visual Basic for Applications (VBA) may only be used in Access 97 and Word 97 to save data in HTML format. Excel 97 and PowerPoint 97 documents may be saved as HTML documents, but not by using VBA. The code snippets below illustrate using VBA to save data in HTML format.

Static HTML from Access using VBA

This example outputs a file in HTML format and immediately starts the default Web browser.

```
DoCmd.OutputTo acOutputTable, "Inventory", acFormatHTML,
  "Inventory.htm", True
```

IDC/HTX from Access using VBA

This example outputs the **Inventory** table to the `INVENTORY.IDC` file and merges the `MC.HTM` template file with the `INVENTORY.HTX` file.

```
DoCmd.OutputTo acOutputTable, "Inventory", acFormatIIS,
  "Inventory",, H:\Office97\Templates\Access\Mc.htm"
```

Static HTML from Word using VBA

Listing 36-4 is an example of an active Word document being saved as a static HTML page using VBA.

LISTING 36-4 Saving the active Word document as static HTML

```
Sub Save_Word_As_HTML
 Dim MyDoc
 Dim intType As Integer
 Dim IntPos as Integer
 intType = FileConverters(:HTML").SaveFormat
 MyDoc = ActiveDocument.Name
 intPos = InStr(myDoc, ".")
 If intPos > 0 Then
  MyDoc = Left(myDoc, intPos -1)
  MyDoc = MyDoc & ".html"
  ActiveDocument.SaveAs FileName:=MyDoc, FileFormat:=intType
 End If
End Sub
```

Access 97 also supports saving a document as an ASP from VBA. This technology is discussed in the next chapter where we dissect the Web site designed for this section.

dbWeb

dbWeb is still Microsoft's second wave of Internet technology. dbWeb is a free ISAPI tool consisting of a dbWeb ISAPI client, a dbWeb Windows NT service, and a dbWeb Administrator. I located my version on CD-ROM 9 of the Microsoft Developer Network (MSDN), Professional Edition. It is also available on the

TechNet CD-ROM subscription starting in July 1996. My July and August Technet copies had decompression errors when trying to load dbWeb 1.1 and September 1996 was the first TechNet issue where a good copy was available. dbWeb was not available as advertised on the Microsoft page `http://www.microsoft.com/intdev/dbweb/`.

Figure 36-7 illustrates the dbWeb architecture.

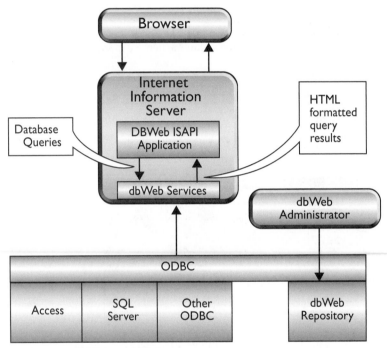

FIGURE 36-7   dbWeb architecture.

After you've installed dbWeb on Windows NT Server 3.51 service pack 4 or better, the proper ODBC drivers and the Internet Information Server (IIS), you must go to the **Services** icon in *Control Panel* and start the dbWeb service. With that accomplished, double-click the dbWeb icon and expand the data sources and schemas. Your expanded image should match Figure 36-8.

A special warning on dbWeb: The DBWEB.MDB repository is an Access 2.0 database, and any repairs or compression by either Access 95 or Access 97 will corrupt DBWEB.MDB.

FIGURE 36-8   dbWeb with the default schema expanded.

dbWeb is not much different than SQL Server Web Assistant. The dbWeb published HTML is static. Selecting *New Schema* from Figure 36-8 followed by selecting *Schema Wizard* creates Figure 36-9.

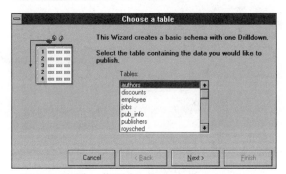

FIGURE 36-9   The dbWeb schema wizard.

An example of a dbWeb application can be found in the dbWeb directory. Ascertain that the Windows NT dbWeb service is running. Use Windows NT Explorer to start DBWTEST.HTM found in the directory where dbWeb is installed. After the page is started in Windows Internet Explorer, select the **Titles** hyperlink. Figure 36-10, which is an example of a dbWeb query, will be displayed.

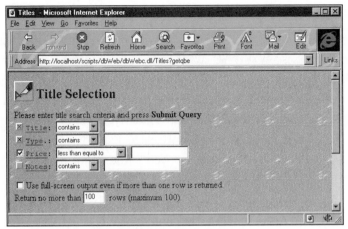

FIGURE 36-10 A sample dbWeb query page.

THE THIRD WAVE

The third wave of Microsoft Internet technology includes Microsoft Internet Explorer 3.0 and beyond, Microsoft FrontPage 98 (a product developed by a company named Vermeer which Microsoft purchased), and ASP of Internet Information Server 3.0 and beyond. The first wave of Microsoft Internet technology involved standalone Internet applications that are primitive by today's standards. The second wave added intelligence to a Web browser, but at the client's expense. The third wave of Microsoft Internet technology moves work directly to the server with ASP. It is not possible to use ASP in an Internet environment unless your Internet service provider supports ASP on its Web host. ASP pages appear to be a natural choice for an intranet where the corporation has control of both the client and server sites.

FrontPage 98

FrontPage 98 is the first tool of the Microsoft third wave of Internet technology. FrontPage 98 is a WYSIWYG (What You See Is What You Get) Web-page creation tool. It provides the essential esthetics and simplifies Web-page generation. If you heard a strange noise recently, that was the transmogrification of a 60-year-old hacker to a 17-year-old Webmaster. (Aaarrrggghhh! I can feel the Web power now!) Figure 36-11 is a view of FrontPage 98 Explorer with a Web site created to illustrate the issues of this chapter. You'll find all the files in the MYWEB directory of your CD-ROM. The Web site expects a SQL Server connection DSN of "ZEUS" and a Microsoft Access 97 connection DSN of "Northwind." FrontPage 98 expects an Access database to be imported into the Web root, the NORTH-WIND.MDB database, and you must use the **Import** command of FrontPage 98 before Web pages using Access will function. Microsoft Visual Interdev also uses both of these database connections.

After the Web site was complete, I attempted to insert a scanned photograph on a page. My first warning of a problem was a dialog box warning me that the server connection was dropped. Things got worse from there. I exited FrontPage 98 and shut everything down. Everything restarted but FrontPage 98 could not load my Web page. My Web page was nearly lost when the configuration file __VTI_PVT, along with other files, was destroyed. Large images cannot be inserted into Web pages with FrontPage 98.

FRONTPAGE TARPITS

Windows NT Server IIS uses HTTP Port 80 for active server pages. So does the Personal Web Server. If you're using FrontPage on Windows NT Server and you've installed the Personal Web Server, you'll want to modify the FrontPage HTTP configuration file. Edit the file:

```
<Server>\FrontPage
  Webs\conf\httpd.cnf
```

Change the statement *Port 80* to *Port 8080*. This places the Personal Web Server on Port 8080 and IIS active server pages on Port 80. A simpler answer is to never install the Personal Web Server when FrontPage is installed on Windows NT Server. If you have an HTTP 501 error, this is probably the problem.

I realize that the Web site cannot be reconstructed by all readers, so as each page of the Web site is presented, I'll also list the essential HTML and scripts.

The configuration for this Web site is:

- Microsoft Windows NT Server 4.0 service pack 3 with system name ZEUS.
- Microsoft FrontPage 98 with FrontPage 98 Server Extensions.
- Microsoft Internet Information Server 3.0.
- Microsoft Office 97 Professional Edition with service release 1.
- Microsoft Visual Studio 97 Enterprise Edition with service release 1.
- Microsoft SQL Server 6.5 service pack 3 with server name THOR.
- ODBC driver versions 3.50.3602.
- DAO 3.5 installed.
- OLE-DB 1.1 installed.
- A server named ZEUS with a DSN of "ZEUS" pointing to the PUBS database of SQL Server.
- A secondary DSN of "NORTHWIND" that points to an imported Access 97 NORTHWIND.MDB in the Web root WWWROOT/MYWEB.
- Microsoft Internet Explorer 3.02. This was installed because it shipped with FrontPage 98. Internet Explorer 4.0 is available, but I elected to not use it.
- A 131MB 133MHz system with two 75MB swap files.

Let's start by taking a quick look at FrontPage 98. Figure 36-11 is a view of FrontPage 98 Explorer showing the architecture of the Web site used for the examples in this chapter.

FrontPage 98 makes it very easy to construct the page, but that is all you want to do using FrontPage. You'll want to design your Web site with FrontPage 98 and then move on to Visual InterDev for your database connections. The other choice is to use Access 97 to create an IDC script and HTX prototype page, and then patch them as necessary into pages created for FrontPage 98.

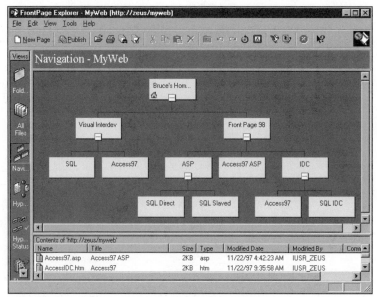

FIGURE 36-11   A view of the FrontPage 98 Explorer.

The implementation of FrontPage 98 is very uneven. The themes and the rich font set deserve an A+ in a graduate course in computer science. (They're hot!) What's not good in FrontPage 98 includes issues that are almost sophomoric in their lack of usefulness and that would not get a passing grade in a graduate computer science class. What's not good in FrontPage 98 includes:

- Microsoft FrontPage development informed me that IDC was being deprecated because service providers didn't universally support it. This is a strange statement to make because it ignores the intranet.

- We know from the JAVA wars that Microsoft wants a Microsoft world. IDC/HTX technology can be platform-independent, where the `HTTPODBC.DLL` of IDC is equivalent to an ISAPI application. Microsoft's current focus is on interactive Web pages of ASP and not IDC/HTX technology, which is not interactive. IDC/HTX doesn't fit into the scheme of active pages with active controls, active scripts, active documents, and an active server that binds you to the Microsoft architecture.

- Field names are not available automatically when using the Database Region Wizard; you have to remember what they are and enter them manually. The same is true for parameter names. I expected to be able to pick a table from the DSN and be able to select column names and parameter names.

- A less than useful (I'm being very polite here) script editing environment. An error occurred in a `MID` function at line 81 during the construction of one of my ASP pages. There are no line numbers and I didn't know where line 81 was located because I didn't know how lines are counted. Is it the total line count or the line count of the server script? I searched the text for the `MID` function and found there were a dozen or more instances. At that time I decided to trash the page and start again.

- FrontPage 98 Database Region Wizard only supports ODBC data sources. A system DSN to an Access 97 `MDB` is not functional in a FrontPage 98 ASP page.

- The ASP code generation in FrontPage 98 is less than adequate. There is duplicated functionality, and the solution appears to be pasted in rather than architected. Remember that these fat pages with superfluous code are being shipped back and forth on the wire. The ASP code from Microsoft Access 97, FrontPage 98, and Visual InterDev have very little similarity. Access 97 uses active data objects (ADO) and is relatively clean, but it doesn't work with FrontPage 98. You can get it to work with hacking. The ASP code in FrontPage 98 uses an ugly creature called a WebBot, while Visual InterDev uses ActiveX controls. You can't hack WebBots and when a FrontPage 98 ASP page doesn't work, there isn't much you can do.

- It is almost as if there are three competing groups within Microsoft, each generating their own version of the technology and not supporting each other. (Examples of the three different types of ASP page types are found in Chapter 37.)

- The FrontPage 98 Database Region Wizard only creates ASP. I am not convinced that service providers will universally support ASP, which is the reason given for the deprecation of the IDC/HTX technology, which repeats the problem. What service provider would want to support ASP when Microsoft currently has three different versions of the technology?

Beyond that, would a service provider want to support something that is not a standard and which Microsoft can capriciously decide to stop supporting? I don't know, but I sometimes feel that Microsoft technology has a half-life on the order of six to nine months.

Microsoft Visual InterDev is easy to use. The recommendation is to construct your pages in FrontPage 98 and build the database connections in Visual InterDev. FrontPage 98 is still a very highly recommended product. Just don't use all the features. What's hot in FrontPage 98 includes:

- *Ease of use* — It is very simple to construct the pages.
- *Fonts and themes* — I've already mentioned them once. They are so good they deserve to be mentioned again.
- *Component renaming* — Hyperlinks are automatically updated when a component is renamed. This is a very helpful feature
- *Design-time controls* — FrontPage 97 has the limitation that once a design-time control is placed on the form, FrontPage 97 cannot be used to reedit the page. This restriction no longer exists in FrontPage 98.
- *Repairing links* — FrontPage 98 automates repairing broken links in a Web page project.

We can't move on without a few passing comments on FrontPage 98 architecture, which consists of an explorer, an editor, and a to-do list. It supports a user interface for *WebBots,* which are automation features. WebBots are features of FrontPage 98-generated HTML code, while ActiveX designer controls are a feature of Microsoft Visual InterDev. WebBots are executed on the Web server and provide many of the features normally relegated to VBA. Figure 36-12 is the FrontPage architecture showing the relationship of all components. You'll see WebBots in the next chapter, where we dissect a Web site.

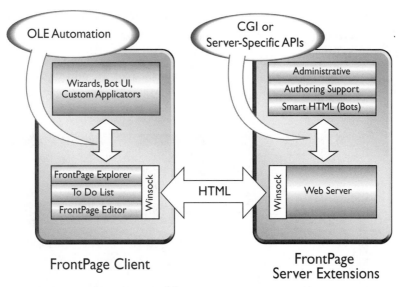

FIGURE 36-12 FrontPage 98 architecture.

Visual InterDev

Another key component of the Microsoft Internet/intranet architecture is Visual InterDev (VI). It is a tool used to create ASP pages and is a component of Visual Studio 97 Enterprise Edition. There are no problems with Visual InterDev. It is clean and very well designed. A few features are a bit obscure, but other than that it is tool which enables the developer to create a Web page in just a few minutes.

Visual InterDev is an integrated development environment contained within Microsoft Visual Studio 97 Enterprise, which itself is an integrated environment. Everything is there and the functionality goes far beyond just creating ASP pages. Additional features include the ability to easily create a query and embed the query on an ASP page, the inclusion of the standard VBA controls such as text boxes and push buttons, the inclusion of design-time controls, and the ability the edit SQL Server stored procedures and to create databases.

Using Visual InterDev is relatively easy if you've ever used Microsoft Access. Many of the Visual InterDev features have counterparts in Microsoft Access.

You start Visual InterDev by selecting *New* from the **File** menu and clicking the **Project** tab in the dialog box. You can import your Web site constructed with FrontPage 98 after you've defined your project. The next logical step is to define your data connections. A Visual InterDev data connection must use a system DSN, which is done from the **Project** menu. To create a project data collection, select **Project** ⇒ **Add to Project** ⇒ **Data Connection**. (You can create a system DSN in your Windows system's Control Panel.)

With the data connections established for the project, select **Data View** and your **Project** view should resemble the left pane of Figure 36-13 below.

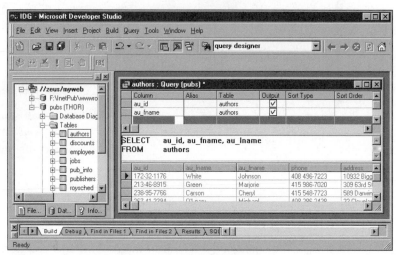

FIGURE 36-13   **Creating a query in Visual InterDev.**

To create an ASP page, follow these steps:

1. Select New from the File menu.

2. Select *Active Server Page* and provide a page name.

3. Close the dialog box and the screen displays the HTML of your new ASP page.

4. Controls are placed on an ASP page by positioning the cursor at the desired point and right-click the mouse. Because this is a new ASP paging the cursor is already positioned at the proper insertion point. Right-click the mouse and select *Insert ActiveX Control* from the menu displayed in Figure 36-14.

5. Click the *Design-Time* tab.

6. Click *DataCommand* control.

7. Select your data connection. The example of Figure 36-13 has a *pubs* database connection.

8. Select *SQL Builder*. At this point your screen should resemble Figure 36-13.

9. You previously placed the Project window in *data view*. If you haven't done this, do so now and expand a data connection to expose the table names. Drag a table to the query pane. The *authors* table of the *pubs* database was selected in Figure 36-13.

10. Select the desired columns.

11. Move to the SQL pane and edit the SQL as necessary.

12. Keep the cursor positioned over the SQL pane and right-click. A pop-up menu is displayed. Select *Verify SQL*. Continue to edit the SQL if necessary. When the SQL is correct, close all windows. An ASP page with a design-time control was created.

To edit an existing ASP page, follow these steps:

1. Place the Project Workspace window in *file mode*.

2. Double-click the ASP page to be edited.

3. Move the cursor over the design-time HTML code and right-click. Select *Edit Design-Time Control* from the pop-up menu and edit the control as necessary.

Creating VBA-type controls is a bit obscure. These controls are different than those found in the *Insert ActiveX Control* entry of Figure 36-14. To add VBA type ActiveX controls to your Web site, follow these steps:

1. Select *New* from the File menu.

2. Select *HTML Layout* and provide a file name. This file will have an .ALX extension.

3. Close the dialog box and you'll see the familiar VBA toolbox. Hack as necessary and save the results when completed.

4. Use the *Insert HTML Layout* entry of Figure 36-14 to insert the controls into an ASP page. Be sure your cursor is properly positioned on the page before inserting the HTML.

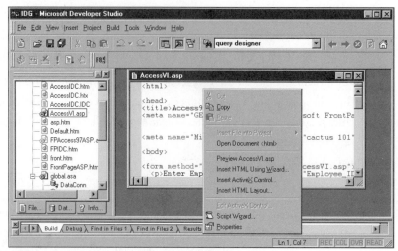

FIGURE 36-14   Editing an existing ASP page.

That was a thumbnail sketch of Microsoft Visual InterDev. There are many more features, but the basic issue here is the role of Visual InterDev in the Microsoft Internet/intranet architecture and not the finer points of Web page development.

The product is integrated with Visual SourceSafe and can be used in a multi-developer environment. Look very carefully at Figure 36-13. The Web site is on the server ZEUS while the *pubs* database is on the Windows NT Server THOR. Visual InterDev is on a separate workstation. Members of this triage use ODBC for communication.

Internet Explorer

Internet Explorer (IE) 3.02 was shipped with FrontPage 98 even though IE 4.0 is available. This makes IE 3.02 my browser of choice for FrontPage 98, and all IE examples in this book are based on IE 3.02.

Microsoft Internet Explorer is the bridge between the desktop and the Internet/intranet. IE does this by being the focal point of different technologies, all of which are ActiveX based. Internet Explorer itself is constructed from two ActiveX controls, the first being the "Microsoft Internet and Shell Control," or SHDOCVW.OCX. This is now called the WebBrowser control, and there are examples of using this control in Chapter 38. The second control is the "Microsoft

Internet Intrinsic Control," or `HTMLCTL.OCX`, which has been renamed to `INTRNSIC.OCX`.

Internet Explorer is the Microsoft de facto Web browser and as such supports HTML documents as a universal standard. However, Internet Explorer also supports:

- *ActiveX controls* — These are controls that are downloaded from a server site as a component of a Web page.

- *Active documents* — The simplest example of this is to drag a Word document into Internet Explorer. The document is hosted with a merging of menu and tool bars, but is not converted to HTML format.

- *Active scripts* — Internet Explorer supports Visual Basic Scripts and Java Scripts.

- *HTML and HTML extensions* — Microsoft goes a bit beyond standard HTML to ease Internet use with HTML extensions.

- *Code downLoad and verification* — A code download service that minimizes download time. Code verification and signing are both significant features of the Microsoft ActiveX Internet architecture.

Much more could be said about Microsoft Internet Explorer. I prefer to call it a bridge in the context of an ODBC bridge. It is the desktop's bridge to the outside world. It recognizes HTML and scripts, but also supports active documents, which translates to supporting any documents created by a Microsoft tool.

KEY POINT SUMMARY

The Internet is not new, but it is new as a public network. The World Wide Web is quite new, and newer World Wide Web technology is spawned before the last wave of technology has gained wide acceptance.

- TCP/IP is the Internet transport protocol. Above that is the HTTP of the World Wide Web. IPX/SPX and TCP/IP are the only protocols in the Microsoft architecture to support sockets.

- HTML is the universal publishing protocol of the WWW. It is a standard and is supported by all WWW browsers and servers. The only issue is that of using HTML technology that is not yet a standard and that can be discarded very quickly when the winds of technology change.

- The common gateway interface is the first and the most primitive Web publishing protocol in the Microsoft architecture. It functions as a standalone application and suffers from not being scalable.

- ISAPI has the advantage of running within the process space of the server. This significantly reduces overhead.

- The next step up in publishing functionality (it's not really a step up because an ISAPI application can be relatively fast) is the IDC. The appeal of IDC is the ease with which an application can be generated. An IDC application is not interactive and is only useful for ODBC-registered data sources.

- The functionality of Internet technology is still moving forward with the inclusion of scripting. The first scripting was limited to only the browser and included both Visual Basic Scripting and Java Scripting. During this time frame, Internet ActiveX controls were introduced.

- Functionality continues to move forward. Now there is the concept of an ASP where portions of the page are executed on the server and other portions are executed on the client browser. A copy of the original page is returned to the browser, which gives the appearance of interaction.

Applying What You've Learned

The review questions measure your comprehension of the issues discussed in this chapter. The questions are a study guide for the Internet and intranet section of the Microsoft Windows Architecture I core examination.

Instant Assessment

1. What advantages does the ISAPI have as compared to the CGI protocol?

2. What is the use of the `<%begin detail%>` and `<%end detail%>` tags? Where are they used and what is their purpose?

3. You wish to publish on the Web. The problem is you want to minimize the Web server load. Which technology is appropriate? (Consider only the Web publishing technologies discussed in this chapter.)

4. FrontPage 98 has automated many facets of Web page creation. One is the IDC wizard, which is started by double-clicking an IDC script. A tool such as Access 97 can generate an IDC script, but that's not always necessary. What are the three essential ingredients of an IDC script that enable FrontPage 98 to automatically generate the .HTX HTML prototype page?

5. What technology can be used to retrieve data from an ODBC data source?

6. There are numerous tags within HTML, and the popular ones should be known. What tag is in error when the browser restarts inadvertently? Within what HTML element would you place buttons or text boxes?

7. The time to load a page is always significant. Microsoft Internet Explorer supports a technology that allows the image to be viewed as it is loaded. What is that technology called?

8. You wish to periodically publish price changes to a parts catalog on a Web page. There is also a requirement to publish a price change immediately when it exceeds a certain threshold. Which Microsoft Internet publishing technology is appropriate?

9. What is the defining difference between ASP and IDC?

 concept link **For answers to the Instant Assessment questions, see Appendix C.**

Lab Exercises

Lab 36.71 *Hosting Active Documents*

WA I

The concept of dynamism within the Microsoft architecture is not well understood. When using the architecture on a daily basis, the subtle nuances are not noticed. I've mentioned several times that the Microsoft architecture consists of active controls, active documents, active scripts, active servers, and active services.

This lab requires Office 97 and Internet Explorer. The following scenario illustrates the concept of an active document:

1. Load Word 97 and place text on a page. Save the page as a regular .DOC file and as an HTML page.

2. Do the same for Microsoft Excel. Start Excel 97 and enter some numbers. Save the spreadsheet as both an HTML page and as a .XLS file.

3. Close both Word 97 and Excel 97.

4. Open Internet Explorer and examine both the Excel-generated and the Word 97-generated HTML documents.

5. Place Internet Explorer on the task bar.

6. Go to *My Computer* and locate the .DOC file or the .XLS file in the appropriate folder. Drag either of these files to the task bar location of Internet Explorer. After Internet Explorer starts, drop the .DOC or .XLS document into Internet Explorer.

7. Note the difference in appearance. This is an active document where menu bars are merged. Note that you can edit the Word and Excel files from within Internet Explorer. Internet Explorer is indeed the bridge between the desktop and the enterprise.

8. Note the differences between an HTML document in Internet Explorer and the native document. Internet Explorer functions both as a native document host and as a container for active documents. (You should have found a surprise when hosting the different documents. The answer is obvious with a few moments of reflection.)

Lab 36.72 *Building your own Web pages*

WA I
WA II

This is not a specific laboratory. Use either Access 97, FrontPage 98, Visual InterDev, or SQL Web Assistant to practice creating Web pages. Use the examples in this chapter as a guide. You can display the resultant HTML in Word 97, Internet Explorer, or FrontPage 98. The wizards are straightforward and you should have no problems. You'll want this experience for Chapter 37 when we add database functionality to our Web site.

About Chapter 37

Chapter 37 explores a working Web site that was specifically constructed for this chapter. It addresses only one Windows Architecture I objective: using the Internet Data Connector (IDC), FrontPage 98, and Active Server Pages (ASP) generated by Microsoft Access, FrontPage 98, and Microsoft Visual InterDev.

The Web site used in this chapter is located in the EXAMPLES\ CHAPTER37\MYWEB folder of the CD-ROM that accompanies this book. The Web site was copied from the path F:\INETPUB\WWWROOT\MYWEB folder of a Windows NT 4.0 Server system. The server is registered as ZEUS and the Web address is `http://zeus/myweb`.

THE WEB SITE

Let's start by looking at the Web site pages shown in Figures 37-1 and 37-2, which is the home page of the site. The Web page examples exhibit a hybrid coding style where manually inserted HTML code, FrontPage 98 HTML, and Visual InterDev ASP HTML are intermixed. This is done to illustrate architectural issues. For example, a parameter query is not created and the HTML is added manually. The reasons for this will become apparent as the examples unfold. The physical file name of each web page is found in the Internet Explorer address window. These Web pages are in the MYWEB directory of the CD-ROM that accompanies this book. You'll want to use Notepad to examine the HTML code.

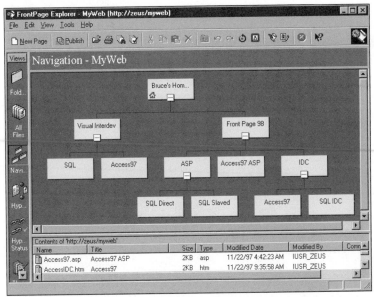

FIGURE 37-1 The Web site architecture displayed in FrontPage98.

Starting the Web site is done by double-clicking the home page in FrontPage 98 Explorer and then selecting *Preview in Browser* from the **File** menu after the page is displayed. Internet Explorer starts, resulting in Figure 37-2 (see Listing 37-1 for HTML code).

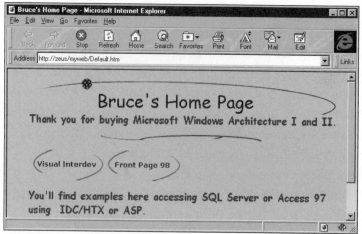

FIGURE 37-2   My home page.

LISTING 37-1 The HTML for Figure 37-2

```
!DOCTYPE HTML PUBLIC "-//IETF//DTD HTML//EN">
<html>

<head>
     <title>Bruce's Home Page</title>
     <meta name="Microsoft Theme"
          content="cactus 101">
     <meta name="Microsoft Border"
          content="tl, default">
</head>

<body>

<h3>Thank you for buying Microsoft Windows
     Architecture I and II.
</h3>

<hr align="center">

<p><!--webbot bot="Navigation" S-Type="children"
     S-Orientation="horizontal" S-Rendering="graphics"
```

```
          B-Include-Home B-Include-Up -->
</p>

<h3>You'll find examples here accessing SQL Server
     or Access 97 using IDC/HTX or ASP.
</h3>

<hr align="center">
 </body>
</html>
```

The Wizard that prompts you when FrontPage 98 is opened generated Figure 37-2 and the subsequent Listing 37-1. After the page was created I selected Format ⇒ Themes to change the page theme. I then selected **Insert** ⇒ **Navigation Bar**. The page was saved and the text comments were added later. Once the **Navigation** bar is embedded, FrontPage 98 maintains all links.

VISUAL INTERDEV AND ACTIVE SERVER PAGES

The next page of the Web site is shown in Figure 37-3 and was created in FrontPage Explorer by first selecting the home page and then selecting *New Page* from the FrontPage 98 toolbar. New pages are automatically attached to the currently selected page. The name was changed from *New Page 1* to *Visual InterDev*. The page was then double-clicked for display in the FrontPage 98 Editor. It was displayed with the theme of the home page, but I still had the opportunity to change it. A navigation bar was added because I knew this page would be the parent of other Web pages. The page was saved. I won't deal with any more minutiae, because the ease of use of FrontPage 98 is obvious.

Both of the examples indicated by the hyperlinks of Figure 37-3 are Active Server Pages. We've already created the *Active Server Pages* (ASP) of this Web site (see Chapter 36, Figures 36-13 and 36-14), and now we're looking at our handiwork. The pages are recursive in that the **Post** method in the **Submit** button points to the current page. We learned in Chapter 36 that the POST method of the HTTP protocol is entity producing. This means the POST method will always create a new page. The name of the new page in the POST method is the same as the current page, and when the same page is returned with changes, a sense of interaction is communicated to the user. The current page is pushed down on the memory stack when the new page is returned. This is understood by considering the actions after the submit button is clicked. The POST method sends the page to the server. The server executes the ASP server-relevant code and sends the page back to the browser. The prior page at the browser is not destroyed, but is simply pushed down on the stack. If the user elects to go to another page, other than the parent of this page, all referenced pages remain on the memory stack until the browser exits. Continually depressing the left-arrow of the browser will pop the pages off the stack until the parent page is exposed. Unfortunately this self-referencing mechanism is what makes the page appear as interactive. It is at the expense of memory. A self-referencing page has the page filename as an argument of the **Post** method such as:

```
<form method="POST" action="/myweb/SQLVI.asp">
```

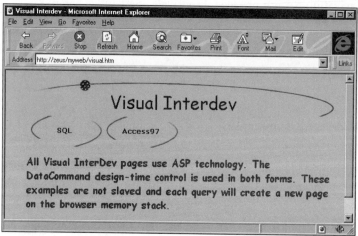

FIGURE 37-3   Branching to Visual InterDev examples on our Web site.

A *slaved* page is an architecture where the results are placed on a separate page and the user must use the **Back** arrow of the browser to return to the query page. The fact that pages may accumulate on the memory stack is not an error with Microsoft implementations of either browser or server software. This is the basic design of the HTTP protocol. Remember that the HTTP protocol is connectionless, and the mechanism that creates the illusion of interaction is to modify the current page.

The HTML of Figure 37-3 is not presented because its only functionality is two hyperlinks to two child pages. Figure 37-4 is a self-referencing ASP created in Visual InterDev. The page retrieves three columns from the *pubs* database of SQL Server.

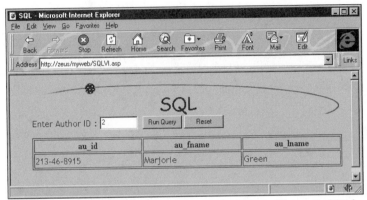

FIGURE 37-4   A Visual InterDev ASP in a FrontPage 98-created Web.

No HTML is listed for Figure 37-4 because it is functionally equivalent to Figure 37-5 (see Listing 37-2 for HTML code). The only differences are the data connection, table name, and column names.

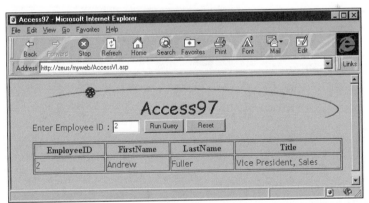

FIGURE 37-5   An ASP of Visual InterDev with an Access database connection.

LISTING 37-2 The HTML code of Figure 37-5

```html
<html>

<head>
        <title>Access97</title>
        <meta name="GENERATOR"
            content="Microsoft FrontPage 3.0">
        <meta name="Microsoft Theme"
            content="cactus 101">
        <meta name="Microsoft Border"
            content="tl, default">
</head>

<body>

<form method="POST" action="/myweb/AccessVI.asp">
        <p>Enter Employee ID :
            <input Name="Employee_ID" size="6"
                VALUE="<%=Request("Employee_ID")%>">
            <input TYPE="SUBMIT"
                VALUE="Run Query" name="B1">
            <input type="reset"
                value="Reset" name="B2"> 
        </p>
</form>

<table WIDTH="100%" BORDER="1">
  <tr>
    <th>EmployeeID</th>
    <th>FirstName</th>
    <th>LastName</th>
    <th>Title</th>
  </tr>
<!    Above is the end of the manual addition. Below is a
    design-time DataCommand control. The code is unchanged
    from the Datacontrol wizard. I did use the Request
```

method in the wizard and verified the syntax before
saving the query. (There are extra spaces in the query
for book formatting purposes.)>

```
<!--METADATA TYPE="DesignerControl" startspan
    <OBJECT ID="DataCommand1" WIDTH=151 HEIGHT=24
        CLASSID="CLSID:7FAEED80-9D58-11CF-8F68-00AA006D27C2">
        <PARAM NAME="_Version" VALUE="65536">
        <PARAM NAME="_Version" VALUE="65536">
        <PARAM NAME="_ExtentX" VALUE="3969">
        <PARAM NAME="_ExtentY" VALUE="635">
        <PARAM NAME="_StockProps" VALUE="0">
        <PARAM NAME="DataConnection" VALUE="DataConn">
        <PARAM NAME="CommandText"
            VALUE="SELECT EmployeeID, LastName, " & _
                "FirstName, Title FROM Employees " & _
                    "WHERE EmployeeID LIKE " & _

"'[Request(&quot;Employee_ID&quot;)] %'">
    </OBJECT>
-->
<%
Set DataConn = Server.CreateObject("ADODB.Connection")
DataConn.ConnectionTimeout = _
  Session("DataConn_ConnectionTimeout")
DataConn.CommandTimeout = _
  Session("DataConn_CommandTimeout")
DataConn.Open Session("DataConn_ConnectionString"),
 Session("DataConn_RuntimeUserName"),
Session("DataConn_RuntimePassword")
Set cmdTemp = Server.CreateObject("ADODB.Command")
Set DataCommand1 = _
  Server.CreateObject("ADODB.Recordset")
cmdTemp.CommandText = "SELECT EmployeeID, " & _
  "LastName, FirstName, Title FROM Employees " & _\
  "WHERE EmployeeID LIKE '" & _
  Request("Employee_ID") & "%'"
```

```
cmdTemp.CommandType = 1
Set cmdTemp.ActiveConnection = DataConn
DataCommand1.Open cmdTemp, , 0, 1
%>
<!--METADATA TYPE="DesignerControl" endspan—>
<!    A manual insertion to display the returned data.>
  <tr>
    <td><%Response.Write DataCommand1("EmployeeID")%>
  </td>
    <td><%Response.Write DataCommand1("FirstName")%>
  </td>
    <td><%Response.Write DataCommand1("LastName")%>
  </td>
    <td><%Response.Write DataCommand1("Title")%>
  </td>
  </tr>
<!    End of manual insertion.>
<!-- Insert HTML here -->
</table>
 </body>
</html>
```

Listing 37-2 is quite simple, although it doesn't look that way at first glance. The code can be explained in sections. At the very top of the listing before the first bold section is the HTML created in FrontPage 98. Included within this section is a FrontPage 98 one-line text box delineated by the <Form and /Form> tags that contain the ASP self reference. Immediately after that is a hand-coded section representing the browser-returned data table headings. This is followed by two sections of ASP code generated by Visual InterDev, the first of which defines the DataCommand ActiveX control. The second ASP section of server code establishes an Active Data Objects (ADO) connection using global variables from the GLOBAL.ASA file created by Visual InterDev (see Listing 37-3). Variables are placed in this file when data connections are added to the Visual InterDev project.

The next bold section, which follows the last Visual InterDev section, is the HTML necessary to display the returned data. The syntax should be self-explanatory because the results are written in the same order as the manually inserted

table entries. The **Write** method of the **Response** object retrieves data from the
DataCommand control.

LISTING 37-3 The GLOBAL.ASA file of the MyWeb Web site

```
<SCRIPT LANGUAGE=VBScript RUNAT=Server>
Sub Session_OnStart
    '==Visual InterDev Generated - DataConnection startspan==
    '--Project Data Connection
        Session("pubs_ConnectionString") =
"DSN=ZEUS;UID=sa;PWD=;
        APP=Microsoft (R) Developer Studio;
        WSID=ZEUS;DATABASE=pubs"
        Session("pubs_ConnectionTimeout") = 15
        Session("pubs_CommandTimeout") = 30
        Session("pubs_RuntimeUserName") = "sa"
        Session("pubs_RuntimePassword") = ""
    '--Project Data Connection
        Session("DataConn_ConnectionString") =
"DSN=Northwind;" & _
        DBQ=F:\InetPub\wwwroot\myweb\Northwind.mdb;" & _
        DriverId=25;FIL=MS Access;MaxBufferSize=512; " & _
        PageTimeout=5;"
        Session("DataConn_ConnectionTimeout") = 15
        Session("DataConn_CommandTimeout") = 30
        Session("DataConn_RuntimeUserName") = ""
        Session("DataConn_RuntimePassword") = ""
    '==Visual InterDev Generated - DataConnection endspan==
End Sub
</SCRIPT>
```

The variables in GLOBAL.ASA are the same variables referenced in the ADO
section of Listing 37-2. This module is not limited to only data connection variables, but it is executed only on the server and is not directly available to browser-
side scripts.

Note that there are two data source names (DSNs) defined within
GLOBAL.ASA. All ASPs of a Web site constructed by Visual InterDev use this module.

Figure 37-4 is an example of a Visual InterDev ASP with a connection to an Open Database Connectivity (ODBC) data source and Figure 37-5 is an example of a Visual InterDev ASP connected to an Access 97 database. Both of these examples work.

Recall from our discussion of FrontPage 98 that Web pages require a system DSN. The other issue is that an Access database must be imported into the root Web directory. This was done for Figure 37-5; the Microsoft NORTHWIND.MDB is not on the CD-ROM. Let's pause and note the status of the different technologies.

What works:

o IDC connecting to an ODBC data source (SQL Server) from FrontPage 98.

o ASP created by FrontPage 98 connecting to an ODBC data source (SQL Server).

o ASP created by Visual InterDev connecting to an ODBC data source (SQL Server).

o ASP created by Visual InterDev connecting to Microsoft Access. (NORTHWIND.MDB is not shipped on your CD-ROM. Your Visual InterDev Access example will not function until you import your own copy of the Microsoft Access NORTHWIND.MDB to the MYWEB directory.)

What doesn't work:

o Microsoft Access 97-generated ASP.

o FrontPage 98-generated ASP connecting to a Microsoft Access 97 MDB.

o IDC from FrontPage 98 connecting to a Microsoft Access 97 MDB.

In summary, FrontPage 98, as shipped, supports both IDC and ASP but only for ODBC data sources. Visual InterDev supports active server pages for both ODBC data sources and the ODBC desktop driver set of Microsoft Access.

FRONTPAGE 98

Figure 37-6 functions only as a linkage page for FrontPage 98 Web pages. No HTML is presented for this page.

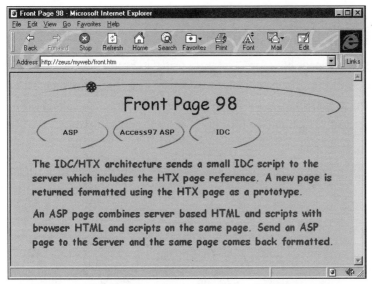

FIGURE 37-6   A Web linkage page to FrontPage 98 Web pages.

Figure 37-7 is another linkage page to Web pages using IDC. No HTML is presented.

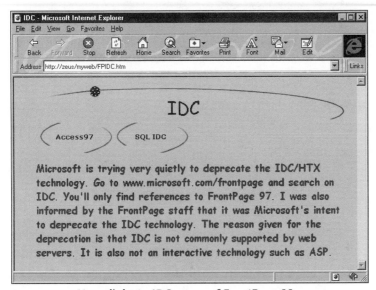

FIGURE 37-7   Hyperlinks to IDC pages of FrontPage 98.

Connecting to Microsoft Access with IDC from FrontPage 98

The Web page of Figure 37-8 was created in FrontPage 98. Other than an apparent ODBC error, the page looks satisfactory. The page consists of three components. The primary page is the image presented in Figure 37-8 along with the supporting IDC and HTX files (see Listings 37-4, 37-5, and 37-6).

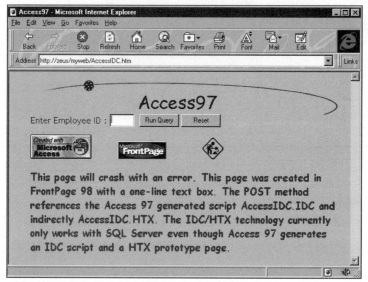

FIGURE 37-8   IDC from a FrontPage 98 Web page.

LISTING 37-4 AccessIDC.HTM, the HTML of Figure 37-8

```
<html>
<head>
        <title>SQL IDC</title>
        <meta name="GENERATOR" content="Microsoft FrontPage
        3.0">
        <meta name="Microsoft Theme" content="cactus 101">
        <meta name="Microsoft Border" content="tl, default">
</head>
<body>
```

```
<form method="POST" action="/myweb/SQLidc.idc">
    <p>Enter Author ID :
            <input type="text" name="user_id" size="6">
            <input TYPE="SUBMIT" VALUE="Run Query" name="B1">
            <input type="reset" value="Reset"
            name="B2">  
        </p>
</form>
<p><img src="images/mslogo.gif" alt="mslogo.gif (9866 bytes)"
 WIDTH="88" HEIGHT="31"></p>
<h3>This page works fine referencing SQL Server. The IDC
        script and HTX page can be generated manually, or
        Access 97 can be used. Create a dummy table with the
        column names you want. Either do a SaveAs HTML from
        table-design or from query-design to create your IDC
        script and HTX prototype page. Create your query page
        in FrontPage 98 and fixup as necessary.  
             <br><br>
</h3>
</body>
</html>
```

LISTING 37-5 AccessIDC.IDC, the IDC file of Figure 37-8

```
Datasource: Northwind
SQLStatement: SELECT EmployeeID, LastName, FirstName, Title
+ FROM [Employees]
Template: AccessIDC.htx
```

LISTING 37-6 AccessIDC.HTX, the HTX template file of Figure 37-8

```
<html>
<head>
        <title>Access IDC</title>
</head>
<body BGCOLOR="#FFFFFF">
```

```
<table BORDER="1" BGCOLOR="#ffffff" CELLSPACING="0">
  <font FACE="Arial" COLOR="#000000"><caption><b>Employee
    Titles</b></caption>
<thead>
  <tr>
    <th BGCOLOR="#c0c0c0" BORDERCOLOR="#000000">
      <font SIZE="2" FACE="Arial"
        COLOR="#000000">Employee ID
      </font>
    </th>
    <th BGCOLOR="#c0c0c0" BORDERCOLOR="#000000">
      <font SIZE="2" FACE="Arial"
        COLOR="#000000">Last Name
      </font>
    </th>
    <th BGCOLOR="#c0c0c0" BORDERCOLOR="#000000">
      <font SIZE="2" FACE="Arial"
        COLOR="#000000">First Name
      </font>
    </th>
   <th BGCOLOR="#c0c0c0" BORDERCOLOR="#000000">
      <font SIZE="2" FACE="Arial"
        COLOR="#000000">Title
      </font>
    </th>
  </tr>
</thead>
<tbody>
<%begindetail%>
   <tr VALIGN="TOP">
    <td BORDERCOLOR="#c0c0c0">
      <font SIZE="2" FACE="Arial"
        COLOR="#000000"><%EmployeeID%><br>
      </font>
```

```
        </td>
        <td BORDERCOLOR="#c0c0c0">
          <font SIZE="2" FACE="Arial"
            COLOR="#000000"><%LastName%><br>
          </font>
        </td>
        <td BORDERCOLOR="#c0c0c0" ALIGN="RIGHT">
          <font SIZE="2" FACE="Arial"
            COLOR="#000000"><%FirstName%><br>
          </font>
        </td>
        <td BORDERCOLOR="#c0c0c0" ALIGN="RIGHT">
          <font SIZE="2" FACE="Arial"
            COLOR="#000000"><%Title%><br>
          </font>
        </td>
      </tr>
    </table>
    <p><br>
      <img src="images/MSACCESS.gif"
        alt="MSACCESS.gif (9400 bytes)" WIDTH="0" HEIGHT="0">
    </p>
    </font>
    </body>
    </html>
```

The FrontPage 98 IDC Wizard created ACCESSIDC.HTX by double-clicking ACCESSIDC.IDC in the *Files View* of FrontPage 98 Explorer. The next IDC example is one that does work.

Connecting to SQL Server with IDC from FrontPage 98

Figure 37-9 is an IDC example that accesses the SQL Server *pubs* database (see Listings 37-7, 37-8, and 37-9).

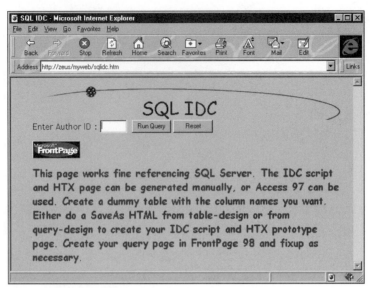

FIGURE 37-9   Using IDC to access SQL Server.

LISTING 37-7   The HTML SQLIDC.HTM file of Figure 37-9

```html
<html>

<head>
  <title>SQL IDC</title>
  <meta name="GENERATOR" content="Microsoft FrontPage 3.0">
  <meta name="Microsoft Theme" content="cactus 101">
  <meta name="Microsoft Border" content="tl, default">
</head>

<body>

<form method="POST" action="/myweb/SQLidc.idc">
    <p>Enter Author ID :
    <input type="text" name="user_id" size="6">
    <input TYPE="SUBMIT" VALUE="Run Query" name="B1">
    <input type="reset" value="Reset" name="B2">
       
  </p>
</form>
```

```
<p><img src="images/mslogo.gif"
  alt="mslogo.gif (9866 bytes)" WIDTH="88" HEIGHT="31">
</p>

<h3>This page works fine referencing SQL Server. The IDC
      script and HTX page can be generated manually, or
      Access 97 can be used. Create a dummy table with the
      column names you want. Either do a SaveAs HTML from
      table-design or from query-design to create your IDC
      script and HTX prototype page. Create your query
      page in FrontPage 98 and fixup as necessary.
        <br><br>
</h3>
</body>
</html>
```

LISTING 37-8 The SQLIDC.IDC file for Figure 37-9

```
Datasource: ZEUS
SQLStatement: SELECT au_id, au_fname, au_lname FROM authors
 where au_id like '%user_id%%%'
Template: sqlidc.htx
Username: sa
```

LISTING 37-9 The SQLIDC.HTX file for Figure 37-9

```
<html>

<head>
  <title>SQL IDC</title>
</head>

<body BGCOLOR="#FFFFFF">

<table BORDER="1" BGCOLOR="#ffffff" CELLSPACING="0">
  <font FACE="Arial"
    COLOR="#000000"><caption><b>Authors</b></caption>
```

```
<thead>
  <tr>
    <th  BGCOLOR="#c0c0c0" BORDERCOLOR="#000000">
      <font SIZE="2" FACE="Arial"
        COLOR="#000000">au_id
      </font>
    </th>
    <th  BGCOLOR="#c0c0c0" BORDERCOLOR="#000000">
      <font SIZE="2" FACE="Arial"
        COLOR="#000000">au_fname
      </font>
    </th>
    <th  BGCOLOR="#c0c0c0" BORDERCOLOR="#000000">
      <font SIZE="2" FACE="Arial"
        COLOR="#000000">au_lname
      </font>
    </th>
  </tr>
</thead>
<tbody>
  <%begindetail%>
    <tr VALIGN="TOP">
      <td BORDERCOLOR="#c0c0c0" ALIGN="RIGHT">
        <font SIZE="2"
          FACE="Arial"
          COLOR="#000000"><%au_id%><br>
        </font>
    </td>
      <td BORDERCOLOR="#c0c0c0" ALIGN="RIGHT">
        <font SIZE="2"
          FACE="Arial"
          COLOR="#000000"><%au_fname%><br>
        </font>
      </td>
      <td BORDERCOLOR="#c0c0c0">
        <font SIZE="2"
```

```
        FACE="Arial"
        COLOR="#000000"><%au_lname%><br>
      </font>
    </td>
    </tr>
  <%enddetail%>
</tbody>
<tfoot>
</tfoot>
</table>
<p><br><br>
</p>
</font>
</body>
</html>
```

The FrontPage 98 SQL IDC of Figure 37-9 is represented by three HTML list-ings. Listing 37-7 is the HTML of Figure 37-9, Listing 37-8 is the IDC script, and Listing 37-9 is the accompanying HTX prototype page.

All that is necessary to use IDC/HTX is the IDC file shown in Listing 37-8. Double-click the IDC file in either *Navigation* or *All Files* mode of FrontPage 98 Explorer. The IDC Wizard starts with a dialog box requesting HTX prototype page parameters.

The remaining issue is creation of the query page of Figure 37-9. This page references the IDC script file in the POST method of the one-line text box. Other embellishments are possible, but this scenario is all that is necessary to build an IDC/HTX web page using FrontPage 98. Unfortunately, this only works for ODBC databases such as SQL server.

Connecting to an Access 97 Database with a FrontPage 98–Generated Active Server Page

Figure 37-10, whose code is shown in Listing 37-10, is one of those dead-ends of FrontPage 98. It is an ASP generated with the FrontPage 98 Database Region Wizard. My calls to Microsoft technical support elicited the information that FrontPage 98 HTML created by the Database Region Wizard would only support ODBC data sources. It is not possible to make this page work by hacking the ASP, which contains that ugly creature called a *WebBot*. Hacking the code is not what it's about. Visual InterDev generates a working active server page that connects to Microsoft Access (and it doesn't use any WebBots).

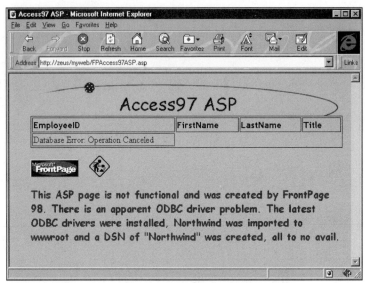

FIGURE 37-10   A nonfunctional Access 97 ASP Web page.

LISTING 37-10   A nonfunctional ASP Web page created by FrontPage 98

```html
<html>

<head>

        <title>Access97 ASP</title>
        <meta name="GENERATOR" content="Microsoft FrontPage
        3.0">
        <meta name="Microsoft Theme" content="cactus 101">
        <meta name="Microsoft Border" content="tl, default">
</head>

<body>

<table width="100%" border="1">
  <tr>
    <td><b>EmployeeID</b></td>
```

```
        <td><b>FirstName</b></td>
        <td><b>LastName</b></td>
        <td><b>Title</b></td>
    </tr>
        <!--webbot bot="DatabaseRegionStart" startspan
        s-columnnames="EmployeeID,FirstName,LastName,Title"
          s-connstring="DSN=Northwind"
        s-password b-tableformat="TRUE"
        s-sql="select EmployeeID FirstName, LastName, Title
              FROM employees"
            local_preview="&lt;tr&gt;&lt;td colspan=8
bgcolor=&quot;#FFFF00&quot; align=&quot;center&quot;
width=&quot;100%&quot;&gt;&lt;font
        color=&quot;#000000&quot;&gt;
        Database Regions do not preview unless this page is
        fetched from a Web server using a web browser. The
        following table will display one row for each query
        result row when the page is fetched from a Web
      server.&lt;/td&gt;&lt;/tr&gt;"
preview clientside s-DefaultFields
        s-NoRecordsFound="No Records Returned"
        i-MaxRecords i-ScriptTimeout tag="BODY" -->
<%
' Substitute in form parameters into the query string
fp_sQry = "select EmployeeID FirstName, LastName, " & _
        "Title FROM employees"
fp_sDefault = ""
fp_sNoRecords = "No Records Returned"
fp_iMaxRecords = 0
fp_iTimeout = 0
fp_iCurrent = 1
fp_fError = False
fp_bBlankField = False
If fp_iTimeout <> 0 Then Server.ScriptTimeout = _
    fp_iTimeout
Do While (Not fp_fError) And _
```

```
(InStr(fp_iCurrent, fp_sQry, "%%") <> 0)
' found a opening quote, find the close quote
fp_iStart = InStr(fp_iCurrent, fp_sQry, "%%")
fp_iEnd = InStr(fp_iStart + 2, fp_sQry, "%%")
If fp_iEnd = 0 Then
    fp_fError = True
    Response.Write "<B>Database Region Error: " & _
        "mismatched parameter delimiters</B>"
Else
    fp_sField = Mid(fp_sQry, fp_iStart + 2, fp_iEnd _
        - fp_iStart - 2)
    If Mid(fp_sField,1,1) = "%" Then
        fp_sWildcard = "%"
        fp_sField = Mid(fp_sField, 2)
    Else
        fp_sWildCard = ""
    End If
    fp_sValue = Request.Form(fp_sField)

    ' note when a named form field doesn't exist.
    If (len(fp_sValue) = 0) Then
        fp_iCurrentField = 1
        fp_bFoundField = False
        Do While (InStr(fp_iCurrentField, fp_sDefault, _
            fp_sField) <> 0) And Not fp_bFoundField
            fp_iCurrentField = InStr(fp_iCurrentField, _
                fp_sDefault, fp_sField)
            fp_iStartField = InStr(fp_iCurrentField, _
                fp_sDefault, "=")
            If fp_iStartField = fp_iCurrentField + _
                len(fp_sField) Then
                fp_iEndField = InStr(fp_iCurrentField, _
                    fp_sDefault, "&")
                If (fp_iEndField = 0) Then _
                    fp_iEndField = len(fp_sDefault) + 1
                fp_sValue = Mid(fp_sDefault, _
```

```
                    fp_iStartField+1, fp_iEndField-1)
                fp_bFoundField = True
            Else
                fp_iCurrentField = fp_iCurrentField + _
                    len(fp_sField) - 1
            End If
        Loop
    End If


    ' this next finds the named form field value, and
    ' substitutes in doubled single-quotes for all single
    ' quotes in the literal value so that SQL doesn't
    ' get confused by seeing unpaired single-quotes
    If (Mid(fp_sQry, fp_iStart - 1, 1) = """") Then
        fp_sValue = Replace(fp_sValue, """", """""")
    ElseIf (Mid(fp_sQry, fp_iStart - 1, 1) = "'") Then
        fp_sValue = Replace(fp_sValue, "'", "''")
    ElseIf Not IsNumeric(fp_sValue) Then
        fp_sValue = ""
    End If

    If (len(fp_sValue) = 0) Then fp_bBlankField = True

    fp_sQry = Left(fp_sQry, fp_iStart - 1) + _
        fp_sWildCard + fp_sValue + _
        Right(fp_sQry, Len(fp_sQry) - fp_iEnd - 1)

    ' Fixup the new current position to be after
    ' the substituted value
    fp_iCurrent = fp_iStart + Len(fp_sValue) + _
        Len(fp_sWildCard)
    End If
Loop

If Not fp_fError Then
    ' Use the connection string directly as entered
```

```
        On Error Resume Next
        set fp_rs = CreateObject("ADODB.Recordset")
        If fp_iMaxRecords <> 0 Then fp_rs.MaxRecords = _
            fp_iMaxRecords
        fp_rs.Open fp_sQry, "DSN=Northwind"
        If Err.Description <> "" Then
            Response.Write "<B>Database Error: " + _
                Err.Description + "</B>"
            if fp_bBlankField Then
                Response.Write "  One or more form fields were
                empty."
            End If
        Else
            ' Check for the no-record case
            If fp_rs.EOF And fp_rs.BOF Then
                Response.Write fp_sNoRecords
            Else
                ' Start a while loop to fetch each record
                Do Until fp_rs.EOF
%>
<!--webbot bot="DatabaseRegionStart"
        i-checksum="5061" endspan -->

    <tr>
      <td>
            <!--webbot bot="DatabaseResultColumn" startspan
        s-columnnames="EmployeeID,FirstName,LastName,Title"
            s-column="EmployeeID"
        b-tableformat="TRUE"
            clientside local_preview="Database: EmployeeID"
        preview="Database: EmployeeID" -->
      <%
            If Not IsEmpty(fp_rs) And Not (fp_rs Is Nothing) _
                Then Response.Write CStr(fp_rs("EmployeeID"))
      %>
            <!--webbot bot="DatabaseResultColumn"
```

```
                             i-checksum="35408" endspan -->
            </td>
        <td>
                <!--webbot bot="DatabaseResultColumn" startspan
            s-columnnames="EmployeeID,FirstName,LastName,Title"
                s-column="FirstName"
                b-tableformat="TRUE"
                clientside local_preview="Database: FirstName"
                preview="Database: FirstName" -->
<%

                If Not IsEmpty(fp_rs) And Not (fp_rs Is Nothing) _
                    Then Response.Write CStr(fp_rs("FirstName"))
%>

                <!--webbot bot="DatabaseResultColumn"
            i-checksum="32411" endspan -->
            </td>
        <td>
                <!--webbot bot="DatabaseResultColumn" startspan
            s-columnnames="EmployeeID,FirstName,LastName,Title"
                s-column="LastName"
                b-tableformat="TRUE"
                clientside local_preview="Database: LastName"
            preview="Database: LastName" -->
<%

                If Not IsEmpty(fp_rs) And Not (fp_rs Is Nothing) _
                    Then Response.Write CStr(fp_rs("LastName"))
%>

                <!--webbot bot="DatabaseResultColumn"
                    i-checksum="29199" endspan
                -->
            </td>
        <td>
                <!--webbot bot="DatabaseResultColumn" startspan
            s-columnnames="EmployeeID,FirstName,LastName,Title"
                s-column="Title" b-tableformat="TRUE"
            clientside local_preview="Database: Title"
```

```
                        preview="Database: Title" -->
        <%

                If Not IsEmpty(fp_rs) And Not (fp_rs Is Nothing) _
                    Then Response.Write CStr(fp_rs("Title"))
        %>

                <!--webbot bot="DatabaseResultColumn"
                    i-checksum="26099" endspan
                -->
            </td>
        </tr>
            <!--webbot bot="DatabaseRegionEnd" startspan
                b-    tableformat="TRUE"
                local_preview preview clientside tag="BODY"
            -->
        <%

                    ' Close the loop iterating records
                    fp_rs.MoveNext
                Loop
            End If
            fp_rs.Close
        ' Close the If condition checking for a connection error
        End If
    ' Close the If condition checking for a
    '       parse error when replacing form field params
    End If
    set fp_rs = Nothing
    %>
    <!--webbot bot="DatabaseRegionEnd"
    i-checksum="55813" endspan -->


    </table>


    <p>
            <img src="images/frontpag.gif"
            alt="frontpag.gif (9866 bytes)"
            WIDTH="88"
```

```
                HEIGHT="31">  
                <img src="images/undercon.gif"
                alt="undercon.gif (293 bytes)"
                WIDTH="40" HEIGHT="38">
</p>

<h3>
                This ASP page is not functional and was created by
                FrontPage 98. There is an apparent ODBC driver
                problem. The latest ODBC drivers were installed,
                Northwind was imported to wwwroot and a DSN of
                &quot;Northwind&quot; was created, all to no avail.
</h3>
</body>
</html>
```

Listing 37-10 is the HTML code of Figure 37-10. Besides not working, it suffers from severe code-bloat.

Let's pause here for some comments on Active Server Page construction. Each of the three listings referenced below illustrates a different type of Active Server Page connecting to Microsoft Access, and only one works. Each represents a different level of the technology, and if another version of Visual InterDev ships before this very long epistle is completed, there may be still another version.

o Listing 37-10 is an active server page, generated by FrontPage 98, which connects to an Access 97 database. It suffers from severe code-bloat and doesn't function.

o Listing 37-11 is an Access 97-generated ASP, connecting to Access 97, which doesn't function.

o Listing 37-2 is a Visual InterDev-created active server page connecting to Microsoft Access 97.

Except for ADO, there are no common components between each of these three types of Active Server Pages, and yet each is supposed to be an ASP. FrontPage 98 has that ugly creature called a WebBot, while Visual InterDev has design-time ActiveX controls. The Access 97 ASP in Listing 37-2 is pretty anemic but could be made to work by hacking the Visual InterDev ADO. But why do it? Just use Visual InterDev and forget about Access 97 ASPs.

LISTING 37-11 A nonfunctional ASP Web page created by Access 97

```
<html>

<head>
    <title>Access97 ASP</title>
</head>

<body BGCOLOR="#FFFFFF">
<%
Param = Request.QueryString("Param")
Data = Request.QueryString("Data")
%>
<%
If IsObject(Session("Northwind_conn")) Then
    Set conn = Session("Northwind_conn")
Else
    Set conn = Server.CreateObject("ADODB.Connection")
    conn.open "Northwind","",""
    Set Session("Northwind_conn") = conn
End If
%>
<%
sql = "SELECT Employees.EmployeeID, Employees.LastName,
  Employees.FirstName, Employees.Title  FROM Employees "
If cstr(Param) <> "" And cstr(Data) <> "" Then
  sql = sql & " WHERE [" & cstr(Param) & _
    "] = " & cstr(Data)
End If
Set rs = Server.CreateObject("ADODB.Recordset")
    rs.Open sql, conn, 3, 3
%>

<table BORDER="1" BGCOLOR="#ffffff" CELLSPACING="0">
  <font FACE="Arial"
      COLOR="#000000"><caption><b>Query1</b></caption>
    <thead>
```

```
      <tr>
        <th BGCOLOR="#c0c0c0"
          BORDERCOLOR="#000000">
          <font SIZE="2" FACE="Arial"
            COLOR="#000000">Employee ID
          </font>
        </th>
        <th BGCOLOR="#c0c0c0"
          BORDERCOLOR="#000000">
          <font SIZE="2" FACE="Arial"
            COLOR="#000000">Last Name
          </font>
        </th>
        <th BGCOLOR="#c0c0c0"
          BORDERCOLOR="#000000">
          <font SIZE="2" FACE="Arial"
            COLOR="#000000">First Name
          </font>
        </th>
        <th BGCOLOR="#c0c0c0"
          BORDERCOLOR="#000000">
          <font SIZE="2" FACE="Arial" \
            COLOR="#000000">Title
          </font>
        </th>
        </tr>
    </thead>
<tbody>
<%
On Error Resume Next
rs.MoveFirst
do while Not rs.eof
%>
  <tr VALIGN="TOP">
    <td BORDERCOLOR="#c0c0c0" ALIGN="RIGHT">
      <font SIZE="2" FACE="Arial" COLOR="#000000">
```

```
<%=Server.HTMLEncode(rs.Fields("EmployeeID").Value)
%><br>
        </font>
    </td>
    <td BORDERCOLOR="#c0c0c0">
        <font SIZE="2" FACE="Arial" COLOR="#000000">
<%=Server.HTMLEncode(rs.Fields("LastName").Value)
%><br>
        </font>
    </td>
    <td BORDERCOLOR="#c0c0c0">
        <font SIZE="2" FACE="Arial" COLOR="#000000">
<%=Server.HTMLEncode(rs.Fields("FirstName").Value)
%><br>
        </font>
    </td>
    <td BORDERCOLOR="#c0c0c0">
        <font SIZE="2" FACE="Arial" COLOR="#000000">
<%=Server.HTMLEncode(rs.Fields("Title").Value)
%><br>
        </font>
    </td>
  </tr>
<%
  rs.MoveNext
loop%>
</tbody>
<tfoot>
</tfoot>
</table>

<p><br>
<br>
<img SRC="msaccess.jpg"> </p>
</font>
</body>
</html>
```

Connecting to SQL Server with a FrontPage 98-Generated Active Server Page

Let's go back to our Web site and look at the active server pages generated by FrontPage 98 that reference an ODBC data source. There are two examples. The first example has no query page and is referenced directly by a hyperlink. The second example uses a Web query page to call the same ASP. In neither example does the ASP call itself, which means it is not interactive. This isn't too bad because extra pages don't build up on the memory stack. The hyperlinks to these two examples are shown in Figure 37-11. No HTML code is presented for this page.

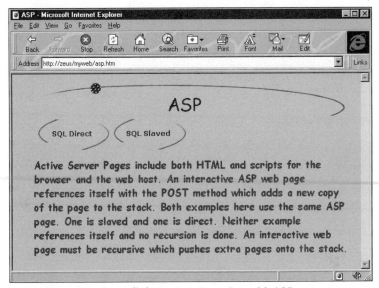

FIGURE 37-11   The hyperlinks to two FrontPage 98 ASPs.

Figure 37-12 is an ASP generated by FrontPage 98 using the Database Region Wizard (see Listing 37-12). No changes were made and the page executes directly. It is an example of an ASP that is not interactive. By that I mean that there is no on-line text box or submit button. It is just a page and it doesn't create an unwanted memory stack entry. Nothing can be done on the page and the user must select the **Back** arrow of the browser to return to the parent page.

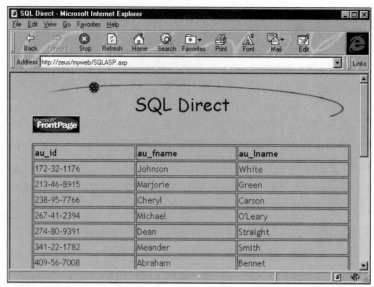

FIGURE 37-12   A FrontPage 98 ASP Web page referenced directly by a hyperlink.

LISTING 37-12 The HTML of Figure 37-12, a FrontPage 98 ASP accessing SQL Server

```html
<html>

<head>
  <title>SQL Direct</title>
  <meta name="GENERATOR" content="Microsoft FrontPage 3.0">
  <meta name="Microsoft Theme" content="cactus 101">
  <meta name="Microsoft Border" content="tl, default">
</head>

<body>

<p>
    <img src="images/mslogo.gif"
    alt="mslogo.gif (9866 bytes)" WIDTH="88" HEIGHT="31">
    <strong>     
    </strong>
</p>

<table width="100%" border="1">
```

```
   <tr>
     <td><b>au_id</b></td>
     <td><b>au_fname</b></td>
     <td><b>au_lname</b></td>
   </tr>
   <!--webbot bot="DatabaseRegionStart"
    startspan s-columnnames="au_id,au_fname,au_lname"
    s-connstring="DSN=ZEUS;UID=sa"
    s-password b-tableformat="TRUE"
    s-sql="select au_id, au_fname, au_lname " & _
       "FROM authors where au_id like '%%user_id%%'"
    local_preview="&lt;tr&gt;&lt;td colspan=6
  bgcolor=&quot;#FFFF00&quot; align=&quot;center&quot;
  width=&quot;100%&quot;&gt;&lt;font color=&quot;
  #000000&quot;&gt;Database Regions do not preview unless
  this page is fetched from a Web server using a web
  browser. The following table will display one row for
  each query result row when the page is fetched from a
  Web server.&lt;/td&gt;&lt;/tr&gt;"
  preview clientside s-DefaultFields
     s-NoRecordsFound="No Records Returned" i-MaxRecords
     i-ScriptTimeout tag="BODY" -->
<%
 ' Substitute in form parameters into the query string
   fp_sQry = "select au_id, au_fname, au_lname from authors "
   fp_sQry = fp_sQry & "where au_id like '%%user_id%%'"
   fp_sDefault = ""
   fp_sNoRecords = "No Records Returned"
   fp_iMaxRecords = 0
   fp_iTimeout = 0
   fp_iCurrent = 1
   fp_fError = False
   fp_bBlankField = False
   If fp_iTimeout <> 0 Then _
      Server.ScriptTimeout = fp_iTimeout
Do While (Not fp_fError) And _
```

```
(InStr(fp_iCurrent, fp_sQry, "%%") <> 0)
' found a opening quote, find the close quote
fp_iStart = InStr(fp_iCurrent, fp_sQry, "%%")
fp_iEnd = InStr(fp_iStart + 2, fp_sQry, "%%")
If fp_iEnd = 0 Then
  fp_fError = True
  Response.Write "<B>Database Region Error: " & _
    "mismatched parameter delimiters</B>"
Else
  fp_sField = Mid(fp_sQry, fp_iStart + 2,
      fp_iEnd - fp_iStart - 2)
  If Mid(fp_sField,1,1) = "%" Then
      fp_sWildcard = "%"
      fp_sField = Mid(fp_sField, 2)
  Else
      fp_sWildCard = ""
  End If
      fp_sValue = Request.Form(fp_sField)

      ' note when a named form field doesn't exist
      If (len(fp_sValue) = 0) Then
        fp_iCurrentField = 1
        fp_bFoundField = False
        Do While (InStr(fp_iCurrentField, fp_sDefault, _
            fp_sField) <> 0) And Not fp_bFoundField
            fp_iCurrentField = InStr(fp_iCurrentField, _
              fp_sDefault, fp_sField)
            fp_iStartField = InStr(fp_iCurrentField, _
              fp_sDefault, "=")
          If fp_iStartField = fp_iCurrentField + _
            len(fp_sField) Then
            fp_iEndField = InStr(fp_iCurrentField, _
              fp_sDefault, "&")
            If (fp_iEndField = 0) Then fp_iEndField = _
              len(fp_sDefault) + 1
            fp_sValue = Mid(fp_sDefault,
```

```
                fp_iStartField+1, _ fp_iEndField-1)
              fp_bFoundField = True
           Else
            fp_iCurrentField = fp_iCurrentField + _
              len(fp_sField) - 1
           End If
        Loop
    End If

  ' this next finds the named form field value, and
  ' substitutes in doubled single-quotes for all
  ' single quotes in the literal value so that SQL
  ' doesn't get confused by seeing unpaired single-quotes
  If (Mid(fp_sQry, fp_iStart - 1, 1) = """") Then
      fp_sValue = Replace(fp_sValue, """", """""")
  ElseIf (Mid(fp_sQry, fp_iStart - 1, 1) = "'") Then
      fp_sValue = Replace(fp_sValue, "'", "''")
  ElseIf Not IsNumeric(fp_sValue) Then
      fp_sValue = ""
  End If

  If (len(fp_sValue) = 0) Then fp_bBlankField = True

  fp_sQry = Left(fp_sQry, fp_iStart - 1) + _
      fp_sWildCard + fp_sValue + _
      Right(fp_sQry, Len(fp_sQry) - fp_iEnd - 1)

  ' Fixup the new current position
  ' to be after the substituted value
  fp_iCurrent = fp_iStart + Len(fp_sValue) + _
      Len(fp_sWildCard)
  End If
Loop

If Not fp_fError Then
  ' Use the connection string directly as entered
```

```
      On Error Resume Next
      set fp_rs = CreateObject("ADODB.Recordset")
      If fp_iMaxRecords <> 0 Then fp_rs.MaxRecords = _
        fp_iMaxRecords
      fp_rs.Open fp_sQry, "DSN=ZEUS;UID=sa"
      If Err.Description <> "" Then
        Response.Write "<B>Database Error: " _
          + Err.Description + "</B>"
        if fp_bBlankField Then
        Response.Write "One or more form fields were empty."
      End If
Else
    ' Check for the no-record case
    If fp_rs.EOF And fp_rs.BOF Then
        Response.Write fp_sNoRecords
     Else
       ' Start a while loop to fetch each record
       Do Until fp_rs.EOF
%>
<!--webbot bot="DatabaseRegionStart"
   i-checksum="45277" endspan -->

   <tr>
     <td><!--webbot bot="DatabaseResultColumn"
       startspan s-columnnames="au_id,au_fname,au_lname"
       s-column="au_id" b-tableformat="TRUE"
       clientside local_preview="Database: au_id"
       preview="Database: au_id" -->
   <%
       If Not IsEmpty(fp_rs) And Not (fp_rs Is Nothing) _
         Then Response.Write CStr(fp_rs("au_id"))
   %>
       <!--webbot
       bot="DatabaseResultColumn"
       i-checksum="24590" endspan -->
     </td>
```

```
    <td><!--webbot bot="DatabaseResultColumn"
      startspan s-columnnames="au_id,au_fname,au_lname"
      s-column="au_fname" b-tableformat="TRUE"
      clientside local_preview="Database: au_fname"
      preview="Database: au_fname" -->
<%
      If Not IsEmpty(fp_rs) And Not (fp_rs Is Nothing) _
        Then Response.Write CStr(fp_rs("au_fname"))
%>
      <!--webbot bot="DatabaseResultColumn"
      i-checksum="28641" endspan -->
    </td>
    <td><!--webbot bot="DatabaseResultColumn"
     startspan s-columnnames="au_id,au_fname,au_lname"
      s-column="au_lname" b-tableformat="TRUE"
      clientside local_preview="Database: au_lname"
      preview="Database: au_lname" -->
<%
      If Not IsEmpty(fp_rs) And Not (fp_rs Is Nothing) _
        Then Response.Write CStr(fp_rs("au_lname"))
%>
      <!--webbot bot="DatabaseResultColumn"
      i-checksum="28647" endspan -->
    </td>
  </tr>
  <!--webbot bot="DatabaseRegionEnd"
    startspan b-tableformat="TRUE" local_preview preview
    clientside tag="BODY" -->
<%
       ' Close the loop iterating records
       fp_rs.MoveNext
     Loop
   End If
   fp_rs.Close
 ' Close the If condition checking for a connection error
 End If
```

```
' Close the If condition checking for a parse error
' when replacing form field params
End If
set fp_rs = Nothing
%>
<!--webbot bot="DatabaseRegionEnd"
  i-checksum="55813" endspan -->

</table>
 </body>
</html>
```

Figure 37-13 references the same ASP as Figure 37-12. The difference is that Figure 37-12 was referenced by a hyperlink from a parent page, whereas Figure 37-13 references the same page with the POST method.

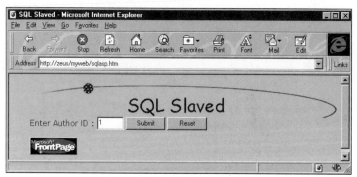

FIGURE 37-13   A Web query page referencing a FrontPage 98 ASP.

Figure 37-14 shows the results of Figure 37-13. As stated previously, this is the same ASP as used in Figure 37-12. The architecture is different with the page referenced by a hyperlink in Figure 37-12 and by a **Submit** command in Figure 37-13.

FIGURE 37-14   The results of Figure 37-13.

Key Point Summary

Active HTML and Active Server Pages are the current focus of Microsoft engineering. New Internet technology is being implemented that supplants the prior technology before the prior technology has gained acceptance. Internet technology is moving too fast to be useful. The only protection an enterprise has is to use Internet technology based on accepted standards, not proposed standards.

The rules of the road are to look carefully at the Microsoft Technology. We learned that there are three unique incarnations of Active Server Pages. The Access 97 ASP pages are not functional but can be hacked to make work. The FrontPage 98 ASP pages suffer severe code bloat and are poorly designed, while the Visual InterDev ASP pages are fine. Create your Web site with FrontPage 98 themes and fonts and do everything else in Visual InterDev.

Applying What You've Learned

The questions below reinforce the material discussed in this chapter. The lab exercise extends the chapter with animation by publishing a PowerPoint kiosk on the Web and adding a marquee control to a Web page.

Instant Assessment

The questions here address issues discussed in this chapter and also serve as a study guide for the Windows Architecture I core examination. A note of caution: Although FrontPage 98 is the Web page generator discussed in this chapter, base your answers to examination questions on FrontPage 97, which was shipping when the Windows Architecture I core examination was released.

1. Which Microsoft Internet publishing technology does FrontPage 98 support?

2. How do I place my Access database on a Web page?

3. How does the Microsoft publishing technology achieve the concept of interaction?

4. What is an issue of active server pages?

5. What is the active server pages issue?

 concept link   **For answers to the Instant Assessment questions, see Appendix E.**

Lab Exercise

Lab 37.73 *Animating a Web page with PowerPoint and a marquee control*

Lab 37.73 is a fun lab in which we illustrate adding animation to a Web page. We do it by hyperlinking to a PowerPoint Internet kiosk presentation. You'll find the example easy to create and very intriguing.

WA I
WA II

1. Create a new Web site in FrontPage 98. A single home page is all this is necessary to illustrate the issue.

2. Place FrontPage 98 on the task bar and start PowerPoint 97.

3. Select *Cancel* for the first dialog box.

4. Select *New* from the File menu.

5. Select the Web Pages tab.

6. Select *Banner2*.

7. Select *OK*.

8. Choose Save As.

9. Save the presentation in your new Web site directory.

10. Exit PowerPoint.

11. Restart FrontPage 98.

12. While in FrontPage 98 Explorer, Navigator view, double-click the page where the animation is to appear.

13. When the selected page is displayed in FrontPage 98 Editor, place the cursor at the position where the hyperlink is to be inserted.

14. Select *Hyperlink* from the Insert menu.

15. Double-click your new PowerPoint file.

16. Select *Active Elements* from the Insert menu to add a marquee.

17. Enter a text message and select *OK*.

18. Select *Preview in Browser* from the File menu. The marquee will start immediately when the page is displayed.

19. Click the hyperlink. The powerpoint animation is played back. (You might want to go back to PowerPoint and examine the animation techniques in the original presentation.)

Windows Architecture I
Windows Architecture II

CHAPTER

Internet Tools for the Trenches

38

About Chapter 38

Choosing the proper Internet technology is split between this chapter and Chapter 39. Here we look at older technologies such as common gateway interface (CGI) and Internet server application programming interface (ISAPI). There are tools for each of these technologies that will smooth the pain of converting from UNIX to Windows NT and the Internet Information Server (IIS). The *Win32 Internet API* is sketched here along with a very interesting ISAPI dynamic link library (DLL). The Microsoft `OLEISAPI.DLL` is a stub for a developer-provided Visual Basic component, which itself is an ActiveX DLL component. This chapter closes with the WebBrowser control, the WinInet control, and WebPost, which are tools for simplifying the life of the developer. The next chapter discusses scripting of both active server pages (ASP) and the Internet Explorer.

The examples for Chapter 38 are located in the CD-ROM that accompanies this book. The EXAMPLES\CHAPTER38 folder of the CD-ROM includes the OLEISAPIWEB folder and the Visual Basic 5.0 Enterprise Edition VBISAPI.VBP, WEBBROWSER.VBP, OLETEST.VBP, and FTP.VBP projects.

BEFORE WE START

As you may have gathered, the code underlying the Microsoft architecture is not unified. It is a patchwork quilt of different technologies. I suspect Microsoft arrived at this point because its growth path was the purchase of software companies with desired technologies.

The different threading models are the issue. Rather than a unified free-threading architecture, Microsoft ActiveX components have four different threading models. The ActiveX threading models discussed below apply to a Web server that supports active server pages, but the information is of general import and is useful in any development context.

- *Single-thread model* — Not recommended for active server pages or for any Web server application. Single-threaded objects only run in one thread. That is the thread that called **CoInitialize**. The Web server creates a parked thread and then marshals object calls to itself. There is only one thread, and only one thread at a time can enter a set of single-threaded objects. Hence the parked thread.

- *Apartment-thread model* — Recommended for active server pages. The Web server creates a new apartment-model object in the same thread that called **CoCreateInstance**. Requests within the same session are not marshaled. Calls to the object are handled by the thread that created the apartment model object.

- *Free-thread model* — This threading technique is not recommended for active server page objects. The reason is that the Web server will create free-thread objects in a thread other than the caller of **CoCreateInstance**. All object calls are then marshaled to the free-thread object, inducing overhead.

- *Objects marked as both* — Both is interpreted to mean free-threaded and apartment-threaded. This is highly recommended for active server pages. The Web server creates an object *marked as both* in the same thread that requested the object. The call to **CoCreateInstance** is not marshaled to another thread.

What's the problem? Obviously the design is ad hoc, but the application developer is not free to implement a free-thread model, which is the best architecture. The behavior of the host environment must be understood when selecting a threading model.

The desirable architecture is a free-thread model where the new object is not created in a new thread, **CoCreateInstance** can be called from that thread, and calls to the object are not marshaled. The very definition of a free-thread model states that there are no thread dependencies. I believe the apartment-model threads should be marshaled and that free-thread model threads shouldn't require marshaling. This is exactly backwards from the Microsoft threading models, which I am certain are carrying the excess baggage of legacy component object model (COM) marshaling. (Surprise, Microsoft also has legacy software.)

We delve a bit deeper in this issue in Chapter 39 when we look at the scope of the **Session** object of active server pages. The threading issue is addressed directly by the Microsoft `OLEISAPI.DLL` used later in the chapter. Threads are locked down to a single-thread environment because the OLEISAPI.DLL cannot trust callers of the DLL. This problem wouldn't exist with a unified thread architecture.

COMMON GATEWAY INTERFACE

We start with the oldest technology first. CGI is really not an issue within the Microsoft architecture, but it is an issue with porting an existing UNIX CGI application to Windows NT. We already know that CGI is not scalable within the Microsoft architecture, but there are some tools that will reduce the angst to a manageable level until the application is completely rewritten. The first step is to obtain the Microsoft ActiveX Development Kit, published by the Microsoft Developer Network (MSDN). The software developer's kit (SDK) can also be found at `http://www.microsoft.con/intdev/sdk`. In the SDK, there are numerous Internet development tools.

IS2WCGI is an interface between Internet Information Server and a CGI 1.2 environment (see Figure 38-1). The main difference between this tool and the normal CGI process is that the tool runs as an in-process server and doesn't incur the overhead of an instantiation for each Hypertext Transport Protocol (HTTP) message. But you're not home-free yet. Even though the tool is an in-process server with reduced overhead, the application still may not be scaleable because of thread limitations. IS2WCGI is only an interim solution until the original application is rewritten. IS2WCGI is not thread-safe, and no critical sections are used to protect data.

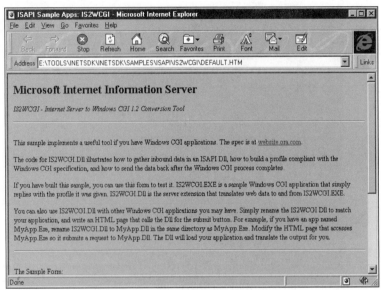

FIGURE 38-1   IS2WCGI from the ActiveX Development Kit.

This topic overlaps with ISAPI, which is discussed next. The problem with creating an in-process DLL is that the server must be stopped and restarted. Debugging also presents special problems. It is next to impossible to debug an ISAPI DLL in a production server. The solution is a wrapper for the ISAPI DLL. The resultant functionality is a CGI interface for debugging purposes that is used as an executable. Figure 38-2 is the DEFAULT.HTM page of CGIWRAP found in the ActiveX Development Kit.

Microsoft will have us believe that dynamic HTML and active server pages are the answer to everything. CGI still has a rightful place in the Internet community. We can't move on to the next topic without saying a few words about Bob Denny. He is the author of WinCGI, a popular CGI application for Visual Basic. Use the AltaVista search engine at http://www.digital.com and search for *WinCGI*. You'll be very surprised at the popularity of this product.

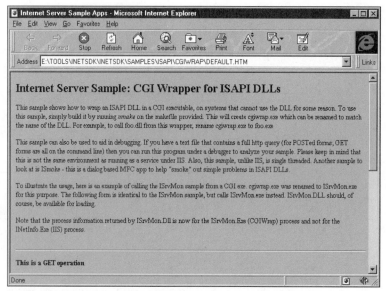

FIGURE 38-2   CGIWrap, or going the other way.

We can see from Figure 38-3 that CGI technologies are still viable. Not every application Web page must be dynamic.

FIGURE 38-3   The O'Reilly Home Page. (Reprinted with permission from the O'ReillyWeb site, O'Reilly & Associates, Inc. http://www.oreilly.com).

INTERNET SERVER APPLICATION PROGRAMMING INTERFACE

ISAPI is as close as we can get to gunmetal with a Web server. (Netscape has a comparable Internet server API appropriately named NSAPI.) An efficient Web site always uses ISAPI, but ISAPI is not interactive in the sense of Microsoft Active Server Pages. ASP technology is interactive but not necessarily efficient. The key difference is in how the communication process occurs between the server and the browser. As a general rule, the Microsoft Internet strategy is to send a page to the server with one section marked for server use and another section marked for browser use. It may be very little text such as an Internet database connector (IDC) script, or it could be a code-bloated ASP page created by FrontPage 98.

An ISAPI application takes a different tack and uses HTML's **Get** or **Post** functions in which parameters and values follow a question mark in a Uniform Resource Locator (URL). The parameter portion of an HTML **Get** or **Post** method is shown here:

```
. . . /lookup.dll?first=dudley+last=doright+age=39
```

This is quite efficient and not interactive. The contents of the returned ISAPI-generated page is determined by the developer, and the new page is independent of the page currently displayed by the client browser. An ISAPI application reads parameters and returns a page formatted with data. This can be compared to ASP architecture, which is a two-way dialog with the same content-rich page.

ISAPI Architecture

We already know that an ISAPI DLL runs in the process space of a Web server and that a CGI application is created in a private address space for each instance of an HTTP message. Calling an ISAPI DLL is almost identical to calling a CGI application from the browser. The only difference is the file extension. The following are two HTML fragments. The first fragment references an ISAPI DLL, and the second fragment references a CGI application. The only change is the executable code reference.

```
http://scripts/lookup.dll?first=dudley+last=doright+age=39
http://scripts/lookup.exe?first=dudley+last=doright+age=39
```

ISAPI uses a structure known as an extension control block (ECB). The relationship of an ECB, an ISAPI application, and a CGI application are illustrated in Figure 38-4.

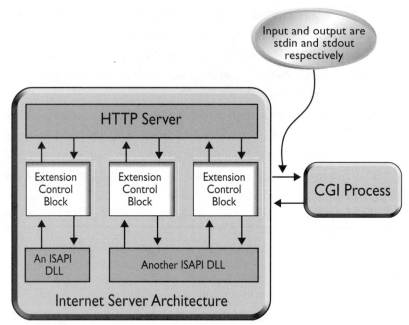

FIGURE 38-4   The relationship of an ECB to the Web server.

Comparing ISAPI and CGI

The ECB supports four callback functions: **GetServerVariable**, **WriteClient**, **ReadClient**, and **ServerSupportFunction**. These functions represent key architectural issues when discussing the difference between an ISAPI application and a CGI application. The comparison points between ISAPI and CGI include:

- A CGI application obtains input from *stdin* while an ISAPI application's data is found at the *lpbData* element of the ECB. Additional ISAPI input is obtained with the **ReadClient** callback function of the ECB.

- The ISAPI application finds most CGI variables in the ECB. Additional server variables are obtained by the ISAPI application using the **GetServerVariable** callback function of the ECB. A CGI application retrieves server variables using **GetEnv**.

- The ISAPI application uses the **WriteClient** callback function of the ECB to send client data back, whereas a CGI application will write the output to *stdout*.

- A CGI completion status of `Status: NNN xxxx...` is sent to *stdout*. ISAPI sends the header directly using the **WriteClient** callback function of the ECB, or it may send `HSE_REQ_SEND_RESPONSE_HEADER` using the ECB callback function **ServerSupportFunction**.

- Redirects of ISAPI and CGI are processed differently. The CGI application writes to *stdout* "Location:" or "URL:". ISAPI issues a redirect by using `HSE_REQ_SEND_URL` when the URL is local. An ISAPI application sends `HSE_REQ_SEND_URL_REDIRECT_RESP` when the URL is remote or unknown using the ECB **ServerSupportFunction** callback function.

An ISAPI Application

An ISAPI application consists of two required entry points, **GetExtensionVersion** and **HttpExtensionProc**, while **TerminateExtension** is an optional entry point. **GetExtensionVersion** is called when the DLL is initially loaded. Both the Internet server and the ISAPI application go through a handshaking process where credentials are exchanged.

Nothing happens until an HTTP message is received. When a message arrives, the server passes control to the **HttpExtensionProc** entry point and program logic processes the client browser input. Callback functions are used to read and write the data and report a status as necessary.

An ISAPI application is loaded in the same process address space as the Internet server, and a faulty ISAPI application can crash the server. Developers are encouraged to implement the *try . . . except* construct of C++ and prevent access violations from bringing down the server.

Developers are also encouraged to include the canonical entry point **DllMain**, which the operating system will call by default the first time a **LoadLibrary** call is made, or the last time a **FreeLibrary** call is made for that DLL, or when a new thread is created or destroyed in the process.

An ISAPI Filter

ISAPI also supports the concept of a filter that can be used for custom authentication, compression, encryption, logging, or traffic analysis. A filter is not necessarily limited to only these functions. Multiple filters can be installed in an Internet server.

An ISAPI filter is not unlike an ISAPI application. It also has two entry points that perform similar functions. **GetFilterVersion** is called when the ISAPI filter DLL is initially loaded. Before the handshaking process is complete, the ISAPI application must choose one or more event notification subscriptions. **HttpFilterProc** is the second entry point. The ISAPI filter uses the same ECB callback functions as the ISAPI application: **GetServerVariable**, **WriteClient**, **ReadClient**, and **ServerSupportFunction**.

The ISAPI filter DLL does nothing until an event occurs, at which time the ISAPI filter DLL is given control at the **HttpFilterProc** entry point. Valid events include: `SF_NOTIFY_SECURE_PORT`, `SF_NOTIFY_NONSECURE_PORT`, `SF_NOTIFY_READ_RAW_DATA`, `SF_NOTIFY_PREPROC_HEADERS`, `SF_NOTIFY_AUTHENTICATION`, `SF_NOTIFY_URL_MAP`, `SF_NOTIFY_SEND_RAW_DATA`, `SF_NOTIFY_LOG`, `SF_NOTIFY_END_NET_SESSION`, and `SF_NOTIFY_ACCESS_DENIED`.

OLEISAPI

OLEISAPI is a Visual Basic interface to ISAPI that uses object linking and embedding (OLE) as the interface. This mechanism is not as efficient as an ISAPI application, but it is much more efficient than a CGI application. Figure 38-5 is the OLEISPI architecture.

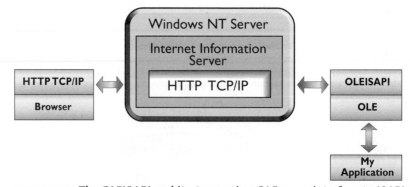

FIGURE 38-5   The OLEISAPI architecture: using OLE as an interface to ISAPI.

MOST COM COMPONENTS ARE SINGLE THREADED

The Microsoft `OLEISAP.DLL` locks everything down to one thread because it assumes, and rightly so, that most COM components are single threads. If you understand the nature of your beast, you might want to modify the Microsoft `OLEISAPI.DLL` and remove that restriction. You might also want to go to the Visual Basic 5.0 Enterprise Edition, Books-on-Line and read the discussions on threading. Threads in the Microsoft architecture are a hoary beast and there are many problems, including cross-threading, which can force an application to lock down to a single thread. The magnitude of thread issues creating performance problems for a component architecture is frightening. Microsoft is trying to add free-threading to an architecture that was designed without a viable thread architecture, and the result is worse than a crazy quilt. In my opinion, Microsoft should stop now with what they have and start over with a new design where single-thread or apartment-thread models don't exist.

 web links
This is older technology, but if you're interested it can be found either in the Internet samples directory of the ActiveX SDK on an MSDN CD-ROM or at `http://www.microsoft.con/intdev/sdk`.

 concept link
As I noted in Chapter 37, Microsoft is quietly deprecating the IDC/HTX technology. An example using OLEISAPI is presented here as an alternative to the IDC/HTX technology.

OLEISAPI is a DLL provided by Microsoft. An ActiveX component is usable with this DLL when these conditions are met:

- The component can have any name, but it must be a public name.

- The component can only accept two arguments, both of which are string values. One argument is the HTML request, and the other argument is the HTML response composed by the ActiveX component.

- Both arguments must be passed by reference and not by value.

- The component must have no user interaction. This permits declaring the DLL as *multiuser*.

`OLEISAPI.DLL` is called in the same manner as a regular ISAPI DLL. The context is slightly different, and the generic prototypes below illustrate the different means of accessing the Microsoft `OLEISAPI.DLL`.

```
<form METHOD="GET" ACTION="/scripts/oleisapi.dll/PROGID.CLASS.
Method">
```

```
<form METHOD="POST" ACTION="/scripts/oleisapi.dll/PROGID.
CLASS.Method">
```

```
<a HREF ="/scripts/oleisapi.dll/PROGID.CLASS.Method?Arg=
value">
Click Here for OLEISAPI</a>
```

The *PROGID* in the generic protypes above represent a Visual Basic 5.0 ActiveX DLL name, *CLASS* represents a .CLS module of the ActiveX DLL, and *Method* represents a method of the .CLS module. The PROGID selected for the upcoming OLEISAPI example is VBISAPI, and the class is VBISAPIClass. The methods are **DoPost**, **DoGet**, and **SimpleCall**. The following steps will make our ActiveX DLL operational:

- The Microsoft OLEISAPI.DLL must be installed in the /SCRIPTS directory of your server. You might want to use C++ and rebuild the DLL. I used Visual C++ 5.0 Enterprise Edition on the ABSHIM project from the ActiveX Developers Kit, and it compiled and linked without errors.

- Start the Internet server manager. Double-click the *wwwroot* icon. Select the *Directories* tab and the *SCRIPTS* subdirectory.

- Click *Edit Properties* and verify that the WWWROOT/SCRIPTS directory allows execution. Set the property accordingly.

- Distributed COM may require a configuration change. Go to the System32 subdirectory for your Internet server and double-click the DCOMCNFG icon. Select the **Default Security** tab, and Figure 38-6 should display.

- Select the **Edit Default** button of *Default Access Permissions,* and you should now see a display similar to Figure 38-7. If you don't have an entry that starts with IUSER_, then select *Add* and add your system name. Close the dialog box.

- Do the same for the *Default Launch Permissions* displayed in Figure 38-8. If you don't have an entry that starts with IUSER_, then select *Add* and add your system name. Close all dialogs.

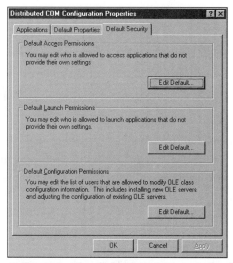

FIGURE 38-6 The dialog box for managing Distributed COM.

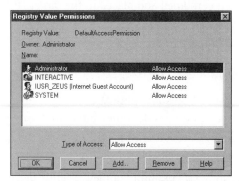

FIGURE 38-7 Internet server default access permissions.

FIGURE 38-8 Internet server default launch permissions.

- We're still in the countdown sequence for our DLL. You'll want to build and link your ActiveX DLL in Visual Basic 5.0. Make sure you select ActiveX DLL and not ActiveX Document DLL when starting the Visual Basic 5.0 project. All the code for the DLL project is shown below in Listing 38-1, and you can type it in or cut and paste the code from the CD-ROM.

- The DLL was developed in sections as standalone modules. ADO code was generated in a separate environment. The HTML text was also generated in a separate environment and written to a file with the code fragment below.

```
Open TestHTML.htm for output as #1
Print #1, html
Close #1
```

- The active data objects code was tested and the HTML page was tested by displaying it in Internet Explorer. The scaffolding was removed from both modules, which were then combined and placed in the target DLL module.

- After you've created your DLL, enter DOS mode and move to the directory where you've stored your DLL. Register the new COM component with:

```
REGSVR32 <Your component Name>.DLL
```

- Editing your DLL presents a unique problem. When recompiling a DLL, the Registry entry must be removed unless the names are changed. (Versions and name changes were not used for the example DLL during the development cycle.) Extreme care should be used in deleting Registry entries because there is always a possibility of inadvertently deleting another entry.

LISTING 38-1 The Visual Basic 5.0 VBISAPIClass ActiveX Class Module

```
Option Explicit
'   (C) 1998 Bruce T. Prendergast
'   DBA Prendergast Consulting
'   DBA PCS
'
'     IDG Books Worldwide ISBN 0-7645-3123-9
'
'     Listing 38-2 Visual Basic 5.0 OLE ISAPI DLL
'
```

```
'   These functions and procedures are elements
'   of the ActiveX VBOLEIsapi.DLL supporting the
'   Microsoft provided OLEISAPI.DLL. The tasks
'   performed are the equivalent of an ISAPI
'   application done through Automation.
'
Function CreateStdResponse(meth As String, Request _
    As String) As String
    CreateStdResponse = "Content-Type: text/html" & _
        vbCrLf & vbCrLf _
        & "<body><h1>" & meth & "</h1>" _
        & "<p><b>Parameters: </b>" & _
        Request & "</body>"
End Function


Function FindEmployee(Request As String)
    Dim MyRS As Recordset
    Dim MyCmd As Command
    Dim MyCon As Connection
    Dim Input_Data
    Dim html As String
    Dim MyErr As Error
    Dim ip As Long
    '
    '   This is a really cheap parser. Just
    '   Find "=" and accept whatever it is.
    '
    On Error GoTo oleDB_error
    ip = InStr(1, Request, "=")
    Input_Data = Mid$(Request, ip + 1)
    '
    '   build my connection. The connection string is
    '   hacked from a Visual InterDev Access connection.
    '   NOTE: NOTE: The Northwind database is in another
    '   local Web, and I didn't want to import it to
    '   every example Web. Do your own fixups here.
```

```
'
Set MyCon = New ADODB.Connection
MyCon.ConnectionString = "DSN=Northwind;" & _
   "DBQ=F:\InetPub\wwwroot\myweb\Northwind.mdb;" & _
   "DriverId=25;FIL=MS Access;MaxBufferSize=512;" & _
   "PageTimeout=5;"
MyCon.Open
Set MyCmd = New ADODB.Command
MyCmd.ActiveConnection = MyCon


MyCmd.CommandText = "SELECT Employees.EmployeeID, " & _
   "Employees.LastName, Employees.FirstName, " & _
   "Employees.Title  FROM Employees  WHERE " & _
   "Employees.EmployeeID= " & Input_Data
Set MyRS = MyCmd.Execute
'
'   I took a NON-FrontPage 98 page (WebBots and
'   smart HTML or the SHTML.DLL won't work here)
'   and went about pasting everything together.
'   There are double quotes where necessary.
'
'   Note that the header is first which is the
'   first line below.
'
html = "Content-Type: text/html" & _
   vbCrLf & vbCrLf & _
   "<body BGCOLOR=""#FFFFFF"">" & vbCrLf & _
   "<table Width=""60%"" BORDER=""1"" " & _
   "BGCOLOR=""#ffffff"" " & _
   "CELLSPACING=""0""> " & vbCrLf & _
   "<font FACE=""Arial"" " & _
   "COLOR=""#000000""><caption>" & _
   "<b>Northwind Employee</b>" & _
   "</caption>" & vbCrLf
html = html & "<thead>" & vbCrLf & _
   "<tr>" & vbCrLf & _
```

```
    "<th BGCOLOR=""#c0c0c0"" " & _
    "BORDERCOLOR=""#000000"">" & _
    "<font SIZE=""2"" FACE=""Arial"" " & _
    "COLOR=""#000000"">" & _
    "EmployeeID</font></th>" & vbCrLf & _
    "<th BGCOLOR=""#c0c0c0"" " & _
    "BORDERCOLOR=""#000000"">" & _
    "<font SIZE=""2"" FACE=""Arial"" " & _
    "COLOR=""#000000"">" & _
    "LastName</font></th>" & vbCrLf & _
    "<th BGCOLOR=""#c0c0c0"" "
html = html & "BORDERCOLOR=""#000000"">" & _
    "<font SIZE=""2"" FACE=""Arial"" " & _
    "COLOR=""#000000"">" & _
    "FirstName</font></th>" & vbCrLf & _
    "</tr>" & vbCrLf & _
    "</thead>" & vbCrLf & "<tbody>" & vbCrLf
html = html & "<tr VALIGN=""TOP"">" & vbCrLf & _
    "<td BORDERCOLOR=""#c0c0c0"" " & _
    "ALIGN=""RIGHT"">" & _
    "<font SIZE=""2"" FACE=""Arial"" " & _
    "COLOR=""#000000"">" & _
    MyRS(0) & "<br>" & vbCrLf & _
html = html & "</font></td>" & vbCrLf & _
    "<td BORDERCOLOR=""#c0c0c0"" " & _
    "ALIGN=""RIGHT""><font SIZE=""2"" " & _
    "FACE=""Arial"" " & _
    "COLOR=""#000000"">" & MyRS(1) & _
    "<br>" & vbCrLf
html = html & "</font></td>" & vbCrLf & _
    "<td BORDERCOLOR=""#c0c0c0"">" & _
    "<font SIZE=""2"" " & _
    "FACE=""Arial"" COLOR=""#000000"">" & _
    MyRS(2) & "<br>" & vbCrLf & _
    "</font></td>" & vbCrLf & _
    "</tr>" & vbCrLf & "</tbody>" & vbCrLf & _
    "</table>" & vbCrLf & vbCrLf & _
```

```
            "</body>" & vbCrLf
        FindEmployee = html
        Exit Function
oleDB_error:
        html = "VB OLEISAP DLL errors: " & vbCrLf
        For Each MyErr In MyCon.Errors
            html = html & MyErr.Number & " — " & _
                MyErr.Description & vbCrLf
        Next MyErr
        Resume Next
        FindEmployee = html
        Exit Function
End Function
Sub DoGet(Request As String, Response As String)
        Response = CreateStdResponse( _
          "GET method not implemented", Request)
End Sub

Sub DoPost(Request As String, Response As String)
        Response = FindEmployee(Request)
End Sub

Sub SimpleCall(Request As String, Response As String)
        Response = CreateStdResponse( _
          "URL invocation not implemented", Request)
End Sub
```

Listing 38-1 is quite simple. The three subroutines **DoPost**, **DoGet**, and **SimpleCall** are the methods supported. The two functions **CreateStdResponse** and **FindEmployee** are for internal operations. **CreateStdResponse** is used by both **SimpleCall** and **DoGet** to return a "Not Implemented" message in HTML. It is also used to return an ADO error message from **FindEmployee** as HTML because a DLL cannot have any user interaction. Remember that your component is a DLL that may be accessed by multiple users. Under no circumstance should it be allowed to crash. All errors must be captured, and the code should be gracious enough to also report the errors.

The **FindEmployee** function locates the employee record and formats the HTML. Standard HTML generated by Microsoft Access was used and hacked to fit. Note that it does not have the `<html /html>` element and has a header at the top. This process can be automated and somewhat represents an HTX page without the `<%begin detail%>` and `<%end detail%>` constructs. The only problem is that the HTML is wired to this module.

The main module of a Visual Basic 5.0 DLL project is trivial and consists of only two lines:

```
Sub main()
End Sub
```

You'll find this DLL example in the CD-ROM EXAMPLES\CHAPTER38 folder as a Visual Basic 5.0 Enterprise Edition VBISAPI.VBP project. Also within that directory is the Web site used in the example below (see Figure 38-9). The Web OLEISAPIWEB folder was copied from the Web root //wwwroot/OLEISAPIWEB. You'll want to recreate this Web on your own system. The OLEISAPI DLL has a local connection to an imported Microsoft Access Northwind .MDB. This MDB is not shipped in this directory and the OLEISAPI DLL must be updated to reflect a local version.

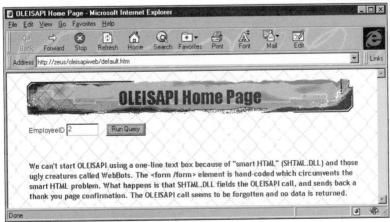

FIGURE 38-9   The Visual Basic 5.0 ISAPI home page in FrontPage 98.

The bold section of Listing 38-2 is the hand-coded HTML FORM element.

LISTING 38-2 The HTML code of Figure 38-9

```html
<html>

<head>
  <title>OLEISAPI Home Page</title>
  <meta name="GENERATOR" content="Microsoft FrontPage 3.0">
  <meta name="Microsoft Theme" content="construc 011">
  <meta name="Microsoft Border" content="tl, default">
</head>

<body>

<form METHOD="POST"
 ACTION="/scripts/oleisapi.dll/VBISAPI.VBISAPIClass.dopost">
  <p>EmployeeID
    <input TYPE="Text"
      NAME="Input_ID" size="8">  
    <input TYPE="Submit"
      VALUE="Run Query">     
  </p>
  <p> </p>
</form>

<h3>We can't start OLEISAPI using a one-line text box
    because of &quot; smart HTML&quot; (SHTML.DLL) and
    those ugly creatures called WebBots. The &lt;form
    /form&gt; element is hand-coded which circumvents
    the smart HTML problem. What happens is that
    SHTML.DLL fields the OLEISAPI call, and sends
    back a thank you page confirmation. The OLEISAPI
    call seems to be forgotten and no data is returned.
</h3>
</body>
</html>
```

The **Post** method is used with the OLEISAPI.DLL. The results of Figure 38-9 are displayed in Figure 38-10.

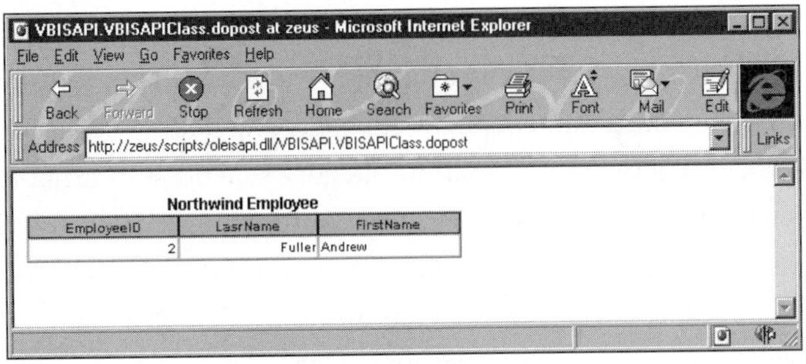

FIGURE 38-10 **The results of Figure 38-9.**

As mentioned previously, do not use a FrontPage 98 one-line text box for an OLEISAPI application. The ugly WebBot creature will give you a nice thank you confirmation page and then proceed to file your OLEISAPI request in its own private black hole. Listing 38-3 is the very polite message returned from SHTML.DLL (smart HTML).

LISTING 38-3 The very polite message from SHTML.DLL

```html
<html>
    <head>
      <meta http-equiv="Content-Type"
      content="text/html; charset=iso-8859-1">
      <title>Form Confirmation</title>
    </head>
    <body>
    <h1>Form Confirmation</h1>
    <p>Thank you for submitting the following information:</p>
    <p><b>T1: </b>1<br><b>B1: </b>Submit<br></p>
    <p><a HREF="/oleisapiweb/default.htm">Return to the form.
      </a>
    </p>
</html>
```

WIN32 INTERNET APPLICATION PROGRAMMING INTERFACE

The Microsoft Win32 Internet API is rich with functionality. A function for almost any conceivable application is available. These functions are sketched below. Review the functions for general functionality and not the details of an individual function call. There are six function categories: general Internet functions; File Transfer Protocol (FTP) functions; Gopher functions; HTTP (World Wide Web) functions; cookie functions; and cache functions. Additional details on the Internet API functions can be found in the MSDN Platform SDK.

Win 32 Internet API handles are managed differently than handles in other APIs. The handles are stored in a hierarchical structure with the handle returned by **InternetOpen** set as the root handle. **InternetConnect** returns the next level's handles with the leaf level populated by handles created by open or find functions such as **FtpFindFirstFile**. **InternetCloseHandle** closes an individual handle or the whole tree.

The first versions of the Win32 Internet API do not support Unicode, but Unicode support will be a standard feature in future releases.

Error handling in the Win 32 Internet API is mixed. Some functions will return a BOOL value of TRUE for a success and FALSE for failure. Other functions will return a value of HINTERNET. A NULL handle indicates the function failed, and anything else represents a failure.

The Win32 Internet API functions are reentrant. When there are multiple requests outstanding, there is no guarantee as to the order in which the requests will be satisfied. It is the responsibility of the application task to synchronize requests.

Win32 General Internet Functions

Following are general Internet utility functions that perform basic services such as URL manipulation, connecting, reading, and terminating an Internet connection. No examples are presented in this section. Instead, refer to the OLEISAPI.DLL found in the ActiveX Development Kit.

In general, returned character string counts do not include the last character or terminating character. When a character string is returned with an error, the character count normally reflects the complete string length.

InternetAttemptConnect	Attempts an Internet connection. Returns ERROR_SUCCESS when successful; otherwise a Win32 error value.
InternetCanonicalizeUrl	Converts a URL to a canonical form. Unsafe characters are converted to escape sequences. Returns TRUE when successful, FALSE otherwise. Use **GetLastError** when FALSE is returned.
InternetCloseHandle	Closes a single Internet handle or a subtree of Internet handles. Returns TRUE when handle is successfully closed, FALSE otherwise. Use **GetLastError** when FALSE is returned.
InternetCombineUrl	A base URL is combined with a relative URL. The resulting URL is in canonical form (see **InternetCanonicalizeUrl**). Returns TRUE when successful, FALSE otherwise. Use **GetLastError** when FALSE is returned.
InternetConnect	Opens an FTP, Gopher, or HTTP session. Returns a valid handle or NULL. When a NULL is returned use **GetlastError** or **InternetGet LastResponseInfo**.
InternetConfirmZoneCrossing	Prompts the user with a dialog box when a URL changes from secure to nonsecure. Returns ERROR_SUCCESS when the user confirmed or no user input was required. ERROR_CANCELLED reflects the user cancelling, and ERROR_NOT_ENOUGH_MEMORY reflects the memory state.
InternetCrackUrl	Cracks a URL into component parts. Returns TRUE when successful, FALSE otherwise. Use **GetLastError** when FALSE is returned.
InternetCreateUrl	Create a URL using a URL_COMPONENTS structure. Returns TRUE when successful, FALSE otherwise. Use **GetLastError** when FALSE is returned. **GetLastError** returns

	ERROR_NO_MORE_FILES when no matching files are found and ERROR_INSUFFICIENT_ BUFFER when the buffer space is inadequate.
InternetErrorDlg	Displays a dialog box explaining why an error occurred with a **HttpSendRequest** function. The user responses result in either ERROR_SUCCESS, ERROR_CANCELLED, or ERROR_INTERNET_FORCE_ENTRY.
InternetFindNextFile	This function continues a file search started by either **FtpFindFirstFile** or **GopherFindFirst File**. FTP returns a WIN32_FIND_DATA structure, and Gopher returns a GOPHER_ FIND_DATA structure. Returns TRUE when successful, FALSE otherwise. Use **GetLastError** when FALSE is returned. ERROR_NO_MORE_ FILES is returned when no matching files are found.
InternetGetLastResponseInfo	Returns the last Win32 Internet function error description or server response for this thread. Returns TRUE when successful, FALSE otherwise. Use **GetLastError** when FALSE is returned. ERROR_INSUFFICIENT_BUFFER is returned when the output buffer is too small.
InternetOpen	Initializes a handle for subsequent Win32 Internet functions. Use **GetLastError** when a NULL is returned.
InternetOpenUrl	Begins reading a complete FTP, Gopher, or HTTP URL. **InternetCanonicalizeUrl** must be used first if the URL contains a relative and a base URL. Returns a valid handle when successful, NULL otherwise. **GetLastError** will retrieve the error code, and **InternetGetLast ResponseInfo** will report the reason for the denial of service.

InternetQueryDataAvailable	Queries for the amount of data available for subsequent **InternetReadFile** function. The file handle for this function is supplied by **FtpOpenFile**, **GopherOpenFile**, or **HttpOpen Request**. Returns TRUE when successful, FALSE otherwise. Use **GetLastError** when FALSE is returned. ERROR_NO_MORE_FILES is returned when there are no matching files.
InternetQueryOption	Queries for the support of a supplied option. Returns TRUE when successful, FALSE otherwise. Use **GetLastError** when FALSE is returned. ERROR_INSUFFICIENT_BUFFER is returned when the output buffer is too small.
InternetReadFile	Reads data from a handle supplied by **InternetOpenUrl**, **FtpOpenUrl**, **GopherOpen Url**, or **HttpOpenRequest**. A transfer is complete when the return value is TRUE and the remaining byte count is zero. Returns TRUE when successful and FALSE otherwise. **GetLastError** will retrieve the error code, and **InternetGetLastResponseInfo** is used when necessary.
InternetSetFilePointer	Sets a file pointer for use by **InternetReadFile**. A synchronous call and subsequent calls to **InternetReadFile** may be blocked when data is not available from cache and the server does not support random access. The file handle is returned from a previous **FtpOpenFile**, **Gopher FileOpen**, **InternetOpenUrl** on an HTTP URL, or to **HttpOpenRequest** using the GET or HEAD method and passed to **HttpSendRequest**. The flags INTERNET_FLAG_DONT_CACHE or INTERNET_FLAG_NO_CACHE must not be set when creating this handle. The function returns the current file position or <-1> when the operation fails.

InternetSetOption	Sets an Internet option on a specified handle. Returns TRUE when successful, FALSE otherwise. Use **GetLastError** when FALSE is returned.
InternetSetOptionEx	Sets an Internet option on a specified handle. Returns TRUE when successful, FALSE otherwise. Use **GetLastError** when FALSE is returned. This function has one more argument than **InternetSetOption**. *dwFlags* gives the option of setting the option globally or in the Registry when applicable.
InternetSetStatusCallback	A placeholder for an application-defined status callback. No status is returned.
InternetStatusCallback	This function is supplied a handle for which the callback function is being called, a reason for the callback, and a buffer with pertinent callback information. No status is returned.
InternetTimeFromSystemTime	Returns a date and time formatted to the current Request for Comments (RFC) format. Returns TRUE when successful, FALSE otherwise. Use **GetLastError** when FALSE is returned.
InternetTimeToSystemTime	An HTTP time/date string is converted to a **SYSTEMTIME** structure. Returns TRUE when successful, FALSE otherwise. Use **GetLastError** when FALSE is returned.
InternetWriteFile	Data is written to an open Internet file. Returns TRUE when successful, FALSE otherwise. Use **GetLastError** when FALSE is returned. **InternetGetLastResponseInfo** is used when necessary. **InternetCloseHandle** will stop application data transfer.

FTP Functions

The File Transport Protocol is used to manage files on remote servers.

FtpCreateDirectory	Creates a new directory on the FTP server. Returns TRUE when successful, FALSE otherwise. Use **GetLastError** when FALSE is returned. The FTP and Gopher protocols support the **InternetGetLast ResponseInfo** method. **InternetGetLastResponseInfo** is used by applications to return error text.
FtpDeleteFile	Deletes a file stored at the FTP server. Returns TRUE when successful, FALSE otherwise. Use **GetLastError** when FALSE is returned.
FtpFindFirstFile	Searches a specified directory of an FTP session. The results are returned in a WIN32_FIND_DATA structure. Returns a valid file handle, NULL otherwise. Use **GetLastError** when a NULL is returned. **GetLast Error** returns ERROR_NO_MORE_FILES when no matching files are found.
FtpGetCurrentDirectory	Retrieves the directory for the current FTP session. Returns TRUE when successful, FALSE otherwise. Use **GetLastError** when FALSE is returned. **InternetGet LastResponseInfo** is used when necessary.
FtpGetFile	Retrieves a file from the FTP server and stores it under the supplied file name. Returns TRUE when successful, FALSE otherwise. Use **GetLastError** when FALSE is returned.
FtpOpenFile	Opens a file at an FTP server for reading or writing, but not both. A handle is returned when the operation is a success, otherwise a NULL is returned. Use **GetLastError** to retrieve the error code. The file is closed with **InternetCloseHandle**, which is also used to terminate current operation. The only other permissible operations are **InternetReadFile**, **Internet WriteFile**, or **FTPFindFirstFile**. Calls to other FTP functions will result in the

	ERROR_FTP_TRANSFER_IN_PROGRESS error code. Only one file may be open in an FTP session. No file handle is returned, and the session uses the FTP session handle as necessary. The *dwContext* parameter is only used when the application has already called **InternetStatusCallback** to set up a callback function.
FtpPutFile	Sends a file to an FTP server. Returns TRUE when successful, FALSE otherwise. Use **GetLastError** to retrieve error information.
FtpRemoveDirectory	Removes the specified directory from the FTP server. Returns TRUE when successful, FALSE otherwise. Use **GetLastError** when FALSE is returned. **InternetGet LastResponseInfo** is used when necessary.
FtpRenameFile	Renames a file stored on an FTP server. Returns TRUE when successful, FALSE otherwise. Use **GetLastError** to retrieve specific error code.
FtpSetCurrentDirectory	Changes the current path to a different working directory on the FTP server. Returns TRUE when successful, FALSE otherwise. Use **GetLastError** to retrieve specific error code. Use **InternetGetLast ResponseInfo** when the request is denied. The FTP and Gopher protocols support the **InternetGetLast ResponseInfo** method. **InternetGetLastResponseInfo** is used by applications to return error text.

Gopher Functions

Gopher functions use a locator and search criteria to locate requested documents, binary files, index servers, or directory trees.

GopherCreateLocator	Creates a Gopher or a Gopher+ locator string from the constituent components. The locator is normally used by **GopherFindFirstFile**. Returns TRUE when successful, FALSE otherwise. Use **GetLastError** or **InternetGetLastResponseInfo** when the request fails.

GopherGetLocatorType	Parses a Gopher locator. No error information is returned.
GopherFindFirstFile	A Gopher locator and a search criterion are used to create a session with a server and locate the documents, binary files, index servers, or directory trees. A GOPHER_FIND_DATA structure is returned. **InternetFindNextFile** retrieves a subsequent object. The Gopher server connection is closed with **InternetCloseHandle**. Returns a valid handle or NULL. When a NULL is returned, use **GetlastError** or **InternetGetLast ResponseInfo**.
GopherGetAttribute	Retrieves a specific attribute, or retrieves all attributes when the supplied attribute name is NULL. Returns TRUE when successful, FALSE otherwise. Use **GetLastError** or **InternetGetLast ResponseInfo** when the request fails. This function optionally installs a callback function for enumerating Gopher server attributes.
GopherAttributeEnumerator	This is a callback function for enumerating Gopher server attributes. The callback function is installed by **GopherGetAttribute**. Returns TRUE to continue the function and FALSE to terminate it. Primarily used for enumerating results of Gopher+.
GopherOpenFile	Starts reading a Gopher server file. The handle used by this operation is supplied by **InternetConnect**. Returns a valid handle or NULL. When a NULL is returned use **GetlastError** or **InternetGetLastResponseInfo**.

HTTP (World Wide Web) Functions

HTTP functions control the transmission and contents of HTTP requests. The headers sent to the server will be RFC822/Multipurpose Internet Mail Extension (MIME)/HTTP compliant.

HttpAddRequestHeaders	Adds request headers to the HTTP request handle. Used by sophisticated clients for finer server control. Returns TRUE when successful, FALSE otherwise. Use **GetLastError** when the request fails.
HttpOpenRequest	Returns an HTTP request header when successful, NULL otherwise. The new HTTP request handle contains all the RFC822/MIME/HTTP headers to be sent as part of the request. Default verb is GET. **InternetCloseHandle** closes the handle. Use **GetLastError** when the request fails.
HttpQueryInfo	Uses the handle returned by **HttpOpenRequest** to return response or to request headers from an HTTP request. Returns TRUE when successful, FALSE otherwise. Use **GetLastError** when the request fails. The function fails with ERROR_HTTP_HEADER_NOT_FOUND when an indexed header is not found. Inadequate space in *lpvBuffer* elicits the error response ERROR_INSUFFICIENT_BUFFER.
HttpSendRequest	Sends the specified request to the HTTP server using the handle opened by **HttpOpenRequest**. Additional RFC822/MIME/HTTP headers can be included with this function. Returns TRUE when successful, FALSE otherwise. Use **GetLastError** when the request fails.

Cookie Functions

Cookies are stored on the client and are used by the server to control state information because HTTP is a stateless protocol.

InternetGetCookie	Retrieves the cookies for the specified URL and all its parent URLs. Microsoft does not publish rules as to what may be stored in a cookie. The developer using cookies should be familiar with cookies as outlined in ftp://ds.internic.net/internet-drafts/draft-ietf-http-state-mgmt-*.txt. An **InternetOpen** is not required to use this function. The function returns TRUE when successful,

FALSE otherwise. Use **GetLastError** when the request fails. ERROR_NO_MORE_ITEMS is returned when no cookies exist for this URL. ERROR_INSUFFICIENT_BUFFER is returned for inadequate cookie storage.

InternetSetCookie   Store a cookie at the specified URL. Returns TRUE when successful, FALSE otherwise. Use **GetLastError** when the request fails.

Cache Functions

Clients with low bandwidth or no Internet access implement caching services. Win32 Internet functions cache by default unless the INTERNET_FLAG_NO_CACHE_WRITE flag is set.

CommitUrlCacheEntry   Caches data in the specified file and associates with the supplied URL. Returns TRUE when successful, FALSE otherwise. Use **GetLastError** when the request fails. ERROR_DISK_FULL can be returned when the disk is full or when the file size is larger than the cache size. ERROR_FILE_NOT_FOUND is returned when the local file is not found.

CreateUrlCacheEntry   Creates a local filename and allocates requested cache storage. Returns TRUE when successful, FALSE otherwise. Use **GetLastError** when the request fails.

GetUrlCacheEntry   Retrieves a cache entry. Returns TRUE when successful, FALSE otherwise. Use **GetLastError** when the request fails. Possible errors include ERROR_INSUFFICIENT_BUFFER and ERROR_FILE_NOT_FOUND.

ReadUrlCacheEntryStream   Reads a cache entry from a stream opened with the **RetrieveUrlCacheEntrySystem** function. Returns TRUE when successful, FALSE otherwise. Use **GetLastError** when the request fails.

RetrieveUrlCacheEntryFile	Retrieves a cache entry in the form of a file which is locked for the caller. The caller is only given read permission. This is not a recommended cache function and may be inefficient. The recommended procedure is to use **RetrieveUrlCacheEntryStream**. Returns TRUE when successful, FALSE otherwise. Use **GetLastError** when the request fails. Possible errors include ERROR_INSUFFICIENT_BUFFER and ERROR_FILE_NOT_FOUND.
RetrieveUrlCacheEntryStream	The most efficient cache access mechanism. A valid handle is returned for use by **ReadUrl CacheEntryStream** and **UnlockUrlCacheEntry Stream**. Returns a valid handle when successful and INVALID_HANDLE_VALUE otherwise. Use **GetLastError** when the request fails. Possible errors include ERROR_INSUFFICIENT_BUFFER and ERROR_FILE_NOT_FOUND.
SetUrlCacheEntryInfo	Sets specified elements of the INTERNET_ CACHE_ENTRY_INFO structure. Returns TRUE when successful, FALSE otherwise. Use **GetLastError** when the request fails. Possible errors include ERROR_INVALID_PARAMETER and ERROR_FILE_NOT_FOUND, which is returned when the cache entry is not found.
UnlockUrlCacheEntryFile	Unlocks the cache entry that was locked while the file was retrieved for use from the cache. The file is no longer accessible after this function is called. Returns TRUE when successful, FALSE otherwise. Use **GetLastError** when the request fails. Possible errors include ERROR_FILE_NOT_FOUND.
UnlockUrlCacheEntryStream	Closes the stream retrieved using the **RetrieveUrlCacheEntryStream** function. Returns TRUE when successful, FALSE

	otherwise. Use **GetLastError** when the request fails.
DeleteUrlCacheEntry	Removes the file associated with a cache entry. The file may not exist. Returns TRUE when successful, FALSE otherwise. Use **GetLastError** when the request fails. Possible errors include ERROR_FILE_NOT_FOUND and ERROR_ ACCESS_DENIED.
FindCloseUrlCache	Closes the cache enumeration handle opened with **FindFirstUrlCacheEntry**. Returns TRUE when successful, FALSE otherwise. Use **GetLastError** when the request fails.
FindFirstUrlCacheEntry	Starts cache enumeration. Returns a handle for use by **FindNextUrlCacheEntry**. Returns a valid handle when successful and NULL otherwise. Use **GetLastError** when the request fails. ERROR_INSUFFICIENT_BUFFER is a possible error.
FindNextUrlCacheEntry	Retrieves the next cache entry. Handle is obtained from a previous call to **FindFirstUrl CacheEntry**. Returns TRUE when successful, FALSE otherwise. Use **GetLastError** when the request fails. Possible errors include ERROR_ INSUFFICIENT_BUFFER and ERROR_NO_ MORE_FILES.

WEBBROWSER CONTROL

Browsing the Internet/intranet is done from Visual Basic 5.0 using the Microsoft Internet Controls (SHDOCVW.OCA) or the WebBrowser control. The control is inserted into a Visual Basic 5.0 application by selecting *References* from the **Project** menu and then checking *Microsoft Internet Controls* and selecting *OK*. Drag the control from the toolbox onto a form and expand it. The one line of code below created Figure 38-11 when the application was started. Note that it is the home page from the Web site of Chapter 37. The Web site is functional within the WebBrowser control, but there are no back links on the page. Because the site is hosted in the WebBrowser control and not in Internet Explorer, there is no method for returning to the home page once you leave it. The developer must supply the missing functionality of Internet Explorer when using the WebBrowser control. You'll find this example on your CD-ROM in the EXAMPLES\CHAPTER38 folder as Visual Basic 5.0 Enterprise Edition BROWSER.VBP project.

```
Private Sub Form_Load()
Me!WebBrowser1.Navigate "HTTP://Zeus/Myweb"
End Sub
```

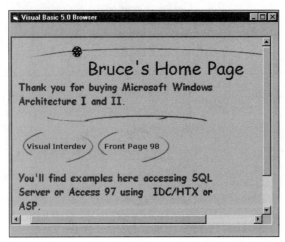

FIGURE 38-11   The WebBrowser control in a Visual Basic 5.0 application.

INTERNET EXPLORER

The WebBrowser control is not the only choice of a browser for the Visual Basic 5.0 developer. Microsoft Internet Explorer is available through Automation as illustrated by the code fragment below, which instantiates Internet Explorer. The WebBrowser control and the Internet Explorer share properties as indicated by the **Navigate** method. The object variable is declared as public variable in a module. You'll find this example in the CD-ROM EXAMPLES\CHAPTER38 folder as Visual Basic 5.0 Enterprise Edition OLETEST.VBP project.

```
Private Sub InternetExplorer_Click()
    Set IEObj = CreateObject("InternetExplorer.Application")
    IEObj.Visible = True
    IEObj.navigate "HTTP://Zeus/MyWeb"
End Sub
```

WININET

A Visual Basic 5.0 application initiates FTP and HTTP file transfers between Web sites with the Microsoft Internet Transfer Control (MSINET.OCA) or the WinInet control (see Figure 38-12). The control is inserted into a Visual Basic 5.0 application by selecting *References* from the **Project** menu and then checking *Microsoft Internet Transfer Control 5.0*. Select *OK* and drop the control onto a form and provide the supporting Visual Basic for Applications (VBA) code. The code in Listing 38-4 responds to the different states of the WinInet control during a transfer operation. Clicking the single command button starts the FTP transfer. You'll find this example in the CD-ROM EXAMPLES\CHAPTER38 folder as Visual Basic 5.0 Enterprise Edition Visual Basic 5.0 FTP.VBP project.

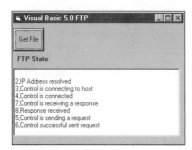

FIGURE 38-12   The WinInet control in a Visual Basic 5.0 Application

LISTING 38-4 The VBA code of Figure 38-12

```
Private Sub cmdSendFile_Click()
    Inet1.Execute "FTP://ZEUS", _
    "GET myFTP/ftpTest.txt e:\idgexamp\ftptest.txt"
End Sub


Private Sub Inet1_StateChanged(ByVal State As Integer)
```

```
'(C) 1998 Bruce T. Prendergast
'   DBA Prendergast Consulting
'   DBA PCS
'   IDG Books Worldwide ISBN 0-7645-3123-9
'
'   Listing 38-4 The WinInet Control
'
    Dim errData
    Select Case State
      Case icNone
        FTPState.Text = FTPState.Text & vbCrLf & _
            "0,None"
      Case icHostResolvingHost
        FTPState.Text = FTPState.Text & vbCrLf & _
            "1,Find the IP address"
      Case icHostResolved
        FTPState.Text = FTPState.Text & _
            vbCrLf & "2,IP Address resolved"
      Case icConnecting
        FTPState.Text = FTPState.Text & _
            vbCrLf & "3,Control is connecting to host"
      Case icConnected
        FTPState.Text = FTPState.Text & _
            vbCrLf & "4,Control is connected"
      Case icRequesting
        FTPState.Text = FTPState.Text & _
            vbCrLf & "5,Control is sending a request"
      Case icRequestSent
        FTPState.Text = FTPState.Text & _
            vbCrLf & "6,Control successful sent request"
      Case icReceivingResponse
        FTPState.Text = FTPState.Text & _
            vbCrLf & "7,Control is receiving a response"
      Case icResponseReceived
        FTPState.Text = FTPState.Text & _
            vbCrLf & "8,Response received"
```

```
        Case icDisconnecting
          FTPState.Text = FTPState.Text &
             vbCrLf & "9,Disconnecting"
        Case icDisconnected
          FTPState.Text = FTPState.Text & _
             vbCrLf & "10, Disconnected"
        Case icError
          FTPState.Text = FTPState.Text & _
             vbCrLf & "11,Error: & _
             Inet1.ResponseCode" & _
             ":" & Inet1.ResponseInfo
        Case icResponseCompleted
          FTPState.Text = FTPState.Text & _
             vbCrLf & "12,Response Completed"
      End Select
  End Sub
```

Listing 38-4 is the code for both the **command** button and the **WinInet** control of Figure 38-12.

WEBPOST

You can create Web sites, but how do you get the Web pages to your service provider? WebPost is the Web Publishing Wizard found in the `ValuPack\` `WebPost` folder of the Office 97 CD-ROM. The purpose of this Wizard is to publish to an FTP or a Web site on an Internet or intranet. The tool can publish pages to Compuserve, Sprynet, America OnLine, and GNN, and to servers running Microsoft Internet Information Server.

WEBPOST API

Of course if you really want to get down to gunmetal, there is always the WebPost API. It is found in the Microsoft Developer Network Platform SDK. It supports the traditional Windows Open Systems Architecture (WOSA) with both an application and a service provider interface. The WebPost API has three basic functions, an advanced binding function to the WebPost SPI functions, and a single element posting function.

- *WpDeleteSite* — Delete a previously configured friendly site name.
- *WpListSites* — Retrieve a list of configured friendly site names.
- *WpPost* — Post a file to the URL at the given site.
- *WpBindToSite* — Return a COM object to the WebPost service provider that supports the given site name or URL. This function allows the client to call into service provider interface (SPI) functions that are not listed here.
- *WpPostFile* — Enable automation and only allow posting of a single file or directory at a time. Very similar to *WpPost*.

KEY POINT SUMMARY

Microsoft believes that the world cannot be without dynamic HTML and Active Server Pages. Many applications do not require the animation and interaction offered by these technologies. An environment that resembles "midnight in the gaslight district" is not necessary for e-mail, and CGI and ISAPI continue to be viable Internet technologies. CGI is very useful; the issue is to remember that it is not scalable. The ISAPI will always have the best performance because its code is executed directly, whereas ASP scripts are interpreted. An ISAPI application has the additional advantage of communicating with parameter values rather than a complete HTML page.

Applying What You've Learned

The questions below primarily address the earlier Internet technologies of CGI and ISAPI. The laboratory recreates the Visual Basic DLL constructed earlier in the chapter. It gives the Visual Basic developer an opportunity to create an ISAPI extension, a task normally reserved for C++ developers.

Instant Assessment

1. Explain the disadvantages of the WebBrowser control.
2. Explain error handling in a Visual Basic DLL.

3. Describe the content of the three parameter fields that follow the OLEISAPI HTML POST or the HTML GET methods.

4. What makes implementing an ISAPI DLL difficult?

5. What is the meaning of the <?> in a GET method?

6. The <?> is syntax signifying that parameters follow. An example might be ?First=sally+last=silly+age=39.

We know that a CGI application runs in its own process space whereas an ISAPI application is a DLL that runs in the process space of the Internet server. What is another operational dissimilarity?

concept link **For answers to the Instant Assessment questions, see Appendix C.**

Lab Exercises

Lab 38.74 *Rolling your own ISAPI DLL*

WA I
WA II

Lab 38.74 is a repeat of the Visual Basic 5.0 VBISAPI.DLL constructed earlier in the chapter. Your first problem is to locate the ActiveX Development Kit. The MSDN ActiveX Development Kit used in this chapter was shipped in 1996. You can start your search for it at http://www.microsoft.com/intdev/ if you are not an MSDN subscriber.

Lab 38.75 *Building an intranet tool*

WA I
WA II

Lab 38.75 is a repeat of creating the WinInet control application of Listing 38-4. The goal is to build a WinInet application that is distributed to users within an intranet. The control is used for downloading from a central location information such as price lists, assembly instructions, or any other document that a user might need. The tool will be started from an icon, an approach that bypasses using a browser.

About Chapter 39

With Chapter 39 we move up a level from Chapter 38. Here we look at scripting for both Internet Information Server (IIS) and Internet Explorer. The chapter closes with a discussion of the Internet download component.

In some ways, this chapter is the closure for many of the issues discussed in this book. One of the last sections of Chapter 10 is **CoGetClassObjectFromURL**. This is the Component Object Model (COM) library interface for the Internet download component; in this chapter, we're tying up a loose end.

A QUICK LOOK BACK AT COM

Scripting uses our old friend COM, the subject of discussion in Chapters 1 to 10. In those chapters, we discussed many generic interfaces, but none were directed at a specific technology. Figure 39-1 is a generic scripting engine. Both Internet Information Server and Internet Explorer use this model for scripting. Our old friend **IDispatch** from Chapter 2 is here. It's old home week for COM!

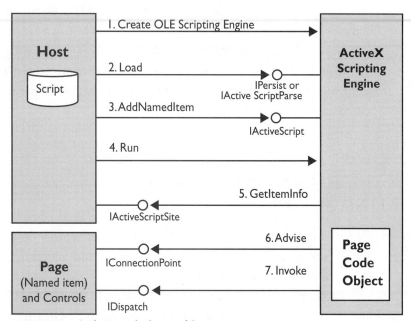

FIGURE 39-1   ActiveX scripting architecture.

Figure 39-1 assumes that the document is already hosted in Internet Explorer (IE) or Internet Information Server. The action starts with the host calling another old friend **CoCreateInstance** (see Chapter 2), which creates a new instance of the ActiveX scripting engine. A class identifier (CLSID) is provided by either IE or IIS (see Listing 39-1). The HTML <OBJECT> tag can also be the source of the CLSID.

The next step is loading the script. This can be done with any of the **IPersist*** interfaces such as **IPersistStorage**, **IPersistFile**, **IPersistStream**, or **IPersist PropertyBag** (see Chapter 4). A NULL script is created with **IPersist*::InitNew** or **IActiveScript::InitNew**. Hosts that maintain a script locally can feed the script to the engine with **IActiveScript::ParseScriptText**, but only after **IActiveScript:: InitNew** is used for initialization.

Name-space items are added when a new top-level item is imported into the scripting engine's name-space. This includes pages and forms. This isn't necessary if the objects are persisted during the load phase (step 2 of Figure 39-1). A host does not use **AddNamedItem** for lower level items such as controls. Lower level items are obtained using the host's **ITypeInfo** and **IDispatch** interfaces.

The next logical step is to run the script. That is done by passing SCRIPT STATE_CONNECTED to **IActiveScript::SetScriptState**. This is an initialization phase that includes static bindings, event hooking, and the execution of initialization code, not unlike a **main()** function.

During execution the script will encounter symbols which are not defined. The host is queried for the unknown item and **IActiveScriptSite::GetItemInfo** will return this information from the host and **IConnectionPoint::Advise** (see Chapter 6) will do the necessary notifications.

INTERNET INFORMATION SERVER SCRIPTING MODEL

We now know what the scripting engine is doing for us, so let's move on to the Microsoft Internet Information Server by reviewing each object of the IIS model. We review client-side scripting later.

IIS objects are like Active Data Objects (ADO) in that a rigid object instantiation is not necessary. There are only five objects and each is associated with a different phase of an Internet Information Server application. The **Application** object is the primary object and all other objects are subservient to it.

- *Application object* — Data common to all users is stored on the server.

- *Request object* — This may be related to the HTML GET and POST methods used to send data to the server.

- *Response object* — An object representing the results to be returned to the user.

- *Server object* — The source for server variables and other configuration information.

- *Session object* — This object represents a client. The server stores client-related variables for later use. Remember, Hypertext Transport Protocol (HTTP) is a stateless protocol and page variables or cookies are used by the server for application management. The **Session** object is very special and if not managed properly, locks the server down to a single thread.

Application Object

The **Application** object is the primary object of the server-side scripting model. It supports:

- *Lock* — A method required when setting or changing application variables.

- *Unlock* — The companion method that releases the **Application** object after an update.

- *Application_OnStart* — A scripting event that occurs at application startup.

- *Application_OnEnd* — A scripting event that occurs at application termination.

The **Application** object is global to all sessions and variables with global scope are stored there. Maintaining a count of page visits is a common example of a global variable:

```
<%
  Application.Lock
  Application("Visits")=Application("Visits")+1
  Application.Unlock
%>
```

The example above has several new concepts when compared to traditional Visual Basic for Applications (VBA) coding. The first new concept is that the `<%` and `%>` tags identify a script. Sending an expression to the browser is accomplished by `<%= expression %>`.

The second new concept is that the **Application** object must be locked when changing variable values. The example used the **Lock** and **Unlock** methods, which are the only methods of the **Application** object. This is a multiuser application and the **Application** object must be locked before variables are changed. The **Response** object, which we discuss later, is not global, but unique to the client, hence a locking mechanism is not required.

Variables are stored in the **Application** object as a collection and not as individual variables. An array may be stored in the **Application** object but may not be updated while stored in the **Application** object. The following code snippet illustrates the *correct* array updating sequence:

```
<%
   Application.Lock
   MyArray=Application("SavedArray")
   MyArray(2)=2
   Application("SavedArray")=MyArray
   Application.Unlock
<%
```

The *incorrect* array updating sequence is shown below. It destroys the third element of the collection and does not replace the third element of the array, assuming that arrays are zero-based.

```
<%
   Application.Lock
   Application("SavedArray")(2)=2 ' This is an error
   Application.Unlock
%>
```

Objects may be stored within the **Application** object. The statement construction is similar to that of VBA and uses the **Set** command. Even though objects may be saved in the **Application** object, attempting to save a **Session** object, **Request** object, **Response** object, **Server** object, or **Application** object will result in an error. This is because the Application object is implemented as a collection.

Objects should not be stored in the **Application** object unless the **ThreadingModel** in the Registry is marked as *both*. *Both* indicates that the component supports both free-threading and apartment-model threading. IIS locks the application down to a single thread when an object with a **ThreadingModel** of other than *both* is stored in the Registry. Because you now understand the issues, this is an example of storing an object in the **Application** object:

```
<%
   Set Application("MyObj")=Server.CreateObject("MyComponent")
%>
```

Scripting may be intermixed with hypertext markup language (HTML) code. Listing 39-1 is the manually inserted section of the SQLASPVI.ASP from the MyWeb Web site of Chapter 37. The bold portions represent the script portion of the code snippet.

LISTING 39-1 Intermixing HTML and scripts

```
<!--METADATA TYPE="DesignerControl" endspan-->
<!    A manual insertion to display the returned data.>
<tr>
<td><!--mstheme--><font face="trebuchet ms, arial, helvetica">
 <%Response.Write DataCommand1("au_id")%>
<!--mstheme--></font></td>
<td><!--mstheme--><font face="trebuchet ms, arial, helvetica">
 <%Response.Write DataCommand1("au_fname")%>
<!---mstheme--></font></td>
<td><!--mstheme--><font face="trebuchet ms, arial, helvetica">
 <%Response.Write DataCommand1("au_lname")%>
<!--mstheme--></font></td>
</tr>
<! End of manual insertion.>
```

The application object supports two events, the **Application_OnEnd** and **Application_OnStart** events. The skeleton below illustrates creating an **Application_OnStart** event.

```
<SCRIPT LANGUAGE=ScriptLanguage RUNAT=Server>
  Sub Application_OnStart
```

```
    .  .  .
    End Sub
</SCRIPT>
```

Microsoft Visual InterDev builds a GLOBAL.ASA file for global variables, **Application** object events, and **Session** object events. Listing 39-2 is the GLOBAL.ASA file from the MyWeb Web project of Chapter 37.

LISTING 39-2 The GLOBAL.ASA from Chapter 37

```
<SCRIPT LANGUAGE=VBScript RUNAT=Server>
Sub Session_OnStart
    '==Visual InterDev Generated - DataConnection startspan==
    '--Project Data Connection
        Session("pubs_ConnectionString") =
        "DSN=ZEUS;UID=sa;PWD=;APP=Microsoft (R) Developer
        Studio;WSID=ZEUS;DATABASE=pubs"
        Session("pubs_ConnectionTimeout") = 15
        Session("pubs_CommandTimeout") = 30
        Session("pubs_RuntimeUserName") = "sa"
        Session("pubs_RuntimePassword") = ""
    '--Project Data Connection
        Session("DataConn_ConnectionString") =
        "DSN=Northwind;DBQ=F:\InetPub\wwwroot\myweb\
        Northwind.mdb;DriverId=25;FIL=MS
        Access;MaxBufferSize=512;PageTimeout=5;"
        Session("DataConn_ConnectionTimeout") = 15
        Session("DataConn_CommandTimeout") = 30
        Session("DataConn_RuntimeUserName") = ""
        Session("DataConn_RuntimePassword") = ""
    '==Visual InterDev Generated - DataConnection endspan==
End Sub
</SCRIPT>
```

Global objects may be created in the GLOBAL.ASA file using the <OBJECT> tag. Declaring objects within GLOBAL.ASA is equivalent to using the **Set** command to store an object. The same caveat regarding threading issues applies to objects defined in GLOBAL.ASA.

Request Object

The **Request** object represents data values that are passed from the client browser to the server in an HTTP request. The object has no methods or events and only consists of collections. The **Request** object collections include:

- *QueryString* — A collection of variables for the HTTP query string.
- *Form* — A collection of form elements in the HTTP request body.
- *Cookies* — A collection of cookie values to be sent in the HTTP packet.
- *ClientCertificate* — A collection of fields stored in the client certificate sent in the HTTP request.
- *ServerVariables* — A collection of predetermined environment variables.

Collections are address by **Request**[.*Collection*](*Variable*). If the optional *Collection* name is missing, the script engine searches the **Request** object collections in this order: **QueryString, Form, Cookies, ClientCertificate,** and **Server Variables.** The developer is advised to adopt a naming convention because different collections may have objects with the same name.

ClientCertificate Collection

The **ClientCertificate** collection is EMPTY when no certificate is sent in the HTTP request. Fields of the **ClientCertificate** are only used when the client connects with https://, which uses the Secure Sockets Layer (SSL) protocol.

Fields with the collection are addressed with **Request.ClientCertificate** (*Key*[*SubField*]). The keys are:

- *Subject* — A comma-delimited list of subfields such as: "C=US, O=MSFT, . . ."
- *Issuer* — A comma-delimited list of subfiles relating to the issuer of the certificate.
- *ValidFrom* — A VBScript formatted date in the U.S. form "12/25/97 11:59:59 PM." International settings apply.
- *ValidUntil* — A VBScript formatted date in the U.S. form "12/25/97 11:59:59 PM." International settings apply.
- *SerialNumber* — A hexadecimal serial number represented in American Standard Code for Information Interchange (ASCII) in the form "AA-02-FC-97-23."

- *Certificate*—A binary stream in Abstract Syntax Notation (ASN) that represents the complete certificate. The certificate format corresponds to the ASN.1 format. ASN is an ISO standard for encoding of human-readable symbols, such as header tags, into condensed binary form. ASN.1 corresponds to CCITT standards X.208 (for the notation) and X.209 (for the encoding rules). In turn it forms part of the specifications for the X.400 and X.500series of standards, as well as for various other specifications.

- *Flags*—A pair of flags representing client certificate information. The two available flags are **ceCertPresent** and **ceUnrecognizedIssuer**.

    Subfields for these keys are:

- *C*—Name of the country of origin.

- *O*—The company or organization name.

- *OU*—Name of the organizational unit.

- *CN*—User common name. Used with "subject" key.

- *L*—Locality.

- *S*—State or province.

- *T*—Organization or person title.

- *GN*—Given name.

- *I*—A set of initials.

    The following example sends a message back to the browser when the user is not recognized:

```
<%
  If Request.ClientCertificate("Flags") and
ceUnrecognizedIssuer then
  Response.Write "Unrecognized issuer"
  End If
%>
```

    The following code issues a welcome message to the user:

```
<%
      If Not IsEmpty(Request.ClientCertificate) then
          Response.Write "Welcome to lala land " & _
              Request.ClientCertificate("SubjectCN")
```

```
        End If
%>
```

Cookies Collection

The Internet Server uses cookies as a management tool because HTTP is a stateless protocol. Using a cookie is illustrated in this generic prototype statement:

```
<%= Request.Cookies(CookieName) %>
```

CookieName can be a cookie dictionary with multiple values or it can have a single value. When there are multiple values, the script line above might produce something similar to the line below at the browser:

```
Name1=Value1&Name2=Value2& . . . NameN=ValueN
```

The **Cookies** collection **HasKeys** attribute will evaluate to TRUE when a **Cookies** collection has keys, or it is a dictionary cookie. Cookies with and without keys are illustrated in Listing 39-3.

LISTING 39-3 Enumerating the Cookie collection

```
<%
   'Enumerate the cookie collection
   For Each cookie in Request.Cookies
        If Not cookie.HasKeys Then
        'Not a dictionary cookie,Print cookie string
%>
        <%= cookie %> = <%= Request.Cookies(cookie)%>
<%
        Else
        'Print cookie collection
        For Each key in Request.Cookies(cookie)
%>
        <%= cookie %> (<%= key %>) =
        <%= Request.Cookies(cookie)(key)%>
<%
        Next
        End If
   Next
%>
```

Forms Collections

The **Forms** collection retrieves the values of FORM elements posted to an HTTP request body by the POST method.

Listing 39-4 is an HTML page created by Microsoft Access 97.

LISTING 39-4 An HTML page created by Access 97

```
<HTML>
<TITLE>Query1</TITLE>
<BODY BGCOLOR="#FFFFFF">
<FORM METHOD="GET" ACTION="Query1_1.ASP">
Input_ID <INPUT TYPE="Text" NAME="Input_ID"><P>
<INPUT TYPE="Submit" VALUE="Run Query">
</FORM>
</BODY>
<BR><BR>
<IMG SRC = "msaccess.jpg">
</HTML>
```

The script below, which is a response to the user after the query is submitted, illustrates the use of the **Forms** collection:

```
The value you submitted is <%= Request.Form("Input_ID") %>
```

Count is the only property of the **Forms** collection. The syntax is **Request.Form**(*Parameter*)[(*Index*)|.**Count**]. The **Forms** collection syntax is illustrated by:

```
Response.Write Request.Form("Parameter")(J) & "<BR>"
```

When an index is not specified and there are multiple values, a comma-delimited string is returned.

The **Forms** collection is easily enumerated. This construct should be very familiar to Microsoft Access and Visual Basic developers:

```
<%
  For Each item in Request.Form("Parameter")
      Response.Write item & "<BR>"
  Next
%>
```

QueryStrings Collection

The **QueryStrings** collection returns the values in the HTTP query string following the ? in the HTTP request using the GET method. A sample request is:

```
http://Inventory.asp?Item=1234
```

The **QueryStrings** collection syntax is identical in structure to that of the **Forms** collection. Syntax for referencing a **QueryString** parameter is **Request. QueryString**(*Parameter*)[(*Index*)|.**Count**]. An example is:

```
/scripts/Employees.asp?name=sally
```

A welcome message can be constructed from this HTML:

```
Good morning & " " & <%= Request.QueryString("name") %>
```

A multivalued string is represented by:

```
/scripts/Employees.asp?name=sally&name=silly
```

The multivalued **QueryStrings** collection is evaluated in the following script example (note the changing of the script notation to output the parameter back to the browser):

```
Good morning
<%
  For each item in Request.QueryString("name")
%>
     " " <%= QueryString(item)%>
<%
  Next
%>
```

ServerVariables Collection

The **ServerVariables** collection is a set of predetermined environment variables. The syntax for retrieving a variable is **Request.ServerVariables**(*Variable*). Members of the **ServerVariable** collection include:

- *AUTH-TYPE* — Authentication method used to validate users.
- *CONTENT_LENGTH* — Client content length.

- *CONTENT_TYPE* — Used with queries that have attached information such as POST and PUT.

- *GATEWAY_INTERFACE* — Format: common gateway interface (CGI)/ revision level.

- *HTTP_<HeaderName>* — Value stored in the header *HeaderName*. Used when the header is not a member of this list (see the example below).

- *LOGON_USER* — Windows NT client user account.

- *PATH_INFO* — Additional path information provided by the client. A script virtual path that is decoded before it is passed to a CGI script.

- *PATH_TRANSLATED* — Translated PATH_INFO.

- *QUERY_STRING* — Information stored after the ? in an HTTP request.

- *REMOTE_ADDR* — Remote host Internet protocol (IP) address.

- *REMOTE_HOST* — Remote host name.

- *REQUEST_METHOD* — For HTTP one of GET, HEAD, or POST.

- *SCRIPT_MAP* — Base portion of a uniform resource locator (URL).

- *SCRIPT_NAME* — Virtual path of the script being executed. Used by self-referencing URLs.

- *SERVER_NAME* — Server's host name, Domain Naming Service (DNS) alias, or IP address as it would appear in self-referencing URLs.

- *SERVER_PORT* — Port number to which the request was sent.

- *SERVER_PORT_SECURE* — 1 if the port is secure; otherwise 0.

- *PROTOCOL* — Format: protocol/revision level.

- *SERVER_SOFTWARE* — Format: name/revision level.

- *URL* — Base portion.

When a client furnishes a header other than one from the foregoing list, the syntax for retrieving the header is

```
<% Request.ServerVariables("HTTP_Warning") %>
```

where *Warning* is the header name in the example below. Headers are HTML elements that must precede the HTML document. The underscore is always translated to a dash and the user-supplied name should *not* have an embedded underscore character:

```
<% Response.AddHeader "WARNING", "HTML is not addictive" %>
<HTML>
Some text on the Web page.
</HTML>
```

Listing 39-5 is an enumeration of the **ServerVariables** collection in a table at the browser.

LISTING 39-5 Enumerating the ServerVariables collection

```
<TABLE>
  <TR>
      <TD><B>Server Variable</B></TD>
      <TD><B>Value</B></TD>
  </TR>
  <% For Each name In Request.ServerVariables %>
      <TR><TD> <%= name %> </TD><TD>
      <%= Request.ServerVariables(name) %> </TD></TR>
  <% Next %>
</TABLE>
```

Response Object

The **Response** object represents information returned to the browser as the result of an HTTP request. Syntax for the **Response** object is **Response.***Collection| Property|Method*. The **Response** object is defined by a cookie collection and these properties and methods:

- *Buffer* — A property set to TRUE when the output to the browser is buffered, FALSE otherwise. The output message is not sent until either the **Flush** or **End** method is called when this property is TRUE.

- *ContentType* — A property with the default value text/HTML. Other possible content types are image/GIF, image/JPEG, and text/plain.

- *Expires* — A property expressing the time in minutes before the current page expires in the browser cache. A zero value implies no caching.

- *ExpiresAbsolute* — A property that is the absolute expiration date of a message conforming to Request for Comments (RFC) 1123. An example: #May 1, 1997 12:59:59#.

- *Status* — A property containing the HTTP status description message (See RFC1945). Examples are 200 OK or 401 Unauthorized.

- *AddHeader* — A method that adds a header name and a value to an HTTP **Response** object. Headers cannot be removed after being added. Headers must be added before content. If **Buffer** is true, however, **AddHeader** may be used at any time in the script. The header name must not contain an underscore.

- *AppendToLog* — A method that appends a string to the Web server log.

- *BinaryWrite* — A method that writes information to the current HTTP output without character conversion.

- *Clear* — A method that clears the response body. The previously written header remains intact.

- *End* — A method that terminates the current script and returns the current results to the browser. The remaining contents are not processed.

- *Flush* — A method that immediately sends the buffered output. An error occurs when **Buffer** is FALSE.

- *Redirect* — A method that causes the browser to attempt a connection to a different URL.

Setting the expiration date shows an example of using a **Response** object property:

```
<% Response.ExpiresAbsolute=#May 1, 1998 12:59:59# %>
```

Adding a header with a **Response** object method is illustrated by:

```
<% Response.AddHeader "WARNING", "HTML is not addictive" %>
```

Attempted unauthorized access is answered with:

```
<% Response.Status = "401 Unauthorized" %>
```

Cookies Collection

The **Cookies** collection of the **Response** object is somewhat richer in content than the **Cookies** collection of the **Request** object, which has only the **HasKeys** attribute. This is because the **Request** object is reading content, whereas the **Response** object is establishing an expiration date, a domain, path, and the security level. The syntax for the **Cookies** collection of a **Response** object is **Response.Cookies**

(Cookie)[*(Key)*|*Attribute*], which has the same structure as the syntax for the **Request** object. The **Cookies** collection of the **Response** object is defined as:

- *Expires* — A write-only attribute that defines the cookie expiration date.

- *Domain* — A write-only attribute that specifies a domain. When set, cookies are only sent to requests of this domain.

- *Path* — A write-only attribute that specifies path. The application path is used when this attribute is not set.

- *Secure* — A write-only attribute. Set to TRUE for a secure link and FALSE otherwise.

- *HasKeys* — A read-only attribute that indicates if the cookie has keys (a dictionary cookie).

When a cookie is created with:

```
<%
  Response.Cookie("MyCookie")("Type1")="Raisins Oatmeal"
  Response.Cookie("MyCookie")("Type2")="PeanutButter"
%>
```

the following header is sent to the browser:

```
Set-Cookie:MYCOOKIE=TYPE1=Raisins+Oatmeal&TYPE2=PeanutButter
```

An example of enumerating the **Cookies** collection of the **Request** object is shown in Listing 39-3.

Server Object

The **Server** object provides access to methods and properties of the server. The syntax for the **Server** object is **Server**.*Property*|*Method(Value)*. The **Server** object is defined as:

- *ScriptTimeout* — A property that defines the time in seconds before a script times out. The default value is 90 seconds.

- *CreateObject* — A method that creates an object based upon a supplied program ID (progID). The threading model issues discussed earlier in this book apply to this method.

- *HTMLEncode* — A method that applies HTML encoding to a supplied string.
- *MapPath* — A method that maps specified relative or virtual path corresponding to the physical directory on the server.
- *URLEncode* — A method for encoding a URL from a string which may have escape characters.

Creating an instance of an object with the **Server** object **CreateObject** method:

```
<% Set MyAd=Server.CreateObject("MSWC.AdRotator") %>
```

Encoding a string with the **HTMLEncode** method:

```
<%= Server.HTMLEncode("This is a paragraph tag: <P>") %>
```

creates this:

```
This is a paragraph tab &lt;P&gt;
```

The browser displays:

```
This is a paragraph tag: <P>
```

Applying URL encoding rules:

```
<%= Server.URLEncode("This is a paragraph tag: <P>") %>
```

creates the following with character in hexadecimal notation:

```
This+is+a+paragraph+tag%3A+%3CP%3E
```

Session Object

This is the last object of the Microsoft Internet Information Server model. The **Session** object variables are not destroyed when a user jumps between pages. A common use of the **Session** object is to store user preferences set on a previous site visit. A **Session** object is only maintained for browsers that support cookies. A **Session** object is defined as:

- *SessionID* — A property that is the assigned user session identification.
- *Timeout* — A property that is the session timeout in minutes.

- *Abandon*—All **Session** object resources are released and the session terminates.

- *SessionOnStart*—An event that is normally found in the GLOBAL.ASA file (see Figure 39-2).

- *SessionOnEnd*—An event, that is normally found in the GLOBAL.ASA file (see Figure 39-2).

The rules of usage as outlined for the **Application** object apply to the **Session** object, with the exception that the **Lock** and **Unlock** methods are not necessary. Variables and arrays are stored in the **Session** object as members of a collection. The value of singular elements may be changed while still members of a collection. The first line in the example below illustrates replacing the value of *UserName* with a string literal. An element of an array cannot be changed as a member of a collection. The complete array must be extracted from the collection, the appropriate array elements changed, with the current array replacing the previous instance as shown below. The following three lines illustrate removing an array from the collection, changing a value, and replacing the array in the collection:

```
<%
    Session("UserName")= "Bruce"
    MyArray=Session("SavedArray")
    MyArray(2)=2
    Session("SavedArray")=MyArray
%>
```

Parallel to the objects discussed thus far in this chapter is a series on C++ interfaces, which supply identical or closely related functionality. These interfaces are not discussed. For a discussion of these interfaces, see the Windows NT Platform Software Development Kit.

SCRIPTING AND YOUR INTERNET/INTRANET APPLICATION

Let's move our focus now to client-side and browser scripting. The context of this section focuses on client-side scripting with Visual Basic Scripting Edition, which is a subset of Microsoft Visual Basic. If you are a Visual Basic developer, you should have no problems because the language constructs are identical to traditional Microsoft Visual Basic. Compiling an executable is the primary feature missing from this version of Visual Basic. Many of the constructs and rules of Visual Basic scripts apply to JScript, which is mentioned only briefly. VBScript and JScript share a common limitation in that system interaction is not permitted with application programming interface (API) calls. This limitation does not extend to Visual Basic components that may use an API. *jscript* defines the concept of *playing in the sandbox* where no local system interaction is permitted, regardless of environment.

Combining Scripts

Internet Information Server supports both *jscript* and *VBScript*. A nice feature of this is that both scripts may be combined in the same module. We've always had some type of language combining before this, but it was typically a high-level language which could revert to assembly language. Listing 39-6 is an example of how *VBScript* and *jscript* are both combined in one module.

The notation <!---, ---> is an HTML comment element. The client browser ignores the script within the HTML comment tags when scripting isn't supported.

LISTING 39-6 Combining jscript and VBScript in the same module

```
<SCRIPT LANGUAGE="VBScript">
<!---
   Visual Basic Script
--->
</SCRIPT>

<SCRIPT LANGUAGE="jscript">
<!---
   Java Script
--->
</SCRIPT>
<SCRIPT LANGUAGE="VBScript" RUNAT="Server">
<!---
   Visual Basic Script
--->
</SCRIPT>
```

A fragment of server-side script is shown in Listing 39-6, but it is decorative because server-side scripts are purged before the page is sent to the browser. The HTML element <%,%> used in previous examples is a shorthand notation for:

```
<SCRIPT LANGUAGE="VBScript" RUNAT="Server">
</SCRIPT>
```

Scripts may be used within controls, and that's what we do next, only we use a different script in each control.

Listing 39-7 has a slightly different twist. One control uses VBScript, while the other control uses JavaScript. JavaScript is the SUN Microsystems implementation of Java, while JScript is the Microsoft implementation of Java.

LISTING 39-7 Controls using different scripting languages

```
<FORM NAME="MyForm">
  <INPUT TYPE="button" NAME="MyButton1" VALUE="VBScript"
      onClick="VBPush" LANGUAGE="VBScript">
  <INPUT TYPE="button" NAME="MyButton2" ="JScript"
      onClick="JavaPush( )" language="Javascript">
</FORM>


<SCRIPT LANGUAGE="VBScript">
  sub VBPush
      document.MyForm.MyButton1.value="Pressed"
      alert "VB did this!"
  end sub
</SCRIPT>


<SCRIPT LANGUAGE="Javascript">
  function JavaPush( )
  {
      document.MyForm.MyButton2.value="Pressed"
      alert("Java did this!")
  }
</SCRIPT>
```

Listing 39-8 is a variation on the syntax of Listing 39-7 where the event scripting occurs within the FORM element.

LISTING 39-8 Event scripting within the HTML FORM element

```
<FORM NAME="MyForm">
  <INPUT TYPE="button" NAME="MyButton" VALUE="Click">
  <SCRIPT FOR="MyButton" EVENT="onClick" LANGUAGE="VBScript">
      document.MyForm.MyButton.value="Pressed"
      alert "VB did this!"
  </SCRIPT>
</FORM>
```

Scripting with ActiveX Controls

You should still be on familiar ground with Figure 39-2. It shows the Visual Basic toolbox, a command button, and the related property page. The property page has all the traditional and expected properties. Now you know that you can position an ActiveX control with the **Top** and **Left** properties (which was a question on one of the Windows Architecture tests).

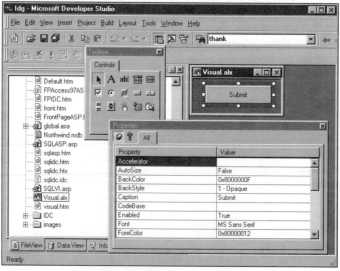

FIGURE 39-2   Visual Basic controls of Visual InterDev.

DEATH SCENE

A few of you may be familiar with the *blue screen of death*, a hexadecimal mishmash presented when Windows NT crashes. I crashed Windows NT server several times trying to capture the screen image of Figure 39-2. The environment was Visual InterDev of Visual Studio 97 Enterprise Edition, service release 1.

The problem started when I had an Access database (`Northwind`) with a master and a working copy which were not synchronized. When starting Visual InterDev, I was asked if I wanted to update my master copy and I answered yes. Big mistake! The project was in the process of loading and the connections were not yet established. I was immediately presented with the *blue screen of death*. I rebooted Windows NT Server 4.0 service pack 3 and was given another *blue screen of death* immediately. The system was recovered quite a few hours later after using my trusty Norton Utilities on the disk from MS-DOS to repair damaged links. I finished the fixing by rebooting to my other trusty system Windows NT 3.51 service pack 5 to finish the cleanup and nothing was lost. In case you are wondering why I didn't use a repair disk, the *blue screen of death* indicated a FAT problem in the partition. It was serious enough that Windows NT could not repair it during the boot process. My system has eight boots with drive letters through <S>.

There are several morals to this pitiful tale. The first we already know is that Microsoft software is unstable. The other moral is to always check objects back into the repository. Better yet, never attempt to update the repository while the project is still loading. Someone really wasn't thinking when that code was implemented.

We know that a file with an `.ASP` extension is an active server page (ASP). We built some ASPs in Chapter 37. A file with an `.ASA` extension contains global variables and was discussed with respect to connection information. The one file type we haven't discussed yet is the `.ALX` extension. Double-clicking the selected `.ALX` file displayed the command button in Figure 39-2. The ActiveX controls are placed in this file and then inserted into the Visual InterDev project using **Insert HTML Layout** from the Visual InterDev menu.

Internet Downloads

Internet downloads are tools that support content. The server must know the client capabilities before a download is possible. Even if one is possible, is it useful? I'll try to integrate the discussion of the Internet Download Component with a practical application. We'll start with Listing 39-9 that looks at the browser type. The second example in Listing 39-10 asks if the browser can support ActiveX controls. The Internet Download Component is invoked only when the browser supports ActiveX controls. This is almost like ADO programming where the developer uses the **Supports** method to verify that the functionality is supported.

LISTING 39-9 Using the marquee control for Internet Explorer

```
<%
  '
  '  Use HTML Marquee if Internet Explorer
  '
  Set MyObj = Server.CreateObject("MSWC.BrowserType")
  if (MyObj.browser = "IE") Then
%>
    <marquee bgcolor="#00005B"
      direction="LEFT"
      behavior="SCROLL">
      Thank you for buying Windows Architecture I & II
    </marquee>
<%
Else
%>
    <center>
      Thank you for buying Windows Architecture I & II
    </center>
<%
End If
%>
```

We're adding some intelligence to our active server page. Listing 39-9 uses the browser capabilities component to determine the type of browser. When Internet Explorer is the client browser, the HTML marquee element is used by the browser, otherwise a text message is displayed. Most browsers probably support the HTML Marquee element, so this example is merely illustrative.

The type of browser is not the only issue. Does the browser support ActiveX controls? Listing 39-10 raises the functionality a notch by deciding between downloading an ActiveX control and displaying a message of the Billboard Rotator Component of Internet Information Server. The Billboard Rotator Component rotates advertising images on a Web page and can be configured so the browser gets a new message each time the ASP is requested. (If that's not clear, then remember that the MWSC.Adrotator control is an Internet Information Server component, and only an image can be downloaded.)

LISTING 39-10 Deciding between the Adrotator control and a custom control

```
<%
   '
   '  Use HTML Marquee if Internet Explorer
   '
   Set MyObj = Server.CreateObject("MSWC.BrowserType")
   if MyObj.ActiveXControls =TRUE Then
%>
<OBJECT
    CODEBASE="/MyWeb/MyBillBoard.CAB#version=8,0,0,8"
    WIDTH=570
    HEIGHT=70
    DATA="/MyWeb/Controls/MyBillBoard.ods"
    CLSID="clsid:11111111-2222-3333-4444-555555555555">
</OBJECT>
<%
   Else
     Set MyAD=Server.CreateObject("MWSC.Adrotator")
     Response.Write(MyAD.GetAdvertisement("/MyWeb/ad.txt"))
   End If
%>
```

The script is busy making download decisions. When the script encounters the CODEBASE attribute of the HTML OBJECT tag, **CoGetClassObjectFromURL** is invoked directly. All the URL Moniker machinations we previously discussed now come into play.

#version-8, 0, 0, 8 is a URL fragment of Listing 39-10 that represents the version number. This portion of the URL is pivotal in the load process because it determines if the component will be downloaded. When this value is -1, -1, -1, -1, a new version of the component is always downloaded. When no version is present, the currently loaded version is considered acceptable, otherwise the Internet download component will download a new version only when the requested version is more recent than the existing version. When no component is loaded, and no version is present, the URL path is searched for the component.

The Internet download component processes three file categories:

- *PE* — A portable executable such as a .OCX, .DLL, or .EXE. A single executable is downloaded, installed, and registered in one operation. The file category may be code-signed. The Internet download component will try to start self-registration for those components marked as such. The Internet download component ignores the OleSelfRegister flag if the main URL code points directly to an .EXE file. This type of file is not platform independent except with HTTP.

- *CAB* — A .CAB file has the advantage of compression and can be code-signed. A .CAB file-required component is an .INF file which contains the packaging instructions. A .CAB file is not platform independent without HTTP format negotiation.

- *INF* — An .INF file that cannot be code-signed, but it is platform independent. The .INF file is a map of all required files. This file download category is useful in an intranet environment but is unsafe on the Internet.

Developers should always use a .CAB file because it uses compression, reduces component download time, and increases client satisfaction.

web links **The** CAB-SDK.EXE, CABVIEW.EXE **tool, and the code-signing tool** AUTH2SDK.EXE **are all downloadable from** http://www. microsoft .com/intdev/sdk/.

Code Signing

Code Signing is used with either a *PE* or a *CAB* file when used with the Internet Download Component. Microsoft support code signing for .exe, .cab, .ocx, and .class files. Code signing is a digital signature that is transmitted with the document to guarantee authenticity. The authenticy is guaranteed by holding either an individual or a corporation accountable for a digitally signed file.

Microsoft calls digital signing Authenticode. Authenticode consists of a public key and a private key. The software publisher applies for a certificate to a Certification Authority (CA), a trusted entity. Before applying, the software publisher generates a key pair that uses either hardware or software. One key will become the public key and the other key will be the private key of the requesting publisher. The CA verifies the credentials of the individual or corporation and a certificate is issued when the credentials are verified. The credentials are a positive identification of the individual or firm along with a pledge not distribute malicious software. The certificate contains the public key and will always be sent with the signed document.

A Local Registering Agency (LRA) assumes some of the responsibilities of a CA, but does not issue certificates. Approved applications are passed on by the LRA to a CA. The CA organization structure is hierarchical with many roots. A root is a CA. Beneath the root CA may be local CAs. A root CA will hold certificates signed by all CAs immediately below the root. Moving down the tree a bit further, the next level of CA will hold certificates for all those CAs immediately below it, and so on. Beneath each CA is one or more LRAs. Based on this hierarchical structure, certificates can be verified for all individuals or entities.

The document itself is not signed. What is signed is a one-way hash of the document. Both the signed hash and the document are transmitted to the recipient. The recipient generates a one-way hash. When the generated one-way hash matches the transmitted hash, the document is valid.

web links   **AUTH2SDK.EXE, the code signing toolkit, is a self extracting file that is downloadable from** `http://www.Microsoft.com/intdev/sdk/`.

Within the sdk the developer will find the following:

- *MakeCert* — Creates a text X.509 certificate. It creates a public/private key pair for digital signatures and associates this key pair with a chosen name.

- *Cert2SPC* — Creates a test Software Publisher Certificate (SPC). This is a test only program since the valid SPC is obtained from a CA.

- *SignCode* — Signs the code using a SPC.

- *PeSigMgr* — A utility to see if the file was signed.

- *ChkTrust* — Tests the validity of the signed file.

tip   **Always sign your code.**

Licensing and the Internet

Licensing with the Internet is very similar to licensing with standard controls. The **IClassFactory2** interface (see Chapter 2) is used at design time. This is the same licensing mechanism currently used for implementing the licensing of existing controls. A developer acquires a license and the authoring tools or utilities call **IClassFactory2::RequestLicKey** to store the run-time licenses for all the controls used on the page as an array of (CLSID, license) tuples. The array is stored in a .LPK file. The HTML page points to the license package via a *relative* URL reference inside the HTML. A relative URL makes pirating inconvenient, but does not stop it.

IClassFactory2::CreateInstanceLic is used at run-time by the web browser to extract the necessary run-time licenses from the license package. The licensed objects are instantiated after the licenses are extracted. Listing 39-10 is updated in Listing 39-11 with a .LPK file illustrating a licensed custom control.

LISTING 39-11 Licensing the custom BillBoard control

```
<%
  '
  '  Use HTML Marquee if Internet Explorer
  '
  Set MyObj = Server.CreateObject("MSWC.BrowserType")
  if MyObj.ActiveXControls =TRUE  Then
%>
  <OBJECT
    CODEBASE=/MyWeb/MyBillBoard.CAB#version=8,0,0,8"
    WIDTH=570
    HEIGHT=70
    DATA="/MyWeb/Controls/MyBillBoard.ods"
    CLSID="clsid:11111111-2222-3333-4444-555555555555">
    <PARAM NAME="LPKPath" VALUE=<relative URL path>
    <EMBED SRC = "BRUCE.LPK">
</OBJECT>
<%
  Else
    Set MyAD=Server.CreateObject("MWSC.Adrotator")
  Response.Write(MyAD.GetAdvertisement("/MyWeb/ad.txt"))
  End If
%>
```

It's Not Pedal to the Metal with the Internet

An intranet does not pose bandwidth, security, or cross-platform issues. The developer has significant latitude in the choice of components. The Internet is a different matter. There are bandwidth considerations, security, and cross-platform issues. Special attention must be given to the browser capabilities. Some of the considerations include:

o Use the **Alternative Text** attribute as shown in the following code sample:

```
<IMG SRC="Earth.bmp" WIDTH=46 HEIGHT=46 ALT="Picture of
the Earth">
```

o Minimize download time for controls with data by specifying a data path for control data. The data will be downloaded asyncronously, minimizing the client writing period. Asynchronous downloading of control data is accomplished by specifying both a DATA and a CODEBASE attribute in an HTML object tag.

o Test the **Browser** property of the ASP **Server** object. The value of this property is *IE* when the browser is Microsoft Internet Explorer (see Listing 39-9).

o Test the **ActiveXControls** property of the ASP **Server** object. This property has a value of TRUE when the browser supports ActiveX controls (see Listings 39-10 and 39-11). Listing 39-11 only examined the **ActiveXControls** property of the Browser Capabilities Component. Other Browser Capabilities Component properties are **Browser**, **Version**, **Frames**, **Tables**, **Tables**, **BackGroundSounds**, **VBScript**, and **JavaScript**.

o Minimize the number of controls on the page. Pure HTML is always the best choice for performance, but it will not have sex appeal.

o Create thumbnail sketches of graphics when necessary. This is an economical alternative to the complete graphic.

o Always sign your code. Code signing and security is not an issue with an intranet, but it is a significant issue with the Internet.

Making Choices

There are no simple answers to selecting the proper technology. You must first understand the Internet technology and then evaluate a Web-based client application based on your knowledge. Often your evaluation will involve adjusting caches or the proper setting of a parameter. When to use a technology often depends on the requirements of the application. Some guidelines include:

- Common Gateway Interface (CGI) can be used for infrequent access where the mode of access is not interactive.

- The Internet Server API (ISAPI) DLL can be used when the Internet application must perform a special function such as monitoring site usage. This is commonly called an ISAPI Filter. Remember that an ISAPI Internet application with an malevolent DLL will crash your Internet Information Server.

- Active Server Pages (ASP) along with ADO can be used for interactive Web site communication. ADO can be used to access a back-end database.

- Static pages can be pushed by any of the Microsoft Office products that are Internet enabled. This is the Internet Assistant technology of Office 95, and the technology is integrated into the products in Office 97.

- Static pages can be published on a regular basis using the SQL Server Web Assistant.

- The retrieving of pages using the IDC/HTX technology. The HTTPODBC.DLL supports this technology and HTTPODBC.DLL functions as an ISAPI DLL.

- The WebBrowser and the WinInet control, both of which are usable from Visual Basic, are two Internet tools not integrated within a product.

The Scripting Choice Is an Architectural Issue

The architectural issue is the relative location of the processing site to the data source. As with client-server applications, the location of processing with respect to the data source is an Internet or intranet architectural issue. Server-side scripting will always yield higher performance than client-side scripting. There are other advantages to server-side scripting, and these include the following:

- Maximum performance is achieved with server-side scripting. Server-side scripts are appropriate for accessing a database, while client-side scripts are appropriate for dealing with the client interface infrastructure.

- Server-side scripts remain hidden from the client browser. Client-side scripts are readable by the user.

- With server-side scripting, objects can have a scope and maintain context beyond a single HTTP request.

- All pages in an Internet/intranet site are kept on disk and loaded as necessary.

BUT MOMMY, HE DOESN'T HAVE ANY CLOTHES EITHER

We left Penelope and her mother Gervia in Chapter 33, where she inadvertently blurted, "Mommy, the Emperor has no clothes." Gervia admonishes Penelope to hush, but she again blurts, "But Mommy, he doesn't have any clothes either." (If you haven't guessed, Penelope is about four years old, a paragon of innocence, and does not yet understand the concept of self-denial.)

Threading Issues

We know the Microsoft threading model is deficient. If you store an object in the **Application** object of IIS, the application is locked down to a single thread. To what extent is Windows NT thread deficient? Properly designed, all threads of an in-process server should be marked as *free-thread*. However, that is not the case because many applications were developed without a viable thread model. Figure 39-3 shows us that the ADO **Recordset** object is an apartment-model thread. If this object is stored in the **Application** object of IIS, the application is locked down to a single thread. The choice is simple. ADO objects can be used but they can never be stored in the **Application** object without dire performance consequences.

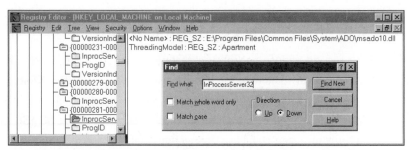

FIGURE 39-3   Locating In-Process Servers in the Windows NT Registry.

Let's look at your system and see what you have for threads. You can then make your own decision as to the viability of Microsoft architecture's threading model. We look at in-process servers that run within the process space of an application and that if properly designed, do not need marshaling, apartment model threads, or single threads, which would be a disaster. The bottom line is that *every* in-process server should be free-threaded, but with the Microsoft crazy quilt thread architecture a desirable thread must be marked as *both*. This translates to a thread supporting both free-threading and the apartment-model threading.

Start your Windows NT registry editor, REGEDT32 and position to the key:

```
HKEY_LOCAL_MACHINE\SOFTWARE\Classes
```

Start a search for "InProcServer32" with neither *Match Case* nor *Match Whole Word Only* selected. Select *Find Next*. The in-process server entries will be displayed. An in-process server is single-thread when there is no **ThreadingModel** value. Note that **ThreadingModel** is a named value and not a Registry key. Continue to select *Find Next* to review the entries. The desirable servers are marked as *Both*. You'll be very surprised at how much software is single-thread. MSRDO20.DLL (RDO) is also an apartment-model threading server, hence it would also lock down the **Application** object of IIS.

It is astounding that ADO, which is a new technology, is apartment-model threading, as are remote data objects (RDO). Both of these are new technologies. RDO is a technology highly touted by Microsoft and prominently featured in Microsoft Press books. ADO is still too new to merit any books. Of course, my opinion of RDO (see Chapters 24 to 26) is that it was only a bridge technology and a preview of things to come. There is now a new class of objects entitled Data Source Objects, which are related to Internet Explorer 4.0. My recommendation is to step back until the technology stabilizes.

Too Many Cooks in the Kitchen

This section on Internet/intranet technology surfaced the fact that three disparate groups appear to be working on active server pages. Chapter 37 steps through the various ASP technologies, including Access 97 ASP, which not only didn't function, but also appear to have never been tested; Front Page 98 ASP which worked, but only for Open Database Connectivity (ODBC) sources; and Visual InterDev of Visual Studio 97 Enterprise fame which was clean and everything worked.

Why do I say Access 97 ASP was never tested? Listing 39-12 is the Structured Query Language (SQL) of a parameter query against the Employees table of the Microsoft `Northwind` database. It is saved as QUERY1.

LISTING 39-12 A Query of the Northwind Employees table

```
SELECT Employees.EmployeeID, Employees.LastName,
 Employees.FirstName, Employees.Title
FROM Employees
WHERE (((Employees.EmployeeID)=[Input_ID]));
```

I opened the query in design mode and did the following:

o Selected Save As HTML, Next

o Selected **Queries**, **Query1**, and **Next**

o Selected **Browse**, double-clicked **default**, **Next**

o Selected **Dynamic ASP**, **Next**

o DSN=**Northwind**, PWD="", UserID="", URL=**ZEUS**

o Next, Next, Next, Finish

The Northwind data source name (DSN) above is a system DSN and anonymous guest is the expected log in.

The four lines below were cut from the generated page `QUERY1_1.HTML`. You'll note that the `GET` method is used but there is no ? on the URL.

```
<FORM METHOD="GET" ACTION="Query1_1.ASP">
[Input_ID] <INPUT TYPE="Text" NAME="[Input_ID]"><P>
<INPUT TYPE="Submit" VALUE="Run Query">
</FORM>
```

The lines below were cut from the corresponding `QUERY1_1.ASP`. At least the ASP module understands that the `GET` method is to be used. We discussed earlier in this section using **Request.QueryString** to retrieve parameters after the ? of a URL. As much as I probably mix my metaphors, the hackers working on this code attached a `GET` method to what looks like a `POST` method construct, and the result is unpalatable code soup.

```
<%
Param = Request.QueryString("Param")
```

```
Data = Request.QueryString("Data")
%>
```

I expected something on the order of:

```
<FORM METHOD="GET" ACTION="Query1_1.ASP?[Input_ID]=foo">
```

The code can be fixed with hacking, but there are other problems such as the ADO connection. All the problems can be fixed and Visual InterDev does it right. Code hacked from Visual InterDev can make this application work. But why do it? The Wizard was supposed to do it.

Internet technology in Access 97 is supposed to be a hot new technology, yet this code appears to have never been tested. This is not the only area of untested code. Earlier in the book I was down for about a week trying to figure out a work-around for problems in Object Word 97. There are many other problem areas, but I think you get the message.

The last question to ask is how can Internet service providers be expected to implement server extensions that are unstable? I would think that in the area of Internet technology, Microsoft would exercise due caution before publishing non-functional server extensions such as those found in FrontPage 98.

It's not just a few minor bugs in FrontPage 98, it is the issue of three different versions of active server pages. Internet service providers need a stable technology or they will not implement the extensions. There is an Access 97 version, an ugly FrontPage 98 version, and a clean Visual InterDev version. Sounds like a shell game and we've got to find the pea. I cheated and picked Visual InterDev. Of course, my house, my rules<g:>.

Deprecation

Corporations take months to make their plans and roll out an upgrade or embrace a new technology. How can a corporation be expected to upgrade to newer technology when the last technology wave is deprecated with the ink still wet on the newest technology? Corporations cannot react to every clever idea that enters the mind of some developer. I use the word developer because, in my opinion, everything appears to be designed from the bottom up. Developers run Microsoft. The first developers are now managers to some degree, and there appears to be too many managers. Unfortunately, bottom-up design is an inherent weakness in any tool company, not just Microsoft. What I mean by bottom-up is the continual invention of new tools without looking at the picture from the top, which is obviously called top-down.

I suspected, and only found out recently, that dbWeb is deprecated. It is a topic in this book. It remains because I know that many of you are using what Microsoft considers ancient software. Good for you! Your systems probably crash less often, but you still must deal with the harangue from users wanting the latest software candy.

I mentioned earlier that Microsoft was quietly trying to deprecate the Internet database connector (IDC/HTX) technology. I did present a very nice example of a Visual Basic 5.0 object linking and embedding (OLE) application using the Microsoft `OLEISAPI.DLL`. I haven't been able to find a newer version, but that, too, may be deprecated.

KEY POINT SUMMARY

Microsoft has created very good Internet software, but there is too much and it comes out too quickly. To compound the issue, the software is rushed to market without thorough testing.

Too many Microsoft programming groups are working on the same technology with mixed results. It is obvious that there is no unifying architecture even though Microsoft would have us believe there is.

What are the rules? The first and foremost rule is to understand what your requirements are. The item in the agenda is to grab the tools you need before they are deprecated. Implement them in your intranet and don't plan any piecemeal or incremental upgrades until you've got your return on investment. At that time, consider stepping up a level in the technology. Remember that software which doesn't have an ISO, ANSI, HTTP, or HTML standard is subject to instant de-support by Microsoft. Wait for supported standards, and then wait some more until the standard has stabilized. Let the motto "Pioneers get arrows in their derrière" be your operational directive.

Applying What You've Learned

The questions here address issues on both the Windows Architecture I and II core examinations. The questions are not limited to topics found in this chapter.

Instant Assessment

1. Which Internet Information Server object is used to retrieve ASP data sent by a user with an HTML form?

2. What is the advantage of a .CAB file?

3. We've discussed both server-side and client-side scripting. What are two advantages of server-side scripting?

4. Which Internet technology provides security and the best performance?

5. Your application may be loaded into browsers that do not support scripting. How do you prevent the script from being displayed at the browser?

6. How do you make data available to an ActiveX component in a Web page?

7. What does the CLSID of the HTML object element refer to?

8. How is an .INF file used in Internet technology?

9. What is a common limitation shared by both VBScript and jscript?

10. How does an active server page application remember user choices as the user moves between pages?

11. You want to monitor performance of your Web site. Which Internet technology is appropriate?

12. Which technology is used to manage scripting with a variety of different browsers?

13. How do you force users to upgrade to the latest version of your component?

concept link **For answers to the Instant Assessment questions, see Appendix C.**

Lab Exercises

Lab 39.76 *Building a downloadable ActiveX control*

WA I
WA II

The rubber hits the road with this lab. Your goal is to build an ActiveX component with code-signing and which is packaged in a .CAB file. You should have all the skills necessary for this task. You built a dynamic link library (DLL) in Chapter 38, and it's time to build another. Think of a simple component such as a calculation that retrieves some data for an application. You can use a variation of the DLL created in Chapter 38.

The primary task for this chapter is to package your new component in a .CAB file with code-signing. You'll need to download CAB-SDK.EXE, the CABVIEW.EXE tool, and the code-signing tool AUTH2SDK.EXE from the Microsoft Web site http://www. microsoft.com/intdev/sdk/. Good luck.

Lab 39.77 *Upgrading a downloadable ActiveX control*

WA II

Upgrading software is always an issue. The simplest technique is to create a new version and control the upgrade. Create several different versions of the example in Lab 39.76. Modify the CODEBASE attribute in an HTML OBJECT by changing the version. Remember that a version of -1,-1,-1,-1 will always force the latest version to be downloaded.

Lab 39.78 *Adding intelligence to the Web page*

WA II

Use the Browser Capabilities Component in creating a Web page. You have learned that the Browser Capabilities Component and the browser supports ActiveX controls. The Browser Capabilities Component returns the characteristics of a client browser. Use this functionality to make the following decisions when creating a Web page:

o ActiveX controls are supported when the **ActiveXControls** property is **True**. Provide alternatives when ActiveX controls are not supported.

o VBScript is supported when the **VBScript** property is **True**. Support only HTML when neither VBScript nor JScript are supported.

o JScript is supported when the **JavaScript** property is **True**. Support only HTML when neither VBScript nor JScript are supported.

Applications

Part V is composed of the following three chapters:

- **Chapter 40: Solutions Design Issues** — Provides a historical perspective of process, data, and business rules. The traditional waterfall architecture is updated and sets the basis for the next chapter.

- **Chapter 41: Designing the Solution** — The emphasis of the chapter is on architecture of the solution. Special emphasis is placed on understanding the business model before the data model is constructed.

- **Chapter 42: Solution Interface Issues** — Numerous interface issues are discussed including control interface guidelines, help and help menus, dialog box guidelines, and menu interface guidelines. Other topics include Windows 95 logo requirements, Office 97 logo requirements, application installation, removal, and Registry usage.

Windows Architecture I
Windows Architecture II

Solutions Design Issues

About Chapter 40

Chapter 40 is the most important chapter of the book. It is divided into three sections. The first section traces the historical forces within the computer industry that created the chaotic situation we have today.

The second section discusses classical data-modeling. It approaches the design of a system by first understanding the problem. This approach is known as a *top-down solution* or the *waterfall method*, which is quite unlike Microsoft Solutions Framework (MSF), which is a bottom-up approach to system design.

This chapter introduces the Zachman Framework (*IBM Systems Journal*, Volume 26, No. 3) and the IDEF1X Information Models, which is a Department of Defense data-modeling standard (see Thomas A. Bruce, *Designing Quality Databases with IDEF1X Information Models*). The application model we use in the chapter is a combination of concepts from IDEF1X and the Zachman Framework. New models are added, and I call the result an Augmented Zachman Framework.

The third section analyzes the computing industry as we know it today. It is very chaotic, and with your understanding of the evolutionary forces and classical data-modeling as a backdrop, I show how we are moving backward on the computing evolutionary scale. Since 1987 there has been a steady decline in information systems productivity, which is the time frame that I characterize as the Microsoft epoch.

For a developer, this is the most important chapter in the book. Formulating a proper problem solution is the key to a successful application deployment. If necessary, read this chapter several times. The concepts are vital to success as a developer.

TRACING THE HISTORY OF THE PROCESS, DATA, BUSINESS RULES, AND PROGRAMMING

This section traces the evolution of computing concepts. Traced are the concepts of a process, of data, of business rules, of programming, and of the programmer. Each is related to the others and some concepts have matured while others have regressed. We revisit these issues in section three after visiting data-modeling.

Evolution of Data

The computer has only been with us for 50 years. We have gone from very simple process automation to sophisticated artificial intelligence programs. The very first uses of computers were for simple process control or repetitive calculations. The concept that data had value was unknown. We can trace the evolution of data in five stages.

In the beginning, there was no data: Stage I

There was no fundamental appreciation for data in this period. Programs were placed at the pinnacle of interest, and there was no perceptible data awareness. Programmers wrote algorithms for the trade journals of the day trying to best a previously published algorithm.

Application programs of this era had only one component, a process component. The programs processed data, but there was no content or business meaning attached to the data.

When an organization purchased a new application, it was selected on the basis of process and functionality rather than on data analysis requirements.

Data dictionaries did not yet exist, and data names were at best cryptic. Hardware was very expensive, so overloading (multiple values) of fields was encouraged.

Dawn breaks for data: Stage II

The distinction between data and programs is made in this period. A very fundamental issue is recognized. The data component is more stable over time than the process component. This recognition brings about the separation of data and the process. Integrity constraints can now be maintained in the data and not in the process.

The evaluation strategy of new applications for purchase also changes. Candidate applications are still evaluated for process and functionality; however, they are also evaluated on the quality of their data structures. An interest in data semantics arises, which leads to the next stage.

Data sees the light: Stage III

In this period, organizations become aware that data semantics exist behind the data. Analysts attempt to build accurate logical representations of business meaning that are not constrained by technological considerations or access requirements.

Logical data-modeling is now added to the product life cycle. Inexpensive computer-aided software engineering (CASE) tools come into use, and analysis techniques and standards emerge on a project-by-project basis. Application development team members now do their own data modeling. The role of database administrator changes as databases house a greater quantity of higher-quality attributes.

An awakening for data: Stage IV

This stage is characterized by the need to understand the data prior to database design so that this understanding can be expressed in the same format across projects.

Programmers have a rude awakening in this stage. They are no longer able to choose or ignore data standards at will. Logical and physical models are now deliverable for a project and must gain formal approval. Design-review sessions are now in place to ensure consistency of the data.

To this point, the information systems departments maintained responsibility for the data. This stage is the first step in a shift from information systems department responsibility to business manager responsibility for data quality.

A new day for data: Stage V

Data is now recognized as a corporate asset. It is leveraged and shared across all project and organizational boundaries. Data quality and shareability are now the responsibility of a business manager.

New data models or databases are not created without justification. Existing models are reused or extended as necessary. Data warehousing, enterprise modeling, object orientation, and business process reengineering can now be done at this stage.

The role of the database administrator expands considerably. Enterprise data is now integrated, and subject-oriented databases can be delivered proactively before an application needs data. A new role of data steward evolves. A data steward is responsible for critical data or for tasks such as ensuring data quality during an early phase of a new project.

Evolution of Data Behavior and Business Rules

The evolution of business rules is quite similar to that of data, but it always lags the evolution of data. Maturity of business rules does not occur simultaneously with maturity of data. We can trace business rule evolution with almost the same five stages we used for data evolution.

Automation or no behavior control – business rules: Stage I

An organization is unaware that data behavior exists. The organization may appreciate the difference between the process component and the data component of application development, but all application development is a function of automation.

Business rules may exist within an application, but they are indistinguishable from the process. The business rules, if any exist, are a function of the target application's nature and intent.

Recognizing behavior – business rules: Stage II

This is the most common level of business rule maturity for organizations today. It is a time of recognition. Programmers and analysts now recognize that *something* exists beyond process and data. This *something* is business rules.

Programmers and analysts also recognize that business rules are more stable than the process component but less stable than the data component. Analysts and developers recognize that business rules can be separate from the programs using them.

Business rule design is now a formal step of the application development life cycle. Database administrators assume the responsibility of implementing these rules. The rules are typically characterized as stored procedures or triggers with each business rule corresponding to a database update event.

A changing of the guard – business rules: Stage III

The recognition process continues. The organization becomes aware that business rules are not the property of programmers or data analysts. Business rules become the property of people charged with running the enterprise — business people.

The representation of business rules also starts to change. The initial implementation of business rules was with stored procedures and triggers as a representation of the rules. Business rules are now defined in natural-language templates that are independent of the underlying database languages.

Formality inches upward with business rule analysis and modeling becoming formal parts of the application life cycle. Business rules can now be distilled from legacy code, but the distillation process is not consistent. This is caused by inconsistent business vocabulary and rule-typing schemes. This is the same problem that occurs when analysts attempt to export business rules across organizational boundaries. At this stage, business rules remain project specific even though the need for enterprise business rules is starting to be recognized.

Another changing of the guard – business rules: Stage IV

The first changing of the guard for business rules was the transferring of business rule ownership from programmers or data analysts to business people. This changing of the guard gave business rule ownership to enterprise-oriented people rather than project-oriented people.

Business rule standards now become important. In the last stage, they were project specific; however, corporate business rule standards must exist for successful enterprise implementation of business rules. Conformity to standards is essential for success at this stage. Developers can no longer develop business rules in their own style. Some unique problems may occur at this level. Even though business rule standards now exist and business rules conform to these standards, not all business rules are sharable or reusable.

Optimal behavior – business rules: Stage V

This is the final stage of business rule evolution. Business rules are now a corporation asset. They may be used for behavioral control with optimal rules inspiring optimal behavior. It should be obvious that less than optimal rules will not inspire optimal behavior. Enlightened corporate leaders can use business rules to:

- Serve customers effectively by understanding their needs and behavior.
- Compete creatively by being able to detect heretofore unknown marketing patterns.
- Avert undesirable organizational behavior.
- Reward productivity by identifying corporate segments with optimal behavior.
- Identify and quickly enable productivity enhancements.
- This new empowerment is enterprise-wide and leads the enterprise to search for additional new and creative business rules.

These are exciting times. The introduction of a tiered architecture by Microsoft with COM/DCOM is epochal. It is the first step in removing business rules from the process. Business rules are still embedded in the process, but now they have been identified and separated from other business functions. With most organizations only at Stage II in the evolutionary cycle, the evolution of business rules is far from complete.

Evolution of the Programmer

Programmers were an absolute necessity in the early days. I don't mean the Commodore or Tandy days, but 30 years before that. Hardware has evolved and so has the concept of a programmer. At the fall 1997 meeting of the Digital Equipment Corporation Users Society (DECUS) in Anaheim, California, Robert Palmer, CEO of Digital Equipment Corporation promised 1GHz Alpha systems by the millennium (700MHz Alpha chips have already been tested). Computer memory continues to get cheaper and as computer power increases, the need for a programmer decreases. This happens because software tools become more powerful allowing users to implement applications directly. Yes, there will always be a need for *real* programmers, but it will be very specialized. The vast majority of programmers will evolve to become developers — that is, users of powerful tools. But it doesn't stop there. Developers will continue to evolve into a new class of users. We already have them. They're called *Power Users* and they've been with us for a while.

In the beginning, hands on bare metal: Stage I

Programming skills matured along with all other aspects of the industry. Programs didn't exist as we know them today, and programming was a process of setting switches or plugging wires into a board. Nothing was easy. Languages were started, but they were very primitive by today's standards. SOAP for the IBM 650 is an example of a primitive language. The IBM 650 was not at the beginning of the computer age, but it is illustrative of the nature of computers from that era because it had only a drum memory.

Tools start to appear: Stage II

Numerous manufacturers are building computers, and each uses their own version of machine assembly language. Efforts are made to create high-level languages, but they are all very specialized and not universally useful. Notable American companies include RCA, GE, Philco, Burroughs, Sperry Rand (Univac), NCR, and IBM. Digital Equipment Corporation wasn't founded until the mid-1960s and only manufactured minicomputers. Companies only supported what they manufactured. All software was proprietary.

In the late 1950s, IBM delivered FORTRAN I and FAP (FORTRAN Assembly Programming). This was the beginning of what might be called the second-generation languages. The language was useful for computation, but data typing and control structures were primitive by today's standards.

Another aspect of this period was that a programmer typically used both an assembly language and FORTRAN. Tool vendors did not yet exist, and programmers from this era became generalists; that is, they became a master of many different skills.

Programming and programmers mature: Stage III

This is the age of third-generation languages. FORTRAN has matured significantly with many enhancements. COBOL (Common Business Oriented Language) has blossomed and is accepted universally. SIMULA, which will eventually provide the seeds for the modern day C++, was a popular language of the day. C was introduced in the 1970s along with UNIX, which became very popular with original equipment manufacturers (OEM). The operating systems and languages of the mainframe manufacturers were proprietary; C and UNIX were the only choices OEMs had for mid-range or minicomputers.

Intercommunication with foreign systems was a hallmark of this period. This was because of the wide acceptance of language standards. Universal standards were accepted for C, COBOL, FORTRAN, and BASIC.

Programming standards became widely accepted. Different consultants of the era espoused different structured programming techniques. This was to rid us of spaghetti code (unstructured programming constructs). All too often, however, the resultant code adhered to the required form, but content was missing. Did you start top-down or bottom-up?

In prior steps of the evolution, programmers were noted for becoming generalists. This changed. The advancement of operating systems and block-structured languages brought about a period of specialization. Jobs became very narrowly defined with definitions such as a JCL (Job Control Language) specialist for IBM operating systems. This era also marked the end of the programming evolution as discussed in the next section.

The programming evolution ends: Stage IV

This era started with the introduction of application generators known as fourth-generation languages (4GL). 4GL systems were introduced in the early to mid-1980s, but they never delivered what they promised. Microsoft popularized the graphical user interface (GUI) in the early 1990s as the interest in 4GL systems waned. The 4GLs were not particularly successful, and it can be argued that the 4GL eventually evolved into the tools we have today, such as Access, Visual Basic, and PowerBuilder. These tools became successful for a number of reasons, but most notable was the use of these tools as a RAD (rapid application development) tool. Prototypes can be delivered very quickly and RAD tools are much easier to use than 4GL systems.

The accepted languages of the day were now proprietary and did not have an American National Standards Institute (ANSI) standard. The industry spent many years evolving language standards, but today we find ourselves dependent on proprietary languages.

That completes the brief sketch of the historical forces that shaped our destiny with a computer today. Let's move on and look at classical data-modeling. Initially, there were different data-modeling technologies competing for the limelight, but the technology presented here won the tug-of-war.

Classical Models

A successful system implementation must be modeled. Every application implementation requires a model to be successful unless it is a trivial system. A model is an abstraction of a real-world phenomenon. Models measure conformance to implementation standards. Models also measure conformance to user requirements. Models place bounds on features thereby preventing *feature-creep*. Models also signal when the application is complete. Models are effective project management tools for keeping a project on schedule and reasonably within budget. When a client wants a feature added, the client could be informed of what other features must be removed to keep the project on schedule and reasonably within budget. Models can be roughly categorized as logical models, physical models, and results models. Many software projects are attempted and fail with models that are wrong or incomplete, or where the problem at hand isn't modeled. The following material provides some insight as to the value of modeling and why software projects fail:

o *A model cannot be built unless the problem is understood.* This sounds reasonable, but the context is the business environment. Developers all too often start with an interim step, which is the information model discussed below. Within that model is the entity-relationship diagram. This diagram will be flawed unless a correct business model exists. The business problem cannot be understood without a business model. Too many projects are started with only an information model whose minimal implementation is an entity-relationship diagram. The information model will be in error unless a business model exists.

o *An application cannot be built without a model.* This is also a deceptively simple statement. The value of a model is incalculable. A model gauges conformance to user requirements and implementation standards. It also serves as a limit on feature-creep.

o *Models prevent us from falling into the trap of thinking about* how *to solve a problem rather than thinking about* what *is the problem.* An example is the image of an engineer who invents a very clever gadget and then looks for a gadget market. The entity established with the engineering approach eventually goes bankrupt. A successful enterprise identifies a market need and then develops a product that satisfies the needs. The engineering approach is to invent a clever gadget and then look for a use for the gadget. Engineers are all too often absorbed by the *how* and not the *what*. You'll learn shortly that distinguishing between the *how* and the *what* is the key to successful software application development (see Figure 40-1).

I believe that programmers work very long hours not because they need to, but because they want to. This explains to some degree why the *how* takes on such importance in the design cycle. This preoccupation with implementation techniques disrupts the design cycle. My own personal experience is that the C/C++ language is one of the most intellectually satisfying languages ever developed but that it is one of the least cost-effective languages. Because of this preoccupation with implementation techniques, systems are designed in terms of the *how* and not in terms of business needs.

This preoccupation with implementation techniques also changes the order of phases in a product life-cycle, with the population of the database occurring after application development. The actual cycle steps should be: design the database, populate it, create reports for it, and then develop the required application. There are third-party tools available today that will let you do this from companies such as InfoModeler from Asymetrix and ER*win*/Desktop from Logic Works, Inc. for Visual Basic/Powerbuilder. A relational database can be designed, and tested with queries and data entry tested without before any coding is done in C/C++, Visual Basic, Power Builder, or Access. The resulting tables can then be exported to a database for application development. This approach puts the *what* before the *how* which is correct. I can recall many instances, including myself, where the application was completed, and then the developer went looking for suitable data.

This preoccupation with the *how* is driven by management that wants immediate results; by a new crop of developers (users) who do not know how to model data or how to normalize it; and by the very nature of the tools, which use the graphical user interface and that promote the *how* aspect with their ease of use.

o   **Models enable the designer to formulate the problem in business terms and not in terms of the resources available or implementation techniques.** This is another deceptively simple statement. Directions are given to implement a system using the current infrastructure. The system fails within a few short months because of performance issues. The other scenario is that client needs are not fulfilled because of inadequate infrastructure.

I offer an architectural model that I call an Augmented Zachman Framework. It is not a single model but a series of models based on the Zachman Framework, with one model replaced by two IDEF1X models and with two added models. The added models are a requirements model and a business rules model. The Zachman objectives/scope model is renamed to the Business Scope Model.

Information Systems Architecture: Zachman Framework

The Zachman Framework is introduced with Figure 40-1. It identifies the *what*, the *how*, and the *where*. The original Zachman Framework names are *data, function,* and *network*. The remainder of this chapter is only interested in the *what* or the Zachman Framework *data*. There is a great deal of detail missing from Figure 40-1, but for now all that is necessary is the identification of the different models.

We discuss the details later in the chapter, but for now, let's borrow some concepts from IDEF1X.

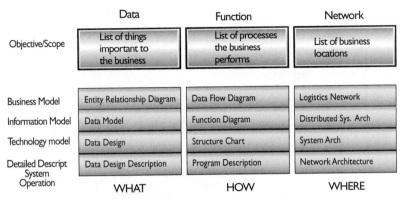

	Data	Function	Network
Objective/Scope	List of things important to the business	List of processes the business performs	List of business locations
Business Model	Entity Relationship Diagram	Data Flow Diagram	Logistics Network
Information Model	Data Model	Function Diagram	Distributed Sys. Arch
Technology model	Data Design	Structure Chart	System Arch
Detailed Descript System Operation	Data Design Description	Program Description	Network Architecture
	WHAT	HOW	WHERE

FIGURE 40-1   The Zachman Framework.

IDEF1X Information Models

As Figure 40-1 shows, there is a clear distinction between the *how* and the *what* within the Zachman Frame. The Zachman Framework gives us that starting point by delineating the difference between the *how* and the *what*. Using it, we focus only on the *what* and develop a methodology for it. The methodology is grounded in the IDEF1X information model, which is illustrated with the hierarchy of models shown in Figure 40-2. Figure 40-2 is a detailed representation of the *what* from a Zachman Framework. The order of the models in the hierarchy is the order of application of our methodology for the application model we are constructing.

Figure 40-2 illustrates the IDEF1X model types. There is no business model within this architecture. That's okay because we're only going to borrow the concept of the key-based model (KBM) and the fully attributed model (FAM).

The 3NF notation of Figure 40-2 represents third normal form, a form of data normalization (see Chapter 41). The KBM of Figure 40-2 consists of entities and primary keys only and is normalized to third normal form. Two other normalization steps precede the third normal form. The three steps are characterized as:

o *First Normal Form* — Groups of repeating data are removed.

o *Second Normal Form* — Duplicate data is removed.

o *Third Normal Form* — Columns of data that do not depend upon the primary key are removed.

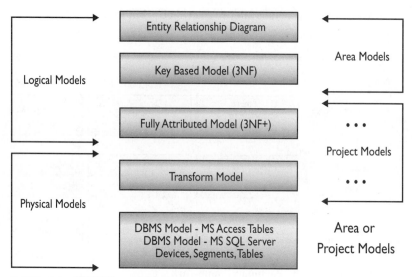

FIGURE 40-2   IDEF1X model types.

The reason for normalizing data is that Structured Query Language (SQL) engines expect a database to be normalized. A SQL engine returns erroneous and incomplete results when the data is not normalized.

There is a significant advantage to partitioning the normalization phase into two models. KBM simplifies the normalization process for a database when there are only entities and primary keys present. Once completed, the transition commences to FAM. Attributes are added, but only a small group at each step. The database is again normalized after each group of attributes is added. When there are no further attributes to add to any table, the model is now considered a FAM.

For now, consider KBM and FAM as notations for the different transitional states the database occupies before it is mapped to the target medium with the transform model. KBM and FAM are only tools to make the normalization of databases manageable. The combination of the IDEF1X KBM and FAM is equivalent to the Zachman Framework information model. Henceforth, we substitute the IDEF1X KBM and FAM for the Zachman Framework information model. This is the first portion of the Augmented Zachman Framework.

 tip   **If you are using a data–design tool, you may not need to break the Zachman Framework information model into two components. I do recommend doing it, however, for manageability.**

Defining the Application Model

The application model consists of a series of models based upon the IDEF1X architecture and the Zachman Framework. When the Augmented Zachman Framework is implemented, there are identifiable deliverables at each level of the architecture. The architecture is designed so that each progressive model has links back to a prior model. This enables an analyst to trace back from a stored procedure, trigger, or intelligent agent to the information model and identify the relevant business rule, constraint, or related entity. If tracing is done back to the requirements model, then the related definition, fact, constraint, or derivation in the requirements model is identified. Tracing back further, we can identify which business rambling caused the creation of the current definition, fact, constraint, or derivation. The last trace back level is the identification of the affected items from the objective/scope level of our Augmented Zachman Framework.

I define the Application Model as the collection of all related models. Application Model deliverables are easily identified. Except for the Requirements Model, the models very closely parallel the Zachman Framework. Table 40-1 outlines the Zachman Framework deliverable models.

TABLE 40-1 ZACHMAN FRAMEWORK DELIVERABLE MODELS

ZACHMAN FRAMEWORK LEVEL	DELIVERABLE
Objectives/scope	Business Scope Model
Business Model	Entity Relationship Model (diagram)
Information Model	Data Model
Technology Model	Access database, SQL Server devices/tables
Detailed Representation Model	Business Implementation Model

The Application Model in Table 40-1 is defined in Zachman Framework terms. I want to redefine it in IDEF1X terms. Redefining simplifies the implementation process. Table 40-2 is the Augmented Zachman Framework or the Applications Model. Let's look at the changes to the Zachman Famework:

- A new Requirements Model is added. The models are arranged in hierarchical order. The Requirements Model is placed between the Business Scope Model and the Entity Relationship Model.

- The Business Rules Model is added in parallel with the Entity Relationship Model.

- The Data Model is decomposed to KBM and FAM, neither of which are deliverables.

- The Technology Model is renamed as the transform model and corresponds to the IDEF1X Transform Model.

That's it! Figure 40-2 represents the Augmented Zachman Framework or Application Model.

TABLE 40-2 AUGMENTED ZACHMAN FRAMEWORK DELIVERABLE MODELS

AUGMENTED ZACHMAN FRAMEWORK	DELIVERABLE
Objectives/scope	Business Scope Model
	Requirements Model
Business Model	Entity Relationship Model (diagram), Business Rules Model
Key-Based Model	
Fully Attributed Model	Data Model
Technology Model	Transform Model (Access database, SQL Server devices/tables, ...)
Detailed Representation Model	Business Implementation Model

Figure 40-3 represents the work we've done so far in constructing the Application Model. That is my name for the aggregation of all models. It is also the Augmented Zachman Framework.

When the methodology is followed, the analyst can trace back through all prior models and identify the dependencies. The Business Scope Model, Requirements Model, Business Rules Model, and Business Implementation Model are all implemented as one or more tables in a relational database. This enables an analyst to identify dependencies between different models.

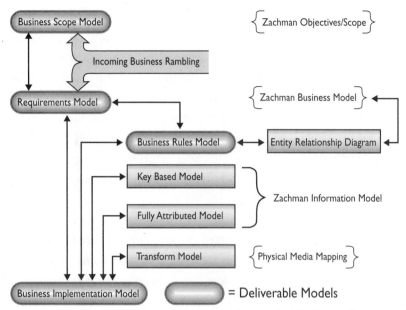

FIGURE 40-3 The application model or the Augmented Zachman Framework.

With the different models, we have made a difficult problem manageable and reduced it to digestible bite-sized chunks. Let's thumbnail-sketch each of the different models before we pause and look back on history and the forces that shaped our computing environment. We step through the different models in a logical order that pursues the *what* well before the *how* is even considered. Note that we're primarily discussing business models; the entity relationship diagram (Data Model). KDM, FAM, and Transform Model are not discussed to any great length until much later in our design methodology. This contrasts with other design methodologies that start with data normalization. By this I mean that the database normalization phase may proceed incorrectly when it is the starting point. The developer is given a list of entities and attributes and is expected to normalize them and commence application development. The developer relies on intuitive judgment that is occasionally wrong, and proceeds to normalize the database. Proper database normalization requires an intimate understanding of the Business Model. All too often database normalization is an intuitive process. Formal database normalization requires knowledge of *functional dependence* (in the mathematical sense). *Something* depends upon *something else*. That dependency cannot be known unless the business model is known and understood, and the very difficult issue is that business models change with time.

Business Scope Model

With the Business Scope Model we try to capture the business essence of constraints. Our goal is the identification of strategies, processes, and constraints that define a scope. The source of this information is the business rambling, and information for this model is captured at the same time that we are capturing information for the requirements model. In computer terms, the incoming user-supplied specifications are parsed, with some information placed in the Business Scope Model and the remainder in the Requirements Model.

Requirements Model

We try to complete our capture of the business essence with this model. The rambling is decomposed into succinct, noncompound English sentences, which are stated in business terms for each of the business rules. The related rambling is placed in a *rambling* table, and the related business rules are placed in a *requirements* table. Within the latter table is our analysis and reasoning for the derived business rule. It, in turn, is linked back to the text of the original business rambling. All business rules from the business rambling appear in this model.

Business Model

We now build an entity relationship diagram (ERD) that must be augmented with a Business Rules Model. The ERD does not contain enough information because we also want to capture the original assumptions, comments, and examples of usage of the attribute or entity. Capturing this type of information is a relatively recent feature of data modeling tools. You'll want to evaluate your data modeling tool in terms of capturing this ancillary information.

ERD and the Business Rules Model comprise the two elements of the Business Model. This is a very key point. ERD is a model of the business and not yet a model of data structures even though there is some resemblance to a data model. Tools such as Erwin confuse the separation of logical models slightly since Erwin supports both the physical and logical models even though the ERD is a logical model.

We really can't store any information in the ERD because it is a structure, so the Business Rules Model is the bridge between the ERD and the Requirements Model. It provides the mapping between the Business Rules Model and the ERD. The Requirements Model gave us definitions, facts, constraints, and derivations. Facts and definitions are the only business rules incorporated in the Business

Rules Model. Not every definition will become an entity, and some definitions may be synonyms for other definitions. To recap, this model is a mapping between the business requirements model's facts and definitions. It also provides the reasoning for the decisions of how this model is implemented. It includes:

o Examples of usage.

o Hidden or underlying assumptions. Documentation is quite often only that information which is stated explicitly in the program implementation. What are the assumptions made when decisions are made? Some of this information is captured in the *reason* attribute of the requirements model database.

o Comments about the attribute or entity.

o Links back to the requirements model. From there a link exists back to the original business rambling and the Business Scope Model.

Business Implementation Model

There are two logical models and one physical intervening model since creation of ERD and the Business Rules Model. These intervening models consist of the Key-Based Model, the Fully Attributed Model, and the Transform Model, which is the physical mapping to the storage media. The Transform Model represents application documentation for all aspects of the application.

o It includes the logical-to-physical mapping of the database.

o It also includes the triggers and procedures (if used) to enforce constraints and derivations from the Business Rules Model.

o It maintains links back to the business rules model to identify the relevant fact, definition, constraint, or derivation, and a second link back to the referenced entity.

o It is the final documentation repository for the application system, so add anything as necessary to complete the system documentation.

Some very important statements are made in the above thumbnail sketches. One of the more profound statements is the importance of capturing the hidden or underlying assumptions that are in place when a model is defined. Because business models do change with time, it is important to know the underlying assumptions when the attribute or entity was defined.

LOOKING BACK

Our primary interest is the quality of our data and the quality of our data structures. Only after the quality of data is established can behavior be detected and managed. These are the business rules we're striving for.

In the beginning, the quality of data was established by separating the data from the process. Focus gradually shifted from the process to the data. Today, focus is, unfortunately, back on the process. You should already have some clues, but if you don't understand why, the reasons are outlined below.

Focusing on data and not the process is not the only issue. There is also the issue of ownership of both the data and business rules. In the primordial days when computers were excruciatingly difficult to use, it's easy to understand why the Information Systems (IS) departments maintained ownership of the data. However, the data belongs to the user and not the IS department. I have witnessed many turf wars over this issue, and it is the primary reason why many marketing organizations hire independent contractors to implement departmental systems. What happens when this is done is that the systems do not always adhere to corporate standards, and the data is orphaned. Orphaned data is best explained by recalling the early 1980s when bootleg PC systems maintained independent copies of data. The corporation no longer had control of the data. It's happening again with corporate intranets. I can't say that Microsoft encourages illegal intranets, but the Microsoft software to create an intranet is relatively easy to use (see Chapters 36 to 39).

There is another ownership problem and this is with business rules. Traditionally developers are the owners of the business rules because they implemented the code manifesting the rule(s). The real problem is that business rules are still embedded in the process. This sense of ownership will continue to exist until such time as business rules are no longer embedded in the process. Two things must happen first. Technology must advance to a point such that business rules are no longer embedded in the process, and the users must acquire full ownership of business rules. Reaching this is some time in the future. The desirable scenario may appear a bit utopian considering our current level of technology is only at Stage II of the data rules evolutionary path: The vice president of sales reviews the weekly reports on Monday morning and decides to implement a new business rule. The vice president wants to change the "2 percent 10 net 30" rule to "3 percent 10 net 30," but only for accounts whose gross sales exceed $100,000 per month. The rule is implemented using the business rule wizard and is in place before the start of business. The goal is to improve collections on the very large accounts. That's not how it's done today. The developer must make a coding change.

Specialization Comes Full Circle

Applications are delivered to the desktop, and too often the user does not have the skill to support it even though the user may know how to use it. Data can be entered, but the necessary infrastructure support skills are missing.

In the very early days of computing, a software developer was a generalist. The developer participated in all facets of application development. Sometimes the job definition extended down to the hardware level, even though it was described as software development. As computing advanced, individuals became specialists. Often the specialties were very narrow. The specialist that I had the most difficulty accepting was the JCL specialist on IBM computers.

Jobs became more and more specialized with time. However, with the advent of RAD tools and a graphical user interface, immense computing power became available on the desktop to either developers or end users. This redefined the legacy concept of centralized computing and centralized administration. End users were quite willing to accept the benefits of distributed computing but were not eager, willing, or able to shoulder the extra burden of distributed administration. A desktop user or developer must accept all the same responsibilities that existed with legacy centralized computer management. A desktop user must be a system manager, a database administrator, and possibly a network administrator. If the desktop user does application development, then there is the extra burden of understanding business processes, data-modeling, and data normalization. If programming is an additional burden, then the desktop user must be able to formulate a problem solution and successfully implement that solution. Along the way, the user must be able to successfully debug the application. The debugging process requires an understanding of the internal process flow and the ability to develop a methodology or approach to the problem resolution.

Skill sets have come full circle. There were generalists in the beginning, with programmers selecting some specialization track. However, placing applications on the desktop now calls for additional skills, and so we enter a new generalization period.

Users Commence Application Development

A very epochal event has occurred. Users commence application development and the *Age of Programming* ends. Applications developed only as a prototype are used for production. The *Age of the User* starts. There is no difference between a developer setting the parameters or properties of a combo box or a text box from that of a user entering accounting information. Each is a different level of user.

Successful application development requires far more skills than simply a mechanical facility with a shrink-wrapped tool. In the legacy world (read that as mainframe), there was a hierarchy of skills. The least-skilled individual was the coder, followed by the programmer, and then the analyst. Within this skill path there were many degrees with many different names such as *Member of Technical Staff-A or Member of Technical Staff-B (MTS-A, MTS-B)*. A database administrator also existed, but not in the same skill path. The least-skilled individual, the coder, eventually became a programmer if the individual developed the required skills and judgment commensurate with the job. I believe that the computer industry today legitimizes the weakest skill set from the legacy world, the coder. A mechanical facility with a GUI tool is recognized as competency for application development. It should be no surprise to anyone that the ease of use of the new tools promotes the use of spaghetti code. This is a step backward and undoes many years of analysis in good, structured program design.

Even after a legacy coder acquired the requisite skills to become a programmer, there was still no need to understand data-modeling or data normalization because that was the exclusive purview of the Database Administrator (DBA). The legacy DBA was almost treated as a god. Today, every developer must understand the many roles of a database administrator, which include data-modeling and data normalization because a full relational database now exists on the desktop.

The user attempting to develop an application is totally unaware of the implied requisite requirements. You can go to your local computer emporium and purchase a complete desktop relational database management system for a few hundred dollars. Successful application development requires the user to be a data-modeler, coder, programmer, analyst, system administrator, and database administrator. The user must know how to formulate a solution, design a database, normalize the database, and then implement the design. The purchaser of such a system may be totally unaware of the implied and requisite skill sets necessary to formulate a successful application. Does a first-time relational database purchaser recognize the need to understand the concept of relational theory to the point of normalizing a database at least through third-normal form? The fact that there are terms such as *natural key, super key, primary key, surrogate key,* and *foreign key* testify to the fact that key selection alone is not always simple.

Process Regains the Spotlight

Process has come full cycle. On the very slow evolutionary path of computing, focus gradually shifted from the process to the quality of data and quality of data structures. The very early systems were purchased based on their capability to process information. It is the *how* factor discussed earlier. Today that evolutionary process is reversed, and the process is again the primary focus. This is because of the graphical user interface, which is not the exclusive purview of Microsoft. Hardware vendors such as Digital Equipment Corporation use a GUI interface, as do UNIX systems. It's not anything that Microsoft started, but the nature of the GUI has created an infatuation with the process and an ignorance of the value of data. Historically, computing evolved, data was eventually recognized to have value, and systems were purchased on the quality of data and quality of data structures. Systems are purchased today based on their process functionality. Developers are hired based on their skills with using the process, and not their ability to analyze data. You don't have a job today unless you have the latest GUI tool skills. Now the picture really isn't that bad yet because we haven't regressed to the very beginning, but we have definitely taken some steps backward. We must regain our focus on the data component of a system and direct our energies in that direction to maintain the data evolution. I believe that the ease of use of a GUI has seduced us.

Microsoft contributes significantly to maintaining the spotlight on the process. Grant for a moment the necessity of making a paradigm shift when moving from a command line metaphor to the Windows 3.1 metaphor. Microsoft didn't let the paradigm shift stabilize. Microsoft keeps the focus on the process with another paradigm shift in Windows 95 and Windows NT 4.0. The Windows 3.1 metaphor is preserved in Windows NT 3.51. This infatuation with the process diverts our focus from the issues of data and business rules and drags us backward on the evolutionary scale. I am certain that Microsoft will continue to keep the focus on the process with Windows 98 and Windows NT 5.0.

THE GUI IS NOT DIRECTLY RESPONSIBLE

In 1967 I witnessed the same problems we have today. The problems occurred with the introduction of the *time sharing option* (TSO) for the IBM 360 model 67. Interaction was with a Teletype, clunky and ancient by today's standards. To that point, all computer work was submitted as a batch job. When presented with the TSO interactive environment, the users appeared to abrogate their responsibility to think.

This was manifested by programmers who did not analyze the reason their program failed and fixed symptoms and not the real problem. They did this because it was too easy to resubmit a task for execution. The logic of the program was eventually destroyed by fixing symptoms and not the real problem. The bottom line is we're apparently all very lazy, and when the interface is too simple we don't think at all.

It's commonly accepted that there is a high failure rate of software. I believe there is a correlation between the high failure rate and the current focus on the process or the *how*. Individuals are hired on the basis of their skills with a GUI tool, and analysts without GUI skills find difficulty in obtaining employment. The analysts without GUI skills are the very ones who can reduce the unusually high failure rate of client server systems.

When Prototypes Become Production Versions

Data have evolved and so have processes. However, processes are now refined to such a degree that end users with little professional software training are developing applications. RAD is seductive in what it offers. A trade journal article stated that Visual Basic applications could be developed in one-tenth the time of a comparable COBOL application. But is application development occurring at the expense of analysis and design? I think so. It is easy to prototype an application with a RAD tool; unfortunately, the prototype often becomes the production version. The same article stated that long-term maintenance costs of a RAD application were ten to twenty times that of a COBOL application. We may not be saving anything; in fact, we may be worse off. We have easier access to data with the new GUI systems, but the GUI systems are notoriously unreliable while mainframe applications are noted for their reliability.

If we look at the situation from the legacy perspective, we note that the percentage of time spent coding during the product development phase represented ten to fifteen percent of the application development life cycle. Twenty percent was considered a pretty high percentage. Today, those numbers are reversed. Because of increased functionality of modern-day tools and the apparent abrogation of the traditional analysis phase, the percentage of time spent on coding during a product's life cycle has actually gone up. This shouldn't be. This reversal comes about at the expense of other phases of the development life cycle such as requirements analysis or functional and detail specifications. Consider these facts:

- A RAD tool reduces the physical coding time of an application.

- A project using a RAD tool has coding as a higher percentage of the total implementation costs. This shouldn't be because the tool is much more efficient than prior methods.

- The conclusion is that some of the savings accrued by using a RAD tool are at the expense of problem analysis. I agree with that conclusion because RAD tools solve apparent problems and not real problems.

The message conveyed by the previous section tells us that every application should be modeled. All of the apparent timesavings accrued with a RAD tool are not attributable to tool ease-of-use; some of the timesaving is attributable to the analysis phase not being performed.

There is a tendency to forgo any analysis when a RAD tool can generate almost immediate results. The problem with this approach is that the solution presented by the RAD tool is usually not scaleable, may be an incomplete solution, or is not a solution to the primary problem as it deals with a tangential issue.

Ignoring the Lessons of the Past

The software industry has spent considerable time and energy organizing and structuring code. That effort has not been completely lost. Professional developers today use high-level objects with inheritance classes. However, the typical RAD tool user knows little of this technology. That user's efforts look more like the spaghetti code the software industry spent many years attempting to eradicate. Do these new RAD tools promote spaghetti code? I believe they do.

ARE APPLICATIONS IMPLEMENTED TOO QUICKLY?

ComputerWorld, May 26, 1997, *Technically Challenged:* "Today's apps can be developed so rapidly that you can have one running before the project plan to do it the old way could be written."

We already had hypertext and hyperlinks, and now we have hyperapplications. As pointed out in the previous sidebar, we stop thinking when the task becomes too easy. Creating an application is now too easy. This hyper-rush to create an application before the project plan is completed accounts in large part for the reduced productivity the computing industry is experiencing.

ComputerWorld, September 15, 1997, *Computers Have Yet to Make Companies More Productive:* "Information costs have risen, not declined, in relation to other production costs. Neither client/server, the Internet nor computer networks have so far improved the productivity of information handling by the premier U.S. industrial corporations. In 1996, $1.1 trillion in cost of goods required $300.5 billion in Sales, General and Administrative Cost (SG&A) expense. This ratio is now lower than it was in the period from 1987 through 1990." Paul A. Strassmann, http://www.strassmann.com.

Are applications generated too quickly and easily? I think they are. Where are the productivity gains promised by RAD tools? There aren't any. Productivity is actually dropping.

Is a RAD Tool Always the Right Choice?

If a RAD tool reduces application implementation costs to one-tenth that of a comparable COBOL application, and the maintenance costs of a RAD tool-developed application are ten to twenty times that of a comparable COBOL application, have we saved anything? Probably not. The only apparent savings incurred by a RAD tool are the deployment costs. The successful deployment of a RAD application is far lower than that of the legacy COBOL applications. RAD applications are fortunate to last a year or more. An application that uses Microsoft technology is considered legacy if it is more than a few years old. An example is an application using dynamic data exchange (DDE) (see Chapter 33). Consider the current year 2000 problem. The programs with the year 2000 problem are 30 years old! I think that's fantastic. A Microsoft application is lucky to have a life of more than a few years. There is almost a vengeance to destroying existing applications. Try to get support for older applications. Microsoft publicly announced that support for SQL Server 4.21 would terminate the day SQL Server 6.0 shipped. There are many other examples but one is sufficient.

Lack of support is not the only issue. There is a factor termed deprecation. Deprecation is the equivalent of the Grim Reaper visiting and warning you that the end is nigh. Microsoft architecture is component-based, and a visit from the Grim Reaper is the annihilation of the dynamic link libraries (DLLs) necessary for your application. The ghost of the Grim Reaper visits every time a new package, package upgrade, or service pack is installed. Updated DLLs always accompany the installation, and DLLs are interrelated. You never know when your time is up, and the only way to avoid the Grim Reaper is to stop installing upgrades and service packs. Of course, this orphans your system, and at some future date you must pay the terrible price of trying to leapfrog several versions to catch-up while not losing any data. This can't happen with a legacy application, which is a compiled and linked immutable binary mass. Yes, there may be a new library and it is installed, but the application is not affected because it was not relinked. Let's consider what we have so far:

- Client Server applications have a very high failure rate.
- Applications developed with RAD tools (used in client-server systems) have very low deployment costs when compared to legacy applications, COBOL being an example.
- Applications developed with RAD tools have a very high maintenance cost.
- RAD applications have a much shorter life span than legacy COBOL applications. Thankfully, the life of a RAD application is short or the total cost would be prohibitive.
- COBOL applications adhere to ANSI standards and are portable.
- RAD tools do not conform to standards and are the clever whims of the supplier.
- COBOL can become a RAD tool by abrogating the analysis phase of application development. Surprise: COBOL is a RAD tool when you fail to do the proper analysis, but the tradeoff is a poor unreliable application.
- Once compiled and linked the COBOL (or FORTRAN) application is an immutable mass. It cannot be changed unless relinked.
- A RAD application can potentially change every time it is loaded. It links to the DLLs present in the system.

Now for a good zinger: We've been operating with the numbers one-tenth and ten to twenty, which are normalized to a unit of time. These are the deployment and life cycle maintenance costs when comparing a RAD-developed application and a COBOL application. Given the same life span for both a RAD-based application and a COBOL application, the total life cycle costs of a RAD-based application become very significant. The RAD application must be very short-lived to realize net savings. The older a RAD-developed application gets, the less significant the savings incurred during the development phase. A RAD application that has a 30-year life span is prohibitively expensive. This, however, is relative and depends on the size of the project. Avoid the high cost of maintenance and build another system with a still better RAD tool. This idea may even have some merit. There is no associated high maintenance cost and deployment is relatively cheap — if it works. What do you think?

You are the CEO of a multibillion dollar corporation. Which course of action do you select? Is it with the RAD tool or COBOL? If you really are a CEO, you apply a rule of thumb. No RAD-based applications with a long life expectancy. The total maintenance costs will be exorbitant. No RAD-based applications for mission-critical operations. The reliability doesn't exist for RAD applications. You are left with short-lived applications that are not mission critical. Isn't that another name for prototyping? Another factor to consider is the project's implementation costs. The high failure rate of RAD-based projects is an additional factor to consider along with the projected life span and total costs. When the total project costs are moderate to small and the life cycle is short, RAD-developed applications are acceptable.

The last issue is that risks must be manageable, and risks cannot be managed with an architecture which forces obsolescence and potential application failure. A COBOL application has a longer life within which to recover costs, the risk of failure is far less, the application is portable, and the risks are manageable because the application is not at the mercy of the vendor.

Let's take the perspective of the developer. COBOL is a boring language to developers. The developer has anxiety about being downsized, wants the latest and greatest ActiveX controls, and is always writing very clever code with a RAD tool. When asked to respond to the question of the RAD tool's suitability for an application, the developer always provides an affirmative answer. I hope you can see the power of marketing here. Marketing is the process of creating false needs. Successful marketing creates a class of consumers who are characterized as conspicuous consumptionists when they purchase inappropriate goods. Using the latest tool is nirvana. You should be able to see the distinction between the *how* and the *what* here. COBOL is *what* based, whereas a RAD tool is *how* based.

As stated previously, information system productivity continues to drop, and the hyperrush with hypertools to build hyperapplications has not changed this.

When new applications can be written faster than a specification can be written the old way, is the application the correct solution? Probably not. The basic philosophy of Microsoft Solutions Framework is that the approach is bottom-up and iterations occur at each step until that segment is correct. Is this managing risk? Certainly not! Isn't it better to completely design the application first? Yes, but in a few years productivity will be a net loss and fundamental changes will occur. What happens then?

Let's go back and look at COBOL a minute. Before I started this book, I did not understand the value of an immutable binary mass. I do now. It is a personal and very fundamental insight for me. I hope the same is true for you.

Another insight related to a COBOL project and the long period of time required to write the specifications is that a gestation period occurs and bad ideas are discarded. So it's not that we should go back to COBOL projects, but that there should be time gaps so that the concepts can gestate and better alternatives can be offered.

Let me wrap this up quickly. I'm not trying to set the clock back to another age, and I don't expect everything to be done in COBOL. Use the right tool for the job. Continue to write COBOL applications because they are robust, which is something that I don't believe the Microsoft component architecture ever will be. Use advanced technologies such as object linking and embedding-database (OLE-DB) to write COBOL application wrappers. This brings the data to the desktop and maintains the best of both worlds. Don't move the corporate jewels to a RAD tool. There might not be any in a few years.

Surprising and fundamental changes should occur when productivity becomes a net loss. Based on the trend lines we have so far, that is probably three to four years away. When it occurs, expect cataclysmic and very fundamental changes within the industry. It should be quite interesting.

The Passing of an Age

There is still another fundamental issue here. The rapid acceptance and growth of the Internet in the last year is testimony to the continuing evolution of the computer industry. It may be that the *Age of Programming* has passed and that we are all only users of different degrees. The concept of a programmer was born of necessity because the very early computers were quite expensive and complex. They were not easy to use. This passing of the *Age of Programming* accounts for the *dumbing down of the programmer* that is occurring today. I know that there may be some disagreement about this, but I do not consider the clicking of a mouse or the setting of a property in a text box to be programming. Welcome to the *Age of Users*. As a programmer since the 1950s, I lament the passing of an age. Unfortunately, the long-term prognosis is not good. We run the risk of becoming a nation of users lacking the fundamental skill sets necessary to develop the very tools we use. Microsoft's apparent goal is to de-skill jobs and automate tasks. Accomplishing this goal broadens its market for software, but it also broadens the labor pool for individuals who heretofore did not possess the requisite skills to enter the computing industry. A good example of this is Visual Basic 5.0, which allows a developer to create an ActiveX control without really understanding the infrastructure issues. Creating an Active control used to be the exclusive purview of a C/C++ programmer.

A secondary problem with the broadening of the labor pool is that the need for developers is shrinking in terms of real need. This is the equivalent of stating that the 1998 dollar is only worth, say 50 cents in terms of the 1988 dollar (I don't know the real ratio). The problem is that as the apparent labor pool expands, the real need for developers diminishes with the automation of tasks. Jobs are still advertised and demand is high. Demand is always high for the very talented developer, and there is always a demand for individuals who will work for lower wages. I had the personal experience of being called by a local placement agency last summer and offered the job of Visual Basic developer. The agency offered me $16 per hour to do Visual Basic development work. There is nothing wrong with this if you just graduated from high school. I didn't take the contract. I was busy on this book. This illustrates the issue that the automating of tasks and de-skilling of jobs broadens the labor pool.

KEY POINT SUMMARY

Nothing of any value is ever free. An analysis of the requirements and a logical design is always required for a successful application. RAD tools are used intuitively with infrequent modeling and with mixed results. Some successful systems are delivered; however, information system productivity continues to decline and has been steadily declining since 1987. I call this time frame the Microsoft epoch. I expect this epoch to end when productivity becomes a net loss. At that time I expect very fundamental changes to occur in the computing industry.

Applying What You've Learned

The Windows Architecture examinations presuppose a knowledge of classical data-modeling and data normalization. The questions below test your understanding of classical data-modeling. There are numerous questions on data normalization in the Windows Architecture II examination, and you'll find additional material on data normalization in Chapter 41.

The material on historical issues within this chapter is not on the Windows Architecture examination. It is placed here to caution you that the Microsoft epoch cannot continue because of steadily declining productivity. It also serves as a warning that fundamental changes will occur within the computing industry.

Instant Assessment

1. What key model is missing from the IDEF1X data-modeling architecture?

2. Explain the role of KBM and FAM in the IDEF1X architecture.

3. What process is accomplished to place a model in first normal form?

4. Explain third normal form.

 concept link   **For answers to the Instant Assessment questions, see Appendix C.**

Lab Exercise

Lab 40.79 *Evaluating client and budget expectations*

WA I

The goal of Lab 40.79 is to identify those RAD application systems which did not meet client expectations. (The laboratory is of no value if the users enthusiastically embraced all RAD application systems.) Review all the projects you've work on in the last two years using RAD tools. Answer each of these questions truthfully for each implementation, because you are the only one who will see the answers. Is there a correlation between modeling and happy users?

1. Was the project a success in terms of fulfilling client needs and expectations?

2. Did you add anything to the project that you thought was needed but which the user did not specifically request?

3. Did you have a budget?

4. How was the budget defined? Was it a time budget or a dollar budget?

5. Was the application on budget?

6. If not on budget, why not?

7. Were you given a budget and then told to complete the application?

8. Did you do any modeling?

9. If you didn't do any modeling, why didn't you?

10. Were you forced to change specifications after code was written?

11. How would you implement the application differently the next time?

12. Were you forced to remove features because of time or monetary constraints?

Windows Architecture II

CHAPTER

Designing the Solution

41

About Chapter 41

Chapter 41 builds the application model using the Augmented Zachman Framework introduced in Chapter 40. The approach is *top-down*, which means that the problem must be fully understood before resources are expended to solve a problem that isn't known. The chapter discusses only those steps necessary to design and construct the application model. *How* is not a topic of discussion for this chapter, although it's been discussed in nearly every chapter of this book.

The previous chapter was the most important chapter in this book; this chapter is the most difficult. There are many complex issues, and data normalization is not commonly understood. Most developers deal with an intuitive sense of what is proper data normalization and have no formal rule mechanism to apply for complex situations. Normalization rules are introduced in this chapter. They can be used when the intuitive sense of data normalization fails. Normalization rules fail when the business rules are not clearly understood.

An intuitive sense of data normalization works well when building a small application on the desktop from scratch. The developer works through all the stages and typically never goes beyond the third normal form. This approach does not work when the developer is trying to place an OLE-DB wrapper around legacy databases. Legacy databases can be flat-file structures where no consideration was given to relational database issues. The intuitive sense of database normalization will often fail with this scenario.

This chapter introduces the concept of functional dependence. It is used in all data normalization phases. The concept of functional dependence is characterized by something *depending on* something else. This dependence may be incorrect unless the business rules are clearly understood.

I have spent more hours on this chapter than any other chapter in the book. If I fail to communicate, I apologize. The issues are complex, and I expect no one to grasp all of the concepts immediately. Please do not feel badly if you get bogged down. Set the chapter aside for several days and then come back. As difficult as this chapter appears, it is still required reading. There are numerous questions on the Windows Architecture II examination that relate to entity relationship diagrams and data normalization.

CAPTURING THE ESSENCE

Let's start with the Augmented Zachman Framework from Chapter 40. Figure 41-1 is the borrowed model from Chapter 40. This is our anchor as we start from the top and build our application model.

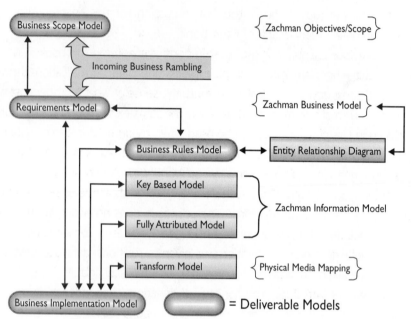

FIGURE 41-1   The application model or the Augmented Zachman Framework.

Problems Obtaining Client Specifications

The first order of business is to understand the client's needs. There are different philosophies of how to acquire the systems specifications. The common technique is to interview the client, and this is not always successful. A failure at this point is often catastrophic. According to *Computerworld* (February 24, 1997), "What many analysts lack . . .are the communication skills and people skills needed for such key tasks as eliciting system requirements from users."

The analyst interviewing the client is faced with these obstacles:

o The client does not correctly understand his or her own role within the corporation. The role is interpreted from a personal perspective.

- The client understands a portion of his or her role correctly, but only as far as the role is known. There may be facets of the role that are not understood because role training was incomplete and informal. The complete picture was not given.

- The interviewer is limited to personal experiences. The interviewer asks questions within the scope of personal experiences and translates client responses in terms of personal experiences.

- The programmer/analyst conducting the interview may lack communication skills. I don't mean in the negative sense, but in the sense of posing questions that lead the client to a particular answer.

- The programmer/analyst often interviews within the context of resources currently available. This includes using favorite rapid application development (RAD) tools, defining the problem within the context of hardware resources, or even encouraging the client to discuss the *How* aspect of the problem.

Having programmer/analysts interview clients doesn't work. An example of good interview techniques is in the artificial intelligence area. A person is specifically trained to interview knowledgeable individuals. This information is then placed in a knowledge base and forms what is known as an expert system. Answers to queries of the expert system represent a composite opinion of the experts in the field. For example, expert systems are used in operating rooms during surgery. A query of an expert system validates the doctor's decision. Expert systems operate at the eighty-five percent correctness level, whereas the best doctors are only right seventy-five percent of the time. This is based on long-term averages. But don't worry. The doctor always makes the ultimate decision. The point of this discussion on expert systems is that care must be taken during the interview.

 note **If you have an interest in expert systems and artificial intelligence, these books can serve as a starter:**

- *The Handbook of Artificial Intelligence*, Volumes 1–4; Barr, Cohen, and Feigenbaum (Addison-Wesley, 1982–1989)

- *Artificial Intelligence*; Luger and StubbleField (Benjamin/Cummings, 1993)

- *Artificial Intelligence*; Rich and Knight (McGraw-Hill, 1991)

Obtaining Client Specifications

The solution to the problem is simple. The client writes the specification. This is the item in Figure 41-1 identified as the *business rambling* ("The Never-Ending Search for Knowledge," Barbara Von Halle, *Database Programming and Design*; February, 1996). The scenario goes like this:

- The client approaches you with an interest in having a system developed.
- You ask the client to place on paper every fact the expected system should solve. No stone is to be left unturned; ask the client to include every small detail relating to the proposed system.
- You emphasize to the client that the required needs are always to be stated in business terms and not implementation terms.
- You also emphasize to the client that the required needs are not to be stated in terms of current resources.
- Also emphasize that this is very informal and not to worry about organization.

Solitary individuals do not plan systems. Everyone who will use the system should construct a business rambling.

Don't expect your user-supplied requirements to make sense. Sentences are unclear, ambiguous, unauthorized, and possibly untrue, and can be incomplete. The sentences probably violate the supplied guidelines. Be prepared to find that the author(s) of the rambling might not understand the enterprise business. To give you an example of what to expect in terms of a requirements model, the following is business rambling from a client. (The names have been changed to protect the innocent.)

Potential fields to include in the ABC Contract Tracking database

I. Areas to track

   A. Name on the file folder and in the current list

   B. Links to other contracts? Do we really want or need this, is it too difficult to do?

      1. By name?

      2. By tracking number?

   C. Tracking Number (assigned by Access)

    1. What procedure do we use if there is a need to put an additional contract into the same folder as the main contract?

    2. What if a codicil is added?

D. Title of contract (which may be different from the name on the folder and in the current list).

E. Address of Party

    1. Address of location if different from the address of the party or principle

        a) (Vendor, Property, etc.)

F. Contract status

    1. Currently in force.

    2. Expired.

        a) What is the disposition of the actual contract after expiration?

            (1) Stored?

            (2) Destroyed?

II. Who are the parties to the contract? (Entities—pull down list of ABC and affiliates—Mexico, H. K., U. K., DRD, etc.)

A. Address of each party

    1. Comes down automatically for the ABC entities?

    2. Capability to modify?

        a) If modified, an automatic indicator to show that it is modified.

B. Principal(s) of each party

C. Signatories (for each party—name(s) and title(s))

    1. Pull-down list of main signatories.

    2. What is the process for adding another name?

        a) Contract administrator?

        b) Data entry person?

        c) Notification to the contract administrator?

III. Is this contract the original?

A. Is it signed?

    1. If it is not signed, where is the signed original or copy?

    2. Is there a copy at all?

B. If it is a copy, where is the original?

C. Are there multiple signed copies?

    1. If so where or who has the other copies?

D. The file folder is empty — apply the above criteria, where, who?

IV. What department is the contract from?

A. Who is the head of the Dept. / or who is responsible for the contract? which/both?

V. Major terms of the contract

A. Dollar value of the contract.

B. Major terms of the contract.

C. Are there specified consequences of noncompliance?

    1. For ABC Corporation.

    2. For other party(ies).

D. Is the contract affected by a change in ownership of either party?

    1. How?

VI. Term of the contract

A. Effective date of the contract.

B. Termination data of the contract (if any).

    1. Has the contract already expired?

C. Terms of renewal

    1. Can it be renewed?

    2. Does it renew automatically?

      a) When does it renew?

      b) What is necessary to prevent it from being renewed?

D. Termination provisions

    1. Automatically expires? (If so, on what date?)

    2. Actions ABC must take to terminate.

      a) Steps.

      b) Timing.

3. Actions other party must take to terminate.

VII. Attachments (note field or fields)

VIII. Other items in the same folder as the main contract that relate to the contract (list)

   A. Law firm(s) involved in writing the contract.

   B. Litigation.

      1. Reference to other contracts.

   C. What?

IX. Fields to flag

   A. Key violations.

   B. Renewal date.

   C. Term date.

   D. Payment either due to or from ABC corporation.

   E. Other?

   F. "Things" to notify Sally Silly about in relation to 10K and other reporting requirements.

X. What else?

XI. Things to cross-relate for reporting

      1. Create a reporting checklist as a guide (see Sally Silly).

   A. What?

   B. Keywords (to provide the ability for a person(s) to sort contracts by type or subject to aid in writing new contracts that address issues that include these topics.

      1. Dividends.

      2. Compensation.

      3. What else?

XII. Fields or determining factors that would indicate that a department action would be in violation of an already existing contract that is in the process of negotiation.

   A. What?

XIII. Key indicators ((((((WHAT))))))

A. What?

XIV. Special "Use" contracts (Set up a window that allows the entry of a preselected type from a pull-down list. This would then bring up a special window(s) for contract specific information).

    A. Banking agreements

        1. Schedules

        2. Amendments

        3. Subsets

    B. Sales rep groups

    C. Leases

    D. What else?

XV. Sales Agreements

XVI. Does this contract need to be serviced in multiple languages?

XVII. What else?

XVIII. Contract tracking (a limited access check list to let all involved with the contract administration program know what the status is of any particular contract or group of contracts.)

    A. It would need to consist of buttons and fields for status and additional information.

        1. It is signed.

        2. Where it is now.

            a) At the lawyers.

            b) At our office.

                (1) With what person or department?

XIX. Future needs

    A. Tracking of status of new contracts.

        1. Who can sign the contract?

        2. What is the approval process?

        3. What is the dollar limit for each signatory?

        4. Who is the key contact?

            a) In ABC corporation.

      b) At the other party.

    5. Autonotification via E-mail.

      a) Flags (discussed above).

      b) What is the routing of the contract in the chain—who, where, for how long, what next, who next?

        (1) New contract administration.

        (2) Renewal of existing contract.

        (3) Changes in terms to an existing contract.

        (4) What else?

B. Is a copy of the executed contract back to our attorney?

C. Is a copy or additional signed original at the office of the other party involved?

D. Log of who accesses the contract.

    1. Who has permission to check a contract out?

    2. What is the approval process for special needs?

    3. Is the original ever to be checked out or only copies?

      a) If so who does the duplicating and has responsibility for the process?

      b) Where is the original?

      c) Where is the copy?

    4. Special situations in which the contract may be read but not copied (restricted access issues).

XX. Reporting

  A. Searching for contract by:

  B. Name.

  C. Date.

  D. Company.

  E. Type of contract.

  F. Key word.

  G. Etc.

XXI. Ease of use is paramount

A. The entire interface to the program needs to be form driven. A learning curve of as close to zero for the person entering the data is what I would like you to strive for.

DISTILLATION REPOSITORIES

Analyzing the business rambling is a distillation process. Two models are created in parallel during the distillation process. The first is the Business Scope Model, which is at the top of our Augmented Zachman Framework. The second model is the Requirements Model, which is also a member of the Augmented Zachman Framework. Figure 41-2 shows how these two models relate to each other.

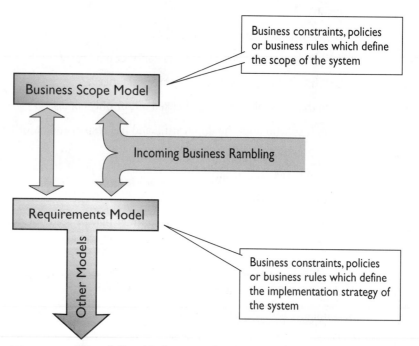

FIGURE 41-2   The relationship between the requirements model and the business scope model.

This section outlines the basic contents of each of these models. There are no hard rules and tables in a relational database represent these models. Feel free to add additional tables or attributes as dictated by your requirements.

The context here is that of supporting a system implementation and not business process reengineering. Consequently, the models may not fulfill all the requirements for business process reengineering, and are not designed to do so.

Business Scope Model

This is the top model in the Augmented Zachman Framework. Although the intent of modeling process is the processing of the *what*, we break the rules slightly and include both the *what* and *how* from the Zachman Framework. The goal of this model is a detailed statement of business strategy, goals, assets, and processes.

There can be more than one goal. Of course, the enterprise can lose focus if there are too many goals. There may be intermediate goals or subgoals. If such goals exist, they are an element of a strategy.

The enterprise may already deliver products so those current products can be categorized as an achieved goal; on the other hand, the increasing of production may be an unachieved goal.

Intangible assets should also be included. These are not dollars and cents in the bank or tangible assets such as equipment, but an enterprise skill-pool enumeration. They are assets in terms of the anticipated system implementation. Enumerating the existing skill pool is enough to question the feasibility of even considering a new system for a business process. The recommendation is to always have the skill pool catalogued and available.

What is wanted is a description of the enterprise. Goals can be stated with various strategies used to achieve the goals. The skill pool implements processes according to a predefined strategy to achieve a goal. This implementation definition provides a natural hierarchy for a database representation. This hierarchy is defined as:

1. Stated goal.

2. Intermediate subgoals.

3. Strategy to implement the goal. There may be multiple strategies.

4. Processes used to realize the goal. There may be multiple processes for a unique strategy.

5. Assets utilized in process. Multiple assets may be used for a process.

A goal of the distillation process is to build a relational database uniquely identifying each goal, strategy, process, or asset. As the requirements models that are discussed next illustrate, a link is made back to this model.

The tables that follow are only suggestions. Any level of detail may be kept. The important issues are that strategies support goal achievement, processes implement a strategy, and assets are consumed in the processing. Tables 41-1, 41-2, 41-3, and 41-4 are elementary and only serve as guidelines. The user is expected to add additional attributes to these tables.

TABLE 41-1 GOALS TABLE DEFINITION

ATTRIBUTE	DATA TYPE	DESCRIPTION
Identifier	Counter	
Description	Text	
Reference	Text	Foreign key. Link to rambling entry in the rambling table.
<Other Attributes>		

TABLE 41-2 STRATEGIES TABLE DEFINITION

ATTRIBUTE	DATA TYPE	DESCRIPTION
Identifier	Counter	
Description	Text	
Goal	Text	Foreign key.
Reference	Text	Foreign key. Link to rambling entry in the rambling table.
<Other Attributes>		

TABLE 41-3 PROCESSES TABLE DEFINITION

ATTRIBUTE	DATA TYPE	DESCRIPTION
Identifier	Counter	
Description	Text	

ATTRIBUTE	DATA TYPE	DESCRIPTION
Strategy	Text	Foreign key.
Reference	Text	Foreign key. Link to rambling entry in the rambling table.
<Other Attributes>		

TABLE 41-4 ASSETS TABLE DEFINITION

ATTRIBUTE	DATA TYPE	DESCRIPTION
Identifier	Counter	
Description	Text	
Process	Text	Foreign key.
Reference	Text	Foreign key. Link to rambling entry in the rambling table.
<Other Attributes>		

Reports from these tables resemble a traditional bill-of-materials expansion.

Reference is the link to the rambling table of the Requirements Model. This is the link between the models of Figure 41-2. The rambling table is defined in the next section.

The incoming business rambling from a user is parsed. Scope parameters move the rambling up toward the Business Scope Model, and implementation of business rules move the rambling down toward the Requirements Model. The Requirements Model provides the input for the subsequent Business Model.

The Business Scope Model is not a model for business process reengineering. If it were, we would attempt to define all business processes within this model. What we use it for is the tracking of requirements within our application model. A business rambling in the requirements model is linked to a business strategy, constraint, or asset in the Business Scope Model. So for our purposes, we will not generate an actual Business Scope Model, but we will augment one with strategies and constraints and possibly assets or process requirements that we encounter in analyzing the business rambling. It is not within our scope to build a Business Scope Model, but only to augment one for tracking purposes. Maybe the correct name is a limited Business Scope Model.

Requirements Model

The Requirements Model is constructed in tandem with the Business Scope Model. You learned in Chapter 40 that the IDEF1X model type does not include a Requirements Model. Other than that, IDEF1X models closely parallel the Zachman Framework. This is the second model in the Augmented Zachman Framework.

Before building our Requirements Model, we should state our goals. The output from the Requirements Model will be used as input for an Information Model. Within that model, you will find the IDEF1X entity relationship diagram (ERD). An interesting transformation occurs with this model. *Facts* from the Requirements Model are transformed into information within the Information Model. We don't do that in this phase. We only catalogue facts within the Requirements Model. Facts with a context and/or relation become information. We discuss the Information Model in greater detail later, but for now let's look at the Requirements Model.

Apart from being an expert on linguistics, building a Requirements Model is difficult. We want to parse both the business requirements and the user requirements. In the business rambling both the user and business requirements are combined. Where do you start? Probably with a high-level list of business functions and then add sentences to that. User requirements are combined with business requirements in business rambling. Once the rambling is complete, we can start construction of a requirements model by defining tables in which to save our information. Just as with the business scope model, there is no limit to the amount of information to be stored in the requirements model. At a minimum, this database should have a derived requirements table and a ramblings table as described in Tables 41-5 and 41-6.

TABLE 41-5 RAMBLING TABLE DEFINITION

Attribute	*Data Type*	*Description*
Identifier	Counter	
Reference	Text	Referenced location within the business rambling text.
Rambling	Text	User supplied statement.

TABLE 41-6 REQUIREMENTS TABLE DEFINITION		
ATTRIBUTE	*DATA TYPE*	*DESCRIPTION*
Identifier	Counter	
Reference	Text	Foreign key.
DerivedSentence	Text	
SentenceIdentifier	Number	Unique. Assigned when derived sentence is accepted. There may be derived sentences that are not accepted. No SentenceIdentifier is assigned for those cases.
Type	Text	Rule type. One of Definition, Fact, Constraint, Derivation, or Implementation.
Reasoning	Text	The analytical reason for accepting or rejecting the derived sentence.

Our analysis of a business rule is very informal; in fact, one of the listed types is not a rule type, but a *How* identifier. Implementation techniques have no place in data-modeling, but they are a hot button with users. This allows easy tracking of the implementation requirements.

These are the rule types as defined within the requirements table. Note that all of them are not business rules, but we declare then as pseudo-rules so we can track all the requirements of the original business rambling. The Requirements Model serves two purposes. The first is as the repository for distilled business rules from the business rambling and the second is to track all issues identified in the business rambling, even if they are not business rules. I offer the following informal business rule categories (feel free to augment these with categories of your own):

- *Definitions* — These will eventually be entities, but for the requirement model they remain definitions.

- *Facts* — Fact business rules may represent connections between definitions or between a definition and attributes.

- *Constraints* — Constraints are mandatory. The condition must be satisfied. "A new client cannot be invoiced for more than $1,000" is an example of a constraint. Constraints as defined here could be, but are not necessarily referential integrity constraints.

- *Inferences/derivations* — This is really a form of a not required constraint. Typical usage might be with "If . . . Then . . .".

- *Implementation (pseudorule)* — This is really not a business rule, but it is an implementation technique. Declaring implementation techniques as informal rules just gives us some way to track them. I am sure you have talked to clients who say, "Yeah, I want a combo box here and a list box over there." Because it is a tracking issue, an implementation technique can be placed in the business requirements model.

- *Process, strategy, asset, or goal (pseudorules)* — These are not business rules, but they are essential elements of a Business Scope Model.

So far we've defined two models: the Business Scope Model and the Business Requirements Model. These models are logically linked to enable tracking.

DISTILLING THE ESSENCE

We've identified the repositories for the business rambling distillation and described the recommended minimal information content. This section provides some guidelines on the distillation and a presentation of the distillation rules. The section closes with a distillation of a few ramblings from the business rambling presented earlier in this chapter.

Distilling the essence of the user-supplied specifications requires significant skill. The ultimate reward is a specification in which:

- The Requirements Model will be business driven.

- Requirements are stated in business terms and not implementation terms.

- It is an unambiguous specification of what is wanted, and not what currently exists.

Unfortunately, these goals listed are still not clear. This is because the enterprise owner, the data modeler, the user, and the programmer/analyst all view the model differently. More than one business rambling may be necessary: one from the enterprise ownership perspective and the other from the user perspective. We only step through the process of analyzing a business rambling once. Additional specifications are applied to the same model because it represents another view of the same business process.

Distillation Guidelines

Viewed casually, the user-supplied specification of the business rambling appears reasonable. However, when looked at closely we find that the business processes are not understood. In particular, near the beginning of the specification a reference to *codicil* is made. This is wrong for a business because a *codicil* is a legal instrument for a will.

There are also too many unanswered questions. This is an indicator that the business process does not yet exist in a manual form. I learned many years ago that if you don't have a good manual system, computerizing the process will not solve the problems.

There are many references to the *how* and this project can be looked upon as an experiment. A good manual system did not exist and the business processes were incomplete.

Are there guidelines that will help us? Yes. Consider these:

1. ***Understand the enterprise.*** You must understand enterprise operations and processes to distill the business rambling accurately. Take it upon yourself to understand the enterprise operations. Always crosscheck your information with more than one source. No single individual always has a complete understanding of all the processes within an enterprise. As demonstrated in the client specification in the business rambling, enterprise operations are not always clearly understood by employees within the enterprise, even when they are in responsible positions. A vice president supplied this rambling.

   I stated in the last chapter that constructing a model of enterprise processes is not possible unless the enterprise processes are understood. A potential problem occurs when the proposed business process does not yet exist and there is no business process model upon which to rely. This issue is addressed in rule 3 below.

2. ***Understand the objectives.*** Clearly understand the objectives or goal of the required task. Go as high as possible within the enterprise to determine the source for the requirement. The CEO may only want one number on a report at the end of the month, but as it filters down through departments, more baggage is added. The original goal becomes obscured and the project may fail because of other infrastructure issues.

3. ***Understand your probabilities for success.*** After you understand the enterprise operations and the stated goal or objective for the endeavor, ask these questions:

- Is there a manual system that the new project replaces? If there is a bad manual system, then computerizing it won't solve any problems. A bad system is always a bad system. A good rule of thumb is that system implementations of bad business process models inevitably fail. Build a good business process first, even if it is manual before attempting a computer-system implementation.

- Is this type of project common within the industry? When you are a pioneer there are always unanticipated problems that threaten the project.

- Has this project been attempted before within the enterprise? Analyze the reason for failure. The real reasons are never obvious and may surprise you.

- What is the success rate for this type of project? If the proposed system is high-risk, why do it unless the life of the corporation is at stake.

- Is the new system a replacement for an existing system? If so, what are the differences in business processes? There is a significant advantage when the business processes are already in place.

4. ***Understand the resource requirements.*** This is an antirule when analyzing the user-supplied specification. Resource requirements are only addressed after the system is designed. One of the more common mistakes is for management to direct that a business process be implemented on existing facilities.

Issues such as five-year business plans are often not considered when implementing WinTel-class systems. What I find amazing is that WinTel-class systems are implemented on an architecture whose growth potential is stated as an aspiration. The WinTel systems are implemented on the blind faith that a faster and bigger box will always be available. If I were a CEO, I would consider it a serious mistake to implement a system that utilizes one hundred percent of an existing architecture and to have future expansions based on aspirations and possibly unreal expectations. Microsoft promises scalability of enterprise applications with a tiered architecture that is a software approach to scalability. The tiered architecture concept holds promise, but the maelstrom of change represented by a component architecture, and the unreliability of Microsoft software, makes a tiered architecture questionable.

An example of a limited architecture is the Compaq Proliant, which is currently the leader in Intel-class boxes for the enterprise. The limit of the Compaq Proliant architecture is where the architecture of the Digital Equipment Corporation Alpha starts.

If the project has been done before, what are the resource requirements? Are there enough resources for the project? This is a very difficult issue. Enterprises have been know to reach too far in building a system and ended up with no funds for ongoing maintenance.

In summary, the project has a high probability of failure when:

- The business processes are not understood when defining the system.

- A Business Model is not constructed before the system is implemented.

- An incomplete Business Model is constructed, which still results in system failure.

- The new system is defined in terms of current resources that are often inadequate. When a system is defined in terms of current resources available, other aspects of the system may not be analyzed at all.

If you followed the steps above, you completed a feasibility study. Management wants the project and the key questions have been answered. The probability for success is reasonable because the resource requirements are not yet known. The next task is to build the Requirements Model and Business Scope Model from a business rambling.

Distillation Rules

I now define informal business rule categorizations. These definitions are quite informal, and new rule types may be added as desired.

The analysis starts by looking at the ramblings that can generate information. A compound rambling is parsed until the rambling is stated as a single sentence that represents a single issue. The sentence must always be stated in business terms and never in implementation terms. The resulting sentence is then categorized as to its content. Sentences are categorized as follows:

- Sentences that contain facts, business terms, or definitions.

- Sentences that identify connections between singular terms. Don't associate a fact with a context yet, but only identify business terms that are related.

- Sentences that identify business rules or policies and that will be constraints upon the business practice.

- Sentences that identify actions or processes.

- Sentences that deal with the infrastructure of implementation of the solution.

   Sentences are constructed in accord these rules:

- Sentences must be atomic and address only one issue such as a fact, definition, constraint, or condition.

- Sentences must not be redundant.

- Sentences must be declarative. Inferred entities are explicitly identified.

- Sentences must be expressed in business terms and not database or implementation terms.

- Sentences must be consistent with each other.

- Sentences must be expressed precisely in terms of other aspects of the data/knowledge environment.

   I enumerate the possible contents of sentences below at the risk of confusing you. Yes, entities do exist within sentences. At this time we only wish to record the business rambling text along with the distilled sentence in the rambling table and requirements table, respectively. Later, when building the information model, we return and examine the rule types and make decisions on entities and attributes. For now, here is the what to expect in a sentence:

- *Entities* — We have a very poor model if it doesn't have any entities. Entities are abstractions of real-world things and are different than real-world things. Entities within a model are only abstractions. An entity may be a person, concept, place, event, or thing. It has lasting value and data about it can be stored. It can be uniquely identified.

- *Inferred entities* — These are entities that are not referenced directly but whose existence may be inferred from context.

- *Entity instances* — There is a difference between an instance of an entity and the entity. Spot the dog is an instance of the entity dog.

- *Attributes* — Attributes describe a specific occurrence of the data (instance). Quite often these are confused with entities. Be careful in your analysis. The list below includes attributes, entities, entity instances, and relationships as *a, e, ei,* and *r,* respectively. Note the differences between each.

animal — *e,ei*	fruit — *e,ei*	mineral — *e,ei*
cabbabe — *ei*	dog — *e,ei*	dog named Spot — *ei*
selling — *r*	car type — *a*	car door — *e,ei*
salesperson — *e*	owner — *e*	Joe the owner — *ei*

- *Implementation techniques* — This is the *how* we discussed above. It falls into the area of user requirements and should not color our thinking. I always give this topic special attention because it is usually a client hot button. Sift out all the implementation issues. They are really not part of the model, but they are important to the user and must be addressed. We can't afford to overlook them or our user will consider us unresponsive. Even though we categorize implementation issues, we must not let them color our thinking or they will confuse the issues.

Parsing the Business Rambling

Let's use the business rambling of presented earlier in this chapter from ABC Corporation to start the construction of our Requirements Model. We build the model by stating the value of each field in the different tables as we progress. The distillation below steps through the first few lines of the business rambling. We are fortunate in that most sentences are already atomic and decomposition isn't necessary. Study the example distillation in Listing 41-1 carefully. Note the inferences that are made. Note also that other interpretations are possible. The goal of the distillation process is context-free facts that are unencumbered with resource issues or implementation techniques. The syntax of the notation is *Model.Table.Field*. The syntax *.Field* assumes the previous model and table. Information is being placed in both the rambling table and requirements table. Table 41-7 represents the distillation of the first five statements of the business rambling.

TABLE 41-7 A PARTIAL DISTILLATION OF LISTING 46-1, THE BUSINESS RAMBLING

MODEL.TABLE.ATTRIBUTE	*VALUE*
ReqModel.Rambling.Reference	I
.Rambling	Areas to track.

continued

TABLE 41-7 *(continued)*	
MODEL.TABLE.ATTRIBUTE	*VALUE*
ReqModel.Requirements.Reference	I
.DerivedSentence	Active contracts exist.
.SentenceIdentifier	1
.Type	Definition.
.Reasoning	Tracking infers that there are active contracts.
.Reference	I
.DerivedSentence	Related contracts exist.
.SentenceIdentifier	2
.Type	Fact.
.Reasoning	An area isn't very specific, so there must be related contracts.
ReqModel.Rambling.Reference	I A
.Rambling	Name on the current folder and in the current list.
ReqModel.Requirements.Reference	I A
.DerivedSentence	Active contracts exist.
.SentenceIdentifier	
.Type	Fact.
.Reasoning	A current list is probably a list of active contracts. The sentence is rejected because it is redundant under rule 2 and SentenceIdentifier 1.
ReqModel.Requirements.Reference	I A
.DerivedSentence	Related contracts exist.
.SentenceIdentifier	
.Type	Fact.
.Reasoning	In doing business with another entity, related contracts are kept in the same file folder. A single contract does not require a folder. Rule 2 and SentenceIdentifier1 reject the sentence.
ReqModel.Rambling.Reference	I B
.Rambling	Link to other contracts. Do we really want or need this? Is it too difficult to do?

MODEL.TABLE.ATTRIBUTE	VALUE
ReqModel.Requirements.Reference	I B
.DerivedSentence	Related contracts exist.
.SentenceIdentifier	
.Type	Fact.
.Reasoning	Redundant under rule 2 and SentenceIdentifier 2.
ReqModel.RamblingReference	I B 1
.Rambling	By name?
ReqModel.Requirements.Reference	I B 1
.DerivedSentence	Contract is identified by name.
.SentenceIdentifier	3
.Type	Fact.
.Reasoning	This is a fact, but eventually it will become an entity attribute.
ReqModel.Rambling.Reference	I B 2
.Rambling	By tracking number.
ReqModel.Requirements.Reference	I B 2
.DerivedSentence	Contract is identified by number.
.SentenceIdentifier	4
.Type	Fact.
.Reasoning	This is a fact that eventually will become an entity attribute.

What have we collected so far from paragraph I of the business rambling? Only the first four sentences listed below. Continuing on derives additional sentences, but the sentences listed below do not constitute a complete list for the business rambling.

Some derived sentences from the business rambling presented earlier:

1. Active contracts exist.

2. Related contracts exist.

3. Contract is identified by name.

4. Contract is identified by number.

5. Group-related contracts.

6. Contract group has a name.

7. Contract party exists.

8. Contract other party exists.

9. Party has address.

10. Other party has address.

11. Real estate contracts exist.

12. Party is a principal.

13. Other party is a principal.

14. Purchase contracts exist.

15. Contract has status.

16. Expired contracts exist.

17. Expired contracts have disposition.

Unfortunately, analyzing paragraph I of the business rambling yielded no Business Scope Model entries. Quite a few of the later rambling entries are candidates for the Business Scope Model, including:

- XIX A 1: Who can sign the contract?
- XIX A 2: What is the approval process?
- XIX A 3: What is the dollar limit for each signatory?

The first and last ramblings are constraints while the second rambling qualifies as a process. These are left as an exercise for you.

We have completed the Requirements Model and now we move to the Business Model in the Zachman Framework. This is where ERD and the Business Rules Model are constructed.

APPLYING THE DISTILLATION

The issue of parsing the business rambling is to obtain facts, definitions, derivations, and constraints that are context-free. The task is not easy because the English language is not context-free. One wishes for a context-free grammar such as used in computer compiler language theory, but such a language is useless to users.

The goal of the parsing phase is to collect the facts in a context-free manner. Here we'll return to the requirements model and analyze each fact, definition, derivation, and constraint. During this review we'll build the Business Rules Model. Output from the Rules Model creates an ERD. The general data flow is shown in Figure 41-3.

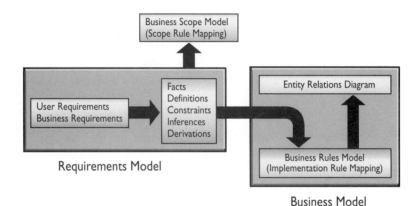

FIGURE 41-3   The requirements model and business model relationship.

Just in case I didn't make the point clear, let me state again that the parsing phase (building the requirements model) is completed before construction of the Business Rules Model is started.

The output of the Business Rules Model completes the distillation phases of building the application model. The output of the Business Rules Model can be directed to a commercial tool and the Key-based Model, Fully Attributed Model, and Transform Model can be generated directly.

Business Rules Model

This is one of the more important models. This model holds all the fact and definition business rules that eventually become either attributes or entities in the entity relationship diagram. The model is represented as a table in a relational database.

Each entry fact or definition entry in this table should parallel an entry in the ERD. Feel free to add anything you wish to the list that will be helpful to you. The table below can be your starting point. The attributes currently defined in Table 41-8 are essential, but others can be added as necessary.

TABLE 41-8 BUSINESS RULES

ATTRIBUTE IDENTIFIER	*DATA TYPE COUNTER*	*DESCRIPTION*
Reference	Text	Foreign key. Link to rambling entry in the rambling table.
EntityDescription	Text	
UniqueIdentifier	Text	Entity or attribute name.
BusinessExamples	Text	Examples of usage.
Comments	Text	Any comments necessary for a complete history.
UnderlyingAssumptions	Text	Assumptions of how used in the enterprise. This may change slowly with time, so the original assumptions are very important.
Type	Text	Rule type. One of Definition, Fact, Constraint, or Derivation. Pseudo-rules do not appear here.

There are several critically important issues here. The first is to document business examples of how the entity is used and where it is used. The second issue is that of identifying and documenting the underlying assumptions. Programs always have two contexts, explicit and implicit. Analyzing the program structure can derive the explicit context. The implicit context is all too often not stated in any program notes and may change with time. Programmers, given enough pressure, will document a program. This quite often isn't enough because they typically document what the program does. The data model is rarely documented, and what documentation that does exist may be buried within a program, which is where a programmer might look for it. There may be some hidden assumptions about the entity. Put that information here. It will be invaluable for maintenance at some future date. (For those who have some legacy experience, this is somewhat analogous to a data dictionary or a data repository on the mainframe.)

When the Distillation Is Complete

One can't take a distillation and proceed to build a system. We've discussed the distillation in terms of a single *business rambling*. There should be more than one rambling if the system has a reasonable size. Each of these ramblings must be distilled. When all distillations are complete, the business model is formally documented. The business analysts report back to the user with a formal statement of the business. The user either states that "yes, that is the correct business model," or he amends his rambling. It is easy to derail a context free distillation with a few hurried questions. It is very important to not ask any questions at this stage. Questions will lead the user and everything must be stated in business terms and not implementation terms. Remember that the user will attain additional insight as the system is being built. You need an initial Business Model that is extremely accurate, since the project scope will creep as the user attains further insight.

All of this sounds fanciful, and to some degree it is. The context of the distillation made no mention of either turf wars or local politics. This will happen. Either return to the top and distill any amendments to the rambling, or continue with the next section and build the data model.

Entity Relationship Diagrams

Let's pause here. You'll want to go back to a previous section ("Distillation Rules") and review the definition of an entity. I placed the definitions there as an admonishment to not consider them during the distillation phase.

DON'T DEPLOY YOUR OBJECTS TOO EARLY

Entities will be your business objects. How the objects are dispersed on the network depends upon the data model. Business rule objects represent the middle tier and can exist at the data source or on business rule servers. Client services exist at the client site while data services exist at the data source.

As you build the entities, don't consider where they will be placed. Your first implementation could quite possibly be a traditional two-tier system. After the system is operation, it can be migrated to multiple tiers. I say this because a very large and elegant system failed recently. It was seven tiers with a very nice design. The basic problem was that the system was deployed before it was complete. As changes were added to the system, new components had to be registered. It took three full-time individuals to maintain object registration. There were too many errors and the complexity was overwhelming. The jury is still out on tiered architectures.

The following list defines the structural properties of a relation. This formal definition of a relation is introduced before the graphical ERD. The graphical ERD oversimplifies a relation and does not accurately portray all properties of a relation.

Structural properties of a relation:

1. Columns represent fields, and each column has a unique name.

2. Each column contains data of the same type; that is, the data is homogeneous.

3. Each column has a domain. This is the set of possible values that can be used in a column.

4. A row is a record. It is also called an *n*-tuple if there are *n* columns.

5. The order of the rows and columns is unimportant.

6. No duplicate rows are allowed. This is not to be confused with *resultsets,* which may have duplicate rows.

7. *Repeating groups* are not allowed. All values are scalar or atomic.

8. A *candidate key* is an attribute or a set of attributes that uniquely identify a row. A candidate key must uniquely identify a row and have the *non-redundancy* property. If a key is *nonredundant*, then no attribute in the key may be discarded without destroying the unique identification property of the key.

9. A primary *key* is a candidate key selected as the unique identifier. Each relation must have a primary key.

10. A *superkey* is any set of attributes that identifies a row. The *non-redundancy* property is not required for a *superkey*. Another name for *superkey* is *natural key.*

11. A *foreign key* is an attribute that appears as a nonkey attribute in one relation and as a *primary key* in another relation.

12. A *composite key* contains more than one attribute.

13. A *relational schema* is a set of attributes, dependencies, and constraints that characterize a relation.

14. An *instance* is a set of rows that populate the *relation*. An update to the *relation* is valid only if all dependencies and constraints are honored.

We now know the properties of a relation and we need a notation to represent the relation. Assume a table with two columns: *A* and *B*. We'll use the notation R(A, B) for the relation where *A* and *B* are the column names in a two-dimensional table and no structural properties of Table 41-10 are violated.

 A data table is not always a relation. An example is a table with a duplicate row.

Let's move on to the construction of an ERD. We have the formal definition of a relation in our pocket and won't be seduced by the simplicity of a diagram. Within the application model I have defined, the ERD is not a standalone model. It is very closely coupled with the business rules model. I did this because there is additional information I wished to capture, such as assumptions, examples of usage, reasoning, and comments. Commercial ERD tools function as standalone models and capturing historical information is not always on their agenda. This explains the maintained between the Business Rules Model and the ERD.

There are numerous tools on the market that can be used to create an ERD. Most data-modeling tools have the capability to create an IDEF1X ERD. I describe the IDEF1X ERD briefly and then show you how to construct one of your own without using a commercial tool. Your company may own a tool such as ERWIN, which costs about $3,000, but that is too much for a small business.

IDEF1X Entity Perspective

The Requirements Model is complete. We have all the business rules and possibly some pseudorules. All rules were placed in the Requirements Model. Rules that mapped to business scope issues are placed in the Business Scope Model, while rules that mapped to business rule implementations are placed in the Business Rules Model. However, we only have facts and definitions. Moving to the Business Model, we will turn facts and definitions into information. We do that with relations. Before we can do that, let's look at the IDEF1X definition of a relation in Figure 41-4.

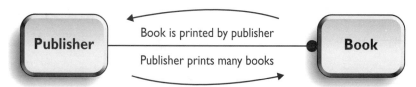

FIGURE 41-4   IDEF1X relationship representation for a publisher that prints books.

From the IDEF1X representation we can discern these business rules:

o **Definition** — Publisher exists.

o **Definition** — Books exist.

o **Fact** — Publisher prints many books.

o **Fact** — Book is printed by publisher.

We see that an IDEF1X relation is a collection of requirements model business rules, in particular definitions and facts. Facts are nothing more than facts until they are associated with definitions. *Book* and *Publisher* are entities within IDEF1X scheme and are definitions in the requirements model. Combining facts and definitions yields a relationship and information.

IDEF1X entities may have unique characteristics and can be classified as follows (symbolic representations of IDEF1X entities are also shown):

o **Independent entity** — An entity that is not dependent upon another entity. It is sometimes referred to as a Kernel entity.

o **Characteristic entity** — A characteristic entity is a group of attributes that occurs many times for an entity. An example is the many sides of a one-to-many relation. The parent entity may be an independent entity, a category entity, an associative entity, or another characteristic entity. The independent entity and the characteristic entity of Figure 41-5 represent a one-to-many relationship.

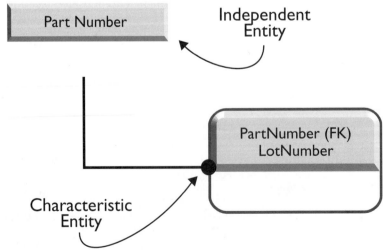

FIGURE 41-5   An independent entity and a characteristic entity.

o *Associative entity* — An associative entity (there is an association) is an entity that inherits its primary keys from two or more entities. This is the mechanism used to resolve what is referred to as a "many-to-many" relationship. Figure 41-6 illustrates two independent entities and an associative entity.

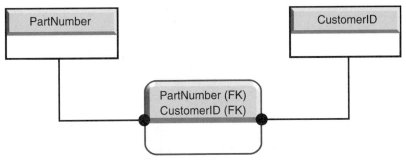

FIGURE 41-6   An associative entity with two independent entities.

o *Category entity* — A category entity is a subset of instances of a generic parent. A *generalization hierarchy* is formed by a category entity. A *category discriminator* is the code that distinguishes the different instances of a generic parent. In Figure 41-7, account *type* is the *category discriminator.*

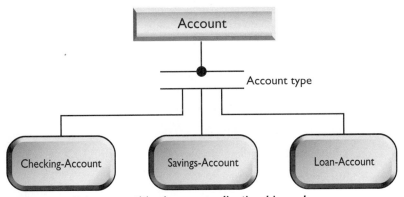

FIGURE 41-7   Category entities in a generalization hierarchy.

Rolling our own ERD

For the definition of a relation, there is the primary definition and the inverse definition. For those of you without a commercial tool for building entity relationship diagrams (ERDs), I'll show you how to make your own, which will have the same characteristics as an IDEF1X ERD. Because this is a manual process, with a large number of entities it isn't feasible to build your own. The concept is very simple. Create an N x N symmetric matrix where each column and row contains the same entity as illustrated below.

Figure 41-8 clearly identifies the two main features of an ERD: the cardinality and the relationships. Using the ERD of Figure 41-8, the business rules along with the cardinality are stated in the following list. Note that nothing is entered on the diagonal.

	Publisher	Author	Book	Employees
Publisher		Pays 1-M	Prints 1-M	Employs 1-M
Author	Is Paid By 1-1		Writes 1-M	
Book	Is Printed By 1-1	Is Written By 1-M		
Employee	Is employed by publisher 1-1			

FIGURE 41-8   A manual ERD of a very small business model.

The business rules of Figure 41-8:

1. Publisher pays many authors.

2. Publisher prints many books.

3. Publisher employs many employees.

4. Author is paid by publisher.

5. Author writes many books.

6. Book is printed by publisher.

7. Book is written by many authors (coauthors).

8. Employee is employed by publisher.

These business rules were applied to a commercial data-modeling tool. The tool is limited to the verb *has* and the results appear in Figure 41-9, which appears to be a distortion of the ERD in Figure 41-8. That is not completely true and the original entities remain; however, the business rule *Publisher pays authors* becomes *Publisher has* authors. Other business rules are also changed. Content is lost. The issue here is that commercial modeling tools are useful in creating the Key-based Model, the Fully Attributed Model, and the Transform Model of Figure 41-1. Commercial modeling tools cannot accurately model the Business Scope Model, the Requirements Model, or the Business Rules Model of Figure 41-1. A commercial modeling tool is not the panacea for all modeling needs. Figure 41-9 illustrates the ERD of Figure 41-8 with lost content.

	Publisher	Author	Book	Employees
Publisher		Has 1-M	Has 1-M	Has 1-M
Author	Has 1-1		Has 1-M	
Book	Has 1-1	Has 1-M		
Employee	Has 1-1			

FIGURE 41-9   An ERD with lost content.

I close this section on ERD by presenting two Microsoft visual modeling aids. Figure 41-10 is presented in Access 97 by opening the `Northwind` database and selecting *Relationships* from the **Tools** menu. Starting Microsoft Visual Modeler and opening the sample model located in the Visual Modeler path . . . `\SAMPLES\ORDERSYSTEM\ORDERSYS.MDL` creates Figure 41-11.

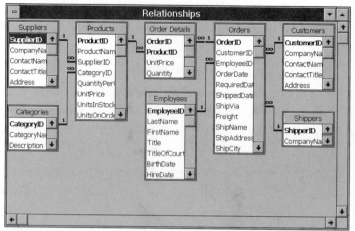

FIGURE 41-10   The Microsoft Access Northwind database relationships.

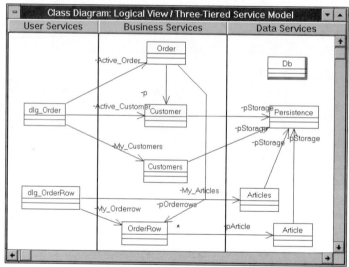

FIGURE 41-11   The three-tiered architecture as viewed from Microsoft Visual Modeler.

BUILDING THE KEY-BASED MODEL

As we traverse the Augmented Zachman Framework of Figure 41-1, the *key-based model* (KBM) is next. The KBM will be constructed from the ERD we defined previously; however, the defined database must be in third normal form (3NF) to qualify as a KBM. We do not add attributes when constructing the KBM, only the primary keys. We only want to create the relationships between all the entities. Building a database is an iterative approach and adding the attributes before they are needed clouds the issues. This approach compartmentalizes normalization into two phases: normalizing the underlying database structure and normalizing the enhanced structure when attributes are added. The data normalization that occurs in the first phase is best for the base structure. When this phase is finished and you move to the next phase, the Fully Attributed Model, you may have to do additional normalization when the attributes are added.

Functional Dependence

A database cannot be normalized unless the Business Model is understood. Figure 41-9 is an example of lost content. Functional dependency requires an understanding of the business process and functional dependency is the tool for normalizing a database. Function dependency is when something *depends on* something else. This relationship may not be inferred accurately when content is missing such as in Figure 41-9. Nearly all developers use an intuitive approach, but this approach fails when faced with complex normalization issues. The intuitive approach works well if you're very experienced. The intuitive approach also works very well when you are designing a new database. The major problems occur when trying to access legacy databases that were implemented as flat-file structures with no normalization considerations.

The problems of normalization and functional dependency centers on the ambiguous nature of the English language and the fact that statements are not context-free. As an example, I had a difficult time with one of my many editors earlier in the book in the Component Technology section. I had a sentence, which read in part: . . . *acquires a pointer (the transfer protocol) to* . . .. Within the context of the dialog, the sentence is precisely correct. The editor proceeded to restructure the sentence. I couldn't understand why until I realized that I had a noun synonym for a verb. There is nothing that I could do.

Functional dependence between attributes in a relation is not unlike functional dependence in mathematics. In the equation $y = x^2 - 2x - x$, we can say that y *depends on* x. x is the independent variable and y is the dependent variable. But functional dependence is not limited to mathematics. Table 41-9 illustrates the concept of functional dependency.

TABLE 41-9 ILLUSTRATING FUNCTIONAL DEPENDENCY WITH AIRPORTS AND CITIES	
AIRPORT NAME	*CITY*
SeaTac	Seattle/Tacoma
Stapleton	Denver
J. F. Kennedy	New York
LaGuardia	New York
LAX	Los Angeles
Portland International	Portland

Airport names are unique, but more than one airport is identified with a city. We can state that city *depends on* name, but name *does not depend on* city. Functional dependence is the key database design tool. As later examples show, primary key determination uses functional dependence.

We need to adopt a notation for functional dependence. We can use mathematical notation for our example above and state city = f(name). I prefer instead to use the notation Airport Name → City, or City depends on Airport Name.

Defining a schema

We have defined a relation (see Table 41-10 and the immediately following paragraph) and a functional dependence. If we combine a relation with a functional dependence, we have a schema. A schema is a relation and the related dependencies and constraints. The schema for our example above is:

R (Airport Name, City), Airport Name → City

Functional dependency inference axioms

A set of functional dependency inference axioms were developed by W. W. Armstrong ("Dependency Structures of Database Relationships," Proceedings, IFIP Congress 1974) and by C. Berri, R. Fagin, and J. H. Howard ("A Complete Axiomatization for Functional and Multivalued Dependencies in Database Relations," Proceedings 1977 ACM SIGMOD International Conference on Management of Data, Toronto, August 1977). These axioms are not on the Windows Architecture examinations, but the axioms are tools that are used in the normalization process. All possible functional dependencies implied by a given set can be generated using these axioms:

o *Reflexivity rule* — If B is a subset of A then A → B. A → A is also implied.

o *Augmentation rule* — If A → B, then AC → BC.

o *Transitivity rule* — If A → B and B → C, then A → C.

o *Union rule* — If A → B and A → C, then A → BC.

o *Decomposition (projection) rule* — If A → C, then A → B where B is a subset of C; or restated as if A → BC then A → B and A → C.

o *Composition rule* — If A → B and C → D, then AC → BD.

o *Pseudotransitivity rule* — If A → B and CB → D, then AC → D.

Rules 1, 2, and 3 are derived from the definition of functional dependence. Rules 4, 5, 6, and 7 are derived from rules 1, 2, and 3.

Finding candidate keys and superkeys with functional dependence

Our discussion now focuses on finding candidate keys and superkeys using functional dependency. This is not an issue for the Key-based Model that contains only primary keys. A Key-based Model only exists if a new database is being constructed. The techniques outlined here using functional dependency fall within the realm of constructing the Fully Attributed Model. I need a vehicle to demonstrate functional dependence, which is used in all normalization steps. These steps can be loosely categorized as:

o Removing groups of repeating data.

o Removing duplicate data.

o Removing columns of a table that do not depend on the primary key.

o Placing independent multiple relationships in separate tables.

o Placing dependent multiple relationships in separate tables.

We'll always use succinct notation. These rules are guides to the notation issues:

o Rather than spelling out a table name, <Rn> is used to indicate a relation. When the table is not a relation or is unknown, a superscript notation is used. For R^{maybe} indicates that the table may not be a relation.

- Functional dependencies are indicated as FD.

- Single uppercase letters indicates columns in a table. Occasionally a superscript will be used to illustrate an issue. An example is $B^{repeats}$. The reader should know immediately that the attribute violates first normal form.

- The primary key of a relation is always underlined. When no underline exists, the primary key has not yet been selected even though one may exist. Consider the relation R(<u>A</u>, B). A is the primary key and B depends upon A.

Let's move on and use our notation and the new notion of functional dependence. The Armstrong axioms have an immediate and practical consequence for key selection. A relation R with attributes A, B, C, D and the functional dependencies illustrate this:

$$A \rightarrow D$$

$$CD \rightarrow B$$

$$AD \rightarrow C$$

This example is artificial and only serves to illustrate the issue. Before proceeding, several definitions must be made so we can understand the objective. These definitions are a repeat of Table 41-10 (structural properties of a relation).

- *Superkey* — An attribute or set of attributes that identify an entity uniquely.

- *Candidate key* — A candidate key is a superkey such that no proper subset of its attributes is itself a superkey.

- *Primary key* — A candidate key that is used to identify tuples (rows) in a relation.

Our interest is in determining candidate keys. We have three choices for a candidate key: A, CD, and AD. We look first at AD to see if it is a candidate key. To do that, we want to compute AD^+ using the following algorithm. The algorithm is iterative, and as long as the result set changes, it loops until there are no further result set changes. The term *determinant* is what is depended on. A is the *determinant* and B is the *dependent* for the functional dependency $A \rightarrow B$.

To determine candidate keys, follow these steps:

1. Initialize the algorithm and place AD in the result set. The selection of the determinant to place in the result set is not arbitrary. We must apply this algorithm to all determinants.

2. Look at the FDs. Is there a FD whose determinant is in the result set? We find that there is a FD whose determinant is in the result set with $AD \to C$. Augment the result set with C. AD is in the result set because we initialized it with AD.

3. Look at the FDs again. The result set is now ACD. Is there another FD whose determinant is found in the result set? The answer is yes, $CD \to B$. Augment the result set with B. The result set AD^+ now contains all attributes of R and we conclude that AD is a superkey.

We have found one superkey. To find the next superkey, we'll need to compute A^+. To do that, we'll use the same algorithm we used above.

1. Assign A to the result set A^+.

2. Look for an FD whose determinant is contained in the result set. We find one in $A \to D$. Augment the result set with D. A^+ now contains AD.

3. Search the FDs for a determinant that is contained in the result set. We find one in $AD \to C$. Augment the result set with C. A^+ now contains ACD.

4. Search the FDs again. $CD \to B$ is an FD whose determinant is contained A^+ so augment A^+ with B. All attributes of R are now in A^+. We conclude that A is a superkey because it has no proper subset that is also a superkey. A is also a candidate key.

AD was the first candidate key we found. We found another candidate key in A. We now know that AD is not a candidate key because the definition of a candidate key is that it has no proper subset of attributes that are superkeys. A is a superkey and is a proper subset of AD. AD still remains a candidate key; it is just not a superkey.

There is one last FD to consider in our search for a candidate key or superkey, the FD $CD \to B$.

1. Initialize CD^+ to CD.

2. Search for an FD whose determinant is contained in CD^+. We find one, $CD \to B$. Augment CD^+ with B.

3. Search for a FD whose determinant is contained in CD⁺. There isn't one, so we can conclude that CD is not a superkey because A is not contained in CD⁺ and therefore is not functionally dependent upon it.

Congratulations. You've just found your first candidate key and your first super key.

A minimal covering: removing redundant functional dependencies

We now have a technique for key determination, but we shouldn't apply our algorithm until a *minimal covering* is built; that is, we remove redundant FDs using the Armstrong axioms. To illustrate removing redundant FDs, consider the relation R with attributes A, B, C, D and FDs:

$A \rightarrow CD$

$A \rightarrow C$

$CD \rightarrow B$

$AD \rightarrow C$

Reducing by *decomposition* we now have:

$A \rightarrow C$

$A \rightarrow D$

$A \rightarrow C$

$CD \rightarrow B$

$AD \rightarrow C$

$A \rightarrow C$ is redundant and the FDs reduce to:

$A \rightarrow C$

$A \rightarrow D$

$CD \rightarrow B$

$AD \rightarrow C$

Let me digress for a moment from the business of removing redundant functional dependencies. A relational database supports the Select, Project, and Join operators. These are features of a relational database; flat-file systems do not support these operators. The decomposition above uses Armstrong Decomposition (axiom 5) but it is also the `Project` operator of a relational database. We'll use the `Project` operator in each of the normalization steps in the remainder of the chapter. This is the formal term; decomposition is the commonly used term.

After the FDs are reduced to a single term by decomposition, we can build the *irreducible* set. We do that with the following algorithm:

Pick an FD. Place the determinant of the selected FD in the result set, but remove that FD from the selection list. Search for a determinant whose value is in the result set. If one is found, include the dependent variable in the new result set. If at any time a determinant is found that is *not* in the result set, then it has been shown that the original dependent variable is not in the result set, and we can conclude that the FD under attack is not redundant. Using the FDs above, this is illustrated as:

1. Select the FD A→C and place A in the result set.

2. Remove the FD A→C from the selection list of candidates. This will be a non redundant FD, if after examining all FDs, the dependent variable is not found in the result set.

3. Locate another FD whose determinant is in the result set. We find the FD A→D. Place D in the result set that now contains AD.

4. Locate another FD whose determinant is in the result set. We find the FD AD→C. Place C in the result set which now contains ACD. However, this variable is the same dependent variable for the FD A→C. The conclusion is that A→C *is redundant* because C is in the result set.

5. Start again and select the FD A→D for evaluation. Place A in the result list and remove the FD from the list of FD candidates.

6. Select A→C because the determinant appears in the result set. Augment the result set so that it now contains AC. Then a search for a determinant that contains AC finds none. It is apparent that the FD A→D *is not redundant* because D is not in the result set.

7. Start again and select the FD CD→B to evaluate. Place CD in the result set.

8. Select a FD whose determinant is in the result set. There is none and the FD CD→B *is not redundant* because B is not in the result set.

9. Start again and select the FD AD→C to evaluate. Place AD in the result set and remove the FD AD→C from the selection list.

10. We find the determinant of A → D is in the result set. However, the dependent variable is already there, and because there are no other FDs with a determinant in the result set, the FD AD → C *is not redundant* because C is not in the result set. We didn't consider A → C because we already know it is redundant. It should also be obvious that A → C is equivalent to AD → C by augmentation (see the Armstrong axioms).

Practicing Recognizing Functional Dependency

Functional dependency is the tool we need to resolve normalization issues. Recognizing functional dependencies is critical and there are a few problems (with answers) that will test your functional dependence recognition skills. It is important that the concept of functional dependency be understood. How about some practice identifying a functional dependency? I used cities and airports in Table 41-9 when I initially introduced functional dependence. Now we'll just use columns of numbers. After all, getting dirty with the data is what it is all about.

We start first with Table 41-10. For part one of the question, identify all possible dependencies. For part two of the question, identify the invalid dependencies. The answers are below so don't peek.

TABLE 41-10 PROBLEM 1

A	B	C
3	5	2
5	5	4
7	5	4
9	4	8
11	2	10

The second problem is to identify all the valid dependencies in Table 41-11.

TABLE 41-11 PROBLEM 2

A	B	C
2	3	4
2	4	5
3	4	6
5	6	6
7	6	6

Our last problem is slightly different. Before you answer the question, go back and reread the 14 structural properties of a relation. Is Table 41-12 a relation?

TABLE 41-12 PROBLEM 3

A	B	C	D
6	7	9	10
2	11	4	3
4	8	21	16
36	23	8	19
6	7	9	10
5	3	2	1

Problem 1 answers: $a \rightarrow b$, $a \rightarrow c$, $ac \rightarrow b$, and $ab \rightarrow c$ are the only valid dependencies. All possible dependencies are $a \rightarrow b$, $a \rightarrow c$, $b \rightarrow a$, $b \rightarrow c$, $c \rightarrow a$, $c \rightarrow b$, $ab \rightarrow c$, $ac \rightarrow b$, $bc \rightarrow a$, $c \rightarrow ab$, $b \rightarrow ac$, and $a \rightarrow bc$.

Problem 2 answers: $ac \rightarrow b$ and $ab \rightarrow c$.

Problem 3 answer: No; rows 1 and 5 are duplicates.

Normalization

Using our newly acquired knowledge of functional dependencies and relations, we can make these statements:

- *First normal form* — All domains must contain atomic values only, be scalar, or contain no repeating groups.
- *Second normal form* — Each nonkey domain must be functionally dependent upon the primary key.
- *Third normal form* — Nonkey domains cannot be functionally dependent on any other nonkey values; transitive dependency.

To help you remember these rules, remember:

```
"The key,
the whole key,
and nothing but the key,
so help me Codd."
```

It pays homage to the inventor of relational database technology, Dr. E. F. Codd and is derived from:

"The rules leading to and including third normal form can be summed up in a single statement: Each attribute must be a fact about the key, the whole key, and nothing but the key." (*DB2 Design and Development Guide*, Wiorkowski and Kull.)

First normal form

First normal form (1NF) requires that all values be atomic or scalar. There are no repeating values. Let's start with the employee table in Table 41-13 that is not in 1NF.

TABLE 41-13 EMPLOYEE TABLE

ID	NAME	PAYDATE
1	Silly, Sally	10 Jan 1995
		10 Feb 1995
		10 March 1995

ID	NAME	PAYDATE
2	Doright, Dudley	10 Jan 1995
		10 Feb 1995
		10 March 1995

Although the personnel record contains more than just the three fields shown above, these three fields are enough to illustrate the issue. Also the repeated values may extend further, but the three values suffice. Recall that a table and a relation are equivalent if the 14 rules we discussed previously are satisfied. Although they are not satisfied in this illustration because rule 7 is violated for repeating groups, we'll describe the table in relation notation for now. Table 41-13 is not a relation, but we'll name it R and script it. The underscore indicates the primary key in our notation. Let's start by defining the relation in terms of the table attributes. The superscripts indicate that the **PayDate** attribute repeats and there is not yet a relation. I illustrate this relation this one time before moving to a succinct notation.

$\text{Relation}^{\text{Maybe}}(\underline{\text{ID}}, \text{Name}, \text{PayDate}^{\text{Repeat}})$.

We move to the succinct notation by using a synonym for the attributes (columns) we have:

$R^{\text{Maybe}}(\underline{I}, N, P^{\text{Repeat}})$.

A relation, the functional dependencies, and constraints determine a schema. There are no constraints here, but there is at least one dependency because there is a primary key, ID. What are the dependencies?

$I \rightarrow NP$ This is the primary key dependency.

So our schema is:

$R^{\text{Maybe}}(\underline{I}, N, P^{\text{Repeat}}), I \rightarrow NP^{\text{repeat}}$

Using decomposition (projection), the dependency $I \rightarrow NP^{\text{repeats}}$ is decomposed to $I \rightarrow N, I \rightarrow P^{\text{repeats}}$. The specific steps of the decomposition are shown below for Tables 41-14 and 41-15. Decomposition is used on all our normalization steps, so it's advantageous to note the decomposition strategies available.

- When the determinant of the dependency that is being decomposed is unique, the determinant becomes the primary key in the new child table and the primary key from the parent table becomes the foreign key in the new child table.

- When the determinant of the dependency is not unique, the primary key of the parent table and the determinant become the primary key in the new child table.

  The determinant in our example is not unique and that requires a projection of both the primary key and the determinant as the new primary key in the child table. Tables 41-14 and Table 41-15 illustrate the decomposition.

- Identify the repeating attribute within the parent relation. In our example, P is the attribute of interest.

  Table 41-14 is the newly created *PayDate* table.

TABLE 41-14 PAYDATE TABLE
PAYDATE
10 Jan 1995
10 Feb 1995
10 Mar 1995
10 Jan 1995
10 Feb 1995
10 Mar 1995

PayDate really isn't a relation yet, just a table. The rows are not unique but creating unique rows will transform the table into a relation. We have decomposed the parent table by removing a column from it. To relate the new table back to the parent table, we add the primary key of the parent relation (see Table 41-15). Attributes within a relation that are primary keys or another relation are foreign keys.

TABLE 41-15	PAYDATE TABLE
ID	**PAYDATE**
1	10 Jan 95
1	10 Feb 95
1	10 Mar 95
2	10 Jan 95
2	10 Feb 95
2	10 Mar 95

In the new *PayDate* table there are no functional dependencies. The table only has a primary key. Because each row is unique we can now call it a relation. We'll name the new relation R1 and provide the new schema. Note that we dropped the script on R because it now a relation.

R(I, N), I → N

R1(I, P)

Both relations are now in 1NF because no repeated values exist.

First normal form in database reengineering

At first glance, Table 41-15 appears to have a first normal form error. This type of normalization error is an example of what can be expected when normalizing legacy databases. *Amount* depends on *PayDate* and gives the appearance of a third normal form error; however, the dependency repeats. This is slightly different than 1NF where an attribute repeats. The solution is to use decomposition again and project the repeating dependency to a new child table.

The situation is actually a little more complicated than it appears at first glance. Note that *Amount* depends on *PayDate*, which is a violation of third normal form, something we haven't discussed yet. You might want to return to this example after reviewing the section below on third normal form. Third normal form corrects transitive dependencies of the form:

A → B, B → C yields the transitive dependency A → C.

Table 41-16 can loosely be classified as a repeating third normal form error; however, by applying a surrogate name to the repeating dependency, it can be treated as a 1NF error. The normalization error illustrated in Table 41-16 is also a form of multivalued dependency discussed below in the advanced normalization forms. We start with the example data of Table 41-16.

TABLE 41-16 EMPLOYEE TABLE

ID	NAME	PAYDATE	AMOUNT
1	Silly, Sally	10 Jan 1995	100
		10 Feb 1995	120
		10 March 1995	100
2	Doright, Dudley	10 Jan 1995	120
		10 Feb 1995	110
		10 March 1995	120

This is almost the same personnel record that we used earlier to illustrate the first 1NF example. All of the stated assumptions as to the use of this table are still in effect. Only the columns necessary to illustrate the issue are exposed. A table and a relation are equivalent if the 14 rules we discussed previously are satisfied. They are not met because rule 7 is violated with repeating groups.

This is a bit more complex than 1NF. To understand it, consider the dependency as a single new attribute with a surrogate name. After all, the definition of functional dependency is a one-many. Considering only the new surrogate name, it is nothing more than a repeating group that we discussed above. So it does indeed violate rule 7 by having repeating values.

We'll use the same relation notation that was used for 1NF to remind us that the table is not really a relation yet. As our reminder that it is not really a relation, we'll name it R and script it as we did for 1NF.

Relation^{Maybe}(<u>ID</u>, Name, PayDate^{repeat}, Amount^{repeats})

If we go a little further and use a synonym for the attributes (columns), we have the succinct notation:

R^{Maybe}(<u>I</u>, N, P^{repeats}, A^{repeats})

Filling in the dependencies we have as our schema:

$R^{Maybe}(\underline{I}, N, P, A), I \rightarrow NP, \{P \rightarrow A\}^{repeats}$

We'll use the *Project* operator to create the new relation and the *Join* operator of a relational database to access the new relation just as we did for the previous 1NF example. We create another table with the dependency and then add the primary key of the parent relation as a foreign key. Let's go through the steps to do that.

o Identify the attributes within the parent relation that are elements of the repeating dependency. In our example, NP is our dependency and the attributes of interest.

o Project the dependency $P \rightarrow A$ to the new *PayRecord* table as represented in Table 41-17.

TABLE 41-17 PAYRECORD TABLE

PayDate	Amount
10 Jan 1995	100
10 Feb 1995	120
10 Mar 1995	100
10 Jan 1995	120
10 Feb 1995	120
10 Mar 1995	120

o *PayRecord* like the table *PayDate* above really isn't a relation yet, just a table. The rows are not unique and creating unique rows will transform the table into a relation. We have decomposed the employee table by removing a dependency from it that consists of more than one attribute. To the new table we'll add the primary key of the parent relation (see Table 41-18). When the projected dependency is unique, project the primary key of the parent relation as the foreign key of the child relation. When the project dependency is not unique, project the primary key of the parent relation as a constituent of the primary key in the new child relation.

TABLE 41-18 PAYRECORD TABLE

ID	PayDate	Amount
1	10 Jan 1995	100
1	10 Feb 1995	120
1	10 Mar 1995	100
2	10 Jan 1995	120
2	10 Feb 1995	120
2	10 Mar 1995	120

In the new *PayRecord* table, there is only one functional dependency, which is $IP \rightarrow A$. Because each row is unique, we can now call it a relation. We'll name the new relation R1 and provide the new schema. Note that we dropped the script on R because it is now a relation.

R($\underline{I}$, N), $I \rightarrow N$

R1($\underline{I}$, $\underline{P}$, A) $IP \rightarrow A$

Both relations are now in 1NF with no repeated values.

Second normal form

A relation is in second normal form (2NF) when it is 1NF and all attributes fully depend on the whole key, not just a portion of it. The simple order detail record shown in Table 41-19 demonstrates this. Table 41-19 has attributes that do not depend upon the complete key.

TABLE 41-19 ITEM TABLE

OrderID	ItemID	Description	OrderDate	Quantity
1	1	Gadget	10 Jan 1995	100
1	2	Widget	10 Jan 1995	120
2	1	Toy	10 Jan 1995	120

We have the relation:

R(<u>OrderID</u>, <u>ItemID</u>, Description, OrderDate, Quantity)

OrderID → OrderDate, OrderID ItemID → Description Quantity

It is obvious that *OrderDate* is functionally dependent upon the order and not the order item. Moving this relation to a more succinct notation we have:

R(<u>A</u>, <u>B</u>, C, D, E) AB → CE, A → D

(where: A = OrderID; B = ItemID; C = Description; D = OrderDate; E = Quantity)

Our solution to this problem is to use the Armstrong's decomposition axiom to create a 2NF schema. We do this by projecting the FD A → D to a new relation. Our new schema becomes:

R(<u>A</u>, <u>B</u>, C, E) AB → CE

R1(<u>A</u>, D) A → D

Third normal form

A relation is in third normal form (3NF) when it is in 2NF and each nonkey attribute depends on the entire key and not another nonkey attribute. Restated, a relation is in 3NF if there are no transitive dependencies. A → B, B → C represents the transitive dependency A → C.

We'll use the 2NF normalization of Table 41-17 and augment the relation R slightly to create a third normal form error. Tables 41-20 and 41-21 represent the 2NF normalization of Table 41-17.

TABLE 41-20 PAYRECORD TABLE

ID	PAYDATE	AMOUNT
1	10 Jan 95	100
1	10 Feb 95	120
1	10 Mar 95	100
2	10 Jan 95	120
2	10 Feb 95	120
2	10 Mar 95	120

TABLE 41-21 EMPLOYEE TABLE	
ID	*NAME*
1	Silly, Sally
2	Doright, Dudley

Augmenting the *Employee* table slightly, we'll create a table that violates 3NF. *Rate* depends upon *Code* and not on the *ID* attribute.

TABLE 41-22 PAYRECORD TABLE		
ID	*PAYDATE*	*AMOUNT*
1	10 Jan 95	100
1	10 Feb 95	120
1	10 Mar 95	100
2	10 Jan 95	120
2	10 Feb 95	120
2	10 Mar 95	120
3	10 Jan 95	120
3	10 Feb 95	120
3	10 Mar 95	120

TABLE 41-23 EMPLOYEE TABLE			
ID	*NAME*	*CODE*	*RATE*
1	Silly, Sally	P	5
2	Doright, Dudley	T	4
3	Whiplash, Snidley	F	3

We start with the schema from the normalized Table 41-21:

R(I, N), I → N

R1(I, P, A) IP → A

That schema is augmented with the new attributes and the additional dependency:

R(I, N, C, R), I → NC, C → R

R1(I, P, A) IP → A

Decomposing (projecting) the C → R dependency into a new child table results in:

R(I, N, C), I → NC

R1(I, P, A) IP → A

R2(C, R) C → R

By now, I hope the benefits of functional notation are obvious.

Steps in Building the Key-based Model

Normalizing a database is an iterative process. We discussed 1NF, 2NF, and 3NF, which is all we need to build a KBM. The following procedure is offered as a guideline for building the Key-based Model. Remember that we are only building the base structure here. This means that attributes that are not keys or foreign keys are not included in the Key-based Model building process. Nonkey attributes are added during the construction of the Fully Attributed Model, which occurs in the next phase. Also recall that a KBM is only normalized through 3NF, so advanced normalization techniques are not yet applied.

- The first step is to define the attributes to be used as keys or foreign keys. You probably already know them from the Business Rules Model and the entity relationship diagram.
- Logically related attributes are grouped into relations.
- Candidate keys are identified for each relation.
- A primary key is selected for each relation.

- The relations are placed in 1NF by identifying and removing all repeating groups.

- Relations with identical foreign keys are combined. This is still 1NF. Look carefully at the primary keys because there may be synonyms.

- Continue the normalization process to 2NF by identifying all functional dependencies. Consider reviewing the "Functional Dependence" section above until you have more experience.

- Decompose (*project*) relations until each nonkey attribute is dependent on all the attributes in the key.

- Complete 2NF normalization by combining all relations with identical primary keys.

- Start 3NF normalization by identifying all transitive dependencies. You want to check for relations where one nonkey attribute depends on another nonkey attribute. Don't limit this checking to just nonkey attributes. Check for instances where an attribute in the key depends upon another attribute in the key.

- Decompose (*project*) relations until there are no transitive dependencies.

- Complete 3NF normalization by combining all relations with identical primary keys *as long as no transitive dependencies occur.*

Fully Attributed Model

Completing the Fully Attributed Model also completes the Zachman Framework. In this phase we add attributes that were not a part of the base structure; that is, they were not primary keys or foreign keys. There is nothing wrong with including all the attributes during the KBM phase, because this phase is only a methodology for developers who do not have database design tools.

The actual normalization process for a FAM proceeds much like that of a KBM. Add some attributes, and then normalize. However, because we are adding only attributes, special situations can develop. We discussed dependencies earlier, but as attributes are added, multivalued dependencies may occur. When this does occur, an additional normalization step must occur.

Boyce Codd Normal Form

We are going beyond our KBM requirement slightly. We've built the KBM, which was only normalized to 3NF. Boyce Codd normal form (BCNF) errors occur with overlapping keys, which are not apparent in 1NF, 2NF, or 3NF normalization. This situation may develop slowly over time as the developer creates new indexes to access the data or to improve performance. Update anomalies occur with BCNF errors.

A relation is in BCNF by ensuring that it is 3NF for any feasible choice of candidate key as a primary key. More formally stated, a relation is in BCNF if for every $X \rightarrow A$, A does not belong to X. In that event, X is a superkey. A relation is in BCNF if and only if each determinant of each dependency in the relation is a candidate key. That is, all attributes are fully determined by each full candidate key and not by any subset of a candidate key. Consider this example in our schema notation:

$R(\underline{A}, \underline{B}, C) \; C \rightarrow A$

This relation is in 3NF because A is a member of a candidate key, but it is not in BCNF because C is not a superkey. In this case, AB is the superkey, candidate key, and primary key.

What about the following example?

$R(\underline{A}, B, C) \; AB \rightarrow C$

This relation is in BCNF because A is the primary key. The relation is also in BCNF if either B or AB is given as the primary key. Note that AB is a superkey even though A is the candidate and primary key.

For those of you who are Star Wars fans, Table 41-24 illustrates a BCNF error.

TABLE 41-24 ILLUSTRATING BCNF ERRORS

CLASS	STUDENT	TEACHER
Planets100	Luke	Anakin
Planets100	Han	Anakin
Planets100	Leia	Winter
Stars100	Lando	Jaina
Stars100	Yoda	Jaina
Stars100	Chewbacca	Jacen

We create two relations. The first is in 3NF and the second is not in 3NF.

Relation 1 (<u>Class</u>, <u>Student</u>, Teacher)   R1(<u>C</u>, <u>S</u>, T)

Relation 2 (<u>Teacher</u>, <u>Student</u>, Class)   R2(<u>T</u>, <u>S</u>, C) T → C

The second relation in not in 3NF because *Class* depends upon *Teacher*. Therefore, the relation is not in BCNF because it is not in 3NF for any feasible choice of candidate keys. We solve this dilemma with a projection, just as we did for 1NF, 2NF, and 3NF normalization.

R2(<u>T</u>, <u>S</u>, C) T → C

becomes

R3(<u>T</u>, C)

R4(<u>T</u>, <u>S</u>)

Fourth Normal Form

Fourth normal form (4NF) is the next logical step after BCNF. 4NF errors are illustrated in Table 41-25. However, before we can discuss 4NF, we must understand the meaning of *multivalued* dependency. Multivalued dependencies occur when there are attributes within a relation that are not logically related. The simplest way to describe a multivalued dependency is to present one.

TABLE 41-25 Illustrating 4NF errors

Name	Occupation	Sports Interest
Tom	Bookkeeper	Hiking
Tom	Bookkeeper	Biking
Tom	Finance	Hiking
Tom	Finance	Biking
Dick	Finance	Running
Dick	Finance	Swimming
Dick	Real Estate	Running
Dick	Real Estate	Swimming

If you look carefully, you'll note that there are two independent dependencies:

Name → Occupation

Name → Sport Interest

These are really multivalued dependencies that can be represented by:

Name > Occupation

The instances of this multivalued dependency are:

Tom → Bookkeeper, Finance

Dick → Finance, Real Estate

The other multivalued dependency is represented by:

Name > Sport Interest

This multivalued dependency has similar instances with:

Tom → Biking, Hiking

Dick → Running, Swimming

The original schema is:

Relation (<u>Name, Occupation, Sports Interest</u>) Name > Occupation, Name > Sports Interest

or

R(<u>N, O, S</u>) N > O, N > S

This is converted to 4NF by using our old friend *projection* (decomposition) to create the new relation:

R1(<u>N, O</u>)

R2(<u>N, S</u>)

which is in 4NF. A relation is 4NF if it is BCNF and there are no independent multivalued dependencies. Another way of saying this is that a relation is in 4NF if the implying set X of every nontrivial multivalued X > Y is a superkey. Here N is a superkey, and the relation is in 4NF.

Fifth Normal Form or Projection–Join Normal Form

This is our last stop in database normalization. Like the earlier discussions, an example illustrates the issues very clearly. A relation is in fifth normal form (5NF) if it has the lossless join property. Recall that a relational database has three operators, a *select,* which determines rows, a *project,* which determines columns, and a *join,* which joins tables (relations). We start first by using a relation that does not exhibit the lossless join property. We start with a relation R1(A, B, C) and create projections R2(A, B), R3(A, C), and R4(B, C), as shown in Table 41-26. We attempt to reconstitute the original relation with the joins (R2 X R3) X R4 and find that the data is invalid. 5NF errors cannot be corrected.

TABLE 41-26 DECOMPOSING A LOSSY RELATION (LOSSLESS JOIN PROPERTY NOT EXHIBITED)

R1(A, B, C)			R2(A, B)		R3(A, C)		R4(B, C)	
A	B	C	A	B	A	C	B	C
3	6	4	3	6	3	4	6	4
3	7	10	3	7	3	10	7	10
4	6	10	4	6	4	10	6	10

The 5NF problem is illustrated by attempting to reconstitute the original relation with the joins (R2 X R3) X R4 to find that the data is invalid. R5 has an extra row that is not valid.

As can be seen, this relation does not exhibit the lossless join property and therefore is not in 5NF (see Table 41-27). Relation R5 is not identical to relation R1.

A relation that exhibits the lossless join property is said to satisfy a projection-join dependency. In our relation R(A, B, C), the projection-join dependency between AB and BC holds if and only if B > A (a multivalued dependency exists). This can only occur if B is a superkey, which it is not, and hence our example does not have the lossless join property and the projection-join dependency is not satisfied. In our example, if A is a primary key, then AB must be a superkey for the join-dependencies to hold. When this is true, 4NF is satisfied by definition. It's not true in our example because neither A nor B are a primary key. For all projection-join dependencies to hold, *each* implying set of multivalued dependencies must be a superkey.

TABLE 41-27 FAILING TO EXHIBIT THE LOSSLESS JOIN PROPERTY

R2(A, B)X		R3(A, C)					X R4(B, C)		=	R5(A, B, C)		
A	B	A	C	A	B	C	B	C		A	B	C
3	6	3	4	3	6	4	6	4		3	6	4
3	7	3	10	3	6	10*	7	10		3	6	10*
4	6	4	10	3	7	4*	6	10		3	7	10
				3	7	10				4	6	10
				4	6	10						

5NF is just an itch to scratch. 5NF normalization errors occur when dealing with multivalued dependencies. However, there is no formal methodology for dealing with the issue. Decomposition can be used with other normalization issues, but you run the risk of losing dependencies when applying decomposition to 5NF normalization problems.

With that said, let's look at a 5NF example. You'll note that the data looks much like that of a BCNF error. Recall that a BCNF error is overlapping keys. A 5NF error is different than a BCNF error and is manifested by paired cyclical dependencies within a compound key. Table 41-28 is an abstract and easy to recognize representation of a 5NF error with paired cyclical dependencies in the primary key.

TABLE 41-28 REPRESENTING 5NF ERRORS

A (PK)	B(PK)	C(PK)	T
A1	B1	C1	T1
A1	B1	C2	T2
A1	B2	C1	T3
A1	B2	C2	T4

continued

	TABLE 41-28 *(continued)*		
A (PK)	**B(PK)**	**C(PK)**	**T**
A2	B1	C1	T5
A2	B1	C2	T6
A2	B2	C1	T7
A2	B2	C2	T8

The pairings in Table 41-28 include (A, B), (A, C), and (B, C). Table 41-28 is artificial and an idealization because I used all combinations. In actual practice, all combinations will not be used and a 5NF error is difficult to detect.

The issue with Table 41-28 is that four updates must be made when any value of the primary key is changed. Using our notation, we can write the schema for Table 41-28 as:

R($\underline{A}$, $\underline{B}$, $\underline{C}$, T) $\underline{ABC} \rightarrow T$

A decomposition will yield:

R1($\underline{A}$, $\underline{B}$)

R2($\underline{B}$, $\underline{C}$)

R2($\underline{A}$, $\underline{C}$)

R($\underline{A}$, $\underline{B}$, $\underline{C}$, T) $\underline{ABC} \rightarrow T$

This reduces the update count to three. This may be good; however, the fact that Table 41-28 has a compound key means that one or more business rules are inferred from the table. As an example, lets rewrite our schema as:

R($\underline{SalesPerson}$, $\underline{Product}$, $\underline{City}$, Quantity) $\underline{SalesPersonProductCity} \rightarrow$ Quantity

We are now stating that a salesperson has access to individual products in a city. This is acceptable, since the original entity R was preserved. In the schema below business rule information may be lost since the original entity was not preserved:

R3($\underline{A}$, $\underline{B}$, T) $\underline{AB} \rightarrow T$

R4($\underline{B}$, $\underline{C}$, T) $\underline{BC} \rightarrow T$

R5($\underline{A}$, $\underline{C}$, T) $\underline{AC} \rightarrow T$

Normalizing to 5NF is not an abstract procedure, but a procedure that must be done with a firm understanding of the business rules. Normalization to 5NF is not a necessity. Knowing that a 5NF error exists should be sufficient for the developer to avoid the lossy joins issue discussed above.

Semantic Disintegrity

Semantic disintegrity refers to result sets with errors that may occur when using database query languages. Semantic disintegrity is the result of joins that are created without the lossless join property. Before we discuss semantic disintegrity, let's review our notation.

- A → B   A function dependency but also a one-to-one mapping.
- A > B   A multivalued dependency.
- A > B/C A multivalued dependency in the context of C.
- A → m B A one-to-many mapping.

If we think carefully about semantic disintegrity, we'll note that there are a number of situations where semantic disintegrity will not occur. Some of them are quite obvious. Semantic disintegrity will not occur when:

- All mappings are one-to-one (for example, A → B, B → C, and C → D).
- The only one-to-many mapping is the first one (for example, A → m B, B → C, and C → D).
- The only one-to-many mapping is the second mapping (for example, A → B, B → m C, and C → D) if B → A *or* B > C/A *or* B > A/C.

I can feel your eyes glazing over right now. There are many other rules associated with semantic disintegrity, but the fact that semantic disintegrity can occur should be of interest. It is not within the scope of this book to pursue the issue other than to state that it exists. You can't always believe what the computer reports.

Domain-key Normal Form

This is the ultimate normalization form. Relations of this form cannot have update, insertion, or deletion anomalies. Even though the concept of domain-key normal form DKNF is easily understood, there is no proven method of converting a design to this form. It remains an academic issue and an ideal. We will not discuss it. If someone tells you that his or her database is normalized to DKNF, then you can assume that he or she is a candidate for the funny farm.

When to Stop Normalization

I've been told many times, "You don't need to go beyond 3NF." This is absolutely *not* true. Although in designing a database you build the KBM to 3NF and the statement is true. You proceed to the point where no further normalization is practical and no normalization errors exist. At that point the database is de-normalized for performance. You want to know the perfect model or something very near to it, because in production you must always de-normalize your database for performance. So when does the normalization process stop? It stops when:

- The number of individual relations becomes too large, and the resulting joins will incur far too much overhead for the database management system.

- Further decomposition will not preserve FDs.

Consider the relation R(<u>Name</u>, City, Street, City, State, Zip). It has the FD Zip → City, State. It becomes a matter of choice to decompose further with the FD Codes(<u>Zip</u>, City, State). A join must occur for each complete address.

Managing De-normalization and the Dependency Model

When our database is de-normalized, we must take special precautions to prevent update anomalies or queries with false output. We can do this by building a complete list of dependencies that exist within the database. The database is normalized to the point where further decomposition will not preserve a FD. We now have our dependency model.

The dependency model is very important for ongoing maintenance and is the schema we discussed earlier, an example being the relation R(<u>A</u>, <u>B</u>, C ,D) with the FD AB → C, D. At this point, de-normalization can start. As we de-normalize, we must "tag" each FD that is no longer valid because of the de-normalization. The database administrator's (DBA) task is to limit/control updates or queries to these

FDs. Either limit access by using a view on SQL Server or a query on Microsoft Access. Both the SQL Server view and the Microsoft Access query can be managed with permissions. An SQL Server trigger is another tool for alerting the user of the invalidity of the query.

Unless you are the architect of a Structured Query Language (SQL) database, maintenance of an existing database is difficult, if not impossible, without a schema that includes the dependencies. Simply having an ERD is not sufficient. The dependencies must also be known. This is because nearly all production database systems are denormalized, and adding dependencies to an existing system where the dependencies are not normalized and are unknown will not necessarily result in proper operation.

BUILDING THE TRANSFORM MODEL

The Transform Model is the creation of tables in the database of your choice. There is no discussion of this model. Data-modeling tools create the required tables automatically.

BUSINESS IMPLEMENTATION MODEL

This is our last stop. I won't bore you with a lot of minutiae, but this is where we place all of the remaining documentation. We captured information for the Business Scope Model, the Requirements Model, and the Business Rules Model, but that information said nothing about the physical implementation. The business Implementation Model is all the documentation required to build the system. In this context, I am not referring to program documentation, but all the requirements, specification, programming notes, and other information. This information is linked to the Requirements Model. Documentation we should consider is:

- Programmatic manifestations of our business rules.
- Physical mapping of the Transform Model and why the choices were made.
- Complete documentation of the De-normalization Model.
- Other issues pertinent to the application.

BUSINESS OBJECTS

This chapter is dedicated to different aspects of entities. Entities are represented in the Transform Model with mappings to database tables. Microsoft represents entities within an application as business objects. Microsoft borrows from other technologies the concept of objects and collections and names this new technology business objects. Entities are now represented as business objects within an application. There is no requirement to map all entities to program constructs (business objects). The one side of a one-to-many relationship is represented by a parent object. The collection of a parent object represents the many side of the one-to-many relationship of an ERD. Unfortunately, this is nearly an unpardonable sin, since it is the embedding of data definitions with process. The very early COBOL programs had a File Definition (FD) section where data definitions were stored. COBOL programs represent an era where definitions of the data was stored in the program. All programs had to be changed whenever the database architecture was changed. A relational database represents an break-through in technology with the data definitions stored within the data and not the program. Microsoft is dragging us backwards to a horrific past where changing the database structure means changing every program that references the database.

Very early in the book is a discussion of Open Database Connectivity (see Chapters 11–14). ODBC is a ubiquitous standard in database connectivity. ODBC also has some very interesting characteristics. The ODBC application knows nothing of the characteristics of the incoming data and uses a very rich ODBC functionality to determine the characteristics of the incoming query (see Listing 14-6 in Chapter 14). The important point is that a properly coded ODBC application is data neutral and contains no data characteristics. I will grant that ODBC has difficulty handling business rules; however, it is my belief that business rules should be handled by a Business Rule Engine much in the same manner that SQL Server has a SQL Engine. Microsoft is on the wrong path with business objects defined as programming constructs.

The other problem with program constructs representing business rules is the sense of ownership. Business rules are owned by business people and not developers. However, since the business rules are manifestations of program constructs, developers have a sense of ownership. With business rules embedded in program constructs, new business rules require program changes.

To be fair, business rules have always been embedded in the process, and Microsoft is not responsible for this paradigm. What is expected of Microsoft, with their unlimited resources, is to take the leadership in removing business rules from the process. This is done with a business rules engine much like the SQL engine of Microsoft SQL Server. On the other hand, Microsoft is re-embedding database architecture in the process with business objects, and that is not tolerable. This represents a regression of technology that is neither desirable nor acceptable.

Removing the Confusion

There are two sets of business objects within the Microsoft architecture. The first set of business objects are the objects that represent entities of an ERD. The second set of business objects are those objects that represent the logical architecture. With an On-Line Transaction Processing (OLTP) system, there are always three tiers. These are not necessarily physical tiers, and the tiers represent client services, business services, and data services. Client services are always placed at the client site. Data services should be placed at the data source, and the business services may be placed at either the client site or the data source. An independent middle hardware tier is optional and can be added for business object support.

A three-tier logical architecture with business rules as the middle tier represents an OLTP system, while a two-tier logical system represents a Decision Support System (DSS). A DSS system does not require business rules because all transactions are queries and there are no updates.

How the physical architecture is derived is the application of experience and common sense. Logical solutions should be designed independent of the existing hardware architecture. A common mistake is to design an application for an existing hardware architecture. Design the solution and then determine the hardware requirements.

Given a solution, it is a matter of deciding where the processing is accomplished and the relative location of the data source with respect to the processing location. Common sense dictates that data processing be accomplished at the data source. This means the creation of stored procedures on SQL Server rather than local procedures at the client site.

The key to a successful system is the understanding of the resources currently available and the expected growth in the use of those resources. Systems should be deployed with a two- to five-year life expectancy. Often that doesn't happen because the growth in system usage is not anticipated. Without room for growth, a successful system at deployment may be an unsuccessful system in as little as six months.

Inviting a Disaster

Microsoft Access represents a single-tier hardware architecture. How individual applications are coded may vary and is not the issue. The issue is upsizing a Microsoft application to SQL Server, and Microsoft has provided free tools for this task. The reason the tools are free may be because upsizing a single-tier architecture to a two-tier architecture is not logical. Unless the application is recoded, the application will have remote data with a local SQL engine. Yes, pass-through queries can be sent to SQL Server and use the remote SQL engine of SQL Server; however, the data processing still occurs locally in the Access application. The real solution, and it's painful, is to redesign the application. DAO procedures in Access must become SQL Server–stored procedures on SQL Server. The general rule is not to move one architecture to another architecture simply because a tool exists. Rethink and redesign the application. The reward will be worth the effort.

KEY POINT SUMMARY

This chapter addresses many of the basic problems associated with application development. Developers abrogate the need to think critically when using powerful RAD tools. There is a quotation in Chapter 40 that states: "an application can be developed quicker than the specification can be written the old way." I take that statement to task and say that the RAD tool can generate output quicker than a specification can be written the old way. No task should be done quickly. If the task can be done quickly, do a portion of the task and set it aside. Time for gestation is required. Taking the time to create models provides the time to think critically. If an application is written faster than its specifications are written, how can the application correctly mirror the requirements?

Data-modeling does not start with purchasing a data-modeling tool and proceeding to normalize relations. The normalization is suspect when the business rules are not understood. Neither is normalization an intuitive ad hoc procedure. Normalization relies on the Armstrong axioms. Normalization uses the concept of functional dependence, which requires an understanding of the business processes.

Database normalization always goes beyond the third normal form. Normally, this isn't required for new databases created from scratch; legacy databases require every trick imaginable.

APPLYING WHAT YOU'VE LEARNED

I started this chapter with a quotation from *ComputerWorld* that illustrates that developers lack the basic communication skills necessary for soliciting application requirements. I can't provide those skills in this book; however, the questions below and the laboratory are designed to address two key issues.

The Instant Assessment questions address the issue of database normalization and there are numerous normalization questions on the Windows Architecture II examination. Understand what each of the normalization errors represents. Also know how to resolve normalization errors. Always use decomposition, and if you write a schema, the required decomposition becomes apparent.

The other issue is to capture context-free information. The laboratory is a continuation of the distillation started earlier in the book.

INSTANT ASSESSMENT

1. What is the schema for the 5-tuple (OrderID, ItemID, Description, OrderDate, Quantity)? You may assume that OrderID and ItemID represent a composite key.

2. What is the normalization error in question 1?

3. Describe a Boyce Codd normal form error.

4. Describe a third normal form error.

5. Describe a second normal form error.

6. Describe a first normal form error.

 concept link   **For answers to the Instant Assessment questions, see Appendix C.**

Lab Exercises

Lab 41.80 *Building a Business Model*

WA II

Lab 41.80 is a difficult lab exercise and is a continuation of the distillation started earlier in this chapter (see "Parsing the Business Rambling"). Partial results are listed in Table 41-7. You'll want to construct the tables for the different models in an Access database. The complete business rambling, which is the source for your distillation, is shown in Listing 41-1. This is not an artificial example and is an example of what can be expected from users. In the other world (read that as legacy), analysts prepared specifications. Welcome to the age of users (see Chapter 40) and the user-written specification.

I cannot emphasize enough the importance of this laboratory. You may analyze the business rambling differently and infer entities that I did not infer. The important issue is that you learn how to distill the information in a context-free manner. As Joe Friday would say, "Just the facts Ma'am!"

Lab 41.81 *Architectural choices*

WA II

This lab exercise assumes that a production Access application exists within the enterprise. An Access application is a single-tier application. The purpose of the laboratory is to estimate the costs of converting a single-tier application to a two-tier architecture versus using the Microsoft Upsizing Tool. Assume for this analysis that performance of the Access application after upsizing is 35 percent of the original performance. Answer these questions:

1. Is performance an issue? Is a 65 percent performance reduction acceptable?

2. What are the conversion costs?

3. What are the costs to develop a new application?

Lab 41.82 *Creating a Business Objects Model*

WA II

Select a small process in your enterprise and write a business rambling. Apply the techniques presented in this chapter to create a distillation. Create an ERD from the distillation. As the final step, create an Business Objects model. Remember that there is no rule that states all entities must be represented by a business object.

Lab 41.83 *Strategic choices*

WA II

This lab exercise assumes that the enterprise has a production SQL Server database. Evaluate the SQL Server database structure and determine what must be done to de-normalize the database in anticipation of creating a DSS database. Anything goes with de-normalization. Consider any trick possible since a DSS is read-only database.

Lab 41.84 *Practicing normalization*

WA II

An application has a single text file with these fields: customer ID, customer name, order ID, order date, total price, tax rate, product ID_1, product_name 1, price_1, quantity_1. Up to ten product ID, product_name, price, and quantity groupings are available per record. Normalize this structure. Hint: You must define at least five tables (entities).

Windows Architecture I
Windows Architecture II

Solution Interface Issues

About Chapter 42

Most of this book concerns the *how*. Chapters 40 and 41 were dedicated to the *what*. We're back to the *how* with Chapter 42, the last chapter of the book.

Chapter 42 is divided into three sections. In the first section, I discuss the user interface. The developer has a wide variety of tools, and the proper tool selection is critical for a successful application.

In the second section, I discuss system interfacing. *System interfacing* includes application installation, startup, termination, and code-signing. Code-signing is expected of any ActiveX control delivered over the Internet. Applications are not monolithic. For example, an Access application may attach a table on the Web.

In the third section, I cover internationalization issues. Very few of us have a need to internationalize our software, but it is still an issue.

THE USER INTERFACE

The goal of the Windows Architecture is to provide a uniform developer environment. This chapter illuminates the Microsoft application interface standards. A successful Windows application is not a clever application; it is an application where controls are used to perform expected tasks.

Placement of the controls and menus is also critical. A rule of thumb is that a clever application is not a good application. Developers are notorious for not documenting applications. When an application is intuitive, the user can adapt readily. A good example is the paradigm of double-clicking an object to start an operation. Change that paradigm and the user is confused.

Figure 42-1 displays the controls available in Visual Basic 4.0 Enterprise Edition.

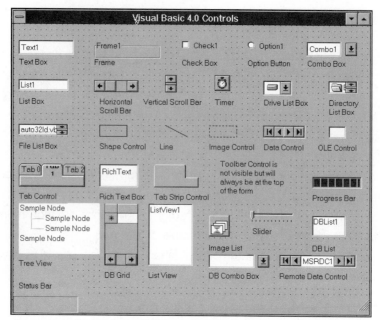

FIGURE 42-1   Controls available to the Visual Basic 4.0 developer.

The primary issue here is look and feel. Clever applications are not acceptable. Your program is acceptable when it appears to be indistinguishable from a Microsoft application. Microsoft Press publishes *The Windows Interface Guidelines of Software Design*. That's too much material for only a few paragraphs, but the items below address some basic issues. We start with window interface guidelines. Other sections include control interface guidelines, dialog box interface guidelines, and menu interface guidelines.

Window Interface Guidelines

The window is the host container for all objects. It is also the environment known as the desktop. Every application has a window except for special cases such as COM windowless controls. These are the most common window interface guidelines. They're not complete, and the issues are only briefly mentioned. The basic interface design guidelines for creating and displaying windows includes:

- Primary window is where most of the editing and viewing takes place.
- Multiple or supplemental secondary windows may be included to enable users to specify parameters or options.

- Primary window components:

  - ***Window Frame*** — A sizable window has a distinct border that provides a control point for resizing the window using direct manipulation with the mouse.

  - ***Title Bar*** — Clicking the title bar with mouse button 2 will display the pop-up menu for the window. Double-clicking will maximize it. Windows are moved by dragging the title bar or using the move command from the window pop-up menu.

  - ***Title bar Icon*** — The title bar icon appears in the upper-left corner of the title bar. If it is a tool (that is, it does not create, load, or save separate date files), then the smaller version of the icon is used. There are two sets of icons and windows buttons when an MDI window is minimized. When maximized, the MDI icon and buttons are merged onto the menu bar.

  - ***Title Text*** — The document name appears in the title bar. A placeholder is supplied in the title text when a document has no name. The full path name is not displayed when the title is a filename. The title can optionally hold the application name in use. For Windows 3.1, the name of the document appears followed by a hyphen and the application name. For Windows 95 and Windows NT the application name is first, followed by the document name. The title text is always kept up to date.

  - ***Task Bar*** — A task bar entry will be created for primary windows when they are opened. Window activation and deactivation is accomplished with a ALT + TAB shift between windows while SHIFT + ALT + TAB shifts between windows in the reverse order.

  - ***Scroll Box*** — Sometimes known as an elevator, thumb, or slider. When scrolling, allow one unit of overlap from previous view. When scrolling horizontally, scroll in units greater than a single character to prevent discontinuous or uneven scrolling. Always scroll in the direction of drag. The scrolling lock is an option for keyboard scrolling.

  - ***Split Box*** — This is typically located at the top of the up arrow or at the left of the right arrow. Pressing ESC cancels the split mode. Split bars must be at least one pixel wide.

Control Interface Guidelines

Controls are graphical objects that represent the properties or operations of other objects. Controls are the vehicle by which a developer expresses a solution for a problem. Appropriate control use is critical in an environment where users do not have the time or desire to study an operations manual, but prefer to "wing it." The following are the common controls with their intended usage:

- *Buttons* — Users change properties or initiate actions with buttons. There are four basic types of buttons: command buttons, menu buttons, option buttons, and check boxes:

  - *Command Buttons* — Include ellipsis points (. . .) as a visual cue for buttons that require additional information. You can use command buttons to enlarge a secondary window and display additional options. Command buttons used in this context are known as *unfold buttons*. When enlarging a secondary window, include the chevron (>) as part of the button's label. A secondary window has neither a menu bar nor min/max buttons.

  - *Menu Buttons* — A menu button displays a pop-up menu; when used for this purpose, it includes a triangular arrow. This triangular arrow is similar to that found in cascading menus.

  - *Option Buttons* — An option button (also known as a radio button) represents a single choice from a set of mutually exclusive choices. The option button can be mixed mode (multiple values), in which case the first click selects, the second click clears, and the third click returns everything to mixed mode. Normally part of a group can have it's own label. Option buttons should be limited to small groups. There should be at least two choices, but never more than six.

  - *Check Boxes* — Check boxes are used for nonexclusive choices. Check boxes do not have labels. Related check boxes should be grouped.

    A check box may be mixed mode. Selecting the check box the first time places a check mark in the check box. The second selection removes the check mark, and the third selection causes the check box to revert to mixed mode.

- *List Boxes* — Used for displaying a large number of choices. List boxes do not include their own label. Keep everything in a natural order. Use numeric or alphabetical when a natural order is not available. Use ellipsis points (. . .) in long text strings to shorten them. Use a horizontal scroll bar if necessary.

- *Single Selection List Box* — The list box is a fixed size, and only one entry may be selected.

- *Drop-down List Box* — Width is a few spaces more than the average width. Normally, there are three to eight entries in a drop-down list box. Use Alt + up arrow and Alt + down arrow for navigation. A drop-down list box is used to conserve screen real estate.

- *Extended Selection* and *Multiple Selection List Boxes* — These list boxes support the selection interface for contiguous and disjoint selection. Extended selection list boxes are optimized for individual item or range selection; multiple selection list boxes are optimized for independent selection. Simple multiple selection list boxes are not visually distinct from extended selection list boxes. You may want to consider designing the multiple selection list box to have the appearance of a scrollable list of check boxes. (See the *Windows Interface Guidelines for Software Design* published by Microsoft Press for additional details.)

- *List View Box* — Displays a set of objects and is often used with a tree control. More than one item may be selected at a time. The list view box is also known as a *Column Headings* control. The list view control supports drag-and-drop.

- *Tree Control Box* — Displays a set of objects in an indented outline based on their logical hierarchical relationship.

- *Text Fields* — No labels included; editing and validation are possible. Can be read-only.

- *Text Boxes* — Individual font or paragraph properties are not supported. Text boxes for fixed-length entry support autoexit.

- *Rich Text Box* — Support for individual character, font, and paragraph formats.

- *Combo Box* — Combines a list box with a text box. Autoscrolling to the nearest entry is supported. Up arrow and down arrow are supported.

- *Drop-Down Combo* — Combines the characteristics of a text box with a drop-down list box. Operates like a combo box.

- **Spin Box** — Similar to a text box but with a limited range of input. The values are ordered and make up a circular loop. The user may enter a value or the buttons can be used to increment or decrement the value. An example of spin boxes is a spin box for setting hours, minutes, and seconds.

- **Static Text Field** — Dates, page number (that is, read-only).

- **Horizontal/Vertical Scroll Bars** — Scroll bars are used for scrolling context only. A common mistake is to set values with a scroll bar.

- **Sliders** — Sliders are used for setting values of a continuous range such as volume or brightness. A slider does not include its own label. The developer should provide a static label to help the user interpret the scale and range of the control.

- **Status Bars** — Status bars only appear at the bottom of the primary window. Secondary windows do not have status bars. A status bar may include controls. Always provide tooltips for controls placed in a toolbar or status bar that does not have labels.

- **Progress Bar** — Progress bars are not interactive. Static text should be provided to indicate the overall purpose of the progress indicator.

- **Tab Control** — Similar to a notebook divider. Used for dividing logical pages. Left arrow or right arrow is used to navigate between tabs. Ctrl+Tab also moves between tabs.

- **Wells** — Used for displaying color, pattern, or image used as a property. An example is the color palette displayed when setting either background or foreground colors.

- **Group Boxes** — Another name for *Frame*. Commonly used to group option buttons.

Dialog Box Interface Guidelines

Whenever possible, common dialog should be used. This goes along with the theme of presenting familiar formats and familiar themes. Common dialog boxes include Open, Save, Find and Replace, Print, Print Setup, and Font. These are the guidelines to follow when using dialog box interfaces:

- Always make the dialog box title "what it is." For example, the *Print* command on the *File* menu should use the title *Print* and not *Print...* or

Print File. From a grammatical sense, provide a descriptive noun phrase and not an action verb phrase.

○ Orient controls in a dialog box in the same way people read information. For the United States this is left-to-right and top-to-bottom.

○ Lay out the major command buttons either stacked along the upper-right border of the dialog box or across the bottom.

○ Make the **Default** button first followed by the **Cancel** button. The **Help** button is last.

○ Optionally, use double-clicking on a selection control to select the option and the **Default** button.

Menu Interface Guidelines

Menus are a means of presenting commands. The user is not faced with the issue of knowing the correct spelling or syntax of a command. A menu bar is not a requirement, although it is a common convention. Interface standards are evolving to unified tool bars where a menu bar is considered a tool bar with menu controls.

Study Microsoft menus before implementing your own. When your menu uses a common command such as **Exit**, ensure that it is placed last. Also ensure that the command is placed in the proper menu. The **Exit** command is always the last entry of the **File** menu. This means that applications must have a **File** menu for an **Exit** command even though there may be no other commands in the file menu.

Be accurate with menu commands. When an object remains active even though the window is closed, use the **Close** command rather than the **Exit** command.

Menus come in three forms: drop-down menus, pop-up menus, and cascading menus:

○ *Drop-Down Menus* — Dragging downward and releasing over an item "chooses" an entry from the menu. Alternately, the Alt key can be used followed by cursor positioning keys. There are five classes of drop-down menus:

○ *File Menu* — Commands such as **Open, Save, Send,** or **Print**. If an **Exit** is used, place it at the end.

○ *Edit Menu* — Commands such as **Undo, Repeat, Find and Replace, Delete,** and **Duplicate.**

- *View Menu* — Includes commands for changing the user's view of data in the window.

- *Window Menu* — Used in multiple-document interface (MDI)-style applications.

- *Help Menu* — Include the **About** *<application name>* here.

- *Pop-Up menus* — A pop-up menu is similar to a drop-down menu except there is no title. A pop-up menu is contextual to the selected object(s). It is not to be used for general purposes. A control can support a pop-up menu. When a pop-up menu is supported, it is contextual to what the control represents, rather than to the control itself. Therefore, do not include commands such as **Set**, **Check,** or **Uncheck**. The exception is in forms design or window layout context, where the commands on the pop-up menu can apply to the control itself.

  Commands in a pop-up menu may not always be supplied by the object but may be a combination of commands from the object and from the container. **Properties** is last in a pop-up menu. **What's This?** is next to last in a pop-up menu.

  Your pop-up menu should follow conventional command ordering. The rule of thumb is that the most frequently referenced items are always placed first in the menu. Some generic pop-up menus are offered below as a design guideline:

  - Pop-up menu command order

    Open, Play, Print

    Cut, Copy, Paste, Paste Link

  - Application file pop-up menu

  - **Cut, Copy, Create Link, Delete, What's This, Properties**

  - MDI application pop-up menu

    Close (or Exit), Save All, Insert New, Find, What's This, Properties

- *Cascading Menus* — Cascading menus should be limited to a single level. The visual cue is the side arrow. User interaction is the same with a cascading menu as with that of a drop-down menu except that the cascading menu displays after a short timeout to avoid a flashing effect.

Help for the User Interface

When a user is at this point, your intuitive interface has failed. This is your last line of defense before the application is relegated to that class of loaded but never used applications.

User help should be simple, efficient, and relevant. But more than that, don't insult the user. (We'll discuss techniques of writing good help dialog shortly.) Remember: at this point the user is quite frustrated, and some of that frustration may be your fault.

Application errors fall into two general categories. The first category is the mechanical errors of spelling, omissions, or incorrect type declarations. The second and most common error category is the developer's perception of the problem does not match the user's perception. The clash is between how the user wants to use the application and how the developer thinks the application should be used. This gap can be huge. In the legacy world, the user had very little choice. The user was forced to accept whatever was provided. The paradigm shift today is that the developer is no longer in control. It's the user who is in control and if the developer doesn't do the application correctly, there is a high probability that the user will implement his or her own version. I've made light of vice presidents to secretaries programming Microsoft Access. It's not a joke — they do!

There are different categories of help. Each is designed for a special purpose. The categories are Context Sensitive, Tooltips, Status Bar Help, Help Command Button, Task Help, and Reference Help. They are outlined as follows:

- **Context Sensitive Help** — Selecting *What's This?* from a menu puts the user in context-sensitive mode. Context-sensitive help is available by clicking *What's This?* from the **Help** menu and then moving the mouse pointer over the object and clicking the left mouse button. During this operation the mouse pointer is considered a contextual pointer. If a user selects a menu title after selecting *What's This?*, keep the mode until something is selected.

  Context-sensitive help is also available by clicking the right mouse button. When the right mouse button is clicked over an object that supports a pop-up menu, maintain the context-sensitive mode until the user chooses something from the menu or cancels the menu.

tip **The developer should always remember that context-sensitive information is written to answer a question. A good practice is to start context-sensitive help with a verb. The information should be brief and reference-related help should be deferred to task-oriented help. Pressing F1 is the shortcut key that presents contextual information for the object that has the input focus.**

- *Tooltips* — Small pop-ups that display the name of a graphical icon. Tooltips do not have a label. Drag the mouse pointer over an object and hesitate for several seconds. The tooltip will display the object name.

- *Status Bar Help* — Use the status bar to provide descriptive information about a menu or toolbar button that the user chooses. Always begin a message with a verb and in the present tense. Use only familiar terms and avoid jargon. Be specific when describing a command. Be constructive and not descriptive. Your goal is to inform the user about the command. The message should be brief, yet not truncated.

- *Help Button* — The help button is different from *What's This?*'s summary assistance, overview, or explanatory information. A help button is used for help from a property sheet, dialog box, or message box. The help button is included in the window. When the user presses the Help command button, the help information is displayed in a Help secondary window and not in a contextual pop-up window. A wizard is always implemented in a secondary window. Selecting a help command from the **Help** command button starts a Help wizard. This, in turn, starts the Help Browser after the indexes and content are initialized.

- *Task Help* — Task help enumerates the steps for carrying out a task. The preferred window type is a primary window that the user can resize, move, maximize, or minimize. The window can support shortcut buttons and has command buttons that support access to the index and content pages of the Help Browser. The developer should use the default system windows colors for the task help window. This distinguishes the task help window from other application windows. The task help window standard has changed slightly. Microsoft added the "Clipit" wizard to the task help menu in Office 97.

- *Reference Help* — Reference help serves as the application's on-line documentation. Reference help is also presented in a primary window, and the developer should use the default system colors for the window. The common use of this help style is from an explicit menu item in the Help drop-down menu with *Contents and Index* as the typical command. The user is initially presented the primary window of the Help Wizard. The bottom of the Help Wizard has the buttons *<Back>*, *Next*, *Finish*, and *Cancel*. Stepping through the different steps initializes the Help Browser. The user is presented with the Help Browser in a primary window and within the primary window are three tabs: Contents, Index, and Find.

Reference help is written in the first person directly to the user. Personal pronouns such as "you" or "your" should be used. The text is written in the user's vernacular and jargon should not be used. The developer should realize that there are two different classes of users. Key words should be provided for beginning users and advanced users. The topic should be described generally and also described specifically. Don't insult the users and keep the writing simple, clear, concise, and not condescending. Be succinct, yet clear, with an economy of style. Watch for unneeded prepositional phrases.

Windows 95 Logo Compliance

Editing and viewing are accomplished in the primary window. Windows 95 and Windows NT reflect the current standards for windows. Let's start by defining the necessary qualifications for a Windows 95 logo. For an application to qualify for the Windows 95 logo it must:

- Support large and small icons. Your application must register 16x16 and 32x32 icons for each file type and application.

- Adhere to the Windows 95 look and not the Windows 3.1 look.

- Support multiple font sizes.

- Support the Windows 95 User Interface Shell Extensions (UI/Shell). The right mouse button is reserved for context and interaction with shell extensions. Windows NT 4.*x*+ and Windows 95 support shell extensions, which are activated by the right mouse button. Developers can also provide their own shell extensions. There are two categories of shell extensions. The first group is registered for each file type:

  - *Context Menu Handlers* — A context menu is displayed when an object is right-clicked.

o *Icon handlers* — Icon handlers add instance-specific icons for file objects. They can also be used to add icons for all files of the same class.

o *Data Handlers* — A data handler provides a type-specific **IDataObject** interface that is passed to a **DoDragDrop** (see Chapter 6) function.

o *Drop Handlers* — A drop handler provides a type-specific behavior to files that can accept drag-and-drop objects.

o *Property Sheet Handlers* — This type of shell extension adds pages to the property sheet dialog box that the shell displays for a file object. The pages are specific to a class of files or a particular file object.

   The second group of shell extensions is associated with file operations such as move, copy, rename, or other file operations:

o *Copy Hook Handlers* — A copy hook handler is called when an operation such as copy, move, or rename is about to occur. A copy hook handler either allows or prevents the operation.

o *Drag-and-Drop Handlers* — A drag-and-drop handler is a context menu handler that the system calls when the user drops an object after dragging it to a new position.

o Colors are not to be hard-coded, and the Win32 application programming interface (API) functions **GetSystemMetrics** and **GetSysColor** are used to determine system colors.

o The application must be developed as a Win32 portable executable (PE). A portable executable is a unique file format. When the application is interpretive, the host interpreter such as Microsoft Access must be a Win32 PE format executable.

o The application must execute successfully on the latest version of Windows NT. This rule will probably be in effect until Windows NT 5.0 is released.

o The application must support long file names. This is not an option.

o Supporting Plug and Play is optional and is not required.

o Applications that work with files should either be a component object model (COM) object or a COM container. If the application is an object linking and embedding (OLE) server, then it must comply with the Windows 95 OLE Self-Registering Server specification:

- Dynamic link library (DLL) servers must support `DllRegisterServer()` and `DllUnregisterServer()`.

- EXE servers must support `/RegServer` and `/UnregServer` command line switches.

- Both DLL and EXE servers must support the `"OLESelfRegister"` `VERSIONINFO` string.

- Applications must also support messaging API (MAPI) to qualify for the Windows 95 logo. This is simple MAPI using common messaging call (CMC) API.

- The application must support drag and drop.

- When compound files are supported, File Summary Information should be provided.

- Support of automation is recommended, but not required.

- Applications using files should support the uniform naming convention (UNC). This is a recommendation and not a requirement.

- Setup and installation should use Registry API functions and not the older **GetPrivateProfileString**. The application must not use either the `WIN.INI` or the `SYSTEM.INI` files and must provide an uninstall capability.

Office 97 Compliance

The Office 97-Compatible Logo program is for applications that have the look and feel of Office 97. There are five basic requirements:

- The application must first qualify for the Windows 95 logo.
- The application must support hypertext markup language (HTML).
- The application must have menus similar to other Office 97 applications.
- The application must have toolbars similar to Office 97 applications.
- The application must support Intellimouse.

Let's take a look at an application that supports the interface guidelines. Figure 42-2 and Figure 42-3 illustrate the Microsoft user interface guidelines with Word 97. Neither Figure 42-2 nor Figure 42-3 follows the interface guidelines precisely. The discrepancies are discussed momentarily.

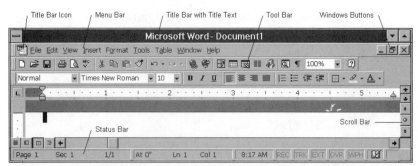

FIGURE 42-2   Word 97 as viewed from Windows NT Workstation 3.51 service pack 5.

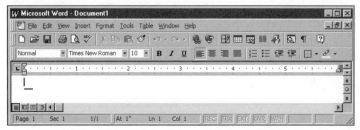

FIGURE 42-3   Word 97 as viewed from Windows NT Server 4.0 service pack 3.

The window is the primary viewing and editing environment. Secondary windows (MDI) provide for editing of parameters or options, or for additional object detail. We'll start with the primary window.

Windows are opened when a task starts execution. Selective activation of loaded windows is controlled by executing Alt + Tab, which shifts focus to another window. Shift + Alt + Tab shifts between windows in the reverse order.

Dragging the title bar or using the move command from the window pop-up menu moves a window.

A task bar entry is created for primary windows when they are opened within Windows NT 4.*x* or Windows 95. The task bar concept does not exist for Windows NT 3.51, Windows NT 3.5, Windows 3.11, or Windows 3.1.

The application window should mimic Microsoft Windows's required features as to placement. Primary window components are listed as follows (a toolbar isn't included because it is a feature of an application and not a basic window requirement):

- **Window Frame** — A sizable window has a distinct border that provides a control point for resizing the window using direct manipulation with the mouse.

- **Title Bar** — Clicking on the title bar with the right mouse button displays the pop-up menu for the window. Double-clicking maximizes it.

- **Title Bar Icon** — The title bar icon appears in the upper-left corner of the title bar. If it is a tool (that is, it does not create, load, or save separate data files), then the smaller version of the icon is used.

- **Title Text** — The document name appears in the title bar when opened. If a document has no name, then it supplies a placeholder in the title. A full path name is not supplied when the title is a filename.

  For Windows 3.1, the title can optionally hold the application name in use. The name of the document appears followed by a hyphen, then the application name. For Windows 95 and Windows NT, the application name is first followed by the document name. What's funny about both Figure 42-2 and Figure 42-3 is that in each case this guideline is violated. Both Figure 42-2 and Figure 42-3 exhibit the Windows 3.1 standard for title bars. The figures both display *Application-Document* while the standard is *Document-Application*. (See *The Windows Interface Guidelines for Software Design,* Microsoft Press.)

- **Windows Buttons** — Windows buttons always appear on the right side of the title bar. This is different than Windows 3.1 or Windows NT 3.51. Figure 42-1 has a control menu in the upper-left corner, while Figure 42-3 has a Windows button on the far upper-right. These buttons replace the control menu of the older Windows 3.1 paradigm.

- **Scroll Bar** — A scroll bar is optional and is sometimes known as an elevator, thumb, or slider. Both Figures 42-2 and 42-3 feature a scroll bar. A scroll bar control consists of scroll arrows, a scroll box, and a scroll bar shaft. When scrolling vertically, allow one unit of overlap from previous view. When scrolling horizontally, scroll in units greater than a single character to prevent discontinuous or uneven scrolling. Always scroll in the direction of drag.

- **Split Box** — If no split box is present, then it is typically located at the top of the up arrow. A split box is a special control contained in the scroll bar. Split bars must be at least one pixel wide.

- **MDI Window** — When an MDI window is maximized, the icon and buttons are merged onto the tool bar of the parent MDI form. Figure 42-4 is an MDI application (Structured Query Language-Distributed Management Object (SQLDMO), Chapters 27 and 28) with a minimized child form. The maximized version is in Figure 42-5, and the tool bars are merged. There is no icon on either the child tool or the parent MDI form.

A child form of a MDI application functions as a primary window in that it can be moved, resized, minimized, or maximized. The only limitation is that all interactions occur within the limits of the parent MDI form.

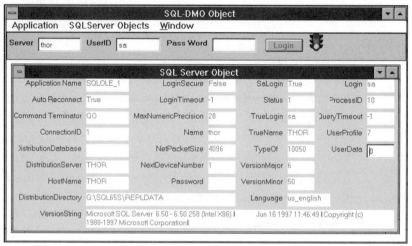

FIGURE 42-4   A MDI form with a minimized child form.

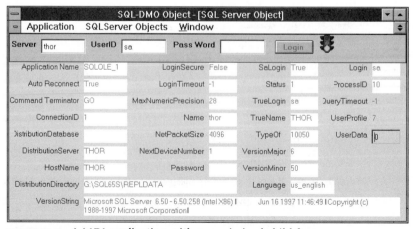

FIGURE 42-5   A MDI application with a maximized child form.

Figures 42-4 and 42-5 certainly will not qualify for the Windows 95 logo because the application has a Windows 3.1 appearance and not a Windows 95 appearance. There are other problems such as no icons and no **File** menu. The user of this application must use the **Control** box to exit the application, which is not a conventional procedure. Logging on to SQL Server is best placed in a dialog box, which isn't done. The **Window** menu is missing. A MDI application is the only application type that supports a Window menu, even though none is shown in either Figure 42-4 or Figure 42-5. Still, the application is clean and simple, and functions well if you're an intuitive person. A MDI application is expected to display the data file name in the title bar at all times, but this requirement isn't applicable to this example.

 Recall that Alt + Tab shifts focus to another primary window, while Shift + Alt + Tab shifts between primary windows in the reverse order. Ctrl + Tab (or Ctrl + F6) moves focus between child windows of an MDI application.

Accessibility Requirements

The last topic of the user interface is accessibility requirements. This is not something the developer must program. Rather, the developer should be aware that there are tools available for impaired individuals. The tools include:

- *Screen Enlargement Utilities* — This is a screen magnifier. The enlarger must track the current position and readjust the screen accordingly.

- *Screen Review Utilities* — A screen reviewer utility scans the screen and renders the information in a different medium. This can be a refreshable Braille display or synthesized speech.

- *Voice Input Utilities* — These utilities are useful when the individual has a mobility impairment. It is also a useful tool for boosting productivity of individuals who are not impaired.

- *In-Screen Keyboards* — There are a number of variations for this type of aid. A Morse code-type system, a system of pointing and clicking, and a system of clicks-only are different types of input systems for impaired individuals. The system that is selected will depend upon the impairment of the individual.

- **Keyboard Filters** — Keyboard filters accommodate impaired dexterity. Windows 95 keyboard filters help by providing some compensation for erratic motion, tremors, or slow response time. In this category of tools are aids such as abbreviation expansion utilities, add-on spelling checkers, and word prediction utilities. These tools are often used to improve the productivity of individuals not impaired.

- **Customizing the Mouse Pointer** — Windows 95 supports a customizable mouse pointer display for the visually impaired. High-contrast color schemes are also an aid for the visually impaired.

- **Keyboard Emulation of the Mouse** — This is another feature of Windows 95.

General Interface Guidelines

The Internet, a Windows 16-bit application, and a Windows 32-bit application each have a different look and feel. The primary rule is to keep the look and feel that is appropriate to the platform. There are no standards for either the Internet or Intranet, and some Internet sites are garish enough to be called *midnight at the gaslight district*. Web developers should use the Browser Capabilities Component (see Chapter 39). Browser functionality is not uniform. For example a browser may support VBScript and not Jscript. The converse may be true. Another consideration is that not all browsers support ActiveX.

There are interface standards for both Windows 95 and Windows 3.1. Windows 95, for example, uses context menus and the right mouse button extensively. There are common interface factors for 16-bit and 32-bit platforms such as the use of controls, control placement, menu placement, and contents.

Each platform also has bandwidth considerations. Internet applications are typically limited to 28.8K or 33.6K for downloading. This means considerations must be give to the amount of information downloaded, and to download asynchronously. Windows 3.1 and 16-bit applications have limitations that are inherent in the platform. This limitation is the 64K GDI, KERNEL, and USER stack sizes. Within Windows 3.1, the "Out of memory" message that occurs is not an exhaustion of physical memory, but the exhaustion of one of the aforementioned stacks. The experienced Windows 3.1user limits the number of windows open simultaneously, thereby avoiding the "Out of memory" message.

32-bit platforms such as Windows 95 and Windows NT utilize a Registry. This is a system-wide database of hardware and software parameters. The corresponding information Windows 3.1 information is stored within the SYSTEM.INI and WIN.INI files, with some applications owning private .INI files.

The bottom line is to stay within the paradigm. Don't add right-context mouse button usage to either Windows 3.1 or Window NT 3.51. It is not an integral feature of the interface and will confuse the user.

LOCALIZING THE APPLICATION

There is no simple answer to internationalization. One of the key steps is language translation. Translating to the target language is never enough. There are also cultural issues to consider. Let's define the character sets before we discuss internationalization issues.

Translating the Character Sets

There are obvious language differences between the United States versions of software and the versions for other countries. The problems extend far beyond mechanical translation of languages and can involve religious and cultural issues. Internationalizing an application is not a simple task for the fainthearted. It is complex, very costly, time consuming, and iterative. The translation starts with an *input method editor* (IME) that translates text entered on a 101-key keyboard to the target character set. When you don't know Japanese, and if you have access to an IME, names like "Toyota" or "Suzuki" can be typed. The appropriate double-byte character is created, and the results are displayed immediately. To understand what's involved in the translation, let's start with the definition of the character sets used today. Table 42-1 maps the support for the different character sets, and Table 42-2 illustrates the various implementations of the character A, each of which are unique.

TABLE 42-1 ANSI, DBCS, AND UNICODE IMPLEMENTATIONS	
ENVIRONMENT	*CHARACTER SET(S)*
Visual basic	Unicode
32-bit object libraries	Unicode
16-bit object libraries	ANSI and DBCS
Windows NT API	Unicode
Automation in Windows NT	Unicode
Windows 95 API	ANSI and DBCS
Automation in Windows 95	Unicode

TABLE 42-2 CHARACTER CODES FOR "A" IN ANSI, UNICODE, AND DBCS	
THE CHARACTER <A>	*HEXIDECIMAL EQUIVALENT*
ANSI character "A"	&H41
Unicode character "A"	&H41 &H00
DBCS character that represents a Japanese wide-width "A"	&H82 &H60
Unicode wide-width "A"	&H21 &HFF

Let's mention a few kind words about each of the character sets:

- **ANSI** — ANSI represents the traditional American Standard Code for Information Interchange (ASCII) character set. It is the most popular and is the legacy character set. The implementation is eight bits.

- **Unicode** — Unicode is a standard and not an invention of Microsoft.

  The Unicode standard is defined in two volumes: *Worldwide Character Encoding* Version 1.0, Volume 1 and Volume 2. Additional Unicode information may be found at `ftp://unicode.org`.

  Unicode is a character-encoding scheme that uses two bytes to represent every character. This scheme is capable of encoding all known characters and is used as a worldwide character-encoding standard. Unicode is supported by all 32-bit versions of Microsoft Windows and by 32-bit OLE technology. All versions of Microsoft Access after Version 2.0 are component-based (OLE) and by definition support Unicode. The same is true for Visual Basic 4.0 and later. Unicode is relatively new even though it is a standard. Legacy applications do not use Unicode.

- **DBCS** — The double-byte character set is used with Windows operating systems that are distributed in most regions of Asia. For example, Japanese has four alphabets, each of which are encoded in DBCS:

  - *Kanji* — Ideograms or meaning not related to pronunciation.

  - *Hiragana* — Phoenetic alphabet that is used for Japanese words.

  - *Katakana* — Phoenetic alphabet used for foreign words.

  - *Romanji* — Latin letter alphabet.

The name *double-byte character set* is a misnomer. It is possible to combine a *single-byte character set* (SBCS) with a DBCS. The result is a character string that is relatively complex to scan. Figure 42-6 illustrates the different character combinations. The current cursor position in each string is noted. Position a cursor at the wrong position in a DBCS string and chaos ensues. The SBCS range is limited to the inclusive values of 20 hexadecimal (hex) to 7F hex. The lead DBCS character is always an extended character that is always greater than 7F hex. The trailing character is not limited in value and may be either a SBCS or a DBCS character.

Character strings 3 and 4 for Figure 42-6 illustrate that the trailing byte may assume any value. This makes DBCS string parsing difficult. Microsoft supplies the function **IsDBCSLeadByte,** which returns a TRUE only when the lead byte is a candidate lead byte. Lead-byte determination is also based on the context of the character. An example is the second character of String 4, which is a candidate lead byte and is a trailing byte. **IsDBCSLeadByte** will return TRUE for this character, but the context is that of a trailing byte. The Visual C++ operators ++ and -- are no longer safe with DBCS character strings. **CharNext** and **CharPrev** are the 32-bit implementations of character positioning, while **AnsiNext** and **AnsiPrev** are the 16-bit implementations. A DBCS is not case sensitive.

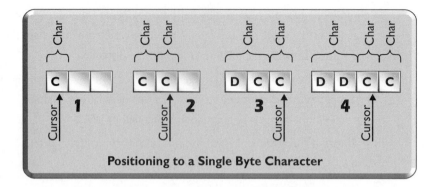

Legend: D > 7F, C >= 20 and <= 7F

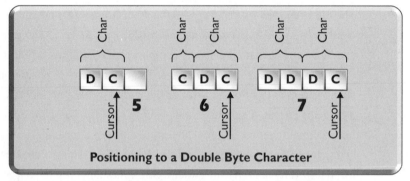

FIGURE 42-6   Double-byte and single-byte character combinations.

Internationalization Issues

Internationalization is almost a litany of what not to do. The internationalization issues mentioned in this section are not inclusive, but should form a starting point for internationalizing your application.

Internationalization starts by isolating localizable resources. This identification of localizable resources is done before the application is completed and is done in tandem with normal application development. The list is more than the traditional bitmaps and character strings, and Table 42-3 lists the program elements that require localization. (Icons are not listed in Table 42-3 and may require localization.)

TABLE 42-3 PROGRAM ELEMENTS REQUIRING LOCALIZATION

Special algorithms	Messages
Constants	Prompts
Dialogs	Sounds
Macro languages	Status bars
Menus	Toolbars

One of the goals of localizing is to reduce production costs of internationalization. Rather than a system per locale, localization isolates the core software from elements that require localization. This means that the core software is compiled independently of resources that must be localized. Resources are normally placed in a .RC file. When the localized resource is placed in a DLL, it need not be linked with the core software, but must be linked at execution time. The goal is one core module and a locale-specific DLL for each locale.

○ Use good coding practices. It is not uncommon to find a statement such as:

```
case '0':
DoClose();
```

This is an example of a literal embedded in code and in general is not a good coding practice. Localize all constants and don't be clever with messages. By that I mean don't try to construct messages on the fly from fragments, but define complete messages that can be localized.

○ Make sure your buffers are large enough to hold the translated text. The word *Edit* in German is *Bearbeiten*. The size consideration doesn't apply to just data buffers. Menu bars, status bars, tool bars, title bars, and dialog boxes should all be designed for an increased text size.

○ Use system functions for sorting, character typing, and string mapping. Always use system dialog boxes.

○ Use extreme caution with keyboard shortcut-key combinations. Not all keyboards are the same and characters map differently. Consider using the function keys such as F4 or F5 rather than a shortcut-key combination.

○ Avoid special effects and be culturally sensitive. The beep of the computer wanting the next installation diskette will embarrass a Japanese user.

- Avoid metaphors. A pointing arrow might be confusing to an Arabic or Hebrew speaker.

- Do not include text in bitmaps unless the text will not be translated. A company name is an example of text that will not be translated.

DEPLOYING THE APPLICATION

Deploying the application requires an understanding of the Registry, which must be used during the installation process. We start the discussion with the Registry and follow with application installation guidelines for Win32 applications.

Understanding the Registry

The Windows 95 logo program requires that information not be added to `WIN.INI` or `SYSTEM .INI` and that an application have install and uninstall capabilities. This requires the use of the Registry, which is a Windows system database. The Registry is a hierarchical database composed of hives. Both Windows 95 and Windows NT support a Registry. All system information is stored in the Registry. This includes hardware parameters, application installation parameters, and information specific to individual users. There are other categories, but it suffices to say that everything is stored in the Registry.

The Windows NT Register supports security, and the hives are a subset of the Windows 95 hives as listed in Table 42-4. A hive is a system-predefined key of the Registry.

There are several characteristics of the Registry, which are worth noting. The first characteristic is that the `HKEY_CLASSES_ROOT` key is an alias for `HKEY_LOCAL_MACHINE/Software/Classes`. The other characteristic is that the `HKEY__CURRENT_USER` key takes precedence over the `HKEY_LOCAL_MACHINE` during execution.

TABLE 42-4 REGISTRY HIVES IN THE WINDOWS ARCHITECTURE				
HIVE	*WIN 95*	*NT 3.51*	*NT 4.x*	*DESCRIPTION*
HKEY_CLASSES_ROOT	yes	yes	yes	Entries define classes or classes of documents and properties. Both conventional and OLE applications use this key. This key provides backward compatibility with the Windows 3.1 registration database.
HKEY_CURRENT_USER	yes	yes	yes	Current user preferences are stored under this key. This key maps to HKEY_USERS, which is the database of all users.
HKEY_LOCAL_MACHINE	yes	yes	yes	This key describes the physical state of the computer. Included is information as to bus type, system memory, central processing unit, and installed hardware and software. This key maintains a subkey for plug and play information, which is currently only a feature of Windows 95.
HKEY_USERS	yes	yes	yes	The key contains the default user configuration and also contains a branch for each computer user.
HKEY_CURRENT_CONFIG	yes	no	yes	This key is mapped to a subkey within HKEY_LOCAL_MACHINE and is used to store nonuser specific information that pertains to hardware such as server names.
HKEY_DYN_DATA	yes	no	no	The source of dynamic data for performance analysis by VxDs. VxDs provide real-time data to Win32 applications, which is not limited to performance data.

Table 42-5 enumerates the Win32 API Registry functions available to the developer. There are a comparable set of Win16 Register API functions, but a Windows 95 logo application must be 32 bits, or at least primarily 32 bits. 32-bit applications can call 16-bit applications using the "thunk" feature of Windows, which translates to and from either 16 or 32 bits.

TABLE 42-5 WIN32 API REGISTRY FUNCTIONS

FUNCTION	DESCRIPTION
RegCreateKeyEx	Creates the specified key.
RegDeleteValue	Deletes a value associated with a key.
RegEnumKeyEx	Enumerates the subkeys of an open key.
RegEnumValue	Enumerates the values of an open key.
RegFlushKey	Writes all attributes of the open key to the Registry.
RegOpenKeyEx	Opens the indicated key.
RegQueryInfoKey	Returns information about the given key.
ReqQueryValueEx	Returns a value of an open key.
RegSetValueEx	Sets the value for an open key.

concept link

Listing 9-1 of Chapter 9 is a simplified example of using the Registry during an installation.

Deployment Alternatives

There are several deployment mechanisms. Some are simple. The list below presents the deployment alternatives available to the developer.

- ○ ***Systems Management Server*** — Only useful when users are connected on a network. SMS clients include Windows 3.1, Windows 95, Windows for Workgroups 3.11, Windows NT Workstation 3.5 or later, MS-DOS 5.0 and later, IBM OS/2 2.x and OS/2 Warp, and Macintosh System 7.

- ○ ***Internet*** — SMS is not Internet enabled. There may be situations where deploying an Access database with e-mail is satisfactory.

- ○ ***Networ*** — The developer builds a network installation and notifies all users.

- ○ ***Setup*** — Build a traditional diskette-based installation with the Setup Wizard of Visual Basic or use the Access Developers Toolkit. A disk installation procedure follows strict guidelines as to where new files will be installed. The Registry must be used for recording installation parameters and WIN.INI or SYSTEM.INI files must not be used. Application files are never to be copied to either the WINDOWS or SYSTEMS directory unless they are system-wide shared files. Application files are placed as follows:

- o *Application Files* — . . . \Program Files\<app>

- o *Shared Files* — . . . \Program Files\Common Files\System

- o *Ancillary Support Files* — . . . \Program Files\<app>\System

- o *Internet* — Software is installed or updated by including a .CAB file reference within the CODEBASE attribute of a HTML OBJECT tag.

  Software deployment on Internet/Intranet is with the Internet Download Component. The component is prepackaged for downloading over the Internet. An Internet download occurs when the CODEBASE attribute in an HTML OBJECT tag points to a COM object (see Chapter 39).

Win32 Application Installation Guidelines

Ease of use is the guideline for the installation of a Win32 application. The purpose of installation guidelines is to present users with a consistent interface during an installation. The scenario is simple enough. Load the CD-ROM, find the root directory, and double-click SETUP.EXE. The uniformity of installation procedures simplifies the user's task. A measure of your success in adhering to installation guidelines is how close your installation mimics a Microsoft installation. The install program has three basic tasks:

- o Determine the user's hardware and software configuration and available disk space. Take into account disk fragmentation. The installation may be quite slow even though there is enough disk space because of the disk fragmentation. The installation should adjust the displayed required disk storage requirements as options are selected or deselected.

note **The installation should verify whether any of the files already exist on the disk. The installation should verify that existing files are current and should not overwrite existing files that have a later version than the installation version.**

- o Copy applicable files to appropriate directories on the hard disk. Files should be copied to appropriate directories. Application files are never to be copied to either the WINDOWS or SYSTEMS directory unless they are systemwide shared files. The Win32 API functions **GetFileTime**, **GetFileVersionInfo**, and **GetFileInformationByHandle** are used to determine whether existing files should be overwritten.

The Win32 API function **MoveFileEx** is used to replace Windows NT DLLs loaded in memory. Replacing loaded DLLs in Windows 95 is a bit more complex. The new DLLs are copied to the target system with a temporary name. The names are mapped in the WININIT.INI file that is executed by WININIT.EXE at Windows 95 startup. WININIT.EXE is a non-Windows application (MS-DOS) that runs before the protected-mode disk system is loaded. This means that the file name in WININIT.INI must conform to the DOS 8.3 convention.

Applications should be copied to the ...\PROGRAM FILES\MY NEW APP directory. When such a directory does not exist, the installation program should create that directory. Ancillary support files such as DLLs should be copied to the ...\PROGRAM FILES\MY NEW APP\SYSTEM directory. The installation program creates the SYSTEM directory when one doesn't exist.

Shared files are to be copied to the directory ...\PROGRAM FILES\COMMON FILES\SYSTEM. The directory is created when such a directory does not exist.

Font installation is different in Windows NT and Windows 95. Windows 95 allows a shared font installation where most system files, including fonts, are stored on a centrally managed server. The type of platform is determined by interrogation of the Registry for the value *SharedDir* in the Registry key:

HKEY_LOCAL_MACHINE\SOFTWARE\Microsoft\Windows\CurrentVersion\Setup

When the key value is *SharedDir*, the system is a Windows 95 platform.

Installed fonts are identified with the Win32 API function **EnumFontFamilies**. Check the version when the font is present by examining the Registry key:

HKEY_LOCAL_MACHINE\SOFTWARE\Microsoft\Windows\
CurrentVersion\Fonts

Before copying a True Type font (.TTF extension) to the system, check that the named font does not already exist. The font is made available to the system with the Win32 API function **AddFontResource**.

- Initialize the execution environment by adding entries to the Registry or modifying existing files. File directories are registered in the Registry under the key:

```
HKEY_LOCAL_MACHINE\SOFTWARE\Microsoft\Windows\CurrentVersion
```

Values for the key are *ProgramFilesDir* and *CommonFilesDir*.

Fonts are registered at:

```
HKEY_LOCAL_MACHINE\SOFTWARE\Microsoft\Windows\
CurrentVersion\Fonts
```

Both Windows 95 and Windows NT use the same key location.

Both the application and the application's install program should exhibit the Windows 95 look and feel. Common responses should be the default, with depressing the Enter key as the only required action for default values. Options and installation status should always be present. The user must be given the option of canceling an installation. The installation program must remove all files installed, remove any Registry settings, and remove any shortcuts installed when the user cancels an installation. This includes removing all directories created. Usage counts on shared DLLs are decremented, and the user is prompted to delete the shared DLL only when the usage count is zero. Application removal from the Control Panel is an automatic process when the following key is defined:

```
HKEY_LOCAL_MACHINE\SOFTWARE\
Microsoft\Windows\CurrentVersion\
Uninstall\application name
DisplayName=product-name
UninstallString=full-path-to-program command-line-parameters
```

The installation program should offer four installation options:

- *Typical Setup* — This is the default setup option with the most common features being installed.

- *Compact Setup* — This installation copies the least number of files necessary for the application. This installation option is suitable for laptops and systems with limited disk space.

- *Custom Setup* — This installation option lets the user select the options including the destination directory. This option should also provide support for installing features omitted in a previous installation.

- *Silent Setup* — This option runs the installation without user interaction. This option should be a command line for installations that will be run within a batch script.

Das ist alles! There is no more. If you're still with me, I award you the Jolt and cold pizza award in absentia. Persevere.

KEY POINT SUMMARY

Microsoft promotes development standards. This is good because one of the more difficult tasks in the world is to get developers to write documentation. The programmer is off the hook for documentation when the application has an intuitive interface and supports the Microsoft-sponsored initiatives.

Standards reduce training costs. Users always expect a context menu with a right-button click. It's not of any value to be a clever fellow.

The issue of localization is a Microsoft issue and an issue of software development companies. I do not market shrink-wrapped software, and I am reasonably sure that you don't either.

Deploying the application is very important. There are guidelines as to where files must be placed; I can assure you, however, from experience that the rules are not followed.

The Microsoft policy is that an application installation has the right to replace a DLL when the supplied DLL is a newer version. I do not accept that. Developers should deliver software for a specific system level such as Windows NT Server 4.0 service pack 3. The consumer does not know in advance what components are to be installed or changed; the knowledge is gained after the fact. My trick is a fresh boot and mapped directories. Install the new package and re-map the directories. It's a lot of work and I shouldn't have to do it. A European newspaper quoted Mr. Bill Gates as stating that service packs were the ideal upgrade mechanism. I do not accept that. I want only fixes in a service pack. My goal is stability, and either the vendor software works with my DLLs or I don't want it. I am sure that you understand by now that the Microsoft software environment is a maelstrom of change, and until that flux is arrested, there can be no stability. (You might want to revisit the Emperor in Chapter 33.)

APPLYING WHAT YOU'VE LEARNED

The questions below and the three lab exercises measure your understanding of this chapter. This chapter contains more answers to questions on the Windows Architecture examination than any other chapter.

Instant Assessment

1. Name two unique characteristics of the double-byte character set.

2. Your application displays characters from the DBCS from the KANJI character set. The text is displayed correctly on the screen. When the printed characters are clicked an error appears. What is the apparent problem?

3. This chapter lists ten resources that potentially must be localized in a DLL. Name four of these resources.

4. What is the difference between the function pairs `AnsiPrev/AnsiNext` and `CharPrev/CharNext`?

5. What control allows multiple selections?

6. What does the double chevron represent on a command button?

7. What is the general rule of command sequence in a menu?

8. What is the common mistake made when using either a horizontal or vertical scroll bar?

9. Where is the Properties command placed in a pop-up menu?

10. Discuss the Windows 95 logo requirements for an application with respect to OLE.

11. Your application must adjust the volume of an audio speaker. Which control do you use?

 concept link **For answers to the Instant Assessment questions, see Appendix C.**

LAB EXERCISES

Each of these laboratories addresses a different topic of this chapter. Two of these laboratories relate your analysis to the costs of compliance.

Lab 42.85 *Evaluating an application for internationalization*

WA II

Take an existing production application and evaluate the changes necessary for localization. Use the guidelines offered in this chapter. Try to estimate the cost of localizing each of the resources that require localization.

Lab 42.86 *Adding the Accessibility option to Windows 95*

WA II

From Windows 95, go to Control Panel and open it. Double-click the **Add/Remove Programs** icon. From the list of components, click **Accessibility Options** and click *OK.* A dialog box should appear with tabs for Keyboard, Sound, Display, Mouse, and General. Each of these tabs represents a different accessibility aid available in Windows 95 to the impaired individual. Investigate and understand what each of these aids offers.

Lab 42.87 *Reviewing Windows 95 logo requirements*

WA II

Review a recently developed application with respect to Windows 95 logo-compliance requirements. Identify each noncompliant or missing feature and estimate the cost of making the application Windows 95 logo compliant.

Lab 42.88 *Building an installable task*

WA II

The SQL-DMO tool is located in the EXAMPLES\CHAPTER28 folder of the CD-ROM that accompanies this book. Copy that complete directory to a temporary directory of your system. Use the Visual Basic 5.0 Application Setup Wizard to create an installable application. Use the floppy disk option. After the setup is built, you'll want to browse your system for SQLOLE65.TLB, which is normally in the BINN subdirectory of your SQL Server installation. Test the results by installing from floppy disk.

Lab 42.89 *Building a downloadable control*

WA II

In Chapter 3, the **ICheckBook** ActiveX control was built. Rebuild that control using the steps provided in Chapter 3, and when finished, use the Visual Basic 5.0 Application Setup Wizard to create a downloadable component.

Lab 42.90 *Building a network installation*

This lab is almost identical to Lab 42.88. The only difference is that the output will be to a directory. This system is Windows NT Workstation 3.51 sp5, and the output was placed in the path I:\SWSETUP. You'll want to copy the contents of that directory to a network directory so that other users can access the installation. Test the results by installing from the network.

Lab 42.91 *Contingency deployment*

Your company has adopted the Microsoft technologies. You have all classes of server installed. The enterprise is not centrally located. Normal software distribution is with Microsoft Systems Management Server (SMS). Develop a contingency deployment plan when either SMS is unavailable or the backing SQL Server used by SMS is unavailable. (You'll find the solution to this problem quite useful on the Windows Architecture II examination.)

Lab 42.92 *Evaluating internationalization issues*

Using the internationalization guidelines stated in this chapter, estimate the cost of localizing a small existing production application. Pay particular attention to coding style. You'll find that the localization problems associated with coding style have much in common with the Year 2000 problem and two digit dates.

Lab 42.93 *Correlating user problems and interface standards*

This lab exercise is for a large enterprise and assumes the presence of a help desk. The lab also assumes that a trouble report is maintained for each application. Identify the application with the highest incident report, the next highest incident report, and the third highest incident report. Analyze each of these applications for adherence to interface standards. Is there a correlation between failure to adhere to standards and incident reporting levels?

Lab 42.94 *Choosing appropriate controls*

Construct a two-column list. In the left column place the common control names. In the right column place a succinct description of the control and the control usage. Memorize this list. This will enhance your developer skills. Memorizing control usage is quite useful for the Windows Architecture II examination.

Lab 42.95 *Correlating user problems and help support*

This lab exercise is for a large enterprise and assumes the presence of a help desk. The laboratory also assumes that a trouble report is maintained for each application. Identify the application with the highest incident report, the next highest incident report, and the third highest incident report. Analyze each of these applications with respect to the type of help available. You'll have to determine your own grading system. General categories will be the common help facilities such as status bars, tool tips, help menu, F1 key, and .hlp files. Within a general category, each application should be ranked. For example, an application may or may not have tool tips, the tool tips may be incomplete on an individual form, and not all forms may support tool tips. Is there a correlation between failure to adhere to help interface guidelines and incident reporting levels?

Lab 42.96 *It's your turn*

This is the last lab exercise of the last chapter. It's your turn to tell me what's wrong! Evaluate the Visual Basic 5.0 CHAPTER28.VBP project found in the EXAM-PLES\CHAPTER28 folder of the CD-ROM that accompanies this book. The evaluation is with respect to Windows interface guidelines. It doesn't adhere to the Windows 95 paradigm, but many issues are common to both the Windows 3.1 and Windows 95 paradigm. Before you get too rude, I intentionally omitted features —the point being that even though the application is very useful, the application usefulness is limited with an interface that does not adhere to Windows interface guidelines.

Resources

Microsoft Windows Architecture I
Exam Objectives

EXAM 70-160: MICROSOFT WINDOWS ARCHITECTURE I

This appendix lists the Microsoft objectives for the Microsoft Windows Architecture I examination. The objectives represent knowledge goals and require a knowledge of Microsoft products, how to use those products, how to apply your other skills while using the products, and the benefits derived by using those products. The Microsoft Architecture Windows Architecture I examination will identify you as a skilled professional.

Credit Toward Certification

A passing score on this exam counts as core credit toward *Microsoft Certified Solution Developer* certification and as core credit toward *Microsoft Certified Product Specialist* certification.

Skills Being Measured

The Microsoft Windows Architecture I certification exam measures your ability to design, build, and implement business solutions by using Microsoft tools and technologies.

Exam Objectives

Component Technologies

- Explain the benefits of the Component Object Model (COM) as a model for developing software.

- Discuss the use of the ActiveX and the OLE technologies as implementations of the Component Object Model (COM).

- Explain the implementation of Automation in the Microsoft Windows operating systems.

- Identify situations in which Remote Automation is an appropriate technology to use in order to provide a desirable solution.

- Compare component architectures on the basis of performance, maintainability, and extensibility.

- Identify which ActiveX technologies are suited for use in implementing a given business solution.

- Assess structured storage as a component of a given solution.

- Discuss the use of Uniform Data Transfer (UDT) as part of a component solution.

- Evaluate the use of one or more of the following in a given component solution: compound documents, OLE embedding and linking, and OLE drag and drop.

- Evaluate the use of Active Documents as a component of a solution for a given business problem.

- Identify the appropriate use of ActiveX controls within component solutions.

Database Access Technologies

- Given a scenario, choose the appropriate data access tool.

- Evaluate Open Database Connectivity (ODBC) as a component of a given business solution.

- Compare solutions that use ODBC on the basis of performance, maintainability, and interoperability.

- Explain the benefits of Active Data Objects (ADO).

- Explain the benefits of Remote Data Objects (RDO).

- Compare Data Access Objects (DAO) with other potential components of a solution, such as ODBC or RDO.

- Explain the benefits of SQL Distributed Management Objects (SQL-DMO).

- Compare OLE Database (OLE-DB) with ODBC and native APIs as a means of retrieving data in a given scenario.

Operating System Awareness

- Identify situations in which it is appropriate to store persisted data in the registry.

- Identify key architectural differences between Microsoft Windows 95 and Microsoft Windows NT.

- Describe the architecture of Windows Open Services Architecture (WOSA) technologies, including Dynamic Link Libraries (DLLs), memory management, and scheduling.

- Describe how the Windows operating systems manage threads, processes, and scheduling.

- Given a scenario, identify the appropriate type of inter-process communication to use. Types of inter-process communication include:

  - DDE (Dynamic Data Exchange)

  - NetDDE (Network Dynamic Data Exchange)

  - Windows Sockets

  - Named pipes

  - Memory-mapped files

  - NetBIOS

- Choose from 16-bit Windows operating systems, Windows 95, Windows NT Workstation, and Windows NT Server for satisfying a set of requirements.

Choosing Development Tools

- Identify situations in which elements of Microsoft Office, Microsoft BackOffice, and Microsoft Visual Tool Suite are components of an appropriate solution.

- Choose appropriate objects from within Microsoft Office, Microsoft BackOffice, and Microsoft Visual Tool Suite as components for a given solution.
- Choose a development system to use as a tool to provide a solution for a given business problem. Development systems include:
  - Microsoft Visual Basic
  - Microsoft Visual J++
  - Microsoft Access
  - Microsoft Visual C++
  - Microsoft Visual FoxPro

Development Methodologies

- Given a scenario, discuss the use of the Microsoft Solutions Framework (MSF) to guide development, testing, and deployment of a business solution.
- Identify strategies for using source-code control to help manage the development process in a given development environment.

Internet and Intranet

- Choose the appropriate protocol for a given application on the Internet or on an intranet.
- Choose an appropriate design for content for an intranet or for the Internet, based on bandwidth and latency considerations.
- Use Internet Data Connector (IDC), Active Server Pages (ASP), or Microsoft FrontPage to provide Internet or intranet database connectivity.
- Choose the appropriate ActiveX technologies for a given Web-based application.
- Given a scenario, evaluate a Web-based client application.

concept link  **See Appendix F on the CD–ROM for a review of each WA I exam objective.**

Exam Objectives Cross-Reference Chart for Study Purposes

Table A-1 lists the objectives for Exam 70-160, Microsoft Windows Architecture I, in a cross-reference chart for study purposes. Use this table to help you determine the specific chapters in this book you should study, as well as the lab exercises you should review to prepare for the exam.

TABLE A-1 WINDOWS ARCHITECTURE I EXAM OBJECTIVES CROSS-REFERENCE CHART

EXAM OBJECTIVE	CHAPTER(S)	LAB(S)
Component Technologies Explain the benefits of the Component Object Model (COM) as a model for the developing of software.	Chapter 1, "COM"	Lab 1.1
Discuss the use of the ActiveX and the OLE technologies as implementations of the Component Object Model (COM).	Chapter 2, "Interface Issues" Chapter 3, "Object Interfacing" Chapter 5, "Monikers"	Lab 2.2 Lab 3.3 Lab 3.4 Lab 3.5 Lab 3.6 Lab 3.7 Lab 3.8 Lab 3.9 Lab 5.12
Explain the implementation of Automation in the Microsoft Windows operating systems.	Chapter 9, "Automation"	Lab 9.22 Lab 9.23 Lab 9.24
Identify situations in which Remote Automation is an appropriate technology to provide a desirable solution.	Chapter 9, "Automation" Chapter 10, "OLE Controls: Using It All (Well, Almost!)"	Lab 9.22 Lab 9.23 Lab 9.24
Compare component architectures on the basis of performance, maintainability, and extensibility.	Chapter 1, "COM"	Lab 10.25
Identify which ActiveX technologies are suited for use in implementing a given business solution.	Chapter 4, "Structured Storage" Chapter 6, "Uniform Data Transfer" Chapter 7, "Document Linking" Chapter 8, "Document Embedding"	Lab 7.14

continued

TABLE A-1 *(continued)*

Exam Objective	Chapter(s)	Lab(s)
Assess OLE structured storage as a component of a given solution.	Chapter 4, "Structured Storage"	Lab 4.11
Discuss the use of Uniform Data Transfer as a part of a component solution.	Chapter 6, "Uniform Data Transfer"	Lab 6.13
Evaluate the use of one or more of the following in a given solution: compound documents, OLE embedding and linking, and OLE drag and drop.	Chapter 7, "Document Linking" Chapter 8, "Document Embedding" Chapter 6, "Uniform Data Transfer"	Lab 8.15 Lab 8.16 Lab 8.17 Lab 8.18 Lab 8.19 Lab 8.20 Lab 8.21
Evaluate the use of ActiveX documents as a component of a solution for a given business problem.	Chapter 7, "Document Linking" Chapter 8, "Document Embedding"	Lab 36.7
Identify the appropriate use of ActiveX controls within component solutions.	Chapter 10, "OLE Controls: Using It All (Well, Almost!)"	Lab 10.26
Database Access Technologies Given a scenario, choose the appropriate data access tool.	Chapters 11–14, ODBC Chapters 15–23, DAO Chapters 24–26, RDO Chapters 27–28, SQL-DMO Chapters 29–31, OLE-DB	Lab 26.48 Lab 16.35
Evaluate Open Database Connectivity (ODBC) as a component of a solution.	Chapter 11, "ODBC"	Lab 11.27 Lab 12.28 Lab 14.31 Lab 14.32
Compare solutions that use ODBC on the basis of performance, maintainability, and interoperability.	Chapter 11, "ODBC"	Lab 14.29 Lab 14.30
Explain the benefits of Active Data Objects (ADO).	Chapter 29, "OLE-DB"	Lab 30.52
Explain the benefits of Remote Data Objects (RDO).	Chapter 24, "RDO"	Lab 25.45 Lab 26.46 Lab 26.47 Lab 26.48

Exam Objective	Chapter(s)	Lab(s)
Compare Data Access Objects (DAO) with other potential components of a solution, such as ODBC and RDO.	Chapter 24, "RDO"	Lab 24.44 Lab 16.33 Lab 16.34 Lab 19.38 Lab 19.39
Explain the benefits of SQL Distributed Management Objects (SQL-DMO).	Chapter 27, "SQL-DMO"	Lab 28.49
Compare OLE Database (OLE-DB) with ODBC and native APIs as a means of retrieving data in a given scenario.	Chapter 31, "Active Data Objects (ADO)"	Lab 29.50 Lab 29.51 Lab 31.53
Operating System Awareness Identify situations in which it is appropriate to store persisted data in the Windows Registry.	Chapter 9, "Automation" Chapter 33, "Operating System Awareness" Chapter 42, "Solution Interface Issues"	Lab 33.56
Identify key architectural differences between Microsoft Windows 95 and Microsoft Windows NT.	Chapter 33, "Operating System Awareness"	Lab 33.57
Describe the architecture of Windows Open Services Architecture (WOSA) technologies, including Dynamic Link Libraries (DLLs), memory management, and scheduling.	Chapter 33, "Operating System Awareness"	Lab 33.58
Describe how the Windows operating systems manage threads, processes, and scheduling.	Chapter 33, "Operating System Awareness"	Lab 33.59
Given a scenario, identify the appropriate type of interprocess communication to use. Types of interprocess communication include: DDE (Dynamic Data Exchange), NetDDE (Net Dynamic Data Exchange), Windows Sockets, Named Pipes, Memory-Mapped Files, NetBIOS.	Chapter 33, "Operating System Awareness"	Lab 33.55

continued

TABLE A-1 *(continued)*		
EXAM OBJECTIVE	*CHAPTER(S)*	*LAB(S)*
Choose from 16-bit Windows operating systems, Windows 95, Windows NT Workstation, and Windows NT Server for satisfying a set of requirements.	Chapter 33, "Operating System Awareness"	Lab 33.63
Choosing Development Tools Identify situations in which elements of Microsoft Office, Microsoft BackOffice, and Microsoft Visual Tool Suite are components of an appropriate solution.	Chapter 34, "Choosing Development Tools"	Lab 34.65
Choose appropriate objects from within Microsoft Office, BackOffice, and Visual Tool Suite as components for a given solution.	Chapter 34, "Choosing Development Tools"	Lab 17.36
Choose a development system to use as a tool to provide a solution for a given business problem. Development tools include: Microsoft Visual Basic, Microsoft J $^{++}$, Microsoft Access, Microsoft Visual C $^{++}$, and Microsoft Visual FoxPro.	Chapter 34, "Choosing Development Tools"	Lab 34.64
Development Methodologies Given a scenario, discuss the use of the Microsoft Solutions Framework to guide development, testing, and deployment of a business solution.	Chapter 35, "Development Methodologies"	Lab 35.68
Identify strategies for using source-code control to help manage the development process in a given development environment.	Chapter 35, "Development Methodologies"	Lab 35.69
Internet and Intranet Choose the appropriate protocol for a given application on the Internet or on an intranet.	Chapter 36, "Internet and Intranet Architecture"	Lab 36.72

Exam Objective	Chapter(s)	Lab(s)
Choose an appropriate design for content for an intranet or for the Internet, based on bandwidth and latency considerations.	Chapter 39, "Internet Applications with Élan"	Lab 39.76
Use IDC (Internet Data Connector), Active Server Pages, or Microsoft FrontPage to provide Internet or intranet database connectivity.	Chapter 37, "Anatomy of a Web Site"	Lab 37.73
Choose the appropriate ActiveX technologies for a given Web-based application.	Chapter 38, "Internet Tools for the Trenches"	Lab 38.74
Given a scenario, evaluate a Web-based client application.	Chapter 39, "Internet Applications with Élan"	Lab 38.75

Microsoft Windows Architecture II
Exam Objectives

EXAM 70-161: MICROSOFT WINDOWS ARCHITECTURE II

The Windows Architecture II examination is much more difficult than the Windows Architecture I examination. Successfully passing this examination marks you as an accomplished professional. Beyond understanding the Microsoft architecture and Microsoft products, the Microsoft Architecture II examination requires knowledge in such areas as data modeling, business rules, and data normalization.

The MCSD professional will have a broad knowledge of all technologies and understand all architectural issues. Creating an application today is not the creation of a monolithic mass, but the melding of components representing different and possibly diverse technologies. The skilled MCSD professional must be a generalist to accomplish the melding.

Credit Toward Certification

A passing score on this exam counts as core credit toward *Microsoft Certified Solution Developer* certification and as core credit toward *Microsoft Certified Product Specialist* certification.

Skills Being Measured

The Microsoft Windows Architecture II certification exam measures your ability to design, build, and implement business solutions by using Microsoft tools and technologies.

Exam Objectives

Deployment Issues

- Identify appropriate information for a solution to store in the Microsoft Windows registry, and specify where in the registry this information should be stored.
- Given a scenario for installing or removing applications, explain the role that the registry should play.
- Given a business solution, develop a strategy for registering the components.
- Identify areas in which a particular business solution is or is not in compliance with the Windows logo requirements or the Office logo requirements.
- Given a scenario for deploying an application, develop an appropriate disk-based, Web-based, or network-based solution for the deployment.
- Given a scenario for upgrading an application, develop an appropriate disk-based, Web-based, or network-based solution for the upgrade.
- Given a scenario, evaluate the use of Microsoft Systems Management Server as an aid to deploying a solution.
- Given a business solution and a deployment scenario, discuss the usefulness of code signing and how code signing is implemented.

Solutions Design Issues

- Describe the benefits of the Windows Open Systems Architecture (WOSA).
- Choose an appropriate replication strategy and technology for a proposed solution.
- Given a solution, evaluate the performance implications of architectural choices.

- Given a particular business process, create an appropriate object model.
- Identify an appropriate multiple-tier application design.
- Given a business scenario, identify what type of solution (single-tier application or multiple-tier application) is appropriate.
- Evaluate a proposed object hierarchy as an appropriate solution in the context of a particular business problem.
- Evaluate Open Database Connectivity (ODBC) as a component of a database application.
- Given a database scenario, evaluate a proposed schema in terms of data normalization.
- Use Entity-Relationship Analysis (ERA) to identify the architecture of the database component for a particular business solution.
- Given a scenario, choose between a local database engine and a remote database engine.
- Evaluate a given architecture as appropriate for a transactional or decision-support system.
- Evaluate the security implications of a proposed business solution.
- Identify appropriate situations for use of a console application.

Internationalization Issues

- Given a business solution, explain the advantages and disadvantages of using the Unicode character representation as a component.
- Analyze the issues involved in developing localized applications.

Choosing Technologies

- Describe the features and capabilities of each Microsoft BackOffice product and use each product as a component of an integrated solution.
- Given a particular business problem, identify potential uses of major APIs, including OLE Messaging, DAO, ODBC, RDO, SQL DMO, and Messaging API (MAPI).
- Describe the features and capabilities of MAPI as a component of a solution.

o Describe the features and capabilities of Windows Telephony API (TAPI) as a component of a solution.

o Describe the features and capabilities of License Service API (LSAPI) as a component of a solution.

o Describe the features and capabilities of Windows SNA API as a component of a solution.

o Describe the features and capabilities of Speech API as a component of a solution.

o Describe the features and capabilities of Crypto API as a component of a solution.

Internet and Intranet

o Compare ActiveX scripting with other technologies as the basis for solving a particular business problem.

o Implement a solution using ActiveX scripting.

o Evaluate a solution using ActiveX controls in terms of performance, capabilities, distribution, security, and multiplatform support.

o Given a business scenario, decide whether Java provides an appropriate solution.

o Given a specification for a Web-based solution, choose between client-side scripting and server-side scripting for components of the solution.

o Compare the Internet Server API (ISAPI) with the Common Gateway Interface (CGI) for use within a specific Internet or intranet application.

o Given a business problem, choose appropriate components and interfaces for developing and deploying an Internet or intranet solution.

User Interface Issues

o Evaluate the interface of a proposed business solution for compliance with the Windows user-interface standards.

o Given a business solution, choose appropriate user-interface components to build the interface.

o Evaluate the various methods of providing help information to users (such as status bars, ToolTips, Help menu, F1 key, and .hlp files).

- Identify the features and benefits of a shell extension as a component of a solution.

- Given accessibility requirements as part of an application design, identify appropriate implementation of these requirements.

- Given a proposed distribution platform (such as 16-bit Windows, 32-bit Windows, the Internet, or an intranet), apply interface design guidelines to evaluate a given interface.

 concept link **See Appendix F on the CD-ROM for a review of the WA II exam objectives.**

Exam Objectives Cross-Reference Chart for Study Purposes

Table B-1 lists the objectives for Exam 70-161, Microsoft Windows Architecture II, in a cross-reference chart for study purposes. Use this table to help you determine the specific chapters in this book you should study, as well as the lab exercises you should review to prepare for the exam.

TABLE B-1 WINDOWS ARCHITECTURE II EXAM OBJECTIVES CROSS-REFERENCE CHART		
EXAM OBJECTIVE	*CHAPTER(S)*	*LAB(S)*
Deployment Issues Identify appropriate information for a solution to store in the Microsoft Windows Registry, and specify where in the Registry this information should be stored.	Chapter 33, "Operating System Awareness"	Lab 42.88
Given a scenario for installing or removing applications, explain the role that the Registry should play.	Chapter 42, "Solution Interface Issues"	Lab 42.89
Given a business solution, develop a strategy for registering the components.	Chapter 42, "Solution Interface Issues"	Lab 38.74

continued

TABLE B-1 *(continued)*

Exam Objective	Chapter(s)	Lab(s)
Identify areas in which a particular business solution is or is not in compliance with the Windows logo requirements or the Office logo requirements.	Chapter 42, "Solution Interface Issues"	Lab 42.87
Given a scenario for deploying an application, develop an appropriate disk-based, Web-based, or network-based solution for deployment.	Chapter 42, "Solution Interface Issues"	Lab 42.90
Given a scenario for upgrading an application, develop an appropriate disk-based, Web-based, or network-based solution for the upgrade.	Chapter 39, "Internet Application with Élan"	Lab 39.77
Given a scenario, evaluate the use of Microsoft Systems Management Server as an aid to deploying a solution.	Chapter 34, "Choosing Development Tools" Chapter 42, "Solution Interface Issues"	Lab 42.91
Solution Design Issues Describe the benefits of Windows Open Systems Architecture (WOSA).	Chapter 1, "COM" Chapter 11, "ODBC" Chapter 33, "Operating System Awareness"	Lab 14.31
Choose an appropriate replication strategy and technology for a proposed solution.	Chapter 34, "Choosing Development Tools"	Lab 34.66
Given a solution, evaluate the performance implications of architectural choices.	Chapter 41, "Designing the Solution"	Lab 41.81
Given a particular business process, create an appropriate object model.	Chapter 41, "Designing the Solution"	Lab 41.82
Identify an appropriate multiple tier application design.	Chapter 41, "Designing the Solution"	Lab 41.81
Given a business scenario, identify what type of solution (single-tier application or multiple-tier solution) is appropriate.	Chapter 41, "Designing the Solution"	Lab 41.83

EXAM OBJECTIVE	CHAPTER(S)	LAB(S)
Evaluate a proposed object hierarchy as an appropriate solution in the context of a particular business problem.	Chapter 41, "Designing the Solution"	Lab 41.83
Evaluate Open Database Connectivity (ODBC) as a component of a database application.	Chapter 11, "ODBC"	Lab 14.31
Given a database scenario, evaluate a proposed schema in terms of data normalization.	Chapter 41, "Designing the Solution"	Lab 41.84
Use Entity-Relationship Analysis (ERA) to identify the architecture of the database component for a particular business solution.	Chapter 41, "Designing the Solution"	Lab 41.82
Given a scenario, choose between a local database engine and a remote database engine.	Chapter 41, "Designing the Solution"	Lab 41.81
Evaluate a given architecture as appropriate for a transactional or decision-support system.	Chapter 41, "Designing the Solution"	Lab 41.81
Evaluate the security implications of a proposed business solution.	Chapter 33, "Operating System Awareness"	Lab 35.70
Identify appropriate situations for use of a console application.	Chapter 33, "Operating System Awareness"	Lab 33.61
Internationalization Issues Given a business solution, explain the advantages and disadvantages of using the Unicode character representation as a component.	Chapter 42, "Solution Interface Issues"	Lab 33.60
Analyze the issues involved in developing localized applications.	Chapter 42, "Solution Interface Issues"	Lab 42.92
Choosing Technologies Describe the features and capabilities of each Microsoft BackOffice product and use each product as a component of an integrated solution.	Chapter 34, "Choosing Development Tools"	Lab 28.49

continued

TABLE B-1 *(continued)*

Exam Objective	Chapter(s)	Lab(s)
Given a particular business problem, identify potential uses of major APIs, including OLE messaging, DAO, ODBC, SQL-DMO, and Messaging API (MAPI).	Chapter 9, "Automation" Chapters 11–14, ODBC Chapters 15–23, DAO Chapters 27–28, SQL–DMO Chapter 33, "Operating System Awareness"	Lab 26.47
Describe the features and capabilities of MAPI as a component of a solution.	Chapter 33, "Operating System Awareness"	Lab 34.67
Describe the features and capabilities of Windows Telephony API (TAPI) as a component of a solution.	Chapter 33, "Operating System Awareness"	Lab 33.62
Describe the features and capabilities of Licensing Service API (LSAPI) as a component of a solution.	Chapter 33, "Operating System Awareness"	Lab 33.63
Describe the features and capabilities of Windows SNA API as a component of a solution.	Chapter 33, "Operating System Awareness"	Lab 14.31
Describe the features and capabilities of Speech API as a component of a solution.	Chapter 33, "Operating System Awareness"	Lab 33.62
Describe the features and capabilities of CryptoAPI as a component of a solution.	Chapter 33, "Operating System Awareness"	Lab 33.62
Internet and Intranet Compare ActiveX scripting with other technologies as the basis for solving a particular business problem.	Chapter 36, "Internet and Intranet Architecture" Chapter 39, "Internet Applications with Élan"	Lab 37.73
Implement a solution using ActiveX scripting	Chapter 39, "Internet Applications with Élan"	Lab 39.76 Lab 38.75
Evaluate a solution using ActiveX controls in terms of performance, capabilities, distribution, and multiplatform support.	Chapter 39, "Internet Applications with Élan"	Lab 39.78
Given a business scenario, decide whether Java provides an appropriate solution.	Chapter 39, "Internet Applications with Élan"	Lab 39.78

Exam Objective	Chapter(s)	Lab(s)
Given a specification for a Web-based solution, choose between client-side scripting and server-side scripting for components of the solution.	Chapter 39, "Internet Applications with Élan"	Lab 36.72
Compare the Internet Server API (ISAPI) with the Common Gateway Interface (CGI) for use within a specific Internet or intranet application.	Chapter 36, "Internet and Intranet Architecture" Chapter 38, "Internet Tools for the Trenches"	Lab 38.74
Given a business problem, choose appropriate components and interfaces for developing and deploying an Internet or Intranet solution.	Chapter 37, " Anatomy of a Web Site" Chapter 38, "Internet Tools for the Trenches"	Lab 38.74
User Interface Issues Evaluate the interface of a proposed business solution for compliance with the Windows user-interface standards.	Chapter 42, "Solution Interface Issues"	Lab 42.93
Given a business solution, choose appropriate user interface components to build the interface.	Chapter 42, "Solution Interface Issues"	Lab 42.94
Evaluate the various methods of providing help information to users (such as status bars, ToolTips, help menus, F1 key, and .hlp files).	Chapter 42, "Solution Interface Issues"	Lab 42.95
Identify the features and benefits of a shell extension as a component of a solution.	Chapter 42, "Solution Interface Issues"	Lab 42.87
Given accessibility requirements as part of an application design, identify appropriate implementation of these requirements.	Chapter 42, "Solution Interface Issues"	Lab 42.86
Given a proposed distribution platform (such as 16-bit Windows, 32-bit Windows, the Internet, or an Intranet), apply interface design guidelines to evaluate a given interface.	Chapter 42, "Solution Interface Issues"	Lab 42.96

Answers to Instant Assessment Questions

This appendix provides the answers to the Instant Assessment questions found at the end of each chapter. The answers are divided by part and listed in chapter order.

PART I: COMPONENT TECHNOLOGIES

Chapter 1: COM

1. **What is the unique difference between a traditional application library service call and that of a client accessing a COM server object interface?**

   A traditional application library publishes service interfaces. This is different than COM, which only publishes generic infrastructure interfaces. Interrogation of the COM object determines the services available.

   COM components do not publish the services available. New features can be added to a COM component and the component installed in the enterprise with no application impact. The installation is transparent to the application. The application cannot interrogate an **IUnknown** interface about features that it doesn't know about. The COM model handles version issues. The server object recognizes an older version of the application and emulates features of a prior version.

2. What interface is required of all COM objects?

IUnknown is the interface which must be supported by all COM objects. The interface supports the **QueryInterface** method for interrogation of services available and the methods **Release** and **AddRef** for object management.

3. What feature does Aggregation or Delegation support?

Aggregation and Delegation support Interface Inheritance. This is a conceptual model that ensures code reusability. Interface Inheritance should not be confused with Implementation Inheritance of C++.

4. What is another name for an Application Programming Interface (API)?

Application Programming Interface (API) is a synonym for Windows Operating System Extensions.

5. What is an SPI and who uses it?

The Service Provider Interface (SPI) is a programming interface that insulates the client application from the different features of various service providers. The client application is written to one API. This model is valuable in a heterogeneous enterprise where there are multiple service providers. The same application program can communicate with Microsoft MSMail, IBM Profs, or Digital Equipment All-In-One.

The SPI model is the other half of the equation and is used by third-party vendors to provide services to a client application. The MAPI model is a good example of service providers and the MAPI SPI. MAPI service providers are free to create and market store, address book, and transport services.

The API/SPI model is a key element of the Microsoft Consistent and Unified Interface. The client uses the API model to develop a Consistent and Unified interface to *use* a MAPI service. The service provider uses the SPI model to *offer* a MAPI service.

6. Name four benefits of the COM model.

- The COM model of component pluggable components reduces software development costs. Off-the-shelf components may be used.

- A component architecture is easy to change as the business model changes.

- The COM model insulates the Enterprise from the traditional problem of updating all applications whenever a library is changed. New or revised

COM components can be installed in the Enterprise with no impact. Older versions are emulated, saving the expense of updating the application.

○ The COM model is a binary interface specification and is language-independent. A COM model may be shared across diverse platforms.

○ COM interfaces are rigid. As new interfaces are added, the original interfaces remain unchanged.

○ All COM objects share the same consistent interface of **IUnknown**. A distributed COM component application can be built since the objects and interfaces are uniquely identified.

7. What is Emulation?

Emulation occurs when the COM server objects detect a prior version of a client application. A prior version of the server is emulated.

8. What is a benefit of Emulation?

Emulation in the COM model is the server object emulating an older server version when it detects a client expecting an older server version. This feature can significantly reduce software costs. Emulation means that not all machines in an enterprise need to be synchronized simultaneously. The logistics are reduced and the enterprise can be upgraded in a controlled manner. Emulation reduces client software updating costs and promotes code reuse.

9. What is Aggregation?

Aggregation is an expression of interface inheritance. An aggregated object is passed to the **IUnknown** reference of the controlling object at creation time. The control object is given the responsibility of managing the services available in the aggregated object. The services of the aggregated object are directly available to the client; however, the client interrogates the **IUnknown** of the control object to determine the services available from the aggregated object. The **IUnknown** of the aggregated object is encapsulated.

10. Describe Delegation?

Delegation is a form of interface inheritance where the control object calls the delegated object. The control object is a client of the delegated object. The delegated object does not know that it plays the role of a delegated object and cannot distinguish between a call from the client or the control object.

The delegated object is a publicly accessible COM object and is also directly accessible from the client. An example is any version of Microsoft Word using a drawing tool. The drawing tool is either an OLE control (OCX) or an ActiveX control in the current technology. Microsoft Word has access to a spell checker object; however, the drawing control also has access to the same spell checker object. I am using Visio as the drawing tool for this book. When I installed Visio, the setup program asked me if I wanted to use the spell checker of Microsoft Word.

11. Describe Containment.

Containment is a variation on delegation where the delegated object is contained within the control object and is not accessible by the client application. Delegation encapsulates the **IUnknown** of the delegated object while containment encapsulates the complete delegated object.

12. Describe Encapsulation.

Encapsulation is the isolation of data or properties from the client. Methods of the object must be used for indirect data access. The client cannot directly access the data. Encapsulation is not limited to data. Containment is an example of object encapsulation.

13. What are the three commonly accepted criteria for object orientation?

I'll assume that the object is a class with methods and properties. Commonly accepted criteria for object orientation are Encapsulation, Inheritance, and Polymorphism. Other answers in this section describe each of these criteria with respect to the COM model.

14. Explain the differences between inheritance in C++ and inheritance in the COM model.

Interface inheritance is a concept of the COM model. By definition all COM objects support the **IUnknown** interface. This does not mean that an object will use existing code for **IUnknown** but that the **IUnknow** methods are always available in any COM object. This technique differs from implementation inheritance where code is inherited from a base class. Each model demonstrates a different type of inheritance; however, both models realize the same goals of reusable code.

15. What is Polymorphism?

Polymorphism is the access of multiple and different objects through the same interface. Aggregation, Delegation, and Containment are examples of Polymorphism.

16. What is the *fragile base-class* problem?

The *fragile base-class* problem is a phenomenon of implementation inheritance associated with an object-oriented language such as C++. Change the base class and the project must be recompiled and relinked.

This problem doesn't occur with COM, which uses generic and universal interfaces and doesn't publish the services available, while C++ class publishes the services available.

17. How does the COM model avoid the *fragile base-class* problem?

COM avoids the fragile base-class problem by not publishing service interfaces. Only generic and universal infrastructure interfaces are published. A client must interrogate the **IUnknown** interface to locate a service.

Chapter 2: Object Interfacing

1. What is a vtable?

A vtable is a virtual function pointer table. The client knows only the address of the table. The interface **IUnknown::QueryInterface** is the first entry and is used to locate other interfaces.

2. What interface must all COM objects support?

All COM objects must support the **IUnknown** interface.

3. What is the minimum number of interfaces for a COM (OLE) object? Name the interfaces.

The minimum number of interfaces that constitutes a COM object is two. They are **IUnknown** and **IClassFactory**. This has been relaxed, with ActiveX™ requiring only the **IUnknown** interface and the ability to be self-registering.

4. Name the three IUnknown methods.

QueryInterface, **AddRef**, and **Release**.

5. Name two unique characteristics of the IDispatch interface.

The **IDispatch** interface is only used by OLE Automation (Automation), and it supports a DISPID for function and parameter referencing.

6. What is a dual interface?

A dual interface is an **IDispatch** interface that supports a vtable entry for a function and a DISPID for the same function.

7. Under what condition might you use a dual interface?

A dual interface is only useful for an in-process server. Marshaling the proxy and stub consumes a disproportionate amount of resources; consequently, a remote or local server will see no benefit from a dual interface.

8. What function is it that the COM library cannot do?

The COM library cannot initialize an object. The object must initialize itself. The client calls **IUnknown::QueryInterface** requesting a pointer to **IPersistFile**. If the request is successful, the client asks the object to initialize itself by calling **IPersistFile::Load**.

9. What is the role of the Service Control Manager?

The Service Control Manager (SCM) is responsible for locating the requested server. This task may involve setting up an RPC. If the request server is not local, SCM sends a message to the target machine and requests the SCM on the target machine to start the server.

10. What is the role of IUnknown::AddRef and IUnknown::Release?

AddRef and **Release** manage the in-use count for an object and the subsequent life of an object. The object cannot be destroyed when the usage count is non-zero.

11. Which component in the COM architecture is responsible for using IUnknown::AddRef and IUnknown::Release?

There really isn't one component responsible for managing **IUnknown:: AddRef**. It is actually the responsibility of any method that creates a pointer. Those methods are **IUnknown::QueryInterface**, **IOleContainer::GetObject**, **IOleContainer::EnumObjects**, and **IClassFactory::CreateInstance**.

12. Identify the COM library component used to start a server.

The COM library function **CoGetClassObject** is the function that starts the server load process. Actually, most of the work is passed off to the Service Control Manager.

13. **Identify the information which must be supplied to the COM library component identified in question 12 in order to successfully start a server.**

    The client must supply the CLSID of the requested server and the IID of the **IClassFactory** interface to COM library function **CoGetClassObject**.

Chapter 3: Interface Issues

1. What is the global name space problem?

The global name space problem is the problem of creating unique names in a global environment. The local directory named *temp* that you'll find in your Windows has the same local name on all Windows systems. Our problem is that each of these directories may be unique locally but not globally.

2. How is the global name space problem solved?

The Open Software Foundation (OSF) proposed a Unique Universal Identifier (UUID) in their Distributed Computing Architecture (DCE) specification. Microsoft adopted that concept.

3. Explain the differences between a UUID, a GUID, and an IID.

The differences are enumerated as follows:

- A Unique Universal Identifier (UUID) is an OSF DCE concept.
- A Globally Unique Identifier (GUID) is the 128-bit Microsoft implementation of a UUID.
- A COM object Class Identifier (CLSID) is a GUID.
- A COM object Interface Identifier (IID) is a GUID.

4. Name three methods of creating a UUID.

A GUID may be created by using the program UUIDGEN, the graphic program GUIDGEN, the COM library function COCreateGUID, or the WIN32 RPC_EntryUuidCreate. Visual Basic 5.0 generates them automatically.

5. What is the unique requirement of an Insertable Object?

All insertable objects require a GUID. Insertable objects are identified by selecting the Insert menu from a Microsoft product such as Word, Access, Excel, or any other product and selecting Object from the resultant menu.

6. When doesn't an object require a GUID?

A GUID is not required for all objects. If an object was not created by the COM library, then it is not required to have a CLSID. However, that does not mean that a non-COM object cannot use COM objects. Indeed they can, and a non-COM object using an OLE Automation server is an example.

7. What is the difference between the ODL compiler MKTYPLIB.EXE and the IDL compiler MIDL?

The MKTYPLIB compiler is now obsolete and has been replaced by the newer Microsoft Interface Definition Language (MIDL). MIDL is the compiler of choice for a 32-bit platform.

8. Name four types of information created by an ODL or IDL compiler.

The MIDL or MKTYPLIB compilers produce a type library, (.TLB extension), C++ header files, proxy code, and stub code. The Proxy and stub code is used for marshaling interfaces for local or remote servers.

9. Name two instances where a GUID is necessary.

A Globally Unique Identifier is required for COM Model object and interface identification.

10. What is Persistent data?

Persistent data is non-volatile data that is available to COM objects. The lifetime of persistent data does not depend upon the lifetime of the object. Data stored in the Registry is persistent since it is still available after the COM object terminates, and the object is released when the usage count goes to zero. Files contain persistent data. The object's type library entry in the registry will have the actual type library file name.

Chapter 4: Structured Storage

1. What is the difference between structured storage and compound files?

Structured storage is a model, and compound files are the implementation of that model.

2. Name the four objects of structured storage.

The structured storage objects are **LockBytes**, **RootStorage**, **Storage**, and the **Stream** object. These objects implement a file system within a file system. The basic functionality can be described as:

- LockBytes — A transparent interface to the underlying file system or global memory

- RootStorage — This object is equivalent to a master directory. Very little functionality is provided at this level.

- Storage — The storage object can be thought of as a directory. It is always a substorage object to a parent storage. Transactions and locking is supported at this level but not at the stream level.

- Streams — Streams are analogous to files. Locking and transactions are not supported in the OLE compound file implementation.

3. Which interface uses the ILockBytes interface?

The **ILockBytes** interface is used transparently by the **IStorage** and **IStream** interfaces. Methods of the **ILockBytes** interface are not used directly.

4. Are there any restrictions on the ILockBytes Interface? If there are, what are they?

As stated above, the **IStream** and **IStorage** interfaces use the **ILockBytes** interface transparently. This means that the marshaling of the **IStream** or **IStorage** interfaces to another process will automatically include the **ILockBytes** interface. This can be prevented by implementing a custom **IMarshal** interface, which will prevent the automatic marshaling of the **ILockBytes** interface.

5. What is the purpose of the one IRootStorage method?

SwitchToFile is the only method of the **IRootStorage** interface. Its purpose is to switch to another file and do a full save when low memory conditions occur. It is not intended to be used as a save-as mechanism, and such an operation may not be supported in future releases of COM.

6. Name two issues when marshaling a stream object to another process.

The first issue is that the current stream pointer is marshaled to the other process. An alternative is using the method **IStream::Clone** with the resulting pointer passed to the other process. There is still one copy of the data; however, there are two different pointers to the data.

The second issue is that the underlying **ILockBytes** interface is also marshaled to the other process. The alternative is a custom **IMarshal** interface.

7. What are the IStream interface limitations?

The OLE implementation of compound files does not support transactions or locking for the **IStream** interface. The **IStream** methods affected by this limitation are **LockRegion**, **UnlockRegion**, **Commit**, and **Revert**.

8. Describe the *data-push* model.

Data-push is a model supported by an asynchronous moniker. It is implemented in the **IStream::Read** interface. The client can return from **IBindStatusCallBack::OnDataAvailable** before reading all the data. The client may elect to skip blocks of data. A seek is available with this model, but only to skip back to missing blocks. In general, a seek is not available with an asynchronous data stream.

9. Describe the *data-pull* model.

Data-pull is a model supported by an asynchronous moniker. It is implemented in the **IStream::Read** interface. The client cannot return from **IBindStatusCallBack::OnDataAvailable** until all the data is read. The client controls the stream. This differs from the data-push model where the source controls the stream.

10. What is the role of IPersistMoniker?

IPersistMoniker signifies an asynchronous object. Binding URL monikers in the background is an example. The synchronous objects interfaces **IPersistFile**, **IPersisnStreamInit**, or **IPersistStorage** use **IMoniker::BindToObject**.

11. Compare the role of IPersistMoniker and persistent data as compared to IMoniker::BindToObject and persistent data.

The difference in techniques is that the **IPersistMoniker** implementation allows control to be given to the object being instantiated. This technique is used for binding URL monikers in the background after the application has regained control.

This compares with the **IPersistStream**, **IPersistStorage**, and **IPersistStream[Init]** interfaces, which use **IMoniker::BindToObject** to bind persistent data to the object.

12. Describe using the IPersistPropertyBag interface.

This is a shared labor. The object decides what to save or load with the **IPersistPropertyBag** interface, and the client saves the information in any manner it deems proper with the **IPropertyBag** interface. The client reports errors back to the object with the **IErrorLog** interface.

13. **What is the primary use of IPersistStream, IPersistStorage, and IPersistMemory?**

    IPersistStorage is associated with files, **IPersistStream** is associated with monikers, and **IPersistMemory** is associated with global memory.

14. **What valuable service does IStorage::CopyTo perform besides performing the utilitarian role of copying a storage object?**

    IStorage::CopyTo defragments a storage object by creating a contiguous stream object in the target compound file. All lost space between stream objects in the source compound file is recovered in the new compound file.

Chapter 5: Monikers

Monikers

1. **Which interface must be supported for all item monikers?**

   The **IOleItemContainer** interface must be supported by all item monikers. The interface includes the functionality necessary for parsing object names and communicating with the object or with the object's storage.

2. **In binding a composite moniker, which moniker is responsible for determining the pointer for the original IID passed in by the client?**

   The simplest answer is the last moniker or the top moniker in the push down stack. The binding process has each item moniker invoking **BindToObject** on the left context object with the IID of the **IOleItemContainer** interface. These addresses are then cascaded back down the stack, and the last item moniker executes the required **QueryInterface**.

3. **When is the first action the client performs related to binding a moniker?**

   The very first action is to create the binding context with the global API **CreateBindCtx**. This allocates and initializes a binding context for later use by the **IMoniker** interface. Simple moniker can be bound directly with the global API **BindMoniker**.

4. **What is the second step?**

   The client starts the binding process by invoking **IMoniker::BindToObject** with the moniker pointer and a pointer to the bind context previously created.

5. **Which important interface does IMoniker inherit besides IUnknown?**

   IMoniker inherits both the **IPerist** and the **IPersistStream** interfaces. These interfaces are necessary for reading and writing monikers to or from a stream.

6. **What is the Running Object Table?**

   The Running Object Table (ROT) is a global table of active objects. The moniker provider is responsible for ROT table maintenance. Entries are removed when objects are no longer running. The ROT table optimizes the binding process. It's not necessary to bind running objects, and **IMoniker** can invoke **IOleItemContainer::GetObject** rather than <LeftContext>::BindToObject.

7. **What restrictions are there on the global API GetRunningObjectTable call?**

   The Running Object Table should only be accessed from within the context of the bind operation. A moniker class will invoke **IBindCtx::GetRunning-ObjectTable**. Failure to do this could result in a severe bug such as the bug that occurred with Access 95 where there were two instances of the same memory data.

8. **What is the unique characteristic of the IOleLink interface?**

   Only a linked object implements this interface. The container object uses this interface for locating the presentation data, activating the link to the native data, and for locating the link source.

9. **What is the unique characteristic of the IOleUILinkContainer interface?**

   The **IOleUILinkContainer** must be implemented by container objects when the global API **OleUIEditLinks** is used to display a dialog box. This includes the Links dialog box, the Change Source dialog box, the Update Links dialog box, and the Object Properties dialog box.

10. **Explain the relationship between MkParseDisplayName, IParseDisplayName, and IMoniker::GetDisplayName.**

    MkParseDisplayName indirectly uses **IParseDisplayName**, which is the inverse of **IMoniker::GetDisplayName**.

Marshaling

1. **What is the general meaning of marshaling within the COM context?**

   Marshaling is the packaging of data by a proxy before being sent by an RPC or LPC to a destination stub.

2. **What are the generic names for the COM functions that perform marshaling?**

The generic names are proxy and stub. The proxy packages the data on the local system and sends it to another site which may be remote. The data is unpacked there by a stub before it is passed to the target server.

3. **What feature of COM requires marshaling?**

Marshaling is required for late binding.

Default marshaling is accomplished with the **IStdMarshal** interface. Name four reasons for custom marshaling.

- ○ Custom marshaling is a consideration when the target server object itself is a proxy for some other object.

- ○ Some objects store their entire state in shared memory. Creating a custom proxy gives immediate access to the storage.

- ○ Some objects have an immutable state after creation — that is, the object cannot change. A custom proxy can create a copy of this immutable state without the overhead of an RPC channel.

- ○ A custom proxy can be used to batch cached data until such time as a commit operation is performed.

Chapter 6: Uniform Data Transfer

Uniform Data Transfer

1. **When is an application using uniform data transfer?**

Any object implementing the **IDataObject** interface is using uniform data transfer.

2. **Discuss the benefits of uniform data transfer.**

Uniform Data Transfer (UDT) provides a wrapper function for the various clipboard protocols and adds support for additional protocols. The most direct benefit to the user is that object I/O is no longer limited to global memory.

3. **Identify the data structures associated with uniform data transfer and describe the contents of each structure.**

There are three data structures associated with Uniform Data Transfer. The first structure is **FORMATETC**, which stores the object format type and the aspect (view), which can be native data, an icon, a thumbnail sketch, or preformatted printer output.

The object storage type is stored in FORMATETC. The type can be global memory, a disk file, a storage object, a stream object, a bitmap, or a metafile.

A pointer to the DVTARGETDEVICE structure is also stored in the FORMATETC structure.

The DVTARGETDEVICE is the second structure that describes the target device with a driver name, a device name, a port name, and a device mode.

The STGMEDIUM structure is the third of the three data structures and stores the filename, a pointer to the stream object, and a pointer to a storage object.

4. Describe the programming restriction when implementing your own version of the IAdviseSink interface.

IAdviseSink is an asynchronous interface. Synchronous methods cannot be called from an asynchronous method.

5. What interfaces are required to implement an advisory connection?

An advisory connection is implemented with the **IDataObject** and **IAdviseSink** interfaces.

6. Explain the role of the interfaces IDataAdviseHolder and IOleAdviseHolder.

IDataAdviseHolder manages the advisory connections for **IDataObject** while **IOleAdviseHolder** manages the advisory connections for **IOleObject**.

7. What interfaces define an embedded object?

Each embedded object requires the interfaces **IOleObject**, **IPersistStorage**, and **IDataObject** for each type of embedded object that is supported.

8. You are building a container application. What are the three nontrivial methods of the IOleObject interface that must be implemented?

This interface has 21 methods, and the three required nontrivial interfaces to implement are **DoVerb**, **SetHostNames, and Close**. **SetExtent, InitFromData, GetClipboardData, SetColorScheme, SetMoniker**, and **GetMoniker** provide optional functionality.

9. What method activates an embedded object?

DoVerb activates an embedded object. Other methods include **SetHostNames** which communicates container application and document names, and **Close** which moves an embedded object from the running state to the loaded state. The **SetExtent, InitFromData, GetClipBoardData, SetColorScheme, SetMoniker,** and **GetMoniker** methods of **IOleObject** are optional and need not be implemented.

10. Explain the difference between IViewData and IDataObject.

The **IViewObject** interface is implemented by object handlers and in-process servers that manage their own presentations. The **IViewObject** is functionally equivalent to **IDataObject**; however, the difference is that **IViewObject** places a data representation on a device context(hDC), while a data representation is placed on a transfer medium by **IDataObject**.

11. What is a limitation of the IViewObject interface?

Device contexts are only valid within the context of a process. This means that **IViewObject** cannot be marshaled. This seems quite logical since a bitmap on the screen is a local rendering dependent upon local attributes and characteristics.

12. What is the relationship between the IAdviseSink and IConnectionPoint interfaces?

IAdviseSink and **IConnectionPoint** are asynchronous communication mechanisms. A client can only pass a single **IAdviseSink** pointer to **IDataObject**. This can be contrasted to the **IContainerPointContainer** interface, which can return a pointer to more than one interface. The client then provides advisory sink pointers to each of the **IConnectionPoint** pointers returned by **IConnectionPointContainer**.

13. What defines a connectable object?

Connecting to a connectable object starts by invoking **IUnknown::Query Interface** with an **IID** of **IID_IconnectionPointContainer**. A pointer is returned to **IConnectionPointContainer** when the object is connectable.

Drag and drop

1. What does drag and drop eliminate?

Drag and drop eliminates traditional application borders. Inter-window dragging moves objects from one application window to another application window.

2. Drag and drop is an extension of what Microsoft operating system feature?

Drag and drop is an extension of the clipboard.

3. Name the two interfaces responsible for drag and drop operations and indicate when they should be implemented.

IDropSource is implemented by any object containing data which can be dropped onto another object.

IDropTarget is implemented by any object which can accept data.

4. What is a requirement of the drag and drop target object?

The drag and drop target object must be registered with **RegisterDragDrop**.

5. What is the function of DoDragDrop?

DoDragDrop is used to initiate a drag and drop operation. Called by the drag source when a drag drop operation starts. **DoDragDrop** calls **IDropTarget::DragEnter** when the mouse pointer passes over a window that is a registered drop target.

DoDragDrop calls **IDropSource::QueryContinueDrag** during each loop iteration to determine if the operation should continue. Consistent operation is assured with **IDropTarget::DragOver** and **IDropSource::GiveFeedback** paired, giving the user the most up-to-date feedback information.

Chapter 7: Document Linking

1. What is an OLE Documents representation?

OLE Documents represents an interaction model. Objects can be spreadsheets, charts, drawings, forms, and video or sound clips. These objects may be linked to or embedded in an OLE Document for interactive use by the user.

2. What is the definition of an OLE component?

An OLE component is an object which uses COM and communicates with other objects.

3. What is the definition of an OLE Document?

An OLE Document is a COM component which supports either or both linking and embedding.

4. Explain COM model compound document embedding.

The persistent state of an object is maintained locally within the document. The document exists within a container and may be nested. Editing this document does not affect other users. An embedded object may be edited in place.

5. Explain COM model compound document linking.

The persistent state of an object is stored with the document source. Only meta-data (presentation data) exists within a container.

A linked object is edited in its own window. Other linked users will see the changes immediately.

6. What is the compelling reason to use linked OLE Documents as compared to embedded documents?

Linked OLE Documents use minimum resources since the original document is stored with the source object. A meta-file presentation copy only exists at the client site.

7. What is an adaptable link?

The linked object can always locate a linked source which has not moved or when both the linked source and object are moved but the same relative path was maintained. Linked source locations are stored in the registry. The Links dialog box can be used when the registry is not current.

8. An object is selected. When can editing start?

Only active objects may be edited.

9. What is outside-in activation?

Outside-in activation is an explicit action by the user such as double-clicking.

10. What is inside-out activation?

Inside-out activation is associated with embedded objects. No overt action on the part of the user is necessary to activate an object. The best example of this is an OLE control (OCX) now known as ActiveX. Inside-out objects are indistinguishable from native data and require very close cooperation between the container and the object.

11. Name an example of a full server.

Microsoft Excel is an example of a full server. It is free-standing, supports both embedded and linked objects, and is implemented as an EXE.

12. When is a mini-server used?

A mini-server only supports embedded objects and runs within the context of a container application as an EXE. It does not access the disk and cannot support linking.

13. What is an in-process server?

An in-process server is a mini-server implemented as a DLL. It runs within the address space of the object application.

14. What is an in-process object handler?

An in-process object handler exists simply to display an object. It reduces the overhead of loading a server.

15. The presence of what interface indicates a linked object?

The object is linked when the **IOleLink** interface is present.

16. What are the three non-trivial interfaces required for an object handler implementation?

The three required non-trivial interfaces for an object handler are:

- **IExternalConnection** — Supports correct shutdown of links to embedded objects.

- **IRunnableObject** — Determines when to transition between running state and when to become a contained object.

- **IOleObject** — The primary interface through which a linked or embedded object provides functionality to the container.

Chapter 8: Document Embedding

1. What is another name for in-place activation?

Visual editing

2. Explain the difference between an embedded document and a linked document.

An embedded object is a copy of the native date. It is edited in-place with visual editing and does not affect other users. A linked document is edited in its own window. The data is maintained at the source, and editing the document will affect all attached users.

3. **What interface does the object request of the container when in-place activation starts?**

The object calls **IOleClientSite::QueryInterface** looking for **IOleInPlaceSite**. The **IOleInPlaceSite** container interface must exist for in-place-activation.

4. **Assume for the moment that the interface IOleInPlaceSite exists. What is the next logical step for in-process activation?**

The next logical step is the object application asking permission to in-place activate by calling **IOleInPlaceSite::CanInPlaceActivate**.

5. **You have implemented an embedded application. The user complains that the screen flashes too much. What interface is faulty, or which did you forget to implement?**

The **IOleInPlaceSiteEx** which inherits from **IOleInPlaceSite** avoids unnecessary screen flashing.

6. **Explain a windowless object implementation.**

A windowless implementation is an object which can be activated without consuming windows resources. The container provides all windows services for the windowless object. A windowless object is an extension of normal compound documents.

7. **What type of object is a candidate for a windowless object implementation?**

A control is a candidate for a windowless object implementation. Small controls do not need a window, and a window prevents the control from being non-rectangular.

8. **What container interface must exist before an object can do a windowless activation?**

The container interface **IOleInPlaceSiteWindowless** must exist before an object can do a windowless activation.

9. **When will a windowless control activate as a normal object?**

The object will activate as a normal compound document when the call **IOleInPlaceSiteWindowless::CanWindowlessActivate** fails.

10. When will edited data of an embedded object be saved?

OLE embedded data is edited in the container. Embedded objects retain their native, full-featured editing and operating capabilities in the new container and are edited in-place within the container. Edits made to the data become a part of the container immediately and automatically, just like edits to native data. OLE embedded objects participate in the undo stack of the window in which they are activated.

Chapter 9: Automation

1. What is the definition of Automation?

Automation is the exposing of methods and properties by an OLE component for manipulation by another OLE component.

2. What distinguishes Automation from OLE Documents?

Automation does not support linking or embedding. Note, however, that a component using Automation may also support the linking and embedding of OLE Documents.

3. Explain a dual interface.

A dual interface is actually the **IDispatch** interface that supports the methods of **IUnknown**, which include **QueryInterface**, **AddRef**, and **Release**. **IDispatch** also supports the methods **GetIDsOfNames**, **GetTypeInfoCount**, **GetTypeInfo**, and **Invoke**. What makes the interface dual is that vtable pointers to private methods are included in the interface as well as the DISPIDs of the methods. Early binding can use a vtable, and late binding can use the dispinterface. Objects without vtable support can use the dispinterface while objects supporting a vtable can use the vtable interface.

4. Explain the term *"Being a good OLE client is a requirement for being an OLE Automation application controller."*

An OLE client exposes numerous interfaces that can be used by the server. The fact that the OLE client can support in-place activation indicates significant support of COM functionality. A good example is the windowless object which uses client services.

5. **Explain why Microsoft Visual Basic cannot be an OLE Automation server.**

   Neither Microsoft Access nor Microsoft Visual Basic can be manipulated. This means they cannot be an OLE Automation server; however, they are both good Automation clients in that they can manipulate an OLE Automation server such as Excel, Project, or Word.

6. **Name the three non-trivial tiers of an architecture which are candidates for Automation.**

   The three non-trivial tiers of an architecture which are candidates for Automation are data services, which is SQL Server or back-end services, business services, which is where business rules are implemented, and user services, which is the client interface. Data services and business services should be shared; however, the sharing of user services is not required.

7. **I mentioned that business rules are very primitive. In what way are they primitive?**

   Business rules are primitive since the business rule is embedded in the process — that is, it is embedded in code. Initially, data was embedded in the process in a dim and distant past. Data has now evolved from being embedded in the process to the point today where the definition of the data is embedded in the data. Business rules always evolve after data and it is reasonable to not expect their evolutionary cycle to be as current as that of data.

Chapter 10: OLE Controls: Using It All (Well, Almost!)

1. **Name a new feature of OLE controls.**

   The new feature of OLE controls is property pages. Properties existed in the COM model before OLE controls, but they were only ad-hoc definitions with no formalized structure and protocol.

2. **OLE controls are considered the pinnacle of COM technology in that they use nearly all COM features. What key COM feature is missing with OLE controls?**

   An OLE control does not support linking.

3. **What is the limitation of using Visual Basic 5.0 for creating ActiveX Controls?**

   Visual Basic 5.0 cannot control threading. Visual Basic 5.0 does not replace Microsoft C++ as the tool for creating an ActiveX control. It functions as a proof of concept until a later implementation is done in either J++ or C++ with thread control.

4. How are events implemented within OLE controls?

Events in an OLE control are a method calling an advisory sink. Events are the formalizing of method calls on a state change.

5. What activation method is used for OLE controls?

In-place activation is used by OLE controls.

6. Explain how DCOM benefits a credit card application?

DCOM benefits a credit card application by decomposing it into at least two components. Verification of the credit is done with a specific component. No interaction occurs with other components when a credit application is rejected.

7. What is the purpose of the IPointerInactive interface?

IPointerInactive enables drag and drop operations over inactive objects. The interface adds intelligence to object activation. A reduced active object count is a performance boost.

8. How does the ICategorizeProperties interface help a container?

A control implements **ICategorizeProperties**. The container interrogates this interface for properties supported.

9. The problem with creating a tiered application architecture is the need for a complete understanding of the application and the supporting infrastructure. What type of object should be implemented for interactive graphical analysis?

Interactive graphical analysis should be implemented as an in-process server. The rule with DCOM is the higher the interaction and computation rate, the closer proximity of the component.

10. What is an ActiveX Document and what are the advantages of using them?

An ActiveX Document is an OLE Document hosted by a browser. The advantage to this is that existing applications can be used on the Web. Non-HTML files can be opened with an ActiveX-aware Web browser. A Word document may be dropped into Microsoft Internet Explorer.

PART II: DATABASE ACCESS TECHNOLOGIES

Chapter 11: ODBC

1. Name the major components of the ODBC architecture.

The major components of ODBC architecture are the application, the driver manager, the driver, and the data source.

2. Name 5 benefits of the ODBC architecture.

o ODBC is vendor neutral. Drivers with the same specifications may be used interchangeably.

o ODBC permits heterogeneous connection of diverse databases from a single application program.

o ODBC insulates the application from data source and network versioning issues.

o ODBC simplifies application development. The same application program can communicate with different databases. The only change necessary is the selection of a different ODBC driver.

o ODBC is a portable application programming interface. The same interface and access technology exists on different platforms.

o ODBC is open. It has the support of the SQL Access Group (SAG) and is the preferred connectivity tool for many Web tools.

3. What role does the ODBC driver play in the Microsoft Windows Architecture?

The ODBC driver has the role of service provider within the framework of the Microsoft Windows Architecture.

4. Explain the roles of each component in the ODBC architecture.

The client uses the application to formulate queries and either display or update data in a data source.

The driver manager is the interface between the application and the ODBC driver. The driver manager communicates with the client and manages the ODBC driver.

The ODBC driver establishes the connection with the data source, issues user formulated queries, and returns result sets to the client application. The driver may manage both cursors and transactions when necessary, but the task will be transparent to the user.

Chapter 12: ODBC Drivers

1. Explain the purpose of conformance levels.

API and SQL grammar conformance exist to guarantee an open architecture. ODBC drivers for the same DBMS may be used interchangeably if the conformance levels agree.

2. Discuss ODBC driver functionality versus client application requirements.

ODBC drivers are written to API and SQL grammar conformance levels. The application must supply the missing functionality when the driver does not support functionality required by the client.

3. The application design requires a time stamp for transactions. Which conformance level is required?

The TIMESTAMP data type is only supported with Extended SQL Grammar.

4. The client wishes to do a browse connect. Which conformance level is required?

This is an API conformance issue and the driver must support a level 2 API conformance level for a browse connect.

5. The client wants optimal performance with prepared SQL statements. Which API conformance level is required?

This is an API conformance issue. Prepared SQL statements are supported by a core API conformance level. This is the minimum API conformance level and is supported by all ODBC drivers.

6. Which ODBC API conformance level supports a scrollable cursor?

A scrollable cursor is supported by the Level 2 API Conformance level.

7. Explain a single-tier driver.

A single-tier driver supports xBase or flat file systems. The driver has the responsibility of converting the SQL statements to file I/O statements. The driver directs the resulting file I/O statements to the data source which may not be local. Results are then returned to the client application. A single-tier driver is the only ODBC driver architecture where the driver processes the SQL requests.

8. What is the difference between a single-tier and a two-tier ODBC driver?

A two-tier driver passes SQL statements to a data source. The statements may be partially parsed; however, the driver takes no responsibility for retrieving the data. That is the responsibility of the data source.

A two-tier driver may be SQL-based or non-SQL-based. The non-SQL-based ODBC driver architecture will have an ODBC bridge, and it may have either a client-based SQL engine or a data source-based SQL engine.

9. What is the basic difference between a two-tier and a three-tier ODBC?

The three-tier driver architecture has gateway software on an intermediary system.

10. What is a driver leveling library?

Not all ODBC drivers adhere to the same conformance level. A driver leveling library presents a uniform interface to the application task by providing missing driver functionality. This gives all drivers the appearance of having the same API and SQL Grammar conformance levels.

Chapter 13: ODBC Applications

1. Explain the concept of a search limited expression. Give several examples of search limited expressions.

A search limited query has an expression which evaluates to a limiting value. The search for equality is search limited since the complete table need not be searched. An obvious corollary is that a table without an index is not search limited. A search limited query requires an index

2. What is the fastest processing technique for a single SQL statement? What about statements that are repeated?

SQLExecDirect will always be the fastest execution technique for a single SQL non-repeated statement. SQLPrepare followed by repeated SQLExecute statements provide the fastest execution for repeated SQL statements.

3. Explain why a SQL query with the NOT IN operator is not search limited.

The issue here is to understand that SQL returns a result set. Members not in the returned result set are by definition in the NOT IN set. The first pass is made creating the result set. Another pass is then made selecting only those elements NOT IN the original result set.

4. What is the problem with calculations in a query expression?

The index can't be used since each row must be retrieved and the required expression calculated before the selection criteria can be applied.

5. What is unique about a SQL expression containing an OR clause?

A SQL expression containing the OR operator is decomposed by the SQL parser into two distinct queries connected with a UNION statement.

6. What advantage does preparing a SQL statement offer?

Microsoft SQL Server and other relational database servers use query optimization. The optimization is cost-based and follows numerous heuristic rules. The resulting query plan is saved and associated with a SQL statement. The advantage to this is that the query plan may be reused, saving recompilation time. This is great stuff; however, there are some occasions where you might not want to use reuse your query plan.

Recall the concept of search limited strings and that the expression LIKE %<character string> is not search limited while the expression like <character string>% is search limited. The issue is client supplied character strings where no control is placed on wild-card characters. Preparing a statement and preserving the query plan is of little value if there are no limits placed on the user provided input. One query may be a specific value which is search limited while the next input value may have a leading wild-card character which is not search limited.

There are other examples such as the data itself. Orders to an order-entry system may be batched. Query plans are made for existing data. New batches of data may skew and invalidate existing query plans. Microsoft is right in recommending that SQL statements should be prepared; however, some thought must be given to creating new query plans when the characteristics of the data change. There is also the related issue of UPDATE STATISTICS on SQL Server, but that is not a topic for this book.

7. What is a state transition error?

A state transition error occurs when API functions are either called in the wrong order or are not in the proper state. The three handles — environment, connection, and statement — each have three states, which are unallocated, allocated, and connected. A state error occurs when calling an API function which is not in the proper state. A simple example is setting connection attributes when not connected to a data source.

8. What is a fat cursor?

A fat cursor is a synonym for a block cursor. A block cursor is a set of rows (result set) that has a cursor that can be positioned to any given row in the result set.

9. What is the unique characteristic of a static cursor?

Static cursors are equivalent to snapshots. It is a copy of a rowset at a point in time. No changes to the underlying tables are detectable.

10. Explain the operating principles of a dynamic cursor?

A dynamic cursor can detect all underlying table changes. It is not an easy cursor to implement. For example, the keyset-driven cursor technique can determine deleted rows in the underlying table. Changed rows can be identified with time stamps, but new rows added are much more complex. A possible implementation mechanism is to notify all attached processes when new rows are added to the underling table. There must be a qualification since an application only wants notification when the newly added row is of interest.

11. What are the limitations of a keyset-driven cursor?

A keyset-driven cursor cannot detect newly added rows, even though it can detect deleted rows. It detects the deleted rows when the cursor is positioned to the row. A read request is issued for the row, and an error status is returned if the row doesn't exist.

12. Name a limitation of the Microsoft implementation of ODBC in C/C++.

Column binding in ODBC utilizes the data types of the implementation language. Microsoft states that the ODBC specification is language-independent; however, the Microsoft implementation of ODBC is C/C++ based, which does not support either the new Unicode or the SQL Server data type VARCHAR. This is by no means a negative statement about ODBC, which is an open and very powerful database connection tool. These issues are only minor irritations, which as you'll see shortly, are solved with wrappers providing a higher level of functionality.

13. What important function must be performed after an environment handle is allocated?

The behavior of ODBC must be established. SQLSetEnvAttr is used to set SQL_ATTR_ODBC_VER before a connection is made to the data source. This is used to change the behavior of ODBC 3.0 to ODBC 2.*x*.

14. **Describe the differences between the ODBC 2.*x* SQLFetch and the ODBC 3.0 SQLFetch.**

The SQLFetch function of ODBC 2.*x* returns a single row while the same function in ODBC 3.0 returns a result set. This could give unexpected results to an application not expecting multiple rows.

15. **Name a new and very useful connection attribute that enhances performance.**

ODBC 3.0 supports connection pooling. The connection example in the topic "Debugging an ODBC Application" illustrates the cost of establishing a connection to a data source.

16. **Describe long data and how to process it.**

Long data is Binary Large Objects (BLOBs). The data can be either characters or binary data. The issue is the stripping of null termination characters before recombining the data buffers.

17. **SQLGetData has a unique property. What is it?**

SQLGetData retrieves data for unbound columns. The function must be called in order of increasing column number. Columns are numbered starting with one on the left.

18. **What new binding feature is not supported for ODBC 2.0? Is it a performance issue?**

ODBC 3.0 provides binding offsets. A pointer to an offset is a parameter, and the client application changes the offset without rebinding the columns. This is not a feature of ODBC 2.0.

19. **What is a catalog function?**

A catalog function is an ODBC API function that returns a result set.

20. **Name the catalog functions.**

The catalog functions are: **SQLTables, SQLColumns, SQLStatistics, SQLSpecialColumns, SQLPrimaryKeys, SQLForeignKeys, SQLTablePrivileges, SQLColumnPrivileges, SQLProcedures, SQLProcedureColumns,** and **SQLGetTypeInfo**.

21. **When is SQLDescribeCols used?**

SQLDescribeCols is used in the column binding loop. The client first invokes **SQLNumResultCols**, which determines the number of result columns. The application then loops on **SQLDescribeCol** and **SQLBindCOL** for the binding. **SQLDescribeCol** isn't necessary when the column attributes are known a priori by the application.

22. **When is the ODBC API function SQLEndTran used?**

The ODBC API function is only used in manual-commit mode.

23. **What happens to a SQL statement which cannot be translated by the ODBC driver?**

A SQL statement which cannot be understood by the ODBC driver is passed directly to the data source without translation. The Microsoft SQL Server statement USE *Pubs* is an example.

24. **What is the scope of a transaction?**

The connection is the scope of a transaction. All statements for the connection will either be committed or rolled back.

25. **Describe using the API function SQLExecute.**

SQLExecute is paired with **SQLPrepare** and executes the query plan prepared by **SQLPrepare**.

26. **What is the default transaction mode for ODBC?**

The default transaction mode for ODBC is auto-commit.

27. **What determines cursor behavior for commit or rollback operations?**

The data source determines cursor behavior for commit or rollback operations. **SQLGetConnectAttr** is interrogated with an attribute of SQL_CURSOR_COMMIT_BEHAVIOR or SQL_CURSOR_ROLLBACK_BEHAVIOR.

28. **When is a cursor closed automatically?**

A cursor is closed automatically when a statement times out or the cursor behavior mode for the connection attribute SQL_CURSOR_COMMIT_BEHAVIOR or SQL_CURSOR_ROLLBACK_BEHAVIOR is set to either SQL_CB_DELETE or SQL_CB_CLOSE.

29. **Describe a performance issue with manual-commit transactions.**

The problem is with the cursor in SQL_CB_PRESERVE mode where the cursor and query plan are preserved even though the transaction has been committed. This leaves a read lock on the server which may block other users.

30. **Discuss optimistic concurrency versus pessimistic concurrency.**

    Optimistic concurrency assumes that few collisions will occur and locks the data only when an update is eminent. Pessimistic concurrency locks the data at the beginning of the transaction.

31. **Describe ODBC cursor library support.**

    ODBC 3.0 cursor library supports only static and forward-only cursors. It supports block scrollable cursors for any driver that is Level 1 API-compliant.

Chapter 15: DAO

1. **Name the four key words which represent the ACID properties of a database and provide a brief phrase describing each property.**

   Atomicity Either all or none of the transaction changes is present when the transaction completes.

   Consistency The transaction will respect all business rules and referential integrity. Inconsistent updates can be done, but will violate system integrity.

   Isolation Transactions are isolated. The isolation is realized by using locks, separate workspaces, and the **IsolateODBCTrans** property.

   Durability Once the commit occurs, the transactions must be present even if the system fails. SQL Server supports this property and Microsoft Access does not. Microsoft Access survives as a server only when transactions are small.

2. **How does Jet and the DAO fail to satisfy the fourth of the ACID properties?**

   Jet does not maintain a log file.

3. **The DAO hierarchy is very rich. What is the rigid restriction which must be imposed on DAO objects?**

   The order of the objects is rigid.

4. **You are developing a complex form with many controls to be used in a Decision Support System (DSS) environment. (A DSS is a read-only database.) In your case it is Microsoft SQL Server. Your choices include ODBC API, DAO, RDO (you have a license), and ODBCDirect. Which database access technology is appropriate for your application?**

The probable choice is DAO since this database does not have transactions and reporting is the only requirement. ODBCDirect does not support bound forms. The ODBC API supports binding, but the binding is only to variables and this will be too much work.

RDO and the Remote Data Control support binding and are a choice with Visual Basic Enterprise; however, this is not a valid answer to this question since our context is the DAO. This is a valid choice after we discuss RDO.

5. **You are tasked with designing a corporate roll-up function. Transactions are gathered from branch offices and posted on a batch basis to a centralized Microsoft SQL Server database. Which database access technology is appropriate?**

   ODBCDirect is the natural choice here. Transaction posting is done on the server, which is assumed to be a registered ODBC data source. RDO is another valid choice, but since the book hasn't discussed this topic yet, we'll let it be a non-choice for now.

6. **Management wishes to create reports in Microsoft Access from an AS/400 system. Which database access technology is correct?**

   It is possible to do this with ODBCDirect, assuming that the AS/400 is a registered ODBC data source. The problem here is heterogeneous enterprise connections. Your best choice is the ODBC API, which removes the application from the vagaries of Microsoft update cycles.

Chapter 16: Working with DAO

1. **Name the first object in the DAO hierarchy.**

   DBEngine is the first object in the DAO hierarchy.

2. **Name a property of all collections.**

   The **Count** property is a property of all collections

3. **Which DAO object does not have a default collection?**

   DBEngine does not have a default collection.

4. **Give an example of a default collection.**

   Numerous examples exist but the most common default collection is the **Fields** collection of the **Recordset** object.

5. Name an object which is automatically appended to a collection.

A **Querydef** object with other than a zero-length name is automatically appended to the **QueryDefs** collection.

6. Discuss the Refresh method of a collection.

The **Refresh** method is used after deleting or appending a new member to a collection. Ordinal numbers for objects may change as a result of the refresh.

7. When does Jet ignore the Close method?

The **Close** method is ignored for the default workspace.

8. Name two methods used to remove a QueryDef from the QueryDefs collection.

The **Close** and **Delete** methods will remove a **QueryDef** object from the **QueryDefs** collection.

9. Name a collection where objects cannot be removed with the Delete method.

The **Recordsets** and **QueryDefs** are examples of collections where objects are removed with the **Delete** method. Object members can only be removed from the **Workspaces** collection with the **Close** method. The default workspace cannot be closed.

10. Name four objects that share the same collection.

All objects except the **Connection** and **Error** object have a **Properties** collection. The **QueryDef**, **Tabledef**, **Recordset**, and **Index** objects all contain a **Fields** collection.

11. What is the purpose of containers?

The **Containers** collection consists of all saved objects which define a database. A **Container** object has a **Documents** collection, and each **Document** object represents a database entity such as a form, module, or query. Permissions and ownership of **Container** and **Document** objects can be managed from VBA.

12. What is a unique characteristic of Container objects?

Container objects are not DAO objects, but are Microsoft Access database objects.

Chapter 17: Working with the DBEngine Object

1. What is another name for a workspace?

A session is another name for a workspace.

2. Name two benefits of compacting a DAO 2.0/3.0/3.5 database.

Compacting a Jet database recovers fragmented space and recomputes table statistics. The Jet Query optimizer uses statistics for creating query plans.

3. Name a DAO 3.0/3.5 benefit of database compacting.

Starting with DAO 3.0, a compacted database will have tables reorganized into primary key order. This is effectively a clustered index, but new rows inserted will not be inserted in key order. New rows are always appended to a table.

4. When should a database be compacted?

The simplest answer is often. I recommend several times a day during the development cycle.

The database should be compacted whenever significant amounts of new data is entered or deleted. At issue is query selectivity. New data may not reflect the actual statistics of a table. As an example, statistics may say that the table is very empty, in which case a table scan is the most efficient access method. The exact opposite can occur with a table scan rather than an indexed search of a large table when statistics are outdated.

5. Name two types of workspaces and identify the basic differences.

There are two types of workspaces: Jet and ODBCDirect. The Jet workspace is the traditional DAO workspace. The ODBCDirect workspace is for connecting to ODBC sources which supports asynchronous operations without the Jet Engine. ODBCDirect does not support bound forms. See later questions on collections or the Connections collection of the Workspace object.

6. Name the DAO entity which contains the methods BeginTrans, CommitTrans, and Rollback.

There is an error in the Microsoft documentation which states that the **BeginTrans**, **CommitTrans**, and **Rollback** methods are methods of the **DBEngine** object. This is not true. **BeginTrans**, **CommitTrans**, and **Rollback** methods are methods of the **Workspace** object.

7. What are the RepairDatabase issues?

The rule with DAO 2.0 was to repair the database and then compact it. This worked fine for DAO 2.0; however, the same technique applied to DAO 3.0 would often corrupt the database. The current rule (DAO 3.5) is to compact the database and don't attempt a repair unless there is a known problem such as logging on.

8. When can a Workspace object be closed?

Any workspace can be closed and deleted from the **Workspaces** collection except the default workspace.

9. What unique feature of VBA can be used to unwind errors?

VBA error handlers cannot handle their own errors. The unwinding process is a mechanism of creating an artificial error in an error handler to force VBA to move back in the call-tree to other error handlers. The technique isn't applicable to smaller applications, but rather to layered applications when simply terminating the application is not appropriate. The technique takes advantage of the fact that an error handler cannot handle its own errors.

Chapter 18: Working with the Connection Object

1. Name four distinct features of an ODBCDirect connection.

ODBCDirect connections have these features:

- The Microsoft Jet Database Engine is not used, reducing the application footprint.
- Server-side cursors are now available.
- Asynchronous queries are supported.
- ODBCDirect supports batch updating.

2. Name four distinct limitations of an ODBCDirect connection.

An ODBCDirect connection does not support:

- Updatable joins
- Heterogeneous joins
- Data Definition Language (DDL) operations
- Bound forms

3. What is a unique feature of creating an ODBCDirect connection?

ODBCDirect connections can only be made to an ODBC data source.

4. Name the two collections of the Connection.

The only two collections of the **Connection** object are the **QueryDefs** and **Recordsets** collections.

5. What Connection object property is useful for checking the validity of a transaction?

RecordsAffected returns the number of rows affected by an action query. This is useful to check the results of a transaction. The application optionally elects to roll the transaction back when the **AffectedRecords** count is incorrect.

6. What is the default collection of a Connection object?

QueryDefs collection

7. Explain the relationship between a Connection object and a Database object.

A **Database** object is created automatically, then the **Connection** object is created within ODBCDirect. The **Database** object assumes the responsibility of managing the **QueryDefs** and **Recordsets** collections of the **Connection** object.

Chapter 19: Working with the Workspace Object

1. What is a characteristic of workspace transactions?

Transactions are global to a workspace, and all transactions on all databases or connections will be rolled back with the **Rollback** method.

2. The Microsoft DAO 3.5 documentation illustrates the transaction methods BeginTrans, CommitTrans, and Rollback as methods of the DBEngine. Can you explain why this is wrong?

It's illogical to roll back transactions from the highest element in the object hierarchy. A session is another name for a workspace, and a rollback at the **DBEngine** level would roll back all transactions in all sessions.

3. What happens to a transaction when a Workspace object is closed?

The transaction is rolled back.

4. What is the difference between SQL Server and DAO transactions?

Jet transactions can be nested while SQL Server transactions cannot be nested. Nested transactions should not be used because of the possibility of an eventual upsizing to SQL Server.

5. What constitutes a poorly constructed transaction?

The simplest answer is poor programming practices. The specific issues are:

- No user interaction
- Use **Parameter** objects for input parameters. User interaction is not required with parameters.
- Never write procedural code. It is subject to Microsoft product level changes. Always use SQL. Write SQL statements which adhere to the ANSI SQL specification.
- Never update the same row twice in the same transaction.

6. What happens when an object is set to Nothing?

Object resources are released.

7. What is the default collection of a Workspace object?

The default collection of a **Workspace** object is the **Databases** collection.

8. What is an inconsistent update?

An inconsistent update is a transaction on a one-to-many relationship which could orphan rows. An example is deleting a parent entity without deleting the corresponding child rows. This problem doesn't exist with cascading deletes.

9. What are the ACID properties?

The ACID properties are:

- *Atomicity* — Either all or none of the transactions changes is present when the transaction completes.
- *Consistency* — The transaction will respect all business rules and referential integrity. Inconsistent updates can be done, but will violate system integrity.
- *Isolation* — Transactions are isolated. The isolation is realized by using locks, separate workspaces, and the IsolateODBCTrans property.
- *Durability* — Once the commit occurs, the transactions must be present even if the system fails.

10. **Which ACID property does Jet and DAO not support?**

    SQL Server supports the **Durability** property but Microsoft Access does not. DAO and Jet do not have a log file.

11. **Explain the actions of the Close method in the following fragment:**

    ```
    Dim MyWS as Workspace
    Set MyWS = DBEngine.Workspaces(0)

    . . .

    MyWS.Close
    ```

    Nothing happens. Normally an object is removed from a collection when it is closed. The default workspace cannot be closed.

12. **What is the meaning of DSN when opening, registering, or connecting to a database?**

    DSN refers to a registered ODBC Data Source Name. SQL Server is registered as a DSN; however, individual databases can still be accessed.

13. **Explain why listing 3.11 uses the DBEngine when it is enumerating the Errors collection of DAO.**

    The reason for the question was to identify the difference between the **DBEngine** object and the Jet Engine. ODBCDirect doesn't use the Jet Engine; however, the **Errors** collection is a component of the **DBEngine** object.

14. **Listing 3.9 uses the Refresh method of a Workspace object to refresh the Groups and the Users collections. Other than exposing new members of these collections, what other action occurs?**

    Ordinal numbers of the elements within the collection may change.

Chapter 20: Working with the Database Object

1. **What collection is a member of every DAO object except the Connection object and the Error object?**

   Properties collection

2. **Explain the difference between the Execute method of a Database or Connection object and the Execute method of a QueryDef object.**

   The **Execute** method of a **Connection** or a **Database** object can only execute an action query. An action query deletes rows, updates rows, or adds new rows.

3. **What is the default collection for the Connection object?**

The default collection for the **Connection** object is the **QueryDefs** collection.

4. **Of what use is the Cancel method?**

The **Cancel** method is used to cancel an asynchronous ODBCDirect operation.

5. **What is unique about a QueryDef object of a Connection object?**

A **Connection** object **QueryDef** object is always temporary.

6. **Explain the difference between the OpenRecordset method of a Connection or Database object and the OpenRecordset method of a QueryDef object, Recordset object, or TableDef object.**

The two types of **OpenRecordset** methods are nearly identical except the first field of the argument list. The **OpenRecordset** method of the **Connection** or **Database** object contains a **Source** field for the database name.

7. **Explain the difference in addressing a user-defined property and a built-in property.**

Built-in properties are addressed with the syntax **Object:Name** while user defined properties are addressed with **Object:Properties!Name**.

8. **What is the purpose of the option dbFailOnError when used with the Execute method?**

An error is not returned when rows are locked. Using this option of the **Execute** method will return an error when rows are locked.

9. **What is the issue of the Connect property of a Jet Querydef object?**

The **Connect** property of a Jet **Querydef** object must be set before setting the **SQL** property of the object. Jet will try to parse the SQL for local use when the **Connect** property is not set. Setting the **Connect** property first stops Jet from statements such as the SQL Server USE statement.

10. **Discuss user-defined properties and the Inherited property.**

User-defined properties do not have inherited properties.

11. **Discuss SQL statements and the QueryDef object.**

Foreign SQL text cannot be placed in the **SQL** text argument of a Jet **QueryDef** object. This field expects Jet SQL.

12. **How is a Jet QueryDef object appended to the QueryDefs collection?**

Automatically

13. How is a temporary jet QueryDef object created?

Use a zero length string for the query name when creating the **QueryDef** object.

14. How is the property ReturnsRecords used?

This property of the **QueryDef** object must be set if the query will return a result set.

15. How can a relation be changed in VBA code?

Relations are read-only. Changes may be made to a created relation, but once appended to the **Relations** collection, it cannot be changed. The only alternate is to delete the relation and recreate it.

This is an issue of extreme risk. **Querydef** objects may have prestored query plans which depend upon the relation that was just changed. Chaos will ensue shortly.

16. What does it mean to *Prepare* a SQL statement?

The SQL Optimizer of SQL Server or the Jet Engine of Microsoft Access prepares a SQL statement by compiling a query plan. The query plan is designed to use the least resources in accessing data. This is why it is so important to have current table statistics. The preparing process also binds parameters.

17. When is an ODBCDirect QueryDef object compiled? When is a Jet QueryDef object compiled?

Query plans for both are created when the **SQL** property is set. The query plan is remembered for a non-temporary **Querydef** object and will not be compiled again.

The ODBCDirect **QueryDef** object can use the **Prepare property** to control query plan compilation. The default value for this property is **dbQPrepare**; however, it may be set to **dbQUnprepare**, which inhibits query plan compilation. At query execution time, the option **dbExecDirect** is user. This is equivalent to the ODBC API function **SQLExecDirect**.

Chapter 21: Working with the TableDef Object

1. What is the fastest access method for retrieving data?

Directly opening a local table is always the fastest.

2. What is the slowest possible access technique to a table?

Opening a remote table

3. What is the limitation of opening a table-type Recordset object from a Database object?

Only a dynaset-type **Recordset** object may be opened from a table-type **Recordset** object.

4. What is the default collection for a TableDef object?

The default collection for a **Tabledef** object is the **Fields** collection.

5. Recordsets may be opened from QueryDef, Recordset, or TableDef objects. What is the restriction on creating a Recordset object from another Recordset object?

It cannot be a forward scrolling snapshot.

6. List the five recordset types with a brief description of each.

- *Table* — One of the original recordset definitions of Microsoft Access and the earlier version of Jet and DAO

- *Snapshot* — Another original Access DAO recordset definition. The data is captured at a point in time, and updates or deletions are not visible to the client. This recordset type is equivalent to an ODBC **Static** cursor.

- *Dynaset* — A keyset recordset which may have either pessimistic or optimistic locking. The last of the original three record set definitions. Deleted rows can be detected but newly added rows will go undetected. This recordset type is equivalent to the ODBC keyset-cursor.

- *Forward-Only* — This is a new recordset which uses the minimalist of resources. If you recall from the last chapter, the ODBC default cursor is forward only with a snapshot type record. This recordset is equivalent to a **Snapshot** without a cursor.

- *Dynamic* — This is a new recordset type which is reserved for access to ODBC registered data sources. It is used by ODBCDirect, which is the name given to using the **Connections** collection and the **Connection** object without the Jet Engine. One very nice feature of ODBCDirect is the ability to define asynchronous operations.

7. What is the only DAO object with an Indexes collection?

The **Table** object is the only DAO object with the **Indexes** collection.

8. Compare tabledef operations in ODBCDirect with tabledef operations in Jet.

ODBCDirect does not support the **TableDefs** collection.

Chapter 22: Working with the QueryDef Object

1. How is an ODBCDirect QueryDef deleted?

It's not deleted since it is temporary. Closing the query is sufficient.

2. What are dbQPrepare and dbQUnprepare and how are they used?

dbQPrepare and **dbQUnprepare** are **Prepare** property values for an ODBCDirect **QueryDef** object. The default value for the **Prepare** property is **dbQPrepare**. Query preparation is the compiling of a minimal resources used query plan.

3. Why would you not want a statement prepared?

The **dbQUnprepare** property is used to inhibit query plan compilation when using the **dbExecDirect** parameter of the **Execute** method. This is equivalent to the ODBC API function and is used when user-provided query parameters will change query selectivity.

4. What is the relationship between the QueryDef object properties Prepare and SQL?

dbUnprepare must be set in the **Prepare** property before the **SQL** property is set to inhibit query plan compilation.

5. What is the default collection for the Field object?

The **Field** object doesn't have a default collection.

6. What is the only object with an Indexes collection?

The **TableDef** object is the only object with an **Indexes** collection.

7. Explain the Clustered property of the Index object.

Jet does not support clustered indexes. The **Clustered** property of an **Index** object merely refers to the existence of a clustered index on the data source.

8. When is an index created automatically by the Jet Engine?

An index is created automatically for enforced referential integrity.

9. When is a Parameter object created?

Parameter objects are created when the **SQL** property is set. The parser doesn't recognize the item as a member of a **Fields** collection and creates a **Parameter** object.

10. What is at risk when cloning tables in a multiuser environment?

Name collisions are the issue in a multiuser environment.

11. What constitutes a good query?

A good query is written in SQL and is not a procedural process using DAO and VBA. However, there are still other problems. The SQL can be deficient. See the *Tarpits* section in Chapter 22.

Chapter 23: Working with the Recordset Object

1. What happens when an AddNew and a Move operation are performed?

All changes are lost.

2. Why must a MoveLast or a FindFirst method be used before executing the AddNew method?

Other rows may be picked up from the base table at the *current record*, effectively corrupting the table.

3. Where are newly inserted rows placed in a table?

Newly inserted rows are always placed at the end of the table. Pessimistic locking is used when a new page must be added.

4. When should the CancelUpdate method be used on a Recordset object?

The **CancelUpdate** method is used to cancel **AddNew** or **Edit** method operations. It replaces the very expensive mechanism **object.move 0**. Do not confuse this method with the **Cancel** method of the ODBCDirect **QueryDef** or the **Connection** object.

5. Explain the RecordCount property.

The **RecordCount** property counts the number of records accessed. This means that row counting requires that the last row must be accessed. Using the SQL COUNT aggregate is a faster mechanism for determining a result set size.

6. **A cloned record can be created with the Clone method of the Recordset object. Name two features of a cloned recordset.**

   A cloned record has no *current record*. A move operation or a bookmark operation will establish a *current record*.

   The **Index** property of a table-type **Recordset** is not copied with the **Clone** method.

7. **What recordset type cannot be cloned?**

   The **Clone** method of a **Recordset** object cannot be used on forward-scrolling snapshots.

8. **When can the FillCache method of a Recordset object be used?**

   The **FillCache** method of a **Recordset** object can only be used by Jet on an ODBC-only dynaset. ODBCDirect has its own caching mechanism.

9. **What is the syntax for retrieving values from a Recordset object when the field names are not known?**

   Recordset.Fields(ordinal)

10. **Name two requirements of the Recordset object Seek method.**

    The **Recordset** object must have an index, and the index type(s) must agree with the search key type(s).

11. **What is a restriction of the Seek method?**

    The **Seek** method is the fastest record access technique but cannot be used on attached tables. The **Seek** method applies to only table-type **Recordset** objects.

Chapter 24: RDO

1. **Name the first object in the RDO hierarchy.**

   The first object in the RDO hierarchy is the rdoEngine. This is a single object and it can only be initialized.

2. **Name a property of all collections.**

   Count is a property of all collections.

3. **Which RDO object does not have a default collection.**

   Neither the rdoColumn object nor the rdoParameter object have a default collection.

4. Give an example of a default collection.

```
MyRS!au_fname
MyRS("au_fname")
MyRS.rdoColumns("au_fname").Value
MyRS.rdoColumns(0).Value
```

5. Name an object which is automatically appended to a collection.

All new objects are automatically appended to a collection.

6. When does RDO ignore the Close method?

RDO ignores the Close method for the default rdoEnvironments(0) object.

7. Name a collection where objects cannot be removed with the Close method.

Nothing can be removed from the rdoTables collection.

8. Name three objects that share the same collection.

The rdoPreparedStatement, rdoTable, and rdoResultset objects have in common the rdoColumns collection.

9. Name two DAO and Jet features not available in RDO.

RDO does not support updatable joins, heterogeneous joins, or DDL statements, all of which are supported in Microsoft Access. RDO uses the DDL statements of the remote server.

Chapter 25: Working with RDO Objects

1. What is the default collection of the rdoEngine object?

The rdoEnvironments collection is the default collection of rdoEngine.

2. Explain the difference in optimistic concurrency in RDO as compared to DAO.

Both DAO and RDO have the same intrinsic constants, although the names differ. DAO requires the intrinsic constant dbSeeChanges to create trappable optimistic concurrency errors, while RDO trappable optimistic concurrency errors occur automatically.

3. **You have two rdoConnection objects, each with a result set. The rdoEnvironment object is not the default environment. What happens when it is closed?**

   You will probably lose data. Objects should always be closed in their inverse hierarchical order. Close the result set, then the connection, and finally the environment.

4. **You are attempting to register a data source using RDO. It fails and you can find nothing wrong with your VB code. What is your probable problem?**

   The SQL Server driver is not registered. This must be registered before the data source can be registered.

5. **You have an error. There are many error messages and it is quite confusing since every layer of the system has its own interpretation of the problem. Where is the primary RDO error message located?**

   The primary error is located at **rdoErrors**(0).

6. **What must be done before accessing the rdoTables collection?**

   It must be populated with the Refresh method.

7. **What is the scope of a transaction?**

   An rdoEnvironment object is the scope of a transaction.

8. **Why is RDO a good choice for heterogeneous connection of the enterprise?**

   RDO is designed to support only ODBC data sources. This gives connectivity to foreign relational databases. RDO is not a good choice for flat-file operations or for Microsoft Access.

9. **You have developed this killer application which uses RDO. What must be done to license the software?**

   RDO cannot be licensed. Your client must purchase Microsoft Visual Basic Enterprise Edition. The exception to this rule is RDO technology encapsulated within an Automation server.

Chapter 26: Working with the rdoPreparedStatement Object

1. The rdoPreparedStatement object has a parallel in the DAO QueryDef object. What unique feature is an option with a DAO QueryDef object and is built-in with the rdoPreparedStatement object?

A DAO **QueryDef** object is prepared automatically when it is saved. The intrinsic constant **dbQPrepare** must be used with ODBCDirect while the **rdoPreparedStatement** object of RDO prepares SQL statements automatically.

2. A Delete method has failed on a row in a result set. Name six reasons for this problem.

A delete may fail for numerous reasons. Factors to consider on a delete failure include:

- There is no current row.
- The rdoConnection object or the rdoResultset object is read-only.
- Columns in the row are not updatable.
- The row doesn't exist; it has already been deleted.
- The row or data page is locked by another user.
- The user permissions do not allow a delete operation.

3. An Edit method has failed on a row of a result set. Name five reasons for this problem.

The **Edit** method will fail when:

- A current row doesn't exist.
- The rdoConnection or rdoResultset object is read-only.
- Columns in the row are not updatable.
- The EditMode property indicates an edit is already in process.
- The row or data page is locked by another user.

Chapter 27: SQL-DMO

1. SQL-DMO has collections that are similar to both RDO and DAO. What is the relationship of a list to a collection?

A list within SQL-DMO is a subset of a collection. It is a mechanism to partition collections down to a managable size.

2. How has SQL-DMO improved property management?

SQL-DMO improves property management by encapsulating properties within a SQL-DMO object, or what is better termed a collection. The SQL-DMO technology calls objects collections, which may confuse the DAO or RDO developer.

3. SQL-DMO has a characteristic shared with RDO. What is that characteristic?

Neither RDO nor SQL-DMO require an engine or a Workspace object. DAO requires both, and ODBCDirect requires a Workspace object.

4. What is the top object in the SQL-DMO object hierarchy? How is it accessed?

The top object in the SQL-DMO hierarchy is the **Application** object. Only one instance of the **Application** object can exist, and each SQL-DMO object contains a reference to this object. The SQL-DMO object cannot be instantiated.

5. All SQL-DMO objects have a very unique property. What is the name of that property and what is it used for?

All SQL-DMO objects have a **UserData** property which is not used by SQL-DMO.

6. Compare using SQL-DMO for connecting to Microsoft SQL versus connecting to Microsoft SQL Server with DAO.

DAO requires an instance of the DBEngine and a **Workspace** object. SQL-DMO is Automation and only requires a **CreateObject** statement or the subclassing of the parent object with the **Set** command. The second step is the connection process.

7. What is a Microsoft C++ limitation with respect to SQL-DMO properties?

Every SQL-DMO object has a **Properties** collection. This does not include the collections themselves. A **Property** object is related to every object property. The Property object is not available to C++.

Chapter 28: Working with Application Scope Objects

1. What is a unique characteristic of Application scope objects?

Application scope objects are temporary and have no persistence.

2. Identify where a Backup object is used in the SQL-DMO architecture.

The **Backup** object is passed to the **Dump**, **Load**, **GenerateBackupSQL** method of a Database or **TransactionLog** object or the SQLServer.**ReadBackupHeader** method.

3. What methods does the Backup object support?

The Backup object supports no methods.

Chapter 29: OLE-DB

1. Name all the different methods which may be used to create a row set. Briefly describe the different characteristics of these rowsets.

The first source for rowsets of OLE-DB is the equivalent of ODBC catalog functions with the **IColumnsRowset::GetColumnsRowset**, **IDBSchemaRowset::GetRowset**, and **ISources::GetSourcesRowset**. These are read-only rowsets for column, schema, and data source metadata.

The second source for OLE-DB rowsets must be supported by all providers. This is **IOpenRowset::OpenRowset** on a session object. This is a simple table interface, and the rowsets are the equivalent of a wild-card select on a table which has the form SELECT * FROM *table*.

The third source of a rowset is from the sequence **IDBCreate:: CreateCommand** on a **Session** object, initializing **Command** object properties and text, and calling **ICommand::Execute** on a **Command** object.

2. What interfaces must all rowsets support?

All rowsets must support **IRowset**, **IAccessor**, **IColumnInfo**, **IRowsetInfo**, and **IConvertType**. **IRowsetLocate** may be exposed even though it is not requested by the consumer. **IRowsetUpdate** cannot be exposed unless specifically requested by the consumer since the presence of this interface changes the behavior of the **IRowsetChange** interface. This is because the IID of **ICommand::Execute** is usually an IID of one of the interfaces listed for the **TRowset** CoType.

3. **Discuss the three roles objects play in the OLE-DB environment.**

Objects in OLE-DB have two basic roles. A *consumer* is any application or system function which consumes an OLE-DB interface. A *provider* is any software component which exposes an OLE-DB interface. A *provider* that owns the data is a *data provider*. *Providers* that do not own the data are *service providers*.

4. **Explain the difference between an Automation error and an OLE-DB error.**

An Automation **Error** object contains a single error message and supports only the **IErrorInfo** interface. An OLE-DB **Error** object supports multiple error records and the interfaces **IErrorInfo** and **IErrorRecords**.

5. **What is a characteristic of the error code DB_S_ERRORSOCCURRED?**

The error code DB_S_ERRORSOCCURRED has memory allocated which must be released by the consumer. DB_S_ indicates a success; however, this code is returned when at least one of the rows or bookmarks was processed successfully.

6. **What is apartment-model threading? How do apartment-model threads communicate? What is the major problem with apartment-model threads?**

Apartment-model threading permits only one thread per object. The thread is managed by the object's parent thread.

Apartment-model threads can only communicate with other apartment model threads by using a stub and a proxy.

The inadvertent mixing of the threads is the major problem of comingling apartment model and free-threading model threads.

7. **When is cache for a rowset released?**

When the row handle is released

8. **What is a *zombie* rowset?**

Microsoft has introduced the concept of a *zombie* state. A rowset is in a *zombie* state when only IUnknown and the release of row handles and rows are functional. Every other interface will return the error code E_UNEXPECTED.

The first situation to consider is the property DBPROP_COMMIT-PRESERVE set to VARIANT_TRUE after returning from **ITransaction:: Commit**. In this situation the rowset is not a *zombie* and remains accessible even though it has been committed. The rowset assumes the *zombie* state when DBPROP_COMMITPRESERVE is set to VARIANT_FALSE after returning from **ITransaction::Commit.**

A parallel situation exists for DBPROP_ABORTPRESERVE being set to VARIANT_FALSE when returning from **ITransaction::Abort**. The rowset is a *zombie* and is not accessible. The rowset is accessible after the **ITransaction::**
Abort when DBPROP_ABORTPRESERVE is set to VARIANT_TRUE.

Chapter 30: Working with OLE-DB Interfaces

1. What is the role of an Accessor object?

All rowsets and commands must implement the **IAccessor** interface, which supplies binding information for rowset data, parameter data, or both. The consumer has the responsibility of verifying that **Accessor** objects created on a command are still valid after the command is changed.

Rowset objects inherit **Accessor** objects from the parent **Command** object. **Accessor** object handles, flags, and bindings are identical for the **Accessor** object of a rowset which was inherited from a **Command** object.

2. Name the interfaces which supply column metadata.

IColumnsInfo is one of two interfaces which exposes column metadata. **IColumnsRowset** provides complete data while **IColumnsInfo** is a simpler interface for the common data. **IColumnsInfo** is a required interface for all commands and rowsets.

3. Name the methods which must be prepared before being called.

When a provider supports command preparation for **IColumnsInfo::GetColumnInfo, IColumnsInfo::MapColumnIDs, IColumnsRowset::GetAvailableColumns**, and **IColumnsRowset::GetColumnsRowset**, all must have the command prepared before being called.

4. What is a unique characteristic of the IErrorLookup interface?

The interface is internal to OLE-DB and should not be called by a consumer.

5. What is a unique characteristic of the IRowsetUpdate interface?

The presence of the **IRowsetUpdate** indicates that changes made to the rowset operate in *deferred* mode.

6. What are the intrinsic constants DBBMK_FIRST and DBBMK_LAST?

These are bookmarks for the first and last rows of a rowset.

7. Describe the mechanism for establishing a notification connection.

o **QueryInterface** is called by the consumer to retrieve a pointer to **ISupportErrorInfo**.

o **ISupportErrorInfo::InterfaceSupportsInfo** is called by the consumer and passed the IID of the OLE-DB object which created the error.

o **GetErrorInfo** is called when S_OK is returned. The result of this call is an **IErrorInfo** interface pointer on the OLE-DB object. Any error object should be discarded by the consumer when S_FALSE is returned by **ISupportErrorInfo::InterfaceSupportsInfo**.

8. What is the relationship between the ITransaction and the ITransactionLocal interfaces?

ITransactionLocal inherits from ITransaction and is the **Session** object interface for transactions.

Chapter 31: Active Data Objects (ADO)

1. It was stated that a memory footprint is not an issue in a virtual memory system such as Windows NT. Can you state why?

DLLs are mapped into system space. There is only one DLL loaded even though there may be dozens or even hundreds of users.

2. What is the default property for the Field, Parameter, and Property objects?

The **Value** property is the default property for the **Field**, **Parameter**, and **Property** objects.

3. Name the collections which support the Append method.

Only the **Parameters** collection supports the **Append** method.

4. What collections or objects support the Delete method?

The **Delete** method is only supported by the **Parameters** collection and the **Recordset** object.

5. Name the collections or objects which support the Clear method.

The **Clear** method is only supported by the **Errors** collection.

Chapter 32: Working with Active Data Objects

1. Name the four ADO collections.

The four ADO collections are the **Errors**, **Fields**, **Parameters**, and **Properties** collections.

2. What is the issue when the Recordset object attribute adApproxPosition is not supported?

Counting records in the **Recordset** object requires the reading of each record, which may be resource intensive.

3. Identify the basic difference between editing a record in DAO and ADO.

An edit mode is not required. The record is edited, and moving to the next record will save the changes.

4. What is batch mode?

Batch mode is a form of record editing where changes are accumulated and submitted collectively. The method **UpdateBatch** submits batch changes while the method **CancelBatch** will revert all changes since the last **UpdateBatch** call.

5. How is batch mode initiated?

Batch mode is initiated by setting the **LockType** property of the **Recordset** object to the intrinsic constant **adLockBatchOptimistic**.

6. What common characteristic does the DAO Errors collection share with the ADO Errors collection?

The ADO **Errors** collection is only for ADO errors, and the DAO Errors collection is only for DAO errors. VBA errors will not be found in either collection.

7. Explain the use of the Supports method.

ADO and OLE-DB are not fully implemented, provider support may be uneven, there are no standards, Microsoft might make unexpected changes, and the **Recordset** object may not be appropriate are some of the reasons the consumer must always verify the support for a particular feature. For example, before deleting a record the consumer should verify that the record can be deleted. Such a prototype statement might be:

```
if MyRS.Supports(adDelete) then
  MyRS.Delete
```

```
else
. . .
```

8. **What is the common issue for the Delete, Resync, UpdateBatch, or CancelBatch methods?**

A run-time error will not occur if at least one operation is performed successfully. As an example, a run-time error will not occur if one record was successfully deleted and 24 records were not deleted. The consumer must check the **Errors** collections for error messages.

PART III: INFRASTRUCTURE

Chapter 33: Operating System Awareness

1. **Name three major issues to consider when deciding between Windows NT workstation and Windows 95.**

Resource requirements for Windows 95 are less. This includes the operating system cost, memory, and the CPU.

Windows 95 does not support security other than file shares.

Windows 95 supports native hardware drivers. Windows NT does not.

2. **Explain the difference between a DLL in Windows 3.1 and a Win32 DLL (either Windows 95 or Windows NT).**

Each task maintains a private copy of the DLL data and only one copy of the DLL is mapped into the address space of each task.

3. **Explain how the Virtual Memory Manager (VMM) allocates task memory.**

The VMM reserves task memory and commits the memory for application use.

4. **What is committed memory and how is it acquired?**

Committed memory is the working set (balance set), which is a collection of swappable task pages. A page is committed when it is written to the swap file. The pages are acquired through page faults with the required pages added automatically by the VMM.

5. What is the primary limitation with DDE?

DDE uses global memory and can be very slow for large data structures. It is considered an older technology.

6. What is the difference between a process and a thread?

A thread executes, while the process object is the task virtual address space and the other objects which constitute the application, such as files or bitmaps.

7. What is a new limitation of Windows NT workstation 4.0?

It is now limited to 10 user connections.

8. Which protocol stack is necessary for your application to use FTP?

FTP is a utility of the TCP/IP protocol. TCP/IP is supported by the Windows Sockets programming interface.

9. Describe thread scheduling in Windows NT.

The thread scheduling is preemptive for higher-priority threads. Threads are given a timeslice, and the thread priority may decrease at the expiration of the timeslice. The Kernel schedules threads on an available resource basis, and threads are not limited to only one CPU. A multithreaded application may have active threads on more than one CPU.

Chapter 34: Choosing Development Tools

1. Which BackOffice product automates the installation of enterprise software?

Systems Management Server (SMS) is the Microsoft BackOffice for managing the software and hardware inventory of an enterprise. Installation of the software can be unattended.

2. SMS requires the cooperation of another Microsoft BackOffice product. What is the name of that product?

Microsoft SQL Server is required for SMS operation. All hardware and software inventory information is maintained in a SQL Server database.

3. You are unable to complete a purchase from a store on the Internet. You believe the Web site is supported by Microsoft Merchant Server. What is the probable problem?

You haven't established a secure link. Microsoft Merchant Server will not honor transactions over an insecure link.

4. How do you establish a secure link on the Web?

Secure hyperlinks begin with https:// instead of the standard http://.

5. You are building a tiered client-server application. What is the suggested development tool to use with Microsoft Transaction Server?

Visual Basic 5.0. ActiveX will have its server plumbing added automatically by Transaction Server, reducing development costs.

6. What is the development tool of choice for building controls in a multiple platform environment?

Microsoft J++ is the recommended tool. There are two possible scenarios. The first is pure JAVA using a JAVA virtual machine, which is hopefully platform independent. The other choice is ActiveX controls and the dependency on the Microsoft infrastructure.

7. You wish to use Jet database replication. Which Microsoft Office tools support Jet replication?

Excel, Visual Basic, Visual C++, and Access. Visual J++ and Visual FoxPro do not support Jet replication.

8. Which BackOffice Server provides connectivity to an AS/400 DB2 relational database?

SNA Server

9. Which Microsoft tools support callback functions?

Visual Basic 5.0 (earlier versions do not support callbacks) and Visual C++

10. There are two definitions of Microsoft Office. The second definition is the composite collection of all objects defined in the Microsoft Office tool collection. What is the most common object?

The Application object which is at the top of the hierarchy for all Office object models

11. Visual FoxPro is a very powerful development tool. What are the two distinguishing characteristics of Visual Foxboro?

Visual Foxboro is object-oriented with polymorphism and inheritance and is the only Microsoft tool to support the dBASE language.

Chapter 35: Development Methodologies

1. Microsoft Solutions Framework (MSF) supports the tiered architecture paradigm. Name the services offered by each of the tiers.

Business services, data services, and user services

2. Name the major milestones of the Process model of MSF.

The milestones are Vision/Scope approval, Functional Specification approval, code complete, and product delivery. A project is not limited to just these milestones; however, when development is iterative it is difficult to quantify a process. The waterfall process is task-based and steps are easily quantified.

3. Microsoft makes a significant issue of ownership within MSF. Describe ownership within MSF.

Team roles within MSF own the milestones. Accountability beyond this must depend upon other tools such as Microsoft Project and the management style of the program manager. No individual is accountable in MSF.

4. You are starting a new Web site with multiple developers, and you know that all the Visual Basic and C++ developers use SourceSafe. Can you use SourceSafe to protect your Web pages?

Yes, Visual SourceSafe can be used on any text or binary file which needs versioning control.

5. Describe the procedure to use with SourceSafe to keep a module under version control.

The Checkout function is used to make a local copy of the module. Changes are made locally and the Checkin function is used when edits are complete. Changes will be merged automatically. A module with merge errors cannot be checked in. The Differences command can be used as a tool in resolving conflicts.

6. A new project is starting which can reuse modules in the current project. How does SourceSafe support different projects with common modules?

SourceSafe always maintains only one master copy. A copy within another project is in reality.

PART IV: INTERNET/INTRANET

Chapter 36: The Internet/Intranet: Architecture, Tools, and Protocols

1. What advantages does the Internet Server Application Programming Interface (ISAPI) have when compared to the Common Gateway Interface (CGI) protocol?

A CGI application runs in its own address space, and a new instance of the application must be started for each HTTP message. The other limiting factor for CGI is that it has no memory between instances. This makes it very difficult to process a transaction on the Internet using CGI.

2. What is the use of the <%begin detail%> and <%end detail%> tags? Where are they used and what is their purpose?

The <%begin detail%> and <%end detail%> tags are elements of a .HTX prototype HTML page from the Internet Data Connector (IDC) technology. The HTTPODBC.DLL at the web server uses these tags to locate where to place the data on the page that is returned to the browser.

3. You wish to publish on the Web. The problem is you want to minimize the web server load. Which technology is appropriate? (Consider only web publishing technologies discussed in this chapter.)

Active Server Pages (ASP) are ruled out since they represent additional server work. The IDC/HTX technology is also ruled out since the HTTPODBC.DLL runs within the server process space. File Transport Protocol (FTP) is ruled out since it doesn't publish but only transfers between file web sites. The only remaining choice is static page publishing using a tool such as Microsoft SQL Web Assistant or any other static page processing mechanism.

4. FrontPage 98 has automated many facets of web page creation. One is the IDC wizard, which is started by double-clicking an IDC script. An IDC script can be generated by a tool such as Access 97, but that's not always necessary. What are the three essential ingredients of an IDC script which enables FrontPage 98 to automatically generate the .HTX HTML prototype page?

The three required IDC parameters are the Data Source Name (DSN), the HTX file name, and a SQL statement.

5. What technology can be used to retrieve data from an ODBC data source?

Active Server Pages (ASP) and the Internet Database Connector (IDC/HTX) can both retrieve data from a registered ODBC source. There are certain limitations which you'll learn about in Chapter 42, but for the purpose of the Windows Architecture I examination, both IDC and ASP are correct answers.

6. There are numerous tags within HTML; however, the popular ones should be known. What tag is in error when the browser restarts inadvertently? Within what HTML element would you place buttons or text boxes?

HREF and FORM, respectively

7. The time to load a page is always significant. Microsoft Internet Explorer supports a technology which allows the image to be viewed as it is loaded. What is that technology called?

The Internet Explorer feature is called progressive rendering, which gives control to the browser before all images are downloaded. Progressive rendering can only be done with a specialized file format. (You and I should both be aware of this, because quite often I am off on a hyperlink before the original images are completely loaded, in which case further downloading is aborted.)

8. You wish to publish price changes to a parts catalog on a web page on a periodic basis. There is also a requirement to publish price changes immediately when they exceed a certain threshold. Which Microsoft Internet publishing technology is appropriate?

This is a natural for Microsoft SQL Server Web Assistant. Price changes can be published both periodically and when a change is significant. Triggers within SQL Server will detect changes, and application logic determines the significance of the price changes. The same tasks in Access 97 require the intervention of a user.

9. What is the defining difference in the technology of ASP and IDC?

ASP is an interactive Internet technology while IDC is not. The sense of interaction comes about because browser HTML and scripts exist on the same page as server HTML and scripts.

Chapter 37: Anatomy of a Web Site

1. Which Microsoft Internet publishing technology is supported by FrontPage 98?

Microsoft FrontPage 98 will create an Active Server Page in the Database region Wizard, or an .HTX prototype web page when an IDC script is double-clicked. As shipped, FrontPage 98 only connects to ODBC sources.

2. How do I place my Access database on a web?

Use Microsoft Visual Interdev which will create an Active Server page. There is an example in Chapter 37.

3. How does the Microsoft publishing technology achieve the concept of interaction?

The common denominator for Internet publishing is that of a file server. A page or a page request is sent, and an HTML-formatted page is returned. Interaction is attained by using the same page at both the browser and the server. Server tags and browser tags delineate the areas where specific code is executed.

4. What is an issue of Active Server Pages?

A page is sent to the server and new HTML is placed on the page. The page is returned and the prior page is pushed down in the local memory stack of the browser. If the client does not use the browser **Back** arrow, the page remains on the stack until the browser exits.

5. What is the Active Server Pages issue?

Three Microsoft tools each generate different Active Server Page coding using different technology. Visual InterDev uses ActiveX controls, FrontPage 98 uses an ugly creature called a WebBot, and Access 97 only uses Active Data Objects. Access 97 Active Server Pages are not functional, and FrontPage 98 Active Server Pages only work with ODBC data sources. Visual InterDev Active Server Pages work with either an ODBC data source or the ODBC Desktop Driver Set.

Chapter 38: Internet Tools for the Trenches

1. Explain the disadvantages of the WebBrowser control.

The control is easy to use. The basic problem is the developer must provide the missing Web browser functionality.

2. Explain error handling in a Visual Basic DLL.

A DLL always runs in the process address space of the host application. An error will crash the application. A DLL must capture all errors and pass that information back to the caller.

3. Describe the content of the three parameter fields following the OLEISAPI HTML POST or GET HTML methods.

The parameters in order can be described as a ProgID, a Class, and a Method. This is a DLL whose ProgID.Class is found in the registry. The ProgID is the DLL name while the Class is the Visual Basic .CLS module name. Method is a public procedure of that .CLS module.

4. What makes implementing an ISAPI DLL difficult?

The server must be brought down, the DLL changed out, and the server restarted. The Visual Basic DLL component suffers similar problems in that the registry entry must be removed before the new version is installed.

5. What is the meaning of the <?> in an HTTP GET method?

The <?> is syntax signifying that parameters follow. An example might be: ?First=sally+last=silly+age=39.

6. We know that a CGI application runs in its own process space while an ISAPI application is a DLL which runs in the process space of the Internet Server. What is another operational dissimilarity?

A CGI application reads all input from stdin and writes all output to stdout. An ISAPI application passes input data in the Extension Control Block (ECB) and uses callback functions of the ECB to read more data and to write data. Invoking a CGI application is nearly identical to invoking an ISAPI DLL. The only difference is the CGI executable name is replaced with the ISAPI DLL name. All other information remains unchanged.

Chapter 39: Internet Applications with Élan

1. Which Internet Information Server object is used to retrieve ASP data sent by a user with an HTML form?

The Internet Information Server **Request** object is used to retrieve user supplied data for an ASP application.

2. What is the advantage of a .CAB file?

It uses compression for packaging components and supporting files for Internet downloads. The compression, which Microsoft states is up to 70 percent, improves download performance. It can be code-signed, which makes it safe.

3. We've discussed both server-side and client-side scripting. What are two advantages of server-side scripting?

The first advantage is that server-side scripts are stripped from the page before it is sent to the client browser. This keeps the scripting private. The other advantage is that server-side scripting is faster than client-side scripting.

4. Which Internet technology provides security and the best performance?

The Internet Server API which runs in the process space of the server.

5. Your application may be loaded into browsers which do not support scripting. How do you prevent the script from being displayed at the browser?

Use the HTML comment element <!--, --> to enclose the script.

6. How do you make data available to an ActiveX component in a Web page?

Declare the file's URL in the DATA attribute of the HTML OBJECT element.

7. What does the CLSID of the HTML Object element refer to?

It does not refer to a .CAB file, but is the CLSID of the component.

8. How is an .INF file used in Internet technology?

A .INF file represents a list of files with packaging information. It is unsafe when downloaded by itself since it cannot be code-signed. However, it can be encapsulated in a .CAB file which supports code-signing.

9. What is a common limitation shared by both VBScript and jscript?

Neither scripting language permits system interaction with an API call.

10. **How does an Active Server Page application remember user choices as the user moves between pages?**

User choices are stored in the Information Server **Session** object.

11. **You want to monitor performance of your Web site. What Internet technology is appropriate?**

An Internet Server API (ISAPI) filter function is appropriate for this task. The ISAPI filter function subscribes to server events and is notified when these events occur.

12. **What technology is used to manage scripting with a variety of different browsers?**

The Browser Capabilities Component identifies the type of browser and whether or not it supports scripting.

13. **How do you force users to upgrade to the latest version of your component?**

Change the CODEBASE property in the HTML Object element referencing your component.

PART V: APPLICATIONS

Chapter 40: Solutions Design Issues

1. **What key model is missing from the IDEF1X data modeling architecture?**

The IDEF1X architecture is missing a Business Model.

2. **Explain the role of the Key Based Model (KBM) and the Fully Attributed Model (FAM) in the IDEF1X architecture.**

The KBM and FAM are transitional steps to creating the Transform Model, which is the mapping to the hardware media. The KBM consists of only keys and entities obtained from the entity relationship diagram (ERD), which are normalized to third normal form. The model is considered a KBM only after all primary key and entities are included and the model is normalized to third normal form.

The FAM represents an interim step. The Fully Attributed Model only exists after all attributes have been added to the KBM. Attributes are added in small groups and the model normalized at that point. This approach makes a difficult problem manageable.

3. What process is accomplished by placing a model in first normal form?

Groups of repeating data are removed.

4. Explain third normal form.

A model is not in third normal form when columns of data do not depend upon the primary key. Removing this dependency places the model in third normal form.

Chapter 41: Designing the Solution

1. What is the schema for the 5-tuple (OrderID, ItemID, Description, OrderDate, Quantity)? You may assume that OrderID and ItemID represent a composite key.

The schema is represented as:

- o R(<u>OrderID</u>, <u>ItemID</u>, Description, OrderDate, Quantity)
- o OrderID ⇒ OrderDate, OrderIDItemID ⇒ DescriptionQuantity

2. What is the normalization error in question 1?

The normalization error is a second normal form error and is the example of Table 41-22.

3. Describe a Boyce Codd Normal Form (BCNF) error.

A BCNF error is a result of overlapping keys. This usually occurs after the database is normalized and the additional keys are being added for performance.

4. Describe a third normal form error.

A third normal form error occurs when an attribute depends upon another attribute and not the primary key. This is also known as transitive dependency.

5. Describe a second normal form error.

A second normal form error occurs when an attribute depends upon a portion of the primary key and not the complete key.

6. Describe a first normal form error.

A repeating group is a first normal form error.

Chapter 42: Solution Interface Issues

1. Name two unique characteristics of the Double Byte Character set.

The first characteristic is that the lead character is always an extended character, and the second characteristic is that SBCS characters may be intermixed with DBCS characters.

2. Your application displays characters from the DBCS from the KANJI character set. The text is displayed correctly on the screen. When the printed characters are clicked, an error appears. What is the apparent problem?

The print routine is using an ANSI character set or is not using the **CharPrev** and **CharNext functions** to position the text.

3. This chapter lists 10 resources that potentially must be localized in a DLL. Name four of these resources.

Program elements requiring localization include special algorithms, constants, dialogs, macro languages, menus, messages, prompts, sounds, status bars, and toolbars.

4. What is the difference between the function pair AnsiPrev/AnsiNext and CharPrev/CharNext?

AnsiPrev and **AnsiNext** are the 16-bit implementations of string traversing while **CharPrev** and **CharNext** are the 32-bit implementations of string traversing.

5. What control allows multiple selections?

The List View control

6. What does the double chevron represent on a command button?

The double chevron is another name for an unfold button. The window unfolds revealing additional detail.

7. What is the general rule of command sequence in a menu?

The most frequent commands always appear first.

8. What is the common mistake made when using either a horizontal or vertical scroll bar?

Scroll bars are not to be used for setting values.

9. Where is the Properties command placed in a pop-up menu?

The Properties command is last in a pop-up menu.

10. **Discuss the Windows 95 Logo requirements for an application with respect to OLE.**

    The Windows 95 Logo-compliant application must either be a COM object or a COM container.

11. **Your application must adjust the volume of an audio speaker. Which control do you use?**

    The slider control

What's on the CD-ROM?

CD-ROM Contents

The CD-ROM included with this book contains the following materials:

- Adobe Acrobat Reader 3.0

- An electronic version of this book, *Windows Architecture I & II MCSD Study Guide,* in Adobe Acrobat format

- An electronic version of three chapters of *MCSE Career Microsoft!* (IDG Books Worldwide, 1997)

- An electronic version of three chapters of *Windows NT 4.0 MCSE Study Guide* (IDG Books Worldwide, 1997)

- Microsoft Internet Explorer version 4.0

- ISG Navigator version 1.5

- Examples from the book of all the technologies required for the Microsoft Windows Architecture I and II examinations

- Electronic resources in Adobe Acrobat format, including a thorough review of all Windows Architecture I and II exam objectives, a mini-lab manual, and a technology-specific glossary.

Installing and Using the CD-ROM

The following sections describe each product included on the CD-ROM and include detailed instructions for installation and use.

Adobe Acrobat Reader and the Adobe Acrobat Version of Windows Architecture I & II MCSD Study Guide

The Adobe Acrobat Reader is a helpful program that will enable you to view the electronic version of this book in the same page format as the actual book.

To install and run Adobe Acrobat Reader and view the electronic version of this book, follow these steps:

1. Start Windows Explorer (if you're using Windows 95) or Windows NT Explorer (if you're using Windows NT), and then open the `Acrobat` folder on the CD-ROM.

2. In the `Acrobat` folder, double-click `ar3230.exe` and follow the instructions presented onscreen for installing Adobe Acrobat Reader.

3. To view the electronic version of this book after you have installed Adobe Acrobat Reader, start Windows Explorer (if you're using Windows 95) or Windows NT Explorer (if you're using Windows NT), and then open the `Books\WinArch I and II` folder on the CD-ROM.

4. In the `WinArch I and II` folder, double-click the chapter or appendix file you want to view. All documents in this folder end with a `.pdf` extension.

MCSE Career Microsoft!® (Sample Chapters in Adobe Acrobat Format)

Most books covering the Microsoft Certified Professional program focus entirely on practice exams and their subject matter. *MCSE Career Microsoft!*® focuses on the professional characteristics involved with obtaining a Microsoft Certification, as well as maintaining and advancing your career once you are certified. This book also provides many practical and essential references to information, training, and tools available to information technology professionals, including Microsoft

Career Professionals (MCPs) and MCP candidates. Included here are excerpts from *MCSE Career Microsoft!*®, including Chapters 1, 2, and 5. These chapters should give you a good impression of how useful and valuable this book can be. No other computer book on the market today provides a comprehensive approach to MCPs and their careers as does *MCSE Career Microsoft!*®

To install and run Adobe Acrobat Reader to view *MCSE Career Microsoft!*®, follow these steps:

1. If you've already installed the Adobe Acrobat Reader to view the electronic version of this book, skip to step 3.

   If you haven't installed Adobe Acrobat Reader, start Windows Explorer (if you're using Windows 95) or Windows NT Explorer (if you're using Windows NT), and then open the `Acrobat` folder on the CD-ROM.

2. In the `Acrobat` folder, double-click `Setup.exe` and follow the instructions presented onscreen for installing Adobe Acrobat Reader.

3. To view the *MCSE Career Microsoft!*® sample chapters after you have installed Adobe Acrobat Reader, start Windows Explorer (if you're using Windows 95) or Windows NT Explorer (if you're using Windows NT), and then open the `Books\Career Microsoft` folder on the CD-ROM.

4. In the `Career Microsoft` folder, double-click the chapter you want to view. All documents in this folder end with a `.pdf` extension.

Windows NT 4.0 MCSE Study Guide (Sample Chapters in Adobe Acrobat Format)

This Microsoft-approved study guide prepares you for three MCSE exams that test implementing and supporting Windows NT products: No. 73 (Workstation 4.0), No. 70-67 (Server 4.0), and No. 70-68 (Server 4.0 in the Enterprise). You'll find three chapters in Adobe Acrobat format on the CD-ROM.

To view *Windows NT 4.0 MCSE Study Guide* chapters, follow these steps:

1. If you've already installed the Adobe Acrobat Reader to view the electronic version of this book, skip to step 3.

   If you haven't installed Adobe Acrobat Reader, start Windows Explorer (if you're using Windows 95) or Windows NT Explorer (if you're using Windows NT), and then open the `Acrobat` folder on the CD-ROM.

2. In the `Acrobat` folder, double-click `ar32e30.exe` and follow the instructions presented onscreen for installing Adobe Acrobat Reader.

3. To view the *Windows NT 4.0 MCSE Study Guide* sample chapters after you have installed Adobe Acrobat Reader, start Windows Explorer (if you're using Windows 95) or Windows NT Explorer (if you're using Windows NT), and then open the `Books\MCSE Windows NT 4.0` folder on the CD-ROM.

4. In the `MCSE Windows NT 4.0` folder, double-click the chapter you want to view. All documents in this folder end with a `.pdf` extension.

Microsoft Internet Explorer Version 4.0

This is a complete copy of Microsoft Internet Explorer. With Internet Explorer you'll be able to browse the Internet if you have an Internet connection, and view the contents of the Microsoft Training and Certification Offline CD-ROM (included on this CD-ROM).

To install and run Microsoft Internet Explorer, follow these steps:

1. Start Windows Explorer (if you're using Windows 95) or Windows NT Explorer (if you're using Windows NT), and then open the `\Msie40` folder on the CD-ROM.

2. In the `Msie40` folder, double-click `Setup.exe` and follow the instructions presented onscreen for installing Microsoft Internet Explorer.

3. To run Microsoft Internet Explorer, double-click the Internet Explorer icon on the desktop.

Transcender Exam Simulation Software

Included on the CD-ROM are demo versions of Transcender's exam simulation for the Windows Architecture I and II exams. Timed, predictive simulations of the actual Microsoft certification exams, the Transcender simulations are timed study tools that model the exams in both the graphical user interface to the difficulty of the questions.

To install and run the Transcender exam simulation software, follow these steps:

1. Start Windows Explorer (if you're using Windows 95) or Windows NT Explorer (if you're using Windows NT).

2. Open the `Transcender` folder on the CD-ROM.

3. In the `Transcender` folder, double-click `Setup.exe` and follow the onscreen prompts.

ISG Navigator

ISG Navigator Universal Data Access software utilizes ADO and OLE-DB and is available for a broad base of platforms, including Windows 95, Windows NT, UNIX and Digital UNIX, Alpha NT, and OpenVMS. ISG Navigator also supports a wide range of relational, object, and other databases.

ISGData Control for ADO data access reduces development cycles by providing Visual Basic 5.0 developers with drag and drop access to local and enterprise data sources. The ISGData Control eliminates most of the manual programming steps needed to connect an application to the databases it uses.

ISG Navigator is located in the ISGSOFT folder of the CD-ROM that accompanies this book. ISG Navigator software is also available from the Download page of the ISGSOFT Web site at `www.isgsoft.com`.

The ISG Navigator version supplied with this book is for Windows 95 and Windows NT. An Alpha NT version is available from ISGSOFT.

To install ISG Navigator, follow these steps:

1. Create a directory on your hard disk.

2. Open the `ISGSOFT` folder of the CD-ROM and drag the file `NAV1529W.EXE` to the newly created directory.

3. Double-click `NAV1529W.EXE` and respond to the prompts.

A Windows NT installation also installs the server (the `NVSERVER.EXE` file). The ISG Navigator Windows/NT server (called `nvServer`) is a multi-threaded ISG Navigator server; it accepts client requests from Windows and non-Windows platforms.

The Examples

All examples used in this book are located on the CD-ROM. The examples are not code fragments, but small working pieces of code that illustrate functionality. They do not modify the registry and are designed to run stand-alone. The `Examples` folder requires 35MB of disk space on your hard drive.

This book represents a quality assurance test of many Microsoft tools and products and not all features work. Features that work for me may not work for you. These examples used the latest service packs available.

To install the Examples, follow these steps:

1. Open File Manager.

2. Drag the Examples folder from the CD-ROM to the root directory of a hard disk (usually the C:\ drive). This places the Examples folder in the root of your hard drive and the book examples may be run from there.

To access and run the Examples, follow these steps:

Running the Access 97 Examples

1. Start Access 97.

2. From the File Menu, select OpenDatabase and browse for the Access 97 MDB of interest.

3. Select Open.

4. After the database is opened, select Forms ⇒ Design Mode.

5. Select Run (the icon immediately below the File menu).

Running the Visual Basic Examples

1. Start Visual Basic 5.0. (You'll need the Enterprise Edition for the RDO examples.)

2. From the File menu select Open Project.

3. Browse for the Visual Basic project of interest.

4. Select a project and choose OK.

5. After the project is loaded, Select *Start with Full Compile* from the Run menu.

TABLE D-1 CD-ROM EXAMPLE INVENTORY	
FOLDER	*DESCRIPTION*
Chapter3	The Visual Basic 5.0 Enterprise Edition project ICHECKBOOK.VBP is located in this folder. This is the ActiveX control example developed within the chapter.

FOLDER	DESCRIPTION
Chapter8	This is not an executable example. The file BLOB.BMP located in this folder is used with the laboratories of Chapter 8.
Chapter9	There are many Automation examples in this folder. The examples are in an Access 97 AUTO.MDB database or in the Visual Basic 5.0 Enterprise Edition AUTO.VBP project.
Chapter14	This chapter is dedicated to the ODBC API examples. The examples were developed using Access 2.0 and SQL Server 6.0. These examples may not run on your system unless you have 16-bit ODBC drivers. In the eventuality that the code does not run, all of the code is included within the chapter. The reason for using Access 2.0 was to avoid the use of Unicode. This facilitates the binding operations of the **SQLExtendedFetch**. There are examples of all ODBC API groups and this code can serve as an aid for using the ODBC API from a VBA environment.
Chapter16	Access 97 CHAPTER16.MDB
Chapter17	Access 97 CHAPTER17.MDB
Chapter18	Access 97 CHAPTER18.MDB
Chapter19	Access 97 CHAPTER19.MDB
Chapter20	Access 97 CHAPTER20.MDB
Chapter21	Access 97 CHAPTER21.MDB
Chapter22	Access 97 CHAPTER22.MDB
Chapter23	Access 97 CHAPTER23.MDB
Chapter24	RDO, Visual Basic Enterprise Edition 5.0 CHAPTER24.VBP
Chapter25	RDO, Visual Basic Enterprise Edition 5.0 CHAPTER25.VBP
Chapter26	RDO, Visual Basic Enterprise Edition 5.0 CHAPTER27.VBP
Chapter27	SQL-DMO, Visual Basic Enterprise Edition 5.0 CHAPTER27.VBP
Chapter28	SQL-DMO tool with 47 forms used in Chapter 28.
Chapter32	ADO, Visual Basic Enterprise Edition 5.0 CHAPTER36.VBP
Chapter33	DDE issues are illustrated with Visual Basic Enterprise Edition 5.0 DDECLIENT.VBP, Access 97 DDESRVR.MDB. The DDE examples support SDQL queries.
Chapter34	Access 97 PRIME_SIEVE.MDB, Visual Basic 5.0 Enterprise Edition PRIME_SIEVE.VBP project.
Chapter36	No executable examples. IDC and ASP files created by Access 97.

continued

TABLE D-1 *(continued)*	
FOLDER	DESCRIPTION
Chapter37	This is a Web site created in the book. The MYWEB Web site is copied complete from the Windows NT Server 4.0 path: <*unit*>\\INETPUB\WWWROOT\MYWEB.
Chapter38	These are loose end examples for the Internet/intranet chapters. An ISAPI DLL is created along with a Web site to support the ISAPI DLL. Tools are Visual Basic 5.0 Enterprise, Visual InterDev, and Window NT Server 4.0 sp3 with Internet Information Server 3.0. Other running examples include a Visual Basic 5.0 Enterprise Edition project using the WinInet control and the WebBrowser control. There is an Automation example of Internet Explorer. The ISAPI Web site is copied complete from the path Windows NT 4.0 Server path: <*unit*>\\INETPUB\WWWROOT\OLEISAPIWEB.
Chapter42	This is not an executable example. It is all the controls from a Visual Basic 4.0 toolbox. Note that I did not say Visual Basic 5.0. VB 4.0 has many desirable features and I prefer the Integrated Development Environment (IDE) of VB 4.0 where I do not have to browse for controls.

If the examples don't work

Many examples require SQL Server. When SQL Server is available, the login to SQL Server must be changed to reflect your SQL Server. Code for the examples is normally behind a command button. In Visual Basic, double-click the command button and modify the login.

The expected problems with Visual Basic will be with missing type libraries, missing controls, or the wrong version when Visual Basic 5.0 is not the Enterprise Edition. If the Visual Basic project reports an error on opening, exit Visual Basic without saving the project. Open the .VBP project in NotePad and examine the first few lines. Some example lines from the CHAPTER24.VBP are shown below:

```
Type=Exe
Reference=*\G{00020430-0000-0000-C000-000000000046}#2.0#0#I:
  \NTWS351\System32\STDOLE2.TLB#OLE Automation
Reference=*\G{EE008642-64A8-11CE-920F-08002B369A33}#2.0#0#I:
  \NTWS351\System32\MSRDO20.DLL#Microsoft Remote Data Object
  2.0
Form=Chapter24.frm
Startup="Chapter24"
```

You can see that Chapter 24 requires the MSRDO20.DLL. In the Tools menu of Visual Basic Code Editor, you'll want to select *References* and browse for MSRDO20.DLL on your own system.

Access 97 examples should work directly and should present no problems except for SQL Server, which will require a login change. To modify the SQL Server login for an example, select the command button of interest, select Click_Event from the properties window for the command button, and proceed to modify the login code.

note ▼ **All examples were testesd at least twice. My e-mail address for this book is** bruce@prendergast.com. **I will provide help with running the examples and updated examples if necessary. (Just remember that I am not a company with a help desk!)**

The host environment

More than one operating system was used while writing this book and creating the Examples. The inventory of the development system includes:

- *Windows NT 3.51 Workstation sp 5* — This system is a 133 MHz and 131MB system. This is the primary development system. There were numerous error messages reported from COM/DCOM error messages that stated "Automation has disappeared." These error messages went away after 131MB was installed.

- *Windows NT 4.0 Workstation sp 3* — No major problems other than an occasional reinstallation. This system is the primary Internet port.

- *Windows NT 4.0 Server sp 3* — All Internet development work was done on this system. Visual Studio 97 Enterprise Edition is installed on this system.

- *Visual Studio 97 Enterprise Edition sp 1* — There are problems with Visual Basic 5.0 Enterprise Edition supporting DAO 3.5. DAO 3.0 was used on many examples. There are also problems with RDO and Visual Basic 5.0 Enterprise Edition (see Chapter 24). DAO 3.5 works fine in Access 97.

- *Access 97* — This product appears to function properly, except that active servers pages generated by the Access 97 Wizard are useless. Access 97 also has a problem in that the transaction methods are exposed on the **DBEngine**. This is a logical error and is not documented as such. The **BeginTrans**, **CommitTrans**, and **Rollback** methods can be browsed from the DBEngine. This is quite unlike Visual Basic 5.0 Enterprise Edition where the errors are documented as features.

o *SQL Server 6.5 sp 3* — No problems with SQL Server, but the SQL-DMO **DBObject** object has a few design problems. Many of the examples require access to the Pubs database of Microsoft SQL Server.

o *FrontPage 98* — No real problems. The themes and fonts are great, but the generated ASP code is almost aboriginal. Use FrontPage 98 themes or fonts and switch to Visual InterDev to finish your Web site.

o *Visual InterDev (Visual Studio 97 Enterprise Edition)* — The only tool that I had no problems with. Don't even think of using Access 97- or FrontPage 98-generated ASPs. The ASPs of Visual InterDev work with no fixups.

Exam Preparation Tips

E

The Microsoft Certified Solution Developer exams are *not* easy, and they require a great deal of preparation. The exam questions measure real-world skills. Your ability to answer these questions correctly will be enhanced by as much hands-on experience with the product as you can get. Appendix E provides you some practical and innovative ways to prepare for the Microsoft Certified Solution Developer exams for Windows Architecture I & II.

 web links

Although the Exam Objectives listed in Appendixes A and B were current when this book was published, you may want to ensure that you have the most current version of the exam objectives by accessing the Microsoft Training and Certification Web site at www. microsoft.com/train_cert.

ABOUT THE EXAMS

An important aspect of passing the MCSD Certification exams is understanding the big picture. This includes understanding how the exams are developed and scored.

Every job function requires different levels of cognitive skills, from memorization of facts and definitions to the comprehensive ability to analyze scenarios, design solutions, and evaluate options. To make the exams relevant in the real world, Microsoft Certified Solution Developer exams test the specific cognitive skills needed for the job functions being tested. These exams go beyond testing rote knowledge—you need to *apply* your knowledge, analyze technical solutions, solve problems, and make decisions—just like you would on the job.

How the Certification Exams Are Developed

To help ensure the validity and reliability of the certification exams, Microsoft adheres to an eight-phase exam-development process:

1. Job analysis
2. Objective domain definition
3. Blueprint survey
4. Item development
5. Alpha review and item revision
6. Beta exam
7. Item selection and cut score setting
8. Exam live

The following paragraphs describe each phase of exam development.

Phase 1: Job analysis

Phase 1 is an analysis of all the tasks that make up the specific job function, based on tasks performed by people who are currently performing the job function. This phase also identifies the knowledge, skills, and abilities that relate specifically to the performance area to be certified.

Phase 2: Objective domain definition

The results of the job analysis provide the framework used to develop objectives. The development of objectives involves translating the job function tasks into a comprehensive set of more specific and measurable knowledge, skills, and abilities. The resulting list of objectives (or the objective domain), is the basis for the development of the certification exams and the training materials.

Phase 3: Blueprint survey

The final objective domain is transformed into a blueprint survey in which con-tributors — technology professionals who are performing the applicable job func-tion — are asked to rate each objective. Contributors may be selected from lists of past Certified Professional candidates, from appropriately skilled exam-develop-ment volunteers, and from within Microsoft. Based on the contributors' input, the objectives are prioritized and weighted. The actual exam items are written accord-ing to these prioritized objectives. Contributors are queried about how they spend their time on the job, and if a contributor doesn't spend an adequate amount of time actually performing the specified job function, his or her data is eliminated from the analysis.

The blueprint survey phase helps determine which objectives to measure, as well as the appropriate number and types of items to include in the exam.

Phase 4: Item development

A pool of items is developed to measure the blueprinted objective domain. The number and types of items written are based on the results of the blueprint sur-vey. During this phase, items are reviewed and revised to ensure that they are:

- o Technically accurate

- o Clear, unambiguous, and plausible

- o Not biased for any population subgroup or culture

- o Not misleading or tricky

- o Testing at the correct level of Bloom's Taxonomy

- o Testing for useful knowledge, not obscure or trivial facts

Items that meet these criteria are included in the initial item pool.

Phase 5: Alpha review and item revision

During this phase, a panel of technical and job function experts reviews each item for technical accuracy and then answers each item, reaching consensus on all technical issues. Once the items have been verified as technically accurate, they are edited to ensure that they are expressed in the clearest language possible.

Phase 6: Beta exam

The reviewed and edited items are collected into a beta-exam pool. During the beta exam, each participant has the opportunity to respond to all the items in this beta-exam pool. Based on the responses of all beta participants, Microsoft performs a statistical analysis to verify the validity of the exam items and to determine which items will be used in the certification exam. Once the analysis has been completed, the items are distributed into multiple parallel forms, or versions, of the final certification exam.

Phase 7: Item selection and cut score setting

The results of the beta exam are analyzed to determine which items should be included in the certification exam. Many factors are taken into consideration, including item difficulty and relevance. Generally, the desired items are those that were answered correctly by anywhere from 25 to 90 percent of the beta-exam candidates. This helps ensure that the exam consists of a variety of difficulty levels — from somewhat easy to extremely difficult.

Also during this phase, a panel of job function experts determines the cut score (minimum passing score) for the exam. The cut score differs from exam to exam because it is based on an item-by-item determination of the percentage of candidates who answered the item correctly, and who would be expected to answer the item correctly. The cut score is determined in a group session to increase the reliability among the experts.

Phase 8: Exam live

Microsoft Certified Solution Developer exams are administered by Sylvan Prometric, an independent testing company. The exams are made available at Sylvan Prometric testing centers worldwide.

Exam Items and Scoring

Microsoft certification exams consist of three types of items: multiple-choice, multiple-rating, and enhanced. The way you indicate your answer and the number of receivable points differ depending on the type of item.

Multiple-choice item

A traditional multiple-choice item presents a problem and asks you to select either the best answer (single response) or the best set of answers (multiple response) to the given item from a list of possible answers.

For a *multiple-choice* item, your response is scored as either correct or incorrect. A correct answer receives a score of 1 point and an incorrect answer receives a score of 0 points.

In the case of a multiple-choice, multiple-response item (for which the correct response consists of more than one answer), the item is scored as correct only if all the correct answers are selected. No partial credit is given for a response that does not include all the correct answers for the item.

For consistency purposes, the question in a multiple-choice, multiple-response item is always presented in singular form (regardless of how many answers are correct). Always follow the instructions displayed at the bottom of the window.

Multiple-rating item

A *multiple-rating* item presents a task similar to those presented in multiple-choice items. In a multiple-choice item, you are asked to select the best answer (or answers) from a selection of several potential answers. In contrast, a multiple-rating item presents a task, along with a proposed solution. Each time the task is presented, a different solution is proposed. In each multiple-rating item, you are asked to choose the answer that best describes the results produced by one proposed solution.

Enhanced item

An *enhanced* item is similar to a multiple-choice item because it asks you to select your response from a number of possible responses. Unlike the traditional multiple-choice item that presents you with a list of possible answers from which to choose, an enhanced item may ask you to indicate your answer in one of three ways:

- Type the correct response, such as a command name.

- Review an exhibit (such as a screen shot, a network configuration drawing, or a code sample), and then use the mouse to select the area of the exhibit that represents the correct response.

- Review an exhibit, and then select the correct response from the list of possible responses.

As with a multiple-choice item, your response to an enhanced item is scored as either correct or incorrect. A correct answer receives full credit of 1 point and an incorrect answer receives a score of 0 points.

PREPARING FOR A MICROSOFT CERTIFIED PROFESSIONAL EXAM

The best way to prepare for an exam is to study, learn, and master the job function on which you'll be tested. For any certification exam, you should follow these important preparation steps:

1. Identify the objectives on which you'll be tested.
2. Assess your current mastery of those objectives.
3. Practice tasks and study the areas you haven't mastered.

This section describes tools and techniques that may be helpful as you perform these steps to prepare for the exam.

Exam Preparation Guides

For each certification exam, an exam preparation guide provides important, specific information about what you'll be tested on and how best to prepare. These guides are essential tools for preparing to take certification exams. You'll find the following types of valuable information in the exam preparation guides:

- **Tasks you should master:** Outlines the overall job function tasks you should master

- **Exam objectives:** Lists the specific skills and abilities on which you should expect to be measured

- **Product resources:** Tells you which products and technologies with which you should be experienced

- **Suggested reading:** Points you to specific reference materials and other publications that discuss one or more of the exam objectives

- **Suggested curriculum:** Provides a specific list of instructor-led and self-paced courses relating to the job function tasks and topics in the exam

You'll also find pointers to additional information that may help you prepare for the exams, such as Microsoft TechNet, *Microsoft Developer Network* (MSDN), online forums, and other sources.

By paying attention to the verbs used in the "Exam Objectives" section of the exam preparation guide, you will get an idea of the level at which you'll be tested on that objective. For more information about which verbs signal each level of the taxonomy, see "About the Exams," in this appendix. It's a good idea to prepare to be tested at the Analysis level or higher for each objective.

 web links

To view the most recent version of the exam preparation guides, which include the exam's objectives, check out Microsoft's Training and Certification Web site at: www.microsoft.com/train_cert.

Assessment Exams

When preparing for the exams, take a lot of assessment exams. Assessment exams are self-paced exams that you take at your own computer. When you complete an assessment exam, you receive instant score feedback so you can determine areas in which additional study may be helpful before you take the certification exam. Although your score on an assessment exam doesn't necessarily indicate what your score will be on the certification exam, assessment exams give you the opportunity to answer items that are similar to those on the certification exams. And the assessment exams use the same computer-based testing tool as the certification exams, so you don't have to learn the tool on exam day.

An assessment exam exists for almost every certification exam.

Test-Taking Tips

Here are some tips that may be helpful as you prepare to take a certification exam:
Before the exam:

- Be sure to read the "What to Expect at the Testing Center," section in this appendix for important information about the sign-in and test-taking procedures you'll follow on the day of your exam.

- Don't study all night before the test. A good night's sleep is often better preparation than the extra studying.

- Try to schedule the exam during your own "peak" time of day. In other words, if you're a morning person, try not to schedule the exam for 3:00 p.m.

- Know your testing center. Call ahead and ask about the hardware they use for their testing computers. If some computers are faster than others, ask for the seat numbers of the faster computers and request one of those seat numbers when scheduling your testing appointment with Sylvan Prometric. Consider visiting a testing center before you schedule an exam there. This will give you an opportunity to see the testing environment.

- Do the Critical Thinking and Hands-on labs for each chapter in this book as you read it. Remember, the exams measure real-world skills that you can't obtain unless you use the product.

- Review the Key Point Summary sections *and* answer the Instant Assessment questions at the ends of the chapters in this book before taking an exam.

- Pay special attention to the exam-preparation pointers scattered throughout this book — these pointers will help you focus on important exam-related topics.

- When you've finished reading all of the chapters (and have done all the labs), take practice tests to assess your readiness for the exam. Most practice tests will reveal your weak areas. Use this information to go back and study.

- Take as many practice exams as you can get your hands on before taking the exam. This will help you in two ways. First, some practice exam questions are quite similar to the real thing, and if you do enough practice exams, some of the questions you see on the exam might look familiar. Second, taking practice exams will make you more comfortable with the computer-based testing environment/process. This will reduce your stress when you take the actual exam. You can't take too many practice exams. It's virtually impossible to be *too* prepared for the exam.

- Take the exam-preparation process seriously. Remember, these exams weren't designed to be easy — they were designed to recognize and certify professionals with specific skill sets.

- Consider joining (or becoming an associate member of) a professional organization or user group in your area that focuses on Internetworking with TCP/IP. Some user groups have a computer lab and/or lending library that can help you with your exam preparation. The meetings are a great place to meet people with similar interests, and potential employers, too.

- Consider subscribing to *Microsoft Certified Professional Magazine*. This magazine, which is an independent publication that is not associated with Microsoft, features an exam spotlight section where new Microsoft Certified Professional exams are critically reviewed as they are released. For more information about this magazine or to subscribe, visit the magazine's Web site at www.mcpmag.com.

- Talk to friends or colleagues who have taken the exam for which you're preparing. Or, check out the Internet for newsgroups or forums where people sometimes share their exam experiences. The experiences of others can shed some light on your potential weak areas that might benefit from further study. The MCSE list server at saluki.com is one example. Don't share (or ask friends to share with you) specific exam questions. It is fair game to share general topics that were strongly emphasized on the exam, and/or areas that had particularly detailed or tough questions.

- Consider forming a study group with friends or coworkers who are also preparing for the TCP/IP exam. As a group you can share hardware and software resources, thus reducing your out-of-pocket costs for exam preparation.

- Do the labs. Do them again for practice.

On exam day:

- Arrive 10 to 15 minutes early, and don't forget your picture ID.

- Dress comfortably. The more comfortable you are, the more you'll be able to focus on the exam.

- If you have any questions about the rules for the exam, ask the exam administrator before the exam begins. The exams are timed, so avoid using valuable test time for questions you could have asked earlier.

- Don't drink a lot of coffee or other beverage before taking an exam. Remember, these tests last 90 minutes, and you don't want to be spending precious exam time running back and forth to the restroom.

During the exam:

- Answer the easy items first. The testing software enables you to move forward and backward through the exam. Go through all the items on the test once, answering those items you are sure of first; then go back and spend time on the harder items.

- Keep in mind that there are no trick items. The correct answer will always be among the list of choices.

- Eliminate the most obvious incorrect answers first. This will make it easier for you to select the answer that seems most right to you.

- Answer all the items before you quit the exam. An unanswered item is scored as an incorrect answer. So, if you're unsure of an answer, it can't hurt to make an educated guess.

- Try to relax. People often make avoidable, careless mistakes when they rush.

- When taking the actual exam, pause every few minutes and take a couple of deep breaths — this will bring more oxygen into your body, and help you to think more clearly. More importantly, this should help you relax and relieve some of the tension created by the testing environment.

After the exam:

- Remember, if you don't pass the first time, you can use your score report to determine the areas where you could use additional study and take the exam again later (for an additional fee).

- Don't get discouraged if you don't pass the test your first time — or second time. Many intelligent, seasoned professionals fail a test once, twice, or more times before eventually passing it. If at first you don't succeed, try, try again . . . perseverance pays.

TAKING A MICROSOFT CERTIFIED PROFESSIONAL EXAM

This section contains information about registering for and taking a Microsoft Certified Professional exam, including what to expect when you arrive at the Sylvan Prometric testing center to take the exam.

How to Find Out Which Exams Are Available

You can find a complete list of MCP exams and their registration costs on the online Microsoft Roadmap to Education and Certification on the CD accompanying this book. To get the latest schedule information for a specific exam, contact Sylvan Prometric at (800) 755-EXAM.

How to Register for an Exam

Candidates may take exams at any of the 700+ Sylvan Prometric testing centers around the world. For the location of a Sylvan Prometric testing center near you, call (800) 755-EXAM (755-3926). Outside the United States and Canada, contact your local Sylvan Prometric Registration Center.

To register for a Microsoft Certified Professional exam:

1. Determine which exam you want to take, and note the exam number.
2. Register with the Sylvan Prometric Registration Center nearest to you. A part of the registration process is advance payment for the exam.
3. After you receive the registration and payment confirmation letter from Sylvan Prometric, call a Sylvan Prometric testing center to schedule your exam.

When you schedule the exam, you'll be provided with instructions regarding the appointment, cancellation procedures, and ID requirements, and information about the testing center location.

Exams must be taken within one year of payment. You can schedule exams up to six weeks in advance, or as late as one working day prior to the date of the exam. You can cancel or reschedule your exam if you contact Sylvan Prometric at least two working days prior to the exam.

Although subject to space availability, same-day registration is available in some locations. Where same-day registration is available, you must register a minimum of two hours before test time.

What to Expect at the Testing Center

As you prepare for your certification exam, it may be helpful to know what to expect when you arrive at the testing center on the day of your exam. The following information gives you a preview of the general procedure you'll go through at the testing center:

- You will be asked to sign the log book upon arrival and departure.
- You will be required to show two forms of identification, including one photo ID (such as a driver's license or company security ID), before you may take the exam.
- The test administrator will give you a Testing Center Regulations form that explains the rules you will be expected to comply with during the test. You will be asked to sign the form, indicating that you understand the regulations and will comply.
- The test administrator will show you to your test computer and will handle any preparations necessary to start the testing tool and display the exam on the computer.
- You will be provided with a set amount of scratch paper for use during the exam. All scratch paper will be collected from you at the end of the exam.
- The exams are all closed book. You may not use a laptop computer or have any notes or printed material with you during the exam session.
- Some exams may include additional materials, or exhibits. If any exhibits are required for your exam, the test administrator will provide you with them before you begin the exam and collect them from you at the end of the exam.
- Before you begin the exam, the test administrator will tell you what to do when you complete the exam. If the test administrator doesn't explain this to you, or if you are unclear about what you should do, ask the administrator before beginning the exam.
- The number of items on each exam varies, as does the amount of time allotted for each exam. Generally, certification exams consist of about 50–100 items and have durations of 60–90 minutes. You can verify the number of items and time allotted for your exam when you register.

Because you'll be given a specific amount of time to complete the exam once you begin, don't hesitate to ask the test administrator if you have any questions or concerns before the exam begins.

As an exam candidate, you are entitled to the best support and environment possible for your exam. In particular, you are entitled to the following:

- A quiet, uncluttered test environment

- Scratch paper

- The tutorial for using the online testing tool, and time to take the tutorial

- A knowledgeable and professional test administrator

- The opportunity to submit comments about the testing center and staff (or the test, itself)

For more information about how to submit feedback about any aspect of your exam experience, see the "If You Have Exam Concerns or Feedback" section in this appendix. The Certification Development Team will investigate any problems or issues you raise and make every effort to resolve them quickly.

Your Exam Results

Once you have completed an exam, you will be given immediate, online notification of your pass or fail status. You will also receive a printed examination score report indicating your pass or fail status and your exam results by section. (The test administrator will give you the printed score report.) Test scores are automatically forwarded to Microsoft within five working days after you take the test. You do not need to send your score to Microsoft.

If you pass the exam, you will receive confirmation from Microsoft, typically within two to four weeks.

If You Don't Receive a Passing Score

If you do not pass a certification exam, you may call Sylvan Prometric to schedule a time to retake the exam. Before retaking the exam, you should review the appropriate exam preparation guide and focus additional study on the topic areas where your exam results could be improved. Please note that you must pay again for each exam retake.

One way to determine areas where additional study may be helpful is to carefully review your individual section scores. Generally, the section titles in your score report correlate to specific groups of exam objectives listed in the exam preparation guide.

Here are some specific ways you can prepare to retake an exam:

- Go over the section-by-section scores on your exam results, noting objective areas where your score could be improved.
- Review the exam preparation guide for the exam, with a special focus on the tasks and objective areas that correspond to the exam sections where your score could be improved.
- Increase your real-world, hands-on experience and practice performing the listed job tasks with the relevant products and technologies.
- Review the suggested readings listed in the exam preparation guide.
- After you review the materials, retake the corresponding assessment exam.

IF YOU HAVE EXAM CONCERNS OR FEEDBACK

To provide the best certification preparation and testing materials possible, we encourage feedback from candidates. If you have any suggestions for improving any of the Microsoft Certified Professional exams or preparation materials, please let us know.

The following sections describe what to do with specific concerns or feedback about the certification exams.

If You Encounter a Problem with the Exam Software or Procedures

Microsoft and Sylvan Prometric make every effort to ensure that your exam experience is a positive one; however, if any problems should occur on the day of the exam, inform the Sylvan Prometric test administrator immediately. The Sylvan Prometric personnel are there to help make the logistics of your exam run smoothly.

If You Have a Concern About the Exam Content

Microsoft Certified Professional exams are developed by technical and testing experts, with input and participation from job function and technology experts.

Through an exhaustive process, Microsoft ensures that the exams adhere to recognized standards for validity and reliability, and are considered by candidates to be relevant and fair. If you feel that an exam item is inappropriate, or if you believe the answer shown is incorrect, write or send a fax to the Microsoft Certification Development Team, using the address or fax number listed in "For More Information."

Although we are unable to respond to individual questions and issues raised by candidates, all input from candidates is thoroughly researched and taken into consideration during development of subsequent versions of the exams. Microsoft is committed to ensuring the validity and reliability of our exams, and your input is a valuable resource.

FOR MORE INFORMATION

To find out more about Microsoft Education and Certification materials and programs, to register with Sylvan Prometric, or to get other useful information, check the following resources. Outside the United States or Canada, contact your local Microsoft office or Sylvan Prometric testing center.

o **Microsoft Certified Professional Program: (800) 636-7544.** Call for information about the Microsoft Certified Professional program and exams, and to order this exam study guide or the Microsoft Roadmap to Education and Certification.

o **Sylvan Prometric testing centers: (800) 755-EXAM.** Call to register to take a Microsoft Certified Professional exam at any of the 700+ Sylvan Prometric testing centers around the world, or to order this exam study guide.

o **Microsoft Sales Fax Service: (800) 727-3351.** Call for Microsoft Certified Professional Exam Preparation Guides, Microsoft Official Curriculum course descriptions and schedules, or this exam study guide.

o **Education Program and Course Information: (800) SOLPROV.** Call for information about Microsoft Official Curriculum courses, Microsoft education products, and the Microsoft Solution Provider *Authorized Technical Education Center* (ATEC) program, where you can attend a Microsoft Official Curriculum course, or to order this exam study guide.

- **Microsoft Certification Development Team: Fax: (206) 936-1311**. Call to volunteer for participation in one or more exam-development phases or to report a problem with an exam. Address written correspondence to: Certification Development Team; Microsoft Education and Certification; One Microsoft Way; Redmond, WA 98052.

- **Microsoft TechNet Technical Information Network: (800) 344-2121**. Call for support professionals and system administrators. Outside the United States and Canada, call your local Microsoft subsidiary for information.

- **Microsoft Developer Network (MSDN): (800) 759-5474**. MSDN is the official source for software development kits, device driver kits, operating systems, and information about developing applications for Microsoft Windows and Windows NT.

- **Online Services: (800) 936-3500**. Call for information about Microsoft Connection on CompuServe, Microsoft Knowledge Base, Microsoft Software Library, Microsoft Download Service, and Internet.

- **Microsoft Online Institute (MOLI): (800) 449-9333**. Call for information about Microsoft's new online training program.

Index

continued

continued

continued

continued

continued

continued

continued

continued

continued

continued

continued

continued

continued

continued

continued

S

continued

continued

continued

IDG BOOKS WORLDWIDE, INC. END-USER LICENSE AGREEMENT

READ THIS. You should carefully read these terms and conditions before opening the software packet(s) included with this book ("Book"). This is a license agreement ("Agreement") between you and IDG Books Worldwide, Inc. ("IDGB"). By opening the accompanying software packet(s), you acknowledge that you have read and accept the following terms and conditions. If you do not agree and do not want to be bound by such terms and conditions, promptly return the Book and the unopened software packet(s) to the place you obtained them for a full refund.

1. **License Grant.** IDGB grants to you (either an individual or entity) a nonexclusive license to use one copy of the enclosed software program(s) (collectively, the "Software") solely for your own personal or business purposes on a single computer (whether a standard computer or a workstation component of a multiuser network). The Software is in use on a computer when it is loaded into temporary memory (RAM) or installed into permanent memory (hard disk, CD-ROM, or other storage device). IDGB reserves all rights not expressly granted herein.

2. **Ownership.** IDGB is the owner of all right, title, and interest, including copyright, in and to the compilation of the Software recorded on the disk(s) or CD-ROM ("Software Media"). Copyright to the individual programs recorded on the Software Media is owned by the author or other authorized copyright owner of each program. Ownership of the Software and all proprietary rights relating thereto remain with IDGB and its licensers.

3. **Restrictions On Use and Transfer.**

   (a) You may only (i) make one copy of the Software for backup or archival purposes, or (ii) transfer the Software to a single hard disk, provided that you keep the original for backup or archival purposes. You may not (i) rent or lease the Software, (ii) copy or reproduce the Software through a LAN or other network system or through any computer subscriber system or bulletin-board system, or (iii) modify, adapt, or create derivative works based on the Software.

(b) You may not reverse-engineer, decompile, or disassemble the Software. You may transfer the Software and user documentation on a permanent basis, provided that the transferee agrees to accept the terms and conditions of this Agreement and you retain no copies. If the Software is an update or has been updated, any transfer must include the most recent update and all prior versions.

4. <u>Restrictions On Use of Individual Programs</u>. You must follow the individual requirements and restrictions detailed for each individual program in Appendix D, "What's on the CD-ROM," of this Book. These limitations are also contained in the individual license agreements recorded on the Software Media. These limitations may include a requirement that after using the program for a specified period of time, the user must pay a registration fee or discontinue use. By opening the Software packet(s), you will be agreeing to abide by the licenses and restrictions for these individual programs that are detailed in Appendix D and on the Software Media. None of the material on this Software Media or listed in this Book may ever be redistributed, in original or modified form, for commercial purposes.

5. <u>Limited Warranty</u>.

(a) IDGB warrants that the Software and Software Media are free from defects in materials and workmanship under normal use for a period of sixty (60) days from the date of purchase of this Book. If IDGB receives notification within the warranty period of defects in materials or workmanship, IDGB will replace the defective Software Media.

(b) IDGB AND THE AUTHOR OF THE BOOK DISCLAIM ALL OTHER WARRANTIES, EXPRESS OR IMPLIED, INCLUDING WITHOUT LIMITATION IMPLIED WARRANTIES OF MERCHANTABILITY AND FITNESS FOR A PARTICULAR PURPOSE, WITH RESPECT TO THE SOFTWARE, THE PROGRAMS, THE SOURCE CODE CONTAINED THEREIN, AND/OR THE TECHNIQUES DESCRIBED IN THIS BOOK. IDGB DOES NOT WARRANT THAT THE FUNCTIONS CONTAINED IN THE SOFTWARE WILL MEET YOUR REQUIREMENTS OR THAT THE OPERATION OF THE SOFTWARE WILL BE ERROR FREE.

(c) This limited warranty gives you specific legal rights, and you may have other rights that vary from jurisdiction to jurisdiction.

6. Remedies.

(a) IDGB's entire liability and your exclusive remedy for defects in materials and workmanship shall be limited to replacement of the Software Media, which may be returned to IDGB with a copy of your receipt at the following address: Software Media Fulfillment Department, Attn.: *Windows Architecture I & II MCSD Study Guide*, IDG Books Worldwide, Inc., 7260 Shadeland Station, Ste. 100, Indianapolis, IN 46256, or call 1-800-762-2974. Please allow three to four weeks for delivery. This Limited Warranty is void if failure of the Software Media has resulted from accident, abuse, or misapplication. Any replacement Software Media will be warranted for the remainder of the original warranty period or thirty (30) days, whichever is longer.

(b) In no event shall IDGB or the author be liable for any damages whatsoever (including without limitation damages for loss of business profits, business interruption, loss of business information, or any other pecuniary loss) arising from the use of or inability to use the Book or the Software, even if IDGB has been advised of the possibility of such damages.

(c) Because some jurisdictions do not allow the exclusion or limitation of liability for consequential or incidental damages, the above limitation or exclusion may not apply to you.

7. U.S. Government Restricted Rights.
Use, duplication, or disclosure of the Software by the U.S. Government is subject to restrictions stated in paragraph (c)(1)(ii) of the Rights in Technical Data and Computer Software clause of DFARS 252.227-7013, and in subparagraphs (a) through (d) of the Commercial Computer — Restricted Rights clause at FAR 52.227-19, and in similar clauses in the NASA FAR supplement, when applicable.

8. General.
This Agreement constitutes the entire understanding of the parties and revokes and supersedes all prior agreements, oral or written, between them and may not be modified or amended except in a writing signed by both parties hereto that specifically refers to this Agreement. This Agreement shall take precedence over any other documents that may be in conflict herewith. If any one or more provisions contained in this Agreement are held by any court or tribunal to be invalid, illegal, or otherwise unenforceable, each and every other provision shall remain in full force and effect.

my2cents.idgbooks.com

Register This Book — And Win!

Visit **http://my2cents.idgbooks.com** to register this book and we'll automatically enter you in our fantastic monthly prize giveaway. It's also your opportunity to give us feedback: let us know what you thought of this book and how you would like to see other topics covered.

Discover IDG Books Online!

The IDG Books Online Web site is your online resource for tackling technology — at home and at the office. Frequently updated, the IDG Books Online Web site features exclusive software, insider information, online books, and live events!

10 Productive & Career-Enhancing Things You Can Do at www.idgbooks.com

- Nab source code for your own programming projects.

- Download software.

- Read Web exclusives: special articles and book excerpts by IDG Books Worldwide authors.

- Take advantage of resources to help you advance your career as a Novell or Microsoft professional.

- Buy IDG Books Worldwide titles or find a convenient bookstore that carries them.

- Register your book and win a prize.

- Chat live online with authors.

- Sign up for regular e-mail updates about our latest books.

- Suggest a book you'd like to read or write.

- Give us your 2¢ about our books and about our Web site.

You say you're not on the Web yet? It's easy to get started with IDG Books' *Discover the Internet,* available at local retailers everywhere.

CD-ROM Installation Instructions

Each software item on the *Windows Architecture I & II MCSD Study Guide* CD-ROM is located in its own folder. To install a particular piece of software, begin by opening its folder with My Computer or Internet Explorer. What you do next depends on what you find in the software's folder:

- Look first for a Readme.txt file or a .doc or .htm document. If this is present, it should contain installation instructions and other useful information.

- If the folder contains an executable (.exe) file, this is usually an installation program. Often it will be called Setup.exe or Install.exe, but in some cases the filename reflects an abbreviated version of the software's name and version number. Run the .exe file to start the installation process.

- In the case of some simple software, the .exe file probably is the software—no real installation step is required. You can run the software from the CD-ROM to try it out. If you like it, copy it to your hard disk and create a Start menu shortcut for it.

Please note that after installing Internet Explorer 4.0 and restarting your machine, a splash screen appears when you click Internet Explorer Setup. This screen lists three options:

1. Click here to start the Internet Connection Wizard.

2. Click here to remove this screen and return to the Windows screen, or

3. Click here to start Internet Explorer.

To run Internet Explorer 4.0, make the first selection. Clicking the third selection will display an error message that says: Internet Explorer cannot open the Internet site. The system cannot find the file specified.

The Readme.txt file in the CD-ROM's root directory may contain additional installation information, so be sure to check it.

For a complete listing of the software on the CD-ROM, see Appendix D, "What's on the CD-ROM."